MODERN CONSTITUTIONAL THEORY

A READER

Fifth Edition

By

John H. Garvey
Dean
Boston College Law School

T. Alexander Aleinikoff
Professor of Law
Georgetown University Law Center

and

Daniel A. Farber
Sho Sato Professor of Law
University of California at Berkeley

AMERICAN CASEBOOK SERIES®

Mat #40165543

610 Opperman Drive
P.O. Box 64526
St. Paul, MN 55164–0526
1–800–328–9352

Printed in the United States of America

ISBN 0–314–14905–8

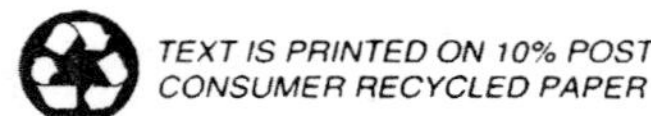

PREFACE

Why a book on constitutional theory? The answer is that today the fundamental premises of constitutional law are sharply challenged, in a way that cannot be ignored by any student of the subject. Supreme Court doctrine is attacked from every direction: from those who argue that text and original intent are more important than precedent, from those who believe the Court has an inflated concept of its authority, from those who think the Court fundamentally misunderstands the nature of race and gender discrimination, and from those who repudiate its abortion and gay rights rulings. These issues are hotly debated in the popular media and on the floor of the Congress. Indeed, they are often contested by the Justices themselves in the pages of the U.S. Reports. To learn constitutional law only as a series of doctrines and multi-prong tests is misleading, for it is the deeper normative disputes that often shape the doctrine.

This normative debate about constitutional law coincides with expanded interest by constitutional scholars in the humanities and social sciences. Moral philosophy, literary theory, economic analysis, and constitutional history are all in a state of ferment. Courses in Constitutional Law cannot ignore this ferment. When there is such widespread disagreement about fundamentals, it is nearsighted to focus only on doctrinal details.

This book is addressed to multiple audiences: students taking introductory constitutional law courses, advanced constitutional law students, and our fellow academics. We also hope that it may find some utility for lawyers and judges who wish to explore constitutional theory. Constitutional theory goes beyond doctrinal analysis to ask deeper normative questions about our constitutional system. We have tried to present some of the leading works of constitutional theory in a form accessible enough for the beginner, but sophisticated enough for the seasoned veteran. The excerpts seek to go deeper than a restatement of the law, to ask what purposes are served by existing rules and whether some other approach would be better. We have selected material taking opposing positions in an effort to give a well-rounded picture of current scholarly disputes.

In terms of coverage, the book tracks what is today the conventional syllabus for introductory constitutional law courses: judicial review, constitutional structure, substantive due process, and equal protection. Because criminal procedure, the First Amendment, and federal jurisdiction are now typically the subjects of separate advanced courses, we do not cover them here. We also slight other significant issues such as taxation of interstate commerce and procedural due process because these topics typically get little attention in introductory courses. Ideally, these subjects should all be treated together with the core materials, but this book would be at least twice as long if we attempted to do so.

We begin in Chapter I with a look at some of the currently influential theories of the Constitution. We then turn in Chapter II to various approaches to interpreting the Constitution, and we round out our study of the foundations of constitutional law by examining debates over judicial review and judicial supremacy in Chapter III. These are issues about which the Justices themselves deeply disagree. They are also issues that set the very terms for debating particular constitutional questions.

The remaining chapters are organized around substantive constitutional issues: federalism (Chapter IV), separation of powers (Chapter V), racial equality (Chapter VI), gender equality (Chapter VII), affirmative action (Chapter VIII), liberty and privacy (Chapter IX), and the state action doctrine (Chapter X). Many of these areas are in a state of doctrinal ferment, with recent judicial opinions on state sovereignty, affirmative action, and gay rights as only the most obvious examples.

Most of the selections have been edited. We have indicated deletions with asterisks ("* * *") or by bracketing (such as "[T]he Court" when we have deleted material preceding that phrase). We have deleted footnotes without indication, retaining the original numbering for the remaining footnotes. Editorial notes, explaining deleted material or adding citations, are included in brackets or in alphabetically labeled footnotes.

Our purpose has been to make each author's thinking as accessible as possible for students. In the end, this book is the vehicle for the work of these scholars, who have done so much to enrich our constitutional discourse. We only regret that space limitations have required the exclusion of so many other fine works; we attempt to make partial amends with bibliographies on each topic, but even the bibliographies are necessarily incomplete. Finally, we also wish to express our gratitude to Laurie Newbauer for her expert and tireless preparation of the manuscript for publication.

John H. Garvey
T. Alexander Aleinikoff
Daniel A. Farber

December 2003

Acknowledgments

We would like to thank the authors and copyright holders of the following works, who permitted their inclusion in this book:

Bruce A. Ackerman, Beyond *Carolene Products*. Reprinted with permission of Bruce A. Ackerman.

Bruce Ackerman, We The People, Volume 1: Foundations. Reprinted with permission of Bruce A. Ackerman and the publishers from We the People: Foundations by Bruce Ackerman, Cambridge, Mass.: Harvard University Press. Copyright © 1991 by the President and Fellows of Harvard College.

T. Alexander Aleinikoff, A Case for Race-Consciousness. This article originally appeared at 91 Colum.L.Rev. 1060 (1991). Reprinted by permission.

Larry Alexander and Frederick Schauer, Defending Judicial Supremacy: A Reply. Reprinted with the permission of the authors and Constitutional Commentary.

Akhil Reed Amar and Neal Kumar Katyal, *Bakke*'s Fate. Reprinted with permission of Akhil Reed Amar; Neal Kumar Katyal, and William S. Hein & Co. Inc.

Akhil Reed Amar and Neal Kumar Katyal, Executive Privileges and Immunities: The Nixon and Clinton Cases. Copyright © 1995 by the Harvard Law Review Association.

Akhil Reed Amar, Foreword: The Document and the Doctrine. Copyright © 2000 by the Harvard Law Review Association.

Elizabeth S. Anderson, Integration, Affirmative Action, and Strict Scrutiny. This article originally appeared at 77 N.Y.U. L.Rev. 1195 (2002). Reprinted with permission of the author and the New York University Law Review.

Lynn Baker and Ernest Young, Federalism and the Double Standard of Judicial Review. This article originally appeared at 51 Duke L.J. 75 (2001). Reprinted with permission of the authors and the Duke Law Journal.

Randy E. Barnett, Justice Kennedy's Libertarian Revolution: *Lawrence v. Texas,* Cato Supreme Court Review (2002-2003). Reprinted with permission of the author and Cato Supreme Court Review.

Derrick Bell, And We Are Not Saved. Copyright © 1987 by Basic Books, Inc. Reprinted by permission of Basic Books, a division of Harper-Collins Publishers, Inc.

Raoul Berger, Government by Judiciary. Reprinted by permission of the Harvard University Press. Copyright © 1977 by the President and Fellows of Harvard College.

Alexander M. Bickel, The Least Dangerous Branch (1962). Reprinted with permission of Josephine A. Bickel.

Charles L. Black, Jr ., The People and the Court (1960). Reprinted with permission of Macmillan Publishing Company. Copyright © 1960 by Charles L. Black, Jr.

Philip Bobbitt, Constitutional Interpretation. Reprinted with permission of Philip C. Bobbit and Blackwell Publishers.

Robert H. Bork, Neutral Principles and Some First Amendment Problems. Reprinted with permission of the Indiana Law Journal and Fred B. Rothman & Company.

Robert Brauneis, "The Foundation of Our 'Regulatory Takings' Jurisprudence": The Myth and Meaning of Justice Holmes's Opinion in *Pennsylvania Coal Co. v. Mahon.* Reprinted with permission of Robert Brauneis and the Yale Law Journal.

Paul Brest, In Defense of the Antidiscrimination Principle. Copyright © 1976 by the Harvard Law Review Association.

Paul Brest, The Misconceived Quest for the Original Understanding. Reprinted with permission of Paul A. Brest and the Boston University Law Review.

Rebecca L. Brown, Accountability, Liberty, and the Constitution. This article originally appeared at 98 Colum.L.Rev. 531 (1998). Reprinted by permission.

Mary Anne Case, "The Very Stereotype The Law Condemns": Constitutional Sex Discrimination Law as a Quest for Perfect Proxies. This article originally appeared at 85 Cornell L.Rev. 1447 (2000). Reprinted with permission of the author and the Cornell Law Review.

Stephen L. Carter, The Political Aspects of Judicial Power: Some Notes on the Presidential Immunity Decision, 131 U.Pa.L.Rev. 1341 (1983) Copyright © 1983 by the University of Pennsylvania.

Erwin Chemerinsky, Rethinking State Action. Reprinted with permission of Erwin Chemerinsky and Northwestern University School of Law, Volume 80, Issue 3, Northwestern University Law Review, (1985), pp. 503.

Edward S. Corwin, The Steel Seizure Case: A Judicial Brick Without Straw. Copyright © 1953 by the Directors of the Columbia Law Review Association, Inc. All rights reserved. This article originally appeared at 53 Colum.L.Rev. 53 (1953). Reprinted by permission.

Kimberle Williams Crenshaw, Race, Reform, and Retrenchment: Transformation and Legitimation in Antidiscrimination Law. Reprinted by permission of Kimberle W. Crenshaw and the Harvard Law Review Association. Copyright © 1988 by the Harvard Law Review Association.

Noel T. Dowling, Interstate Commerce and State Power. Reprinted with permission of the Virginia Law Review and Fred B. Rothman & Company.

Ronald H. Dworkin, Freedom's Law: The Moral Reading of the American Constitution. Reprinted by permission of the Harvard University Press. Copyright © 1996 by the President and Fellows of Harvard College.

John Hart Ely, Democracy and Distrust, Reprinted by permission of the Harvard University Press. Copyright © 1980 by the President and Fellows of Harvard College.

John Hart Ely, The Wages of Crying Wolf: A Comment on *Roe v. Wade.* Reprinted with permission of John Hart Ely.

John Hart Ely, War and Responsibility: Constitutional Lessons of Vietnam and Its Aftermath. Copyright © 1993 by Princeton University Press. Excerpts reprinted with permission of Princeton University Press.

Richard Fallon, The "Conservative" Paths of The Rehnquist Court's Federalism Decisions. 69 U.Chi.L.Rev. (2002). Copyright © 2002 by The University of Chicago. All rights reserved.

Richard A. Fallon, How to Choose a Constitutional Theory. This article originally appeared at 87 Cal.L.Rev. 537 (1999). Reprinted with permission of the author and the California Law Review.

John M. Finnis, Law, Morality, and "Sexual Orientation." This article originally appeared at 9 Notre Dame J.L. Ethics & Pub. Pol'y (1995). Reprinted with permission of the author and the Notre Dame Journal of Law, Ethics & Public Policy.

Owen M. Fiss, Groups and the Equal Protection Clause, Philosophy & Public Affairs 5, no. 2 (Winter 1976). Copyright © 1976 Princeton University Press, Excerpts reprinted with permission by Princeton University Press.

Martin S. Flaherty, The Most Dangerous Branch. Reprinted by permission of The Yale Law Journal Company and Fred B. Rothman & Company from The Yale Law Journal, Vol. 105, pages 1725-1839.

Barry Friedman, Valuing Federalism. This article originally appeared at 82 Minn. L.Rev. 317 (1997). Reprinted with permission of the author and the Minnesota Law Review.

John H. Garvey, Control Freaks. Reprinted with permission of John H. Garvey and the Drake Law Review.

John H. Garvey, What Are Freedoms For? Reprinted with permission of John H. Garvey and the Harvard University Press.

Ruth Bader Ginsburg, Some Thoughts on Autonomy and Equality in Relation to *Roe v. Wade.* Reprinted by permission of the Honorable Ruth Bader Ginsburg and the North Carolina Law Review.

Neil Gotanda, A Critique of "Our Constitution is Color-Blind." Reprinted by permission of Neil Gotanda.

Thomas C. Grey, Do We Have an Unwritten Constitution?, 27 Stan. L. Rev. 703 (1975). Reprinted with permission of the Stanford Law Review and Fred B. Rothman & Co. Copyright © 1975 by the Board of Trustees of the Leland Stanford Junior University.

Janet E. Halley, Sexual Orientation and the Politics of Biology: A Critique of the Argument From Immutability. Republished with permission of the Stanford Law Review, 559 Nathan Abbott Way, Palo Alto, CA 94305. Sexual Orientation and the Politics of Biology: A Critique of the Argument from Immutability, Janet E. Halley, 1994, Vol. 46. Reproduced by permission of the publisher via Copyright Clearance Center, Inc.

John Harrison, Substantive Due Process and the Constitutional Text. Reprinted with permission of John Harrison and the Virginia Law Review.

Vicki C. Jackson, Federalism and the Uses and Limits of Law: *Printz* and Principle. Copyright © 1998 by the Harvard Law Review Association.

Richard S. Kay, Adherence to the Original Intentions in Constitutional Adjudication: Three Objections and Responses. 82 Nw.U.L.Rev. 226 (1988). Copyright © 1988 by Northwestern University.

Michael J. Klarman, *Brown*, Racial Change, and the Civil Rights Movement. Reprinted with permission of Michael J. Klarman and the Virginia Law Review.

Larry Kramer, We The Court. Copyright © 2001 by the Harvard Law Review Association.

Charles R. Lawrence III, The Id, The Ego, and Equal Protection: Reckoning With Unconscious Racism. Copyright © 1987 by the Board of Trustees of the Leland Stanford Junior University.

Gary Lawson, The Rise and Rise of the Administrative State. Copyright © 1994 by the Harvard Law Review Association.

Lawrence Lessig, Fidelity and Constraint. Reprinted with permission of Lawrence Lessig and the Fordham Law Review.

Sanford Levinson, Law as Literature. Published originally in 60 Texas Law Review 373 (1982). Copyright © 1982 by the Texas Law Review. Reprinted by permission.

Catharine A. MacKinnon, Difference and Dominance: On Sex Discrimination, from Feminism Unmodified: Discourses on Life and Law (1987). Reprinted by permission of Rowman & Littlefield Publishers.

Thurgood Marshall, Reflections on the Bicentennial of the United States Constitution. Copyright © 1987 by the Harvard Law Review Association.

William.P. Marshall, Diluting Constitutional Rights: Rethinking "Rethinking State Action." Reprinted by permission of William P. Marshall and The Northwestern University Law Review.

Robert G. McCloskey, Economic Due Process and the Supreme Court: An Exhumation and Reburial. Reprinted with permission of the University of Chicago Press.

Michael W. McConnell, The Importance of Humility in Judicial Review: A Comment on Ronald Dworkin's "Moral Reading" of the Constitution. Reprinted with permission of Michael W. McConnell and the Fordham Law Review.

Michael W. McConnell, The Right to Die and the Jurisprudence of Tradition. Reprinted with permission of Michael W. McConnell and the Utah Law Review.

Gillian Metzger, Privatization as Delegation. Copyright © 2003 by the Directors of the Columbia Law Review Association, Inc. All rights reserved. This article originally appeared at 103 Colum.L.Rev. 543 (2003). Reprinted by permission.

Henry P. Monaghan, The Protective Power of the Presidency. This article originally appeared at 93 Colum.L.Rev. 1 (1993). Reprinted by permission.

Robert F. Nagel, The Future of Federalism. Reprinted with permission of Robert F. Nagel and the Case Western Reserve Law Review.

John T. Noonan, Jr., The Root and Branch of *Roe v. Wade*. Reprinted with permission of the Nebraska Law Review.

Victoria Nourse, The Vertical Separation of Powers. This article originally appeared at 49 Duke L.J. 749 (1999). Reprinted with permission of the author and the Duke Law Journal.

Richard A. Posner, Against Constitutional Theory. This article originally appeared at 73 N.Y.U. Rev. 1 (1998). Reprinted with permission of the author and the New York University Review.

Richard A Posner, The *DeFunis* Case and the Constitutionality of Preferential Treatment of Racial Minorities, 1974 Sup.Ct.Rev. 1. Copyright © 1975 by The University of Chicago. All rights reserved.

Richard Posner, Economic Analysis of Law (3rd ed. 1986). Reprinted with permission of Richard A. Posner.

Richard A. Posner, Pragmatic Adjudication. This article originally appeared in 18 Cardozo L.Rev. 1 (1996). Reprinted with permission of Richard A. Posner and the Cardozo Law Review.

Robert Post and Reva Siegal, Legislative Constitutionalism and Section Five Power: Poliocentric Interpretation of the Family and Medical Leave Act. Reprinted with permission of the authors and the Yale Law Journal.

H. Jefferson Powell and Jed Rubenfeld, Laying It on the Line: A Dialogue on Line Item Vetoes and Separation of Powers. Reprinted with permission of H. Jefferson Powell, Jed Rubenfeld, and the Duke Law Journal.

Jack Rakove, Making Hash of Sovereignty, Part II. This article originally appeared at 3 Green Bag 2d 51 (1999). Reprinted with permission of the author and Green Bag.

Donald H. Regan, The Supreme Court and State Protectionism: Making Sense of the Dormant Commerce Clause. Reprinted with permission of the Michigan Law Review Association.

Edward L. Rubin and Malcolm Feeley, Federalism: Some Notes on a National Neurosis. Reprinted with permission of Edward L. Rubin, Malcolm Feeley, and William S. Hein & Co. Inc.

Jed Rubenfeld, Of Constitutional Self-Government. Reprinted with permission of Jed Rubenfeld and the Fordham Law Review.

Jed Rubenfeld, The Right of Privacy. Copyright © 1989 by the Harvard Law Review Association.

Lawrence Gene Sager, The Legal Status of Underenforced Constitutional Norms. Copyright © 1978 by the Harvard Law Review Association.

Frederick Schauer, Easy Cases, 58 S.Cal.L.Rev. 399 (1985). Reprinted with permission of the Southern California Law Review.

Michael Seidman, Our Unsettled Constitution: A New Defense of Constitutionalism and Judicial Review. Reprinted by permission of Michael Seidman and the Yale University Press. © 2003.

Suzanna Sherry, Civic Virtue and the Feminine Voice in Constitutional Adjudication. Reprinted with permission of the Virginia Law Review.

Girardeau A. Spann, The Dark Side of *Grutter*. This article is scheduled to appear in Constitutional Commentary. Reprinted with permission of the author and Constitutional Commentary.

Girardeau A. Spann, Pure Politics. Reprinted with permission of Girardeau A. Spann and the Michigan Law Review Association.

Peter J. Spiro, War Powers and the Sirens of Formalism. This article originally appeared at 68 N.Y.U. L.Rev. 1338 (1993). Reprinted with permission of the author and the New York University Law Review.

David A. Strauss, Common Law, Common Ground, and Jefferson's Principle. Reprinted by permission of the Yale Law Journal Company and Fred B. Rothman & Company from the Yale Law Journal, Vol. 112 (2003).

David A. Strauss, Abortion, Toleration, and Moral Uncertainty, 1992 Sup.Ct.Rev. 1. Copyright © 1992 by The University of Chicago. All rights reserved.

David A. Strauss, What is Constitutional Theory. This article originally appeared at 87 Cal.L.Rev. 581 (1999). Reprinted with permission of the author and the California Law Review.

Cass R. Sunstein, The Partial Constitution. Reprinted with permission of Cass R. Sunstein and the publishers from The Partial Constitution by Cass Sunstein. Cambridge, Mass: Harvard University Press. Copyright © 1993 by the President and Fellows of Harvard College.

Judith Jarvis Thomson, A Defense of Abortion, Philosophy & Public Affairs 1, no. 1 (Fall 1971). Copyright © 1971 by Princeton University Press. Excerpts reprinted with permission of Princeton University Press.

William Michael Treanor, Jam for Justice Holmes: Reassessing the Significance of *Mahon*. This article originally appeared at 86 Geo. L.J. 813 (1998). Reprinted with permission of the author and the Georgetown Law Journal.

Laurence H. Tribe, "In What Vision of the Constitution Must the Law Be Color-Blind?" Reprinted with permission of the John Marshall Law Review.

Laurence H. Tribe, The Puzzling Persistence of Process-Based Constitutional Theories. Reprinted by permission of the Yale Law Journal, Vol. 89, pp. 1064-1080.

Mark Tushnet, New Forms of Judicial Review and the Persistence of Rights- and Democracy-Based Worries. This article originally appeared at 38 Wake Forest L.Rev. (2003). Reprinted with permission of the author and the Wake Forest Law Review.

William Van Alstyne, Rites of Passage: Race, The Supreme Court, and the Constitution. Reprinted with permission of William W. Van Alstyne and the University of Chicago Law Review.

Jeremy Waldron, Banking Constitutional Rights: Who Controls Withdrawals. This article originally appeared at 52 Ark.L.Rev. (1999). Reprinted with permission of the author and the Arkansas Law Review.

Richard A. Wasserstrom, Racism and Sexism. From Philosophy and Social Issues by Richard A. Wasserstrom. Copyright © 1980 by the University of Notre Dame Press. Reprinted by permission.

Herbert Wechsler, The Political Safeguards of Federalism: The Role of the States in the Composition and Selection of the National Government. Copyright © 1954 by the Directors of the Columbia Law Review Association, Inc. All rights reserved. This article originally appeared at 54 Colum.L.Rev. 543 (1954). Reprinted by permission.

Robin L. West, Constitutional Skepticism. Reprinted by permission of Robin L. West and the Boston University Law Review.

Joan C. Williams, Deconstructing Gender. Reprinted by permission of Joan C. Williams and the Michigan Law Review Association.

Wendy W. Williams, The Equality Crisis: Some Reflections on Culture, Courts, and Feminism. Reprinted with permission of the Women's Rights Law Reporter.

Summary of Contents

Table of Contents

MODERN CONSTITUTIONAL THEORY

A READER

Fifth Edition

Chapter I

THEORIES OF THE CONSTITUTION

Does the Constitution have a theme? How do we go about interpreting its various provisions? Why is it the business of the Supreme Court to answer these questions? These overarching theoretical questions are addressed in the first three Chapters.

It should be apparent that these are related questions, and authors addressing one issue frequently make explicit or implicit claims about the other issues. For example, if the Constitution is largely about specifying a fair process for making political decisions, one might justify judicial review by charting a role for the Supreme Court of ensuring an open and well-functioning political process; such a perspective might take a dim view of attempts by the Court to read substantive values into the document (such as a right to decide whether or not to terminate a pregnancy). Or, if one believes that judicial review can be justified only if the Court is enforcing decisions by "the people" to constitutionalize certain values, one might support interpretative strategies aimed at uncovering the "original meaning" of the text's provisions.

Many other possible linkages are imaginable. What interpretative methods, for example, might be favored by a theorist who believes that the Supreme Court can contribute to the moral growth of our polity, or by a theorist who understands the Constitution as primarily concerned with ensuring deliberative decision-making by elected officials? In short, as you read each selection in one of the first three Chapters, keep asking yourself how the author might answer the questions raised in the other two Chapters.

Is the Constitution a collection of provisions directed at topical concerns of the late 18th century, a compromise among competing regional and economic interests? Or is there a political theory that lies behind the specific bits of text, supplying a unifying theory to the whole? Assuming we can identify an animating theory of the Constitution, is our Constitution, so understood, a good constitution? These questions are the primary focus of this Chapter.

Before turning to these questions, however, it seems useful to begin a book on constitutional theory by asking a few preliminary questions: What kinds of constitutional arguments are currently part of our legal culture? What exactly is a constitutional theory? And how important is it to have one? We start with Phillip Bobbitt's survey of the modes of constitutional argument. Constitutional theories are nearly always efforts to develop one of these modes into a systematic framework. David Strauss gives us a working definition of the subject: a constitutional theory is an effort to provide a general justification for particular solutions to controversial constitutional issues. Such an effort, he says, proceeds by showing how these solutions flow from a unifying framework and how that framework best justifies our most central constitutional tenets. Richard Posner questions whether such theoretical arguments are likely to prove useful for judges and lawyers, as opposed to academics addressing each other. Richard Fallon argues, in response to Posner and other critics of constitutional theory, that judges need at least a tacit constitutional theory if they are to provide a principled, consistent legal fabric. From this perspective, the diverse constitutional arguments discussed by Bobbitt offer too much leeway for judges, who need the discipline provided by theory.

After these preliminary discussions about the nature of constitutional theory, we consider some of the most noteworthy efforts to provide a theory of the Constitution. In *Democracy and Distrust* (probably the most influential book on constitutional law in the past few decades), John Hart Ely argues that the Constitution is primarily concerned with process and structure—not the identification and preservation of specific substantive values. He suggests that the open-ended provisions of the document—such as the Fourteenth Amendment—be read to further process-based goals. Exercised in this way, judicial review can be seen as enhancing, rather than frustrating, democratic governance. Laurence Tribe's review of Ely's book—*The Puzzling Persistence of Process-Based Constitutional Theories*—is skeptical of a reading of the document simply in "process" terms. Indeed, he argues, even Ely's approach ultimately requires a commitment to substantive values (such as a theory of which groups need special protection in the political process).

To many Americans, the Constitution embodies fundamental moral principles, such as equality, fairness, and justice, that find their expression in the protection of individual rights from oppressive majorities. Ronald Dworkin, a leading advocate of a "moral reading" of the Constitution, argues that judges instinctively rely upon moral judgments in interpreting the document. The "moral reading" is constrained, according to Dworkin, by the requirements that constitutional interpretation "begin in what the framers said" and be fitted to the structure of the Constitution as a whole and the dominant lines of past interpretations. Michael McConnell's critique of Dworkin notes the tension between Dworkin's twin goals of seeking "right answers" and ensuring that judgments "fit" constitutional text and history. He also takes issue with Dworkin's "moral reading" of the Fourteenth Amendment, arguing that Dworkin does not adequately defend the abstract principle of equality that he ascribes to the equal protection clause.

Some important recent constitutional theories view the Constitution as being "about" democracy, but not merely in the commonplace sense of majority rule. We include an excerpt from the first volume of Bruce Ackerman's massive revisionist study of constitutional history. Ackerman argues for a "dualist" understanding of democracy. This two-track model distinguishes between constitutional decisions made by the People and ordinary political decisions reached by the People's elected representatives. Judicial review, from this perspective, presents no "counter-majoritarian difficulty" to the extent it is enforcing a prior higher-track decision by the People against a lower-track decision of the People's agents.

Cass Sunstein contributes another effort to enrich our concept of democracy. According to Sunstein, central to our constitutional system is an "impartiality principle": the idea that government is prohibited from acting on the basis of pure self-interest, power, or whim. Judicial review in service of the impartiality principle furthers the framers' plan to create a system of government—a "deliberative democracy"—that would counteract the dangers of the legacy of monarchy, self-interested representation, and majority tyranny.

The third of these efforts to reconceptualize democracy comes from Jed Rubenfeld. He argues that much of constitutional theory is based on the misguided view that democracy means rule by the current majority. He argues instead that true self-governance includes the ability of a people to make commitments across generations. By embodying such commitments, the Constitution is not a restraint on democracy but a paradigm of its exercise. Note that this theory is directly contrary to Ackerman's argument, which posits that at any given time "The People" retain the prerogative of revamping the Constitution as they see fit. Rubenfeld is similarly at odds with Sunstein, who views the Constitution as empowering contemporary deliberative democracy rather than constraining it.

The Chapter concludes with two "critical perspectives" on the Constitution and constitutionalism. Justice Thurgood Marshall casts a dissenting vote on the Constitution's 1987 Bicentennial celebration. He argues that the constitutional system constructed in Philadelphia was "defective from the start" because of its unwillingness to condemn slavery and other abridgments of fundamental rights. Robin West's article notes the absence of "an explicitly normative debate about the Constitution's value." She argues that the combined claims of the "constitutional faithful" (liberal theorists who urge that the Constitution can be read to achieve liberal ends) and the "constitutional sceptics" (who maintain that the text is indeterminate) have impeded the development of a "progressive constitutional faith" (which challenges a constitutional tradition that fails to condemn unjust concentrations of private power).

A. THE NATURE OF CONSTITUTIONAL THEORY

PHILIP BOBBITT, THE MODALITIES OF CONSTITUTIONAL ARGUMENT

CONSTITUTIONAL INTERPRETATION 12–22 (1991).

I will be speaking of *constitutional modalities*—the ways in which legal propositions are characterized as true from a constitutional point of view. * * * [The] six modalities of constitutional argument are: the historical (relying on the intentions of the framers and ratifiers of the Constitution); textual (looking to the meaning of the words of the Constitution alone, as they would be interpreted by the average contemporary "man on the street"); structural (inferring rules from the relationships that the Constitution mandates among the structures it sets up); doctrinal (applying rules generated by precedent); ethical (deriving rules from those moral commitments of the American ethos that are reflected in the Constitution); and prudential (seeking to balance the costs and benefits of a particular rule). Now let us look at some examples, and a somewhat more formal statement of each form of argument.

Consider the question whether a state may validly enforce a law that makes it a crime to procure an abortion. An *historical* modality may be attributed to constitutional arguments that claim that the framers and ratifiers of the Fourteenth Amendment intended, or did not intend, or that it cannot be ascertained whether it was their intention, to protect pregnant women from a state's coercion, through threats of fines and imprisonment, to bear children. Similarly, an historical modality might approach the abortion question as: did the framers and ratifiers of the Fourteenth Amendment intend to countenance, or to overturn by means of the Amendment, or are their intentions unclear as to the effect of the Amendment regarding, those state laws that existed at the time of ratification that prohibited abortions?

Oftentimes this modality is confused with textual argument since both can have reference to the specific text of the Constitution. Historical, or "originalist" approaches to construing the text, however, are distinctive in their reference back to what a particular provision is thought to have meant to its ratifiers. Thus, when Justice Taney in the *Dred Scott* case was called upon to construe the scope of the diversity jurisdiction in Article III, which provides for suits "between citizens of the several states," so that he might decide whether a slave could seek his freedom in a diversity suit before a federal court, he wrote:

> It becomes necessary to determine who were the citizens of the several states when the constitution was adopted. And in order to do this we must recur to the governments and institutions of the colonies. We must inquire who at the time were recognized as citizens of the states, whose rights and liberties [had been] outraged by the English government and who declared their independence and assumed the powers of government to defend their rights [by force] of arms. We refer to these historical facts for the purpose of showing the fixed opinions concerning the Negro race upon which the statesmen of that day spoke and acted.[7]

Now consider the same question—who are the "citizens" of the phrase that provides for suits in federal court "between citizens of different states" ("diversity" suits)—from another point of view. A *textual* modality may be attributed to arguments that the text of the Constitution would, to the average person, appear to declare, or deny, or be too vague to say whether, a suit between a black American citizen resident in a state and a white American citizen resident in another state, is a "controversy between citizens of different states." I would imagine that the contemporary meaning of these words is rather different than that which Taney found them to mean to the framers and ratifiers of 1789. One should not be tempted to conclude, however, that textual approaches are inevitably more progressive than originalist approaches. Sometimes the text can be a straitjacket, confining the judge to language that would have been different if its drafters had foreseen later events. Thus consider whether wiretapping is prohibited by the Fourth Amendment, which guarantees "the right of the people to be secure in their persons, houses, papers and effects against unreasonable searches and seizures." Here is Chief Justice Taft in a case in which incriminating information was largely obtained by federal prohibition officers intercepting messages on the telephones of the conspirators:

> The amendment itself [he says] shows that the search is to be of material things—the person, the house, his papers or his effects. The amendment does not forbid what was done here for there was no seizure. The evidence was secured by the sense of hearing and that only. There was not entry of the houses. The language of the amendment cannot be extended and expanded.[9]

By contrast, a later court had no trouble finding that wiretapping came within the Amendment. It simply relied upon historical argument—the intentions that animated the adoption of the amendment—and concluded that:

---

[7]Dred Scott v. Sandford, 60 U.S. (19 How.) 393, 407 [, 409] (1856).

[9]Olmstead v. United States, 277 U.S. 438, 464 (1928).

> The purpose of the . . . Fourth Amendment [is] to keep the state out of constitutionally protected areas until it has reason to believe that a specific crime has been or is being committed.[10]

Consider another constitutional question: can a court issue a subpoena (or should it enjoin some other subpoena) for the disclosure of the President's working notes and diaries? To say that the institutional relationships promulgated by the Constitution require or are incompatible with or tolerate a particular answer to this question is to use a *structural* mode of argument. There are many recent, celebrated examples of this form of argument to be found in the cases of the US Supreme Court; indeed the 1980s were particularly notable for the Court's focus on structural issues. But structural argument is hardly a recent invention. *McCulloch v. Maryland,* the principal foundation case for constitutional analysis, relies almost wholly on structural approaches. In determining whether a Maryland tax on the Federal Bank of the United States could be enforced, Chief Justice Marshall studiedly refuses to specify the particular text that supports his argument, and explicitly rejects reliance on historical arguments, preferring instead to state the rationale on inferences for the structure of federalism. Such a structure could not be maintained, he concluded, if the states, whose officials are elected by a state's constituency, could tax the agencies of the federal government present in a state and thereby tax a nationwide constituency. The constitutional structure would not tolerate such a practice.

* * *

Structural arguments are a little less intuitively obvious than arguments from the text or history of the Constitution, so perhaps it would be well to briefly outline their characteristic form. Usually, arguments in this modality are straightforward: first, an uncontroversial statement about a constitutional structure is introduced [for example, * * * the statement that the right to vote for a member of Congress is provided for in the Constitution]; second, a relationship is inferred from this structure [that this right, for example, gives rise to the federal power to protect it and is not dependent on state protection]; third, a factual assertion about the world is made [that, if unprotected, the structure of federal representation would be at the mercy of local violence]. Finally a conclusion is drawn that provides the rule in the case. * * *

Consider whether the state can require mandatory testing for the AIDS virus antibodies. To say that it is wise, or unwise, or simply unclear on the present facts whether or not it is wise to permit such testing is to propose an evaluation from a *prudential* point of view. In the first half of this century, this mode of constitutional argument was principally associated with

[10] Berger v. New York, 388 U.S. 41, 59 (1967).

doctrines that sought to protect the political position of the courts. But the dramatic national crises of depression and world war soon provided ample reason to introduce the practical effects of constitutional doctrine into the rationales underpinning doctrine. For example, one such case arose when, in the depths of the midwestern farm depression, the Minnesota legislature passed a statute providing that anyone who was unable to pay a mortgage could be granted a moratorium from foreclosure. On its face such a statute not only appeared to realize the fears of the framers that state legislatures would compromise the credit market by enacting debtor relief statutes, but also plainly to violate the Contracts Clause that was the textual outcome of such concerns. Moreover, the structure of national economic union strongly counseled against permitting states to protect their constituents by exploding a national recovery program that depended on restoring confidence to banking operations. Nevertheless the Supreme Court upheld the statute, observing that:

> An emergency existed in Minnesota which furnished a proper occasion for the exercise of the reserved power of the state to protect the vital interests of the community.[16]

Very simply, the Court recognized the political expediency of the legislature's action and acquiesced in it. * * *

[P]rudential argument * * * is by no means confined to the extremes a nation undergoes in emergencies. Of course in such circumstances prudential arguments are likeliest to be decisive. But, as one of prudentialism's most eloquent practitioners argued, such an approach has a place in every decision:

> The accomplished fact, affairs and interests that have formed around it, and perhaps popular acceptance of it—these are elements * * * that may properly enter into a decision * * *; and they may also enter into the shaping of the judgment, the applicable principle itself.[18]

Prudential argument is actuated by facts, as these play into political and economic policies as to which the Constitution is itself agnostic. The legal rule to be applied is derived from a calculus of costs and benefits, when the facts are taken into account. Accordingly, this often gives rise to a "balancing test" (the balance being a scales, not a tightrope.)

By contrast, when we say that a neutral, general principle derived from the caselaw construing the Constitution should apply, does not apply or may apply, we make an appeal in a *doctrinal* mode. * * *

To familiarize oneself with this form of argument, let us take up this question: to what extent can a state constitutionally aid parochial schools? Suppose, for example, that parochial school students whose schools are not

---

[16] Home Building and Loan Assoc. v. Blaisdell, 290 U.S. 398, 444 (1934).

[18] A. Bickel, The Least Dangerous Branch (1962), 116.

on the route of free public school buses are given a cash allowance by the state to provide for their transportation. Does this offend the Establishment Clause of the First Amendment because the state is bearing the burdens of costs that would otherwise be borne by church members, in much the way that the government in Great Britain, a country that has an established church, provides funds to supplement the income of the Church of England? A judge confronting such a case would probably begin, not by reading the text of the First Amendment which states a rule in rather general terms but by turning to precedent to find similar cases in which authoritative decisions would govern the present one. Not surprisingly, in the area of Establishment jurisprudence there is a great deal of constitutional doctrine, developed in many cases. The standards these cases develop and apply can be stated as legal rules; the case "on point"—that is, whose facts are similar in those aspects that are relevant to the legal question being posed—is probably *Everson v. Board of Education,* which sustained the power of local authorities to provide free transportation for children attending church schools. In *Everson* the Supreme Court treated the provision of transportation as a form of public welfare legislation, noting that it was being extended by the state "to all its citizens without regard to their religious belief." The Court wrote:

> It is undoubtedly true that children are helped to get to church schools. There is even a possibility that some of the children might not be sent to the church schools if the parents were compelled to pay their children's bus fares out of their pockets when transportation to a public school would have been paid for by the State.[21]

Transportation, however, benefited the child in the same way as did police protection at crossings, fire protection, connections for sewage disposal, public highways, and sidewalks. Based on this rationale, subsequent cases have developed a three-pronged test: does the state program have a secular purpose; is its principal effect neither to advance nor inhibit religion; does its administration excessively entangle the state in religious affairs?[22]

Applying this test to the question above, the judge might write: "*Everson* must be distinguished from the instant case because the program in *Everson* provided transportation common to all students, whereas here only some students—the parochial ones—are given cash allowances. While we do not question that the legislature had a secular purpose in mind, we think the evidence indicated that the effect of these allowances was in fact to make the parochial schools more attractive to parents than their secular counterparts, and thereby advance the cause of religious institutions.

[21][330 U.S. 1, 17 (1947).]

[22]Lemon v. Kurtzman, 403 U.S. 602 (1971).

Moreover, the oversight required of the state to ensure that the allowances are in fact spent on providing a system of parochial school transportation intrudes the administrative apparatus of the state into the affairs of the church schools. This can only lead to the interference with budgets and an insistence on allocations for transportation that will excessively entangle the state in the administration of church affairs. Accordingly the program must be held unconstitutional."

Or a judge might write: "*Everson,* which also involved public transportation to parochial school students, governs this case. Here as there, the state's program provides aid to students and their parents, and not—as in cases that have applied *Everson* and struck down state assistance in this area—direct assistance to church-related schools. Its secular purpose, to provide school transportation at greater efficiency and less cost to the state than expanding its own bus fleets, is apparent. Like school lunches, public health services, and secular textbooks, the transportation provided here confers a benefit on the parochial student that is at parity with what the secular student receives. Thus its effect is neither to advance nor inhibit religion, but rather to avoid exacting a penalty from the parochial student. Finally, whatever state management is required to administer the program will be limited to the oversight of transportation; such involvement as there may be need not, therefore, excessively entangle the state in those religious matters with regard to which it has no role."

In either case, the hypothetical judge has applied a rule derived from the relevant caselaw. The rule is neutral as to the parties; that is, it applies equally to Catholics and Jews and atheist claimants and does not vary depending on who is bringing or defending the suit. And the rule is general, that is, it applies to all cases in which the state is arguably giving assistance to religious institutions, and is not confined to the facts of the original case that gave birth to the rule. One more point, however, should be made about this modality: its operation is not confined to the application of *stare decisis,* that is, the strict adherence to previously decided cases. On the contrary, in the American system one of the principles of doctrinalism is that the Supreme Court may reverse the relevant precedent. This would appear to follow from the family of modalities—that provide alternative legal rules—and the supremacy of the Constitution to the acts of government (including, of course, the judicial branch). The Court is entitled, indeed obligated, to overrule itself when it is persuaded that a particular precedent was wrongly decided and should not be applied.

Finally, let us consider the modality of ethical argument. This form of argument denotes an appeal to those elements of the American cultural ethos that are reflected in the Constitution. The fundamental American constitutional ethos is the idea of limited government, the presumption of which holds that all residual authority remains in the private sphere. Thus when we argue that a particular constitutional conclusion is obliged by, or permitted, or forbidden by the American ethos that has allocated certain decisions to the individual or to private institutions, we are arguing in an *ethical* mode.

Ethical arguments arise as a consequence of the fundamental constitutional arrangement by which rights, in the American system, can be defined as those choices beyond the power of government to compel. Thus structural and ethical arguments share some similarities, as each is essentially an inferred set of arguments. Like structural arguments, ethical arguments do not depend on the construction of any particular piece of text, but rather on the necessary relationships that can be inferred from the overall arrangement expressed in the text. Structural argument infers rules from the powers granted to governments; ethical argument, by contrast, infers rules from the powers denied to government. The principal error one can make regarding ethical argument is to assume that any statute or executive act is unconstitutional if it causes effects that are incompatible with the American cultural ethos. This equates ethical argument, a constitutional form, with moral argument generally.

Let us review a hypothetical example that shows the basic pattern of ethical argument. Note that while the American cultural ethos may encompass cheeseburgers, rock and roll, and a passion for Japanese electronics, the American *constitutional* ethos is largely confined to the reservation of powers not delegated to a limited government.

It was recently reported that a state judge in South Carolina had given the choice of thirty-year prison sentences or castration to three convicted sex offenders. Suppose a convicted man accepted the bargain and was released on probation terms that incorporated this pledge (as by drug-induced impotence). Then suppose that he ceased taking the prescribed drug. If his probation were revoked, a constitutional challenge to the terms of his probation might take this form:

1. The reservation to the individual of the decision to have children is deeply rooted in the American notion of autonomy; there is no express constitutional power to implement a program of eugenics.
2. Moreover, such programs are not a conventionally appropriate means to any express power.
3. Those means denied the federal government are also denied the states.
4. The South Carolina sentence amounted to ordering a man to comply with a eugenics scheme that deemed him ineligible to procreate.

The element of the American ethos at stake is the reservation to individuals and families of the freedom to make certain kinds of decisions. Similar sorts of arguments are to be found in cases in which a state attempted to bar schools from teaching foreign languages;[26] in which a state passed a compulsory education act requiring every school-age child to attend public school (that is, implicitly outlawing private schools);[27] in which a local zoning ordinance was applied to prohibit a grandmother from living with her grandchildren;[28] in which a hospital sought authority to amputate a gangrenous limb from an elderly man who refused his consent;[29] in which a man allegedly suffering from delusions (but concededly harmless) was confined to a mental hospital for almost twenty-five years without treatment.[30] One may test one's mastery of this form of argument by taking each of these examples and stating an ethical argument to resolve it, e.g., (1) There is no express constitutional power to monopolize education; (2) Moreover, a statute outlawing private education is not an appropriate means to any express power (such as regulating commerce or providing for armed forces); (3) The decision to educate one's children privately or parochially or publicly is reserved to the family; (4) A statute compelling attendance exclusively at public schools amounts to a scheme to coerce families into a particular educational choice and destroy private educational options.

These then are the six modalities of constitutional argument in the United States. [E]ach of these forms of argument can be used to construct an ideology, a set of political and practical commitments whose values are internally consistent and can be distinguished, externally, from competing ideologies. * * * [T]he reader should not conclude that, because of this relationship—because, for example, some persons may believe that one particular modality represents the only legitimate means of interpreting the Constitution (e.g., historical argument) since it is verifiable by a resort to materials (e.g., the intentions of the ratifiers) that are mandated according to a particular political theory of interpretation (e.g., "originalism")—the modalities of argument are no more than instrumental, rhetorical devices to be deployed in behalf of various political ideologies. The modalities of constitutional argument are the ways in which law statements in constitutional matters are assessed; standing alone they assert nothing about the world. But they need only stand alone to provide the means for making constitutional argument.

There is no constitutional legal argument outside these modalities. Outside these forms, a proposition about the U.S. constitution can be a fact, or be elegant, or be amusing or even poetic, and although such assessments

---

[26] Meyer v. Nebraska, 262 U.S. 390 (1923).
[27] Pierce v. Society of Sisters, 268 U.S. 510 (1925).
[28] Moore v. City of East Cleveland, 431 U.S. 494 (1977).
[29] In re Quackenbush, 156 N.J.Super. 282, 383 A.2d 785 (1978).
[30] O'Connor v. Donaldson, 422 U.S. 563 (1975).

exist as legal statements in some possible legal world, they are not actualized in our legal world.

DAVID A. STRAUSS, WHAT IS CONSTITUTIONAL THEORY?

87 CAL. L. REV. 581, 582–584, 587–588 (1999).

We can best understand constitutional theory, I believe, if we see it as an exercise in justification. Specifically, a constitutional theory is an effort to justify a set of prescriptions about how certain controversial constitutional issues should be decided. The justification is addressed to people within a particular legal culture (in the case of the United States Constitution, of course, the legal culture of the United States). A constitutional theory justifies its prescriptions about controversial issues by drawing on the bases of agreement that exist within the legal culture and trying to extend those agreed-upon principles to decide the cases or issues on which people disagree. This is the conception of justification given by John Rawls in *A Theory of Justice*:

> [J]ustification is argument addressed to those who disagree with us, or to ourselves when we are of two minds. It presumes a clash of views between persons or within one person, and seeks to convince others, or ourselves, of the reasonableness of the principles upon which our claims and judgments are founded. Being designed to reconcile by reason, justification proceeds from what all parties to the discussion hold in common. . . . [T]he argument . . . proceed[s] from some consensus. This is the nature of justification.[7]

There are many points of agreement within the American legal culture. Some are quite abstract; some are highly concrete. No one denies that the text of the Constitution matters, indeed matters a lot. [T]his is simply a fact about our legal culture. The reason the Constitution is law is not that it declares itself to be law; if that were the reason, any document that declared itself to be law would have to be treated that way. The Constitution enjoys a legal status in our society that the Articles of Confederation—or, for that matter, the Declaration of Independence—does not; but at bottom, that is just because our culture has come to treat the Constitution that way.

Our legal culture agrees on other fundamental matters as well. On the abstract level, probably everyone agrees that the Framers' intentions count for something, although there is of course a great deal of disagreement about how much they count. Nearly everyone also acknowledges that in interpreting the Constitution, precedent counts for something. There is also agreement about relatively concrete matters. Today, for example, everyone

---

[7] John Rawls, A Theory of Justice 580-581 (1971).

agrees that *Brown v. Board of Education*[11] was rightly decided (or at least was not a usurpation or a lawless act by the judiciary). No one seems to question any more that, for the most part, the Bill of Rights applies to the states. And there is general agreement on the basic contours of, for example, First Amendment doctrine: a theory of judicial restraint that required judges to defer across the board to legislation restricting speech—a theory embraced by Justice Felix Frankfurter a few decades ago—would not be acceptable today.

* * *

A constitutional theory tries to take such points of agreement and organize them in a way that will satisfy at least two criteria. First, the theory cannot contradict any of the points of agreement within the legal culture that are absolutely rock solid, such as the relevance of the Constitution's text or, today, the legitimacy of *Brown*. Second, the theory should say something about how to approach controversial issues. Otherwise, there is little point in constructing a theory.

But what about the suspicion that there is something unprincipled about a constitutional theory if it does not "bind [an] . . . adherent to at least some results that she would otherwise reject?"[31] Perhaps this widely held intuition can be understood in the following way. While there is a great deal of agreement within our society, and our legal culture, on certain moral matters, there is also a great deal of disagreement. One reason we have legal systems—indeed, government generally—is so that society can decide how to act with respect to issues on which there is great moral disagreement. Citizens might disagree about the morality of, say, affirmative action; but if the legislature duly adopts an affirmative action measure and the courts uphold it, everyone agrees that the measure is to be carried out until it is repealed or otherwise lawfully undone.

One thing we do, then, when we accept a legal system, is in effect to say to our fellow citizens that we are not going to insist on having everything our way. More precisely, we are saying that we recognize that there is intense disagreement about certain moral matters; that if society is to function, some of those matters must be authoritatively resolved, and everyone must live with the resolution; and that we understand that the institutions we establish to resolve those disagreements might sometimes reach the result we do not favor. In any large and heterogeneous society—that is, a society that must confront many different issues, and in which there are many different views—nearly everyone will lose occasionally.

---

[11] 347 U.S. 483 (1954).

[31] Fallon, [*How to Choose a Constitutional Theory*, 87 Calif. L. Rev. 535], 539 [(1999)].

A constitutional theory prescribes something about the results a legal system should reach in controversial cases. If that theory always produces the results in controversial cases that the theory's adherents would have favored anyway, we are entitled to suspect that the theory has been rigged. That is, we might suspect that the theory does not represent a serious effort to gather together widely shared bases of agreement and use them to resolve controversial issues, but instead slights views that do not support the outcomes desired by the proponent of the theory.

RICHARD A. POSNER, AGAINST CONSTITUTIONAL THEORY

73 NYU L. Rev. 1–4, 11–12 (1998)

Constitutional theory, as I shall use the term, is the effort to develop a generally accepted theory to guide the interpretation of the Constitution of the United States. It is distinct on the one hand from inquiries of a social scientific character into the nature, provenance, and consequences of constitutionalism—the sort of thing one associates mainly with historians and political scientists, such as Charles Beard, Jon Elster, and Stephen Holmes—and on the other hand from commentary on specific cases and doctrines, the sort of thing one associates with legal doctrinalists, such as Kathleen Sullivan, Laurence Tribe, and William Van Alstyne. A number of scholars straddle this divide, such as Ronald Dworkin and Lawrence Lessig, and although I mean to keep to one side of it in this lecture, the straddle is no accident. Constitutional theorists are normativists; their theories are meant to influence the way judges decide difficult constitutional cases; when the theorists are law-trained, as most of them are, they cannot resist telling their readers which cases they think were decided consistently with or contrary to their theory. Most constitutional theorists, indeed, believe in social reform through judicial action. Constitutional theory that is strongly influenced by moral theory has additional problems, as I have discussed recently and will not repeat here.

I must stress at the outset the limited domain of constitutional theory. Nothing pretentious enough to warrant the name of theory is required to decide cases in which the text or history of the Constitution provides sure guidance. No theory is required to determine how many Senators each state may have. Somewhat more difficult interpretive issues, such as whether the self-incrimination clause should be interpreted as forbidding the prosecutor to comment on the defendant's failure to take the stand, can be resolved pretty straightforwardly by considering the consequences of rival interpretations. Were the prosecutor allowed to argue to the jury that the defendant's refusal to testify should be taken as an admission of guilt, it would be extremely difficult for defense counsel to counter with some plausible explanation consistent with his client's being innocent. So allowing comment would pretty much destroy the privilege—at least as it is currently understood. That is an important qualification. It has been strongly argued that the current understanding is incorrect, that the purpose of the privilege is merely to prevent improper methods of interrogation; and if this is right then there is no basis for the rule of no comment. Maybe, as this example suggests, when fully ventilated no issue of constitutional law not founded on one of the numerical provisions of the Constitution is beyond contestation. But as a practical matter there are large areas of constitutional law that the debates over constitutional theory do not touch and that consequently I shall ignore.

Constitutional theory in the sense in which I am using the term is at least as old as the Federalist papers. And yet after more than two centuries no signs of closure or even, it seems to me, of progress, are visible. The reason is that constitutional theory has no power to command agreement from people not already predisposed to accept the theorist's policy prescriptions. It has no power partly because it is normative, partly because interpretation, the subject of constitutional theory, is not susceptible of theoretical resolution, and partly because normativists in general and lawyers (and as I said most constitutional theorists are lawyers, albeit professors of law rather than practicing lawyers) do not like to be backed into a corner by committing themselves to a theory that might be falsified by data, just as no practicing lawyer wants to take a position that might force him to concede that his client has no case. Neither type of lawyer wants the validity of his theory to be a hostage to what a factual inquiry might bring to light. But as a result, constitutional theory, while often rhetorically powerful, lacks the agreement-coercing power of the best natural and social science.

* * *

The leading theorists are intelligent people, and it is possible that their lively debates have a diffuse but cumulatively significant impact on the tone and texture and occasionally even on the outcomes of constitutional cases. (Whether it is a good impact is a different question, and one that cannot be answered on the basis of existing knowledge.) If the theorists do not have a large audience among judges, and I do not think they do, they have a large audience among their own students and hence among the judges' law clerks, whose influence on constitutional law, though small, is not completely negligible. Yet the real significance of constitutional theory is, I believe, as a sign of the increased academification of law school professors, who are much more inclined than they used to be to write for other professors rather than for judges and practitioners. The causes of this academification are beyond the scope of this Article, but a particularly mundane cause is simply that there are so many more law professors than there used to be that it has become possible for them to have a nonnegligible audience for their work even if their work is read only by other law professors, as I believe is largely the case with regard to constitutional theory. In addition, as constitutional theory becomes more "theoretical," less tethered to the practice of law, it becomes increasingly transparent to professors in other fields, such as political theory and moral philosophy; and by this means the ranks of the constitutional theorists grow to the point of self-sufficiency. Constitutional theory today circulates in a medium that is largely opaque to the judge and the practicing lawyer.

RICHARD H. FALLON, HOW TO CHOOSE A CONSTITUTIONAL THEORY

87 CAL.L.REV. 537, 573–579 (1999)

[One] related argument against traditional constitutional theory focuses specifically on whether constitutional theory is valuable to judges. As Cass Sunstein points out, the Supreme Court has never made an "official choice" among competing theories.[215] Arguing "[a]gainst theories, [a]gainst rules,[216] Sunstein maintains that judges are unlikely to have any special aptitude for theory.[217] He further asserts that we are frequently likely to get better decisions if Supreme Court Justices resolve issues on a case-specific, shallowly theorized basis.[218] According to Sunstein, the Court should avoid entanglement with large, confusing, and often divisive abstractions, such as the claims of constitutional theories.[219]

I agree with Professor Sunstein that a judge does not need a fully articulated theory in order to do her job. A judge or Justice can proceed case by case. Indeed, in the best tradition of the common law, she may have good reason to avoid theoretical commitments that may prove untenable in light of events and arguments that she cannot foresee. Nonetheless, a judge's work cannot be innocent of constitutional theory, nor can a judge escape obligations of theoretical consistency.

For a judge as much as for anyone else, it is impossible to engage in constitutional argument without making at least implicit assumptions about appropriate methodology. For example, to adopt an argument based on precedent is to presuppose the validity of a theory that makes precedent at least relevant and possibly controlling. Theoretical commitments are also

---

[215] [Cass R. Sunstein, The Supreme Court, 1995 Term–Foreword: Leaving Things Undecided, 110 Harv. L. Rev. 4], at 13 [(1996)].

[216] Id. at 14.

[217] See Cass R. Sunstein, Legal Reasoning and Political Conflict 46 (1996)(citing the "limited capacities of judges" as a reason why constitutional adjudication should generally turn on "low-level principles: rather than abstract, general theories).

[218] See id. at 35-58.

[219] See id. at 171-82; cf. id. at 56-57 ("Judges should adopt a presumption rather than a taboo against high-level theorization.")

implied when a judge or Justice either appeals to the original understanding or rejects such appeals.

Moreover, in offering arguments that reflect theoretical assumptions, participants in constitutional debates assume obligations of consistency. Suppose that Justice A, dissenting in one case, argues that the Supreme Court is bound to follow the original understanding of constitutional language, but that Justice A herself refuses to be bound by the original understanding in another case. Or suppose that Justice B criticizes Justice A for deciding an unnecessary constitutional issue, but then herself decides an unnecessary issue in a subsequent case. Unless the cases are persuasively distinguishable, Justices A and B have both fallen short of professional ideals. Judicial inconsistency affronts the rule of law. A substantive injustice may also occur if relevant similar cases are treated differently. More insidiously, a failure of judges and Justices to behave consistently may breed a destructive, spiraling cynicism. The practice of constitutional adjudication depends for its integrity on an assumption of good faith:

> There must be a sense that [judges and Justices with opposing views] are advancing legal arguments because they believe in them deeply and not as a stratagem for imposing their will on the law. There must be a sense that reasons matter more than results. The power to interpret carries the responsibility of good faith and self-denial. When these are destroyed, nothing remains but counting votes and the exercise of raw power.[223]

Again, by suggesting that judges and Justices have obligations of methodological consistency, I do not imply that each needs to, or indeed should, begin by endorsing a comprehensive constitutional theory. I do mean to claim, however, that issues of constitutional theory are unavoidable, especially for judges. Every judge and Justice therefore needs at least parts of a constitutional theory, even if not a complete one. Commitments to theoretical tenets occur willy-nilly in the decision of cases.

* * *

We should assess constitutional theories in light of their capacity to promote the rule of law, political democracy, and a scheme of individual rights consonant with substantive justice. The last of these criteria, in particular, is substantive rather than formal. For those who would choose a constitutional theory, ultimate questions of political morality therefore cannot be avoided. But neither can the choice of a constitutional theory occur solely by reference to ideals. A crucial practical question is how any particular theory would probably be employed—for good or for ill—by those who are likely to be judges in particular historical contexts.

---

[223] Edward Lazarus, Closed Chambers 249 (1998).

In light of the complexity of the issues on which choice of a constitutional theory appropriately depends, many will wish to avoid opting definitively for one theory and renouncing all others. They will instead prefer a case-by-case approach, similar to that of common law judges. This can indeed be a responsible stance. Nonetheless, taking positions on issues of constitutional theory is ultimately unavoidable. It is impossible to engage in constitutional argument without making methodological assumptions. Moreover, anyone who engages in good-faith argumentation assumes obligations of methodological consistency. The enterprise of constitutional justification requires consistent application of fair standards of valid argument.

To recognize that a constitutional theory should be chosen partly on instrumental grounds is, therefore, not to license unprincipled manipulations. Once adopted, a constitutional theory ought to impose constraints on those who accept it. Nonetheless, it would reflect a deep mistake—a misunderstanding of what constitutional theory is for—not to evaluate constitutional theories based on the results that they are likely to produce.

B. PROCESS THEORY

JOHN HART ELY, POLICING THE PROCESS OF REPRESENTATION: THE COURT AS REFEREE

DEMOCRACY AND DISTRUST 73–84, 86–95, 97–101 (1980).

[In earlier chapters, Professor Ely discusses "interpretivism" and "noninterpretivism"—"the former indicating that judges deciding constitutional issues should confine themselves to enforcing norms that are stated or clearly implicit in the written Constitution, the latter the contrary view that courts should go beyond that set of references and enforce norms that cannot be discovered within the four corners of the document." He argues that "clause-bound interpretivism" (the claim that constitutional phrases be given content solely on the basis of their language and surrounding legislative history) is both impossible and unwise; yet "noninterpretivism" appears to invite judicial value imposition.]

All this seems to leave us in a quandary. An interpretivist approach—at least one that approaches constitutional provisions as self-contained units—proves on analysis incapable of keeping faith with the evident spirit of certain of the provisions. When we search for an external source of values with which to fill in the Constitution's open texture, however—one that will not simply end up constituting the Court a council of legislative revision—we search in vain. Despite the usual assumption that these are the only options, however, they are not, for value imposition is not the only possible response to the realization that we have a Constitution that needs filling in. A quite different approach is available, and to discern its outlines we need look no further than to the Warren Court.

* * *

Many of the Warren Court's most controversial decisions concerned criminal procedure or other questions of what judicial or administrative process is due before serious consequences may be visited upon individuals—process-oriented decisions in the most ordinary sense. But a concern with process in a broader sense—with the process by which the laws that govern society are made—animated its other decisions as well. Its unprecedented activism in the fields of political expression and association obviously fits this broader pattern. Other Courts had recognized the connection between such political activity and the proper functioning of the democratic process: the Warren Court was the first seriously to act upon it. That Court was also the first to move into, and once there seriously to occupy, the voter qualification and malapportionment areas. These were certainly interventionist decisions, but the interventionism was fueled not by a desire on the part of the Court to vindicate particular substantive values it had determined were important or fundamental, but rather by a desire to ensure that the political process—which is where such values *are* properly identified, weighed, and accommodated—was open to those of all viewpoints on something approaching an equal basis.

Finally there were the important decisions insisting on equal treatment for society's habitual unequals: notably racial minorities, but also aliens, "illegitimates," and poor people. But rather than announcing that good or value X was so important or fundamental it simply had to be provided or protected, the Court's message here was that insofar as political officials had chosen to provide or protect X for some people (generally people like themselves), they had better make sure that everyone was being similarly accommodated or be prepared to explain pretty convincingly why not. * * *

THE *CAROLENE PRODUCTS* FOOTNOTE

The Warren Court's approach was foreshadowed in a famous footnote in *United States v. Carolene Products Co.,* decided in 1938. Justice Stone's opinion for the Court upheld a federal statute prohibiting the interstate shipment of filled milk, on the ground that all it had to be was "rational" and it assuredly was that. Footnote four suggested, however, that mere rationality might not always be enough:

> There may be narrower scope for operation of the presumption of constitutionality when legislation appears on its face to be within a specific prohibition of the Constitution, such as those of the first ten amendments, which are deemed equally specific when held to be embraced within the Fourteenth * * *.
>
> It is unnecessary to consider now whether legislation which restricts those political processes which can ordinarily be expected to bring about repeal of undesirable legislation, is to be subjected to more

exacting judicial scrutiny under the general prohibitions of the Fourteenth Amendment than are most other types of legislation * * *.

Nor need we enquire whether similar considerations enter into the review of statutes directed at particular religious * * * or national * * * or racial minorities * * *; whether prejudice against discrete and insular minorities may be a special condition, which tends seriously to curtail the operation of those political processes ordinarily to be relied upon to protect minorities, and which may call for a correspondingly more searching judicial inquiry.[7]

* * *

For all its notoriety and influence, the *Carolene Products* footnote has not been adequately elaborated. Paragraph one has always seemed to some commentators not quite to go with the other two. Professor Lusky, who as Stone's law clerk was substantially responsible for the footnote, has recently revealed that the first paragraph was added at the request of Chief Justice Hughes. Any implied substantive criticism seems misplaced: positive law has its claims, even when it doesn't fit some grander theory. It's true, though, that paragraphs two and three are more interesting, and it is the relationship between those two paragraphs that has not been adequately elaborated. Popular control and egalitarianism are surely both ancient American ideals; indeed, dictionary definitions of "democracy" tend to incorporate both. Frequent conjunction is not the same thing as consistency, however, and at least on the surface a principle of popular control suggests an ability on the part of a majority simply to outvote a minority and thus deprive its members of goods they desire. Borrowing Paul Freund's word, I have suggested that both *Carolene Products* themes are concerned with participation: they ask us to focus not on whether this or that substantive value is unusually important or fundamental, but rather on whether the opportunity to participate either in the political processes by which values are appropriately identified and accommodated, or in the accommodation those processes have reached, has been unduly constricted. But the fact that two concepts can fit under the same verbal umbrella isn't enough to render them consistent either, and a system of equal participation in the processes of government is by no means self-evidently linked to a system of presumptively equal participation in the benefits and costs that process generates; in many ways it seems calculated to produce just the opposite effect. To understand the ways these two sorts of participation join together in a coherent political theory, it is necessary to focus more insistently * * * on the American system of representative democracy.

[7] 304 U.S. 144, 152–53 n. 4 (1938) (citations omitted).

REPRESENTATIVE GOVERNMENT

Representative democracy is perhaps most obviously a system of government suited to situations in which it is for one reason or another impractical for the citizenry actually to show up and personally participate in the legislative process. But the concept of representation, as understood by our forebears, was richer than this. Prerevolutionary rhetoric posited a continuing conflict between the interests of "the rulers" on the one hand, and those of "the ruled" (or "the people") on the other.[10] A solution was sought by building into the concept of representation the idea of an association of the interests of the two groups. Thus the representatives in the new government were visualized as "citizens," persons of unusual ability and character to be sure, but nonetheless "of" the people. Upon conclusion of their service, the vision continued, they would return to the body of the people and thus to the body of the ruled. In addition, even while in office, the idea was that they would live under the regime of the laws they passed and not exempt themselves from their operation: this obligation to include themselves among the ruled would ensure a community of interest and guard against oppressive legislation. The framers realized that even visions need enforcement mechanisms: "some force to oppose the insidious tendency of power to separate * * * the rulers from the ruled" was required.[17] The principal force envisioned was the ballot: the people in their self-interest would choose representatives whose interests intertwined with theirs and by the critical reelection decision ensure that they stayed that way, in particular that the representatives did not shield themselves from the rigors of the laws they passed.

Actually it may not matter so much whether our representatives are treating themselves the way they treat the rest of us. Indeed it may be precisely because in some ways they treat themselves better, that they seem so desperately to want to be reelected. And it may be that desire for reelection, more than any community of interest, that is our insurance policy. If most of us feel we are being subjected to unreasonable treatment by our representatives, we retain the ability—irrespective of whether they are formally or informally insulating themselves—to turn them out of office. What the system, at least as described thus far, does *not* ensure is the effective protection of minorities whose interests differ from the interests of most of the rest of us. For if it is not the "many" who are being treated unreasonably but rather only some minority, the situation will not be so comfortably amenable to political correction. Indeed there may be political pressures to *encourage* our representatives to pass laws that treat the majority coalition on whose continued support they depend in one way, and

[10]L. Lusky, By What Right? 110–11 (1975).

[17][Buel, "Democracy and The American Revolution: A Frame of Reference," 21 Wm. & M.Q. 165, 184 (1964).]

one or more minorities whose backing they don't need less favorably. Even assuming we were willing and able to give it teeth, a requirement that our representatives treat themselves as they treat most of the rest of us would be no guarantee whatever against unequal treatment for minorities.

This is not to say that the oppression of minorities was a development our forebears were prepared to accept as inevitable. The "republic" they envisioned was not some "winner-take-all" system in which the government pursued the interests of a privileged few or even of only those groups that could work themselves into some majority coalition, but rather—leaving slavery to one side, which of course is precisely what they did—one in which the representatives would govern in the interest of the whole people. Thus every citizen was said to be entitled to equivalent respect, and equality was a frequently mentioned republican concern. Its place in the Declaration of Independence, for example, could hardly be more prominent. When it came to describing the actual mechanics of republican government in the Constitution, however, this concern for equality got comparatively little explicit attention. This seems to have been largely because of an assumption of "pure" republican political and social theory that we have brushed but not yet stressed: that "the people" were an essentially homogenous group whose interests did not vary significantly. Though most often articulated as if it were an existing reality, this was at best an ideal, and the fact that wealth redistribution of some form—ranging from fairly extreme to fairly modest proposals—figured in so much early republican theorizing, while doubtless partly explainable simply in terms of the perceived desirability of such a change, also was quite consciously connected to republicanism's political theory. To the extent that existing heterogeneity of interest was a function of wealth disparity, redistribution would reduce it. To the extent that the ideal of homogeneity could be achieved, legislation in the interest of most would necessarily be legislation in the interest of all, and extensive further attention to equality of treatment would be unnecessary.

The key assumption here, that everyone's interests are essentially identical, is obviously a hard one for our generation to swallow, and in fact we know perfectly well that many of our forebears were ambivalent about it too. Thus the document of 1789 and 1791, though at no point explicitly invoking the concept of equality, did strive by at least two strategies to protect the interests of minorities from the potentially destructive will of some majority coalition. The more obvious one may be the "list" strategy employed by the Bill of Rights, itemizing things that cannot be done to anyone, at least by the federal government (though even here the safeguards turn out to be mainly procedural). The original Constitution's more pervasive strategy, however, can be loosely styled a strategy of pluralism, one of structuring the government, and to a limited extent society generally, so that a variety of voices would be guaranteed their say and no majority coalition could dominate. As Madison—pointedly eschewing the approach of setting up an undemocratic body to keep watch over the majority's values—put it in *Federalist* 51:

> It is of great importance in a republic not only to guard the society against the oppression of its rulers, but to guard one part of the society against the injustice of the other part * * *. If a majority be united by a common interest, the rights of the minority will be insecure. There are but two methods of providing against this evil: the one by creating a will in the community independent of the majority * * * the other, by comprehending in the society so many separate descriptions of citizens as will render an unjust combination of a majority of the whole very improbable, if not impracticable. The first method prevails in all governments possessing an hereditary or self-appointed authority. This, at best, is but a precarious security; because a power independent of the society may as well espouse the unjust views of the major, as the rightful interests of the minor party, and may possibly be turned against both parties. The second method will be exemplified in the federal republic of the United States.

The crucial move from a confederation to a system with a stronger central government was so conceived. Madison has been conspicuously attacked for not understanding pluralist political theory, but in fact there is reason to suppose he understood it rather well. His theory, derived from David Hume and spelled out at length in *The Federalist,* was that although at a local level one "faction" might well have sufficient clout to be able to tyrannize others, in the national government no faction or interest group would constitute a majority capable of exercising control. The Constitution's various moves to break up and counterpoise governmental decision and enforcement authority, not only between the national government and the states but among the three departments of the national government as well, were of similar design.

It is a rightly renowned system, but it didn't take long to learn that from the standpoint of protecting minorities it was not enough. Whatever genuine faith had existed at the beginning that everyone's interests either were identical or were about to be rendered so, had run its course as the republic approached its fiftieth birthday. Significant economic differences remained a reality, and the fear of legislation hostile to the interests of the propertied and creditor classes—a fear that of course had materialized earlier, during the regime of the Articles of Confederation, and thus had importantly inspired the constitutional devices to which we have alluded—surely did not abate during the Jacksonian era, as the "many" began genuinely to exercise political power. * * *

Also relevant was the persistence of the institution of slavery. So long as blacks could conveniently be regarded as subhuman, they provided no proof that some people were tyrannizing others. Once that assumption began to blur, there came into focus another reason for doubting that the protection of the many was necessarily the protection of all.

Simultaneously we came to recognize that the existing constitutional devices for protecting minorities were simply not sufficient. No finite list of entitlements can possibly cover all the ways majorities can tyrannize minorities, and the informal and more formal mechanisms of pluralism cannot always be counted on either. The fact that effective majorities can usually be described as clusters of cooperating minorities won't be much help when the cluster in question has sufficient power and perceived community of interest to advantage itself at the expense of a minority (or group of minorities) it is inclined to regard as different, and in such situations the fact that a number of agencies must concur, and others retain the right to squawk, isn't going to help much either. If, therefore, the republican ideal of government in the interest of the whole people was to be maintained, in an age when faith in the republican tenet that the people and their interests were essentially homogeneous was all but dead, a frontal assault on the problem of majority tyranny was needed. The existing theory of representation had to be extended so as to ensure not simply that the representative would not sever his interests from those of a majority of his constituency but also that he would not sever a majority coalition's interests from those of various minorities. Naturally that cannot mean that groups that constitute minorities of the population can never be treated less favorably than the rest, but it does preclude a refusal to *represent* them, the denial to minorities of what Professor Dworkin has called "equal concern and respect in the design and administration of the political institutions that govern them."[34] The Fourteenth Amendment's Equal Protection Clause is obviously our Constitution's most dramatic embodiment of this ideal. Before that amendment was ratified, however, its theory was understood, and functioned as a component—even on occasion as a judicially enforceable component—of the concept of representation that had been at the core of our Constitution from the beginning.

It's ironic, but the old concept of "virtual representation" is helpful here. The actual term was anathema to our forefathers, since it was invoked to answer their cries of "taxation without representation." But the concept contained an insight that has survived in American political theory and in fact has informed our constitutional thinking from the beginning. The colonists' argument that it was wrong, even "unconstitutional," to tax us when we lacked the privilege of sending representatives to Parliament was answered on the British side by the argument that although the colonies

[34] R. Dworkin, Taking Rights Seriously 180 (1977).

didn't actually elect anyone, they were "virtually represented" in Parliament. * * *

Although the term understandably has not been revived, the protective device of guaranteeing "virtual representation" by tying the interests of those without political power to the interests of those with it, was one that importantly influenced both the drafting of our original Constitution and its subsequent interpretation. Article IV's Privileges and Immunities Clause was intended and has been interpreted to mean that state legislatures cannot by their various regulations treat out-of-staters less favorably than they treat locals. "It was designed to insure to a citizen of State A who ventures into State B the same privileges which the citizens of State B enjoy."[37] Article IV conveys no set of substantive entitlements, but "simply" the guarantee that whatever entitlements those living in a state see fit to vote themselves will generally be extended to visitors. An ethical ideal of equality is certainly working here, but the reason inequalities against nonresidents and not others were singled out for prohibition in the original document is obvious: nonresidents are a paradigmatically powerless class politically. And their protection proceeds by what amounts to a system of virtual representation: by constitutionally tying the fate of outsiders to the fate of those possessing political power, the framers insured that their interests would be well looked after. The Commerce Clause of Article I, Section 8 provides simply that Congress shall have the power to regulate commerce among the states. But early on the Supreme Court gave this provision a self-operating dimension as well, one growing out of the same need to protect the politically powerless and proceeding by the same device of guaranteed virtual representation. Thus, for example, early in the nineteenth century the Court indicated that a state could not subject goods produced out of state to taxes it did not impose on goods produced locally. By thus constitutionally binding the interests of out-of-state manufacturers to those of local manufacturers represented in the legislature, it provided political insurance that the taxes imposed on the former would not rise to a prohibitive or even an unreasonable level.

These examples involve the protection of geographical outsiders, the literally voteless. But even the technically represented can find themselves functionally powerless and thus in need of a sort of "virtual representation" by those more powerful than they. From one perspective the claim of such groups to protection from the ruling majority is even more compelling than that of the out-of-stater: they are, after all, members of the community that is doing them in. From another, however, their claim seems weaker: they do have the vote, and it may not in the abstract seem unreasonable to expect them to wheel and deal as the rest of us (theoretically) do, yielding on issues about which they are comparatively indifferent and "scratching the

[37] Toomer v. Witsell, 334 U.S. 385, 395 (1948).

other guy's back" in order to get him to scratch theirs. "[N]o group that is prepared to enter into the process and combine with others need remain permanently and completely out of power."[41] Perhaps not "permanently and completely" if by that we mean forever, but certain groups that are technically enfranchised *have* found themselves for long stretches in a state of persistent inability to protect themselves from pervasive forms of discriminatory treatment. Such groups might just as well be disenfranchised.

* * * Whatever may have been the case before, the Fourteenth Amendment quite plainly imposes a judicially enforceable duty of virtual representation of the sort I have been describing. My main point in using the examples has been to suggest a way in which what are sometimes characterized as two conflicting American ideals—the protection of popular government on the one hand, and the protection of minorities from denials of equal concern and respect on the other—in fact can be understood as arising from a common duty of representation. * * *

* * * [C]ontrary to the standard characterization of the Constitution as "an enduring but evolving statement of general values," * * * the selection and accommodation of substantive values is [in fact] left almost entirely to the political process and instead the document is overwhelmingly concerned, on the one hand, with procedural fairness in the resolution of individual disputes (process writ small), and on the other, with what might capaciously be designated process writ large—with ensuring broad participation in the processes and distributions of government. An argument by way of *ejusdem generis* seems particularly justified in this case, since the constitutional provisions for which we are attempting to identify modes of supplying content, such as the Ninth Amendment and the Privileges or Immunities Clause, seem to have been included in a "we must have missed something here, so let's trust our successors to add what we missed" spirit. On my more expansive days, therefore, I am tempted to claim that the mode of review developed here represents the ultimate interpretivism.[48] Our

[41] A. Bickel, The Supreme Court and the Idea of Progress 37 (1970).

[48] As I've indicated, I don't think this terminological question is either entirely coherent or especially important. Obviously the approach recommended is neither "interpretivist" in the usual sense (of treating constitutional clauses as self-contained units) nor "noninterpretivist" in the usual sense (of seeking the principal stuff of constitutional judgment in one's rendition of society's fundamental values rather than in the document's broader themes). What counts is not whether it is "really" a broad interpretivism or rather a position that does not fall entirely in either camp, but whether it is capable of keeping faith with the document's promise in a way I have argued that a clause-bound interpretivism is not, and capable at the same time of avoiding the objections to a value-laden form of noninterpretivism, objections rooted most importantly in democratic theory. In that regard the two arguments that close this chapter, those addressed explicitly to consistency with democratic theory and the relative institutional capacities of legislatures and courts, seem at least as important as the argument from the nature of the Constitution (which given the complexity of the document must be a

review will tell us something else that may be even more relevant to the issue before us—that the few attempts the various framers *have* made to freeze substantive values by designating them for special protection in the document have been ill-fated, normally resulting in repeal, either officially or by interpretative pretense. This suggests a conclusion with important implications for the task of giving content to the document's more open-ended provisions, that preserving fundamental values is not an appropriate constitutional task.

* * *

THE NATURE OF THE UNITED STATES CONSTITUTION

Many of our colonial forebears' complaints against British rule were phrased in "constitutional" terms. Seldom, however, was the claim one of deprivation of some treasured good or substantive right: the American colonists, at least the white males, were among the freest and best-off people in the history of the world, and by and large they knew it. "Constitutional" claims thus were often jurisdictional—that Parliament lacked authority, say, to regulate the colonies' "internal commerce"—the foundation for the claim being generally that we were not represented in Parliament. (Obviously the colonists weren't any crazier about being taxed than anyone else is, but what they damned as tyrannical was taxation *without representation.*) Or they were arguments of inequality: claims of entitlement to "the rights of Englishmen" had an occasional natural law flavor, but the more common meaning was that suggested by the words, a claim for equality of treatment with those living in England. Thus the colonists' "constitutional" arguments drew on the two participational themes we have been considering: that (1) their input into the process by which they were governed was insufficient, and that (partly as a consequence) (2) they were being denied what others were receiving. The American version of revolution, wrote Hannah Arendt, "actually proclaims no more than the necessity of civilized government for all mankind; the French version * * * proclaims the existence of rights independent of and outside the body public * * *."[53]

* * *

I don't suppose it will surprise anyone to learn that the body of the original Constitution is devoted almost entirely to structure, explaining who among the various actors—federal government, state government; Congress, executive, judiciary—has authority to do what, and going on to fill in a good bit of detail about how these persons are to be selected and to conduct their business. Even provisions that at first glance might seem

qualified one in any event).

[53]H. Arendt, [On Revolution] 147 [(1963)].

primarily designed to assure or preclude certain substantive results seem on reflection to be principally concerned with process. Thus, for example, the provision that treason "shall consist only in levying War against [the United States], or in adhering to their Enemies, giving them Aid and Comfort," appears at least in substantial measure to have been a precursor of the First Amendment, reacting to the recognition that persons in power can disable their detractors by charging disagreement as treason. The prohibitions against granting titles of nobility seem rather plainly to have been designed to buttress the democratic ideal that all are equals in government. The Ex Post Facto and Bill of Attainder Clauses prove on analysis to be separation of powers provisions, enjoining the legislature to act prospectively and by general rule (just as the judiciary is implicitly enjoined by Article III to act retrospectively and by specific decree). And we have seen that the Privileges and Immunities Clause of Article IV, and at least in one aspect—the other being a grant of congressional power—the Commerce Clause as well, function as equality provisions, guaranteeing virtual representation to the politically powerless.

* * *

* * * [M]y claim is * * * that the original Constitution was principally, indeed I would say overwhelmingly, dedicated to concerns of process and structure and not to the identification and preservation of specific substantive values. Any claim that it was exclusively so conceived would be ridiculous (as would any comparable claim about any comparably complicated human undertaking). And indeed there are other provisions in the original document that seem almost entirely value-oriented, though my point, of course, is that they are few and far between. Thus "corruption of blood" is forbidden as a punishment for treason. Punishing people for their parents' transgressions is outlawed as a substantively unfair outcome: it just can't be done, irrespective of procedures and also irrespective of whether it is done to the children of all offenders. The federal government, along with the states, is precluded from taxing articles exported from any state. Here too an outcome is simply precluded; what might be styled a value, the economic value of free trade among the states, is protected. This short list, however, covers just about all the values protected in the original Constitution—save one. And a big one it was. Although an understandable squeamishness kept the word out of the document, *slavery* must be counted a substantive value to which the original Constitution meant to extend unusual protection from the ordinary legislative process, at least temporarily. Prior to 1808, Congress was forbidden to prohibit the slave trade into any state that wanted it, and the states were obliged to return escaping slaves to their "homes."

The idea of a bill of rights was not even brought up until close to the end of the Constitutional Convention, at which time it was rejected. The reason is not that the framers were unconcerned with liberty, but rather that by their lights a bill of rights did not belong in a constitution, at least not in the one they had drafted. As Hamilton explained in *Federalist* 84, "a minute detail of particular rights is certainly far less applicable to a Constitution like that under consideration, which is merely intended to regulate the general political interests of the nation * * *." Moreover, the very point of all that had been wrought had been, in large measure, to preserve the liberties of individuals. "The truth is, after all the declamations we have heard, that the Constitution is itself, in every rational sense, and to every useful purpose, *a Bill of Rights.*" "The additional securities to republican government, to liberty, and to property, to be derived from the adoption of the plan under consideration, consist chiefly in the restraints which the preservation of the Union will impose on local factions * * * in the prevention of extensive military establishments * * * in the express guarantee of a republican form of government to each [state]; in the absolute and universal exclusion of titles of nobility * * *."[72]

Of course a number of the state ratifying conventions remained apprehensive, and a bill of rights did emerge. Here too, however, the data are unruly. The expression-related provisions of the First Amendment—"Congress shall make no law * * * abridging the freedom of speech, or of the press; or the right of the people peaceably to assemble, and to petition the Government for a redress of grievances"—were centrally intended to help make our governmental processes work, to ensure the open and informed discussion of political issues, and to check our government when it gets out of bounds. We can attribute other functions to freedom of expression, and some of them must have played a role, but the exercise has the smell of the lamp about it: the view that free expression per se, without regard to what it means to the process of government, is our preeminent right has a highly elitist cast. Positive law has its claims, and I am not suggesting that such other purposes as are plausibly attributable to the language should not be attributed: the amendment's language is not limited to political speech and it should not be so limited by construction (even assuming someone could come up with a determinate definition of "political"). But we are at present engaged in an exploration of what sort of document our forebears thought they were putting together, and in that regard the linking of the politically oriented protections of speech, press, assembly, and petition is highly informative.

The First Amendment's religious clauses—"Congress shall make no law respecting an establishment of religion, or prohibiting the free exercise thereof"—are a different matter. Obviously part of the point of combining these cross-cutting commands was to make sure the church and the government gave each other breathing space: the provision thus performs a

[72]The Federalist no. 85, at 542 (B. Wright ed. 1961) (Hamilton).

structural or separation of powers function. But we must not infer that because one account fits the data it must be the only appropriate account, and here the obvious cannot be blinked: part of the explanation of the Free Exercise Clause has to be that for the framers religion was an important substantive value they wanted to put significantly beyond the reach of at least the federal legislature.

* * *

Amendments five through eight tend to become relevant only during lawsuits, and we tend therefore to think of them as procedural—instrumental provisions calculated to enhance the fairness and efficiency of the litigation process. That's exactly what most of them are: the importance of the guarantees of grand juries, criminal and civil petit juries, information of the charge, the right of confrontation, compulsory process, and even the assistance of counsel inheres mainly in their tendency to ensure a reliable determination. Unconcerned with the substance of government regulation, they refer instead to the ways in which regulations can be enforced against those they cover.

* * *

With one important exception, the Reconstruction Amendments do not designate substantive values for protection from the political process. The Fourteenth Amendment's Due Process Clause, we have seen, is concerned with process writ small, the processes by which regulations are enforced against individuals. Its Privileges or Immunities Clause is quite inscrutable, indicating only that there should exist some set of constitutional entitlements not explicitly enumerated in the document: it is one of the provisions for which we are seeking guides to construction. The Equal Protection Clause is also unforthcoming with details, though it at least gives us a clue: by its explicit concern with equality among the persons within a state's jurisdiction it constitutes the document's clearest, though not sole, recognition that technical access to the process may not always be sufficient to guarantee good-faith representation of all those putatively represented. The Fifteenth Amendment, forbidding abridgment of the right to vote on account of race, opens the process to persons who had previously been excluded and thus by another strategy seeks to enforce the representative's duty of equal concern and respect. The exception, of course, involves a value I have mentioned before, slavery. The Thirteenth Amendment can be forced into a "process" mold—slaves don't participate effectively in the political process—and it surely significantly reflects a concern with equality as well. Just as surely, however, it embodies a substantive judgment that human slavery is simply not morally tolerable. Thus at no point has the Constitution been neutral on this subject. Slavery was one of the few values the original document singled out for protection from the political branches; *non*slavery is one of the few values it singles out for protection now.

What has happened to the Constitution in the second century of our nationhood, though ground less frequently plowed, is most instructive on the subject of what jobs we have learned our basic document is suited to. There were no amendments between 1870 and 1913, but there have been eleven since. Five of them have extended the franchise: the Seventeenth extends to all of us the right to vote for our Senators directly, the Twenty-Fourth abolishes the poll tax as a condition of voting in federal elections, the Nineteenth extends the vote to women, the Twenty-Third to residents of the District of Columbia, and the Twenty-Sixth to eighteen-year-olds. Extension of the franchise to groups previously excluded has therefore been the dominant theme of our constitutional development since the Fourteenth Amendment, and it pursues both of the broad constitutional themes we have observed from the beginning: the achievement of a political process open to all on an equal basis and a consequent enforcement of the representative's duty of equal concern and respect to minorities and majorities alike. Three other amendments—the Twentieth, Twenty-Second, and Twenty-Fifth—involve Presidential eligibility and succession. The Sixteenth, permitting a federal income tax, adds another power to the list of those that had previously been assigned to the central government. That's it, save two, and indeed one of those two did place a substantive value beyond the reach of the political process. The amendment was the Eighteenth, and the value shielded was temperance. It was, of course, repealed fourteen years later by the Twenty-First Amendment, precisely, I suggest, because such attempts to freeze substantive values do not belong in a constitution. In 1919 temperance obviously seemed like a fundamental value; in 1933 it obviously did not.

What has happened to the Constitution's other value-enshrining provisions is similar, and similarly instructive. Some surely have survived, but typically because they are so obscure that they don't become issues (corruption of blood, quartering of troops) or so interlaced with procedural concerns they seem appropriate in a constitution (self-incrimination, double jeopardy). Those sufficiently conspicuous and precise to be controvertible have not survived. The most dramatic examples, of course, were slavery and prohibition. Both were removed by repeal, in one case a repeal requiring unprecedented carnage. Two other substantive values that at least arguably were placed beyond the reach of the political process by the Constitution have been "repealed" by judicial construction—the right of individuals to bear arms, and freedom to set contract terms without significant state regulation. Maybe in fact our forebears did not intend very seriously to protect those values, but the fact that the Court, in the face of what must be counted at least plausible contrary arguments, so readily read these values out of the Constitution is itself instructive of American expectations of a constitution. Finally, there is the value of religion, still protected by the Free Exercise Clause. Something different has happened here. In recent years that clause has functioned primarily to protect what must be counted as discrete and insular minorities, such as the Amish, Seventh Day Adventists, and Jehovah's Witnesses. Whatever the original conception of the Free Exercise Clause, its function during essentially all of its effective life has been one akin to the Equal Protection Clause and thus entirely appropriate to a constitution.

Don't get me wrong: our Constitution has always been substantially concerned with preserving liberty. If it weren't, it would hardly be worth fighting for. The question that is relevant to our inquiry here, however, is how that concern has been pursued. The principal answers to that, we have seen, are by a quite extensive set of procedural protections, and by a still more elaborate scheme designed to ensure that in the making of substantive choices the decision process will be open to all on something approaching an equal basis, with the decision-makers held to a duty to take into account the interests of all those their decisions affect. (Most often the document has proceeded on the assumption that assuring access is the best way of assuring that someone's interests will be considered, and so in fact it usually is. Other provisions, however—centrally but not exclusively the Equal Protection Clause—reflect a realization that access will not always be sufficient.) The general strategy has therefore not been to root in the document a set of substantive rights entitled to permanent protection. The Constitution has instead proceeded from the quite sensible assumption that an effective majority will not inordinately threaten its own rights, and has sought to assure that such a majority not systematically treat others less well than it treats itself—by structuring decision processes at all levels to try to ensure, first, that everyone's interests will be actually or virtually represented (usually both) at the point of substantive decision, and second, that the processes of individual application will not be manipulated so as to reintroduce in practice the sort of discrimination that is impermissible in theory. [There are] a few provisions that do not comfortably conform to this pattern. But they're an odd assortment, the understandable products of particular historical circumstances—guns, religion, contract, and so on—and in any event they are few and far between. To represent them as a dominant theme of our constitutional document one would have to concentrate quite single-mindedly on hopping from stone to stone and averting one's eyes from the mainstream.

The American Constitution has thus by and large remained a constitution properly so called, concerned with constitutive questions. What has distinguished it, and indeed the United States itself, has been a process of government, not a governing ideology. Justice Linde has written: "As a charter of government a constitution must prescribe legitimate processes, not legitimate outcomes, if like ours (and unlike more ideological documents elsewhere) it is to serve many generations through changing times."[95]

LAURENCE H. TRIBE, THE PUZZLING PERSISTENCE OF PROCESS-BASED CONSTITUTIONAL THEORIES

59 YALE L.J. 1063, 1065–73, 1075–1077 (1980).

I. THE CONSTITUTION'S OPENLY SUBSTANTIVE COMMITMENTS

One difficulty that immediately confronts process theories is the stubbornly substantive character of so many of the Constitution's most crucial commitments: commitments defining the values that we as a society, acting politically, must respect. Plainly, the First Amendment's guarantee of religious liberty and its prohibition of religious establishment are substantive in this sense. So, too, is the Thirteenth Amendment, in its abolition of slavery and repudiation of the Constitution's earlier, ostensibly procedural, protections of that institution.

In many of its parts, the Constitution also evinces a substantive commitment to the institution of private property and to the contractual expectations that surround it. The just compensation clause of the Fifth Amendment is an obvious example. The contracts clause of article I, section 10 is another. The old substantive due process, which is obviously an important part of our constitutional history and thus significant for our understanding of what the Constitution is about, also served to protect the transactions and expectations to which the institution of private property gives rise. Whatever our views of the substantive due process heyday, most of us would readily concede that the framers of the 1787 Constitution adopted a federal system of government organization in order to, among other goals, help secure the institution of private property. When Madison, in his theory of faction, suggested that shifting the legislative responsibility for certain problems from the state to the national level could help assure that majorities would not trample minority rights, the problems he had in mind were largely economic; the minority rights the federal system would protect were, for the most part, rights of property and contract.

Religious freedom, antislavery, private property: much of our constitutional history can be written by reference to just these social institutions and substantive values. That the Constitution has long addressed such matters, and often with beneficial effect, ought to surprise no one. What is puzzling is that anyone can say, in the face of this reality, that the Constitution is or should be predominantly concerned with *process* and *not* substance.

---

[95] Linde, "Due Process of Lawmaking," 55 Neb.L.Rev. 197, 254 (1975).

But our constitutional reality poses even deeper problems for process theorists. Even the Constitution's most procedural prescriptions cannot be adequately understood, much less applied, in the absence of a developed theory of fundamental rights that are secured to persons against the state—a theory whose derivation demands precisely the kinds of controversial substantive choices that the process proponents are so anxious to leave to the electorate and its representatives.

II. THE SUBSTANTIVE ROOTS OF PROCEDURAL NORMS

Much of the Constitution does indeed appear to address matters of procedure. Sometimes the subject is *adjudicative* process—the process due to individuals who become defendants in criminal or civil litigation or targets of administrative actions. Elsewhere, the Constitution focuses on *representative* process—including the process that governs the election of Congress, of the President, or of state representative bodies. That the *subject* in all these cases is procedure, however, is not to say that the *meaning* and *purpose* of the Constitution's prescriptions on each such subject are themselves merely procedural. There is no reason to suppose that "constitutive" rules—rules defining the basic structure of political and legal relations—can or should be essentially neutral on matters of substantive value.

* * *

The question of whether adjudicative or representative process is required in a given context simply cannot be analyzed in terms of how fairly and accurately various participatory processes reflect the interests and inputs of those governed by them. Deciding what *kind* of participation the Constitution demands requires analysis not only of the efficacy of alternative processes but also of the character and importance of the interest at stake—its role in the life of the individual as an individual. That analysis, in turn, requires a theory of values and rights as plainly substantive as, and seemingly of a piece with, the theories of values and rights that underlie the Constitution's provisions addressing religion, slavery, and property.

Once one has decided whether the Constitution requires adjudicative or representative process in a particular setting, one must again rely on substantive values in elaborating the requirements of either procedural form. Consider first the problem of adjudicative process. Certainly the Fifth Amendment's self-incrimination and double jeopardy clauses embody concerns for protecting individual dignity in the criminal process. A substantive concern for individual "privacy" necessarily underpins the Fourth Amendment. Other superficially procedural provisions of the Constitution, such as the rights to counsel, confrontation, bail, and jury trial, echo similar themes; they function, often at some cost to the efficiency and accuracy of fact-finding, to prevent the government from treating individuals in the criminal process as though they were objects.

Even outside the criminal context, elaborating rights of adjudicative process requires recourse to a substantive theory. Procedural due process rights are not simply means of protecting whatever "entitlements" happen to be conferred by legislation or administrative regulation. Otherwise, the drafters of an entitlement could frame it in the procedural terms of their choice, and the constitutional guarantee would be reduced to a right to receive whatever process the drafters had defined as due. But that view has been repeatedly rejected by the Supreme Court, which has never fully embraced a purely positivist theory of procedural due process. The only alternative theories, however, are ones that posit a right to individual dignity, or some similarly substantive norm, as the base on which conceptions of procedural fairness are constructed.

* * *

III. The Quandary of Whom to Protect

For those who would fill the gaps left by the Constitution's ambiguities and silences with representation-reinforcing principles, perhaps the core "process value" is the value of protecting certain minorities from perennial defeat in the political arena. The theme was anticipated by John Marshall;[44] it assumed a central role for Harlan Fiske Stone;[45] it signally motivated Earl Warren;[46] and it has been elaborated by numerous scholars, most powerfully in the work of John Ely. The idea seems as simple as it sounds reasonable: governmental action that burdens groups effectively excluded from the political process is constitutionally suspect. In its most sophisticated form, the resulting judicial scrutiny is seen as a way of invalidating governmental classifications and distributions that turn out to have been motivated either by prejudiced hostility or by self-serving stereotypes.

It all sounds pretty good—until we ask how we are supposed to distinguish such "prejudice" from principled, if "wrong," disapproval. Which groups are to count as "discrete and insular minorities"? Which are instead to be deemed appropriate losers in the ongoing struggle for political acceptance and ascendancy?

---

[44]*See* McCulloch v. Maryland, 17 U.S. (4 Wheat.) 316, 435–36 (1819) (state has no power to tax federal instrumentality because it would thereby act on national population, not represented in its legislature).

[45]United States v. Carolene Prods. Co., 304 U.S. 144, 152 n. 4 (1938) (strict judicial review for statutes that are directed against "discrete and insular minorities"); South Carolina State Highway Dep't v. Barnwell Bros., 303 U.S. 177, 184 n. 2 (1938) (commerce clause may prohibit legislation burdening political outsiders).

[46]*See* Ely, *The Chief,* 88 Harv.L.Rev. 11, 12 (1974) (Warren sought to ensure that machinery of democratic process does not become self-serving organ of privileged class).

* * *

Consider several illustrations. Burglars are subject to widespread hostility: indeed, the activity that defines the group is everywhere legislatively prohibited. Are burglars therefore a "suspect class"? Of course not. Suspect status is unthinkable—but only because of the substantive value we attach to personal security, and the importance for us of the system of private property and its rules of transfer, which the burglary prohibition preserves. If we speak of burglars as a class, we do so as a way of giving form to our view that burglary *is* a "different" activity, different not so much because burglars visibly define a group as because we disapprove of the activity, deny it any claim to protection as a right.

Homosexuals, too, are subject to widespread hostility; legislation penalizing homosexuals and homosexual practices is common. Homosexuals often do not identify themselves by sexual preference when acting politically, and generally do not "come out of the closet" to refute the traditional stereotypes. But even if they did, legislation might be unaltered. Coming out of the closet could dispel ignorance, but it may not alter belief. Legislators may see homosexuals as "different" not out of ignorance, but on principle—on the basis of a morality that treats certain sexual practices as repugnant to a particular view of humanity, and thus regards people who engage in those practices as "other." Such legislation can be rejected only on the basis of a principle that is equally substantive: a view of what it means to be a person, and to have a sexual identity. Process and prejudice thus seem profoundly beside the point. Any constitutional distinction between laws burdening homosexuals and laws burdening exhibitionists, between laws burdening Catholics and laws burdening pickpockets, must depend on a substantive theory of which groups are exercising fundamental rights and which are not.

Indeed, even laws putting blacks and women "in their place"—banning racial intermarriage, say, or excluding women from combat—are likely to reflect neither simple hostility nor self-serving blindness but *a substantive vision of proper conduct*—a vision that no amount of attention to flaws in the political process could condemn or correct. Accordingly, the idea of blacks or women as properly segregated beings can be rejected *only* by finding a constitutional basis for concluding that, in our society, such hierarchical visions are substantively out of bounds, at least as a justification for government action. And such a finding would in turn entail a theory of unenumerated substantive rights, rights at best *suggested* by constitutional text and history, rights whose necessarily controversial elaboration the process theorists seek to eschew.

The crux of any determination that a law unjustly discriminates against a group—blacks, or women, or even men—is not that the law emerges from a flawed process, or that the burden it imposes affects an independently fundamental right, but that the law is part of a pattern that denies those subject to it a meaningful opportunity to realize their humanity. Necessarily, such an approach must look beyond process to identify and proclaim fundamental substantive rights. Whatever difficulties this may entail, it seems plain that important aspects of constitutional law, including the determination of which groups deserve special protection, can be given significant content in no other way. Thus it is puzzling indeed that process-based approaches—designed to deny the need for, and legitimacy of, any such substantive theory—should nonetheless continue to find such articulate proponents and persist in attracting such perceptive adherents.

C. MORALITY-BASED APPROACHES

RONALD DWORKIN, INTRODUCTION: THE MORAL READING AND THE MAJORITARIAN PREMISE

FREEDOM'S LAW: THE MORAL READING OF THE AMERICAN CONSTITUTION 2–4, 7–11 (1996).

[This book] illustrates a particular way of reading and enforcing a political constitution, which I call the *moral* reading. Most contemporary constitutions declare individual rights against the government in very broad and abstract language, like the First Amendment of the United States Constitution, which provides that Congress shall make no law abridging "the freedom of speech." The moral reading proposes that we all—judges, lawyers, citizens—interpret and apply these abstract clauses on the understanding that they invoke moral principles about political decency and justice. The First Amendment, for example, recognizes a moral principle—that it is wrong for government to censor or control what individual citizens say or publish—and incorporates it into American law. So when some novel or controversial constitutional issue arises—about whether, for instance, the First Amendment permits laws against pornography—people who form an opinion must decide how an abstract moral principle is best understood. They must decide whether the true ground of the moral principle that condemns censorship, in the form in which this principle has been incorporated into American law, extends to the case of pornography.

The moral reading therefore brings political morality into the heart of constitutional law. But political morality is inherently uncertain and controversial, so any system of government that makes such principles part of its law must decide whose interpretation and understanding will be authoritative. In the American system judges—ultimately the justices of the Supreme Court—now have that authority, and the moral reading of the Constitution is therefore said by its critics to give judges absolute power to impose their own moral convictions on the public. I shall shortly try to explain why that crude charge is mistaken. I should make plain first, however, that there is nothing revolutionary about the moral reading in practice. So far as American lawyers and judges follow any coherent strategy of interpreting the Constitution at all, they already use the moral reading. * * *

That explains why both scholars and journalists * * * find it reasonably easy to classify judges as "liberal" or "conservative": the best explanation of the differing patterns of their decisions lies in their different understandings of central moral values embedded in the Constitution's text. Judges whose political convictions are conservative will naturally interpret abstract constitutional principles in a conservative way, as they did in the early years of this century, when they wrongly supposed that certain rights over property and contract are fundamental to freedom. Judges whose convictions are more liberal will naturally interpret those principles in a liberal way, as they did in the halcyon days of the Warren Court. The moral reading is not, in itself, either a liberal or a conservative charter or strategy. It is true that in recent decades liberal judges have ruled more statutes or executive orders unconstitutional than conservative judges have. But that is because conservative political principles for the most part either favored or did not strongly condemn the measures that could reasonably be challenged on constitutional grounds in those decades. There have been exceptions to that generalization. Conservatives strongly disapprove, on moral grounds, * * * affirmative action programs * * * which give certain advantages to minority applicants for universities or jobs, and conservative justices have not hesitated to follow their understanding of what the moral reading required in such cases. That reading helps us to identify and explain not only these large-scale patterns, moreover, but also more fine-grained differences in constitutional interpretation that cut across the conventional liberal-conservative divide. Conservative judges who particularly value freedom of speech, or think it particularly important to democracy, are more likely than other conservatives to extend the First Amendment's protection to acts of political protest, even for causes that they despise, as the Supreme Court's decision protecting flag-burners shows.

So, to repeat, the moral reading is not revolutionary in practice. Lawyers and judges, in their day-to-day work, instinctively treat the Constitution as expressing abstract moral requirements that can only be applied to concrete cases through fresh moral judgments. * * * [T]hey have no real option but to do so. But it would indeed be revolutionary for a judge openly to recognize the moral reading, or to admit that it is his or her strategy of constitutional interpretation, and even scholars and judges who come close to recognizing it shrink back, and try to find other, usually metaphorical, descriptions of their own practice. There is therefore a striking mismatch between the role the moral reading actually plays in American constitutional life and its reputation. It has inspired all the greatest constitutional decisions of the Supreme Court, and also some of the worst. But it is almost never acknowledged as influential even by constitutional experts, and it is almost never openly endorsed even by judges whose arguments are incomprehensible on any other understanding of their responsibilities. On the contrary, the moral reading is often dismissed as an "extreme" view that no really sensible constitutional scholar would entertain. It is patent that judges' own views about political morality influence their constitutional decisions, and though they might easily explain that influence by insisting that the Constitution demands a moral reading, they never do. Instead, against all evidence, they deny the influence and try to explain their decisions in other—embarrassingly unsatisfactory—ways. They say they are just giving effect to obscure historical "intentions," for example, or just expressing an overall but unexplained constitutional "structure" that is supposedly explicable in nonmoral terms. * * *

The clauses of the American Constitution that protect individuals and minorities from government are found mainly in the so-called Bill of Rights—the first several amendments to the document—and the further amendments added after the Civil War. (I shall sometimes use the phrase "Bill of Rights," inaccurately, to refer to all the provisions of the Constitution that establish individual rights, including the Fourteenth Amendment's protection of citizens' privileges and immunities and its guarantee of due process and equal protection of the laws.) Many of these clauses are drafted in exceedingly abstract moral language. The First Amendment refers to the "right" of free speech, for example, the Fifth Amendment to the process that is "due" to citizens, and the Fourteenth to protection that is "equal." According to the moral reading, these clauses must be understood in the way their language most naturally suggests: they refer to abstract moral principles and incorporate these by reference, as limits on government's power.

There is of course room for disagreement about the right way to restate these abstract moral principles, so as to make their force clearer for us, and to help us to apply them to more concrete political controversies. I favor a particular way of stating the constitutional principles at the most general possible level. * * * I believe that the principles set out in the Bill of Rights, taken together, commit the United States to the following political and legal ideals: government must treat all those subject to its dominion as having equal moral and political status; it must attempt, in good faith, to treat them all with equal concern; and it must respect whatever individual freedoms are indispensable to those ends, including but not limited to the freedoms more specifically designated in the document, such as the freedoms of speech and religion. Other lawyers and scholars who also endorse the moral reading might well formulate the constitutional principles, even at a very general level, differently and less expansively than I just have however[.]

[Therefore] I should say something about how the choice among competing formulations should be made.

Of course the moral reading is not appropriate to everything a constitution contains. The American Constitution includes a great many clauses that are neither particularly abstract nor drafted in the language of moral principle. Article II specifies, for example, that the President must be at least thirty-five years old, and the Third Amendment insists that government may not quarter soldiers in citizens' houses in peacetime. The latter may have been inspired by a moral principle: those who wrote and enacted it might have been anxious to give effect to some principle protecting citizens' rights to privacy, for example. But the Third Amendment is not itself a moral principle: its *content* is not a general principle of privacy. So the first challenge to my own interpretation of the abstract clauses might be put this way. What argument or evidence do I have that the equal protection clause of the Fourteenth Amendment (for example), which declares that no state may deny any person equal protection of the laws, has a moral principle as *its* content though the Third Amendment does not?

This is a question of interpretation or, if you prefer, translation. We must try to find language of our own that best captures, in terms we find clear, the content of what the "framers" intended it to say. (Constitutional scholars use the word "framers" to describe, somewhat ambiguously, the various people who drafted and enacted a constitutional provision.) History is crucial to that project, because we must know something about the circumstances in which a person spoke to have any good idea of what he meant to say in speaking as he did. We find nothing in history, however, to cause us any doubt about what the framers of the Third Amendment meant to say. Given the words they used, we cannot sensibly interpret them as laying down any moral principle at all, even if we believe they were inspired by one. They said what the words they used would normally be used to say: not that privacy must be protected, but that soldiers must not be quartered in houses in peacetime. The same process of reasoning—about what the framers presumably intended to say when they used the words they did—yields an opposite conclusion about the framers of the equal protection clause, however. Most of them no doubt had fairly clear expectations about what legal consequences the Fourteenth Amendment would have. They expected it to end certain of the most egregious Jim Crow practices of the Reconstruction period. They plainly did not expect it to outlaw official racial segregation in school—on the contrary, the Congress that adopted the equal protection clause itself maintained segregation in the District of Columbia school system. But they did not say anything about Jim Crow laws or school segregation or homosexuality or gender equality, one way or the other. They said that "equal protection of the laws" is required, which plainly describes a very general principle, not any concrete application of it.

The framers meant, then, to enact a general principle. But which general principle? That further question must be answered by constructing different elaborations of the phrase "equal protection of the laws," each of which we can recognize as a principle of political morality that might have won their respect, and then by asking which of these it makes most sense to attribute to them, given everything else we know. The qualification that each of these possibilities must be recognizable as a political *principle* is absolutely crucial. We cannot capture a statesman's efforts to lay down a general constitutional principle by attributing to him something neither he nor we could recognize as a candidate for that role. But the qualification will typically leave many possibilities open. It was once debated, for example, whether the framers intended to stipulate, in the equal protection clause, only the relatively weak political principle that laws must be enforced in accordance with their terms, so that legal benefits conferred on everyone, including blacks, must not be denied, in practice, to anyone.

History seems decisive that the framers of the Fourteenth Amendment did not mean to lay down only so weak a principle as that one, however, which would have left states free to discriminate against blacks in any way they wished so long as they did so openly. Congressmen of the victorious nation, trying to capture the achievements and lessons of a terrible war, would be very unlikely to settle for anything so limited and insipid, and we should not take them to have done so unless the language leaves no other interpretation plausible. In any case, constitutional interpretation must take into account past legal and political practice as well as what the framers themselves intended to say, and it has now been settled by unchallengeable precedent that the political principle incorporated in the Fourteenth Amendment is not that very weak one, but something more robust. Once that is conceded, however, then the principle must be something *much* more robust, because the only alternative, as a translation of what the framers actually *said* in the equal protection clause, is that they declared a principle of quite breathtaking scope and power: the principle that government must treat everyone as of equal status and with equal concern.

* * * [T]his brief discussion has mentioned two important restraints that sharply limit the latitude the moral reading gives to individual judges. First, under that reading constitutional interpretation must begin in what the framers said, and, just as our judgment about what friends and strangers say relies on specific information about them and the context in which they speak, so does our understanding of what the framers said. History is therefore plainly relevant. But only in a particular way. We turn to history to answer the question of what they intended to say, not the different question of what *other* intentions they had. We have no need to decide what

they expected to happen, or hoped would happen, in consequence of their having said what they did, for example; their purpose, in that sense, is not part of our study. That is a crucial distinction * * *. We are governed by what our lawmakers said—by the principles they laid down—not by any information we might have about how they themselves would have interpreted those principles or applied them in concrete cases.

Second, and equally important, constitutional interpretation is disciplined, under the moral reading, by the requirement of constitutional *integrity* * * *. Judges may not read their own convictions into the Constitution. They may not read the abstract moral clauses as expressing any particular moral judgment, no matter how much that judgment appeals to them, unless they find it consistent in principle with the structural design of the Constitution as a whole, and also with the dominant lines of past constitutional interpretation by other judges. They must regard themselves as partners with other officials, past and future, who together elaborate a coherent constitutional morality, and they must take care to see that what they contribute fits with the rest. (I have elsewhere said that judges are like authors jointly creating a chain novel in which each writes a chapter that makes sense as part of the story as a whole.[7] Even a judge who believes that abstract justice requires economic equality cannot interpret the equal protection clause as making equality of wealth, or collective ownership of productive resources, a constitutional requirement, because that interpretation simply does not fit American history or practice, or the rest of the Constitution.)

Nor could a judge plausibly think that the constitutional structure commits any but basic, structural political rights to his care. He might think that a society truly committed to equal concern would award people with handicaps special resources, or would secure convenient access to recreational parks for everyone, or would provide heroic and experimental medical treatment, no matter how expensive or speculative, for anyone whose life might possibly be saved. But it would violate constitutional integrity for a judge to treat these mandates as part of constitutional law. Judges must defer to general, settled understandings about the character of the power the Constitution assigns them. The moral reading asks them to find the best conception of constitutional moral principles—the best understanding of what equal moral status for men and women really requires, for example—that fits the broad story of America's historical record. It does not ask them to follow the whisperings of their own consciences or the traditions of their own class or sect if these cannot be seen as embedded in that record. Of course judges can abuse their power—they can pretend to observe the important restraint of integrity while really ignoring it. But generals and presidents and priests can abuse their powers,

[7] See Law's Empire, p. 228 [(Harvard University Press).]

too. The moral reading is a strategy for lawyers and judges acting in good faith, which is all any interpretive strategy can be.

I emphasize these constraints of history and integrity, because they show how exaggerated is the common complaint that the moral reading gives judges absolute power to impose their own moral convictions on the rest of us. Macauley was wrong when he said that the American Constitution is all sail and no anchor,[8] and so are the other critics who say that the moral reading turns judges into philosopher-kings. Our constitution is law, and like all law it is anchored in history, practice, and integrity. Most cases at law—even most constitutional cases—are not hard cases. The ordinary craft of a judge dictates an answer and leaves no room for the play of personal moral conviction. Still, we must not exaggerate the drag of that anchor. Very different, even contrary, conceptions of a constitutional principle—of what treating men and women as equals really means, for example—will often fit language, precedent, and practice well enough to pass these tests, and thoughtful judges must then decide on their own which conception does most credit to the nation.

MICHAEL W. MCCONNELL, THE IMPORTANCE OF HUMILITY IN JUDICIAL REVIEW: A COMMENT ON RONALD DWORKIN'S "MORAL READING" OF THE CONSTITUTION

65 FORDHAM L. REV. 1269–74, 1276–83 (1997).

INTRODUCTION

In recent writings, Professor Ronald Dworkin advocates what he calls "The Moral Reading of the Constitution."[1] This approach, he says, cuts across the usual categories of "liberal" or "conservative" decisionmaking. Its distinguishing characteristic is that judges must decide cases on the basis of how the "abstract moral principle[s]" of the Constitution are "best understood." This means that judges should decide, frankly, on the basis of their "own views about political morality" rather than purporting to decide on the basis of such "metaphorical" notions as "historical 'intentions'" or "constitutional 'structure.'"

Many arguments can be made, some more persuasive than others, that judges are superior to legislatures in making decisions of moral importance. It is easy to see why these arguments would appeal to law professors, who

[8]Thomas Babington, Lord Macauley, letter to H.S. Randall, May 23, 1857.

[1]See Ronald Dworkin, Freedom's Law: The Moral Reading of the American Constitution (1996) [hereinafter Dworkin, Freedom's Law]; Ronald Dworkin, *The Arduous Virtue of Fidelity: Originalism, Scalia, Tribe, and Nerve*, 65 Fordham L. Rev. 1249 (1997) * * *; *see also* Ronald Dworkin, The Moral Reading of the Constitution, Robert L. Levine Lecture Series at Fordham University School of Law (September 18, 1996) (transcript on file with the Fordham Law Review) [hereinafter Dworkin, Levine Lecture].

share with federal judges a common background, social class, and education. In other writings, I have questioned the validity of such arguments.[4] But Dworkin does not make these arguments. Instead, Dworkin makes the claim that "The Moral Reading" is necessary if we are to show proper "fidelity" to the Constitution. In other words, he claims that his approach is the most faithful interpretation of the constitutional text. * * * In this Response, I will explain why this claim is not convincing.

Before making the argument, it is necessary to achieve greater clarity about the nature of Dworkin's argument. Running through Dworkin's account is a profound ambivalence toward arguments based on history (text, history, practice, and precedent). It is not too much to say that there are two Dworkins, with two quite different versions of "The Moral Reading." I will call these "the Dworkin of Fit" and "the Dworkin of Right Answers." According to the Dworkin of Fit, judges are, and should be, seriously constrained by what has come before—by text, history, tradition, and precedent—and should exercise their moral-philosophical faculties only within the limits set by history. The Dworkin of Fit recognizes that the constraints of history are an indispensable part of the "principle" that governs judicial decision making. The Dworkin of Right Answers, by contrast, distinguishes sharply between "the party of history" (bad) and "the party of principle" (good). He insists that text, history, and unwelcome precedent must be interpreted at a sufficiently abstract level that they do not interfere with the judge's ability to make the Constitution "the best it can be." The "best reading" is the reading that, in the judge's own opinion, will produce the best answers, defined philosophically and not historically.

The relation between the Dworkin of Fit and the Dworkin of Right Answers is unclear at a theoretical level. One would expect the Dworkin of Fit to attack the Dworkin of Right Answers for the latter's lack of respect for the distinctive qualities of judging within the American tradition (what he calls elsewhere "integrity"), and the Dworkin of Right Answers to charge the Dworkin of Fit with sacrificing "principle" to "history." Each Dworkin seems to refute the other. But the two work together harmoniously at a practical level. The division of labor is as follows: The Dworkin of Right Answers decides all important contested cases, while the Dworkin of Fit defends against charges of judicial imperialism. The Dworkin of Fit is allowed to resolve hypothetical cases, but in all of Dworkin's writings I am unable to discover an actual, important, controversial case in which "fit" ever precluded the Dworkin of Right Answers from having his way.

---

[4]See Michael W. McConnell, *A Moral Realist Defense of Constitutional Democracy*, 64 Chi.-Kent L. Rev. 89, 105–09 (1988)* * *; Michael W. McConnell, *The Role of Democratic Politics in Transforming Moral Convictions into Law*, 98 Yale L.J. 1501, 1534–38 (1989) (book review) * * *.

Let us consider each of these versions of "The Moral Reading" on its own terms.

I. THE DWORKIN OF FIT

The Dworkin of Fit sounds mainstream, even conservative. This Dworkin is attentive to the problem of judicial overreaching and respectful of the constraints of constitutional text and history. The essence of his position is that a judge is not writing on a blank slate, free to decide every question according to his own view of the best answer. Rather, he is seriously constrained by what has come before: by text, history, practice, and precedent. This is what he calls "fit." Only within the bounds set by text, history, practice, and precedent may the judge use the tools of moral philosophy to determine what is best.

* * *

* * * [Dworkin's] approach can be seen as a three-stage filtering process. Out of the entire universe of moral principles, the text of the Constitution embraces some principles, and excludes others. The linguistic intentions of the Framers provide a second filter, excluding some interpretations that are textually plausible but that do not fit the historical circumstances. Practice and precedent provide a third filter, but even these leave the judge, in many cases, with a range of possible answers.

It is at this stage in the analysis that Dworkin departs from mainstream constitutional practice. When different conceptions of the constitutional principle satisfy the tests of "language, precedent, and practice," he says, "*thoughtful judges must then decide on their own which conception does most credit to the nation.*" In other words, after the backward-looking process of examining text, history, practice, and precedent is completed, the judge decides among the remaining possible answers on philosophic, normative, non-interpretive grounds. Dworkin sometimes calls this stage in the process "justification." By contrast, mainstream practice treats any decision of the representative branches that survives the filters of text, history, practice, and precedent *as constitutional*. Indeed, properly enacted legislation enjoys a presumption of constitutionality, and can be overturned only when the alleged constitutional violation is tolerably clear. The notion that in unclear cases judges may substitute "their own views about political morality" for the considered judgments of representative bodies, turns settled constitutional practice—as articulated by such revered figures as Marshall,[22] Brandeis,[23] Holmes,[24] Stone,[25] and Harlan[26]—on its head.

---

[22]See, e.g., Trustees of Dartmouth College v. Woodward, 17 U.S. (4 Wheat.) 518, 625 (1819) (Marshall, C.J.) ("On more than one occasion, this Court has expressed the cautious circumspection with which it approaches the consideration of [a constitutional] question, and has declared, that in no doubtful case, would it pronounce a legislative act to be contrary to

The theory underlying this more modest view of constitutional judicial review is that the Constitution is not designed to produce the one "best answer" to all questions, but to establish a framework for representative government and to set forth a few important substantive principles, commanding supramajority support, that legislatures are required to respect. The job of the judge is to ensure that representative institutions conform to the commitments made by the people in the past, and embodied in text, history, tradition, and precedent. Another way to express the point is: "Fit is everything." When the dictates of "fit" are satisfied, the judge's role is at an end. Within the range of discretion established by the various conceptions that are consistent with text, history, practice, and precedent, the people through their representative institutions—not the courts—have authority to decide which course of action "does most credit to the nation." There may be many different answers to that question, and none is constitutionally privileged. It is the right, privilege, and obligation of the people to deliberate about such questions through their elected representatives.

* * *

II. THE DWORKIN OF RIGHT ANSWERS

In other recent writings, Dworkin draws a sharper dichotomy between the constraints of history and the search for "the right answer" to constitutional questions, arguing that fidelity to history is antithetical to principled decision making.[33] The "party of history," he says, looks to whether a putative right has been historically recognized either through original understanding at the time of the framing or by past practice—whether it is "deeply rooted in this Nation's history and tradition."[34] The "party of principle," by contrast, "argues that the abstract constitutional rights acknowledged for one group be extended to others if no moral ground

---

the constitution.").

[23]See, e.g., Ashwander v. Tennessee Valley Auth., 297 U.S. 288, 354 (1936) (Brandeis, J., concurring) (discussing and applying the "long established presumption in favor of the constitutionality of a statute").

[24]See, e.g., Missouri, Kansas & Texas Ry. v. May, 194 U.S. 267, 270 (1904) (Holmes, J.) ("[I]t must be remembered that legislatures are ultimate guardians of the liberties and welfare of the people in quite as great a degree as the courts.").

[25]See, e.g., United States v. Butler, 297 U.S. 1, 83 (1936) (Stone, J., dissenting) ("The presumption of constitutionality of a statute is not to be overturned by an assertion of its coercive effect which rests on nothing more substantial than groundless speculation.").

[26]See, e.g., Poe v. Ullman, 367 U.S. 497, 542 (1961) (Harlan, J., dissenting) (emphasizing that courts must interpret "due process" in accordance with "the balance struck by this country" rather than the "unguided speculation" of judges).

[33][Ronald Dworkin, *Sex, Death, and the Courts*, N.Y. Rev. Books, Aug. 8, 1996,] 44.

[34]Id. (quoting Bowers v. Hardwick, 478 U.S. 186, 192 (1986)).

distinguishes between them."[35] The Dworkin of Right Answers criticizes judges who allow the apparent constraints of history and tradition to distract them from the most "principled" answer.

According to this view, the words of the Constitution should be read as abstractions having meaning independent of any meaning that the Framers and Ratifiers, or the people, may have intended to communicate. For example, in interpreting the Equal Protection Clause, Dworkin advises that we should not ask what the framers and ratifiers meant by "equal citizenship;" nor what "we think" about the issue. "I am interested in the *right answer* to the question, what is equal citizenship properly understood."[37] * * *

Especially revealing is Dworkin's depiction of Justice Scalia's affirmative action decisions as an example of a conservative "Moral Reading"—one with which he would disagree, but which is a "principled" interpretation nonetheless. Dworkin maintains—accurately or not—that Scalia's "color blind" interpretation of the Equal Protection Clause "is not to be found in history," but is, instead, the Justice's "emotional and moral reaction."[40] One might think that would be a criticism, but it is not. In Dworkin's view, this establishes that Scalia is giving a "Moral Reading," even if it is one with which Dworkin would not agree. The defining characteristic of "The Moral Reading," as this example shows, is not that the interpretation is correct or well-reasoned, but simply that it *does not rest on historical authority*. If Scalia's view were, in fact, historically grounded, it would not be deemed a "Moral Reading." This suggests that "The Moral Reading" is nothing but a repudiation of "fit"—any reading is a "Moral Reading" so long as it is based on the judge's own "moral and emotional reaction" to the problem rather than on the nation's historical understanding of constitutional principle. Indeed, it suggests that by "The Moral Reading," Dworkin means nothing other than judicial willfulness.

That this is Dworkin's position is further evident from his conclusion that the death penalty is unconstitutional. There is no serious argument that the framers of either the Eighth or the Fourteenth Amendment deemed death, in all cases, a cruel and unusual punishment; indeed, the very language of the constitutional text belies this. Nor is there any serious argument that the tradition of the nation has judged capital punishment to be immoral. Nor do the precedents of the Supreme Court support that position. In a case where the democratically accountable branches have prescribed the death penalty, therefore, the only conceivable ground for Dworkin's legal conclusion is that the interpreter's own opinion of what is "cruel and unusual" is entitled to prevail. "Fit" counts for nothing. The

[35] Id.

[37] [See Dworkin, Symposium, supra note 32] at 89 (emphasis added).

[40] [Dworkin, Levine Lecture (Q & A), supra note 1,] at 55.

same must be said of Dworkin's constitutional positions on euthanasia and abortion, at least at the time of *Roe v. Wade*. In neither of these cases can a persuasive argument be made that the constitutional text, history, practice, tradition, or precedent required invalidation of the state statutes in question. Nonetheless, on the basis of independent moral judgment, Dworkin contends that the courts should declare these statutes unconstitutional. This version of "The Moral Reading," then, is the argument that courts must read the language of the Constitution abstractly, in light of their own judgment of the best answer, with only slight constraint, if any, from text or history.

If I seem to belabor this point, it is solely because Dworkin declares "exaggerated" the "common complaint that the moral reading gives judges absolute power to impose their own moral convictions on the rest of us."[42] The reason the complaint is exaggerated, Dworkin says, is because judges are bound by fit. If the constraints of fit are illusory, as they turn out to be, the complaint is not exaggerated.

III. "FIDELITY" AND "THE MORAL READING"

As noted above, Dworkin defends his approach to constitutional interpretation not explicitly on the basis that courts are more virtuous decision makers, but on the ground that it is the only way to show "fidelity" to the constitutional text. "The Moral Reading," he contends, is simply faithful interpretation. Let us examine his argument, as it applies to text, history, precedent, and deference to representative institutions.

A. Text and Semantic Intention

Dworkin professes to deem text, interpreted in accordance with the semantic intention of its Framers, as authoritative and dispositive. Contrary to some of his admirers, he does not take the view that constitutional principles are independent of, or unaffected by, their particular expression in the document we call the Constitution. Rather, he says, judges must be faithful to the text, and judging must be understood as an interpretive enterprise, fundamentally distinct from legislation.

I wish Dworkin would elaborate on his reasons for taking this position. I suspect that if we knew the reason for treating the text, interpreted in light of the semantic intention of its Framers, as authoritative, we would find it difficult to account for Dworkin's readiness to depart from the Framers' understanding of constitutional principles. If the Framers' words have authority for us today, this is because, in Chief Justice Marshall's words, "the people have an original right to establish, for their future government, such principles as, in their opinion, shall most conduce to their own

[42]Dworkin, Freedom's Law, supra note 1, at 11.

happiness."[46] This, he said, "is the basis on which the whole American fabric has been erected."[47] It would seem to follow that it is the principles to which the people assented, understood as nearly as is possible as they understood them, which should guide us today. There are good reasons not to follow the principles of people many generations ago, but I can think of no good reasons to pretend to adhere to their words, if those words are stripped of the principles they sought to express.

* * *

I believe Dworkin's embrace of "semantic intention" brings him closer to the mainstream originalist view than he realizes. In the context of directive or prohibitory language, what the authors intend to "say" is precisely what they intend to require, authorize, or prohibit; thus, what they intend to "say" is what they intend to have happen "in consequence of their having said what they did." It is not possible to isolate "semantic intentions" from the broader context of their purpose and political theory.

* * *

A genuine commitment to the semantic intentions of the Framers requires the interpreter to seek the level of generality at which the particular language was understood by its Framers. * * * If "cruel and unusual punishment" was understood to mean something like "punishments that are widely regarded as excessively cruel and therefore have passed out of common accepted use," then the interpreter would apply that standard, rather than the interpreter's own moral judgment, to the issue of capital punishment. It is perfectly possible that, upon dispassionate historical investigation, the interpreter would discover that some provisions of the Constitution were understood at a high level of generality, or that judges would be expected to apply their own moral judgments. But such a conclusion must be based on a serious examination of the context, linguistic conventions, and historical purposes of the provision in question, and not on *a priori* preferences for abstract interpretations.

It is emblematic of Dworkin's ambiguity that I do not know whether he would agree or disagree with the preceding paragraph. To be sure, he "favor[s] a particular way of stating the constitutional principles at the most general possible level."[55] This is his rationale for increasing judicial discretion. But he claims to derive this high level of generality as a matter of "fidelity" to the constitutional text and the semantic intentions of the Framers. He thus tries to have it both ways: to liberate judges to achieve their own vision of the "best answers" to controversial questions without

---

[46]Marbury v. Madison, 5 U.S. (1 Cranch) 137, 176 (1803).

[47]Id.

[55]Dworkin, Freedom's Law, supra note 1, at 7.

regard to the Framers' opinions, while simultaneously claiming to be faithfully carrying out the Framers' intentions. Let us see if he carries off this happy feat persuasively.

He offers the example of the Equal Protection Clause. He suggests that we begin our interpretation of this clause by "constructing different elaborations of the phrase 'equal protection of the laws,' each of which we can recognize as a principle of political morality that might have won [the framers'] respect," and then ask "which of these it makes most sense to attribute to them, given everything else we know."[56] So far, so good. "It was once debated," he continues, "whether the framers intended to stipulate, in the equal protection clause, only the relatively weak political principle that laws must be enforced in accordance with their terms, so that legal benefits conferred on everyone, including blacks, must not be denied, in practice, to anyone." This, he points out, "would have left states free to discriminate against blacks in any way they wished so long as they did so."[57]

* * *

Now comes the key step in Dworkin's logic:

> Once that is conceded, however, then the principle [of equal protection] must be something *much* more robust, because the only alternative, as a translation of what the framers actually *said* in the equal protection clause, is that they declared a principle of quite breathtaking scope and power: the principle that government must treat everyone as of equal status and with equal concern.[58]

This is a textbook example of what logicians call the fallacy of black-and-white reasoning. The fallacy consists of falsely positing that there are only two alternatives, and then purporting to prove one by disproving the other.

It should be obvious that the two alternatives Dworkin explores do not exhaust the possible meanings of "equal protection of the laws." Indeed, as an historical matter, neither of these two meanings is plausible. I have already explained why the "weak" reading is unsupportable. There is not much more historical support for Dworkin's theory of "equal concern." That certainly was not the language of the day. The notion of "equal concern" is so subjective and indeterminate that it is highly unlikely that the practical statesmen of the 39th Congress, who deeply distrusted the courts, would have employed it.

There were, however, a number of competing conceptions of equality that "might have won [the Framers'] respect," each with some degree of

---

[56] Id. at 9.

[57] Id.

[58] Id. at 10.

historical support. The principle of equal protection of the laws can be understood as a rule of strict formal equality, requiring all citizens to be treated without regard to race or other morally irrelevant distinctions. (This interpretation differs sharply from Dworkin's notion of "equal concern" because "equal concern" might well require unequal treatment.) Alternatively, it might mean what Earl Maltz has called "limited absolute equality"—absolute equality of all citizens with respect to a limited category of rights (civil rights, but not social or political rights).[60] It might be rooted in the Jacksonian abhorrence of "class legislation" or "special legislation." It could be limited to discrimination that partakes of "caste," something akin to modern anti-subordination theories.

If Dworkin wishes to base his interpretation on the principle that "makes most sense to attribute to [the Framers]," then he needs to do more serious historical work. He is simply wrong when he posits two extreme alternatives and purports to prove one by disproving the other. The level of generality of the constitutional principle can be determined only by examining the context of the constitutional decision and the intellectual history of the terms employed. Even then, more than one alternative interpretation may emerge as plausible. But there is no logical basis for assuming that constitutional provisions should be read at the highest level of generality.

D. RECONCEPTUALIZING DEMOCRACY

BRUCE ACKERMAN, WE THE PEOPLE, VOLUME 1: FOUNDATIONS

6–14, 16–17, 40–44, 47–50 (1991).

DUALIST DEMOCRACY

THE BASIC IDEA

Above all else, a dualist Constitution seeks to distinguish between two different decisions that may be made in a democracy. The first is a decision by the American people; the second, by their government.

Decisions by the People occur rarely, and under special constitutional conditions. Before gaining the authority to make supreme law in the name of the People, a movement's political partisans must, first, convince an extraordinary number of their fellow citizens to take their proposed initiative with a seriousness that they do not normally accord to politics;

[60]Earl M. Maltz, Civil Rights, the Constitution, and Congress, 1863–1869, at 68, 157–58 (1990).

second, they must allow their opponents a fair opportunity to organize their own forces; third, they must convince a majority of their fellow Americans to support their initiative as its merits are discussed, time and again, in the deliberative fora provided for "higher lawmaking." It is only then that a political movement earns the enhanced legitimacy the dualist Constitution accords to decisions made by the People.

Decisions made by the government occur daily, and also under special conditions. Most importantly, key officials must be held accountable regularly at the ballot box. In addition, they must be given incentives to take a broad view of the public interest without the undue influence of narrow interest groups. Even when this system of "normal lawmaking" is operating well, however, the dualist Constitution prevents elected politicians from exaggerating their authority. They are not to assert that a normal electoral victory has given them a mandate to enact an ordinary statute that overturns the considered judgments previously reached by the People. If they wish to claim this higher form of democratic legitimacy, they must take to the specially onerous obstacle course provided by a dualist Constitution for purposes of higher lawmaking. Only if they succeed in mobilizing their fellow citizens and gaining their repeated support in response to their opponents' counterattacks may they finally earn the authority to proclaim that *the People* have changed their mind and have given their government new marching orders.

Such a brief statement raises many more questions than answers. One set involves issues of institutional design. First, we must consider the design of a good higher lawmaking system: How to organize a process that will reliably mark out the rare occasions when a political movement rightly earns the special recognition accorded the outcomes of mobilized deliberation made in the name of We the People? Second, there is the question of normal lawmaking: How to create incentives for regularly elected officials to engage in public-spirited deliberation despite the pressures of special interests? Third, there is the design of preservation mechanisms: How to preserve the considered judgments of the mobilized People from illegitimate erosion by the statutory decisions of normal government?

And then there are the ultimate issues that transcend institutional mechanics: Is dualist democracy a good form of government for America? The best? If not, what's better?

This chapter does not aim for final answers. It simply describes how the very questions provoked by dualist democracy suggests inquiries different from those now dominant in the academy. Although each academic competitor differs from dualism in a different way, it may help to begin with the one thing they have in common. For all their luxuriant variety, they ignore the special importance dualists place upon *constitutional politics:* the series of political movements that have, from the Founding onward, called upon their fellow Americans to engage in acts of citizenship that, when successful, culminates in the proclamation of higher law in the name of We the People.

But let me be more specific.

MONISTIC DEMOCRACY

Of the modern schools, the monistic democrats have the most impressive pedigree: Woodrow Wilson,[1] James Thayer,[2] Charles Beard,[3] Oliver Wendell Holmes,[4] Robert Jackson,[5] Alexander Bickel,[6] John Ely.[7] These, and many other distinguished thinkers and doers, have made monism dominant amongst serious constitutionalists over the course of the last century. As with all received opinions, complexities abound. But, at its root, monism is very simple: Democracy requires the grant of plenary lawmaking authority to the winners of the last general election—so long, at least, as the election was conducted under free and fair ground rules and the winners don't try to prevent the next scheduled round of electoral challenges.

This idea motivates, in turn, a critical institutional conclusion: during the period between elections, all institutional checks upon the electoral victors are presumptively antidemocratic. For sophisticated monists, this is only a presumption. Perhaps certain constitutional checks may prevent the victors from abrogating the next scheduled election; perhaps others might be justified once one considers the deeper ways normal elections fail to satisfy our ideals of electoral fairness. While these exceptions may have great practical importance, monists refuse to let them obscure the main point: when the Supreme Court, or anybody else, invalidates a statute, it suffers from a "countermajoritarian difficulty" which must be overcome before a good democrat can profess satisfaction with this extraordinary action.

* * *

The monist begs a big question when he asserts that the winner of a fair and open election is entitled to rule with the full authority of We the People. It is much better, of course, for electoral winners to take office

---

[1]Woodrow Wilson, Congressional Government (1885); Woodrow Wilson, Constitutional Government in the United States (1907).

[2]James Thayer, "The Origin and Scope of the American Doctrine of Constitutional Law," 7 Harv.L.Rev. 129 (1893).

[3]Charles Beard, An Economic Interpretation of the Constitution of the United States (1913).

[4]Lochner v. New York, 198 U.S. 45, 74 (1905) (Holmes, J., dissenting).

[5]Robert Jackson, The Struggle for Judicial Supremacy (1941); Railway Express Co. v. New York, 336 U.S. 106, 111 (1949) (Jackson, J., concurring).

[6]Alexander Bickel, The Least Dangerous Branch (1962).

[7]John Ely, Democracy and Distrust: A Theory of Judicial Review (1980).

rather than suffer an authoritarian putsch by the losers. But it does not follow that all statutes gaining the support of a legislative majority in Washington, D.C., represent the considered judgment of a mobilized majority of American citizens. Instead, the dualist sees a profoundly democratic point to many of the distinctive practices that baffle the monist. For her, they express our Constitution's effort to require elected politicians to operate within a two-track system. If politicians hope to win normal democratic legitimacy for an initiative, they are directed down the normal lawmaking path and told to gain the assent of the House, Senate, and President in the usual ways. If they hope for higher lawmaking authority, they are directed down a specially onerous lawmaking path—whose character and historical development will be the subject of the next chapter. Only if a political movement successfully negotiates the special challenges of the higher lawmaking system can it rightfully claim that its initiative represents the constitutional judgment of We the People.

Once the two-track character of the system is recognized, the Supreme Court appears in a different light. Consider that all the time and effort required to push an initiative down the higher lawmaking track would be wasted unless the Constitution prevented future normal politicians from enacting statutes that ignored the movement's higher law achievement. If future politicians could so easily ignore established higher law, why would any mass movement take the trouble to overcome the special hurdles placed on the higher lawmaking track?

To maintain the integrity of higher lawmaking, all dualist constitutions must provide for one or more institutions to discharge a preservationist function. These institutions must effectively block efforts to repeal established constitutional principles by the simple expedient of passing a normal statute and force the reigning group of elected politicians to move onto the higher lawmaking track if they wish to question the judgments previously made by We the People. Only after negotiating this more arduous obstacle course can a political elite earn the authority to say that We the People have changed our mind.

It follows, then, that the dualist will view the Supreme Court from a very different perspective than the monist. The monist treats every act of judicial review as presumptively antidemocratic and strains to save the Supreme Court from the "countermajoritarian difficulty" by one or another ingenious argument. In contrast, the dualist sees the discharge of the preservationist function by the courts as an essential part of a well-ordered democratic regime. Rather than threatening democracy by frustrating the statutory demands of the political elite in Washington, the courts serve democracy by protecting the hard-won principles of a mobilized citizenry against erosion by political elites who have failed to gain broad and deep popular support for their innovations.

This is not to say that any particular decision by the modern Supreme Court can be justified in preservationist terms. The key point is that dualists cannot dismiss a good-faith effort by the Court to interpret the Constitution as "antidemocratic" simply because it leads to the invalidation of normal statutes; this ongoing judicial effort to look backward and interpret the meaning of the great achievements of the past is an indispensable part of the larger project of distinguishing the will of We the People from the acts of We the Politicians.

RIGHTS FOUNDATIONALISTS

In confronting monism, the dualist's main object is to break the tight link monists construct between two distinct ideas: "democracy" on the one hand and "parliamentary sovereignty" on the other. Like monists, dualists are democrats—they believe that the People are the ultimate authority in America. They disagree only about the easy way in which normally elected politicians claim to legislate with the full authority of the People.

In contrast, the primacy of popular sovereignty is challenged by a second modern school. While none of these theorists completely denies a place for democratic principles, their populist enthusiasms are constrained by deeper commitments to fundamental rights. Unsurprisingly, members of this school differ when it comes to identifying the rights that are fundamental. Conservatives like Richard Epstein emphasize the foundational role of property rights;[13] liberals like Ronald Dworkin emphasize the right to equal concern and respect;[14] collectivists like Owen Fiss, the rights of disadvantaged groups.[15] These transparent differences should not blind us to the idea that binds them together. Whatever rights are Right, all agree that the American constitution is concerned, first and foremost, with their protection. Indeed, the whole point of having rights is to trump decisions rendered by democratic institutions that may otherwise legislate for the collective welfare. To emphasize this common thread, I shall group these thinkers together by calling them *rights foundationalists.*

As with the monists, this school is hardly a trendy creation of yesterday. There is, however, an interesting difference in the intellectual lineage they construct for themselves. While monists refer to a series of Americans from Wilson and Thayer to Frankfurter and Bickel, foundationalists favor philosophical writers further removed in time and space—with Kant (via Rawls)[16] and Locke (via Nozick)[17] presently serving as the most important sources of inspiration. Right now, I am not interested in these internal

[13]Richard Epstein, Takings: Private Property and the Power of Eminent Domain (1985).

[14]Ronald Dworkin, Taking Rights Seriously, ch. 5 (1978); Ronald Dworkin, Law's Empire, chs. 10–11 (1986).

[15]Owen Fiss, *Groups and the Equal Protection Clause,* 5 J.Phil. & Pub.Aff. 107 (1976).

[16]John Rawls, *Kantian Constructivism in Moral Theory,* 77 J.Phil. 515 (1980).

[17]Robert Nozick, Anarchy, State, and Utopia (1974).

debates. My aim is to describe how foundationalists as a group differ from more democratic schools.

Begin with the monists. It is fair to say that they are hostile to rights, at least as foundationalists understand them. Indeed, it is just when the Supreme Court begins to invalidate statutes in the name of fundamental rights that the monist begins to worry about the "countermajoritarian difficulty" that renders judicial review presumptively illegitimate.

This "difficulty" does not seem so formidable to the foundationalist. Instead, she is more impressed by the fact that a democratic legislature might endorse any number of oppressive actions—establish a religion, or authorize torture, or * * *. When such violations occur, the foundationalist demands judicial intervention despite the breach of democratic principle. Rights trump democracy—provided, of course, that they're the Right rights.

* * *

How does the introduction of dualism change the shape of this familiar conversational field? By offering a framework which allows both sides to accommodate some—if not all—of their concerns. The basic mediating device is the dualist's two-track system of democratic lawmaking. It allows an important place for the foundationalist's view of "rights as trumps" without violating the monist's deeper commitment to the primacy of democracy. To grasp the logic of accommodation, suppose that a rights-oriented movement took to the higher lawmaking track and successfully mobilized the People to endorse one or another Bill of Rights. Given this achievement, the dualist can readily endorse the judicial invalidation of later statutes that undermine these rights, even when they concern matters, like the protection of personal freedom or privacy, that have nothing much to do with the integrity of the electoral process so central to monistic democrats. As we have seen, the dualist believes that the Court furthers the cause of democracy when it preserves constitutional rights against erosion by politically ascendant elites who have yet to mobilize the People to support the repeal of previous higher lawmaking principles. Thus, unlike the monist, she will have no trouble supporting the idea that rights can properly trump the conclusions of normal democratic politics. She can do so, moreover, without the need for non-democratic principles of the kinds proffered by the rights foundationalist. Thus, the dualist can offer a deeper reconciliation of democracy and rights to those who find a certain amount of truth in both sides of the debate.

* * *

The clash between monists and foundationalists dominates the present field of constitutional debate and has moved beyond the classroom to the courtroom. The sharp split between the two schools mimics the split between plaintiff and defendant in the typical lawsuit—the plaintiff insisting that a statute has violated her fundamental rights, the defendant responding that courts should defer to the democratic authority of Congress. Little wonder that thoughtful judges and citizens are drawn to reflections about democracy and rights—creating an audience for the work of the two competing schools.

Dualism expresses a more hopeful possibility. Perhaps the conflict between plaintiff and defendant is not a sign of unremitting conflict between the democratic and rights-oriented aspects of our tradition. Instead, both the enactment of normal statutes *and* the judicial protection of constitutional rights are part of a larger practice of dualist democracy. This abstract synthesis, of course, is hardly enough to decide concrete cases. But it points in a particular direction—toward a reflective study of the past to determine when the People have spoken and what they have said during their historic moments of successful constitutional politics.

* * *

THE SHAPE OF THE CONSTITUTIONAL PAST

When modern lawyers and judges look to the deep past, they tell themselves a story that has a distinctive structure. Though special problems may lead them to appreciate the relevance of one or another aspect of America's constitutional history, three historical periods stand out from the rest. These eras have a pervasive significance: the lessons a judge draws from each of them organizes her entire approach to concrete cases. The first of these jurisgenerative[2] eras is the Founding itself—the framing of the original Constitution and the Bill of Rights, the Supreme Court's initial assertion of judicial review in *Marbury v. Madison.* A second great period occurs two generations later, with the bloody struggles that ultimately yield the Reconstruction amendments. Then there is another pause of two generations before a third great turning point. This one centers on the 1930's and the dramatic confrontation between the New Deal and the Old Court that ends in the constitutional triumph of the activist welfare state.

This three-part story defines the legal meaning of modernity: All of us live in the modern era that begins with the Supreme Court's "switch in time" in 1937, in which an activist, regulatory state is finally accepted as an unchallengeable constitutional reality. For a modern judge, one of the worst insults is that she is reenacting the sin originally committed by the pre-New Deal Court in cases like *Lochner v. New York.* Of course, different moderns define the nature of original sin differently. What is important is not the

[2] I borrow this term from Robert Cover, *The Supreme Court 1982 Term—Foreword: Nomos and Narrative,* 97 Harv.L.Rev. 4, 11 (1983).

competing diagnoses but the universal recognition that the constitutional world before the Roosevelt era was profoundly different from our own.

In contrast, today's lawyers and judges experience no similar estrangement in dealing with more recent history: the New Deal Court that digs itself out of the wreckage of laissez-faire jurisprudence in the late 1930's is recognizably *our* Court. Just as it struggled to define a new conception of individual rights in a burgeoning bureaucratic state, so do modern constitutionalists. While the New Deal Court's early confrontations with these questions differ from more recent encounters, we still think we can learn from these early cases in very positive ways. Rather than functioning as negative precedents like *Lochner,* these early decisions of the New Deal Court mark the very dawning of the modern world.

So much, I think, is shared by all competent constitutional lawyers, regardless of their more particular political or philosophical convictions. I believe, moreover, that the profession's selective concentration upon these three historical turning points is fundamentally sound. Though other periods have contributed a lot to the modern practice of American government, lawyers and judges are right to look upon the Founding, Reconstruction, and the New Deal as decisive moments at which deep changes in popular opinion gained authoritative constitutional recognition. The problem comes only when we consider the way the profession has transformed this selective chronology into a meaningful narrative that roots the modern age in the deep past.

* * *

The problem is this: the stories lawyers tell about each of the three turning points do not invite them to reflect upon the common features of these great transformative exercises. Instead, each of these three jurisgenerative events is cabined by a set of lawyerly categories that emphasize how different one episode is from the next.

Of the three, the Founding is treated as if it were the most radical break with the past. Modern lawyers are perfectly prepared to admit that the Constitutional Convention was acting illegally in proposing its new document in the name of We the People. The Founding Federalists, after all, were not prepared to follow the ratification procedures set out in the Articles of Confederation that had been solemnly accepted by all thirteen states only a few years before. The Articles required the unanimous consent of all thirteen state legislatures before any new amendment could come into effect. In contrast, the Federalists blandly excluded state legislatures from *any* role in ratification, and went on to assert that the approval of special constitutional conventions meeting in only nine of the thirteen states would suffice to validate the Convention's effort to speak for the People.

Illegalities like these may not be among the first things that surface in the legal mind, but modern lawyers show no great resistance coming to terms with them. Indeed, there is a conceptual sense in which our very identification of the Founding as a Founding presupposes that the Philadelphia Convention acted without legal warrant under the preexisting Articles. If this were not the case, the *real* Founders of our Republic were the folks who wrote and ratified the Articles of Confederation; the Philadelphia Convention simply gained the ratification of some sweeping "amendments" to the Founding document. Since modern lawyers do not trace the origin of the Republic to the Articles of Confederation but to *the* Constitution of 1787, the discovery of some Founding illegalities confirms, rather than denies, their sense of the overall shape of our constitutional past.

Things are different when the subject turns to the constitutional amendments enacted after the Civil War. Here modern law-talk exhibits a sharp dichotomy between substance and procedure. Substantively, everybody recognizes that these three amendments profoundly transformed preexisting constitutional principles. But if we turn to the process by which they became part of our higher law, a remarkable silence descends on the legal community. While it has no trouble admitting the dubious legality of the Founding, professional talk contains no hint that Reconstruction might be similarly tainted. If asked to explain why the Civil War amendments are part of the Constitution, the modern American lawyer or judge would almost certainly point to the rules for constitutional amendment contained in Article Five of the 1787 Constitution. According to received opinion, the Civil War amendments are just that: ordinary amendments which, like all the others, owe their legality to their conformity with the formal rules for constitutional revision established by the Federalists in the 1787 Constitution. To put this point in a formula: while the professional narrative insists that Reconstruction was *substantively creative,* it supposes that it was *procedurally unoriginal.*

Even this much originality is denied the New Deal. While all lawyers recognize that the 1930's mark the definitive constitutional triumph of activist national government, they tell themselves a story which denies that anything deeply creative was going on. This view of the 1930's is obtained by imagining a Golden Age in which Chief Justice Marshall got things right for all time by propounding a broad construction of the national government's lawmaking authority. The period between Reconstruction and the New Deal can then be viewed as a (complex) story about the fall from grace—wherein most of the Justices strayed from the path of righteousness and imposed their laissez-faire philosophy on the nation through the pretext of constitutional interpretation. Predictably, these acts of judicial usurpation increasingly set the judges at odds with more democratic institutions, which acutely perceived the failure of laissez-faire to do justice to an increasingly interdependent world.

* * *

Founding Federalists → Illegal Constitution; Reconstruction Republicans → Formal Amendments; New Deal Democrats → Judicial Rediscovery of Ancient Truths: this schema suggests a subtle but unmistakable decline in the constitutionally generative capacities of the American people. Apparently, We the People have never again engaged in the sweeping kind of critique and creation attempted by the Founding Federalists. We have made substantive revisions in the original structure of the Constitution, but we have never gone so far as to revise the very process of constitutional revision. A similar loss is implied by a comparison between the nineteenth and twentieth centuries: while the Reconstruction Republicans gained the consent of the American people to fundamental changes in governing principles, the sweeping transformations won by the New Deal Democrats represent nothing more than a return to the wisdom of the early Founders.

* * *

My counterthesis: Like the Reconstruction Republicans, the New Deal Democrats relied on the national separation of powers between Congress, President, and Court to create a new institutional framework through which the American People might define, debate, and finally decide their constitutional future. The key institutional difference between the two periods involves the Presidency. Franklin Roosevelt remained at the helm of the reformist coalition throughout the Democrats' period of constitutional transformation, whereas Lincoln's assassination deprived Republican reformers of Presidential support during the critical struggle over the Fourteenth Amendment. Roosevelt's long tenure had fundamental, if unsurprising, implications for the Presidency's role in the process of higher lawmaking. While the Republicans successfully experimented with Presidential leadership in the process of legitimating the Thirteenth Amendment, they could not build on this experience once Andrew Johnson declared war on the Fourteenth Amendment. In contrast, the Democrats were in a position to develop the power of the Presidency in a far more incisive fashion.

When due allowances are made for the defection of President Johnson from the Republican coalition, however, it will be possible to identify remarkable similarities in the way in which the separation of powers tested, and finally legitimated, the constitutional revisions proposed by nineteenth-century Republicans and twentieth-century Democrats. Each higher lawmaking exercise began with the reformers in control of only part of the national government—in the case of the Republicans, it was Congress that took on the mantle of reform leadership with Johnson's defection; in the case of the Democrats, the Presidency was the leading reform branch. In both cases, the constitutional reformers' proposals were exposed to an initial period of incisive critique by conservative branches, which publicly appealed to the People to decisively reject the dangerous innovations proposed by the reformers. In the case of the Republicans, the leading conservative branch was the Presidency; for the Democrats, it was the Supreme Court.

These institutional differences were important, of course, in explaining the different dynamics of constitutional debate and decision. But it is even more important to see the deeper similarities. In both cases, the institutional deadlock in Washington forced both sides to mobilize their supporters in the country at large. These remarkable efforts at popular mobilization, in turn, gave extraordinary constitutional meaning to the next regularly scheduled election. If one or another side could win a decisive victory at the polls, it would try to use its popular support to break the institutional impasse.

This process of interbranch struggle and popular mobilization made the elections of 1866 and 1936 decisive events in constitutional history. On both occasions, the reformers returned to Washington with a clear victory at the polls. They proceeded to proclaim that the election results gave them a "mandate from the People," and that the time had come for the conservative branches to end their constitutional resistance.

This demand by the electorally victorious reformers inaugurated the period of ratification—in which the conservative branches considered whether to continue their resistance or to recognize that the People had indeed given their fixed support to the reformist movement. In both cases, this decision was not made in silent contemplation but in response to a challenge by the reformist branches to the conservatives' continued legitimacy. During Reconstruction, the reformist Congress finally threatened President Johnson with impeachment if he continued to use his office to sabotage ratification of the Fourteenth Amendment. During the New Deal, it was the reformist President's threat of packing the Court that provoked the conservative Justices to consider the wisdom of continued resistance. In both cases, however, the question was very much the same: Should the conservatives in the dissenting branches finally recognize that *the People had spoken?*

In both cases, the conservatives' answer was the same. Rather than escalating the constitutional crisis further, they decided, with evident reluctance, that further resistance would endanger too many of the very values they held fundamental. They made the "switch in time": Johnson called off his effort to prevent the formal ratification of the Fourteenth Amendment; the Supreme Court repudiated its doctrinal defense of laissez-faire capitalism and began to build new constitutional foundations for activist national government.

In turn, the victorious reformers responded in the same way. The Republicans refused to convict the President, allowing Johnson to remain in office to proclaim the validity of the Fourteenth Amendment; the Democrats called off the threat of court-packing, allowing the Old Court to proclaim that activist New Deal government was constitutionally legitimate.

As a consequence of these "switches in time," all three branches emerge from the period of democratic testing once again united, and the separation of powers remains intact for use by the next constitutional regime. But it is now in the service of the new constitutional solution that had previously been so controversial.

Interbranch Impasse → Decisive Election → Reformist Challenge to Conservative Branches → Switch in Time: This separation of powers schema will require lots of elaboration before it can gain legal credibility. There is no way to avoid the hard historical work required to appreciate the functional similarities between President Johnson's veto of Congress's Civil Rights Act and the Supreme Court's veto of the NIRA; between the critical election of 1866 and the critical election of 1936; between the Republican effort to impeach the President and the Democratic effort to pack the Court; between the final ratification of the Fourteenth Amendment by Johnson's Secretary of State and the final ratification of the welfare state by the New Deal Court; and so forth. Fortunately, many of these fascinating events have attracted the sustained attention of generations of historians; and I will try to make use of their insights as best I can. An even more formidable challenge will be to set each particular episode into the larger context of higher lawmaking—and thereby grasp the evolving constitutional process through which the separation of powers first forced the contending parties to refine their constitutional vision and counter-vision, then presented the key issues in dramatic form to a mobilized electorate, and then provided a further period during which thoughtful conservatives could consider whether the time had not come to recognize that the People had indeed spoken.

In elaborating these striking parallels between Reconstruction and the New Deal, I shall be building upon the insights of the protagonists of the 1930's. Time and again, the New Dealers invoked Reconstruction precedents in their efforts to build a modern model of Presidential leadership in the higher lawmaking process. The challenge is to *listen* to these voices, not insist upon viewing the New Deal reformers as if they were exhausted epigones, capable only of returning to the forgotten wisdom of the Founders.

CASS R. SUNSTEIN, A REPUBLIC OF REASONS

THE PARTIAL CONSTITUTION 18–34, 38–39 (1993).

MONARCHY, SELF-INTEREST, FACTIONS

The framers of the American Constitution sought to create a system of government that would simultaneously counteract three related dangers: the legacy of monarchy; self-interested representation by government officials; and the power of faction, or "majority tyranny." The impartiality principle was part of the attempt to respond to all these problems.

* * *

The impartiality principle is conspicuously connected with the desire, traceable to the early period of the founding, to limit the potential arbitrariness of the king and indeed of everything entailed by the institutions of monarchy. The Constitution should be understood against the backdrop set by prerevolutionary America, which had been pervaded by monarchial characteristics, including well-entrenched patterns of deference and hierarchy. In the prerevolutionary period, many of these patterns were attributed to nature itself. These included not merely the institution of slavery but also existing family structures, relations between employers and employees, occupational categories, education, the crucial concept of the gentleman, and of course the structures of government. Indeed, those very structures were thought to be modeled on the family and to grow out of the same natural sources.

A large element in the American Revolution consisted of a radical rebellion against the monarchical legacy. The rebellion operated with special force against the traditional belief in a "natural order of things." Thus the Americans insisted, in direct opposition to their English inheritance, that "culture" was "man-made." In America, social outcomes had to be justified not by reference to nature or to traditional practices, but instead on the basis of reasons.

The American framers were alert not only to the legacy of monarchy, but also to the general risk that public officials would act on behalf of their own self-interest rather than the interests of the public as a whole. Actual corruption in government was the most dramatic illustration of this danger. But self-interested representation could be found in many places in which officials seek to aggrandize their own powers and interests at the expense of the people as a whole. The responsibility of the public official was to put personal interest entirely to one side. The impartiality principle, requiring public officials to invoke public-regarding reasons on behalf of their actions, was a check on self-interested representation.

Finally, the framers sought to limit the power of self-interested private groups, or "factions," over governmental processes. For Madison, this was the greatest risk in America: "[I]n our Governments the real power lies in the majority of the Community, and the invasion of private rights is chiefly to be apprehended, not from acts of Government contrary to the sense of its constituents, but from acts in which the Government is the mere instrument of the major number of the constituents."[3] Hence majority rule was, for the framers, a highly ambiguous good. On their view, even an insistent majority should not have its way, if power was the only thing to be invoked on its behalf.

It is relevant here that the framers operated in the light of their experiences under the Articles of Confederation. Under the Articles, powerful private groups appeared to dominate state and local government, obtaining measures that favored them but no one else, and that could be explained only by reference of private self-interest. The new Constitution was intended to limit this risk.

Above all, the American Constitution was designed to create a deliberative democracy. Under that system, public representatives were to be ultimately accountable to the people; but they would also be able to engage in a form of deliberation without domination through the influence of factions. A law based solely on the self-interest of private groups is the core violation of the deliberative ideal.

The minimal condition of deliberative democracy is a requirement of reasons for governmental action. We may thus understand the American Constitution as having established, for the first time, a republic of reasons. A republic of this sort is opposed equally to outcomes grounded on self-interest and to those based solely on "nature" or authority. Where the monarchical system saw government as an outgrowth of a given or natural order, the founding generation regarded it as "merely a legal man-made contrivance having little if any natural relationship to the family or to society."[5]

FOUNDING INSTITUTIONS

The general commitment to deliberative democracy, and the belief in a republic of reasons, echo throughout the founding period. In *The Federalist* No. 10—James Madison's most outstanding contribution to political thought—the system of national representation is defended as a mechanism with which to "refine and enlarge the public views by passing them through the medium of a chosen body of citizens, whose wisdom may discern the true interest of their country and whose patriotism and love of justice will be least likely to sacrifice it to temporary or partial considerations." On this

---

[3]Madison to Jefferson, Oct. 17, 1788, in 11 J. Madison, *The Papers of James Madison* 298 (R. Rutland & C. Hobson eds. 1977).

[5]Gordon Wood, *The Radicalism of the American Republic* 167 (1992).

view, national officials, selected from a broad territory, would be uniquely positioned to operate above the fray of private interests.

In their aspirations for deliberative government, the framers modernized the classical republican belief in civic virtue. The antifederalists, critics of the proposed Constitution, had invoked traditional republican ideas in order to challenge the Madisonian belief that a large territory was compatible with true republicanism. In the antifederalist view, a genuine republic required civic virtue, or commitment to the public good. Civic virtue, they insisted, could flourish only in small communities united by similar interests and by a large degree of homogeneity.

The framers fully accepted the goal; but they firmly rejected the prescription. For the framers, as for those in the classical tradition, virtue was indispensable; and the framers continued to understand virtue as a commitment to the general good rather than to self-interest or the interest of private factions. Thus Hamilton urged that the "aim of every political constitution is, or ought to be, first to obtain for rulers men who possess most wisdom to discern, and most virtue to pursue the common good of the society; and in the next place, to take the most effectual precautions for keeping them virtuous whilst they continue to hold their public trust."[7] But for the framers, a large republic would be more, rather than less, likely to serve republican aspirations. It would do so precisely because in a large republic, national representatives would be in an unusually good position to engage in the deliberative tasks of government. A small republic, as history had shown, would be buffeted about by the play of factions. In a large republic, the various factions would offset each other.

In recent years, there has been an extraordinary revival of interest in republican thought. The revival is directed above all against two groups: people who think that the Constitution is designed only to protect a set of identified "private rights," and people who treat the document as an effort to provide the rules for interest-group struggles among selfish private groups.

The framers' aspirations were far broader. They attempted to carry forward the classical republican belief in virtue—a word that appears throughout the period—but to do so in a way that responded realistically, not romantically, to likely difficulties in the real world of political life. They continued to insist on the possibility of a virtuous politics. They tried to make a government that would create such a politics without indulging unrealistic assumptions about human nature. We might understand the Constitution as a complex set of precommitment strategies, through which the citizenry creates institutional arrangements to protect against political

[7] *The Federalist* No. 63.

self-interest, factionalism, failures in representation, myopia, and other predictable problems in democratic governance.

The commitment to these ideas explains many of the founding institutions. It helps explain why, in the original system, the Senate and the President were to be chosen by deliberative representatives rather than directly elected by the people. It helps with the mystery of the Electoral College, which was, at the inception, to be a deliberative body, one that would discuss who ought to be President, rather than simply register votes. It helps explain why the framers favored long terms of service and large election districts. All these ideas about government structure were designed to accomplish the same goals, that is, to promote deliberation and to limit the risk that public officials would be mouthpieces for constituent interests. It was in this vein that Madison attacked Congress in 1787 as "advocates for the respective interests of their constituents" and complained of "the County representatives, the members of which are everywhere observed to lose sight of the aggregate interests of the Community, and even to sacrifice them to the interests or prejudices of their respective constituents."[10] The new Constitution was designed to reduce this risk. The framers designed a system in which representatives would have the time and temperament to engage in a form of collective reasoning.

* * *

The basic institutions of the resulting Constitution were intended to encourage and to profit from deliberation, thus understood. The system of checks and balances—the cornerstone of the system—was designed to encourage discussion among different governmental entities. So too with the requirement of bicameralism, which would bring different perspectives to bear on lawmaking. The same goals accounted for the notion that laws should be presented to the President for his signature or veto; this mechanism would provide an additional perspective. The federal system would ensure a supplemental form of dialogue, here between states and the national government.

Judicial review was intended to create a further check. Its basic purpose was to protect the considered judgments of the people, as represented in the extraordinary law of the Constitution, against the ill-considered or short-term considerations introduced by the people's mere agents in the course of enacting ordinary law. As we will see, many of the original individual rights can be understood as part of the idea of deliberative democracy. Indeed, the goals of protecting rights and of promoting deliberation were understood to march hand in hand. The special status of property rights was

[10]Letter to Jefferson, Oct. 3, 1785, reprinted in 8 *The Papers of James Madison* 374 (Robert Rutland & William Rachal eds. 1975); Remarks on Mr. Jefferson's Draft of a Constitution, in *The Mind of the Founder* 35 (Marvin Meyers rev. ed. 1981).

an effort to ensure against precipitous, short-sighted, or ill-considered intrusions into the private sphere. Deliberative government and limited government were, in the framers' view, one and the same.

I have said that the framers' belief in deliberative democracy drew from traditional republican thought, and that it departed from the tradition in the insistence that a large republic would be better than a small one. It departed even more dramatically in its striking and novel rejection of the traditional republican idea that heterogeneity and difference were destructive to the deliberative process. For the framers, heterogeneity was beneficial, indeed indispensable; discussion must take place among people who were different. It was on this score that the framers responded to the antifederalist insistence that homogeneity was necessary to a republic.

Drawing on the classical tradition, the antifederalist "Brutus," complaining of the theory behind the proposed nationalist Constitution, wrote, "In a republic, the manners, sentiments, and interests of the people should be similar. If this be not the case, there will be a constant clashing of opinions; and the representatives of one part will be continually striving against those of the other."[16] Hamilton, by contrast, thought that heterogeneity, as part of the deliberative process, could be a creative and productive force. Thus he suggested that the "differences of opinion, and the jarrings of parties in [the legislative] department * * * often promote deliberation * * *."[17] As the framers saw it, the exchange of reasons in the public sphere was a condition for this process.

IMPARTIALITY, THE REPUBLIC OF REASONS, AND INTEREST-GROUP PLURALISM

Read against this background, the principle of impartiality requires government to provide reasons that can be intelligible to different people operating from different premises. The requirement might be understood in this respect as a check on government by fiat, helping to bar authoritarianism generally. Drawing from our founding aspirations, we might even define authoritarian systems as all those that justify government outcomes by reference to power or will rather than by reference to reasons. At the heart of the liberal tradition and its opposition to authoritarianism lies a requirement of justification by reference to public-regarding explanations that are intelligible to all citizens. The principle of impartiality is the concrete manifestation of this commitment in American constitutional law.

Described in this way, the impartiality requirement might seem trivial and therefore uncontroversial. But the requirement turns out to be in severe tension with one of the most influential approaches to both modern government and American constitutionalism: interest-group pluralism.

---

[16] 2 *The Complete Antifederalist* 369 (Herbert Storing ed. 1980).

[17] *The Federalist* No. 70.

There are many different forms of pluralism, but the unifying pluralist claim is that laws should be understood not as a product of deliberation, but on the contrary as a kind of commodity, subject to the usual forces of supply and demand. Various groups in society compete for loyalty and support from the citizenry. Once groups are organized and aligned, they exert pressure on political representatives, also self-interested, who respond to the pressures thus imposed. This process of aggregating and trading off interests ultimately produces law, or political equilibrium.

Whether pluralist ideas accurately describe current American politics is a subject of much dispute. There can be little doubt that the American framers were not pluralists. Some people also think that contemporary real-world government outcomes actually reflect reasons and justifications, and that those outcomes diverge from legislative and constituent self-interest (unless the concept of self-interest is understood so broadly as to be trivialized—as in the idea that altruism reflects self-interest, because altruists are interested in altruism). As we will see, interest-group pluralism is not an attractive political ideal. But if interest-group pluralism does describe contemporary politics, a requirement of impartiality, understood as a call for public-regarding justifications for government outcomes, is inconsistent with the very nature of government. It imposes on politics a requirement that simply cannot be met.

In the discussion to follow, I explore the relationship between the principle of impartiality and contemporary constitutional law. I show the extraordinary persistence of the principle across many generations and many constitutional provisions. I do not defend the requirement here; my purpose is descriptive. I claim only that the antiauthoritarian impulse, understood as a requirement of reasons, lies at the heart of American constitutional law.

THE BAN ON NAKED PREFERENCES

Judicial interpretation of many of the most important clauses of the Constitution reveals a remarkably common theme. Although the clauses have different historical roots and were originally directed at different problems, they appear to be united by a concern with a single underlying evil: the distribution of resources or opportunities to one group rather than to another solely on the ground that those favored have exercised the raw political power to obtain what they want. I will call this underlying evil—a violation of the impartiality requirement—a *naked preference.*

The commerce clause, for example, allows one state to discriminate against commerce from another state only if that discrimination is a means of promoting some goal unrelated to helping self-interested insiders. The privileges and immunities clause prohibits a state from preferring its citizens over outsiders, unless the preference is supported by reasons independent of protecting the insiders. The equal protection clause permits laws treating two classes of people differently only if there is a good connection between the distinctions and legitimate public purposes. The due process clause requires all government action to be justified by reference to some public purpose. The contract clause allows government to break or modify a contract only if the action is intended to promote a general public goal and does not reflect mere interest-group power. The eminent domain clause protects private property against self-interested private groups, both by demanding that a "public use" be shown to justify a taking of private property and by distinguishing between permissible exercises of the government power and prohibited takings.

The prohibition of naked preferences therefore underlies a wide range of constitutional provisions. The prohibition is connected with the original idea that government must be responsive to something other than private pressure, and with the associated notion that politics is not the reconciling of given interests but instead the product of some form of deliberation about the public good. As it operates in current constitutional law, the prohibition of naked preferences—like Madison's approach to the problem of factionalism—focuses on the motivations of legislators, not of their constituents. The prohibition therefore embodies a particular conception of representation. Under that conception, the task of legislators is not to respond to private pressure but instead to select values through deliberation and debate.

The notion that governmental action must be grounded in something other than political power is of course at odds with pluralism. Naked preferences are common fare in the pluralist conception; interest-group politics invites them. The prohibition of naked preferences stands as a repudiation of theories claiming that the judicial role is only to police the processes of representation to ensure that all affected interest groups may participate. In this respect, the prohibition of naked preferences reflects a distinctly substantive value and cannot easily be captured in procedural terms. Above all, it presupposes that constitutional courts will serve as critics of the pluralist vision, not as adherents striving only to "clear the channels" for political struggle.[23] And if a judicial role seems odd here, we should recall that the founding generation itself regarded courts as an important repository for representation and preservation of republican virtue, standing above the play of interests.

THE BASIC FRAMEWORK

We might distinguish between two bases for treating one group or person differently from another. The first is a naked preference. For

[23]On this question, the influential treatment in John Hart Ely, *Democracy and Distrust* (1980), is untrue to the original constitutional structure or to current law.

example, state A may treat its own citizens better than those of state B—say, by requiring people of state B to pay for the use of the public parks in state A—simply because its own citizens have the political power and want better treatment. Or a city may treat blacks worse than whites—say, by denying them necessary police and fire protection—because whites have the power to restrict government benefits to themselves. In these examples, the political process is a mechanism by which self-interested individuals or groups seek to obtain wealth or opportunities at the expense of others. The task of the legislator is to respond to the pressures imposed by those interests.

Contrast with this a political process in which outcomes are justified by reference not to raw political power, but to some public value that they can be said to serve. For the moment we can define a public value extremely broadly, as any justification for government action that goes beyond the exercise of raw political power. (I describe later how the Constitution limits permissible public values.) For example, a state may relieve a group of people from a contractual obligation because the contract called for an act—say, the sale of heroin—that violated a public policy. Or state A may treat its own citizens better than those of state B—say, by limiting welfare payments to its own citizens—because it wants to restrict social spending to those who in the past have made, or in the future might make, a contribution to state revenues. In these examples, the role of the representative is to deliberate rather than to respond mechanically to constituent pressures. If an individual or group is to be treated differently from others, it must be for a reason that can be stated in public-regarding terms.

These competing portraits of the political process are of course caricatures of a complex reality. It is rare that government action is based purely on raw political power. Losers in the political process may have lost for a very good reason that has little to do with the power of their adversaries. Belief that an action will promote at least some conception of the public good almost always plays at least some role in government decisions. Sometimes people motivated to vote for certain legislation cannot easily disentangle the private and public factors that underlie the decision.

It is also rare for government action to be based on a disembodied effort to discern and implement public values, entirely apart from considerations of private pressure. Representatives are almost always aware of the fact that their vote will have electoral consequences. What emerges is therefore a continuum of government decisions, ranging from those that are motivated primarily by interest-group pressures to those in which such pressures play a very minor role. In any particular case, it may well be difficult to see which of these is dominant. But the occasional or even frequent difficulty should not be taken to obscure the existence of a real distinction. There is all the difference in the world between a system in which representatives try to offer some justification for their decisions, and a system in which political power is the only thing that is at work.

* * *

The equal protection clause, part of the Fourteenth Amendment, forbids a state to deny to any person "the equal protection of the laws." The clause is not concerned solely with the special case of discrimination between in-staters and out-of-staters. Its prohibition is far broader. Indeed, in many respects the clause may be understood as a generalization of the central concerns of the dormant commerce and privileges and immunities clauses, applying to all classifications their prohibition of naked preferences at the behest of in-staters. In this way, the basic requirement of impartiality is applied to everything.

Disadvantaged groups, impermissible ends, and heightened scrutiny. Discrimination against blacks, the central evil at which the clause was aimed, is the equal protection analogue of discrimination against out-of-staters under the commerce and privileges and immunities clauses. When a statute discriminates on its face against blacks, the Court applies a strong presumption of invalidity. One reason for heightened scrutiny is a belief that when a statute discriminates on its face against members of racial minority groups, a naked preference is almost certainly at work. Here a familiar idea—the relative political powerlessness of members of minority groups—helps to account for that belief. The central notion is that the ordinary avenues of political redress are much less likely to be available to minorities. The danger that such statutes will result from an exercise of (what is seen as) raw political power is correspondingly increased.

Current equal protection law also treats a number of government ends as impermissible. Notably, these prohibited ends involve a wide range of justifications that do not involve the exercise of raw political power in the ordinary sense. The point becomes clearest in cases involving classifications drawn on the basis of gender, alienage, and legitimacy. For example, when a statute provides that the spouses of male workers automatically qualify for social security benefits, but that spouses of female workers must show dependency, the classification hardly reflects an exercise of raw political power—narrowly understood—but instead embodies certain conceptions about the nature of female participation in the labor market. Invalidation of such statutes cannot be explained only on the basis of the minimal requirement that classifications rest on something other than raw power. Although the Court has not provided a clear rationale for its decisions here, the central ideas seem to be that the relevant groups are politically weak and that the traditional justifications for discrimination both reflect and perpetuate existing injustice.

* * *

[T]here can be no question that current legal doctrines reject interest-group pluralism as a constitutional creed. They point instead to a conception of politics that demands a measure of deliberation from government representatives, deliberation that has some autonomy from private pressures. Many provisions of the Constitution are thus aimed at a single evil: the distribution of resources to one person or group rather than to another on the sole ground that those benefited have exercised political power in order to obtain government assistance.

To be sure, the prohibition rarely results in invalidation. But the cases are strikingly unanimous in their version of the prohibited end. In this way, the impartiality principle lies at the core of American constitutional law.

JED RUBENFELD, OF CONSTITUTIONAL SELF-GOVERNMENT

71 FORDHAM L. REV. 1749 (2003)

Is constitutional law democratic?

If democracy means government by the living will of the people, the answer seemingly has to be no. Why should we cavil at this answer? Constitutional law checks the excesses of popular rule; that was and is its point. Europeans, by and large, are content to say so; the entire ideology of "universal human rights," which is orthodoxy in the "international community" today, presents these rights, enforced by constitutional tribunals throughout the world, as a supra-national, supra-political imperative to which every nation, including democratic nations, must equally bend.

But Americans have never wanted to concede that their Constitution or its rights are anti-democratic. For over a hundred years, American constitutionalists have offered ever more ingenious theories reconciling constitutional law with the principle of government by the living will of the people. This is a prestigious, central line of American constitutional thought, linking such prominent figures as Tiedeman, Thayer, Holmes, Meiklejohn, Bickel and Ely.

* * *

Majority rule is one way to operationalize the democratic imperative of governance by the present will of the governed. According to some, it is the best way; according to others, it is only a fair way. But whatever is said for it, the idea behind majority rule is clearly governance by present popular will or judgment.

Why is democracy understood—so frequently that it is often stated without argument or assumed without even being stated—as governance by the present will (or preferences, consent, judgment, values, etc.) of the people? The answer is that governance by the present will of the governed is thought to be nothing other than the principle of self-government itself. What else could self-government be if not that? * * *

In short, to be governed by "principles laid down long ago" is not self-government at all. It is rule by "the dead hand of the past."

It is not, however, self-evident that self-government consists of governance by the self's present will. There is another way of thinking about self government, which restores to self-government the dimension of time. On this view, self-government consists of living under self-given commitments laid down in the past to govern the future.

The easiest and strongest way for me to bring home this alternative picture of self-government is by invoking the case of individuals who aspire to be self-governing. This strategy of argument, as many readers have told me, runs the risk of overly anthropomorphizing the subject of democratic self-government. But it remains the clearest argument, so I will pursue it, notwithstanding the risks.

Most of us live lives deeply inscribed by commitments we have made for ourselves, large or small, professional or intimate. We do not live our lives by asking what we most want to do at each moment. Nor do we ask ourselves, at each moment, what we ought to do, all things considered. We live within the terms of our commitments—our jobs, our families, the goals we have set out to achieve—asking what we ought to do given these commitments. We reserve, to be sure, the right to repudiate some or all of these commitments. Nevertheless, in the way we actually live our lives—we who enjoy more freedom than almost any who ever lived—we exercise our capacity for self-government by living out purposes and engagements that occupy us, that govern us, for extended periods of time.

It is possible to see in this a failure of courage. To be really free, someone might say, we would cast off all commitments, if we only had the nerve. We would live in a state of pure ungovernedness. We would recognize no prior restraints. We would live "in the present."

* * *

[T]he ideal of living in the present fails to do justice to our most distinctively human capacity for self-government: the capacity to give our lives purposes of our own devising. To give purpose to what we do takes time. To be self-governing takes time. Animal freedom may properly consist of the freedom to act on present will; that is the freedom, presumably, of a stray dog. An animal, then, may be free for and in a moment. Human freedom is something more. And the something more, I suggest, lies in the human capacity to give one's life direction, purpose, and commitment over time.

The self that aspires to self-government, in short, does not aspire to a state of pure ungovernedness. This self aspires to be governed as well as governing; it aspires to be governed by self-given commitments. What is a commitment? It is, essentially, an act of autonomy—of self-law-giving. The self-governing self aspires not to be free from all governance, and hence free from the past and future, but to be governed by law of its own making.

These observations apply, if anything, even more clearly to democratic self-government than to individual self-government. There is no political freedom without law. There is no possibility of a purely unconstrained society. Without law, there can be only anarchy, not democracy. To the extent that a people would be self-governing, it must make law for itself, and this law must project itself over time.

Yes, I am assuming here that a people can act collectively—that there is such a thing as rational, purposive collective decision-making. And yes, I am also assuming that a people can continue to exist over time, indeed over generations, so that the American people today are in an important sense, the same people that made the Constitution two hundred years ago and remade it after the Civil War. These assumptions I will not try to defend here. But if a nation does have a temporally extended existence, then its self-government must also be temporally extended. Self-government for a people, no less than a person, can be a matter of laying down and living up to self-given commitments over time.

Once self-government is so understood, the whole question of constitutionalism's relationship to democracy changes radically. For on this view, in order to make constitutional self-government intelligible, there is no longer any need to deny constitutional law's historicity. There is no longer any need to struggle, against all appearances, to depict constitutional law as a vehicle for present popular will. There is no longer any need to suppress the judicial tendency, when ruling a statute unconstitutional, to cite the Constitution's text, enacted long ago, or the history that underlay that text, or the past decisions of the Court, or the fact, most fundamentally, that the Court is trying to honor a commitment the nation laid down for itself long ago.

None of this need be denied or suppressed, because it is just what judges should be doing, if they are to keep the nation to its constitutional commitments, which, in turn, is just what they should be doing in the name of constitutional self-government. For constitutional law, from this perspective, is not opposed to democracy. It is democracy—or at least it holds itself out as, it promises to be democracy—over time. Constitutionalism is an institution through which a democratic nation tries to lay down and hold itself to its own fundamental legal and political commitments. And that is self-government.

This line of argument * * * solves the counter-majoritarian difficulty. American written constitutionalism rejects the present-oriented speech-modeled conception of self-government—a conception underlying the New England town meeting, the Rousseauian republic, and every society based on the ideal of governance responsive to the "voice of the people." Whenever judges are said to "speak for" the people, this present oriented, speech-modeled conception is in play.

Against and in place of this speech-modeled democracy, American constitutionalism launched the idea of self-government through foundational texts. Americans would govern themselves by laying down their own fundamental commitments in a constitution and holding themselves to these commitments over time, unless or until these commitments are repudiated, and even at times when they happen to run contrary to popular will.

Unelected judges are called on to interpret this constitutional text precisely because these judges will not be responsive to present popular will or opinion. Judges are called on not to represent "the actual people of the here and now," nor to "respond to the interests and opinions of all the people." That is a job for politicians and administrators. It may be the job of the people's elected representatives. But the judicial task is to hold the nation to its self-given commitments, even at times when these commitments do not enjoy popular appeal. Or so at least Americans have always understood it, producing, I suggest, a better picture of constitutional self-government than the one made available by a good deal of highly sophisticated constitutional theory.

E. CRITICAL PERSPECTIVES

THURGOOD MARSHALL, REFLECTIONS ON THE BICENTENNIAL OF THE UNITED STATES CONSTITUTION

101 Harv.L.Rev. 1–5 (1987).

The year 1987 marks the 200th anniversary of the United States Constitution. A Commission has been established to coordinate the celebration. The official meetings, essay contests, and festivities have begun.

The planned commemoration will span three years, and I am told 1987 is "dedicated to the memory of the Founders and the document they drafted in Philadelphia."[1] We are to "recall the achievements of our Founders and the knowledge and experience that inspired them, the nature of the government they established, its origins, its character, and its ends, and the

[1] Commission on the Bicentennial of the United States Constitution, Preparation for a Commemoration: First Full Year's Report 6 (Sept. 1986).

rights and privileges of citizenship, as well as its attendant responsibilities."[2]

Like many anniversary celebrations, the plan for 1987 takes particular events and holds them up as the source of all the very best that has followed. Patriotic feelings will surely swell, prompting proud proclamations of the wisdom, foresight, and sense of justice shared by the framers and reflected in a written document now yellowed with age. This is unfortunate—not the patriotism itself, but the tendency for the celebration to oversimplify, and overlook the many other events that have been instrumental to our achievements as a nation. The focus of this celebration invites a complacent belief that the vision of those who debated and compromised in Philadelphia yielded the "more perfect Union" it is said we now enjoy.

I cannot accept this invitation, for I do not believe that the meaning of the Constitution was forever "fixed" at the Philadelphia Convention. Nor do I find the wisdom, foresight, and sense of justice exhibited by the framers particularly profound. To the contrary, the government they devised was defective from the start, requiring several amendments, a civil war, and momentous social transformation to attain the system of constitutional government, and its respect for the individual freedoms and human rights, that we hold as fundamental today. When contemporary Americans cite "The Constitution," they invoke a concept that is vastly different from what the framers barely began to construct two centuries ago.

For a sense of the evolving nature of the Constitution we need look no further than the first three words of the document's preamble: "We the People." When the Founding Fathers used this phrase in 1787, they did not have in mind the majority of America's citizens. "We the People" included, in the words of the framers, "the whole Number of free Persons."[3] On a matter so basic as the right to vote, for example, Negro slaves were excluded, although they were counted for representational purposes—at three-fifths each. Women did not gain the right to vote for over a hundred and thirty years.[4]

These omissions were intentional. The record of the framers' debates on the slave question is especially clear: the Southern states acceded to the demands of the New England states for giving Congress broad power to regulate commerce, in exchange for the right to continue the slave trade. The economic interests of the regions coalesced: New Englanders engaged in the "carrying trade" would profit from transporting slaves from Africa as

[2]Commission on the Bicentennial of the United States Constitution, First Report 6 (Sept. 17, 1985).

[3]U.S. Const. art. I, § 2, cl. 3.

[4]*See id.* amend. XIX (ratified in 1920).

well as goods produced in America by slave labor. The perpetuation of slavery ensured the primary source of wealth in the Southern states.

Despite this clear understanding of the role slavery would play in the new republic, use of the words "slaves" and "slavery" was carefully avoided in the original document. Political representation in the lower House of Congress was to be based on the population of "free Persons" in each state, plus three-fifths of all "other Persons."[5] Moral principles against slavery, for those who had them, were compromised, with no explanation of the conflicting principles for which the American Revolutionary War had ostensibly been fought: the self-evident truths "that all men are created equal, that they are endowed by their Creator with certain unalienable Rights, that among these are Life, Liberty and the pursuit of Happiness."

It was not the first such compromise. Even these ringing phrases from the Declaration of Independence are filled with irony, for an early draft of what became that declaration assailed the King of England for suppressing legislative attempts to end the slave trade and for encouraging slave rebellions. The final draft adopted in 1776 did not contain this criticism. And so again at the Constitutional Convention eloquent objections to the institution of slavery went unheeded, and its opponents eventually consented to a document which laid a foundation for the tragic events that were to follow.

Pennsylvania's Gouverneur Morris provides an example. He opposed slavery and the counting of slaves in determining the basis for representation in Congress. At the Convention he objected that

> the inhabitant of Georgia [or] South Carolina who goes to the coast of Africa, and in defiance of the most sacred laws of humanity tears away his fellow creatures from their dearest connections and damns them to the most cruel bondages, shall have more votes in a Government instituted for protection of the rights of mankind, than the Citizen of Pennsylvania or New Jersey who views with a laudable horror, so nefarious a practice.[8]

And yet Gouverneur Morris eventually accepted the three-fifths accommodation. In fact, he wrote the final draft of the Constitution, the very document the bicentennial will commemorate.

As a result of compromise, the right of the Southern states to continue importing slaves was extended, officially, at least until 1808. We know that it actually lasted a good deal longer, as the framers possessed no monopoly on the ability to trade moral principles for self-interest. But they nevertheless set an unfortunate example. Slaves could be imported, if the commercial interests of the North were protected. To make the compromise even

---

[5] *Id.* art. I, § 2, cl. 3.

[8] The Records of the Federal Convention of 1787, at 222 (M. Farrand rev. ed. 1966).

more palatable, customs duties would be imposed at up to ten dollars per slave as a means of raising public revenues.[9]

No doubt it will be said, when the unpleasant truth of the history of slavery in America is mentioned during this bicentennial year, that the Constitution was a product of its times, and embodied a compromise which, under other circumstances, would not have been made. But the effects of the framers' compromise have remained for generations. They arose from the contradiction between guaranteeing liberty and justice to all, and denying both to Negroes.

The original intent of the phrase, "We the People," was far too clear for any ameliorating construction. Writing for the Supreme Court in 1857, Chief Justice Taney penned the following passage in the *Dred Scott* case,[10] on the issue of whether, in the eyes of the framers, slaves were "constituent members of the sovereignty," and were to be included among "We the People":

> We think they are not, and that they are not included, and were not intended to be included. . . .
>
> . . .
>
> They had for more than a century before been regarded as beings of an inferior order, and altogether unfit to associate with the white race * * *; and so far inferior, that they had no rights which the white man was bound to respect; and that the negro might justly and lawfully be reduced to slavery for his benefit. . . .
>
> . . .
>
> . . . [A]ccordingly, a negro of the African race was regarded * * * as an article of property, and held, and bought and sold as such * * *. [N]o one seems to have doubted the correctness of the prevailing opinion of the time.[11]

And so, nearly seven decades after the Constitutional Convention, the Supreme Court reaffirmed the prevailing opinion of the framers regarding the rights of Negroes in America. It took a bloody civil war before the thirteenth amendment could be adopted to abolish slavery, though not the consequences slavery would have for future Americans.

While the Union survived the civil war, the Constitution did not. In its place arose a new, more promising basis for justice and equality, the fourteenth amendment, ensuring protection of the life, liberty, and property of *all* persons against deprivations without due process, and guaranteeing equal protection of the laws. And yet almost another century would pass

[9]U.S. Const. art. I, § 9, cl. 1.

[10]Dred Scott v. Sandford, 60 U.S. (19 How.) 393 (1857).

[11]*Id.* at 405, 407–08.

before any significant recognition was obtained of the rights of black Americans to share equally even in such basic opportunities as education, housing, and employment, and to have their votes counted, and counted equally. In the meantime, blacks joined America's military to fight its wars and invested untold hours working in its factories and on its farms, contributing to the development of this country's magnificent wealth and waiting to share in its prosperity.

What is striking is the role legal principles have played throughout America's history in determining the condition of Negroes. They were enslaved by law, emancipated by law, disenfranchised and segregated by law; and, finally, they have begun to win equality by law. Along the way, new constitutional principles have emerged to meet the challenges of a changing society. The progress has been dramatic, and it will continue.

The men who gathered in Philadelphia in 1787 could not have envisioned these changes. They could not have imagined, nor would they have accepted, that the document they were drafting would one day be construed by a Supreme Court to which had been appointed a woman and the descendent of an African slave. "We the People" no longer enslave, but the credit does not belong to the framers. It belongs to those who refused to acquiesce in outdated notions of "liberty," "justice," and "equality," and who strived to better them.

And so we must be careful, when focusing on the events which took place in Philadelphia two centuries ago, that we not overlook the momentous events which followed, and thereby lose our proper sense of perspective. Otherwise, the odds are that for many Americans the bicentennial celebration will be little more than a blind pilgrimage to the shrine of the original document now stored in a vault in the National Archives. If we seek, instead, a sensitive understanding of the Constitution's inherent defects, and its promising evolution through 200 years of history, the celebration of the "Miracle at Philadelphia" will, in my view, be a far more meaningful and humbling experience. We will see that the true miracle was not the birth of the Constitution, but its life, a life nurtured through two turbulent centuries of our own making, and a life embodying much good fortune that was not.

Thus, in this bicentennial year, we may not all participate in the festivities with flag-waving fervor. Some may more quietly commemorate the suffering, struggle, and sacrifice that has triumphed over much of what was wrong with the original document, and observe the anniversary with hopes not realized and promises not fulfilled. I plan to celebrate the bicentennial of the Constitution as a living document, including the Bill of Rights and the other amendments protecting individual freedoms and human rights.

ROBIN L. WEST, CONSTITUTIONAL SCEPTICISM

72 B.U.L.REV. 765–70, 774–79 (1992).

CONSTITUTIONAL MEANING AND VALUE

Interpretive constitutional debate over the last few decades has centered on two apparently linked questions: whether the Constitution can be given a determinate meaning, and whether the institution of judicial review can be justified within the basic assumptions of liberalism. Two groups of scholars have generated answers to these questions. The "constitutional faithful" argue that meaning can indeed be determinately affixed to constitutional clauses, by reference to the plain meaning of the document, the original intent of the drafters, evolving political and moral norms of the community, or the best political or moral philosophical theory available and that, because of that determinacy, judicial review can indeed be brought within the rubric of liberalism. Taking issue with the constitutional faithful is a group who might be called "constitutional sceptics." Scholars in this group see, in every constitutional phrase or doctrine, the possibility of multiple interpretations, and in the application of every constitutional method the possibility of multiple outcomes. It follows from this indeterminacy that judicial review cannot be easily justified by reference to liberal assumptions, because the power of the interpreting judge irreparably compromises the stability and rationality of the "Rule of Law" so central to liberal ideals.

As important as the debate over constitutional determinacy may be, its prominence in modern constitutional theory over the last thirty years has carried with it serious opportunity costs. Specifically, the prominence of the debate over the Constitution's meaning, whether it can be said to have one, and the implications for the coherence of liberalism that these questions of interpretation seem to raise, has pushed to the background an older and possibly more important debate about the Constitution's value. By asking relentlessly whether the Constitution's meaning can be made sufficiently determinate to serve the Rule of Law—by focusing almost exclusively on whether constitutionalism is possible within liberal theory and whether liberalism is possible, given an indeterminate Constitution—we have neglected to ask whether our Constitution is desirable. Does it further the "good life" for the individuals, communities, and subcommunities it governs?

We might pose these evaluative questions in any number of ways. Has the Constitution or the Bill of Rights well served the communities and individuals they are designed to protect? Are the visions of individualism, community, and human nature on which the Bill of Rights rests, and the balances it strikes between rights and responsibilities, or civic virtue and freedoms, noble conceptions of social life, true accounts of our being, hospitable to societal and individual attempts to live the good life? More specifically, does the First Amendment, for example, well serve its core values of free expression, individual actualization, and open political debate? Assuming that it does, are those values good values to have? Are they worth the damage to our social cohesion, our fragile sense of fraternity with others, and our attempts at community that they almost undeniably cause? Are the Fourteenth Amendment's sweeping and majestic guarantees of "liberty" and "equal protection of the law," appearances notwithstanding, in fact unduly stingy? Do they simply, and cruelly, fail to guarantee a liberty that would meaningfully protect against the most serious constraints on peoples' liberties, or an equality that would even begin to address the grotesque material inequities at the very heart of our social and economic life? Do those guarantees perversely protect, rather than guarantee against, those constraints and inequities? Similarly, but from a quite different political orientation, are Fourth Amendment guarantees simply not worth their cost in law enforcement? Is it unwise to let eighteen-year-olds vote? Is the Second Amendment the height of foolishness?

These questions—about the value, wisdom, decency, or sensibility of constitutional guarantees—do of course receive some attention in contemporary legal scholarship, but nevertheless, it seems fair to say that in spite of the legal academy's supposed obsession with "normativity," normative questions about the Constitution have not been at the heart of constitutional discourse of the last thirty years. By contrast, normative questions of precisely this sort constitute the great bulk of scholarship in other areas of law. Scholars question the value of the holder in due course doctrine in commercial transactions, the negligence doctrine or strict liability in tort law, the rules governing acceptance of unilateral contracts in contract law, and insanity defenses in criminal law. But normative questions are neither the subject of constitutional "grand theory" nor, more revealingly perhaps, the subject of doctrinal constitutional scholarship. Instead, while theoretical constitutional scholarship centers on questions about the meaningfulness of the Constitution and its implications for the possibility or impossibility of liberalism, doctrinal constitutional scholarship centers on questions of the Constitution's meaning, rather than questions of its value. Thus, for example, rather than debate whether the First or the Fourteenth Amendment is a good idea, doctrinalists debate what the First Amendment or the Fourteenth Amendment means, and theorists debate whether they have any meaning and what it means to assert that they do or do not have meaning. In short, neither theoretical nor doctrinal constitutional scholarship places the value, rather than either the meaningfulness or the meaning, of the Constitution at the heart of constitutional analysis.

That we lack an explicitly normative debate about the Constitution's value might be evidenced by the visible effects of that absence in our substantive constitutional arguments. Let me cite a few examples, simply to convey the flavor of what I suggest is missing. One debate between constitutional scholars arising over the last few years, and of great interest to political progressives, concerns the constitutionality under the First Amendment of the attempts made by some cities and universities to control, through disciplinary sanctions, the intimidation and subordination of racial, ethnic, and sexual minorities by use of "hate speech." Those contributing to the small explosion of scholarly writing on this topic have generally taken one of two polar positions: one group of scholars and litigators (generally liberal) argues that hate speech regulations are simply unconstitutional under the First Amendment while a second, more or less minority (and generally progressive), position argues that they are constitutional, either by virtue of the similarity between hate speech regulations and traditionally accepted limits on the First Amendment, or because of limits we should imply into that amendment through the "penumbral" and balancing, or counterbalancing, effect of the Fourteenth Amendment's equality clause. The position that seems to have no adherents is that hate speech regulations are desirable, for progressive reasons, but are nevertheless unconstitutional, but shouldn't be, and that this shows that, at least from a progressive perspective, the First Amendment is morally flawed. But again, this position seems to have no adherents. Instead, those who think hate speech regulations are a good idea generally think they are constitutional while those who think they are not a good idea generally find them unconstitutional. No one seems to find them both desirable and unconstitutional, and hence exemplary of a problem with the First Amendment. No one, in other words, is led by a commitment to the desirability of hate speech regulations and a fair reading of the Constitution to take a progressive and morally sceptical stance toward the Constitution.

* * *

PROGRESSIVE CONSTITUTIONAL SCEPTICISM

Progressives have both substantive and methodological reasons to be sceptical about the Constitution's value. I define "progressivism," in part, by its guiding ideal: progressives are loosely committed to a form of social life in which all individuals live meaningful, autonomous, and self-directed lives, enriched by rewarding work, education, and culture, free of the disabling fears of poverty, violence, and coercion, nurtured by life-affirming connections with intimates and co-citizens alike, and strengthened by caring communities that are both attentive to the shared human needs of its members and equally mindful of their diversity and differences. Much of this guiding ideal, however, is shared by liberals. What distinguishes progressives from liberals is that while liberals tend to view the dangers of an over-oppressive state as the most serious obstacle to the attainment of such a world, progressives, while agreeing that some obstacles emanate from the state, argue that for the most part the most serious impediments emanate from unjust concentrations of private power—the social power of whites over blacks, the intimate power of men over women, the economic power of the materially privileged over the materially deprived. From a progressive perspective, it is those concentrations of private power, not state power, that presently riddle social life with hierarchic relationships of mastery and subjection, of sovereignty and subordination. Hence, it is those concentrations of private power that must be targeted, challenged, and reformed by progressive political action. That action, in turn, will often involve state intervention into the private spheres within which hierarchies of private power are allowed to thrive, and that simple fact will commonly pit the progressive strategy of ending private domination against the liberal goal of minimizing the danger of an oppressive state.

* * *

If that progressive insight is basically correct, then at least two problems exist with the scheme of individual rights and liberties protected by the Constitution. First, the Constitution does not prohibit the abuse of private power that interferes with the equality or freedom of subordinated peoples. The Constitution simply does not reach private power, and therefore cannot possibly prohibit its abuse. Even the most far reaching liberal interpretations of the Reconstruction Amendments—the only amendments that seemingly reach private power—refuse or fail to find either a constitutional prohibition of private societal racism, intimate sexual violence, or economic coercion or a constitutional imperative that the states take affirmative action to eradicate it. Justice Harlan's famous liberal dissent in *Plessy v. Ferguson*, for example, makes painfully clear that, even on his reading of the amendment (which, of course, would have outlawed Jim Crow laws), the Fourteenth Amendment does not challenge the sensed or actual cultural and social superiority of the white race. More recently, Justices Brennan and Marshall's argument in their dissent in *City of Richmond v. J.A. Croson Co.*,[20] that the state may remedy private discrimination if failure to do so would enmesh the state in those discriminatory practices, did not suggest that the Constitution requires the state to address private discrimination. Similarly, virtually no liberal judges or commentators have read the Constitution and the Reconstruction Amendments to require that states take affirmative action to address the unconstitutional maldistribution of household labor, with its serious, well-proven, and adverse effects on women's liberty and equality. No liberal court or commentator reads the Constitution to require that states or Congress take

[20] 488 U.S. 469, 528 (1989) (Marshall, J., joined by Brennan & Blackmun, JJ., dissenting) (arguing that the program setting aside a percentage of contracts for minorities is constitutional).

action to protect against homophobic violence and rage, or to protect against the deadening, soul-murdering, and often life-threatening effects of homelessness, hunger, and poverty. The Constitution apparently leaves untouched the very conditions of subordination, oppression, and coercion that relegate some to "lesser lives" of drudgery, fear, and stultifying self-hatred. For that reason alone, the Constitution appears to be fundamentally at odds with progressive ideals and visions.

The incompatibility, however, of progressivism and the Constitution goes deeper. Not only does the Constitution fail to prohibit subordinating abuses of private power, but, at least a good deal of the time, in the name of guaranteeing constitutional protection of individual freedom, it also aggressively protects the very hierarchies of wealth, status, race, sexual preference, and gender that facilitate those practices of subordination. Thus, the Constitution seemingly protects the individual's freedom to produce and consume hate speech, despite its propensity to contribute to patterns of racial oppression. It also clearly protects the individual's right to practice religion, despite the demonstrable incompatibility of the religious tenets central to all three dominant mainstream religions with women's full civic and political equality. It protects the individual's freedom to create and use pornography, despite the possible connection between pornography and increases in private violence against women. It protects the privacy and cultural hegemony of the nuclear family, despite the extreme forms of injustice that occur within that institution and the maldistribution of burdens and benefits visited by that injustice upon women and, to a lesser degree, children. Finally, it protects, as a coincidence of protecting the freedom and equal opportunities of individuals, both the system of "meritocracy" and the departures from meritocracy that dominate and constitute the market and economy, despite the resistance of those systems to full participation of African Americans and hence despite the subordinating effects of those "markets" upon them. * * *

Finally, this incompatibility of the Constitution with progressive ideals is neither momentary nor contingent. It is not a product of false or disingenuous interpretation by a particular court or Justice hostile to progressive politics. Rather, the Constitution's incompatibility with progressive ideals stems from at least two theoretical and doctrinal sources that lie at the heart of our constitutional structure: first, the conception of liberty to which the Constitution is committed and, second, its conception of equality.

First, as is often recognized, the Constitution protects a strong and deeply liberal conception of what Isaiah Berlin has termed the "negative liberty"[21] of the individual to speak, think, choose, and labor within a

[21]Sir Isaiah Berlin, Two Concepts of Liberty, in Four Essays on Liberty 118 (1969)

sphere of noninterference from social, community, or state authority. As is less often recognized, however, the Constitution creates and protects these spheres of noninterference not only in preference to, but also at the cost of, the more positive conceptions of freedom and autonomy necessary for progressive change. The cultural, intimate, private, and economic spheres of noninterference protected by the Constitution are the very spheres of private power, control, and coercion within which the positive liberty of subordinated persons to live lives of meaning is most threatened. Thus, the Constitution protects the rights of producers and consumers of racial hate speech and pornography so as to protect the negative liberty of those speakers and listeners. By doing so, it not only fails to protect, but also actively threatens, the positive freedom of women and African Americans to develop lives free from fear for one's safety, the seeds of racial bitterness, the "clouds of inferiority,"[22] the interference with one's movements, and the crippling incapacities to participate fully in public life occasioned by the constitutionally protected cultures of racism and misogyny. The negative liberty of the individual heralded and celebrated by liberalism is not only inconsistent with, but also hostile to the positive liberty central to progressivism, simply because protection of "negative liberty" necessarily creates the sphere of noninterference and privacy within which the abuse of private power can proceed unabated. The Constitution is firmly committed to this negative rather than positive conception of liberty, and is thus not only not the ally, but also a very real obstacle, to progressive ideals.

Second, the Fourteenth Amendment's mandate of equality, rather than being a limit to the Constitution's celebration of liberty, is also a bar to progressive progress, the heroic efforts of progressive litigators, judges, and commentators to prove the contrary notwithstanding. The "equal protection of the laws" guaranteed by the Fourteenth Amendment essentially guarantees that one's membership in a racially or sexually defined group will not adversely affect one's treatment by the state. As such, the mandate powerfully reinforces the liberal understanding that the only attributes that matter to the state are those shared universally by all members of the community: the possession of equal dignity, the power to form one's own plan of life, and the universal aspirations to autonomy and so forth. Precisely this understanding of equality, grounded in the liberal claim and promise of universality and equal treatment, however, renders the Equal Protection Clause an obstacle to progressive progress. The need to acknowledge and compensate for the individual's membership in pro-

---

(distinguishing the "negative" liberty to do as one pleases within a designated sphere from the "positive" liberty to live a particular kind of life).

[22]Martin Luther King, Jr., Why We Can't Wait 83 (1963) (describing the impact of racism on the self image of African American children).

foundly non-universal subordinate groups—whether racially, sexually, or economically defined—is what distinguishes the progressive political impulse from the liberal. It is precisely that membership in non-universal groups, and the centrality of the non-universal attributes that distinguish them, that both liberalism and the liberally defined constitutional mandate of equality are poised not simply to ignore, but also to oppose. It is, then, both unsurprising and inevitable that the Fourteenth Amendment's Equal Protection Clause is understood as not requiring, and indeed forbidding, the state and public interventions into private, intimate, and economic spheres of life needed to interrupt the patterns of domination, subordination, and inequality that continue to define the lives of those within these protected private realms.

Methodologically, the Constitution is also hostile to political and moral progressivism, simply because it elevates one set of moral values above others, relegating non-constitutional ideals or visions to the sphere of the "merely political." The Constitution's peculiar status as a bridge between liberal morality and aspirations and positive law, although much heralded by liberal philosophers and constitutionalists, poses a triple danger to progressive ideals. First, because the Constitution is indeed law, and law in the ordinary as well as extraordinary sense, it imprints upon the liberalism on which it rests the imprimatur of positive legal authority. One set of political convictions hence receives not only the persuasive authority derived from its merits, but also the political, willed authority of the extant, empowered, positive sovereign. These ideals simply are, as well as ought to be; and they are in a way that makes compliance mandatory. Second, because the Constitution is law in the extraordinary as well as ordinary sense, the positive political authority imprinted upon the liberal morality of the Constitution is of a higher, permanent, and constitutive sort. It severely constrains moralities and aspirations with which it is inconsistent in the name of the community from which it purportedly draws its sovereign authority. Thus, it is not just "the law" that is hostile to non-liberal moral aspirations, such as progressivism. It is also, more deeply and meaningfully, "we the people"—all of us, the inter-generational community of citizens—for whom the Constitution speaks and from whom it draws its authority that is hostile to the ideals with which it is inconsistent. Third, because the Constitution is also undeniably a moral as well as legal document, the authority it embodies is exercised not only coercively—telling us who we must be—but also instructively—telling us who we ought to be. It defines and confines not just our options—as does any law, higher or lower—but our aspirations as well. For all three reasons, the Constitution is not just a peculiarly authoritarian legal document, but is also authoritarian in a peculiarly parental way. Like a parent's authority over the identity of his or her children, the Constitution both persuades us to be a certain way and it constitutes us in a certain way. It creates us as it defines a morality to which we will and should subscribe.

For all of these reasons, the Constitution is methodologically as well as substantively hostile to progressive politics. The moral authoritarianism at its core is in many ways conducive to the reverence for the individual and distrust of the mass so central to liberalism, but it is inimical to the egalitarian, inclusive, and largely communitarian methods—the grass roots politics at the local level and the participatory democracy at the national and state level—that must form the foundation of genuine progressive change. Effective political challenges to the subordination of some groups by others must rest on a fundamental change of human orientation in both the dominated and oppressing groups: the dominated must come to see their interests as both shared with each other and opposed to the interests of the stronger; and the stronger must come to embrace empathetically the subordinated as sufficiently close to their own identities to be "of their concern." Neither progressive end—the mounting of sufficient power within the ranks of the subordinated through cross-group organizing or the challenge to the received self-identity of the strong—is attainable through the legal, coercive imposition of a particular moral paradigm that characterizes constitutional methodology. In fact, the moral and legal authoritarianism at the heart of our constitutional method will almost invariably frustrate it.

BIBLIOGRAPHY

General

Amar, *The Bill of Rights as a Constitution,* 100 Yale L.J. 1131 (1991).

Balkin, *Agreements with Hell and Other Objects of Our Faith,* 65 Fordham L.Rev. 1703 (1997).

Balkin, *What is a Post-Modern Constitutionalism?,* 90 Mich.L.Rev. 1966 (1992).

Barnett, *Constitutional Legitimacy,* 103 Colum.L.Rev. 111 (2003).

Breyer, *Our Democratic Constitution,* 77 N.Y.U.L.Rev. 245 (2002).

Eisgruber, *The Fourteenth Amendment's Constitution,* 69 S.Cal.L.Rev. 47 (1995).

Fleming and McClain, *In Search of a Substantive Republic,* 76 Tex.L.Rev. 509 (1997).

Kramer, *Madison's Audience,* 112 Harv.L.Rev. 611 (1999).

Symposium, *Contemporary Perspectives on Constitutional Interpretation,* 72 B.U.L.Rev. 681–799 (1992).

Symposium, *One Hundred Years of Judicial Review: The Thayer Centennial Symposium,* 88 Nw.U.L.Rev. 1–461 (1993).

The Role of Theory

Dorf, *Create Your Own Constitutional Theory,* 87 Colum.L.Rev. 593 (1999).

Farber, D. and Sherry, S., DESPERATELY SEEKING CERTAINTY: THE MISGUIDED QUEST FOR CONSTITUTIONAL FOUNDATIONS (2002).

Posner, R., THE PROBLEMATICS OF MORAL AND LEGAL THEORY (1999).

Process Theories

Klarman, *The Puzzling Resistance to Political Process Theory,* 77 Va.L.Rev. 747 (1991).

McGinnis and Rappaport, *Our Supermajoritarian Constitution,* 80 Tex.L. Rev. 703 (2002).

Sager, *The Incorrigible Constitution,* 65 N.Y.U.L.Rev. 893 (1990).

Symposium, *Judicial Review versus Democracy,* 42 Ohio St.L.J. 1–434 (1981).

Tushnet, *Darkness on the Edge of Town: The Contributions of John Hart Ely to Constitutional Theory,* 89 Yale L.J. 1037 (1980).

Morality Based Theories

Brest, *The Fundamental Rights Controversy: The Essential Contradictions of Normative Constitutional Scholarship,* 90 Yale L.J. 1063 (1981).

Fleming, *Fidelity to Our Imperfect Constitution,* 65 Fordham L.Rev. 1335 (1997).

Foley, *Interpretation and Philosophy: Dworkin's Constitution,* 14 Const.Comm. 151 (1997).

Richards, D., TOLERATION AND THE CONSTITUTION (1986).

Schauer, *Constitutional Invocations,* 65 Fordham L.Rev. 1295 (1997).

Symposium, *Individual Rights and the Powers of Government,* 27 Ga.L.Rev. 343–501 (1993).

Tushnet, *An Essay on Rights,* 62 Tex.L.Rev. 1363 (1984).

West, *Integrity and Universality: A Comment on Ronald Dworkin's Freedom's Law,* 65 Fordham L.Rev. 1313 (1997).

Reconceptualizing Democracy

Eisgruber, *Dimensions of Democracy*, 71 Fordham L.Rev. 1723 (2003).

Fallon, *What is Republicanism, and Is It Worth Reviving?,* 102 Harv.L.Rev. 1695 (1989).

Flaherty, *The Practice of Faith,* 65 Fordham L.Rev. 1565 (1997).

Fleming, *The Missing Selves in Constitutional Self-Government,* 71 Fordham L.Rev. 1789 (2003).

Fleming, *We the Exceptional American People,* 11 Const.Comm. 355 (1994).

Appleby, J., LIBERALISM AND REPUBLICANISM (1992).

Diggins, J., THE LOST SOUL OF AMERICAN POLITICS (1986).

Rubenfeld, J., FREEDOM AND TIME: A THEORY OF CONSTITUTIONAL SELF-GOVERNMENT (2001).

Klarman, *Constitutional Fact/Constitutional Fiction: A Critique of Bruce Ackerman's Theory of Constitutional Moments,* 44 Stan.L.Rev. 759 (1992).

Michelman, *Law's Republic,* 97 Yale L.J. 1493 (1988).

Pangle, T., THE SPIRIT OF MODERN REPUBLICANISM (1988).

Pope, *Republican Moments: The Role of Direct Popular Power in the American Constitutional Order,* 139 U.Pa.L.Rev. 287 (1990).

Posner, R., LAW, PRAGMATISM, AND DEMOCRACY (2003).

Sherry, *Civic Virtue and the Feminine Voice in Constitutional Adjudication,* 72 Va.L.Rev. 543 (1986).

Sunstein, *Beyond the Republican Revival,* 97 Yale L.J. 1539 (1988).

Tushnet, *Constituting We the People,* 65 Fordham L.Rev. 1557 (1997).

Critical Perspectives

Becker, *The Politics of Women's Wrongs and The Bill of "Rights": A Bicentennial Perspective,* 59 U.Chi.L.Rev. 453 (1992).

Bell, D., FACES AT THE BOTTOM OF THE WELL: THE PERMANENCE OF RACISM (1992).

Farber, D., and Sherry, S., BEYOND ALL REASON: THE RADICAL ASSAULT ON TRUTH IN AMERICAN LAW (1997).

Cook, *Beyond Critical Legal Studies: The Reconstructive Theology of Dr. Martin Luther King, Jr.,* 103 Harv.L.Rev. 985 (1990).

Culp, *Toward a Black Legal Scholarship: Race and Original Understandings,* 1991 Duke L.J. 39.

Matsuda, *Looking to the Bottom: Critical Legal Studies and Reparations,* 22 Harv.C.R.–C.L.L.Rev. 323 (1987).

Tushnet, M., RED, WHITE, AND BLUE (1988).

Peller, *Race Consciousness,* 1990 Duke L.J. 758.

Williams, P., THE ALCHEMY OF RACE AND RIGHTS (1991).

Chapter II

METHODS OF CONSTITUTIONAL INTERPRETATION

Constitutional lawyers have traditionally employed a variety of methods to interpret the Constitution. They have consulted the constitutional text; the intent of the drafters of the constitutional provision at issue; the structure of the Constitution as a whole; precedent; and deeply held values or notions of social policy. Today, theorists debate the merits of three main methods of interpretation: originalism (based on the intentions or purposes of the Framers); textualism (which stresses the precise language used in the Constitution); and evolutionary approaches (which view constitutional law as changing with the times).

Originalism: A familiar claim in constitutional law is that the original intent of the framers ought to control constitutional interpretation. Robert Bork's article is an influential statement of this position. Paul Brest offers both a practical and a normative critique of this view. In turn, Richard Kay provides responses to the prevailing criticisms of original intentions adjudication (that is, that it is impossible and that it is normatively objectionable).

How would the arguments of Brest and Kay apply in the interpretation of the Equal Protection Clause? Can one reasonably ascertain the "original understanding" of the Clause? Should it be read to cover gender discrimination? Indeed, is the decision in *Brown v. Board of Education* consistent with "original intent"? Does it matter if it is not?

Textualism: Frederick Schauer suggests that there are far more "easy cases" in constitutional adjudication than one might suppose from reading casebooks and Supreme Court opinions. He contends that language (either from the constitutional text or from a rule in a case or a series of cases) can be a significant, even if unappreciated, constraint on constitutional interpretation. Akhil Amar presents a detailed blueprint for an especially ambitious form of textualism. Sanford Levinson turns textualist claims on their head. He argues that texts don't constrain interpretation; rather, interpretation creates texts. Drawing on modern literary theory, Levinson doubts that one can sensibly talk about extracting a "true" or "correct" meaning from a constitutional provision.

One way to finesse the tension between textualism and the idea of a "living Constitution" is to understand constitutional interpretation as a process akin to translation: the goal of the interpreter is to be true to the original text in a new context. Sketching such a theory, Lawrence Lessig argues that translation can satisfy demands for fidelity in constitutional law while recognizing that the meanings of constitutional texts can change over time.

Evolutionary Approaches: Thomas Grey distinguishes between interpretivist approaches, like those we have already discussed, in which constitutional values are generated only by the Framers, and non-interpretivist approaches in which judges also play a role in generating constitutional values. David Strauss's article explains his "common law" view of constitutional law. He attempts to reconcile this approach with the distinctive importance placed on the constitutional text and on the views of the Framers in American constitutional practice. Richard Posner propounds a more adventuresome form of constitutional interpretation: "a pragmatist judge always tries to do the best he can do for the present and the future, unchecked by any felt duty to secure consistency in principle with what other officials have done in the past." Posner argues that pragmatic judging is more constrained than one might initially think, and, in any event, is likely to spur more thoughtful inquiry and better results. After considering these approaches, you should reread the critiques of dynamic interpretations in earlier excerpts by originalists and textualists.

Of course, the distinction between static and dynamic theories of interpretation is more of a spectrum than a dichotomy, so that a relatively dynamic textualist like Lessig need not be far away from a moderate doctrinal evolutionist like Strauss. But Posner's view of the judicial role is obviously far removed from Bork's. As this contrast shows, these disputes about methodology cannot be reduced simply to ideology: both Posner and Bork are well-known political conservatives.

A. ORIGINALISM

ROBERT H. BORK, NEUTRAL PRINCIPLES AND SOME FIRST AMENDMENT PROBLEMS

47 IND.L.J. 1–11 (1971).

The subject of the lengthy and often acrimonious debate about the proper role of the Supreme Court under the Constitution is one that preoccupies many people these days: when is authority legitimate? I find it convenient to discuss that question in the context of the Warren Court and its works simply because the Warren Court posed the issue in acute form.

The issue did not disappear along with the era of the Warren Court majorities, however. It arises when any court either exercises or declines to exercise the power to invalidate any act of another branch of government. The Supreme Court is a major power center, and we must ask when its power should be used and when it should be withheld.

Our starting place, inevitably, is Professor Herbert Wechsler's argument that the Court must not be merely a "naked power organ," which means that its decisions must be controlled by principle.[1] "A principled decision," according to Wechsler, "is one that rests on reasons with respect to all the issues in a case, reasons that in their generality and their neutrality transcend any immediate result that is involved."[2]

Wechsler chose the term "neutral principles" to capsulate his argument, though he recognizes that the legal principle to be applied is itself never neutral because it embodies a choice of one value rather than another. Wechsler asked for the neutral application of principles, which is a requirement, as Professor Louis L. Jaffe puts it, that the judge "sincerely believe in the principle upon which he purports to rest his decision." "The judge," says Jaffe, "must believe in the validity of the reasons given for the decision at least in the sense that he is prepared to apply them to a later case which he cannot honestly distinguish."[3] He must not, that is, decide lawlessly. But is the demand for neutrality in judges merely another value choice, one that is no more principled than any other? I think not, but to prove it we must rehearse fundamentals. This is familiar terrain but important and still debated.

The requirement that the Court be principled arises from the resolution of the seeming anomaly of judicial supremacy in a democratic society. If the judiciary really is supreme, able to rule when and as it sees fit, the society is not democratic. The anomaly is dissipated, however, by the model of government embodied in the structure of the Constitution, a model upon which popular consent to limited government by the Supreme Court also rests. This model we may for convenience, though perhaps not with total accuracy, call "Madisonian."[4]

A Madisonian system is not completely democratic, if by "democratic" we mean completely majoritarian. It assumes that in wide areas of life majorities are entitled to rule for no better reason [than] that they are majorities. We need not pause here to examine the philosophical underpinnings of that assumption since it is a "given" in our society; nor need we worry that "majority" is a term of art meaning often no more than the

---

[1] H. Wechsler, *Toward Neutral Principles of Constitutional Law,* in Principles, Politics, and Fundamental Law 3, 27 (1961)[.]

[2] *Id.*

[3] L. Jaffe, English and American Judges as Lawmakers 38 (1969).

[4] *See* R. Dahl, A Preface to Democratic Theory 4–33 (1956).

shifting combinations of minorities that add up to temporary majorities in the legislature. That majorities are so constituted is inevitable. In any case, one essential premise of the Madisonian model is majoritarianism. The model has also a counter-majoritarian premise, however, for it assumes there are some areas of life a majority should not control. There are some things a majority should not do to us no matter how democratically it decides to do them. These are areas properly left to individual freedom, and coercion by the majority in these aspects of life is tyranny.

Some see the model as containing an inherent, perhaps an insoluble, dilemma.[5] Majority tyranny occurs if legislation invades the areas properly left to individual freedom. Minority tyranny occurs if the majority is prevented from ruling where its power is legitimate. Yet, quite obviously, neither the majority nor the minority can be trusted to define the freedom of the other. This dilemma is resolved in constitutional theory, and in popular understanding, by the Supreme Court's power to define both majority and minority freedom through the interpretation of the Constitution. Society consents to be ruled undemocratically within defined areas by certain enduring principles believed to be stated in, and placed beyond the reach of majorities by, the Constitution.

But this resolution of the dilemma imposes severe requirements upon the Court. For it follows that the Court's power is legitimate only if it has, and can demonstrate in reasoned opinions that it has, a valid theory, derived from the Constitution, of the respective spheres of majority and minority freedom. If it does not have such a theory but merely imposes its own value choices, or worse if it pretends to have a theory but actually follows its own predilections, the Court violates the postulates of the Madisonian model that alone justifies its power. It then necessarily abets the tyranny either of the majority or of the minority.

This argument is central to the issue of legitimate authority because the Supreme Court's power to govern rests upon popular acceptance of this model. Evidence that this is, in fact, the basis of the Court's power is to be gleaned everywhere in our culture. We need not canvass here such things as high school civics texts and newspaper commentary, for the most telling evidence may be found in the U.S. Reports. The Supreme Court regularly insists that its results, and most particularly its controversial results, do not spring from the mere will of the Justices in the majority but are supported, indeed compelled, by a proper understanding of the Constitution of the United States. Value choices are attributed to the Founding Fathers, not to the Court. The way an institution advertises tells you what it thinks its customers demand.

---

[5] *Id.* at 23–24.

This is, I think, the ultimate reason the Court must be principled. If it does not have and rigorously adhere to a valid and consistent theory of majority and minority freedoms based upon the Constitution, judicial supremacy, given the axioms of our system, is, precisely to that extent, illegitimate. The root of its illegitimacy is that it opens a chasm between the reality of the Court's performance and the constitutional and popular assumptions that give it power.

I do not mean to rest the argument entirely upon the popular understanding of the Court's function. Even if society generally should ultimately perceive what the Court is in fact doing and, having seen, prove content to have major policies determined by the unguided discretion of judges rather than by elected representatives, a principled judge would, I believe, continue to consider himself bound by an obligation to the document and to the structure of government that it prescribes. At least he would be bound so long as any litigant existed who demanded such adherence of him. I do not understand how, on any other theory of judicial obligation, the Court could, as it does now, protect voting rights if a large majority of the relevant constituency were willing to see some groups or individuals deprived of such rights. But even if I am wrong in that, at the very least an honest judge would owe it to the body politic to cease invoking the authority of the Constitution and to make explicit the imposition of his own will, for only then would we know whether the society understood enough of what is taking place to be said to have consented.

Judge J. Skelly Wright, in an argument resting on different premises, has severely criticized the advocates of principle. He defends the value-choosing role of the Warren Court, setting that Court in opposition to something he refers to as the "scholarly tradition," which criticizes that Court for its lack of principle.[6] A perceptive reader, sensitive to nuance, may suspect that the Judge is rather out of sympathy with that tradition from such hints as his reference to "self-appointed scholastic mandarins."[7]

The "mandarins" of the academy anger the Judge because they engage in "haughty derision of the Court's powers of analysis and reasoning."[8] Yet, curiously enough, Judge Wright makes no attempt to refute the charge but rather seems to adopt the technique of confession and avoidance. He seems to be arguing that a Court engaged in choosing fundamental values for society cannot be expected to produce principled decisions at the same time. Decisions first, principles later. One wonders, however, how the Court or the rest of us are to know that the decisions are correct or what they portend for the future if they are not accompanied by the principles

[6] Wright, *Professor Bickel, The Scholarly Tradition, and the Supreme Court,* 84 Harv.L.Rev. 769 (1971).

[7] *Id.* at 777.

[8] *Id.* at 777–78.

that explain and justify them. And it would not be amiss to point out that quite often the principles required of the Warren Court's decisions never did put in an appearance. But Judge Wright's main point appears to be that value choice is the most important function of the Supreme Court, so that if we must take one or the other, and apparently we must, we should prefer a process of selecting values to one of constructing and articulating principles. His argument, I believe, boils down to a syllogism. I. The Supreme Court should "protect our constitutional rights and liberties." II. The Supreme Court must "make fundamental value choices" in order to "protect our constitutional rights and liberties." III. Therefore, the Supreme Court should "make fundamental value choices."

The argument displays an all too common confusion. If we have constitutional rights and liberties already, rights and liberties specified by the Constitution, the Court need make no fundamental value choices in order to protect them, and it certainly need not have difficulty enunciating principles. If, on the other hand, "constitutional rights and liberties" are not in some real sense specified by the Constitution but are the rights and liberties the Court chooses, on the basis of its own values, to give to us, then the conclusion was contained entirely in the major premise, and the Judge's syllogism is no more than an assertion of what it purported to prove.

If I am correct so far, no argument that is both coherent and respectable can be made supporting a Supreme Court that "chooses fundamental values" because a Court that makes rather than implements value choices cannot be squared with the presuppositions of a democratic society. The man who understands the issues and nevertheless insists upon the rightness of the Warren Court's performance ought also, if he is candid, to admit that he is prepared to sacrifice democratic process to his own moral views. He claims for the Supreme Court an institutionalized role as perpetrator of limited coups d'etat.

Such a man occupies an impossible philosophic position. What can he say, for instance, of a Court that does not share his politics or his morality? I can think of nothing except the assertion that he will ignore the Court whenever he can get away with it and overthrow it if he can. In his view the Court has no legitimacy, and there is no reason any of us should obey it. And, this being the case, the advocate of a value-choosing Court must answer another difficult question. Why should the Court, a committee of nine lawyers, be the sole agent of change? The man who prefers results to processes has no reason to say that the Court is more legitimate than any other institution. If the Court will not listen, why not argue the case to some other group, say the Joint Chiefs of Staff, a body with rather better means for implementing its decisions?

* * *

It follows that the choice of "fundamental values" by the Court cannot be justified. Where constitutional materials do not clearly specify the value to be preferred, there is no principled way to prefer any claimed human value to any other. The judge must stick close to the text and the history, and their fair implications, and not construct new rights. The [*Griswold* case[a]] illustrates the point. The *Griswold* decision has been acclaimed by legal scholars as a major advance in constitutional law, a salutary demonstration of the Court's ability to protect fundamental human values. I regret to have to disagree, and my regret is all the more sincere because I once took the same position and did so in print.[15] In extenuation I can only say that at the time I thought, quite erroneously, that new basic rights could be derived logically by finding and extrapolating a more general principle of individual autonomy underlying the particular guarantees of the Bill of Rights.

The Court's *Griswold* opinion, by Justice Douglas, and the array of concurring opinions, by Justices Goldberg, White and Harlan, all failed to justify the derivation of any principle used to strike down the Connecticut anti-contraceptive statute or to define the scope of the principle. Justice Douglas, to whose opinion I must confine myself, began by pointing out that "specific guarantees in the Bill of Rights have penumbras, formed by emanations from those guarantees that help give them life and substance."[16] Nothing is exceptional there. In the case Justice Douglas cited, *NAACP v. Alabama,*[17] the State was held unable to force disclosure of membership lists because of the chilling effect upon the rights of assembly and political action of the NAACP's members. The penumbra was created solely to preserve a value central to the first amendment, applied in this case through the fourteenth amendment. It had no life of its own as a right independent of the value specified by the first amendment.

But Justice Douglas then performed a miracle of transubstantiation. He called the first amendment's penumbra a protection of "privacy" and then asserted that other amendments create "zones of privacy."[18] He had no better reason to use the word "privacy" than that the individual is free within these zones, free to act in public as well as in private. None of these penumbral zones—from the first, third, fourth or fifth amendments, all of which he cited, along with the ninth—covered the case before him. One more leap was required. Justice Douglas asserted that these various "zones of privacy" created an independent right of privacy,[19] a right not lying

---

[a]Griswold v. Connecticut, 381 U.S. 479 (1965).

[15]Bork, *The Supreme Court Needs a New Philosophy,* Fortune, Dec., 1968, at 170.

[16]381 U.S. at 484.

[17]357 U.S. 449 (1958).

[18]381 U.S. at 484.

[19]*Id.* at 485, 486.

within the penumbra of any specific amendment. He did not disclose, however, how a series of specified rights combined to create a new and unspecified right.

The *Griswold* opinion fails every test of neutrality. The derivation of the principle was utterly specious, and so was its definition. In fact, we are left with no idea of what the principle really forbids. Derivation and definition are interrelated here. Justice Douglas called the amendments and their penumbras "zones of privacy," though of course they are not that at all. They protect both private and public behavior and so would more properly be labelled "zones of freedom." If we follow Justice Douglas in his next step, these zones would then add up to an independent right of freedom, which is to say, a general constitutional right to be free of legal coercion, a manifest impossibility in any imaginable society.

Griswold, then, is an unprincipled decision, both in the way in which it derives a new constitutional right and in the way it defines that right, or rather fails to define it. We are left with no idea of the sweep of the right of privacy and hence no notion of the cases to which it may or may not be applied in the future. The truth is that the Court could not reach its result in *Griswold* through principle. The reason is obvious. Every clash between a minority claiming freedom and a majority claiming power to regulate involves a choice between the gratifications of the two groups. When the Constitution has not spoken, the Court will be able to find no scale, other than its own value preferences, upon which to weigh the respective claims to pleasure. Compare the facts in *Griswold* with a hypothetical suit by an electric utility company and one of its customers to void a smoke pollution ordinance as unconstitutional. The cases are identical.

In *Griswold* a husband and wife assert that they wish to have sexual relations without fear of unwanted children. The law impairs their sexual gratifications. The State can assert, and at one stage in that litigation did assert, that the majority finds the use of contraceptives immoral. Knowledge that it takes place and that the State makes no effort to inhibit it causes the majority anguish, impairs their gratifications.

The electrical company asserts that it wishes to produce electricity at low cost in order to reach a wide market and make profits. Its customer asserts that he wants a lower cost so that prices can be held low. The smoke pollution regulation impairs his and the company's stockholders' economic gratifications. The State can assert not only that the majority prefer clean air to lower prices, but also that the absence of the regulation impairs the majority's physical and aesthetic gratifications.

Neither case is covered specifically or by obvious implication in the Constitution. Unless we can distinguish forms of gratification, the only course for a principled Court is to let the majority have its way in both cases. It is clear that the Court cannot make the necessary distinction. There is no principled way to decide that one man's gratifications are more deserving of respect than another's or that one form of gratification is more worthy than another.[20] Why is sexual gratification more worthy than moral gratification? Why is sexual gratification nobler than economic gratification? There is no way of deciding these matters other than by reference to some system of moral or ethical values that has no objective or intrinsic validity of its own and about which men can and do differ. Where the Constitution does not embody the moral or ethical choice, the judge has no basis other than his own values upon which to set aside the community judgment embodied in the statute. That, by definition, is an inadequate basis for judicial supremacy. The issue of the community's moral and ethical values, the issue of the degree of pain an activity causes, are matters concluded by the passage and enforcement of the laws in question. The judiciary has no role to play other than that of applying the statutes in a fair and impartial manner.

One of my colleagues refers to this conclusion, not without sarcasm, as the "Equal Gratification Clause." The phrase is apt, and I accept it, though not the sarcasm. Equality of human gratifications, where the document does not impose a hierarchy, is an essential part of constitutional doctrine because of the necessity that judges be principled. To be perfectly clear on the subject, I repeat that the principle is not applicable to legislatures. Legislation requires value choice and cannot be principled in the sense under discussion. Courts must accept any value choice the legislature makes unless it clearly runs contrary to a choice made in the framing of the Constitution.

It follows, of course, that broad areas of constitutional law ought to be reformulated. Most obviously, it follows that substantive due process, revived by the *Griswold* case, is and always has been an improper doctrine. Substantive due process requires the Court to say, without guidance from the Constitution, which liberties or gratifications may be infringed by majorities and which may not. This means that *Griswold's* antecedents were also wrongly decided, *e.g., Meyer v. Nebraska,*[21] which struck down a statute forbidding the teaching of subjects in any language other than English; *Pierce v. Society of Sisters,*[22] which set aside a statute compelling all Oregon school children to attend public schools; *Adkins v. Children's Hospital,*[23] which invalidated a statute of Congress authorizing a board to fix minimum wages for women and children in the District of Columbia;

[20]The impossibility is related to that of making interpersonal comparisons of utilities. *See* L. Robbins, The Nature and Significance of Economic Science, ch. 4 (2d ed. 1969); P. Samuelson, Foundations of Economic Analysis 243–52 (1965).

[21]262 U.S. 390 (1922).

[22]268 U.S. 510 (1925).

[23]261 U.S. 525 (1923).

and *Lochner v. New York,*[24] which voided a statute fixing maximum hours of work for bakers. With some of these cases I am in political agreement, and perhaps *Pierce's* result could be reached on acceptable grounds, but there is no justification for the Court's methods. In *Lochner,* Justice Peckham, defending liberty from what he conceived as a mere meddlesome interference, asked, "[A]re we all * * * at the mercy of legislative majorities?"[25] The correct answer, where the Constitution does not speak, must be "yes."

PAUL BREST, THE MISCONCEIVED QUEST FOR THE ORIGINAL UNDERSTANDING

60 B.U.L.REV. 204, 204–09, 214–24, 231–34 (1980).

By "originalism" I mean the familiar approach to constitutional adjudication that accords binding authority to the text of the Constitution or the intentions of its adopters.[1] At least since *Marbury,* in which Chief Justice Marshall emphasized the significance of our Constitution's being a written document, originalism in one form or another has been a major theme in the American constitutional tradition. The most widely accepted justification for originalism is simply that the Constitution is the supreme law of the land. The Constitution manifests the will of the sovereign citizens of the United States—"we the people" assembled in the conventions and legislatures that ratified the Constitution and its amendments. The interpreter's task is to ascertain their will. Originalism may be supported by more instrumental rationales as well: Adherence to the text and original understanding arguably constrains the discretion of decisionmakers and assures that the Constitution will be interpreted consistently over time.

The most extreme forms of originalism are "strict textualism" (or literalism) and "strict intentionalism." A strict textualist purports to construe words and phrases very narrowly and precisely. For the strict intentionalist, "the whole aim of construction, as applied to a provision of the Constitution, is * * * to ascertain and give effect to the intent of its framers and the people who adopted it."[2]

---

[24] 198 U.S. 45 (1905).

[25] *Id.* at 59.

[1] John Ely uses the term "interpretivism" to describe essentially the same concept. J.H. Ely, Democracy and Distrust: A Theory of Judicial Review, chs. 1–2 (1980). At the cost of proliferating neologisms I have decided to stick with "originalism." Virtually all modes of constitutional decisionmaking, including those endorsed by Professor Ely, require interpretation. The differences lie in what is being interpreted, and I use the term "originalism" to describe the interpretation of text and original history as distinguished, for example, from the interpretation of precedents and social values.

[2] Home Bldg. & Loan Ass'n v. Blaisdell, 290 U.S. 398, 453 (1934) (Sutherland, J., dissenting).

Much of American constitutional interpretation rejects strict originalism in favor of what I shall call "moderate originalism." The text of the Constitution is authoritative, but many of its provisions are treated as inherently open-textured. The original understanding is also important, but judges are more concerned with the adopters' general purposes than with their intentions in a very precise sense.

Some central doctrines of American constitutional law cannot be derived even by moderate originalist interpretation, but depend, instead, on what I shall call "nonoriginalism." The modes of nonoriginalist adjudication defended in this article accord the text and original history presumptive weight, but do not treat them as authoritative or binding. The presumption is defeasible over time in the light of changing experiences and perceptions.

* * *

PART ONE: THE CONCEPTS AND METHODS OF ORIGINALISM

* * *

I. Textualism

Textualism takes the language of a legal provision as the primary or exclusive source of law (a) because of some definitional or supralegal principle that only a written text can impose constitutional obligations, or (b) because the adopters intended that the Constitution be interpreted according to a textualist canon, or (c) because the text of a provision is the surest guide to the adopters' intentions. The last of these, probably the central rationale for an originalist-based textualism, is sometimes stated as a preamble to textualist canons. For example:

> It is a cardinal rule in the interpretation of constitutions that the instrument must be so construed as to give effect to the intention of the people, who adopted it. This intention is to be sought in the Constitution itself, and the apparent meaning of the words employed is to be taken as expressing it, except in cases where that assumption would lead to absurdity, ambiguity, or contradiction.[8]

Implicit in the preceding quotation is a canon of interpretation paradigmatic of textualism—the so-called "plain meaning rule." Chief Justice Marshall invoked this canon in *Sturges v. Crowningshield:*

> [A]lthough the spirit of an instrument, especially of a constitution, is to be respected not less than its letter, yet the spirit is to be collected chiefly from its words * * *. [I]f, in any case, the plain meaning of a provision, not contradicted by any other provision in the same instrument, is to be disregarded, because we believe the framers of that instrument could not intend what they say, it must be one in which the

[8] H. Black, Handbook on the Construction and Interpretation of the Laws 20 (1911).

> absurdity and injustice of applying the provision to the case, would be so monstrous that all mankind would, without hesitation, unite in rejecting the application.[9]

The plain meaning of a text is the meaning that it would have for a "normal speaker of English" under the circumstances in which it is used. Two kinds of circumstances seem relevant: the linguistic and the social contexts. The linguistic context refers to vocabulary and syntax. The social context refers to a shared understanding of the purposes the provision might plausibly serve.

A tenable version of the plain meaning rule must take account of both of these contexts. The alternative, of applying a provision according to the literal meanings of its component words, misconceives the conventions that govern the use of language. Chief Justice Marshall argued this point eloquently and, I think, persuasively, in *McCulloch v. Maryland,*[13] decided the same year that he invoked the plain meaning rule in *Sturges*. The state had argued that the necessary and proper clause authorized only legislation "indispensable" to executing the enumerated powers. Marshall responded with the observation that the word "necessary," as used "in the common affairs of the world, or in approved authors, * * * frequently imports no more than that one thing is convenient, or useful, or essential to another."[14] He continued:

> Such is the character of human language, that no word conveys to the mind, in all situations, one single definite idea; and nothing is more common than to use words in a figurative sense. Almost all compositions contain words, which, taken in their rigorous sense, would convey a meaning different from that which is obviously intended. It is essential to just construction that many words which import something excessive, should be understood in a more mitigated sense—in that sense which common usage justifies * * *. This word, then, like others, is used in various senses; and, in its construction, the subject, the context, the intention of the person using them, are all to be taken into view.[15]

As Marshall implied, to attempt to read a provision without regard to its linguistic and social contexts will either yield unresolvable indeterminacies of language or just nonsense. Without taking account of the possible purposes of the provisions, an interpreter could not, for example, decide whether singing, flag-waving, flag-burning, picketing, and criminal conspiracy are within the protected ambit of the first amendment's "freedom of speech," or whether the "writings" protected by the copyright

---

[9] 17 U.S. (4 Wheat.) 202–03 (1819).
[13] 17 U.S. (4 Wheat.) 316 (1819).
[14] *Id.* at 413.
[15] *Id.* at 414–15.

clause include photographs, paintings, sculptures, performances, and the contents of phonograph records. She would not know whether the phrase, "No person except a natural born Citizen * * * shall be eligible to the Office of President," disqualified persons born abroad or those born by Caesarian section. We understand the range of plausible meanings of provisions only because we know that some interpretations respond to the kinds of concerns that the adopters' society might have while others do not.

That an interpreter must read a text in the light of its social as well as linguistic context does not destroy the boundary between textualism and intentionalism. Just as the textualist is not concerned with the adopters' idiosyncratic use of language, she is not concerned with their subjective purposes. Rather, she seeks to discern the purposes that a member of the adopters' society would understand the provision to encompass.

Suppose that phrases such as "commerce among the several states," or "freedom of speech," or "equal protection of the laws," have quite different meanings today than when they were adopted. An originalist would hold that, because interpretation is designed to capture the original understanding, the text must be understood in the contexts of the society that adopted it: "The meaning of the constitution is fixed when it is adopted, and it is not different at any subsequent time when a court has occasion to pass upon it."[21]

When a provision is interpreted roughly contemporaneously with its adoption, an interpreter unconsciously places the provision in its linguistic and social contexts, which she has internalized simply because she is of that society. But she cannot assume that a provision adopted one or two hundred years ago has the same meaning as it had for the adopters' society today. She must immerse herself in their society to understand the text as they understood it. Although many provisions of the Constitution may pose no serious interpretive problems in this respect, the textualist interpreter cannot be sure of this without first understanding the ordinary usage at the time of adoption. Did "commerce" include manufacture as well as trade? Did the power to "regulate" commerce imply the power to prohibit it? Did the power to "regulate commerce among the several states" include the power to regulate intrastate transactions which affected interstate commerce? With what absoluteness did 18th century Americans understand the prohibitions against "impairing" contractual obligations and "abridging the freedom of speech?" What did the words "privileges," "immunities," "due process," "equal protection of the laws," "citizen," and "person" mean to those who adopted the fourteenth amendment in 1868?

---

[21] T.M. Cooley, A Treatise on the Constitutional Limitations Which Rest Upon the Legislative Power of the States of The American Union 124 (Carrington's 8th ed. 1927) (n.p. 1868). * * *

Despite the differences between textualism and intentionalism, placing a constitutional provision in its original contexts calls for a historical inquiry quite similar to the intentionalist interpreter's. * * *

II. Intentionalism

By contrast to the textualist, the intentionalist interprets a provision by ascertaining the intentions of those who adopted it. The text of the provision is often a useful guide to the adopters' intentions, but the text does not enjoy a favored status over other sources. * * *

* * *

1. Who Are the Adopters?

The adopters of the Constitution of 1787 were some portion of the delegates to the Philadelphia Convention and majorities or supermajorities of the participants in the ratifying conventions in nine states. For all but one amendment to the Constitution,[35] the adopters were two-thirds or more of the members of each House of Congress and at least a majority of the legislators in [three-fourths] of the state legislatures.

For a textual provision to become part of the Constitution, the requisite number of persons in each of these bodies must have assented to it. Likewise, an intention can only become binding—only become an institutional intention—when it is shared by at least the same number and distribution of adopters. (Hereafter, I shall refer to this number and distribution as the "adopters.")

If the only way a judge could ascertain institutional intent were to count individual intention-votes, her task would be impossible even with respect to a single multimember law-making body, and a fortiori where the assent of several such bodies were required. Therefore, an intentionalist must necessarily use circumstantial evidence to educe a collective or general intent.

Interpreters often treat the writings or statements of the framers of a provision as evidence of the adopters' intent. This is a justifiable strategy for the moderate originalist who is concerned with the framers' intent on a relatively abstract level of generality—abstract enough to permit the inference that it reflects a broad social consensus rather than notions peculiar to a handful of the adopters. It is a problematic strategy for the strict originalist.

As the process of adoption moves from the actual framers of a constitutional amendment to the members of Congress who proposed it to the state legislators who ratified it, the amount of thought given the provision surely diminishes—especially if it is relatively technical or uncontroversial, or one

---

[35]The twenty-first amendment was ratified by state conventions.

of several of disparate provisions (*e.g.,* the Bill of Rights) adopted simultaneously. This suggests that there may be instances where a framer had a determinate intent but other adopters had no intent or an indeterminate intent. For example, suppose that the framers of the commerce clause considered the possibility that economic transactions taking place within the confines of a state might nonetheless affect interstate commerce in such a way as to come within the clause, and that they intended the clause to cover such transactions. But suppose that most of the delegates to the ratifying conventions did not conceive of this possibility and that either they "did not intend" that the clause encompass such transactions or else their intentions were indeterminate. Under these circumstances, what is the institutional intent, *i.e.,* the intent of the provision?

If the intent of the framers is to be attributed to the provision, it must be because the other adopters have in effect delegated their intention-votes to the framers. Leaving aside the question whether the adopters-at-large had any thoughts at all concerning this issue of delegation, consider what they might have desired if they had thought about it. Would they have wanted the framers' intentions to govern without knowing what those intentions were? The answers might well differ depending on whether the adopters had "no intent" or "indeterminate intent."

A delegate to a ratifying convention might well want his absence of intention (*i.e.,* "no-intent") regarding wholly intrastate transactions to be treated as a vote against the clause's encompassing such transactions (*i.e.,* "intent-not"): Since no-intent is the intentionalist equivalent of no-text, to accede to the framers' unknown intentions would be tantamount to blindly delegating to them the authority to insert textual provisions in the Constitution.

Where the framers intend that the activity be covered by the clause, and the adopters' intentions are merely indeterminate, the institutional intent is ambiguous. One adopter might wish his indeterminate intent to be treated as "no intent." Another adopter might wish to delegate his intention-vote to those whose intent is determinate. Yet another might wish to delegate authority to decisionmakers charged with applying the provision in the future. Without knowing more about the mind-sets of the actual adopters of particular constitutional provisions, one would be hard-pressed to choose among these.

2. The Adopters' Interpretive Intent

The intentionalist interpreters' first task must be to determine the interpretive intentions of the adopters of the provision before her—that is the canons by which the adopters intended their provisions to be interpreted. The practice of statutory interpretation from the 18th through at least the mid-19th century suggests that the adopters assumed—if they assumed anything at all—a mode of interpretation that was more textualist than intentionalist. The plain meaning rule was frequently invoked: judicial recourse to legislative debates was virtually unknown and generally considered improper. Even after references to extrinsic sources became common, courts and commentators frequently asserted that the plain meaning of the text was the surest guide to the intent of the adopters.

This poses obvious difficulties for an intentionalist whose very enterprise is premised on fidelity to the original understanding.

3. The Intended Specificity of a Provision

I now turn to an issue that lies at the intersection of what I have called interpretive and substantive intent: How much discretion did an adopter intend to delegate to those charged with applying a provision? Consider, for example, the possible intentions of the adopters of the cruel and unusual punishment clause of the eighth amendment. They might have intended that the language serve only as a shorthand for the Stuart tortures which were their exemplary applications of the clause. Somewhat more broadly, they might have intended the clause to be understood to incorporate the principle of *ejusdem generis*—to include their exemplary applications and other punishments that they found or would have found equally repugnant.[41]

What of instances where the adopters' substantive intent was indeterminate—where even if they had adverted to a proposed application they would not have been certain how the clause should apply? Here it is plausible that—if they *had* a determinate interpretive intent—they intended to delegate to future decisionmakers the authority to apply the clause in light of the general principles underlying it. To use Ronald Dworkin's terms, the adopters would have intended future interpreters to develop their own "conceptions" of cruel and unusual punishment within the framework of the adopters' general "concept" of such punishments.[42]

What of a case where the adopters viewed a certain punishment as not cruel and unusual? This is not the same as saying that the adopters "intended not to prohibit the punishment." For even if they expected their laws to be interpreted by intentionalist canons, the adopters may have intended that their own views not always govern. Like parents who attempt to instill values in their child by both articulating and applying a moral principle, they may have accepted, or even invited, the eventuality that the principle would be applied in ways that diverge from their own views.[43] The adopters may have understood that, even as to instances to which they believe the clause ought or ought not to apply, further thought by themselves or others committed to its underlying principle might lead them

[41]On a rather restrictive view, "would have found" means that, although the adopters did not advert to a punishment, they nonetheless intended that it be prohibited.

[42]R. Dworkin, Taking Rights Seriously 135 (1977).

[43]See id. at 134.

to change their minds. Not believing in their own omniscience or infallibility, they delegated the decision to those charged with interpreting the provision. If such a motivation is plausible with respect to applications of the clause in the adopters' contemporary society, it is even more likely with respect to its application by future interpreters, whose understanding of the clause will be affected by changing knowledge, technology, and forms of society.

The extent to which a clause may be properly interpreted to reach outcomes different from those actually contemplated by the adopters depends on the relationship between a general principle and its exemplary applications. A principle does not exist wholly independently of its author's subjective, or his society's conventional exemplary applications, and is always limited to some extent by the applications they found conceivable. Within these fairly broad limits, however, the adopters may have intended their examples to constrain more or less. To the intentionalist interpreter falls the unenviable task of ascertaining, for each provision, how much more or less.

* * *

IV. The Interpreter-Historian's Task

The interpreter's task as historian can be divided into three stages or categories. First, she must immerse herself in the world of the adopters to try to understand constitutional concepts and values from their perspective. Second, at least the intentionalist must ascertain the adopters' interpretive intent and the intended scope of the provision in question. Third, she must often "translate" the adopters' concepts and intentions into our time and apply them to situations that the adopters did not foresee.

The first stage is common to originalists of all persuasions. Although the textualist's aim is to understand and apply the language of a constitutional provision, she must locate the text in the linguistic and social contexts in which it was adopted. * * * The intentionalist would ideally count the intention-votes of the individual adopters. In practice, she can at best hope to discover a consensus of the adopters as manifested in the text of the provision itself, the history surrounding its adoption, and the ideologies and practices of the time.

The essential difficulty posed by the distance that separates the modern interpreter from the objects of her interpretation has been succinctly stated by Quentin Skinner in addressing the analogous problem facing historians of political theory:[52]

---

[52]Skinner, *Meaning and Understanding in the History of Ideas,* 8 Hist. & Theory 3[, 6] (1969). * * *

> [I]t will never in fact be possible simply to study what any given classic writer has *said* * * * without bringing to bear some of one's own expectations about what he must have been saying * * *. [T]hese models and preconceptions in terms of which we unavoidably organize and adjust our perceptions and thoughts will themselves tend to act as determinants of what we think or perceive. We must classify in order to understand, and we can only classify the unfamiliar in terms of the familiar. The perpetual danger, in our attempts to enlarge our historical understanding, is thus that our expectations about what someone must be saying or doing will themselves determine that we understand the agent to be doing something which he would not—or even could not—himself have accepted as an account of what he *was* doing.

To illustrate the problem of doing original history with even a single example would consume more space than I wish to here. Instead, I suggest that a reader who wants to get a sense of the elusiveness of the original understanding study some specific areas of constitutional history, reading both works that have been well received,[54] and also the controversy surrounding some of those that have not.[55]

The intentionalist interpreter must next ascertain the adopters' interpretive intent and the intended breadth of their provisions. That is, she must determine what the adopters intended future interpreters to make of their substantive views. Even if she can learn how the adopters intended contemporary interpreters to construe the Constitution, she cannot assume they intended the same canons to apply one or two hundred years later. Perhaps they wanted to bind the future as closely as possible to their own notions. Perhaps they intended a particular provision to be interpreted with increasing breadth as time went on. Or—more likely than not—the adopters may have had no intentions at all concerning these matters.[57]

For purposes of analytic clarity I have distinguished between (1) the adopters' interpretive intent and the intended scope of a provision and (2) their substantive intent concerning the application of the provision. If

[54]*See, e.g.,* C. Fairman, Reconstruction and Reunion, 1864–88, Pt. 1 (1971); L. Levy, Origins of the Fifth Amendment (1968); L. Levy, Legacy of Suppression (1960). *See also* I. Brandt, The Life of James Madison (1941–61); G. Wood, The Creation of the American Republic, 1776–87 (1969).

[55]A recent example is Raoul Berger's Government by Judiciary: The Transformation of the Fourteenth Amendment (1977), which argues that almost of all the Supreme Court's decisions under the fourteenth amendment are incorrect. *See, e.g.,* Kutler, *Raoul Berger's Fourteenth Amendment: A History or Ahistorical,* 6 Hastings Const.L.Q. 511 (1979); Murphy, Book Review, 87 Yale L.J. 1752 (1978); Soifer, Review Essay, 54 N.Y.U.L.Rev. 651 (1979). *But see* Perry, Book Review, 78 Colum.L.Rev. 685 (1978).

[57]In any case, the adopters' sense of time and change—of the relationship between present and future—was almost certainly not the same as ours, which has been affected by such phenomena as the industrial revolution, theories of evolution, relativity and quantum mechanics, and the possibility of annihilation.

interpretive intent and intended scope can be ascertained at all, they may instruct the interpreter to adopt different canons of interpretation than she would prefer. Under these circumstances, the intentionalist interpreter may wish to ignore these intentions and limit her inquiry to the adopters' substantive intentions. Leaving aside the normative difficulty of such selective infidelity, this is a problematic strategy: To be a coherent theory of interpretation, intentionalism must distinguish between the adopters' personal *views* about an issue and their *intentions* concerning its constitutional resolution. And it is only by reference to their interpretive intent and the intended scope of a provision that this distinction can be drawn.

The interpreter's final task is to translate the adopters' intentions into the present in order to apply them to the question at issue. Consider, for example, whether the cruel and unusual punishment clause of the eighth amendment prohibits the imposition of the death penalty today. The adopters of the clause apparently never doubted that the death penalty was constitutional. But was death the same event for inhabitants of the American colonies in the late 18th century as it is two centuries later? Death was not only a much more routine and public phenomenon then, but the fear of death was more effectively contained within a system of religious belief.[60] Twentieth-century Americans have a more secular cast of mind and seem less willing to accept this dreadful, forbidden, solitary, and shameful event.[61] The interpreter must therefore determine whether we view the death penalty with the same attitude—whether of disgust or ambivalence—that the adopters viewed their core examples of cruel and unusual punishment.[62]

Intentionalist interpretation frequently requires translations of this sort. For example, to determine whether the commerce clause applies to transactions taking place wholly within the boundaries of one state, or whether the first amendment protects the mass media, the interpreter must abstract the adopters' concepts of federalism and freedom of expression in order to find their analogue in our contemporary society with its different technology, economy, and systems of communication. The alternative would be to limit the application of constitutional provisions to the particular events and transactions with which the adopters were familiar. Even if such an approach were coherent, however, it would produce results that even a strict intentionalist would likely reject: Congress could not regulate any item of commerce or any mode of transportation that did not

---

[60] *See* P. Aries, Western Attitudes Toward Death 11–13 (1974); D. Stannard, The Puritan Way of Death 93 (1977).

[61] *See* Death in American Experience 102 (A. Mack ed. 1973); P. Aries, *supra* note 60, at 85–86.

[62] *See* Granucci, *"Nor Cruel and Unusual Punishment Inflicted": The Original Meaning*, 57 Calif.L.Rev. 839 (1969).

exist in 1789; the first amendment would not protect any means of communication not then known.

However difficult the earlier stages of her work, the interpreter was only trying to understand the past. The act of translation required here is different in kind, for it involves the counterfactual and imaginary act of projecting the adopters' concepts and attitudes into a future they probably could not have envisioned. When the interpreter engages in this sort of projection, she is in a fantasy world more of her own than of the adopters' making.

* * *

Even when the interpreter performs the more conventional historian's role, one may wonder whether the task is possible. There is a hermeneutic tradition, of which Hans-George Gadamar is the leading modern proponent, which holds that we can never understand the past in its own terms, free from our prejudices or preconceptions.[65] We are hopelessly imprisoned in our own world-views; we can shed some preconceptions only to adopt others, with no reason to believe that they are the conceptions of the different society that we are trying to understand. One need not embrace this essentially solipsistic view of historical knowledge to appreciate the indeterminate and contingent nature of the historical understanding that an originalist historian seeks to achieve.

None of this is to disparage doing history and other interpretive social science. It suggests, however, that the originalist constitutional historian may be questing after a chimera. The defense that "We're doing the best we can" is no less available to constitutional interpreters than to anyone else. But the best is not always good enough. The interpreter's understanding of the original understanding may be so indeterminate as to undermine the rationale for originalism. Although the origins of some constitutional doctrines are almost certainly established, the historical grounding of many others is quite controversial. It seems peculiar, to say the least, that the legitimacy of a current doctrine should turn on the historian's judgment that it seems "more likely than not," or even "rather likely," that the adopters intended it some one or two centuries ago.

V. Two Types of Originalism

The originalist interpreter can approach her task with different attitudes about the precision with which the object of interpretation—the text [or] intentions * * *—should be understood. In this section I describe the

---

[65] *See* Hans-Georg Gadamer, Truth and Method (Eng. trans. 1975). *See also* P. Winch, The Idea of a Social Science and its Relation to Philosophy (1958); Taylor, *Interpretation and the Sciences of Man,* 25 Rev. of Metaphysics 3 (1971). For a sharply critical review of Gadamer's work, see E.D. Hirsch, Validity in Interpretation 245 (1967).

attitudes of "strict" and "moderate" originalism—two areas, not points, on a spectrum—and briefly survey the practices of American constitutional decisionmaking in terms of them.

I have devoted very little attention to the most extreme form of strict textualism—literalism. A thorough-going literalist understands a text to encompass all those and only those instances that come within its words read without regard to its social or perhaps even its linguistic context. Because literalism poorly matches the ways in which we speak and write, it is unable to handle the ambiguity, vagueness, and figurative usage that pervade natural languages, and produces embarrassingly silly results.

Strict intentionalism requires the interpreter to determine how the adopters would have applied a provision to a given situation, and to apply it accordingly. The enterprise rests on the questionable assumption that the adopters of constitutional provisions intended them to be applied in this manner. But even if this were true, the interpreter confronts historiographic difficulties of such magnitude as to make the aim practicably unattainable.

Strict textualism and intentionalism are not synergistic, but rather mutually antagonistic approaches to interpretation. The reader need only consider the strict textualist's and intentionalist's views of the first amendment protection of pornographic literature. By contrast, moderate textualism and intentionalism closely resemble each other in methodology and results.

A moderate textualist takes account of the open-textured quality of language and reads the language of provisions in their social and linguistic contexts. A moderate intentionalist applies a provision consistent with the adopters' intent at a relatively high level of generality, consistent with what is sometimes called the "purpose of the provision." Where the strict intentionalist tries to determine the adopters' actual subjective purposes, the moderate intentionalist attempts to understand what the adopters' purposes might plausibly have been, an aim far more readily achieved than a precise understanding of the adopters' intentions.

* * *

Strict originalism cannot accommodate most modern decisions under the Bill of Rights and the fourteenth amendment, or the virtually plenary scope of congressional power under the commerce clause. Although moderate originalism is far more expansive, some major constitutional doctrines lie beyond its pale as well.

A moderate textualist would treat almost all contemporary free speech and equal protection decisions as within the permissible ambit of these clauses, though not necessarily entailed by them. Because of our uncertainty about the original understanding, it is harder to assess the legitimacy of these doctrines from the viewpoint of a moderate intentionalist. For example, the proper scope of the first amendment depends on whether its adopters were only pursuing "representation reinforcing" goals,[70] or were more broadly concerned to promote a free marketplace of ideas or individual autonomy.[71] The level of generality on which the adopters conceived of the equal protection clause presents a similar uncertainty, but whether or not a moderate intentionalist could accept all of the "new" or "newer" equal protection,[72] she could read the clause to protect "discrete and insular minorities" besides blacks.

On the other hand, a moderate originalist, whether of textualist or intentionalist persuasion, would have serious difficulties justifying (1) the incorporation of the principle of equal protection into the fifth amendment,[73] (2) the incorporation of provisions of the Bill of Rights into the fourteenth amendment,[74] (3) the more general notion of substantive due process, including the minimal rational relationship standard,[75] and (4) the practice of judicial review of congressional legislation established by *Marbury v. Madison.*[76] * * *

* * *

Moderate originalism is a perfectly sensible strategy of constitutional decisionmaking. But its constraints are illusory and counterproductive. Contrary to the moderate originalist's faith, the text and original understanding have contributed little to the development of many doctrines she accepts as legitimate. Consider the relationship between the original understanding of the fourteenth amendment and current doctrines

---

[70]*See* J.H. Ely, *supra* note 1, at chs. 4–6. *See also* Mills v. Alabama, 384 U.S. 214, 218–20 (1966) * * *.

[71]*See, e.g.,* J.S. Mill, On Liberty (1859); Richards, *Free Speech and Obscenity Law: Toward a Moral Theory of the First Amendment,* 123 U.Pa.L.Rev. 45 (1974); Scanlon, *A Theory of Free Expression,* 1 Phil. & Pub. Affairs 204 (1972).

[72]*See generally,* [P. Brest, Processes of Constitutional Decisionmaking 809–93 (1975)]; Gunther, *In Search of Evolving Doctrine on a Changing Court: A Model for a Newer Equal Protection,* 86 Harv.L.Rev. 1 (1972).

[73]*See, e.g.,* Frontiero v. Richardson, 411 U.S. 677 (1973); Bolling v. Sharpe, 347 U.S. 497 (1954); Linde, *Judges, Critics, and the Realist Tradition,* 82 Yale L.J. 227, 233–34 (1972).

[74]Compare Justice Black's and Justice Frankfurter's views in Adamson v. California, 332 U.S. 46 (1947). *See also* L. Levy, *The Fourteenth Amendment and the Bill of Rights* in Judgments: Essays on American Constitutional History 64 (1972); Fairman, *Does the Fourteenth Amendment Incorporate the Bill of Rights? The Original Understanding,* 2 Stan.L.Rev. 5 (1949); Morrison, *Does the Fourteenth Amendment Incorporate the Bill of Rights? The Judicial Interpretation,* 2 Stan.L.Rev. 140 (1949).

[75]*See, e.g.,* R. Berger, *supra* note 55; C. Fairman, *supra,* note 54, at 1207 * * *.

[76]*See* L. Boudin, Government by Judiciary (1932); A. Westin, Introduction and Historical Bibliography to C. Beard, The Supreme Court and the Constitution (1912); Judicial Review and the Supreme Court 1–12 (Levy ed. 1967). *But see* R. Berger, Congress v. The Supreme Court (1969); E. Corwin, Court Over Constitution (1938); Corwin, *Marbury v. Madison and the Doctrine of Judicial Review,* 12 Mich.L.Rev. 538 (1914) * * *.

prohibiting gender-based classifications[103] and discriminations in the political process.[104] For the moderate originalist these may be legitimately premised on the equal protection clause. But to what extent have originalist sources *guided* the evolution of these doctrines? The text is wholly open-ended; and if the adopters had any intentions at all about these issues, their resolution was probably contrary to the Court's. At most, the Court can claim guidance from the general notion of equal treatment reflected in the provision. I use the word "reflected" advisedly, however, for the equal protection clause does not establish a principle of equality; it only articulates and symbolizes a principle defined by our conventional public morality. Indeed, because of its indeterminacy, the clause does not offer much guidance even in resolving particular issues of discrimination based on race.[105]

* * *

In sum, if you consider the evolution of doctrines in just about any extensively-adjudicated area of constitutional law—whether "under" the commerce, free speech, due process, or equal protection clauses—explicit reliance on originalist sources has played a very small role compared to the elaboration of the Court's own precedents. It is rather like having a remote ancestor who came over on the Mayflower.

RICHARD S. KAY, ADHERENCE TO THE ORIGINAL INTENTIONS IN CONSTITUTIONAL ADJUDICATION: THREE OBJECTIONS AND RESPONSES

82 NW.U.L.REV. 226, 228–30, 236, 242–57, 259, 284–92 (1988).

This essay will critically examine the reasons given by modern scholars for rejecting the conventional norm of judicial review—adherence to the original intentions of the Constitution's enactors. While variously phrased, their reasons may be subsumed under three general objections: 1) Adherence to the original intentions is impossible; 2) It is self-contradictory; and 3) It is wrong.

While there is some force in each of these objections, I conclude that the first two are unconvincing and the third depends on personal judgments ultimately not susceptible to rational resolution. My objective is to provide responses to these objections and not to make a complete affirmative case for original intentions adjudication. * * *

---

[103] *E.g.*, Craig v. Boren, 429 U.S. 190 (1976).

[104] *E.g.*, Harper v. Virginia Bd. of Elections, 383 U.S. 663 (1966).

[105] *See* Brown v. Board of Educ., 347 U.S. 483, 489–91 (1954); Bickel, *The Original Understanding and the Segregation Decision*, 69 Harv.L.Rev. 1 (1955); Kelly, *The Fourteenth Amendment Reconsidered: The Segregation Question*, 54 Mich.L.Rev. 1049 (1956).

I also do not intend to argue that, historically, adjudicated constitutional law is in any significant way an actual reflection of the original intentions. Clearly it is not. Rather my goal is to clarify the arguments for one or another approach to constitutional adjudication as an abstract matter. Moreover, the practical consequences of accepting the propriety of original intentions adjudication may be extremely limited. The legal, social and economic impacts of judicial review cannot be wished away, nor may we want them to be. An abrupt and complete adoption of original intentions adjudication might inflict injuries that far transcend the kinds of specifically legal considerations I discuss here. I am convinced, however, that we cannot intelligently discuss these practical matters until we have a clear sense of the underlying theoretical positions and disagreements.

* * *

* * * Adherence to the conventional view of constitutional adjudication is sometimes associated with the idea that judges should be tethered to the intentions of those who enacted the relevant constitutional provisions, and sometimes with the idea that judges should be restrained by the *text itself,* independent of the particular historical intentions of those who created it. The model I discuss will require further elaboration, but, briefly put, it calls for judges to apply the rules of the written constitution *in the sense in which those rules were understood by the people who enacted them.* Probably the purest judicial exposition and application of this understanding can be found in Justice Sutherland's dissenting opinion in the Minnesota Mortgage Moratorium case.[17] He said the "aim of construction" is to "discover the meaning," that is to "ascertain and give effect to the intent of its framers and the people who adopted it."[18] The view discussed here, therefore, rejects the idea that judicial allegiance is owed only to the mere words of the Constitution.

* * *

III. First Objection: It's Impossible

* * *

A. It's Really Impossible

The objection that original intentions adjudication is really impossible is founded on an extreme and general proposition about the capacity of human beings to communicate a determinate meaning through the medium of language. The argument suggests that because linguistic communication is impossible, it is futile for judges to attempt to learn the intentions of the

[17] Home Building & Loan Ass'n v. Blaisdell, 290 U.S. 398, 448 (1934) (Sutherland, J., dissenting).

[18] *Id.* at 453.

constitution-makers by studying what they said or what other people said about them.

Some legal scholars have taken positions similar to this by adopting the views of writers in the fields of philosophy and literary criticism.[50] * * *

* * *

The most glaring problem with the extreme position that interpretation according to original intentions is impossible, when applied to the use of language in general, is that it is wildly counterintuitive. It is inconsistent with the way people carry on their lives every day. We all confidently proceed on the assumption that we are capable of communicating through words a single determinate intention and that we are capable of understanding the single, determinate intentions of others. Most of the time our confidence is well-founded. We arrive at the right place for the right meetings at more or less the right time. We read and discuss articles with the impression that we are talking about the same thing. We stop at stop signs, file our tax returns, and obey subpoenas. All these commonplace experiences testify powerfully against the claim that the inference of a determinate meaning from a sequence of words uttered in a particular context is essentially, and always, impossible. * * *

The most telling response to this objection is simply that no one really believes it, not even the writers who make the objection. If they did, they would not use language to advance the argument. * * *

B. It's Too Hard

The more moderate form of the impossibility objection to original intentions adjudication—It's too hard—appears much more plausible. It concedes that language is sometimes capable of communicating a speaker's or writer's intentions, but holds that interpretation of the American Constitution creates peculiar problems which make the relevant original intentions inaccessible.

* * *

Before addressing [this criticism], it is necessary to explain precisely what original intentions adjudication requires of judges in the context of actual litigation. No judge is ever required to answer the abstract question: "What did the enactors intend by the phrase 'due process of law'?" Rather, judges must decide in a specific case whether or not, given the original intentions of the constitution-makers, a particular governmental action deprives someone of liberty or property without due process of law. The difference between the two questions is critically important. It is much

---

[50] *See, e.g.*, Garet, *Comparative Normative Hermeneutics: Scripture, Literature, Constitution,* 58 S.Cal.L.Rev. 35 (1985); Levinson, *Law As Literature,* 60 Tex.L.Rev. 373 (1982); Peller, *The Metaphysics of American Law,* 73 Calif.L.Rev. 1151 (1985).

easier to answer the second than the first because the alternatives are binary. The question can and can only be answered "yes" or "no," and since the judge must give some answer, it follows that he need not answer with certainty. All he needs to do is decide which of the two possible answers in that case is *more likely* correct.

Defining the judge's task as that of choosing which of two outcomes is more likely consistent with original intentions is particularly important in light of criticisms that stress the impossibility of ascertaining those intentions with sufficient certainty. It is true that we can never know the original intentions with certainty, but then we can never know any speaker's or writer's intent with certainty. Nevertheless, it is almost always possible to examine the constitutional text and other evidence of intent associated with it and make a reasonable, good faith judgment about which result is more likely consistent with that intent. Of course confidence in these judgments will be different in different situations, but one answer will almost always appear better than the other. Indeed, one of the two possible responses will be obviously incorrect because, while it is theoretically possible that the lawmakers held such an intention, the available historical evidence will be overwhelmingly against it. Thus, we can be uncertain about the intended meaning of a constitutional provision at the same time we are convinced that it is not consistent with one of the two contesting positions in a lawsuit. And, given that we have only two options, that conviction will decide the case.

There is nothing extraordinary in making important decisions this way. Almost every decision we make and action we take is based on a judgment of probabilities, often as to the probable intended meaning of what we read or hear. To insist on certainty would lead to paralysis. In asking judges to make decisions in this way we demand nothing more or less than the same kinds of decisions everyone makes everyday.

1. *The Problem of Multiple Intentions.* * * * The first problem concerns the difficulty of discerning a single intention when there are multiple constitution-makers.[82]

In one sense this argument is a variant of the more extreme claim discussed above. To speak of an intention is to speak of a human mind. A joint intention cannot be the simple analog of an individual intention because we cannot easily conceive of a joint or group mind. But intent can

[82] *See* R. Dworkin, [Law's Empire] 315–21 (1986); Brennan, [*The Constitution of the United States: Contemporary Ratification,* 27 S.Tex.L.J. 433, 435 (1986)]; Brest, [*The Misconceived Quest for the Original Understanding,* 60 B.U.L.Rev. 204, 212–13 (1980)]; Dworkin, *The Forum of Principle,* 56 N.Y.U.L.Rev. 469, 480–81, 487–88 (1981); Radin, [*Statutory Interpretation,* 43 Harv.L.Rev. 863, 870–71 (1930)]; Saphire, *Judicial Review in the Name of the Constitution,* 8 U.Dayton L.Rev. 745, 772–80 (1983); Hancher, *Dead Letters: Wills and Poems,* 60 Tex.L.Rev. 507 (1982).

be attributed to a group without positing the idea of a group mind. When we speak of such an intention we usually mean that each member of the group holds an identical individual intention. If a husband and wife discuss and settle on a list of invitations to a dinner party it seems perfectly proper to say that they have "an intention" about who their guests will be. This phenomenon would only be impossible if the couple could not articulate and communicate their intentions to each other in a way that let each one know those intentions coincided. I have already discussed why I believe such communication is not only possible but common.

Nevertheless, ascertaining the intention of a group is more complicated than discovering the intention of a single person. Many individuals in different capacities were involved in making the Constitution. In investigating the original intentions of these individuals, one problem lies in identifying those people whose coincident intentions created the relevant original intent. This problem is two-fold. First, every constitutional provision is the product of consideration and approval by different groups; therefore, we must identify which groups should be counted in defining the original intention. Second, within a specific group, there will be a variety of individual intentions and we will have to decide whose intentions define the intention of the group. Each of these aspects will be considered in turn.

a. *Which groups?*—In answering the first question, it is useful to recall the reason for being concerned with intention in the first place. * * * Recourse to intention is necessary because only certain people have the authority to make law. Thus, in constitutional law, we must identify which groups could, by their approval, give the Constitution the sanction of law.

It is necessary at this point to distinguish between the original Constitution of 1787 and subsequent amendments. We ordinarily treat amendments as law because they were created in accordance with Article V. An amendment becomes law when it is ratified by the legislatures of three-fourths of the States. The intentions of these legislatures is, thus, essential. But knowing those intentions is not sufficient. According to Article V, state legislatures may only ratify amendments that have been proposed by Congress with a two-thirds majority in each House. Thus, the Senate and House of Representatives are indispensable actors in the law-making process. In sum, constitutional amendments require identical intentions in the two Houses of Congress and in thirty-eight state legislatures.

When we consider the Constitution of 1787, of course, there is no governing law analogous to Article V that informs us who must agree before the Constitution acquires the force of law. The Constitution was a clean break with prior existing law. This does not mean, however, that we have no idea whose judgments and approval gave the Constitution authority. Like any supreme law, the legal character of the Constitution will depend on political beliefs and attitudes in a society about who has the final right to make law. This is a complex matter I have addressed at some length elsewhere.[89] It is sufficient here to note that the authority of the Constitution is conventionally and popularly premised on the understanding that it was the work of "the People" in their original, sovereign capacity. Actually, the role of "the People" was played by the special ratifying conventions in the individual states. The drafters at the Philadelphia Convention could claim no such mandate from "the people." Some supporters of the Constitution went so far as to disparage the importance of the Convention, except insofar as it was able to place a proposal before the state conventions.[91] The inquiry into original intent, therefore, should focus on the intentions of the various ratifying bodies who possessed the constituent authority.

With regard to both the body of the Constitution and its amendments, then, the only valid original intentions will be those held in common by a number of legislative bodies. This conclusion raises an obvious problem: What if we discover that, though they approved the same texts, different groups held different intentions so that no single intention can be applied to a particular question of interpretation? I will return to this question shortly.

b. *Which individuals within groups?*—The very same problem arises in answering the second question. Once we have found the authoritative groups, we must find a single intention for each group. Which individuals' intentions in, say, the Senate or in the Virginia Ratifying Convention should be considered?

The reasoning employed above can be applied to this problem. We wish to obtain the group intention because we deem it capable of establishing an authoritative rule. A given body acts when some number of its members agree to act. In the ordinary course that number is a majority. In the case of the Houses of Congress proposing amendments it is—by virtue of prior governing law—a two-thirds majority. The intention of the body, therefore, is embodied in the shared intentions of the appropriate majority of its members.

One consequence of this reasoning is that only the intentions of those voting in favor of the constitutional provision at issue will be relevant. The intentions of dissenters may be useful in illuminating the intention of the proponents, but they are not a part of the authoritative intention. Dissenters neither contributed nor were necessary to the event which made the text law and, for reasons already discussed, our concern is with the intentions of the

---

[89]*See* Kay, [*Preconstitutional Rules,* 42 Ohio St.L.J. 187 (1981)]; Kay, *The Creation of Constitutions in Canada and the United States,* 7 Can.–U.S.L.J. 111 (1984).

[91]*See* 1 M. Farrand, Records of the Federal Convention of 1787 295 (remarks of A. Hamilton), 253 (remarks of J. Wilson) (1966); The Federalist No. 40 at 247–48 (J. Madison) (C. Rossiter ed. 1961) * * *.

lawmakers. Proper inquiry, therefore, is restricted to the members of the majority.

As we saw earlier when there were numerous law-making bodies, however, there may be more than one intention in the majority that approves the very same act of legislation. The difficulty will be even greater here because the number of potential intentions will be larger. When we multiply the number of possible intentions in a legislature by the number of possible intentions among legislative bodies the task of determining one original intention might appear hopeless.

c. *Summing different intentions.*—The possibility of multiple, varying intentions is not, however, fatal to the enterprise of original intentions adjudication. The difficulty is intractable only if there are multiple and totally *contradictory* intentions. This could happen if, for example, a constitutional provision was created with some constitution-makers intending it to mean *X* and only *X*, while other constitution-makers intended it to mean not-*X* and only not-*X*. Such contradiction is extremely unlikely, however, because though the intentions involved are held by different people, those intentions are associated with the adoption of identical language. The use of the same language suggests a common core of meaning shared by all. Any different intentions are, therefore, likely to be overlapping not contradictory. Thus, if an ordinance prohibits "vehicles in the park," it is safe to assume that all of the enactors intended it apply to ordinary automobiles. Similarly, in a constitutional context, probably all of the enactors of the fifth and fourteenth amendments understood that incarceration would be a deprivation of liberty requiring due process of law. The differences in intention will arise in cases beyond the obvious situations suggested by the language, as that language was ordinarily used and understood. Where there is disagreement it will be with respect to the outer reach or scope of the rule. To use the terminology of some modern philosophers of language, these differences will be attributable to the vagueness, not the ambiguity, of the words adopted.[95]

Originally, I stated the problem in this section to be the combination of disparate intentions into one authoritative intention of the group with authority to make law. But, given the kind of differences likely to occur, we should be able to accumulate enough *identical* intentions to compose an authoritative lawmaker. By discerning the language's central paradigm, we can define an area of application that was intended by virtually all the relevant individuals who together constitute the lawmaker. As we move out from this core idea to somewhat less obvious applications, we can expect to find fewer individuals who intend the law to extend so far. Still, as long as

---

[95] *See* W. Quine, Word and Object 125–34 (1960); Young, *Equivocation in the Making of Agreements,* 64 Colum.L.Rev. 619, 626–32, 646–47 (1964). * * *

it is probable that a necessary law-making majority shared a particular understanding it will be appropriate to so interpret the provision. This approach, therefore, requires the judge to ask whether the challenged action falls within a meaning intended by an authoritative lawmaker. Idiosyncratic meanings held by individuals within the majority (or by individual law-making bodies) falling outside that shared, core intention will not have the force of law because they lack such an authoritative source. They may be ignored for the same reasons that we ignore the intentions of the dissenters.

This argument assumes that individuals do not employ the same words to mean entirely opposite things, especially in circumstances where they discuss and debate the meaning of those words before adopting them. Therefore, there will almost always be some core meaning that reflects the intentions of the constitution-makers. This is true even when there is no controlling intention with respect to other, fringe meanings.

* * *

2. *The Problem of Historical Understanding.*—Another argument against original intentions adjudication suggests that it is very difficult, if not impossible, to understand intentions formed and expressed a very long time ago.[103] * * * This claim is based on a "fatal" gap between the moment of expression and the moment of understanding. But all interpretation—contemporary as well as ancient—is historical in this sense. And, if it is conceded that some immediate communication is possible, then the difficulty is not different in kind simply because the time between speaking and listening or writing and reading is changed from minutes or days to decades or centuries.

* * *

The very breadth of this claim makes it implausible. It is essentially an attack on the possibility and validity of historical investigation. While some students of history deny the possibility of objectively correct historical conclusions, the contrary view is also widely and firmly held. Indeed, the force of the latter position is strengthened by the fact that history is a well-established discipline to which thousands of sensible people have devoted and continue to devote their energy and intelligence. These scholars proceed on the assumption that, with varying degrees of effort, it *is* possible to ascertain and adopt the viewpoint of another person, even if that other person is remote in place, culture or time.

* * *

---

[103]*See* Brennan, *supra* note 82, at 435; Powell, *Rules for Originalists,* 73 Va.L.Rev. 659, 673–74 (1987); Tushnet, *Following the Rules Laid Down: A Critique of Interpretivism and Neutral Principles,* 96 Harv.L.Rev. 781, 793–804 (1983).

Finally, as I noted when considering the problem of multiple intentions, original intentions adjudication only calls for decisions regarding which of two proposed interpretations is more likely to be consistent with those original intentions. In most cases, it should be possible to recapture enough of the past to make that choice.

3. *The Probabilities in Balance.*—The discussion thus far has omitted one significant possibility. A judge, after considering the evidence of the relevant intentions, could decide that neither of the contesting propositions about the original intention is more likely than the other—that is, he might conclude that the evidence exactly balances. In such cases, we might have a supplemental rule that, for example, places the burden of proof on the party claiming that constitutional rules have been violated.[115] But unless such a rule itself could be inferred from the original intentions of the enactors, this would result in cases being decided on grounds independent of the original intentions. There may exist, therefore, certain cases in which original intentions adjudication will yield no answer.

In practice, however, these "ties" will be exceedingly rare. This is because the available information about the creators of the constitutional rules is so plentiful. Given the usual denseness of the historical record, a competent person is unlikely to come across many cases where the evidence that the original intentions did and the evidence that it did not extend to the act in question is precisely equal. The strength of an interpreter's convictions may depend on the relative strength of the two cases, but he will almost always be able to say that one is better than the other.

* * *

* * * [S]ome things may fall outside the categories established by the constitution-makers * * * because they are so different from those the enactors knew about. In such cases, we cannot assume they made any provision for them at all. But do such cases really result in a 0–0 tie with original intentions adjudication providing no solution? I believe the Constitution, as intended by its creators, provides a decision on constitutionality for every possible action no matter how different it is from the things and circumstances the constitution-makers had in mind. Implicit in the Constitution are "back-up rules" which cover all things not provided for in the explicit rules. It must be stressed these back-up rules are *not* new constructs created in order to make original intentions adjudication feasible. Rather, they are legitimate inferences from the enactment of the constitutional text. They are an inherent part of what the constitution-makers did when they created the Constitution.

---

[115] *See, e.g.*, Metropolitan Cas. Ins. Co. v. Brownell, 294 U.S. 580, 584 (1935) (heavy burden of proof rests on party claiming unconstitutionality of statutes); Brown v. Maryland, 25 U.S. (12 Wheat.) 419, 436 (1827) (same).

These back-up rules are a necessary consequence of the federal system of granted and residual powers established by the Constitution. The Constitution created a national government against a background of pre-existing states. That government exists *only* by virtue of the enactment of the Constitution. Therefore, we must find in the Constitution all of its features and all of its powers. There is nowhere else to look. Consequently, any action of the federal government not traceable to the enumerated institutions and powers is an exercise of power not granted to it and is contrary to the Constitution. Any truly *new* thing done by the federal government is unauthorized and therefore void.

On the other hand, the United States Constitution was enacted on the assumption that the existing states would continue to exist. The states necessarily derived their governmental institutions and powers from sources outside the new Constitution. Therefore, the absence of a reference to a state power is not equivalent to a lack of authorization. The Constitution declares itself to be and was, no doubt, intended to be supreme over the states, but only insofar as it specifically limited state powers. Any truly *new* thing done by a state must be outside of those prohibitions, and must, therefore, be constitutional.

This conclusion is itself an interpretation of the Constitution. It is, therefore, subject to rebuttal by persuasive historical evidence to the contrary. The case for it, however, is very strong. The constitution-makers differed among themselves about the appropriate scope of the powers of the new national government, but there is no serious evidence that these powers (whatever their extent) were not entirely granted by the new constitution or that state power was altered except insofar as affirmatively limited by the Constitution. The Tenth Amendment makes this explicit. The Civil War amendments significantly altered the constitutional allocation of national and state powers by enlarging federal legislative authority and especially by placing new and broad limits on state power. But it did not alter the underlying scheme of granted and residuary powers. Debate about power in the federal system, therefore, must turn on what the Constitution gave to the federal government and what it took away from the States. So long as that is true, there is an answer to the validity of every new thing. There are no omitted cases.

* * *

* * * Original intentions adjudication may not achieve [its] goals perfectly, but to conclude that it is, therefore, useless "is like saying that as a perfectly aseptic environment is impossible, one might as well conduct surgery in a sewer."[137] When honestly applied, original intentions

---

[137] C. Geertz, The Interpretation of Cultures 30 (1973) (attributed to Robert Solow). * * *

adjudication seems to reduce the influence of the personal and idiosyncratic aspects of a judge's personality or ideology more than do alternative theories that rely on ill-defined standards of one kind or another. Such rule-governed adjudication may or may not be appealing, but, for the reasons suggested, it is possible.

* * *

IV. SECOND OBJECTION: IT'S SELF-CONTRADICTORY

The second principal objection to original intentions adjudication is that the enactors themselves did not want their intentions to govern judicial exposition on the lawfulness of certain governmental action. Proponents of this argument suggest that the constitution-makers intended judges to look elsewhere for guides to decision and (depending on the proponent) wanted judges to possess varying degrees of discretion.

* * *

[This] * * * objection assumes that the interpretative intentions of the enactors ought to control constitutional interpretation and that those intentions were that substantive intentions should not control. The latter can be reduced to a mere (although certainly difficult) question of historical fact. We know that the constitution-makers thought it was important to enact written constitutional rules. We know they took great pains to choose the terms they did and that they argued about the best language and about the merits of the proposals before them as if their decisions on these things would make a difference. We would not expect such deliberation from people who wanted their intentions to be ignored or to play a minor role in the future application of the rules they made. A strong case would seem in order from those who would impute such a desire to them. I do not contend that such a claim could never be proven. But [for reasons not included in these excerpts] it does not seem to me to have been proven yet.

V. THIRD OBJECTION: IT'S WRONG

* * * [E]ven if [original intentions] adjudication is both possible and coherent, it must face a final objection: that [it] makes for bad government and bad law. While rarely put so bluntly, this is the most potent of the three objections that I have listed. Its power derives from the fact that, unlike the first two, refuting it requires more than simply an appeal to facts, history, or ordinary experience. This objection is the expression of a political and moral judgment about the best way for people to live in society. As such, conventional argument can take us only so far.

To evaluate this objection, we cannot consider original intentions adjudication in isolation, as we were able to do with the first two objections. The judgment here is necessarily relative: original intentions adjudication must be worse than *some other* system in which constitutional decisions are made according to some standards or processes other than fidelity to the original intentions.

* * *

* * * [This] third objection to original intentions adjudication might be put this way: limiting government by fixed rules intended by people in the more or less distant past will yield less satisfactory political and social consequences than will some other limiting technique. The exact nature of the objection depends on the proffered alternative, but most versions find similar problems with submission to the original intentions. These problems involve the incapacity of set, abstract rules to respond over time to our collective and individual well-being. * * *

* * *

* * * [A fair] response is to affirm the values inherent in "inflexibility"—the values of stability and clarity. Constitutional government exists to limit the sphere of appropriate government activity. It rests on the premise that there should be a realm of action and private decision-making immune from public coercion. The value of dividing human activity into exclusively private and potentially public zones would be severely diminished if the boundary between the two areas could be frequently and unpredictably altered. It is not merely the ability to contest, and sometimes successfully resist, government impositions that benefit those living under a constitutional government. It is, at least as much, the ability to "count on" government being constrained by certain procedures and within certain limits. Such stability permits us confidently to plan our lives, a freedom which is at the core of our capacity for self-definition. The opposite kind of existence, where we live in perpetual dread of the secret decree and the surprise order becomes, at the extreme, totalitarianism—the opposite of government under law.

This characteristic of government under law is not the only important value in the relationship of government and the individual, but it is difficult to overestimate its importance. * * * When life-plans are at stake, we are "risk-averse." Indeed, it may be the securing of a class of expectations from undefined and unpredictable interferences that is the peculiar contribution of law to society, a contribution particularly important when it is applied to the potential dangers of abuse by government.

* * *

But recognition of this value does not rebut the initial objection to original intentions adjudication that static constitutional rules are unsuitable for a constantly changing society. It is merely a counter-weight. Whether it is sufficient depends on an evaluation of the relative importance of the competing values: the value of flexibility and adaptability on the one hand, and the value of predictability and stability on the other.

Moreover, in specific cases, these concerns cannot be considered in isolation. How we view their competing advantages will be influenced by the substantive content of the constitutional rules at issue, and our regard for the individuals who, as judges, will undertake whatever revisions are allowed. Our enthusiasm for stable rules will be reduced if we think the rules protected are oppressive and unfair. Our taste for responsive and up-to-date rules will be diminished if we know they will be "improved" by people we regard as ignorant or immoral. Thus the preconstitutional decision must be largely empirical, depending on facts that may be disputed and it must, therefore, be only provisional.

Even if we could agree about the quality of the substantive rules and the credentials of the judges who would supervise their evolution, we would probably still disagree on the desirability of adhering to the original intentions because the weights we assign these competing sets of values are different. Those preferences, in turn, would depend on our confidence in the capacity of government officials, including judges, to discover and act on the public good without well-defined prior rules and on the risk that, without strict prior limits, such officials might cause suffering, unrest, and injury. Our choice of the governing norm of constitutional adjudication, then, will turn on the kinds of chances we are willing to take in living together in society, and, what comes to the same thing, on our judgment as to the kind of people we are.

B. TEXTUALISM

FREDERICK SCHAUER, EASY CASES

58 S.Cal.L.Rev. 399, 414–423, 430–31 (1985).

* * * [It is] clear that there *are* easy cases in constitutional law—lots of them. The parties concerned know, without litigating and without consulting lawyers, that Ronald Reagan cannot run for a third term; that the junior Senator from Virginia, who was elected in 1982, does not have to run again in 1984 or 1986 even though the Representative from the First Congressional District does; that bills receiving less than a majority of votes in either the House or the Senate are not laws of the United States; that the Equal Rights Amendment, the District of Columbia Representation in the Senate Amendment, and the Balanced Budget Amendment are not now part of the Constitution; and that a twenty-nine year-old is not going to be President of the United States. I have equivalent confidence that I will not receive a notice in the mail informing me that I must house members of the armed forces in my spare bedroom; that criminal defendants in federal courts cannot be denied the right to be represented by a qualified lawyer for whom they are willing to pay; and that the next in line to succeed to the Presidency in the event of the President's death is the Vice-President, and

not the Secretary of the Interior, the Congressman from Wyoming, or the quarterback for the Philadelphia Eagles.

The foregoing is only a small sample of the legal events that are "easy" constitutional cases. Once free from the lawyer's preoccupation with close cases—those in which the lawyer *qua* lawyer is a necessary actor in the play[39]—we begin to comprehend the enormous quantity of instances in which the legal results are commonly considered obvious. But why is this? What makes the easy case easy?

In searching for the sources of easiness, it is perhaps best to look for the sources of hardness, and then define easy cases as those without any of the characteristics of hard cases. Such definition by exclusion is not the only approach, but it seems particularly appropriate because it is the exception, the hard case, that most commonly commands our attention.

Prototypically, a vague, ambiguous, or simply opaque linguistic formulation of the relevant rule generates a hard case. Such a linguistic phenomenon may be caused by questions about the result announced by a clearly applicable rule, questions about which rule, if any, is in fact relevant, or both. Regardless of the cause, the result is the same: one cannot find the answer to a question (which is not the same as a controversy) by a straightforward reading of rules.

To the extent that one *can* find an answer to a question by a straightforward reading of rules, other factors may make a case hard. A case that seems linguistically easy may be hard if the result announced by the language is inconsistent with the "purpose" of the rule. In such cases the tension between the plain meaning of the words and the reason for using those words creates a hard case, in much the same way that linguistic imprecision creates a hard case.

Even if a rule seems plainly applicable, and even if that application is consistent with the purpose behind a rule, it may be that two or more rules, dictating different results, will be applicable. If one rule suggests answer *A* to the question, and another suggests answer *B,* then it is as if no answer had been provided. In the calculus of rules, too many rules are no better than none at all.

Finally, and perhaps most importantly, there may be only one relevant rule, it may be quite straightforwardly applicable, and its application would be consistent with its purpose. Yet it may still be morally, socially, or politically hard, however, in the sense of *hard* to swallow. * * *

---

[39]Part of the problem, of course, is that legal theory in general is undertaken largely by those who train lawyers. We will have made considerable strides when we recognize that not only hard cases, but also all litigation and all lawyers, are in important respects epiphenomenal.

There may very well be other sources of hardness, but this sample seems sufficiently large. With these types of hard cases in mind, we can tentatively define an easy case as one having *none* of these characteristics of hardness, one in which a clearly applicable rule noncontroversially generates an answer to the question at hand, and one in which the answer so generated is consistent both with the purpose behind the rule and with the social, political, and moral climate in which the question is answered.

There is clearly more involved than merely describing an easy case. Perhaps easy cases are like unicorns, quite capable of definition and description, but not to be found in the real world. Thus, my list of seemingly easy cases purported to fill this argumentative gap, to show that easy cases not only can be imagined, but in fact exist if we only know where to look. And, as should be apparent from the particular examples offered, my thesis here is that language is a significant and often underappreciated factor in the production of easy cases. I am *not* claiming that only language can generate easy cases. Various other legal, cultural, and historical phenomena can create those shared understandings that will clarify a linguistically vague regulation, statute, or constitutional provision. And, as the foregoing taxonomy of hard cases was designed to demonstrate, language alone is insufficient to generate an easy case. Neither of these qualifications, however, is inconsistent with my central claim that language is significantly important in producing easy cases—that language can and frequently does speak with a sufficiently clear voice such that linguistically articulated norms themselves leave little doubt as to which results are consistent with that command.

One way of supporting the claim that language is important in producing easy cases is to engage in an extended and most likely incomprehensible discussion of numerous theories of meaning, attempting to demonstrate by some collage of philosophical and behavioral arguments the way in which the use of certain artificially created symbols can and does enable us to communicate with each other. In this context, however, and indeed in most others, such an excursus seems to ignore the most significant piece of evidence supporting a claim about meaning, which is that even the discussion of meaning would take place in English. The discussion itself would thus irrefutably prove the very hypothesis at issue, just as this Article is right now doing the same thing.

When Wittgenstein remarked that "[l]anguage must speak for itself,"[47] he was not claiming that language existed in a vacuum, or that meaning could be disassociated from context. Rather, he was pointing out that the ability of language to function ought to be self-evident, and that the inability to explain all or even any of the sources of this phenomenon does

---

[47] L. Wittgenstein, Philosophical Grammar 40 (1974).

not detract from the conclusion that language does function. Thus, to demonstrate that language works with a typical-looking argument would be possible only because of the conclusion of that very argument. If language didn't "work," the world would be so different from the world in which we live as to be beyond both description and comprehension. Regardless of how understandable this Article may be, it is certainly more understandable to this audience than it would be if it were written in Hungarian, in Chinese, or in semaphore signals. Whether our ability to understand each other in language is biological, behavioral, sociological, or some combination of these is less important than the fact that we can do it.

This is not meant to be the end of an argument, but only the beginning of one. Because law operates with language, understanding the way in which law works requires starting with the proposition that language works. In many instances, some of which I will deal with presently, it may be important to know *why* or *how* language works. In many other instances, however, it is sufficient to do less thinking and more looking, and at least take certain observable facts about language as a possible starting point in the analysis.

It is thus worthwhile to note that the Constitution is, even if nothing else, a use of language. By virtue of being able to speak the English language, we can differentiate between the Constitution and a nursery rhyme, between the Constitution and a novel, and between the Constitution and the Communist Manifesto. Let us construct a simple thought experiment involving a person who is fluent in English (even the English of 1984, and not necessarily the English of 1787 or 1868), but who knows nothing of the history, politics, law, or culture of the United States. If we were to show this person a copy of the Constitution, would that person glean from that collection of marks on a piece of paper alone at least some rudimentary idea of how *this* government works and of what types of relationships exist between the central government and the states, between the different branches of government, and between individuals and government? Although the understanding would be primitive and significant mistakes would be made, it still seems apparent that the answer to the question would be, "Yes." However sketchy and distorted the understanding might be, it would still exceed the understanding produced by a document written in a language not understood by our hypothetical reader, and surpass as well the understanding gained from no information at all.

This general intelligibility of language enables us to understand immediately the mandate of numerous constitutional provisions without recourse to precedent, original intent, or any of the other standard interpretive supplements. We need not depart from the text to determine the rudiments of how a bill becomes a law, the age and other qualifications for various federal offices, the permissible and impermissible limits on the franchise, the number of terms that may be served by the President, the basic procedure for amending the Constitution, the mechanics of admitting a new state, the number of witnesses necessary in a trial for treason, and the permissibility of calling the defendant as a prosecution witness in a federal criminal case.

In some of these and other instances, some noncontroversial technical knowledge may be necessary for understanding. In order to appreciate the clarity of some of the requirements of the fourth, fifth, and sixth amendments, for example, one must understand what a trial is, how it is conducted, and so on. In order to understand some of the structural provisions, it is useful to have at least some preconstitutional understanding of what a state is. These shared background understandings, however, virtually a part of understanding *this* language, do not make the notion of a clear meaning implausible. Words themselves are nothing other than marks or noises, transformed into vehicles for communication by virtue of those rules of language that make it possible for the listener to understand the speaker in most cases. But these rules are not contained in a set of maroon volumes, the linguistic equivalent to the United States Code. These rules are made and continuously remade by the society that uses the language, and different rules may prevail in different segments of that society at different times.

Thus, language cannot be divorced from its context, because meanings become clear if and only if certain understandings are presupposed. Language cannot and does not transcend completely the culture of which it is a part. It is not something that has been delivered packaged, assembled, and ready-to-use to a previously nonlinguistic culture. Language and society are part and parcel of each other; understanding a language, even at its clearest, requires some understanding of the society that has generated it.

But what does this tell us? Certainly not that the notion of plain meaning is worthless, or that questions of interpreting language collapse completely into questions about a culture. That a rosebush springs from and cannot exist without earth, sun, and water does not mean that the notion of a rosebush is not distinguishable from the concepts earth, sun, and water. Similarly, that language requires context does not mean that language *is* context. Language operates significantly because of and as a system of rules that enable people within a shared context to understand each other. At times these rules may be vague, and thus may produce hard cases, but at other times the rules can and do operate to produce the very kinds of "easy" cases I have been describing.

* * *

I am * * * quite willing to concede that it is impossible to have an entirely clear constitutional clause, for the same reason that it is impossible to have an absolutely airtight legal provision of any kind, or an absolutely airtight definition in any field. This is merely a recasting of the well-known message that all terms and all laws have fringe as well as core applications.[60] That there are fringe meanings of words, or fringe applications of laws, for which one can make a reasonable argument for either inclusion or exclusion, does not mean that there are no core cases in which an argument on one side would be almost universally agreed to be compelling, and an argument on the other side would be almost universally agreed to be specious. That I am unsure whether rafts and floating motorized automobiles are "boats" does not dispel my confidence that rowboats and dories most clearly are boats, and that steam locomotives, hamburgers, and elephants equally clearly are not.

This is not to deny that determining the contents of the core, the fringe, and what is wholly outside are contextually and culturally contingent. I can imagine a world in which "elephant" is a fringe (or core) example of a boat, and I can imagine a set of circumstances in *this* world in which a floating hamburger might legitimately present us with a definitional problem vis-à-vis the class "boats." The mere possibility of such circumstances does not eliminate our ability to make sense out of the words as standardly applied, however. If it did, we would have no way of communicating with each other.

The lesson of open texture, then, is that every use of language is potentially vague * * *. The precision of language is necessarily limited by the lack of omniscience of human beings, and thus any use of language is bounded by the limitations of human foresight. The *non sequitur,* however, is the move from the proposition that language is not perfectly precise to the proposition that language is useless. * * *

Although linguistic nihilism seems scarcely comprehensible as a general statement about language, nihilistic tendencies have had a surprising vitality in legal and constitutional theory. The attractions of nihilism seem to be largely attributable, however, to a crabbed view of the legal world, a view that focuses almost exclusively on those hard cases that wind up in court. If we focus only on the marginal cases, only on the cases that a screening process selects largely because of their very closeness, it should come as no surprise that we would have a skeptical view of the power of language to draw distinctions. The cases that wind up in court are not there solely because they lie at the edge of linguistic distinctions, but this is at least a significant factor. Thus the cases that are in court are hardly a

---

[60] *See* Hart, *Scandinavian Realism,* 17 Cambridge L.J. 233, 239 (1959); Williams, *Language and the Law—II,* 61 Law Q.Rev. 179 (1945); *see generally* M. Black, *Reasoning with Loose Concepts,* in Margins of Precision: Essays in Logic and Language 1 (1970); I. Scheffler, Beyond the Letter: A Philosophical Inquiry into Ambiguity, Vagueness, and Metaphor in Language (1979).

representative sample of the effects of legal language. But if we focus instead on easy as well as hard cases, and thus take into our comprehension the full legal world, we see that the cases at the margin are but a small percentage of the full domain of legal events; the bulk of the remaining cases are those in which we can answer questions by consulting the articulated norm. * * *

* * *

The perspective described above views linguistically articulated rules as excluding wrong answers rather than pointing to right ones. From this perspective, there is no longer any justification to view the specific and the general clauses in the Constitution as fundamentally different in kind. Since no clause can generate a uniquely correct answer, at least in the abstract rather than in the context of a specific question, the best view of the specific clauses is that they are merely less vague than the general clauses. The language of a clause, whether seemingly general or seemingly specific, establishes a boundary, or a frame, albeit a frame with fuzzy edges. Even though the language itself does not tell us what goes within the frame, it does tell us when we have gone outside it.

It is best to view the role of language in setting the size of the frame as presumptive rather than absolute. Factors other than the language of the text, or the language of a specifically articulated rule in a case or series of cases, often influence the size and shape of the frame of permissible argument. The language of the text itself is still, however, commonly not only the starting point, but also a constant check long after leaving the starting point. When we look at an uninterpreted clause (in the sense of a series of authoritative judicial interpretations), we commonly focus quite closely on the text. Even in those cases in which an established body of precedent exists, reference to the text is never considered illegitimate.

The language of the text, therefore, remains perhaps the most significant factor in setting the size of the frame. Those clauses that look quite specific are those where the frame is quite small, and thus the range of permissible alternatives is equivalently small. Those clauses that look much more general are those with a substantially larger frame, giving a much wider range of permissible alternatives. This, however, is a continuum and not a dichotomy. Those clauses that seem specific differ from those that seem general in that the former exclude as wrong a larger number of answers than do the latter. * * *

* * * If we consider the text to be informative about boundaries, or limits, rather than about centers, or cores, then the text appears far less irrelevant than is commonly assumed. The text presumptively constrains us, or should, from overstepping what are admittedly pretheoretical and almost

intuitive linguistic bounds, and thus serves as one constraint on constitutional interpretation.

We can thus view these linguistic frames as telling an interpreter, *for example* the Supreme Court, which areas are legitimately within the province of interpretation, which subjects are properly the business of the interpretation. An interpretation is legitimate (which is not the same as correct) only insofar as it purports to interpret some language of the document, and only insofar as the interpretation is within the boundaries at least suggested by that language.

AKHIL REED AMAR, FOREWORD: THE DOCUMENT AND THE DOCTRINE

114 HARV.L.REV. 26–31, 43–44, 49–53, 79–88 (2000).

From the Founding to the Millennium, the Constitution has often proved more enlightened and enlightening than the case law glossing it. The millennial year itself has exemplified this general pattern. Indeed, the year's prominent Court decisions and political controversies provide a rather nice set of detailed case studies allowing us to measure the document against the doctrine.

The document, of course, must be interpreted. But some modes of constitutional interpretation focus more directly on the Constitution than do others. Consider, then, two broad camps of constitutionalists transcending the divide between liberals and conservatives. Those in the first camp—call them documentarians—seek inspiration and discipline in the amended Constitution's specific words and word patterns, the historical experiences that birthed and rebirthed the text, and the conceptual schemas and structures organizing the document. I have in mind interpreters like Justice Hugo Black, Dean John Hart Ely, and Professors Steven Calabresi and Douglas Laycock. Those in the second camp—call them doctrinalists—rarely try to wring every drop of possible meaning from constitutional text, history, and structure Instead, they typically strive to synthesize what the Supreme Court has said and done, sometimes rather loosely, in the name of the Constitution. For them, the elaborated precedent often displaces the enacted text. Prominent doctrinalists include the younger Justice Harlan, Dean Kathleen Sullivan, and Professors Richard Fallon and David Strauss.

The difference lies in emphasis and attitude. Those who privilege the document do not ignore precedent altogether. (How could they, given that the text itself suggests a role for judicial exposition?) Conversely, those who privilege precedent concede that the text does sometimes matter—on rare occasions, they have even been caught reading the Constitution. (Hasn't the Court itself suggested that constitutional precedents must often yield if later adjudged contrary to the document?) In some sense, we are all documentarians; we are all doctrinalists.

But some of us are documentarians first, and doctrinalists second. And rightly so, I shall argue. What the American People have said and done in the Constitution is often more edifying, inspiring, and sensible than what the Justices have said and done in the case law. Even if we are not legally bound by every scrap of meaning that can be mined from the document, we would do well to study our amended Constitution with care, because it can teach us a great deal about who We are as a People, where We have been, and where We might choose to go. Conversely, to put doctrine first is to miss the point of many constitutional rights and structures—to spend too much time pondering arid formulas and not enough time recalling the world the Constitution rejected and imagining the world it promised. Even worse than doctrine's regular sterility is its recurrent perversity. Judges have often transformed sound and widely accepted constitutional principles into normatively insensitive or outlandish lines of case law. Genuine doctrinal improvements on the document have been less common.

* * * Granted, even after close study the document itself will often be indeterminate over a wide range of possible applications. Within this range, judicial doctrine can work alongside practical resolutions achieved by other branches to specify particular outcomes and thereby concretize the Constitution. Judicial precedent and nonjudicial practice can also serve important epistemic and default functions, helping us to find the best documentarian reading in cases of doubt. Moreover, pure textualism can risk serious instability if not chastened by attention to the legal status quo. Thus, even the best documentarian reading must sometimes yield in court to brute facts born of earlier judicial and political deviations. It may even be that today's Justices are institutionally ill-equipped to be good documentarians, and that matters would be even worse, in our second-best world, if they tried to be more documentarian. If so, this sobering fact might suggest that some of the rest of us, especially law professors and law students, can play useful roles in helping our fellow citizens learn things about the document that they cannot learn merely by reading the United States Reports.

* * *

I mean to defend a spacious but not unbounded version of constitutional textualism. On this view, textual analysis dovetails with the study of enactment history and constitutional structure. The joint aim of these related approaches is to understand what the American People meant and did when We ratified and amended the document.

This is not the only way to define textualism, but it seems the best way. Epic events gave birth to the Constitution's words—the American Revolution, the Civil War, the Woman Suffrage Movement, the 1960s Voting Rights and Youth Movements. The document's words lose some of their meaning—some of their wisdom, some of their richness, some of their nuance, some of their rigor—if read wholly apart from these epic events. Textualism presupposes that the specific constitutional words ultimately enacted were generally chosen with care. Otherwise, why bother reading closely? By pondering the public legislative history of these carefully chosen words, we can often learn more about what they meant to the American People who enacted them as the supreme law of the land. Thus, good historical narrative, in both a broad (epic-events) sense and a narrow (drafting/ratification) sense, should inform good textual analysis; with uncanny economy, the text often distills hard-won historical lessons and drafting insights. Although one could imagine a brand of textualism that seeks only the present-day meaning of words, severing textual from historical argument, I endorse a different approach. What counts as text is the document as understood by the American People who ratified and amended it, and what counts as history is accessible public meaning, not secret private intent.

Similarly, although some might seek to divorce textual from structural arguments, there are sound reasons to keep them wed. The American People ratified the Philadelphia Constitution not clause by clause, but as a single document. Later generations of Americans have added amendments one by one, but no amendment stands alone as a discrete legal regime. Each amendment aims to fit with, and be read as part of, the larger document. Indeed, because the People have chosen to affix amendments to the end of the document rather than directly rewrite old clauses, a reader can never simply look to an old clause and be done with it. Rather, she must always scour later amendments to see if they explicitly or implicitly modify the clause at hand. To do justice to these basic facts about the text, we must read the document holistically and attend to its overarching themes.

For example, the phrases "separation of powers" and "checks and balances" appear nowhere in the Constitution, but these organizing concepts are part of the document, read holistically. Each of the three great departments—legislative, executive, judicial—is given its own separate article, introduced by a separate vesting clause. To read these three vesting clauses as an ensemble (as their conspicuously parallel language and parallel placement would seem to invite is to see a plain statement of separated powers. And a close look at the interior of these three articles reveals a variety of interbranch checks, such as the executive's veto check on the legislature's lawmaking in Article I and the legislature's advice and consent check on the executive's appointments in Article II. For present purposes it matters little whether we label such readings "textual" (because they begin by parsing language), "structural" (because they seek larger organizing schemas), or "historical" (because ratifiers generally understood the document to embody these schemas). The key point is that these readings are documentarian, aiming to mine as much meaning as possible from the Constitution itself.

Documentarian analysis ponders important word patterns in the Constitution, even if such patterns emerged over the course of centuries rather than at a single moment. Both Article IV and the Fourteenth Amendment, adopted eighty years apart, speak of "privileges" and "immunities" of "citizens," though in different textual formations. Are these similarities and differences significant? The words "the People" chime boldly in the Preamble, then echo in Article I and reverberate five more times in the later-adopted Bill of Rights—more frequently than any other phrase in the Bill. What are we to make of this musical motif? Four separate amendments, adopted over the course of a century, proclaim in virtually identical words that "[t]he right of citizens of the United States . . . to vote . . . shall not be denied or abridged by the United States or by any State on account of [X]." How do these amendments fit together? Several amendments authorize Congress to "enforce" their respective provisions in almost identical language. Shouldn't these provisions be read in pari materia, as having similar meanings? Whether we call such observations and inquiries "intratextual," "structural," or something else, they are all documentarian—textual in a broad sense,.

This is the sense in which most self-described textualists (myself included) understand our interpretive practice. Most of us seek to braid arguments from text, history, and structure into an interpretive rope whose strands mutually reinforce. By contrast, doctrinalists aim to do something rather different. They start with decisions found in the United States Reports, decisions often penned decades or centuries after the relevant constitutional texts were enacted, and sometimes authored by Justices indifferent or even hostile to the vision originally inscribed in these texts.

* * *

Two heads are often better than one, and multitudes may be far wiser than five or nine. We should envision the People who have written and rewritten the document not merely as America's Supreme Legislature, but also as our Ultimate Court and Grandest Jury. The Constitution should be read as collecting the solemn judgments of this Court, inscribing the lived experiences and wisdom—the reason and not merely the will or whim—of a great many people. We should study this document with care, even if we are not strictly bound to follow it, because we can learn from it. Even if Justices were free at the end of the day to deviate from this document—and as a practical matter, there is little to stop them—they miss much when they race past the greatest opinion of the Highest Court to spend their time musing on the lesser opinions of their own lesser court.

This is an epistemic argument on behalf of the document. Later, I shall offer an epistemic argument on behalf of judicial precedent. The Court may presumptively adhere to its past constitutional precedents not because precedent, right or wrong, binds, but because precedent can teach and help find the right answer. Justices may properly accord prior Supreme Court precedents a rebuttable presumption of correctness because the circumstances under which the precedents were rendered give the Justices plausible epistemic grounds for this presumption. The precedents reflect the earnest efforts of thoughtful members of the nation's highest court deliberating together about important issues with their minds focused by the real-world facts before them.

But all this is generally true in spades of the judgments collected in the Constitution itself. The American People who birthed and rebirthed this text did so with their minds wonderfully concentrated by the epic events they experienced and the palpable evils they endured: an arrogant monarchy that gave way to an armed Revolution and an unsatisfactory regime under early state constitutions and the Articles of Confederation; an 1801 electoral crisis spawned by the failure to anticipate the rise of national presidential parties; a bloody Civil War triggered by a repressive slaveocracy that at the war's end posed an ongoing threat to the liberty of all and the equality of blacks; a series of lingering disfranchisements that mocked the democratic promise of the Preamble; an out-of-touch gerontocracy obliging teenagers to fight in Vietnam while barring them from voting on the war's wisdom; and so on. Judges who did not see all these evils with their own eyes and feel them deep in their bones have often missed the basic point of words born in blood, toil, tears, and sweat. An inspired document has thus regularly given rise to obtuse doctrine. * * *

* * *

* * * Despite its grand claims, the document in 1788 was deeply flawed—indeed, conceived in the sin of slavery. The document is still flawed. But it has improved over time. Virtually every amendment has genuinely made amends, even if imperfectly and incompletely, for the sins and flaws of the prior system.

There is nothing logically inevitable about this. There is no supernatural destiny driving America toward a guaranteed happy ending. We the People could backslide tomorrow. But to read the actual amendments as they have in fact accreted over two centuries is to see successive generations of Americans repeatedly and consciously choosing to redeem and expand some of the inspiring promises made (or at least suggested) but not kept by the 1788 Preamble. Over time, the American People have been helping the document "work itself pure," to borrow a phrase.

This borrowed phrase has usually been used to describe the process by which case law becomes refined over time. But along what dimensions, and using what criteria, can it be said that the Taney Court's case law was better than the Marshall Court's, and that the Fuller Court's was better still? That the Rehnquist Court is better than the Warren Court, which was in turn better than all its predecessors? By contrast, with the exception of the Prohibition and anti-Prohibition Amendments, which simply cancel out, I think it is fair to say that virtually every amendment has made the Constitution better. The Bill of Rights cured various lapses in the Philadelphia document; the Eleventh Amendment (rightly read) reined in an overreaching judiciary that had overprotected moneyed interests against a state that had violated no federal law; the Twelfth Amendment adjusted the system of presidential election to accommodate the unforeseen emergence of presidential political parties; the Reconstruction Amendments began the long process of making amends for slavery and racism; and the twentieth-century amendments made America more democratic, inclusive, equal, and just.

When we read the document as a whole, it makes sense to construe ambiguous Founding language so as to redeem the vision of later amendments that are more inclusive in both process and result. For example, at the Founding, the ideal of republican government could be read narrowly or broadly. Narrowly, it might be said that the republican ideal is static, fixed in 1788: if a given group—such as free blacks, or women, or propertyless citizens—did not have the right to vote in 1788 in state A, then A's continued exclusion of this group in the future could never be deemed unrepublican. Broadly, it might be countered that the goal of constitutional republicanism (implicit in the Preamble and many other constitutional references to "the people," the "public," and "republican" government is to have the most participatory regime the world has ever seen, subject only to obvious constraints imposed by practicality. On this dynamic view, the republican ideal might sometimes require the abolition of various 1788 disfranchisements if their original real-world justifications later lose force, or if they mutate into exclusions more reactionary than the original ones. For example, the enfranchising experiences of sister states might ultimately prove that some of state A's continued disfranchisements are not in fact necessary to maintain stable government. Or state A's continued disfranchisements might end up excluding more citizens than at the Founding, say, because the percentage of free blacks or propertyless citizens sharply increases. In such situations, a dynamic approach might condemn state A's exclusions despite their pedigree. Howsoever we might resolve this ambiguity if we merely consulted the Founders' story, later chapters of the constitutional saga shed strong light on the problem. Many amendments have explicitly expanded suffrage to include the once excluded, and no amendments go the other way. Indeed, the very enactment of the Civil War Amendments visibly pivoted on procedural improvisations explicitly based on a dynamic reading of the republican ideal. (As with the Constitution itself, we must understand an amendment as an embodied act as well as a written text. Thus we must attend to the theory implicit in what the American People did, as well as said, when enacting the Civil War Amendments.) Given all this, shouldn't we read republicanism broadly rather than narrowly, dynamically rather than statically, with the grain of the document rather than against the grain? We the People today must be expansive even if We the People at one time were less so.

The entire Bill of Rights takes on new meaning when viewed through the prism of the later Fourteenth Amendment, but the Constitution's story hardly ends there. For example, the Fourteenth Amendment itself must be read in light of the later Nineteenth Amendment. If we simply parsed the Fourteenth in isolation, the status of women's equal civil rights might be unsure. On one hand, the Amendment's opening section affirms the rights of all "citizens" and "persons" and says nothing in particular about "race" as distinct from "sex." Its language in fact resembles language that Elizabeth Cady Stanton herself endorsed in 1865, which she in turn borrowed from the Seneca Falls Declaration of 1848. The Amendment's first sentence proclaims that all Americans are "born" free and equal "citizens," implicitly discountenancing laws heaping disadvantage upon a person because of that person's birth status—as slave, black, poor, female, or illegitimate, for example. Some of the basic concepts organizing the Amendment—full and equal "civil rights" as opposed to "political rights" (like voting and jury service)—themselves drew upon the model of women's rights: Unmarried white women enjoyed most civil rights but not political rights, and the Fourteenth Amendment can thus be seen as giving blacks the historic rights of these women. On the other hand, it is doubtful that all discriminations against women were henceforth to be viewed in exactly the same way as discriminations against blacks. Traditional marriage law subordinated the woman to the man; but a law allowing a black and a white to join together as business partners only so long as the white was the senior partner would plainly violate the Amendment. Regardless of this original ambiguity, after the Nineteenth Amendment becomes part of the document, we have strong documentarian warrant to construe the Fourteenth Amendment in favor of women's rights. Once the Constitution vests women with full and equal political rights, shouldn't entitlement to the full and equal enjoyment of lesser civil rights follow a fortiori? Discriminations that might once have seemed legitimate based on an old-fashioned view of woman's role and capacities become illegitimate when the Constitution itself, in a later amendment, affirms a very different and more robust vision of women as full and equal members of the political People who govern America.

Arguments based on the Constitution's chronological trend and the tug of later amendments on earlier clauses reflect the textual architecture of the document itself. Instead of directly rewriting Articles I through VII via deletions and insertions, later generations of Americans have chosen to make amends at the end of the document in a series of postscripts inscribed in chronological order. Although this mode of textual alteration has generated certain ambiguities that direct rewriting might have avoided, there is an offsetting virtue in the postscript approach: The practice of inscribing amendments in chronological order visually dramatizes the distinct improvements of each generation and makes the temporal trajectory of the overall document much easier to identify at a glance. The document itself thus takes pains to draw attention to the vector of constitutional change, to highlight the arc of constitutional history. Sensitive documentarians should not ignore this arc.

* * *As the preceding examples illustrate, constitutional textualism (broadly defined) is not mechanical. It requires judgment, and good interpreters will often disagree. On this count, the document is neither better nor worse than the doctrine; good doctrinalists will often disagree about how best to read a given case or a broad line of cases. To interpret the document, or the doctrine for that matter, is to engage in an act of construction; the interpreter tries to weave together a coherent account from tangled data. Further wrinkles arise when the faithful interpreter tries to apply the document's precepts to a world that is in many respects different from the world that generated the constitutional texts in question. * * *

Though not wholly determinate, documentarianism is nonetheless disciplined. It seeks not merely a modestly plausible reading of the Constitution, but the most plausible reading, the reading that best fits the entire document's text, enactment history, and general structure. Considerations of justice are not wholly foreign to the enterprise of close reading and the goal of tight fit. The document itself begins by trumpeting its aim to "establish justice" and we fail to best fit the document if we simply ignore this aim. But a proper justice-seeking reading of the document does not warrant an interpreter to invent his own theory of justice and call it "the Constitution." The documentarian quests after the American People's particular sense of justice as embodied in the unfolding words, deeds, and spirit of the Constitution and its Amendments

* * *

What, then, is the proper role for judicial doctrine? A thoroughgoing commitment to the document would leave vast space for judicial doctrine, but doctrine would ultimately remain subordinate to the document itself.

Case law would work to concretize the Constitution, not to amend or eclipse it.

Article III proclaims that the Constitution is to be enforced as justiciable law in ordinary lawsuits. The document thus envisions that in deciding cases arising under it, judges will offer interpretations of its meaning, give reasons for those interpretations, develop mediating principles, and craft implementing frameworks enabling the document to work as in-court law. These interpretations, reasons, principles, and frameworks are, in a word, doctrine.

Because the document does not and cannot properly partake of the prolixity of a legal code, doctrine helps fill in the gaps, translating the Constitution's broad dictates into law that works in court, in keeping with the vision of Article III. For example, the Fourth Amendment's central command is that all searches and seizures must be reasonable. * * * Judicial doctrines, working alongside rules laid down and practices built up by other branches, properly fill in the document's outline, making broad principles workably specific in a court and in the world.

Free speech provides another example of the large role for doctrine even under a strict documentarian regime. A proper understanding of the document gives us some clear paradigm cases of the kinds of speech that must be protected and the sorts of laws that cannot stand. But exactly how far should these paradigm cases be extended by analogy? How should judges treat cases involving a mixture of expression and conduct? Even if judges properly agree that political speech ranks higher than purely literary speech, which in turn ranks higher than corporate commercial speech, exactly how should doctrine reflect this documentarian ranking in a world where the lines between these forms of speech are often blurred? A documentarian judge does not begin and end with the document. Rather, she begins with the document and then ponders how best to translate its wisdom into workable in-court rules, as contemplated by Article III.

Article III authorizes these doctrinal decisions to be made by "one supreme Court," which presides over various "inferior" federal courts and state courts in federal question cases. The document's import is that "inferior" courts should generally be bound by the interpretations, reasons, mediating principles, and implementing frameworks—the doctrine—of the "[S]upreme" Court. This is so even if lower courts think that the higher court is wrong about the meaning of the document. Lower courts are free to say that the high court has erred, and to offer their reasons for so believing, but disagreement does not justify a general right of disobedience; an inferior may tell his boss that she is wrong, but must nevertheless follow her instructions.

What weight should erroneous Supreme Court doctrine carry in the Court itself? If the current Court now believes that a past decision misconstrued the document, should this belief be prima facie grounds for overruling the past decision? If so, what might overcome this prima facie showing? In seeking to answer these hard questions, a documentarian should begin—where else?—with the document itself. Though it does not provide all the details, here too it gives us the broad outlines of the proper approach.

Article III envisions the Court as a continuous body. The Court never automatically turns over, as the House turns over every two years and the Presidency every four. A continuing body would seem intentionally structured so as to give some weight to its past and some thought to its future. It does not invent itself anew each day. Given the Court's clear constitutional design, it seems permissible for the Court to give its past decisions a rebuttable presumption of correctness. A past case may properly control until proved wrong, with those challenging it saddled with the burden of proof. Furthermore, a Justice may rightly give a precedent epistemic weight in deciding whether the burden is met. Even if her first reaction is that the precedent is wrongly decided as a documentarian matter, the very fact of the prior decision may persuade her that her first reaction is mistaken: "If John Marshall and his brethren thought X, perhaps X is right after all, despite initial appearances to the contrary." (For similar reasons, a deferential Justice might choose to give Congress, a coequal branch, the benefit of the doubt in certain cases.) The precise epistemic weight of a past case will vary. Not all Justices are John Marshall, and it may be relevant that a particularly sound Justice dissented in the allegedly erroneous case. Sometimes, a later Court will find wisdom in certain language of a past case even if its result seems wrong on the facts. Other times, its fact-specific result may distill great wisdom even if its language, on reflection, does not persuade. Both as a default rule and as an epistemic weight, a prior Supreme Court case counts for much more than, say, a typical law review article or lower court opinion.

But should it count for even more? Should the Court generally feel permitted or bound to follow a past case even after it has been shown to reflect an erroneous understanding of the document

* * *

Does a documentarian view, then, require that erroneous precedents always be tossed aside and treated as nullities? No. The guiding structural principle may be stated as follows. Once We the People have struggled to put something in the document, it should not be altered except by the People themselves; erroneous precedents may stand if they have in effect been ratified not merely by the Court, but also by the People.

* * *

Yet several modern developments are conspiring to elevate doctrine over document. Even the most faithful documentarian must confront many issues on which the document is silent and the key issues are specified by doctrine. As doctrine becomes increasingly extensive and elaborate, it becomes easier to forget that all this exposition exists in subordinate relation to the document. Besides, Justices cannot be expected to constantly reinvent the wheel. For reasons of economy and vanity, they often begin thinking about a constitutional problem by considering what they or their colleagues have already said about it. Most of the recent appointments to the Supreme Court have come from lower courts. A lower court judge's job is not to think directly about the Constitution, but rather to follow the dictates of the Supreme Court. And so these judges typically come to the Court with a clearer sense of Supreme Court doctrine than of the Constitution itself. When they arrive on a Court whose more senior members are all talking doctrine, it is natural for the new appointees to do the same. In their first few years, they must take positions on a great range of issues they had not previously considered in detail—issues that their colleagues have long pondered—and they may naturally defer. Later in their tenure, they may have doubts about some of their early votes, but it is awkward to admit error. As they mature, the doctrine increasingly comes to reflect their own contributions, and their self-love is thus bound up with it.

* * *

At the dawn of a new millennium, constitutional law is at risk of losing touch with the Constitution itself. A dense doctrinal grid threatens to obscure the document, with generally unfortunate consequences. The Constitution is wiser than the Court.

SANFORD LEVINSON, LAW AS LITERATURE

60 TEX.L.REV. 373, 376–89 (1982).

I

* * *

Constitutions, of the written variety especially, are usefully viewed as a means of freezing time by controlling the future through the "hardness" of language encoded in a monumental document, which is then left for later interpreters to decipher. The purpose of such control is to preserve the particular vision held by constitutional founders and to prevent its overthrow by future generations. The very existence of written constitutions with substantive limitations on future conduct is evidence of skepticism, if not outright pessimism, about the moral caliber of future citizens; else why not simply enjoin them to "be good" or "do what you think best"? Writers of constitutions must have a very high confidence in the ability of language both to "harden" and to control.

* * *

Any writer, including a framer of constitutions, presumably imagines the following relationship between text and reader: "The reader sets himself to make out what the author has designed and signified through putting into play a linguistic and literary expertise that he shares with the author. By approximating what the author undertook to signify the reader understands what the language of the work means."[14] And, of course, in the case of those particular texts called legal, by understanding the meaning the conscientious adjudicator-reader becomes authorized to enforce it.

The remark just quoted comes from an essay vigorously attacking certain strains of contemporary literary criticism that Abrams finds insufficiently respectful of determinate meanings allegedly generated by disciplined study of texts. The disputes currently raging through literary criticism precisely mirror some of the central problems facing anyone who would take law seriously; the basis of this parallelism is the centrality to law of textual analysis.[15] If we consider law as literature, then we might better understand the malaise that afflicts all contemporary legal analysis, nowhere more severely than in constitutional theory.

II

* * *

Two classic approaches to understanding a written constitution involve emphasizing either the allegedly plain words of the text or the certain meaning to be given those words through historical reconstruction. I think it fair to say that these particular approaches are increasingly without defenders, at least in the academic legal community. Even so capable an analyst as Professor Monaghan, who is eager to return to the confines of a

---

[14]Abrams, *How to Do Things with Texts,* 46 Partisan Rev. 566 (1979). I owe my familiarity with this comment to Richard Rorty. *See* R. Rorty, *Nineteenth-Century Idealism and Twentieth-Century Textualism,* in Consequences of Pragmatism 139 (1982), *reprinted from* 64 Monist 155 (1981).

[15]The best short treatment of these disputes is Culler, *Issues in Contemporary American Critical Debate,* in American Criticism in the Poststructuralist Age 1–18 (I. Konigsberg ed. 1981). A very illuminating book-length study is F. Lentricchia, After the New Criticism (1980). The commonality of some of the problems of law and literary analysis are touched on in Abraham, *Three Fallacies of Interpretation: A Comment on Precedent and Judicial Decision,* 23 Ariz.L.Rev. 771 (1981); Abraham, *Statutory Interpretation and Literary Theory: Some Common Concerns of an Unlikely Pair,* 32 Rutgers L.Rev. 676 (1980); Michaels, *Against Formalism: The Autonomous Text in Legal and Literary Interpretation,* 1 Poetics Today 23 (1979), *reprinted with minor changes as* Michaels, *Against Formalism: Chickens and Rocks,* in The State of the Language 410 (1980); and Yeazell, *Convention, Fiction, and Law,* 13 New Literary Hist. 89 (1981).

knowable "originalist" Constitution, admits that he has no way of handling the authority of judicial precedents that (he argues) violate initial understandings.[19]

There is not time in this essay to canvass the problems of originalism. Suffice it to say that the plain meaning approach inevitably breaks down in the face of the reality of disagreement among equally competent speakers of the native language. Intentionality arguments, on the other hand, face not only the problem of explaining why intentions of long-dead people from a different social world should influence us, but also, perhaps more importantly, the problem of extracting intentions from the collectivity of individuals and institutions necessary to give legal validity to the Constitution. Even literary critics most committed to the existence of objective meaning through recovery of authorial intent, like E.D. Hirsch, admit that their approach applies only to individually authored works, and therefore cannot be used to analyze a document like the Constitution.[22]

As Richard Rorty has pointed out, however, there are at least two options open to critics who reject the two approaches outlined above but who, nonetheless, remain interested in interpreting the relevant texts. The first option involves the use of an allegedly more sophisticated method to extract the true meaning of the text. Thus Rorty refers to "the kind of textualist who claims to have gotten the secret of the text, to have broken its code," as a "weak" textualist,[23] where the term is seemingly a metaphor for the power of the individual critic. Whatever pyrotechnics might come from a critic who "prides himself on not being distracted by anything which the text might previously have been thought to be about or anything its author says about it,"[24] there remains the infatuation—110 years after Langdell—with the possibility of a science of criticism. A "weak" textualist "is just doing his best to imitate science—he wants a *method* of criticism and he wants everybody to agree that he has cracked the code. He wants all the

---

[19]Monaghan, *Our Perfect Constitution,* 56 N.Y.U.L.Rev. 353, 382 (1981). Like Raoul Berger, *see* R. Berger, Government by Judiciary 412–13 (1977), Monaghan does not really counsel turning back the clock by instantly overruling all putatively misdecided cases. Both offer what might uncharitably be regarded as an "adverse possession" approach to constitutional interpretation, whereby precedents that should at one time have been properly overruled (as wrongly decided) become entitled to recognition as authoritative after the passage of enough time and after the citizenry has come to rely on them. Neither offers the slightest guidance for recognizing the terms of such possession. To be fair, no other theorist of precedent does any better. Perhaps the central difference between law and literature is the lack in the latter of the notion of stare decisis.

[22]*See* E. Hirsch, Validity in Interpretation 123 & n. 53 (1967); *see also* E. Hirsch, The Aims of Interpretation 1–13 (1976).

[23]R. Rorty, *supra* note 14, at 152.

[24]*Id.* at 151–52.

comforts of consensus, even if only the consensus of readers of the literary quarterlies" (or law reviews).[25]

Perhaps the best current example of such a "weak" textualist is John Hart Ely, whose *Democracy and Distrust,* however radical some of its criticisms of so-called "interpretivism" purport to be, is merely the latest effort to crack the code of the United States Constitution and discover its true essence. As James E. Fleming pointed out in a recent review, Ely is engaged in a "quest for the ultimate constitutional interpretivism" which would in effect foreclose further debate about the genuine meaning of the Constitution.[27]

* * *

No one can read Ely and miss his anger at those who merely read their own views into the Constitution. Indeed, most of Ely's reviewers agree with him at least on this last point, even as they criticize him for reading *his* preferred views into the Constitution. What unites Ely and most of his critics, though, is the continued belief that there is something "in" the Constitution that can be extracted if only we can figure out the best method to mine its meaning.

Against such weak textualists—the decoders, whatever the fanciness of their methods of decoding—Rorty posits "strong" textualists, who reject the whole notion of questing for the essential meanings of a text. "Strong," it should be emphasized, refers to the power of the critic, not the power of the text (or of its author). According to Stanley Fish, one of the leading proponents of this approach, "Interpretation is not the art of construing but the art of constructing. Interpreters do not decode poems; they make them."[30] Fish has argued that "[t]he objectivity of the text is an illusion and, moreover, a dangerous illusion, because it is so physically convincing. The illusion is one of self-sufficiency and completeness. A line of print or a page is so obviously *there* . . . that it seems to be the sole repository of whatever value and meaning we associate with it."[31]

* * *

The view endorsed by Fish regards "human beings as at every moment creating the experimental spaces into which a personal knowledge flows."[35] Meaning is created rather than discovered, though the source of creative energy is the particular community within which one finds him- or herself. Critics more Emersonian in their inspiration, like Harold Bloom, are willing

---

[25] *Id.* at 152 (emphasis in original).

[27] Fleming, *A Critique of John Hart Ely's Quest for the Ultimate Constitutional Interpretivism of Representative Democracy* (Book Review), 80 Mich.L.Rev. 634 (1982).

[30] S. Fish, Is There a Text in This Class? 327 (1980) * * *.

[31] [*Id.*] at 43. * * *

[35] [*Id.*] at 94. * * *

to credit individual acts of creativity, though Bloom's emphasis on the ubiquity of "misreadings," rather than "truthful" renderings of what is inside texts, links him to Rorty's "strong" textualists.[36] All such readers could well join the Whitmanian anthem, where all readings, whether of life or of texts, become songs of oneself.

The patron saint of all strong textualists is Nietzsche:

> [W]hatever exists, having somehow come into being, is again and again reinterpreted to new ends, taken over, transformed, and redirected by some power superior to it; all events in the organic world are a subduing, a *becoming master,* and all subduing and becoming master involves a fresh interpretation, an adaptation through which any previous "meaning" and "purpose" are necessarily obscured or even obliterated.[37]

And the argument of Fish, Bloom, and other strong textualists, whether American or continental, is *not* that they prefer to do their thing as an alternative to the more banal work of "truthseekers" like Abrams or Hirsch, but rather that the project of ultimate truth-seeking is based on philosophical error. At the very least it presumes a privileged foundation for measuring the attainment of truth, and it is precisely this foundation that Nietzsche and most of the more radical literary theorists deny. Like Rorty, they do not substitute a new candidate for a winning method of how to recognize literary truth when one sees it; rather, they reject the very search for finality of interpretation.

To be sure, none of the radical critics defends the position that any interpretation is just as good as any other. Stanley Fish, for example, notes that he genuinely believes in the validity of any given view that he happens to hold, and he can present reasons for rejecting the views of his opponents on the interpretation of a given text.[38] In this regard Fish seems similar to Ronald Dworkin, who views judging as including the phenomenological experience of feeling oneself to have achieved the uniquely correct solution even to a hard case.[39] But Fish, more candid than Dworkin on this point, admits that his own conviction of rightness will provide no answer at all to anyone who happens to disagree with him, and that there is no way to resolve the dispute. It is at this point that he retreats to his Kuhnian[40] emphasis on communities of understanding and shared conventions. It may be true that these communities will share, at any given moment, a sense of what distinguishes "on the wall" from "off the wall" arguments, but Fish is

---

[36]*See, e.g.,* H. Bloom, A Map of Misreading (1975).

[37]F. Nietzsche, On the Genealogy of Morals 77 (W. Kaufmann trans. 1967) (emphasis in original).

[38]S. Fish, *supra* note 30, at 338–71.

[39]*See* R. Dworkin, Taking Rights Seriously 279–90 (1977) * * *.

[40]*See* T. Kuhn, The Structure of Scientific Revolutions (2d ed. 1970).

acutely aware of the contingency of such judgments. They describe only our own temporal sense of what is currently acceptable, rather than anything genuinely mirroring the essential characteristics of the texts being discussed.

III

Presumably only those professionally interested in literature are forced to wrestle with the issues presented by Abrams * * * and Fish regarding poetics or the interpretation of fiction. But if law is, in some meaningful sense, a branch of literature, then the problems discussed above take on new and bothersome implications. And nowhere is this more true within our own culture than in constitutional interpretation and its emphasis on writtenness.

The role of our Constitution is not only to enable us to pretend that past linguistic acts can control future action. It is also presumably to prevent the rise of Nietzschean "masters." Nietzsche seems to suggest, however, that a massive exercise in social deception is necessary if we are not to recognize the way that "interpretation" inevitably implies a struggle for mastery in the formation of political consciousness. For a Nietzschean reader of constitutions, there is no point in searching for a code that will produce "truthful" or "correct" interpretations; instead, the interpreter, in Rorty's words, "simply beats the text into a shape which will serve his own purpose."[43]

* * * If one takes seriously the views articulated by Nietzsche, Rorty, and Fish (among others), one must give up the search for principles and methods of constitutional interpretation. Instead, one assesses the results of an interpretive effort by something other than the criterion of adherence to an inner essence of the text being interpreted * * *.

To put it mildly, there is something disconcerting about accepting the Nietzschean interpreter into the house of constitutional analysts, but I increasingly find it impossible to imagine any other way of making sense of our own constitutional universe. For some years I have organized my own courses in constitutional interpretation around the central question, "But did the Court get it right?", as if one could grade any given opinion by whether or not it measured up to the genuine command of the Constitution. Answering such a question, of course, requires the development of a full set of "principles and methods of correct interpretation," and my courses have involved a search for such principles and methods.

I still spend a great deal of time examining various approaches, ranging from the linguistic to the historical, from the structural to what my colleague Philip Bobbitt calls the "ethical,"[46] but I have less and less confidence that this is a sensible enterprise. At the very least there is no

---

[43] R. Rorty, *supra* note 14, at 151.

[46] See P. Bobbitt, Constitutional Fate (1982) * * *.

reason to believe that the community of persons interested in constitutional interpretation will coalesce around one or another of these approaches. Moreover, insofar as one accepts the plausibility of an analysis like Rorty's, there is no reason to regret this, for it is the result of a genuine plurality of ways of seeing the world, rather than of the obdurate recalcitrance of those who refuse to bend to superior argument.

Yet there are obvious difficulties in adopting Rorty's metaphor of the conversation (rather than the argument), for the principal social reality of law is its coercive force vis-à-vis those who prefer to behave other than as the law "requires." As Chairman Mao pointed out, a revolution is not a tea party, and the massive disruption in lives that can be triggered by a legal case is not a conversation. The legal system presents a conversation from which there may be no exit, and there are certainly those who would define hell as the vision of their least favorite constitutional interpreter, whether the Court or a benighted law professor.

What does one do, then, when studying opinions, if one gives up the enterprise of determining whether or not they are "correct"? Are cases simply historical fragments which should be studied for insight into the ideology of the time?[48] One no longer would say, for example, that *Dred Scott*[49] or *Lochner v. New York,*[50] or any other case, was "wrongly" decided, for that use of language presupposes belief in the knowability of constitutional essence. One *can* obviously show that constitutional tastes and styles shift over time, but this retreat into historicism has nothing to do with the legal science so desperately sought by Langdell and his successors.

* * *

Consider * * * the way we treat the innovative judges of our legal tradition, particularly as they appear in law school courses. Do we really wish to argue that John Marshall or Earl Warren (or the most recent dynamic innovator, William Rehnquist) got the essence right in their interpretations of the Constitution, or do we recognize instead the extent to which we have been subdued by their political visions?

Perhaps the most significant example of this dilemma is John Marshall himself, or rather I should say our response to Marshall. I have little trouble stating that I consider his major opinions to run the gamut from the intellectu-

---

[48]This seems to be the approach taken by some of the most fruitful practitioners of "critical legal studies." *See, e.g.,* M. Horwitz, The Transformation of American Law, 1780–1860 (1977); M. Tushnet, The American Law of Slavery 1810–1860 (1981).

[49]Dred Scott v. Sandford, 60 U.S. (19 How.) 393 (1856).

[50]198 U.S. 45 (1905). There is obviously not space here to consider in depth the complexity of our responses to these two cases. One might begin, though, by asking whether Taney's or Peckham's arguments in the two cases are really "off-the-wall" in terms of the conventions of American legal discourse; it seems clear that the answer is no.

ally dishonest[60] to the majestically visionary,[61] and rarely to contain the only (or even the most) plausible rendering of the Constitution. Yet there is also a profound irrelevance to such a criticism. Not only does it assume the existence of a privileged discourse that allows me to dismiss Marshall as "untruthful" rather than merely different, it also ignores the fundamental fact that John Marshall is as much a "founder" of the American legal system as those who wrote the Constitution he purported to interpret. He is, perhaps, the great Nietzschean judge of our tradition.

LAWRENCE LESSIG, FIDELITY AND CONSTRAINT

65 FORDHAM L.REV. 1365, 1367, 1371–72, 1376–80, 1414–19, 1424, 1431 (1997).

I. FIRST STEPS

Readings of the Constitution have changed. A theory of fidelity must explain at least this. It must explain, that is, why readings change, whether such changes are changes of fidelity, and more generally, how we could know whether such changes are changes of fidelity.

A theory modeled on translation is one such account. It uses "translation" as a heuristic for suggesting just how changed readings could be changes of fidelity. It uses this heuristic for guiding this change to assure that they are. The heuristic is modeled upon linguistic translation, or what we ordinarily mean by "translation," but the pattern it invokes is much broader than that. As George Steiner puts it, "[w]hen we read or hear any language-statement from the past . . . we translate."[2] Translation, in this sense, is a practice to understand a contextually distant text, whether a text written in a different language, or a text written at a different time. It is translation in this broader sense that I mean to model, and the ethic that this practice invokes that I mean to draw upon.

* * *

In its simplest, perhaps crudest form, the translator's task is this: She is presented with a text that is written in one language. This is the source text; the language is the source language. Her aim is to write another text in a second language—the target language, and her text, the target text. If the translation succeeds—if it is a good translation—then there is an important relation between the two texts, in these two contexts: naively put, their "meaning" is to be "the same." Different texts; different contexts; same meaning.

---

[60] *See* Marbury v. Madison, 5 U.S. (1 Cranch) 137 (1803) (presentation and construction of § 13 of the Judiciary Act of 1789).

[61] *See* McCulloch v. Maryland, 17 U.S. (4 Wheat.) 316 (1819) (invocation of American nationalism).

[2] See George Steiner, After Babel: Aspects of Language and Translation 28 (1975).

My claim is that judges face a similar task. Like the linguistic translator, the judge is faced with a text (say, the Constitution), written in an original or source context (America, late eighteenth century); she too must write a text (a decision, or an opinion) in a different context (America, today); this decision, in its context, is to have the same meaning as the original text in its context. Of course, unlike the linguistic translator, the judge can't simply rewrite the original text. That text must remain the same. But the judge does change readings of that original text: The judge gives a reading of the original text that in the current context yields the same meaning as the original text in its original context. For the legal translator, the reading is to the original text as, to the linguistic translator, the target text is to the source text.

This process is not automatic. But neither is it automatic for the linguistic translator. There is no obvious, or complete, mapping of one language onto another; no simple formula will carry meaning from one to another. Always the linguistic translator, like the legal translator, makes a certain judgment about how best to carry the meaning of one world into second. And always this judgment requires choice.

* * *

[One] choice is about the constraints on the practice * * *. And here the links with linguistic translation are quite rich. For translators struggle with a tension that defines the tension confronted by the judge: If translation requires creativity—if there is no such thing as "mechanical" translation—then some counsel the translator to a kind of humility. Humility means this: to avoid translations that the translator believes make the text a better text; to choose instead translations that will carry over a text's flaws as well as its virtues. This counsel to humility is offered as a virtue in the translator's practice. It is an integrity—to be faithful to the strengths of a text as well as the vice; to exercise the power of the translator in a sense not to change the text translated, while in a sense changing the text translated fundamentally.[14] On this view of the translator's task, fidelity requires a certain restraint—the restraint to minimize the voice of the translator in the text being translated.

* * *

C. How Much Translation Explains

So much for theory and for pedigree: The test of translation as a practice of interpretation in constitutional theory hangs upon the results—upon

---

[14]See Lawrence Lessig, *Fidelity in Translation*, 71 Tex. L. Rev. 1165, 1189–1211 (1993) for a discussion of the parallels between translation and legal interpretation.

how well it fits, and justifies, the history of our constitutional practice; and upon how well it helps us understand how best to go on. * * *

1. TVs and Airforces

The Constitution doesn't speak much about televisions or airforces. The First Amendment speaks of the freedom of the "press"; and Article I speaks of the "army" and "navy." How should these words—"press," "army," "navy"—be read today?

The originalist might puzzle the question. Since his method is single step, he might survey the doctrine, and the text, and say, with a bit of impatience, something like this: "the text of the First Amendment makes no distinction between print, broadcast, and cable media, but we have done so."[24]

The translator, however, can well understand this apparent anomaly. For her method takes two steps. First, she notes this: At the time all three ("press," "army," and "navy") were written, all three marked out the full range of each kind. There were no televisions, but likewise, there was no device of publication in 1791 that was not within the reach of "the press." There was no airforce, but "army" and "navy" marked out the full range of the armed forces. Both terms when written were exhaustive of the category that they described.

The second step is to carry these exhaustive terms into the present. No reason presents itself for not including televisions or airforces into the terms of the original grant. The translator, therefore, includes them. The "text" now is about an army, navy and airforce, or about the press and the broadcasting media. The Framers gave every reason to believe such terms would be included; they could not at the time exclude them; therefore, they should be included.

Everyone agrees with these conclusions, so it is useful to remark how sharply they diverge from what a plain language jurist might say. They force the plain language jurist to account for the significance of time. These words were "plain," but the change in circumstance justifies our looking beyond them to understand their meaning now.

It is useful as well to mark some limits: It is because the category of TVs and Airforces did not exist that it is an easy case to include them. If our Constitution were drafted today with the very same words, the interpretive question would be quite different and difficult. To make it easy, two steps to reading must be taken.

---

[24]Denver Area Educ. Telecomm. Consortium v. FCC, 116 S. Ct. 2374, 2419–20 (1996) (Thomas, J., concurring in part, dissenting in part).

2. Commerce I

A second easy case is a bit less easy. The Framers gave Congress the power "to regulate Commerce . . . among the several States." They also gave Congress the power "to make all Laws . . . necessary and proper" to the regulation of "commerce . . . among the several States." The extent of both powers turns upon something important in the world—viz., the extent of "commerce" "among" the several states. To the extent that there is more interstate commerce, there is a greater reach to Congress's power. To the extent that there is less, there is less. In either case, the power is contingent upon some fact in the world.

This understanding of the nature of the clause is original—meaning from the origin, at least if Marshall is original. It is the understanding sketched in *Gibbons v. Ogden* and *McCulloch v. Maryland*; and it is the practice of the early cases. From the start, it was the interplay between commerce and the Necessary and Proper Clause that defined the scope of Congress's power to regulate commerce. As the extent of that commerce expanded, so too did the power.

Of course, how one measures the extent of commerce; how one knows what is interstate versus intrastate; how one relates these economic notions to constitutional ideals—all these are tough questions, poorly answered over the past two centuries. But the point is that however they are answered, the relationship between economics and power stands. The Framers were realists in this sense about the Necessary and Proper Clause at least, ceding to Congress the judgment about whether a measure was really necessary and proper. And despite some honorable and understandable formalism in the late middle republic * * * , we can't help but be the same sort of realists today. We can't help but conclude (as a partial solution at least) that the scope and reach of the commerce power expands as the economy it tracks expands.

3. Privacy

Before there were televisions and airforces, there were also no telephones, and therefore, no wiretaps. One lived one's life face to face; what one wrote—in letters or diaries—and kept a hold of, was protected. One was protected because all this was one's property; and one's property—person, home, papers and effects—could not unreasonably be searched.

When telephones and wiretaps came around, this formula for protection got challenged. For one could tap my telephone without violating my property rights. Thus the question: Was such a violation within the scope of the Fourth Amendment?

In its first consideration of the question, the Supreme Court said no. Said the Court, the Fourth Amendment protected against trespass; wiretapping was not a trespass; so the Fourth Amendment didn't protect against wiretapping. This was, for the Chief Justice, an easy case; and with that opinion, life on the wire became life in public.

This is classic one-step originalism.[33] But matched with that classic is a paradigm of two-step translation—the dissent of Justice Brandeis. Said Brandeis, the Fourth Amendment was meant to protect the privacy of people, not the sanctity of property. To that end, given the technologies of the late eighteenth century, it selected the means it did. But as the technologies of invasion have changed, Brandeis said, so too should the techniques of protection change. The Fourth Amendment (we might paraphrase, or better, translate) had to be translated to give citizens in the twentieth century the sort of protection that the Framers gave citizens in the Eighteenth.

The Court eventually followed the intuition of Brandeis's dissent. In *Katz v. United States*, it held that the Constitution protected "people, not places."[37] And while one could well question the technique used by *Katz* in this effort at translation, one can't mistake its motive. Its aim was a certain equivalence, forged between worlds that had become quite distinct.

4. Federalism, Herein Commerce II

I said above that it was an easy case that the power of Congress under the Commerce Clause (tied to the Necessary and Proper Clause) would increase over time, tracking, as the clause suggests it should, an increasingly integrated national economy. Taken in isolation, that is true. But the power clauses don't stand in isolation. In context, they have an effect upon a second aspect of the framing design—federalism. As the scope of federal authority is enriched, by an expanding commerce power, the reach of exclusive state authority is impoverished. Granting the growth of federal power means yielding to the withering of the power of the state.

This conflict raises a second question of translation. For the question now is how best to read the commerce power, to preserve something of the original balance in the federal design. Of course one might argue that there is no conflict at all; one might say, that is, that this growth of federal power was originally intended. Perhaps. But assume for the moment it was not. The question for the translator is how to accommodate this conflict.

The history of the Commerce Clause (both negative and positive) tells a nice story of this conflict. At first federal power grows quite extensively—a function of the easy translation I sketched above. But in a second stage, the Court engages in a bold, if abortive effort to cut back. This was the "Old Court," in the struggle that ended in 1935. In a series (though not many) of cases, it imposed artificial and formal limitations on the scope of Con-

[33]See Olmstead v. United States, 277 U.S. 438 (1928).

[37][389 U.S. 347, 351 (1967).]

gress's power in the name of constitutional federalism. These limitations were said to flow from the Constitution itself; they were driven by the observation that the Framers gave us a Constitution of enumerated powers, yet now power seemed unlimited. But however true this motive may have been, the Framers didn't give us the kinds of tools that the Old Court used to cabin federal power. These tools that Court made up, at least in the sense that they are nowhere found in the Framers' text.

This is not to criticize, for I am a big fan of makings-up in the name of fidelity. But it is to emphasize what we have been led to forget: That while the ends of this Court may have been conservative, its means certainly were not. In its effort to impose limits on federal power, in the name of preserving something of the Framing balance, it put firm and wholly constructed limits on Congress's power; it dissembled about the original and historical understandings of that power; and it pretended to find firmness and clarity in a practice that was anything but. But it did this to restore—to reclaim a balance that time had shifted.

* * *

II. THE CONSTRAINTS OF CONTEXT

* * *

[*D.*] *Equal Protection*

[In this section I discuss] the Equal Protection Clause. The vitality of this most important Civil War amendment was affirmed, to a limited degree, just last term in * * * *United States v. Virginia*[.][145]

[The decision in *Virginia*] puzzled, and perhaps disgusted the Court's most conservative justices. Some think the disgust pure prejudice. I don't believe it is that. My view is that the frustration of the most principled among these dissenters comes from their view that these changes in the reach of the Equal Protection Clause cannot be changes of fidelity; that the continuing productivity of the Equal Protection Clause is just so much judicial lawmaking; that at some point the transformative power of this clause must come to an end, and if anywhere, certainly here: with a class who has long been the target of animus and discrimination by America.

* * *

In his lone dissent in *Virginia*, Justice Scalia stated the question in a way that links directly with the analysis that I have sketched so far. As he is the principal, and principled, dissenter that I am considering, consider what he wrote, introducing his opinion:

---

[145] 116 S. Ct. 2264 (1996).

> Much of the Court's opinion is devoted to deprecating the closed-mindedness of our forebears with regard to women's education and even with regard to the treatment of women in areas that have nothing to do with education. Closed-minded they were—as every age is, including our own, with regard to matters it cannot guess, because it simply does not consider them debatable. The virtue of a democratic system with a First Amendment is that it readily enables the people, over time, to be persuaded that what they took for granted is not so, and to change their laws accordingly. That system is destroyed if the smug assurances of each age are removed from the democratic process and written into the Constitution. So to counterbalance the Court's criticism of our ancestors, let me say a word in their praise: they left us free to change.[147]

Scalia frames the question just right. When the Fourteenth Amendment was passed, the framers took many things for granted. These things taken for granted—what Scalia calls, "not debatable"—change. * * * [T]he discourses that constitute them become contested. Sometimes these contested questions become again uncontested, and sometimes uncontested in just the opposite way as before. The not "debatable" change, both by becoming debatable, and by becoming not debatable in a very different way. The question that Scalia rightly poses is this: What does fidelity require, when what they presupposed is no longer presupposed by us?

This, I believe, is the central question for fidelity theory, but a question for which we haven't yet a good answer. We might imagine three sorts of responses. The first is the extreme one-step originalist response. For the one-step originalist, the question is: What would the Framers have thought? To understand that, one must presuppose what they presupposed. So the fact that we consider just nuts the stuff that they considered not even debatable is not, for the one-step, relevant. The question is what they think, not what we think. They, after all, were the Framers.

This one-step originalist response is not Scalia's. He does not argue that we should decide these questions as if we had the presuppositions of the Framers. But neither does he argue for the opposite response—the translator, or two-step response. His response is between the one-step, and two-step. To see its place, consider the two-step, or translator's, response first.

The translator reads what the Framers did, understanding it relative to that framing context; she then locates in this context the equivalent to their deeds there. So about the question of sex discrimination, the translator might argue (in a very crude form): The framers of the Fourteenth Amendment plainly thought that race should not matter to one's civil rights.

---

[147][Id.] at 2291–92 (Scalia, J., dissenting).

But about sex, they had a different view. In Scalia's terms, they didn't even think it "debatable" whether sex discrimination was justified. Indeed, for many, the discriminations of the time would not have appeared as "discriminations," just as for us, the discriminations in the minimum driving age don't appear to us as "discrimination" against children.

But we, the translator would argue, have a different view. It is not just the case that for us the matter of sex discrimination is debatable; if it were debatable, then perhaps there may be good reason for judicial deference. For us the matter is no longer debatable. Or better, it is as undebatable for us that sex discrimination is a violation of equality as it was for the framers of the Fourteenth Amendment that racial discrimination was a violation of equality. No doubt what sex discrimination is, or how it applies in a particular case, is debatable. But that's the same with racial discrimination. Fray at the border does not of necessity undo the cloth.

The translator might then argue that because it is not debatable that sex discrimination is a violation of equality, we should read the Fourteenth Amendment to apply to sex just as we have read it to apply to race.

Scalia's view is in-between these two. He rejects the one-step originalist view in principle (though in effect the result might be the same): We are not tied to what they considered undebatable. But neither does he embrace the translator's view, which would update the amendment to reflect (at a minimum) what we now treat as non-debatable. His position is more agnostic: Those issues that the Framers took for granted but which now are debatable or non-debatable in a different way are matters to which the Constitution does not speak. They are left to democratic politics. Any attempt now to constitutionalize them, by recognizing today a new set of undebatable beliefs, is illegitimate: Fundamentally, Scalia charges, "illiberal."

* * *

[W]hat this abstract debate about equality forgets is the presumption—the "trump"—of a rights claim (or at least, of an equal protection rights claim). The burden for those who would discriminate is to demonstrate a sufficiently strong reason for that discrimination. They must offer, that is, a justification for this discrimination. But in offering a justification, the "undebatable" is critical. If the justification rests on what people think is undebatable, the justification is relatively strong. If the justification rests on what people think is debatable, or contested in my terms, then the justification is relatively weak. Thus, if the justification for a discrimination rests upon what the Framers thought non-debatable, then when that undebatable becomes debatable, so too does the justification. When the undebatable changes, it weakens the justification for the discrimination.

Contestation is in this sense transitive; it weakens what its absence supported.

At some point this contestation matters. * * * As in rights cases perhaps generally, * * * the contestation of a justification for invading a right yields a more active defense of that right. Contestation tilts to the default, and the default is active support of the right.

This is, I want to argue, the pattern in the history of the Fourteenth Amendment. Or better, it is a history that can be understood in light of this pattern. * * *

* * *

My model, then, of fidelity as translation can be specified as follows: That translation proceeds subject to the constraints of contested discourses, and uncontested discourses. Sometimes these constraints explain shifts of deference, where the court backs away from creatively translating limits on federal or state power. Sometimes they explain shifts of activism, where the court rejects justifications for limiting the scope of a right because contest has infected these justifications.

C. EVOLUTIONARY THEORIES

THOMAS C. GREY, DO WE HAVE AN UNWRITTEN CONSTITUTION?

27 STAN.L.REV. 703–717 (1975).

In reviewing laws for constitutionality, should our judges confine themselves to determining whether those laws conflict with norms derived from the written Constitution? Or may they also enforce principles of liberty and justice when the normative content of those principles is not to be found within the four corners of our founding document? Excluding the question of the legitimacy of judicial review itself, that is perhaps the most fundamental question we can ask about our fundamental law.

I. THE PURE INTERPRETIVE MODEL

For many years this most basic question has not much engaged the explicit attention of constitutional scholars or of the courts or judges themselves, with at least one important exception. That exception was Mr. Justice Black. Throughout his long and remarkable career on the bench, the most consistently reiterated theme of his constitutional jurisprudence was the need for fidelity to the constitutional text in judicial review, and the illegitimacy of constitutional doctrines based on sources other than the explicit commands of the written Constitution.[1]

---

[1] *See, e.g.*, *In re* Winship, 397 U.S. 358, 377 (1970) (Black, J., dissenting); Griswold v.

It now appears that as a final mark of Mr. Justice Black's achievement, his jurisprudential view of constitutional adjudication may be returning to favor. In the last few years, distinguished commentators on constitutional law have begun to echo Mr. Justice Black's central theme, criticizing constitutional developments in terms that have scarcely been heard in the scholarly community for a generation.

* * *

The truth is that the view of constitutional adjudication that [these commentators] share with Mr. Justice Black is one of great power and compelling simplicity. That view is deeply rooted in our history and in our shared principles of political legitimacy. It has equally deep roots in our formal constitutional law; it is, after all, the theory upon which judicial review was founded in *Marbury v. Madison*.

The chief virtue of this view is that it supports judicial review while answering the charge that the practice is undemocratic. Under the pure interpretive model (as I shall henceforth call the view in question), when a court strikes down a popular statute or practice as unconstitutional, it may always reply to the resulting public outcry: "We didn't do it—you did." The people have chosen the principle that the statute or practice violated, have designated it as fundamental, and have written it down in the text of the Constitution for the judges to interpret and apply. The task of interpretation of the people's commands may not always be simple or mechanical; there is no warrant to condemn Mr. Justice Black or his allies with the epithet "mechanical jurisprudence." But the task remains basically one of interpretation, the application of fixed and binding norms to new facts.[9]

II. BEYOND INTERPRETATION

The contrary view of judicial review, the one that I espouse and that

---

Connecticut, 381 U.S. 479, 507 (1965) (Black, J., dissenting); Rochin v. California, 342 U.S. 165, 174 (1952) (Black, J., concurring); Adamson v. California, 332 U.S. 46, 68 (1947) (Black, J., dissenting).

[9] The pure interpretive model should not be confused with *literalism* in constitutional interpretation, particularly with "narrow" or "crabbed" literalism. The interpretive model, at least in the hands of its sophisticated exponents, certainly contemplates that the courts may look through the sometimes opaque text to the purposes behind it in determining constitutional norms. Normative inferences may be drawn from silences and omissions, from structures and relationships, as well as from explicit commands. Thus I do not see the sort of constitutional reasoning described by Professor Charles Black in his Structure And Relationship In Constitutional Law (1969) as necessarily going beyond the interpretive model.

What distinguishes the exponent of the pure interpretive model is his insistence that the only norms used in constitutional adjudication must be those inferable from the text—that the Constitution must not be seen as licensing courts to articulate and apply contemporary norms not demonstrably expressed or implied by the framers.

seems to me implicit in much of the constitutional law developed by the courts, does not deny that the Constitution is a written document, expressing some clear and positive restraints upon governmental power. Nor does it deny that part of the business of judicial review consists of giving effect to these explicit commands.

Where the broader view of judicial review diverges from the pure interpretive model is in its acceptance of the courts' additional role as the expounder of basic national ideals of individual liberty and fair treatment, even when the content of these ideals is not expressed as a matter of positive law in the written Constitution. It must at once be conceded that such a role for our courts is more difficult to justify than is the role assigned by the pure interpretive model. Why, one asks, are the courts better able to discern and articulate basic national ideals than are the people's politically responsible representatives? And one recalls Learned Hand's remark that he would find it "most irksome to be ruled by a bevy of Platonic Guardians, even if I knew how to choose them, which I assuredly do not."[10]

These grave difficulties no doubt explain, although they do not excuse, the tendency of our courts—today as throughout our history—to resort to bad legislative history and strained reading of constitutional language to support results that would be better justified by explication of contemporary moral and political ideals not drawn from the constitutional text. Of course, this tendency of the courts in no way helps to establish the legitimacy of noninterpretive judicial review. Indeed, standing alone it tends to establish the opposite; for if judges resort to bad interpretation in preference to honest exposition of deeply held but unwritten ideals, it must be because they perceive the latter mode of decisionmaking to be of suspect legitimacy.

However, the tendency to slipshod history and text-parsing does not stand alone. The courts do not only effectuate unwritten ideals and values covertly. Rather, in a very large proportion of their important constitutional decisions, they proceed in a mode that is openly noninterpretive. If this assertion seems at first glance surprising, it may be so partly because of the way in which constitutional law is taught in our law schools.

In the academic teaching of constitutional law, the general question of the legitimacy of judicial review is addressed largely through the vehicle of *Marbury v. Madison.* Students examine the arguments made for judicial review by Chief Justice Marshall, and perhaps contrast them with some of the counterarguments of later judges or commentators. The discussion concludes with the point that, whatever the validity of those arguments as an original matter, history has firmly decided in favor of judicial review.

---

[10] L. Hand, The Bill of Rights 73 (1958).

Thereafter, debates about judicial review focus on the question of how "activist" or how "deferential" *it* should be. *It* is always assumed to be the single unitary practice established and justified in *Marbury*.

This seems to me a seriously misleading way of proceeding. *Marbury* defends (and its detractors attack) what I have here called the pure interpretive model of judicial review. The case itself involves the close interpretation of a technical and explicit constitutional provision, which is found, upon conventional linguistic analysis, to conflict with a statute. The argument for judicial review as a general matter is made in terms appropriate to that sort of case. Chief Justice Marshall's stress is on the *writtenness* of the Constitution, and on its supremacy in cases of clear conflict with ordinary law.[11] His heuristic examples all involve obvious conflicts between hypothetical (and unlikely) statutes on the one hand, and particularly explicit constitutional commands on the other.[12]

All this makes *Marbury* a most atypical constitutional case, and an inappropriate paradigm for the sort of judicial review that has been important and controversial throughout our history, from *Dred Scott*[13] to the *Legal Tender Cases*[14] to *Lochner*[15] to *Carter Coal*[16] and on to *Brown v. Board of Education,*[17] *Baker v. Carr,*[18] and the Death Penalty[19] and Abortion[20] cases in our own day. In the important cases, reference to and analysis of the constitutional text plays a minor role. The dominant norms of decision are those large conceptions of governmental structure and individual rights that are at best referred to, and whose content is scarcely at all specified, in the written Constitution—dual federalism, vested rights, fair procedure, equality before the law.

The question of the legitimacy of this very different sort of judicial review is scarcely addressed, much less concluded, by the arguments of *Marbury v. Madison.* To approach that question, we might better examine

---

[11]5 U.S. (1 Cranch) 137, 176–78 (1803). Although the argument proceeds in terms of instances of purely interpretive judicial review, the underlying principle—that the courts must give precedence to constitutional law over ordinary law—is not itself found in or easily inferred from the text. Nevertheless, the argument for that principle still seems to be in the interpretive mode, based as it is on the intentions inferable from the framers' adoption of a written constitution.

[12]For example, Marshall asks rhetorically whether the courts should enforce a statute generally imposing a duty on exports from a state, or an avowed bill of attainder or ex post facto law. *Id.* at 179.

[13]Dred Scott v. Sanford, 60 U.S. (19 How.) 393 (1857).

[14]79 U.S. (12 Wall.) 457 (1871).

[15]Lochner v. New York, 198 U.S. 45 (1905).

[16]Carter v. Carter Coal Co., 298 U.S. 238 (1936).

[17]347 U.S. 483 (1954).

[18]369 U.S. 186 (1962).

[19]Furman v. Georgia, 408 U.S. 238 (1972).

[20]Roe v. Wade, 410 U.S. 113 (1973), Doe v. Bolton, 410 U.S. 179 (1973).

the debate between Justices Chase and Iredell in *Calder v. Bull.*[21] And if exposure to the matchless rhetoric of John Marshall is desired, *Fletcher v. Peck*[22] provides an excellent example. In that case, the Georgia statute is struck down on two alternative grounds. The first is a strained interpretation of the contract clause, comparable in flimsiness to some of the poorer interpretive efforts of the Warren Court. The second ground is expressed in the Court's conclusion that the statute violates "general principles which are common to our free institutions"—in particular, the principle of the inviolability of vested rights. Conspicuously absent is a dissent arguing that this principle is nowhere stated in the constitutional text. Indeed, the other opinion in the case—that of Justice Johnson—expresses agreement with the result on the ground of "general principles," but disavows the strained reading of the contract clause.

The parallel between *Fletcher* and most contemporary judicial review is striking. Today, the Court will formally invoke one of the majestic generalities of the Constitution, typically the due process or equal protection clause, as the textual basis for its decision. Even this much specificity is not always vouchsafed us. Thus we are told of the constitutional "right to travel" that the Court has "no occasion to ascribe the source of this right to * * * a particular constitutional provision."[25] And in the Abortion Cases, the Court's reference to the textual cover for the "right of privacy" is strikingly casual:

> This right of privacy, whether it be founded in the Fourteenth Amendment's concept of personal liberty and restrictions upon state action, as we feel it is, or, as the District Court determined, in the Ninth Amendment's reservation of rights to the people, is broad enough to encompass a woman's decision whether or not to terminate her pregnancy.[26]

---

[21] 3 U.S. (3 Dall.) 386 (1798). Chase: "I cannot subscribe to the omnipotence of a state legislature, or that it is absolute and without control, although its authority should not be expressly restrained by the Constitution, or fundamental law of the State. . . There are certain vital principles in our free republican governments, which will determine and overrule our apparent and flagrant abuse of legislative power. . . " *Id.* at 387–88 (majority opinion).

Iredell: "It is true, that some speculative jurists have held, that a legislative act against natural justice must, in itself, be void; but I cannot think, that under such a government, any court of justice would possess a power to declare it so. . .

"[T]he ideas of natural justice are regulated by no fixed standard; the ablest and the purest men have differed upon the subject; and all that the court could properly say, in such an event, would be, that the legislature, possessed of an equal right of opinion, had passed an act which, in the opinion of the judges, was inconsistent with the abstract principles of natural justice." *Id.* at 398–99 (concurring opinion).

[22] 10 U.S. (6 Cranch) 87 (1810).

[25] Shapiro v. Thompson, 394 U.S. 618, 630 (1969) (footnote omitted).

[26] Roe v. Wade, 410 U.S. 113, 153 (1973). Students of the aesthetics of pseudo-interpretation may debate whether or not this formulation is preferable to the Court's

It should be clear that in these cases the Court is quite openly *not* relying on constitutional text for the content of the substantive principles it is invoking to invalidate legislation. The parallel reliance on the ninth amendment and the due process clause in the Abortion Cases is instructive on the point. The ninth amendment on its face has no substantive content. It is rather a license to constitutional decisionmakers to look beyond the substantive commands of the constitutional text to protect fundamental rights not expressed therein. In this case at least, the due process clause is being used in the same way.

Much of our substantive constitutional doctrine is of this kind. Where it arises "under" some piece of constitutional text, the text is not invoked as the source of the values or principles that rule the cases. Rather the broad textual provisions are seen as sources of legitimacy for judicial development and explication of basic shared national values. These values may be seen as permanent and universal features of human social arrangements—natural law principles—as they typically were in the 18th and 19th centuries. Or they may be seen as relative to our particular civilization, and subject to growth and change, as they typically are today. Our characteristic contemporary metaphor is "the living Constitution"—a constitution with provisions suggesting restraints on government in the name of basic rights, yet sufficiently unspecific to permit the judiciary to elucidate the development and change in the content of those rights over time.

This view of constitutional adjudication is at war with the pure interpretive model. As Mr. Justice Black said often and forcefully enough, he had no truck with the notion of changing, flexible, "living" constitutional guarantees.[28] The amendment process was the framers' chosen and exclusive method of adopting constitutional values to changing times; the judiciary was to enforce the Constitution's substantive commands as the framers meant them.

This is not to say that the interpretive model is incompatible with one limited sense of the concept of a "living" constitution. The model can contemplate the application of the framers' value judgments and institutional arrangements to new or changed *factual* circumstances. In that sense, its proponents can endorse Chief Justice Marshall's view of the Constitution as "intended to endure for ages to come, and consequently, to be adapted to the various crises of human affairs."[30]

But the interpretive model cannot be reconciled with constitutional doctrines protecting unspecified "essential" or "fundamental" liberties, or

---

celebrated shuffle in Griswold v. Connecticut, 381 U.S. 479 (1965), through the "emanations" and "penumbras" of the Bill of Rights.

[28] *See, e.g.,* Harper v. Virginia Bd. of Elections, 383 U.S. 663, 670 (1966) (Black, J., dissenting).

[30] McCulloch v. Maryland, 17 U.S. (4 Wheat.) 415, 427 (1819).

"fair procedure," or "decency"—leaving it to the judiciary to give moral content to those conceptions either once and for all or from age to age. That sort of "interpretation" would drain from the interpretive model its animating strength. Once it was adopted, the courts could no longer honestly defend an unpopular decision to a protesting public with the transfer of responsibility: "We didn't do it—you did." No longer would the Court's constitutional role be the technical and professional one of applying *given* norms to changing facts; instead the Court would assume the large and problematic role of discerning a society's most basic contemporary values.

III. THE IMPLICATIONS OF THE PURE INTERPRETIVE MODEL

Let me now give some examples, confined to the area of individual rights, of the numerous and important substantive constitutional doctrines which seem to me unjustified under a consistently applied pure interpretive model of judicial review. First and most obvious is virtually the entire body of doctrine developed under the due process clauses of the 5th and 14th amendments. If those clauses can be seen as having any specific normative content attributable to their framers, it is probably only that given to them by Mr. Justice Black.[31] In his view, due process requires only that deprivations of life, liberty or property be authorized by law duly enacted, rather than carried out by arbitrary executive action. A slightly more ambitious, though highly implausible, narrow interpretation is that adopted by the pre-Civil War Supreme Court—that the clause prohibits departures from the settled course of procedure familiar in the English courts in 1791.[32]

On the interpretive model, then, all the rest of due process doctrine must go. First, what many regard as the core of due process doctrine—its flexible requirement of "fundamentally fair" procedures in criminal and civil proceedings—cannot be reconciled with the interpretive model. These doctrines are developments of the "living constitution" concept *par excellence.*[33] In addition, everything that has been labeled "substantive due process" would be eliminated. It is these doctrines on which the proponents of the interpretive model have most often focused their attacks. Much of the force behind their position derives from the deeply felt opposition to the

[31] *See In re* Winship, 397 U.S. 358, 377–85 (1970) (dissenting opinion). As Mr. Justice Black notes in that opinion, his separate position that the 14th amendment incorporates the Bill of Rights is not based on construction of the due process clause alone, but on "the language of the entire first section of the Fourteenth Amendment, as illuminated by the legislative history surrounding its adoption." *Id.* at 382 n. 11.

[32] Murray's Lessee v. Hoboken Land & Improvement Co., 59 U.S. (18 How.) 272, 277 (1856).

[33] *See, e.g., In re* Winship, 397 U.S. 358, 377 (1970) (Black, J., dissenting); Goldberg v. Kelly, 397 U.S. 254 (1970) (Black, J., dissenting).

constitutionalization of laissez-faire economics epitomized by *Lochner v. New York,*[34] and they typically unite in opposition to contemporary doctrinal developments that remind them too much of *Lochner.*[35]

A striking point often overlooked by contemporary interpretivists is that the demise of substantive due process must constitutionally free the federal government to engage in explicit racial discrimination. There is no textual warrant for reading into the due process clause of the fifth amendment any of the prohibitions directed against the states by the equal protection clause.[36]

Equally strikingly, the application of the provisions of the Bill of Rights to states cannot be justified under an interpretive model—unless one strains to accept, as the Court clearly has declined to do, the flimsy historical evidence that the framers of the 14th amendment intended this result.[37] Freedom of speech, freedom of religion, and the requirement of just compensation in the taking of property, as well as the procedural provisions

---

[34]198 U.S. 45 (1905).

[35]It now seems that the ultimate punchline in the criticism of a constitutional decision is to say that it is "like *Lochner.*" Professor Ely has even minted a generic term, "to *Lochner,*" to describe whatever-it-was-so-awful-the-Court-did-in-*Lochner.* Ely, [*The Wages of Crying Wolf: A Comment on* Roe v. Wade, 82 Yale L.J. 920, 944 (1973).]

Lochner is only one of thousands of decisions in the history of the Court that invoke a noninterpretive mode of constitutional adjudication; if it was a bad decision, as I think it was, it by no means follows that the general mode of adjudication it represents is illegitimate. There are many bad decisions in the mode of pure interpretation.

It is an often overlooked point that Mr. Justice Holmes in his classic *Lochner* dissent did not use the case as an occasion to reject noninterpretive adjudication generally, or even substantive due process as such; quite the contrary: "I think that the word liberty in the Fourteenth Amendment is perverted when it is held to prevent the natural outcome of a dominant opinion, *unless it can be said that a rational and fair man necessarily would admit that the statute proposed would infringe fundamental principles as they have been understood by the traditions of our people and our law.*" 198 U.S. at 76 (emphasis added).

[36]*See* Bolling v. Sharpe, 347 U.S. 497, 499 (1954). Since *Bolling,* the Court has often applied equal protection doctrine to the federal government "under" the fifth amendment due process clause. *See, e.g.,* Shapiro v. Thompson, 394 U.S. 618 (1969), in which the Court invalidated a District of Columbia statute as a violation of due process, while relying upon the equal protection clause to invalidate similar state statutes. Since *Bolling*—at least as far as I have been able to discover—the Court has never even seriously discussed the possibility that the fifth amendment due process clause might not fully incorporate the requirements progressively imposed on the states under the equal protection clause.

[37]The Court's refusal to adopt the "incorporation" theory is clear both from its refusal to apply the requirements of grand jury indictment and civil jury trial to the states, and from its statements in "selective incorporation" cases. *See, e.g.,* Duncan v. Louisiana, 391 U.S. 145, 149 (1968), which held that due process required the states to provide jury trial in serious criminal cases *because* "trial by jury in criminal cases is fundamental to the American scheme of justice * * *." For the controversy over the intent of the framers, *compare* Fairman, *Does the Fourteenth Amendment Incorporate the Bill of Rights?,* 2 Stan.L.Rev. 5 (1949), *with* Adamson v. California, 332 U.S. 46, 68 (1947) (Black, J., dissenting).

of the fourth, fifth, sixth, and eighth amendments must then no longer be seen as federal constitutional restraints on state power.

All of the "fundamental interests" that trigger "strict scrutiny" under the equal protection clause would have to be discarded, if the interpretive model were to control constitutional adjudication. Most obviously, the large body of doctrine that has grown up around the interests in the franchise and in participation in the electoral process could not stand. If the values implicit in the equal protection clause are limited only to those that its framers intended at the time of enactment, the clause clearly does not speak to questions of eligibility for the franchise or of legislative apportionment.[38]

Thus far, it seems to me there is little room for disagreement that the premises of the pure interpretive model would require the conclusions I have drawn from it. For those who have not yet had enough, and coming to slightly more doubtful matters, there is serious question how much of the law prohibiting state racial discrimination can survive honest application of the interpretive model. It is clear that the equal protection clause was meant to prohibit *some* forms of state racial discrimination, most obviously those enacted in the Black Codes. It is equally clear from the legislative history that the clause was *not* intended to guarantee equal political rights, such as the right to vote or to run for office, and perhaps including the right to serve on juries.[39]

It is at least doubtful whether the clause can fairly be read as intending to bar any form of state-imposed racial segregation, so long as equal facilities are made available. Professor Bickel's careful study of the legislative history revealed little evidence of intent to prohibit segregation, which at the time was widespread in the North.[40] Professor Bickel did conclude that the original understanding of the amendment was consistent with the decision in the School Segregation Cases, but only in the sense that the general language of the clause *licensed* the courts (and Congress) to enforce evolving ideals of racial justice.[41] Yet this is a classic invocation of the notion of the "living constitution," and as such is not permitted by the interpretive model.

Finally, under the interpretive model, modern applications of the provisions of the Bill of Rights based on their capacity to grow or develop with changing social values would have to be discarded. Prominent among the discarded doctrines would be the prevailing view that the eighth amend-

---

[38]The numerous dissenting opinions of Mr. Justice Harlan in voting and reapportionment cases put the point beyond doubt. *See, e.g.,* Carrington v. Rash, 380 U.S. 89, 97 (1965) (Harlan, J., dissenting); Reynolds v. Sims, 377 U.S. 533, 589 (1964) (Harlan, J., dissenting).

[39]*See generally* Bickel, *The Original Understanding and the Segregation Decision,* 69 Harv.L.Rev. 1 (1955).

[40]*Id.* at 58.

[41]*Id.* at 62–65.

ment's prohibition of cruel and unusual punishments must be "interpreted" in light of society's "evolving standards of decency."[42] It is doubtful that much of modern first amendment doctrine could be defended on the basis of value choices attributable to the framers,[43] and similar doubts must cast a shadow on some of the law of the fourth amendment.[44] The doctrine that the sixth amendment guarantees appointed counsel for indigent defendants[45] is likewise in serious jeopardy, if historically intended meaning must be the only legitimate guide in constitutional adjudication.[46]

While one might disagree with this rough catalogue on points of detail, it should be clear that an extraordinarily radical purge of established constitutional doctrine would be required if we candidly and consistently applied the pure interpretive model. Surely that makes out at least a prima facie practical case against the model. Conservatives ought to be cautious about adopting any abstract premise which requires so drastic a change in accepted practice, and liberals presumably will be dismayed by the prospect of any major diminution in the courts' authority to protect basic human rights.

---

[42]*See, e.g.*, Trop v. Dulles, 356 U.S. 86, 101 (1958).

[43]*See generally* L. Levy, Legacy of Suppression (1960).

[44]*See, e.g.*, Katz v. United States, 389 U.S. 347 (1967), in which the Court extended fourth amendment coverage to the recording of oral statements by electronic devices. Justice Black filed a lone dissent arguing—from an interpretive stance—"[s]ince I see no way in which the words of the Fourth Amendment can be construed to apply to eavesdropping, that closes the matter for me * * *. I will not distort the words of the Amendment in order to 'keep the Constitution up to date' or 'to bring it into harmony with the times.'" *Id.* at 373 (dissenting opinion).

[45]Johnson v. Zerbst, 304 U.S. 458 (1938).

[46]The instances of noninterpretive judicial review I have mentioned fall into three general groups. First are those instances where the courts have created (or found) independent constitutional rights with almost no textual guidance. Examples are the contemporary right of privacy, and the older liberty of contract. Second are those instances where the courts have given general application to norms that the constitutional text explicitly applies in a more limited way. Examples are the application of equal protection and contract clause principles to the federal government, and the application of the Bill of Rights to the states—"under" the conveniently all-embracing due process clauses. The third type is the extension or broadening of principles stated in the Constitution beyond the normative content intended for them by the framers. Examples are the School Segregation Cases, and the extension of the fourth amendment to cover eavesdropping.

Most of the ire of proponents of the pure interpretive model has been directed against the first of these types of noninterpretive review. However the other two types are equally illegitimate, given the logic of the interpretive model. The advantage of placing a controverted case in the third rather than the first grouping is that it is usually possible to argue, with at least a shadow of plausibility, that extension of a specific constitutional prohibition really involves only the application of old norms to changed facts, and not a change in the norms themselves. *See, e.g.*, the majority opinion in Griswold v. Connecticut, 381 U.S. 479 (1965), for an implausible attempt to base a non-textual right of marital privacy on an "interpretation" of various provisions of the Bill of Rights—thus converting a Type 1 case into a "less suspect" Type 3 case.

IV. BEYOND INTERPRETATION: A PROGRAM OF INQUIRY

The uncomfortable results of adopting the interpretive model do not by themselves make a wholly satisfying argument for judicial review that goes beyond interpretation. Constitutional adjudication going beyond the norms implicit in text and original history requires its own affirmative justification. In this short Essay, I can only suggest the several levels on which this inquiry might proceed, and hint at some of the directions it might take.

A. The Question of Practical Wisdom

First, one must consider the question of the wisdom and prudence of putting—or more accurately *leaving*—in the hands of judges the considerable power to define and enforce fundamental human rights without substantial guidance from constitutional text and history. How one views this question depends largely on how one evaluates the practical results, over the long run, of the exercise of this power. Arguments about institutional competence and the general propensities of judges become relevant here. Familiar in this context is the argument made in varying forms by constitutional commentators from Alexander Hamilton to Alexander Bickel that it makes some sense to give the final—or nearly final—say over the barrier between state and individual to the "least dangerous branch," the one that possesses neither purse nor sword.[47] But much can be said the other way, particularly through assignment in the name of popular sovereignty, and through allusion to *Lochner* and its ilk.

B. The Jurisprudential Question

Second, one can ask the jurisprudential question whether as a general matter the defining and enforcing of basic rights without external textual guidance is essentially a judicial task. Judges may be fine folk, but if what they are doing when they engage in judicial review on the basis of changing and unwritten moral principles is not adjudication, then they are sailing under false colors. For they have consistently told us that judicial review is genuinely incident to their traditionally assigned task of deciding litigated cases according to law.

A rigorously positivist jurisprudence would hold that judicial decision not directed by the articulate command of a determinate external sovereign is not truly adjudication. Rather it is a species of legislation. But this sort of positivist also views the entirely traditional judicial task of common law development through case-by-case decision as a form of legislation.[48] If

---

[47] *See* The Federalist No. 78, at 504–05 (E. Earle ed.) (A. Hamilton); A. Bickel, The Least Dangerous Branch 23–28 (1962).

[48] I do not endorse this positivist analysis. It seems to me that traditional common law decision and constitutional decision according to the noninterpretive mode both can be seen as decision of cases according to law. The law in question consists of the generally accepted social norms applied in the decision of the cases, norms that are—contrary to the positivists'

common law development is an appropriate judicial function, falling within the traditionally accepted judicial role, is not the functionally similar case-by-case development of constitutional norms appropriate as well? Granted that the supremacy of constitutional law over legislation, when contrasted with the formally inferior status of common law, makes a great difference. But the difference is in the hierarchical status of the judicial decision—which turns on a question of *authority*—and not in the intrinsic nature of the task.

C. The Question of Lawful Authority

The question of authority is the third level of inquiry into the justification for noninterpretive judicial review. Even if this mode of judicial review produces good results in the eyes of some beholders, and even if it is not intrinsically unjudicial, there remains the question whether in our Constitution we have actually granted this large power to our judges.

In resolving this issue of legal authority, there seems to me only one plausible method of inquiry. We must apply the conventional and accepted categories of legal argument—original understanding, judicial precedent, subsequent history, and internal consistency—and see if they support judicial review that goes beyond interpretation.

I believe that when these tests are applied, constitutional adjudication of the sort objected to by Mr. Justice Black and the other proponents of the pure interpretive model will be seen to be a lawful and legitimate feature of our system of judicial review. Full development of the argument must await another occasion; it necessarily requires lengthy and detailed historical documentation. But a brief sketch may be useful here.[49]

For the generation that framed the Constitution, the concept of a "higher law," protecting "natural rights," and taking precedence over ordinary positive law as a matter of political obligation, was widely shared and deeply felt. An essential element of American constitutionalism was the reduction to written form—and hence to positive law—of some of the principles of natural rights. But at the same time, it was generally recognized that written constitutions could not completely codify the higher law. Thus in the framing of the original American constitutions it was

---

position—best seen as "part of the law," quite independent of their promulgation through defined lawmaking procedures. *See* Dworkin, *The Model of Rules,* 35 U.Chi.L.Rev. 14 (1967); Wellington, *Common Law Rules and Constitutional Double Standards: Some Notes on Adjudication,* 83 Yale L.J. 221 (1973).

[49] I have set out my sketch as a simple narrative, lacking the detail, the qualifications, and the analysis of conflicting evidence that the full argument requires. I have also left out any documentation, on the theory that incomplete and necessarily misleading citation of sources is worse than none at all. [For a] full-scale development of the historical argument sketched here [see Grey, *Origins of The Unwritten Constitution: Fundamental Law in American Revolutionary Thought,* 30 Stan.L.Rev. 843 (1978)].

widely accepted that there remained unwritten but still binding principles of higher law. The ninth amendment is the textual expression of this idea in the federal Constitution.

As it came to be accepted that the judiciary had the power to enforce the commands of the written Constitution when these conflicted with ordinary law, it was also widely assumed that judges would enforce as constitutional restraints the unwritten natural rights as well. The practice of the Marshall Court and of many of its contemporary state courts, and the writings of the leading constitutional commentators through the first generation of our national life, confirm this understanding.

A parallel development during the first half of the 19th century was the frequent attachment of unwritten constitutional principles to the vaguer and more general clauses of the state and federal constitutions. Natural-rights reasoning in constitutional adjudication persisted up to the Civil War, particularly with respect to property and contract rights, and increasingly involving "due process" and "law of the land" clauses in constitutional texts. At the same time, an important wing of the antislavery movement developed a natural-rights constitutional theory, built around the concepts of due process, of national citizenship and its rights, and of the human equality proclaimed in the Declaration of Independence.

Though this latter movement had little direct effect on pre-Civil War judicial decisions, it was the formative theory underlying the due process, equal protection, and privileges and immunities clauses of the 14th amendment. Section 1 of the 14th amendment is thus properly seen as a reaffirmation and reenactment in positive law of the principle that fundamental human rights have constitutional status.

The late 19th century saw the most controversial phase in our history of unwritten constitutional law, with the aggressive development by state and federal judges of constitutional principles protecting "liberty of contract" against labor regulation, and restraining taxation and the regulation of prices charged by private business. The reaction to this tendency marked the beginning of sustained intellectual and political attack on the whole concept of unwritten constitutional principles.

Politically, emergent and eventually dominant social forces continued to press for the legislation that was being invalidated under these constitutional principles. Intellectually, the 18th-century philosophical framework supporting the concept of immutable natural rights was eroded with the growth of legal positivism, ethical relativism, pragmatism, and historicism.

Under the combined assault of these social and intellectual forces, the courts retreated from the doctrines of "economic due process," abandoning them in the 1930's. However, although the more sweeping attack on the whole tradition of unwritten constitutional principles gained some important adherents within the judiciary and still more among academic critics, it did not ultimately prevail.

For at almost the same time as the doctrines protecting the laissez-faire economy were passing out of constitutional law, the judiciary began the active development of new civil libertarian constitutional rights whose protection was deemed "essential to the concept of ordered liberty"—for example, rights against state governments of freedom of speech and religion, rights to "fundamentally fair" proceedings, and rights to familial autonomy in childrearing and education.

The last generation has seen further development of constitutional rights clearly—and sometimes avowedly—not derived by textual interpretation, notably the right of privacy, the right to vote, the right to travel, and generally the rights resulting from application of "equal protection of the laws" to the federal government. The intellectual framework against which these rights have developed is different from the natural-rights tradition of the founding fathers—its rhetorical reference points are the Anglo-American tradition and basic American ideals, rather than human nature, the social contract, or the rights of man. But it is the modern offspring, in a direct and traceable line of legitimate descent, of the natural-rights tradition that is so deeply embedded in our constitutional origins.

To summarize, there was an original understanding, both implicit and textually expressed, that unwritten higher law principles had constitutional status. From the very beginning, and continuously until the Civil War, the courts acted on that understanding and defined and enforced such principles as part of their function of judicial review. Aware of that history, the framers of the 14th amendment reconfirmed the original understanding through the "majestic generalities" of section 1. And ever since, again without significant break, the courts have openly proclaimed and enforced unwritten constitutional principles.

DAVID A. STRAUSS, COMMON LAW, COMMON GROUND, AND JEFFERSON'S PRINCIPLE

112 YALE L.J. 1717 (2003).

Why do we care about the Framers of the Constitution? After all, they lived long ago, in a world that was different in countless ways from ours. Why does it matter what their views were, for any reasons other than purely historical ones? And if we don't care about the Framers, why do we care about their handiwork, the Constitution itself? It was the product of the Framers' times and the Framers' sensibilities. What possible reason can we have for allowing its provisions to rule us today? Even if the Founding generation was exceptionally visionary and enlightened, we would not allow ourselves to be ruled by even the most extraordinary group of people if they lived in another country halfway across the world today. Why do we allow ourselves to be ruled by the decisions of people who lived in a time that was, in every relevant respect, much further away than that?

These might seem to be the most academic of questions. No one seriously disputes that the Constitution is supreme law, and nearly everyone acknowledges that the views of the Framers matter to some degree. Academic or not, though, these questions are important because throughout constitutional law, the role of text and original understandings remains uncertain. Until we have tried to answer the most fundamental skeptical question—why do we care at all about the Framers?—we will not know what role the text and the original understandings should play.

The role of the text and the original understandings may be as much in dispute today as it has ever been. In some areas—federalism, the right to keep and bear arms under the Second Amendment, the Eighth Amendment's protection against cruel and unusual punishment, the Religion Clauses of the First Amendment—there is a concerted effort underway, by advocates and sometimes by judges and Justices, to make constitutional law conform more closely to what are said to be the dictates of the text and the original understandings. To what extent should the original understandings govern the interpretation of those provisions, or of the Free Speech Clause of the First Amendment, or the Fourth Amendment, or the Self-Incrimination or Just Compensation Clauses of the Fifth Amendment, or the Due Process and Equal Protection Clauses of the Fourteenth Amendment, or the structural provisions of the original Constitution? Critics have powerfully attacked the notion that constitutional interpretation can rely exclusively on the text and the original understandings; but as long as the text and original understandings play some role in constitutional interpretation—as essentially everyone agrees they must—these issues about the role of text and original understandings will remain with us, and we will have to address the fundamental question of why the Framers matter at all.

There is no agreed-upon answer to that question. It has been asked before: It was Thomas Jefferson's question at the time of the Founding. "[T]he earth belongs to the living, and not to the dead," he wrote to James Madison from Paris in 1789; [3] so how can any constitution purport to bind later generations? Jefferson was not alone in raising the question at that time—he was not even the most extreme skeptic—but his formulation was the most memorable.

The problem is that Jeffersonian skepticism is very difficult to rebut, on one level, but wholly unpersuasive on another. It is, in fact, hard for anyone

[3] Letter from Thomas Jefferson to James Madison (Sept. 6, 1789), in 15 The Papers of Thomas Jefferson 392, 396 (Julian P. Boyd & William H. Gaines, Jr., eds., 1958) [hereinafter Letter of Sept. 6, 1789].

who believes in self-government to come up with an explanation for why long-ago generations should have such a decided effect on our law today, whether they are the generation of the Founding, or the Civil War, or any other. But at the same time, Jeffersonian skepticism about the Constitution seems out of touch with the reality of our political and legal culture, or even our culture more generally. Many people revere the Constitution. Many Americans consider themselves connected, in some important way, to earlier generations. American law today seems like a chapter in a multigenerational project, and its multigenerational character is part of the reason it is valued. To many people, allegiance to the Constitution and a certain kind of respect for the Founding, and for crucial episodes in our history, are central to what it means to be an American. All of those attitudes are deeply incompatible with Jefferson's kind of skepticism, and as long as those attitudes remain widespread, Jefferson's skepticism will always seem to many to be a little like a debating point—clever and hard to answer, but somehow deeply wrong.

In this Essay, I want to address these issues in a way that responds to Jefferson—that gives a reason for paying attention to the Constitution that ought to satisfy even a Jeffersonian skeptic—but that also accommodates more deeply held views about the Constitution and American traditions, rather than dismissing those views as mysticism or ancestor worship in the way that Jefferson's skepticism seems to dismiss them. The first part of the answer to Jefferson is confession and avoidance: To a large extent, American constitutional law has developed in a way that is independent of the views of the Founding generation. Much of American constitutional law consists of precedents that have evolved in a common-law-like way, with a life and a logic of their own. But it would be a mistake to say that American constitutional law consists entirely of precedents and is independent of the text and the Framers. The text, unquestionably, and the original understandings, to a lesser degree, continue to play a significant role. We cannot escape Jefferson's question by saying that we have left the Framers behind.

The central answer to Jefferson is that the text of the Constitution provides a common ground among people, and in that way it facilitates the resolution of disputes that might otherwise be intractable. Sometimes, in the familiar formulation, it is more important that things be settled than that they be settled right, and the provisions of the Constitution settle things. The Constitution tells us how long a President's term will be, how many senators each state will have, whether there are to be jury trials in criminal cases, and many other things. Even if the rules the Constitution prescribes are not the best possible rules, they serve the very valuable function of providing an answer so that we do not have to keep reopening those issues all the time.

These justifications, as I will explain, ought to satisfy even the most iconoclastic Jeffersonian skeptic. Equally important, they fit with our current practices of constitutional interpretation. The common law and common ground justifications make sense of the way we interpret the Constitution, including aspects of our practice of constitutional interpretation that otherwise seem quite problematic. The common law and common ground justifications should therefore be acceptable to anyone who finds our current constitutional order generally acceptable, even if that person wants to reject, à la Jefferson, anything that might remotely look like ancestor worship.

But at the same time, the common law and common ground justifications do not require anyone to reject more reverential views of the Constitution and the Framers. People who believe, as some do, that the Framers were divinely inspired can accept the common law and common ground justifications; in fact, they have an especially strong reason for accepting those justifications. People who, less dramatically, see themselves as part of an ongoing American tradition that embraces earlier generations also have good reasons to accept those justifications. But people who want to debunk all of that—or who identify with other traditions, religious or ethnic traditions perhaps, that have nothing to do with the Framers—can also accept the common law and common ground justifications. The key idea here is Rawls's famous notion of the overlapping consensus. People who adhere to widely and fundamentally different belief systems, such as different religions, can nonetheless all embrace certain common principles, as can people who reject any religious belief system. That is the kind of justification that adherence to the Constitution and the original understandings requires, and the common law and common ground justifications can, I believe, provide it.

* * *

III. CONFESSION AND AVOIDANCE: THE COMMON LAW ANSWER TO JEFFERSON

The text and the original understandings unquestionably play a significant role in constitutional law, but it is far from a dominant role. Part of the answer to Jefferson's question about why we should adhere to the Framers' decisions is: Often, we don't. To a large extent our constitutional law has solved Jefferson's problem by becoming a common law system in which cases are decided on the basis of precedents, not the text. The dispute in controverted cases is over the best reading of the precedents, and—consistent with the approach common law courts have historically taken—over what is fairer or more sensible policy. The common law approach is central to many of the most important areas of constitutional law: freedom of expression, race and gender discrimination, property rights, procedural due process, federalism, capital punishment, police interrogation, the limits of congressional power, implied fundamental rights, the "case or controversy" requirement in the federal courts, state power over interstate commerce, and state sovereign immunity.

The constitutional law governing freedom of expression is an illustration. Today, this law consists of an elaborate doctrinal structure. One asks whether a restriction on speech is content-based, content-neutral, or incidental; whether the speech that is restricted is high-value or low-value; whether the measure in question is a restriction or a subsidy. Depending on the answers, there are further tests to be applied. (If the speech is incitement, a version of the "clear and present danger" test; if the speech is defamatory, a version of the standard established by *New York Times Co. v. Sullivan*;[27] and so on.) This body of doctrine is based in precedent and developed over time. The spare text of the First Amendment of course could not, by itself, generate such an elaborate set of rules, and while it is common to impute to the Framers views about freedom of expression that agree with modern conceptions, actual investigation of the Framers' views has played essentially no role in the development of the law.

The same pattern holds in all the other areas I mentioned. A lawyer who needs to learn constitutional law in an area generally learns the cases or, in some areas, the nonjudicial precedents. In one of the most active areas in recent constitutional law—the principles governing the relationship between the states and the federal government—even some of the Supreme Court's most relentless advocates of relying on the text of the Constitution have found themselves forced to concede that their conclusions are based on something other than the text.[29]

Of course, the use of precedent itself might be challenged by a Jeffersonian skeptic. The common law of England was a favorite target of Tom Paine and others who made arguments like Jefferson's. But the use of precedent is much more easily defended against such a skeptical attack than is the use of the original understandings, or even the use of the text. The practice of following precedent can be justified in fully functional terms, without relying on a controversial conception of national identity or intergenerational obligation.

To some degree, the use of precedent is simply unavoidable. Neither legal doctrine nor anything else can be created anew every day. That is a principal lesson of the failure of Jefferson's sunset solution. The work of the previous generation will, to some degree at least, inevitably be our

[27] 376 U.S. 254 (1964).

[29] See, e.g., Alden v. Maine, 527 U.S. 706, 713 (1999) (Kennedy, J., joined by Rehnquist, C.J., and O'Connor, Scalia, and Thomas, JJ.); Printz v. United States, 521 U.S. 898, 905 (1997) (Scalia, J.); Seminole Tribe v. Florida, 517 U.S. 44, 54 (1996) (Rehnquist, C.J., joined by O'Connor, Scalia, Kennedy, and Thomas, JJ.).

starting point, in law and elsewhere. To that extent, we have no choice but to follow precedent. A system of constitutional law that did not build on what has been done before may be literally inconceivable and is certainly entirely impracticable.

In addition, there are well-known justifications for the use of precedent that do not require the kind of ancestor worship that Jefferson attacked and that do not appeal to sectarian conceptions of American traditions. The most familiar justification is often (if perhaps misleadingly) called Burkean. In modern terms, the basis of this justification is that human rationality is bounded. The problems confronted by the legal system are complex and multifaceted; an individual's capacity to solve them is limited. It therefore makes sense to take seriously what has been done before, both because it may reflect an accumulation of wisdom that is not available to any one individual and because it provides a storehouse of trial-and-error information on how the problems might be solved.

These justifications for a common law approach—which relies on precedent while gradually updating it to take account of new conditions and to embody new insights—should be enough to satisfy a Jeffersonian skeptic. The common law approach does not treat past decisions as binding commands; it adheres to those decisions only because, and to the extent that, it makes good functional sense to do so. Jefferson himself seems to have recognized that such an evolutionary system would not present the problems he identified. In one of his famous later letters, in which he again endorsed periodic revisions of the Constitution, his remarks took on a common-law-like tone, endorsing a practice of "wisely yielding to the gradual change of circumstances" and "favoring progressive accommodation to progressive improvement."[34] To the very considerable extent that our constitutional law is a common law system, based on precedent rather than text, Jefferson's challenge can be met with relative ease.

IV. COMMON GROUND AND CONVENTIONALISM

Our constitutional system is not entirely a common law system, however. This is a fixed point of our legal culture. In particular, no one says that the text of the Constitution does not matter or is only advisory. You cannot make an argument for any constitutional principle without purporting to show, at some point, that the principle is consistent with the text of the Constitution. And no provision of the Constitution—even an indefensible one (like the requirement that a President be a natural born citizen)—can be overruled in the way a precedent can.

On many important issues, the text is followed exactly, even when substantial arguments can be made that the judgments reflected in the text

[34] [Letter from Thomas Jefferson to Samuel Kercheval (July 12, 1816), in Thomas Jefferson, Writings 1395, 1401 (Merrill D. Peterson ed., 1984).]

have been superseded. No one seriously suggests that the age limits specified in the Constitution for Presidents and members of Congress should be interpreted to refer to other than chronological (earth) years because life expectancies now are longer, that a President's term should be more than four years because a more complicated world requires greater continuity in office, or that states should have different numbers of senators because they are no longer the distinct sovereign entities they once were. This seems to reintroduce Jefferson's puzzle. Why do we universally accept that the words written by earlier generations are binding?

The answer is that we accept those words, not because we acknowledge the authority of earlier generations over us, but because they serve as common ground in the way I described earlier. This matters, potentially greatly, because it affects how we interpret these words in controversial cases. For Jefferson's reason, the objective of interpretation is not—and should not be—"fidelity," in any meaningful sense, to the people who drafted or adopted the Constitution. Their judgments, including the judgments reflected in the words they adopted, are entitled to respectful consideration as precedents, but no more; and we have overridden their judgments on a number of important issues. Rather, the objective, in interpreting the text, is to make sure that the text can continue to serve as common ground. This can be called the conventionalist justification for relying on the text. The text serves as a convention, a focal point of agreement.

* * *

Our Constitution is, in certain important ways, very well designed to serve as common ground. It is sometimes objected that the conventionalist justification is too cold-blooded: It seems to reduce the Constitution from being a quasi-sacred document, the product of the Framers' genius, to being a desiccated focal point. If this were true, then the conventionalist justification might be another sectarian account, not something that can serve as part of an overlapping consensus among different conceptions of American citizenship. But it is by no means an implication of conventionalism that the Constitution is "merely" a focal point. On the contrary, it takes a certain kind of genius to construct a document that uses language specific enough to resolve some potential controversies entirely and to narrow the range of disagreement on others, but also uses language general enough not to force on a society outcomes that are so unacceptable that they discredit the document.

The genius of the Constitution is that it is specific where specificity is valuable, general where generality is valuable—and that it does not put us in unacceptable situations that we can't plausibly interpret our way out of. There is reason to think the Framers were self-conscious about this, for example in their elliptical (albeit doomed) treatment of slavery in the original document. Edmund Randolph gave essentially this advice to the Committee on Detail at the Constitutional Convention: "[T]he draught of a fundamental constitution," he said, should include "essential principles only; lest the operations of government should be clogged by rendering those provisions permanent and unalterable, which ought to be accommodated to times and events."[41]

Our political culture today seems to have internalized the requirements of conventionalism: that there is a time for specificity in the Constitution, but there is also a time for generality that will allow interpretive flexibility in the future. People seem to recognize, for example, that when constitutional amendments address large-scale problems, they should be written in general terms; it is commonly said that the Constitution should not be "cluttered up" with amendments that are too specific or that respond too narrowly to particular current controversies. But at the same time, we are willing to add highly specific amendments to the Constitution, such as the Twenty-Fifth Amendment, providing for presidential disability, or the Twentieth Amendment, specifying the dates when the President will be inaugurated and Congress will convene.

One important implication of conventionalism is that this choice between generality and specificity is a crucial constitutional decision. That is why originalism is, despite its pretensions, inconsistent with the true genius of the Constitution. At least this is so if originalism means that whenever the text of a constitutional provision is unclear, the understandings of those who adopted the provision will govern until the provision is formally amended. That approach takes provisions that the Framers left general and makes them specific. The drafters and ratifiers of the First Amendment may well have thought that blasphemy could be prohibited; the drafters and ratifiers of the Fourteenth Amendment thought that racial segregation and gender discrimination were acceptable. Had the amendments said those things, in terms that could not be escaped by subsequent interpreters, our Constitution would work less well today.

But the text does not express those specific judgments. As a result, instead of having to read the First or Fourteenth Amendments out of the Constitution, we are able to read our own content into them—following a common law approach—and then use those provisions, interpreted in that way, to enhance the prestige of the Constitution as a whole. That, in turn, more thoroughly entrenches the specific, focal provisions of the Constitution. The Constitution as a whole commands allegiance more readily when the Equal Protection Clause is interpreted to outlaw state-enforced

---

[41] See Supplement to Max Farrand's The Records of the Federal Convention of 1787, at 183 (James H. Hutson ed., 1987).

segregation rather than in the way the ratifiers of that Clause understood it. Making the general provisions specific, as originalists would, undoes this ingenious project.

* * *

Someone who believes that being an American means joining an ongoing tradition that began with the Framers can—indeed, should—fully embrace the common law and common ground justifications. The common law approach provides a way to understand the idea of an ongoing American tradition. The common ground approach can be understood to assert precisely that one thing Americans have in common is allegiance to the text of the Constitution. The skeptic would adhere to the text (in the way required by the common ground argument) just because it is useful and fair to do so. People with more elaborate views about the provenance of the Constitution will have other reasons for adhering to the text. But those people can also fully endorse the common ground arguments without feeling that they must regard their more elaborate views about American traditions as irrational. Those more elaborate views just give them additional, strong reasons to endorse the common ground arguments.

The common law and common ground justifications might, of course, require some people to modify views they hold about the Constitution. Someone who believed that the Framers were divinely inspired would find much to accept in the common law and common ground accounts, but—depending on exactly what it means to be divinely inspired—might have to forgo some claims, as well. The common law and common ground accounts do not justify an uncritical adherence to the original understandings, for example. But for two reasons, it is acceptable for the common law and common ground accounts to require people to modify their understandings of the Constitution, so long as those accounts allow room for a wide range of conceptions of American traditions and American identity and do not require skepticism of Jefferson's kind.

First, the common law and common ground justifications provide reasons to adhere to the Constitution that can be, and should be, accepted by everyone. To go beyond those justifications is to impose a particular quasi-ethnic (or quasi-religious) conception of American identity. That should not be the basis for governing a diverse liberal society. People are entitled to hold such a conception of American identity and not to have their views disparaged, but people cannot insist that others comply with that conception. They can insist that others go as far as the common law and common ground justifications dictate, but they cannot insist on more.

Second, the common law and common ground accounts are consistent with current practices in the way that a more thoroughgoing commitment to the original understandings, for example, is not. As I have said, much of current constitutional law conforms to the common law model. Someone who wanted to reject the common law model in favor of an original understanding approach not only would be relying on a sectarian justification but would be overturning important and thoroughly settled constitutional principles about race and gender discrimination, freedom of expression, and a number of other subjects. * * *

* * *

Finally, there is an issue that is not currently controverted but that could arise, were the Constitution to be amended again. Even Jefferson did not deny that the current generation may govern itself. But the common law and common ground views do not seem to leave any room for that. Does the Austinian view—that the Constitution is, in some sense, a legitimate command that people are obligated to obey—have any remaining significance?

All the provisions of our Constitution that give rise to litigation are quite old. In recent years there appear to have been no significant cases decided under any amendment more recent than the Twenty-First, added in 1933. (There was litigation under the Twenty-Fourth Amendment, outlawing poll taxes, soon after its adoption, but such litigation seems unlikely to recur, at least on a large scale.) As a result, constitutional law today does not really illustrate the intertemporal nature of interpretation. Everything is more than a generation old, however generations are counted; the common law and common ground justifications for obedience therefore predominate.

But things do not have to remain that way. If an amendment were added to the Constitution, the Austinian justification could reassert itself, for a time. In virtually every session of Congress, for example, a constitutional amendment is proposed that would specify, in one way or another, that "voluntary prayer" is to be permitted in the public schools. It is generally understood that the purpose of such an amendment is to overrule a series of Supreme Court decisions beginning with *School District v. Schempp*,[81] which held that it was unconstitutional for a public school to conduct teacher-led devotional Bible reading in the classroom. Under *Schempp* and other decisions, the fact that a student could leave the classroom during the prayer was not enough to make the practice constitutional.

Suppose such a constitutional amendment were adopted, after a debate in which it was generally acknowledged that the purpose of the amendment was to overrule the Supreme Court's decisions. How should a court, or any other conscientious official (or citizen) interpret such an amendment? The answer to this question should change over time.

---

[81] 374 U.S. 203 (1963). The development began with Engel v. Vitale, 370 U.S. 421 (1962).

Immediately after the amendment was adopted, it seems clear that the correct interpretation of the amendment would be that it permits school prayer of the kind banned by Schempp. This is true even though the text, read in isolation, does not compel such a result. It is certainly plausible to say that school prayer of that kind is not "voluntary." Indeed, that is probably the best way to understand the basis of the Supreme Court's decisions (although it is not quite what the opinions said). But if the public debate on the amendment proceeded on the assumption, generally shared by all involved, that the issue was whether the Court's decision should be overruled, then it seems quite clear that it would be wrong for the courts or anyone else to interpret the amendment differently. In those circumstances, seizing on the term "voluntary" to produce a different result immediately after the amendment was adopted would be a kind of trickery, an action taken in bad faith.

If this is so, then one consequence is that originalism is, to a degree, rehabilitated from various attacks other than Jefferson's. Obviously there will be some problems in asserting that "everyone knows" or "everyone understood" that the purpose of the amendment was to overrule *Schempp*. Some people, somewhere, might not have understood that. In fact, during the debate some people would undoubtedly have made the argument that the amendment, as drafted, did not accomplish the effect the drafters sought, because it referred only to "voluntary" prayer. But it would still be possible for people living at the time to say, with confidence, that the provision was generally understood to overrule *Schempp*. To that extent, one of the common criticisms of originalism—that it is impossible in principle to identify an original understanding—seems mistaken.

Over time, though, the interpretation of a voluntary prayer amendment could appropriately change. For Jefferson's reason, it would be acceptable for an interpreter to say, a few decades down the road, that although teacher-led school prayer was considered "voluntary" when the amendment was adopted, we have now come to understand, in the light of experience, that such prayer is never really voluntary, and that therefore the amendment should be understood only to allow prayer that is not officially sponsored. This would be inconsistent with the original understanding of the amendment, but consistent with its language. Such an explicit reversal and rejection of the acknowledged original intent might seem jarring. But this is, in substance, no different from the most generally accepted justification for *Brown v. Board of Education*.[82] At one time it was thought that school segregation was consistent with equality; now we understand otherwise. * * * The hypothetical school prayer amendment would be different to the extent that it reversed an earlier Supreme Court decision, and this would be

[82]See, e.g., Planned Parenthood v. Casey, 505 U.S. 833, 863 (1992) (plurality opinion) (discussing *Brown*).

an additional reason for caution in moving away from the original understanding of the amendment. But otherwise the cases are parallel.

The justification for such a break with original understandings would have to be, as usual, a common law one. One would have to show that, even giving due deference to the judgment of those who adopted the provision, the conclusion they reached should now be overturned. That showing would be easier to make if there were a progression of cases in which the criterion of "voluntariness," understood to permit school prayer, became more and more difficult to apply and was gradually eroded. In any event, one could not say that the language was irrelevant; under the hypothetical amendment, if school prayer were to be banned, it would have to be on the basis of an argument that was consistent with the text in some way.

One problem, of course, would be to identify the point at which a court would be justified in abandoning the original intentions—the point comparable to Jefferson's nineteen years. Obviously this cannot be done with precision. The problem of defining this point is less severe than it might seem—less severe than it was for Jefferson, who had to choose an expiration date—because the text continues to be honored (for conventionalist reasons), and even the original understanding has the force of a precedent. And as with many things in a common law system, the judgment will depend on factors that cannot be reduced to a rule: not just the passage of time but the extent to which circumstances have changed or new facts have emerged, the difficulty in administering the old rule in contested cases, and so on. The one thing that seems clear is that the interpretation of legal provisions cannot remain static. That is one overriding lesson of Jefferson's principle.

RICHARD A. POSNER, PRAGMATIC ADJUDICATION

18 Cardozo L. Rev. 1, 2–5, 9–15, 16, 18 (1996).

[I want to consider] whether adjudication—particularly appellate adjudication—can or should be pragmatic.

The issue is at once spongy and, for me at least, urgent. It is spongy because "pragmatism" is such a vague term. Among the Supreme Court Justices who have been called "pragmatists" are Holmes, Brandeis, Frankfurter, Jackson, Douglas, Brennan, Powell, Stevens, White, and now Breyer;[3] others could easily be added to the list. Among theorists of adjudication, the label has been applied not only to those who call themselves pragmatists, of whom there are now quite a number, but also to Ronald Dworkin,[5] who calls pragmatism, at least Rorty's conception of

[3]See, e.g., Daniel A. Farber, *Reinventing Brandeis: Legal Pragmatism for the Twenty-First Century*, 1995 U. Ill. L. Rev. 163.

[5]See Richard Rorty, *The Banality of Pragmatism and the Poetry of Justice*, in Pragmatism in Law and Society 89 (Michael Brint & William Weaver eds., 1991).

pragmatism, an intellectual meal fit only for a dog[6] (and I take it he does not much like dogs). Some might think the inclusion of Frankfurter in my list even more peculiar than the inclusion of Dworkin. But it is justified by Frankfurter's rejection of First Amendment absolutism, notably in the flag-salute cases, and by his espousal of a "shocks the conscience" test for substantive due process. This is a refined version of Holmes's "puke" test—a statute or other act of government violates the Constitution if and only if it makes you want to throw up. Can it be an accident that Frankfurter announced his test in a case about pumping a suspect's stomach for evidence?[8]

[I]

[P]ragmatic adjudication will have to be defended—pragmatically—on its own terms * * *. But what exactly is to be defended? I do not accept Dworkin's definition: "[t]he pragmatist thinks judges should always do the best they can for the future, in the circumstances, unchecked by any need to respect or secure consistency in principle with what other officials have done or will do."[13] That is Dworkin the polemicist speaking. But if his definition is rewritten as follows—"a pragmatist judge always tries to do the best he can do for the present and the future, unchecked by any felt *duty* to secure consistency in principle with what other officials have done in the past"—then I can accept it as a working definition of the concept of pragmatic adjudication. On this construal the difference between, say, a judge who is a legal positivist in the strong sense of believing that the law is a system of rules laid down by legislatures and merely applied by judges, and a pragmatic judge, is that the former is centrally concerned with securing consistency with past enactments, while the latter is concerned with securing consistency with the past only to the extent that such consistency may happen to conduce to producing the best results for the future.

II

What does the pragmatic approach to judging entail? What are the pros and cons (pragmatically evaluated, of course)? And is it, on balance, the right approach for judges to take?

Consider, to begin with, the differences in the way the judicial positivist and the judicial pragmatist might weight or order the materials bearing on the decision of a case. By "judicial positivist" I mean a judge who believes not only that the positivist account of law is descriptively

[6]Ronald Dworkin, *Pragmatism, Right Answers, and True Banality*, in Pragmatism in Law and Society, supra note 5, at 359, 360.

[8]Rochin v. California, 342 U.S. 165 (1952).

[13]Ronald Dworkin, Law's Empire 161 (1986).

accurate—that the meaning of law is exhausted in positive law—but also that the positivist account *should* guide judicial decision-making, in the strong sense that no right should be recognized or duty imposed that does not have its source in positive law. * * * The judicial positivist would begin and usually end with a consideration of cases, statutes, administrative regulations, and constitutional provisions—all these and only these being "authorities" to which the judge must defer in accordance with Dworkin's suggestion that a judge who is not a pragmatist has a duty to secure consistency in principle with what other officials have done in the past. If the authorities all line up in one direction, the decision of the present case is likely to be foreordained, because to go against the authorities would—unless there are compelling reasons to do so—violate the duty to the past. The most compelling reason would be that some other line of cases had adopted a principle inconsistent with the authorities directly relevant to the present case. It would be the judge's duty, by comparing the two lines and bringing to bear other principles manifest or latent in case law, statute, and constitutional provision, to find the result in the present case that would promote or cohere with the best interpretation of the legal background as a whole.

The pragmatist judge has different priorities. That judge wants to come up with the best decision having in mind present and future needs, and so does not regard the maintenance of consistency with past decisions as an end in itself but only as a means for bringing about the best results in the present case. The pragmatist is not uninterested in past decisions, in statutes, and so forth. Far from it. For one thing, these are repositories of knowledge, even, sometimes, of wisdom, and so it would be folly to ignore them even if they had no authoritative significance. For another, a decision that destabilized the law by departing too abruptly from precedent might have, on balance, bad results. There is often a trade-off between rendering substantive justice in the case under consideration and maintaining the law's certainty and predictability. This trade-off, which is perhaps clearest in cases in which a defense of statute of limitations is raised, will sometimes justify sacrificing substantive justice in the individual case to consistency with previous cases or with statutes or, in short, with well-founded expectations necessary to the orderly management of society's business. Another reason not to ignore the past is that often it is difficult to determine the purpose and scope of a rule without tracing the rule to its origins.

The pragmatist judge thus regards precedent, statutes, and constitutions both as sources of potentially valuable information about the likely best result in the present case and as signposts that must not be obliterated or obscured gratuitously, because people may be relying upon them. But because the pragmatist judge sees these "authorities" merely as sources of information and as limited constraints on his freedom of decision, he does not depend upon them to supply the rule of decision for the truly novel case. For that he looks also or instead to sources that bear directly on the wisdom of the rule that he is being asked to adopt or modify.

* * *

III

I want to examine a little more systematically the objections to the pragmatic approach to judging. One objection to inviting the judge * * * to stray beyond the boundaries of the orthodox legal materials of decision is that judges are not trained to analyze and absorb the theories and data of social science. The example of Brandeis is not reassuring. Although Brandeis was a brilliant man of wide intellectual interests, his forays into social science—whether as advocate or as judge—were far from an unqualified success. Indeed, most social scientists today would probably agree that Brandeis's indefatigable industry in marshaling economic data and viewing them through the lens of economic theory was largely misguided. It led him to support (and to try to make a part of the law) such since discredited policies as limiting women's employment rights, fostering small business at the expense of large, and encouraging public utility and common carrier regulation. Holmes * * * had reservations about the reliability of social scientific theories, but his unshakable faith in the eugenics movement, an early twentieth-century product of social and biological theory, undergirds his most criticized opinion (incidentally one joined by Brandeis)—*Buck v. Bell.*[20] One of the deformities of the majority opinion in *Roe v. Wade* is the opinion makes it seem that the issue of abortion rights is a medical one and that the reason for invalidating state laws forbidding abortion is simply that they interfere with the autonomy of the medical profession—a "practical" angle reflecting Justice Blackmun's long association with the Mayo Clinic. The effects of abortion laws on women, children, and the family, which are the effects that are important to evaluating the laws, are not considered.

A second and related objection to the use of nonlegal materials to decide cases is that it is bound often to degenerate into "gut reaction" judging. I think that this appraisal is basically correct—provided the phrase "gut reaction" is taken figuratively rather than literally—but that the word "degenerate" is too strong. Cases do not wait upon the accumulation of some critical mass of social scientific knowledge that will enable the properly advised judge to arrive at the decision that will have the best results. The decisions of the Supreme Court in the area of sexual and reproductive autonomy, for example, came in advance of reliable,

[20] 274 U.S. 200, 207 (1927) ("three generations of imbeciles are enough.")

comprehensive, and accessible scholarship on sexuality, the family, and the status of women. The Court had to decide whether capital punishment is cruel and unusual punishment at a time when the scientific study of the deterrent effects of capital punishment was just beginning. When the Court decided to redistrict the nation according to the "one man, one vote" principle it cannot have had a clear idea about its effects, on which political scientists still do not agree more than thirty years later. * * * When judges try to make the decision that will produce the "best results," without having any body of organized knowledge to turn to for help in making that decision, it seems they must rely on their intuitions.

The fancy term for the body of bedrock beliefs that guide decision is natural law. Does this mean that the pragmatic approach to adjudication is just another version of the natural law approach? I think not. The pragmatist does not look to God or other transcendental sources of moral principle to validate his departures from statute or precedent or other conventional "sources" of law. He does not have the confidence of secure foundations and this should make him a little more tentative, cautious, and piecemeal in imposing his vision of the Good on society in the name of legal justice. If Holmes really thought he was applying a "puke" test to statutes challenged as unconstitutional rather than evaluating those statutes for conformity with transcendental criteria, it would help explain his restrained approach to constitutional adjudication. On the other hand, a pragmatic Justice such as Robert Jackson, who unlike Holmes had a rich background of involvement in high-level political questions, was not bashful in drawing upon his extrajudicial experience for guidance to the content of constitutional doctrine.[22] The pragmatic judge is not always a modest judge.

The reason that using the "puke" test or one's "gut reactions" or even one's pre-judicial high-governmental experiences to make judicial decisions sounds scandalous is that the legal profession, and particularly its academic and judicial branches, want the added legitimacy that accrues to the decisions of people whose opinions are grounded in expert knowledge. The expert knowledge of another discipline is not what is wanted, although it is better than no expert knowledge at all. Both the law professor and the judge feel naked before society when the positions they take on novel

---

[22]Quite the contrary. As he said in his famous concurrence in the steel-seizure case,

> That comprehensive and undefined presidential powers hold both practical advantages and grave dangers for the country will impress anyone who has served as legal adviser to a President in time of transition and public anxiety. While an interval of detached reflection may temper teachings of that experience, they probably are a more realistic influence on my views than the conventional materials of judicial decision which seem unduly to accentuate doctrine and legal fiction.

Youngstown Sheet & Tube Co. v. Sawyer, 343 U.S. 579, 634 (1952) (Jackson, J., concurring).

cases—however carefully those positions are dressed up in legal jargon—are seen to reflect unstructured intuition based on personal and professional (but nonjudicial) experiences, and on character and temperament, rather than on disciplined, rigorous, and articulate inquiry.

Things are not quite so bad as that. It is not as if American judges were chosen at random and made political decisions in a vacuum. Judges of the higher American courts are generally picked from the upper tail of the population distribution in terms of age, education, intelligence, disinterest, and sobriety. They are not tops in all these departments but they are well above average, at least in the federal courts because of the elaborate pre-appointment screening of candidates for federal judgeships. Judges are schooled in a profession that sets a high value on listening to both sides of an issue before making up one's mind, on sifting truth from falsehood, and on exercising a detached judgment. Their decisions are anchored in the facts of concrete disputes between real people. Members of the legal profession have played a central role in the political history of the United States, and the profession's institutions and usages reflect the fundamental political values that have emerged from that history. Appellate judges in nonroutine cases are expected to express as best they can the reasons for their decision in signed, public documents (the published decisions of these courts); this practice creates accountability and fosters a certain reflectiveness and self-discipline. None of these things guarantees wisdom, especially since the reasons given for a decision are not always the real reasons behind it. But at their best, American appellate courts are councils of wise elders and it is not completely insane to entrust them with responsibility for deciding cases in a way that will produce the best results in the circumstances rather than just deciding cases in accordance with rules created by other organs of government or in accordance with their own previous decisions, although that is what they will be doing most of the time.

Nor do I flinch from another implication of conceiving American appellate courts in the way I have suggested: these courts will tend to treat the Constitution and the common law, and to a lesser extent bodies of statute law, as a kind of putty that can be used to fill embarrassing holes in the legal framework. Such an approach is not inevitable. In the case of property rights in oil and gas, a court could take the position that it had no power to create new rules and must therefore subsume these newly valuable resources under the closest existing rule, the rule governing wild animals. It might even take the position that it had no power to enlarge the boundaries of existing rules, and in that event no property rights in oil and gas would be recognized until the legislature created a system of property rights for these resources. Under this approach, if Connecticut has a crazy law (as it did until *Griswold v. Connecticut* struck it down) forbidding married couples to use contraceptives, and no provision of the Constitution limits state regulation of the family, the crazy law will stand until it is repealed or the Constitution amended to invalidate it. Or if the Eighth Amendment's prohibition against cruel and unusual punishments has reference only to the *method* of punishment or to the propriety of punishing at all in particular circumstances (for example, for simply being poor, or an addict), then a state can with constitutional impunity sentence a sixteen-year old to life imprisonment without possibility of parole for the sale of one marijuana cigarette—which in fact seems to be the Supreme Court's current view,[25] one that I find very difficult to stomach. I do not think a pragmatic Justice of the Supreme Court *would* stomach it, although he or she would give due weight to the implications for judicial caseloads of bringing the length of prison sentences under judicial scrutiny, and to the difficulty of working out defensible norms of proportionality. The pragmatic judge is unwilling to throw up his hands and say "sorry, no law to apply" when confronted with outrageous conduct that the Constitution's framers neglected to foresee and make specific provision for.

Oddly, this basic principle of pragmatic judging has received at least limited recognition by even the most orthodox judges in the case of statutes. It is accepted that if reading a statute the way it is written would produce absurd results, the judges may in effect rewrite it.[26] Most judges do not put it quite this way—they say statutory interpretation is a search for meaning and Congress can't have meant the absurd result—but it comes to the same thing. And, at least in this country, common law judges reserve the right to "rewrite" the common law as they go along. I am merely suggesting that a similar approach, prudently employed, is the pragmatic approach to constitutional adjudication as well.

I do not belittle the dangers of the approach. People can feel very strongly about a subject and be quite wrong. Certitude is not the test of certainty. A wise person realizes that even his unshakable convictions may be wrong—but not all of us are wise. In a pluralistic society, moreover, which America seems to be more and more every year, a judge's unshakable convictions may not be shared by enough other people that he can base a decision on those convictions and be reasonably confident it will be accepted. So the wise judge will try to check his convictions against those of some broader community of opinion, as suggested by Holmes in his dissent in *Lochner*. It was not irrelevant, from a pragmatic standpoint, to the outcome of *Brown v. Board of Education* that official racial segregation had been abolished outside the South and bore a disturbing resemblance to Nazi racial laws. It was not irrelevant to the outcome of *Griswold v. Connecticut*

---

[25]See Harmelin v. Michigan, 501 U.S. 957 (1991).

[26]See, e.g., Burns v. United States, 501 U.S. 129, 136–37 (1991); Green v. Bock Laundry Mach. Co., 490 U.S. 504, 527 (1989) (Scalia, J., concurring).

that, as the Court neglected to mention, only one other state (Massachusetts) had a similar law. If I were writing an opinion invalidating the life sentence in my hypothetical marijuana case I would look at the punishments for this conduct in other states and in the foreign countries, such as England and France, that we consider in some sense our peers. If a law could be said to be contrary to world public opinion I would consider this a reason, not compelling but not negligible either, for regarding a state law as unconstitutional even if the Constitution's text had to be stretched a bit to cover it. The study of other laws, or of world public opinion as crystallized in foreign law and practices, is a more profitable inquiry than trying to find some bit of eighteenth-century evidence that maybe the framers of the Constitution wanted courts to make sure punishments prescribed by statute were proportional to the gravity, or difficulty of apprehension, or profitability, or some other relevant characteristic of the crime. If I found such evidence I would think it a valuable bone to toss to a positivist or formalist colleague but I would not be embarrassed by its absence because I would not think myself duty-bound to maintain consistency with past decisions.

I would even think it pertinent to the pragmatic response to my hypothetical marijuana case to investigate or perhaps even just to speculate (if factual investigation proved fruitless) about the psychological and social meaning of imprisoning a young person for his entire life for the commission of a minor crime. What happens to a person in such a situation? Does he adjust? Deteriorate? What is the likely impact on his family, and on the larger society? How should one feel as a judge if one allows such a punishment to be imposed? And are these sentences "for real," or are preposterously severe sentences soon commuted? Could it be that the deterrent effect of so harsh a sentence will be so great that the total number of years of imprisonment for violation of the drug laws will be reduced, making the sacrifice of this young person a utility-maximizing venture after all? Is utility the right criterion here? Is the sale of marijuana perhaps far more destructive than some ivory-tower judge or professor thinks? Do judges become callous if a large proportion of the criminal cases they review involve very long sentences? Need we fear that if a defendant appealed who received "only" a five-year sentence the appellate judge's reaction would be: "Why are you complaining about such a trivial punishment?"

The response to the hypothetical case of the young man sentenced to life for selling marijuana is bound in the end to be an emotional rather than a closely reasoned one because so many imponderables enter into that response, as my questions were intended to indicate. But emotion is not pure glandular secretion. It is influenced by experience, information, and imagination, and can thus be, to some extent anyway, disciplined by fact.

Indignation or disgust founded on a responsible appreciation of a situation need not be thought a disreputable motive for action, even for a judge; it is indeed the absence of any emotion in such a situation that would be discreditable. It would be nice, though, if judges and law professors were more knowledgeable practitioners or at least consumers of social science (broadly defined to include history and philosophy), so that their "emotional" judgments were better informed.

* * *

The greatest danger of judicial pragmatism is intellectual laziness. It is a lot simpler to react to a case than to analyze it. The pragmatic judge must bear in mind at all times that he is a judge and that this means he must consider all the legal materials and arguments that can be brought to bear upon the case. If legal reasoning is modestly defined as reasoning with reference to distinctive legal materials such as statutes and legal doctrines and to the law's traditional preoccupations, for example with stability, the right to be heard, and the other "rule of law" virtues, then it ought to be an ingredient of every legal decision, though not necessarily the decision's be-all and end-all. Just as some people think an artist must prove he is a competent draftsman before he can be taken seriously as an abstract artist, so I believe that a judge must prove—anew in every case—that he is a competent legal reasoner before he can be taken seriously as a pragmatic judge.

* * *

If intellectual laziness is a danger of pragmatic adjudication, and I think it is, it is also a danger of not being pragmatic. The conventional judge is apt not to question his premises. If he thinks that "hate speech" is deeply harmful, or that banning hate speech would endanger political liberty, he is not likely to take the next step, which is to recognize that he may be wrong and to seek through investigation to determine whether he is wrong. The deeper the belief—the closer it lies to our core values—the less likely we are to question it. Our disposition will be not to question but to defend. As Pierce and Dewey emphasized, doubt rather than belief is the spur to inquiry; and doubt is a disposition that pragmatism encourages, precisely in order to spur inquiry. One reason that attitudes toward hate speech are held generally as dogmas rather than hypotheses—one reason that so little is known about the actual consequences of hate speech—is that a pragmatic approach has not been taken to the subject.

BIBLIOGRAPHY

Interpreting the Constitution: General

Bobbitt, P., CONSTITUTIONAL FATE (1982).

Bobbitt, P., CONSTITUTIONAL INTERPRETATION (1991).

Fallon, R., IMPLEMENTING THE CONSTITUTION (2001).

Farber, D. and Sherry, S., DESPERATELY SEEKING CERTAINTY: THE MISGUIDED QUEST FOR CONSTITUTIONAL FOUNDATIONS (2002).

Greenawalt, *The Enduring Significance of Neutral Principles,* 78 Colum.L.Rev. 982 (1978).

Komesar, *Back to the Future—An Institutional View of Making and Interpreting Constitutions,* 81 Nw.U.L.Rev. 191 (1987).

Michelman, *The Supreme Court, 1985 Term—Foreword: Traces of Self-Government,* 100 Harv.L.Rev. 4 (1986).

Sherry, *Judges of Character*, 38 Wake Forest L.Rev. 793 (2003).

Tushnet, M., THE NEW CONSTITUTIONAL ORDER (2003).

Young, *Judicial Activism and Conservative Politics*, 73 Colo.L.Rev. 1139 (2002).

Wechsler, *Toward Neutral Principles of Constitutional Law,* 73 Harv.L.Rev. 9 (1959).

Originalism

Ackerman, *Robert Bork's Grand Inquisition* [reviewing R. Bork, THE TEMPTING OF AMERICA: THE POLITICAL SEDUCTION OF THE LAW (1990)], 99 Yale L.J. 1419 (1990).

Berger, R., GOVERNMENT BY JUDICIARY (1977).

Dorf, *The Case of Original Meaning*, 85 Geo.L.J. 1857 (1997).

Dworkin, *The Forum of Principle,* 56 N.Y.U.L.Rev. 469 (1981).

Farber, *Disarmed by Time: The Second Amendment and the Failure of Originalism*, 76 Chi.-Kent L.Rev. 167 (2000).

Farber, *The Originalism Debate: A Guide for the Perplexed,* 49 Ohio St.L.J. 1085 (1989).

Flaherty, *History "Lite" in Modern American Constitutionalism*, 95 Colum.L.Rev. 523 (1995).

Fleming, *We the Unconventional American People*, 65 U.Chi.L.Rev. 1513 (1998).

Gedicks, *Conservatives, Liberals, Romantics: The Persistent Quest for Certainty in Constitutional Interpretation*, 50 Vand.L.Rev. 613 (1997).

Klarman, *Constitutional Fact/Constitutional Fiction: A Critique of Bruce Ackerman's Theory of Constitutional Moments,* 44 Stan.L.Rev. 759 (1992).

Maltz, *Some New Thoughts on an Old Problem—The Role of the Intent of the Framers in Constitutional Theory,* 63 B.U.L.Rev. 811 (1983).

Monaghan, *Our Perfect Constitution,* 56 N.Y.U.L.Rev. 353 (1981).

Nelson, *History and Neutrality in Constitutional Adjudication,* 72 Va.L.Rev. 1237 (1986).

Nelson, *Originalism and Interpretive Conventions*, 70 U. Chi.L.Rev. 519 (2003).

Powell, *The Original Understanding of Original Intent,* 98 Harv.L.Rev. 885 (1985).

Powell, *Rules for Originalists,* 73 Va.L.Rev. 659 (1987).

Rakove, J., ORIGINAL MEANINGS: POLITICS AND IDEAS IN THE MAKING OF THE CONSTITUTION (1996).

Scalia, A., A MATTER OF INTERPRETATION: FEDERAL COURTS AND THE LAW (1997).

Segall, *A Century Lost: The End of the Originalism Debate*, 15 Const.Comm. 411 (1998).

Simon, *The Authority of the Framers of the Constitution: Can Originalist Interpretation Be Justified?,* 73 Calif.L.Rev. 1482 (1985).

Solum, *Originalism as Transformative Politics,* 63 Tulane L.Rev. 1599 (1989).

Textualism

Amar, *Intratextualism*, 112 Harv.L.Rev. 747 (1999).

Balkin & Levinson, *Constitutional Grammar*, 72 Texas L.Rev. 1771 (1994).

Black, C., STRUCTURE AND RELATIONSHIP IN CONSTITUTIONAL LAW (1969).

Calabresi, *The Tradition of the Written Constitution: A Comment on Professor Lessig's Theory of Translation,* 65 Fordham L.Rev. 1435 (1997).

Greene, *Discounting Accountability,* 65 Fordham L.Rev. 1489 (1997).

Klarman, *Antifidelity,* 70 S. Cal.L.Rev. 381 (1997).

Lessig, *Understanding Changed Readings: Fidelity and Theory,* 47 Stan.L.Rev. 395 (1995).

Levinson, *Translation: Who Needs It?,* 65 Fordham L.Rev. 1457 (1997).

Schauer, *An Essay on Constitutional Language,* 29 UCLA. L.Rev. 797 (1982).

Symposium, *Interpretation,* 58 S.Cal.L.Rev. (1985).

Symposium, *Textualism and the Constitution*, 66 Geo.Wash.L.Rev. 1085 (1998).

Vermeule and Young, *Hercules, Herbert, and Amar: The Trouble with Intratextualism*, 113 Harv.L.Rev. 730 (2000).

Winter, *Indeterminacy and Incommensurability in Constitutional Law*, 78 Cal.L.Rev. 1441 (1990).

Evolutionary Approaches

Aleinikoff, *Constitutional Law in the Age of Balancing,* 96 Yale L.J. 943 (1987).

Alexander, *Constrained by Precedent,* 63 S.Cal.L.Rev. 1 (1989).

Corwin, *The "Higher Law" Background of American Constitutional Law,* 42 Harv.L.Rev. 149, 365 (1928–29).

Eisgruber, C., CONSTITUTIONAL SELF-GOVERNMENT (2001).

Farber, *Reinventing Brandeis: Legal Pragmatism for the 21st Century*, U.Ill.L.Rev. 163 (1995).

Farber, *The Inevitability of Practical Reason: Statutes, Formalism, and the Rule of Law,* 45 Vand.L.Rev. 533 (1992).

Farber, *Legal Pragmatism and the Constitution*, 72 Minn.L.Rev. 1331 (1988).

Grey, *Judicial Review and Legal Pragmatism*, 38 Wake Forest L.Rev. 473 (2003).

Grey, *Origins of the Unwritten Constitution: Fundamental Law in American Revolutionary Thought,* 30 Stan.L.Rev. 843 (1978).

Lawson, *The Constitutional Case Against Precedent*, 17 Harv.J.L. & Pub. Pol'y 23 (1994).

Monaghan, *Stare Decisis and Constitutional Adjudication*, 88 Colum.L.Rev. 723 (1988).

Nichol, *Children of Distant Fathers: Sketching an Ethos of Constitutional Liberty,* 1985 Wis.L.Rev. 1305.

Perry, M., THE CONSTITUTION, THE COURTS, AND HUMAN RIGHTS (1982).

Posner, R., LAW, PRAGMATISM, AND DEMOCRACY (2003).

Rehnquist, *The Notion of a Living Constitution,* 54 Tex.L.Rev. 693 (1976).

Richards, *Human Rights as the Unwritten Constitution: The Problem of Change and Stability in Constitutional Interpretation,* 4 U.Dayton L.Rev. 295 (1979).

Schauer, *Precedent,* 39 Stan.L.Rev. 571 (1987).

Sherry, *The Founders' Unwritten Constitution,* 54 U.Chi.L.Rev. 1127 (1987).

Strauss, *The Irrelevance of Constitutional Amendments*, 114 Harv.L.Rev. 1457 (2001).

Sunstein, C., ONE CASE AT A TIME: JUDICIAL MINIMALISM ON THE SUPREME COURT (1998).

Symposium, *The Revival of Pragmatism*, 18 Cardozo L.Rev. 1–180 (1996).

Chapter III

JUDICIAL REVIEW

Marbury v. Madison continues to be viewed as one of the central texts in constitutional law, because it establishes the principle of judicial review. At the same time, *Marbury* is regularly subjected to scathing criticism in introductory constitutional law classes. It is commonplace to note that alternative interpretations of the Judiciary Act of 1789 and Article III of the Constitution were available to Chief Justice Marshall, interpretations that would have avoided holding the statute unconstitutional. Indeed, some suggest that John Marshall should have recused himself from the case because of his involvement in the underlying events. Finally, it is fairly easy to show that while Marshall's opinion admirably establishes the supremacy of the Constitution, it does not adequately demonstrate that the Supreme Court must be the final interpreter of what the Constitution means.[1]

Poking holes in Supreme Court opinions is the mainstay of scholarly work and classroom discussion. But finding fault with *Marbury v. Madison* is not merely sport or a demonstration of legal acuity. *Marbury* is the fount of the Supreme Court's role in explicating constitutional law. To say that the case rests on unsteady legal foundations may be to undermine two centuries of judicial review.

Part A begins by considering some critical perspectives on judicial review. The classic criticism, articulated by Jeremy Waldron, is that judicial review impairs democratic self-government. Waldron considers, but rejects, what he considers to be the most plausible rebuttal to this criticism, which is that judicial review provides a form of pre-commitment through which the public can protect itself from ill-advised future actions. Girardeau Spann also argues that judicial review impairs democratic politics, but he puts a different spin on this argument. Rather than arguing that judicial review interferes with majority rule, he argues that it really

[1]For elaborations of these and other familiar criticisms of the opinion in *Marbury,* see Van Alstyne, *A Critical Guide to* Marbury v. Madison, 1969 Duke L.J. 1., and Sanford Levinson, *Why I do Not Teach* Marbury *(Except to Eastern Europeans) and Why You Shouldn't Either*, 38 Wake Forest L.Rev, 553 (2003). For a defense of *Marbury*, see Louise Weinberg, *Our* Marbury, 89 Va.L.Rev. 1235 (2003).

tends to favor majority interests, distracting minority groups from more vigorous use of the political process. Finally, Mark Tushnet explores some alternatives to the American version of judicial review. These alternatives allow courts to make determinations of unconstitutionality but give the legislature the final word on statutory validity. Tushnet raises questions about the long-term viability of these alternatives, but you should consider whether they would provide the benefits of judicial review at lower cost.

Part B explores several attempts by scholars to provide a firmer foundation for judicial review, and to test the limits of the practice. The justifications are "non-textual"; that is, they rely not on the specific language of the Constitution (compare Marshall's partial reliance on the Supremacy Clause and the Oath Clause[2]), but rather on the structure of government created by the Constitution, the principles and purposes that underlie the Constitution, democratic theory, or functional considerations. We consider four such efforts.

1. Charles Black's defense of judicial review derives from the theory of limited powers that underlies our political system. In order to maintain the legitimacy of government, some institution must be authorized to decide whether or not governmental action transgresses constitutional limits. Black suggests that an independent, precedent-respecting, learned tribunal could best carry out this function. Not surprisingly, he views the Supreme Court as such an institution.

2. Alexander Bickel argues that, due to the counter-majoritarian nature of judicial review, the practice can be justified only if it serves a function that is (a) distinct from legislative and executive activities and (b) consistent with the basic democratic principles upon which our system of government is based. He identifies that function as the identification and protection of "enduring values."

3. Rebecca Brown thinks that Bickel's notion of the "counter-majoritarian difficulty" has haunted modern constitutional scholarship to its detriment. She argues that the idea of democratic accountability has been wrongly rendered as meaning that representatives should reflect the preferences of their electorates. Brown suggests that accountability is better understood as a structural feature of our "constitutional architecture" that serves the protection of liberty (like judicial review).

4. Michael Seidman argues that the key function of judicial review is to undo political settlements of issues, especially when those settlements exclude individuals holding certain viewpoints. By providing a forum in

---

[2]Herbert Wechsler also offers a largely textual justification for judicial review in *Toward Neutral Principles of Constitutional Law,* 73 Harv.L.Rev. 1, 2–5 (1959). For a historical defense of judicial review, see Daniel Farber, *Judicial Review and its Alternatives: An American Tale*, 38 Wake Forest L.Rev. 415 (2003).

which politically excluded viewpoints can seek reconsideration, he contends, judicial review provides disaffected political minorities with reasons to remain connected with political society.

Part C turns to the issue of judicial supremacy. Judicial review (in its American version) dictates that courts have the ultimate authority to determine the constitutionality of a particular statute or executive action. But this may or may not mean that others—executives, legislatures, and voters—should regard the Court's opinions as definitively settling the meaning of the Constitution in future cases. Larry Alexander and Frederick Schauer provide an argument in favor of granting the Court this form of authority. They also consider a variety of criticisms of their position. In contrast, Lawrence Sager offers a caution against confusing our theory of judicial review with our theory of what the Constitution means. There are times when courts will decline to invalidate unconstitutional laws—because of doubts about their own competence, respect for separation of powers, concerns about federalism, and similar reasons. When they do, Sager says, other institutions of government may still be obliged to give the full measure of respect to the Constitution's directions. Finally, Larry Kramer makes a broader argument that constitutional meaning is also the domain of popular institutions, whose views should receive judicial respect.

A. CRITICAL VIEWS

JEREMY WALDRON, BANKING CONSTITUTIONAL RIGHTS: WHO CONTROLS WITHDRAWALS?

52 ARK.L.REV. 533–549, 556, 561 (1999).

People who deal with compulsive gambling know that one of the worst things for a problem gambler is the ready availability of cash twenty-four hours a day from automated teller machines (ATMs), using either a bank card to access one's checking account or, still worse, a credit card to access cash advances. Gamblers tell terrible stories of having run through all their savings and having accumulated thousands of dollars of credit card debt in a single night at a casino. It is in the interests of casino operators to facilitate this, and of course they do. In August 1996, casino regulators in Atlantic City voted to allow players to purchase chips or slot tokens using their credit cards or ATM cards right at the table. They do not even need to walk out to the lobby to use a cash machine: they can buy more chips to chase their losses right then and there in the heat of the moment. Of course, the New Jersey Council on Compulsive Gambling opposed the change. I guess they thought there was something valuable in preserving that long walk to the cash machine: indeed why not put it out in the parking lot, so that one has to walk out in the dark and the cold, away from the crowds, the light, and the glamour that are feeding one's gaming frenzy?

There are other safeguards of course. Eventually, the ATM machine will decline one's request for more cash, as the gambler exhausts his funds or his line of credit. * * * Some banks even allow customers to set for themselves a lower-than-usual limit—$100 or even $50. If they ever want more money than that, they have to present a check at a teller window at a branch of the bank. Such a customer will have the consolation, as he curses the machine at the casino, that the lower limit was actually set by him—in a cool hour—and not by the bureaucrats at the bank.

My topic in this lecture is not gambling or banking law or the law relating to automated teller machines. What I have said about gambling, ATMs, and daily limits is a metaphor for the real topic I want to address: constitutional constraints, particularly the constraints on legislation laid down in the Bill of Rights. I want to examine a particular theory of those constraints—a theory that assimilates them to self-imposed limitations like the lower daily limit we imagined a compulsive gambler securing for himself at the bank.

Constitutional constraints come in all shapes and sizes. Some of them represent what we might call the due process of legislation: to enact a law, the legislature must go through certain specified steps, like first and second readings, hearings, committee stages, notifications that a vote will be held, and so on. These procedural requirements are rather like the 'grammar' of legislation. Unless there were some such requirements to frame a procedure, there would be nothing that counted formally as 'passing a law.' They are like the requirements for the ATM example that you actually have to insert your card the right way up and key in your personal identification number (PIN) and the amount you want to withdraw, before you can actually get any cash. Other constitutional requirements flow over from the grammatical structure of legislation to the imposition of safeguards: bicameral structures slow things down, and the requirement of the president's or the governor's consent (or a super-majority override) adds an extra layer of protection. An analogy might be the following: if I deposit a check at the ATM and then ask to withdraw money, the machine will cue me to re-enter my PIN, as a safeguard. And then there are substantive constraints, like those imposed by the First Amendment[.]

* * *

In countries that do not allow legislation to be invalidated [by courts], the people themselves can decide by ordinary legislative procedures whether they want an established church, laws prohibiting pornography, flag-burning, the expression of racial hatred, or laws protecting celebrities from press intrusion. If they disagree about it, they may deliberate both directly and through their representatives, and settle the matter finally by voting. In the United States, with its system of constitutional constraints, the people do not have that power: they are disabled constitutionally from settling matters like these for themselves. Any decision they reach by popular or representative democratic procedures will be checked against formulas that have been pre-ordained for issues of this sort, and struck down if the members of an unelected and unaccountable tribunal decide that they do not match up.

No one can properly take pride in our constitutional arrangements without confronting this difficulty, and without trying to develop a theory or an explanation which reconciles the ideal of democratic self-government with our system of constitutional constraint. We are proud of our constitution; but we are also proud of our democratic ideals: 'Here, the people rule.' And we want the two to fit more comfortably together.

The image with which we began—the compulsive gambler and his own pre-set ATM limit—seems to offer us a way of effecting this reconciliation. The gambler draws $100 out of his account, loses it at the tables, and tries to withdraw another $100. The machine informs him that he has several thousand in his account, but it refuses to give him any more of it. At the time, he feels this as a frustration, a limit on his freedom, an impediment blocking his access to that which is rightfully his. But on reflection, he reminds himself that it was he who went to the bank and asked for the lower withdrawal limit, and that he did this as part of a process of taking control of his life, not as a way of submitting blindly to external coercion. It feels like a constraint at the moment it kicks in. But in fact it is a precommitment, something that he has entered into himself. In just the same way, a chronic over-sleeper with a weakness for the 'snooze' button may place his alarm clock out of reach on the other side of the bedroom; a smoker may hide his cigarettes; and a heavy drinker may give his car keys to a friend at the beginning of a party with strict instructions not to return them when they are requested at midnight. It is not just we moderns who have to do this, to combat our fin de siecle self-indulgence: in the Odyssey, we are told that Ulysses decided that he should be bound to the mast of his boat in order to resist the charms of the Sirens, and he instructed his crew that, 'if I beg you to release me, you must tighten and add to my bonds.'

* * *

So, similarly, it may be said, a whole people may decide collectively to bind themselves in advance to resist the siren charms of rights-violations. Aware, as much as the gambler, of the temptations of wrong or irrational action, the people as a whole in a lucid moment may put themselves under certain constitutional disabilities—disabilities which serve the same function in relation to democratic values as are served by ATM withdrawal limits in relation to the gambler's autonomy. The gambler does not really want to draw out the rest of his money. Ulysses does not really want to leap over the side of the boat and swim to the Sirens. The drinker does not really want to drive under the influence of alcohol at the end of the party. The mechanisms they adopt enable them to secure the good that they really want and avoid the evil which, occasionally despite themselves, they really want to avoid. Similarly, the people do not really want to restrict free speech, abridge press freedom, or set up an established church. They are aware, however, that on occasion they may be panicked into doing something like this. So they take precautions in advance, instituting legal constraints as safeguards to prevent them from doing in a moment of fever what in their cooler, more thoughtful moments they are sure they do not want to do.

* * *

It is a plausible and attractive model, and it holds out a promise of reconciling constitutional constraint and democratic self-government in an illuminating way. It does not try to explain away the tension. As in the case of our gambler, we acknowledge the existence of constraint at the moment when the decision in question is being made: the people or their legislative representatives will feel limited and frustrated when the courts strike down their enactments. It will seem to them at that moment as though they are not really their own masters. But when they reflect on how we came to have a constitution, they will understand these constraints as an aspect of their self-mastery, not as a derogation of it.

I believe that this is the most promising case that can be made for representing constitutional constraints as ultimately compatible with democracy. But is it a watertight case? I fear it is not; and in the rest of this article, I would like to explore some of its more obvious difficulties.

* * *

But of course we disagree even in our lucid moments about what counts in politics as pathological. What one man calls 'greed,' another will call 'entitlement.' What one party calls 'envy,' another will call 'social justice.' And what one faction calls 'rage' or 'panic,' another will call 'righteous anger' or 'prudence.' In the previous paragraph, I said that the history of political thought is replete with warnings against the irrationality of democratic politics. But those warnings are themselves contested: are they wise and appropriate cautions or are they self-serving ideological denunciations dressed up in the garb of precommitment? That contestation is as fierce in the area of constitutional framing as it is anywhere in politics. Ideologues have a habit of branding one another's proposals as 'crazy,' not merely 'inadvisable' or 'wrong.' (Indeed, in the culture generally, 'You're crazy' has become increasingly the standard way of expressing straightforward disagreement.) Now, the precommitment model of constitutional constraints offers a huge pay-off to any group that can get such a characterization of its opponent's policies accepted in the community: if the policies it opposes can be stigmatized in advance as crazy, then putting a constraint in place now to prevent their being implemented later, even if they acquire majority support, can be represented as a triumph for and not an abrogation of democracy. I wonder, therefore, whether it is altogether wise to take akrasia—pathological weakness, craziness—as our model for the circumstances in which the imposition of a constitutional constraint is appropriate.

All this is reinforced by our understanding of the way in which constitutional constraints are actually framed and operated. In most cases the situation looks something like this: there is a vehement disagreement in the community about a particular type of political proposal, X. (X may be 'the introduction of paper money,' 'the abolition of trial by jury,' 'the permitting of school prayer' or whatever.) Opponents of X routinely stigmatize its supporters as crazy and irrational: their support for X is taken in itself to be conclusive evidence of their irresponsibility, corruption, or incapacity for thinking straight in politics. Needless to say the supporters of X repudiate these imputations (some no doubt tossing them back at their opponents).

One day (Day 1) the opponents of X become aware that their side happens to have achieved a very large measure of popular support. Opportunists that they are, they take advantage of this temporary ascendancy to commit the society (by a supermajority) to some vaguely-worded constitutional constraint, which they hope will have the effect of excluding any policy of type X. Most opponents of X support the constraint, but not all: some think that it is ill-advised to settle this by constitutional, rather than ordinary, political means. And most supporters of X oppose the constraint, because they don't think that X or anything like it ought to be ruled as crazy in this way. But again, not all do: some vote for the constraint because they think it may be vague enough to let some version of X through, and they favor the formulation on grounds unrelated to X.

Some years later (Day 2), the balance of political forces has changed. The legislature passes a measure which is a version of X, and which therefore arguably violates the constraint imposed on Day 1. The legislative measure is supported by a majority of representatives (and their constituents), some of them longtime supporters of X, who never accepted its stigmatization (on Day 1) as crazy; others new converts to the cause of X, who are now persuaded that something they used to think crazy is in fact eminently sane. They are all aware that the bill before them is arguably unconstitutional. But they vote for it anyway, some because they do not believe the constitutional text actually covers the current version of X, others because they oppose the constitutional constraint and always have.

A little later still (Day 3), the validity of the legislation is challenged and the issue comes before the society's highest court. The court, deciding by a simple majority, holds that the legislature's enactment is unconstitutional. Four out of the nine judges argue, however, in dissent, that the legislation should not be struck down. They maintain that the interpretation of the constraint that would be required to sustain a finding of unconstitutionality is implausible, mainly on the ground that such interpretation would make the relevant constitutional provision quite unattractive from a moral political point of view. Needless to say, their brethren on the bench do not agree with this.

Now, it is important to emphasize that the disagreement among the judges on Day 3 inevitably involves a disagreement about the rationality or irrationality of proposal X. It is probably not the whole of the judges' disagreement: maybe they also dispute the meanings of words in the constitutional provision and the historical facts about original intent on Day 1. But interpretive questions almost always end up engaging the interpreter's own substantive convictions as well, if only because one way of discrediting an interpretation is to show that it makes the text under consideration look completely wrong-headed. Thus, if two judges disagree about whether proposals like X are crazy or irrational, then they are likely to disagree about whether the particular version of X under consideration is prohibited by the constraint. The constraint is clearly meant to be a prophylactic against craziness in this sort of area, i.e., the sort of area in which questions about X arise. Someone who thinks that X is crazy will think, then, that an interpretation of the constraint that does not cover X is patently absurd. Others who think X is sane will regard any interpretation which precludes X as evidently unacceptable. The issue of the craziness of X, then, will be part of what the judges have to decide on Day 3.

But of course that is also exactly what the members of the legislature were disagreeing about on Day 2 when they voted on the bill. They were debating (and voting on) the merits—the sanity or craziness—of the type X proposal. And it was also one of the focuses of disagreement among the people when the constitutional provision was originally adopted on Day 1. It is the same disagreement all the way through, though the weight of opinion has shifted back and forth over time: a supermajority of the people against X on Day 1; a simple majority of their legislative representatives in favor of X on Day 2; and a simple majority of judges back in the original direction again on Day 3. (This of course is what we should expect when a complex and highly charged moral issue is put in slightly different forms to somewhat different constituencies for decision at different times.)

I cannot see why anyone should think that a narrative like this is appropriately modeled by the hypothetical case of the gambler or the story of Ulysses and the Sirens. Our gambler was in no doubt about wanting to limit his ATM withdrawals; and when he came up against the machine's obduracy, he could recognize that as exactly the steadfastness he was trying to create for himself. Similarly with the story from the Odyssey. Ulysses was sure that he wanted to hear, but not respond to, the Sirens' song; the people in our constitutional example are torn. If Ulysses were somehow to untie himself and get ready to dive over the side of the boat and swim to the Sirens, it would be clear to his crew that this was exactly the action he commanded them to restrain; but in most constitutional cases, opinions differ among the citizens as to whether the legislation in question is the sort of thing they wanted (or would or should have wanted) in a founding moment to pre-empt. What is more, all the judges and all the legislators know in our constitutional example that the issue they are facing is one on which reasonable people disagree, whereas in the Odyssey the crew members know for certain that Ulysses' straining at his bonds is the product of a decisional pathology that is perfectly well understood by everyone involved, including Ulysses.

* * *

Clearly there are dangers in any simplistic analogy between the rational autonomy of individuals and the democratic governance of a community. The idea of a society binding itself against certain legislative acts in the future is problematic in cases where members disagree with one another about the need for such bonds, or if they agree abstractly about the need, but disagree about their content or character. It is particularly problematic where such disagreements can be expected to persist and to develop and change in the community in unpredictable ways. And it becomes ludicrously problematic in cases where the form of precommitment is to assign the decision, procedurally, to another body whose members are just as torn and just as conflicted about the issue as the members of the first body were.

If, moreover, the best explanation of these persisting disagreements is that the issues the society is addressing are themselves very difficult issues, then we have no justification whatever for regarding the temporary ascendancy of one or other party to the disagreement as an instance of full and rational precommitment on the part of the entire society. In these circumstances the logic of precommitment must be simply put aside, and we must leave the members of the community to work out their differences and, if necessary, to change their minds back and forth in collective decision-making over time, the best way they can.

* * *

Early in our tradition, political theorists developed a taxonomy of various forms of constitution, of which the most familiar is the Aristotlean distinction between government by one man, government by a few men, and government by the many. The distinction was not necessarily a matter of whose will was to prevail in a society. According to Aristotle, the distinction was needed even in a society ruled by law, since the application of law required judgment and there was a question about who should apply the laws. Judgment foreshadows disagreement, and in politics the question is always how disagreements among the citizens are to be resolved. It is, I think, important to remember that this includes disagreements about rights and justice and thus disagreements about the things covered by the abstract moral principles to which the people have committed themselves in their constitution. Different forms of government amount to different answers to the question: whose judgment is to prevail when citizens disagree in their judgments about matters as important as this?

Now there may be good reasons for the people to offer as their answer to this question: 'Not us, or our representatives, but the judiciary.' But if that is their answer, it amounts pro tanto to a refusal of self-government. * * *

Of course such a system is not wholly aristocratic, for the few best are to exercise their judgment on the interpretation and application of principles which, initially at any rate and in their most general form, are chosen by the people. The fact that authority is accorded to the people's choice as to which abstract principles are to be considered by the judges makes this a mixed Constitution. Nevertheless the aristocratic nature of the arrangement is not diminished by the fact that the judicial 'aristocrats' are exercising judgment rather than will. For in our best understanding, politics is always a matter of judgment, even at the most abstract level. The democratic claim is that the people are entitled to govern themselves by their own judgments. So, to the extent that we invest the unelected and unaccountable judiciary with an overriding power of judgment as to how something as basic as equal protection is to be understood, allowing that judgment to override the judgment of the people or their representatives on this very issue, it is undeniable that in terms of the Aristotlean taxonomy we have set up what would traditionally be described as a non-democratic arrangement.

Under these circumstances, then, the constitutional arrangements we have been discussing cannot really be regarded as a form of autonomous precommitment by a person A ('We, the People. . .') on Day 1 to a decision (for Day 2) which A itself has chosen. They are not like the gambler's precommitment: his own decision locked into a machine. Instead our constitutional arrangements involve a form of submission by A on Day 1 to whatever judgment is made on Day 3 by another person, B, in the application of very general principles which A has instructed B to take into account.

What follows from the difficulties of the precommitment model? What do we learn from the failure of this way of characterizing constitutional rights? Does it mean we should give up the institution of constitutional rights and judicial review?

That is certainly not what I intend. For one thing, there may be other good arguments for this institution, besides the argument we have been examining. One does not undermine institutions like the Bill of Rights and judicial review simply by undermining the force of this precommitment characterization. It was a promising gambit, and its failure is a disappointment, albeit, as I shall suggest in a moment, an instructive one. But as any logician will tell you, it is a fallacy to think that a position is falsified simply because one particular argument for it is discredited.

Anyway, it is, I think, a mistake to approach legal or jurisprudential argument purely in terms of the bottom line, purely in terms of what we should change or abolish or close down if the argument is correct. I am not urging us in this lecture to give anything up. At most, I would urge some reconsideration of the spirit in which this practice—to which the United States is undoubtedly committed—should be understood. For it matters not only whether we have judicial review, but how we engage in it (as advocates, lawyers, law professors and judges). In what spirit should we participate in this practice? A spirit of moral certainty? Or a spirit of hesitation and humility? What should be the ethos of constitutional constraint and judicial review? What place should they have in judicial culture, lawyerly culture, the culture of our law schools, and political culture generally? And then there is the issue of the rest of the world. Should we trumpet our constitutional practice abroad—try and sell it to the English and the New Zealanders and for all I know the Hungarians and the Bosnians, as the epitome of a good political procedure? Or should we be a little more troubled than that, thinking perhaps that this is our institution which we have a responsibility to make the best of, but that other countries may quite properly consider different arrangements for addressing this problematic cusp between genuine disagreement about rights and dysfunctional or pathological majority decisions.

GIRARDEAU A. SPANN, PURE POLITICS

88 MICH.L.REV. 1971, 1975, 1990–94, 2012–17 (1990).

I. MAJORITARIAN JUDICIAL REVIEW

The traditional model of judicial review, which emanates from the Supreme Court decision in *Marbury v. Madison,* is premised upon the belief that the Court is capable of performing its adjudicatory function in a countermajoritarian manner. The viability of this countermajoritarian model ultimately rests upon the ability of doctrinal principles to constrain judicial discretion in a manner sufficient to prevent domination of the judicial process by the majoritarian preferences embodied in the socialized values of individual justices. However, the level of judicial discretion inescapably entailed in the process of principled adjudication seems to preclude continued adherence to the countermajoritarian assumption. In fact, that discretion actually implicates the Court in the majoritarian exploitation of minority interests, rather than permitting it to serve as the guardian of minority rights. * * *

* * *

Majoritarian preferences reside in the socialized attitudes and values of Supreme Court justices, and they find expression in the exercise of judicial discretion. Although a justice may be prompted by the formal safeguards of life tenure and salary protection consciously to guard against majoritarian influences, such efforts cannot be effective against the unconscious operation of those influences. Moreover, the operational safeguard of principled adjudication cannot guard effectively against majoritarianism because many legal principles incorporate majoritarian preferences into their meanings. In addition, the ambiguity inherent in both the selection and application of governing principles is too great to permit the principles to serve as meaningful constraints on the exercise of judicial discretion. Rather than protecting minority interests from majoritarian abrogation, as envisioned by the traditional model of judicial review, the Supreme Court appears actually to serve the function of advancing majority interests at minority expense, while operating behind the veil of countermajoritarian adjudication. Assuming that the traditional model has in fact failed, racial minorities must consider novel strategies to deal with the essentially majoritarian nature of the Court.

II. RACE AND POSITIVE POLITICS

Contemporary minority attraction to judicial review has been premised on the belief that the Framers' political safeguards against factionalism could not adequately protect the interests of racial minorities who would effectively be under-enfranchised by their discrete and insular character.[57] Moreover, the substantial dilution of the structured safeguards during the New Deal eliminated any effectiveness they may have had initially. Reexamination of these assumptions in light of the majoritarianism inherent in judicial review, however, suggests that, whatever their defects, the political safeguards hold more promise for contemporary racial minorities than continued reliance on judicial review. * * *

* * *

In a contest between competing societal interests that is ultimately to be judged by political considerations, minorities might well prefer to compete in an arena that is openly political, rather than one from which political concerns nominally have been excluded. In an overtly political process,

[57] See J. Ely, [Democracy and Distrust] 77–88, 145–70 (describing representation-reinforcement theory of judicial review).

minority interests will receive whatever degree of deference their innate strength can command, subject only to limitations in the bargaining and organizational skills of minority politicians. In a positive sense, therefore, the overt political process is pure. Outcomes are determined by counting votes, with no need to consider the reasons for which those votes were cast. The process purports to be nothing more than what it is—a pluralistic mechanism for generating binding results. Although rhetorical principles may accompany the solicitation of political support, the principles themselves are inconsequential. No one cares much about their content, and their meaning is measured only by the extent to which their rhetorical invocation proves to be effective.

For racial minorities, the overt political process has two attractions. First, the political process is definitionally immune from distortion because it has essentially no rules that can be violated. In the film *Butch Cassidy and the Sundance Kid,* Butch Cassidy prevailed in a knife fight over one of his adversaries by exploiting the absence of formal rules. Butch first suggested that he and his adversary needed to clarify the rules of the knife fight. As the adversary—put off-guard by Butch's suggestion—protested that there were no such things as "rules" in a knife fight, Butch kicked the adversary very hard in a very sensitive part of his anatomy. With this one action, Butch was able both to establish the truth of the proposition being asserted by his adversary and to capitalize on that proposition in order to win the fight.

As a positive matter, the pure political process is nothing more than the process of casting and counting votes. Outcomes cannot be right or wrong, nor can they be just or unjust. They are simply the outcomes that the process produces. Although outcomes may be determined by how the issues are framed, how support for those issues is secured, and even by who is permitted to vote, minorities should not be distracted by considerations relating to whether the process is operating fairly. The process simply works the way it works. What minorities should focus on is how best to maximize their influence in that process. Minority participation in pluralist politics can, of course, take the form of voting, running for office, or making campaign contributions, but it is not limited to those forms of involvement. Minority participation can also take the form of demonstrations, boycotts and riots. Although such activities may be independently illegal, for purposes of positive politics their significance is limited to their potential for increasing or decreasing political strength. This is not to say that no rules at all govern the positive political process. Operative rules determine which strategies will increase and which will decrease political power. However, the operative rules are not only too complex and contingent to permit them to be articulated accurately, but those rules need never be articulated, because the selective responsiveness of the political process itself will promote adherence to those rules without regard to the accuracy of their formal expression. The process of positive politics—like a knife fight—cannot be distorted because it has no formal rules. In addition, the operative rules that do govern the process tend to be self-enforcing.

The second attraction of the overt political process is that it permits minorities to assume ultimate responsibility for their own interests. [T]here are inherent limits on the political strength of any interest group. Within those limits, however, positive politics gives minorities themselves control over the degree to which minority interests are advanced. Minorities determine how important it is for minorities to engage in political activity; minorities determine how much political activity is appropriate; and minorities decide what minority priorities should be in selecting among competing political objectives. Positive politics gives minorities both the credit for minority advances and the blame for minority failures. By thus promoting minority self-determination, positive politics elevates minority dignity and self-esteem in a way that is likely to be of more long-term significance than minority success in advancing any particular interest.

The politics inherent in the process of judicial review is of a different order. Where the overt political process is transparent and unassuming, the Supreme Court political process is opaque and pretentious. The Court requires its political bargaining to be conducted in the vernacular of legal principle, and its referenda to be cloaked in the mantle of reasoned deliberation. Moreover, because judicial convention requires the justices to camouflage the political preferences that ultimately govern their applications of principle, political negotiation with the Court is haphazard and imprecise. Judicial opinions must be deciphered for clues regarding the concessions for which a justice will commit his or her vote. And once a commitment is made, members of the Court are largely impervious to any leverage through which future fidelity to that commitment could be enforced. Unlike the positive political process that is effectively immune from distortion, the Supreme Court process is itself a distortion that renders the outcomes of ordinary politics uncertain. Because it is the Court rather than the pluralist process that has the final say over which of the competing political interests will prevail, it is the Court, rather than the affected minority group, that retains ultimate control over the fate of the minority group's interests.

The positive reasoning that permits one to conceive of the overt political process as immune from the possibility of distortion also makes it possible to characterize the Supreme Court political process in such terms. However, this does not undermine the reasonableness of a minority preference for a simple process that does not involve the Supreme Court over a complex process that does. Less experienced players can master more easily the skills required for effective participation in a simple process than acquire the skills demanded of a complex process. A preference for simplicity is particularly sensible if complexities are differentially beneficial to participants depending on whether they wish to maintain or to change the status quo. Supreme Court political complexity creates just such a differential benefit, working to the disadvantage of minorities who typically wish to alter rather than preserve the socioeconomic status quo.

The Supreme Court adjudicatory process is political, but its political dimensions are complex and obscure. Even though every interest group competing for Supreme Court endorsement will be burdened similarly by the complexities of the Supreme Court process, a rational minority response to those complexities nevertheless would be to prefer the candor and elegance of representative politics. Pluralist politics is, of course, no panacea. Its historical loss of favor reflects genuine grounds for concern. Nevertheless, pluralist negotiation offers more to minorities than continued reliance on judicial review. * * *

MARK TUSHNET, NEW FORMS OF JUIDICIAL REVIEW AND THE PERSISTENCE OF RIGHTS- AND DEMOCRACY-BASED WORRIES

38 WAKE FOREST L.REV. 813–815, 820–835, 837–838 (2003).

Two models of constitutionalism were on offer in the last century. One was the so-called Westminster model of parliamentary supremacy, in which democratically elected legislatures had power unconstrained by anything other than the cultural presuppositions embedded in a majority's will. The other was the United States ("U.S.") model of constrained parliamentarianism, as Bruce Ackerman has labeled it.[2] In this model, the legislature's powers are limited by the terms of a written constitution that courts will enforce. Each model promoted some values of liberal constitutionalism and raised worries about others. The Westminster model maximally advanced democratic self-governance, but made it possible for empowered democratic majorities to violate rights that liberal systems should protect. The U.S. model gave the courts a wide-ranging power to invalidate legislation on the ground that the legislation violated those rights, but made it possible for reckless courts to interfere needlessly with policy choices democratic majorities should be allowed to make.

For all practical purposes, the Westminster model has been withdrawn from sale. This Article examines some aspects of the situation that have resulted. Do the versions of liberal constitutionalism presently available do an acceptable job of reconciling empowered democracy with protected rights? First, I describe what I call strong-form judicial review, for which

---

[2]Bruce Ackerman, *The New Separation of Powers*, 113 Harv.L.Rev. 633, 664-87 (2000) (describing some components of some systems of constrained parliamentarianism). I use the somewhat more graceful term parliamentarism here.

the United States provides the primary example. Strong-form judicial review generated a set of debates over judicial activism and judicial restraint, which threaten to reproduce themselves in newer systems of constrained parliamentarism. * * * Weak-form systems hold out the promise of protecting liberal rights in a form that reduces the risk of wrongful interference with democratic self-governance.

* * *

Every constitution-maker in the past generation has adopted some form of constrained parliamentarism, and at present Australia and New Zealand provide the only significant examples of nations committed to something even approaching the Westminster model.[5] For years, the only real alternative to parliamentary supremacy appeared to be U.S.-style strong-form judicial review. Strong-form judicial review generated its own debate, this one between advocates of what was labeled judicial restraint and what was labeled judicial activism. Advocates of judicial restraint argued that restrained courts would interfere with democratic self-governance only when doing so was truly necessary; advocates of judicial activism argued that a more aggressive posture was necessary to ensure that liberal rights were protected. The extended U.S. experience, coupled with the force of the U.S. example in worldwide constitutional deliberations, has produced debates over activism and restraint in constitutional systems that have moved toward constrained parliamentarism.

* * *

The [Canadian] "notwithstanding" clause provides the most studied example of weak-form judicial review, and the one with which there has been the most experience. [Subject to some exceptions, Canadian parliaments may reenact statutes that courts have previously held unconstitutional, but the reenactment must say that it is being adopted "notwithstanding" the constitutional provision in question.] There are other types of weak-form review, however. Stephen Gardbaum has identified

---

[5]Even this has to be qualified. Australia's High Court does enforce the federalist limitations on legislative power in the nation's constitution, and has toyed with doctrines that would allow it to enforce some human rights on the ground that the written constitution's commitment to government responsible to the people presupposes such rights. Austl. Capital Television Proprietary, Ltd. v. Australia (1992) 177 C.L.R. 106, 107–08 (Austl.) (invalidating a campaign finance law as inconsistent with Australia's constitutional commitment to representative government); Lange v. Austl. Broad. Corp. (1997) 189 C.L.R. 520, 520–21 (Austl.) (limiting Australian Capital Television Proprietary, Ltd.). As for New Zealand, James Allan has argued perhaps a bit too forcefully that New Zealand's judges have made that nation's Human Rights Act, which on its face simply instructs judges to interpret statutes to be consistent with basic human rights, into a document that gives judges authority to displace legislative authority quite broadly. See, e.g., James Allan, *The Effect of a Statutory Bill of Rights Where Parliament is Sovereign: The Lesson from New Zealand*, in Sceptical Essays on Human Rights 375 (Tom Campbell et al. eds., 2001).

several, which he calls the "new Commonwealth model" of constitutionalism.[25] The "new Commonwealth model" consists of instructions to courts that they should construe legislation whenever fairly possible to be consistent with constitutional norms, without giving them the power to displace legislation that, once interpreted, is inconsistent with those norms. Gardbaum identifies the possibility that there may be a variety of types of judicial review, lying along a continuum measuring the strength of the judicial role relative to that of the legislature.

The weakest form within the "new Commonwealth model" is the pure interpretive requirement, for which the New Zealand Bill of Rights Act is the prime example. Here courts are charged only with the new interpretive task. The British Human Rights Act 1998[28] is a somewhat stronger version. It directs courts to interpret statutes in a manner that makes them consistent with the European Convention on Human Rights ("the Convention"), if such a construction is possible. Courts unable to do so may declare the statute incompatible with the Convention. The minister responsible for the statute's enforcement is then authorized to invoke a fast-track procedure for enacting a new statute that would be compatible with the Convention or even, in special circumstances, to place in force a revised statute pending its enactment by Parliament.

That the pure interpretive requirement is a form of judicial review can be seen by comparing what happens to a statute in a system without such a requirement to what happens in a system with one. Suppose the courts, without an interpretive requirement, routinely interpret statutes according to their plain language on the theory that the statute's language is the surest guide to the purposes the legislature sought to achieve. That is, the courts say, in effect, "You told us what you wanted to do in the statute's plain language, and that's what we will do." Add on the interpretive requirement, and the courts say something quite different:

> The language of this statute tells us what you wanted to do, but if we did that you would be violating constitutional norms. You've also told us that you don't want to do that. So, we'll interpret the statute to be consistent with constitutional norms, even though that leads us to enforce a statute that does something other than what the statutory language says you wanted to do. Weak-form judicial review in the form of an interpretive mandate gives the courts an effect on policy that

[25]Stephen Gardbaum, *The New Commonwealth Model of Constitutionalism*, 49 Am.J.Comp.L. 707, 710 (2001). I prefer to use the more general label weak-form for the variants Gardbaum describes, largely because I do not think that there is an intrinsic connection between the form of review and the fact that the nations that have adopted weak-form systems of judicial review are, or were, members of the British Commonwealth.

[28]Human Rights Act, 1998, c. 42 (Eng.).

is different from the effect they have using their traditional methods of statutory interpretation.

* * *

Accustomed to strong-form judicial review, U.S. scholars may be particularly attracted to the idea that weak-form judicial review is fundamentally a sham, parliamentary supremacy parading under the guise of effective judicial review. The Human Rights Act might offer such skeptics a strong example, but the problem can arise in all systems of weak-form review. Consider a statute adopted after a minister makes a statement of compatibility, reflecting the government's judgment that the statute is consistent with the European Convention. A court comes along and issues a declaration of incompatibility. True, the minister now has the authority to introduce fast- track legislation to modify the statute, and the commentary routinely asserts that everyone expects such a response. But, why should a minister use that authority? If the statute is one to which the government is committed in principle, the minister and the government can express their disagreement with the courts on the interpretive question—as to which they had already expressed their views in the statement of compatibility—and insist on enforcing the statute as adopted.

* * *

The Canadian cases illustrate a problem common to weak-form and strong-form systems, but which takes on particular resonance in weak-form systems. The problem is that courts are not insensitive to the political responses to their actions. Sometimes they retreat from advanced positions but attempt to conceal their capitulation to political disagreement by insisting that the new cases are truly and fairly distinguishable from the older ones. These retreats can be described as reinstituting systems of parliamentary supremacy with respect to the rights at issue. In strong-form systems of judicial review, perhaps such retreats are sometimes necessary if the courts are to retain their power to overturn other legislation. What is striking is that weak-form systems purport to make such retreats unnecessary, because legislatures have the means at hand to reject the courts' decisions. Perhaps we can describe weak-form systems as degenerating when the retreats occur in such systems nonetheless.

The section 33 power suggests another way in which weak-form systems can degenerate. Defenders of Canada's system of judicial review have asserted that it promotes dialogue between the courts and the legislature. I discuss some aspects of that dialogue below. For now, consider two types of "dialogue"—really, different monologues. First, sometimes a legislature will pass a statute that, on reflection, its members think ill-considered. The courts can invalidate the statute, and the legislature will do nothing in response even though it has the power to override the courts' decision. The reason is that the legislature, on reflection, agrees with the courts. This, sometimes called the "sober second thought" effect, is a real benefit of judicial review, whether strong- or weak-form. Second, suppose that the legislature routinely invoked its power to override the courts whenever a court invalidated a statute. Weak-form review, under those circumstances, would be indistinguishable from parliamentary supremacy. Weak-form review supports true dialogue only when the legislature actually does respond to judicial decisions, but only on occasion.

There are, then, predictable ways in which weak-form systems of judicial review can be ineffectual. Next, I consider some predictable ways in which such systems can become strong-form systems in effect, if not in formal, law.

* * *

[For example, Canadian legislatures] might not use the section 33 power because they agree with the courts' interpretations, it is true, but they may also fail to use the power because they are unable to use it. The reason lies in the structure of the legislative process. That structure is more clearly exposed in a separation-of-powers system than in a parliamentary system, but, after making the point in the easier context, I will show how the argument goes in parliamentary systems. The general problem is that the legislative process has a number of what political scientists call "veto points," places where less than a majority of the legislature can stop legislative proposals from going forward. In the United States, legislative committees, or even sub-committees, can be veto points. Forty Senators constitute a veto point for most legislation as well, given recent changes in Senate norms regarding the propriety of filibusters. And, of course, the President has a formal veto power. Legislative inaction—of any sort, including the failure to invoke the override power—thus cannot be taken to represent a legislative judgment that the proposal (to override a court decision, for example) is ill-considered. Inaction may result from the exercise of power by a minority strategically located at a veto point.

Canada's parliamentary system appears—but only appears—to have fewer veto points. As a matter of formal law, a government can impose party discipline on its members and deploy its majority to enact anything the Prime Minister and Cabinet care enough about. So, one might think, the failure to invoke section 33 in Canada does indeed show that legislatures do not disagree strongly enough with court interpretations to do anything about them. But, here the formal law is misleading. Parliamentary majorities are actually coalitions, sometimes formal but sometimes informal. Imposing party discipline is politically costly—which means that a prime minister who does so with respect to one proposal will inevitably find it more difficult to assemble a legislative majority for some other proposal. Failure to invoke the section 33 power does not mean that a majority approved of the courts' interpretation. It means only that the government surveyed the political terrain and decided that it would lose more on other important issues if it imposed party discipline to override the courts. Weak-form judicial review is supposed to impose political costs on the government by drawing public attention to the possibility that the government has violated constitutional rights. But, it imposes other political costs as well, not inherent in the theory of weak-form review but inherent in the structure of policy-making, as it induces the government to change its policy priorities. These costs may be sufficient to convert a decision that nominally can be overridden into one that is effectively final.

* * *

Weak-form systems of judicial review are intriguing. With the demise of parliamentary supremacy as a system constitutionalists are willing to defend forcefully, weak-form judicial review provides constitution designers a new choice within the universe of constrained parliamentarism. I have suggested here some reasons for thinking that weak-form systems of judicial review might not provide a permanent resolution of the worry that unconstrained parliamentarism is insufficiently attentive to human rights, or of the worry that strong-form systems of judicial review are in tension with the values of democratic self-governance. Still, thinking about weak-form systems is certainly more interesting than reproducing the discussion of judicial activism and restraint in the context of new institutions. * * *

B. JUSTIFICATIONS FOR JUDICIAL REVIEW

CHARLES L. BLACK, JR., THE BUILDING WORK OF JUDICIAL REVIEW

THE PEOPLE AND THE COURT 37–42, 47–53 (1960).

* * * Whatever else may be said about the intention of the Framers, there can be no question whatever that * * * they intended to found [a government of limited powers]. The powers of the branches of government were enumerated, and it would be pretty hard to see this enumeration as merely playful, or as an elaborate hoax. But if there were any doubt on this score, one might turn to the explicit limitations, worded as such, both in the constitutional text and in some of the Amendments. Perhaps more important (for we are talking about the generation of a conviction of governmental legitimacy among the people) the conception of our government as one of limited powers is and since the beginning has been at the very center of American political belief. It is an essential part of the picture the American has of his government.

* * *

Now, for a government based on the theory of limited powers the problem of the legitimation of governmental action is one of special difficulty. * * *

First, and perhaps most important, the fact of limitation itself generates doubt and debate on the legitimacy of particular actions. In Britain, no one can argue that a particular measure oversteps the bounds of Parliament's power, for the plain reason that there are no such bounds; an argument of that *form* is impossible. Where, on the other hand, limitations are built into government and into the theory underlying government, it is certain that particular interests will from time to time discern in the limitations a forbidding of some action to which they are about to be subjected. No matter what the nature of the limitations may be, such claims will always arise, for there will be a borderline somewhere. Given the theory of limitation, these claims cannot be brushed aside as political solecisms, but must be met and answered in some fashion.

Secondly, it is to be expected (and certainly is true in the case of our Constitution) that the language in which limitations on government are expressed will be broad, and hence will invite competing constructions, supported in entire good faith. This breadth of language is not accidental. It is inherent in the very concept of limitation, for, paradoxically, a limitation which is specific often fails effectively to limit. Our Bill of Rights, for example, prohibits the imposition of "cruel and unusual" punishments. It would have been possible to omit the general phrase, and to list the punishments specifically forbidden. But it is plain that such a technique would have failed to implement the purpose behind the provision, for if a government were specifically shut off from nose-docking and boiling in oil, it could surely find some punishment equally cruel that was not on the list.

To look at the matter from another side, the affirmative powers of government, to which it is confined, must also be expressed in general, and hence in vague, language. Here again there is no question of intellectual sloppiness; it is impossible to calculate or list, in advance, the concrete and specific measures which a government is to be authorized to take, and if you tried to do so you would unquestionably leave out some that were vital. So constitutional draftsmen, in granting powers as well as in limiting them, are driven, whether they like it or not, to do their work in relatively imprecise language. And it is inevitable that such language will lend itself to conflicting interpretations.

* * *

Thirdly (and this is beyond question the most delicate point), the resolution of doubts as to the legitimacy of governmental action must be undertaken, and bindingly effected, by the government itself. There is no other viable possibility. The alternatives may be briefly stated: judgment by an outsider, and individual judgment by the people and institutions subject to the exercise of the disputed power of government. There is no outsider to judge, and nobody would stand for his judging if there were. The other alternative has been seriously, even passionately put forward, in a limited form, but it seems plain (to cite the classic example) that if South Carolina is to decide whether Congress is empowered to levy a protective tariff, while Massachusetts comes to an opposite decision, we have neither a nation nor a government. Yet there is, in the referral of decision on governmental power to the government itself, a flavor of setting up a party as judge in his own cause. There must always be something of a miracle, as well as much sound political intuition and wisdom, in the overcoming of this difficulty, and what must be looked for is success in satisfactory measure, rather than complete success.

* * *

* * * I have tried to show how a government founded on the theory of limited powers faces and must solve the problem of legitimacy—it must devise some way of bringing about a feeling in the nation that the actions of government, even when disapproved of, are authorized rather than merely usurpative. There are several hopeless ways to go about this, and just one, I think, that has some hope in it.

First, the determinations of Congress and the President could simply have been made final on all questions affecting their own power. I have already indicated the chief objection to that: It is wholly incompatible with the notion of limited power. It might have been acquiesced in, after a while, and a consensus reached on a British-style legitimacy, though conflicts between the President and Congress, and between the nation and the states, would have made that process a highly problematic one. In any case, it is not what happened, and I venture to say there is nothing in the history of this country to indicate it ever could have succeeded.

Trust could have been placed in "appeal to reason"; it could have been tried whether, in the end, people could not be persuaded of the legitimacy of governmental actions by argument alone. This, we can say confidently, would have been doomed. First, there is no finite set of "constitutional questions"; each new period generates new ones, and they are always charged with emotion and tied in with deep political strivings. Secondly, there is no single "reasonable" view of any of the great questions of the Constitution, if by "reasonable" we mean "capable of being held, after mature reflection and study, by an intelligent and relevantly well-informed person." The test of this is objective. Such persons have, in fact, differed on all great constitutional questions—that is what made them questions. But even if we didn't know this as a fact, we'd know it must be so. Words, preeminently the great vague words of the Constitution, have no single fixed meaning, and had no single fixed meaning at the time of adoption. Difference of private opinion was and is inevitable.

The last expedient, the one that was partly planned and that partly happened, is the one suggested by all of human experience in dealing with disputes. Where consensus on the *merits* of a question cannot be attained, it is sometimes possible to get consensus on a procedure for submitting the question for decision to an acceptable tribunal. If this were not true, no baseball game could be played to the end.

The difficulty here, as we have already seen, is that, where the questions concern governmental power in a sovereign nation, it is not possible to select an umpire who is outside government. Every national government, so long as it is a government, must have the final say on its own power. The problem, then, is to devise such governmental means of deciding as will (hopefully) reduce to a tolerable minimum the intensity of the objection that government is judge in its own cause. Having done this, you can only hope that this objection, though theoretically still tenable, will practically lose enough of its force that the legitimating work of the deciding institution can win acceptance. Reliance here must be on the common sense of the people, who may be expected to see that all has been done that can be done, in the nature of the case, to ensure fair disposition of questions of governmental power.

I would suggest that the first step is to give such a decision-making institution a satisfactory degree of independence from the active policy-making branches of government. It is in these that controversial exercises of governmental power will originate, and the umpire on questions of power must have such measure of detachment from them as will convince those whose claims are being decided that he is not practically, even though he may be theoretically, deciding his own case.

Secondly, I should want my umpire to be a specialist in tradition—not in sudsy, out-of-focus tradition, but in tradition's concrete minutiae and accurate ground plan. I would recognize that the decisions I was asking him to make were not open-and-shut arithmetic examples, soluble on the basis of precedent alone. But I would be sure that wiser and more acceptable work in deciding would be done by someone with respect for precedent, with an instilled feeling of responsibility to precedent, with a trained skill in following precedent—and in discerning when it ought not to be followed.

I would want to assure that my institution would be manned by people who had had training in the orderly presentation of evidence and argument, and who had absorbed the habit, through professional inveteration, of sifting carefully and then deciding firmly. I would want people who were experienced in the handling of masses of data of all sorts, people who were schooled to deal with little things carefully while keeping big issues clearly in sight. I should want people who were accustomed enough to the concept of attachment to a cause that it could be expected that, having been assigned the supremely important task of decision that I proposed giving them, they would perceive with clarity that they were now attached to the cause of learned and wise constitutional exposition, in the long-range interest, as best they could see it, of the whole people.

I have been using the plural, and of course we would want more than one man. It would obviously be prudent to reduce the risk of the impact of personal idiosyncrasy by composing the tribunal of enough men to check one another, and to provide that institutional continuity through time which is vital to the establishment of independence and a sound tradition of work.

Finally, having set up these requirements, I would not be astounded, or overly disappointed, if the fact fell short sometimes of perfection. No institution can be as perfect, in men or work, as its ideal model, though the very mark of the truly living institution is that it has an ideal model which is always there nudging its elbow.

* * *

What makes the final difference between success and failure of such a legitimating device, between its contemptuous rejection on theoretical grounds and its acceptance as being the substantial best that can be done toward following out in practice the principle of limitation of power? Who can tell? Something clicks into place. When you have done the best you can, it may be good enough. No tree knows whether it will bear fruit; its job is to stand up tall and wait.

In our history, it did work, in sufficient measure. The institution I have described is, as you will have perceived, a court, manned by skillful lawyers steeped in the judicial tradition, and, with the added caveat of imperfection, it is our own Supreme Court. Pretty clearly, it had been foreseen by the Founders that the courts would decide "constitutional" questions where these arose in litigation. Surprising nobody, Congress and the Supreme Court early confirmed this understanding. And the Court took up the umpiring job.

Popular acceptance of this role was not a foregone conclusion. If it had not been forthcoming, no amount of theoretical or historical argument could have enabled the Court to fill this need. But acceptance did come, in sufficient amount and with sufficient reliability.

Now it will have been observed that I have described the function of the Supreme Court in a way which turns the usual account upside down. The role of the Court has usually been conceived as that of *invalidating* "hasty" or "unwise" legislation, of acting as a "check" on the other departments. It has played such a role on occasion, and may play it again in the future.

But a case can be made for believing that the prime and most necessary function of the Court has been that of *validation,* not that of invalidation. What a government of limited powers needs, at the beginning and forever, is some means of satisfying the people that it has taken all steps humanly possible to stay within its powers. That is the condition of its legitimacy, and its legitimacy, in the long run, is the condition of its life. And the Court, through its history, has acted as the legitimator of the government. In a very real sense, the Government of the United States is based on the opinions of the Supreme Court.

* * *

The power to validate is the power to invalidate. If the Court were deprived, by any means, of its real and practical power to set bounds to governmental action, or even of public confidence that the Court itself regards this as its duty and will discharge it in a proper case, then it must certainly cease to perform its central function of unlocking the energies of government by stamping governmental actions as legitimate. If everybody gets a Buck Rogers badge, a Buck Rogers badge imports no distinction. The Court may go thirty or forty years without declaring an Act of Congress unconstitutional; that means nothing, for it is scarcely to be looked for that Congress will pass any given annual or decennial quota of statutes that the Court will regard as invalid. But if it ever so much as became known—even as a matter of tacit understanding in the profession and on the Court, for such a secret could not be kept from the people—that the Court would not seriously ponder the questions of constitutionality presented to it and declare the challenged statute unconstitutional if it believed it to be so, then its usefulness as a legitimatizing institution would be gone.

ALEXANDER M. BICKEL, ESTABLISHMENT AND GENERAL JUSTIFICATION OF JUDICIAL REVIEW

THE LEAST DANGEROUS BRANCH 16–26 (1962).

The root difficulty is that judicial review is a counter-majoritarian force in our system. There are various ways of sliding over this ineluctable reality. Marshall did so when he spoke of enforcing, in behalf of "the people," the limits that they have ordained for the institutions of a limited government. And it has been done ever since in much the same fashion by all too many commentators. Marshall himself followed Hamilton, who in the 78th *Federalist* denied that judicial review implied a superiority of the judicial over the legislative power—denied, in other words, that judicial review constituted control by an unrepresentative minority of an elected majority. "It only supposes," Hamilton went on, "that the power of the people is superior to both; and that where the will of the legislature, declared in its statutes, stands in opposition to that of the people, declared in the Constitution, the judges ought to be governed by the latter rather than the former." But the word "people" so used is an abstraction. Not necessarily a meaningless or a pernicious one by any means; always charged with emotion, but nonrepresentational—an abstraction obscuring the reality that when the Supreme Court declares unconstitutional a legislative act or the action of an elected executive, it thwarts the will of representatives of the actual people of the here and now; it exercises control, not in behalf of the prevailing majority, but against it. That, without mystic overtones, is what actually happens. It is an altogether different kettle of fish, and it is the reason the charge can be made that judicial review is undemocratic.

* * *

It is true, of course, that the process of reflecting the will of a popular majority in the legislature is deflected by various inequalities of representation and by all sorts of institutional habits and characteristics, which perhaps tend most often in favor of inertia. Yet it must be remembered that statutes are the product of the legislature and the executive acting in concert, and that the executive represents a very different constituency and thus tends to cure inequities of over- and underrepresentation. Reflecting a balance of forces in society for purposes of stable and effective government is more intricate and less certain than merely assuring each citizen his equal vote. Moreover, impurities and imperfections, if such they be, in one part of the system are no argument for total departure from the desired norm in another part. A much more important complicating factor—first adumbrated by Madison in the 10th *Federalist* and lately emphasized by Professor David B. Truman and others[13]—is the proliferation and power of what Madison foresaw as "faction," what Mr. Truman calls "groups," and what in popular parlance has always been deprecated as the "interests" or the "pressure groups."

No doubt groups operate forcefully on the electoral process, and no doubt they seek and gain access to an effective share in the legislative and executive decisional process. Perhaps they constitute also, in some measure, an impurity or imperfection. But no one has claimed that they have been able to capture the governmental process except by combining in some fashion, and thus capturing or constituting (are not the two verbs synonymous?) a majority. They often tend themselves to be majoritarian in composition and to be subject to broader majoritarian influences. And the price of what they sell or buy in the legislature is determined in the biennial or quadrennial electoral marketplace. It may be, as Professor Robert A. Dahl has written, that elections themselves, and the political competition that renders them meaningful, "do not make for government by majorities in any very significant way," for they do not establish a great many policy

[13]See D.B. Truman, *The Governmental Process* (New York: Knopf, 1951).

preferences. However, "they are a crucial device for controlling leaders." And if the control is exercised by "groups of various types and sizes, all seeking in various ways to advance their goals," so that we have "minorities rule" rather than majority rule, it remains true nevertheless that only those minorities rule which can command the votes of a majority of individuals in the legislature who can command the votes of a majority of individuals in the electorate. In one fashion or another, both in the legislative process and at elections, the minorities must coalesce into a majority. Although, as Mr. Dahl says, "it is fashionable in some quarters to suggest that everything believed about democratic politics prior to World War I, and perhaps World War II, was nonsense," he makes no bones about his own belief that "the radical democrats who, unlike Madison, insist upon the decisive importance of the election process in the whole grand strategy of democracy are essentially correct."[14]

The insights of Professor Truman and other writers into the role that groups play in our society and our politics have a bearing on judicial review. They indicate that there are other means than the electoral process, though subordinate and subsidiary ones, of making institutions of government responsive to the needs and wishes of the governed. Hence one may infer that judicial review, although not responsible, may have ways of being responsive. But nothing can finally depreciate the central function that is assigned in democratic theory and practice to the electoral process; nor can it be denied that the policy-making power of representative institutions, born of the electoral process, is the distinguishing characteristic of the system. Judicial review works counter to this characteristic.

* * *

* * * Besides being a counter-majoritarian check on the legislature and the executive, judicial review may, in a larger sense, have a tendency over time seriously to weaken the democratic process. Judicial review expresses, of course, a form of distrust of the legislature. "The legislatures," wrote James Bradley Thayer at the turn of the century,

> . . . are growing accustomed to this distrust and more and more readily inclined to justify it, and to shed the considerations of constitutional restraints,—certainly as concerning the exact extent of these restrictions,—turning that subject over to the courts; and what is worse, they insensibly fall into a habit of assuming that whatever they could constitutionally do they may do,—as if honor and fair dealing and common honesty were not relevant to their inquiries. The people, all this while, become careless as to whom they send to the legislature; too often they cheerfully vote for men whom they would not trust with an important

---

[14] R.A. Dahl, *A Preface to Democratic Theory* (Chicago: University of Chicago Press, 1956), pp. 125, 132.

> private affair, and when these unfit persons are found to pass foolish and bad laws, and the courts step in and disregard them, the people are glad that these few wiser gentlemen on the bench are so ready to protect them against their more immediate representatives * * *. [I]t should be remembered that the exercise of [the power of judicial review], even when unavoidable, is always attended with a serious evil, namely, that the correction of legislative mistakes comes from the outside, and the people thus lose the political experience, and the moral education and stimulus that comes from fighting the question out in the ordinary way, and correcting their own errors. The tendency of a common and easy resort to this great function, now lamentably too common, is to dwarf the political capacity of the people, and to deaden its sense of moral responsibility. It is no light thing to do that.[18]

To this day, in how many hundreds of occasions does Congress enact a measure that it deems expedient, having essayed consideration of its constitutionality (that is to say, of its acceptability on principle), only to abandon the attempt in the declared confidence that the Court will correct errors of principle, if any? It may well be * * * that any lowering of the level of legislative performance is attributable to many factors other than judicial review. Yet there is no doubt that what Thayer observed remains observable. * * *

Finally, another, though related, contention has been put forward. It is that judicial review runs so fundamentally counter to democratic theory that in a society which in all other respects rests on that theory, judicial review cannot ultimately be effective. We pay the price of a grave inner contradiction in the basic principle of our government, which is an inconvenience and a dangerous one; and in the end to no good purpose, for when the great test comes, judicial review will be unequal to it. The most arresting expression of this thought is in a famous passage from a speech of Judge Learned Hand, a passage * * * "of Browningesque passion and obscurity," voicing a "gloomy and apocalyptic view." Absent the institution of judicial review, Judge Hand said:

> I do not think that anyone can say what will be left of those [fundamental principles of equity and fair play which our constitutions enshrine]; I do not know whether they will serve only as counsels; but this much I think I do know—that a society so riven that the spirit of moderation is gone, no court *can* save; that a society where that spirit flourishes, no court *need* save; that in a society which evades its re-

[18][J.B. Thayer, *John Marshall* (Boston: Houghton Mifflin, 1901), pp. 103–04, 106–07.]

sponsibility by thrusting upon the courts the nurture of that spirit, that spirit in the end will perish.[22]

* * *

Such, in outline, are the chief doubts that must be met if the doctrine of judicial review is to be justified on principle. Of course, these doubts will apply with lesser or greater force to various forms of the exercise of the power. For the moment the discussion is at wholesale, and we are seeking a justification on principle, quite aside from supports in history and the continuity of practice. The search must be for a function which might (indeed, must) involve the making of policy, yet which differs from the legislative and executive functions; which is peculiarly suited to the capabilities of the courts; which will not likely be performed elsewhere if the courts do not assume it; which can be so exercised as to be acceptable in a society that generally shares Judge Hand's satisfaction in a "sense of common venture"; which will be effective when needed; and whose discharge by the courts will not lower the quality of the other departments' performance by denuding them of the dignity and burden of their own responsibility. It will not be possible fully to meet all that is said against judicial review. Such is not the way with questions of government. We can only fill the other side of the scales with countervailing judgments on the real needs and the actual workings of our society and, of course, with our own portions of faith and hope. Then we may estimate how far the needle has moved.

The point of departure is a truism; perhaps it even rises to the unassailability of a platitude. It is that many actions of government have two aspects: their immediate, necessarily intended, practical effects, and their perhaps unintended or unappreciated bearing on values we hold to have more general and permanent interest. It is a premise we deduce not merely from the fact of a written constitution but from the history of the race, and ultimately as a moral judgment of the good society, that government should serve not only what we conceive from time to time to be our immediate material needs but also certain enduring values. This in part is what is meant by government under law. But such values do not present themselves ready-made. They have a past always, to be sure, but they must be continually derived, enunciated, and seen in relevant application. And it remains to ask which institution of our government—if any single one in particular—should be the pronouncer and guardian of such values.

Men in all walks of public life are able occasionally to perceive this second aspect of public questions. Sometimes they are also able to base their decisions on it; that is one of the things we like to call acting on

[22]L. Hand, "The Contribution of an Independent Judiciary to Civilization," in I. Dilliard, ed., *The Spirit of Liberty* (New York: Knopf, 1953), pp. 155–65.

principle. Often they do not do so, however, particularly when they sit in legislative assemblies. There, when the pressure for immediate results is strong enough and emotions ride high enough, men will ordinarily prefer to act on expediency rather than take the long view. Possibly legislators—everything else being equal—are as capable as other men of following the path of principle, where the path is clear or at any rate discernible. Our system, however, like all secular systems, calls for the evolution of principle in novel circumstances, rather than only for its mechanical application. Not merely respect for the rule of established principles but the creative establishment and renewal of a coherent body of principled rules—that is what our legislatures have proven themselves ill equipped to give us.

Initially, great reliance for principled decision was placed in the Senators and the President, who have more extended terms of office and were meant to be elected only indirectly. Yet the Senate and the President were conceived of as less closely tied to, not as divorced from, electoral responsibility and the political marketplace. And so even then the need might have been felt for an institution which stands altogether aside from the current clash of interests, and which, insofar as is humanly possible, is concerned only with principle. We cannot know whether, as Thayer believed, our legislatures are what they are because we have judicial review, or whether we have judicial review and consider it necessary because legislatures are what they are. Yet it is arguable also that the partial separation of the legislative and judicial functions—and it is not meant to be absolute—is beneficial in any event, because it makes it possible for the desires of various groups and interests concerning immediate results to be heard clearly and unrestrainedly in one place. It may be thought fitting that somewhere in government, at some stage in the process of law-making, such felt needs should find unambiguous expression. Moreover, and more importantly, courts have certain capacities for dealing with matters of principle that legislatures and executives do not possess. Judges have, or should have, the leisure, the training, and the insulation to follow the ways of the scholar in pursuing the ends of government. This is crucial in sorting out the enduring values of a society, and it is not something that institutions can do well occasionally, while operating for the most part with a different set of gears. It calls for a habit of mind, and for undeviating institutional customs. Another advantage that courts have is that questions of principle never carry the same aspect for them as they did for the legislature or the executive. Statutes, after all, deal typically with abstract or dimly foreseen problems. The courts are concerned with the flesh and blood of an actual case. This tends to modify, perhaps to lengthen, everyone's view. It also provides an extremely salutary proving ground for all abstractions; it is conducive, in a phrase of Holmes, to thinking things, not words, and thus to the evolution of principle by a process that tests as it creates.

Their insulation and the marvelous mystery of time give courts the capacity to appeal to men's better natures, to call forth their aspirations, which may have been forgotten in the moment's hue and cry. This is what Justice Stone called the opportunity for "the sober second thought."[26] Hence it is that the courts, although they may somewhat dampen the people's and the legislatures' efforts to educate themselves, are also a great and highly effective educational institution. * * * The educational institution that both takes the observation to correct the dead reckoning and makes it known is the voice of the Constitution: the Supreme Court exercising judicial review. The Justices, in Dean Rostow's phrase, "are inevitably teachers in a vital national seminar."[28] No other branch of the American government is nearly so well equipped to conduct one. And such a seminar can do a great deal to keep our society from becoming so riven that no court will be able to save it. Of course, we have never quite been that society in which the spirit of moderation is so richly in flower that no court need save it.

REBECCA L. BROWN, ACCOUNTABILITY, LIBERTY, AND THE CONSTITUTION

98 COLUM.L.REV. 531–33, 535, 539–43, 552–54, 556, 564–65, 568–74 (1998).

Honk if you are tired of constitutional theory. More than ever before thought, the blame lies with Alexander Bickel. At his instigation, contender after contender has stepped forward to try a hand at pulling the sword of judicial review from the stone of illegitimacy. Each suggests a different way to ease the discomfort of unaccountable decisionmaking in a democracy. Some have argued that judicial review is not *countermajoritarian*, but is more supramajoritarian[1] or paramajoritarian,[2] others that it is not *counter*majoritarian,[3] still others that it is not counter*majoritarian*.[4] The

---

[26]H.F. Stone, "*The Common Law in the United States,*" 50 Harvard Law Review 4, 25 (1936).

[28]See E.V. Rostow, "*The Democratic Character of Judicial Review,*" 66 Harvard Law Review 193, 208 (1952).

[1]See Bruce Ackerman, We The People: Foundations 6–7 (1991) (setting forth dualist theory in which constitutional limitations are democratically justified by fact that they were themselves agreed to by the people acting at a higher level of lawmaking).

[2]See John Hart Ely, Democracy and Distrust 87–88 (1980) (setting forth "representation-reinforcing" approach to judicial review which limits courts' involvement to policing the process of representation).

[3]See Barry Friedman, *Dialogue and Judicial Review*, 91 Mich.L.Rev. 577, 590–607 (1993) (arguing that courts do not really act in opposition to majority will); Michael J. Klarman, *Rethinking the Civil Rights and Civil Liberties Revolutions*, 82 Va.L.Rev. 1, 16 n.72 (1996) (noting that "the Court strays relatively little from majoritarian impulses because the justices are embedded in majoritarian culture"); Christopher J. Peters, *Adjudication as Representation*, 97 Colum.L.Rev. 312, 314 (1997) (arguing that accusations of judicial illegitimacy are wrong because courts are not undemocratic).

[4]See, e.g., Frank H. Easterbrook, *The Supreme Court, 1983 Term—Foreword: The Court and the Economic System*, 98 Harv.L.Rev. 4, 15–18 (1984) (demonstrating

curious thing about these defenses of judicial review, however, is that they suggest not that unaccountable decisionmaking is legitimate, but only that it is not really unaccountable. The arguments take the form of a confession and avoidance, rather than a rebuttal, of Bickel's charge.

The vast majority of theorists have failed to challenge Bickel's basic assumption, that political accountability is the sine qua non of legitimacy in government action. As a consequence, that assumption for decades framed the debate in constitutional law. Even the most sympathetic theorists tended to assume the role of apologist for judicial review,[5] while the unsympathetic made concerted efforts to exploit that widespread assumption in order to engender profound skepticism about judging itself.[6] Judgment was no longer the proper and revered sphere of judges, but was recast as the unforgivable "value imposition."[7] These attacks on the legitimacy of judgment in a democracy have left their mark not only on the academy, but also on the public understanding of the judicial role and on the Supreme Court's understanding of its own role. These effects, in turn, have had palpable implications for the recognition and enforcement of individual rights.

* * * It seems to me that too much effort has been expended in the quest to solve Bickel's difficulty, especially since efforts to "solve" the difficulty serve rather to entrench the insidious assumption underlying it. Instead, I seek to contribute to the budding effort to resist the siren song of popular sovereignty as the foundation of constitutional thought. I do so by examining the character of accountability itself.

* * *

This Article posits that accountability is best understood, not as a utilitarian means to achieve maximum satisfaction of popular preferences, but as a structural feature of the constitutional architecture, the goal of

---

nonmajoritarian aspects of modern lawmaking practice); Michael J. Klarman, *Majoritarian Judicial Review: The Entrenchment Problem*, 85 Geo.L.J. 491, 495 & n.22 (1997) (suggesting that the political process does not produce majoritarian results). * * *

[5]See, e.g., Jesse H. Choper, Judicial Review and the National Political Process 9–10 (1980) ("[T]he procedure of judicial review is in conflict with the fundamental principle of democracy—majority rule under conditions of political freedom."); Laurence H. Tribe, American Constitutional Law § 3–6, at 51 (1978) (arguing that the American system of rights protection is "an imperfectly antidemocratic judicial process and an imperfectly democratic political process").

[6]See Robert H. Bork, The Tempting of America 173–76, 191 (1990) (critiquing theories that allow judgment, on the ground that judges are no better at taking long-term principle into account than are citizens: "There is no objectively correct balance between principle and expediency."); Antonin Scalia, *Originalism: The Lesser Evil*, 57 U.Cin.L.Rev. 849, 863 (1989) ("[T]he main danger in judicial interpretation of the Constitution . . . is that the judges will mistake their own predilections for the law.").

[7]Erwin Chemerinsky, *The Supreme Court, 1988 Term—Foreword: The Vanishing Constitution*, 103 Harv.L.Rev. 43, 62 (1989).

which is to protect liberty. In this respect it is much like the other structural constitutional features such as separation of powers, checks and balances, and federalism—all of which are more comfortably accepted as devices for protecting individual rights. It may seem counterintuitive to consider that a system of electorally accountable government might also be designed to serve the end of individual liberty. We have been trained to view popular will as antithetical to the protection of rights. But it is counterintuitive only because we have not properly honed our intuitions about the Constitution that we have.

The resolution of this conundrum asks the reader to abandon the deeply entrenched prejudices that haunt a generation weaned on the countermajoritarian difficulty. It asks the reader to turn Bickel's difficulty on its head and wonder instead how one might justify a system of *majority rule* in a government whose final cause is the protection *of individual rights*. The resolution lies in the almost instinctive realization that unless a government is politically accountable, an independent judiciary that vigorously protects rights from government encroachment could not survive.

I. DELEGATION AND DISTRUST * * *

* * *

For adherents to the majoritarian paradigm, democratic government means that decisions affecting the polity will be made by accountable officials; anything else runs counter to the very defining principles of this nation. This commitment leads the more extreme of their number to be suspicious of any type of public decisionmaking that does not lie with accountable public officials. Courts are the primary targets for their skepticism. In the most extreme version of this modern majoritarianism, the skepticism extends to the concept of rights itself, because rights are nothing but exogenous limits on the power of the people, necessarily determined by some metric other than the people's current preferences.

The most salient proponent of this rights skepticism, [Robert] Bork, goes so far as to contend that there is simply no hierarchy of values in a society such that one could be said to have to yield to another. Everything is but a "form of gratification," and, because there is no objective way to put one form of gratification ahead of another, the majority of the people should have the freedom to choose whichever of these indistinguishable preferences they collectively wish.[29] Although Bork offers an example of "sexual gratification" versus "moral gratification," it is clear that his analysis would apply equally, say, to a society's desire to enslave pitted

---

[29]See Robert H. Bork, *Neutral Principles and Some First Amendment Problems*, 47 Ind.L.J. 1, 8–10 (1971).

against an individual's desire to live free. This moral leveling is the direct consequence of the majoritarian paradigm carried to its extreme.

* * *

* * * [W]here did the fixation on accountability come from, such that institutions that depart from it are immediately suspect? It might be thought that the fixation on majoritarian decisionmaking and democracy that took hold during and after the Warren Court era was the direct result of Progressive thinking in the early 1900s. Common wisdom paints the twentieth century as simply one continuous movement toward a majoritarian paradigm, with the severe moral skeptics emerging as the almost inevitable result of the thinking that had dominated the century. Indeed, the skeptics tend to describe their critique of the judiciary's lack of accountability as "conservative," as if it were based on conserving principles that have long been entrenched in American jurisprudence and political philosophy. This turns out to be wrong.

The theorists that are usually invoked as precursors to the skeptics of the later decades are in fact very different. While the Progressive-era utilitarians criticized judicial review and advocated broad latitude for the actions of the legislature, they did so without, for the most part, any accusation that the Court was in some fashion inherently evil or deficient. Rather, their approach was generally instrumental in that they believed that a better result would be reached if the legislature could have the greater role in governing. The goal was always for "better laws" and a "progressive" society searching for ways to achieve the greater good, including a strong commitment to liberty and individual rights. This is not a position of skepticism, but of idealism.

A look back at those associated with the early beginnings of the democratic obsession shows that critics of judicial review did not disparage the concept of individual rights or the exercise of judgment in the way that the modern critics do. James Bradley Thayer is often mentioned as the initiator of a modern-era "countermajoritarian critique" of the Court,[37] and indeed Bickel relied on Thayer in developing his theory. Thayer advocated a judicial "rule of clear mistake," under which an act of a legislature would be upheld unless "those who have the right to make laws have not merely made a mistake, but have made a very clear one—so clear that it is not open to rational question."[39] But it was Bickel, and not Thayer, who tied this principle to the imperatives of democracy. Bickel wrote, "[t]he principle [Thayer's rule of clear mistake] continues to possess dignity and utility. It

---

[37]See, e.g., Morton J. Horwitz, *Republicanism and Liberalism in American Constitutional Thought,* 29 Wm. & Mary L. Rev. 57, 61 (1987).

[39]James B. Thayer, *The Origin and Scope of the American Doctrine of Constitutional Law*, 7 Harv. L. Rev. 129, 144 (1893).

is crucial to any accommodation between judicial review and the democratic faith."[40]

For Thayer, there were important structural and pragmatic reasons for a principle of deference to legislative judgment, analogous to the reasons that a judge does not set aside a jury verdict merely because she disagrees with it. In Thayer's expectation, every act of legislation includes a conscious legislative determination of its constitutionality, and the legislature should be encouraged to engage seriously in this undertaking for the public good. His is a rationale based on the equality and separation of coordinate branches, and also on the deleterious effect on legislators and their constituents of denying representatives the responsibility for determining constitutional principle and relegating it to the courts. "The checking and cutting down of legislative power, by numerous detailed prohibitions in the constitution, cannot be accomplished without making the government petty and incompetent."[44]

These arguments are about how best to achieve the highest national accomplishments of government, not about the hegemony of popular will. Nowhere in his article does Thayer even mention the principle of accountability as that which distinguishes legislatures from courts. Nor does he denigrate courts for what they are or what they appropriately do. Quite to the contrary, he unapologetically asserts that "[t]he ultimate arbiter of what is rational and permissible is indeed always the courts, so far as litigated cases bring the question before them. This leaves to our courts a great and stately jurisdiction."[45] Thus, while he would not expand the role of the courts, Thayer did not seek to condemn them either. Rather, he sought to encourage judgment in legislators, which is a goal far removed from a worship of popular will and vastly remote from a skepticism about individual rights.

* * *

II. THE PREMISE OF THE MAJORITARIAN PARADIGM

Proponents of the majoritarian paradigm have been vague about whether their belief that all public policy must be made according to majority rule derives from their understanding of the Constitution or comes from some other source. Bickel used terms like "democratic faith."[97] A starting place for inquiry into the source should be the Constitution itself, for presumably it either creates, or is the creature of, the democratic faith.

---

[40][See Alexander M. Bickel, The Least Dangerous Branch 37 (2d ed. 1986).]

[44]Thayer, supra note 39, at 156.

[45]Id. at 152.

[97]Bickel, supra note [40], at 37.

The Constitution provides in several ways for electoral accountability. It specifies that representatives shall be chosen by "the People of the several States," that senators from each state shall be "elected by the People thereof," and that the President shall be selected as the "person having the greatest number of votes" of electors, "if such number be a majority of the whole number of Electors appointed." There is also a requirement that the United States "guarantee to every State in this Union a Republican Form of Government," which may be thought implicitly to ensure a majoritarian form of public decisionmaking in the states. Notice that the only place in which majority rule is explicitly invoked is in the provision for election of the President by the electoral college. In other places the text refers only to selection, without specifying the rule by which selection would be accomplished. But there is no serious dispute that the understanding of the time and continuously since has been that a majority vote will govern both in the election of officials by the public and in the passage of legislation in Congress.

A major problem for majoritarians has been extending the examples of accountability or majority rule in our constitutional system to a general presumption that majorities should control decisionmaking. Much work has been done to demonstrate that the republic established by the Constitution simply cannot be explained by a belief in the "agency" theory of representation, which is an essential belief if one is to translate the accountability provisions into a general principle of majority rule. "If the Constitution's Framers were keen on majority rule, they certainly had a bizarre manner of demonstrating their affection."[106] At every turn, they buffered majority will, insulated representatives from direct influence of majority factions, and provided checks on majority decisionmaking. The framers of the Constitution were afraid of government, even if made up of officials elected by the people. Madison's renowned invective against faction, defined to include a numerical majority of the people,[108] suggests a real difference between the goal of representative government, on the one hand, and the translation of popular will into law, on the other.

* * *

The Federalist Papers do not suggest that the authors feared that representatives would not be responsive *enough* to popular desires with regard to political choices, but rather that they might listen too closely to the ill-considered voice of constituent passion. Indeed, the two-year term for members of the House of Representatives was challenged as being too infrequent to keep the representatives in touch with popular will, and

---

[106]Julian N. Eule, *Judicial Review of Direct Democracy*, 99 Yale L.J. 1503, 1522 (1990).

[108]See The Federalist No. 10 * * *.

Madison responded in The Federalist No. 53 to a then-current proverb, "that where annual elections end, tyranny begins." The response was that a longer time period was necessary to allow members to acquire knowledge and to ensure a system that was "safe to the liberties of the people." That comment establishes a clear dichotomy between the implementation of popular will, on the one hand, and liberty, on the other. The majoritarians have not demonstrated any basis for claiming that "liberty" was understood in the founding period of history, or should be understood today, to mean freedom of the majority of the people to have their policy preferences enacted into law. Liberty had—and retains—quite a separate meaning.

* * *

If one is bothered by the idea that judicial review entails a countermajoritarian or undemocratic type of decisionmaking, if one views this as deviant, troubling, or even "difficult" to reconcile with one's vision of American government, then one has approached the question with a presumption that majority rule is the starting point of inquiry. That presumption is not justified by the text of the Constitution, nor has it been justified by extrinsic theoretical arguments. Majority rule has a place under the Constitution, but that document does not purport to elevate popular will to a position of even presumptive primacy. Indeed, popular political will is a force to be tempered at every turn.

* * *

III. The Evolution of Accountability

* * *

In the debates that led to the drafting of the Constitution, some Federalists defended the absence of a bill of rights on the ground that the government and the people were one—the English view of popular sovereignty. A bill of rights was necessary only when wrested as a concession from a tyrant, as in the case of the Magna Carta. There was no need to wring concessions from "ourselves." But the antifederalist argument on this point ultimately prevailed: Government and people could not be the same, no matter what view of popular sovereignty one took. It was simply too dangerous. Past abuses of representative government in the name of the people were too stark to overlook, especially those which had been inflicted on the American colonies who enjoyed "virtual representation" in Parliament. Thus, the American Constitution implemented a form of the strategy offered by the Levellers in England a hundred years before, endowing a government with limited powers, but still allowing the people to retain a degree of sovereignty sufficient to enforce the terms of that endowment.

My claim is that the key to understanding the principle of accountability in our constitutional system today is to be found in this view of popular sovereignty. Accountability is the means by which the entire people stands apart from the government, in all its segments, and enforces the people's compact with its government. It is not designed solely as a means to implement popular preferences on points of ordinary governance, except in the roughest sense, nor is it designed to eliminate the judgment expected of elected representatives. It is a means to enforce the trust placed in the representatives. The accountability provisions do not establish a preference-maximizing constitution. They create a tyranny-minimizing constitution.

Indications from the time surrounding the drafting and ratification of the Constitution suggest that this is the view of accountability that the founding community held. It is a view of accountability as a notion of blame. Elections provide the people with an opportunity to punish those who have violated their duty by invading the liberties of the people. The problem with unaccountable government is that there is no one to blame if oppression ensues.

* * *

While there had for a time been a dominant view of representatives as true agents of the people, and of representation as a means for implementing a real mutuality of interest between representatives and constituents, that view broke down in the period just prior to the Constitutional Convention. In its place came a renewed emphasis on election as "the sole basis of representation,"[182] and a removal of the people themselves from actual governance. The people's voice in government would be heard on election day.

Madison, as Publius, suggested that the goal of elections, or at least one such goal, is to keep rulers "virtuous whilst they continue to hold their public trust."[184] Jefferson made a similar point regarding the goal for representation in the Senate: "I had two things in view: to get the wisest men chosen, *and to make them perfectly independent when chosen*."[185] Thus, while of course a purpose of choosing representatives was to allow them to govern, a principal purpose of keeping them responsible to the people was to allow the people to check any abuse of that power.

Gordon Wood observed that the American use of the concept of representation in the design of government redefined the notion of liberty. "[T]he liberty and security of the people, as Americans had thought in

---

[182][Gordon S. Wood, The Creation of the American Republic, 1776–1787, at 388 (1969).]

[184]The Federalist No. 57 * * * .

[185]Letter from Thomas Jefferson to Edmund Pendleton (Aug. 26, 1776) in 1 Papers of Thomas Jefferson, 1760–1776, at 503 (J. Boyd ed., 1950) (emphasis added).

1776, *no longer came from their participation* in one part of the government, as the democracy balanced against the monarchy and aristocracy, 'but from the responsibility, and dependence of each part of the government, upon the people.'"[187] The possibility of displacement at election time created a dependence on the people that created a substitute for participation.

Both "liberty" and "tyranny" underwent changes of meaning that mirrored the change in the understanding of representation. Liberty had once been understood as the people's right to participate in the government, to share in it. But with the establishment of the constitutional government, the "liberty that was now emphasized was personal or private, the protection of individual rights against all governmental encroachments, particularly by the legislature, the body which the Whigs had traditionally cherished as the people's exclusive repository of their public liberty and the surest weapon to defend their private liberties."[190] Liberty was, that is, a sphere of protection, not the affirmative power to enact laws of one's own choosing.

Tyranny was understood as the abuse of power by government—even by representative government acting on the basis of what a majority of its constituents wanted. Institutional structures, rather than popular participation, became the principal defense against tyranny. Thus, the design of government itself took on a new purpose—instead of merely promoting the collective happiness of the people, the government was designed to "protect the citizens in their personal liberty, and in their property, even against the public will."[192] That means, in more modern parlance, that the people did not establish primarily a utility-maximizing constitution, but rather a tyranny-minimizing one. As Madison emphatically put it, "Justice"—not happiness or prosperity, but justice, the absence of government oppression—"is the end of government. It is the end of civil society."[194]

The historical evidence relied on by Wood, coupled with the overall preeminence, throughout The Federalist, of evident concern for the vital need to check abuse of power, supports the conclusion that the accountability of government officers to the people was one of the structures, along with separation of powers, federalism, and checks and balances, employed to accomplish that end. Electoral responsibility is a means for meting out consequences for violations of the public trust, for ferreting out corruption,

[187]Wood, supra note [182], at 603 (quoting Samuel Williams, The Natural and Civil History of Vermont 342–43 (Walpole, N.H., Isaiah Thomas and David Carlisle 1794)) (emphasis added).

[190]Wood, supra note [182], at 609.

[192][Id.](quoting State of Rhode–Island and Providence–Plantations, In General Assembly, Act of October 1789, *in* The Providence Gazette and Country Journal, Nov. 7, 1789, at 1). * * *

[194]The Federalist No. 51 * * *.

and for limiting entrenchments and accretion of excessive power over time—transgressions that ultimately threaten the liberty of the people. Accountability is a structural notion of blame whose final cause is liberty.

IV. Accountability and Liberty

* * *

If one's commitment is to liberty, then the theoretical starting point for government should be a body whose duty it is to protect the liberty of the people and whose inclination to infringe liberty is institutionally at its weakest. In Hamilton's view, the judiciary was indisputably the "weakest of the three departments of power . . . [I]t can never attack with success either of the other two; . . . and the general liberty of the people can never be endangered from that quarter. . . ." Thus, the judiciary was entrusted with the primary responsibility for guarding the value that underlay the entire constitutional structure: The courts were expected to commit to "inflexible and uniform adherence to the rights of the Constitution, and of individuals. . . ."

This body, entrusted with such an indispensable role, "must ultimately depend upon the aid of the executive arm even for the efficacy of its judgments."[199] It is not enabled to go out and take life, liberty, or property from people, and, given its political insulation, would have very little reason to do so. Thus, the judiciary does not present a "difficulty," but is by far the easiest branch to reconcile with a government devoted to the preservation of liberty.

* * *

The judgments of the rights-protecting branch, the judiciary, must be enforced by someone if liberty is to be preserved. Moreover, the members of this judicial branch must be subject to some scheme for selection and removal. And most importantly, this branch must nonetheless remain truly independent of those whose exercises of power it reviews, or its value in protecting individual rights will be lost. Consider the possibility that, to support the independent, rights-protecting judiciary, the Constitution provided that the power to govern would be placed in the hands of a hereditary monarch or unaccountable despot. The despot's exercise of power would be reviewed by the independent courts for conformity with constitutional limitations. Quite quickly, one would expect to see the unaccountable government seeking to take over the independent court, to control its judgments, or at the very least to resist any unwanted orders issuing from the court. There would be no structural incentive for this government to enforce or support the independence of the court. It is

[199][The Federalist No. 78.]

unimaginable that such an unaccountable government would allow the court to survive as a truly independent reviewer of its actions, because there would be no external check to prevent the government from disregarding the court's judgments. The stronger branch would simply cannibalize the weaker.

* * *

Thus, it is essential to the security of the courts that government have a mechanism that keeps it within its proper bounds and forces it to resist the temptation to swallow up the judiciary in pursuit of its own ends. One way of achieving this security derives from the distinctively American conception of representation. One of the genuinely unique aspects of the Constitution was its dependence on a principle of representation "'where all authority flows from and returns at stated periods to, the people.'"[204] Representation, while having ancient roots, was redefined when it came to America as the pervasive principle on which the entire government rested, even as it comprised only a limited delegation of power. "All parts of the government were equally responsible but limited spokesmen for the people, *who remained as the absolute and perpetual sovereign, distributing bits and pieces of power to their various agents*."[205] Thus, in America, it became obvious that there was no supreme power except what the people themselves held. "The powers of the people were thus never alienated or surrendered to a legislature. Representation, in other words, never eclipsed the people-at-large, as apparently it did in the English House of Commons."[206] They delegated a portion of their power in whatever manner, and for whatever time, they chose.

This unique structure of American government, then, does not divide all power amongst the branches. It divides all *delegated* power amongst the branches, always retaining the role of the people as an overseer of the entire system. Thus, if the executive refused to enforce the orders of the court, or if the legislature tried to impeach the members of the court without warrant, the people would still stand outside of those actions and could pass judgment on them through their retained political powers by holding elected officials accountable for any such breach of trust. Thus, the encroachment into the independence of the judiciary that seemed inevitable under any form of autocratic government is subject to an extrinsic check by the people under their own Constitution. And this role for the people gives meaning to the Constitution's commitment to accountability, without making it necessary to jettison its equally clear commitment to liberty.

---

[204]Wood, supra note [182], at 596 (quoting Charles Pinckney in 4 The Debates in the Several State Conventions on the Adoption of the Federal Constitution 331 (Jonathan Elliot ed., Philadelphia, J.B. Lippincott & Co. 1876)).

[205]Wood, supra note [182], at 599 (footnote omitted).

[206]Id. at 599–600.

There lies the hard answer to the question why, in a system whose final cause is liberty, the powers of government should be housed in an accountable body, elected by the people: to support the existence of the judiciary and thus to allow for the continual protection of liberty. John Hart Ely's theory[a] leads to the conclusion that the Bill of Rights exists to support majoritarian government. If he is right, the Constitution is a miserable failure. The government is not majoritarian and does not even come close to enabling pure majority preferences to prevail in the policymaking process. But Ely had it exactly backwards. A better understanding of the system we have is that *majoritarian government exists to support the Bill of Rights*.

MICHAEL SEIDMAN, OUR UNSETTLED CONSTITUTION: A NEW DEFENSE OF CONSTITUTIONALISM AND JUDICIAL REVIEW

1–11 (2001)

We live in an age of growing doubt as to the utility of any normative theory of constitutional law, much less a new one. Thinkers spanning a political spectrum anchored by Richard Posner on the right and Richard Rorty on the left agree that constitutional theory leads to a dead end. Rebecca L. Brown began a recent article by asking her readers to "honk if you are tired of constitutional theory." If the resulting sound was less than deafening, that was only because many legal academics are too bored with constitutional theory to bother to read her fine article.

* * *

The short of the matter, then, is that this hardly seems like the moment to propose a new, comprehensive constitutional theory that defends an expansive version of judicial review. Yet paradoxically, the current pessimism about constitutional theory in general and hostility to judicial review in particular can also be seen as laying the necessary foundations for a new approach. Three interrelated points provide the reasons why a new theory may be useful after all.

First, whatever the doubts of the critics, the fact remains that the Supreme Court continues to begin a new term on the first Monday of every October. Not only has the Court stubbornly refused to go out of business; it is more activist than ever. "Conservative" and "liberal" justices alike regularly vote to invalidate laws on a wide range of subjects. Although politicians occasionally grumble about judges who "make" rather than "enforce" the law, the country is far from open revolt against this practice. Judges and lawyers frequently accuse constitutional theorists of being out of touch with the "real world." This charge may be aimed at the wrong target. It is the anti-theorists who seem to hold themselves arrogantly aloof

[a]See Ely, supra note 2. [Eds.]

from a practice that people in the real world take for granted.

Perhaps judicial review is simply illegitimate. Yet it is a striking fact that even after *Bush v. Gore*, many Americans who thought that the decision was politically biased and wrong nonetheless continued to support the Court as an institution. Isn't it at least worth asking whether there is some intellectually respectable way to justify a practice that is so widely accepted? In the spirit Robert Nozick gracefully expressed in his book *Philosophical Explanations*, we might ask how these beliefs are *possible* even as we avoid the temptation to "[try] to get someone to believe something whether he wants to believe it or not." I think that there is a coherent explanation for judicial review, an explanation that the anti-theorists should engage with, even if they are not ultimately persuaded by it.

The second point is that however unfashionable, constitutional theory is in some sense inevitable.* After all, judicial restraint is itself a theory of constitutional law, and a controversial one at that. Why should elected officials, who may be short-sighted, poorly informed, or venal, have the final say on constitutional disputes? There may be good reasons for judicial restraint, but they should be put on the table just like the justifications for any other constitutional theory.

Consider, in this light, Judge Posner's recent attack on constitutional theory. Posner complains that it "has no power to command agreement from people not already predisposed to accept the theorist's policy prescriptions." Yet in the same article that asserts the worthlessness of constitutional theory, Posner advances a theory of his own, which he labels "pragmatism." Posner is too intelligent to miss this irony, so he takes pains to argue that pragmatism is really an anti-theory. Apparently, pragmatism amounts to no more than careful attention to empirical facts and the ways in which judicial decisions interact with those facts. How could anyone be against this?

Yet to precisely the extent that pragmatism is an anti-theory, it begs questions that only theory can answer. The instrumental rationality that Posner favors yields determinate outcomes only if we first agree on what it is that we are trying to accomplish. But even the most careful and comprehensive empirical study cannot settle disputes about ends.**

---

*This statement should not be confused with an assertion that any particular version of constitutional law is inevitable. In particular, I do not want to insist that there is anything inevitable about the American system of judicial review. A defense of the system is necessary precisely because it is not inevitable.

**For example, Posner faults the Supreme Court for its inattention to scientific evidence that might demonstrate that homosexuality is spread "from flaunting or public endorsement of the homosexual way of life." Richard A. Posner, *Against Constitutional Theory*, 73 NYU L. Rev. 1, 20 (1998). But this evidence (which, by the way, Posner himself considers

Posner, also candidly directs attention to a second question that his pragmatism begs. As he admits at the end of his essay, often the facts are unknown or even unknowable. When this is true, judges must nonetheless resolve disputes. Which resolution they choose will depend upon who bears the burden of proof, and surely this decision requires some theoretical justification.

Although Posner is less than crystal clear on this point, apparently he would place the burden on those who wish to reverse political outcomes on constitutional grounds. He expresses "considerable sympathy" with the view that judges should "take a back seat to the other branches of government," and should intervene only if their "sense of justice is sufficiently outraged." Moreover, although he may not realize it, the very structure of Posner's argument reflects this stance. It is telling that Posner chooses constitutional adjudication as the target for his complaint about the failure to attend to facts on the ground. There is no a priori reason to suppose that judges are more guilty of this sin than legislators or executive branch officials. Posner's choice of target strongly suggests that his default position is respect for decisions made by the political branches.

This position has the virtue of answering one of the questions that pragmatism begs, but it does so only by advancing the kind of theory that Posner wants to avoid. As I have already noted, "judicial restraint" is also a theory of constitutional adjudication, which should enjoy no more presumptive correctness than the theories that Posner attacks. If his general thesis is right, then it must be that this theory, like any other constitutional theory, "has no power to command agreement from people not already predisposed to accept the theorist's policy prescriptions."

One can hardly fault Judge Posner for falling into this trap. Being a thoroughgoing and consistent theoretical skeptic is hard work. Sometimes, anti-theorists try to make the job easier by relying on some of the negative connotations contingently associated with the word *theory*. The theoretical enterprise is treated as if it were necessarily abstruse, metaphysical, and impractical. To be sure, some theorists are guilty of these sins, but there is nothing about theory itself that requires their commission. Stripped of these negative connotations, all that *theory* amounts to is the offering of justifications for the decisions that one makes that are comprehensible to the audience to whom they are offered.

Anti-theorists are surely correct when they maintain that this enterprise can never be wholly successful. There will always be some people excluded

nonexistent) would be relevant only if homosexuality were a moral or social evil. This question, in turn, cannot be answered by empirical data. As Posner himself acknowledges, "There is no way to assess the validity of [the belief that homosexuality is morally blameworthy] and what weight if any such a belief should be given in a constitutional case [is] an equally indeterminate question." Id.

from the intended audience. I am reasonably confident that St. Thomas Aquinas, Josef Stalin, Frederich Nietzsche, and Antonin Scalia would be unmoved if exposed to the theory that I offer in this book. It does not follow that theory is worthless or unnecessary, however. To give up on the theoretical enterprise merely because it will never be wholly successful is to give up on the possibility of communicating with others about the reasons for one's actions.[***] And that is something that most people are simply unwilling or unable to do. We need to consider the implications of the fact that Steven Smith's intelligent and original book-length attack on the role of reason in constitutional theory is, itself, carefully reasoned or that Judge Posner not only advances a theory of his own, but also ends up articulating a theoretical argument against constitutional theory.

All of which leads to the third point: Although I cannot demonstrate that it is true, my guess is that the real target of the anti-theorists is not constitutional theory per se, but rather a particular kind of tendentious and unconvincing constitutional theory. The sort of theory that rubs skeptics the wrong way is one that dresses up controversial policy prescriptions in the garb of timeless and acontextual principle—a theory that tries to "command agreement" in Posner's words. Posner and his fellow critics are right to object to this sort of theory, and there is plenty of it around to object to. Consider, for example, John Rawls' notorious assertion that "any comprehensive doctrine that leads to a balance of political values excluding [a] duly qualified right [to an abortion] in the first trimester is to that extent unreasonable." Are we really to expect that abortion opponents will give up on their deepest moral and political commitments because of this claim?[****] And Rawls is hardly alone. Constitutional theories offered by scholars as diverse and talented as Frank Michelman, Ronald Dworkin, Michael Perry, John Hart Ely, Michael Sandel, and Richard Epstein, all claim that the theoretical enterprise can resolve some of our deepest political and moral disagreements.

There is a sense in which these efforts are quite noble. They reflect a faith in the power of reason and persuasion that is admirable. At their best,

***I do not mean to suggest that this communication must be in the form of reasoned argument in the philosophically rigorous sense of the term. We often successfully communicate by methods that are not "reasonable" in this sense—for example, by moral demonstration or empathic connection. In any event, the boundaries of "reasoned argument" are themselves unclear and contested. I use the term "reasons" more loosely to include any account of one's actions that is comprehensible to its audience.

****John Rawls, *Political Liberalism* 243 n. 32 (1993). To his great credit, Rawls himself has retracted this assertion. See John Rawls, *The Idea of Public Reason Reconsidered,* 64 U.Chi. L. Rev. 808 n. 80 (1997). As Rawls himself has written, "[I]t is often thought that the task of philosophy is to uncover a form of argument that will always prove convincing against all other arguments. There is, however, no such argument. People may often have final ends that require them to oppose one another without compromise." John Rawls, *The Law of Peoples* 123 (1999).

such theories can help us to understand positions that we might otherwise reject out of hand and build empathetic and intellectual bridges to political opponents. Unfortunately, though, constitutional theorists, like the rest of us, are not always at their best. Sometimes, theorists claim that their work shows not just that their views are possible or plausible, but that opposing views are irrational or illegitimate. When theorists try to command agreement rather than begin discussions, they are bound to be unsuccessful —and to enlarge, rather than shrink, the political and moral gulf that separates us.

Through a kind of guilt by association, the failures of these theories have brought into question not only the theoretical enterprise more generally, but also the practice of judicial review. Instead of legitimating exercises of judicial power, tendentious theories have tended to discredit them. Anti-theorists argue that if judicial decisions on controversial subjects like abortion, religion, gender, or sex really rest on the weak normative foundations supplied by academic theorists, then there is no good reason why these decisions should be entitled to our respect or obedience. Because these theories cannot justly command dissenters to give up their positions on these topics, decisions based on the theories amount to no more than an exercise of raw power masquerading as disinterested reason. Modern skepticism about theory and modern hostility to judicial review are therefore linked by a common worry about elitism and authoritarianism in constitutional analysis.

These concerns are legitimate and healthy. There is, indeed, a problem with most *theories* of constitutional law. It does not follow, however, that there is a problem with constitutional *theory.* The criticisms of the anti-theorists should provide a goad to do better, not an excuse for giving up. The challenge for a modern theorist is to formulate a general approach to constitutional law that takes into account the intractable nature of our political disagreements instead of attempting to suppress them. Our efforts should be directed toward building a new theory of constitutional law that starts by acknowledging the very weakness that has so often bedeviled the theoretical enterprise.

[W]e can accomplish this task by reversing the two central assumptions upon which most prior theory has been based: that principles of constitutional law should be independent of our political commitments and that the role of constitutional law is to settle political disagreement. It is just these assumptions that have discredited so much prior theory. To critics, it is obvious that theories offered by academic constitutionalists are not apolitical. Rather, they serve as rationalizations for a set of political commitments that precede the theory. It is obvious as well that these commitments are appropriately contestable and that disagreements with regard to them cannot be settled by any theoretical construct.

It does not follow, however, that all theories are subject to these criticisms. Suppose that we start by acknowledging that the critics are right. Just as they claim, the content of constitutional law does and must reflect contestable political views. And just as they claim, no constitutional theory will settle our disagreement about these views. Might we build a successful theory of constitutional law that rests on these concessions?

We can start by relaxing the first assumption. Judges regularly insist on the political neutrality of their role, but most ordinary citizens are not fooled. According to polling data, a large number of Americans think that the decision in *Bush v. Gore* was influenced by politics, and they are surely right. Are we really supposed to believe that it "just so happened" that the Court's most conservative Justices read the equal-protection clause in a way that favored George W. Bush while their more liberal colleagues read the same words so as to favor Al Gore? Of course, *Bush v. Gore* was an extraordinary case, but the point can be made more generally. It requires more faith than most people can muster to suppose that it is mere coincidence when Justice Antonin Scalia, a conservative Republican, finds conservative principles embedded in the Constitution, while Justice Ruth Bader Ginsburg, a liberal Democrat, regularly discovers liberal principles lurking in the same document.

Does this obvious fact discredit constitutional law? Viewed from one perspective, perhaps it does. It means that opinions about the content of constitutional law cannot be separated from political opinions. People will therefore favor or oppose particular interpretations of constitutional law based upon their political positions.

Suppose, though, that we try to view constitutional law from the outside. Instead of thinking of ourselves as participants in our political disputes, we might imagine that we are anthropologists investigating the function served by a particular practice in an alien culture. Viewed from this perspective, the political contestability of Supreme Court decisions is hardly fatal. To be sure, it would be fatal if one thought that the function of constitutional law was to settle ordinary political disagreements, for we can hardly expect constitutional law to resolve these disagreements if it simply reflects them. But it is precisely because most judges and constitutional theorists are committed to a settlement theory that they must insist on an Alice-in-Wonderland world where judicial interpretation of the Constitution is uninfluenced by politics.

On the other hand, if we relax the second assumption—if we assume that the function of constitutional law is not to settle disputes, but to unsettle any resolution reached by the political branches—then the political contestability of constitutional doctrine is much less troubling. To see why this is so, we need to consider what we should expect from constitutional law in the first place.

Like its rivals, unsettlement theory begins with the premise that in a free and diverse society, there is bound to be political conflict. Like its rivals, unsettlement theory takes the purpose of constitutional law to be the maintenance of a just community in the face of this conflict. Our ultimate objective should be to provide a just reason why individuals who lose political battles should nonetheless maintain their allegiance to the community. Unsettlement theory differs from its rivals by making the paradoxical claim that constitutional law can help build such a community by creating, rather than settling political conflict.

Any constitutional settlement is bound to produce losers who will continue to nurse deep- seated grievances, and we would be hard put to offer reasons, convincing within their own normative frameworks, for why these losers should abide by a settlement that they deeply oppose. But a constitution that unsettles creates no permanent losers. By destabilizing whatever outcomes are produced by the political process, it provides citizens with a forum and a vocabulary that they can use to continue the argument. Even when they suffer serious losses in the political sphere, citizens will have reason to maintain their allegiance to the community—not because constitutional law settles disputes, but because it provides arguments grounded in society's foundational commitments, for why the political settlement they oppose is unjust. In short, an unsettled constitution helps to build a community founded on consent by enticing losers into a continuing conversation.

It is important to understand that unsettlement theory does not preordain any particular outcome to this conversation. In particular, it provides no guarantee that the conversation will result in the reversal of the initial decision. A preordained outcome entails a settlement; it is the very indeterminacy of the outcome that makes the constitution unsettled. Thus, an unsettled constitution is different from a system with a settled mechanism for power sharing. Unsettlement does not promise losers that they will necessarily get their way. It promises them only that they will have a continued opportunity to engage their opponents in a good-faith and open ended discussion about what is to be done.

Of course, standing alone, this argument provides no reason why judges should play a special role in implementing the unsettled constitution. If the content of constitutional law is indeed inseparable from contestable, political commitments, one might fairly ask why a tiny number of unelected judges should be able to exercise political power over the rest of us?

In order to tackle this objection, it is necessary to emphasize, once again, the distinction between a community member and an anthropologist. If constitutional law is not politically neutral, then of course it follows that any individual's opinion about constitutional law will turn on the politics of the law in question. For example, my own views about judicial authority to invalidate laws restricting abortion or providing for affirmative action depend upon my substantive beliefs about the morality and wisdom of these practices and on my empirical judgment about whether judges are likely to share those beliefs. This fact is a necessary implication of the claim that constitutional law cannot settle political disputes.

It does not follow, however, that there is nothing to be gained from attempting to abstract from the disputes. From the perspective of an anthropologist, it still makes sense to ask whether a particular form of constitutional law allows a community to live in peace by offering reasons that make sense to its members for why political divisions should not lead to a severing of ties. When we ask this question, it turns out that there is a strong argument to be made for vigorous judicial review. Judges have the potential to play a special role, not because they can settle our disputes, but because they stand astride a series of contradictions that can unsettle any resolution of them. The best way to see this is to examine some of the criticisms that have been made of judicial review.

Sometimes, critics argue that judges are not accountable to the people. These critics start with the assumption that our disputes should be settled by democratic means. On other occasions, however, critics complain about the "myth" of judicial independence, pointing out that judges do not effectively protect individual rights because they have neither the inclination nor the ability to depart much from the contemporary popular consensus. At first, it would seem that these criticisms cannot both be right. Oddly, though, it is the very fact that both *are* that provides the justification for judicial power. Precisely because judges are both public and private, both independent and accountable, they are able to police a boundary that is never fixed.

The point missed by the critics is that both a democratic, collective mechanism for resolving our disputes and a private, individualist mechanism are contestable settlements. Losers have no more obligation to accept these outcomes than any other settlement. A large part of what divides us is precisely the question whether particular issues should be resolved publicly and democratically, or privately and individually. There is no reason to expect this argument to be finally resolved to everyone's satisfaction by simply assuming the primacy of a one settlement or the other. Because judges straddle the public-private line—because they are both independent from the political branches, and in some sense accountable to them—they are well suited to the job of keeping the division between public and private permanently unsettled.

Another set of criticisms of judicial review points to the supposed indeterminacy—some would say incoherence—of the standard tools of liberal constitutionalism. For someone skilled at the relevant moves, open-ended constitutional text and vague judicial precedent can be made to support a wide variety of arguments. Moreover, the core distinctions around which constitutional law is organized—the difference between freedom and coercion, public and private, or feasance and nonfeasance—are easily deconstructed. Many skeptics have complained that this manipulability of constitutional doctrine means that judicial judgments are inevitably political. To the extent that one thinks of constitutional law as providing a politically neutral method of resolving our disputes, this criticism is on target.

But the skeptics have often failed to notice that this fact about constitutional argument can also be a virtue. An odd feature of constitutional rhetoric is that it is at once analytically empty and uniquely powerful. For example, no matter how persuasive the demonstration that the private can be collapsed into the public or the free into the coerced, very few people are able to give up on these fundamental concepts around which most of us organize our experience of the world. If one believes that judicial decisions are legitimate not because they settle disputes, but because they utilize an analytic technique well suited to unsettling them, then we should celebrate the fact that constitutional rhetoric provides very powerful support for virtually any outcome to any argument.

C. THE ISSUE OF JUDICIAL SUPREMACY

LAWRENCE GENE SAGER, FAIR MEASURE: THE LEGAL STATUS OF UNDERENFORCED CONTITUTIONAL NORMS

91 HARV.L.REV. 1212, 1213–1227 (1978)

A. Judicial Underenforcement of Constitutional Norms

When we think about matters of constitutional interpretation in our legal system * * * our attention is drawn to the federal judiciary in general and the Supreme Court in particular. In applying the provisions of the Constitution to the challenged behavior of state or federal officials, the federal courts have modeled analytical structures; I will call these models or structures of analysis *constructs*. These resemble conceptions of the various constitutional concepts from which they derive. But the important difference between a true constitutional conception and the judicially formulated construct is that the judicial construct may be truncated for reasons which are based not upon analysis of the constitutional concept but upon various concerns of the Court about its institutional role. These concerns operate to produce some judicial constructs which are not at all exhaustive of the constitutional concepts they reflect. Thus, a federal judicial construct may not be a true constitutional conception because it may not exhaust the concept from which it derives when this is the case, the construct will let, go unchecked some official behavior which may well be in conflict with the concept itself.

A prominent example of this phenomenon is by the equal protection clause of the fourteenth amendment. Views of equal protection may vary, but a reasonable statement of the concept for purposes of this discussion is: "A state may treat persons differently only when it is fair to do so."

Under this federal judicial construct of the equal protection clause, only a small part of the universe of plausible claims of unequal and unjust treatment by government is seriously considered by the federal courts; the vast majority of such claims are dismissed out of hand. Thus, for example, claims that classifications made in the fashioning of schemes of taxation or business regulation are arbitrary or unfair simply are not congenial to the federal courts, and will occasion in the federal courts only the purely nominal review of the traditional rational relationship test. There are reasons which explain and to some degree justify federal judicial restraint in the application of the equal protection clause to state regulatory and taxation measures; these reasons have been extensively rehearsed in the literature of judicial restraint.[11] In the most general of terms, the claims for restraint typically turn on the propriety of unelected federal judges' displacing the judgments of elected State officials,[12] or upon the competence of federal courts to prescribe workable standards of state conduct and devise measures to enforce them.[13]

What these arguments do not typically include are claims to the effect that the very concept of equal protection should be understood to exclude from its boundaries the tax or regulatory measures enacted by state or municipal officials. As an historical matter, it could be argued that racial equality was the exclusive ingredient of the concept of equal protection. But that conceptual check has long since been rejected by the federal judiciary.

What I want to distinguish between here are reasons for limiting a judicial construct of a constitutional concept which are based upon questions of propriety or capacity and those which are based upon an understanding of the concept itself. The former I will refer to as "institutional," the latter as "analytical." Institutional rather than analytical reasons have prompted the broad exclusion of state tax and regulatory measures from the

---

[11]Prominences in this terrain include A. Bickel, The Least Dangerous Branch 34–72 (1962); * * * McCloskey, *Economic Due Process and the Supreme Court: An Exhumation and Reburial* 1962 Sup. Ct. Rev. 34; Thayer, *The Origin and Scope of the American Doctrine of Constitutional Law*, 7 Harv. L. Rev. 129 (1893).

[12]*See, e.g.*, A. Bickel *supra* note 11 at 16–23; L. Hand, The Bill of Rights 73–74 (1958); J. Thayer, John Marshall 103–04, 106–07 (1901).

[13]*See, e.g.*, * * * San Antonio Independent School Dist. v. Rodriquez, 411 U.S. 1, 41–43 (1973).

reach of the equal protection construct fashioned by the federal judiciary. This is what creates the disparity between this construct and a true conception of equal protection, and thus substantiates the claim that equal protection is an underenforced constitutional norm.

* * *

The equal protection clause is offered here as a prominent example of a constitutional norm which is underenforced to a significant degree by the federal judiciary, but there are certainly other norms which are significantly underenforced. While there is no litmus test for distinguishing these norms, there are indicia of underenforcement. These include a disparity between the scope of a federal judicial construct and that of plausible understandings of constitutional concept from which it derives, the presence in court opinions of frankly institutional explanations for setting particular limits to a federal judicial construct, and other anomalies such as the disparity in thirteenth and fourteenth amendment analysis between the independent reach of amendments and the scope of congressional authority which they confer. On this basis, the following are among the likely candidates for characterization as underenforced: the fifth amendment's prohibition against takings of property without just compensation,[22] the privileges or immunities clause of the fourteenth amendment,[23] and the due process clause of the fourteenth amendment, particularly in its substantive application.[24]

B. Legal Status of Judicially Underenforced Constitutional Norms

Conventional analysis does not distinguish between fully enforced and underenforced constitutional norms; as a general matter, the scope of a constitutional norm is considered to be coterminous with the scope of its judicial enforcement. Thus, when the Supreme Court declines to inquire seriously into an arguably unjust distinction drawn between classes of persons or enterprises in a state tax or regulatory statute, this decision is

---

[22]The line between those economic injuries inflicted on property owners by government which are compensable and those which are not has been remarkably elusive, and courts have been led to draw distinctions at apparently arbitrary points. [This may be because] courts are institutionally incapable of making the routine "fairness" determinations required for a satisfactory answer to the question of when compensation should be awarded. As a consequence they may tend to focus only on core cases]—those fitting the paradigm of physical seizure or virtual destruction.

[23]The privileges or immunities clause was greatly restricted in its infancy by the Supreme Court's holding in the Slaughter–House Cases, 83 U.S. (16 Wall.) 36 (1873), that the only rights secured therein were those peculiar to national citizenship. Consequently, the clause never lived up to the hopes of its Radical proponents. * * *

[24]The argument for characterizing substantive due process as a judicially underenforced norm is based on the proposition that only institutional concerns can justify the Court's total retreat from the enforcement of economic due process rights in even quite extreme contexts. The case for this proposition is made convincingly in McCloskey, *supra* note 11, at 40–62.

generally expressed and understood as an authoritative determination that the distinction does not violate the equal protection clause.

Where a federal judicial construct is found not to extend to certain behavior because of institutional concerns rather than analytical perceptions, it seems strange to regard the resulting decision as a statement about the meaning of the constitutional norm in question. After all, what the members of the federal tribunal have actually determined is that there are good reasons for stopping short of exhausting the content of the constitutional concept with which they are dealing; the limited judicial construct which they have fashioned or accepted is occasioned by this determination and does not derive from a judgment about the scope of the constitutional concept itself.

From this observation flows the thesis which I want to advance here: constitutional norms which are underenforced by the federal judiciary should be understood to be legally valid to their full conceptual limits, and federal judicial decisions which stop short of these limits should be understood as delineating only the boundaries of the federal courts' role in enforcing the norm: By "legally valid," I mean that the unenforced margins of underenforced norms should have the full status of positive law which we generally accord to the norms of our Constitution, save only that the federal judiciary will not enforce these margins. Thus, the legal powers or legal obligations of government officials which are subtended in the unenforced margins of underenforced constitutional norms are to be understood to remain in full force.

* * *

The idea that the judicially enforced norm may be narrower than its scope as legal authority in other contexts may be unconventional today, but it enjoys a venerable provenance. James Bradley Thayer's essay on *The Origin and Scope of the American Doctrine of Constitutional Law*[31] is an important intellectual fount of the judicial restraint thesis. Thayer argued for the rule of clear mistake—that is, that "'an Act of the legislature is not to be declared void unless the violation of the constitution is so manifest as to leave no room for reasonable doubt.'" The heart of Thayer's argument is that the legislature is charged with the responsibility of measuring its own conduct against the Constitution and that the judiciary should therefore not lightly reach a judgment on the constitutionality of a legislative act contrary to the prior constitutional judgment of the legislature. * * * The rule of clear mistake, therefore, is not founded on the idea that only manifestly abusive legislative enactments are unconstitutional, but rather on the idea that only such manifest error entitles a court to displace the prior constitu-

[31]Thayer, *supra* note 11.

tional ruling of the enacting legislature. It is a rule of judicial behavior—or, in Thayer's words, a "rule of administration." * * *

* * *

The judicial restraint thesis has retained its vitality, and continues to be instrumental in the judicial enforcement of the Constitution, as the federal judicial enforcement of the equal protection clause so clearly indicates. But, under the influence of a vigorous tradition of Supreme Court enforcement of constitutional norms, we have come to lose sight of the fact that some judicial decisions reflect the tradition of judicial restraint and should not be understood to be exhaustive statements of the meaning of the implicated constitutional norms.

* * *

In sum, these arguments support the proposition that judicially underenforced constitutional norms should be regarded as legally valid to their conceptual limits. When the federal courts restrain themselves for reasons of competence and institutional propriety rather than reasons of constitutional substance, it is incongruous to treat the products of such restraint as authoritative determinations of constitutional substance. This view is further reinforced by early formulations of the judicial restraint thesis, to which the idea of the scope of constitutional norms extending beyond the scope of their judicial enforcement is intrinsic. Finally, this view is consistent with our understanding of the political question doctrine, which operates in some contexts that closely parallel those which produce the underenforcement of some constitutional norms.

But the force and meaning of this revised view of the legal status of judicially underenforced constitutional norms can best be assessed by considering what, as a practical matter, will change in our legal system if we adopt it. The most direct consequence of adopting this revised view is the perception that government officials have a legal obligation to obey an underenforced constitutional norm which extends beyond its interpretation by the federal judiciary to the full dimensions of the concept which the norm embodies. This obligation to obey constitutional norms at their unenforced margins requires governmental officials to fashion their own conceptions of these norms and measure their conduct by reference to these conceptions. Public officials cannot consider themselves free to act at what they perceive or ought to perceive to be peril to constitutional norms merely because the federal judiciary is unable to enforce these norms at their margins. At a minimum, the obligation of public officials in this context, as in any other, is one of "best efforts" to avoid unconstitutional conduct. The observation that public officials have an obligation in some cases to regulate their behavior by standards more severe than those imposed by the federal judiciary constitutes a significant claim on official behavior and, if accepted, should alter discourse among and about officials.

[In the later part of his article Sager suggests two further implications of his thesis. One is that judicial interpretation of equal protection, due process, and the other guarantees of the Fourteenth Amendment may not exhaust the legal meaning of those clauses. If it does not, then Congress may have authority under section 5 of the Amendment to do more than the Court does to enforce its guarantees. See *Katzenbach v. Morgan*.[a] A second and more novel suggestion is this: state courts may go further than federal courts in sustaining federal constitutional claims. Federal courts often decline for institutional reasons to enforce the norms at their margins. But state courts in these cases, if they are not bound by the same institutional constraints, should be free to enforce the norms to the limits of their conceptual boundaries. In Sager's view, the Supreme Court should not review and reverse such state decisions, even though it would reach an opposite result.]

LARRY ALEXANDER AND FREDERICK SCHAUER, DEFENDING JUDICIAL SUPREMACY: A REPLY

17 Const.Comment. 455–473, 481–482 (2002)

In *On Extrajudicial Constitutional Interpretation*,[1] we put forth and defended the position that the Supreme Court's interpretations of the Constitution should be taken by all other officials, judicial and non-judicial, as having an authoritative status equivalent to the Constitution itself. We argued, to put it starkly, that "the Constitution is what the judges say it is" may well be bad jurisprudence because it is incomprehensible as an attempt to explain what it means to argue to the Supreme Court, but that it is nonetheless a desirable attitude for non-judicial officials to have towards the Court and its product, in much the same way, but far less controversially, that it is a desirable attitude for lower court judges to have towards the Court and its opinions.

This position, commonly associated with the Supreme Court's opinions in *Cooper v. Aaron*[5] and, more recently, in *City of Boerne v. Flores*,[6] has long been subject to withering criticism. Some of this criticism has come from academics, but even more has come from officials of the executive

---

[a]384 U.S. 641 (1966).

[1]Larry Alexander and Frederick Schauer, *On Extrajudicial Constitutional Interpretation*, 110 Harv.L.Rev. 1359 (1977).

[5]358 U.S. 1 (1958).

[6]521 U.S. 507, 536 (1997) ("When the political branches of the Government act against the background of a judicial interpretation of the Constitution already issued, it must be understood that in later cases and controversies the Court will treat its precedents with the respect due them under settled principles, including stare decisis, and contrary expectations must be disappointed."). * * *

and legislative branches of government who see little reason to take their own interpretations of the Constitution as being subject to override or nullification just because of a prior claim by a branch of government—the judiciary—that is given no interpretative priority in the constitutional text itself. The raw assertion of judicial supremacy in the task of interpreting the Constitution, so the critics of *Cooper* and *City of Boerne* have insisted, is unsupported by history, unsupported by the structure of our own constitutional system, and unsupported by persuasive normative arguments of political theory or institutional design.

That *Cooper* and *City of Boerne* announce the supremacy of the Supreme Court and its interpretations of the Constitution is largely beside the point, for the Supreme Court's bald assertion of its own interpretive supremacy begs the question whether other branches and other officials, to say nothing of the public at large, should accept the consequences of that assertion. Nevertheless, and without relying on the bootstrapping argument that the Supreme Court's assertion of its own supremacy establishes that supremacy, we argued that a central moral function of law is to settle what ought to be done. A constitution, because of the difficulty of altering it, attempts to effect a more permanent settlement of what ought to be done than do statutes and common law decisions. Where the meaning of a legal settlement, including a constitutional one, is itself controverted, it is a central moral function of judicial interpretation to settle the meaning of that (attempted) settlement. The undeniable fact that a judicial interpretation of an attempted legal settlement may be incorrect does not and should not call into question its authority, for it is inherent in all legal settlements of what ought to be done that such settlements claim authority even if those subject to them believe the settlements to be morally and legally mistaken. Moreover, the authority of a mistaken second-order settlement of the meaning of a first-order settlement of some moral question is less problematic than the authority of the first-order settlement itself. So if we expect people to obey the Constitution even when they morally disagree with it, we can, for the same reasons but at one remove, expect them to obey the Supreme Court's interpretation of the Constitution even when they believe that interpretation to be erroneous.

Perhaps gratifyingly, our article has in the past three years become the target for many of those who take the central claims of *Cooper* and *City of Boerne*, and the claims of judicial interpretive supremacy more generally, to be misguided. In half a dozen extended published responses,[12] and additional

---

[12]See Neal Devins and Louis Fisher, *Judicial Exclusivity and Political Instability*, 84 Va.L.Rev. 83 (1998); Edward Hartnett, *A Matter of Judgment, Not a Matter of Opinion*, 74 N.Y.U. L.Rev. 123 (1999); Robert F. Nagel, *Judicial Supremacy and the Settlement Function*, 39 Wm. & Mary L.Rev. 849 (1998); Bruce G. Peabody, *Nonjudicial Constitutional Interpretation, Authoritative Settlement, and a New Agenda for Research*, 16

commentary contained in less targeted books and articles,[13] we have been seen as ahistorical defenders of Supreme Court arrogance, and equally ahistorical denigrators of the constitutional interpretive capabilities of Congress and the executive branch. To our critics, our claims of judicial supremacy represent ignorance of history, bad constitutional law, misguided institutional design, and impoverished democratic theory.

These criticisms have been thoughtful and troubling, but our aim here is not to engage in the kind of acrimonious debates between critics and "misunderstood" authors that one normally associates with the letters section of the *New York Review of Books*. Rather, we take the existence of this volume of criticism as an occasion for joining issue, and continuing a debate that goes to the central questions of the role of a constitution and the role of the courts in a democratic society.

* * *

An essential preliminary is to consider the nature of the question we are asking when we ask whether the Supreme Court should be the supreme interpreter of the Constitution, its interpretations consequently binding on others even when their own interpretations strike them as better than the Supreme Court's. Even before we ask what the question is, we must ask what kind of question it is we are asking.

We frame the preliminary question in this way to make clear that we are not asking a question that can be answered from the Constitution itself. John Harrison, Edward Hartnett, Neal Devins, and Louis Fisher all devote considerable attention to the way in which we have ignored the non-designation of the Supreme Court as supreme interpreter in the Constitution itself as a dispositive datum, and have ignored as well the constitutional history explaining and supporting the view that the Constitution does not and was not intended to grant the Supreme Court supreme interpretive power over the Constitution's terms.

We accept for the sake of argument (and also because we have no reason to doubt it) the rich historical evidence that Harrison, Hartnett, Devins, and Fisher have adduced. We thus accept that the Framers did not

---

Const.Comment. 63 (1999); Emily Sherwin, *Ducking* Dred Scott*: A Response to Alexander and Schauer*, 15 Const.Comment. 65 (1998); Mark Tushnet, *Two Versions of Judicial Supremacy*, 39 Wm. & Mary L.Rev. 945 (1998); see also John Harrison, Coordination, the Constitution, and the Binding Effect of Judicial Opinions, University of Virginia School of Law Working Papers.

[13]See Mark Tushnet, Taking the Constitution Away from the Courts 27–29 (Princeton U. Press, 1999); William G. Buss, *Federalism, Separation of Powers, and the Demise of the Religious Freedom Restoration Act*, 83 Iowa L.Rev. 391, 429-31 (1998); Joel K. Goldstein, *The Presidency and the Rule of Law: Some Preliminary Reflections*, 43 St. L. L.J. 791, 818–19, 833-35 (1999); Suzanna Sherry, *Justice O'Connor's Dilemma: The Baseline Question*, 39 Wm. & Mary L.Rev. 865, 903–05 (1998).

intend the Supreme Court to be the Constitution's supreme interpreter, that the ratifiers in the states did not understand the Supreme Court to be the Constitution's supreme interpreter, and that the text does not designate the Supreme Court as the Constitution's supreme interpreter. Consequently, we accept that such a role for the Supreme Court cannot itself be based on the Constitution textually or historically understood. Indeed, we shall go even further and assume, for the sake of argument, that the Constitution actually repudiates such a role. But we nevertheless maintain that our argument is not simply one about hypothetical systems, but one that pertains to this Constitution in this constitutional system.

We are able to make this claim, even with the assumptions we accept, because we are arguing for a preconstitutional norm, a norm that determines not what was adopted then, but how what was adopted then should be regarded now. The Constitution's authority—its status as fundamental law—ultimately rests not on facts about the past, but on the Constitution's acceptance as authoritative in the present. This is a logical and not a historical point, and it is a logical point that undergirds our entire approach.

* * *

It is for these reasons that we take the illuminating historical and textual analyses of Devins, Fisher, Hartnett, and Harrison to be far less conclusive than they take them to be. The question of how we are to ground the Constitution is preconstitutional and extraconstitutional, and so the question of how we are to understand the Constitution is likewise preconstitutional and extraconstitutional. Our inquiry into whose interpretations, if anyone's, of the Constitution are to be regarded as authoritative and supreme is just this kind of preconstitutional and extraconstitutional inquiry, and thus a historical or textual focus strikes us as missing the point. If when asked why we drive in the direction of the tip of the arrow and not the tail we were to respond that the arrow tells us to go in the direction of its tip, we would be rightfully accused of failing to understand the conditions, external to the arrow itself, that enable us to understand what the arrow means. Similarly, to say that we should look conclusively to the Constitution's text and history to determine what that text and history are to tell us is to make the same conceptual error. Our inquiry is into the conditions that determine what the Constitution is to be understood as meaning, and it will be of no help to presuppose a meaning as a way of answering the question of what the meaning is.

* * *

That what Madison and others thought does not settle the question is premised, again, on the problem of self-reference. Suppose, to vary slightly an example that one of us has used previously, that we were to write a constitution establishing us—Larry Alexander and Fred Schauer—as its supreme interpreters, and suppose we were to provide in this document that it would become valid and effective upon our signing of it and upon notice of that signing appearing, as it now is with these very words, in *Constitutional Commentary*. Under these circumstances, our constitution's own internally specified conditions for its validity would have been satisfied, and thus our constitution's own claim to be the Constitution of the United States would be valid according to the conditions contained within the document.

As should be clear, however, the satisfaction of the document's internal and self-specified conditions for its own validity would be woefully inadequate to establish the document as the Constitution of the United States. And that is because a constitution's status as the constitution is dependent upon its (empirical) acceptance by a polity as their constitution. Without this empirical acceptance—acceptance as social fact—no amount of formal internal validity will make a document a constitution.

What follows from this is that what makes James Madison's constitution and not Alexander and Schauer's constitution the Constitution of the United States is not something that is contained in the document, and not something that could have been determined in 1787, but is rather something that is determined now by the American people. Without the social fact of acceptance by the American people in 2000 that the document that Madison and his compatriots wrote in 1787 is the Constitution of the United States, that document is no more authoritative than the constitution that we purported to make effective on the pages of this volume.

If what makes the 1787 Constitution the 2000 Constitution is dependent on 2000 social facts, then so is the 2000 status of what James Madison and the other framers intended in 1787 dependent on a 2000 decision and not on a 1787 decision. The relevance of history is not determined historically, but by a present political and social decision. As a consequence, the determination of 1787 preconstitutional questions is necessarily a non-historical question, although it is of course possible that the non-historical question might be answered by giving a role to history.

This is the sense in which we claimed that our inquiry was not historical. What Madison thought about the question of judicial supremacy, if indeed he thought about it at all, is no more dispositive than what the text says about judicial supremacy, for the point about preconstitutionality is as germane to the question of the authority of history as it is to the authority of the text. Thus, our argument is that the *Cooper* rule is normatively superior to what we tendentiously call institutional anarchy. If the original Constitution lacks the *Cooper* rule, then our claim is that the original Constitution is normatively inferior to a constitution that contains the *Cooper* rule. We could, of course, obtain the *Cooper* rule by amending the Constitution through the formal processes it prescribes in Article V. But that is not what we are advocating. Rather, we are advocating that we obtain the *Cooper* rule (or recognize the existence and validity of the *Cooper* rule) in the same way that we have obtained the original Constitution itself, namely, by accepting it as authoritative. In *Cooper*, the Supreme Court ran that rule up the flagpole. If we like it, all we have to do is salute. And it appears that most of us have in fact done so. And if that is so, then that makes the *Cooper* rule as "constitutional" as the Constitution itself.

* * *

Once we turn from meta-questions about the nature of the question to the question itself, we arrive at our claim that one of the chief functions of law in general, and constitutional law in particular, is to provide a degree of coordinated settlement for settlement's sake of what is to be done. In a world of moral and political disagreement, law can often provide a settlement of these disagreements, a settlement neither final nor conclusive, but nevertheless authoritative and thus providing for those in first-order disagreement a second-order resolution of that disagreement that will make it possible for decision to be made, actions to be coordinated, and life to go on.

But what is so special about settlement? Here our critics come in two varieties. Some, especially Mark Tushnet but most of the others as well, and indeed a vast tradition surrounding them, sees an independent virtue in public constitutional discourse, and thus sees a virtue in the kind of discourse that will never come to pass without some degree of continuous public dispute and debate about constitutional meaning. For an entire contemporary movement stressing the Constitution as a forum and a focal point for public deliberation, a cardinal virtue of the Constitution is that it provides the locus for desirable public debate about crime control, affirmative action, gender equality, sexual orientation, devolution of authority to the states, presidential conduct, the role of religion in public life, and innumerable other topics that combine undeniable public interest and importance with a plain connection to the kinds of topics that the Constitution designates as fundamental. And if we overly stress the settlement function of the Constitution, so the argument appears to go, we truncate precisely the public debate and deliberation that lies, or should lie, at the heart of the constitutional tradition.

We demur. Although we do not deny the virtues of public discourse, it strikes us as the conceit of American constitutionalists to think that Americans need the Constitution in order to debate affirmative action, criminal justice, abortion, religion and the state, privacy, or capital punishment. These debates have flourished in countries in which there is no single written constitutional document (primarily Great Britain, New Zealand, and Israel), and they have flourished in countries in which the written constitutions have not constitutionalized these particular topics. Although it would take serious comparative deliberative research, using various dimensions of constitutionalism as variables, to answer this question with any authority, and although such research does not yet exist, it appears to us far from certain that a constitution is either a necessary or a sufficient condition, or even a significant causal contributor, to fruitful public debate about matters of great political and moral moment.

To put the point differently, our argument is premised not on the assumptions that agreement is better than disagreement, or that settlement is better than keeping things open, even though both of these are plausible world-views. Rather, our argument is premised on the special functions that law serves, and that agreement and settlement appear to be the peculiar and special province of law, and the peculiar and special province of constitutions that have been written down and understood in substantially law-like ways. There are other forms of discourse-focusing public documents, but our argument is premised on there being something important about the difference between the American Constitution and the writings of Confucius or Chairman Mao (to take two prominent examples of discourse-focusing non-legal documents), and about the difference between the Constitution and the Declaration of Independence.

Moreover, although constitutions typically deal with matters of greater moral moment than determining whether people should drive on the right or on the left, to take the classic example of law's coordinating function, the value of settlement for settlement's sake is hardly absent from the functions of a constitution. Although people could well have serious moral and political disagreements about whether to have proportional or "first past the post" representation, about whether there should be an established state religion, about whether there should be trial by jury in civil (or criminal) cases, about whether criminal defendants should be compelled (upon pain of punishment for contempt of court, or a permissible inference of guilt to testify), or about whether Presidents should serve as many four-year terms as the electorate is willing to permit, all of these areas of plausible political and moral disagreement are pretty much settled in the American constitutional text, thus taking them off the agenda, even for those who disagree with the substance of the settlement. The authority of law, when it is taken to be authoritative, provides, for those who disagree with the terms of the settlement, content-independent reason for obeying the terms of the settlement even when they disagree with their substance. If, as Justice Brandeis claimed, "in most matters it is more important that the applicable rule of law be settled than that it be settled right,"[36] the settlement qua

[36] Burnet v. Coronado Oil & Gas Co., 285 U.S. 393, 406 (1932) (Brandeis, J., dissenting); see also Sheddon v. Goodrich, 8 Ves. 481, 497, 32 Eng. Rep. 441, 447 (1803) ("better the Law should be certain, than that every Judge should speculate upon improvements").

settlement serves important social functions. And as the examples we just gave illustrate, the value of settlement for settlement's sake is hardly absent from the realm of constitutional settlements. * * *

The examples we have just used, of course, represent a biased sample, for they are all examples in which the constitutional text makes moderately clear what the settlement is. With a text as indeterminate as the American Constitution, however, it is far more common to find disputes with a constitutional dimension in which the text itself provides no settlement for that dispute. Does the establishment clause prohibit teacher-organized non-denominational prayer in the public schools or student-led non-denominational prayer at public school graduations? Does the equal protection clause prohibit states from maintaining single-sex colleges and universities? Does the Fourth Amendment's warrant requirement prohibit use at trial of probative evidence obtained without a warrant? * * *

In these and countless other instances, there exists in the United States plausible moral and political disagreement and the absence of a clear textual settlement. In place of this textual settlement, however, we have Supreme Court opinions attempting to resolve the issue, but whose resolutions certainly do not eliminate the underlying disagreement. In such cases, our central claim is that the value of settlement for settlement's sake is such that bodies other than the Supreme Court, especially lower courts, state legislatures, Congress, and the President, ought to take the resolution as authoritative even as these bodies continue to disagree with the substance of the resolution. By recognizing the authority and thus the interpretive supremacy of the Supreme Court, we argue, these other bodies will contribute to stability and social harmony in just the same way that they do when they recognize the authoritative and supremacy of the constitutional text itself. * * *

* * *

Implicit in our argument, however, is something we should make explicit—we do not believe that law, or courts, or constitutions, are or should be the repositories for all that is good in institutional design. Just as we ought not to design the brakes on a car in order to maximize speed, acceleration, or ease of steering, even as we recognize these other goals as relevant, so too do we rely on the proposition that law-based institutions serve stability and settlement fostering functions more than do other social institutions, and that that is not necessarily a bad way to think about the separation of functions in a complex and differentiated society. So when we claim that settlement for settlement's sake is the special brief of the law, we do not claim, and should not be understood as claiming, that all social institutions have the same brief as does the law, or that settlement should loom as large in the pantheon of social values as it properly does in that subset of society we call the law. To see judicial supremacy in settlement terms, as we do, is thus to see constitutional law as serving an essentially stabilizing and constraining function. Were stability and constraint not preeminent among constitutional values, we wonder why it is seen as important in the first instance to impose second-order constitutional constraints on first-order political decisions. But if stability and constraint are central to explaining constitutionalism itself, then the argument for a single authoritative interpreter is an argument that flows directly from the deepest values of constitutionalism.

* * *

In cases in which a Supreme Court interpretation is believed by the political branches to be not only incorrect but also iniquitous or bad policy, should settlement then take a back seat to substantive correctness? From the standpoint of institutional design, which is the standpoint that pervades our project, we continue to believe that the answer is "no." Many, perhaps most, constitutional issues touch on matters of substantive importance, so that practically all interpretive disagreements with the Court will be accompanied by policy disagreements. That means that without authoritative settlement, most constitutional issues will remain open in the sense that any governmental actor who disagrees with a Supreme Court constitutional decision will feel free, legally and morally even if not always politically or prudentially, to ignore that decision. The police officer who disagrees with the prevailing state of Fourth Amendment warrant law will likely bypass seeking a warrant if he believes he might achieve his ends in doing so; and his chances of doing so will be enhanced if, for example, lower court judges are under no legal obligation to follow Supreme Court decisions with which they disagree. So too with state legislatures that would prefer organized prayer in the public schools, municipalities that seek to regulate indecency as well as obscenity, and the panoply of executive officials who might wish to use their powers to discourage women from having abortions.

Perhaps because of examples like these, none of our critics take the position that lower courts need not follow the Supreme Court, nor even the position, central to Attorney General Meese's claim a dozen years ago, that the states, whether in their executive, legislative, law enforcement, or judicial capacities, were free to take Supreme Court decisions as being limited to the case in which they arose, and thus not setting out law for other actors. That our critics are unwilling to come out strongly in support of dispersal of the interpretive authority among the 50 states suggests that the debate is narrower than might at first appear, and that our arguments for national interpretive supremacy of the national constitution is well-accepted. Still, Devins and Fisher, Nagel, Peabody, and Tushnet all argue that the need for authoritative settlement does not dictate which institution should possess that authority. A democratically constituted body can settle constitutional issues, they argue, and thus for some or many issues Congress might be superior to a court in performing the settlement function.

* * *

It is fashionable to dismiss John Marshall's claim that the province of the judiciary is "to say what the law is" as typical Marshallian hubris, unnecessary to the result in *Marbury*, unsupported by the Constitution, and unwise as a matter of policy. Yet if a multiplicity of bodies says what the law is, then there is likely to be a multiplicity of laws, or, more precisely, a multiplicity of interpretations of the same law. And if, as Lon Fuller maintained, knowing what the law is and knowing how to comply are necessary conditions for legality itself,[77] then multifarious law and multifarious interpretation are at odds with the rule of law itself. Although diversity of opinion is a valuable social phenomenon, law exists primarily because diversity of opinion and diversity of action may sometimes produce more harm than good. When we value coordination and settlement more than we value diversity, we employ law, and John Marshall's claim is nothing less than the observation, later refined by Fuller, that without a single and authoritative interpreter there would be little difference between law and the numerous non-enforced directives we find in philosophy books and advice columns.

As a judge, Marshall not surprisingly moved too quickly from the need for a single authoritative interpreter to the claim that the judiciary was the only institution that could serve this role. But although there are other candidates, none of them contain the institutional constraints that could enable them to speak with the same degree of consistency as the Supreme Court. As long as this is so, and there is no evidence that it is not, then it will and should be the function of the Supreme Court to say what the law is. For those arguing to the Supreme Court or evaluating its work, there will always remain some conceptual space between what the Supreme Court says and the law the Court purports to interpret. For those to whom the Supreme Court speaks, however, the functions of law have been better served, and will be better served in the future, if the Constitution is what the Supreme Court says it is.

LARRY KRAMER, WE THE COURT

115 HARV.L.REV. 4–15, 157–169 (2001)

For all his genius, John Marshall is seldom included among American's great political or legal rhetoricians. He penned some decent enough lines, but nothing with the power routinely displayed by a Holmes or a Lincoln, or, even among his contemporaries, by a Jefferson or a Paine. There is one

[77] See Lon L. Fuller, The Morality of Law (Yale U. Press, 2d ed. 1969).

line, though, that every lawyer and law student knows by heart, almost by instinct: "It is, emphatically, the province and duty of the judicial department, to say what the law is." There supposedly, in one pithy sentence, is the Supreme Court's own Declaration of Independence.

But what does Marshall's statement mean—on the ground, in operation? In 1958, the Court insisted in the almost-as-famous case of *Cooper v. Aaron* that *Marbury* "declared the basic principle that the federal judiciary is supreme in the exposition of the law of the Constitution," adding that this idea "has ever since been respected by this Court and the Country as a permanent and indispensable feature of our constitutional system." Well, hardly. As we shall see below (though it is by now conventional wisdom), *Marbury* staked out a considerably more modest position, venturing only that it was proper for the Court to interpret the Constitution without in any way suggesting that its interpretations were superior to those of the other branches. And certainly, as we shall also see below (though this, too, is conventional wisdom), the idea of judicial supremacy was not cheerfully embraced in the years after *Marbury*. The Court's periodic tugs of war with the likes of Jefferson, Jackson, Lincoln, the Reconstruction Congress, and FDR, to name only a few, are familiar terrain even to non-historians.

But here is the striking thing: in the years since *Cooper v. Aaron*, the idea of judicial supremacy—the notion that judges have the last word when it comes to constitutional interpretation and that their decisions determine the meaning of the Constitution for everyone—has finally found widespread approbation. The Court's decisions are often still controversial. State legislatures sometimes enact laws they know the Justices will strike down, and compliance with the Court's most contentious rulings, like those on abortion and school prayer, is willfully slack in many places. But these incidents of non-compliance have become forms of protest more than claims of interpretive superiority. Outright defiance in the shape of denying that Supreme Court decisions define constitutional law has, quite simply, disappeared. Witness the conniptions evoked when former Attorney General Edwin Meese dared to suggest in 1986 that Supreme Court decisions might be binding only on the parties to a case, an argument made (albeit with greater subtlety) by Abraham Lincoln in the 1850s. Meese was accused of inviting anarchy and of "making a calculated assault on the idea of law in this country."[6] He quickly backed down, softening his criticism to concede that judicial decisions "are the law of the land" and "do indeed have general applicability,"[7] and no public servant since has presumed to

[6] Anthony Lewis, Law or Power?, N.Y. Times, Oct. 27, 1986, at A23; see also Ronald J. Ostrow, Meese's View that Court Doesn't Make Law Scored, L.A. Times, Oct. 24, 1986, at I13 (quoting Ira Glasser describing Meese's speech as an "invitation to lawlessness").

[7] Edwin Meese III, The Tulane Speech: What I Meant, Wash. Post, Nov. 13, 1986, at A21.

pick the argument up again. It seems fair to say that, as a descriptive matter, judges, lawyers, politicians, and the general public today accept the principle of judicial supremacy—indeed, they assume it as a matter of course.

I am certain that the vast majority of law professors also shares this view, though no one has taken any polls of which I am aware. A minority disagrees, and perhaps because its views are outside the mainstream, most of its members apparently feel compelled to write about it. There is, as a result, a not insubstantial literature decrying the Court's pretensions to have the final say on constitutional meaning. Yet with but one exception,[10] the authors all ultimately accept some version of judicial supremacy. They all (but one) agree, for example, that particular judgments must be enforced—even knowing that, for practical purposes, this gives the Court the last word so long as it adheres to its judgments as a matter of stare decisis. Nor do the critics stop there. Ultimately, they defend models in which the other branches remain subservient to the Supreme Court, albeit with small enclaves of interpretive independence or the capability of pushing the Court by exploiting ambiguities in its opinions or urging the Justices to overrule themselves. The political branches are permitted, in effect, to behave like naughty lower courts, free to ignore the spirit though not the letter of judicial precedent. Bottom line: all the hullabaloo notwithstanding, the Court remains the preeminent institution in establishing constitutional meaning even among the academic critics of judicial supremacy.

A second observation follows directly from this first one: what is evident in the literature challenging judicial supremacy is that its authors see themselves as a beleaguered minority, fighting an uphill battle. The Supreme Court's authority to interpret is given; the question is whether space can be found for the other branches to have a say. * * *

There is, I believe, a simple explanation both for the general acceptance of judicial supremacy and for the defensiveness of its critics. Put simply, everyone—friend or foe of supremacy—begins with a shared understanding of the Constitution as ordinary law. It is "supreme," meaning it is superior to other forms of positive law and so trumps them when conflicts arise. But in every other respect, the Constitution is just "law" in the conventional sense in which lawyers use the word. It follows, naturally and ineluctably, that judges should be the ones to interpret it. Law is, after all, the stuff of judges; it is what they do. If the law is unclear, interpreting it to clarify its

---

[10] Michael Stokes Paulsen defends a position allowing each branch to interpret the Constitution independently, with no requirement of deference to any other. If the Court renders a judgment based on one understanding of the Constitution and the Executive disagrees, Paulsen says, the Executive need not enforce the judgment. See Michael Stokes Paulsen, *The Merryman Power and the Dilemma of Autonomous Executive Branch Interpretation*, 15 Cardozo L. Rev. 81, 81-82 (1993).

meaning is among the judiciary's central missions. It follows, almost as ineluctably, that judicial interpretations should be treated as conclusive by the other branches. Insofar as questions arise about what a legal text means, courts are where we go to get answers. And once a court has spoken, or at least once the Supreme Court has done so, its interpretations are supposed to trump those of other political actors unless and until the law is formally changed This is universally acknowledged when it comes to statutes, and insofar as the Constitution shares the same status as these of positive law, there is no reason suddenly to abandon the practice.

For friends of judicial supremacy, recognizing the Constitution's pedigree as ordinary law practically ends the argument. Take the recent defense made by Larry Alexander and Fred Schauer, which despite its many nuanced and complicated arguments, ultimately rests entirely on this single premise. * * *

* * * Placing something in a "law" box thus shifts our expectations and assumptions about authority to interpret. If the Constitution is law, then it is those who would argue that courts should not be its authoritative expositor who bear the burden of justifying what amounts to an exception to our normal practice.

The Founding generation did not see the Constitution this way and, as a result, had very different views about the role of the judiciary. Their Constitution was not ordinary law, not peculiarly the stuff of courts and judges. It was * * * a special form of popular law, law made by the people to bind their governors, and so subject to rules and considerations that made it qualitatively different from (and not just superior to) statutory or common law.

Americans of the Founding era felt the wonder of popular government in a way that we, who take so much for granted, do not. The United States was then the only country in the world with a government founded explicitly on the consent of its people, and the people who gave that consent were intensely, profoundly conscious of the fact. And proud. This pride, this awareness of the fragility and importance of their venture in popular government, informed everything the Founders did. It was, as Gordon Wood said, "the deeply felt meaning of the Revolution."[26] Modern commentators, especially legal commentators, read the Founders' letters and speeches anachronistically, giving too much weight, or the wrong kind of weight, to complaints about "the excess of democracy." We depict the men who framed the Constitution as striving to create a self-correcting system of checks and balances whose fundamental operations would all take place from within the government itself, with minimal involvement or interference from the people. Our political grammar is saturated with this

[26] Gordon S. Wood, The Creation of the American Republic 1776-1787, at 47 (1969).

reading of the Founding, which sees the movement to write a new Constitution almost exclusively in anti-democratic terms.

There is, of course, some truth to this characterization. Having overvalued the capacity of an unchecked legislature to govern during the wave of romantic enthusiasm that swept the country with the Declaration of Independence, American's leadership relearned the hard way in the 1780s why it was necessary to fragment and separate power within the government. Yet we must be careful, lest we exaggerate the extent of the reaction by focusing too narrowly on its direction. The Federalist "counterrevolution" was not a rejection of republicanism so much as an effort to save republicanism from itself. The Founding generation's ideas about constitutional reform remained thoroughly embedded in a political ideology that celebrated the central role of "the people" in supplying the government with its energy and direction. Preserving liberty demanded a constitution whose internal architecture was carefully arranged to check power, just as it demanded leaders of sufficient "character" and "virtue." But structural innovations and virtuous leadership were devices to channel and control popular politics, not to isolate or eliminate it. The people remained responsible for making things work.

This was particularly true when it came to a constitution, the most direct expression of the people's voice. Listen to St. George Tucker, in an appendix to his 1803 edition of Blackstone's Commentaries:

> [T]he American Revolution has formed a new epoch in the history of civil institutions, by reducing to practice, what, before, had been supposed to exist only in the visionary speculations of theoretical writers. . . . The world, for the first time since the annals of its inhabitants began, saw an original written compact formed by the free and deliberate voices of individuals disposed to unite in the same social bonds; thus exhibiting a political phenomenon unknown to former ages. . . . [T]he powers of the several branches of government are defined, and the excess of them, as well in the legislature, as in the other branches, finds limits, which cannot be transgressed without offending against that greater power from whom all authority, among us, is derived; to wit, the people.[29]

When Tucker and his contemporaries invoked "the people," they were not conjuring an empty abstraction or describing a mythic philosophical justification for government. "The people" they knew could speak, and had done so. "The people" they knew had fought a revolution, expressed dissatisfaction with the first fruits of independence, and debated and

---

[29] St. George Tucker, On Sovereignty and Legislature, in Blackstone's Commentaries app. A, reprinted in St. George Tucker, View of the Constitution of the United States with Selected Writings 18, 19 (Liberty Fund 1999) (1803).

adopted a new charter to govern itself. Certainly the Founders were concerned about the perils of popular government, some of them obsessively so. But they were also captivated by its possibilities and in awe of its importance. Their Constitution remained, fundamentally, an act of popular will: the people's charter, made by the people. And, as we shall see, it was the people themselves—working through or responding to their agents in the government—who were responsible for seeing that the Constitution was properly interpreted and implemented. The idea of turning this responsibility over to judges was unthinkable.

* * * The Founders possessed a substantial body of inherited wisdom, to which they had already made their own unique contributions. But most of their theory was just that: theory. The American people learned a great deal during the early years of their Republic—including that many of their most cherished beliefs and firmly held ideas were either wrong or unworkable (which makes one wonder why any sensible person, even a lawyer, would privilege the speculative writings of the 1780s over the hard-earned experience of subsequent decades).

Among the lessons they learned * * * were first, that it was difficult to keep courts out of the business of interpreting a written constitution, and second, that popular constitutionalism of the eighteenth-century variety was not well suited for American's new circumstances. That courts might play a role enforcing the Constitution had been understood by some even before Ratification; by the time *Marbury* was decided in 1803, this role had expanded to permit courts routinely to act on their own best understanding of the Constitution's meaning. That it might extend further, that judges might be assigned the final word in disputes over how to interpret the Constitution, was already being debated by the early decades of the nineteenth century. It may have taken until some time after *Cooper v. Aaron* for this proposition to achieve acceptance, but the idea of judicial supremacy had entered American's political lexicon by the 1830s.

Many factors contributed to these developments, but two in particular deserve mention. First, the conceptual and linguistic framework shifted as the Constitution was "legalized" and came to be seen more and more as ordinary positive law. Second, and more pragmatically, experience demonstrated the potentially destabilizing effects of leaving constitutional disputes to be worked out through politics alone. The Founders had expected disputes to arise over the meaning of the Constitution. But, perhaps näively, they thought these would lead to some sort of constitutional settlement (like the one reached in England during the Glorious Revolution), after which things would settle down. What they learned instead was that controversies did not fade. The Federalist Party might fade, but the underlying divisions that had made early politics so dyspeptic remained, reappearing or popping up in new guises. And so, with experience, the idea of settling constitutional controversies through politics alone gradually gave way to the need for someone more definite to have the final word. To many, particularly as the Constitution came to be identified with ordinary law, the Court seemed to be a natural choice.

There is, nevertheless, a world of difference between having the last word and having the only word: between judicial supremacy and judicial sovereignty. We may choose to accept judicial supremacy, because we need someone to settle certain constitutional questions and, for a variety of historical and jurisprudential reasons, the Supreme Court seems like our best option. But it does not follow either that the Court must wield its authority over every question or that, when it does, the Court can dismiss or too quickly supplant the views of other, more democratic institutions. Nothing in the doctrine of judicial supremacy, in other words, requires denying either that the Constitution has qualities that set it apart from ordinary law, or that these qualities confer legitimate interpretive authority on political actors as a means of ensuring continued popular input in shaping constitutional meaning.

* * *

Perhaps the argument should be stated more strongly. History may not compel us to embrace the Founders' exact understanding of popular constitutionalism, but it does suggest that one position at least is not plausible: the one embraced by the Rehnquist Court, which denies that popular constitutionalism is even a valid concept. In fact, both our theory and our practice have always reserved substantial space for the people to have a say in interpreting their Constitution, albeit in complex ways that have changed over time. Popular constitutionalism is not some quaint curiosity from the Founders' world. It is a vital principle that has been part of our constitutional tradition all along. To deny that there are spaces outside the Court where constitutional decisions are made, decisions to which judges are subservient, is a radical and unprecedented idea. There is a place for judicial supremacy, but it has bounds. There is no place for the totalizing claims of judicial sovereignty.

Ultimately, concern about congressional excess may help to explain the uneasiness that provoked the Justices to act, but it does not explain their actions. The members of the conservative majority on the Rehnquist Court are constitutional fundamentalists, acting to restore the Constitution to what they believe is its true form. Like most forms of fundamentalism, their belief rests on an imagined past that never existed. How long must we let them continue fantasizing at our expense?

* * *

History may not tell us what to do. But it can tell us who we were and in this way help us understand who we have become. Legend has it that, as he left the Constitutional Convention, Benjamin Franklin was approached by a woman who asked him, "What have you given us, Dr. Franklin?" "A republic," he replied, "if you can keep it." Have we? For all the disagreement about what we mean by "republic," no one has ever doubted that self-government is its essence and a constitution the purest distillate. What kind of republic removes its constitution from the process of self-governing? Certainly not the one our Founders gave us. Is it one we prefer? The choice, after all, is ours. The Supreme Court has made its grab for power. The question is: will we let them get away with it?

Bibliography

General Background on Judicial Review

Bailyn, B., THE IDEOLOGICAL ORIGINS OF THE AMERICAN REVOLUTION (1967).

BEYOND CONFEDERATION: ORIGINS OF THE CONSTITUTION AND AMERICAN NATIONAL IDENTITY (R. Beeman, S. Botein & E. Carter II eds. 1987).

Clinton, R., *MARBURY V. MADISON* AND JUDICIAL REVIEW (1989).

Corwin, E., CORWIN ON THE CONSTITUTION (R. Loss ed., 2 vols., 1981, 1987).

Cox, A., THE ROLE OF THE SUPREME COURT IN AMERICAN GOVERNMENT (1976).

Friedman, *The Birth of an Academic Obsession: The History of the Countermajoritarian Difficulty, Part Five*, 112 Yale L.J. 153 (2002).

Harrison, *The Constitutional Origins and Implications of Judicial Review,* 84 Va.L.Rev. 333 (1998).

Jackson, R., THE STRUGGLE FOR JUDICIAL SUPREMACY (1941).

McCloskey, R., THE AMERICAN SUPREME COURT (1960).

MacDonald, F., NOVUS ORDO SECLORUM: THE INTELLECTUAL ORIGINS OF THE CONSTITUTION (1985).

Rakove, *The Origins of Judicial Review: A Plea for New Contexts,* 49 Stan.L.Rev. 1031 (1997).

Treanor, *The Case of the Prisoners and the Origins of Judicial Review,* 143 U.Penn.L.Rev. 491 (1994).

Tribe, L., AMERICAN CONSTITUTIONAL LAW (2d ed. 1988).

Warren, C., THE SUPREME COURT IN UNITED STATES HISTORY, 3 vols. (1922–24).

Wood, G., THE CREATION OF THE AMERICAN REPUBLIC, 1776–1787 (1969).

Symposium, *Judicial Review: Blessing or Curse? Or Both?*, 38 Wake Forest L.Rev. 313 (2003).

Critical Perspectives on Judicial Review

Bork, R., THE TEMPTING OF AMERICA: THE POLITICAL SEDUCTION OF THE LAW (1990).

Gardbaum, *The New Commonwealth Model of Constitutionalism*, 49 Am.J.Comp. L. 707 (2001).

Graglia, *Judicial Review on the Basis of "Regime Principles": A Prescription for Government by Judges,* 26 S.Tex.L.J. 435 (1985).

Lawson & Moore, *The Executive Power of Constitutional Interpretation,* 81 Iowa L.Rev. 1267 (1996).

McCleskey, *Judicial Review in a Democracy: A Dissenting Opinion,* 3 Hous.L.Rev. 354 (1966).

Paulsen, *The Most Dangerous Branch: Executive Power to Say What the Law Is,* 83 Geo.L.J. 217 (1994).

Presser, *Some Alarming Aspects of the Legacies of Judicial Review and of John Marshall,* 43 Wm. & Mary L.Rev. 1495 (2002).

Strauss, *Presidential Interpretation of the Constitution,* 15 Cardozo L.Rev. 113 (1993).

Symposium, *Judicial Review versus Democracy,* 42 Ohio St.L.J. 1–434 (1981).

Tushnet, M., TAKING THE CONSTITUTION AWAY FROM THE COURTS (1999).

Tushnet, *Politics, National Identity, and the Thin Constitution,* 34 U.Rich.L.Rev. 545 (2000).

Justifications for Judicial Review

Ackerman, *The Storrs Lectures: Discovering the Constitution,* 93 Yale L.J. 1013 (1984).

Bickel, A., THE SUPREME COURT AND THE IDEA OF PROGRESS (1970).

Bishin, *Judicial Review in Democratic Theory,* 50 S.Cal.L.Rev. 1099 (1977).

Brown, *A Government* For *the People*, 37 U.S.F. L.Rev. 5 (2002).

Carter, *Constitutional Adjudication and the Indeterminate Text: A Preliminary Defense of an Imperfect Muddle,* 94 Yale L.J. 821 (1985).

Casto, *James Iredell and the American Origins of Judicial Review,* 27 Conn.L.Rev. 329 (1995).

Chemerinsky, *Wrong Questions Get Wrong Answers: An Analysis of Professor Carter's Approach to Judicial Review,* 66 B.U.L.Rev. 47 (1986).

Choper, J., JUDICIAL REVIEW AND THE NATIONAL POLITICAL PROCESS (1980).

Corwin, *Marbury v. Madison and the Doctrine of Judicial Review,* 12 Mich.L.Rev. 538 (1914).

Dahl, *Decision–Making in a Democracy: The Supreme Court as National Policy–Maker,* 6 J.Pub.L. 279 (1975).

Eisgruber, *Justice and the Text: Rethinking the Constitutional Relation Between Principle and Prudence,* 43 Duke L.J. 1 (1993).

Fallon, *Judicial Legitimacy and the Unwritten Constitution: A Comment on* Miranda *and* Dickerson, 45 N.Y.L.Sch. L.Rev. 119 (2000–2001).

Fiss, *The Supreme Court, 1978 Term—Foreword: The Forms of Justice,* 93 Harv.L.Rev. 1 (1979).

Friedman, *Dialogue and Judicial Review,* 91 Mich.L.Rev. 577 (1993).

Klarman, *Majoritarian Judicial Review: The Entrenchment Problem,* 85 Geo.L.J. 491 (1997).

Llewellyn, *The Constitution as an Institution,* 34 Colum.L.Rev. 1 (1934).

Nelson, *Changing Conceptions of Judicial Review: The Evolution of Constitutional Theory in the United States,* 1790–1860, 120 U.Pa.L. Rev. 1166 (1972).

O'Fallon, *Marbury,* 44 Stan.L.Rev. 219 (1992).

Peters, *Adjudication as Representation,* 97 Colum.L.Rev. 312 (1997).

Rostow, *The Democratic Character of Judicial Review,* 66 Harv.L.Rev. 193 (1952).

Thayer, *The Origin and Scope of the American Doctrine of Constitutional Law,* 7 Harv.L.Rev. 129 (1893).

Wellington, *The Nature of Judicial Review,* 91 Yale L.J. 486 (1982).

Wright, *Professor Bickel, The Scholarly Tradition and the Supreme Court,* 84 Harv.L.Rev. 769 (1971).

Judicial Supremacy

Alexander and Schauer, *On Extrajudicial Constitutional Interpretation,* 110 Harv.L.Rev. 1359 (1997).

Balkin and Levinson, *Understanding the Constitutional Revolution*, 87 Va.L.Rev. 1045 (2001).

Chang, *A Critique of Judicial Supremacy,* 36 Vill.L.Rev. 281 (1991).

Devins and Fisher, *Judicial Exclusivity and Political Instability,* 84 Va.L.Rev. 83 (1998).

Farber, *Judicial Review and its Alternatives: An American Tale*, 38 Wake Forest L.Rev. 415 (2003).

Ferejohn and Kramer, *Independent Judges, Dependent Judiciary: Institutionalizing Judicial Restraint*, 77 NYU L.Rev. 962 (2002).

Chapter IV

FEDERALISM

In recent years, one of the areas of greatest Supreme Court activity has been federalism. The Rehnquist Court has proved much more interested than its immediate predecessors in limiting federal authority and protecting state immunities. National authority was paramount from 1937 to about 1990, but states' rights have now reemerged. The readings in this Chapter explore the theoretical issues raised by these developments.

We begin in part A with the question whether the Court should be enforcing federalism norms at all. Herbert Wechsler's influential article, written in the 1950s, contends that judicial protection of federalism is unnecessary, because adequate protections for states are built into the political process. Going further, Edward Rubin and Malcolm Feeley argue that federalism as a constitutional value serves no useful social purpose. In contrast, Lynn Baker and Ernest Young argue that federalism is valuable and deserves the same respect from courts as other aspects of the Constitution.

Part B turns to the scope of congressional power under Article I and the Reconstruction amendments. After decades in which the federal commerce power was virtually unlimited, the Rehnquist Court has held that some important social issues do not involve interstate commerce. Robert Nagel views the Court's recent efforts to cut back on the Commerce Clause as only the most recent chapter in the Court's long-running effort to be true to two conflicting constitutional norms: a broad federal commerce power and a government of enumerated powers. The Rehnquist Court has also cut back on congressional power over civil rights. Robert Post and Reva Siegel are critical of the Supreme Court's current interpretation of the grant of congressional power in section 5 of the Fourteenth Amendment. They argue that the Court has limited congressional power under a mistaken vision of separation of powers, rather than making a direct case for federalism-based limits on civil rights legislation. This excerpt brings together issues of federalism, separation of powers, and judicial supremacy.

In Part C, we consider the related question of state immunities. Under current doctrine, regulations that might otherwise be within congressional power are trumped by states' rights, in much the same way that such legislation might be trumped by the Bill of Rights. For example, Congress cannot coerce state officials to assist in administering federal programs, and it cannot make States liable for damages except in narrow circumstances. Vicki Jackson, though sympathetic to some federalism limitations, is critical of the Court's bright-line rule against "commandeering" of state officials. Historian Jack Rakove probes the concept of state sovereignty, the fundamental underpinning of these immunity doctrines. Finally, Richard Fallon brings the themes of Parts B and C together by asking why the Court has been so aggressive with respect to state immunities (especially immunity from suit), moderately active with respect to congressional regulatory powers, and completely inactive in protecting states in other areas such as preemption doctrine and the dormant Commerce Clause. Fallon explores a number of explanations for this uneven pattern of activism.

Picking up on Fallon's discussion of the dormant Commerce Clause, Part D focuses on that limitation on the states. Noel Dowling proposed the use of a balancing test in an important early article. But more recent scholarship evinces dissatisfaction with both the theory and practice of balancing. Donald Regan argues that the main target of the dormant Commerce Clause should be protectionist legislation. Finally, Barry Friedman contends that the Court's modern rulings are actually deeply at odds with basic principles of federalism.

A. FEDERALISM AS A CONSTITUTIONAL VALUE

HERBERT WECHSLER, THE POLITICAL SAFEGUARDS OF FEDERALISM: THE ROLE OF THE STATES IN THE COMPOSITION AND SELECTION OF THE NATIONAL GOVERNMENT

54 COLUM.L.REV. 543–552, 557–560 (1954).

I

Our constitution makers established a central government authorized to act directly upon individuals through its own agencies—and thus they formed a nation capable of function and of growth. To serve the ends of federalism they employed three main devices:

> They preserved the states as separate sources of authority and organs of administration—a point on which they hardly had a choice.
>
> They gave the states a role of great importance in the composition and selection of the central government.
>
> They undertook to formulate a distribution of authority between the nation and the states, in terms which gave some scope at least to legal processes for its enforcement.

Scholarship—not only legal scholarship—has given most attention to the last of these enumerated mechanisms, perhaps because it has been fascinated by the Supreme Court and its interpretations of the power distribution clauses of the Constitution. The continuous existence of the states as governmental entities and their strategic role in the selection of the Congress and the President are so immutable a feature of the system that their importance tends to be ignored. Of the Framers' mechanisms, however, they have had and have today the larger influence upon the working balance of our federalism. The actual extent of central intervention in the governance of our affairs is determined far less by the formal power distribution than by the sheer existence of the states and their political power to influence the action of the national authority.

The fact of the continuous existence of the states, with general governmental competence unless excluded by the Constitution or valid Act of Congress, set the mood of our federalism from the start. The first Congress did not face the problem of building a legal system from the ground up; it started with the premise that the standing *corpus juris* of the country was provided by the states. * * *

National action has thus always been regarded as exceptional in our polity, an intrusion to be justified by some necessity, the special rather than the ordinary case. This point of view cuts even deeper than the concept of the central government as one of granted, limited authority, articulated in the Tenth Amendment. National power may be quite unquestioned in a given situation; those who would advocate its exercise must none the less answer the preliminary question why the matter should not be left to the states. Even when Congress acts, its tendency has been to frame enactments on an *ad hoc* basis to accomplish limited objectives, supplanting state-created norms only so far as may be necessary for the purpose. Indeed, with all the centralizing growth throughout the years, federal law is still a largely interstitial product, rarely occupying any field completely, building normally upon legal relationships established by the states. * * *

* * *

II

If I have drawn too much significance from the mere fact of the existence of the states, the error surely will be rectified by pointing also to their crucial role in the selection and the composition of the national authority. * * *

Despite the rise of national parties, the shift to popular election of the Senate and the difficulty of appraising the precise impact of such provisions on the legislative process, Madison's analysis has never lost its thrust:

> The State governments may be regarded as constituent and essential parts of the federal government; whilst the latter is nowise essential to the operation or organization of the former.[7]
>
> A local spirit will infallibly prevail much more in the members of Congress, than a national spirit will prevail in the legislatures of the particular States.[8]
>
> Even the House of Representatives, though drawn immediately from the people, will be chosen very much under the influence of that class of men, whose influence over the people obtains for themselves an election into the State legislatures.[9]

To the extent that federalist values have real significance they must give rise to local sensitivity to central intervention; to the extent that such a local sensitivity exists, it cannot fail to find reflection in the Congress. Indeed, the problem of the Congress is and always has been to attune itself to national opinion and produce majorities for action called for by the voice of the entire nation. It is remarkable that it should function thus as well as it does, given its intrinsic sensitivity to any insular opinion that is dominant in a substantial number of the states.

III

The point is so clear in the Senate that, as Madison observed of the equality accorded to the states, it "does not call for much discussion."[11] The forty-nine votes that will determine Senate action,[a] even with full voting, could theoretically be drawn from twenty-five states, of which the combined population does not reach twenty-nine millions, a bare 19% of all state residents. The one-third plus one that will defeat a treaty or a resolution of amendment could, equally theoretically, be drawn from seventeen states with a total population little over twelve millions, less than that of New York. I say theoretically since, short of a combination to resist an effort to impair state equality within the Senate (which the Constitution purports to place beyond amendment) or to diminish the political power of the smaller states in other ways, a coalition in these terms is quite unthinkable. The fact remains that in more subtle ways the Senate cannot fail to function as the guardian of state interests as such, when they are real enough to have political support or even to be instrumental in attaining other ends. And if account is taken of the operation of seniority within the Senate, of the opportunity of Senators to marshal individual authority, not to speak of the possibility of filibuster, this power of negation, vested in the

[7]The Federalist, No. 45 at 288 (Lodge ed. 1888).
[8]*Id.*, No. 46 at 294.
[9]*Id.*, No. 45 at 288–89.
[11]The Federalist, No. 62, at 385 (Lodge ed. 1888).
[a]Alaska and Hawaii were admitted as states in 1959.

states without regard to population, multiplies in many ways. Given a controversy that has any sectional dimension, it is not long before the impact of this power is perceived.

* * *

IV

Even the House is slanted somewhat in the same direction, though the incidence is less severe. * * * [Here it stems from] the states' control of voters' qualifications, on the one hand, and of districting, on the other.

The position with respect to voters' qualifications derives from the constitutional provision that fixes the electorate of Representatives (and of Senators as well since the Seventeenth Amendment) as those persons who "have the qualifications requisite for electors of the most numerous branch of the State Legislature." Subject, then, to the prohibition of the denial of franchise because of color, race or sex, embodied in the Fifteenth and Nineteenth Amendments and the radiations of the equal protection clause of the Fourteenth, the states determine—indirectly it is true—the electorate that chooses Representatives. The consequences of contracting the electorate by such devices as a poll-tax are, of course, incalculable, but they tend to buttress what traditionally dominant state interests conceive to be their special state position; that is the point of the contraction. This sentiment, reflected in the Representatives that these constituencies send to Congress, is not ordinarily conducive to support for an adventurous expansion of the national authority, though there have been exceptions, to be sure.

* * *

State control of congressional districting derives from the constitutional provision that the "times, places and manner of holding elections for Senators and Representatives, shall be prescribed in each State by the Legislature thereof." * * *

It is well known that there are great discrepancies in district size in many multi-district states, paralleling for Congress the discrepancies, to forego harsher terms, that prevail in districting for the state legislatures. A recent study estimates that in the spring of 1952, 115 of the 435 congressional districts showed variation as to size larger than 15% above or below the state average, the maximum above the average being 129.8% in Texas and, below the average, 51.3% in South Dakota (where there are only two districts). * * *

It may be said, and perhaps rightly, that the situation with respect to districting, while detracting from the equality of popular representation in the House, has little bearing on the role of Congress in preserving federalist values. I am not so sure. It is significant, for one thing, that it is the states that draw the districts; one can hardly think the district lines would be the same had they been drawn from the beginning by Congress. Beyond this, however, the general motive and tendency of district deviations has quite clearly been to reduce urban power, not in the meaning of the census classification but in the sense of the substantial cities. The tendency is so appreciable that a recent article assures the readers of a small town magazine that while cities or towns of under 10,000 coupled with the farms account for only 51% of the entire population, residents of such areas are numerically dominant in 265 of the 435 congressional districts, accounting for the choice of 61% of the House (including 18 of the 21 committee chairmen) in addition to their numerical dominance in the choice of 75% of the Senate. Traditionally, at least, a more active localism and resistance to new federal intrusion centers in this 51% of Americans than in the other 49%. I should suppose that this is likely to continue; and that the figures, therefore, have some relevancy to an understanding of why presidential programs calling for the extension of national activity, and seemingly supported by the country in a presidential election, may come a cropper notwithstanding in the House. Such hostility to Washington may rest far less on pure devotion to the principle of local government than on opposition to specific measures which Washington proposes to put forth. This explanation does not make the sentiment the less centrifugal in its effects. Federalism would have few adherents were it not, like other elements of government, a means and not an end.

V

If Congress, from its composition and the mode of its selection, tends to reflect the "local spirit" predicted by Madison, the prime organ of a compensating "national spirit" is, of course, the President—both as the Chief Executive and as the leader of his party. Without the unifying power of the highest office, derived from the fixed tenure gained by his election and the sense that the President speaks for and represents the full national constituency, it would be difficult to develop the centripetal momentum so essential to the total federal scheme. * * *

* * *

Federalist considerations * * * play an important part even in the selection of the President, although a lesser part than many of the Framers must have contemplated. A presidential candidacy must be pointed towards the states of largest population in so far as they are doubtful. It must balance this direction by attention to the other elements of the full coalition that is looked to for an electoral majority. Both major parties have a strong incentive to absorb protest movements of such sectional significance that their development in strength would throw elections to the House. Both must give some attention to the organized minorities that may approach balance of power status in important states, without, however, making promises that will outrun the tolerance of other necessary elements of their required strength. Both parties recognize that they must appeal to some total combination of allegiance, choice or interest that will yield sufficient nation-wide support to win elections and make possible effective government.

The most important element of party competition in this framework is the similarity of the appeal that each must make. This is a constant affront to those who seek purity of ideology in politics; it is the clue, however, to the success of our politics in the elimination of extremists—and to the tolerance and basic unity that is essential if our system is to work.

The President must be, as I have said above, the main repository of "national spirit" in the central government. But both the mode of his selection and the future of his party require that he also be responsive to local values that have large support within the states. And since his programs must, in any case, achieve support in Congress—in so far as they involve new action—he must surmount the greater local sensitivity of Congress before anything is done.

VI

If this analysis is correct, the national political process in the United States—and especially the role of the states in the composition and selection of the central government—is intrinsically well adapted to retarding or restraining new intrusions by the center on the domain of the states. Far from a national authority that is expansionist by nature, the inherent tendency in our system is precisely the reverse, necessitating the widest support before intrusive measures of importance can receive significant consideration, reacting readily to opposition grounded in resistance within the states. Nor is this tendency effectively denied by pointing to the size or scope of the existing national establishment. However useful it may be to explore possible contractions in specific areas, such evidence points mainly to the magnitude of unavoidable responsibility under the circumstances of our time.

It is in light of this inherent tendency, reflected most importantly in Congress, that the governmental power distribution clauses of the Constitution gain their largest meaning as an instrument for the protection of the states. Those clauses, as is well known, have served far more to qualify or stop intrusive legislative measures in the Congress than to invalidate enacted legislation in the Supreme Court.

* * *

The prime function envisaged for judicial review—in relation to federalism—was the maintenance of national supremacy against nullification or usurpation by the individual states, the national government having no part in their composition or their councils. This is made clear by the fact that reliance on the courts was substituted, apparently on Jefferson's suggestion, for the earlier proposal to give Congress a veto of state enactments deemed to trespass on the national domain. And except for the brief interlude that ended with the crisis of the thirties, it is mainly in the realm of such policing of the states that the Supreme Court has in fact participated in determining the balances of federalism.[56] This is not to say that the Court can decline to measure national enactments by the Constitution when it is called upon to face the question in the course of ordinary litigation; the supremacy clause governs there as well. It is rather to say that the Court is on weakest ground when it opposes its interpretation of the Constitution to that of Congress in the interest of the states, whose representatives control the legislative process and, by hypothesis, have broadly acquiesced in sanctioning the challenged Act of Congress.

Federal intervention as against the states is thus primarily a matter for congressional determination in our system as it stands. So too, moreover, is the question whether state enactments shall be stricken down as an infringement on the national authority. For while the Court has an important function in this area, as I have noted, the crucial point is that its judgments here are subject to reversal by Congress, which can consent to action by the states that otherwise would be invalidated. The familiar illustrations in commerce and in state taxation of federal instrumentalities do not by any means exhaust the field. The Court makes the decisive judgment only when—and to the extent that—Congress has not laid down the resolving rule.[59]

---

[56]Of the great controversies with respect to national power before the Civil War, only the Bank and slavery within the territories were carried to the Court and its participation with respect to slavery was probably its greatest failure. The question of internal improvements, for example, which raised the most acute problem of constitutional construction, was fought out politically and in Congress. After the War only the Civil Rights Cases and income tax decisions were important in setting limits on national power—until the Child Labor Case and the New Deal decisions. The recasting of constitutional positions since the crisis acknowledges much broader power in the Congress—as against the states—than it is likely soon or ever to employ.

[59]The judicial function in relation to federalism thus differs markedly from that performed in the application of those constitutional restraints on Congress or the states that are designed to safeguard individuals. In this latter area of the constitutional protection of the individual against the government, both federal and state, subordination of the Court to Congress would defeat the purpose of judicial mediation. For this is where the political processes cannot be relied upon to introduce their own correctives—except to the limited extent that individuals or small minorities may find a champion in some important faction. See Stone, J., in United States v. Carolene Products Co., 304 U.S. 144, 152–53 n. 4 (1938).

EDWARD L. RUBIN AND MALCOL[…] FEDERALISM: SOME NOTES O[…] NATIONAL NEUROSIS

41 UCLA L. REV. 903, 906–15, 927–34, 936, 937, 940-[…]

* * * We Americans love federalism or, as the Cour[…] Federalism."[26] It conjures up images of Fourth of July […] Street, drugstore soda fountains, and family farms witl[…] front yard. Imagery aside, a number of appealing arguments have been made on its behalf * * *. Federalism, Justice O'Connor states, "increases opportunity for citizen involvement in democratic processes," it "makes government more responsive by putting the States in competition for a mobile citizenry," and "it allows for more innovation and experimentation in government."[27] But its principal virtue is that it constitutes "a check on abuses of government power" by diffusing power among separate sovereigns.[28] Justice O'Connor thus invoked all the familiar themes regularly cited by legal scholars in support of federalism. The only one she missed was the newly fashionable concept of community. But she did add that federalism "assures a decentralized government that will be more sensitive to the diverse needs of a heterogenous society."[30] This, together with the reference to citizen involvement, resonates with themes sounded in recent communitarian scholarship.[31]

In our view, federalism in America achieves none of the beneficial goals that the Court claims for it. * * * The current Court can proclaim the virtues of federalism with a straight face only because it does not know what federalism is. Its current usage may well correspond to "Our Federalism," if that term is taken to mean whatever it is we have, but it does not correspond to any coherent political concept.

In fact, federalism is America's neurosis. We have a federal system because we began with a federal system; the new nation consisted of a group of self-governing units that had to relinquish some of their existing powers to a central government. We began with a federal system because of some now uninteresting details of eighteenth century British colonial administration. We carry this system with us, like any neurosis, because it is part of our collective psychology, and we proclaim its virtues out of the universal desire for self-justification. But our political culture is essentially

---

[26] Younger v. Harris, 401 U.S. 37, 44 (1971).

[27] [Gregory v. Ashcroft, 111 S. Ct. 2395, 2399 (1991).]

[28] *Gregory*, at 2399–2400.

[30] [Id. at 2399]

[31] See, e.g., Adeno Addis, *Individualism, Communitarianism and the Rights of Ethnic Minorities*, 67 Notre Dame L. Rev. 615 (1991); Akhil R. Amar, *Of Sovereignty and Federalism*, 96 Yale L.J. 1425 (1987); Andrzej Rapaczynski, *From Sovereignty to Process: The Jurisprudence of Federalism After Garcia*, 1985 Sup. Ct. Rev. 341.

healthy, and we do not let our neuroses control us. Instead, we have been trying to extricate ourselves from federalism for at least the last 130 years. When federalism is raised as an argument against some national policy, we generally reject it by whatever means are necessary, including, in one case, killing its proponents.[35] This Article describes that process, and asserts that, on grounds of political morality, it has been exactly the right thing to do.

We are not arguing for the abolition of the states. States fulfill the important governmental function of facilitating decentralization, as we will discuss below. Yet there is no policy reason why other subdivisions of the nation could not fulfill this function, or why state lines could not be redrawn on a functional, rather than historical basis. To be sure, this would be costly and disruptive; hence, in the final analysis, it is probably best to use the existing states as our primary means of decentralization. What we do argue is that decentralization is the only purpose states serve, and that they do not embody any important normative principle at this juncture in our history. The Supreme Court should never invoke federalism as a reason for invalidating a federal statute or as a principle for interpreting it. Thus, we subscribe to the conclusion stated in *Garcia v. San Antonio Metropolitan Transit Authority*. Our rationale for this conclusion, however, is not that the states are capable of protecting themselves, as Justice Blackmun's opinion argues,[37] but that there is no normative principle involved that is worthy of protection.

* * *

I. Federalism and Decentralization

* * *

"Federalism," like most broad political or legal terms, can mean many different things, but any definition that would justify judicial enforcement, to say nothing of the emotional freight that we Americans attach to it, must distinguish federalism from decentralization. Decentralization is a managerial concept; it refers to the delegation of centralized authority to subordinate units of either a geographic or a functional character. Setting aside the political context for the moment, and focusing on the concept of decentralization as a matter of organization or systems theory, the main reason to decentralize is to achieve effective management. Very often, an administrator who is relatively close to the subject matter will be more knowledgeable, more responsive, and more involved than a higher ranking person ensconced in some distant central office. An industrial corporation might decentralize authority to factory managers, or a state university

[35] The Civil War.

[37] [469 U.S. 528,] 547–55 [(1985)]. See Jesse H. Choper, Judicial Review and the National Political Process (1980).

system might decentralize authority to the head of each constituent campus. * * *

But none of this has anything to do with federalism. All these decentralized systems are hierarchically organized and the leaders at the top or center have plenary power over the other members of the organization. Decentralization represents a deliberate policy that the leaders select, or at least approve, based on their view of the best way to achieve their goals. A decentralized system can be, and often is, the product of a purely managerial decision by a centralized authority.

The essence of federalism, as a coherent political concept, is quite different. To be sure, federal systems share certain structural features with decentralized ones. The most basic is that, within a single system of governance, decisions are made by subsidiary units and the central authority defers to those decisions. But in a federal system, the subordinate units possess prescribed areas of jurisdiction that cannot be invaded by the central authority, and leaders of the subordinate units draw their power from sources independent of that central authority. Federalism is not a managerial decision by the central decision-maker, as decentralization can be, but a structuring principle for the system as a whole.

* * *

The point of granting partial independence in this way, and thus the point of federalism, is to allow normative disagreement amongst the subordinate units so that different units can subscribe to different value systems. Purely instrumental disagreements can be resolved within a unitary system because the criteria for judgment are shared by or imposed on those within the system. Similarly, the adaptation of a single norm or goal to different circumstances can be readily achieved by managerial decentralization. Once everyone agrees that the goal is to produce more wheat, there may nonetheless be disagreement about whether one growing method is better than another. But the standard way to resolve this question is to investigate the merits of each method, not to give different farmers the right to grow wheat any way they please. When the investigation is complete, it may turn out that the growing conditions are crucial and that these vary markedly from place to place. A natural resolution would be to decentralize the regulation of wheat growing, enabling farm administrators to adapt to the differing conditions of each region. Federalism becomes relevant only when the people in one region want to grow wheat, while those in another want to build factories on farmland or turn all the wheat fields into ecological preserves. It is possible, and indeed quite common, to resolve such normative disagreements by a centralized decision-maker's fiat. The point is that it is also possible to resolve this problem by federalism, that is, by recognizing that each area has a right to control the use of its own land. More importantly, federalism only makes sense in this context; there is no need to grant such rights in order to choose more effective instrumentalities or to adapt the selected instrumentalities to local circumstances.

* * *

[O]nly federalism can operate as a bar to national policy, and only federalism can justify the imposition of that bar by the judiciary. Decentralization, being an instrumental, managerial strategy, is no different in degree from any other policy; like cost or administrative convenience, it is simply one factor that political decision-makers should take into account. Their failure to do so could lead to the charge that they are unwise, but everyone agrees that such debates over policy alternatives are consigned to the ordinary political process. To place a policy beyond the power of the central government, and to enforce that policy by judicial action, requires the assertion that a right has been infringed. That right, in the case of federalism, is the right of states to act independently, in furtherance of goals the national government does not share. The notion that an admittedly valid national policy is best implemented by decentralizing its administration cannot support either the rhetoric of federalism or the remedy of judicial intervention.

* * *

Once we recognize the distinction between federalism and decentralization, we can see that many standard arguments advanced for federalism are clearly nothing more than policy arguments for decentralization. These are the claims that some nationally-defined policy is best achieved by permitting regional variation. * * *

Of the standard arguments[,] [four are of this variety:] these are public participation, effectuating citizen choice through competition among jurisdictions, achieving economic efficiency through competition among jurisdictions, and encouraging experimentation. All four reflect policies that are applicable to the American political context; while questions can certainly be raised about their desirability, they are at least plausible strategies for governing our country. They are national strategies, however, linked to federalism only by confusing that concept with decentralization, and by the airy, flag-waving-in-the-breeze rhetoric that characterizes the entire subject.

* * *

II. FEDERALISM AND THE DIFFUSION OF POWER

* * * There remain, however, two important arguments that genuinely support the basic principle of federalism: an older one, which emphasizes

federalism's role in diffusing governmental power, and a more recent one, which emphasizes its protection of communitarian values. These arguments, unlike the argument for participation, citizen choice, governmental competition, or experimentation, do not champion one substantive policy; instead they favor the rights of political sub-units to adopt whatever policy they choose, and they justify this position on the basis of overarching moral values like liberty or community. Concern about the concentration of power was one of the guiding forces in the design of our entire political system. The Founders of our nation, according to the current view, were motivated by their commitment to liberty and defined themselves as revolutionaries because of their opposition to the unchecked authority that Britain exercised over their lives. Federalism can be seen as responding to this basic concern because it insulates certain decisions from the power of the central government. By doing so, the argument goes, power is diffused among different governmental entities; in particular, the central government is disabled from imposing norms upon the states, at least in certain subject areas. The enormous growth of the national government during the course of the last century is thus seen as a threat to liberty, a threat that can be counteracted by the principle of federalism.

* * *

The functional argument regarding the dispersion of power is that it secures liberty by protecting the populace from the unconstrained control of a single governmental actor. But to assess the relationship between the doctrine of federalism and the diffusion of governmental power, one needs to know precisely what is meant by power, and how the process of diffusion operates. As an initial, and perhaps obvious, matter, power cannot mean the physical power of the state. If it does, the United States does not have a federal regime, and it is inconceivable that we would develop one. There is no period of history when a central government possessed such overwhelming physical power, compared to its governmental sub-units, as the present time. Our federal armed forces have the capacity to turn any state, any segment of humanity, or humanity in general into a thin gas, and to do so, like the seventh seal's silence, in "about the space of half an hour."[87] This situation will not change. Even the rapidly dispersing republics of the former Soviet Union quailed before the possibility that they would secure their independence from the center by maintaining nuclear arsenals of rival strength; the likelihood that, within our infinitely more cohesive union, Nebraska would develop a deterrent force of nuclear missiles, or New Jersey would launch a fleet of nuclear submarines to patrol its seacoasts, is not particularly great.

---

[87]Revelations 8:1.

If the power that federalism is intended to diffuse is not physical power, perhaps it is political power—the power of the central government to carry out its policies. Federalism grants governmental sub-units the right to choose their own officials and to develop their own policies within their areas of jurisdiction. In a fully centralized regime, sub-unit officials are appointed by a central authority and all policies emanate from that authority. Clearly, political power is more diffused in a federal regime because the leaders and representatives of each sub-unit possess a legally-protected political base from which they can voice their opposition to the central authority.

While there is an undeniable validity to this argument for federalism, it can readily be overstated. Like other constitutional doctrines, federalism memorializes a deeply-felt element in our political culture, rather than creating it by fiat. The election of chief administrators, lawmaking bodies, and other officials is our instinctive approach to government at any level, not a result of the legal rights that federalism grants our states. City and county officials are also chosen by election. These local officials do not owe their independence from state government to federalism or any other juridical principle, however; as stated above, a basic tenet of American federalism is that the national government will not interfere with a state's supervision of its counties or municipalities. The autonomy of local officials is the product of American political culture, not of the Constitution.

In any event, political power cannot be the subject of our concern about the growth of the national government, or serve as a basis for invoking federalism. The political power of the states, whether cultural or constitutional in origin, is not under attack. No one is suggesting that state governors be appointed by the President, or that the U.S. Department of Agriculture cancel elections for the state legislatures in rural areas. The political independence of the states has not changed over the course of this century and has not been challenged since the Reconstruction Era.

* * *

The issue of federalism arises, and the jeremiads about its demise seem plausible, because of concerns about administrative, rather than physical or political power. If physical power is control over soldiers, airplanes, missiles, and artillery, and political power is control over votes, offices, and public opinion, then administrative power is control over appointed officials, public resources, and regulatory rules. While complaints about the demise of federalism often speak in terms of political power, they invoke the centralization of administrative power as their principal evidence. The vast growth of federal regulatory programs, from the banking, antitrust, and conservation programs of the Progressive Era, through the labor, agricultural, and social security programs of the New Deal, to the consumer, environmental, social welfare, and civil liberties programs of the 1960s and 1970s, all involved administrative power. These programs left the political structure of the states entirely intact; their effect was to expand the central government's administrative apparatus.

Having identified the nature of the power that is at issue in debates about federalism, it is now necessary to determine what the concept of diffusion means. The image that seems to underlie this concept is that there exists some fixed amount of power—administrative power in this case—which can either be concentrated in the central government or spread between the central government and the states. In fact, there is no fixed supply of administrative power such that increases in federal power necessarily cause decreases in state power through a zero sum exchange. Rather, the power of government at all levels has been steadily increasing in our culture for a substantial period of time. One hundred years ago, the workplace was essentially unregulated other than by judicial enforcement of individual contracts. Now, a formidable panoply of labor, health, and safety regulations emanates from both the federal government and the states. Similarly, the government's involvement in environmental matters once consisted essentially of selling off the environment in hundred-acre parcels; now, governments at all levels monitor the quality of air and water, and regulate the emissions of factories which once spewed their fumes into the air with laissez-faire abandon.

One cannot even be certain that this increasing power of government at all levels has necessarily led to a reduction in the power of private entities. The power of human beings in general has increased immeasurably in our modern age. We have changed the physical features of our planet, which for so long, under the designation "nature," were assumed to be predominant and immutable. While the deforestation of the Spanish Meseta and the Indo-Gangnetic plain attest to the rapacity of prior eras, we have far surpassed these feats, raising the Earth's temperature, punching photo-chemical holes through its ozone layer, transforming large lakes into porridges of synthetic substances, and covering the landscape with vast networks of asphalt and plastic. To this may be added the less concrete phenomena that Weber noted, whereby control of economic behavior has been transferred from ritual and tradition to self-conscious, bureaucratic enterprises.[100] Thus, there is much more human activity for governments to govern, and it is entirely conceivable that the power of the federal government, of the state governments that complain about its usurpations, and of the private enterprises that complain about them both, are all increasing at a rapid and roughly proportional rate.

---

[100]Max Weber, *Bureaucracy*, in On Charisma and Institution Building 66 (S.N. Eisenstadt ed., 1968).

But even if we assume that the administrative power of the federal government is growing at the direct expense of states and private enterprises, we cannot conclude that this growth reduces the dispersion of governmental control over the people, and thereby threatens liberty. The crucial question is not the gross aggregation of power, but the way power is exercised in each area of human life. Once we focus on particular areas, it becomes apparent that the growth of the national government often increases the diffusion of administrative power by adding a second decision-maker to the previously comprehensive power of the state.

* * *

[F]ederal intervention generally means that two governmental hierarchies will be involved in a particular area of governance instead of one. This is sometimes described as cooperative federalism; Milton Grodzins invokes the image of marble cake, with state and federal power intertwined in innumerable, complex ways.[105] Of course, the federal government can preempt state authority in its entirety, but this is not the typical pattern; more often, federal action alters state governance, or simply adds to it. Whether one regards our political system as cooperative, competitive, or simply a mess—whether it resembles marble cake or mush—there is little doubt that state and national powers overlap, and that national policy is regularly implemented by state officials. All the advantages associated with power dispersion can flow from this intervention. The second decision-maker can introduce new standards, subject old ones to debate, increase popular awareness, decrease arbitrary power, restrain corruption and thereby expand liberty—the liberty of individuals from excessive or inappropriate government control.

To be sure, the federal government might take complete control of a particular area, thus transferring exclusive jurisdiction from the state to itself. This would mean that federal intervention neither increased nor decreased the dispersion of power. In our system, however, federal intervention has almost always resulted in increased dispersion, because the expansion of federal power into areas that were previously the exclusive province of the states has generally involved the sharing of power between federal and state officials. Even congressional action follows this pattern; federal courts are still more securely committed to it. Thus, diffusion of power virtually never provides a rationale for courts to stay their hand or to strike down national legislation.

Perhaps it could be argued that the aggregation of federal power across a broad range of governmental areas represents a dangerous concentration

---

[105] See [Morton Grodzins, The American System (Daniel J. Elazar ed., 1966)], at 60–88; Morton Grodzins, *The Federal System*, in American Federalism in Perspective (Aaron B. Wildavsky ed., 1967).

of power, even if its effect, in individual areas, is to disperse power among multiple authorities. But this assumes the point at issue—whether federalism has moral force that justifies its invocation as a constraint on governmental action. If one wants to argue this point, rather than asserting it, one must show that federal aggrandizement impinges on some independent value, such as individual liberty. As indicated, however, federal intervention tends to increase liberty in each area of governance, and thus with respect to each group of people. * * *

* * *

III. FEDERALISM AND COMMUNITY

* * *

Many different types of community are possible, but there are two that seem particularly relevant for present purposes. First, a group of people may be regarded as a community because its members feel a personal or emotional connection to one another. Borrowing a term from Robert Wolff, this may be called an "affective community."[124] Alternatively, the members of a group may function as a community because they engage in a collective decision-making process regarding major questions of self-governance. This is sometimes referred to as a "dialogic" community, by emphasizing the element of public debate; Wolff uses the term "rational" community because he, like Jurgen Habermas, regards uncoerced persuasion as essential to true collective decision-making.[125] A safer term might be political community; this acknowledges the sense of a shared enterprise, while not imposing such high standards that it precludes historical examples.

* * *

[In assessing the claim that federalism is justified by the value of community and thus should operate as a principle for judicial decision-making, we] can begin with affective community, and assume that fostering such

---

[124][Robert P. Wolff, The Poverty of Liberalism (1968)], at 187–92. Wolff's use of this term is somewhat different: he states that affective community "is the reciprocal consciousness of a shared culture." Id. at 187. In exploring the possibility of an affective community, however, he refers to reciprocal relationships between individuals. Id. at 182–83. We use his term to describe the set of such relationships within a group.

[125]Id. at 192–93; Jurgen Habermas, The Theory of Communicative Action 8–42, 273–337 (Thomas McCarthy trans., 1984). Wolff would call this one form of affective community, reserving the term political community for a society in which "each member of society must recognize his fellow citizens as rational moral agents and must freely acknowledge their right (and his) to reciprocal equality in the dialogue of politics." Wolff, supra note [124], at 192. As Wolff acknowledges, this is an aspiration. Since it refers to a null set, we adopt the term political community for actually existing societies that engage in collective decision-making.

communities is a desirable goal. This is by no means self-evident; small, tightly-knit groups of people with strong affective bonds among themselves are likely to be xenophobic, intolerant, and repressive. But even if they behave more the way that proponents of community envision, that is, like the people in contemporary beer and wine commercials, such communities do not support an argument for federalism. Federalism, unlike the more general principle of managerial decentralization, only protects the rights of states, and all, or virtually all, American states are far too large to function as affective communities. If we take the notion of mutual bonds of emotional attachment seriously, it seems clear that we are speaking about small towns or urban neighborhoods, not about our nation-size political subdivisions. It may be true that smaller American states are often controlled by a narrow political elite that operates as a community for certain purposes. But since communities tend to be exclusionary, and elites remain elite by that same mechanism of exclusion, a political elite of this sort is unlikely to instill communitarian feelings among its state's excluded millions. When proponents of affective community become specific, they tend to speak about volunteer groups, PTAs, church congregations, farm cooperatives, and urban self-help programs—all entities that are considerably smaller than a state.

Because of the obvious disjunction between affective communities and states, the communitarian argument for federalism tends to emphasize a different claim: that state governments are more likely to protect and foster local communities than a remote federal government. But no theoretical argument or empirical evidence supports this proposition. Indeed * * * the only reliable way to establish a program of this sort throughout the nation is to have the national government implement it. Left to their own devices, some states might foster community, while others might attempt to extirpate it. Affective community, like any other uniform policy, is more likely to be achieved through comprehensive nation-wide action.

Empirical evidence confirms that there is no necessary link between states and affective communities. Much of the supplementary funding for local governments comes directly from the federal government, rather than the states. More importantly, since most local governments are themselves too large to constitute affective communities, efforts to involve neighborhood leadership in government program operation have often issued from the national government. This was particularly true during the War on Poverty, when federal initiatives like Model Cities and the Elementary and Secondary Education Act required participation from what was explicitly referred to as "the Community."

If federalism does not protect or foster affective communities, perhaps it plays this role for political communities. There is no particular constraint on the size of such communities; indeed, looking around the world, or across the course of history, there appear numerous political communities as large as or larger than our states. One finds, moreover, impressive empirical evidence to indicate that federalism protects political communities. Many current nations are alliances of political communities, with the existence of each community being secured by the rights that it can assert against the central government. These political communities often preserve linguistic, religious, and cultural features that would be disrupted or submerged by central control—a control that tends to be exercised quite rigorously in diverse nations unless the political communities have a legal right to resist. Conversely, political rights often contribute to people's sense of identity with each other and to their ability to constitute a political community.

An example of a political community that exists within a larger state is Catalonia. * * *

* * *

A political community like Catalonia can advance a powerful demand for autonomy upon the central government.[153] From the Catalans' perspective, of course, this demand may express itself in the desire for total independence, thus rejecting centralized authority in any form. But from the central government's perspective, the demand provides an argument for federalism. Creating a federal structure, and thus preserving Catalonia's right to function as a political community, would recognize and foster a language, a culture, and a shared historical experience. In pragmatic terms, it might also secure the unity of the nation by acceding to some measure of independence for its constituent communities. Of course, a particular regime might reject such a claim, as the Bourbons, the nineteenth century Liberal government, and Franco's dictatorship all did with respect to Catalonia. But the point remains that, in Spain, federalism is genuinely supported by a normative argument based on the principle of political community.

This is not true of the United States. There are no regions in our nation with a separate history or culture like Catalonia's. Most of our states, the alleged political communities that federalism would preserve, are mere administrative units, rectangular swatches of the prairie with nothing but

[153] The province of Quebec provides a similar example. Unlike any American state, the majority of Quebec's citizens speak a different language from the remainder of their nation, and feel their strongest cultural ties to a different European parent. The vigor and perceived legitimacy of their separatism may be one reason why Canadian courts have been more solicitous of federalism concerns, despite the relatively weak support for this position in the Canadian constitution. See [Edwin R. Black, Divided Loyalties: Canadian Concepts of Federalism (1975)]; Martha A. Field, *The Differing Federalisms of Canada and the United States*, 55 Law & Contemp. Probs. 107 (1992).

their legal definitions to distinguish them from one another.[155] Although some of the original thirteen states had unique political communities resulting from their separate origins, their uniqueness has long since given way to the national culture. Of course, citizens of Nebraska know that they live in Nebraska, and can identify themselves as Nebraskans * * *. But this level of identification does not exceed that which people naturally establish with a governmental sub-unit that administers numerous decentralized services. If that is counted as a political community, then such communities are not only ubiquitous, but virtually unavoidable in any moderate-size nation. This dilutes the concept to the point of insignificance.

* * *

To be sure, there are affective communities to be found in various parts of the United States: religious groups, Native American tribes, even towns with relatively homogeneous populations. Because of the necessarily small size of such communities, they are generally located within the borders of a single state. But they have no particular relationship to the state itself, and we cannot identify any of our states as being uniquely composed of, or identified with, such communities, with the possible exception of Utah. Indeed, states are often hostile to the presence of such communities and the national government is required to intervene on their behalf. Native Americans are perhaps the prime example. Given how cruel our national government has been to Native Americans, the fact that it is nonetheless their principal protector testifies to the truly abysmal attitudes that state governments often display toward affective communities within their midst.

This nation-wide dispersion of ethnic and cultural identities, paralleling the dispersion of economic or ideological identities, does not mean that the concept of political community is inapplicable to the United States. What it means, rather, is that the United States has one political community, and that political community is the United States. The arena in which our political consciousness takes shape and our crucial decisions are made is a national one. It is the nation as a whole that constructs our sense of self and that provides a sense of participation in a larger group. Thus, American

---

[155] As Glazer points out, Utah is something of an exception, having been founded, and continuing to be dominated, by members of a distinct religion. See [Nathan Glazer, *The Constitution and American Diversity*, in Forging Unity out of Diversity (Robert Goldwin et al. eds., 1989)], at 64. But the Mormons are a recent group, who emerged from a period of general turmoil in American Protestantism and have no distinguishing features apart from their religious commitment. Thus, while they undoubtedly represent a true community, there are many bonds linking them to the national community as well. Guam and Puerto Rico, on the other hand, are genuine political communities, with their own language, culture, and history. They are not, however, part of the United States; they are simply ruled by the United States. If we were to grant them statehood status (something they apparently do not want, precisely because of their separate identity), there would be a strong argument for allowing them to follow separate norms—that is, for genuine federalism.

federalism is nothing more than decentralization bec claim of political community is not available to it. meaningful sense, belongs only to the nation as a single

LYNN BAKER AND ERNEST YOUNG, FEDI THE DOUBLE STANDARD OF JUDICIA

51 DUKE L.J. 75, 887–88, 96–98, 105–106, 117–126, 133–137, 14

fed has value

The Court's abandonment of many aspects of federalism after 1937—in particular, the Court's refusal to enforce substantive limits on the scope of Congress's commerce power—is often justified in terms of institutional concerns about judicial competence. * * *

These arguments draw their persuasive power from an extended history of judicial efforts to define and monitor exclusive spheres of state and federal regulatory authority. Certainly the graveyard of failed distinctions that these efforts left behind—"commerce" versus "police" regulation "inherently national" versus "inherently local" matters, "manufacturing" or "mining" versus "commerce," "direct" versus "indirect" effects—does not speak well for the judicial ability to develop doctrinal limits on national power that are at once meaningful and workable. But the question is not whether a revival of these failed doctrines would be a good thing * * *. Rather, the issue for the present day is whether the Court is somehow institutionally incapable of fashioning new rules that would constrain Congress while at the same time constraining the courts.

In answering that question, it is instructive to look to the present fate of dual federalism's pre-1937 partner in crime: substantive due process. Certainly similar charges of institutional incapacity were made about *Lochner* and its progeny; critics have argued that doctrinal formulae like "freedom of contract" were insufficiently constraining to prevent the judges from simply enforcing their own policy preferences for laissez-faire economics. And yet, the Court has rehabilitated substantive due process in more recent years and used it to strike down a relatively wide range of social legislation. Critics of these more recent decisions have not hesitated to cry "*Lochner*!" or to doubt the institutional competence of the courts to render these judgments. And yet a fairly consistent majority of the Court—including, frequently, those Justices most incensed about the illegitimacy of judicial review in the federalism area—generally has rejected judicial competence concerns when due process rights affecting personal autonomy are at stake. * * *

* * *

A frank appraisal of the pervasive line-drawing problems throughout constitutional law suggests that the double standard must be defended—if it can be defended—on grounds other than judicial competence. * * * The

Court never has articulated a comprehensive theory of substantive due process; instead, the doctrinal development in that area has been an incremental process of inclusion and exclusion. Justice Harlan's argument in *Poe* that the right to use contraceptives can be derived from the intersection of two lines of precedent—cases recognizing the sanctity of the marital relationship and cases recognizing a privacy interest in one's home—typifies this process.[110]

So, too, there is no reason to believe that a workable doctrine cannot emerge from the Court's recent efforts to define the limits of the federal commerce power. The Court's decisions in *Lopez* and *Morrison*, for example, represent a significant refinement of the pre-1937 law in that they accept the principle of an integrated national market; rather than attempting to distinguish intra-from inter-state commerce, the Court's more recent decisions simply draw a line between what is "commercial" and what is not. The Court's refusal to frame this distinction in a categorical way, on the other hand, represents a recognition that further doctrinal refinement may be necessary. To the extent that this development traces an "unsteady path," that unsteadiness simply reflects the nature of common law incrementalism rather than the illegitimacy of the enterprise.

* * *

To say that the judiciary may not decline to enforce federalism constraints on competence grounds is not, of course, to determine the appropriate rigor of judicial review. In any number of instances, courts have articulated deferential standards of review in response to concerns about the relative institutional competence of courts vis-à-vis the political branches. But this problem of doctrinal design recurs throughout constitutional law, and the relevant considerations—which surely include the necessity of judicial enforcement and the normative appeal of the relevant values, as well as the issue of judicial competence—may play out differently in different situations even within the same general doctrinal context. We cannot address here the broader question of how federalism doctrine should be designed. Our narrow point, rather, is that judicial competence concerns cannot justify a categorical distinction between federalism and other constitutional principles.

* * *

Even if the state-based apportionment of representation within the federal government did ensure that "the States as States" are protected against federal overreaching [which the authors doubt], this is only one facet of the problem. Most of the literature on political safeguards has focused solely on this vertical aspect of federalism, but the horizontal

[110]Poe v. Ullman, 367 U.S. 497, 543-44 (1961) (Harlan, J., dissenting) * * *

dimension is at least as important. The concern here is that in the absence of judicial review, some states will harness the federal lawmaking power to impose their policy preferences on other states to the former states' own advantage. Not only does the state-based allocation of congressional representation sometimes fail to protect minority states against this majoritarian use of the federal lawmaking power, it often facilitates it.

It is important to appreciate that arguments about horizontal threats to state autonomy presume that the Wechslerian political safeguards are sometimes effective vis-à-vis some vertical aspects of federalism. That is, horizontal arguments rest on the assumption that federal institutions are sometimes responsive to the preferences and interests of state governments or (more often) of interest groups geographically concentrated in particular states. It is this very responsiveness that creates the problem: to the extent that Congress responds to the preferences of a majority of states, it may take action that encroaches on the autonomy of a minority of dissenting states. Such encroachment minimizes the benefits of federalism by creating a federally imposed homogenization of preferences.

* * *

The net result of the federal legislation in each of the scenarios discussed above is a reduction in the diversity among the fifty states in the package of taxes and services, including constitutional rights and other laws, that each offers its residents and potential residents. Some individuals (and corporations) may no longer find any state that provides a package (including the permissibility of polygamy, a minimum drinking age of eighteen, the availability of various family benefits for homosexual partners, or free soil laws) that suits their preferences, while other individuals and corporations may confront a surfeit of states offering a package (including prohibitions on polygamy, a minimum drinking age of twenty-one, laws restricting various family benefits to married couples of different genders, or fugitive slave laws) they find attractive.

In many instances, this reduced diversity is likely to mean a decrease in aggregate social welfare, since the loss in welfare to those with the minority preference is unlikely to yield a comparable gain in welfare for those who favor it. But it is important to understand that, although we have deliberately chosen unattractive (especially to liberals) examples for our initial exposition, we also could cite horizontal encroachments, both historical and hypothetical, that seem much more legitimate and appealing. The northern states' efforts to end slavery, for example, are surely an instance of our first type of scenario: the North did not attack slavery primarily in Virginia or Georgia or Alabama because it harmed citizens of Massachusetts or, due to some collective action problem, undermined Massachusetts's ability to enact an effective free soil regime in its own state. Rather, the North sought to impose its antislavery preferences on the South because its citizens firmly believed slavery was wrong and were unwilling to tolerate diversity on that point.

Likewise, states sometimes may have a legitimate interest in having certain conditions imposed on federal funds offered to the states. If an outlier state is pursuing policies that tend to undermine the efficacy of moneys provided for a federal program, other states legitimately might object that the common federal funds are not being efficiently spent and impose a funding condition to redress the problem. A majority of states could insist, for example, that federal highway funding be reserved for those states that adhere to certain minimum safety standards in roadway design.

Finally, the need to overcome externalities and other collective action problems—our third scenario—is one of the classic justifications for federal action. We have tried to suggest that such federal action is not always a good thing, but there surely are many examples where it is beneficial. Two states sharing a border may have different preferences regarding the regulation of pollution; where smog from the more permissive state crosses the border, it is not obviously illegitimate for the more restrictive state to seek federal regulation that would eliminate the externality-producing disparity. Our point is simply that elimination of externalities is not intrinsically good; adoption of a uniform federal rule in such circumstances does not generally require only that the externality-producing state internalize the costs of those externalities, but also that the state conform to the regulatory preferences of the majority. [That] is not always a good thing.

* * *

Telling the difference between good horizontal encroachments and bad ones will not always be an easy task. The important point for present purposes, however, is that we cannot necessarily expect the national political process to distinguish accurately between the two types. The traditional literature on federalism provides no reason to think that the aspects of the federal structure that usually are identified as guarding against vertical aggrandizement—particularly the responsiveness of Congress and the president to interests concentrated at the state level—will provide a bulwark against horizontal aggrandizement. * * *

* * *

At the end of the day, changing normative preferences may provide a more convincing descriptive explanation for the double standard than any principled distinctions among constitutional values. Economic rights like property and contract seem so, well, bourgeois today—especially to typically left-of-center academics. So too with federalism. Edward Rubin and Malcolm Feeley, for instance, boldly assert that "there is no normative principle involved [in federalism] that is worthy of protection." * * *

We doubt that these changed preferences provide a legitimate justification for ceasing to enforce particular aspects of the constitutional order. A constitution, after all, is supposed to place certain values off limits to alteration not only by populist sentiment but by intellectual fashion as well. If a particular principle is part of the Constitution, then there can be no legitimate justification for putting it in "exile" other than a subsequent—and fairly direct—constitutional amendment. The current unpopularity of states' rights in the academy thus cannot itself justify the double standard of judicial review.

We consider the normative argument for the double standard at some length here because we find the widespread conviction that states' rights are normatively unattractive somewhat puzzling. We think this conviction ultimately springs from some combination of four different sources. First, the significance of the term "states' rights" and its relation to traditional liberal appreciation for diversity frequently are not appreciated or understood. Second, the historical linkage of states' rights to slavery and segregation tends to obscure the fact that federalism is largely irrelevant to those issues under current constitutional law. Third, liberals seem to assume that a particular historical configuration of political forces—i.e., Democratic party dominance of the federal government; more conservative regimes in the states—will endure forever. And finally, most observers have overlooked the distinctive interaction between federalism, individual rights, and economic regulation in contemporary law.

* * *

One crucial feature of a system of institutional checks and balances is that the various participants in the system have rights against one another—that is, that each institution has certain trumps that it can exercise to protect its position against encroachments by other entities. No one is confused when we speak of Congress's "rights" vis-à-vis the president or vice versa. No one thinks we are "anthropomorphizing" Congress by such language, or that any of these institutions exists for any purpose other than to protect the freedom and welfare of individual human beings. The point is simply that, to act as an effective check on executive power for the benefit of the people, Congress must have certain prerogatives that are enforceable as a matter of legal "right." So, too, with states' rights: if the states are to be an effective component of Madison's "double security" for individual liberty, then the states must have certain "rights" that the national government is bound to respect.

* * * State autonomy ultimately exists to safeguard the liberty of individuals in at least three ways. First, it creates a set of intermediary institutions that exist as a buffer between the individual and the central government. State institutions are large, well established, and provide a rallying point for opposition to federal policies. As a result, they often will raise a far more serious obstacle to illiberal measures at the federal level than could individuals acting alone or even through private associations. Extensive political theory and social science literatures long have linked the decline of intermediary institutions such as churches, unions, and families to the centralization and accumulation of government power. To the extent that state institutions play a role in filling this gap, they provide an important safeguard for individual liberty.

The role of the states in resisting the accumulation of power in Washington, D.C., sometimes is viewed as important only in implausible "worst case scenarios" involving the ascension of a dictator in Washington. Yet the states play a more prosaic checking role on a regular basis. An important element of political liberty is the openness of the system to changes in leadership, reform of government institutions, and changes in official policy. The states provide critical staging grounds for such movements; groups that are out of power at the national level nonetheless may develop political experience and support, as well as a successful record for their policies, in individual states before competing for power at the national level.

* * *

In any event, federalism's current bad odor is a historically contingent function of the uses to which federalism's advocates sometimes have put state autonomy—specifically, as a sanctuary for slavery and segregation. To leap from this history to a condemnation of federalism in general is to misunderstand that states' rights are a form of negative freedom. As we explained in the previous Section, the freedom of local political communities to choose their own visions of the good society, like any other form of "diversity," predictably produces a mixed bag of results. We therefore should not be surprised that the vision of the "good" that some communities choose to pursue is, well, bad. Anyone who (a) believes that diversity is an important value but (b) is not a complete moral skeptic—i.e., believes that at least some moral questions have "right answers"—must live with these sorts of contradictions. Diversity always entails the freedom to make wrong choices.

The way that American society has dealt with this tension is to place certain fundamental values off limits to diversity by enshrining them in the Constitution itself. Society does not, for example, allow local communities to organize themselves along aristocratic lines by granting titles of nobility.

So, too, has society dealt with the past failure of some states adequately to protect individual freedom and equality: the Thirteenth, Fourteenth, and Fifteenth Amendments go directly to the issue of racial equality, while the gradual incorporation of the Bill of Rights ensures that other freedoms society has come to regard as basic are respected in all American jurisdictions. While the actual realization of all these values no doubt remains incomplete, states' rights are no longer a barrier to these constitutional values. * * *

* * *

It may be that the federalist "turn" in the Supreme Court's jurisprudence also suffers from the fact that it is, in fact, a turn. Federalism has labored under the double standard for so long that any proponents of judicial review in federalism cases—no matter how mild that review ultimately might be in its application—are easily tarred as "extremists."

We have attempted, in this Article, to help "normalize" debates about federalism and judicial review. We have questioned the longstanding assumption that states' rights are somehow importantly different from other areas of constitutional law in which the necessity and value of judicial review are taken for granted. We have argued, therefore, that concerns about judicial competence, necessity, and the normative value of federalism are all insufficient to justify a double standard of judicial review between federalism and other constitutional principles. To say that, of course, is merely to begin a long and complex discussion about what sort of judicial review we should have in this area. That conversation cannot move forward, however, until we welcome constitutional federalism home from its long "exile."

B. FEDERAL POWERS

ROBERT F. NAGEL, THE FUTURE OF FEDERALISM

46 CASE W. RES. L. REV. 643, 645–54 (1996).

I

Is the United States about to undergo a significant transformation of the legal relationship between the national government and the states?

* * *

The sense that we may be on the verge of important alterations in the federal system * * * is entirely understandable. Even sophisticated observers, who are not inclined to overreact to every lurch in the case law or to overestimate the actual capacity of the Court to achieve its objectives, might well take the view that serious change is at hand. After all, the fact that we are all accustomed to living under a fairly centralized administrative state does not foreclose dramatic revisions to that structure. Periods of radical transformation do occur. When intellectual themes in judicial decisions are not only potentially far-reaching but persistent and when those themes reflect wider social movements, it is possible that the Supreme Court may be signaling—or even helping to induce—one of those transformations.

But I do not think so. I can begin to explain why not by focusing on what seems to me to be potentially the most expansive aspect of [*United States v.*] *Lopez*.[a]

II

The formal doctrine adopted by the *Lopez* majority "requires an analysis of whether the regulated activity 'substantially affects' interstate commerce."[18] Like many judicial "tests," this one has the ring of relevance and realism. Anyone reassured by this formulation would be consternated to discover a page or two later in the opinion that the Court does not actually engage in the required analysis. I do not mean that the Justices engaged in the inquiry superficially or unsatisfactorily; I mean they did not make the inquiry at all.

This failure is not something that requires subtle analysis to discover. It is apparent on the face of the opinion. The Court first summarizes the Government's "essential contention."[19] That contention was that the possession of firearms in school zones can be expected to result in violence and that such violence can be expected to have economic consequences because it is costly in itself and also reduces the willingness of economic actors to travel into dangerous areas. The Court also summarizes the Government's contention that violence threatens the educational process and thus reduces productivity. Because the Court states these claims as if it is going to deny them, it is possible to miss the fact that it does not do so. Instead, the Justices "pause to consider the implications of the Government's arguments." Those implications are, according to the majority, that under the Commerce Clause the national government could regulate "all activities that might lead to violent crime . . . (or affect) the economic productivity of individual citizens." Thus, the Court concluded that "if we were to accept the Government's arguments, we are hard-pressed to posit any activity by an individual that Congress is without power to regulate."[24]

My point in detailing this part of the *Lopez* opinion is not to quarrel with the Court's conclusion, which seems to me to be accurate. My point is the entirely obvious one that the Court's conclusion is not an application of

---

[a][115 S. Ct. 1624 (1995).]
[18][Id.] at 1630.
[19]Id. at 1632.
[24]Id.

its announced test. In fact, the reason why there is force to the Court's claim that the Government's contention would prove too much is because it is logically possible—even as a practical matter highly likely—that such everyday matters as the quality of family life (or public schooling) do affect productivity. If these activities did not have economic consequences, their regulation would be readily distinguishable from the circumstance depicted by the Government in *Lopez*. In short, the Court's analysis effectively concedes that regulation of guns near schools would have a substantial effect on commerce.

Thus, in my view, the *Lopez* decision is potentially far-reaching not because it authoritatively announces the "substantial effects" test, but because at a crucial point the Justices abandon that test. To appreciate the full implications of the Court's approach, consider how it would have affected the outcome of *Katzenbach v. McClung*, in which the Court upheld the public accommodations provisions of the Civil Rights Act of 1964.[25] Under the analysis actually utilized in *Lopez*, it would not have mattered in *Katzenbach* that racial integration of public accommodations might have had—in fact, did have, as it turned out—a very substantial effect on the economies of Southern states. Even in the face of this strong connection to commerce, the *Lopez* logic would have required invalidation of the Civil Rights Act because it is difficult to conceive of any aspect of race relations, including private racist acts and beliefs, that does not have the potential to sour human interactions and depress economic activity.

I recognize that *Katzenbach* is formally different from *Lopez* in certain respects. The restaurant at issue in *Katzenbach* served food that had moved across state lines while there is no such "jurisdictional tie" regarding the guns regulated in *Lopez*. But any conceivable object of regulation will necessarily involve something that has traveled in interstate commerce. Everyone knows that schools, police departments, and families all purchase goods that have been a part of commerce. Therefore, the much-heralded jurisdictional tie is itself subject to the logic of *Lopez*—that is, the asserted tie to commerce would potentially allow national regulation of any imaginable activity.

It is also possible to depict cases like *Katzenbach* as different from *Lopez* by saying that they involved commercial enterprises, like restaurants, rather than education. But the *Lopez* approach, fully applied, would devour the distinction between commercial and noncommercial activities in the same way that it would demolish the significance of the jurisdictional tie. Even if the word "commerce" is used to mean only the production and sale of goods, there is no end to the local activities, such as a child's lemonade stand, that potentially could be subject to national regulation. Moreover, the

[25] 379 U.S. 294, 304 (1964).

majority itself points out that "depending on the level of generality, any activity can be looked upon as commercial."[28] This is true, of course. Schools and families, for instance, can be viewed as producers of economic participants that eventually sell themselves in the market. Under the analysis employed in *Lopez*, the identification of this kind of conceptual slide means that the Court is not obliged to examine the scale of economic effects. This leads to the absurd conclusion that commercial activities themselves are beyond the commerce power even when the Court is unable to demonstrate that they do not have sizable economic consequences.

Certainly, it is possible to criticize the Court both for failing to apply its own announced test and for the expansive potential that arises from that failure. However, that is not my purpose. In fact, the point that I want to develop is that the Court's behavior is quite understandable and, indeed, is even built into the interpretive process. I hope to show that what we are witnessing is an aspect of normal, predictable doctrinal gyrations, not the beginning of a significant political transformation.

III

The aspects of the *Lopez* decision that I have been focusing on are understandable and predictable as soon as we consider the problem faced by the Court. That problem is that our Constitution only authorizes certain enumerated powers for the national government, but also authorizes some enumerated powers that are broad enough to allow congressional control over any aspect of human affairs. This dilemma has various subparts or versions. The best-known is that Congress is delegated not only enumerated powers but also those extra powers necessary and proper for accomplishing its objectives. Another is that, while it is possible to insist on a superficial distinction between commercial and other kinds of activities, noncommercial behavior has substantial effects on the economy. Another is that there inevitably are both commercial and noncommercial effects and purposes involved in any wise policy. These dilemmas are known to virtually all educated observers, but their insuperability is usually not fully acknowledged because most of those observers are committed to judicial review.

If, as the practice of judicial review requires, constitutional meaning is to be determined as a part of the adjudicative process, it is necessary that the content of the Constitution be coherent enough to yield singular answers. Puzzles, contradictions, omissions, mistakes, parallel truths, and similar blemishes must be disregarded because the enterprise of interpretation is subordinate to the enterprise of authoritative dispute settlement. For obvious reasons, it simply will not do for a judge to say, "The Constitution is a mess on this point and cannot provide any single answer." The lawyer's task, therefore, is to help obliterate multiple meanings. Substantive

[28] *Lopez*, 115 S. Ct. at 1633.

dilemmas are the occasion for our work, not the objects of our curiosity. Lawyers are so accustomed to this great intellectual constraint imposed by judicial review that we hardly notice it.

Suppose that we were not a part of the adjudicative process and we were studying the Constitution just to try to understand it. We would have to admit that under our system, Congress may regulate any imaginable activity, but that it has only defined, limited powers. We could, perhaps, attribute this contradiction to the Framers' lack of economic sophistication, to changes in social circumstances, or to the nature of collective decision-making. If we were inclined to trust in central planning, we might be concerned that the fundamental charter places substantive limits on national regulatory power, but if we were in favor of decentralization we might worry about the limitless power to regulate commerce. We probably would end with an accurate but banal insight into the extreme fallibility of human efforts to structure public decision-making. What we could not do, if we were only interpreting and not adjudicating, is talk as if either horn of the dilemma were absent or unimportant.

Now, litigators and judges do not have the luxury of bemused inspection or full understanding. What alternatives are available to them? A number of options can be seen in the case law that has been built up over the decades.

First of all, lawyers can pretend that one horn of the dilemma does not exist. The Court did this when it denied that labor unrest in the nation's coal fields was linked directly enough to commerce to justify national regulation of working conditions at the mines.[29] This position, which focused on the ends for which national power may be exercised, ignored the existence of the Necessary and Proper Clause and the undeniable, brute fact that instability in the mining industry had had an enormous impact on commerce. As the ultimate abandonment of the distinction between "direct" and "indirect" effects suggests, the strategy of denial is difficult to sustain for long. It is, if my assumptions are correct, fundamentally and demonstrably untrue to the meaning of the document. Moreover, when applied rigidly in the real world, this strategy is likely to have disastrous consequences because there can be practical reasons for either centralization or decentralization depending on the time and the setting.

A second tactic is more flexible and also more credible. Using conventional legal justifications, the Court often devalues one or the other of the competing propositions. Common as it is, the overall logic of this approach is still worth examining. Conventional legal explanations, whether based on old-fashioned metaphors or modern balancing, acknowledge both horns of the dilemma and then provide various reasons why in a particular case they

[29]See Carter v. Carter Coal Co., 298 U.S. 238, 307–10 (1936).

are not of equivalent importance. You will recall, for example, that it used to be the position of the Court that Congress could not prohibit shipment of goods produced by child labor.[30] This case acknowledged but devalued the proposition that the commerce power allowed regulation for moral purposes; it explained that national regulation was appropriate only when shipment of the good created the moral harm or "polluted" the channels of commerce. The same method can be couched in more modern and realistic terms. For instance, the "substantial effects" test announced in *Lopez* concedes that commercial regulations can have non-commercial consequences and that prohibiting guns near schools could have some effects on commerce. Under the test as announced, however, these points are devalued for the reason that the demonstrated effects on commerce are not large enough. The strategy of devaluation can, of course, also be used to uphold legislation. For example, the Court approved national regulation of agricultural production that admittedly might otherwise be defined as "local" (because the wheat was meant for home consumption) on the ground that the regulatory program in question was generally aimed at wheat destined for interstate shipment.[33] In that instance, the practical necessities of administering a national program were a reason for devaluing the proposition that there is some regulatory authority that is beyond the power of Congress.

These kinds of explanations are familiar to us all and therefore have a certain plausibility. But ultimately, each depends on the assumption that "federalism" can be said to require one outcome or another in a particular case. To the extent that the underlying dilemma is, as I have claimed, unresolvable, the truth is that either outcome would be equally constitutional and, at the same time, equally unconstitutional. Hence, legalistic devaluation of either of the two relevant constitutional propositions will always be intellectually unsatisfactory if examined carefully. This dilemma, I think, is one reason the "substantial effects" test was only announced—and not applied—in *Lopez*. Although most people are not accustomed to thinking about the connection between conditions in public schools and robust commercial activity, there surely is such a connection and in the future that connection might become as intuitive to the general public as the idea that working conditions in the mines affect interstate commerce. Moreover, even if the connection between public schooling and commerce were limited, nothing in the commerce clause dictates that Congress may regulate only those activities that have large effects on commerce.

The weaknesses in the strategy of denial and the strategy of legalistic devaluation create natural pressures toward what I will call "successive

[30]See Hammer v. Dagenhart, 247 U.S. 251, 272 (1918), overruled in part by United States v. Darby, 312 U.S. 100 (1941).

[33]See Wickard v. Filburn, 317 U.S. 111, 128 (1942).

validation," which is the method actually used in *Lopez*. Under this approach, one horn of the dilemma is subordinated in the case at hand but the equivalency of the competing constitutional proposition is reasserted by a stated commitment to enforce that proposition in some future case. In its pure form, this strategy would take the form of randomized outcomes and thus, is not compatible with traditional legal norms. Nevertheless, muted versions of this tactic can be seen at work in the cases. As the *Lopez* opinion reminds us, each of the post-1937 cases approving congressional regulatory authority contained admonitions about the limited scope of the commerce power and indications that the Court might someday intervene if necessary to enforce those limits.[34] These admonitions were, in my view, mostly incompatible with the logic of the opinions in which they appeared, but they did serve to reassert the overall equivalency of the proposition subordinated in those cases. Of course, *Lopez* also contains its own commitments emphasizing the continuing validity of the principle that it subordinated, namely, that under the commerce authority Congress can regulate all aspects of life. The Court strongly suggests, for instance, that Congress could regulate guns at schools if it would only make some factual findings or link its regulation to the movement of something across state lines.[35]

By promising future enforcement, these kinds of commitments reduce the pressure to devalue either of the competing propositions. Moreover, from a systemic perspective, the strategy of successive validation allows some realization over time of both propositions. The great difficulty, however, is that the method is inconsistent with the legalistic ideals of consistency and authoritativeness. As I explained earlier, the *Lopez* opinion employs logic that is incompatible with finding virtually any of the statutes approved since 1937 to be a valid exercise of the commerce power. *Lopez* is written this way because it is an effort to enforce a constitutional principle that is irreconcilably at odds with the principle that was validated in the post-1937 cases. That is, precisely because under the method of successive validation the cases as a whole are true to the complexity of the Constitution, no one decision can be reconciled with all the others and each is partially (but deeply) unjustified.

The embarrassments created by these techniques force consideration of more extreme measures. One option would be for the Court to withdraw from enforcing both horns of the dilemma. Indeed, until *Lopez*, many academic observers thought that the definition of "commerce among the states" was effectively a matter for congressional judgment.[36] Judicial

---

[34] 115 S. Ct. at 1628–30.

[35] Id. at 1631–32.

[36] See, e.g., Jesse H. Choper, Judicial Review and the National Political Process 175–84 (1980) (discussing the "Federalism Proposal," namely, that questions concerning the division

abdication, especially if explicit, would have its intellectual advantages. It would be consistent with the admission, as accurate as it is foreign to the legal mind, that either outcome of any particular case would be equally constitutional. Nevertheless, abdication is difficult to sustain over time because it conflicts with strong preferences in favor of judicial review.

The difficulties with all these strategies suggest a final option. Weary of all efforts to enforce or to withdraw from enforcing the principle of enumerated powers, the Court can claim to uphold that principle while substituting for it some other, more tractable value, such as democratic accountability.[38] The strategy of substitution has, obviously, considerable potential for intellectual embarrassment, but it is nevertheless sustainable to the extent that the courts' critics prefer whatever value the judiciary is enforcing over the values represented by federalism.

There is nothing inevitable about any of the five adjudicatory strategies that I have outlined. In varying degrees and combinations, the Court can and has used all of them in attempting to domesticate the unresolvable dilemma presented by the principle of enumerated powers. The method of legalistic devaluation is no doubt the one most congenial to our profession, but the Court's history is littered with one failed and discarded doctrine after another. This strongly suggests that the intellectual deficiencies connected with this strategy are, as my assumptions about the contradictory nature of the relevant constitutional propositions would predict, unavoidable and profound. Of the remaining three approaches that involve judicial enforcement of some constitutional value, the strategy of successive validation has been used, I think, most frequently, and is truest to our actual, confused Constitution.

Given the intellectual and practical advantages of this method and given its wide use, *Lopez* is not at all surprising. In many cases since 1937, the Court has acknowledged both horns of an unresolvable dilemma and has repeatedly committed itself to the validation (in some future case) of the principle of limited national power that it was subordinating in the cases it was deciding. Although it would have been possible, of course, for the Court to have simply continued this pattern, the full intellectual and practical advantages of the strategy of successive validation require at least some variation in outcome. In short, that the Court in *Lopez* should have eventually redeemed its pile of pledges seems a natural part of the most

---

of power between the federal government and the states should be left to the political branches); William Van Alstyne, Comment, *The Second Death of Federalism*, 83 Mich. L. Rev. 1709, 1722 (1985) (stating that it has been the province of Congress to determine the degree to which enumerated powers displace state action).

[38]See New York v. United States, 505 U.S. 144, 168–69 (1992) (discussing the problem of accountability in order to justify its conclusion that a state's legislative process cannot be commandeered).

attractive interpretive strategy available. Although the opinion in which the redemption occurs is starkly inconsistent with many other cases, it is not necessarily a signal of radical change, for the inconsistency is a necessary part of the strategy and flows ultimately from the content of the Constitution itself.

ROBERT POST AND REVA SIEGEL, LEGISLATIVE CONSTITUTIONALISM AND SECTION FIVE POWER: POLIOCENTRIC INTERPRETATION OF THE FAMLIY AND MEDICAL LEAVE ACT

112 YALE L.J. 1945–1947, 1952–1966, 2039–2041, 2048–2059 (2003)

Because Section 5 of the Fourteenth Amendment vests in Congress "power to enforce, by appropriate legislation, the provisions of this article the great rights contained in Section 1 of the Fourteenth Amendment are enforced by both Congress and the Court. How to conceive of the relationship between the legislative power established in Section 5 and the judicial power authorized by Section 1 is one of the deep puzzles of American constitutional law. This Article argues that Section 5 is a structural device that fosters the democratic legitimacy of our constitutional order. It links the legal interpretations of courts to the constitutional understandings of the American people, as expressed through their chosen representatives.

The history of Section 5 doctrine has been one of turmoil and revision. In the early years of the Fourteenth Amendment the Court was quite hostile to Section 5 power, fearing that it might "authorize Congress to create a code of municipal law for the regulation of private rights" that would displace "the domain of State legislation."[2] In the 1960s, during the so-called Second Reconstruction, the Court adopted a deliberately permissive stance and began to review Section 5 legislation with the same deference that it extended to every other exercise of national authority in the aftermath of the New Deal. In recent years the Rehnquist Court has turned the tables once again. In addition to reviving concerns about federalism, it has discovered an entirely new reason to renew judicial hostility to Section 5 authority: separation of powers.

The Rehnquist Court now views Section 5 power as a potential threat to the Court's role as "the ultimate expositor of the constitutional text."[4] Beginning with its 1997 decision in *City of Boerne v. Flores*,[5] the Court has repeatedly affirmed that Section 5 does not authorize Congress "to determine what constitutes a constitutional violation" or "to rewrite the Fourteenth

---

[2]The Civil Rights Cases, 109 U.S. 3, 11 (1883)

[4]United States v. Morrison, 529 U.S. 598, 616 n.7 (2000).

[5]521 U.S. 507 (1997).

Amendment law laid down by this Court."[8] * * * Condemning Section 5 legislation that might establish Congress as an independent interpreter of the Constitution, the Court has announced that "Congress' power under § 5 . . . extends only to 'enforc[ing]' the provisions of the Fourteenth Amendment," and that "Congress does not enforce a constitutional right by changing what the right is."[10]

We call this view of separation of powers the "enforcement model." The Rehnquist Court has used the enforcement model to strike down path-breaking civil rights legislation enacted under the quite different understanding of Section 5 that prevailed during the thirty years that preceded *Boerne*. * * * Disagreement with the enforcement model would seem possible only on the basis of a popular constitutionalism that would virtually abandon judicial review. It is no surprise that the enforcement model presently enjoys widespread support on all sides of the political spectrum.

We contend, however, that there is no need to choose between judicial review and innovative Section 5 legislation based on congressional interpretations of the Fourteenth Amendment. Both are possible, but only if we can break the hold that the enforcement model has on our common sense. The model seeks to exclude Congress from the process of constitutional lawmaking because it regards the integrity of our system of constitutional rights as dependent upon its complete insulation from the contamination of politics. Although we agree that there are many circumstances when constitutional law requires separation from politics, we also believe that a legitimate and vibrant system of constitutional law requires institutional structures that will ground it in the constitutional culture of the nation. Our Constitution contains a variety of structures and arrangements that facilitate these necessary connections between constitutional law and constitutional culture. These mechanisms range from the amendment procedures of Article V to the political appointment of Article III judges. Section 5 is best conceived as another such mechanism.

We therefore propose an account of Section 5 power that would enable it to perform this function. We call this account the model of policentric constitutional interpretation. The policentric model holds that for purposes of Section 5 power the Constitution should be regarded as having multiple interpreters, both political and legal. The model attributes equal interpretive authority to Congress and to the Court. The model thus entails (1) that Congress does not violate principles of separation of powers when it enacts Section 5 legislation premised on an understanding of the Constitution that differs from the Court's, and (2) that Congress's action does not bind the

---

[8][Bd. Of Trustees of the Univ. of Ala. v. Garrett, 531 U.S. 356, 374 (2001).]

[10][*City of Boerne*, 521 U.S. at 536].

Court, so that the Court remains free to invalidate Section 5 legislation that in the Court's view violates a constitutional principle requiring judicial protection. This account of Section 5 power combines a robust legislative constitutionalism with a vigorous commitment to rule-of-law values.

In advancing the policentric model of Section 5 authority, we do not understand ourselves to be proposing some novel or innovative constitutional regime. To the contrary, the policentric model more accurately reflects the understandings and practices that make up our constitutional practice than does the enforcement model. During the period between the Second Reconstruction and *Boerne*, for example, Section 5 doctrine actually fostered a policentric practice of Section 5 authority. Our thesis in this Article is that Section 5 jurisprudence has been, and ought to remain, policentric. We draw on both history and theory to show that Section 5 legislation has in the past helped to establish democratic foundations for the Court's own articulation of constitutional rights.

* * *

The enforcement model is a recent innovation. In the nineteenth century the Court severely restricted Section 5 power in order to maintain what it believed were proper principles of federalism. But in 1997 the Rehnquist Court added an entirely new chapter to the interpretation of Section 5. It declared that the reach of Section 5 power was constrained not merely by federalism, but also, and primarily, by the requirements of separation of powers Because the Court understood Section 5 to regulate the relationship between Congress and the Court, it held that Congress had power to "enforce" the provisions of the Fourteenth Amendment, but not to "interpret" their meaning * * *

We call this account the "enforcement" model. At the heart of the enforcement model lies a particular view of separation of powers, which holds that the constitutional function of courts is to declare the substance and nature of Fourteenth Amendment rights, whereas the constitutional function of Section 5 legislation is to "enforce" those rights. The central premise of the enforcement model is that courts are the only legitimate source of authoritative constitutional meaning. Courts hold this privilege because the Constitution is a form of law and "the province of the Judicial Branch . . . embraces the duty to say what the law is."

* * *

Both the Court and Congress interpret the Constitution from the perspective of a particular institution. The point is not immediately obvious only because we tend to accept uncritically the fiction that the Constitution speaks abstractly, as though pronounced on high by some ideal interpreter in some unspecified space. When we accept this fiction, we ask whether the

Court or Congress is more likely to read the Constitution accurately, to ascertain its "true" meaning. But once we see that interpretation is always practiced by particular persons who seek to understand the Constitution in particular institutional settings and for particular institutional purposes, we can see that claims about constitutional meaning are always embedded in contexts.

By prohibiting Congress from using its Section 5 power to remedy or deter violations of constitutional rights until it has first "identified a history and pattern of unconstitutional . . . state transgressions," *Garrett* essentially subjects Congress to this paradigm of judicial power. *Garrett* holds that Congress has no power to deter future constitutional violations unless it first finds that constitutional rights have been violated. We may ask, however, why Congress should be constrained by limitations that derive from the particular institutional function of courts. What principle of legislative power would prohibit Congress from preventing future violations of constitutional rights, even if the record of actual or potential violations were inadequate to authorize a court to exercise equitable jurisdiction to order declaratory or injunctive relief? Congress does not derive its legitimacy from the practice of adjudication; it is not an institution designed to settle disputes between parties. Congress is instead a legislature that derives legitimacy from its democratic responsiveness to the values and commitments of the nation. Section 5 is a grant of legislative power, not a grant of judicial power. Why, then, should congressional authority under Section 5 be constrained by the limitations that reflect the specific institutional characteristics of Article III courts?

The enforcement model, in short, is rendered highly vulnerable once we understand that constitutional interpretation always proceeds within specific institutional contexts that inform both the substance of constitutional rights and the procedural framework within which they are enforced. The thesis of the enforcement model is that Section 5 power should be circumscribed by the pragmatic horizon of adjudication. But because Section 5 is a grant of legislative power, rather than of judicial power, it is puzzling why the enforcement model would limit Section 5 authority by the institutional norms applicable to courts, rather than by the institutional norms applicable to legislatures. Even if this normative constraint could be justified, moreover, there would remain the conceptual difficulty of articulating exactly what it might mean for a legislature to act according to norms appropriate for courts. In many circumstances it may be both incoherent and improper to require Congress to behave in this way. Because it does not take account of institutional differentiation, the enforcement model will typically import extrinsic principles to determine when legislative action is sufficiently "like" judicial action to count as the enforcement of judicially defined rights.

* * *

The distinct political dimensions of legislative constitutionalism enable Congress to articulate constitutional aspirations in a manner that consolidates constitutional values, and hence that enhances the likelihood that judicial interpretations of the Constitution will receive the political allegiance that is frequently necessary for their full legitimation. [F]or example, even so profound a constitutional vision as *Brown v. Board of Education* was not "firmly law" until it was able to inspire the political support of Congress and the President. Similarly, the vibrant legislative constitutionalism of the Ninety-Second Congress helped to ensure the legitimacy of the Court's new constitutional doctrine of sex equality.

* * *

The model of policentric constitutional interpretation does not imply that all Section 5 legislation is constitutional. The model asserts only that Section 5 legislation should not be deemed unconstitutional merely because it enforces R_c [Congress's conception of rights] as distinct from R_j [the judiciary's conception]. The model leaves open any and every other reason to find Section 5 legislation unconstitutional.

The most obvious reason for striking down Section 5 legislation is that it violates constitutional rights. The model of policentric constitutional interpretation attributes to Section 5 legislation the same structural relationship between power and rights as that which obtains for every other form of federal legislation. Courts assessing a federal statute normally ask two logically distinct questions: (1) Does Congress have the power to enact the statute? (2) Does the statute violate any constitutional rights? Thus Congress may have power to enact a statute under the Commerce Clause, but the existence of this power does not settle the question whether the statute violates a distinct constitutional provision like the First Amendment.

The same structure of analysis applies to the model of policentric constitutional interpretation. The model asks, first, whether Congress has the power to enact Section 5 legislation. The answer to this question turns on whether Congress intends to enforce its understanding of Section 1 of the Fourteenth Amendment, and not upon whether Congress has correctly anticipated how courts will enforce Section 1 of the Fourteenth Amendment. The model thus addresses the question of power through ordinary techniques of statutory interpretation. The model then asks a second and logically distinct question, which is whether Section 5 legislation violates any rights that courts will enforce against Congress. The source of congressional power is not generally determinative of this question. If legislation enacted pursuant to the Commerce Clause violates the First Amendment, so will that same legislation if enacted under Section 5.

The Court sometimes invalidates federal statutes not because they violate rights, but because they infringe what the Court has called "'essential postulates'" that define "the structure of the Constitution." One such postulate is federalism, which the Court has used to strike down statutes that Congress would otherwise have power to enact. An objection to the policentric model might be that independent congressional authority to interpret the Constitution might transform Section 5 power into a vehicle of unlimited power, capable of imposing boundless burdens on states. If one were inclined to fear such an outcome because one did not trust the political safeguards of federalism, then the policentric model might seem unacceptable. It is therefore important to stress that nothing in the policentric model prevents the Court from using postulates of federalism in appropriate circumstances to strike down a statute that Congress would otherwise have power under Section 5 to enact. * * *

* * *

We wish to be clear that the policentric model does not itself contain any implications about the relationship between Section 5 legislation and federalism. The model addresses only issues of separation of powers. The model would thus not require the Court to ignore the effects of Section 5 legislation on the values of federalism. But because the model would abandon the congruence-and-proportionality test, and because it would substitute a rather easy and clear set of tests for the establishment of Section 5 power, it would require the Court explicitly to articulate and defend the conclusion that particular Section 5 statutes, which are otherwise legitimate, so compromise essential principles of federalism as to be unconstitutional.

* * *

Distinguishing the question of Section 5 power from the constraints of federalism would allow the Court to apply the model of policentric constitutional interpretation without fear that it would lead to the oppression of the states or to the loss of indispensable aspects of their sovereignty. The Court could protect the values of federalism it thought essential, while nevertheless authorizing Congress to participate in the formation of constitutional culture through the enactment of Section 5 legislation reflecting a legislative vision of constitutional meaning. Even if the Court were to strike down such legislation on federalism grounds, the recognition of Congress's authority to articulate its underlying constitutional beliefs would still contribute to the ongoing dialogue between Congress and the Court that in the past has proved so important for the development of our understanding of the Constitution.

* * *

Although we regard the federalism values at issue in *Morrison* to be weak and ultimately indefensible, the Court evidently disagrees. It so strongly believes in these values that it is willing to use them to limit congressional power. We contend that in such circumstances it is especially important that the Court conceive federalism according to the states' rights approach, as a limitation on otherwise legitimate Section 5 power. The Court ought to be put to the test of explicitly articulating and defending the values of federalism that it believes are significant enough to circumscribe Section 5 power. Perhaps the Court in *Morrison* might have contended, along with Chief Justice Rehnquist, that VAWA contravenes postulates of federalism because it constitutes a federal intrusion into the family Or perhaps it might have believed that, despite the nearly forty-year history of Title VII of the Civil Rights Act of the 1964, regulating private discrimination is inconsistent with proper limitations on federal authority. Whatever reasons the Court might ultimately develop, they ought to be explicitly articulated and defended. They ought to be persuasive enough to withstand clear and crisp formulation, and they ought not to be allowed to masquerade as principles of separation of powers.

C. STATE IMMUNITIES

VICKI C. JACKSON, FEDERALISM AND THE USES AND LIMITS OF LAW: *PRINTZ* AND PRINCIPLE?

111 HARV.L.REV. 2180, 2213–28, 2246–47, 2251–58 (1998).

Although the Constitution is silent on enclaves for state regulation, the Constitution is explicit on state governments: first, that they exist;[276] second, that they exist in the form of a legislature,[277] an "executive authority,"[278] and courts;[279] and third, that they have affirmative responsi-

[276]See U.S. Const. art. IV (protecting territorial boundaries of states)[.]

[277]See U.S. Const. art. I, § 2, cl. 1 (linking qualifications for voters for representatives to those for members of the most numerous branch of the state legislature); id. amend. XVII (requiring popular election of senators by voters having the same "qualifications requisite for electors of the most numerous branch of the State legislatures"); id. art. I, § 8, cl. 17 (referring to the "Consent of the [state] Legislature" for federal purchases of property); id. art. II, § 1, cl. 2 (directing each state to appoint presidential electors "in such Manner as the Legislature thereof may direct"); id. art. IV, § 3, cl. 1 (forbidding states to be formed out of the territory of existing states without the consent of legislatures of the affected states); id. art. V (specifying state legislatures' involvement in amending the Constitution).

[278]Id. art. I, § 2, cl. 4 (requiring the "Executive Authority" of the state to call an election to fill House vacancies); id. art. IV, § 2, cl. 2 (requiring fugitives from justice to be returned on demand of "executive authority,"); id. art. IV, § 4 (providing protection against "domestic violence" on the application of state legislature or, if necessary, "of the Executive"); id. amend. XVII (requiring the "executive authority" of the state to call a special election for Senate vacancies, unless empowered by the state legislature to make temporary appointments).

[279]See id. art. VI, § 2; id. art. VI, § 3 (requiring state judicial and executive officers and

bilities (1) to participate in the selection of federal officials, (2) at least as to courts, to "be bound [ ]by" valid federal laws,[280] and (3) as to all state officials, to be bound by oath to support the Constitution.[281]

So, the Constitution clearly does contemplate and require two levels of sovereign government—joined in acting under the Constitution, but with separate sources of sovereignty arising from different, though overlapping, constituencies. This structure suggests a commitment to the viability of those governments, and hence a constitutional basis for special rules concerning federal interferences with the functioning of state governments and their constitutionally contemplated legislative, executive, and judicial branches.

* * *

Three features of legislative action may justify treating it as peculiarly protected from "outside" mandates for action—whether by federal courts or by federal legislative mandates for positive legislation. First, the front-line enforcement mechanisms for "law" in our legal system and culture are courts, and judicial enforcement of judgments against collective bodies like legislatures poses difficulties less likely to be present in the enforcement of orders against the executive or judicial officials. Second, there is a close association in our legal culture between voting and speech; compelled voting by legislative representatives thus bears a disquieting similarity to governmentally compelled speech, a constitutional anathema. Finally, and returning to the idea of accountability, legislatures are more closely bound up with public understandings of self-governance than either executive officers or courts. Compelled legislation may therefore have greater potential for voter confusion than mandates directed to other branches of state government. Although both courts and executive officials are commonly understood to carry out or apply laws or mandates given by others, legislatures are understood to behave (and to be authorized to behave), to a larger extent than courts or executives, as creators and initiators of law. When another body requires the legislature to act, the requirement may contradict widely held assumptions about the legislature's generative role and create uncertainty as to the source of the action in question.

Would these three characteristics support a bright-line rule against federal "commandeering" of state legislative bodies? I am not sure. But a strong presumption against interpreting federal laws enacted under Article I to so require would clearly be justified as a matter of federal common law,

---

state legislators to take an oath to support the Constitution)[.]

[280] U.S. Const. art. VI, § 2.

[281] See id. art. VI, § 3.

and a reasonable case can be made against the constitutionality of such laws.

However, historical evidence and other aspects of our constitutional tradition do not support the line drawn in *Printz v. United States*, extending as it does to all executive action. [S]ome kinds of federal "commandeering" of state executive functions may have higher potential than others for politically irresponsible and unaccountable behavior, confusing the relationships between state and federal representatives and their constituents. Although the Constitution might reasonably be construed to prohibit such acts, it cannot bear the construction presented in *Printz*.

Given the constitutional status of states and state governments, there is some basis for a more substantive form of review when a federal statute imposes duties or obligations on state governments in their governmental capacities. If such a statute is challenged as unconstitutional, it would be proper for a court to examine whether the statute is inconsistent with the constitutionally contemplated functions of state governments and with their constitutionally independent relationships with their own constituents. Such review could take a number of doctrinal forms.

Instead of a bright-line rule against "legislative commandeering," courts could adopt a presumption that federal directives to state legislatures are not "Necessary and Proper" if the same goal can be accomplished through other means, such as direct federal regulation.[309] It is hard to imagine circumstances in which national purposes could be served only by requiring state legislatures to adopt federally mandated legislation, and thus such an approach would be similar in effect to a flat prohibition on legislative commandeering.

It is less difficult to imagine circumstances in which a national purpose could be well served only by utilizing available state or local law enforcement officers—for example, the need quickly to implement a federal draft, or to combat a health emergency. Yet it is not clear that the best approach is one that simply permits such executive commandeering whenever Congress wants. Rather, an important or legitimate government interest test might be imposed, or an inquiry under the Necessary and Proper Clause that focuses both on the reasons for the federal action and the degree of interference with the performance of duties under state law might

[309]This approach could draw on versions of a "compelling," or "legitimate," government interest test articulated in other areas of constitutional law. See, e.g., Adarand Constructors, Inc. v. Pena, 515 U.S. 200, 227 (1995) (holding that the Constitution prohibits government use of race to award contracts unless measures are "narrowly tailored . . . [to] further compelling governmental interests"); Maine v. Taylor, 477 U.S. 131, 151 (1986) (rejecting a dormant commerce clause challenge to a state law that discriminated against an out-of-state product because the law met "legitimate local purposes that could not adequately be served by available nondiscriminatory alternatives").

be imposed. Under either formulation, constitutional inquiry might consider the size of the burden or amount of state time and resources needed to perform the federally mandated tasks—thereby permitting distinctions between relatively minor recordkeeping, record-checking, or information-providing and more substantial impositions on state resources involving matters that (even if directed at executive officials) come close to the core of legislative responsibilities.

[A] focus on whether a federal statute interferes with constitutionally contemplated functions of state governments may require developing a theory of core state government functions, an enterprise begun in *National League of Cities* and abandoned in *Garcia*. Professor Merritt has argued that certain state governmental functions should be protected from federal regulation, even if the regulation is identical to that of private activities. Such functions include setting voter qualifications, organizing the internal structure of state government, and determining qualifications and wages for state office when the employee performs "executive, judicial, or legislative tasks essential to a republican government."[313] These latter categories correspond to what I claim are constitutionally contemplated structures and functions of state governance under the federal Constitution.

Yet the demands of federalism do not lend themselves to decontextualized, formalist rulemaking by courts. For example, despite Merritt's powerful arguments that police forces should be treated as core aspects of the state's constitutionally protected executive function, courts should not absolutely protect state or local police from being required to carry out federal duties if the need is sufficiently urgent, or the duties are small and similar enough in character to duties imposed under state law, or the duration of the imposition is sufficiently limited. Conversely, I would not suggest that all "generally applicable" laws necessarily could be applied to state governments just as they are to private employers. * * * [T]here are persuasive bases to distinguish the question of compelling state governments to carry out uniquely governmental functions, as in *Printz* or *New York v. United States*, from that of extending laws like the Fair Labor Standards Act to the states. But at the same time, state governments are not fully situated like private employers. States should thus be permitted to challenge particular applications of generally applicable laws in order to avoid undue interference with state constitutional functions.

My goal here is not to articulate a fully developed doctrine, but rather to suggest that federal regulation of state governments can threaten constitutional values related to maintaining the states as independent sources and locations of government authority. Although the political

---

[313] [Deborah Jones Merritt, *The Guarantee Clause and State Autonomy: Federalism for a Third Century*, 88 Colum. L. Rev. 1, 53 (1988).]

process may be able to correct itself on these issues as well, under whatever test is developed there are substantive acts that one could fairly say are inconsistent with the Constitution—for example, congressional abolition of state legislatures (or, possibly, preemption of all state law enforcement). In this respect * * *, the Constitution itself imposes some barriers intended to be firm and capable of judicial enforcement, should the political process spin far enough out of control.

JACK RAKOVE, MAKING HASH OF SOVEREIGNTY, PART II

3 GREEN BAG 2d 51–58 (1999)

In the first installment of this essay,[1] I proposed that Americans should long since have banished the word sovereignty from their political vocabulary (at least as it is applied to issues of domestic governance, as opposed to the usage which sees all nation-states as equally sovereign jurisdictions). The traditional definition of sovereignty—which emphasized its unitary and absolute character, and its ultimate power to command obedience—simply has little descriptive value for our federal system, which parcels out the sovereign powers of government between the nation and the states in discrete, untidy, and often overlapping ways. Divided sovereignty has been the reality of American practice since Independence. Although the Constitution shifted the existing balance of power away from the states and toward the Union, it did not establish anything like the concentration of authority necessary to establish an unequivocal, much less univocal, repository of sovereignty. The effort pioneered by James Wilson in 1787 to preserve the unitary nature of sovereignty by locating it in the people only confirms the futility of the project. Popular sovereignty may express a noble idea, but as an analytical principle, it is vacuous.

Yet as the Supreme Court likes to remind us with its periodic federalism bombshells, the discourse of (state) sovereignty remains an active component of our constitutional jurisprudence. More than two centuries after the adoption of the Constitution, the location and definition of sovereignty still perplex us. The Tenth Amendment has enthusiastic proponents who see its truism as an affirmation of state sovereignty, while (pace Hobbes) advocates of Native American self-government similarly equate the power to maintain gambling casinos with the badge of sovereignty.

In this second installment of the essay, then, I propose to offer some speculations and reflections on the curious persistence of sovereignty talk in American usage. These speculations take the form of mere provocations to which readers can give as much or as little credit as they deserve. I ask

[1] *Making a Hash of Sovereignty*, Part I, 2 Green Bag 2d 35-44 (1998).* * *

only that you consider sympathetically the genuine puzzle on which these speculations rest: Why should sovereignty, a word which outlived its usefulness long ago, have instead discovered the marvelous recuperative and self-inflating powers that keep it alive today?

* * *

THE USEFUL FICTION ARGUMENT

Edmund Morgan, the distinguished historian of early America, offered one partial answer to this question in his stimulating book, *Inventing the People: The Rise of Popular Sovereignty in England and America*, which traced the concept from its origins in the political controversies of Stuart England to its appropriation by the American revolutionaries and constitutionalists of the eighteenth century. Taking his cue from David Hume's observation that it is "on opinion only that government is founded," Morgan argued (with a characteristic blend of light irony and deep insight) that popular sovereignty was a "fiction," and that appeals to its authority were so many acts of rhetorical "make-believe," no less contrived than the equally fictive notion of divine-right monarchy that it sought to replace, or the Jeffersonian affirmation "that all men are created equal" with which it was closely associated. Of course the people can never really rule in their own name, nor should they be so naive as to think that they and their elected representatives are truly identical in the power they share or the interests on which they act. Belief in this fictive popular sovereignty created the opinion upon which representative government was founded.[4]

This image of sovereignty as useful fiction nicely captures the clever way in which James Wilson wiggled out of the Antifederalist trap by proclaiming the sovereignty of the people. During the ratification debate of 1787–1788, Antifederalists repeatedly argued that adoption of the Constitution would vest real sovereignty in a consolidated national government; if the states survived at all, it would be as hollow jurisdictions, exercising only vestigial functions at best. To the zero-sum, slippery-slope mode of Antifederalist thinking, the idea that sovereignty could be permanently divided, with both Union and the states exercising specific powers of sovereignty, was not so much useful fiction as rank heresy.

Wilson responded to this criticism by arguing that the Antifederalist conception of sovereignty rested on a category error. Speaking to the Pennsylvania ratification convention on December 4, 1787, Wilson agreed with the conventional wisdom "that there cannot be two sovereign powers

---

[4]Edmund S. Morgan, Inventing The People: The Rise of Popular Sovereignty in England and America 13-15 (1988). Morgan is not so cynical as to suggest that only 'happy slaves' are foolish enough to take the fiction seriously. 'Although fictions enable the few to govern the many, it is not only the many who are constrained by them,' he concludes; for once established, they constitute the beliefs upon which the entire polity may come to act.

on the same subject," and further, that in every society there "of necessity must be, a supreme, absolute and uncontrollable authority." So sovereignty must indeed remain unitary and absolute. But in the United States it was fundamentally wrong, he observed, to think of sovereignty as a property or attribute of any government—national or state. The Antifederalist "position is, that the supreme power resides in the states, as governments; and mine is, that it resides in the PEOPLE, as the fountain of government." This people was divided into two communities ("one great [national] community," and within the states "on a lesser scale"), but "the fee simple" of sovereignty "continues, resides, and remains with the body of the people." That people could always choose how to delegate different portions of their sovereignty to whichever level of government they favored.[5]

At first glance, Wilson's sleight of hand in relocating sovereignty from state (or states) to people illustrates the striking Federalist capacity to expropriate but also transform seemingly familiar ideas, leaving their antagonists, in Gordon Wood's wonderful image, to "stand amazed with confusion, left holding remnants of thought that had lost their significance."[6] To take sovereignty out of government entirely, Antifederalists thought, and to vest it in a people who, Wilson conceded, would themselves have a dual (not unitary) character, was to rob the concept of its substance while preserving only the name (much as the Constitution would strip the states of real power while conceding them only a nominal sovereignty). If the concept of sovereignty initially survived the radical mitosis that the Constitution imposed on its traditional meaning, then, it was because Wilson and other Federalists seized the rhetorical advantage, creating a fiction that had little descriptive power, but which at least satisfied the accepted criterion of locating a "supreme, absolute, and uncontrollable power" somewhere in the polity.

Wilson's efforts to answer Antifederalist objections left a second major legacy for American constitutional theory. In an earlier, even more influential public speech, he had rebutted the charge that the Constitution was fatally flawed because its framers had conspicuously omitted anything resembling a declaration or bill of rights. Wilson's famous response was that the federal government was one of specific enumerated powers, and that the addition of a declaration affirming particular rights might be misconstrued to imply that powers (to infringe the freedom of the press, for example, or of conscience) were granted to the national government which in fact had not been.

---

[5]James Wilson, Speech of Dec. 4, 1787, 2 Documentary History of the Ratification of the Constitution 471-74 (J. Kaminski & G. Saladino, eds., 1976).

[6]Gordon S. Wood, The Creation of the American Republic, 1776-1787 at 524 (1969); and see Wood's discussion of the sovereignty question and Wilson's role in its reformulation that immediately follows.

Wilson's argument had its strong echo in the Tenth Amendment, with its reminder that "powers not delegated" to the Union "are reserved to the States respectively, or to the people." As James Hutson has noted, the Tenth Amendment was "a kind of anti-bill of rights" which simply "repeated the stock Federalist charge" used to deny the necessity for rights-affirming amendments. * * * Far from explicitly (or "expressly") confirming the sovereignty of the states, as Antifederalists would have wished, the Tenth Amendment restated the basic premise that the powers of sovereignty had been divided—some reallocated to the Union, others reserved to the states. If the Tenth Amendment implicates any theory of unitary sovereignty, that implication is to be found in its final four words, "or to the people."

For the question of which level of government would gain the advantage in wielding the powers of sovereignty would finally depend not on formal constitutional design but rather on the essentially political determinations that Americans, as members of two communities, would make, as they organized and reorganized in coalitions intent on bending the exercise of particular powers to their own advantage. Wilson's appeal to popular sovereignty, in other words, was not just a rhetorical fillip or fiction; it recognized that the federal balance of power between the Union and the states would always depend upon the political preferences of their citizens. But under the American electoral system, this was a people who could rarely if ever act as a unitary sovereign. In nearly every case, their shifting preferences would register only gradually, as they filtered through the complicated political mechanisms that Wilson and his colleagues at Philadelphia had contrived.

THE SOVEREIGN AS UNCHECKED

Wilson's rhetorical move helps us to understand why Federalists in 1787 had to coopt rather than abandon sovereignty, but it cannot explain its long-term persistence in the American political vocabulary. We must also consider whether sovereignty has survived not merely as a rhetorical legacy, but because it in fact acquired a new meaning which somehow fit the distinctive oddities of American federalism.

Here it is important to begin by noting that the most important appeals to sovereignty in American usage have historically been made not in the name of determining where the supreme, absolute, irresistible power to command finally resided, but for exactly the opposite purpose: to deny some other locus of authority—either the evil empire in London, or the new Leviathan in the federal district—that power. The American concept of sovereignty, that is, has always had a profoundly negative, defensive, reactive character. That concept has survived not because it accurately enables us to map the active sources of legal and political power, but because it ironically expresses the dominant anti-statist currents that have swirled through our political culture since the eighteenth century.

That American thinking about sovereignty should have taken this course is not especially surprising, for serious concern with the concept entered American consciousness only with the Stamp Act controversy of 1765–1766. It was the assertion of parliamentary sovereignty to legislate for the colonies "in all cases whatsoever" (in the Declaratory Act accompanying repeal of the stamp tax) that sent American thinking off on its distinctive trajectory. Americans were driven to discuss sovereignty not because they were meeting frustration in their own efforts to consolidate and exercise authority, but simply because British defenders of parliamentary power over the colonies left them no choice. By playing the sovereignty card, the British evidently hoped to trump the Americans' reliance on the principle of no taxation without representation and customary practice.

Instead the Americans tackled the daunting problem of demonstrating why they were exempt from parliamentary jurisdiction without completely renouncing the concept of sovereignty itself. Under their emerging theory of empire, the colonial assemblies were to be regarded as virtually equivalent to Parliament, while the bond uniting the colonies to the empire would lie to the king, the common sovereign who would serve, in Jefferson's phrase, as "the balance of a great, if a well poised empire." But even here, a sovereign king was hardly a Hobbesean sovereign, for George III would have to rule in America as he did "at home"—with the consent of his subjects' elected representatives.

For the American colonists, then, the dispute about sovereignty involved an effort to define and justify exemptions from the one institution which had the strongest claim to possess it. To the American way of thinking, it was much more important to explain why Parliament could not exercise legislative sovereignty over the colonies than to map the exact dimensions of the sovereign powers the colonies wished to retain for themselves. Rather than offer constructive alternatives to the abyss into which the empire was lurching, or propose the terms of an American "bill of rights," the First Continental Congress of 1774 simply asked for a restoration of a status quo ante in which the colonies would retain their customary powers of self-government while Parliament abjured any authority to legislate for America.

Later controversies in which the appeal to state sovereignty played a prominent role—the debate over ratification of the Constitution; the promulgation of the Virginia and Kentucky resolutions of 1798; the nullification dispute of the early 1830s; the crisis of the Union in 1860–1861—reinforce the point. In each case the argument from sovereignty was mounted not in behalf of a state's (or the states') fundamental authority or capacity to exercise paramount, positive authority over the contested area of governance, but rather to identify the dangers, imagined or real, that would arise from conceding a national authority to act. It was the prospective fear of the future consequences of conceding a national authority, not the urgency of the threat to immediate interests, that gave the appeal to state sovereignty its rhetorical effect. At no point was this more evident than during the secession winter and spring of 1861, when the Republican capture of the presidency drove the states of the South to reclaim their primordial sovereignty, notwithstanding Lincoln's promise to respect the municipal law of slavery as an appropriate exercise of the residual sovereign powers of the states.

Sovereignty had thus acquired a new meaning in American usage. To acknowledge state sovereignty was to accord the states a final say, not in exercising the power to command obedience, but in nullifying the commands of an authority perceived, in particular cases, to be external and illegitimate. The effect was to invert the original formulation. Sovereignty now lay much closer to a theory of resistance than of command—closer to Locke, in a sense, than to Hobbes. The states, in the final analysis, would act as an unchecked checker, the court of last resort in determining when an exercise of national supremacy had gone a measure or two too far.

THE ALLURE OF REDUCTIONISM

Had James Madison been able to play the part of philosopher-king or Enlightenment Lawgiver, imposing a constitution on a deferential people, the sovereignty problem might in fact have been definitely resolved for Americans. Such at least was the promise implicit in his most radical (or reactionary) proposal, to establish a congressional negative on all state laws. By effectively making the national government a third branch of the state assemblies, the negative would have sharply undercut any claim that the states retained even the legislative dimensions of sovereignty; their subordination and inferiority to the Union would have been apparent.

Absent the negative, the Constitution created a system in which the powers of sovereignty were both divided between and shared by the national and state governments. How could the potential for conflict that existed where national and state powers inevitably overlapped be managed or alleviated, in the interest of maintaining constitutional equilibrium? Madison understood that the principal responsibility for policing the boundaries of federalism would devolve upon the judiciary, but he also doubted whether the judiciary, even with life tenure, would be up to the task.[11] Judicial resolution of disputes might be necessary, but it would also

[11]See the brief but trenchant comments in his letter to Jefferson of October 24, 1787, in 10 The Papers of James Madison 211 (R. Rutland, ed., 1977).

be useful, even preferable, to do as much as possible to prevent them from arising.

It was Madison's early and mature view, I believe, that the fate of the federal system would ultimately depend upon the willingness of Americans to puzzle through its nuances and complexities in good faith. The prolegomena to any such effort would require an acceptance of the principles he first laid down in Federalist 39, where he took up the Antifederalist objection that the Constitution would create a consolidated national government rather than preserve the confederation of sovereign states. Madison answered this objection in terms very different from James Wilson's earlier responses to the same challenge. Rather than invoke the panacea of popular sovereignty, Madison offered a five-pronged analysis of the mixed "federal" and "national" elements of the American compound republic. In this discussion, the word "sovereignty" appears only once, when Madison concedes that the Constitution "leaves to the several States a residuary and inviolable sovereignty over all other objects" of legislation not among the enumerated powers of the national government. But sovereignty, as a mode of analysis, is otherwise conspicuous in this discussion by its absence. Madison asks good-faith readers to think of the problem in other terms: as an exercise requiring an explicit, empirical, and pragmatic mapping of the actual distribution of power, not an appeal to the heavy artillery of a killer definition.

Ten years later, it is true, Madison verged close to invoking the ultimate sovereignty of the states when he drafted the Virginia Resolutions protesting the Alien and Sedition Acts of 1798. But that appeal rested on the belief that the nation faced a constitutional crisis so grave that the states, as the parties to the federal compact, had a right to act (at least in a political capacity) to sound the tocsin. But a principle to be invoked only in extremis cannot, by definition, provide a sound rule for conducting the ordinary business of federalism. In later years—and especially amid his long retirement from 1817 to 1836—Madison repeatedly returned to the principle of Federalist 39. Not only did he defend the Supreme Court's role as umpire of federalism; he also reminded inquiring correspondents, anxious for his wisdom, that the American federal system could be understood only by grasping its uniqueness, by realizing that it was a system without precedent, and accordingly by resisting the temptation to resort to simplistic principles to explain its inner logic.

Thus in one of his various letters denouncing the South Carolina nullifiers, Madison ridiculed "those who now Contend that the States have never parted with an Atom of their sovereignty" before proceeding to explain the fallacy of their position.

> Our political system is admitted to be a new Creation—a real non-descript. Its character therefore must be sought within itself; not in

> precedents, because there are none; not in writers who are guided by precedents. Who can tell at present how Vattel and others of that class, would have qualified (in the Gallic sense of the term) a Compound & peculiar system with such an example of it as ours before them[?][12]

He had made much the same point to Daniel Webster in 1830. The American federal system "is so unexampled in its origin, so complex in its structure, and so peculiar in some of its features, that in describing it the political vocabulary does not furnish terms sufficiently distinctive and appropriate, without a detailed resort to the facts of the case."[13]

A Madisonian interpretation of the Constitution would certainly allow some room to acknowledge that the states retained certain sovereign powers, but it would have little tolerance for deductive arguments from the talisman of sovereignty. Such an interpretation would come encumbered with distinctions, nuances, qualifications, and above all, closely reasoned efforts to allocate powers according to the essential design of the Constitution. Madison recognized that appeals to sovereignty were dangerous because they were inherently absolutist and preclusive of the patience and flexibility that the enterprise of making federalism work demanded. In that sense, the resurgence of sovereignty talk in southern reactions against the Marshall Court or during the nullification controversy was ominous indeed. To invoke sovereignty was to reason not descriptively or empirically but formulaically, invoking a doctrine or "precedent" that had only the authority of its prior history to commend it.

But of course, reasoning from a simplistic principle like sovereignty was much easier than doing the heavy if prosaic lifting of making federalism work by avoiding the allure of extreme formulations. Nor was every constitutional polemicist a Madison, willing and able to maintain his quizzical approach to the messiness of political life.

LINGUISTIC CREEP

A final source of the persistence and periodic resurgence of sovereignty in the vocabulary of American politics can also be proposed to lie in the nature of political language itself. For sovereignty is one of those terms that is inherently inflationary. It begs to be borrowed and assigned new and surprising uses, beckoning would-be consumers to take it down from the shelf and put it to work. In this sense, it closely resembles another word whose inflationary properties have been the subject of much recent dispute: rights.

---

[12]Madison to William Cabell Rives, March 12, 1833, in James Madison: Writings 863-64 (J. Rakove, ed., 1999).

[13]Madison to Daniel Webster, May 27, 1830, in 4 Letters and Other Writings of James Madison 84, 85 (Worthington 2d ed., 1884).

Here we can take a cue from the ongoing controversy that surrounds the prevalence of "rights talk" in contemporary jurisprudence and political theory more generally. * * * To advance our claims, as individuals or as members of social groups, in the language of our interests or the benefits to be rendered to the public good is one thing; to stake them as assertions of rights is another matter entirely. For rights talk is by its nature absolutist and preemptive; once the card of rights is played as a trump (to use Ronald Dworkin's famous metaphor), what room is left for the presumably normal give-and-take of democratic bargaining? It is in this sense that rights talk can be described as an inherently inflationary currency. It may not offer the most accurate way to characterize the interest or activity you happily wish to pursue, but if you can expropriate the term and make it work for you, an advantage will be gained.

Sovereignty is subject to the same inflationary or expropriative processes. Even in its residuary, debased (because of inflation) form, the vestigial aura of ultimate authority that still clings to the term offers a measure of rhetorical or polemical advantage. Sovereignty talk is also a trump; play that card successfully, and your opponent either has to fold his hand or lose this round. Indeed, in the most drastic circumstances—Charleston in 1861—the invocation of sovereignty means that the game is over.

Under this theory of "linguistic creep," as I like to label it, sovereignty survived in American usage not because it retained any analytical or descriptive power, but rather because it promised rhetorical and political advantage to those who sought to use it. Madison could not have been especially surprised by this development, which he lived long enough to witness. In Federalist 37, he had noted that one of the inherent difficulties of reasoning about politics lay in the nature of language itself. "No language is so copious as to supply words and phrases for every complex idea," he observed, "or so correct as not to include many equivocally denoting different ideas." Hence the pursuit of "perspicuity"—one of his own favorite words—was doomed to fall short of perfect success. Yet that did not stop Madison—as it should not stop us—from pursuing accuracy in political reasoning, especially when the essential character of the federal system appeared to be at stake. And to accord the principle of state sovereignty a respect it no longer deserved was to preserve a term that could only be invoked, Madison came to realize, in extremis, as a means not of restoring the federal equilibrium but of threatening its demise.

We should therefore not be surprised that sovereignty talk is still with us, but neither should we rejoice in its curious persistence.

A CONCLUDING HISTORICAL REFLECTION

When Antifederalists beat the drum of sovereignty in 1787–1788, they did so because they anticipated that adoption of the Constitution would lead, sooner or later, to the evil of "consolidation." Twenty-one decades later, the national government obviously exercises legislative and administrative powers well beyond the eighteenth-century imagination, and the balance of power between the Union and the states has equally clearly shifted sharply toward the nation. Yet the states do not seem to have withered away. At last report, they were still collecting steady revenues, enacting laws that regulate much of our domestic life, and even enjoying a modest resurgence of authority in the wake of the devolutionist politics of welfare reform. Nor is there much evidence that either the current president or his successor will unleash federal janizaries to seize the public radio stations in the state capitals, depriving citizens of one of their few remaining sources of information as to what their state governments are actually doing.

Yet concern persists, at least among a majority of the Supreme Court, that real dangers to state sovereignty exist. That the Court is responsible for adjudicating the boundaries of federalism is beyond question; indeed, one could argue that this responsibility is itself the single most important element of the original constitutional design for the federal republic. That it should reason about the exercise of this responsibility on the basis of a principle as foggy as Justice Kennedy's statement that the Constitution "reserves to [the States] a substantial portion of the Nation's primary sovereignty, together with the dignity and essential attributes inhering in that status,"[15] is something else again. Sovereignty is too vague and anachronistic a term to allow us to reason about anything more than our propensity to keep using it.

RICHARD FALLON, THE "CONSERVATIVE" PATHS OF THE REHNQUIST COURT'S FEDERALISM DECISIONS

69 U.CHI.L.REV. 429–437, 486–493 (2002)

It seems agreed on all sides now that the Supreme Court has an agenda of promoting constitutional federalism. Since the appointment of Clarence Thomas in 1991 to fill the seat formerly occupied by Thurgood Marshall, the Court has maintained a relatively stable five-justice majority—consisting of Chief Justice Rehnquist and Justices O'Connor, Scalia, Kennedy, and Thomas—committed to enforcing limits on national power and to protecting the integrity of the states. Over that period, the Court has held at least ten federal statutes to be constitutionally invalid, either in whole or in part, on grounds involving federalism. By contrast, the Court

[15] Alden v. Maine, 119 S. Ct. 2240, 2247 (1999).

had found only one federal statute to violate principles of constitutional federalism during the previous span of more than fifty years,[3] and it actually reversed the single anomalous decision less than ten years later.[4] Commentators unhesitatingly refer to a federalism "revival." Law reviews echo with discussion of whether the Court has yet achieved, or is likely to effect, a federalism "revolution."

In the Rehnquist Court's federalism revival, as it has developed so far, three categories of cases dominate the foreground. The first consists of cases restraining Congress's power to regulate private conduct under the Commerce Clause. By limiting Congress's regulatory capacity, decisions such as *United States v Lopez*[7] preserve spheres in which state and local governments are the exclusive lawgivers. The second prominent line of federalism cases establishes limits on Congress's authority directly to regulate state and local governments. Widely noted decisions have struck down legislation that attempted to "commandeer" state and local officials and compel their execution of a federally mandated agenda. A third line of decisions involves the Eleventh Amendment and state sovereign immunity. Subject only to narrow exceptions, these cases establish that Congress cannot compel the states to submit to private suits for money damages even when they violate federal rights.

Given these well-known lines of cases and the Court's recent record of invalidating federal statutes, no one should doubt that the Rehnquist Court has made the promotion of federalism an important priority. Surprisingly, however, few if any scholars have carefully examined the overall pattern of Rehnquist Court decisions involving constitutional federalism. My first goal in this Article is to fill the resulting gap in the literature. Looking beyond the three categories of cases that have dominated recent discussions, this Article surveys a broader sample of doctrines involving, for example, the constitutionally permissible scope of state regulatory authority, federal preemption of state law, Supreme Court review of state court judgments, federal judicial "abstention" in favor of state adjudication, and canons of statutory interpretation and judicially fashioned rules of "official immunity" which protect governments and their officials from legal liability.

When the lens is thus broadened, three notable conclusions emerge. First, the Court's federalism revolution includes what I shall describe as a

[3]See National League of Cities v Usery, 426 US 833, 852 (1976) (invalidating minimum wage and overtime provisions of the FLSA as applied to certain functions of state and local governments).

[4]See Garcia v San Antonio Metropolitan Transit Authority, 469 US 528, 531 (1985) (holding that states are not exempt from complying with the minimum wage and overtime requirements of the FLSA).

[7]514 US 549 (1995) (invalidating the Gun Free School Zones Act on the ground that it exceeded congressional power and invaded the states' regulatory power).

number of "quiet fronts"—areas in which the Court has done little or nothing to promote federalism, despite having the opportunity to do so. For example, the Court has done more to tighten than to loosen the restrictions that the so-called dormant Commerce Clause imposes on state and local governments. Moreover, some of the Court's most prominently pro-federalism justices are quick to find that federal regulatory statutes displace or preempt state regulations.

Second, among the three lines of cases widely thought to constitute the federalism revival, there is an interesting divergence of approaches. Although the Court has imposed limits on Congress's general regulatory powers, its decisions in that domain have displayed a cautious tentativeness. Notably, the Court has not overruled a single case upholding congressional power to regulate commercial activities. Recent cases have put regulation of noncommercial activity largely off-limits to Congress, but it remains unclear whether this restriction will have broad significance. Similarly, cases restricting Congress's power directly to regulate state and local governments have taken a narrow approach. Although the Court has erected prohibitions against federal legislation that singles out state and local governments and compels the performance of distinctively governmental functions, it has not questioned Congress's authority to impose other kinds of regulatory burdens. Perhaps most significantly, the Court has left standing the holding of *Garcia v San Antonio Metropolitan Transit Authority*,[17] under which federal statutes generally regulating terms and conditions of employment can apply to state and local governments on the same basis as to other employers.

In comparison, recent decisions involving state sovereign immunity have effected bold revisions in the doctrinal structure. Trumpeting the value of state sovereignty, the Court has overruled at least two precedents within the past five years.[18] In another recent case, the justices broke new ground by holding that the Constitution incorporates a principle of state sovereign immunity that applies as much in state courts as in federal courts.[19]

Third, the Rehnquist Court's efforts to advance federalism are by no means limited to constitutional rulings. On the contrary, many of the most important protections that the Court has afforded to state, and especially to local, governments and their officials formally involve statutory interpreta-

---

[17]469 US 528 (1985).

[18]See College Savings Bank, 527 US at 680 (permitting constructive waiver of state immunity under the Federal Employers' Liability Act), overruling Parden v Terminal Railway of the Alabama State Docks Department, 377 US 184 (1964); Seminole Tribe, 517 US at 66, overruling Pennsylvania v Union Gas Co, 491 US 1 (1989) (granting Congress the power to abrogate state sovereign immunity under the Commerce Clause).

[19]See Alden v Maine, 527 US 706, 754 (1999).

tion. Through equitable doctrines, interpretive canons, and other devices of statutory construction, the Court has conferred protections that would be difficult if not impossible to derive directly from the Constitution. If the Court's federalism revival has some quiet fronts, it also includes some areas of important activity that have largely escaped public notice.

Against the background of these empirical conclusions, my second principal aim in this Article is to account for the variegated, sometimes puzzling, pattern of the Rehnquist Court's federalism decisions. My explanatory thesis includes three main themes, which roughly correspond with my three principal descriptive claims.

The first explanatory theme involves judicial conservatism. In some senses of the term, the current Court is indisputably a conservative one, and a commitment to protecting federalism constitutes a core component of conservative judicial philosophies. As I shall emphasize, however, the "conservative" label is easier to apply than to define. In particular, the relationship between a commitment to constitutional federalism and other conservative values is by no means always obvious. In many if not most cases, judicial protection of federalism has the effect of limiting liberal forces and doctrines. Sometimes, however, state and local decisionmaking produces outcomes that judicial conservatives find substantively objectionable—for example, restrictive zoning schemes, or complex tangles of regulations for interstate businesses to navigate, or interpretations of the federal Constitution that give broad protections to criminal defendants.

To put my conclusion in a nutshell, the substantive conservatism of the Court's majority explains most, if not all, of the quiet fronts in the federalism revival. The Court's pro-federalism majority is at least as substantively conservative as it is pro-federalism. When federalism and substantive conservatism come into conflict, substantive conservatism frequently dominates.

My second explanatory theme involves the crucial, albeit limited, significance of path dependence in Supreme Court adjudication. As I shall use the term, "path dependence" functions as a capsule reference to various ways in which history and surrounding attitudes and expectations influence judicial decisionmaking. Within my usage, the phenomenon of path dependence encompasses the legal concept of stare decisis—the basic idea that past decisions must generally (though not always) be accepted as binding authorities, even by the Supreme Court, and that legal reasoning in current cases should be consistent with judicial precedents. But the notion of path dependence also links the legal force of precedent with an implication that the Court feels constrained by surrounding attitudes in the public and political culture. Absent unusually strong foundations in constitutional text and the evolving public sense of fairness or necessity, the Court may believe that it would risk public confidence if, especially by a narrow margin, it were simultaneously to reverse its own precedent and to dramatically alter settled schemes of rights and responsibilities.

Also encompassed within my capacious conception of path dependence is the idea that as the Court proceeds along a doctrinal path, both it and the attentive public assess what the justices may properly do next in light of past experiences. * * * By contrast, the Court may believe that it has made and can continue to make steady, even if meandering, progress along paths where it has previously proceeded without palpable misstep.

Among my theses in this Article is that considerations of path dependence must loom large in any plausible explanation of why the Court has acted with such relative caution in reshaping constitutional doctrines involving Congress's general regulatory powers and its related authority to impose obligations on state and local governments under the Commerce and Spending Clauses. The Court's effort to restrict Congress's general regulatory powers occasioned embarrassment and near disaster during the economic and political crises of the 1930s. Then, when the Court shifted course and authorized broad assertions of congressional power, patterns of reliance developed. The Court's more recent efforts to enforce broadly applicable restrictions on Congress's regulation of state and local governments also ended in a sharp reversal. Although eager to promote federalism through modest doctrinal reform and to shape new options for the future, the Court now hesitates to take aggressive steps, threatening entrenched regulatory regimes back into territory that it previously abandoned. By contrast, the path of sovereign immunity doctrine now appears to the Court as one along which it has so far progressed successfully and can travel without serious hazard.

My third explanatory theme involves what might be called the Court's doctrinal opportunism in promoting federalism and, in particular, in protecting governmental treasuries from damages liability. Especially when considerations of path dependence have made it difficult for the Court to protect its vision of federalism through direct constitutional rulings, the pro-federalism majority has relied on an array of other devices, including judge-made equitable doctrines, pro-federalism principles of statutory construction, and official immunity rules. The result is an inelegant patchwork of protective doctrines that makes it exceedingly difficult—even when not constitutionally impossible—for private plaintiffs to recover money damages from state and local governments and their officials.

* * *

In implementing its federalism revival, the Supreme Court has not pursued a single methodology in either constitutional or statutory cases. For example, in construing Section 5 of the Fourteenth Amendment * * *, the Court rested heavily on an originalist examination of language and legislative history. By contrast, in cases involving the scope of Congress's power to regulate private conduct under the Commerce Clause, only Justice Thomas has called for the Court to pursue originalist inquiries.

In limiting Congress's powers to regulate state and local governments directly in *New York* and *Printz*, the Court depended on inferences from the Constitution's structure not tied tightly to particular constitutional language. The opinions discussed the original constitutional understanding, but in *Printz* Justice Scalia acknowledged that the most directly relevant historical evidence was "not conclusive."[374] Although he found support for the Court's ruling in a number of sources, he termed judicial precedent "most conclusive( ) in the present litigation." [375]

An interesting disparity thus arises. As Professor Tribe has noted, in cases involving substantive rights, the conservative justices commonly scorn arguments based on inferences from the Constitution's structure and otherwise supported principally by judicial precedent.[376] By contrast, in federalism cases, the conservatives themselves rely on structural inferences supported by judicial precedent, with other kinds of argument—including those based on the Constitution's plain language—sometimes relegated to subordinate roles.

The Court's sovereign immunity cases betray methodological inconsistencies even among themselves. In *Seminole Tribe*, Chief Justice Rehnquist framed the Court's holding as based on the Eleventh Amendment—even though he recognized that the Amendment's plain text would not support the result. Instead the Chief Justice relied on the view of the original understanding adopted in *Hans* and, in response to challenges to that view, on stare decisis. *Hans* was a Nineteenth Century case holding that the Amendment reaffirmed a broad concept of sovereign immunity. With minimal engagement, he derided the principal dissenting opinion for "disregard(ing) our case law in favor of a theory (of the original understanding) cobbled together from law review articles and its own version of historical events." In *Alden*, the Court sought a new foundation for its sovereign immunity jurisprudence, not in the Eleventh Amendment but in the Tenth Amendment and the original understanding of the Constitution's structure.

Overall, a defender of the Court's approach might assert that the five-justice, pro-federalism majority has followed the original understanding except when considerations of path dependence make that course infeasible:

---

[374] *Printz*, 521 U.S at 905-23, *New York [v. United States]*, 505 U.S. [144], 163-166 [(1992)].

[375] *Printz*, 521 U.S. [898], 925 [(1997)].

[376] See Laurence H. Tribe, *Saenz Sans Prophecy: Does the Privileges or Immunities Revival Portend the Future – Or Reveal the Structure of the Present?*, 113 Harv. L. Rev. 110, 158-72 (1999).

only in defining Congress's power under the Commerce Clause has the Court not tried to reach results consistent with originalist principles. But this explanation is too neat. Among other things, it cannot account for why the Court has so regularly fractured along the same 5–4 line, even when the dissenting justices, as much as the majority, have engaged in evidently sincere originalist argumentation. Nor can this defense explain why the Court has paid so little heed to the original understanding along some of the quiet fronts of the federalism revolution—for example, with respect to the dormant Commerce Clause.

* * *

Overall, the pattern of the federalism revival confirms that ideology is relevant to Supreme Court decisionmaking, but does not establish precisely how the influence occurs. Despite its apparent methodological inconsistencies, the Court operates within the conventions of legal argumentation. Never does the majority simply impose its will in the absence of colorable supporting arguments. Nevertheless, the key to understanding the federalism revival does not lie in any particular methodology.

* * *

Although it is sometimes said that judicial conservatives believe in a narrow, deferential judicial role, the Rehnquist Court's federalism revival constitutes a counterexample to that claim. In cases involving federalism, the Court—led by its most conservative justices—has either wholly or partly invalidated at least ten acts of Congress within the past seven years. My point here is not to accuse the pro-federalism majority of failing to adhere to a consistent conservative philosophy. As I have said, there are multiple strands of diverse judicially conservative philosophies. In addition, principles that apply in one context may have exceptions or may simply be outweighed in others. My point, instead, is that the Court, determined to limit congressional power in the name of federalism, has not been deferential. Nor, given the nature of its federalist agenda, could it be.

* * *

In implementing a federalism revival, the Court has struggled to reconcile competing goals. One is to afford a decent respect to stare decisis. Another is to effect significant doctrinal reform to promote constitutional federalism. In some doctrinal areas, the Court has tipped discernibly in one or the other direction. For example, the Court has moved cautiously in restricting Congress's general regulatory powers under the Commerce Clause; in this doctrinal area, stare decisis and related considerations of path dependence have had a significant constraining effect. By contrast, in the domain of sovereign immunity jurisprudence, the Court has felt freer to overrule cases and otherwise revise the doctrinal landscape.

Often, however, the Court has attempted to achieve significant change without overruling cases. Instead, the Court's pro-federalism majority has purported to leave leading cases undisturbed, while at the same time surrounding them with exceptions and qualifications. * * * In the tension between a commitment to pro-federalism change and to respect for stare decisis, exception builds on exception.

Yet a further level of complexity comes into the picture as a result of the Court's third, partly distinct goal of creating doctrines that either promote or accord with its substantive conservatism. Consider the Court's relatively recent practices in recognizing exceptions to *Hans*. As noted above, the Court has developed exceptions—seemingly unrelated to federalism—for suits to recover coercively collected taxes and apparently to compel the payment of just compensation for "takings" of private property.

When the Court's reluctance to overrule cases is coupled with a readiness to create exceptions and draw fine distinctions, and sometimes to advance substantive as well as structural goals, federalism doctrine inevitably grows complex, and occasionally bewildering. In creating and sustaining a complex doctrinal structure, the current Court has not necessarily performed worse than its predecessors. Doctrinal complexity bordering on contradiction has long persisted in federal courts doctrine. But if the Rehnquist Court's federalism revival has not rendered federal courts law dramatically less coherent, neither has it arrested the slide into Byzantine complexity.

* * *

In commentary on the Court's federalism agenda, three lines of cases have dominated attention. That attention is merited, but it should not obscure surrounding developments. If the federalism revolution has proceeded along three main paths, important developments have also occurred along a variety of subpaths. Moreover, the rates of advance along the various paths have varied widely. Indeed, there are some available paths for the promotion of constitutional federalism along which nothing has occurred.

In seeking to explain this pattern, I have emphasized the widely recognized judicial conservatism of the current Supreme Court, in particular the relation between "substantive" and "methodological" conservatism and a commitment to constitutional federalism. The term "conservatism" does not denote a single philosophy so much as encompass a family of related, but occasionally mutually inconsistent, dispositions. Amid the competition internal to judicial conservatism, a commitment to federalism by no means always predominates. In order to make sense of the overall structure of federalism jurisprudence, it is crucial to understand that the Court's prevailing majority is at least as substantively conservative as it is pro-federalism. The Court's substantive conservatism helps to explain the existence of what I have called "quiet fronts" in the federalism revolution. It also helps to explain otherwise puzzling exceptions to the general rule that sovereign immunity protects the states from unconsented private suits for damages. This rule must yield, the Court has suggested, in cases involving takings and coercive collections of taxes—two types of "old property" rights of which substantive conservatives tend to be solicitous.

My second explanatory theme involves path dependence. The Court has proceeded cautiously along doctrinal paths where previous efforts to protect federalism occasioned embarrassment, where reliance interests make dramatic change difficult, and where the attentive public has conspicuously embraced prevailing doctrine. By contrast, the Court has proceeded most vigorously in sovereign immunity cases, in which the way has appeared clear for notable reforms.

* * *

Overall, there is both less and more to the federalism revolution than generally meets the eye. There is less consistency; the federalism revolution has not advanced equally along all fronts. In addition, two of the main paths have exhibited fewer grand developments than some might have predicted. But a broadened perspective also reveals more than is sometimes noticed, as the Court has pushed its federalism agenda along a myriad of subpaths, mostly involving subconstitutional doctrines and statutory interpretation. Individually, the steps may be small, but their cumulative impact is large.

If the Supreme Court is implementing a federalism revolution, it is thus distinctively a lawyers' revolution. Though the rhetoric is sometimes audacious, few landmarks have toppled. Much of the significance, if not the devil himself, inhabits the details.

D. LIMITS ON STATES

NOEL T. DOWLING, INTERSTATE COMMERCE AND STATE POWER

27 VA.L.REV. 1–6, 19–24 (1940).

PRIOR THEORIES

The views which have been entertained as to the effect of the commerce clause on state power may be summarized under four heads. Each of them has been held by the Court, or a number of Justices, at one time or another, and one of them contains in substance, as I will try to show, the desirable doctrine for the future. They are:

1. That the clause impliedly prohibits all state regulation or taxation of interstate commerce;

2. That the clause itself prohibits nothing, the states being free to regulate and tax as they see fit unless and until they are stopped by Congressional action;

3. That the clause prohibits some, but not all, state regulation and taxation—that is, sometimes it prohibits and sometimes it does not;

4. That though the clause itself prohibits nothing an impediment may arise from the express or implied will of Congress.

The first is of historical interest as that to which the Court inclined at the beginning. In *Gibbons v. Ogden,* counsel contended that "as the word 'to regulate' implies in its nature full power over the thing to be regulated, it excludes, necessarily, the action of all others that would perform the same operation on the same thing," and further that "regulation is designed for the entire result, applying to those parts which remain as they were, as well as to those which are altered." "Great force" was conceded to this argument by Chief Justice Marshall, and the Court was "not satisfied that it has been refuted." But it was unnecessary in that case to decide whether the power of the states was surrendered by the mere grant to Congress, or is retained until Congress shall exercise the power, for the reason that the power had been exercised, and the regulations which Congress deemed it proper to make were in full operation. And the narrow holding was that the Act of Congress prevailed over the inconsistent regulation of the New York statute. As to taxation, *Brown v. Maryland* all but committed the Court to the first view. * * *

The second view is, in substance, the one expounded by Chief Justice Taney, particularly in the *License* cases. Though his opinion did not win the support of a full majority of the Court, there was agreement in the conclusion to which it led. In general, this view would remove the commerce clause from judicial consideration. * * *

The third view, a compromise between the two earlier views, represents the first definite position taken by the Court on the commerce clause; and this occurred in *Cooley v. The Board of Wardens,* in 1851. In the course of the opinion the Court undertook to explain the cause of its prior diversities of opinion, saying that they arose "from the different views taken of the nature of the power." But when, the Court added, the nature of a power like this is spoken of, when it is said that the nature of the power requires that it should be exercised exclusively by Congress, "it must be intended to refer to the subjects of that power, and to say they are of such a nature as to require exclusive legislation by Congress." For the power to regulate commerce, the Court observed, embraces a vast field, containing not only many, but exceedingly various subjects, quite unlike in their nature; some imperatively demanding a single uniform rule, and some as imperatively demanding that diversity which alone can meet local necessities. * * *

The fourth view may be described as a composite of the second and third, and a limited version of it was announced by the Court in 1890. It originally covered only interstate commerce in intoxicating liquors, though it was later enlarged. This view squares with the second in the sense that no prohibition inheres in the commerce clause itself, and it preserves the results of the third in that some state action would be upheld—*e.g.,* where "matters of local concern" are involved—and some overturned. Also it calls for the same kind of inquiry as under *Cooley v. The Board,* but with this difference in result: if the subject were held "national," a congressional negative would be presumed rather than a constitutional prohibition applied. This view admitted the power of Congress to exercise complete control in both fields: to supersede state action in local matters, to permit it in national. The significant and salutary effect was to take constitutional rigidity out of the commerce clause problem and substitute the flexible and adaptable will of Congress. At the same time it recognized a definite function for the courts in the ascertainment of that will. * * *

In the intervening period up to 1938 no distinctive theory appears to have been formulated or urged. New terminology crept into the opinions, and the Court talked increasingly of "direct" and "indirect" effects or burdens on interstate commerce, the former being held invalid and the latter valid. The "direct-indirect" test had this much at least in common with *Cooley v. The Board,* that it upheld some and overturned other state action; but it was far from satisfying since it offered so little of a criterion for determining on which side a case would fall. Quarantine laws, for example, which hit interstate commerce head-on and stopped it dead in its tracks at the border, surely would have to be classed as "direct," yet they were sustained. The oleomargarine laws of Massachusetts had a no less direct impact on traffic than did Iowa's liquor laws, but Massachusetts won and Iowa lost. * * *

* * *

WHAT OF THE FUTURE?

From what has gone before, a doctrine can be drawn which offers, I believe, desirable and helpful guidance for the Court in the future. It is, that in the absence of affirmative consent a Congressional negative will be presumed in the courts against state action which in its effect upon interstate commerce constitutes an unreasonable interference with national interests, the presumption being rebuttable at the pleasure of Congress. Such a doctrine would free the states from any constitutional disability but at the same time would not give them license to take such action as they see fit irrespective of its effect upon interstate commerce. With respect to such commerce, the question whether the states may act upon it would depend upon the will of Congress expressed in such form as it may choose. State action falling short of such interference would prevail unless and until superseded or otherwise nullified by Congressional action.

[Several] reasons support the foregoing:

1. The congressional consent aspect of the doctrine would entail no sharp break with the past, and its adoption would constitute the acceptance of some of the best efforts of the Court. * * * I have always thought that it was implicit in *Cooley v. The Board* [.] * * * [The] doctrine was slow in taking form and did not acquire definite proportions until *Leisy v. Hardin* in 1890. The fact that the Court's arrival at this position culminated a long consideration accentuates the burden upon those who would depart from it. * * *

2. The substantive standard embodied in the doctrine, "unreasonable interference with national interests," would commit the Court to no new or untried principle. It would, to be sure, involve an avowal that the Court is deliberately balancing national and local interests and making a choice as to which of the two *should* prevail. That, as I see the matter, is a policy judgment. But the test of reasonableness in interstate commerce cases is not the same as, for example, in due process cases. Additional factors are involved. In a sense, a state law must take the hurdle of due process before it comes to the interstate barrier. The blow-post-law case from Georgia affords a striking illustration. The requirement that trains slow down at crossings was deemed, as well as it can be gleaned from the report and with regard to the situation in Georgia, an appropriate and permissible means for securing safety of life and property notwithstanding the inconvenience to local traffic and to the companies. At that stage the judicial scales tipped in favor of the statute. But other factors thrown into the other side of the scales—*e.g.,* convenience and economy of time in through traffic, more efficient and less expensive operation of railway systems—tipped them back against the statute.[35]

As already indicated, *Cooley v. The Board* comprehended a certain balancing of state and national interests, though the Court did not go into the subject in detail. And it was just there, in an effort to discover the relevant considerations for answering the question whether the "national interest in maintaining freedom of commerce across state lines" has been infringed, that Mr. Justice Stone tackled the problem in his *Di Santo* dissent.[a] His approach in that opinion appears to be well calculated to produce a "realistic" judgment whether any given state action constitutes an unreasonable interference with national interests. * * * He essayed no

[35]Seaboard Air Line R.R. v. Blackwell, 244 U.S. 310 (1917).

[a]Di Santo v. Pennsylvania, 273 U.S. 34, 43 (1927).

exhaustive list, nor would he exclude such factors as the desirability of uniform regulation (the principal point of *Cooley v. The Board*); or the consequences to the state if its action were disallowed—how serious and widespread the evil and what the prospect for national action; or the intangible but nevertheless real benefits to be had from giving the people of the states the satisfaction of, and stimulus to responsibility from, home government as against distant government. And in order to bring all such considerations into the judicial forum, could not the rules of evidence be made more generous and elastic? It is true that the litigation is between private parties, but the issue touches the relative jurisdictions of nation and state. After all, this is statecraft in which the courts are engaged.

3. This doctrine would provide flexibility in the adjustment and accommodation of national and state interests, at the same time preserving the judicial and amplifying the legislative function. From the judicial point of view it would preserve a role which the Court, beginning with the leadership of Marshall, has worked out for itself and which has conspicuously contributed to the functioning of the federal system. That role brings to constitutional cases the best of the common law methods in the building up of principles from specific decisions. The trial courts would operate out on the front line, where the impact of state action on interstate commerce is first felt, and they could appraise at close range the conflicting state and national interests. Furthermore, the judicial sifting of the facts would have the manifest merit of sharpening the issues and facilitating legislative efforts in the event that Congress, dissatisfied with the judicial results, should desire to take corrective action of its own.

* * *

There is no assurance that the commerce problem would be as well handled by Congress alone as where both Congress and the courts participate in its solution. I say "would", drawing a distinction between what seems likely and what is theoretically possible. Congress is a big and heavy machine to set in motion, and its progress is sometimes impeded even when national interests of the highest order are at stake. Meanwhile much damage to interstate commerce, to say nothing of the otherwise amicable relationships among the states, might be caused by unrestrained state action. * * *

Even if Congress should accept the task it would not find it an easy one. It would have to labor with much of the same evidence that would be offered in the courts, as well as other matters bearing upon various phases of policy (including sheer political pressures); and perhaps more often than not the solution would have to be stated in general terms. And then, after all that were done, it is not at all unlikely that the whole thing would be thrown into the courts for final settlement, but with this difference, that whereas formerly the courts could turn to the judicially developed principles and feel their way along, henceforth they would have to interpret and apply new and general formulas from Congress.

DONALD H. REGAN, THE SUPREME COURT AND STATE PROTECTIONISM: MAKING SENSE OF THE DORMANT COMMERCE CLAUSE

84 MICH.L.REV. 1091, 1094–1095, 1112–1118, 1124–1125, 1160–1166 (1986).

WHAT IS "PROTECTIONISM"?

* * *

I shall say that a state statute (or administrative regulation, or local ordinance, or whatever) is protectionist if and only if:

(a) the statute (or whatever) was adopted for the purpose of improving the competitive position of local (in-state) economic actors, just because they are local, vis-à-vis their foreign (by which I mean simply out-of-state) competitors; and

(b) the statute (or whatever) is analogous in form to the traditional instruments of protectionism—the tariff, the quota, or the outright embargo (all of which can be on imports or exports).[a]

The doctrine that states may not engage in protectionism (may not adopt protectionist legislation as I have defined it) I shall refer to as the "anti-protectionism principle."

* * *

There are three objections to state protectionism, which I shall call the "concept-of-union" objection, the "resentment/retaliation" objection, and the "efficiency" objection.

The concept-of-union objection is so obvious that it is easily overlooked. State protectionism is unacceptable because it is inconsistent with the very idea of political union, even a limited federal union. Protectionist legislation is the economic equivalent of war. It is hostile in its essence.

In saying protectionist legislation is hostile, I do not mean that the harm to the foreign victims is necessarily valued for itself. The ultimate goal may be only promotion of local well-being. But the harm to foreign interests is also not merely incidental. The immediate intended means to improvement of local well-being is the transfer of certain profitable activities from

---

[a]Regan states that part (b) of the definition "is necessary in part to account for the Court's recent decisions on the state-as-market-participant; but it is necessary for other reasons as well, and it has its own theoretical justification * * *. As it happens, all the state laws involved in what the reader would think of as standard cases under the dormant commerce clause satisfy part (b) of the definition * * *." Regan's full discussion of part (b) is omitted.

foreign to local hands. Protectionism does not merely harm some foreign interests in the process of conferring an independent local benefit. Rather, it takes away from the foreigners in order to give to local residents exactly what has been taken away. Nations under arms are often no more hostilely disposed to their enemies than this. Such behavior has no place in a genuine political union of any kind.

Notice I have not said that all legislation that distinguishes between locals and foreigners is objectionable. A state does have a special relationship to its own citizens. Alaska may provide that only Alaskans can run for governor or share in the distribution of the state's oil royalties. Such legislation is not hostile to non-Alaskans in the way protectionism is hostile. It takes nothing away from non-Alaskans that we would normally think they have as much right to as Alaskans have.

The reader might wonder whether protectionist legislation is any more hostile than ordinary competitive economic behavior. When the Coca-Cola Company introduced its new flavor of Coke, it was trying to take business away from Pepsi-Cola and transfer that business to itself. We would not normally characterize Coca-Cola's behavior as hostile. We even tend to assume behavior like this is socially valuable.

Now, states do not ordinarily compete with each other for customers in the way Coca-Cola and Pepsi-Cola compete, but states do sometimes try to help local businesses compete by what we would think of as normal marketing techniques. Thus, the State of Michigan advertises Michigan as a vacation paradise for boaters and fishermen, hoping thereby to benefit the Michigan tourist industry, and recognizing that any benefit will come at least in part at the expense of other states' tourist industries.

Such behavior by Michigan is perfectly permissible. * * * [D]eveloping our war analogy, we might say that protectionism takes over a market share by force; it is like acquiring territory by armed conquest. Advertising, like product improvement and other standard market ploys, uses no force; it encourages a free transfer of allegiance. It is like acquiring territory by plebiscite of the inhabitants.

The next objection to protectionism is the resentment/retaliation objection. If protectionism is conceptually inconsistent with political union, it is also practically inconsistent. Protectionist impositions cause resentment and invite protectionist retaliation. If protectionist legislation is permitted at all, it is likely to generate a cycle of escalating animosity and isolation (and even of hostility in the strongest sense, where the harm to foreign interests *is* valued as such), eventually imperiling the political viability of the union itself.

* * *

The third objection to protectionism is that it is inefficient. Now, "efficiency" is a treacherous notion. Let us pause to be sure we know what we are saying. Why exactly is protectionism inefficient? The obvious answer is that tariffs, embargoes, quotas, and the like interfere with efficiency in the production of goods; they divert business from low-cost (foreign) to high-cost (local) producers.

For some purposes, the statement that protectionism is inefficient because it diverts business from low-cost (foreign) to high-cost (local) producers would be perfectly adequate. But for our purposes, it is inadequate. It tells part of the story, but not the whole story, of why classical protectionist measures seem so self-evidently objectionable on efficiency-related grounds.

The first problem with the statement as it stands is this: It suggests that *every* law which diverts business away from the producers who currently have it is necessarily diverting business from low-cost to high-cost producers and impairing efficiency. But that need not be so.

Consider the Oregon bottle law.[b] That law diverted business from can manufacturers to bottle manufacturers and, because of the increased transportation cost associated with heavier containers, from out-of-state bottlers to in-state bottlers. But there is no reason to think the Oregon bottle law impaired productive efficiency. The object of the law was to discourage a mode of production, the packaging of beverages in nonreusable and nonreturnable cans, that created costs (in the form of litter) not accounted for by market mechanisms. In other words, the object of the law was to improve productive efficiency by correcting an inefficiency that resulted from an external cost of the existing productive process.

* * *

Our discussion of the Oregon bottle law makes it clear that we cannot be satisfied with a statement of the efficiency objection to protectionism that suggests that every law that diverts business away from (foreign) producers who currently have it impairs productive efficiency and thus shares the evil of protectionism. How shall we reformulate the efficiency objection in order to avoid this suggestion?

We could say that protectionism is inefficient because it diverts business from producers who are the low-cost producers under the cost-assignment scheme implicit in the legal status quo, without the state's even claiming the justification, which Oregon claimed for its bottle law, that that cost-assignment scheme is defective. Or, compressing what we have just said: protectionism is inefficient because it diverts business away from

---

[b]In 1971 Oregon passed a law to protect the environment by discouraging the use of nonreturnable cans.

presumptively low-cost producers without any colorable cost-based justification.

This reformulation of the efficiency objection is an improvement, but it is still not fully acceptable. The change we have made, focusing as it does on cost-based justification, responds too exclusively to the Oregon bottle law. We can see the need for further reformulation by considering a somewhat different case, *Exxon Corp. v. Maryland.* If we give the Maryland legislature the benefit of any doubts about its purpose, the object of the Maryland law forbidding ownership of retail service stations by producers or refiners of petroleum was to secure fairer treatment of independent service station operators. Is that a "cost-based justification" for the diversion of retail business away from vertically integrated oil refiners? There may be room for someone to argue that this fairness justification for the Maryland law is not cost-based; but if there is room, that merely shows that a formulation of the efficiency objection in terms of cost-based justification is still not the right formulation. Whether or not we regard the claimed justification for the Maryland law as cost-based, the justification prevents the law from being self-evidently and unambiguously objectionable in the way a classical tariff is. (Remember we are assuming innocent purpose.) To be certain we exclude the Maryland law from the scope of the efficiency objection, we need to state the efficiency objection to protectionism more narrowly still, if we can find a way to do so.

Here is the proper formulation: protectionism is inefficient because it diverts business away from presumptively low-cost producers without any colorable justification in terms of a benefit that deserves approval from the point of view of the nation as a whole. Or, again compressing slightly: protectionism is inefficient because it diverts business away from presumptively low-cost producers without any colorable justification in terms of a "federally cognizable benefit."

Consider once more the classical tariff, and see how this reformulated efficiency objection fits it. The classical protectionist tariff diverts business away from those producers who currently have it, and the only benefit sought by the state imposing the tariff is a transfer of welfare from foreign producers (firms or workers) to their local counterparts. This transfer is a benefit from the narrowly self-interested viewpoint of the state imposing the tariff; but by its very nature this benefit to the imposing state is balanced by an equal loss to some other state or states. From the point of view of the nation as a whole, such a bare transfer of welfare between similarly situated parties in different states creates no benefit at all.

It is clear, then, that a classical tariff aims at no federally cognizable benefit, no benefit that deserves approval from the point of view of the nation as a whole. But what about the Oregon bottle law, or the Maryland law about service stations? Must there be a national policy in favor of reducing the litter in Oregon's parks and highways, or must we be able to say there should be such a national policy, before we can say the Oregon law seeks a federally cognizable benefit? No. The states are independent entities. Part of the point of federalism is to allow states to make their own decisions about such matters as what sort of an environment they value and want to maintain. So long as there is no constitutionally stipulated policy against minimizing litter (that is, no constitutionally stipulated policy in favor of litter *as such*), the elimination of litter from Oregon's parks and highways is a good thing from the federal viewpoint if Oregon says it is. Similarly, so long as there is no constitutional policy against fairer treatment (or what Maryland views as fairer treatment) for independent service stations, securing fairer treatment for independent service stations in Maryland is a good thing from the federal viewpoint if Maryland says it is.

* * *

I have put the efficiency objection last, even though it would occur first to many constitutional scholars, because it deserves to be downplayed. The relevant sense of "efficiency" turns out to be much weaker than one might at first assume; and the objection also was not primary in the framers' thinking. The people who wrote our Constitution were by no means thoroughgoing free traders. They envisaged a mercantilist foreign trade policy for the United States as a whole. One reason they wanted to locate the power to regulate commerce with foreign nations in Congress was that independent regulation of such commerce by the states prevented the implementation of an optimal national mercantilist policy. The framers did have some efficiency-related objection to interstate protectionism. They argued that eliminating preferential state regulation of trade would encourage agriculture and industry. But that is a much narrower claim than is suggested by modern apostles of efficiency, who operate with a strong presumption in favor of total economic *laissez-faire.* The framers would have recognized many good reasons for state economic regulation, and they would have recognized that the states must be the primary judges of what are good reasons. To the extent the framers were concerned with efficiency, it seems reasonable to think of their objection as being the objection I have formulated.

The structural argument against state protectionism is now complete. It remains only to consider whether there is a textual argument as well. In my opinion, the structural argument does not need to be supported by an argument from any single short bit of text (which is what lawyers normally mean by a "textual" argument), so long as there is no short bit of text that contradicts the structural argument (and there is none). Even so, let us see what we make of the text in bits.

Does the constitutional text include any bit that prohibits state protectionism? That depends, not surprisingly, on how the bits are approached. If we ask whether there is any bit of text that, taken by itself, naturally suggests to a modern reader that the states are forbidden to engage in protectionism against other states, the answer is easy: No, there is not. But there is another question, still about bits of text, that may be of interest. Is there any bit of text that might have suggested to a reader in 1787 that state protectionism was forbidden? Or, what is almost the same question, is there any bit of text that we could reasonably take to embody a final intention of the framers to forbid state protectionism, if we have independent reason to think the framers intended to forbid it and intended the text to say so? Here, the answer is: Yes. The relevant bit of text is the words, "The Congress shall have power * * * to regulate commerce * * * among the several states * * *."

There is much evidence that the main point of this grant (unlike the grant of power over foreign commerce) was not to empower Congress, but rather to disable the states from regulating commerce among themselves. The type of commercial regulation uppermost in the framers' minds was what we might categorize generally as mercantile regulation—regulation of navigation, customs regulation, and the like. The framers wanted commerce among the states to be free of state-originated mercantilist impositions. Giving Congress the power to regulate internal commerce was one way of denying states that power, under the view, much more natural to the framers than to us, that granted regulatory powers were exclusive. I have remarked previously that as Congress' power over interstate commerce is now understood, we cannot treat that power as exclusive. But that does not mean the framers could not have regarded as exclusive the much narrower power they were thinking of. There is considerable evidence that they did so regard it.[68]

Against the Carolene Products *Theory of the Dormant Commerce Clause and Open-Ended Private Interest Balancing*

The basic idea of the *Carolene Products* theory of the dormant commerce clause is simple enough: When states adopt economic regulations that affect out-of-state interests, those out-of-state interests are likely to be

[68] * * *Of course, if the commerce clause forbids state mercantilist legislation, then it also provides a ground for judicial review to prevent such legislation. But notice that this argument for judicial review extends only so far as state legislation is flatly prohibited, which is to say, only so far as Congress' power is exclusive. This argument provides no ground for judicial review of all state legislation which is "commercial" in the sense that it duplicates what Congress might do under its (largely nonexclusive) commerce power as presently interpreted. (It is a very natural extension of the mercantilist exclusion, however, to say the Court may suppress what is superficially ordinary commercial legislation if that legislation has a protectionist purpose.)

shortchanged because they are not represented in the political process that produces the regulations. But everyone who is affected ought to be represented. Therefore we have judicial review of state economic regulation that affects out-of-state interests in order to give those interests "virtual representation."

* * *

Now, in discussing the *Carolene Products* theory of the dormant commerce clause (which I shall refer to hereafter as just the "*Carolene Products* theory," leaving the limitation to the dormant commerce clause understood), the first thing we need to do is to be clear about the scope of judicial review that the theory is supposed to justify.

The *Carolene Products* theorist might argue only for judicial application of the anti-protectionism principle as I have developed it. This would put him on solid ground, but it would rob his theory of any interest. Certainly the *Carolene Products* theory entails the anti-protectionism principle as a consequence. There would be no protectionist legislation (in my sense) if foreign interests were represented equally with the local interests they compete against. However, the idea of virtual representation is not necessary to justify the anti-protectionism principle. My own argument for the anti-protectionism principle made no use of the idea of virtual representation. (The idea that one state may not behave hostilely to another is a much more limited idea, as is the idea that state regulation producing protectionist effect must aim at some federally cognizable benefit.) If virtual representation is the central idea of the *Carolene Products* theory, then the *Carolene Products* theory is not necessary to ground the anti-protectionism principle, and acceptance of the anti-protectionism principle does not commit us to the *Carolene Products* theory.

The *Carolene Products* theory is interesting only if it entails more than the anti-protectionism principle—specifically, if it entails that economic regulation that affects foreign interests should be reviewed by courts applying a balancing methodology. Open-ended private interest balancing is what virtual representation requires, and it is what most *Carolene Products* theorists have argued for.[c] (The balancing that is required is private interest balancing because it is private interests that are supposed to deserve virtual representation.)

Now, one problem with the *Carolene Products* theory is that if it justifies balancing at all, it requires balancing over a much broader range of

[c] "Open-ended private interest balancing," Regan explains elsewhere, is the view "that any cost imposed by a statute on a private party can be advanced as an argument against the constitutionality of the statute[.]" Not every such cost will invalidate a law, but every cost counts in the scale used to measure validity.

cases than its proponents usually recognize. Justice Stone, the original *Carolene Products* theorist (in the dormant commerce clause area as elsewhere), suggested that judicial review would not be necessary if there were in-state interests functionally equivalent to the damaged out-of-state interests. * * * But if any foreigners are harmed, then representation of those foreigners in the political process of the enacting state might have shifted the political balance and prevented the adoption of the regulation. This is true even if there are already similarly burdened local interests, and even if these local interests are more heavily burdened than the foreign. * * *

This means the *Carolene Products* theory requires review of laws no one would normally think of as requiring judicial scrutiny. If Minnesota adopts an advertising campaign to try to discourage smoking among its population, or if it forbids smoking in enough stores, offices, and places of public assembly to affect significantly the total number of cigarettes smoked, then the law should be judicially inspected to see that it does not unjustly harm tobacco growers in North Carolina. If a major city adopts a rent control ordinance, judicial review is required to protect the interests of people living elsewhere who might have moved to the city except for the increased difficulty of securing housing.[131] If a state has a stingy workmen's compensation program that attracts employers, the courts must stand ready to consider whether representation in that state's legislature of foreign workers might not have produced a program that was more generous.

My last example might elicit the response that review is not required because the foreign workers are not objecting to the program as it exists so much as they are objecting to the state's failure to have a more generous program. This raises an interesting question about what counts as action by a state and what is a mere omission. But even if we could make that distinction perfectly clear, it would not help the *Carolene Products* theorist. On his theory, the courts ought to review legislative omissions as freely as they review positive legislative action. After all, representation of foreign interests would not result only in blocking legislation. Sometimes it would tip the balance in favor of legislation where none was otherwise forthcoming. * * *

Overbreadth, however, is not the most fundamental problem with the *Carolene Products* theory of the dormant commerce clause. The *Carolene Products* theory assumes that out-of-state interests really ought to be represented—the theory assumes it is a defect in our system that the system denies foreigners representation, as it is a defect if racial minorities or women are unrepresented or represented ineffectively. But that assumption

[131]This example is borrowed from Kitch, [*Regulation and the American Common Market,* in Regulation, Federalism, and Interstate Commerce 31 (A. Tarlock, ed. 1981).]

is not warranted. Nonrepresentation of foreign interests follows from the simple fact that there are separate states; and the existence of separate states, while it might be a defect in an ideal political system, can hardly be treated as a defect in ours.

I suggest that with regard to treatment by the states of out-of-state interests, our system embodies the following compromise between unlimited state autonomy and perfect national unity. The states may not single out foreigners for disadvantageous treatment just because of their foreignness. But, provided they do not single out foreigners, the states need not attend positively to the foreign effects of laws they adopt nor to the distribution between locals and foreigners of the benefits and burdens of those laws. "Singling out" foreigners does not necessarily involve explicitness. It does involve purpose. The state legislature that simply fails to attend to foreign interests or to any local/foreign distinction may do as it pleases. This is the message of the dormant commerce clause, as it is the general message of the privileges and immunities clause of article IV.

Clearly, this is a compromise. If the states were perfectly autonomous, they would be free to single out foreigners for disadvantageous treatment. If, on the other hand, we had perfect national unity, there would be no states at all, except perhaps as administrative departments, and all interests throughout the nation would be taken into account in any significant legislative decision. Giving foreign interests virtual representation in the actual independent state legislatures may be thought of as an attempt to mimic a regime of perfect national unity. But in view of the compromise I have described, such "virtual" perfect unity is not required.

The autonomy interest of the states that we protect by not requiring virtual representation may seem like just a freedom to harm foreigners with impunity so long as it is done by inadvertence. This is not an interest one can feel much enthusiasm for. But in fact, there is more at stake.

By not requiring state lawmakers to be always looking over their shoulders for foreign interests and always calculating the proportionate incidence of benefits and burdens, we make legislation a possible task for lawmakers with less expertise and less administrative support available to them than Congress has. We also avoid a massive transfer of power to the courts, federal and state. And we avoid the tendency to homogenization of values that commitment of economic regulation to the courts, under the general supervision of the Supreme Court, would tend to bring about. It is worth remembering that states can disagree about issues with significant interstate aspects for reasons having nothing to do with hostility to, or even indifference to, foreigners as such.

BARRY FRIEDMAN, VALUING FEDERALISM

82 MINN.L.REV. 317, 347–360 (1997)

* * *

At least with regard to preemption there is the appearance that Congress intended state law to give way to federal interests; in the final doctrinal area—the dormant Commerce Clause—this appearance disappears entirely. Under the dormant Commerce Clause courts strike down state enactments on the ground that they interfere with the concerns underlying the Commerce Clause, despite the fact that Congress has been completely silent on the subject. In other words, in dormant Commerce Clause cases the courts alone do the work of displacing state law, in the name of furthering national interests.

The Constitution itself provides no indication that courts are to strike state laws under the dormant commerce power. The Constitution says only that "*Congress* shall have the Power . . . [t]o regulate Commerce . . . among the several States." Congress not having regulated, one might conclude the states are free to (as the Court itself would say) "occupy the field." * * * Partly for reasons of history, and partly because there is no coherent understanding of the values of federalism, the doctrine has evolved quite differently.

* * *

The high point for the states may have been right before the fall, in *South Carolina State Highway Department v. Barnwell Bros.*[136] The *Barnwell* Court upheld a state law regulating the weight of trucks on state highways, the Court stating that "[t]he fact that many states have adopted a different standard is not persuasive."[137] [T]he *Barnwell* Court recognized the importance of state regulatory authority even if it was commerce that was being regulated: "It is not any the less a legislative power committed to the states because it affects interstate commerce, and courts are not any the more entitled, because interstate commerce is affected, to substitute their own for the legislative judgment."[138]

The modern doctrine of the dormant Commerce Clause, born shortly after *Barnwell*, purports to accommodate both national and state interests. Eschewing the earlier formalism that divided the world into commerce on the one hand, and the police power on the other, the modern-day doctrine focuses instead on the evils that can arise when states regulate in a way that affects the national market. The modern test comes in two parts. First, the Court asks if a state law "discriminates" against interstate commerce. The

[136]303 U.S. 177 (1938).

[137]Id. at 195.

[138]Id. at 191.

concern here is protectionist legislation, which can lead to retaliation and balkanization among the states. Discriminatory, or protectionist, legislation is per se invalid. Second, if a state law does not discriminate against interstate commerce, then the courts look further to ensure that the burdens on commerce do not outweigh the benefits to the state of regulating.

Among the members of the Court and among commentators there is some confusion about this second step. Some see it as a way only of smoking out more subtle protectionist legislation: if the burdens are high and the benefits illusory, then one suspects a protectionist purpose motivated the law. Others see true benefit-burden balancing, concluding that when the burdens are too high, interstate commerce simply is jeopardized to the extent that judicial invalidation of state law is necessary. As will be evident, the Court's weighing of interests under the second step has not been uniform.

On its face, the doctrine of the dormant Commerce Clause appears to be respectful of state authority. Protectionism is construed simply to mean "differential treatment of in-state and out-of-state economic interests that benefits the former and burdens the latter."[147] Under benefit-burden balancing, the state regulation supposedly will be upheld so long as the benefits to the state are not "illusory," the Court sometimes taking the view that a nondiscriminatory state law with any actual benefits will be upheld. The opinions are rife with language praising the importance of state regulation to protect the health, safety, and welfare of state citizens.

Although the rhetoric of the dormant Commerce Clause decisions sounds out favorably for state autonomy, in reality this line of cases may be the most devastating to state authority. While purporting to act with deference to the regulatory authority of the states, in reality the Supreme Court pursues a course of enforcing uniformity and a free market in trade, concepts that have the potential to level state authority. As Justice Stevens said in a somewhat different context, "uniformity is an ungovernable engine."[150] By its very nature an insistence on uniformity has the potential to spell the end of state regulatory autonomy. [T]here is a significant difference between a prohibition on protectionism and an insistence on free trade, the latter necessarily running flat against countless state regulatory choices.

The Court's free-trade tendencies were evident in the recent decision *in C & A Carbone, Inc. v. Town of Clarkstown,* [152] in which the Court struck down a city's flow-control ordinance. In order to handle solid waste, Clarkstown had entered into a contract with a company that would build

[147]*Oregon Waste,* 511 U.S. at 99 (defining discrimination as used in the phrase "discrimination against interstate commerce").

[150]Michigan v. Long, 463 U.S. 1032, 1070 (1983)(Stevens, J., dissenting).

[152]511 U.S. 383 (1994).

and operate a transfer station at which goods were separated into recyclables and nonrecyclables. Construction of the facility was financed by a "tipping fee" charged at the transfer station. At the end of a five-year period, the town would purchase the facility for one dollar in order to ensure the flow of goods sufficient to finance the facility over the initial five-year period, Clarkstown passed an ordinance requiring that all nonhazardous solid waste in the town be brought to the transfer station. The ordinance was challenged by another waste processor when the town sought an injunction enforcing the tipping law. The question was whether the flow-control ordinance requiring all waste to be tipped at the town facility violated the dormant Commerce Clause.

As the dissent in the case made clear, the Clarkstown ordinance did not follow the pattern of laws typically struck down as protectionist. The hallmark of protectionism, according to the Court, is differential treatment of in-state and out-of-state entities. Here, all were treated alike: every individual and company was required to tip waste at the municipal facility. Indeed, the municipal ordinance clearly disadvantaged one group of insiders more than it disadvantaged anyone else, that being the people of Clarkstown who voted to impose the tipping rule on themselves, thus raising their own costs for the disposal of solid waste. As the dissent understood matters, the law at issue was simply a nonprotectionist way for the municipality to fund a solution to the solid waste problems facing all communities.

The majority nonetheless struck down the law in an opinion that clearly privileged the idea of free trade, rather than simply eliminating protectionism. In the face of the dissent's careful analysis, it is difficult to accept the majority's repeated assertion that the flow-control ordinance discriminated against out-of-state interests in favor of in-state interests. It is true that only one company benefited from the ordinance, to the exclusion of out-of-state interests that might have sought to dispose of Clarkstown's waste. But the same was true vis-à-vis in-state interests, and as the dissent pointed out in a footnote, the record was silent as to whether the owner of Clarkstown's facility was from within or without the state. Yielding better insight into the Court's thinking were repeated references in the *Carbone* decision suggesting that the Court saw the Commerce Clause as guaranteeing a free national market. It particularly is significant that in its central claim that the Commerce Clause promotes the "free flow" of commerce, the Court cited not a dormant Commerce Clause case, but the decision in *Jones & Laughlin Steel.*[164] Undoubtedly Congress could decide in favor of an entirely free market, but it has not done so, and the Court's limited antidiscrimination and antiprotectionism decisions do not justify the result in Carbone.

---

[164]See *Carbone*, 511 U.S. at 389 (citing NLRB v. Jones & Laughlin Steel Corp., 301 U.S. 1, 31 (1937)).

For all its talk of deferring to state police regulations that provide nonprotectionist benefits to the state, in recent decisions the Court looks more toward ensuring national uniformity, a quite different approach and one far more devastating to state regulatory authority. This was evident in *Kassel v. Consolidated Freightways*,[165] in which the Supreme Court struck an Iowa state law limiting the length of double trucks on its highways. *Kassel* is best understood as a case in which uniformity was the Court's primary concern. The law in *Kassel* was challenged by trucking companies because it forced those companies to either divert shipments around Iowa or move them to smaller trucks to ship through Iowa. The record as to the safety of the longer double trucks was distinctly mixed, and could been seen in quite different ways, as the plurality and dissent made clear. Yet, as the dissent demonstrates, the safety benefits arguably achieved by the state regulation were far from "illusory." Thus under the Court's own formulation of the second step of its dormant Commerce Clause doctrine, the law should have been upheld.

Despite its troubling facts, *Kassel* can only awkwardly be viewed as a protectionism case. True, the Governor had vetoed a law passed by the legislature to raise the length limit, questioning (in the veto message) why Iowa should subject itself to additional through-state traffic. In addition, the older law did contain exceptions that seemed designed to favor longer truck lengths for traffic that benefited Iowa, such as an exception for agricultural vehicles, or a "border-cities" exception. The problem with the protectionist rationale, however, was that Iowa had clearly not enacted the law to frustrate interstate commerce, it had simply failed to change its law to accommodate the interests of the trucking industry. The law at issue was enacted long before it was challenged, at a time when it imposed no disuniformity of regulation. Many other states had laws similar to Iowa's. The trucking companies could have gone to Congress to obtain a national uniform law, but appeared to prefer picking the state laws off one by one in litigation.

Moreover, the Iowa law should have fared pretty well under some prior decisions of the Supreme Court. In *Barnwell* the Court had upheld a differential weight limit for trucks on state highways, stating that "[f]ew subjects of state regulation are so peculiarly of local concern as is the use of state highways."[175] And in *Cooley* the law at issue also was riddled with exceptions that suggested some protectionist purpose, but the Court there recognized that so long as the law generally achieved its aim, some such exceptions were permissible.[176] The *Cooley* Court found these exemptions

[165]450 U.S. 662 (1981).

[175]South Carolina State Highway Dep't v. Barnwell Bros., 303 U.S. 177, 187 (1938).

[176]Cooley v. Bd. of Wardens, 53 U.S. (12 How.) 299, 313 (1851) ("[F]air objects of a law imposing half-pilotage when a pilot is not received, may be secured, and at the same time some classes of vessels exempted from such charge.").

nothing but appropriate "legislative discretion." Deriving the benefits of the general rule was appropriate in cases in which the harm followed, but the legislature could also generalize about vessels that might be exempted without causing such harm.

On the other hand, *Kassel* closely resembles another dormant Commerce Clause case in which the Court clearly chose the benefits of uniformity over the protection of state regulatory authority. That case was *Southern Pacific Co. v. Arizona ex rel. Sullivan*,[178] in which the Court struck down a state law limiting the length of railroad trains. In *Southern Pacific*, as in *Kassel*, the safety evidence was surely a matter of fair dispute. Although the Court claimed the safety benefits were small, it was clear in *Southern Pacific*, as it was in *Kassel*, that the real concern was the obstruction of commerce created by disuniformity: "Enforcement of the law in Arizona, while train lengths remain unregulated or are regulated by varying standards in other states, must inevitably result in an impairment of uniformity of efficient railroad operation because the railroads are subjected to regulation which is not uniform in its application."[181]

These cases clearly suggest that the Supreme Court's dormant commerce jurisprudence is tending toward requiring national uniformity. It could be, as Donald Regan suggests, that *Kassel* and *Southern Pacific* are transportation cases and should be understood as sui generis. Regan distinguishes transportation cases from movement of goods cases, arguing that the needs for uniformity are greater in transportation, and that antiprotectionism should be the only rule in movement of goods cases. It is true that the courts have tolerated some greater disuniformity in movement of goods cases. Yet, the argument is not entirely persuasive, because increasingly, in contexts outside of transportation, the Court is coming to rely on the language of uniformity and on a less-deferential balancing of burdens and benefits.[185]

---

[178] 325 U.S. 761 (1945)

[181] Id. at 773.

[185] See, e.g., Healy v. Beer Inst., 491 U.S. 324, 336-37 (1989) ("[T]he practical effect of the statute must be evaluated not only by considering the consequences of the statute itself, but also by considering how the challenged statute may interact with the legitimate regulatory regimes of other States and what effect would arise if not one, but many or every, State adopted similar legislation. Generally speaking, the Commerce Clause protects against inconsistent legislation arising from the projection of one state regulatory regime into the jurisdiction of another state."); Brown-Forman Distillers Corp. v. New York Liquor Auth., 476 U.S. 573, 583 (1986) (noting that proliferation of affirmation laws had increased the likelihood that a seller would be subjected to inconsistent obligations in different states); Edgar v. MITE Corp., 457 U.S. 624, 642 (1982) (observing that if all states enacted similar legislation, "interstate commerce in securities transactions generated by tender offers would be thoroughly stifled"); cf. CTS Corp. v. Dynamics Corp. of America, 481 U.S. 69, 88-89 (1987).

The dormant commerce cases represent a clear and energetic effort by the Supreme Court to pursue a doctrinal line that accords very little value to federalism. Unlike the other doctrinal areas examined above, the Supreme Court is moving on its own here, with little guidance from Congress. Moreover, unlike the other areas, in which the Court has little sense of why national regulation must be preferred over state regulation, the Court here does advance strong national interests, certainly in antiprotectionism, but also in free trade and national uniformity. Yet it is ironic, to say the least, that the Court evidences no theory of national regulation when it reviews an explicit act of the national Congress, but when it acts alone the Court adopts a theory more aggressively nationalizing than any Congress has pursued. At the same time, the Court pays lip service to the police power, but strikes down many state laws that come its way.

BIBLIOGRAPHY

Background Reading on the American Federal System

Althouse, *Federalism, Untamed,* 47 Vand.L.Rev. 1207 (1994).

Beer, *Federalism, Nationalism, and Democracy in America,* 72 Am.Pol. Sci.Rev. 9 (1978).

Briffault, *"What About the 'Ism'?" Normative and Formal Concerns in Contemporary Federalism,* 47 Vand.L.Rev. 1303 (1994).

Cushman, *Continuity and Change in Commerce Clause Jurisprudence*, 55 Ark.L.Rev. 1009 (2003).

Dorf and Sabel, *A Constitution of Democratic Experimentalism,* 98 Colum.L.Rev. 267 (1998).

Elazar, D., THE AMERICAN PARTNERSHIP (1962).

Eskridge and Ferejohn, *The Elastic Commerce Clause: A Political Theory of American Federalism,* 47 Vand.L.Rev. 1355 (1994).

Farber, D., LINCOLN'S CONSTITUTION (2003).

Flaherty, *More Apparent Than Real: The Revolutionary Commitment to Constitutional Federalism,* 45 U.Kan.L.Rev. 993 (1997).

Friedman, *Federalism's Future in the Global Village,* 47 Vand.L.Rev. 1441 (1994).

Friedman, *The Sometimes-Bumpy Stream of Commerce,* 55 Ark.L.Rev. 981 (2003).

Kaczorowski, *The Tragic Irony of American Federalism: National Sovereignty Versus State Sovereignty in Slavery and in Freedom,* 45 U.Kan.L.Rev. 1015 (1997).

Kramer, *Understanding Federalism,* 47 Vand.L.Rev. 1485 (1994).

McConnell, *Federalism: Evaluating the Founders' Design,* 54 U.Chi.L.Rev. 1484 (1987).

Storing, *What the Anti-Federalists Were For,* in H Storing, ed., THE COMPLETE ANTI-FEDERALIST (1981).

THE FEDERALIST, Nos. 10, 14, 39, 44–46, 51.

Tushnet, *Federalism and the Traditions of American Political Theory,* 19 Ga.L.Rev. 981 (1985).

Federalism as a Constitutional Value

Barron, *A Localist Critique of the New Federalism*, 51 Duke L.J. 377 (2001).

Cross, *The Folly of Federalism*, 24 Cardozo L.Rev. 1 (2002).

Bednar and Eskridge, *Steadying the Court's "Unsteady Path": A Theory of Judicial Enforcement of Federalism*, 68 S. Cal.L.Rev. 1447 (1995).

McGinnis, *Reviving Tocqueville's America: The Rehnquist Court's Jurisprudence of Social Discovery*, 90 Cal.L.Rev. 487 (2002).

Prakash and Yoo, *The Puzzling Persistence of Process-Based Federalism Theories*, 79 Tex.L.Rev. 1459 (2001).

Federal Power

Baker, *Conditional Federal Spending After Lopez,* 95 Colum.L.Rev. 1911 (1995).

Barnett, *Necessary and Proper,* 44 UCLA.L.Rev. 745 (1997).

Barnett, *The Original Meaning of the Commerce Clause*, 68 U.Chi.L.Rev. 101 (2001).

Calabresi, *"A Government of Limited and Enumerated Powers": In Defense of* United States v. Lopez, 94 Mich.L.Rev. 752 (1995).

Caminker, *"Appropriate" Means-Ends Constraints on Section 5 Powers*, 53 Stan. L. Rev. 1127 (2001).

Engdahl, *Casebooks and Constitutional Competency,* 21 Seattle U.L.Rev. 741 (1998).

Engdahl, *The Spending Power,* 44 Duke L.J. 1 (1994).

Farber, *The Constitution's Forgotten Cover Letter; An Essay on the New Federalism and the Original Understanding,* 94 Mich.L.Rev. 615 (1995).

Frickey and Smith, *Judicial Review, the Congressional Process, and the Federalism Cases: An Interdisciplinary Critique*, 111 Yale L.J. 1707 (2002).

Jackson, *Holistic Interpretation:* Fitzpatrick v. Bitzer *and Our Bifurcated Constitution*, 53 Yale L.J. 1259 (2001).

Lessig, *Translating Federalism: United States v. Lopez,* 1995 Sup.Ct.Rev. 125.

Maggs, *Translating Federalism: A Textualist Reaction,* 66 Geo.Wash.L. Rev. 1198 (1998).

McConnell, *Institutions and Interpretation: A Critique of* City of Boerne v. Flores, 111 Harv.L.Rev. 153 (1997).

Merritt, *The Third Translation of the Commerce Clause: Congressional Power to Regulate Social Problems,* 66 Geo.Wash.L.Rev. 1206 (1998).

Post and Siegel, *Equal Protection by Law: Federal Antidiscrimination Legislation After* Morrison *and* Kimmel, 110 Yale L.J. 441 (2000).

Regan, *How to Think About the Federal Commerce Power and Incidentally Rewrite* United States v. Lopez, 94 Mich.L.Rev. 554 (1995).

State Immunities

Caminker, Printz, *State Sovereignty, and the Limits of Formalism,* 1997 Sup.Ct.Rev. 199.

Caminker, *State Sovereignty and Subordinacy: May Congress Commandeer State Officers to Implement Federal Law?,* 95 Colum.L.Rev. 1001 (1995).

Chemerinsky, *Against Sovereign Immunity*, 53 Stan. L. Rev. 1201 (2001).

Field, Garcia v. San Antonio Metropolitan Transit Authority: *The Demise of a Misguided Doctrine,* 99 Harv.L.Rev. 84 (1985).

Hills, *The Political Economy of Cooperative Federalism: Why State Autonomy Makes Sense and "Dual Sovereignty" Doesn't,* 96 Mich.L.Rev. 813 (1998).

Merritt, *Republican Governments and Autonomous States: A New Role for the Guarantee Clause,* 65 U.Colo.L.Rev. 815 (1994).

Noonan, J., NARROWING THE NATION'S POWER: THE SUPREME COURT SIDES WITH THE STATES (2002).

Post, *Chief Justice William Howard Taft and the Concept of Federalism,* 9 Const.Comm. 199 (1992).

Reagan, M., THE NEW FEDERALISM (1972).

Smith, *States as Nations: Dignity in Cross-Doctrinal Perspective,* 89 Va.L.Rev. 1 (2003).

Soifer, *Truisms That Never Will Be True: The Tenth Amendment and the Spending Power,* 57 Colo.L.Rev. 793 (1986).

Limits on States

Abel, *The Commerce Clause in the Constitutional Convention and in Contemporary Comment*, 25 Minn.L.Rev. 432 (1941).

Coenen, *Business Subsidies and the Dormant Commerce Clause*, 107 Yale L.J. 965 (1998).

Coenen, *Untangling the Market-Participant Exemption to the Dormant Commerce Clause,* 88 Mich.L.Rev. 395 (1989).

Coenen and Hellerstein, *Suspect Linkage: The Interplay of State Taxing and Spending Measures in the Application of Constitutional Antidiscrimination Rules,* 95 Mich.L.Rev. 2167 (1997).

Cohen, *Congressional Power to Validate Unconstitutional State Laws,* 35 Stan.L.Rev. 387 (1983).

Gardbaum, *New Deal Constitutionalism and the Unshackling of the States*, 64 U.Chi.L.Rev. 483 (1997).

Goldsmith, *Statutory Foreign Affairs Preemption*, 2000 Sup.Ct.Rev. 175.

Gey, *The Political Economy of the Dormant Commerce Clause,* 17 N.Y.U.Rev.L. & Soc. Change 1 (1989).

Gillette, *Business Incentives, Interstate Competition, and the Commerce Clause,* 82 Minn.L.Rev. 447 (1997).

Goldsmith and Sykes, *The Internet and the Dormant Commerce Clause,* 110 Yale L.J. 785 (2001)

Hellerstein, *Is "Internal Consistency" Foolish?: Reflections on an Emerging Commerce Clause Restraint on State Taxation,* 87 Mich.L.Rev. 138 (1988).

Hellerstein, *Justice Scalia and the Commerce Clause: Reflections of a State Tax Lawyer,* 12 Cardozo L.Rev. 1763 (1991).

Hudec and Farber, *Free Trade and the Regulatory State: A GATT's-Eye View of the Dormant Commerce Clause,* 47 Vand.L.Rev. 1401 (1994).

Kitch, *Regulation and the American Common Market,* in REGULATION, FEDERALISM, AND INTERSTATE COMMERCE 9 (Tarlock ed. 1981).

Lockhart, *A Revolution in State Taxation of Commerce?,* 65 Minn.L.Rev. 1025 (1981).

Manheim, *New-Age Federalism and the Market Participant Doctrine,* 22 Ariz.St.L.J. 559 (1990).

Maltz, *How Much Regulation Is Too Much—An Examination of Commerce Clause Jurisprudence,* 50 Geo.Wash.L.Rev. 47 (1981).

McGreal, *The Flawed Economics of the Dormant Commerce Clause,* 39 Wm. & Mary L.Rev. 1191 (1998).

O'Fallon, *The Commerce Clause: A Theoretical Comment,* 61 Ore.L.Rev. 395 (1982).

Powell, *The Still Small Voice of the Commerce Clause,* Proceedings Nat. Tax Ass'n 337 (1938).

Schoettle, *Commerce Clause Challenges to State Taxes,* 75 Minn.L.Rev. 907 (1991).

Tushnet, *Scalia and the Dormant Commerce Clause: A Foolish Formalism?,* 12 Cardozo L.Rev. 1717 (1991).

Chapter V

SEPARATION OF POWERS

Like federalism, separation of powers doctrine deals with relations among the institutions of American government. While federalism addresses the "vertical" division of authority between national and state governments, separation of powers doctrine concerns the "horizontal" division among the national executive, legislature, and judiciary. The Supreme Court has played an active supervisory role in this area during the last twenty years.

This Chapter begins with a discussion of general theoretical approaches. We then turn to issues of presidential power—first the president's domestic powers, and then his power to wage war. The Chapter closes with a discussion of executive immunities.

A. GENERAL THEORETICAL APPROACHES

We cannot deal intelligently with separation issues without first thinking about the purposes served by a division of authority within the national government. One reason ("efficiency") for creating a strong executive was that the Framers viewed legislative government—with which they had some experience under the Articles of Confederation—as too fragmented and episodic. They thought that the national government would be more efficient if they separated executive from legislative functions. A second reason for dividing power—one mentioned prominently by Madison[1]—is the prevention of tyranny. Lest one institution become too powerful the Constitution confers on others the ability to check and balance its authority. So, for example, the President can veto legislation, the Congress can impeach the President and cut his budget, and the courts can invalidate executive and legislative actions. But the objectives of tyranny-prevention and efficiency may conflict with one another (checks and balances will weaken a strong executive).

The controversy over purposes is entwined with a second theme that is important today in all areas of constitutional law—the conflict over methods of interpreting the Constitution. One approach, labelled "formalist," urges that the text and structure of the Constitution and the intentions

[1]The Federalist No. 47.

of its authors provide clear answers to many conflicts about separation of powers. By way of contrast, a second approach might be called "functional." Under this view, categories of legislative and executive power overlap, especially in the complex administrative state. The key idea is one of maintaining balance among the branches. The excerpt in this section represent this conflicting viewpoints.

Gary Lawson, adopting a formalist perspective, contends that the post-New Deal administrative state is unconstitutional. He argues that foundational ideas such as a limited national government, non-delegation of legislative power, and a "unitary" executive power have been abandoned; this is best exemplified by the fact that the constitutionality of modern administrative agencies is not seriously questioned today.

Unlike Lawson, Martin Flaherty advances a decidedly "functionalist" approach to separation of powers issues during the founding period. He identifies three goals important to the framers: balance, accountability and energy. These values, translated to today's world, provide a new perspective on questions such as the removal power and the constitutionality of the legislative veto.

H. Jefferson Powell and Jed Rubenfeld, in an entertaining dialogue between two fictional constitutional pundits, seek a coherent schema for the Court's recent separation of powers issues. They find it by being formalists when the question is one of congressional overreaching and functionalists when the question concerns the powers of the other branches. Their analysis leads them to conclude that a strong case can be made for the constitutionality of the line item veto statute invalidated in *Clinton v. New York.*[2]

GARY LAWSON, THE RISE AND RISE OF THE ADMINISTRATIVE STATE

107 HARV.L.REV. 1231–45, 1248–49 (1994).

The post-New Deal administrative state is unconstitutional,[1] and its validation by the legal system amounts to nothing less than a bloodless constitutional revolution. The original New Dealers were aware, at least to some degree, that their vision of the national government's proper role and structure could not be squared with the written Constitution: The Administrative Process, James Landis's classic exposition of the New Deal model

---

[2]524 U.S. 417, 118 S.Ct. 2091, 141 L.Ed.2d 393 (1998).

[1]I use the word "unconstitutional" to mean "at variance with the Constitution's original public meaning." That is not the only way in which the word is used in contemporary legal discourse. On the contrary, it is commonly used to mean everything from "at variance with the private intentions of the Constitution's drafters" to "at variance with decisions of the United States Supreme Court" to "at variance with the current platform of the speaker's favorite political party." * * *

of administration, fairly drips with contempt for the idea of a limited national government subject to a formal, tripartite separation of powers.[4] Faced with a choice between the administrative state and the Constitution, the architects of our modern government chose the administrative state, and their choice has stuck.

* * *

I. THE DEATH OF CONSTITUTIONAL GOVERNMENT

The United States Congress today effectively exercises general legislative powers, in contravention of the constitutional principle of limited powers. Moreover, Congress frequently delegates that general legislative authority to administrative agencies, in contravention of Article I. Furthermore, those agencies are not always subject to the direct control of the President, in contravention of Article II. In addition, those agencies sometimes exercise the judicial power, in contravention of Article III. Finally, those agencies typically concentrate legislative, executive, and judicial functions in the same institution, in simultaneous contravention of Articles I, II, and III.

In short, the modern administrative state openly flouts almost every important structural precept of the American constitutional order.

A. The Death of Limited Government

The advocates of the Constitution of 1789 were very clear about the kind of national government they sought to create. As James Madison put it: "The powers delegated by the proposed Constitution to the federal government are few and defined." Those national powers, Madison suggested, would be "exercised principally on external objects, as war, peace, negotiation, and foreign commerce," and the states would be the principal units of government for most internal matters.[12]

The expectations of founding-era figures such as James Madison are instructive but not controlling for purposes of determining the Constitution's original public meaning: the best laid schemes o' mice, men and framers gang aft a-gley. The Constitution, however, is well designed to limit the national government essentially to the functions described by Madison.

Article I of the Constitution vests in the national Congress "[a]ll legislative powers *herein* granted," and thus clearly indicates that the national government can legislate only in accordance with enumerations of power. Article I then spells out seventeen specific subjects to which the federal

[4]See James M. Landis, The Administrative Process passim (1938).

[12][The Federalist No. 45, at 292–93 (James Madison)(Clinton Rossiter ed., 1961).]

legislative power extends: such matters as taxing and borrowing, interstate and foreign commerce, naturalization and bankruptcy, currency and counterfeiting, post offices and post roads, patents and copyrights, national courts, piracy and offenses against the law of nations, the military, and the governance of the nation's capital and certain federal enclaves. Article IV further grants to Congress power to enforce interstate full-faith-and-credit requirements, to admit new states, and to manage federal territories and property. Article V grants Congress power to propose constitutional amendments.

This is not the stuff of which Leviathan is made. None of these powers, alone or in combination, grants the federal government anything remotely resembling a general jurisdiction over citizens' affairs. The Commerce Clause, for example, is a grant of power to regulate "Commerce . . . among the several States," not to regulate "all Activities affecting, or affected by, Commerce . . . among the several States." The Commerce Clause clearly leaves outside the national government's jurisdiction such important matters as manufacturing (which is an activity distinct from commerce), the terms, formation, and execution of contracts that cover subjects other than the interstate shipment of goods, and commerce within a state's boundaries.

Nor does the Necessary and Proper Clause, which the founding generation called the Sweeping Clause, grant general legislative powers to the national government. This clause contains two significant internal limitations. First, it only validates laws that "carry[ ] into Execution" other granted powers. To carry a law or power "into Execution" means to provide the administrative machinery for its enforcement; it does *not* mean to regulate unenumerated subjects in order to make the exercise of enumerated powers more effective. Second, and more fundamentally, laws enacted pursuant to the Sweeping Clause must be both "necessary and *proper*" for carrying into execution enumerated powers. As Patty Granger and I have elsewhere demonstrated at length, the word "proper" in this context requires executory laws to be distinctively and peculiarly within the jurisdictional competence of the national government—that is, consistent with background principles of separation of powers, federalism, and individual rights.[22] Thus, the Sweeping Clause does not grant Congress power to regulate unenumerated subjects as a means of regulating subjects within its constitutional scope.

* * *

Admittedly, some post-1789 amendments to the Constitution expand Congress's powers beyond their original limits. For example, the Thirteenth and Fifteenth Amendments authorize Congress to enforce prohibitions

---

[22]See Gary Lawson & Patricia B. Granger, *The "Proper" Scope of Federal Power: A Jurisdictional Interpretation of the Sweeping Clause*, 43 Duke L.J. 267, 335–36 (1993).

against, respectively, involuntary servitude and racially discriminatory voting practices; the Fourteenth Amendment gives Congress power to enforce that Amendment's numerous substantive constraints on states; and the Sixteenth Amendment permits Congress to impose direct taxes without an apportionment requirement. These are important powers, to be sure, but they do not fundamentally alter the limited scope of Congress's power over private conduct.

Of course, in this day and age, discussing the doctrine of enumerated powers is like discussing the redemption of Imperial Chinese bonds. There is now virtually no significant aspect of life that is not in some way regulated by the federal government. This situation is not about to change. Only twice since 1937 has the Supreme Court held that a congressional statute exceeded the national government's enumerated powers,[33] and one of those holdings was overruled nine years later.[34]

Furthermore, both cases involved the direct regulation of state governments in their sovereign capacities. To the best of my knowledge, the post-New Deal Supreme Court has never invalidated a congressional intrusion into private affairs on ultra vires grounds; instead the Court has effectively acquiesced in Congress's assumption of general legislative powers.[a]

* * *

B. The Death of the Nondelegation Doctrine

The Constitution both confines the national government to certain enumerated powers and defines the institutions of the national government that can permissibly exercise those powers. Article I of the Constitution provides that "[a]ll legislative Powers herein granted shall be vested in a Congress of the United States, which shall consist of a Senate and House of Representatives." Article II provides that "[t]he executive Power shall be vested in a President of the United States of America." Article III specifies that "[t]he judicial Power of the United States, shall be vested in one supreme Court, and in such inferior Courts as the Congress may from time to time ordain and establish." The Constitution thus divides the powers of the national government into three categories—legislative, executive, and judicial—and vests such powers in three separate institutions. To be sure, the Constitution expressly prescribes some deviations from a pure tripartite

[33]See New York v. United States, 112 S.Ct. 2408, 2428–29 (1992); National League of Cities v. Usery, 426 U.S. 833, 852 (1976).

[34]See Garcia v. San Antonio Metro. Transit Auth., 469 U.S. 528, 531 (1985) (overruling *Usery*).

[a]This article was written before the Supreme Court's decision in United States v. Lopez, 514 U.S. 549 (1995). It also predates Boerne v. Flores, 521 U.S. 507 (1997), and Printz v. United States, 521 U.S. 98 (1997). Eds.

scheme of separation,[41] but this only underscores the role of the three Vesting Clauses in assigning responsibility for governmental functions that are not specifically allocated by the constitutional text.

* * *

Although the Constitution does not tell us how to distinguish the legislative, executive, and judicial powers from each other, there is clearly some differentiation among the three governmental functions, which at least generates some easy cases. Consider, for example, a statute creating the Goodness and Niceness Commission and giving it power "to promulgate rules for the promotion of goodness and niceness in all areas within the power of Congress under the Constitution." If the "executive power" means simply the power to carry out legislative commands regardless of their substance, then the Goodness and Niceness Commission's rulemaking authority is executive rather than legislative power and is therefore valid. But if that is true, then there never was and never could be such a thing as a constitutional principle of nondelegation—a proposition that is belied by all available evidence about the meaning of the Constitution. Accordingly, the nondelegation principle, which is textually embodied in the command that all executory laws be "necessary and proper," constrains the substance of congressional enactments. Certain powers simply cannot be given to executive (or judicial) officials, because those powers are *legislative* in character.

A governmental function is not legislative, however, merely because it involves some element of policymaking discretion: it has long been understood that some such exercises of discretion can fall within the definition of the executive power. The task is therefore to determine when a statute that vests discretionary authority in an executive (or judicial) officer has crossed the line from a necessary and proper implementing statute to an unnecessary and/or improper delegation of distinctively legislative power. While I cannot complete that task here, the core of the Constitution's nondelegation principle can be expressed as follows: Congress must make whatever policy decisions are sufficiently important to the statutory scheme at issue so that Congress must make them. Although this circular formulation may seem farcical, it recognizes that a statute's required degree of specificity depends on context, takes seriously the well-recognized

---

[41]The President, through the presentment and veto provisions, see U. S. Const. art. I, § 7, cls. 2–3, is given a sui generis role in the legislative process that defies classification along tripartite lines. See Gary Lawson, *Territorial Governments and the Limits of Formalism*, 78 Cal.L.Rev. 853, 858 n. 19 (1990). The Vice President is made an officer of the Senate and is given the power to break ties in that body. See U.S. Const. art. I, § 3, cl. 4. The Senate is given the seemingly judicial power to try impeachments. See id. art. I, § 3, cl. 6. Certain other powers, such as the power to make treaties and to appoint national officers, are shared among the various departments. See id. art. II, § 2, cl. 2.

distinction between legislating and gap-filling, and corresponds reasonably well to judicial application of the nondelegation principle in the first 150 years of the nation's history. If it does not precisely capture the true constitutional rule of nondelegation, it is a plausible first approximation.

In any event, it is a much better approximation of the true constitutional rule than is the post-New Deal positive law. The Supreme Court has not invalidated a congressional statute on nondelegation grounds since 1935. This has not been for lack of opportunity. The United States Code is filled with statutes that create little Goodness and Niceness Commissions—each confined to a limited subject area such as securities,[51] broadcast licenses,[52] or (my personal favorite) imported tea.[53] These statutes are easy kills under any plausible interpretation of the Constitution's nondelegation principle. The Supreme Court, however, has rejected so many delegation challenges to so many utterly vacuous statutes that modern nondelegation decisions now simply recite these past holdings and wearily move on.[54] Anything short of the Goodness and Niceness Commission, it seems, is permissible.

The rationale for this virtually complete abandonment of the nondelegation principle is simple: the Court believes—possibly correctly—that the modern administrative state could not function if Congress were actually required to make a significant percentage of the fundamental policy decisions. Judicial opinions candidly acknowledge this rationale for permitting delegations. For example, the majority in *Mistretta v. United States* declared that "our jurisprudence has been driven by a practical understanding that in our increasingly complex society, replete with ever changing and more technical problems, Congress simply cannot do its job absent an ability to delegate power under broad general directives."[57] When faced with a choice between the Constitution and the structure of modern governance, the Court has had no difficulty making the choice.

* * *

---

[51]See 15 U.S.C. § 78j(b) (1988) (proscribing the use or employment, "in connection with the purchase or sale of any security . . ., [of] any manipulative or deceptive device or contrivance in contravention of such rules and regulations as the [Securities and Exchange] Commission may prescribe as necessary or appropriate in the public interest or for the protection of investors").

[52]See 47 U.S.C. § 307(a) (1988) (prescribing that the Federal Communications Commission shall grant broadcast licenses to applicants "if public convenience, interest, or necessity will be served thereby").

[53]See 21 U.S.C. § 41 (1988) (forbidding the importation of "any merchandise as tea which is inferior in purity, quality, and fitness for consumption to the standards" set by the Secretary of Health and Human Services).

[54]See, e.g., Touby v. United States, 111 S.Ct. 1752, 1756 (1991); Skinner v. Mid–America Pipeline Co., 490 U.S. 212, 218–24 (1989); Mistretta v. United States, 488 U.S. 361, 378–79 (1989).

[57][488 U.S. 361, 372 (1989).]

C. The Death of the Unitary Executive

Article II states that "[t]he executive Power shall be vested in a President of the United States of America." Although the precise contours of this "executive Power" are not entirely clear, at a minimum it includes the power to execute the laws of the United States. Other clauses of the Constitution, such as the requirement that the President "take Care that the Laws be faithfully executed," assume and constrain this power to execute the laws, but the Article II Vesting Clause is the constitutional source of this power—just as the Article III Vesting Clause is the constitutional source of the federal judiciary's power to decide cases.

Significantly, that power to execute the laws is vested, not in the executive department of the national government, but in "a President of the United States of America." The Constitution thus creates a *unitary executive*. Any plausible theory of the federal executive power must acknowledge and account for this vesting of the executive power in the person of the President.

Of course, the President cannot be expected personally to execute all laws. Congress, pursuant to its power to make all laws "necessary and proper for carrying into Execution" the national government's powers, can create administrative machinery to assist the President in carrying out legislatively prescribed tasks. But if a statute vests discretionary authority directly in an agency official (as do most regulatory statutes) rather than in the President, the Article II Vesting Clause seems to require that such discretionary authority be subject to the President's control.

This model of presidential power is not without its critics. Indeed, most contemporary scholars believe that Congress may vest discretionary authority in subordinate officers free from direct presidential control,[66] and early American history and practice reflect this view to a considerable extent.[67] Nonetheless, the Vesting Clause inescapably vests "the executive Power" directly and solely in the person of the President. Accordingly, scholars sometimes deny that the Article II Vesting Clause is a grant of

---

[66]See, e.g., Thomas O. McGarity, Presidential Control of Regulatory Agency Decisionmaking, 36 Am.U.L.Rev. 443, 465–72 (1987) (arguing that Congress "may provide that the President may not substitute his judgment . . . for that of the official to whom Congress has delegated decisionmaking power"); *cf.* Lawrence Lessig & Cass R. Sunstein, *The President and the Administration*, 94 Colum.L.Rev. 1, 55 (1994) (claiming that, under an originalist interpretation of the Constitution, "Congress has wide discretion to vest [administrative powers] in officers operating under or beyond the plenary power of the President").

[67]Several legal scholars have compiled impressive lists of historical materials suggesting that many early legal actors and writers did not contemplate any wide-ranging presidential power of supervision. See Lessig & Sunstein, supra note 66, at 15–17; Morton Rosenberg, *Presidential Control of Agency Rulemaking: An Analysis of Constitutional Issues That May Be Raised by Executive Order 12,291*, 23 Ariz.L.Rev. 1199, 1205–10 (1981).

power to the President to execute the laws,[68] but none has yet adequately rebutted the compelling textual and structural arguments for reading the Vesting Clause as a grant of power—a grant of power specifically and exclusively to "a President of the United States."

* * *

The death of the unitary executive cannot be traced to the New Deal revolution. The First Congress, in the so-called Decision of 1789, engaged in one of the most spirited and sophisticated debates on executive power in the nation's history, but did not once focus on a presidential power to make discretionary decisions or to veto actions by subordinates. Moreover, many Attorneys General in the nineteenth century affirmatively denied that the President must always have the power to review decisions by subordinates. The absence of a functioning unitary executive principle, however, may well have made the Revolution of 1937 possible. Judging from the political conflict that is often generated by disputes between Congress and the President, it is at least arguable that Congress would never have granted agencies their current, almost-limitless powers if Congress recognized that such power had to be directly under the control of the President.

* * *

E. The Death of Separation of Powers

The constitutional separation of powers is a means to safeguard the liberty of the people. In Madison's famous words, "[t]he accumulation of all powers, legislative, executive, and judiciary, in the same hands, whether of one, a few, or many, and whether hereditary, self-appointed, or elective, may justly be pronounced the very definition of tyranny."[93] The destruction of this principle of separation of powers is perhaps the crowning jewel of the modern administrative revolution. Administrative agencies routinely combine all three governmental functions in the same body, and even in the same people within that body.

Consider the typical enforcement activities of a typical federal agency—for example, of the Federal Trade Commission. The Commission promulgates substantive rules of conduct. The Commission then considers whether to authorize investigations into whether the Commission's rules have been violated. If the Commission authorizes an investigation, the investigation is conducted by the Commission, which reports its findings to the Commission. If the Commission thinks that the Commission's findings warrant an enforcement action, the Commission issues a complaint. The Commission's complaint that a Commission rule has been violated is then

---

[68]See Lessig & Sunstein, supra note 66, at 46–52; McGarity, supra note 66, at 466; Rosenberg, supra note 67, at 1209.

[93]The Federalist No. 47, at 301 (James Madison) (Clinton Rossiter ed., 1961).

prosecuted by the Commission and adjudicated by the Commission. This Commission adjudication can either take place before the full Commission or before a semi-autonomous Commission administrative law judge. If the Commission chooses to adjudicate before an administrative law judge rather than before the Commission and the decision is adverse to the Commission, the Commission can appeal to the Commission. If the Commission ultimately finds a violation, then, and only then, the affected private party can appeal to an Article III court. But the agency decision, even before the bona fide Article III tribunal, possesses a very strong presumption of correctness on matters both of fact and of law.

This is probably the most jarring way in which the administrative state departs from the Constitution, and it typically does not even raise eyebrows. The post-New Deal Supreme Court has never seriously questioned the constitutionality of this combination of functions in agencies.

MARTIN S. FLAHERTY, THE MOST DANGEROUS BRANCH

105 YALE L.J. 1725, 1727–30, 1802–10, 1816–22, 1824–28, 1832–36 (1996).

The dominance of executive power ought by now, to lift a phrase from Charles Black, to be a matter of common notoriety not so much for judicial notice as for background knowledge of educated people who live in this republic.[6] The point holds, moreover, notwithstanding Congress's recent resurgence, especially when the larger historical context is kept in mind. Over one hundred years ago, Woodrow Wilson could still write that "[t]he balances of the Constitution are for the most part only ideal. For all practical purposes . . . Congress [is] predominant over its so-called co-ordinate branches."[7] Nor, ordinarily, did this state of affairs produce constitutional conflict or appreciable case law. But the government Wilson knew, "congressional government," is long gone, and with it the inter-branch harmony that once prevailed. Today the President can treat even the most meager electoral victory as a national mandate to a degree unthinkable in Wilson's day. Even after the Cold War, the President commands the largest military establishment on earth and the massive security apparatus that goes with it. Finally, the President maintains either direct or primary control over the "administrative state," the colossal array of agencies that legislate and adjudicate under any but the broadest definition of "executing" the laws. The Supreme Court has little legitimately to say about claims to electoral mandates. It has chosen to say little about executive deployment of the military. Thanks to repeated congressional challenges, however, it

---

[6]Charles L. Black, Jr., *The Lawfulness of the Segregation Decisions*, 69 Yale L.J. 421, 426 (1960).

[7]Woodrow Wilson, Congressional Government: A Study in American Politics 52 (The Legal Classics Library 1993) (1885).

has said a great deal about the President's authority to carry out laws at home. The more it has said, however, the less it has made clear.

* * *

* * * The Founders embraced separation of powers to further several widely agreed-upon goals. Among these were certain ends or values that today are commonly at the center of separation of powers debates, including balance among the branches, responsibility or accountability to the electorate, and energetic, efficient government. Currently, these goals are seen to be almost necessarily in tension, with balance cutting against a unitary presidency but accountability and energy cutting in its favor. The light shed by the Founding suggests that this need not be the case. On the one hand, an examination of the period only confirms the foundational importance of balance. In this light, the emergence of the administrative state renders congressional regulation of the executive branch more crucial than ever before, especially since Congress enjoyed extensive regulatory authority even when it was still the most dangerous branch. On the other hand, a better understanding of the Founding undermines current thinking about accountability and energy. Contrary to the usual scholarly assumptions—including those of Lessig and Sunstein[a]—the Founders sought to tame, not further empower, those divisions of government that claim a special responsiveness to the electorate. On this basis, the need for congressional regulation becomes imperative precisely because of the modern presidency's claim to electoral accountability. Conversely, many of the Founders did extol separation of powers as a way to accord government greater energy, much as modern constitutional thinkers do today. Viewed in context, however, that commitment was modest, especially given the sheer scope of modern governmental activity.

These basic strategies—first, a faithful reconstruction of the doctrine's origins, and second, the attendant reconciliation of the purposes underlying separation of powers—confirm the initial intuition that there is something anomalous about the judiciary shielding what is now the most powerful office in the nation. These approaches refute the idea that the Founders had developed a thoroughgoing, tripartite baseline capable of resolving modern controversies. They demonstrate that balance favors a flexible approach, that accountability bolsters this view, and that energy in the modern context is largely irrelevant. They point, finally, toward doctrinal bases for congressional regulation that are more thoroughgoing than anything currently mooted in separation of powers scholarship.

* * *

[a]Lawrence Lessig & Cass R. Sunstein, *The President and the Administration*, 94 Colum. L. Rev. 1 (1994). Eds.

III. THE FOUNDING: INVENTING SEPARATION OF POWERS

1. The Federalist "Case" for Functionalism

More than any other argument, the Federalists defended the Constitution's at times quirky division of powers as the surest way to achieve the elusive goal of balance. In doing this, they assumed an object that by now nearly every American valued, however much they disagreed about the scope of the powers being divided or the extent of the division. Federalists and Anti-Federalists, both famous and obscure, proclaimed over and over that separation of powers would prevent the concentration of too much authority in any one branch of government and thus prevent tyranny. Hamilton put the point concisely at the New York Convention, declaring: "The true principle of government is this—make the system complete in its structure, give a perfect proportion and balance to its parts, and the powers you give it will never affect your security." "Brutus," an Anti-Federalist, concurred:

> The judgment of the learned Montesquieu will be found analogous to these [separation of powers clauses] of Virginia and Massachusetts. This able writer says, "whenever the legislative and executive powers are united in the same person or in the same body of magistracy, there can be then no liberty; because apprehensions may arise that the same monarch or senate should enact tyrannical laws to execute them in a tyrannical manner. Again, there is no liberty if the power of judging be not separated from the legislative and executive powers."

"A gentleman in New-York," another Anti-Federalist, put the matter more tersely, stating, "To vest judicial, legislative, and executive powers in the same body, is admitted by all constitutional writers as parental of aristocratic tyranny, or single despotism." James Wilson did not disagree, declaring in almost identical terms that, "[t]o have placed in the [Confederation Congress], the legislative, the executive, and judicial authority, all of which are essential to the general government, would indubitably have produced the severest despotism."

Where the Federalists and Anti-Federalists parted company was on the question of whether the Constitution's approach to the doctrine struck the proper balance. The Federalists had no doubt, at least in public. Much of the time they preached to their own choir, praising the Constitution's enhancement of the executive and judiciary as a response to the legislative excesses that had prompted the Federal Convention in the first place. Madison sounded this theme in classic fashion in The Federalist. Noting that "[t]he legislative department is everywhere extending the sphere of its activity and drawing all power into its impetuous vortex,"[412] he lamented

---

[412]The Federalist No. 48 * * *.

the comparative disadvantages of both the executive and judiciary. The remedy for this was not absolute separation of governmental power. Instead, it was "to divide the legislature into different branches;. . . . [a]s the weight of the legislative authority requires that it should be thus divided, the weakness of the executive may require, on the other hand, that it should be fortified," in particular, by the President's qualified veto.[414] To this prescription, Hamilton would add his famous defense of the Constitution's enhancement of judicial power in The Federalist No. 78.

At the same time, the Federalists also argued that the Constitution's remedies did not make the legislature too weak. Many Anti-Federalists, unconvinced that the state legislatures had gotten out of hand to begin with, raised fears that the proposed framework tipped the balance toward the newly fortified branches, especially the executive. Against this charge, Federalists typically contrasted the President's limited powers with those of their former monarch. Tench Coxe, for example, argued that "[t]he king of England has legislative power, while our President can only use it when the other servants of the people are divided," and later concluded that "[f]rom such a servant with powers so limited and transitory, there can be no danger, especially when we consider the solid foundations on which our national liberties are immovably fixed by other provisions of this excellent Constitution." Here, as before, the Federalist defense did not assume that a complete division of powers, precisely delineated, was an end in itself. Rather, the Federalist argument turned on whether the division actually made advanced the functional goal of balance.

Balance was just the beginning. Federalists contended that their new Constitution also promoted accountability—not the simple, legislative accountability of the first state constitutions but the more complex, joint accountability advocated by the reformers who sought to change those early frameworks. In part for this reason, Federalists like Tench Coxe wasted no time in pointing out that under their approach to separation of powers, "[t]he people will remain . . . the fountain of power and public honour." "The president, the Senate, and the House of Representatives," Coxe continued, "will be the channels through which the stream will flow—but it will flow from the people, and from them only." Moreover, Wilson noted,

> The executive, and judicial power are now drawn from the same source, are now animated by the same principles, and are now directed to the same ends, with the legislative authority: they who execute, and they who administer the laws, are so much the servants, and therefore as much the friends of the people, as those who make them.

As Wood observes, the consequences of this system not only contributed to balance but to a new type of shared, interbranch, governmental

[414]The Federalist No. 51 * * *.

responsiveness: "Because the Federalists regarded the people as 'the only legitimate fountain of power,' . . . no department was theoretically more popular and hence more authoritative than any other."[420] More specifically, no longer could any department claim an exclusive popular mandate to justify ill-considered or oppressive measures, as legislative departments had done in the preceding decade.

[T]he diffusion of accountability represented by the Federalist separation of powers meant that only a sustained and widespread popular desire could serve as the legitimate basis for government action.

But the Federalists sought more than gridlock. For all that it promoted balance and expanded accountability, separation of powers was also intended to ensure that government had enough energy to do what it had to do once it did decide to act. As Hamilton told the New York Convention, "[T]o secure ourselves from despotism . . . certainly was a valuable [object]." He continued, "but, sir, there is another object, equally important . . .: I mean a principle of *strength* and *stability* in the organization of our government, and *vigor* in its operations." Though Hamilton was perhaps the best exponent of vigorous government, Federalists generally agreed with his diagnosis.

Separation of powers, at least the Constitution's version, advanced governmental efficiency mainly though the executive. Toward this end, Wood notes, "[n]ot only was the president to be made independent of the legislature, but he was to be granted an extraordinary amount of power."[425] * * *

Perhaps the most thorough expression of the Federalist position came from Hamilton in The Federalist No. 70: "The ingredients which constitute energy in the executive are unity; duration; an adequate provision for its support; and competent powers" (as opposed to some fixed notion of "executive power"). * * * Hamilton praised the Constitution for creating a single President, because "[d]ecision, activity, secrecy, and dispatch will generally characterize the proceedings of one man in a much more eminent degree than the proceedings of any greater number." * * * Nowhere, however, did he argue that the need for energy requires absolute unity below the unitary Chief Executive. In fact, later in The Federalist he assumed that the approval of the Senate is required before the President can remove executive appointees, even though the document is silent on the matter.[431] In the end, the constitutional goal was not complete unity but sufficient energy. Against the failures of the state governments and the Articles, a unitary President with enhanced powers sufficed. Too many

[420][Gordon S. Wood, The Creation of the American Republic, 1776–1787, at 550 (1969).]

[425][Id. at 551.]

[431]The Federalist No. 77 * * *.

people retained too many Whiggish fears for widespread agreement on anything more.

2. The Federalist "Case" Against Formalism

Little in the ratification debates supports the view that either the Federalists or the Anti-Federalists presupposed that the Constitution reflected a more thoroughgoing, formalist approach to separation of powers. Much refutes it. As with the Convention, the records yield nothing approaching a consensus either as to what separation of powers entailed or what the powers themselves included beyond the basic values the doctrine was to serve. Perhaps more than the Convention, the evidence suggests that the goal of dividing powers no longer commanded the support it once did, even assuming that it was possible to define those powers with precision. Challenged by their opponents, many leading Federalists not only acknowledged but celebrated the ways in which the Constitution mixed powers, the better to serve such more fundamental ends as balance, accountability, and energy.

Especially striking is the lack of direct evidence for the formalist position. As had been true for over a decade, the Americans who debated the Constitution freely tossed about such terms as "legislative power," "executive power," "judicial power," "executive unity," and "separation" or "division" of powers. As had also been true, rarely did anyone define what these terms meant with any precision. Still less frequently did they address issues that today are at the center of separation of powers disputes. It could be, of course, that silence on these matters simply means that there existed such a deep-seated consensus on these terms that no one thought elaboration was necessary. Or it could be that these general terms signalled only the most basic agreement while masking profound disputes and uncertainties. Given the historical context, the formalist possibility is untenable.

But the point hardly needs to rest on negative inference. Madison, for one, recognized precisely the true state of affairs when he remarked to Jefferson that, "[e]ven the boundaries between the Executive, Legislative and Judiciary powers, though in general so strongly marked in themselves, consist in many instances of mere shades of difference." Time and time again, Federalists and Anti-Federalists alike pointed to the numerous ways that the Constitution violated a strict separation of powers even on the assumption that the powers to be divided could be clearly defined. * * * The Anti-Federalists keenly understood this and cried foul. Typical were the remarks of an "Officer of the Late Continental Army," who criticized the Constitution on the ground that "the LEGISLATIVE and EXECUTIVE powers are not kept separate as every one of the American constitutions declares they ought to be; but they are mixed in a manner entirely novel and unknown, even to the constitution of Great Britain."

[T]he Federalists extolled mixture as a means that at points better served the purposes attributed to separation of powers. "Is there any one branch," Hamilton asked the New York Convention, "in which the whole legislative and executive powers are lodged?" The answer:

> No. The legislative authority is lodged in three distinct branches, properly balanced; the executive is divided between two branches; and the judicial is still reserved for an independent body, who hold their office during good behavior. This organization is so complex, so skillfully contrived, that it is next to impossible that an impolitic or wicked measure should pass the scrutiny with success.

* * *

It would fall to "Publius," in this case Madison, to develop the point most powerfully. A rigid formalist separation of powers, he explained, misconstrued Montesquieu, the British Constitution on which he drew, and the early state constitutions:

> [Montesquieu's] meaning, as his own words import, and still more conclusively as illustrated by the example in his eye, can amount to no more than this, that where the *whole* power of one department is exercised by the same hands which possess the *whole* power of another department, the fundamental principles of a free constitution are subverted. . . .
>
> . . . .
>
> If we look into the constitutions of the several States we find that, notwithstanding the emphatical and, in some instances, the unqualified terms in which this axiom has been laid down, there is not a single instance in which the several departments of power have been kept absolutely separate and distinct.[441]

The trick of government was not to assign three clearly conceived types of governmental authority to three discrete branches, but to seek the most sensible degree of division and linkage. As Madison put it, "[U]nless these departments be so far connected and blended as to give to each a constitutional control over the others, the degree of separation which the maxim requires, as essential to a free government, can never in practice be duly maintained."[442] But it was impossible to achieve the proper blend through setting it out extensively in advance (and still less, it follows, by presuming it implicitly). The Critical Period showed that "a mere demarcation on parchment of the constitutional limits of the several departments is not a sufficient guard against those encroachments which lead to a tyrannical

---

[441] The Federalist No. 47 * * *.

[442] The Federalist No. 48 * * *.

concentration of all the powers of government in the same hands."[443] Ultimately, the solution lay not in any particular division, express or presumed, but sounded mainly in process. "[T]he defect must be supplied," Madison concluded, "by so contriving the interior structure of the government as that its several constituent parts may, by their mutual relations, be the means of keeping each other in their proper places." In this way separation of powers would ensure that the government "will be controlled by itself."[445] So long as the system did this, it was doing its job.

IV. FOUNDING VALUES TWO HUNDRED YEARS LATER

* * *

B. Changed Circumstances

As a general matter, developments in American government over the past two centuries undercut the modern formalist case still further. For starters, "more than 200 years of practice under the Constitution suggest that the inherent fluidity and the system of checks and balances render a strict separation impossible,"[477] a point that scholars as diverse as McDonald, Corwin, Lessig and Sunstein, and Susan Low Bloch have suggested.[478] That phenomenon would be dispositive assuming that evolving custom should count as a source for constitutional norms. For present purposes, however, more important are the ways "more than 200 years of practice" affect the application of norms derived from the Founding itself. Those two centuries of change have profoundly reshaped the context in which each of the principal Founding values so far considered are to be implemented today if they are to be implemented at all.

1. Balance in an Executive Vortex

By far the greatest changes concern the goal of balance, the Founding's most important separation of powers value. As Forrest McDonald recently observed, "[i]t is a commonplace among students of the presidency that the two-plus centuries of American experience under the Constitution have been characterized by a general if irregular drift of authority and responsibility toward the executive branch."[480] This is not to say that Congress cannot, on occasion, still seize the initiative when, as now, it benefits from an effective leadership and a rudderless Chief Executive. But from a larger

---

[443]Id. * * *

[445][The Federalist No. 51.]

[477][Forrest McDonald, The American Presidency: An Intellectual History 180 n.35 (1994).]

[478]See [Edward S. Corwin, The President: Office and Powers 76–84 (1940)], McDonald, supra note [477], at 180 n.35; Susan Low Bloch, *The Early Role of the Attorney General in Our Constitutional Scheme: In the Beginning There Was Pragmatism*, 1989 Duke L.J. 561, 618–51; Lessig & Sunstein, supra note 17, at 14–22.

[480]McDonald, supra note [477], at 277. * * *

perspective the overall drift has been inexorable and shows few signs of any long-term shift. It often surprises students to discover Madison's statement * * * that "[t]he legislative department is . . . drawing all power into its impetuous vortex."[482] Were Madison to consider the same problem in light of subsequent developments, he would have little choice but to conclude that if there were any one branch against which "the people ought to indulge all their jealousy and exhaust all their precautions,"[483] it would be the executive.

* * *

* * * [The most clearcut shift toward presidential power] is, of course, the grand-scale emergence of executive and independent agencies, the "fourth branch of government" also known as the "administrative state." As the nation's problems grew, Progressives and New Dealers believed that so too should the federal response. * * * Once more the net beneficiary would be the President, the nominal head of the agencies that would both execute and make policy. But unlike many of the transfers considered so far, this one crossed bright doctrinal lines. Previously, a formalist-minded Supreme Court had held that, while Congress could enact laws that required execution, it could not franchise away its legislative power by passing laws that required broad-scale policymaking. Twice the Court invoked this "nondelegation doctrine" to strike down congressional giveaways.[506] These were, however, the last times the Court tried to keep the floodgates shut.

* * *

* * * With the New Deal, and the attendant death of the nondelegation doctrine, the giveaway of what had been seen as legislative authority (or something close) became massive. Between 1934 and 1936 alone, Congress established the Securities and Exchange Commission, the National Labor Relations Board, the Bituminous Coal Commission, and the United States Maritime Commission, to name a few. This trend, moreover, has generally accelerated during the five decades since F.D.R.'s death. At least as important as the scope of modern delegation, however, is to whom the power has been delegated. If there has been any net beneficiary of Congress's abdication of authority, it has been the President. In formal terms, Presidents ultimately exercise the appointments and removal powers over the heads of both executive and independent agencies (a distinction that is becoming increasingly difficult to maintain). Informally, Presidents influence agencies through ex parte and secret contacts and through executive agencies established to coordinate agency activities. This is not to

[482]The Federalist No. 48 * * *.

[483][Id.]

[506]A.L.A. Schechter Poultry Corp. v. United States, 295 U.S. 495, 541–42 (1935); Panama Refining Co. v. Ryan, 293 U.S. 388, 430 (1935).

say that Congress lacks methods of influencing agency conduct. It is to say, however, that a substantial measure of power that under the nondelegation doctrine would by definition have resided in Congress has since fallen to the President.

Any approach that ignores changes bearing upon ongoing constitutional commitments overlooks them not so much at its own peril, but at the peril of the commitments it purports to further. Where the commitment is balance, even the most glancing survey indicates that the executive branch long ago supplanted its legislative counterpart as the most powerful—and therefore most dangerous—in the sense that the Founders meant. This shift toward presidential government suggests that at a minimum we need an approach that would permit Congress to maintain some control over the authority the Court now permits it to delegate away to the administrative state. More broadly, this shift implies that invoking separation of powers to invalidate congressional attempts to keep pace with the presidency is not only wrong headed but, more important still, fundamentally unfaithful to our founding values.

* * *

2. Accountability and the Populist Presidency

Two hundred years of practice have also affected the Founding commitment to accountability, properly recaptured. On this view, accountability should no longer be the province of one branch of government but instead should rest with both houses of the legislature, the executive, and, less directly, even the judiciary. In this way, separation of powers tamed accountability by ensuring that government, or any part of it, could threaten liberty in the name of last year's election results. It also refined accountability by ensuring that government action could not proceed legitimately only if it rested on sustained, widespread, and deliberative support as reflected in the agreement of several components of the government, in turn reflecting several soundings of popular will through staggered congressional and presidential elections.

If any branch at first seemed the most likely to claim electoral mandates for tyrannical or precipitous actions, it was the legislature. By contrast, the Founders generally conceived of the presidency not first and foremost as a representative post, but as a relatively apolitical award for men who had demonstrated extraordinary virtue and character through selfless public service. No longer. As unitarians are quick to point out, at present no elected official plausibly claims to be more representative or accountable than the President. He, or one day she, can do this on the strength of elections that, far from filtered affairs envisioned by the electoral college process, long ago evolved into tournaments that are in part plebiscite, in larger part popularity contests.

* * *

In this light, accountability appears as nearly the opposite of the trump card that proponents, and even many opponents, of the unitary executive take it to be. As with balance, the changes in government practice since the Founding cut against, not for, executive power. In each case the trick is to avoid confusing original applications of a constitutional norm with the norm itself, properly reconstructed. Contrary to the usual assumption, here was not the rudimentary accountability that modern unitarians extol. Instead, the Founders reconceptualized the idea to render it more safe and more reflective of considered popular choice. Initially, Congress put the greatest pressure on this more sophisticated commitment by virtue of its superior representativeness. As unitarians are the first to argue, this is exactly the area in which the President now advances a comparable, if not more compelling, claim. Any response faithful to the Founding, therefore, should greet this development not as a cause for celebration but concern.

* * *

3. Energy and Governmental Activity

Modern government at its most lethargic is energetic beyond the Founders' most reckless speculations. To take one not entirely symbolic measure, from 1789 to 1861 Congress on average enacted 60 public bills and 6.4 public joint resolutions per year—and each of these averaged less than a single page. By 1992 the number had climbed to 609 bills and 50 resolutions, with one act alone running over 1000 pages. * * *

* * *

An incalculable number of these policies could not exist without one segment of government yet to be directly considered in this regard—the administrative state. Here the not-entirely-symbolic measure is the Code of Federal Regulations (CFR). In its first year of publication, significantly 1939, the CFR consisted of sixteen volumes; last year it had expanded to 200 volumes, exceeding 60,000 pages combined. As these numbers suggest, delegation may have come about because the world became too complicated for Congress to handle alone, but it also enabled Congress to address more than it ever otherwise would have on its own. In this regard, the Progressives and New Dealers who advocated agencies for their expertise, efficiency, and, in turn, energy were right all along. This is not to ignore that in several other regards they were not. An enormous literature chronicles the ways in which agencies have not lived up to their original billing. They can be "captured" by the industries they purport to regulate. They are subject to "triangulation," by which the agency, Congress, and the President produce stalemate. They are, more simply, often overstaffed, wasteful, and inert. All of this may well be accurate, but it begs the relevant question. If the issue is fidelity to Founding concerns about energy, agencies—warts and all—provide one more reason for constitutional scholars to look elsewhere for problems to lose sleep over.

* * *

C. Separation of Powers Doctrine Restored

* * *

2. Applications

* * *

a. The Legislative Veto

Many who defended the legislative veto suggested that the mechanism comported with "original intent," but few if any among them realized how strong their case was—strong enough, in fact, to merit the device's resurrection. As Justice White made clear in *Chadha*, the legislative veto was a classic response to the administrative state.[546] In scores of instances, Congress realistically had to, and constitutionally could, relinquish substantial policymaking authority that could variously be termed legislative, executive, adjudicative, administrative, or "quasi" variants of all of the above. Yet fearful of ceding too much power, particularly to the executive branch, Congress reserved vestigial authority to reverse policy determinations made by whatever entity now exercised the power delegated away. In practical terms, this type of reservation meant that Congress—or more problematically, either House—no longer needed a two-thirds vote to rescind certain decisions but could instead do so with a mere majority. The question remains: Is what was once a classic response a constitutional one from the viewpoint of fidelity?

There is no reason why it should not be, least of all a formalist one. Then again, this dispute, unlike others, does implicate fairly precise requirements. Article I, Section 7 provides that "Every Bill which shall have passed the House of Representatives and the Senate, shall, before it become a Law, be presented to the President of the United States." The strictures of bicameralism and presentment, however, do not apply just because they exist. To the contrary, fidelity points the other way on at least two counts—one contingent, the other, unconditional. As many have argued before and after *Chadha*, it is difficult to find an analytic difference between the power Congress may permissibly give away in general and the portion of that same power it opts to reserve in certain instances. Absent some other reason, either power should qualify as "legislative," and thus trigger bicameralism and presentment, or neither should. Since the Supreme

---

[546] INS v. Chadha, 462 U.S. 919, 967–74 (White, J., dissenting) (tracing historical use of legislative veto to resolve major constitutional and policy differences).

Court long ago gave up subjecting delegated policymaking to Article I, Section 7, so too should it abandon doing the same to reservations of this same authority.

In addition, and perhaps overlooked, the Bicameralism and Presentment Clauses cut against application here precisely because they are express. Recall that the developments leading to the Constitution's text indicate that its drafters at most offered a sketch of separation of powers, inked in only at the top of each branch, and even then not fully filled in. This context in turn suggests that the two clauses at issue are best read as speaking not to every governmental action that changes the legal relations between parties, which even in the eighteenth century would have been incalculable. Rather, it suggests that the clauses address departures in policy—including a system of joint oversight for the implementation of those departures—which by virtue of their novelty would be important enough to require the attention of both political branches. Put another way, neither the text nor its history specifies the exact relationship among the branches apart from certain requirements at the framework's apex. It follows that those requirements should not be extended below that apex to such matters as implementation, which the document in most other areas leaves to the political branches to work out among themselves.

Conversely, there is every functionalist reason to look favorably upon the legislative veto, at least with regard to those functions championed at the Founding. First, consider balance, the centerpiece of the system. Given that balance was a primary purpose for dividing government authority, and given further that the executive has supplanted the legislature as the branch posing the greatest threat to this balance, it follows that any jurist faithful to the past should applaud, not deride, legislative attempts to maintain that balance, especially when those attempts appear in part of a package delegating still more power to the executive.

Now turn to accountability, ostensibly the unitarian strong suit. Yet here, contrary to unitarians left and right, the given from history is not unmediated responsiveness to a single electorate by a single branch, but coordinate responsibility to the people as reflected in several elections. On this score, the last thing on a judge's mind should be preventing Congress from exercising some vestigial control over policymaking decisions rendered by executive and administrative officials who are otherwise answerable to the President, the officer who today makes the most plausible yet problematic claim to an electoral mandate. * * *

Nor, finally, does a concern for energy preclude the device. For all of their worries about "democratic despotism," the Constitution's supporters to be sure prized a government that would possess sufficient vigor to act. As an initial matter, it is far from clear that a legislative veto necessarily frustrates this goal. It may just as easily block executive attempts to suspend an action as impede decision to take them, as *Chadha* itself demonstrates. But suppose that the legislative veto did spell gridlock. In light of the governmental activity made possible by the administrative state, the inefficiency wrought by the legislative veto would have to be crippling before it raised a concern of constitutional proportion. Fifty years of practice under the device suggests that this was hardly the case.

b. Removal

* * *

The removal issue, in fact, exposes formalist analysis at its least grounded. Unlike the legislative veto, arguably no specific text serves as a candidate to determine matters. Absent a "Removals Clause," or something reasonably close, opponents of legislative involvement must retreat to an originalist baseline that assumes that the removal of government officials is categorically an executive task. In this way, unitarians can claim that the removal authority is inherently executive, bootstrap the power to the all-purpose Executive Vesting Clause, or both. Yet such an originalist baseline is precisely what the original understanding does not support. While some of the Founders may have believed that removal was necessarily an executive act, many, including the proexecutive Hamilton, did not—too many to assume sufficient agreement on the matter. Rather, the Constitution's silence left the issue, as it did so many others, to the political processes that it explicitly set forth.

By contrast, limitations on executive removal authority comport with those values that did initially command widespread support—or at least they comport with modern values. Start again by considering balance. As the *Humphrey's* Court recognized, preventing Congress from imposing neutral restrictions on the dismissal of "independent" agency officials would accord the President a powerful weapon for controlling administrative policymaking, even as Congress was ceding even more policymaking control to such officials.[554] As Brandeis earlier recognized[555]—and as the Court came to appreciate in *Morrison*—a similar threat to balance may arise from unrestricted presidential control over "purely executive" officials as well. In the abstract, policymaking by officials subject to congressional approval may well present a closer case. In the real world of presidential dominance, however, such arrangements should not necessarily trigger constitutional concern. They may even function to maintain interbranch balance, especially when Congress limits its own removal authority to neutral, "for cause" reasons.

---

[554]See Humphrey's Ex'r v. United States, 295 U.S. 602, 629 (1935).

[555]See Myers v. United States, 272 U.S. 52, 291–95 (1926) (Brandeis, J., dissenting).

As with the legislative veto, a proper reconstruction of accountability turns this value against its usual champions. When the goal is diffusing accountability rather than concentrating it, and when the presidency lays the most plausible claim to the concentrated version, congressional involvement in the critical area of removal should meet with approval instead of invalidation. Moreover, the case is even more compelling than that of the legislative veto. Here, Congress would have no other way of checking officials who, to follow the example, promulgated massive environmental legislation at the President's behest, in a manner consistent with a general statutory delegation but not reflective of an electorate that has yet to back the President's approach fully by returning a compliant House and Senate. Admittedly, the value of joint accountability provides less support for arrangements in which, as in *Bowsher*, Congress itself wields removal authority absent presidential involvement. In this situation, even a "for cause" limitation on removals would not expand the input of the elected branches. That said, the restriction to neutral criteria would at least lessen concern about the concentration of unlimited authority.

As a final matter, efficiency concerns again may not support the device in question, but they do not undermine it either. Once more, it is not clear that removal limitations will always work to produce less government rather than more. Insulated officials may just as easily resist presidential attempts to reduce governmental activity as expand it, a discovery made by President Reagan much to his chagrin. But even if they did produce stasis, removal limitations would not rise to the level of constitutional concern. As with the legislative veto, post-New Deal experience suggests that the mechanism has not exactly impeded the government's ability to act with sufficient energy. Short of that, the extent to which it hampers the President's efficient "chain of command" is simply the price of balance and joint accountability.

H. JEFFERSON POWELL AND JED RUBENFELD, LAYING IT ON THE LINE: A DIALOGUE ON LINE ITEM VETOES AND SEPARATION OF POWERS

47 DUKE L.J. 1171, 1201–09 (1998).

[In this Dialogue two constitutional pundits, **Confident** and **Doubtful**, debate the constitutionality of the Line Item Veto Act of 1996 (struck down by the Supreme Court in *Clinton v. City of New York*, 524 U.S. 417, 118 S.Ct. 2091, 141 L.Ed.2d 393 (1998)). As the Dialogue proceeds, **Confident** becomes **No-Longer-So-Confident** that the Act should be judged unconstitutional.]

No-Longer-So-Confident: * * *. The Line Item Veto Act, for all practical purposes, gives the President substantial lawmaking power. Its hard to believe that that could be constitutionally acceptable. I want to know how that result is constitutionally acceptable. This is the kind of case that requires us to go back to first principles.

Doubtful: Are you prepared to conclude that the entire administrative state is unconstitutional?

No-Longer-So-Confident: No. I didn't mean to go back that far into first principles.

Doubtful: Good. But perhaps we had better say that the constitutionality by and large of the administrative state will be one of our first principles.

No-Longer-So-Confident: Okay.

Doubtful: Perhaps it will also be helpful to clarify the debate we are trying to resolve. I will understand the so-called "formalist" position to hold that the correct approach to separation of powers cases is for a court to look at the governmental action at issue, to decide whether that governmental action is legislative, executive or judicial in nature, and then to make sure that only legislators are performing legislative actions, only executive officers are performing executive actions, and so on. Is that fair?

No-Longer-So-Confident: I think so.

Doubtful: And I will understand the "functionalist" position to hold that the proper approach is not to make these conceptual determinations, but rather to favor overlapping, concurrent jurisdictions among the branches and to ensure that no one branch is vested with too much unilateral power. All right?

No-Longer-So-Confident: All right.

Doubtful: So that we might call formalism a separation of powers approach and functionalism a checks and balances approach. Do you follow me?

No-Longer-So-Confident: Yes, and that's why I've always preferred formalism. Call me old-fashioned, but I think there should be a separation of powers approach to separation of powers cases.

Doubtful: Perhaps so, but what if I now said that the administrative state effectively puts an end to the whole debate between formalism and functionalism in the area of separation of powers? What if I said that you can't be a separation of powers formalist and accept the constitutionality of executive officers performing legislative functions?

No-Longer-So-Confident: I wouldn't be happy with that conclusion at all. There are a lot of formalist cases out there, and I'm not prepared to accept that it follows as a logical matter from the administrative state that they were all wrongly decided. *Chadha* held that legislative vetoes were unconstitutional because they were legislative in nature and therefore had to comply with Section 7.[66] *Bowsher* held that Congress could not retain a removal power over officers exercising executive functions.[67] *Youngstown* held that the President could not unilaterally order his subordinates to take over American steel mills because his doing so was essentially presidential lawmaking.[68] *Metropolitan Washington* held that Members of Congress cannot exercise executive powers.[69] I told you before: I think these cases may have been rightly decided, and I can't believe that the constitutionality of the administrative state somehow dictates a contrary result.

Doubtful: Know what? I think they may have been rightly decided too.

No-Longer-So-Confident: You do?

Doubtful: I really do.

No-Longer-So-Confident: Well, then, don't go defending the Line Item Veto Act by invoking *Morrison*[a] and *Mistretta*.[b] If you accept the formalist cases, you have to admit that the Act vests in the President an essentially legislative function.

Doubtful: On the contrary. [Recall the Court's decision in *Bowsher*, where it] held—as a formalist matter—that the power to exercise budget-cutting discretion over the entire range of federal spending programs was an executive function[.]

No-Longer-So-Confident: * * * How can that function be executive when we know that if Congress performed the very same function, it would be legislative? I mean, if we accept the formalist cases, how can a given governmental action be legislative when Congress performs it, but executive when the executive performs it? And if we can't solve that problem, why isn't the administrative state unconstitutional after all? Now I'm totally perplexed * * *.

Doubtful: I may have an answer to all your riddles. But I have to tell you in advance that I can't agree with you about dismissing *Morrison* and *Mistretta*. I think they may have been rightly decided too.

No-Longer-So-Confident: But you can't. Unless you mean they were rightly decided but wrongly reasoned at a deep level. Is that what you mean?

---

[66]See INS v. Chadha, 462 U.S. 919, 953 (1983).

[67]See Bowsher v. Synar, 478 U.S. 714, 732–34 (1986).

[68]See Youngstown Sheet & Tube Co. v. Sawyer, 343 U.S. 579, 588–89 (1952).

[69]See [Metropolitan Washington Airports Authority v. Citizens for the Abatement of Aircraft Noise, 501 U.S. 252, 277 (1991)].

[a]Morrison v. Olson, 487 U.S. 654 (1988) (upholding constitutionality of the Ethics in Government Act). Eds.

[b]Mistretta v. United States, 488 U.S. 361 (1989) (upholding constitutionality of the United States Sentencing Commission). Eds.

Doubtful: No. I mean that I accept the checks and balances approach to separation of powers questions. And I do so in part because otherwise the administrative state would indeed be unconstitutional.

No-Longer-So-Confident: But you said you thought the formalist cases might have been rightly decided too. I don't understand.

Doubtful: Everyone seems to think that "formalism" and "functionalism," or the separation of powers and checks and balances approaches, are mutually exclusive. I don't.

No-Longer-So-Confident: But they are mutually exclusive. If you took a rigorous separation of powers approach to *Mistretta*, the case would have come out the other way, wouldn't it?

Doubtful: I imagine so.

No-Longer-So-Confident: But you think *Mistretta* was rightly decided?

Doubtful: I do.

No-Longer-So-Confident: But that means you reject the formalist, separation of powers approach.

Doubtful: Definitely not. * * * Here's the key to the riddle. I believe in the formalist separation of powers approach to separation of powers cases when Members of Congress are the governmental actors whose reaching or overreaching is in question.

No-Longer-So-Confident: What? I've never heard of such a thing.

Doubtful: I understand that, but it entirely solves all the difficulties at once. Look at the great formalist cases. In *Chadha*, as you noted, Members of Congress were trying to decide whether an individual alien was deportable under established law. In *Bowsher*, a congressional removal power was at stake. In *Metropolitan Washington*, it was Members of Congress again, trying to sit on an airport authority board. The same point can be about other formalist cases, too. Congressmen cannot exercise executive or judicial powers, but executive and judicial officers may exercise legislative powers. Hence the administrative state is perfectly constitutional, but courts must continue to exercise formalist separation of powers vigilance whenever Congress tries to give its own Members any powers outside the Article I, Section 7 lawmaking process.

No-Longer-So-Confident: But what possible basis is there for drawing such a distinction between Congressmen and the officials of other branches?

Doubtful: The best possible basis: the command of the Constitution. In Article I, Section 6, the Constitution expressly provides that no Member of Congress may serve as an Officer of the United States. And in Article II, Section 2, the Constitution excludes Congress from appointing Officers of the United States. An "Officer of the United States" is a federal official exercising any significant executive or judicial powers. It follows that Members of Congress cannot exercise such powers; nor can they appoint themselves to do so. There is an excellent reason why the Constitution should prevent Members of Congress from serving as officers. The reason comes back to checks and balances.

When an executive or judicial officer exercises legislative power, he can do so only through an authority delegated by Congress and with monies appropriated by Congress. Moreover, when executive officers perform lawmaking functions in administrative agencies, they act not only within confines set forth by Congress, but subject to review by the judiciary. But if Members of Congress were able to give themselves the power to execute, interpret, or adjudicate their own laws, then Congress would have no check on its powers at all. The administrative state is full of checks and balances guarding against an accumulation of excessive unilateral power in the President. But without the distinction on which I insist and which Article I, Section 6 polices, Congress could arrogate to itself unilateral power.

The Constitution erects no similar bar against executive or judicial officers. Of course they cannot serve as Members of Congress, but there is no bar against an executive officer holding a judicial office (remember Chief Justice Marshall) or performing lawmaking duties if such duties have been duly delegated to the officer by Congress.

I think that with this rule in mind, you should be able to solve all your perplexities about modern separation of powers doctrine.

No-Longer-So-Confident: I still have at least one. You neglected to mention *Youngstown*. In *Youngstown*, it was the President—not the Congress—whose actions were at issue, and the opinion of the Court concluded that the President had violated the Constitution by acting legislatively.

Doubtful: Which is why the official opinion of the Court in *Youngstown* has been so entirely superseded in authority by Justice Jackson's much better reasoned concurrence.[80] It's hard to even make sense of the idea that the President acted "legislatively" by seizing the nation's steel mills. Justice Jackson had it right: the President acted unconstitutionally in *Youngstown* because he acted in defiance of congressional directives, without any sustainable claim in the Constitution that he could act unilaterally in such a matter. Indeed, Justice Jackson's opinion in *Youngstown*, which has been so influential, may be said to be the very cornerstone of the anti-unilateral-power, checks and balances approach I have been describing. The President's steel seizure was unconstitutional not because he acted "legislatively," which Presidents may do when so

[80]See id. at 592–655 (Jackson, J., concurring); see also, e.g., Bowsher v. Synar, 478 U.S. 714, 721 (1986) (citing Jackson concurrence).

authorized by Congress, but because he had acted in such a way as to circumvent or ignore any possible check from Congress.

No-Longer-So-Confident: Well, you are too many for me. I can't object to your solution to the separation of powers debate, but I'm not entirely sure I accept it, either. Can you just tell me how things play out for the Line Item Veto Act?

Doubtful: Here is how I think things stand. First, if you accept unquestioningly the formalist cases, your objection to the Act will primarily be that the President has been made into a lawmaker, but this objection is substantially undermined by *Bowsher*, a formalist case holding that the power to go through the federal budget and make discretionary, program-by-program cuts is executive in nature.

Second, if you accept unquestionably the functionalist cases, or if you accept my solution to the debate between formalism and functionalism in separation of powers cases, you will not have much of an objection either, because then the only question will be whether the Act "disrupts the proper balance between the coordinate branches" or whether it "prevents [the affected] Branch from accomplishing its constitutionally assigned function"[83]—tests that are not hard to satisfy and that, I think, the Act quite easily satisfies. Have we come, then, to the end of our conversation?

No-Longer-So-Confident: No, not yet. I admit that my efforts to bring the Act down on formalist grounds have not succeeded. But I'm not prepared to agree with you on your last point. Even if I accept the checks and balances approach, and the more nebulous standards from *Morrison* and *Mistretta*, I think there is still a case to be made against the Line Item Veto Act. The Act vests unilateral power in the President to make budget-cutting decisions. It prevents Congress from accomplishing its constitutionally assigned function of determining the content of federal law.

Doubtful: I don't agree. Congress's ability to determine the content of federal law is entirely unimpaired, including its power to present the President with a take-it-or-leave-it taxing or spending bill. Moreover, the Act is fairly tightly circumscribed. The fact that the President can exercise his line item veto only within the first five days after signing a bill into law is an important restriction. Otherwise, the President would have a weapon he could wield against individual congressmen at any time, by threatening to cancel their favorite spending measures if they don't do his bidding. The limited category of provisions to which the line item power applies is another important restriction. And, Congress is perfectly free to forbid the exercise of the line item veto as to any particular provision, or any particular bill. True, to do so requires the mustering of enough political will to enact legislation, but that's the case any time Congress delegates power

[83]Mistretta v. United States, 488 U.S. 361, 382 (1989).

to the executive and doesn't include an automatic sunset provision. And anyway, even if you put more weight than I think you should on the Act's "imposition" on Congress, it is clear from the modern cases that mere interference with the freedom of action of one of the branches doesn't violate the separation of powers.

B. THE EXECUTIVE POWER: DOMESTIC AFFAIRS

Unlike Article I of the Constitution, which states in some detail the powers given to Congress, Article II is fairly laconic about the President's authority. This generates frequent conflict about the limits of executive power in domestic affairs[1] (which we address in this Section) and foreign affairs[2] (which we take up in Section C).

Henry Monaghan and Edward Corwin discuss the scope of the President's inherent authority in domestic affairs—an issue raised by President Truman's seizure of the nation's steel mills during the Korean War. Monaghan argues that there is no such thing as inherent executive power.[3] He asserts that the text and history of the Constitution envision only a "law enforcement" executive: except for those functions expressly named in Article II, the President gets his power to act from Congress alone. Monaghan concedes that nowadays (since the nondelegation barrier has fallen) the congressional authorization may be exceedingly broad and vague. But as the *Steel Seizure Case* illustrates, we have held fast to the idea that executive officials must have some statutory warrant for their actions. Corwin disagrees. He contends that the President has fairly broad inherent authority. He does not deny the fact of congressional supremacy: the President may not do what Congress has forbidden. But the courts should not try to enforce legal limits on the President's authority through a narrow definition of the idea of "executive power."

HENRY P. MONAGHAN, THE PROTECTIVE POWER OF THE PRESIDENCY

93 COLUM.L.REV. 1, 3–5, 9–10, 12–18, 20–22 (1993).

The Constitution seemingly contemplates only a "law enforcement" Executive; that is, the President simply "executes" the will of Congress.

---

[1]Youngstown Sheet & Tube Co. v. Sawyer, 343 U.S. 579, 72 S.Ct. 863, 96 L.Ed. 1153 (1952).

[2]Dames & Moore v. Regan, 453 U.S. 654, 101 S.Ct. 2972, 69 L.Ed.2d 918 (1981); United States v. Curtiss–Wright Export Corp., 299 U.S. 304, 57 S.Ct. 216, 81 L.Ed. 255 (1936).

[3]In a part of the article not reproduced here, he qualifies this point in one significant way. There is, he concedes, an inherent executive "protective" power which gives the President authority to protect and defend the personnel, property, and instrumentalities of the United States from harm. For examples see In re Neagle, 135 U.S. 1, 10 S.Ct. 658, 34 L.Ed. 55 (1890), and In re Debs, 158 U.S. 564, 15 S.Ct. 900, 39 L.Ed. 1092 (1895).

* * * This conception recognizes little independent presidential authority, at least when presidential authority would directly interfere with pre-existing private rights. * * * *Youngstown Sheet & Tube Co. v. Sawyer (Steel Seizure)*[17] provides the classic illustration of this conception of presidential authority. There, the Supreme Court invalidated President Truman's attempt to seize the nation's steel mills in the face of a threatened strike that Mr. Truman feared would jeopardize the national defense and military operations in the Korean conflict. The Court said that "[i]n the framework of our constitution, the President's power to see that the laws are faithfully executed refutes the idea that he is to be a lawmaker." While the Court did not see the issue before it as involving in any significant way presidential authority in foreign affairs, its premise is fully applicable to presidential conduct in foreign as well as domestic affairs: no independent, free-standing presidential law-making authority exists insofar as the rights of American citizens are concerned.

Well before *Steel Seizure,* however, the reality behind the constitutional theory of the law enforcement Executive had been transformed. Alexander Hamilton wrote that "[t]he *essence of the legislative authority* is to enact laws, or in other words, *to prescribe rules for the regulation of the society.*"[22] In theory, this congressional authority was nondelegable, but—and the "but" is pretty nearly everything—the nondelegation barrier, never very sturdy, has collapsed. Only the fiction remains. The reality is that frequently executive officials shape and reshape the relevant legal rules. Congress itself is no longer required to "prescribe [the] rules for the regulation of society;" it can, instead, transfer much of that task to the executive. As *Steel Seizure* illustrates, what remains of the old constitutional jurisprudence is the quite different requirement that, from the President on down, all executive officials must exhibit some statutory warrant at least when their conduct invades the private rights of American citizens.

* * *

* * * My primary focus is the extent of presidential authority to invade the "private rights" of American citizens *absent legislative authority*—that is, presidential authority independently to alter negatively what in common legal understanding would be viewed as a prior liberty or property baseline. I do not, of course, refer to presidential invasions of constitutionally protected interests, because Congress could confer no such authorization. But the President is not Congress, and so the question persists: to what extent can the President, acting on his or her own, invade the rights of

[17]343 U.S. 579 (1952).

[22]The Federalist No. 75, at 504 (Alexander Hamilton) (Jacob E. Cooke ed., 1961) (emphasis added)[.]

American citizens in circumstances which Congress could—but did not—authorize. As used here, the term "private rights" is conventional in nature. The point of reference is to contemporary legal understanding. * * *

* * *

SOURCES OF THE CONCEPT OF "THE EXECUTIVE POWER"

* * *

A. Historical Antecedents and Textual Sources of Executive Authority

The rich tradition out of which the concept of "The executive Power" sprang is best explored through Locke's notion of executive power, which was in place nearly a full century before ratification of the American Constitution. This vantage point provides insight into the concepts of executive that the Framers understood and transformed.

1. *John Locke's Taxonomy of Executive Power.*—Eighteenth-century English conceptions of legislative authority did not include many of the substantive powers now held wholly or partially by Congress. Moreover, English conceptions did not include the notion of a Parliament actively shaping policy so much as that of a Parliament either assenting to or rejecting policy formulated by the Executive. As St. George Tucker recognized, "the laws do in fact originate with the executive."[46] In allocating the powers of their new national government, the framers of the American Constitution clearly broke new ground; indeed, the American Constitution can be seen as a revolutionary document both in the powers it assigned to Congress and in the "active" role it contemplated for that body. In the process, the Constitution's terminology displaced that of Locke.

In 1690, John Locke described three kinds of powers possessed by the executive department,[47] powers, I should add, that were thought to be compatible with the Glorious Revolution's principle of parliamentary supremacy. First, Locke mentioned executive power in what, for us, is its "law enforcement" sense: "Execution of the Laws." Second, Locke described the federative power: "This therefore contains the Power of War and Peace, Leagues and Alliances, and all the Transactions, with all Persons and Communities without the commonwealth, and may be called Federative, if any one pleases. So the thing be understood, I am indifferent as to the name." Third, and finally, Locke referred to "prerogative" power. This term is not now common in American legal discourse because, for the founding generation, it was invariably a term of opprobrium. While pre-

[46]St. George Tucker, Blackstone's Commentaries with Notes of Reference to the Constitution and Laws of the Federal Government of the United States and of the Commonwealth of Virginia 324 (1970)[.]

[47]See John Locke, Second Treatise of Civil Government §§ 144–148, 155–168, at 106–08, 113–25 (Gateway Editions 1955) (1690).

rogative is often simply a synonym for the exercise of lawfully conferred discretion, Locke posited two other troublesome formulations. Prerogative, he said, is "nothing but the Power of doing public good without a Rule," that is, without statutory authority. Indeed, he went further: "This Power to act according to discretion, for the publick good, without the prescription of the Law, and sometimes even against it, is that which is called Prerogative." Three-quarters of a century later, Blackstone endorsed similar conceptions of prerogative power, although apparently not including the authority to disregard legislation.[55]

Behind the Lockean taxonomy stood important conceptions of the nature of what powers were inherent in the "Executive." With the exception of taxation, most of the great governmental powers were held by the Executive, including the legal right to make treaties, to decide on war and peace, to lay embargoes, to create offices, to raise armies and navies, to act in emergencies, and so on. And, as noted, "laws" generally originated in the Executive. Even after the Glorious Revolution, the Executive remained the dominant figure in government[.] But even advocates of a strong American Chief Executive distanced themselves from the Crown as an acceptable conception of executive authority. This is reflected in the disappearance of Lockean terminology from American legal discourse.

2. *The Constitution and the "Law Enforcement" Executive.*—In the overwhelming majority of cases, presidential conduct is defended on the straightforward ground that the President has simply "executed" identifiable congressional commands. This is the "law enforcement" President—a President who simply executes the authority (however open-ended) conferred by Congress.

When, however, no readily identifiable legislative warrant exists, and arguably the President is implementing presidential policy alone, a different constitutional vocabulary surfaces. The Vesting Clause,[59] the Take Care Clause,[60] the Presidential Oath to "preserve, protect and defend the constitution of the United States,"[61] and the President's "inherent," "implied" or "aggregate" powers are all invoked in defense of the President's conduct.

With one exception, each of these terms is simply a different formulation of the fundamental claim that the President's conduct is valid even though no statutory authority exists. Like the term "The executive Power," terms such as "inherent" and "aggregate" presidential power derive their substantive content from some external reference points, express or implied. Accordingly, one may assign all such claims of inherent, implied,

[55]See 1 William Blackstone, Commentaries * 243–44.

[59]"The executive Power shall be vested in a President of the United States of America." U.S. Const. art. II, § 1.

[60]"[H]e shall take Care that the Laws be faithfully executed." Id. § 3.

[61]Id. § 1.

or aggregate presidential power to the Vesting Clause, that is, "The executive Power." Moreover, the same seems true of both the Take Care and Oath Clauses; at bottom, they are simply expressions of the constitutional nature of "The executive Power."

* * *

3. *Early American Constitutional History.*—We turn now from terminology to the substance behind the terminology. Whatever other uncertainties may exist about the founding generation's vision of the American presidency, no reasonable doubt existed on one point: the President possessed no independent law-making power. A good deal of the relevant evidence is negative in character, inferable simply from the complete absence of any claims. The silence is, however, fully consistent with what was said. Jefferson's Proposed Constitution for Virginia, drafted in 1783, contains perhaps the best statement of the limited nature of American conceptions of "executive power":

> By executive powers, we mean no reference to those powers exercised under our former government by the crown as of its prerogative, nor that these shall be the standard of what may or may not be deemed the rightful powers of the Governor. We give them those powers only, which are necessary to execute the laws (and administer the government), *and which are not in their nature either legislative or judiciary.* The application of this idea must be left to reason.

This is, of course, the "Whig" theory of executive power, one that is incompatible with the recognition of an independent executive regulatory power, or indeed with much of the modern presidency, because the modern Executive quite plainly executes laws that "are * * * in their nature * * * [both] legislative or judiciary." Jefferson went on, moreover, to reject specific substantive attributes of the Crown's federative and prerogative powers:

> We do however expressly deny him the prerogative powers of *erecting* courts, *offices,* boroughs, corporations, fairs, markets, ports, beacons, light-houses, and sea marks; of laying embargoes, of establishing precedence, of retaining within the State, or *recalling to it any citizen thereof,* and of making denizens, except so far as he may be authorized from time to time by the legislature to exercise any of those powers.

* * *

Not surprisingly, * * * the most important datum—the Constitution itself—contains no hint of an independent presidential regulatory power. The great powers of the national government are vested in Congress. Some of the Crown's important powers—to create offices, to declare war—were transferred outright to Congress; other formerly important "executive" powers, such as making appointments and treaties, were shared with the Senate. * * *

Federalist, the great canonical authority, is fully consistent with this view. Hamilton expressly disclaimed the Crown's powers as a model for the American presidency. While he emphasized that "[e]nergy in the executive is a leading character in the definition of good government,"[78] that energy largely consisted in authority to use the military, when necessary, to enforce national law and for the common defense. * * *

* * *

B. The Residuum Argument

The view that the "executive Power" lacks independent substantive content has not gone unchallenged. Implicitly taking the Crown's powers (or Locke's description) as a bench-mark, some commentators have insisted that, in 1789, "The executive Power" had a substantive content. Accordingly, unless the Constitution reallocates formerly "executive" powers to Congress generally, or to the Senate particularly, whatever power was held by the "Executive" in 1789 must have been understood to inhere in the President.

Writing as "Pacificus," Hamilton first articulated the public foundation for this "residuum" argument in June 1793 in his well-known defense of Washington's Proclamation of Neutrality in the conflict between Great Britain and France.[95] Emphasizing the language differences between the Constitution's grants of "all legislative Powers hereinafter granted" and "The executive Power," Hamilton insisted that the Constitution embodied an independent, substantive conception of executive power. Article II's subsequent "enumerations" of specific executive powers were, he insisted, only "intended by way of greater caution, to specify and regulate the principal articles implied in the definition of Executive Power."

In *Myers v. United States,*[97] Chief Justice Taft appeared to endorse the Hamiltonian conception: "The executive power was given in general terms, strengthened by specific terms where emphasis was regarded as appropriate, and was limited by direct expressions where limitation was needed." Taft attacked the notion that the subsequent grants of power to the Executive were unnecessary if the Vesting Clause possessed an independent substantive content. He insisted that much of Article II, such as the treaty and appointments powers, limited powers that otherwise would have been plenary in the Executive. Taft's endorsement was, however, limited,

---

[78]The Federalist No. 70, at 471 (Alexander Hamilton) (Jacob E. Cooke ed., 1961).

[95]See Pacificus No. 1 (June 29, 1793), reprinted in 15 The Papers of Alexander Hamilton, June 1793–January 1794, at 33–43 (Harold C. Syrett et al. eds., 1969)[.]

[97]272 U.S. 52 (1926) (Taft, C.J.).

focusing only on presidential control over public administration, specifically on the President's power to remove subordinates he appointed. * * *

Moreover, the "legislative history" of the difference in language between the legislative powers "herein granted" and "The executive Power" provides no basis for ascribing any importance to this difference. That discrepancy occurred late in the Convention, on September 12, 1787, as a result of a Report of the Committee on Style, which had narrowed Congress' legislative powers to those "herein granted," but left unchanged "The executive Power." This change seemed designed only to reflect the limits of federalism on national regulatory power, not to ratify or to recognize substantive executive power.

EDWARD S. CORWIN, THE STEEL SEIZURE CASE: A JUDICIAL BRICK WITHOUT STRAW

53 COLUM.L.REV. 53–61, 66 (1953).

President Truman's seizure of the steel industry without specific statutory warrant[1] brings to a new pitch a developing reliance on the "Executive Power" which began almost at the inception of the Federal Government. True, this development has not always proceeded at the same pace; while at times it has seemed to be arrested, during the last fifty years its maturation has been virtually uninterrupted. Moreover, the forces, interests and events which have energized the development are today more potent than ever.

The opening clause of Article II of the Constitution reads: "The executive Power shall be vested in a President of the United States of America." The records of the Constitutional Convention make it clear that the purposes of this clause were simply to settle the question whether the executive branch should be plural or single and to give the executive a title.[2] Yet, in the very first Congress to assemble under the Constitution, the opening clause of Article II was invoked by James Madison and others in order to endow the President with power to remove officers whose appointments had been made with the advice and consent of the Senate. Madison's view prevailed, and was finally ratified by the Supreme Court in 1926.[4] The same theory was invoked by Hamilton in support of President Washington's Proclamation of Neutrality upon the outbreak of war between France and Great Britain. This time the Court's acquiescence was not long delayed. Even in the act of asserting the power of the Court to pass upon the constitutionality of acts of Congress, Chief Justice Marshall said: "By the Constitution of the United States the President is invested with certain important political powers, in the exercise of which he is to use his own discretion, and is accountable only to his country in his political character,

---

[1]Youngstown Sheet & Tube Co. v. Sawyer, 343 U.S. 579 (1952).

[2]2 Farrand, Records of the Federal Convention 171, 185 (rev. ed. 1937).

[4]Myers v. United States, 272 U.S. 52 (1926).

and to his own conscience."[6] Even Thomas Jefferson, cousin and congenital enemy of Marshall, had said of the executive power in an official opinion as Secretary of State in 1790: "The Executive [branch of the government], possessing the rights of self-government from nature, cannot be controlled in the exercise of them but by a law, passed in the forms of the Constitution."[7]

Throughout the last half century the theory of presidential power has recruited strength from a succession of "strong" presidents, from an economic crisis, from our participation in two world wars and a "cold" war, and finally from organization of the labor movement. Moreover, the constitutional basis of the doctrine has shifted somewhat since the early nineteenth century. It no longer relies exclusively, or even chiefly, on the opening clause of Article II. To the terminology of political disputation in the Jacksonian period it is indebted for such concepts as "residual," "resultant" and "inherent" powers. Thanks to Lincoln, it is able to invoke the president's duty to "take care that the laws," i.e., all the laws, "be faithfully executed," and his power as commander-in-chief of the armed forces. * * *

* * *

The Facts of the Youngstown Case. To avert a nation-wide strike of steel workers which he believed would jeopardize the national defense, President Truman, on April 8th, 1952, issued Executive Order 10340 directing the Secretary of Commerce to seize and operate most of the country's steel mills. The order cited no specific statutory authorization, but invoked generally the powers vested in the president by the Constitution and laws of the United States. Secretary Sawyer forthwith issued an order seizing the mills and directing their presidents to operate them as managers for the United States in accordance with his regulations and directions. The President promptly reported these events to Congress, conceding Congress' power to supersede his order; but Congress failed to take action either then or a fortnight later, when the President again raised the problem in a special letter. Of course, in the Defense Production Act of 1950, the Labor Management Relations (Taft-Hartley) Act of 1947 and the Selective Service Act of 1948, Congress had in fact provided other procedures for dealing with such situations; and in the elaboration of these statutory schemes it had repeatedly declined to authorize governmental seizures of property to settle labor disputes. The steel companies sued the Secretary in a federal district court, praying for a declaratory judgment and injunctive relief. The district judge issued a preliminary injunction, which the court of appeals stayed. On certiorari to the court of appeals, the Supreme Court

[6] Marbury v. Madison, 1 Cranch 137, 166 (U.S.1803).

[7] 5 Writings of Jefferson 209 (Ford ed. 1895).

affirmed the district court's order by a vote of six to three. Justice Black delivered the opinion of the Court in which Justices Frankfurter, Douglas, Jackson and Burton concurred * * *. The Chief Justice, speaking for himself and Justices Reed and Minton, dissented.

The Doctrine of the Opinion of the Court. The chief point urged in Justice Black's opinion is that there was no statute which expressly or impliedly authorized the President to take possession of the steel mills. On the contrary, in its consideration of the Taft-Hartley Act in 1947, Congress refused to authorize governmental seizures of property as a method of preventing work stoppages and settling labor disputes. Authority to issue such an order in the circumstances of the case was not deducible from the aggregate of the executive powers under Article II of the Constitution; nor was the Order maintainable as an exercise of the president's powers as commander-in-chief of the armed forces. The power sought to be exercised was the lawmaking power. * * *

The pivotal proposition of the opinion is, in brief, that inasmuch as Congress could have ordered the seizure of the steel mills, there was a total absence of power in the president to do so without prior congressional authorization. To support this thesis no proof in the way of past opinion, practice or adjudication is offered. * * *

The somewhat different truth of the matter is that the framers of the Constitution were compelled to defend their handiwork against the charge that it violated "the political maxim that the legislative, executive, and judicial departments ought to be separate and distinct."[27] To meet this charge Madison sought to show in the *Federalist* that the three departments ought not to be so far separated as to have no control over each other.[28] In his opinion for the Court in *Ex parte Grossman,*[29] decided 137 years later, Chief Justice Taft adopted the same point of view: the fact that when two departments both operate upon the same subject matter the action of one may cancel that of the other *affords no criterion of the constitutional powers of either.* Rather the question is what does *the pertinent historical record* show with regard to presidential action in the field of congressional power?

The Historical Record. Our history contains numerous instances in which, contrary to the pattern of departmental relationship assumed in the Black opinion, presidential action has occurred within a recognized field of congressional power and has, furthermore, fully maintained its tenancy until Congress adopted superseding legislation. And Congress' right to supersede was not contested. In brief, the mere existence in Congress of

[27]The Federalist, No. 47 at 245 (Everyman's ed. 1929).
[28]The Federalist, No. 48 (Madison).
[29]267 U.S. 87 (1925). * * *

power to do something has not, of itself, excluded the president from the same field of power until Congress finally acted. But once this happened, its legislation was forthwith recognized as governing the subject and as controlling presidential action in the area.

* * *

[One] field which the President and Congress have occupied successively is extradition. In 1799 President Adams, in order to execute the extradition provisions of the Jay Treaty, issued a warrant for the arrest of one Jonathan Robbins. As Chief Justice Vinson recites in his opinion:

> This action was challenged in Congress on the ground that no specific statute prescribed the method to be used in executing the treaty. John Marshall, then a member of the House of Representatives, in the course of his successful defense of the President's action, said: "Congress, unquestionably, may prescribe the mode, and Congress may devolve on others the whole execution of the contract; but, till this be done, it seems the duty of the Executive department to execute the contract by any means it possesses."[32]

Not until 1848 did Congress enact a statute governing extradition cases and conferring on the courts, both State and Federal, the duty of handling them.

The power of the president to act until Congress acts in the same field is also shown in these instances. The first Neutrality Proclamation, issued by President Washington in 1793, was also without congressional authorization. The following year Congress enacted the first neutrality statute, and subsequent proclamations of neutrality have been based on an act of Congress governing the matter. The president may, in the absence of legislation by Congress, control the landing of foreign cables in the United States and the passage of foreign troops through American territory, and has done so repeatedly. Likewise, until Congress acts, he may govern conquered territory[37] and, "in the absence of attempts by Congress to limit his power," may set up military commissions in territory occupied by the armed forces of the United States.[38] He may determine in a manner binding on the courts whether a treaty is still in force as law of the land, although again the final power in the field rests with Congress.[39] One of the president's most ordinary powers and duties is that of ordering the prosecution of supposed offenders against the laws of the United States.

[32]Youngstown Sheet & Tube Co. v. Sawyer, 343 U.S. 579, 684 (1952), citing 10 Annals of Congress 619 (1948).

[37]Santiago v. Nagueras, 214 U.S. 260 (1909).

[38]Madsen v. Kinsella, 343 U.S. 341 (1952).

[39]Charlton v. Kelly, 229 U.S. 447 (1913). See also Botiller v. Dominguez, 130 U.S. 238 (1889).

Yet Congress may do the same thing under the "necessary and proper" clause.[40] On September 22, 1862, President Lincoln issued a proclamation suspending the privilege of the writ of habeas corpus throughout the Union in certain classes of cases. By an act passed March 3, 1863, Congress ratified his action and at the same time brought the whole subject of military arrests in the United States under statutory control. Conversely, when President Wilson failed in March, 1917, to obtain Congress' consent to his arming American merchant vessels with defensive arms, he went ahead and did it anyway, "fortified not only by the known sentiments of the majority in Congress but also by the advice of his Secretary of State and Attorney General."[42]

* * *

The doctrine dictated by the above considerations as regards the exercise of executive power in the field of legislative power was well stated by Mr. John W. Davis, principal counsel on the present occasion for the steel companies, in a brief which he filed nearly forty years ago as Solicitor General. The brief defended the action of the president in withdrawing certain lands from public entry, although his doing so was at the time contrary to express statute. "Ours," the brief reads, is a "self-sufficient Government within its sphere." (*Ex parte Siebold,* 100 U.S. 371, 395; *In re Debs,* 158 U.S. 564, 578.) "Its means are adequate to its ends" (*McCulloch v. Maryland,* 4 Wheat. 316, 424), and it is rational to assume that its active forces will be found equal in most things to the emergencies that confront it. While perfect flexibility is not to be expected in a Government of divided powers, and while division of power is one of the principal features of the Constitution, it is the plain duty of those who are called upon to draw the dividing lines to ascertain the essential, recognize the practical, and avoid a slavish formalism which can only serve to ossify the Government and reduce its efficiency without any compensating good. The function of making laws is peculiar to Congress, and the Executive can not exercise that function to any degree. But this is not to say that all of the *subjects* concerning which laws might be made are perforce removed from the possibility of Executive influence. The Executive may act upon things and upon men in many relations which have not, though they might have, been actually regulated by Congress. In other words, just as there are fields which are peculiar to Congress and fields which are peculiar to the Executive, so there are fields which are common to both, in the sense that the Executive may move within them until they shall have been occupied by legislative action. These are not the fields of legislative prerogative, but fields within which the lawmaking power may enter and dominate

[40]See Sinclair v. United States, 279 U.S. 263, 289, 297 (1929).

[42]Berdahl, War Powers of the Executive in the United States 69 (1921).

whenever it chooses. This situation results from the fact that the President is the active agent, not of Congress, but of the Nation. As such he performs the duties which the Constitution lays upon him immediately, and as such, also, he executes the laws and regulations adopted by Congress. He is the agent of the people of the United States, deriving all his powers from them and responsible directly to them. In no sense is he the agent of Congress. He obeys and executes the laws of Congress, not because Congress is enthroned in authority over him, but because the Constitution directs him to do so.

Therefore it follows that in ways short of making laws or disobeying them, the Executive may be under a grave constitutional duty to act for the national protection in situations not covered by the acts of Congress, and in which, even, it may not be said that his action is the direct expression of any particular one of the independent powers which are granted to him specifically by the Constitution. Instances wherein the President has felt and fulfilled such a duty have not been rare in our history, though, being for the public benefit and approved by all, his acts have seldom been challenged in the courts.

* * *

* * * [T]he moral from all this is plain: namely, that escape must be sought from "presidential autocracy" by resort not to the judicial power, but to the legislative power—in other words, by resort to timely action by Congress and to procedures for the meeting of emergency situations so far as these can be intelligently anticipated.

And—not to give the thing too fine a point—what seems to be required at the present juncture is a new Labor Disputes Act which ordains procedures for the handling of industry-wide strikes in terms so comprehensive and explicit that the most headstrong president cannot sidestep them without manifest attaint to the law, the Constitution and his own oath of office. "Presidential autocracy," when it is justified, is an inrush of power to fill a power vacuum. Nature abhors a vacuum; so does an age of emergency. Let Congress see to it that no such vacuum occurs.

C. THE EXECUTIVE POWER: WAGING WAR

The Gulf War of 1990, NATO's air assault on Yugoslavia in 1999, and the Iraq war of 2003 recalled the public's attention to an issue that has never really receded from view since the Viet Nam War. The Constitution makes the President Commander in Chief of the armed forces. But it also grants Congress the authority to declare war; to raise, support, and regulate the army and navy; and a number of related powers. Suppose, as is often the case, that the President is more willing to commit forces to combat than Congress is. What independent authority does he have? When must he get

Congress's permission before acting? And how may Congress rein him in if he acts in ways that it finds objectionable?

We include here portions of the first Chapter of John Hart Ely's important book, *War and Responsibility: Constitutional Lessons of Vietnam and Its Aftermath*. Ely argues that the Constitution's commitment to Congress of the power to "declare war" should be taken seriously; that is, prior congressional approval is required before the President leads the nation into war. Ely would allow a limited exception for a President to respond militarily (while seeking simultaneous congressional approval) to serious threats to U.S. national security. But he finds unpersuasive the claims that modern needs or historical practice have diluted the constitutional requirement of prior congressional approval of war-making.

In his review of Ely's book, Peter Spiro argues that Ely inappropriately undervalues the role of historical practice in interpretation of the Constitution's war powers. He warns of the risks of a formal approach to such questions, suggesting that neither adherence to the War Powers Resolution[1] nor judicial involvement offers a promising course of action.

JOHN HART ELY, THE CONSTITUTIONAL FRAMEWORK

WAR AND RESPONSIBILITY: CONSTITUTIONAL LESSONS OF VIETNAM AND ITS AFTERMATH 3–10 (1993).

One of the recurrent discoveries of academic writing about constitutional law—an all but certain ticket to tenure—is that from the standpoint of twentieth-century observers, the "original understanding" of the document's framers and ratifiers can be obscure to the point of inscrutability. Often this is true. In this case, however, it isn't. The power to declare war was constitutionally vested in Congress. The debates, and early practice, establish that this meant that all wars, big or small, "declared" in so many words or not—most weren't, even then—had to be legislatively authorized. Indeed, only one delegate to either the Philadelphia convention or any of the state ratifying conventions, Pierce Butler, is recorded as

[1]The War Powers Resolution was adopted over President Nixon's veto in 1973. 50 U.S.C.A. §§ 1541–1548. The Resolution tries to encourage consultation between the President and Congress when hostilities are imminent. It is also designed to require Congressional approval within 60 (or 90) days any time the President commits armed forces to real or imminent hostilities.

The Resolution has not succeeded in either aim. It is difficult to legislate a requirement of consultation. And the mechanism designed to trigger congressional approval has malfunctioned. Congress is required to act within 60 days after the President files a report under § 1543(a)(1). But recent presidents have simply avoided filing such reports, so the 60–day clock never started running. The Resolution also authorizes Congress to direct the removal of forces by concurrent resolution. But the validity of that provision has been in doubt since the Supreme Court held the legislative veto invalid in INS v. Chadha, 462 U.S. 919, 103 S.Ct. 2764, 77 L.Ed.2d 317 (1983).

suggesting that authority to start a war be vested in the president. Elbridge Gerry, backed by others, responded that he "never expected to hear in a republic a motion to empower the Executive alone to declare war, and Butler subsequently disowned his earlier view."

There were several reasons for the founders' determination to vest the decision to go to war in the legislative process. The one they mentioned most often is the most obvious, a determination not to let such decisions be taken easily. The founders assumed that peace would (and should) be the customary state of the new republic—James Madison characterized war as "among the greatest of national calamities"—and sought to arrange the Constitution so as to assure that expectation. Their assumption was not that Congress was any more expert on the subject of war than the executive—if anything they assumed the contrary—but rather that requiring its assent would reduce the number of occasions on which we would become thus involved. There were various statements by influential framers to the effect that executives tended to be more warlike than legislative bodies. Madison's is typical: "The constitution supposes, what the History of all Governments demonstrates, that the Executive is the branch of power most interested in war, and most prone to it. It has accordingly with studied care, vested the question of war in the Legislature." Patently the point was not to exclude the executive from the decision—if the president's not on board, we're not going to have much of a war—but rather to "clog" the road to combat by requiring the concurrence of a number of people of various points of view. Justice Story wrote in 1833, "[T]he power of declaring war is not only the highest sovereign prerogative; but . . . it is in its own nature and effects so critical and calamitous, that it requires the utmost deliberation, and the successive review of all the councils of the nation." To invoke a more contemporary image, it takes more than one key to launch a missile: It should take quite a number to start a war.

Two other rationales that played a role can be highlighted by examining the (debated) decision to involve the House of Representatives in the decision to go to war. The House was certainly not included because of any perceived expertise: Indeed, because of its assumed lack thereof it was excluded from such foreign policy processes as the approval of treaties. Rather, authorization by the entire Congress was foreseeably calculated, for one thing, to slow the process down, to insure that there would be a pause, a "sober second thought," before the nation was plunged into anything as momentous as war. Thus in defense of including the House, Story wrote that "[l]arge bodies necessarily move slowly; and where the co-operation of different bodies is required, the retardation of any measure must be proportionately increased." (Occasionally there won't be time for such deliberation, but we shall see that that is something the framers foresaw and accommodated.)

The House was included for another reason as well, that it was conceived as "the people's house": Given the way the burdens of war get distributed, it was felt that the people's representatives should have a say. (It was felt further that the involvement of "the people's representatives" would increase the participation of the people themselves in the debate.) The requirement of authorization by both houses of Congress was thus also calculated to increase the probability that the American people would support any war we entered into. The founders didn't need a Vietnam to teach them that wars unsupported by the people at large are unlikely to succeed. (Indeed, the difficulties of keeping the colonial troops in the field during the Revolution provided the beginnings of a similar lesson.)

This point applies a fortiori to the legislature. Unless Congress has unequivocally authorized a war at the outset, it is a good deal more likely later to undercut the effort, leaving it in a condition that satisfies neither the allies we induced to rely on us, our troops who fought and sometimes died, nor for that matter anyone else except, conceivably, the enemy. Admiral James Stockdale, who spent seven and a half years as a prisoner of war in Hanoi, put it well: "Our Constitution as written protected our fighting men from shedding blood in pointless exercises while a dissenting Congress strangled the effort. But what has evolved . . . affords them no such protection." Thus, he concludes, we cannot afford "to fight any more wars without a thoroughgoing national commitment in advance.'" * * *

It is true that an early draft of the Constitution vested the power "to make war" in Congress, and this language was changed during the editing process to the power "to declare war." This change was made for two reasons. The first was to make clear that once hostilities were congressionally authorized, the president, as "commander in chief," would assume tactical control (without constant congressional interference) of the way they were conducted. (Proponents of broad executive authority to involve the nation in military hostilities often rely on the constitutional designation of the president as "Commander in Chief of the Army and Navy of the United States," but the record is entirely clear that all this was meant to convey was command of the armed forces once Congress had authorized a war, that it did not carry authority to start one.) The second reason for the change in language was to reserve to the president the power, without advance congressional authorization, to "repel sudden attacks."

THE COUNTERARGUMENT FROM OBSOLESCENCE

The clarity of the Constitution on this question leaves two strategies open to advocates of executive authority to start wars—though it can be demonstrated quite rapidly that neither will work. The first is simply to assert that the Constitution does not fit today's world—that it is, in a word, obsolete. In fact this is a line that is rarely taken in so many words, as the conventions of constitutional discourse do not recognize it as a legitimate move. For good reason: The most archaic-sounding provisions of our founding document, their purposes intelligently unpacked, generate commands of complete contemporary relevance. If there is a consensus that one of those commands has become unworkably burdensome—their point, of course, is to be at least somewhat burdensome—the appropriate response is repeal by the constitutionally prescribed method, not a unilateral declaration by the burdened official that the provision no longer applies, at least not to him.

In any event, the constitutional requirement that Congress express its formal approval before the president leads the nation into war is not remotely obsolete: The purposes that underlay it were rendered sufficiently transparent to permit their mapping onto contemporary conditions. Occasionally—though nowhere near as often as enthusiasts would have us—military emergencies can develop faster than Congress can convene and react. That was also true, however, in the late eighteenth century—in fact it was probably truer then than it is today, given that (a) Congress was out of session most of the time and it took weeks, not hours, to round its members up, and (b) its members and committees did not have significant staffs. The founders understood this, though, and consequently reserved to the president authority to respond on his own to "sudden attacks" until there was time for Congress to convene and confer: In such situations the president could respond militarily and seek authorization simultaneously.

It probably is the case, however, that enemy actions not actually amounting to attacks on the United States can more obviously threaten our national security now than they could when the Constitution was agreed to. This raises the question whether the reserved emergency presidential authority to "repel sudden attacks" should be (1) limited to actual attacks on United States territory or (2) "functionally" extended to other situations where a clear danger to our national security has developed so unexpectedly, and immediate military response is so imperative, that advance congressional authorization to respond militarily simply cannot be awaited (though such authorization must be requested, at the latest, simultaneously with the issuance of the order dispatching the troops, our military response discontinued if such authorization is not promptly forthcoming).

At first blush the language seems mildly helpful: "attack" might or might not mean "attack on the United States," but "sudden" does seem to suggest that time urgency is the point. This is building too much on too little, however, as the phrase appears not in the document but in Madison's notes on the debates. We therefore will make better progress by inquiring into the purpose of the reservation of authority to repel sudden attacks. One animating idea could have been that there would in the event of an attack on the United States inevitably be a consensus that a military response was in order, and thus a requirement of congressional approval would be a needless formality. If that was the idea, however, a limitation to actual attacks on U.S. territory seems highly questionable: The *preclusion* of such an attack by a preemptive strike seems likely to garner a similar consensus, as for that matter would an American military response to, say, a Soviet invasion of Mexico or Canada. But then how about Guatemala, Great Britain, or Japan? Thus if we construe the reservation in "likely consensus" terms we confront two choices, each unacceptable. Either we limit it to actual attacks on the United States, which seems to undershoot the posited rationale and thus constitute a questionable approach to constitutional language, or we expand it to all cases where the executive believes that "all sensible people" would agree with his response, in which case we can be quite certain it would be invoked whenever the executive himself thought a military response appropriate. (The tendency of virtually everyone to assume that all rational people, properly advised, would agree with him is one I assume I need not annotate.)

The most natural alternative construction of the reservation would focus on the word "sudden" and assume the point was to give the president authority to respond without advance authorization when there has not been time to secure it (so long as he seeks it simultaneously and subsides if it is not promptly forthcoming). This path appears more promising. In the first place, it fits a general theory of emergency power entertained by some of the founders, that under emergency conditions the executive can properly act in excess of legislative authorization, so long as he makes swift and full disclosure to the legislature and subsides if they do not approve. Second, it parallels a similar reservation of extraordinary military authority another section of Article I made in favor of the *states*: "No State shall, without the Consent of Congress . . . engage in War, unless actually invaded, *or* in such imminent Danger as will not admit of delay." Finally, unlike the "most sensible persons would agree" rationale, "there wasn't time to secure advance authorization so we had to seek it simultaneously" seems susceptible to principled limitation and thus may be given the sort of functional construction we are accustomed to according constitutional language. Thus although the point is arguable, I am inclined to construe the president's reserved authority to go ahead and respond militarily (and seek congressional authorization simultaneously) as extending to genuine and serious threats to our national security beyond actual attacks on United States territory.

Thus construed, the constitutional command is certainly not obsolete: In fact other changes have made it more urgent than ever. In the nineteenth century—indeed, up until World War II—the nation took quite seriously the founders' fear of a "standing army": Thus in order to lead the nation into combat the president needed not only a declaration of war or comparable statement of authorization, but also statutory authority to raise an army and a congressional appropriation of the funds needed to support it. Now, of course, we do effectively have a standing army, which means that today the requirement of congressional authorization is all that stands in the way of unfettered executive discretion to commit it to combat.

* * *

Of course, if he asked, the president probably would usually receive rather readily the support of both Congress and the American people when he decided to have a war. (Admittedly this is somewhat hard to judge, as of late congressional and popular opinion has generally not been permitted to register until the war is under way, at which point support notoriously increases.) From childhood we Americans are programmed to fall in when the bugle sounds, a fact that has caused no small percentage of my friends to ask me why, if approval is a foregone conclusion, I'm wasting my time worrying about increasing participation in such decisions. Is there any reason to suppose, given their respective performances, that Congress will prove wiser on issues of war and peace than the president? Actually I think our history does support, if slightly, the founders' judgment that Congress (if only because it is necessarily more deliberate) tends to be more responsible in this area than the executive. To answer the question on its own (comparative) terms, however, is to miss the point. The constitutional strategy was to require more than one set of keys to open the Pandora's box of war. As usual, Alexander Bickel said it well: "Singly, either the President or Congress can fall into bad errors. . . .So they can together too, but that is somewhat less likely, and in any event, together they are all we've got."[47]

THE COUNTERARGUMENT FROM PRACTICE

The other argument that we can ignore the original demand of the Constitution here—this one is made more explicitly—is an argument from post-ratification practice, that the behavior of various presidents, and the acquiescence of various congresses, during the 200 years since the document was adopted have in essence amended it, effectively eliminating the requirement of congressional authorization. The most obvious answer here is one the Supreme Court has given many times, that past violations are only that—violations—and cannot change the meaning of the Constitution: "That an unconstitutional action has been taken before surely does not render that same action any less unconstitutional at a later date."[48] Though that's got to be generally right, it may oversimplify somewhat,

[47]Hearings on War Powers, Libya, and State–Sponsored Terrorism before the Subcomm. on Arms Control, International Security and Science of the House Comm. on Foreign Affairs, 99th Cong., 2d Sess. 88 (1986)(quoted by J. Brian Atwood).

[48]Powell v. McCormack, 395 U.S. 486, 546–47 (1969).

unduly assimilating constitutional provisions of relevantly different types. If, for example, the question before the Court were whether a certain action was appropriately classified as within the "legislative power" or the "executive power"—*and* there were no more precise provision suggesting an answer—one would rightly expect the judges to be interested in how various presidents and congresses, most particularly *early* presidents and congresses, had by action and acquiescence effectively classified it. Our question, however, does not present a case of one or more vague documentary vessels that must receive their meaning from subsequent experience. In language and recorded purpose the War Clause made an unmistakable point that needed no further gloss: Acts of war must be authorized by Congress. In cases like this the Court is quite right: Usurpation isn't precedent, it's usurpation.

Assume this were not so, however, and that on some oddly repotted "adverse possession" theory, post-ratification practice in violation of the Constitution could change it, still the argument could not work in this context. At the very least we would require "a systematic, unbroken, executive practice, long pursued to the knowledge of the Congress and never before questioned",[53] a pattern that on every count is manifestly lacking here. Of course real life is never entirely neat and clean, but the original constitutional understanding was quite consistently honored from the framing until 1950. And when certain presidents did play a little fast and loose with congressional prerogatives—Polk at the start of the Mexican War; Wilson and Roosevelt, respectively, in the events leading up to the First and Second World Wars—they obscured or covered up the actual facts, pledging public fealty to the constitutional need for congressional authorization of military action. It is therefore impossible to build the occasional nonconforming presidential actions of this period into an argument that they had gradually altered the constitutional plan. Shifts of constitutional power, to the extent they are possible at all, must be accomplished in the open.

> In the case of executive wars, none of the conditions for the establishment of constitutional power by usage is present. The Constitution is not ambiguous. No contemporaneous congressional interpretation attributes a power of initiating war to the President. The early Presidents, and indeed everyone in the country until the year 1950, denied that the President possessed such a power. There is no sustained body of usage to support such a claim. It can only be audacity or desperation that leads the champions of recent presidential usurpations to state that "history had legitimated the practice of presidential war-making."[58]

[53]Youngstown Sheet & Tube Co. v. Sawyer, 343 U.S. 579, 610 (1952)(Frankfurter, J., concurring). * * *

[58]Hearings on Assignment of Ground Forces of the U.S. to Duty in the European Area

PETER J. SPIRO, WAR POWERS AND THE SIRENS OF FORMALISM

(Review of JOHN HART ELY, WAR AND RESPONSIBILITY: CONSTITUTIONAL LESSONS OF VIETNAM AND ITS AFTERMATH)
68 N.Y.U. L. REV. 1338, 1355–65 (1993).

HISTORY AS LAW

[W]ar powers law does not lend itself to refined parchment solutions. It is rather the "court of history,"[70] an accretion of interactions among the branches, that gives rise to basic norms governing the branches' behavior in the area. The process is marked by debate and disagreement, accommodation and acquiescence. Controversies become precedents. There may be no final word or neutral treatment on the significance of each, nothing in the way of a court's opinion, but that does not make custom unworkable as the basis of law. While demanding more facets than the common law methodology of judicial decisionmaking, interbranch episodes can be meaningfully disentangled so as to define the line between acceptable and unacceptable action on war powers questions.

To follow Professor Glennon in borrowing from the international legal doctrine of *opinio juris*,[71] the legal significance of any such episode will hinge on three elements. First, it is actions that count, not words; mere assertions of executive or legislative authority are largely irrelevant in the long run, the chaff of institutional bravado. Second, in order to take on lawmaking significance, the conduct must be known to the other branch; secret operations will have no constitutional significance until they are made known to Congress and it has had an opportunity to respond. Third, the other branch must have accepted or acquiesced in the action. Any conduct that satisfies (or even arguably satisfies) these requirements will become part of the precedential mix; a single historical episode can create incremental elements of custom in the same way that a single judicial decision will incrementally change court-made doctrine.

Individual episodes will, of course, have more or less weight in the same way that decisions from some courts are more meaningful than from others, and in this respect such factors as frequency, consistency, and regularity will be important to determining the constitutional probity of a particular practice. By itself, congressional acquiescence in the invasion of Grenada may have been of middling significance; but added to dozens of similar cases spanning almost the full length of American history, it served to confirm the President's capacity to undertake such incursions without

---

before the Senate Comms. on Foreign Relations and Armed Services, 82d Cong., 1st Sess. 88–93 (1951)(testimony of Secretary Acheson).

[70] New York Times v. Sullivan, 376 U.S. 254, 276 (1964). * * *

[71] See [Michael J. Glennon, Constitutional Diplomacy 59 (1990)].

prior legislative approval. Likewise, the invasion of Panama added a new element insofar as it was justified by the arrest of a foreign leader for violation of U.S. drug laws and itself could thus be used to justify similar operations in the future. The near-uniform practice of securing congressional approval for large-scale operations sets another line of precedent, as does the emerging phenomenon of accepted congressional constraints on defensive deployments. * * *

* * * Ely appears to allow no room for the significance of historical practice, at least not in this context. His answer to those who would interpose custom for the clarification of constitutional norms is * * * premised on the notion that the constitutional text is itself unequivocal: "In language and recorded purpose the War Clause made an unmistakable point that needed no further gloss: Acts of war must be authorized by Congress." Customs to the contrary are "past violations and are only that—violations—and cannot change the meaning of the Constitution."[79] The arguably more ambiguous definition of "war" aside, this defensive rejection of historical practice is lamentable given that the book itself focuses on history. Indeed, Ely's treatment of the "secret" wars would have been considerably strengthened with an acknowledgment of the role of custom. Instead of finding simply that covert operations in Laos and Cambodia were unconstitutional on formalist grounds alone, Ely might also have noted that the incursions were without even remote historical precedent. Where many pages are devoted to rebutting contemporaneous military and policy justifications for the secret operations, the public and congressional uproar sparked by their revelation, including legislation restricting subsequent U.S. activities in the two countries, goes almost ignored. Congress did not accept the incursions as constitutionally legitimate, and hence the incursions cannot now comprise authority for similar exercises in secret presidential warmaking. No President would ever highlight the examples of Cambodia and Laos by way of constitutional defense for secrecy. On the contrary, Congress could well exploit the two episodes to its institutional advantage were an executive so foolish as to attempt their replication.

Ely's refusal to accept some place for historical precedents sets him apart even from other commentators who favor further statutory and judicial constraint of executive action.[84] Not that those commentators place custom high on the legal hierarchy. They too remain true to the lawyerly urge for formalist resolution which Ely typifies. One might pose the other extreme with the proposition that texts, even where they exist, do not

[79][John Hart Ely, War and Responsibility: Constitutional Lessons of Vietnam and Its Aftermath 9 (1993).]

[84]See, e.g., M. Glennon, supra note [71], at 55 (describing custom as "judicially cognizable precedent"); [Harold Hongju Koh, The National Security Constitution 70–71(1990)] (acknowledging "quasi-constitutional custom"). * * *

necessarily prevail over practice. Statutes and judicial decisions will not perforce trump the tide of history; rather, they become a part of that history, one source (more often a reflection) of law but not necessarily a higher one. Where accepted or acquiesced in by the executive branch and specific to a particular use of force, they may memorialize the outcome of a certain dispute; where accepted or acquiesced in by the executive branch and purporting to govern interbranch relationships prospectively, they may affect marginally the historical mix to the extent they regularize and entrench actual practice. In this area as in all others, texts may reduce decisionmaking friction to the extent they are specific and thus reduce uncertainty. In the war powers context, however, such specificity may increase the text's "rate of decay"[87]—the speed with which it comes no longer to govern actual practice—and hence diminish its overall utility.

In any event, where the relevant branches do not acquiesce in the textual instrument, its content will by itself be of little consequence to interbranch norms and behavior. The War Powers Resolution is a statute, but it has never been the law. Far from setting the balance of war powers, the Resolution has established what is *not* the balance; it has become a sort of historical foil. The same would hold true of any judicial pronouncement which inflexibly attempted to rearrange the evolutionary constitutional construct.

Moreover, there is a harm in the perpetuation of text that neither reflects nor governs behavior. The War Powers Resolution * * * continues to bring the legislative branch into institutional disrepute. Congress looks toothless to the extent that it has not, loosely speaking, lived up to its responsibilities or exploited its prerogatives under the Resolution. At the same time, the presidency seems bold in defiance. Insofar as it has not come to be ignored altogether, the Resolution may play into the hands of executive branch partisans by serving as a lingering reminder that Congress, even as equipped with statutory tools, has acquiesced in the sometimes uncurbed exercise of presidential discretion. This acquiescence, in turn, may fuel the more extreme claims of exclusive presidential powers, as was true of some of President Bush's pronouncements leading up to the Gulf War. Alternatively, the continued formal validity of the Resolution may drive the executive branch to overcompensate rhetorically in defending what it considers to be its exclusive powers unconstitutionally reallocated by the Act. Worse, the disjunction of text and practice could distort the

---

[87]The phrase is Professor Reisman's, although I use it here in a slightly different fashion than does he. See W. Michael Reisman, International Incidents: Introduction to a New Genre in the Study of International Law, in [International Incidents: The Law That Counts in World Politics 12–13 (W. Michael Reisman & Andrew R. Willard eds, 1988)] (noting that rate of decay of sociopolitical context will always be greater than that of text, creating incongruence between formal law and actual "operational code").

decisionmaking process so as to result in presidential attempts to broaden the range of action undertaken without legislative approval.

Judicial intervention would be to similar effect. The courts would be no better able to make good on an inflexible statutory mandate. The stakes are too high, as is the risk of error, and, unlike mistakes in more pedestrian settings, errors here are not so easily corrected. Proponents of judicial participation in war powers disputes, Ely included, are wont to note that courts are used to dealing with issues of war and peace, as in considering war-risk insurance clauses. The step from one to the other is grossly understated. A mistake in the insurance context might implicate the survival of a company; a mistake in a case involving the use of U.S. forces abroad could well jeopardize the lives of our troops and might conceivably implicate the survival of the nation. The gravity of combat-related decisions in turn greatly magnifies the risk of noncompliance with judicial decrees, a risk no less real for its repeated recitation as a pillar of the political question doctrine. The political branches have demonstrated a capacity to circumvent the judiciary where the courts have assumed a formalist stance against well-established practice,[95] a disrespect that could be far more obvious, and institutionally damaging, in the war powers context.

* * *

Supporters see the War Powers Resolution and the prospect of its enforcement by the courts as a leap towards order in a sphere otherwise characterized by disarray, hence their almost stubborn defense of a law that has long lost relevance to reality. But war powers possibly is a context in which statutory refinements and the tidiness of *Marbury* simply do not work, at least not where they try to rearrange the weight of history. This does not mean that there is no place for lawyers, statutes, and the courts in the war powers context; rather, only that they may not be preeminent, and that the law here may be molded to a greater degree by battles fought by political actors in the political arena. * * *

If lawyers are instead seduced by the sirens of formalism, they will be forgotten by those who decide. As Professor Reisman notes in the context

---

[95]This capacity has been demonstrated most notably with respect to Immigration & Naturalization Service v. Chadha, 462 U.S. 919 (1983), in which the Supreme Court held the longstanding mechanism of the legislative veto unconstitutional. Notwithstanding *Chadha*, Congress has continued to enact legislative veto mechanisms into law, by one count more than 200 since the decision was handed down. See Louis Fisher, *The Legislative Veto: Invalidated, It Survives*, Law & Contemp. Probs., Autumn 1993, at 273, 273. In perhaps the most celebrated violation of the spirit if not the letter of *Chadha*, the Bush administration and Congress resolved the issue of aid to the contras in Nicaragua by resort to a "political" legislative veto mechanism, i.e., one negotiated and agreed to but not enacted into law. See Bipartisan Accord on Central America, 25 Weekly Comp. Pres. Doc. 420–21 (Mar. 24, 1989); Baker Plan: A New Deal, N.Y. Times, Mar. 25, 1989, at A1, A6 * * *).

of international law, "One is as unlikely to seek and pay for the advice of the votaries of a demonstrably ineffective legal system as one is to seek and pay for the blessings of the high priests of a sect manifestly out of favor with the pertinent divinity."[107] * * * This is a danger here in the law of war powers, a context in which dangers are not to be taken lightly.

D. EXECUTIVE PRIVILEGES AND IMMUNITIES

Another set of separation of powers problems concerns efforts by one branch of government to interfere in the internal affairs of another. Sometimes Congress or the courts will thrust themselves into executive affairs. Impeachment is one (serious) example; lawsuits and congressional demands for information are more typical. Sometimes the judiciary and the executive will pry into the affairs of Congress. Here the Constitution offers some explicit protection—in the Speech or Debate Clause—though its scope is uncertain.[1]

The articles in this section discuss interference in executive affairs, in the context of actions against Presidents Nixon and Clinton. Does the President, like Congress, have some protection against such action? In particular, may he assert executive privileges (against production of evidence)[2] and immunities (from suit)?[3]

Stephen Carter argues that the Supreme Court was right in *Nixon v. Fitzgerald*,[4] although he suggests an alternative interpretive route for upholding President Nixon's immunity from suit. Akhil Amar and Neal Katyal contend that, despite Supreme Court decisions to the contrary,[5] President Clinton had a stronger case for (at least temporary) immunity from suit during his term in office than President Nixon had for immunity from suit after leaving office.

Victoria Nourse offers an alternative perspective on separation of powers issues. She argues that Congress represents local constituencies, while the President represents a national constituency. For this reason, she suggests that courts should attend more to the balance of political power

[107]W. Reisman and A. Willard, supra note [87], at 6.

[1]Hutchinson v. Proxmire, 443 U.S. 111, 99 S.Ct. 2675, 61 L.Ed.2d 411 (1979); Eastland v. United States Servicemen's Fund, 421 U.S. 491, 95 S.Ct. 1813, 44 L.Ed.2d 324 (1975); Doe v. McMillan, 412 U.S. 306, 93 S.Ct. 2018, 36 L.Ed.2d 912 (1973); Gravel v. United States, 408 U.S. 606, 92 S.Ct. 2614, 33 L.Ed.2d 583 (1972); United States v. Brewster, 408 U.S. 501, 92 S.Ct. 2531, 33 L.Ed.2d 507 (1972).

[2]Nixon v. Administrator of General Services, 433 U.S. 425, 97 S.Ct. 2777, 53 L.Ed.2d 867 (1977); United States v. Nixon, 418 U.S. 683, 94 S.Ct. 3090, 41 L.Ed.2d 1039 (1974).

[3]Clinton v. Jones, 520 U.S. 681, 117 S.Ct. 1636, 137 L.Ed.2d 945 (1997); Nixon v. Fitzgerald, 457 U.S. 731, 102 S.Ct. 2690, 73 L.Ed.2d 349 (1982); Mississippi v. Johnson, 71 U.S. (4 Wall.) 475, 18 L.Ed. 437 (1866).

[4]457 U.S. 731, 102 S.Ct. 2690, 73 L.Ed.2d 349 (1982).

[5]Compare Clinton v. Jones, 520 U.S. 681, 117 S.Ct. 1636, 137 L.Ed.2d 945 (1997), with Nixon v. Fitzgerald, 457 U.S. 731, 102 S.Ct. 2690, 73 L.Ed.2d 349 (1982).

between national and local constituencies. She uses this theory to illuminate issues concerning independent prosecutors and presidential immunity. Compare the methods of constitutional interpretation adopted by Carter, Amar and Katyal, and Nourse. Do the kinds of questions addressed here argue for a formalist attention to text and original intent, or a more functionalist understanding of balance and the modern presidency?

STEPHEN L. CARTER, THE POLITICAL ASPECTS OF JUDICIAL POWER: SOME NOTES ON THE PRESIDENTIAL IMMUNITY DECISION

131 U.PA.L.REV. 1341, 1353–1371 (1983).

[In the first part of his article Carter reviews the Supreme Court's decision in *Nixon v. Fitzgerald.*[a] The plaintiff in that case sued President Nixon for damages, claiming that he had been fired for exercising his right to freedom of speech. The Court held, 5–4, that the President was immune from suit for damages.]

The conclusion that the federal courts lack authority to punish the President of the United States may at first seem somewhat startling, but after a little thought, it makes more sense. One may begin by hypothesizing the contrary. Suppose a court did try to hold the President of the United States in contempt for disobeying an order addressed to him. Would federal marshals arrive at the White House, demanding that the Secret Service agents let them seize the President? Suppose the President—with the assistance of the security personnel—decided to resist arrest. Aside from a definite air of lese majesty about the whole thing, there is also the undeniable fact that should matters come to a showdown, the President has more guns at his command than a federal court does. The Supreme Court has never pretended otherwise. During the Reconstruction Era, the Court in *Mississippi v. Johnson,*[53] took explicit note of the difficulties it would encounter in trying to "force" a President to comply with an order, and dismissed a complaint against President Andrew Johnson. Earlier opinions included dicta to similar effect.[56]

The mere fact that forcing the President to pay damages might not be easy does not by itself justify a constitutional rule against trying. After all, President Nixon did turn over the Watergate tapes, even though the federal courts probably could not have enforced a contempt citation against him. Besides, resistance to judicial decrees is hardly new. Had the President not decided to send troops to Little Rock in the wake of *Cooper v. Aaron,*[60] the

[a]457 U.S. 731 (1982).

[53]71 U.S. (4 Wall.) 475 (1867).

[56]*Cf.* Chisholm v. Georgia, 2 U.S. (2 Dall.) 419, 476–78 (1793) (dictum) (sovereign immunity derives from ability to resist judicial process).

[60]358 U.S. 1 (1958).

schools in that city might be segregated to this day. The Court's inability to enforce its order without the assistance of the executive branch did not mean that the Justices had no power to issue the order. Thus the claim that the Court lacks power to punish the President must be defended on some ground other than the Court's lack of enforcement power.

In supporting its conclusion in *Nixon v. Fitzgerald,* the majority focused on what it considered the public policy reasons militating in favor of an immunity rule. Justice White's dissent at least showed that these arguments have two sides. The malleability of public policy arguments makes the majority's reasoning suspect, but need not vitiate the result. In order to tie its decision more closely to the Constitution, the Court could have relied on something other than public policy.

* * *

Provisions describing the functions and powers of the government may demand a different interpretive approach from provisions describing the rights of the people. A strict textual approach, focusing on the understanding of the Framers, may be a more sensible method to use in interpreting the structural clauses of the Constitution. * * *

1. The Original Understanding Approach

* * * The original understanding—when one can be discerned—is more likely to be important in a case involving the system of checks and balances than it is in a case involving individual rights. The reason should be obvious. In protecting individuals against government mistreatment, those who drafted the 1787 Constitution and its amendments took pains to use language so broad as fairly to beg to be filled with substantive content from external sources. They used words sparingly, an approach that makes sense when one begins with a conception of rights as broad and government power as narrow. In structuring the government, however, the drafters set themselves rather a different task and used dramatically different language.

The 1787 Constitution set forth with painstaking attention to detail the powers and functions of the federal government. Despite a few glaring errors,[72] the document reflects an obsessive concern for the minutiae of government operation. Words were used cautiously so as to leave little room for interpretation. Thus although some wanted to make the President

---

[72] A good example concerns the role of the Vice President. The Vice President serves as President of the Senate. U.S. Const. art. I, § 3. When the President of the United States is tried in the Senate following impeachment by the House of Representatives, the Chief Justice of the United States presides. *Id.* That is the only provision in the Constitution requiring the Vice President to turn over the gavel to another individual. Yet the Vice President himself is also impeachable, and if impeached by the House, he would be tried in the Senate. It appears, therefore, that the Vice President could preside at his own impeachment trial, should he choose to do so.

impeachable for any reason, the delegates in Philadelphia finally voted to limit impeachable offenses to "Treason, Bribery, or other high Crimes and Misdemeanors," in the hope of limiting congressional power over him. The Constitution also does not include a requirement that members of the House of Representatives be "mature"—although maturity emerged as a major concern in the debates—but only that they be at least twenty-five years old. One can imagine a Constitution providing that elected representatives be "mature" or "of good character," but there is something disturbing, perhaps counterintuitive, about such provisions, as there would be about a provision for congressional overriding of the President's veto "by an extraordinary majority," unless the provision specified what the majority must be. These hypothetical provisions seem counterintuitive for a good reason, and that good reason probably explains their absence from the Constitution: in determining such matters as the qualifications for elected officials, the Framers were structuring a government, not setting forth rights. In the Framers' view, the former called for more precise language than did the latter. The precise wording of the structural provisions reflects an effort to define the structure of government carefully and circumscribe the powers of government narrowly. This purpose should not be ignored when construing the structural provisions of the Constitution.

It therefore makes sense to try to determine the way that the Framers hoped that the Presidency would be controlled. * * * The great weight of the historical evidence suggests the existence of a consensus at the time of ratification to the effect that those checks on presidential abuse of power expressly set forth in the document were the only checks available.

This consensus emerges from the nature of the disputes among the drafters and ratifiers over the proper functions and powers of the President. The intense debate surrounding the Presidency induced the Framers to define their views with rare precision. Those who favored a loose confederation of quasi-independent states argued that the President was too strong and not sufficiently accountable for wrongdoing; those who thought the central government should be strong argued that the President was too weak, that he was subject to too many controls and potential punishments to be able to do his job properly. Supporters of the Constitution had ready responses to each objection.

The President was not too strong, supporters contended, because he was subject to several specific checks on abuses of his authority. The supporters always listed the checks appearing in the document: the power of the purse rested with Congress, the President could be impeached, his veto could be overridden, he could make no appointments or treaties without Senate consent, he was subject to reelection every four years. Hamilton went to great lengths in *The Federalist* to assure the worried public that these provisions were adequate to control presidential misconduct.[97] At the same time, Hamilton and other supporters of ratification repeatedly warned that no additional checks should be permitted, lest the President become too weak.

The Constitution's supporters made, with slightly different emphasis, the same argument to those who thought the Constitution made the executive too weak. In reassuring those who feared presidential weakness, supporters emphasized that the limitations actually stated in the Constitution were the only limitations placed on the President, and these, the opponents were assured, would not impair the President's ability to do his job. Some provision had to be made against the possibility of presidential tyranny, supporters pointed out, and the drafters had done the best they could without limiting the Chief Executive's powers too greatly.

There is no reason to belabor this; attempts to piece together an original "understanding" from the fragments of history tend to end up looking silly. What is rather startling in this instance is that the same questions and answers occur again and again in the surviving records. That is why it may be safe to assume that a consensus existed. At the very least, it cannot fairly be asserted that the history points in some other direction.

2. THE STRUCTURAL APPROACH

The Constitution's relatively precise clauses describing the operation of the federal government are designed to fit together to form a coherent structure. This purpose distinguishes them from the open-ended clauses, many of which were designed to address particular problems and bear little relation to the other parts of the document. * * *

The system of checks and balances is a delicate one, and the Constitution sets forth with some degree of care the checks that each branch may apply to the others. Thus the President may nominate and, if the Senate consents, appoint Justices to the Supreme Court and judges to the lower federal courts, but only Congress, through impeachment and conviction, may remove them. Congress may propose legislation (including legislation channeling the President's discretion), but absent extraordinary majorities in both Houses, the proposals do not become law if the President objects. Congress may go through the motions of enacting legislation that violates the Constitution, but the federal courts, in a case properly brought, may strike those statutes down. Congress holds exclusive power of the purse, and Congress alone can impeach the President and remove him from office. A few other checks, mostly in the form of congressional powers, are scattered through the document. In addition, because all members of Congress as well as the President are elected, popular sentiment provides a powerful and constant check on the operation of the entire system. Outside

[97] * * *The Federalist No. 69 at 444–45 (A. Hamilton) (B. Wright ed. 1961)[.]

the interplay of these powers, the Constitution provides no further express controls on misconduct.

* * *

The balance of powers among the three branches of the federal government is a delicate construct, and if any one of the branches is empowered to create new checks on the others that branch will be in the position to upset the very balance that it purports to protect. Thus the system requires placing the narrowest possible reading on the authority of each branch of government to act in the name of preserving that system. Attention to the original understanding and a strict view of constitutional language are both merely means to the end of maintaining the balance of power among the branches of the federal government.

* * *

The arguments set out above are arguments that the majority could have made, but failed to make in any detail, in support of the theory that the decision is constitutionally based. The arguments share a simple conclusion: in determining the role that each branch should play in the system of checks and balances, all judgments on proper policy must be subordinated to the most important policy, preserving that selfsame system of checks and balances. Permitting one branch to create fresh remedies will upset the balance. Anything that upsets the balance is wrong. That is why the federal courts cannot create a cause of action for damages running against a President or former President on the basis of misconduct in office.

Had it explained *Nixon v. Fitzgerald* that way, the Court would presumably have gone on to explain why the theory that all other interests must be subordinated to the need to preserve the system of checks and balances does not do violence to precedent. A distinction must be drawn between the two very different roles the federal courts play in the system of checks and balances. To paraphrase Felix Frankfurter, when the courts settle a dispute between the two more overtly political branches, they act as "referees at prize fights;" but when they act affirmatively to vindicate an individual claim of right against a representative of another branch, they act as "functionaries of justice." In *Nixon v. Fitzgerald,* an individual asked the Court to make him whole, and the Justices hesitated. The majority's reasoning suggests constitutional limitations on the judicial power to act as functionaries of justice by creating fresh remedies. Nothing in the decision is inconsistent with the cases in which the Court has acted as a referee.

United States v. Nixon[109] does not fall squarely into either category, but it is probably best viewed as a "court-as-referee" decision. The Justices were not settling a dispute between the other two branches, but they were

[109] 418 U.S. 683 (1974).

also not protecting the rights of any individual against government excess. The Court was called upon instead to act as referee *within* a particular branch of government.[110] The Court accepted the task, and its resolution of the dispute required the President to comply with an order. The result in *Nixon v. Fitzgerald* suggests that had the President defied the Court's order in *United States v. Nixon,* the Justices would not have created a fresh remedy through which to try and punish him. The risk of presidential defiance, however, although much bandied-about at the time, was probably close to nil. President Nixon was politically helpless and the Justices must have known that. Had he refused to comply with the Court's "definitive" decision, he would almost certainly have been impeached and removed from office. The federal court could not, under the logic of the presidential immunity decision, have acted against him directly, but a punishment for disobedience would have been imposed all the same. The order would simply have been enforced by a branch other than the one that issued it.

That inability to act against the President directly is hardly inconsistent with other cases in which the federal courts have, in evaluating the legitimacy of presidential actions, evinced reluctance to deal with the President directly. With rare exception, the courts have reviewed presidential activities through suits naming as a defendant not the President himself, but some lower executive functionary. The same theory—that no punishment question was involved and the courts were merely acting as referees—may explain these results, but another theory fits them even better. The President was not a defendant, and it is only to the President himself, with his special place in the constitutional scheme and history, that immunity attaches. The Supreme Court acknowledged as much when, on the same day that it decided the presidential immunity case, it ruled in *Harlow v. Fitzgerald* that no similar immunity attaches to the President's aides.[116] Because the President almost always acts through his subordinates, a non-immune defendant will generally be available in any case brought to contest the validity of a presidential directive.

If the President's aides are not immune from suit as he is, they may be placed in an uncomfortable position when he orders them to do something that they believe to be wrong. There is a temptation to say flippantly that an executive functionary placed in that position may resign, tell his story to the *Washington Post,* and write a bestselling book. More seriously, the position may be uncomfortable, but the choice should not be difficult. The employees of the executive branch work for the United States of America,

---

[110]Acting as a referee *within* a particular branch is a power that the Court exercised previously in 1969 when it issued its controversial decision in Powell v. McCormack, 395 U.S. 486 (1969), invalidating a congressional attempt to exclude a member on grounds other than the "Qualifications" that the Court said are set forth expressly in the Constitution. * * *

[116]* * *457 U.S. 800 (1982) * * *.

not for the person who happens to occupy the office of President. Faced with an order they believe to be illegitimate, executive functionaries should state their belief and refuse to carry the order out. They may be dismissed for that refusal, but they will have acted in accord with the requirements of the Constitution.

AKHIL REED AMAR AND NEAL KUMAR KATYAL, EXECUTIVE PRIVILEGES AND IMMUNITIES: THE NIXON AND CLINTON CASES

108 HARV. L. REV. 701–17, 719, 726 (1995).

In 1978, Ernest Fitzgerald sued Richard Nixon, and in 1994, Paula Jones sued Bill Clinton. In a landmark but closely divided 1982 opinion, *Nixon v. Fitzgerald*, the Supreme Court sided with Nixon and against Fitzgerald.[1] What does this mean for Jones and Clinton today?[a] Ed Meese speaks for many when he insists that Nixon protects Presidents only for presidential conduct and that extending immunity to Clinton's pre-presidential conduct would be a huge and unprincipled stretch that would place Bill Clinton above the law.[3] Other commentators aren't so sure that *Nixon* itself was rightly decided but are sure that Clinton's claim is much weaker. Terry Eastland has argued that, if you reject Nixon's immunity claim, you presumably must reject Clinton's a fortiori.[4]

We will show that all of this is dead wrong. Bill Clinton's claim for immunity is actually much stronger than Richard Nixon's—supported by crisper arguments from constitutional text and structure, by more historical evidence from the Founding and early Republic, and by better modern-day policy arguments. Nixon sought absolute and permanent immunity from a civil damage action after he left office; Clinton seeks only temporary immunity from litigating a civil damage suit while he serves as President. We will show that the Arrest Clause of Article I, Section 6 and the democratic structural principles underlying this Clause cast light on Article II, and provide a sturdy constitutional basis for temporary presidential immunity. In the process of elaborating the best argument for Clinton, we will also show how all nine Justices in *Nixon* missed the point and in

---

[1]457 U.S. 731 (1982). The suit alleged that Nixon had unlawfully fired Fitzgerald in retaliation for his testimony before Congress about military aircraft cost overruns.

[a]This article was written before the Supreme Court's decision in *Clinton v. Jones*, 520 U.S. 681 (1997). Eds.

[3]*Nightline: Presidential Immunity* (ABC television broadcast, June 13, 1994) (transcript on file with the Harvard Law School Library); *Crossfire: Justice Delayed for the President?* (CNN television broadcast, May 25, 1994) (transcript on file with the Harvard Law School Library); *Morning Edition: Sexual Harassment Suit Questions Presidential Immunity* (National Public Radio broadcast, June 15, 1994) (transcript on file with the Harvard Law School Library).

[4]See Terry Eastland, *No Immunity for Clinton from Paula Jones's Charges*, Wall St. J., June 8, 1994, at A17.

particular misread a key quote from the great Justice Joseph Story. We will outline a new theory of limited executive immunity that protects a sitting President and (most importantly) the American people he serves, yet does not put the President above the law, as *Nixon* did, despite the Court's protestations to the contrary.

I. UNTANGLING IMMUNITY

* * *

In a lengthy and important footnote, the *Nixon v. Fitzgerald* majority properly rejected a wooden *expressio unius* reading of Article I, Section 6, arguing that "a specific textual basis has not been considered a prerequisite to the recognition of immunity."[29] But the Court's desire to find a quick answer to Nixon's problem blinded it to the architecture of Section 6. To see this, we must carefully pull apart the two types of immunity mentioned in Article I. One type is "Immunity From Arrest": legislators' *temporary* immunity from litigating even *private* lawsuits while "at the Session" of Congress as public officers. The other type is "Immunity For Speech or Debate": *permanent* immunity from liability in lawsuits that arise out of the performance of *public* duties of democratic deliberation. This latter form is what all nine Justices in *Nixon* conceptualized as "immunity."

I. Permanent *Immunity*.—The Court's application of *permanent* immunity in *Nixon* was hard to justify by analogy to the Speech or Debate Clause or by other basic structural principles of constitutional law. Richard Nixon did not speak out against Ernest Fitzgerald in public debate; Nixon fired Fitzgerald from a civil service position. Worse still, Fitzgerald alleged that Nixon fired him because of Fitzgerald's speech activities—whistleblowing testimony before the Congress. A broad commitment to the constitutional ideals of democratic self-government and citizen speech argued against Nixon's immunity, not for it. According to Fitzgerald's complaint, Richard Nixon violated the Constitution itself (the First Amendment no less), and yet the Court shielded Nixon with permanent immunity.

* * *

[T]he Framers would have been shocked by the notion that, as a general matter, executive officials could violate the Constitution and yet be held permanently immune. The modern judicial proliferation of various qualified immunities for constitutional torts is a twentieth century betrayal of founding principles. These immunities should be sources of concern—things to be minimized or, ideally, eliminated—rather than springboards for further violations of *Marbury*. The *Nixon* five's complacent apologetics

[29] 457 U.S. 731, 750 n. 31 (1982)[.]

here are embarrassing, at least to those who value the Framers' first principles.

* * *

2. Temporary *Immunity*.—The other half of immunity, temporary immunity akin to Article I immunity from arrest, went wholly unnoticed by *Nixon*'s nine Justices. As Article I makes clear, members of Congress are privileged from arrest while Congress is in session. The Framers intended "Arrest" in this Clause to mean civil arrest, not criminal arrest. The Arrest Clause explicitly exempts cases of "Treason, Felony and Breach of the Peace"; and both the clear language of Blackstone's Commentaries and English debates well known to the Framers stressed that this exempting phrase was a term of art encompassing all crimes.

The real question is whether civil arrest should be understood strictly and formally, or more functionally. Technical civil arrest—commencing a lawsuit by seizing the civil defendant's person—is all but dead today, and so the Arrest Clause, when strictly construed, shrinks to a virtual nullity. But "Arrest" may also be understood more functionally as extending to various civil cases that interfere with—that arrest—a person's performance of her duties in public office. This functional immunity avoids undemocratic results: functional civil arrests of members of Congress while it is in session might skew votes in Congress and penalize innocent third parties, namely, the American people. As Joseph Story put the point in his Commentaries, explicitly building on Thomas Jefferson's famous Congressional Manual:

> When a representative is withdrawn from his seat by a summons, the people, whom he represents, lose their voice in debate and vote. . . . When a senator is withdrawn by summons, his state loses half its voice in debate and vote. . . . The enormous disparity of the evil admits of no comparison.[45]

But Article I prohibits civil arrests only while Congress is in session; it implicitly permits the arrests when Congress is not in session. (And here we see a less wooden and more proper application of the *expressio unius* maxim.) Arrest Clause immunity is thus *temporary* immunity—stopping the clock on a lawsuit until litigation can occur without disruption of the defendant's public duties.

* * *

The structural constitutional logic undergirding temporary immunity applies with * * * [great] force to the President. Unlike federal lawmakers and judges, the President is at "Session" twenty-four hours a day, every

[45][2 Joseph Story, Commentaries on the Constitution of the United States, § 857 (Boston, Hilliard, Gary & Co. 1833)].

day. Constitutionally speaking, the President never sleeps. The President must be ready, at a moment's notice, to do whatever it takes to preserve, protect, and defend the Constitution and the American people: prosecute wars, command armed forces (and nuclear weapons), protect Americans abroad, negotiate with heads of state, and take care that all the laws are faithfully executed. We should hesitate before arming each citizen with a kind of legal assault weapon enabling him or her to commandeer the President's time, drag him from the White House, and haul him before any judge in America.

What's more, the President is the only person for whom the entire nation—We the People of the United States—votes. There are over 500 federal lawmakers—the House and Senate can function if one member is absent, as the quorum rules of Article I, Section 5 make clear[49]—but there is only one President, in whom all executive power is vested by Article II. Thus, the democratic skew that can result if civil suits impede—arrest—the President is far more dramatic than for a typical Representative or Senator. To be sure, the Vice President always remains at hand, ready to step in for the President in emergency situations, but the elaborate provisions of the Twenty-Fifth Amendment and past practice indicate that these emergencies should be the exception, not the rule. Yet they could well become the rule if a handful of citizens—acting independently or in concert—could functionally arrest the President in his performance of the people's business and trigger his temporary inability "to discharge the Powers and Duties of . . . Office" under Article II and the Twenty-Fifth Amendment.

This approach does not mean that the President is above the law. It simply means that, in cases seeking compensation for past wrongs, a President should be able to request temporary immunity to avoid interference with his duties. Whereas *Nixon* eliminated all remedies against the President, at least for constitutional torts committed qua President, arrest immunity would only "toll"—stop the clock on—a lawsuit and would preserve the plaintiff's ultimate remedy and vindicate the ideal of *Marbury*. Because of the Twenty-Second Amendment, the Constitution itself assures that plaintiffs will not have to wait more than eight years.

But eight years is a long time—much longer than any "Session" of Congress under Article I, Section 6—and so perhaps the Section 6 analogy breaks down at precisely that point. On the other hand, eight years is a lot shorter than eternity, which is how long the *Nixon* Court said Ernest Fitzgerald had to wait. * * *

If sensible structural inferences lead us to think that a President, under the logic of Article II, merits an immunity akin to Section 6 "Arrest"

---

[49]See [U.S. Const.] art. I, § 5, cl. 1 ("[A] Majority of each [House] shall constitute a Quorum to do Business").

immunity, it becomes important to refine further the functional concept of civil arrest. Our legal order has long distinguished between damage suits for past, discrete wrongs, and injunctive suits to end ongoing harm. In effect, we should distinguish between civil damage arrests and ongoing harm injunctions. In arrest scenarios, plaintiffs may be obliged to wait, but interest payments presumably can make up for lost time. Civil actions arising out of ongoing harms—continuing possession of a steel mill in *Youngstown*,[57] or a hypothetical divorce or child custody suit involving a sitting President—are quite different. Putting the point more textually, perhaps one could say that an ongoing harm is functionally one kind of "Breach of the Peace" and thus lies outside the proper scope of arrest immunity.

C. *Nixon* Revisited

Not only does temporary immunity from "civil arrest" make good sense from the perspective of constitutional structure and policy, but it also makes the most sense of the historical evidence offered up by the *Nixon* majority. The best evidence that the *Nixon* five had for their position, Justice White's dissent conceded, was from Justice Story. But now that we have tipped our hand and identified two types of immunity, listen to Story's words with fresh ears:

> There are . . . incidental powers, belonging to the executive department, which are necessarily implied from the nature of the functions, which are confided to it. Among these, must necessarily be included the power to perform them, without any obstruction or impediment whatsoever. The president cannot, therefore, be liable to arrest, imprisonment, or detention, while he is in the discharge of the duties of his office; and for this purpose his person must be deemed, in civil cases at least, to possess an official inviolability.[60]

Let us note carefully Story's moves. First, Story believes that Section 6 does not exclude immunities for coordinate federal branches. In particular there are "incidental" presidential powers, not textually spelled out but "necessarily implied" by the spare words of Article II. Next, Story hints that these immunities should be understood functionally, not formally—they are deducible from the nature of presidential "functions." Third, Story articulates presidential immunity as an immunity from "arrest"—obviously conjuring up an analogy to the Arrest Clause of Article I, rather than the Speech or Debate Clause. Fourth, this immunity is explicitly temporary, once again in keeping with arrest immunity rather than speech or debate immunity. It is immunity "*while* he is in the discharge of the duties of his office"—while he is in "Session," in the analogous language of Section 6.

[57]See Youngstown Sheet & Tube Co. v. Sawyer, 343 U.S. 579, 585 (1952).
[60]3 Story, supra note [45], § 1563.

Fifth, it is immunity even for certain lawsuits based on a President's private conduct—immunity for his "person." Once again, this tracks arrest immunity rather than speech or debate immunity. Finally, Story carefully limits this immunity to "civil cases"—just as the Arrest Clause (but not the Speech or Debate Clause) is limited to civil cases.

This quote from Story could be challenged, or narrowly construed, were we writing on a clean slate. Perhaps Story is referring only to technical civil arrests, rather than to broader litigation impediments. In any event, Story is not speaking in his judicial capacity, but only as a commentator on the Constitution (though perhaps its most distinguished commentator), and is writing almost fifty years after the document's ratification.

Today, however, we do not write on a clean slate. We write in the wake of *Nixon*. A very broad reading of Story is inscribed in the United States Reports—it is the rock on which *Nixon* is built. If Story was enough to win for Nixon, why not for Clinton? * * *Indeed, as should be clear by now, a careful reading of Story does *not* support the result in *Nixon*, contrary to Justice White's glib concession in dissent.[64] But a close reading of Story does support Clinton and our Arrest Clause methodology today.

* * *

[T]he fact that the evidence fails to support *Nixon* doesn't mean that the same goes for Clinton. On the contrary, even if *Nixon* is a twisted stretch of history and text, the historical evidence does provide sturdy support for temporary immunity from arrest.[73] Despite what the pundits are saying, Clinton has a far stronger case than Nixon had.

VICTORIA NOURSE, THE VERTICAL SEPARATION OF POWERS

49 DUKE L.J. 749, 750–752, 758–760, 768–775 (1999).

Tell a lawyer to take out a pen and paper and to write down the power the Constitution provides to the Congress, the President, and the courts. No doubt she will provide you with something that looks vaguely like the Vesting Clauses or a list of governmental functions, emphasizing the executive, legislative, and judicial. What you will not have is a working government—or at least, there will be no one running it, no one voting for it, and no one representing anyone else. You may excise the words

[64]See *Nixon*, 457 U.S. at 776 (White, J., dissenting) (conceding that the Story passage "clearly supports [Nixon's] position but it is of such a late date that it contributes little to understanding the original intent").

[73]To put the point slightly differently, we are suggesting that President Clinton's immunity should not turn on whether his alleged conduct towards Jones was an "official" duty or not (a holdover of viewing immunity through the prism of the Speech or Debate Clause), but rather should turn on whether the Jones suit and others like it * * *could functionally "Arrest" the President while at "Session."

"executive," "legislative," and "judicial" from the Vesting Clauses, replace them with other adjectives, or strike the Vesting Clauses altogether. People will still vote, Congress will still convene, the Supreme Court will still decide cases, and the President will still direct his administration. The Constitution describes our government as a compendium of executive, legislative, and judicial powers, but it also creates that government by constituting electoral relationships that confer political authority.

If this is right, then it is time to reconsider a basic assumption relied upon by scholars, courts, and lawyers in analyzing separation of powers controversies. It is a commonplace of structural theory that we have three branches of government arranged horizontally along "functional" lines, separating judicial from executive from legislative power. In this Article, I urge that this image of horizontal separation is incomplete if it does not take into account the "vertical" aspects of political power, aspects that are intimately connected with notions of constitutional risk and institutional incentive. By vertical power, I mean those relationships between government and constituency that create and, in this sense, constitute the three different branches of our government. The power created by our Constitution comes from more than constitutional description; it comes from the people, aggregated in different kinds of constituencies, commonly distinguished as districts, states, and nation. Thus, every shift in governmental function or task can be reconceived, not simply as a shift in tasks but also as a shift in the relative power of popular constituencies. For example, rather than asking whether a shift in power is really executive or legislative, we might ask from which constituency the power comes, and to which constituency it is given, and what relative risks and incentives that shift entails for those constituencies. The risk on which we would focus would not be the fuzziness of a functional label, but, instead, the risk that a shift in power would create substantial incentives for government actors to silence a majority or to oppress a minority. There may be no easy answers here; indeed, the calculus may be quite complex, but at the same time it may represent an "angle of vision" that is distinctly more realistic than much legal discussion on structural matters. Indeed, I believe that a vertical approach may lead us toward a functionalism that frees us from the standard battles about whether we really can define the legislative, the judicial, and the executive.

* * *

The premise of the vertical approach is simple: if, as the constitutional text makes quite clear, the departments are created by various political relationships—by voting, by representation, by appointment—then we must pay attention to those relationships in considering shifts in power. In one sense, this is obvious: shifting the war power to the Supreme Court shifts political relationships as well as tasks; it significantly weakens the people's power to decide whether to go to war. This reflects an equally obvious but broader principle that changing the nature of the constituencies that control government can change the form of that government. Put decisionmaking power in the hands of the few, and you lurch toward aristocracy; put it in the hands of the many, and you invite the mob; take away the representative relationship altogether, and you risk anarchy or autocracy. The vertical approach asks whether and how the shifting of tasks among government players affects "who" will decide, where the "who" appears as the constituencies creating the departments, and where the risks are not descriptive impurities, but structural incentives likely to change political relationships between the governed and their governors.

Verticality seeks to identify constitutional harm in something more than the transcendental—more than "too much" power, "balance" disrupted, or "functions mixed." The vertical approach posits that the constitutional danger in shifting functions lies in popular silences and amplifications, in empowering some constituencies at the expense of others. Under this view, the problem with sending the war decision to the Court is not the bad descriptive fit between war and judicial function but the silencing of national and local constituencies on such an important issue—that the Court will go to war without the people. As the Founders might have said, the fear is that, if we give the war power to the Court, we will have traded the people's decision for one by an elite, that we will have exchanged democracy for aristocracy.

Rather than looking for a description to impose from the "top-down," the vertical approach considers power from the "bottom-up"—as a function of the people who grant it to the government—and thus is an explicitly populist approach. It takes seriously, as a matter of constitutional law and theory, what Hannah Arendt made clear so long ago—that "when we say of somebody that he is 'in power' we actually refer to his being empowered by a certain number of people to act in their name." With this shift from the categorical to the relational idea of political power, the question is not what power has changed hands, where the power belongs, or whether the power shifted is too much, but who will wield that authority and what comparative risks that shift in decisionmaker entails for constitutional relationships between the people and their government.

The vertical approach, then, locates constitutional risk, quite literally, in constituent harm—in the relationship between changing constituencies and forms of government. The Framers knew that a republic depends for its form upon the ways in which it "mixes" countervailing forms of representation. Indeed, the unique genius of the constitutional plan was its ability to mediate self-interest through three forms of popular sovereignty, government by three differently aggregated constituencies: the states, the localities, and the nation. It is in changing the relative strength of these political relationships that we shift power in the sense of changing the form of our government. It is this that the law of the separation of powers should illuminate.

* * *

If the vertical approach helps to give us a new perspective on separation of powers controversies, it must help in a real constitution, not simply a hypothetical one. Recent events have suggested that there is a broad gap between the nation's political life and the Supreme Court's analysis of the risks of structural change. In this part, I explain why I believe that the vertical approach may help us ask questions that bridge that "realism" gap in the separation of powers. To flesh out an alternative vertical approach, I consider what it might have told us about the Supreme Court's decisions in *Clinton v. Jones*[68] and *Morrison v. Olson*,[69] as well as in the Court's recent federalism cases. * * *

Clinton v. Jones is known as a case about executive function and presidential immunity. Faced with the question whether the President could be sued by a private party, Paula Jones, the Supreme Court rejected the President's arguments that the judicial consideration of this suit would violate the separation of powers, concluding that the suit would in no way impair executive or judicial "functions." As the Court put it: "[t]he litigation of questions that relate entirely to the unofficial conduct of the individual who happens to be the President poses no perceptible risk of misallocation of either judicial power or executive power."[72]

Read today, with the knowledge that the Jones suit led to the impeachment of a sitting President, it seems difficult to understand the Supreme Court's confidence that "there is no possibility that [its] decision will" have a significant effect upon the presidency.[73] And, yet, from a functional perspective, the Court's analysis seems perfectly plausible. This proposal, like the ones in our hypothetical constitution, does not require that the President perform any new or incompatible function; nor does it seem to require the courts to take on executive responsibilities. Indeed, the Supreme Court seems quite right to conclude that the President's inconvenience was insufficient to overcome the plaintiff's right to be heard. Balancing the "inconvenience" of a private suit against the "rule of law," the Court not surprisingly decided that the suit should go forward.

The issue remains whether the functional inquiry identifies all the constitutional risks at stake. No one was really claiming in *Clinton v. Jones* that the President could not be sued, only that he could not be sued while in

[68] 520 U.S. 681 (1997).

[69] 487 U.S. 654 (1988).

[72] [*Jones*, 520 U.S.] at 701.

[73] Id. (emphasis added).

office. That should have raised, for the Court, the question of constituency and political relationship. For what is the difference between a President after his term and a President during his term but the interests of those who empower him? In a republic, a President does not "happen []" (as the Court put it); he is elected, and, as an elected official, he exercises the political authority granted him by a national constituency. From the vertical perspective, then, the question in *Clinton* is not simply about inconvenience or even the rule of law, but the risks to the people the President represents. Put more colloquially, a civil lawsuit against a sitting President may be problematic not because the President is in any sense above the law (he is not), but because the courts, which are political outsiders in our system, are not above the people.

To see the risks, it is important to remember that a President sued is a President who may lose a suit and that a President who may lose a suit is a President who will do political battle over that loss. No matter how trivial or private the suit may seem—from a bad debt to a slip-and-fall—if the President is adjudged to be negligent or to defalcate, his loss will not simply be the loss of a private citizen but the loss of a President, a player in that institutional competition we know as the separation of powers. It is not too difficult to predict how a presidential loss in a suit about drunk driving or bad debts might create an incentive for the President's political opponents to step up their attacks or even lead to impeachment. What may be more difficult to see is how a judicial ruling changes the President's fate in that political battle. It is the judicial proceeding that transforms public denials into claims of perjury, that transforms a private matter of a debt or a slip-and-fall into a violation of the "rule of law." With or without a judicial ruling, the facts that led to the *Jones* suit might well have been the subject of an impeachment proceeding. With a court ruling, however, the case for impeachment changes: whether the court says it is avoiding politics or not, its decision puts the judicial imprimatur, institutional legitimacy, even the rule of law, on one side of the political debate. And, with this, the court risks acquiring power to determine (even if in small part) the political fate of the nation and its President.

Traditionally, the separation of powers issue in *Jones* is seen as one of executive power, but, if this is right, the question turns out to be less about the *executive* than about the *judiciary*. Indeed, it is a question less about the relation of the President to the courts than that of the *Congress* to the courts. The separation of powers risk is that the court is (inadvertently, perhaps, or even against its wishes) acquiring a political role in "checking" the President, a role typically left to Congress. As a general rule, our constitutional system leaves it to the politically responsive branches to do battle by means of oversight and impeachment. Shifting even a small part of that power to the courts, relative political outsiders, and away from

Congress and its direct constituency relations, should represent a serious separation of powers question. Why? Because it risks shifting a matter of great public import to those least responsive to the people.

There are, of course, important countervailing interests at stake in the *Jones* case—the interests of the plaintiff and private litigants generally. Indeed, it is these interests that make many appeal reflexively to notions of the "rule of law" and "individual rights." The vertical approach suggests, however, that this kind of move may be a bit too easy; indeed, that these very concerns might be more likely to be satisfied by postponing, rather than proceeding with, the lawsuit. [S]hifts in constituency typically do not simply lead to one kind of risk. Shifts from a more to a less politically tied body tend to increase minoritarian risk—the risk that a minority may silence a majority; at the same time, shifts from a less to a more politically tied body tend to increase majoritarian risk—that a majority will silence a minority or individual. *Jones* raises not only the question whether the Court's ruling will place the unelected in charge of the nation's political life (minoritarian risk) but also whether it will subject individual litigants to the vagaries of the nation's political life (majoritarian risk). Put another way, if one is really concerned about Paula Jones's fate, one must worry that, if the suit is to proceed while the President is still in office, politics might inevitably affect the judgment in her case. There is always the risk that any judge empowered to rule against the nation's leading political figure will be influenced by majoritarian politics in making her ruling, whether it is in rejecting such politics too strenuously or in coddling it too nervously. And if the judge rules for or against the President or Jones because of majoritarian concerns, rather than the demands of the lawsuit, one can hardly call this "the rule of law."

* * * *Morrison v. Olson*,[84] the IC case, presents difficult questions for the Court's future approach in separation of powers cases (even though the IC statute has not been renewed). To many, today, in light of concerns about Kenneth Starr's IC investigation, it seems difficult to accept the majority's conclusion that the statute did not "unduly trammel[] on executive authority."[87]At the same time, although many have come to newly admire Justice Scalia's dissent in *Morrison*, few are willing to accept the implications of its formalism—that independent agencies are unconstitutional.

The vertical approach may, however, provide some clues about what went wrong in *Morrison*—how functionalism could have turned out to be

[84]487 U.S. 654 (1988).

[87]*Morrison*, 487 U.S. at 691; see also id. at 693 ("The final question to be addressed is whether the Act, taken as a whole, violates the principle of separation of powers by unduly interfering with the role of the Executive Branch.").

so unrealistic despite its contrary pretensions, and yet how the dissent's formalism failed to cure this problem. *Morrison* is traditionally perceived as a case about executive power and the constitutionality of independent executive agents. As I explain more fully below, there were other important issues left unaddressed in *Morrison*. From a vertical perspective, *Morrison* raises questions about the relationship of the IC not only to the President but also to the Congress. Indeed, the vertical approach suggests that both the majority and dissent in *Morrison* may well have been trying to answer the wrong question by focusing so heavily on questions of removal. In the end, the most serious issue *Morrison* poses may not be about the status of independent agencies or the unitary executive but about whether the statute permits Congress and the President to sever from the people, even in small part, their power to choose their own government.

Consider a statute in which Congress delegated part of its impeachment authority to an independent agent. The problem with this proposal would not depend upon the independence of the agent alone, but upon the fact that an agent, with no constituency, is deciding the ultimate constituency issue in a republic—the political fate of a sitting President. The committed functionalist would no doubt argue that a partial delegation of the impeachment power does not interfere with the functioning of the executive or the Congress. But such an approach betrays the oddity of the conventional functionalists' realism. Perhaps a partial delegation of a function seems to matter little in the abstract, but, in real life, it may matter quite a good deal. Indeed, it is precisely because it would matter to the people that many would find it quite unconstitutional for Congress to hand over its impeachment authority to an independent entity; in such a world, "we the people" do not decide who governs but, instead, "we the investigating authority" decides. The constitutional risk of elitism is obvious: that a willful bureaucrat will investigate and prompt the removal of a President that the nation does not really want removed.

I am not arguing that the IC statute should have been held unconstitutional because the statute delegated Congress's power to impeach the President. But I am arguing that the IC is not a standard "independent agent," raising only questions analogous to those raised by the status of the Federal Trade Commission or the Nuclear Regulatory Commission. The important point here, lost in the Court's focus on executive power and removal, is the degree to which the IC statute shifts constituencies on the question of executive misconduct and impeachment and, as a result, creates significant incentives for majority will to be thwarted. Traditionally, Congress (and its state and local audiences) is responsible for policing presidential misconduct; the Constitution itself seals this by granting the impeachment power to the House initially and then to the Senate. The statute not only permits the IC to investigate and prosecute the President but also requires the IC to inform the Congress of grounds for impeachment. As Julie O'Sullivan has noted, "[t]his mandatory impeachment referral provision arguably makes impeachment proceedings far more likely to be initiated, and when initiated, far more threatening to the administration," because it may allow "an IC to control the timing, scope, and content of impeachment inquiries."[97] The IC statute thus shifts at least some of the responsibilities ordinarily committed to the Congress to an official who is not only independent of the President but also independent of the Congress, and whose incentives may dispose him toward, rather than against, impeachment.

At the same time as the IC statute shifts power away from Congress, it also shifts important powers to Congress. Traditionally, the power to prosecute is remitted to the executive department, not to the Congress. However, under the IC statute, the decision to prosecute is granted, in part, to members of Congress. The statute specifically contemplates that "[t]he Committee on the Judiciary of either House of the Congress, or a majority of majority party members or a majority of all non-majority party members of either such committee, may request in writing that the Attorney General apply for the appointment of an independent counsel." That application must identify the persons and subject of the proposed investigation. The mere power to identify misconduct and its targets surely increases Congress's power, and the power of particular members of Congress, to target individuals relative to the powers Congress would have without the IC statute. Indeed, there is no greater power of a prosecutor than to decide the targets of an investigation and potential prosecution.

* * *

A functional approach might tell us that, since this exercise of congressional authority does not undermine the prosecutorial function in general, it is permissible. A vertical approach, however, suggests that this should be constitutionally controversial. The Constitution grants no power to Congress to prosecute criminal behavior; indeed the Constitution bars bills of attainder explicitly. There is a good reason for this bar: the incentives of congressional leaders to punish the politically unpopular or simply their political enemies. Those very same risks inhere in the IC statute. By granting members of Congress the power to target individuals, and without substantial room for the Attorney General to reject investigations, the IC statute clearly creates incentives to politicize the decision of whom to prosecute. And those incentives are likely to be greater than if the decision rested in the hands of a career prosecutor. This is precisely because the political incentives of members of Congress, with their smaller and more

[97]Julie R. O'Sullivan, The Interaction Between Impeachment and the Independent Counsel Statute, 86 Geo.L.J. 2193, 2195 (1998).

local audiences, are likely to be stronger than those of a federal prosecutor, whose political incentives are dispersed across a national constituency, a broad range of prosecutions, and are limited by scarce resources. In shifting a decision from a relatively less to a more local political audience, the IC statute increases risks to minorities and individuals—risks that the decision to prosecute may depend upon the political whims not only of Congress, but of a few minority members of a congressional committee.

To summarize, the IC statute poses two distinct structural risks—separate and apart from the traditional question the statute raises about independent agents and the unitary executive. Shifting influence over the question of impeachment from state and local constituencies to an actor without constituency (i.e., the IC) takes a very public, political act and hands it, in part, to an actor without public constituency. The second risk in *Morrison* raises a very different issue—risk not to the public but to individuals. Shifting part of the decision to prosecute from the executive to the Congress increases the risks that individuals will be targeted for their politics, not their crimes. Events have suggested that both of these risks were more real than anticipated either by *Morrison*'s dissenting or majority opinions.

* * *

The separation of powers debate is, in the end, a debate as much about the structure of our government as about an idea of law and political power. To a lawyer, political power is created in the image of law. Power is not the power to speak on behalf of others, as political theorists tell us; instead, power is the power to command legitimately. Shifts in power do not shift constituencies or political voice, but they shift the legal authority to do something. This view, when applied to the separation of powers, has kept our gaze on rather lawyerly questions. Scholars are obsessed with answering questions about departmental hierarchy and the best interpretation of the terms of the departments' grants of authority, the Vesting Clauses. Even functionalists, who aim toward a more critical stance, borrow this lawyerly assumption. They simply wish to soften its implications.

The problem for this lawyerly ideal is the one with which I began this Article: it does very little actually to create a government. Neither the Vesting Clauses nor enumerated powers authorize the vote or create constituencies. As a result, they cannot create the kind of relationships that lawyers describe somewhat disdainfully as "political" power. Law's vision of power as authority or command may be necessary to understand governmental structure, but it is not sufficient. The Constitution not only limits the exercise of political power but also creates political power. In a sense, we should know this. The Founders knew it: Madison understood that political order depends upon channeling public opinion. The moderns know it: political philosophers of various stripes have argued that power is public voice and relationship. Indeed, in an age of resurgent interest in republicanism, it seems particularly odd that lawyers would continue to invest unreflectively in the notion that political power is only function or authority. Surely, to believe that power is decreed from somewhere on high, transcending public voice, is antithetical to the notion that "we the people" constitute our government.

The great danger here is not that the Supreme Court will make the wrong decision. We have survived two hundred years of structural controversy, some true crises, and more than a few difficult judicial decisions. But it is tempting to wonder whether we would be better off if the Court did not base its decisions on a view of the world in its own image. Like most institutions, courts have a tendency toward institutional self-regard, and this affects the ways in which they think about concepts. Function, as law, sees the world of political power in the image of law, and it sustains the courts' idea of their own legitimacy by placing in their hands the rule of law. But this kind of self-regard, however important in some respects, also poses risks. For in such a world, it is possible to sever the people from their Constitution, to believe, as the Supreme Court so recently said, that it is possible to have a government in which a man simply "happens" to be President. "[A] legal order cannot in the long run be true to itself and at the same time be better than the values or vision of its beneficiaries."[218] In the end, a constitution disembodied is no constitution at all.

---

[218] [James Willard Hurst, Law and Conditions of Freedom 5 (1956)].

BIBLIOGRAPHY

General Theoretical Approaches

Barber, S., THE CONSTITUTION AND THE DELEGATION OF CONGRESSIONAL POWER (1975).

Brown, *Separated Powers and Ordered Liberty,* 139 U.Pa.L.Rev. 1513 (1991).

Calabresi & Rhodes, The *Structural Constitution: Unitary Executive, Plural Judiciary,* 105 Harv.L.Rev. 1155 (1992).

Casper, *An Essay in Separation of Powers: Some Early Versions and Practices*, 30 Wm. & Mary L. Rev. 211 (1989).

Chemerinsky, *A Paradox Without a Principle: A Comment on the Burger Court's Jurisprudence in Separation of Powers Cases,* 60 S.Cal.L.Rev. 1083 (1987).

Choper, J., JUDICIAL REVIEW AND THE NATIONAL POLITICAL PROCESS ch. 5 (1980).

Currie, *The Distribution of Powers after Bowsher*, 1986 Sup.Ct.Rev. 19.

THE FEDERALIST Nos. 47–48, 51 (Madison).

Feld, *Separation of Political Powers: Boundaries or Balance?,* 21 Ga.L.Rev. 171 (1986).

Fisher, L., CONSTITUTIONAL CONFLICTS BETWEEN CONGRESS AND THE PRESIDENT (1985).

Fisher, L., THE POLITICS OF SHARED POWER (1981).

Krent, *Separating the Strands in Separation of Powers Controversies,* 74 Va.L.Rev. 1253 (1988).

Lessig & Sunstein, *The President and the Administration,* 94 Colum.L.Rev. 1 (1994).

Lowi, T., THE END OF LIBERALISM ch. 5 (2d ed. 1979).

Merrill, *The Constitutional Principle of Separation of Powers,* 1991 Sup.Ct.Rev. 225.

Osgood, *Governmental Functions and Constitutional Doctrine: The Historical Constitution,* 72 Cornell L.Rev. 553 (1987).

Rakove, J., ORIGINAL MEANINGS: POLITICS AND IDEAS IN THE MAKING OF THE CONSTITUTION (1996).

Sargentich, *The Limits of the Parliamentary Critique of the Separation of Powers,* 34 Wm. & Mary L.Rev. 679 (1993).

Schoenbrod, *The Delegation Doctrine: Could the Court Give It Substance?,* 83 Mich.L.Rev. 1223 (1985).

Sharp, *The Classical American Doctrine of "The Separation of Powers",* 2 U.Chi.L.Rev. 385 (1935).

Sherry, *Separation of Powers: Asking a Different Question*, 30 Wm. & Mary L. Rev. 287 (1989).

Stith, *Congress' Power of the Purse,* 97 Yale L.J. 1343 (1988).

Strauss, *Formal and Functional Approaches to Separation-of-Powers Questions—A Foolish Inconsistency?,* 72 Cornell L.Rev. 488 (1987).

Strauss, *The Place of Agencies in Government: Separation of Powers and the Fourth Branch*, 84 Colum.L.Rev. 573 (1984).

The Administrative State

Bruff, *Legislative Formality, Administrative Rationality*, 63 Texas L.Rev. 207 (1984).

Bruff, On the Constitutional Status of the Administrative Agencies, 36 Am.U.L.Rev. 491 (1987).

Eskridge & Ferejohn, *The Article I, Section 7 Game*, 60 Geo.L.J. 523 (1992).

Elliott, INS v. Chadha: *The Administrative Constitution, the Constitution, and the Legislative Veto,* 1983 Sup.Ct.Rev. 125.

Louis Fisher, CONSTITUTIONAL CONFLICTS BETWEEN CONGRESS AND THE PRESIDENT (1985).

Krent, *Fragmenting the Unitary Executive: Congressional Delegations of Administrative Authority Outside the Federal Government*, 85 Nw.U.L.Rev. 62 (1990).

Miller, *Independent Agencies,* 1986 Sup.Ct.Rev. 41.

Nagel, *The Legislative Veto, the Constitution, and the Courts*, 3 Const.Comm. 61 (1986).

Smolla, *Bring Back the Legislative Veto: A Proposal for a* Constitutional Amendment, 37 Ark.L.Rev. 509 (1984).

Spann, *Deconstructing the Legislative Veto*, 68 Minn.L.Rev. 473 (1984).

Strass, *Was There a Baby in the Bathwater? A Comment on the Supreme Court's Legislative Veto Decision,* 1983 Duke L.J. 789.

Tribe, *The Legislative Veto Decision: A Law by Any Other Name?*, 21 Harv.J.Legis. 7 (1984).

Verkuil, *The Status of Independent Agencies After Bowsher v. Synar,* 1986 Duke L.J. 779.

Presidential Power

Bruff, *Judicial Review and the President's Statutory Powers,* 68 Va.L.Rev. 1 (1982).

Calabresi, *Some Normative Arguments for the Unitary Executive,* 48 Ark.L.Rev. 23 (1995).

Calabresi, *The Vesting Clauses as Power Grants,* 88 Nw.U.L.Rev. 1377 (1994).

Calabresi & Yoo, *The Unitary Executive During the First Half-Century,* 47 Case W.Res.L.Rev. 1451 (1997).

Corwin, *Tenure of Office and the Removal Power Under the Constitution,* 27 Colum.L.Rev. 353 (1927).

Easterbrook, *Presidential Review,* 40 Case W.Res.L.Rev. 905 (1990).

THE FEDERALIST Nos. 67–77 (Hamilton).

Farber, D., LINCOLN'S CONSTITUTION (2003).

Fitts, *The Paradox of Power in the Modern State: Why a Unitary, Centralized Presidency May Not Exhibit Effective or Legitimate Leadership,* 144 U.Pa.L.Rev. 827 (1996).

Flaherty, *Relearning Founding Lessons: The Removal Power and Joint Accountability,* 47 Case W.Res.L.Rev. 1563 (1997).

Froomkin, *The Imperial Presidency's New Vestments,* 88 Nw.U.L.Rev. 1346 (1994).

Lessig & Sunstein, *The President and the Administration,* 94 Colum.L.Rev. 1 (1994).

MacDonald, F., THE PRESIDENCY: AN INTELLECTUAL HISTORY (1994).

Shane, *Independent Policymaking and Presidential Power: A* Constitutional *Analysis,* 57 Geo. Wash.L.Rev. 596 (1989).

Shane, P., and Bruff, H., SEPARATION OF POWERS LAW: CASES AND MATERIALS (1996).

Sidak, *The President's Power of the Purse,* 1989 Duke L.J. 1162 (1989).

Westin, A., THE ANATOMY OF A CONSTITUTIONAL CASE (1958).

Foreign Affairs and the Constitution

Casper, *Constitutional Constraints on the Conduct of Foreign and* D*efense Policy: A Nonjudicial Model,* 43 U.Chi.L.Rev. 463 (1976).

Glennon, M., CONSTITUTIONAL DIPLOMACY (1990).

Glennon, *Too Far Apart: Repeal the War Powers Resolution,* 50 U.Miami L.Rev. 17 (1995).

Goldwin, R. and Licht, R., FOREIGN POLICY AND THE CONSTITUTION (1990).

Henkin, L., CONSTITUTIONALISM, DEMOCRACY, AND FOREIGN AFFAIRS (1990).

Henkin, L., FOREIGN AFFAIRS AND THE CONSTITUTION (1972).

Koh, H., THE NATIONAL SECURITY CONSTITUTION (1990).

Koh, *Why the President (Almost) Always Wins in Foreign* Affairs*: Lessons of the Iran-Contra Affair,* 97 Yale L.J. 1255 (1988).

Lobel, *"Little Wars" and the Constitution*, 50 U.Miami L.Rev. 61 (1995).

Powell, J., THE PRESIDENT'S AUTHORITY OVER FOREIGN AFFAIRS: AN ESSAY IN CONSTITUTIONAL INTERPRETATION (2002).

Sofaer, *The Power Over War*, 50 U.Miami L.Rev. 33 (1995).

Trimble, P., INTERNATIONAL LAW: UNITED STATES FOREIGN RELATIONS LAW (2002).

War Powers

Adler, *The Constitution and Presidential Warmaking: The Enduring Debate,* 103 Pol.Sci.Q. 1 (1988).

Berger, *War-Making by the President,* 121 U.Pa.L.Rev. 29 (1972).

Bickel, *Congress, the President and the Power to Wage War,* 48 Chi.-Kent L.Rev. 131 (1971).

Ely, *The American War in Indochina (Parts I & II),* 42 Stan.L.Rev. 876, 1092 (1990).

Koh, *The Coase Theorem and the War Power: A Response*, 41 Duke L.J. 122 (1991).

Lofgren, *On War-Making, Original Intent, and Ultra-Whiggery,* 21 Val.U.L.Rev. 53 (1986).

Lofgren, *War-Making Under the Constitution: The Original Understanding,* 81 Yale L.J. 672 (1972).

Ratner, *The Coordinated Warmaking Power—Legislative,* Executive, *and Judicial Roles,* 44 S.Cal.L.Rev. 461 (1971).

Reveley, W.T., WAR POWERS OF THE PRESIDENT AND CONGRESS (1981).

Rostow, *"Once More Into the Breach:" The War Powers Resolution Revisited,* 21 Val.U.L.Rev. 1 (1986).

Rubner, *The Reagan Administration, the 1974 War Powers Resolution, and the Invasion of Grenada,* 100 Pol.Sci.Q. 627 (1986).

Scigliano, *The War Powers Resolution and the War Powers,* in THE PRESIDENCY IN THE CONSTITUTIONAL ORDER 124 (J. Bessette & J. Tulis eds. 1981).

Sidak, *To Declare War*, 41 Duke L.J. 27 (1991).

Sofaer, A., WAR, FOREIGN AFFAIRS AND CONSTITUTIONAL POWER (1976).

Stromseth, *Understanding Constitutional War Powers Today: Why Methodology Matters*, 106 Yale L.J. 845 (1996).

Treanor, *Fame, the Founding, and the Power to Declare War*, 82 Cornell L.Rev. 695 (1997).

Van Alstyne, *Congress, the President, and the Power to Declare War: A Requiem for Vietnam,* 121 U.Pa.L.Rev. 1 (1972).

Vance, *Striking the Balance: Congress and the President Under* the *War Powers Resolution,* 133 U.Pa.L.Rev. 79 (1984).

Wormuth, F. and Firmage, E., TO CHAIN THE DOG OF WAR: THE WAR POWER OF CONGRESS IN HISTORY AND LAW (1986).

Yoo, *The Original Understanding of the War Powers*, 84 Cal. L. Rev. 167 (1996).

Presidential Impeachment

Berger, R., IMPEACHMENT: THE CONSTITUTIONAL PROBLEMS (1973).

Black, C., IMPEACHMENT: A HANDBOOK (1974).

Brant, I., IMPEACHMENT: TRIALS AND ERRORS (1972).

Committee on Federal Legislation of the Bar Association of the City of New York, THE LAW OF PRESIDENTIAL IMPEACHMENT (1974).

Fenton, *The Scope of the Impeachment Power,* 65 Nw.U.L.Rev. 719 (1971).

Freedman, *The Law as King and the King as Law: Is a President Immune from Criminal Prosecution Before Impeachment?,* 20 Hastings Const.L.Q. 7 (1992).

Garvey, *Foreword: Judicial Discipline and Impeachment,* 76 Ky.L.J. 633 (1988).

Gerhardt, M., THE FEDERAL IMPEACHMENT PROCESS: A CONSTITUTIONAL AND HISTORICAL ANALYSIS (2d ed. 2000).

Gormley, *Impeachment and the Impeachment Counsel: A Dysfunctional Union*, 51 Stan.L.Rev. 309 (1999).

HIGH CRIMES AND MISDEMEANORS (Funk & Wagnalls 1973).

Pollitt, *Sex in the Oval Office and Cover-Up Under Oath: Impeachable Offense?*, 77 N.C.L.Rev. 259 (1998).

Presidential Privileges and Immunities

Berger, R., EXECUTIVE PRIVILEGE: A CONSTITUTIONAL MYTH (1974).

Cox, *Executive Privilege,* 122 U.Pa.L.Rev. 1383 (1974).

Freund, *Foreword: On Presidential Privilege,* 88 Harv.L.Rev. 13 (1974).

Mishkin, *Great Cases and Soft Law: A Comment on* United States v. Nixon, 22 UCLA L.Rev. 76 (1974).

Peterson, *Prosecuting Executive Branch Officials for Contempt of Congress,* 66 N.Y.U.L.Rev. 563 (1991).

Shane, *Legal Disagreement and Negotiation in a Government of Laws: The Case of Executive Privilege Claims Against Congress,* 71 Minn.L.Rev. 461 (1987).

Symposium, *The Independent Counsel Act: From Watergate to Whitewater and Beyond*, 86 Geo.L.J. 2011–2419 (1998).

Tiefer, *The Specially Investigated President*, 5 U.Chi.L.Sch. Roundtable 143–204 (1998).

Chapter VI

EQUALITY AND RACE

The next three Chapters are designed to explore several controversial themes concerning the Constitution's guarantee of equality. The Equal Protection Clause declares that "No State shall . . . deny to any person within its jurisdiction the equal protection of the laws." As the materials on interpretation in Chapter II suggest, there may be more than one approach to understanding those few words.

One way of interpreting the Clause might be: "The laws shall treat all persons alike." But there is surely no constitutional harm in denying drivers' licenses to persons under 16. People are different in many ways, and the law can take account of some of those differences. One problem in reading the Equal Protection Clause is deciding what differences matter. *Who* must be treated alike?

We might instead restate the Clause this way: "People who are alike (in whatever way matters) shall be treated alike by the laws." But what does it mean to be treated alike? A welfare program may treat the poor alike by giving each person what he needs—the difference between his income and some minimum standard of living. Here the end result is "equal." A medical assistance program like Medicaid may treat the poor alike by giving everyone 14 days of free medical care. (This may be less than some need to be cured.) Here the stipend is "equal." A program for granting broadcast licenses (or drafting soldiers) may treat all persons alike by picking the winners (or losers) at random. Here the process gives each person an opportunity that is "equal." Thus another problem in reading the Equal Protection Clause is deciding what *equal* protection means.

As a general matter, courts do not look too hard at legislative decisions about classification and similar treatment.[1] But there is general agreement that assuring equal treatment to blacks is a value that lies at the core of the Equal Protection Clause. Scholars tend to theorize about equal protection by generalizing from the case of blacks. But what are the salient features of that case? What counts, for example, as equal treatment on the basis of race? Must we make no distinctions based on race? Why, for that matter, is

---

[1]New York City Transit Authority v. Beazer, 440 U.S. 568, 99 S.Ct. 1355, 59 L.Ed.2d 587 (1979).

treatment of blacks a core value of the Clause? Because that was the Framers' intent? Because there is something special about racial discrimination? Because blacks are an oppressed group in American society? Because the political process does not work for them? Getting the theory right on these questions is of the greatest importance if we are to get it right in other cases. The readings in this Chapter present a number of different answers.

We begin with historical treatments. Derrick Bell sends noted civil rights attorney Geneva Crenshaw (a fictional character) back in time to the Philadelphia Convention, where she gives the stunned delegates a look into the future. This literary technique permits Bell to explore the fundamental contradiction of our Constitution—that a document dedicated to freedom and self-government could not bring itself to condemn the most brutal denial of freedom and self-government: slavery. Raoul Berger focusses on the framing of the Fourteenth Amendment. He believes that those who wrote the Amendment intended the Equal Protection Clause to produce much less in the way of equal treatment than we usually suppose. It was, he contends, no more than a constitutional confirmation of the 1866 Civil Rights Act; and given the racism of Republicans and Democrats alike, Berger finds it unthinkable that Congress would have desired to go further. Michael Klarman examines the third watershed event in the history of American race relations—the Supreme Court's decision in *Brown v. Board of Education*.[2] Conventional wisdom holds that racial change in the latter half of the twentieth century was brought about largely by the courts, through reinterpretation and enforcement of the Equal Protection Clause. Not so, says Klarman. *Brown* had far less impact than people suppose, and the good it did came about almost perversely, by crystalizing southern white resistance to integration.

The next set of selections seeks to identify the theory that animates Equal Protection analysis. Paul Brest and Owen Fiss both start from the premise that racial classifications produce special harm. But they disagree about whether we should focus on individuals or on groups in assessing the harm the Clause forbids. Brest seeks to explain the intuitive appeal of an antidiscrimination principle concerned with individual harm. He then addresses a difficult problem for devotees of that principle: what to do with laws that make no discriminatory classification but have a disparate racial impact. Fiss responds that the antidiscrimination principle, because of its focus on individual harm and the lawmaking process, cannot deal satisfactorily with the problem of disparate impact. He proposes instead that we read into the Equal Protection Clause a group-disadvantaging principle. Such a principle might, for example, invalidate civil service job tests simply because blacks failed in disproportionately high numbers.

---

[2] 347 U.S. 483, 74 S.Ct. 686, 98 L.Ed. 873 (1954).

Charles Lawrence offers a different solution to the problem of disparate impact. Many effects that we treat as innocent may result from unconscious racism, a problem that is more like a disease than a crime. It is a mistake to insist on a showing of individual responsibility before addressing these effects. But the law need not go as far as Fiss suggests in order to combat them. We can accommodate the problem of unconscious racism within the framework of a "stigma" theory like Brest's or a "process" theory like Ely's.

John Hart Ely and Bruce Ackerman disagree about whether the rule of equality is concerned with process or with some more substantive value. Ely believes that the Equal Protection Clause should be used to perfect the democratic process. As Justice Stone said in *United States v. Carolene Products Co.,*[3] "prejudice against discrete and insular minorities" can cause the political process to malfunction. Racial classifications that disadvantage minorities are a signal that that has happened.

Ackerman responds that the process-oriented approach of *Carolene Products* fails on all counts. It ignores anonymous and diffuse minorities (homosexuals and women), who are less able to protect themselves politically than discrete and insular minorities (blacks). More fundamentally, despite its focus on process and its claim to value-neutrality, it ends by imposing substantive values on the political branches of government.

The final selection of the Chapter is by Kimberlé Crenshaw, a leading Critical Race Theorist. She argues that racist ideology is a central factor in the continued subordination of African Americans; like Derrick Bell, she maintains that white race consciousness has cemented ties among whites with arguably conflicting interests by defining blacks as "other." Antidiscrimination law may have eradicated formal barriers based on race but it has done little to remedy the deteriorating material conditions of most blacks, nor has it undermined the race consciousness that makes such inequality appear unproblematic.

[3] 304 U.S. 144, 152 n. 4, 58 S.Ct. 778, 783 n. 4, 82 L.Ed. 1234 (1938).

A. RACE AND THE CONSTITUTION IN HISTORICAL PERSPECTIVE

DERRICK BELL, THE CHRONICLE OF THE CONSTITUTIONAL CONTRADICTION

AND WE ARE NOT SAVED 26–44 (1987).

AT THE END of a journey back millions of light-years, I found myself standing quietly at the podium at the Constitutional Convention of 1787. It was late afternoon, and hot in that late summer way that makes it pleasant to stroll down a shaded country lane, but mighty oppressive in a large, crowded meeting room, particularly one where the doors are closed and locked to ensure secrecy.

The three dozen or so convention delegates looked tired. They had doubtless been meeting all day and now, clustered in small groups, were caucusing with their state delegations. So intense were their discussions that the few men who looked my way did not seem to see me. They knew this was a closed meeting, and thus could not readily take in the appearance, on what had just been an empty platform, of a tall stranger—a stranger who was not only a woman but also, all too clearly, black.

Though I knew I was protected by extraordinary forces, my hands were wet with nervous perspiration. Then I remembered why I was there. Taking a deep breath, I picked up the gavel and quickly struck the desktop twice, hard.

"Gentlemen," I said, "my name is Geneva Crenshaw, and I appear here to you as a representative of the late twentieth century to test whether the decisions you are making today might be altered if you were to know their future disastrous effect on the nation's people, both white and black."

For perhaps ten seconds, there was a shocked silence. Then the chamber exploded with shouts, exclamations, oaths. I fear the delegates' expressions of stunned surprise did no honor to their distinguished images. A warm welcome would have been too much to expect, but their shock at my sudden presence turned into an angry commotion unrelieved by even a modicum of curiosity.

The delegates to the Constitutional Convention were, in the main, young and vigorous. When I remained standing, unmoved by their strong language and dire threats, several particularly robust delegates charged toward the platform, determined to carry out the shouted orders: "Eject the Negro woman at once!"

Suddenly the hall was filled with the sound of martial music, blasting trumpets, and a deafening roll of snare drums. At the same time—as the delegates were almost upon me—a cylinder composed of thin vertical bars of red, white, and blue light descended swiftly and silently from the high ceiling, nicely encapsulating the podium and me.

* * *

"Gentlemen," I began, "delegates"—then paused and, with a slight smile, added, "fellow citizens, I—like some of you—am a Virginian, my forefathers having labored on the land holdings of your fellow patriot, the Honorable Thomas Jefferson. I have come to urge that, in your great work here, you not restrict the sweep of Mr. Jefferson's self-evident truths that all men are equal and endowed by the Creator with inalienable rights, including 'Life, Liberty and the pursuit of Happiness.'" It was, I thought, a clever touch to invoke the name of Thomas Jefferson who, then serving as American minister to France, was not a member of the Virginia delegation. But my remark could not overcome the offense of my presence.

"How dare you insert yourself in these deliberations?" a delegate demanded.

"I dare," I said, "because slavery is an evil that Jefferson, himself a slave owner and unconvinced that Africans are equal to whites," nevertheless found involved "a perpetual exercise of the most boisterous passions, the most unremitting despotism on the one part, and degrading submissions on the other." Slavery, Jefferson has written, brutalizes slave owner as well as slave and, worst of all, tends to undermine the "only firm basis" of liberty, the conviction in the minds of the people that liberty is "the gift of God."

"Gentlemen, it was also Thomas Jefferson who, considering the evil of slavery, wrote: 'I tremble for my country when I reflect that God is just; that his justice cannot sleep forever.'"

There was a hush in the group. No one wanted to admit it, but the ambivalence on the slavery issue expressed by Jefferson obviously had meaning for at least some of those in the hall. It seemed the right moment to prove both that I was a visitor from the future and that Jefferson's troubled concern for his country had not been misplaced. In quick, broad strokes, I told them of the country's rapid growth, of how slavery had expanded rather than withered of its own accord, and finally of how its continued presence bred first suspicion and then enmity between those in the South who continued to rely on a plantation economy and those Northerners committed to industrial development using white wage workers. The entry into the Union of each new state, I explained, further dramatized the disparity between North and South. Inevitably, the differences led to armed conflict—a civil war that, for all its bloody costs, did not settle those differences, and they remain divisive even as we celebrate our two-hundredth anniversary as one nation.

"The stark truth is that the racial grief that persists today," I ended, "originated in the slavery institutionalized in the document you are drafting. Is this, gentlemen, an achievement for which you wish to be remembered?"

Oblivious to my plea, a delegate tried what he likely considered a sympathetic approach. "Geneva, be reasonable. Go and leave us to our work. We have heard the petitions of Africans and of abolitionists speaking in their behalf. Some here are sympathetic to these pleas for freedom. Others are not. But we have debated this issue at length, and after three months of difficult negotiations, compromises have been reached, decisions made, language drafted and approved. The matter is settled. Neither you nor whatever powers have sent you here can undo what is done."

I was not to be put off so easily. "Sirs," I said, "I have come to tell you that the matter of slavery will not be settled by your compromises. And even when it is ended by armed conflict and domestic turmoil far more devastating than that you hope to avoid here, the potential evil of giving priority to property over human rights will remain. Can you not address the contradiction in your words and deeds?"

"There is no contradiction," replied another delegate. "Gouverneur Morris of Pennsylvania, the Convention's most outspoken opponent of slavery, has admitted that 'life and liberty were generally said to be of more value, than property, . . . [but] an accurate view of the matter would nevertheless prove that property was the main object of Society.'"

"A contradiction," another delegate added, "would occur were we to follow the course you urge. We are not unaware of the moral issues raised by slavery, but we have no response to the delegate from South Carolina, General Charles Cotesworth Pinckney, who has admonished us that 'property in slaves should not be exposed to danger under a Govt. instituted for the protection of property.'"

"Of what value is a government that does not secure its citizens in their persons and their property?" inquired another delegate. "Government, as Mr. Pierce Butler from South Carolina has maintained here, 'was instituted principally for the protection of property and was itself . . . supported by property.' Property, he reminded us, was 'the great object of government; the great cause of war; the great means of carrying it on.' And the whole South Carolina delegation joined him in making clear that 'the security the Southern states want is that their negroes may not be taken from them.'"

"Your deliberations here have been secret," I replied. "And yet history has revealed what you here would hide. The Southern delegates have demanded the slavery compromises as their absolute precondition to forming a new government."

"And why should it not be so?" a delegate in the rear called out. "I do not represent the Southern point of view, and yet their rigidity on the slavery issue is wholly natural, stemming as it does from the commitment of their economy to labor-intensive agriculture. We are not surprised by the determined bargaining of the Georgia and South Carolina delegations, nor distressed that our Southern colleagues, in seeking the protection they have gained, seem untroubled by doubts about the policy and morality of slavery and the slave trade."

"Then," I countered, "you are not troubled by the knowledge that this document will be defended by your Southern colleagues in the South Carolina ratification debates, by admissions that 'Negroes were our wealth, our only resource'?"

"Why, in God's name," the delegate responded, "should we be troubled by the truth, candidly stated? They have said no less in these chambers. General Charles Cotesworth Pinckney has flatly stated that 'South Carolina and Georgia cannot do without slaves.' And his cousin and fellow planter, Charles Pinckney, has added, 'The blacks are the laborers, the peasants of the Southern states.'"

At this, an elderly delegate arose and rapped his cane on his chair for attention. "Woman, we would have you gone from this place. But if a record be made, that record should show that the economic benefits of slavery do not accrue only to the South. Plantation states provide a market for Northern factories, and the New England shipping industry and merchants participate in the slave trade. Northern states, moreover, utilize slaves in the fields, as domestics, and even as soldiers to defend against Indian raids."

I shook my head. "Here you are then! Representatives from large and small states, slave states and those that have abolished slavery, all of you are protecting your property interests at the cost of your principles."

* * *

I asked, "Are you not concerned with the basic contradiction in your position: that you, who have gathered here in Philadelphia from each state in the confederacy, in fact represent and constitute major property holders? Do you not mind that your slogans of liberty and individual rights are basically guarantees that neither a strong government nor the masses will be able to interfere with your property rights and those of your class? This contradiction between what you espouse and what you here protect will be held against you by future citizens of this nation."

"Unless we continue on our present course," a delegate called out, "there will be no nation whose origins can be criticized. These sessions were called because the country is teetering between anarchy and bankruptcy. The nation cannot meet its debts. * * * "

* * *

"Do you recognize," I asked, "that in order to gain unity among yourselves, your slavery compromises sacrifice freedom for the Africans who live amongst you and work for you? Such sacrifices of the rights of one group of human beings will, unless arrested here, become a difficult-to-break pattern in the nation's politics."

* * *

"I expect," [said a man I decided must be James Madison,] "that many will question why I have agreed to the Constitution. And, like General Washington, I will answer: 'because I thought it safe to the liberties of the people, and the best that could be obtained from the jarring interests of States, and the miscellaneous opinions of Politicians; and because experience has proved that the real danger to America & to liberty lies in the defect of *energy & stability* in the present establishments of the United States.'"

"Do not think," added a delegate from Massachusetts, "that this Convention has come easily to its conclusions on the matter that concerns you. Gouverneur Morris from Pennsylvania has said to us in the strongest terms: 'Domestic slavery is the most prominent feature in the aristocratic countenance of the proposed Constitution.' He warned again and again that 'the people of Pennsylvania will never agree to a representation of Negroes.'"

"Many of us shared Mr. Morris's concern about basing apportionment on slaves as insisted by the Southern delegates. I recall with great sympathy his questions:

> Upon what principle is it that the slaves shall be computed in the representation? Are they men? Then make them citizens & let them vote? Are they property? Why then is no other property included? * * *
>
> The admission of slaves into the Representation when fairly explained comes to this: that the inhabitant of Georgia and S.C. who goes to the Coast of Africa, and in defiance of the most sacred laws of humanity tears away his fellow creatures from their dearest connections & damns them to the most cruel bondages, shall have more votes in a Govt. instituted for protection of the rights of mankind, then the Citizen of Pa or N. Jersey who views with a laudable horror, so nefarious a practice.

"I tell you, woman, this Convention was not unmoved at these words of Mr. Morris's only a few weeks ago."

* * *

To pierce the delegates' adamant front, I called on the oratorical talents that have, in the twentieth century, won me both praise and courtroom battles: "The real crisis you face should not be resolved by your recognition of slavery, an evil whose immorality will pollute the nation as it now stains your document. Despite your resort to euphemisms like *persons* to keep out of the Constitution such words as *slave* and *slavery,* you cannot evade the consequences of the ten different provisions you have placed in the Constitution for the purpose of protecting property in slaves.*"

* * *

Finally, a delegate responded to my challenge. "You have, by now, heard enough to realize that we have not lightly reached the compromises on slavery you so deplore. Perhaps we, with the responsibility of forming a radically new government in perilous times, see more clearly than is possible for you in hindsight that the unavoidable cost of our labors will be the need to accept and live with what you call a contradiction."

The delegate had gotten to his feet, and was walking slowly toward me as he spoke. "This contradiction is not lost on us. Surely we know, even though we are at pains not to mention it, that we have sacrificed the rights of some in the belief that this involuntary forfeiture is necessary to secure the rights for others in a society espousing, as its basic principle, the liberty of all."

He was standing directly in front of the shield now, ignoring its gentle hum, disregarding its known danger. "It grieves me," he continued, "that your presence here confirms my worst fears about the harm done to your people because the Constitution, while claiming to speak in an unequivocal voice, in fact promises freedom to whites and condemns blacks to slavery.

---

*The historian William Wiecek has listed the following direct and indirect accommodations to slavery contained in the Constitution:

1. Article I, Section 2: representatives in the House were apportioned among the states on the basis of population, computed by counting all free persons and three-fifths of the slaves (the "federal number," or "three-fifths," clause);

2. Article I, Section 2, and Article I, Section 9: two clauses requiring, redundantly, that direct taxes (including capitations) be apportioned among the states on the foregoing basis, the purpose being to prevent Congress from laying a head tax on slaves to encourage their emancipation;

3. Article I, Section 9: Congress was prohibited from abolishing the international slave trade to the United States before 1808;

4. Article IV, Section 2: the states were prohibited from emancipating fugitive slaves, who were to be returned on demand of the master;

5. Article I, Section 8: Congress empowered to provide for calling up the states' militias to suppress insurrections, including slave uprisings;

6. Article IV, Section 4: the federal government was obliged to protect the states against domestic violence, including slave insurrections;

7. Article V: the provisions of Article I, Section 9, clauses 1 and 4 (pertaining to the slave trade and direct taxes) were made unamendable;

8. Article I, Section 9, and Article I, Section 10: these two clauses prohibited the federal government and the states from taxing exports, one purpose being to prevent them from taxing slavery indirectly by taxing the exported product of slave labor.

[William Wiecek, The Sources of Antislavery Constitutionalism in America: 1760–1848 (1977), pp. 62–63.]

But what alternative do we have? Unless we here frame a constitution that can first gain our signatures and then win ratification by the states, we shall soon have no nation. For better or worse, slavery has been the backbone of our economy, the source of much of our wealth. It was condoned in the colonies and recognized in the Articles of Confederation. The majority of the delegates to this convention own slaves and must have that right protected if they and their states are to be included in the new government."

He paused and then asked, more out of frustration than defiance, "What better compromise on this issue can you offer than that which has been fashioned over so many hours of heated debate?"

The room was silent. The delegate, his statement made, his question presented, turned and walked slowly back to his seat. A few from his state touched his hand as he passed. Then all eyes turned to me.

I thanked the delegate for his question and then said, "The processes by which Northern states are even now abolishing slavery are known to you all. What is lacking here is not legislative skill but the courage to recognize the evil of holding blacks in slavery—an evil that would be quickly and universally condemned were the subjects of bondage members of the Caucasian race. You fear that unless the slavery of blacks is recognized and given protection, the nation will not survive. And my message is that the compromises you are making here mean that the nation's survival will always be in doubt. For now in my own day, after two hundred years and despite bloody wars and the earnest efforts of committed people, the racial contradiction you sanction in this document remains and threatens to tear this country apart."

"Mr. Chairman," said a delegate near the podium whose accent indicated that he was from the deep South, "this discussion grows tiresome and I resent to my very soul the presence in our midst of this offspring of slaves. If she accurately predicts the future fate of her race in this country, then our protection of slave property, which we deem essential for our survival, is easier to justify than in some later time when, as she implies, negroes remain subjugated even without the threats we face."

"Hear! Hear!" shouted a few delegates. "Bravo, Colonel!"

"It's all hypocrisy" the Colonel shouted, his arms flailing the air, "sheer hypocrisy." Our Northern colleagues bemoan slavery while profiting from it as much as we in the South, meanwhile avoiding its costs and dangers. And our friends from Virginia, where slavery began, urge the end of importation—not out of humanitarian motivations, as their speeches suggest, but because they have sufficient slaves, and expect the value of their property will increase if further imports are barred.

* * *

"This, Mr. Chairman, is nothing but hypocrisy or, worse, ignorance of history. We speak easily today of liberty, but the rise of liberty and equality in this country has been accompanied by the rise of slavery. The negress who has seized our podium by diabolical force charges that we hold blacks slaves because we view them as inferior. Inferior in every way they surely are, but they were not slaves when Virginia was a new colony 150 years ago. Or, at least, their status was hardly worse than the luckless white indentured servants brought here from debtors' prisons and the poverty-ridden streets of England. Neither slave nor servant lived very long in that harsh, fever-ridden clime."

The Colonel, so close to the podium, steadfastly refused to speak to me or even to acknowledge my presence.

"In the beginning," he went on, "life was harsh, but the coming of tobacco to Virginia in 1617 turned a struggling colony into a place where great wealth could be made relatively quickly. To cultivate the labor-intense crop, large numbers of mainly white, male servants, indentured to their masters for a period of years, were imported. Blacks, too, were brought to the colony, both as slaves and as servants. They generally worked, ate, and slept with the white servants.

"As the years passed, more and more servants lived to gain their freedom, despite the practice of extending terms for any offense, large or small. They soon became a growing, poverty-stricken class, some of whom resigned themselves to working for wages; others preferred a meager living on dangerous frontier land or a hand-to-mouth existence, roaming from one county to another, renting a bit of land here, squatting on some there, dodging the tax collector, drinking, quarreling, stealing hogs, and enticing servants to run away with them.

"It is not extraordinary to suggest that the planters and those who governed Virginia were caught in a dilemma—a dilemma more like the contradiction we are accused of building into the Constitution than may at first meet the eye. They needed workers to maintain production in their fields, but young men were soon rebellious, without either land of their own or women, who were not seen as fit to work the fields. Moreover, the young workers were armed and had to be armed to repel attacks from Indians by land and from privateers and petty-thieving pirates by sea.

"The worst fears of Virginia's leaders were realized when, in 1676, a group of these former servants returned from a fruitless expedition against the Indians to attack their rulers in what was called Bacon's Rebellion. Governor William Berkeley bemoaned his lot in terms that defined the problem: 'How miserable that man is that Governes a People where six parts of seaven at least are Poore Endebted Discontented and Armed.'

"The solution came naturally and without decision. The planters purchased more slaves and imported fewer English servants. Slaves were more expensive initially, but their terms did not end, and their owners gained the benefits of the slaves' offspring. Africans, easily identified by color, could not hope to run away without being caught. The fear of pain and death could be and was substituted for the extension of terms as an incentive to force the slaves to work. They were not armed and could be held in chains.

"The fear of slave revolts increased as reliance on slavery grew and racial antipathy became more apparent. But this danger, while real, was less than that from restive and armed freedmen. Slaves did not have rising expectations, and no one told them they had rights. They had lost their freedom. Moreover, a woman could be made to work and have children every two years, thereby adding to the income of her master. Thus, many more women than indentured servants were imported.

"A free society divided between large landholders and small was much less riven by antagonisms than one divided between landholders and landless, masterless men. With the freedmen's expectations, sobriety, and status restored, he was no longer a man to be feared. That fact, together with the presence of a growing mass of alien slaves, tended to draw the white settlers closer together and to reduce the importance of the class difference between yeoman farmer and large plantation owner.

"Racial fears tended to lessen the economic and political differences between rich and poor whites. And as royal officials and tax collectors became more oppressive, both groups joined forces in protesting the import taxes on tobacco which provided income for the high and the low. The rich began to look to their less wealthy neighbors for political support against the English government and in local elections.

"Wealthy whites, of course, retained all their former prerogatives, but the creation of a black subclass enabled poor whites to identify with and support the policies of the upper class. With the safe economic advantage provided by their slaves, large landowners were willing to grant poor whites a larger role in the political process."

"So, Colonel," I interrupted, "you are saying that slavery for blacks not only provided wealth for rich whites but, paradoxically, led also to greater freedom for poor whites. One of our twentieth-century historians, Edmund Morgan, has explained this paradox of slave owners espousing freedom and liberty:

> Aristocrats could more safely preach equality in a slave society than in a free one. Slaves did not become leveling mobs, because their owners would see to it that they had no chance to. The apostrophes to equality were not addressed to them. And because Virginia's labor force was

composed mainly of slaves, who had been isolated by race and removed from the political equation, the remaining free laborers and tenant farmers were too few in number to constitute a serious threat to the superiority of the men who assured them of their equality."[32]

"In effect," I concluded, "what I call a contradiction here was deemed a solution then. Slavery enabled the rich to keep their lands, arrested discontent and repression of other Englishmen, strengthened their rights and nourished their attachment to liberty. But the solution, as Professor Morgan said, 'put an end to the process of turning Africans into Englishmen. The rights of Englishmen were preserved by destroying the rights of Africans.'"[33]

"Do you charge that our belief in individual liberty is feigned?" demanded a Virginian, outraged.

"It was Professor Morgan's point," I replied, "not that 'a belief in republican equality had to rest on slavery, but only that in Virginia (and probably in other southern colonies) it did. The most ardent American republicans were Virginians, and their ardor was not unrelated to their power over the men and women they held in bondage.'"[34]

And now, for the first time, the Colonel looked at me, amazed. "My thoughts on this slavery matter have confounded my mind for many years, and yet you summarize them in a few paragraphs. I must, after all, thank you." He walked back to his seat in a daze, neither commended nor condemned by his colleagues. Most, indeed, were deep in thought—but for a few delegates I noticed trying desperately to signal to passersby in the street. But I could not attend to them: my time, I knew, must be growing short.

* * *

I longed to continue the debate, but never got the chance. Apparently someone outside had finally understood the delegates' signals for help, and had summoned the local militia. Hearing some commotion beyond the window, I turned to see a small cannon being rolled up, pointing straight at me. Then, in quick succession, the cannoneer lighted the fuse; the delegates dived under their desks; the cannon fired; and, with an ear-splitting roar, the cannonball broke against the light shield and splintered, leaving me and the shield intact.

I knew then my mission was over, and I returned to the twentieth century.

---

[32][Edmund Morgan, American Slavery, American Freedom (1975), pp. 380–81.]

[33][Edmund Morgan, "Slavery and Freedom: The American Paradox," Journal of American History 59 (1972); 1, 24.]

[34][Morgan, supra note 32, p. 381.]

GENEVA had related the Chronicle of the Constitutional Contradiction as though she were living it again—and, indeed, I felt, as she talked, as though I, too, were in that hot and humid hall arguing along with her. Now she sat back in her chair and looked toward me in anticipation * * *

* * * "I hope you have not missed the real point of the Chronicle[," she said.] "It was not a debate. The Chronicle's message is that no one could have prevented the Framers from drafting a constitution including provisions protecting property in slaves. If they believed, as they had every reason to do, that the country's survival required the economic advantage provided by the slave system, than it was essential that slavery be recognized, rationalized, and protected in the country's basic law. It is as simple as that."

"And not so simple, to judge by the Colonel's revelations," I suggested. "As a result of your aggressive advocacy, you forced him and the rest of the Convention to think through motivations for the slavery compromises that went beyond the Southern delegates' refusal to compromise on this issue."

"The Colonel's reaction surprised me," Geneva admitted, "but his insight into the political as well as the economic importance of slavery simply added more compelling reasons for recognizing and providing protection for slavery in the Constitution."

"The implications for current civil rights work are a bit too close for comfort."

"Exactly right." Geneva leaned forward in her chair to give emphasis to her words. "Even in that extraordinary setting, what struck me as I fought for their attention was how familiar it all was. You know, friend, we civil rights lawyers spend our lives confronting whites in power with the obvious racial bias in their laws or policies, and while, as you know, the litany of their possible exculpatory responses is as long as life, they all boil down to: 'That's the way the world is. We did not make the rules, we simply play by them, and you really have no alternative but to do the same. Please don't take it personally.' The Colonel's speech revealed components of those rules far more complex than ignorant prejudice."

* * *

RAOUL BERGER, GOVERNMENT BY JUDICIARY

Pp. 10–14, 22–24, 27, 30–31, 169–172, 176 (1977).

Background

The key to an understanding of the Fourteenth Amendment is that the North was shot through with Negrophobia, that the Republicans, except for a minority of extremists, were swayed by the racism that gripped their constituents rather than by abolitionist ideology. At the inception of their crusade the abolitionists peered up at an almost unscalable cliff. Charles Sumner, destined to become a leading spokesman for extreme abolitionist views, wrote in 1834, upon his first sight of slaves, "My worst preconception of their appearance and their ignorance did not fall as low as their actual stupidity * * * They appear to be nothing more than moving masses of flesh unendowed with anything of intelligence above the brutes." Tocqueville's impression in 1831–32 was equally abysmal. He noticed that in the North, "the prejudice which repels the negroes seems to increase in proportion as they are emancipated," that prejudice "appears to be stronger in the States which have abolished slavery, than in those where it still exists."

Little wonder that the abolitionist campaign was greeted with loathing! In 1837 Elijah Lovejoy, an abolitionist editor, was murdered by an Illinois mob. How shallow was the impress of the abolitionist campaign on such feelings is graphically revealed in a Lincoln incident. A delegation of Negro leaders had called on him at the White House, and he told them,

> There is an unwillingness on the part of our people, harsh as it may be, for you free colored people to remain with us * * *. [E]ven when you cease to be slaves, you are far removed from being placed on an equality with the white man * * * I cannot alter it if I would. It is a fact.

Fear of Negro invasion—that the emancipated slaves would flock north in droves—alarmed the North. The letters and diaries of Union soldiers, [C. Vann] Woodward notes, reveal an "enormous amount of antipathy towards Negroes"; popular convictions "were not prepared to sustain" a commitment to equality. Racism, David Donald remarks, "ran deep in the North," and the suggestion that "Negroes should be treated as equals to white men woke some of the deepest and ugliest fears in the American mind."

One need not look beyond the confines of the debates in the 39th Congress to find abundant confirmation. Time and again Republicans took account of race prejudice as an inescapable fact. George W. Julian of Indiana referred to the "proverbial hatred" of Negroes, Senator Henry S. Lane of Indiana to the "almost ineradicable prejudice," Shelby M. Cullom of Illinois to the "morbid prejudice," Senator William M. Stewart of Nevada to the "nearly insurmountable" prejudice, James F. Wilson of Iowa to the "iron-cased prejudice" against blacks. These were Republicans, sympathetic to emancipation and the protection of civil rights. Then there were the Democratic racists who unashamedly proclaimed that the Union should remain a "white man's" government. In the words of Senator Garrett Davis of Kentucky, "The white race * * * will be proprietors of the land, and the blacks its cultivators; such is their destiny." Let it be regarded as political propaganda, and, as the noted British historiographer Sir Herbert

Butterfield states, it "does at least presume an audience—perhaps a 'public opinion'—which is judged to be susceptible to the kinds of arguments and considerations set before it." Consider, too, that the Indiana Constitution of 1851 excluded Negroes from the State, as did Oregon, that a substantial number of Northern States recently had rejected Negro suffrage, that others maintained segregated schools. It is against this backdrop that we must measure claims that the framers of the Fourteenth Amendment swallowed abolitionist ideology hook, line, and sinker.

* * *

THE CIVIL RIGHTS ACT OF 1866

The meaning and scope of the Fourteenth Amendment are greatly illuminated by the debates in the 39th Congress on the antecedent Civil Rights Act of 1866. As Charles Fairman stated, "over and over in this debate [on the Amendment] the correspondence between Section One of the Amendment and the Civil Rights Act is noted. The provisions of the one are treated as though they were essentially identical with those of the other." George R. Latham of West Virginia, for example, stated that "the 'civil rights bill' which is now a law * * * covers exactly the same ground as this amendment." In fact, the Amendment was designed to "*constitutionalize*" the Act, that is, to "embody" it in the Constitution so as to remove doubt as to its constitutionality and to place it beyond the power of a later Congress to repeal. An ardent advocate of an abolitionist reading of the Amendment, Howard Jay Graham, stated that "virtually every speaker in the debates on the Fourteenth Amendment—Republican and Democrat alike—said or agreed that the Amendment was designed to embody or incorporate the Civil Rights Act."

Section 1 of the Civil Rights Bill provided in pertinent part,

> That there shall be *no discrimination in civil* rights or immunities * * * on account of race * * * but the inhabitants of every race * * * shall have the *same* right to make and enforce contracts, to sue, be parties, and give evidence, to inherit, purchase, lease, sell, hold and convey real and personal property, and to full and *equal benefit* of all laws and proceedings for the *security* of person and property, and shall be subject to *like* punishment * * * and no other.[14]

* * *

The explanations of the Civil Rights Bill by the respective committee chairmen made its limited objectives entirely clear. Speaking to "civil rights and immunities," House Chairman Wilson asked,

[14][Cong. Globe, 39th Cong., 1st Sess. 474 (1866) (emphasis added).]

What do these terms mean? Do they mean that in all things, civil, social, political, all citizens, without distinction of race or color, shall be equal? By no means can they be so construed * * * Nor do they mean that all citizens shall sit on juries, or that their children shall attend the same schools. These are not civil rights and immunities. Well, what is the meaning? What are civil rights? I understand civil rights to be simply the absolute rights of individuals, such as "The right of personal security, the right of personal liberty, and the right to acquire and enjoy property." * * *

* * *

* * * [Senator Lyman] Trumbull [of Illinois] stated that the Bill "has nothing to do with the right of suffrage, or any other political rights." When Senator Willard Saulsbury, a Democrat of Delaware, sought specifically to except "the right to vote," Trumbull replied: "that is a political privilege, not a civil right. This bill relates to civil rights only." And he reiterated that the Bill "carefully avoided conferring or interfering with political rights or privileges of any kind." The views of Trumbull and Wilson were shared by fellow Republicans. The "only effect" of the Bill, said Senator Henderson, was to give the blacks the enumerated rights. "These measures did not pretend to confer upon the Negro the suffrage. They left each State to determine the question for itself." Senator Sherman said the Bill "defines what are the incidents of freedom, and says that these men must be protected in certain rights, and so careful is its language that it goes on and defines those rights, the rights to sue and be sued [etc.] * * * and other universal incidents of freedom." [Martin] Thayer [of Pennsylvania] stressed that the Bill did not "extend the right of suffrage," that suffrage was not a "fundamental right." That the purpose of the Bill was to *prevent discrimination with respect to enumerated,* fundamental *not political or social rights,* was also stated in one form or another by Cook and Moulton of Illinois, Hubbell, Lawrence, and Shellabarger of Ohio, and Windom of Minnesota.

* * *

WHAT WAS EQUAL PROTECTION TO PROTECT?

The Civil Rights Act * * * secured to blacks the *same* right to contract, to hold property, and to sue, as whites enjoyed, and the "*equal* benefit of all laws *for security of person and property.*" "Political rights" were excluded. In describing these aims the framers interchangeably referred to "equality," "equality before the law," and "equal protection" (but always in the circumscribed context of the rights enumerated in the Bill), so that it is reasonable to infer that the framers regarded these terms as synonymous. What is required, said Moulton of Illinois, is "that each State shall provide for equality before the law, equal protection to life, liberty, and property, equal right to sue and be sued." A leading Radical, Samuel Shellabarger of Ohio, said, of the Civil Rights Bill, "whatever rights *as to each of these enumerated* civil (not political) matters the State may confer upon one race * * * shall be held by all races in equality * * *. It secures * * * *equality of protection in those enumerated civil rights* which the States may deem proper to confer upon any races." So it was understood by Senator Hendricks, an Indiana Democrat: "To recognize the civil rights of the colored people as equal to the civil rights of the white people, I understand to be as far as Senators desire to go; in the language of the Senator from Massachusetts [Sumner] to place all men upon an equality before the law; and that is proposed in regard to their civil rights." He objected that "in the State of Indiana we do not recognize the civil equality of the races." When Andrew Johnson combed the Bill for objections and vetoed it, he noted that § 1 "contains an enumeration of the rights to be enjoyed" and that "perfect equality" was sought with respect to "these enumerated rights." Thomas T. Davis, a New York Republican, expressed a widely shared feeling in stating, Negroes "must be made equal before the law, and be permitted to enjoy life, liberty, and the pursuit of happiness [property]," but he was against "the establishment of perfect equality between the colored and the white race of the South." While James W. Patterson of New Hampshire was "opposed to any law discriminating against [blacks] in the security and protection of life, liberty, person and property," "beyond this," he stated, "I am not prepared to go," explicitly rejecting "political and social equality." Windom declared that the Civil Rights Bill conferred an "equal right, nothing more * * * to make and enforce contracts," and so on, but no "social privileges." Thus, the concept of "equal protection" had its roots in the Civil Rights Bill and was conceived to be limited to the enumerated rights.

What reason is there to conclude that when the words "equal protection of the laws" were embodied in the Amendment they were freighted with a new cargo of meaning—unlimited equality across the board? The evidence points the other way. In an early version of the Amendment, provision was made for both "the same political rights and privileges and * * * equal protection in the enjoyment of life, liberty and property," an indication that "equal protection" did not include "political rights and privileges," but was confined to "life, liberty, or property." [John] Bingham [of Ohio] proposed a substitute, H.R. No. 63, that would empower Congress "to secure * * * all privileges and immunities * * * (Art. IV, Sec. 2); and * * * equal protection in the rights of life, liberty and property (5th Amendment)." "Political rights and privileges" had disappeared; in its place was "privileges and immunities." Neither "privileges and immunities," nor its antecedent, "civil rights" had included "political privileges." Bingham explained that his proposal was aimed at "confiscation statutes * * * statutes of unjust imprisonment" of the "rebel states," the objects of the Civil Rights Bill. * * *

Among the statements indicating that § 1 was considered to embody the objectives of the Civil Rights Act is that of Latham of West Virginia: "The 'civil rights bill,' which is now a law * * * covers exactly the same ground as this amendment." [Thaddeus] Stevens [of Pennsylvania] explained that the Amendment

> allows Congress to correct the unjust legislation of the States *so far* that the law which operates upon one shall operate *equally* upon all. Whatever law punishes a white man for a crime shall punish the black man precisely in the same way * * *. Whatever law protects the white man shall afford *equal protection* to the black man. Whatever means of redress is afforded to one shall be afforded to all. Whatever law allows the white man to testify in court shall allow the man of color to do the same. These are great advantages over their present [Black] codes * * *. I need not enumerate these partial and oppressive laws * * *. Your civil rights bill secures the same thing. * * *

* * *

But, it may be asked, does not the differentiation in § 1 between "due process" protection of "life, liberty, and property" and "equal protection of the laws" indicate that "equal protection" was now divorced from the earlier limitation to "life, liberty, and property?" Nothing in the debates indicates such a purpose. "Equal protection of the laws" expressed the central object of the framers: to prevent *statutory* discrimination with respect to the rights enumerated in the Civil Rights Act. That purpose had been loosely expressed in Bingham's earlier formulation: "equal protection in the rights of life, liberty, and property," which he mistakenly identified with the "5th Amendment." Possibly some more perceptive lawyer restored the words "life, liberty, and property" to their Fifth Amendment association with due process, thus insuring access to the courts. At the same time, the established association of due process with judicial procedure made it necessary to block what Stevens denominated "partial and oppressive laws," a purpose succinctly expressed by "equal protection of the laws" to which reference had been made during the debate on the Civil Rights Bill.

A number of scholars have offered critical reviews of Berger's historical research and interpretive conclusions.[3] Historian Eric Foner

[3]*See, e.g.*, Soifer, *Review Essay—Protecting Civil Rights: A Critique of Raoul Berger's History*, 54 N.Y.U.L.Rev. 651, 657 (1979); Kutler, *Raoul Berger's Fourteenth Amendment: A History or Ahistorical?*, 6 Hast. Const.L.Q. 511 (1979); Murphy, *Book Review—Constitutional Interpretation: The Art of Historian, Magician or Statesman?*, 87 Yale L.J.

argues that to reduce the aims of framers of the Fourteenth Amendment to invalidation of the Black Codes and validation of the Civil Rights Act of 1866 "is to misconstrue the difference between a statute and a constitutional amendment." The Fourteenth Amendment was a "broad [statement] of principle, giving constitutional form to the resolution of a national cris[i]s, and permanently altering American nationality":

> [Even moderate Republicans] understood Reconstruction as a dynamic process, in which phrases like "privileges and immunities" were subject to changing interpretation. They preferred to allow both Congress and the federal courts maximum flexibility in implementing the Amendment's provisions and combatting the multitude of injustices that confronted blacks in many parts of the South. * * *
>
> * * * [I]t is abundantly clear that Republicans wished to give constitutional sanction to states' obligation to respect such key provisions [of the Bill of Rights] as freedom of speech, the right to bear arms, trial by impartial jury, and protection against cruel and unusual punishment and unreasonable search and seizure. The Freedmen's Bureau had already taken steps to protect these rights, and the Amendment was deemed necessary, in part, precisely because every one of them was being systematically violated in the South in 1866.[4]

MICHAEL J. KLARMAN, *BROWN*, RACIAL CHANGE, AND THE CIVIL RIGHTS MOVEMENT

80 VA. L. REV. 7, 8–13, 77–84 (1994).

Brown v. Board of Education is commonly deemed to be one of the most important decisions in the history of the United States Supreme Court. Yet virtually no scholarly attention has been devoted to corroborating this conventional estimation of *Brown's* significance. While nearly everyone assumes that *Brown* has had momentous implications for American race relations, nobody has bothered to identify the precise channels through which *Brown* effected change.

This scholarly oversight appears all the more peculiar in light of the uncontested fact, well known to informed observers though perhaps not to the general public, that *Brown* was *directly* responsible for only the most token forms of southern public school desegregation. In North Carolina, for example, just 0.026% of black schoolchildren attended desegregated schools in 1961—seven years after the original *Brown* decision—and that figure did not rise above 1% until after passage of the 1964 Civil Rights Act. Likewise in Virginia, a grand total of 208 blacks, out of a statewide school population of 211,000 (or 0.09%), were attending desegregated

---

1752 (1978).

[4]E. Foner, Reconstruction 257–259 (1988).

schools as of May 1961; that number had risen to only 1.63% in 1964. Such figures actually would have represented a stunning success by comparison with desegregation rates in the deep South; *not a single* black child attended an integrated public grade school in South Carolina, Alabama or Mississippi as of the 1962–1963 school year. Across the South as a whole, just over 0.15% of black schoolchildren in 1960 and 1.2% in 1964 were attending school with whites. Only after the 1964 Civil Rights Act threatened to cut off federal educational funding for segregated school districts and the Department of Health, Education, and Welfare in 1966 adopted stringent enforcement guidelines did the integration rate in the South rise to 32% in 1968–1969 and 91.3% in 1972–1973. As one commentator has rightly observed: "The statistics from the Southern states are truly amazing. For ten years, 1954–1964, virtually nothing happened."[8]

That *Brown* failed to desegregate southern schools without the assistance of federal legislation does not mean, of course, that the decision was unimportant. After all, conventional wisdom holds that such legislation was attainable only because *Brown* had first laid the groundwork for it. My objective in this Article is to reconsider the question of *indirect* causation—namely, the relationship between *Brown* and the landmark civil rights legislation of the mid-1960s. I shall also investigate, more generally, the connection between *Brown* and the transformation of race relations in the United States.

Briefly stated, my argument consists of two parts. First, I argue that from a long-range perspective (by which I mean decades, not centuries) racial change in America was inevitable owing to a variety of deep-seated social, political, and economic forces. These impulses for racial change, I shall suggest, would have undermined Jim Crow regardless of Supreme Court intervention; indeed, the *Brown* decision was judicially conceivable in 1954 only because the forces for change had been preparing the ground for decades.

To say that transformative racial change was ultimately inevitable, though, is not to say that it had to transpire when it did—largely in the 1960s. Judged from a narrower time horizon, *Brown* did play a vital role in the enactment of landmark civil rights legislation in the mid-1960s. The precise chain of causation linking *Brown* with this transformative racial change, however, is very different from what has been commonly supposed. The conventional view is that *Brown* instigated racial change either by pricking the conscience of northern whites or by raising the hopes and expectations of southern blacks. [But] surprisingly little evidence supports either of these claims regarding *Brown's* contribution to the civil rights

---

[8][Gerald N. Rosenberg, The Hollow Hope: Can Courts Bring About Social Change? 52 (1991).]

movement of the 1960s. The crucial link between *Brown* and the mid-1960s civil rights legislation inheres, rather, in the decision's crystalizing effect on southern white *resistance* to racial change. By propelling southern politics dramatically to the right on racial issues, *Brown* created a political climate conducive to the brutal suppression of civil rights demonstrations. When such violence occurred, and was vividly transmitted through the medium of television to national audiences, previously indifferent northern whites were aroused from their apathy, leading to demands for national civil rights legislation which the Kennedy and Johnson administrations no longer deemed it politically expedient to resist.

One final point must be made by way of introduction. It is my view that revolutionary racial change took place in the United States in the quarter century following World War II. Formal state-sponsored racial segregation has been eradicated; racially-motivated lynchings, which remained an all too common feature of 1960s Mississippi and Alabama, are virtually unheard of today (and when they do occur, are vigorously investigated, condemned, and prosecuted by public authorities); southern blacks have advanced from nearly universal exclusion from the political community to participation rates roughly comparable to those of southern whites of similar economic class, with concomitant increases in the responsiveness of public officials to the interests of the black community; many areas of public life, including schools, public accommodations, and employment have been de facto as well as de jure integrated to a significant degree; and per capita income and educational disparities between *middle class* whites and blacks have been largely eliminated. Yet there is no denying that in many contexts racial change has been far less substantial than the civil rights movement once aspired to achieve. Residential segregation has increased in nearly every American city since the civil rights revolution began; relatedly, de facto school segregation in all large urban school districts has intensified since the late 1960s, with the Northeast now possessing the most racially segregated (and usually unequal) schools in the country; an urban minority underclass has grown in size, for whom differentials in education, income, and job opportunities have been widening, rather than narrowing; and black political participation has failed to produce either proportionate numbers of black officeholders or remedies for the relative material deprivation of many blacks. I wish to emphasize that nothing in my argument turns on whether one accepts my judgment that racial change in this country has been transformative. My claims are simply that, *whatever change did occur* (whether judged to be revolutionary, superficial, or somewhere in between) was (1) inevitable over the long haul, and (2) substantially facilitated by *Brown* in the short term, albeit in an indirect, almost perverse, manner. * * *

A. The Conventional View of Brown's Connection to the 1960's Civil Rights Legislation

* * * Two conventional arguments are made regarding *Brown's* importance to the civil rights movement. First, it is often said that *Brown* increased the salience of the civil rights issue, pricking the conscience of northern whites and converting many of them into civil rights enthusiasts. Second, and even more fundamentally, the conventional wisdom holds that *Brown* raised the hopes and expectations of (mainly southern) blacks, prodding them to adopt a more aggressive civil rights posture by rendering more realistic the possibility of genuine racial change. While neither of these traditional accounts is flatly wrong (the second, I believe, having greater merit than the first), both of them substantially overstate *Brown's* impact in certain directions, while missing one key to the decision's significance—its crystalization of southern white resistance.

Brown no doubt did focus the attention of some northern whites on civil rights issues in a novel manner. But the historical record belies the notion that *Brown* was tremendously significant in this regard. Analyses of print media coverage of civil rights *"events"* suggest that court decisions, including *Brown,* attracted relatively little attention as compared with demonstrations producing confrontation and violence, such as the Montgomery bus boycott of 1955–1956, which had very little connection to the *Brown* decision. The New York Times actually provided greater coverage to civil rights issues in 1952 than in 1954 or 1955 (the years of *Brown I* and *Brown II,* respectively). Moreover, it seems clear that *Brown* attracted considerably more attention in the South than in the North. One study found that in 1955 northerners were far less likely than southerners to have recently discussed the *Brown* decision. Only 6% of northerners interviewed that year, as compared with 30% of southerners, regarded segregation as an issue of equal importance with atomic bombs, crime, and high taxes.

Even to the extent that *Brown* propelled the segregation issue into the consciousness of northerners, there is little evidence that it made them more sympathetic to the civil rights cause. One opinion poll conducted in July 1959 recorded only a five percentage point increase (to 59%) in public support for the *Brown* decision over the preceding five years. The number of congressional sponsors for civil rights legislation, having risen steadily through the late 1940s and peaked in 1951–1952, declined throughout the remainder of the 1950s, *Brown* notwithstanding, reaching a new low in 1959–1960. There is little evidence that politicians, either locally or nationally, discerned any critical awakening of civil rights consciousness among their white constituents in the post-*Brown* years. [T]he civil rights policies of the Eisenhower administration in the 1950s and the Kennedy administration in the early 1960s indicate a political perception that white racial attitudes had undergone no dramatic transformation in the wake of *Brown,* as they clearly would after Birmingham and Selma. There may well have been more talk about civil rights in the wake of *Brown,* but there was very little in the way of action.

The second conventional claim regarding *Brown's* influence upon the civil rights movement is that the Court's decision energized (especially southern) blacks by demonstrating that at least one important governmental institution was genuinely committed to the cause of racial justice. Anecdotal evidence supports this proffered link between *Brown* and an emerging black civil rights consciousness, and the claim does possess a certain inherent plausibility. For example, we know that *Brown,* at the very least, had a marked impact on the form, if not the existence, of civil rights activity in Birmingham, where court challenges to various aspects of public segregation were launched in the wake of *Brown,* largely owing to the fact that direct action demonstrations were too dangerous in the South's most violent city. In Greensboro, North Carolina, as well, *Brown* seems to have heightened black insurgency in the form of efforts to desegregate the city golf course and more insistent demands by black parents for improved educational facilities. Moreover, it seems plausible that the abysmal record of southern compliance with *Brown* crystalized black frustration with the racial status quo, ultimately leading to the civil rights explosion of the early 1960s.

Nevertheless, while it would be mistaken to deny *Brown's* inspirational impact on American blacks, alternative factors account equally well for the emergent black civil rights consciousness. First, *Brown* obviously cannot account for the burst of civil rights activity in the middle and late 1940s. Sit-in demonstrations, Freedom Rides, and voter registration drives were not invented in the 1960s; these forms of civil rights activity flourished in the immediate postwar years. But such activity slowed to a trickle during the early 1950s, before rising dramatically in the year of the Montgomery bus boycott, and then falling precipitately again in 1957–1959.

One plausible explanation for the relative quiescence in civil rights activity during the 1950s focuses on the rise of the Cold War and its domestic counterpart, McCarthyism. With the country widely perceived to be under both internal and external attack, any social, political, or cultural movement challenging the status quo was susceptible to being labeled communist-inspired. The battle against communism, in the words of one civil rights historian, "virtually commanded an unquestioning acceptance of the righteousness of the American way." Indeed, southern traditionalists constantly charged (and seem genuinely to have believed) that the civil rights movement was communist-inspired, and many southern states launched legislative antisubversion investigations of the NAACP. By reining in the aggressive civil rights campaign of the late 1940s, the black leadership, consciously or subconsciously, avoided the tincture of communist complicity. The virtual demise of domestic anticommunism as a serious concern by 1960 rendered possible the reemergence of a social movement critical of the racial status quo. On this view, then, the civil rights revolution of the 1960s had less to do with *Brown* than with the dissipation of McCarthyism as a temporary impediment to a civil rights movement that had been spawned by World War II.

Even setting aside the question of *pre-Brown* antecedents, alternative factors account about as well as does *Brown* for the timing of the 1960s civil rights revolution. Historians frequently identify the Greensboro sit-ins of 1960 as the inaugural event of the modern civil rights revolution. While similar demonstrations had occurred before, "never in the past had they prompted such a volcanic response." The speed with which the sit-in demonstrations spread, first through Greensboro, then through North Carolina, and finally through more than fifty cities in nine southern states, makes it clear that the time was ripe for large-scale civil rights protest activity. It is not obvious that *Brown,* decided six years earlier, was a crucial factor in laying the groundwork.

Two other factors seem to explain equally well the explosion of civil rights activity in the early 1960s—the decolonization of Africa, and the rise of a well-educated, relatively prosperous black middle class. In 1957, Ghana became the first black African nation to achieve its independence from colonial rule; within roughly half a dozen years, over thirty other countries had followed suit. Many civil rights leaders identified the changing international status of blacks as an important impetus for America's civil rights movement. One such leader observed that to witness black African statesmen participating in world decisionmaking processes at the United Nations "can cause you to swell with pride." The stunning successes of nonwhite independence movements around 1960 demonstrated to American blacks the feasibility of racial change. It also heightened their sense of frustration by widening the gap between black status at home and abroad. As one leading civil rights historian has observed, by 1963 thirty-four African nations had freed themselves from colonial bondage, while more than two thousand southern American school districts remained segregated. Or, as James Baldwin explained the operative psychological dynamic, American blacks observed the rapidly unfolding international events and concluded that "[a]ll of Africa will be free before we can get a lousy cup of coffee."[360]

Another explanation for the civil rights explosion of the early 1960s focuses upon the gradual emergence of a well-educated, relatively prosperous southern black middle class, many of whom had performed

[360][Harvard Sitkoff, The Struggle for Black Equality 1954–1980, at 83, 128 (1981).]

military service. World War II had ignited economic growth which fostered the rise of a substantial southern black educational and economic elite, but postwar changes in racial practices had failed to keep pace with the underlying socioeconomic reality. For this group, identifiably middle class according to most social and economic indices, Jim Crow practices must have appeared egregiously anachronistic. Moreover, advances in black education had failed to produce jobs commensurate with risking skill levels. To take just one example, during a four-year period in the late 1950s, only 7 of 124 black graduates from the Atlanta University School of Social Work could find a local job in their chosen profession. On this view, then, the emergence of a well-educated, relatively prosperous black middle class rendered an explosion of civil rights protest activity inevitable, and the Greensboro sit-ins simply provided a spark to the powder.

In sum, evidence that *Brown* inspired the 1960s civil rights movement is considerably less persuasive than the conventional wisdom would have us believe. Alternative factors, having nothing to do with the Supreme Court, appear to account at least as well as *Brown* does for the timing of the civil rights revolution. Yet even if I am wrong about this, [I maintain] that the civil rights movement achieved transformative racial change only when it intersected, at places like Birmingham and Selma, with the southern political backlash that *Brown* produced. Thus, even if *Brown* did provide (as I believe it did not) critical inspiration for the modern civil rights movement, the decision's most important ramification may still have been the crystalization of southern resistance to racial change and the consequent rightward lurch of southern politics.

B. EQUAL PROTECTION THEORIES

PAUL BREST, IN DEFENSE OF THE ANTIDISCRIMINATION PRINCIPLE

90 HARV.L.REV. 1, 5–10, 22–26, 28–29, 31, 33, 43–52 (1976).

By the "antidiscrimination principle" I mean the general principle disfavoring classifications and other decisions and practices that depend on the race (or ethnic origin) of the parties affected.

* * *

I. THE ANTIDISCRIMINATION PRINCIPLE

The antidiscrimination principle rests on fundamental moral values that are widely shared in our society. Although the text and legislative history of laws that incorporate this principle can inform our understanding of it, the principle itself is at least as likely to inform our interpretations of the laws. This is especially true with respect to the equal protection clause of the fourteenth amendment. The text and history of the clause are vague and ambiguous and cannot, in any event, infuse the antidiscrimination principle with moral force or justify its extension to novel circumstances and new beneficiaries. Therefore, the argument of this section does not ultimately turn on authority, but on whether it comports with the reader's reflective understanding of the antidiscrimination principle.

Stated most simply, the antidiscrimination principle disfavors race-dependent decisions and conduct—at least when they selectively disadvantage the members of a minority group. By race-dependent, I mean decisions and conduct (hereafter, simply decisions) that would have been different but for the race of those benefited or disadvantaged by them. Race-dependent decisions may take several forms, including overt racial classifications on the face of statutes and covert decisions by officials.

A. Rationales for the Antidiscrimination Principle

The antidiscrimination principle guards against certain defects in the *process* by which race-dependent decisions are made and also against certain harmful *results* of race-dependent decisions. Restricting the principle to a unitary purpose vitiates its moral force and requires the use of sophisticated reasoning to explain applications that seem self-evident.

1. *Defects of Process*.—The antidiscrimination principle is designed to prevent both irrational and unfair infliction of injury.

Race-dependent decisions are irrational insofar as they reflect the assumption that members of one race are less worthy than other people. Not all such decisions are necessarily irrational, however. For example, if black laborers tend to be absent from work more often than their white counterparts—for whatever reason—it is not irrational for an employer to prefer white applicants for the job. If Americans of Japanese ancestry were more prone to disloyalty than Caucasians during World War II, it was not irrational for the United States government to take special precautions against sabotage and espionage by them. Regulations and decisions based on statistical generalizations are commonplace in all developed societies and essential to their functioning. And it is often rational for decision-makers to rely on weak and even dubious generalizations. Consider, for example, a fire department's or airline's policy against employing over-weight personnel, based on the rather slight probability that they will suffer a heart attack while on duty.

In short, the mere fact that most blacks are industrious and most Japanese-Americans loyal does not make the employer's or the Government's decision irrational. Indeed, if all race-dependent decisions were irrational, there would be no need for an antidiscrimination principle, for it would suffice to apply the widely held moral, constitutional, and practical principle that forbids treating persons irrationally. The antidiscrimination principle fills a special need because—as even a glance at history indicates—race-dependent decisions that are rational and purport to be based solely on legitimate considerations are likely in fact to rest on assumptions of the differential worth of racial groups or on the related phenomenon of racially selective sympathy and indifference.

Mr. Justice Black focused on the first of these dangers in *Korematsu v. United States,*[33] the case in which the Government sought to justify its policy of interning Japanese-Americans, and in which the Court first enunciated the modern "suspect classification" doctrine. He wrote for the majority:

> [A]ll legal restrictions which curtail the civil rights of a single racial group are immediately suspect * * *. [C]ourts must subject them to the most rigid scrutiny. Pressing public necessity may sometimes justify the existence of such restrictions; racial antagonism never can.

Mr. Justice Black chose the word "suspect" advisedly. For, although a court often cannot ascertain the true motives underlying a decision, our history and traditions provide strong reasons to suspect that racial classifications ultimately rest on assumptions of the differential worth of racial groups. These racial value judgments appear in forms besides "racial antagonism"—for example in paternalistic assumptions of racial inferiority.

By the phenomenon of racially selective sympathy and indifference I mean the unconscious failure to extend to a minority the same recognition of humanity, and hence the same sympathy and care, given as a matter of course to one's own group.

Although racially selective sympathy and indifference (hereafter, just indifference) is an inevitable consequence of attributing intrinsic value to membership in a racial group, it may also result from a desire to enhance our own power and esteem by enhancing the power and esteem of members of groups to which we belong. And it may also result—often unconsciously—from our tendency to sympathize most readily with those who seem most like ourselves. Whatever its cause, decisions that reflect this phenomenon, like those reflecting overt racial hostility, are unfair; for by hypothesis, they are decisions disadvantaging minority persons that would not be made under the identical circumstances if they disadvantaged members of the dominant group. The unequal treatment could be justified only if one group were in fact more worthy than the other. This justification failing, such treatment violates the cardinal rule of fairness—the Golden Rule.

2. *Harmful Results.*—A second and independent rationale for the antidiscrimination principle is the prevention of the harms which may result from race-dependent decisions. Often, the most obvious harm is the denial of the opportunity to secure a desired benefit—a job, a night's lodging at a

[33] 323 U.S. 214 (1944).

motel, a vote. But this does not completely describe the consequences of race-dependent decisionmaking. Decisions based on assumptions of intrinsic worth and selective indifference inflict psychological injury by stigmatizing their victims as inferior. Moreover, because acts of discrimination tend to occur in pervasive patterns, their victims suffer especially frustrating, cumulative and debilitating injuries.

* * *

Recognition of the stigmatic injury inflicted by discrimination explains applications of the antidiscrimination principle where the material harm seems slight or problematic. For example, it fully explains the harmfulness of de jure school segregation without the need to invoke controversial social science evidence concerning the effects of segregation on achievement, interracial attitudes, and the like, and thus explains the Supreme Court's casual extension of *Brown* [*v. Board of Education*] to prohibit the segregation of public beaches, parks, golf courses and buses. It also explains how present practices that are racially neutral may nonetheless perpetuate the harms of past de jure segregation.

Racial generalizations usually inflict psychic injury whether or not they are in fact premised on assumptions of differential moral worth. Although all of us recognize that institutional decisions must depend on generalizations based on objective characteristics of persons and things rather than on individualized judgments, we nonetheless tend to feel unfairly treated when disadvantaged by a generalization that is not true as applied to us. Generalizations based on immutable personal traits such as race or sex are especially frustrating because we can do nothing to escape their operation. These generalizations are still more pernicious, for they are often premised on the supposed correlation between the inherited characteristic and the undesirable voluntary behavior of those who possess the characteristic—for example, blacks are less industrious, trustworthy or clean than whites. Because the behavior is voluntary, and hence the proper object of moral condemnation, individuals as to whom the generalization is inaccurate may justifiably feel that the decisionmaker has passed moral judgment on them.

The psychological injury inflicted by generalizations based on race is compounded by the frustrating and cumulative nature of their material injuries. Racial generalizations are pervasive and have traditionally operated in the same direction—to the disadvantage of members of the minority group. A person who is denied one opportunity because he or she is short or overweight will find other opportunities, for in our society height and weight do not often serve as the bases for generalizations determining who will receive benefits. By contrast, at least until very recently, a black was not denied *an* opportunity because of his or her race, but denied virtually *all* desirable opportunities. As door after door is shut in one's face, the individual acts of discrimination combine into a systematic and grossly inequitable frustration of opportunity.

* * *

II. RACIALLY DISPROPORTIONATE IMPACT

Race-dependent decisions typically produce a racially disproportionate impact—a disproportion between the number of blacks and whites on the voting rolls, in an employer's work force, on a jury, or in a school. Because race-dependent decisions are so often concealed, racially disproportionate impact has customarily been offered as evidence that ostensibly nondiscriminatory decisions are in fact race-dependent. * * *

* * *

[I]n *Washington v. Davis,*[105] an action challenging the verbal ability test required of applicants by the District of Columbia Police Department, the Supreme Court held that * * * only official conduct having a "discriminatory purpose" violates the equal protection clause. * * *

* * *

Davis reflects both the centrality of race-dependence to the equal protection clause and the judicial unmanageability of a general rule requiring an extraordinary justification for practices that produce racially disproportionate effects. The following discussion identifies and evaluates five possible rationales for the disproportionate impact doctrine. The first three are rooted in the antidiscrimination principle and involve remedies for present, past, and future discrimination. I believe that the disproportionate impact doctrine can continue to play a useful role, for courts as well as for legislatures, in enforcing the antidiscrimination principle. The fourth rationale is concerned with remedying "race-specific harms" produced by disproportionate impact. Although legislatures may properly ameliorate race-specific harms, I argue that the Constitution provides no basis for judicial intervention. The fifth rationale embodies a theory that accords moral status to groups and holds that it is intrinsically unjust for one racial group to be appreciably worse off than others. I believe that this theory is fundamentally misconceived and should not serve as the basis of policymaking by any institution.

A. Suspected Race-Dependency

Federal courts have used the disproportionate impact doctrine to avoid the unique difficulties of dealing with discriminatory intent or motive. * * *

[105] [426 U.S. 229 (1976).]

* * *

* * * If courts may grant relief only when plaintiffs have made a clear case [of discriminatory motivation] on the record, many instances will remain where race-dependent decisions are strongly suspected but cannot be proved. Although this is not essentially different from the difficulty facing the proponents in most litigation seeking to overturn government policies, it is especially troubling in the race area. The accumulation of suspected but unproved race-dependent conduct, such as decisions to zone out low income housing, may systematically deprive minorities of important benefits. And the very existence of a state of affairs which "everyone knows" is based on racial discrimination but no one will remedy is demoralizing and stigmatic.

The disproportionate impact doctrine thus acts as a safeguard against improper race-dependent decisions. But * * * the doctrine cannot reasonably be applied across the board. If disproportionate impact is to remain a useful device, it must be used selectively and perhaps be modified to create rebuttable rather than conclusive presumptions of discriminatory intent. * * *

B. *The Effects of Past and Remote Discrimination*

The effects of discrimination may attenuate over time or be submerged in superseding events. But the injuries inflicted by discrimination can place its victims at a disadvantage in a variety of future endeavors, and discrimination can also perpetuate itself by altering the social environment to harm new generations of victims. Discrimination often works its injuries through practices, not themselves race-dependent, implemented by institutions that have not themselves discriminated. Past and remote discrimination often manifest themselves in racially disproportionate impact, and the antidiscrimination principle may therefore support its amelioration or elimination.

* * *

The causal connection between past discrimination and present states of affairs has * * * received the Court's attention in school segregation litigation. *Green v. County School Board*[156] involved a small Virginia school district which, like many rural areas, was not residentially segregated. The district had only two schools, which were de jure segregated—first pursuant to state law, later by local practice. In 1965, in order to remain eligible for federal financial aid, the school board adopted a "freedom of choice" plan of desegregation, which required each pupil to choose which school to attend each year. After three years under the plan,

[156] 391 U.S. 430 (1968).

fifteen percent of the black pupils attended the formerly all-white school; no whites attended the all-black school.

* * *

In *Green* the causal connection between past discrimination and the current racial composition of the schools was as clear as such matters ever can be. It is not plausible, and the school board did not try to argue, that the county school system would have been substantially segregated in 1968 had children never been assigned by race. * * *

* * *

C. *Preventing Future Remote Discrimination*

The disproportionate absence of minorities from certain positions—whether or not itself the result of racial discrimination—may conduce to discrimination in other areas. Such a link underlies the special legislative and judicial concern to protect the political power of minorities. * * *

The Supreme Court's constitutional doctrine concerning multimember legislative districts seems responsive to [this] concern[.] A 1966 opinion indicated that constitutional problems would arise if "designedly or otherwise, a multi-member constituency apportionment scheme * * * operate[d] to minimize or cancel out the voting strength of racial or political elements of the voting population."[201] In *White v. Regester,*[202] a unanimous Court struck down two multimember districts in Texas, on the ground that black and Mexican-American minorities were effectively excluded from political processes. Mr. Justice White's opinion assigned plaintiffs a heavy burden, but not one requiring proof of discriminatory intent:

> [I]t is not enough that the racial group allegedly discriminated against has not had legislative seats in proportion to its voting potential. The plaintiffs' burden is to produce evidence to support findings that the political processes leading to nomination and election were not equally open to participation by the group in question—that its members had less opportunity than did other residents in the district to participate in the political processes and to elect legislators of their choice.[203]

The Court did not imply that the multimember districts had been discriminatorily designed. It noted, however, that both counties involved had histories of discrimination in the provision of public services and that

---

[201]Burns v. Richardson, 384 U.S. 73, 88 (1966). In Whitcomb v. Chavis, 403 U.S. 124 (1971), the Court scrutinized, but upheld, multimember districts in Marion County, Indiana.

[202]412 U.S. 755 (1973).

[203]*Id.* at 765–66.

in one the major political organization had intentionally excluded minorities.

D. *Race-Specific Harms*

The disproportionate disadvantage or exclusion, or the segregation, of the members of a racial minority may give rise to individual and social costs produced solely because of the race of the people affected—costs that would not arise from the identical practices if their impact was random with respect to race. These "race-specific harms" can result from practices that are not race-dependent.

The disproportionate absence of minorities from juries is an example. The principle that juries should represent a cross-section of the community reflects a belief that jurors from different racial, ethnic, and socioeconomic groups tend to have different viewpoints which affect their perceptions of fact and exercise of discretion, and that the system will function most accurately and fairly if a variety of viewpoints is brought to bear on the decision. For this reason, although it would be impossible to assure the proportional representation of the many relevant social groups on jury panels, some legislatures and courts have taken measures to assure that salient groups are not systematically underrepresented. * * *

* * * [O]ther putative race-specific harms do not violate definite constitutional provisions. This is true, for example, of the harms that may result from de facto segregation and from the depressed socioeconomic status of certain minorities.

School segregation, whatever its cause, has been said to reduce the self-esteem, aspirations, motivations, and achievement of black children and to encourage racial fears, hostility, and prejudice. But although these hypotheses have been tested in hundreds of studies, none has been established or disproved to the satisfaction of disinterested social scientists. * * *

* * *

The existence, degree, and nature of these and most other race-specific harms arguably produced by non-race-dependent practices are seldom self-evident. The independent significance of race, as distinguished from poverty, will likely remain unknown for the immediate future. Assuming, however, that significant race-specific harms do exist, by what authority may they be ameliorated?

Much race-specific harm in contemporary American society may be traceable to present or past violations of the antidiscrimination principle. It seems improbable that most lower-class, isolated, and intradependent minority communities would possess these vulnerable characteristics to nearly the same degree were it not for longstanding and pervasive patterns of discrimination. The antidiscrimination principle provides sufficient authority for ameliorating race-specific harms to the extent that they depend on conditions caused by discrimination.

An institution enjoying more or less plenary policymaking authority may remedy race-specific harms that are *not* traceable to violations of the antidiscrimination principle, just as it may remedy any number of other kinds of injuries wholly unrelated to race. For example, a school board might focus on the special needs of minority children today, and deal with blind and retarded children a decade later—as claims come to its attention through interest groups, social upheavals, personal experience, and the like. But where the very authority of the judiciary is based on its ability to expound and apply general principles, it cannot act on such an ad hoc basis. Apart from the antidiscrimination principle, does there exist a coherent principle that requires remedy of race-specific harms but not other equally severe injuries—a principle, for example, under which a school district must spend $*X* to prevent *Y* amount of race-specific harm by integrating the schools, but need not spend the same amount of money to prevent the same amount of harm to mentally or physically handicapped children or to white children from impoverished environments?

To be sure, race-specific harms may produce serious individual and social costs. But these costs seem neither different in kind nor of a greater order of magnitude to the individuals affected than many others that might be ameliorated by changing school assignment schemes, employment criteria, and the like. * * *

E. *Justice for Racial Groups*

The most pernicious feature of racial prejudice and discrimination is their underlying premise that members of some racial groups are less worthy than members of others. The antidiscrimination principle holds that this assumption is fallacious because race has no moral salience. For administrative purposes, some remedies for racial discrimination are triggered by disproportionate racial impact or treat persons according to membership in racial groups; but group membership is always a proxy for the individual's right not to be discriminated against. Similarly, remedies for race-specific harms recognize the sociological consequences of group identification and affiliation only to assure justice for individual members.

In contrast to the theories considered so far, some commentators have suggested that racial groups should be treated as moral entities, holding rights as groups to distributive and compensatory justice. The distributive theory assumes the moral permissibility of unequal distributions of welfare among individuals, but holds that it is at least prima facie unjust for one racial or ethnic group to be substantially worse off than others. Like many individual-oriented theories of distributive justice, a group theory is essentially indifferent to the history that led to the unequal distribution. For example, Owen M. Fiss proposes a noncompensatory, purely redistributive principle—a "group disadvantaging principle"—that requires relief for any group that constitutes a "perpetual underclass." He argues that "[t]he redistributive strategy could give expression to an ethical view against caste, one that would make it undesirable for any social group to occupy a position of subordination for any extended period of time."[218] * * *

The arguments supporting the theories of group distributive justice are difficult to discern. Professor Fiss states that his "group disadvantaging principle" is justified primarily by its intuitive correctness: "visions about how society should be structured may be as irreducible as visions about how individuals should be treated—for example, with dignity." * * *

If a society can be said to have an underlying political theory, ours has not been a theory of organic groups but of liberalism, focusing on the rights of individuals, including rights of distributive justice. Of course, we recognize the sociological fact that people desire to affiliate and associate with others who share common interests or characteristics. The religion and association clauses of the first amendment are responsive to such desires. But though groups and associations may benefit incidentally from these guarantees, the amendment is designed to protect the individual's freedom to associate. We grant rights to associations or treat them as fictitious persons only to protect the rights of their individual members and for other instrumental purposes. Otherwise, the rights of associations and groups are no greater than the sum of those of their members. Indeed, under our received—albeit philosophically inadequate—metaphor of the social contract, the state itself does not enjoy rights greater than those of its citizens.

To say that we generally embrace the liberal tradition is, of course, no response to the claim that we should modify the theory and restructure our institutions accordingly. But without derogating from competing political traditions, they have implications that vie with, if they are not inconsistent with, principles that we hold fundamental—including the antidiscrimination principle, which attributes no moral significance to membership in racial groups, and notions of individual autonomy. Moreover, although the practices of nations—including our own—often fall short of their aspirations, most societies in which power is formally allocated among racial and national groups are strikingly oppressive, unequal, and unstable. In view of all of this, it seems reasonable to place the burden on proponents of a theory of group racial justice to show that it is morally tenable and consistent with other values that we cherish. To my knowledge, this has not yet been done.

---

[218] [Fiss, *Groups and the Equal Protection Clause,* 5 Phil. & Pub.Aff. 107 (1976).]

Several commentators, who concede that racial groups have no intrinsic moral salience, assert that they acquire moral rights once the members of a group have suffered racial discrimination. * * *

> [T]here need be no contradiction involved in claiming that being black is both morally irrelevant for discriminating against people and morally relevant in discriminating in favour of people to provide reparations * * *. One may hold that people have an obligation to give reparations to groups they have wronged. By using the characteristic of being black as an identifying characteristic to discriminate against people, a person has wronged the group, blacks. He thus has an obligation to make reparations to the group. Since the obligation is to the group, no specific individual has a right to reparation. However, since the group is not an organized one like a state, church, or corporation, the only way to provide reparations to the group is to provide them to members of the group.[225]

A similar view may be implicit in some judicial decisions requiring employers and unions to adopt hiring and admission quotas to compensate for their past discrimination, even though the remedies are not likely to benefit the victims. * * *

* * *

The notion that the treatment of individuals as a group for malign purposes requires their treatment as a group for benign compensatory purposes has the superficial appeal of all such symmetries. But, unless one adopts a notion of group rights such as that examined and rejected above, the fact is that most injuries of discrimination—even indirect or secondary ones—were inflicted on particular persons and only they are entitled to compensation. Where discrimination has undermined the unity or culture of a group, it may be appropriate to characterize the injury as one to the group; but the appropriate remedy then is one that reestablishes the group, an end that is not promoted by the fiction of treating individual members as its agents.

OWEN M. FISS, GROUPS AND THE EQUAL PROTECTION CLAUSE

5 PHIL. & PUB.AFF. 107, 108, 129, 141–142, 144–156 (1976).

One purpose of this essay is simply to underscore the fact that the antidiscrimination principle is not the Equal Protection Clause, that it is nothing more than a mediating principle. I want to bring to an end the identification of the Clause with the antidiscrimination principle. But I also have larger ambitions. I want to suggest that the antidiscrimination

---

[225] Bayles, *Reparations to Wronged Groups,* 33 Analysis 182, 183 (1973).

principle embodies a very limited conception of equality, one that is highly individualistic and confined to assessing the rationality of means. I also want to outline another mediating principle—the group-disadvantaging principle—one that has as good, if not better, claim to represent the ideal of equality, one that takes a fuller account of social reality, and one that more clearly focuses the issues that must be decided in equal protection cases.

* * *

THE LIMITATIONS OF THE ANTIDISCRIMINATION PRINCIPLE

* * * The antidiscrimination principle has structural limitations that prevent it from adequately resolving or even addressing certain central claims of equality now being advanced. For these claims the antidiscrimination principle either provides no framework of analysis or, even worse, provides the wrong one. * * *

* * *

The Problem of Facially Innocent Criteria

* * * [One such] problem area arises from state conduct that does in fact discriminate among persons, but not on the basis of a suspect criterion. The discrimination is based on a criterion that seems innocent on its face and yet nonetheless has the effect of disadvantaging blacks (or other minorities). For example, when the state purports to choose employees or college students on the basis of performance on standardized tests, and it turns out that the only persons admitted or hired are white.

As originally conceived[,] * * * the antidiscrimination principle promised to evolve a small, finite list of suspect criteria, such as race, religion, national origin, wealth, sex. These would be presumptively impermissible. The great bulk of other criteria may ultimately be deemed arbitrary in some particular instances because of ill-fit, but they would be presumptively valid. For these criteria—which I call *facially innocent*—the mere rational-relation test would suffice, and the probability would be very high that the statute or administrative action incorporating or utilizing such criteria would be sustained.

In some instances the presumption of validity may be dissolved, and the contrary presumption created, through the use of the concept of the *real* criterion. The plaintiffs can charge cheating: while the state says that it is selecting on the basis of an innocent criterion (such as performance on a written test), in truth the selection is being made on the basis of a suspect criterion (race). The substantiation of this charge confronts the plaintiffs with enormous evidentiary burdens. No one can be expected to admit to charges of cheating, and rarely is the result so striking * * * as to permit only one inference—discrimination on the basis of a suspect criterion. But if the charge could be substantiated (perhaps with an assist from the reallocation of the burdens of proofs when the criterion had almost the same effect as a suspect one), then there would be no problem of using the strict-scrutiny branch of the antidiscrimination principle: the real criterion, as opposed to the stated criterion, is a suspect one, and there the court should insist upon a very tight fit between purpose and criterion. The troublesome cases arise, however, when the charge of cheating cannot be substantiated, where, for example, the court finds that in truth the jobs were allocated or students selected on the basis of academic performance. What then?

* * *

A second, and seemingly more modest way of rationalizing the judicial treatment of facially innocent criteria, is to introduce the concept of past discrimination. Strict scrutiny should be given, so the argument runs, to state conduct that perpetuates the effects of earlier conduct (it might be state or private) that was based on the use of a suspect classification. Conduct that perpetuates the effects of past (suspect-criterion) discrimination is as presumptively invalid as the present use of suspect criteria. An objective civil service test is presumptively impermissible whenever it perpetuates the past discrimination of the dual school system (the dual school system put the blacks at a competitive disadvantage and the test perpetuates that disadvantage). The use of geographic proximity is an impermissible criterion of school assignment whenever it perpetuates the past discrimination of the dual school system. The racial assignments of that school system led to the present residential segregation and account for the location and size of the school buildings, and both of these factors in turn explain why the use of geographic proximity as a criterion of assignment results in segregated patterns of school attendance today.

A ban on "the perpetuation of past arbitrary discrimination" looks like a close cousin of the ban on "arbitrary discrimination." But this tie can only be maintained at great expense to important institutional values—those that cluster around the ideal of objectivity, an ideal the antidiscrimination principle is supposed to serve. A true inquiry into past discrimination necessitates evidentiary judgments that are likely to strain the judicial system—consume scarce resources and yield unsatisfying results. It would require the courts to construct causal connections that span significant periods of time, periods greater than those permitted under any general statute of limitations (a common device used to prevent the judiciary from undertaking inquiries where the evidence is likely to be stale, fragmentary, and generally unreliable). The difficulties of these backward-looking inquiries are compounded because the court must invariably deal with aggregate behavior, not just a single transaction; it must determine the causal explanation for the residential patterns of an entire community, or the skill levels of all the black applicants.

* * *

The third move designed to deal with the problem of facially innocent criteria—the introduction of the concept of de facto discrimination (or discriminatory effect)—does not focus on the past. Instead it shifts the trigger for strict scrutiny from the *criterion* of selection to the *result* of the selection process, and the result is stated in terms of a *group* rather than an individual. What triggers the strict scrutiny is not the criterion of selection itself, but rather the result—the fact that a minority group has been especially hurt. (This special hurt is sometimes described as a "differential impact.")

This concept of de facto discrimination also involves a basic modification of the antidiscrimination principle. The trigger is no longer classification, but rather group-impact. * * * The concern with the result reveals to me that what is ultimately at issue is the welfare of certain disadvantaged groups, not just the use of a criterion, and if that is at issue, there is no reason why the judicial intervention on behalf of that group should be limited to an inquiry as to the degree of fit between a criterion and a purpose.

THE GROUP-DISADVANTAGING PRINCIPLE

* * *

In attempting to formulate another theory of equal protection, I have viewed the Clause primarily, but not exclusively, as a protection for blacks. In part, this perspective stems from the original intent—the fact that the Clause was viewed as a means of safeguarding blacks from hostile state action. The Equal Protection Clause (following the circumlocution of the slave-clauses in the antebellum Constitution) uses the word "person," rather than "blacks." The generality of the word chosen to describe those protected enables other groups to invoke its protection; and I am willing to admit that was also probably intended. But this generality of coverage does not preclude a theory of primary reference—that blacks were the intended primary beneficiaries, that it was a concern for their welfare that prompted the Clause.

* * *

Starting from this perspective, a distinctively racial one, it strikes me as odd to build a general interpretation of the Equal Protection Clause * * * on the rejection of the idea that there are natural classes, that is, groups that have an identity and existence wholly apart from the challenged state statute or practice. There are natural classes, or social groups, in American society and blacks are such a group. Blacks are viewed as a group; they view themselves as a group; their identity is in large part determined by membership in the group; their social status is linked to the status of the group; and much of our action, institutional and personal, is based on these perspectives.

I use the term "group" to refer to a social group, and for me, a social group is more than a collection of individuals, all of whom, to use a polar example, happen to arrive at the same street corner at the same moment. A social group, as I use the term, has two other characteristics. (1) It is an *entity* (though not one that has a physical body). This means that the group has a distinct existence apart from its members, and also that it has an identity. It makes sense to talk about the group (at various points of time) and know that you are talking about the same group. You can talk about the group without reference to the particular individuals who happen to be its members at any one moment. (2) There is also a condition of *interdependence.* The identity and well-being of the members of the group and the identity and well-being of the group are linked. Members of the group identify themselves—explain who they are—by reference to their membership in the group; and their well-being or status is in part determined by the well-being or status of the group. * * *

I would be the first to admit that working with the concept of a group is problematic, much more so than working with the concept of an individual or criterion. It is "messy." For example, in some instances, it may be exceedingly difficult to determine whether particular individuals are members of the group; or whether a particular collection of persons constitutes a social group. I will also admit that my definition of a social group, and in particular the condition of interdependence, compounds rather than reduces, these classificatory disputes. But these disputes do not demonstrate the illegitimacy of this category of social entity nor deny the validity or importance of the idea. They only blur the edges. Similarly, the present reality of the social groups should not be obscured by a commitment to the ideal of a "classless society" or the individualistic ethic—the ideal of treating people as individuals rather than as members of groups. Even if the Equal Protection Clause is viewed as the means for furthering or achieving these individualistic ideals (and I am not sure why it should be), there is no reason why the Clause—as an instrument for bringing about the "good society"—must be construed as though it is itself governed by that ideal or why it should be assumed that the "good society" had been achieved in 1868, or is so now.

The conception of blacks as a social group is only the first step in constructing a mediating principle. We must also realize they are a very special type of social group. They have two other characteristics as a group that are critical in understanding the function and reach of the Equal

Protection Clause. One is that blacks are very badly off, probably our worst-off class (in terms of material well-being second only to the American Indians), and in addition they have occupied the lowest rung for several centuries. In a sense, they are America's perpetual underclass. It is both of these characteristics—the relative position of the group and the duration of the position—that make efforts to improve the status of the group defensible. This redistribution may be rooted in a theory of compensation—blacks as a group were *put* in that position by others and the redistributive measures are *owed* to the group as a form of compensation. The debt would be viewed as owed by society, once again viewed as a collectivity. But a redistributive strategy need not rest on this idea of compensation, it need not be backward looking (though past discrimination might be relevant for *explaining* the identity and status of blacks as a social group). The redistributive strategy could give expression to an ethical view against caste, one that would make it undesirable for any social group to occupy a position of subordination for any extended period of time. What, it might be asked, is the justification for that vision? I am not certain whether it is appropriate to ask this question, to push the inquiry a step further and search for the justification of that ethic; visions about how society should be structured may be as irreducible as visions about how individuals should be treated—for example, with dignity. But if this second order inquiry is appropriate, a variety of justifications can be offered and they need not incorporate the notion of compensation. Changes in the hierarchical structure of society—the elimination of caste—might be justified as a means of (a) preserving social peace; (b) maintaining the community as a community, that is, as one cohesive whole; or (c) permitting the fullest development of the individual members of the subordinated group who otherwise might look upon the low status of the group as placing a ceiling on their aspirations and achievements.

It is not just the socioeconomic status of blacks as a group that explains their special position in equal protection theory. It is also their political status. The power of blacks in the political arena is severely limited. For the last two centuries the political power of this group was circumscribed in most direct fashion—disenfranchisement. The electoral strength of blacks was not equal to their numbers. That has changed following the massive enfranchisement of the Voting Rights Act of 1965, but structural limitations on the political power of blacks still persist. These limitations arise from three different sources, which can act either alternatively or cumulatively and which, in any event, are all interrelated. One source of weakness is their numbers, the fact that they are a numerical minority; the second is their economic status, their position as the perpetual underclass; and the third is that, as a "discrete and insular" minority, they are the object of "prejudice"—that is, the subject of fear, hatred, and distaste that make it particularly difficult for them to form coalitions with others (such as the white poor) and that make it advantageous for the dominant political parties to hurt them—to use them as a scapegoat.

* * *

Hence, despite recent demographic shifts in several large cities, I think it appropriate to view blacks as a group that is relatively powerless in the political arena and in my judgment that political status of the group justifies a special judicial solicitude on their behalf. When the product of a political process is a law that hurts blacks, the usual countermajoritarian objection to judicial invalidation—the objection that denies those "nine men" the right to substitute their view for that of "the people"—has little force. For the judiciary could be viewed as amplifying the voice of the powerless minority; the judiciary is attempting to rectify the injustice of the political process as a method of adjusting competing claims. The need for this rectification turns on whether the law is deemed one that harms blacks—a judgment that is admittedly hard to make when the perspective becomes a group one, for that requires the aggregation of interests and viewpoints, many of which are in conflict. It is important to emphasize, however, that the need for this rectification does not turn on whether the law embodies a classification, racial or otherwise; it is sufficient if the state law simply has the *effect* of hurting blacks. Nor should the rectification, once triggered by a harmful law, be confined to questions of fit—the judicial responsibility is more extensive than simply one of guarding against the risk of imprecise classifications by the political agencies. The relative powerlessness of blacks also requires that the judiciary strictly scrutinize the choice of ends; for it is just as likely that the interests of blacks as a group will not be adequately taken into account in choosing ends or goals. Maximizing goals such as reducing transportation costs (a goal that might account for the neighborhood-school plan) or having the most brilliant law students (a goal that might account for requiring a [high score] on the LSAT) are constitutionally permissible goals in the sense that there is no substantive constitutional provision (or implied purpose lying behind some provision) that deny them to the state. On the other hand, these maximizing goals are obviously not in any sense constitutionally compelled goals and there is a chance—a most substantial one—that they would not be chosen as *the* goals (without any modification) if the interests of the blacks as a group were adequately taken into account—if the goal-choosers paid sufficient attention to the special needs, desires, and views of this powerless group.

The injustice of the political process must be corrected, and perhaps as a last resort, that task falls to the judiciary. But this claim does not yield any basis for specifying what the corrected process would look like, or what the court should say when it amplifies the voice of the powerless minority. A just political process would be one in which blacks would have "more" of a voice than they in fact do, but not necessarily one in which they would "win." In a sense there is a remedial lacuna; a pure process claim cannot determine substantive outcomes. * * * But this processual theory focusing on the relative powerlessness of blacks in the political arena need not stand alone. The substantive standards can be supplied by the other critical characteristics of this social group—perpetual subordination. The political status of the group justifies the institutional allocations—our willingness to allow those "nine men" to substitute their judgment (about ends as well as means) for that of "the people." The socioeconomic position of the group supplies an additional reason for the judicial activism and also determines the content of the intervention—improvement of the status of that group.

I would therefore argue that blacks should be viewed as having three characteristics that are relevant in the formulation of equal protection theory: (a) they are a social group; (b) the group has been in a position of perpetual subordination; and (c) the political power of the group is severely circumscribed. Blacks are what might be called a specially disadvantaged group, and I would view the Equal Protection Clause as a protection for such groups. Blacks are the prototype of the protected group, but they are not the only group entitled to protection. There are other social groups, even as I have used the term, and if these groups have the same characteristics as blacks—perpetual subordination and circumscribed political power—they should be considered specially disadvantaged and receive the same degree of protection. What the Equal Protection Clause protects is specially disadvantaged groups, not just blacks. A concern for equal treatment and the word "person" appearing in the Clause permit and probably require this generality of coverage.

Some of these specially disadvantaged groups can be defined in terms of characteristics that do not have biological roots and that are not immutable; the Clause might protect certain language groups and aliens. Moreover, in passing upon a claim to be considered a specially disadvantaged group, the court may treat one of the characteristics entitling blacks to that status as a sufficient but not a necessary condition; indeed the court may even develop variable standards of protection—it may tolerate disadvantaging practices that would not be tolerated if the group was a "pure" specially disadvantaged group. Jews or women might be entitled to less protection than American Indians, though nonetheless entitled to some protection. Finally, these judicial judgments may be time-bound. Through the process of assimilation the group may cease to exist, or even if the group continues to retain its identity, its socioeconomic and political positions may so improve so as to bring to an end its status as specially disadvantaged.

All this means that the courts will have some leeway in identifying the groups protected by the Equal Protection Clause. I think, however, it would be a mistake to use this flexibility to extend the protection to what might be considered artificial classes, those created by a classification or criterion embodied in a state practice or statute, for example, those classes created by tax categories (those having incomes between $27,000 and $30,000, or between $8,000 and $10,000) or licensing statutes (the manufacturers of filled milk). By definition those classes do not have an independent social identity and existence, or if they do, the condition of interdependence is lacking. It is difficult, if not impossible, to make an assessment of their socioeconomic status or of their political power (other than that they have just lost a legislative battle). And, if this is true, neither redistribution nor stringent judicial intervention on their behalf can be justified. It is not that such arguments are unpersuasive, but that they are almost unintelligible. Thus, in only one sense should the group-disadvantaging strategy be viewed as conducive to "more equality": it will get more for fewer. It will get more for the specially disadvantaged groups but will not provide any protection for artificial classes, those solely created by statute or a state practice. Of course, this loss may be more formal than real. Artificial classes constitute part of the universe that the antidiscrimination principle *purports* to protect, but in truth almost never does protect given the permissibility of the minimum-scrutiny inquiry.

[In the concluding portion of his article Fiss explains how he would implement his proposal for a group-disadvantaging principle. He admits that it would reach the same results as the antidiscrimination principle in what he calls "first-order" situations—exclusion of blacks from public institutions. The choice of a principle would matter more in "second-order" cases—challenges to the use of facially innocent criteria such as test performance. And in "third-order" cases—preferential treatment—the differences would be most evident. The antidiscrimination principle, with its individualistic character, tends to prohibit such treatment; a focus on disadvantaged groups tends to allow (perhaps even require) it.

[Not every instance of disparate impact is a "second-order" case. A sales tax, because of its diffuse impact, may harm individuals but not aggravate the subordinate status of blacks as a group. But in any true "second-order" case the state practice would be presumptively invalid. The state could overcome the presumption by showing that its practice was necessary to produce a compelling benefit. It could, for example, insist on certain minimum levels of competence for its employees or students.

[In "third-order" cases Fiss's principle would require only a rational basis for preferential policies. The reason is that the Equal Protection Clause is not concerned with fairness (e.g., to individual whites), but with group harm. For the same reason, it would not matter that some individual beneficiaries (e.g. rich blacks) were not victims.]

CHARLES R. LAWRENCE III, THE ID, THE EGO, AND EQUAL PROTECTION: RECKONING WITH UNCONSCIOUS RACISM

39 STAN.L.REV. 317, 321–323, 328, 331–339, 344–355 (1987).

Much of one's inability to know racial discrimination when one sees it results from a failure to recognize that racism is both a crime and a disease.[15] This failure is compounded by a reluctance to admit that the illness of racism infects almost everyone. Acknowledging and understanding the malignancy are prerequisites to the discovery of an appropriate cure. But the diagnosis is difficult, because our own contamination with the very illness for which a cure is sought impairs our comprehension of the disorder.

* * *

Americans share a common historical and cultural heritage in which racism has played and still plays a dominant role. Because of this shared experience, we also inevitably share many ideas, attitudes, and beliefs that attach significance to an individual's race and induce negative feelings and opinions about nonwhites. To the extent that this cultural belief system has influenced all of us, we are all racists. At the same time, most of us are unaware of our racism. We do not recognize the ways in which our cultural experience has influenced our beliefs about race or the occasions on which those beliefs affect our actions. In other words, a large part of the behavior that produces racial discrimination is influenced by unconscious racial motivation.

There are two explanations for the unconscious nature of our racially discriminatory beliefs and ideas. First, Freudian theory states that the human mind defends itself against the discomfort of guilt by denying or refusing to recognize those ideas, wishes, and beliefs that conflict with what the individual has learned is good or right. While our historical experience has made racism an integral part of our culture, our society has more recently embraced an ideal that rejects racism as immoral. When an individual experiences conflict between racist ideas and the societal ethic that condemns those ideas, the mind excludes his racism from consciousness.

Second, the theory of cognitive psychology states that the culture—including, for example, the media and an individual's parents, peers, and authority figures—transmits certain beliefs and preferences. Because these beliefs are so much a part of the culture, they are not experienced as

[15] "Immorality" and "criminality" are thought of in terms of blameworthiness. In contrast, Chester Pierce, a black psychiatrist, has described racism as a "public health problem." Pierce, *Psychiatric Problems of Black Minority,* in 2 American Handbook of Psychiatry 512, 513 (G. Caplan 2d ed. 1974). * * *

explicit lessons. Instead, they seem part of the individual's rational ordering of her perceptions of the world. The individual is unaware, for example, that the ubiquitous presence of a cultural stereotype has influenced her perception that blacks are lazy or unintelligent. Because racism is so deeply ingrained in our culture, it is likely to be transmitted by tacit understandings: Even if a child is not told that blacks are inferior, he learns that lesson by observing the behavior of others. These tacit understandings, because they have never been articulated, are less likely to be experienced at a conscious level.

I. "THY SPEECH MAKETH THEE MANIFEST": A PRIMER ON THE UNCONSCIOUS AND RACE

* * *

Psychoanalytic Theory: An Explanation of Racism's Irrationality

The division of the mind into the conscious and the unconscious is the fundamental principle of psychoanalysis. Psychoanalytic theory explains the existence of pathological mental behavior as well as certain otherwise unexplained behavior in healthy people by postulating two powerful mental processes—the primary and the secondary—which govern how the mind works. The primary process, or Id, occurs outside of our awareness. It consists of desires, wishes, and instincts that strive for gratification. It follows its own laws, of which the supreme one is pleasure. The secondary process, or Ego, happens under conscious control and is bound by logic and reason. We use this process to adapt to reality: The Ego is required to respect the demands of reality and to conform to ethical and moral laws. On their way to gratification, the Id impulses must pass through the territory of the Ego where they are criticized, rejected, or modified, often by some defensive measure on the part of the secondary process. Defensive mechanisms such as repression, denial, introjection, projection, reaction formation, sublimation, and reversal resolve the conflicts between the primary and secondary processes by disguising forbidden wishes and making them palatable.

* * *

An examination of the beliefs that racially prejudiced people have about out-groups demonstrates their use of * * * mechanisms observed by both Freudian and nonFreudian behavioralists. For example, studies have found that racists hold two types of stereotyped beliefs: They believe the out-group is dirty, lazy, oversexed, and without control of their instincts (a typical accusation against blacks), or they believe the out-group is pushy, ambitious, conniving, and in control of business, money, and industry (a typical accusation against Jews). These two types of accusation correspond to two of the most common types of neurotic conflict: that which arises when an individual cannot master his instinctive drives in a way that fits into rational and socially approved patterns of behavior, and that which arises when an individual cannot live up to the aspirations and standards of his own conscience. Thus, the stereotypical view of blacks implies that their Id, the instinctive part of their psyche, dominates their Ego, the rationally oriented part. The stereotype of the Jew, on the other hand, accuses him of having an overdeveloped Ego. In this way, the racially prejudiced person projects his own conflict into the form of racial stereotypes.

The preoccupation among racially prejudiced people with sexual matters in race relations provides further evidence of this relationship between the unconscious and racism. Taboos against interracial sexual relations, myths concerning the sexual prowess of blacks, and obsessions with racial purity coexist irrationally with a tendency to break these taboos. Again, psychoanalytic theory provides insights: According to Freud, one's sexual identity plays a crucial role in the unending effort to come to terms with oneself. Thus, the prominence of racism's sexual component supports the theory that racial antagonism grows in large part out of an unstable sense of identity.

* * *

Thus far we have considered the role the unconscious plays in creating overtly racist attitudes. But how is the unconscious involved when racial prejudice is less apparent—when racial bias is hidden from the prejudiced individual as well as from others? Increasingly, as our culture has rejected racism as immoral and unproductive, this hidden prejudice has become the more prevalent form of racism. The individual's Ego must adapt to a cultural order that views overtly racist attitudes and behavior as unsophisticated, uninformed, and immoral. It must repress or disguise racist ideas when they seek expression.

* * *

A Cognitive Approach to Unconscious Racism

Cognitive psychologists offer a contrasting model for understanding the origin and unconscious nature of racial prejudice. This is essentially a rational model. The cognitivists acknowledge the importance of emotional and motivational factors, but they do not embrace the Freudian belief that instinctive drives dominate individuals' concepts, attitudes, and beliefs. Instead, they view human behavior, including racial prejudice, as growing out of the individual's attempt to understand his relationship with the world (in this case, relations between groups) while at the same time preserving his personal integrity. But while the ultimate goal of the cognitive process is understanding or rationality, many of the critical elements of the process occur outside of the individual's awareness. This is especially true when there is tension between the individual's desire for simplification and the complexity of the real world or conflict between an understanding of a situation that preserves the individual's self-image and one that jeopardizes a positive view of himself.

Cognitivists see the process of "categorization" as one common source of racial and other stereotypes. All humans tend to categorize in order to make sense of experience. Too many events occur daily for us to deal successfully with each one on an individual basis; we must categorize in order to cope. When a category—for example, the category of black person or white person—correlates with a continuous dimension—for example, the range of human intelligence or the propensity to violence—there is a tendency to exaggerate the differences between categories on that dimension and to minimize the differences within each category.

The more important a particular classification of people into groups is to an individual, the more likely she is to distinguish sharply the characteristics of people who belong to the different groups. Here, cognitivists integrate the observations of personality theorists and social psychologists with their own. If an individual is hostile toward a group of people, she has an emotional investment in preserving the differentiations between her own group and the "others." Thus, the preservation of inaccurate judgments about the out-group is self-rewarding. This is particularly so when prejudiced judgments are made in a social context that accepts and encourages negative attitudes toward the out-group. In these cases, the group judgment reinforces and helps maintain the individual judgment about the out-group's lack of worth.

The content of the social categories to which people are assigned is generated over a long period of time within a culture and transmitted to individual members of society by a process cognitivists call "assimilation." Assimilation entails learning and internalizing preferences and evaluations. Individuals learn cultural attitudes and beliefs about race very early in life, at a time when it is difficult to separate the perceptions of one's teacher (usually a parent) from one's own. In other words, one learns about race at a time when one is highly sensitive to the social contexts in which one lives.

* * *

Furthermore, because children learn lessons about race at this early stage, most of the lessons are tacit rather than explicit. Children learn not so much through an intellectual understanding of what their parents tell them about race as through an emotional identification with who their parents are and what they see and feel their parents do. Small children will adopt their parents' beliefs because they experience them as their own. If we do learn lessons about race in this way, we are not likely to be aware that the lessons have even taken place. If we are unaware that we have been taught to be afraid of blacks or to think of them as lazy or stupid, then we may not be conscious of our internalization of those feelings and beliefs.

* * *

Case studies have demonstrated that an individual who holds stereotyped beliefs about a "target" will remember and interpret past events in the target's life history in ways that bolster and support his stereotyped beliefs and will perceive the target's actual behavior as reconfirming and validating the stereotyped beliefs. While the individual may be aware of the selectively perceived facts that support his categorization or simplified understanding, he will not be aware of the process that has caused him to deselect the facts that do not conform with his rationalization. Thus, racially prejudiced behavior that is actually the product of learned cultural preferences is experienced as a reflection of rational deduction from objective observation, which is nonprejudicial behavior. The decisionmaker who is unaware of the selective perception that has produced her stereotype will not view it as a stereotype. She will believe that her actions are motivated not by racial prejudice but by her attraction or aversion to the attributes she has "observed" in the groups she has favored or disfavored.

* * *

II. A Tale of Two Theories

* * *

Two theories have attempted to specify the central function of suspect classification doctrine. The first, the "process defect" theory, sees the judicial intervention occasioned by strict scrutiny of suspect classifications as an appropriate response to distortions in the democratic process. The second theory cites racial stigma as the primary target of suspect classification doctrine. * * * [R]ecognizing the presence of unconscious motive furthers the central rationale of each theory.[115]

[115] A third substantive theory of equal protection suggests that racial groups should be treated as moral entities with group rights to distributive and compensatory justice. It holds that it is prima facie unjust for one racial or ethnic group to be substantially worse off than another. This "group disadvantaging principle" requires relief for any group that constitutes a "perpetual underclass" and argues that such redistribution would express an ethical view disfavoring caste. *See* Fiss, [*Groups and the Equal Protection Clause,* 5 Phil. & Pub.Aff. 107 (1976)]. This article will not discuss this approach. Fiss' theory is essentially indifferent to the motives and history that have led to unequal distribution and is, therefore, sufficiently sensitive to the correction of disadvantage resulting from unconscious racism without the assistance of my analysis.

The Process Defect Theory

The chief proponent of the process defect theory has been John Ely.[116] He identifies the systematic exclusion of a group from the normal workings of the political process as the harm that heightened judicial scrutiny for suspect classifications seeks to prevent or remedy.

* * *

Motive and intent are at the center of Ely's theory. The function of suspect classification doctrine is to expose unconstitutional motives that may have distorted the process. A statute that classifies by race is strictly scrutinized, because the requirement of "close fit" between end sought and means used will reveal those instances where the actual motive of the legislature was to disadvantage a group simply because of its race.

Under present doctrine, the courts look for Ely's process defect only when the racial classification appears on the face of the statute or when self-conscious racial intent has been proved * * * But the same process distortions will occur even when the racial prejudice is less apparent. Other groups in the body politic may avoid coalition with blacks without a conscious awareness of their aversion to blacks or of their association of certain characteristics with blacks. They may take stands on issues without realizing that their reasons are, in part, racially oriented. Likewise, the governmental decisionmaker may be unaware that she has devalued the cost of a chosen path, because a group with which she does not identify will bear that cost. Indeed, because of her lack of empathy with the group, she may have never even thought of the cost at all.

Process distortion exists where the unconstitutional motive of racial prejudice has influenced the decision. It matters not that the decisionmaker's motive may lie outside her awareness. For example, in *Village of Arlington Heights v. Metropolitan Housing Development Corp.*,[127] a predominantly white, upper middle class Chicago suburb prevented the construction of a proposed housing development for low and moderate income families by refusing to rezone the projected site to allow multi-family units. The Supreme Court agreed that the decision not to rezone had racially discriminatory effects, but it rejected the black plaintiffs' equal protection claim on the ground that they had "simply failed to carry their burden of proving that discriminatory purpose was a motivating factor in the Village's decision." The Court focused on the lack of any evidence of conscious intent to discriminate on the part of either the city council in enacting the zoning ordinance that restricted use to single family homes or the planning commission in administering the ordinance.

---

[116] *See* J. Ely, Democracy and Distrust 135–79 (1980). * * *

[127] 429 U.S. 252 (1977).

We can envision several possible scenarios that demonstrate the possible process-distorting effects of unconscious racism on a governmental decision like that in *Arlington Heights:*

(1) The city council refused to rezone for the sole purpose of stigmatizing and denying housing to blacks. This case resembles *Plessy v. Ferguson*[131] and *Gomillion v. Lightfoot,*[132] in which the only motives were unconstitutional, and the ordinances were, therefore, per se unconstitutional.

(2) The city claims a legitimate economic or environmental purpose, but evidence shows that it sought to exclude blacks in order to achieve that purpose. This case is the same as a classification by race on the face of a statute for which a legitimate goal is claimed. It is the case Ely describes where blacks are consciously excluded from the political process and devalued in the assessment of costs and benefits. When this self-conscious motive can be proved, the resulting classification is subject to strict scrutiny under existing doctrine.

(3) The purpose of the ordinance was economic—i.e., to keep property values up by keeping poor people out—but the decisionmakers associated poverty with blacks and would have weighed the costs and benefits differently if the poor people they envisioned excluding were elderly white people on social security. This "selective sympathy or indifference" could have occurred at a conscious or unconscious level. It is more than likely that the decisionmakers knew that the poor people they were excluding were black, but they would not be likely to have known that they undervalued the cost to poor people because they thought of them as black rather than white.

(4) A constituency within Arlington Heights—for example, elderly whites—did not actively campaign for the rezoning because of aversion to blacks who might have benefited from it. This occurred despite the fact that this constituency's interest in low income housing would otherwise have outweighed its interest in property values. This inability or unwillingness to apprehend and act upon an overlapping interest is precisely the kind of process distortion through group vilification that Ely describes. It is as likely as not that these elderly voters are largely unaware of the vilification and resulting aversion that preempted their potential coalition with blacks.

(5) No one in Arlington Heights thought about blacks one way or the other—i.e., it was a fight between environmentalists and developers—but an inadvertent devaluing of black interests caused inattention to the costs blacks would have to bear. If one asked the decisionmakers how they had valued the cost to blacks of the exclusionary zoning, they might have

---

[131] 163 U.S. 537 (1896).

[132] 364 U.S. 339 (1960).

responded, "I never thought of that." This is an example of selective indifference or misapprehension of costs that occurs entirely outside of consciousness.

The process defect theory sees suspect classification doctrine as a roundabout way of uncovering unconstitutional motive by suspecting those classifications that disadvantage groups we know to be the object of widespread vilification. But by only suspecting laws that classify by race on their face or are the result of overtly self-conscious racial motivation, the theory stops an important step short of locating and eliminating the defect it has identified. Where a society has recently adopted a moral ethic that repudiates racial disadvantaging for its own sake, governmental decision-makers are as likely to repress their racial motives as they are to lie to courts or to attempt after-the-fact rationalizations of classifications that are not racial on their face but that do have disproportionate racial impact. Unconscious aversion to a group that has historically been vilified distorts the political process no less than a conscious decision to place race hatred before politically legitimate goals.

* * *

The Stigma Theory

A second theory posits elimination of racially stigmatizing actions as the central concern of the equal protection clause. Under this theory, racial classifications should be strictly scrutinized when they operate to shame and degrade a class of persons by labeling it as inferior. Stigmatization is the process by which the dominant group in society differentiates itself from others by setting them apart, treating them as less than fully human, denying them acceptance by the organized community, and excluding them from participating in that community as equals. * * *

The prevention of stigma was at the core of the Supreme Court's unanimous declaration in *Brown v. Board of Education* that segregated public schools are inherently unequal. In observing that the segregation of black pupils "generates a feeling of inferiority as to their status in the community," Chief Justice Warren recognized what a majority of the Court had ignored almost sixty years earlier in *Plessy v. Ferguson:* The social meaning of racial segregation in the United States is the designation of a superior and an inferior caste, and segregation proceeds "on the ground that colored citizens are * * * inferior and degraded."

Stigmatizing actions harm the individual in two ways: They inflict psychological injury by assaulting a person's self-respect and human dignity, and they brand the individual with a sign that signals her inferior status to others and designates her as an outcast. The stigma theory recognizes the importance of both self-esteem and the respect of others for participating in society's benefits and responsibilities.

* * *

The injury of stigmatization consists of forcing the injured individual to wear a badge or symbol that degrades him in the eyes of society. But in most cases the symbol is not inherently pejorative. Rather, the message obtains its shameful meaning from the historical and cultural context in which it is used and, ultimately, from the way it is interpreted by those who witness it. Thus the woman who is asked to use a separate public bathroom from her husband is unlikely to be stigmatized by that action: Our society does not ordinarily interpret sex-segregated toilet facilities as designating the inferiority of women. By contrast, the black who is asked to use a different public bathroom from that of a white companion of the same gender is stigmatized. * * * [R]acially segregated bathrooms were an important part of the system of segregation. That system's ideology held not only that blacks were less than fully human but also that they were dirty and impure. Racially segregated bathrooms ensured that blacks would not contaminate the facilities used by whites.

If stigmatizing actions injure by virtue of the meaning society gives them, then it should be apparent that the evil intent of their authors, while perhaps sufficient, is not necessary to the infliction of the injury. For example, a well-meaning if misguided white employer, having observed that her black employees usually sat together at lunch, might build a separate dining room for them with the intent of making them more comfortable. This action would stigmatize her black employees despite her best intentions. Similarly, when the city of Jackson, Mississippi closed its public pools after a federal court ordered it to integrate them, the action stigmatized blacks regardless of whether the government's purpose was racial or economic.

Given that stigma occurs whether there is racial animus or not, the answer to our initial question, "Is knowledge about the intent of the governmental actor significant to the achievement of the equal protection clause's purpose?" would seem an obvious "No." But many of the stigma theory's advocates find themselves in a quandary when faced with the question of how the Court should approach laws that are not apparently "race-dependent" but that result in disparate and stigmatizing effects. * * *

* * * Paul Brest, having persuasively argued the need to eliminate racially disproportionate impact that stigmatizes, cautions that the impact doctrine "cannot reasonably be applied across the board" and urges that the doctrine be used "selectively."[168] He warns that "remedies for

[168] [Brest, *Foreword: In Defense of the Antidiscrimination Principle,* 90 Harv.L.Rev. 1 (1976).]

disproportionate impact may impose heavy costs on institutions and individuals, and cannot be tailored narrowly to compensate all those and only those whose present situation is the result of past discrimination." Brest's reference to the overbreadth of remedies for disproportionate impact adds to the general concern about unduly limiting legislative discretion and the particular concern about the legitimacy of courts imposing costs on "blameless" individuals and conferring benefits on those who have not been directly harmed.

The consideration of unconscious intent responds to both of these concerns. Identifying stigmatizing actions that were affected by the actor's unconscious racial attitudes achieves two benefits. First, it significantly decreases the absolute number of impact cases subject to heightened scrutiny without eviscerating the substantive content of the equal protection clause. The bridge toll, the sales tax, and the filing fee can no longer be numbered among the parade of horribles that Justice White suggested in [*Washington v.*] *Davis.*[171] At the same time, cases where racially discriminatory impact results directly from past intentional discrimination or from current but unprovable racial animus will be well within judicial reach. A law does not stigmatize blacks simply because exclusion itself is stigmatizing, and, in this instance, they are disproportionately represented among the excluded group. Instead, the stigma stems at least in part from society's predisposition to exclude blacks. The fact that unconscious racial attitudes affected a governmental action is evidence that the racially stigmatizing symbolism preexisted the present impact.

Second, consideration of unconscious motivation provides a neutral principle for judicial intervention—i.e., the identification of a process defect. This counters the argument made against the impact test that the judiciary has no principled basis for imposing a priority for the removal of racial stigma over other social goods to which the political branch might choose to give preeminence. In short, stigma often occurs regardless of the intent of those who have engaged in the stigmatizing action. Thus, it is arguable that under the stigma theory neither conscious nor unconscious intent should be considered, and heightened judicial scrutiny should apply in all cases when governmental action produces a stigmatizing effect. Nonetheless, recognizing unconscious racism provides a mechanism for effectively responding to continuing race-based inequalities while minimizing the costs of judicial overreaching.

[In the concluding portion of his article Lawrence deals with the most obvious objection to his theory: how courts can identify cases where unconscious racism is operating. He proposes that we should look not at individual actions but at the "cultural meaning" of allegedly discriminatory

[171][426 U.S. 229, 248 & n. 14 (1976).]

acts as the best evidence of the collective unconscious. This test would evaluate governmental conduct to see whether it conveys a symbolic message to which the culture attaches racial significance. If it does, the court should apply heightened scrutiny.

[For example, the building of a wall between white and black communities in *Memphis v. Greene*[a] has a cultural meaning because of the long history of whites separating themselves from blacks as a symbol of superiority. It would not matter that individual members of the city council were unconscious of their failure to empathize with how blacks felt.

[Lawrence stresses that the task of interpreting cultural meaning is not foreign to courts. In Establishment Clause cases the courts decide whether a practice advances religion by asking what meaning we attach to a practice—*e.g.* a Christmas creche. In sex discrimination cases the courts ask whether laws tend to perpetuate a "stereotyped view" of men and women—*e.g.* as breadwinners and homemakers. Lawrence argues that the task he sets for the judiciary in race cases would not be essentially different.]

JOHN HART ELY, FACILITATING THE REPRESENTATION OF MINORITIES

DEMOCRACY AND DISTRUST 145–146, 148–161 (1980).

[In the opening part of the chapter from which this selection is drawn Ely argues that the Equal Protection Clause is primarily concerned with the process by which the government allocates various harms and benefits. This means that the constitutionality of any particular allocation will depend in part on why it was undertaken—*i.e.* on the motives of the actors involved. Ely notes, however, that the courts have generally been reluctant to inquire into legislative or administrative motivation.

[Ely then turns to the doctrine of "suspect classifications." He contends that the real point of this doctrine is to serve as a handmaiden of motivation analysis.]

The [suspect classification and motivation] doctrines support each other in this way. The goal the classification in issue is likely to fit most closely, obviously, is the goal the legislators actually had in mind. If it can be directly identified and is one that is unconstitutional, all well and good: the classification is unconstitutional. But even if such a confident demonstration of motivation proves impossible, a classification that in fact was unconstitutionally motivated will nonetheless—thanks to the indirect pressure exerted by the suspect-classification doctrine—find itself in serious constitutional difficulty. For an unconstitutional goal obviously cannot be invoked in a statute's defense. That means, where the real goal

---

[a] 451 U.S. 100, 101 S.Ct. 1584, 67 L.Ed.2d 769 (1981).

was unconstitutional, that the goal that fits the classification best will not be invocable in its defense, and the classification will have to be defended in terms of others to which it relates more tenuously. Where the requirement is simply the Court's standard call for a "rational" relation between classification and goal, that will seldom matter: even if the goal the classification fits best is disabled from invocation, there will likely be other permissible goals whose relation to the classification is sufficiently close to be called rational. The "special scrutiny" that is afforded suspect classifications, however, insists that the classification in issue fit the goal invoked in its defense more closely than any alternative classification would. There is only one goal the classification is likely to fit *that* closely, however, and that is the goal the legislators actually had in mind. If that goal cannot be invoked because it is unconstitutional, the classification will fall. Thus, functionally, special scrutiny, in particular its demand for an essentially perfect fit, turns out to be a way of "flushing out" unconstitutional motivation, one that lacks the proof problems of a more direct inquiry and into the bargain permits courts (and complainants) to be more politic, to invalidate (or attack) something for illicit motivation without having to come right out and say that's what they're doing.

* * *

During the Warren era, the Supreme Court was quite adventurous in expanding the set of suspect classifications beyond the core case of race. Laws classifying to the comparative disadvantage of aliens, persons of "illegitimate" birth, even poor people, were all at one time or another approached as suspect. The Burger Court has also paid lip service to the general idea. In fact Justice Blackmun was the first ever—apart, of course, from Justice Stone's original *Carolene Products* footnote[a]—to indicate in an Opinion of the Court that "discrete and insular" minorities are entitled to special constitutional protection from the political process. However, the Burger Court's performance on this score has not matched its rhetoric. Since he came on the Court, Justice Rehnquist has been campaigning to reduce the set of suspect classifications to race and "its first cousin," national origin, and his campaign seems to be succeeding. * * *

The reason Justice Rehnquist gives for wanting to cut the list back to race and national origin is one allegedly grounded in original intent, that those are the classifications the framers of the Fourteenth Amendment would have wanted to subject to unusual scrutiny. * * * The justice thinks he sees a family resemblance between national origin and race, but

[a]In United States v. Carolene Products, 304 U.S. 144, 152 n. 4 (1938), Justice Stone suggested in dictum that "prejudice against discrete and insular minorities may be a special condition, which tends seriously to curtail the operation of those political processes ordinarily to be relied upon to protect minorities, and which may call for a correspondingly more searching judicial inquiry."

classifications aren't really the same thing as people and it takes a theory to make one classification the "first cousin" of another. It's true, only "racelike" classifications should be regarded as suspect, but we have to figure out what "racelike" should mean in this context.

It's probably because Court and commentator alike have failed here, at the level of theory, that Justice Rehnquist is steadily gaining his way. Factors are frequently mentioned in the literature that in an intuitive way do seem to have something to do with the point—and on further analysis we'll see that in oblique ways some of them do—but somehow none is quite capable of convincing us that it *is* the point. Thus, for example, it is often said that the immutability of the classifying trait ought to make a classification suspect. * * * [But] no one has bothered to * * * tell us exactly *why* we should be suspicious of legislatures that classify on the basis of immutable characteristics. Surely one has to feel sorry for a person disabled by something that he or she can't do anything about, but I'm not aware of any reason to suppose that elected officials are unusually unlikely to share that feeling. Moreover, classifications based on physical disability and intelligence are typically accepted as legitimate, even by judges and commentators who assert that immutability is relevant. The explanation, when one is given, is that *those* characteristics (unlike the one the commentator is trying to render suspect) are often relevant to legitimate purposes. At that point there's not much left of the immutability theory, is there?

A number of commentaries, purporting to find support in *Brown v. Board of Education,* argue that classifications disfavoring racial minorities are suspect because they "will usually be perceived as a stigma of inferiority and a badge of opprobrium." This confuses two issues and thus misreads *Brown.* Feelings of opprobrium *are* relevant to determining whether a classification the state claims is "harmless," such as "separate but equal" schooling, in fact inflicts harm on one or the other class. But *Brown* was unusual in that respect: the existence of comparative harm to one of the classes distinguished by a governmental classification is rarely an issue. Neither can the idea be that the presence of stigma is necessary in order to establish some requisite *amount* of harm. That account would make sense if the Court followed the practice of reviewing more strenuously those distinctions that hurt more, which it doesn't. A taxation distinction worth $1,000,000 receives about the same review as one worth $100—that is, virtually none.

An account that seems more to the point, one to which I've alluded several times, is that attributed to Justice Stone's *Carolene Products* footnote and recently paraphrased for the Court * * * by Justice Blackmun: "Aliens as a class are a prime example of a 'discrete and insular' minority

* * * for whom * * * heightened judicial solicitude is appropriate * * * "[59] * * * In a sense the complainant in every case speaks for such a group: he wouldn't be in court if the class in which the legislature had placed him had not been, on at least one occasion, a political minority (they lost), both discrete (they're the ones on the disfavored side of the statutory line) and insular (they couldn't gather enough allies to defeat the legislation). But obviously that isn't what Justice Stone meant. His reference was rather to the sort of "pluralist" wheeling and dealing by which the various minorities that make up our society typically interact to protect their interests, and constituted an attempt to denote those minorities for which such a system of "mutual defense pacts" will prove recurrently unavailing.

* * *

* * * [T]hough the general idea here may be clear enough—courts should protect those who can't protect themselves politically—the justification for it isn't. In a way it is of the essence of democracy to allow the various persons and groups that make up our society to decide which others they wish to combine with in shaping legislation. We are not all the same in all respects, and on certain subjects our interests in fact do differ substantially. There is thus no way to exclude a priori—as the theory as elaborated so far does—the possibility that there may exist groups or interests with which others will refuse to combine politically for perfectly respectable reasons.

An added element is therefore needed, that the minority in question be one that is barred from the pluralist's bazaar, and thus keeps finding itself on the wrong end of the legislature's classifications, for reasons that in some sense are discreditable. Standard renditions of what we think of as the *Carolene Products* approach, such as the one by Justice Blackmun quoted above, do not include this element: "discrete and insular minorities" are simply entitled to "heightened judicial solicitude." Justice Stone's original, however, was richer than this, indicating that "*prejudice against discrete and insular minorities* may be a special condition, which tends to curtail the operation of those political processes ordinarily to be relied upon to protect minorities * * *." Now "prejudice" is a mushword in its own right, one we shall have to clarify, but it does supply the element that is missing in the usual rendition. For whatever else it may or may not be, prejudice is a lens that distorts reality. We are a nation of minorities and our system thus depends on the ability and willingness of various groups to apprehend those overlapping interests that can bind them into a majority on a given issue; prejudice blinds us to overlapping interests that in fact exist. As Frank Goodman put it so well eight years ago: "Race prejudice divides groups that have much in common (blacks and poor whites) and unites groups

[59] Graham v. Richardson, 403 U.S. 365, 372 (1971).

(white, rich and poor) that have little else in common than their antagonism for the racial minority. Race prejudice, in short, provides the 'majority of the whole' with that 'common motive to invade the rights of other citizens' that Madison believed improbable in a pluralistic society."[63]

Switching the principal perspective thus, from the purely political to one that focuses more on the psychology of decision, possesses the additional virtue of relating rather directly to what we found to be the functional significance of a theory of suspect classifications, one of flushing out unconstitutional motivations. "Prejudice" has a lot to do with that; discreteness and insularity don't seem to (except derivatively, to the extent that they are likely to reflect and engender prejudiced behavior). That connection also puts us in a position to begin to specify the meanings of prejudice relevant in this context. If the doctrine of suspect classifications is a roundabout way of uncovering official attempts to inflict inequality for its own sake—to treat a group worse not in the service of some overriding social goal but largely for the sake of simply disadvantaging its members—it would seem to follow that one set of classifications we should treat as suspicious are those that disadvantage groups we know to be the object of widespread vilification, groups we know others (specifically those who control the legislative process) might wish to injure.

Note that the inquiry suggested is not whether there exists *unjustified* widespread hostility toward the group disadvantaged by the official act in issue—that would constitute a straightforward invitation to second-guess the legislative judgment—but simply whether there exists widespread hostility. There is a good deal of discretion in that inquiry too, of course, and courts must be scrupulous not simply to legislate there either. Later on I shall suggest a refinement that should help bridle the inquiry. For the moment, though, it may help to recall that all that labeling a classification "suspect" means functionally is that a prima facie case has been made out and that the inquiry into its suspiciousness should continue. If it turns out directly to pursue a substantial goal (other than the impermissible one of simply disadvantaging those it disadvantages), it will survive. Thus, for example, burglars are certainly a group toward which there is widespread societal hostility, and laws making burglary a crime certainly do comparatively disadvantage burglars. Such laws plainly should survive, however. There is so patently a substantial goal here, that of protecting our homes by penalizing those who break and enter them, and the fit between that goal and the classification is so close, that whatever suspicion such a classification might under other circumstances engender is allayed so immediately it doesn't even have time to register.

---

[63] Goodman, [*De Facto School Segregation: A Constitutional and Empirical Analysis,* 60 Calif.L.Rev. 275, 315 (1972).]

Although there is more to be said about what factors properly give rise to suspicion, we have reached a point where the appeal (and limitations) of a reference to the immutability of the classifying characteristic can begin to be put in perspective. A law making burglary a crime is not suspicious—or, if you prefer, the suspicion is immediately allayed—because the goal of making life unpleasant for burglars is immediately translatable into the goal of discouraging people from breaking into our homes. It would not make sense, however, to defend a law disadvantaging blacks on the ground that we are trying to discourage people from being black. The ability to frame the point of a classification harming (or subsidizing) a certain group in terms of a desire to discourage people from joining (or encourage people to join) that group obviously depends on the mutability of the characteristic that forms the basis of classification. We shouldn't go overboard and conclude that classification on the basis of an immutable characteristic is always suspicious: that would follow only if increasing or decreasing the incidence of the classifying characteristic were the only legitimate governmental end. Forbidding blind people to pilot airplanes will do little to encourage eyesight, but such a prohibition will obviously stand nonetheless, since the classification fits perfectly a different goal, one I need hardly argue is important. Immutability thus cannot be the talisman that some have tried to make it, but it isn't entirely irrelevant either, since classifications geared to characteristics it is not within the power of the individual to change will not be amenable to immediate and innocent explanation in terms of altering the classifying characteristic's incidence.

An account mentioned with increasing frequency, and indeed it does seem more to the point, is that classifications rooted in "stereotypes" should be regarded as suspicious. Stated this way, without elaboration, it cannot do. The dictionary tells us that a stereotype is "a fixed or conventional notion or conception, as of a person, group, idea, etc., held by a number of people, and allowing for no individuality * * *." Legislation on the basis of "stereotype" is thus legislation by generalization, the use of a classification believed in statistical terms to be generally valid without leaving room for proof of individual deviation. That, however, is the way legislation ordinarily proceeds, as in most cases it must. * * *

* * * If the concept is to provide us with anything beyond a basis for begging questions, it has to be refined, so as to separate, if you will, the acceptable stereotypes from the unacceptable. The approach that may initially seem most attractive would be to treat as suspicious those stereotypical generalizations to which there exist unusually high numbers or percentages of counterexamples. * * * It won't work, though; generalizations cannot be intelligibly evaluated simply in terms of the number or percentage of false-positives they entail. Sometimes, as in the case of capital punishment, any nontrivial incidence of counterexample

would be intolerable. Other times, as where we are trying to keep those susceptible to heart attacks from piloting commercial airliners, a quite high percentage, surely sometimes more than half, is entirely appropriate. A determination of the acceptable incidence of counterexample must therefore involve, at a minimum, a comparison of the costs to those "wrongfully" excluded or included with the costs to the rest of us, sometimes in time and money but often also in increased risk, of trying to tune the system more finely. A mode of review geared to whether the incidence of counter-examples is "too high" is thus indistinguishable from the unacceptable theory that courts should intervene in the name of the Constitution whenever they disagree with the cost-benefit balance the legislature has struck.

* * * The cases where we ought to be suspicious are not those involving a generalization whose incidence of counterexample is "too high," but rather those involving a generalization whose incidence of counterexample is significantly higher than the legislative authority appears to have thought it was. No matter how many considerations may have entered into the cost-benefit balance, a misapprehension regarding the incidence of counterexample (or for that matter the cost of individualized determination) will have distorted the entire decision. Just as we would want reconsidered any important decision that was made under the influence of an erroneous assumption about the relevant facts, so should we here. * * *

The rub comes in how the Court should go about identifying such situations. Just leaving it to their gestalt judgment seems obviously unacceptable, too close to simply handing over an unbridled power of substantive review. (I am not suggesting bad faith here, but a justice whose instinct is to disagree with the legislative cost-benefit balance is likely in all good faith to suppose the legislature "must have" overestimated the statistical validity of the generalization on the basis of which it appears to have acted.) The Court should therefore look not simply to the legislative product here, but to the process that generated it, to see whether it can identify some factor or factors that suggest the likelihood of such legislative misapprehension. * * *

In deciding how much presumptive credit to extend a given generalization in our everyday lives, we would want to know where it came from—who came up with it and whether it is one that serves their interests. This commonsense insight, again tempered with others, seems relevant to the constitutional inquiry as well. The choice between classifying on the basis of a comparative generalization and attempting to come up with a more discriminating formula always involves balancing the increase in fairness that greater individualization will produce against the added costs it will entail. Where the generalization involved is one that serves the interests of the decision-makers, however, certain dangers that are inherent in any balancing process are significantly intensified. Where it tangibly enhances their fortunes, the dangers may be most obvious—on the one hand that the costs of treating others as they are treating themselves are likely to be overestimated, and on the other that the validity of the generalization being proffered as the basis of classification is likely to be overestimated, thus resulting in an underevaluation of the interest in individual fairness. But even where no tangible gain can be identified, there are psychic rewards in self-flattering generalizations. * * *

Thus generalizations to the effect, say, that whites in general are smarter or more industrious than blacks, men more stable emotionally than women, or native-born Americans more patriotic than Americans born elsewhere, are likely to go down pretty easily—and in fact we know they have—with groups whose demography is that of the typical American legislature. Few will suppose there aren't counterexamples, but the overall validity of such a generalization is likely to be quite readily accepted. By seizing upon the positive myths about the groups to which they belong and the negative myths about those to which they don't, or for that matter the realities respecting some or most members of the two classes, legislators, like the rest of us, are likely to assume too readily that not many of "them" will be unfairly deprived, nor many of "us" unfairly benefited, by a classification of this type. Generalizations of the opposite sort, which attribute superiority to a group to which most legislators do not belong—say, that blacks are better basketball players or that Jews are better students—are a different matter. A generalization of this sort may occasionally find grudging acceptance, but here we can be sure that the imperfect, statistical nature of the claim will be well appreciated, and in addition that there will be explanations—in both these examples, that it has to do with "the way they are brought up"—that will prevail in the legislature to assure an individualized test or at least that the statutory presumption will be rebuttable. A statutory distinction built on a comparison of the qualifications of optometrists and opticians occupies an in-between position, since neither of the groups being compared is one to which most of the legislators belong. Such a law—and most legislative classifications are of this "they-they" contour—may lack the special safeguard that a self-deprecating generalization seems to provide, but it also lacks the unusual dangers of self-serving generalization and is consequently correctly classified as constitutionally unsuspicious.

We have seen already how the mutability of the classifying characteristic will often render a classification immediately defensible in terms of a legitimate social goal and thus allay any incipient suspicion. We are now in a position to understand how mutability (or something like it) may be relevant in another way as well, one that bears on the likelihood that the decision-maker's ability to generalize will be distorted by his or her perspective. For example it is at least arguable that the facts that all of us once were young, and most expect one day to be fairly old, should neutralize whatever suspicion we might otherwise entertain respecting the multitude of laws (enacted by predominantly middle-aged legislatures) that comparatively advantage those between, say, 21 and 65 vis-à-vis those who are younger or older. It is not quite the same thing as immutability, of course: alienage generally is an escapable condition, so in theory are poverty and perhaps even gender. But nonetheless, and it is this that seems more relevant, most legislators have never been alien, poor, or female. They all were young, though, a fact that may enhance their objectivity about just what the difference entails.

One can empathize without having been there, though, and at this point a reference to discreteness and insularity reasserts its relevance. Though theoretically indefensible in its usual free-standing form, it can quite sensibly augment and qualify an approach geared to the distorting effect of perspective. To render the concept useful, though, we have to recognize and break apart its two components, the political and the social. Political access is surely important, but (so long as it falls short of majority control) it cannot alone protect a group against the first type of prejudice we examined, out-and-out hostility, nor will it even serve effectively to correct the subtler self-aggrandizing biases of the majority. If voices and votes are all we're talking about, prejudices can easily survive (and even on occasion be exacerbated): other groups may just continue to refuse to deal, and the minority in question may just continue to be outvoted. Discreteness and insularity have a social component as well, however—of course the two will often go hand in hand—and it is that component that seems more relevant to the amelioration of cooperation-blocking prejudice. Increased social intercourse is likely not only to diminish the hostility that often accompanies unfamiliarity, but also to rein somewhat our tendency to stereotype in ways that exaggerate the superiority of those groups to which we belong. The more we get to know people who are different in some ways, the more we will begin to appreciate the ways in which they are not, which is the beginning of political cooperation.

BRUCE A. ACKERMAN, BEYOND *CAROLENE PRODUCTS*

98 HARV.L.REV. 713, 713–715, 717–739 (1985).

I. THE PROMISE OF *CAROLENE PRODUCTS*

*"[P]rejudice against discrete and insular minorities may be a special condition * * * curtail[ing] the operation of those political processes ordinarily to be relied upon to protect minorities, and*

[so] may call for a correspondingly more searching judicial inquiry."[1]

These famous words, appearing in the otherwise unimportant *Carolene Products* case, came at a moment of extraordinary vulnerability for the Supreme Court. They were written in 1938. The Court was just beginning to dig itself out of the constitutional debris left by its wholesale capitulation to the New Deal a year before. With the decisive triumph of the activist welfare state over the Old Court, an entire world of constitutional meanings, laboriously built up over two generations, had come crashing down upon the Justices' heads. Indeed, the Court had been so politically discredited by its constitutional defense of laissez-faire capitalism that it was hardly obvious whether *any* firm ground remained upon which to rebuild the institution of judicial review. How, then, to begin the work of reconstruction?

* * *

* * * *Carolene* promises relief from the problem of legitimacy raised whenever nine elderly lawyers invalidate the legislative decisions of a majority of our elected representatives. The *Carolene* solution is to seize the high ground of democratic theory and establish that the challenged legislation was produced by a profoundly defective process. By demonstrating that the legislative decision itself resulted from an undemocratic procedure, a *Carolene* court hopes to reverse the spin of the countermajoritarian difficulty. For it now may seem that the original legislative decision, not the judicial invalidation, suffers the greater legitimacy deficit.

* * *

* * * I shall argue, however, that the *Carolene* formula cannot withstand close scrutiny.

* * *

To demonstrate the need for doctrinal reorientation, I shall examine separately each of *Carolene*'s four operative terms: (1) prejudice, (2) discrete, (3) insular, and (4) minorities. It is by means of these four terms that *Carolene* hopes to identify groups that have been unconstitutionally deprived of their fair share of democratic influence. * * *

II. DISCRETE AND INSULAR *MINORITIES?*

* * *

---

[1]United States v. Carolene Prods. Co., 304 U.S. 144, 152 n. 4 (1938). * * *

A. The Principle of Minority Acquiescence

* * * [M]inorities are *supposed* to lose in a democratic system—even when they want very much to win and even when they think (as they often will) that the majority is deeply wrong in ignoring their just complaints. This principle—call it the principle of minority acquiescence—is absolutely central to democratic theory. Of course, a minority may not be denied its right to participate within a democratic framework. Although it must acquiesce in current legislative decisions, it is fully entitled to use all its political resources to induce a future legislative majority to accede to its demands. But *Carolene* promises minorities more than formal rights: it asserts that they are sometimes entitled to demand substantive victory now, not merely the chance of victory later.

The problem this promise raises is all the more acute because *Carolene* refuses to accept the solution that countless others have embraced. It is easy to solve the problem of majority rule by positing the existence of minority rights that are so fundamental as to trump the value of democratic rule itself. Indeed, as the *Carolene* Court was well aware, it is *too* easy to solve the problem in this way. Faced with the political repudiation of *Lochner*'s natural rights jurisprudence, the Court was determined to build another foundation for the protection of minority rights: why not redefine the concept of democracy itself in a way that would support the notion that minorities *do* have a right to win some of the time?

B. The Pluralist Solution

While the courts speak vaguely of "those political processes ordinarily relied upon to protect minorities," generations of American political scientists have filled in the picture of pluralist democracy presupposed by *Carolene*'s distinctive argument for minority rights. According to this familiar view, it is a naive mistake to speak of democracy as if it involved rule by a single, well-defined majority over a coherent and constant minority. Instead, normal American politics is pluralistic: myriad pressure groups, each typically representing a fraction of the population, bargain with one another for mutual support.

Once this picture of pluralistic politics is accepted, the stage has been set for the rehabilitation of *Carolene*'s concern with ineffective minorities. We may now find that there is something about certain minority groups—call them *Carolene* or *C*-groups—that makes it especially difficult for them to strike bargains with potential coalition partners. As a consequence, *C*-groups will find themselves in politically ascendant coalitions much less often than will otherwise comparable groups. Over time, then, *C*-groups will achieve less than their "fair share" of influence upon legislation. And it is for this reason, the pluralist concludes, that *Carolene* rightly suggests that judicial protection for *C*-groups can be defended in a manner responsive to the countermajoritarian difficulty afflicting judicial review. By intervening on behalf of *C*-groups, a *Carolene* court merely produces the substantive outcomes that the *C*-group would have obtained through politics if it had not been so systematically disadvantaged in the ongoing process of pluralist bargaining.

* * *

* * * In the common legal understanding, *Carolene* is generally taken to imply that the same level of strict judicial scrutiny should apply to legislation affecting each and every *C*-group. But the pluralist model cannot justify such a uniform judicial approach.

Consider, for example, an American constituency that includes 12 percent blacks and .5 percent Jehovah's Witnesses among its population. Doubtless, both groups will be encouraged by the pluralist vision of democracy, since it suggests that neither group will inexorably be excluded from the pluralist bazaar. Nonetheless, it should be plain that these two groups have absolutely no reason to find the prospect of pluralist bargaining *equally* gratifying. To the contrary, the fact that blacks greatly outnumber Witnesses is bound to play an important role in any plausible bargaining theory. Thus, even if the two groups could somehow be compensated for their *Carolene* disadvantages, the Witnesses could not reasonably expect to win substantive victories nearly as often as the blacks.

To put the point more generally, a bargaining approach to *Carolene* does not suggest that each *C*-group has a right to be treated identically to all other *C*-groups in the legislative process. Instead, the decisive thought-experiment should involve the comparison of a particular *C*-group with a hypothetical minority that I shall call an unencumbered or *U*-group. In each comparison, the relevant *U*-group should be supposed to contain the same proportion of the population as the *C*-group that invokes the Court's protection; the *U*-group differs, however, in that it is unencumbered by the bargaining disadvantages that unconstitutionally burden the *C*-group. Thus, the *Carolene* question for blacks entails a comparative analysis of the bargaining expectations of a 12 percent minority unencumbered by those structural impediments that unconstitutionally impair blacks' bargaining position in the ongoing pluralist process, while the question for Jehovah's Witnesses involves a comparison with a much smaller *U*-group.

Such thought-experiments will most naturally result in a sliding scale of *Carolene* concern. On one end of the scale are groups consisting of ineffective majorities or very large minorities that find themselves disadvantaged in the political process by some constitutionally impermissible barrier to bargaining. In cases involving these "major minorities," a court can be quite confident that a comparable *U*-group would have a decisive impact on the terms of pluralistic legislation. In the middle of the *Carolene* scale are "middling minorities" in the 10 to 20 percent range. Here there is less reason for a court to expect that a *U*-group of comparable size would radically change the terms of political trade, though its influence would be very substantial in many plausible contexts. And finally, on the other end of the scale, there are groups so small as to elicit little solicitude from courts concerned with correcting the failures of democratic bargaining. When faced with "minor minorities" of .01 percent, for example, a judge might well be unmoved by the enumeration of *Carolene* factors that would generate substantial concern in the case of middling minorities, not to mention major minorities. For the fact is that a *U*-group of .01 percent has little to expect from a democratic political process, unless it is very lucky, or exceptionally adept, in the bargaining process. This point is essential to the responsible elaboration of *Carolene Products*—whose promise, be it recalled, is to permit courts to evade the thrust of the countermajoritarian difficulty by appealing over the heads of real-world legislatures to the hypothetical outcomes of a purified democratic process.

There is, then, an inevitably uneasy relationship between *Carolene*'s pluralist approach to democracy and the judicial protection of minority rights. The tension reaches the breaking point in the proverbial case of a minority of one: when the solitary citizen, having little to expect from pluralist bargaining, challenges the invasion of his fundamental rights by the normal political process.

My aim here, though, is to work out the doctrinal implications of the *Carolene* formula rather than to criticize its foundations. So let us focus our attention upon those groups, ranging from middling minorities to encumbered majorities, whose role in the bargaining process might well have a significant impact on the ongoing stream of legislative decisions. How does *Carolene* propose to determine whether a group suffers from severe enough bargaining disadvantages to merit special protection? In other words, how are we supposed to distinguish a *C*-group from a *U*-group?

III. DISCRETE AND *INSULAR* MINORITIES?

* * *

* * * Other things being equal, "discreteness and insularity" will normally be a source of enormous bargaining advantage, not disadvantage, for a group engaged in pluralist American politics. Except for special cases, the concerns that underlie *Carolene* should lead judges to protect groups that possess the opposite characteristics from the ones *Carolene* emphasizes—groups that are "anonymous and diffuse" rather than "discrete and insular." It is these groups that both political science and American history indicate are systematically disadvantaged in a pluralist democracy.

A. The Free-Rider Problem

To see my point, start with insularity and consider a thought-experiment suggested by the previous argument. Imagine two groups, *I* and *D,* of equal size (say each accounts for 12 percent of the population). The members of one group, the *I*'s, are distributed in an insular way, concentrated in a single massive island within the sea of American life; the *D*'s, on the other hand, are diffused evenly throughout the sea. Is it really so clear that, by virtue of their diffusion throughout American life, the *D*'s will gain systematic advantages over the *I*'s in the normal course of pluralist politics?

Hardly. To begin with the basics, a political interest gains a great advantage if its proponents can form a well-organized lobby to press their cause in the corridors of power. Yet the construction of a pressure group is no easy task. The main obstacle is the familiar free-rider problem. Simply because a person would find his interests advanced by the formation of a pressure group, it does not follow that he will spend his own scarce time and energy on political organization. On the contrary, from each individual's selfish viewpoint, abstaining from interest-group activity is a "heads-I-win-tails-you-lose" proposition. If only a few people adopt the do-nothing strategy, the do-nothings will free-ride on the successful lobbying effort of others. If free-riding becomes pervasive, things will not improve much if a single member of the group adds his money and time to the floundering political effort. Either way, it pays for a selfish person to remain a free rider even if he has a lot to gain from concerted lobbying. For this reason, many interests remain ineffectively organized even in pressure-group America. How, then, does a minority's insularity affect the probability that it will break through the free-rider barrier and achieve organizational effectiveness?

Far from being a patent disadvantage, insularity can help *I*-groups in at least four different ways[.] * * *

First, insularity will help breed sentiments of group solidarity. Given an *I*'s daily immersion in social realities that reaffirm his group identity, the typical *I* will conceive his *I*-ness as something much more than an incidental fact about himself. Instead, *I*-ness will serve as a fundamental feature of self-identity—one that will encourage each *I* to view the political activities of the group from a perspective that transcends the purely instrumental. Thus, when a black or a Jew gives $25 to the NAACP or the Anti-Defamation League, he is not merely, or even principally, gambling that his small bit of money will perceptibly increase his chance of enjoying the fruits of future lobbying victories. Rather, the contribution is a means by which the donor can symbolize the seriousness of his own commitment to his *I*-ness. By contributing to the group cause, I demonstrate to myself, as well as others, that I am serious about the values I profess to hold. Here, at last, is one commodity—group identification—that is immune from the free-rider problem: for if I do not give even a few dollars to the group cause, can I plausibly say, even to myself, that I take my *I*-ness seriously?

But insularity * * * also aids the *I*-group in a second way by providing it with a new range of social sanctions to impose upon would-be free riders. An *I* who refuses to contribute to his interest group cannot expect this fact to be kept secret from his fellow *I*'s—news travels fast along the grapevine in an insular community. * * * In contrast, a member of a diffuse *D*-group need not suffer such severe dislocation in order to avoid the disapproval of his fellow group members. Instead, he may insulate himself from their displeasure by assimilating into the majoritarian mainstream—undoubtedly a costly process, but typically less costly than the social stigma heaped on the free-riding *I*. * * *

B. Organizational Costs

It follows, then, that the average *I* is more likely to contribute his time and money to the group cause than is an otherwise comparable *D*. Yet this conclusion tells only half the story: not only will an *I*-group receive more resources from its constituency, but *I*'s will also find it cheaper to organize themselves for effective political action. First, the dense communications network generated by insularity dramatically reduces one of the heaviest costs involved in effective political lobbying: the cost of communicating with a mass membership. To get its messages out to its constituency, an insular political group can often avail itself of the communications channels already established by the group's churches, businesses, or labor unions. In contrast, a *D*-group must somehow locate and reach people who interact with one another much less frequently and who have fewer channels already established for the cheap transmission of *D*-group concerns.

Second, the organic character of insular life greatly reduces the costs of selecting credible political leaders. The *I*-group can draw upon a pool of people who have already earned the respect of their fellow *I*'s in other communal contexts: ministers and rabbis, successful lawyers, businessmen, union leaders. In contrast, even if *D*-group members manage to overcome the communications barrier, they must often take the risk of selecting political leaders who have not been tested and observed in other leadership settings.

C. Insularity and Congressional Influence

* * *

We have reached a point, however, where it is necessary to introduce an explicitly geographic concept of insularity into the discussion—for the simple reason that geography is of the first importance in assessing a group's influence within the American political system. For present purposes, it will suffice to restrict our speculations to two simple geographic alternatives. On the one hand, our sociologically insular minority might also be geographically insular: concentrated in a relatively small number of places in the United States. On the other hand, geographic insularity might not accompany sociological insularity. Indeed, at the limit, the *I*-group might be evenly spread over the fifty states and 435 congressional districts. For heuristic purposes, let us begin with the alternative that is empirically less common, but analytically more tractable. Suppose that an *I*-group is distributed in a geographically diffuse way: if it contains 12 percent of the national population, it accounts for 12 percent of each congressional district. Now compare this geographically diffuse *I*-group with a *D*-group that is both sociologically and geographically diffuse. Other things being equal, which group is more likely to succeed in influencing Congressmen?

The previous analysis suggests that the *I*-group will probably have greater influence. Such a group is more likely to form a political lobby peopled by credible leaders who remain in close touch with the insular constituency they represent. When such lobbyists threaten a Congressman with electoral retribution, they can expect a respectful hearing. * * * In short, even if the *I*-group is distributed evenly throughout the nation, it has a greater ability to exert political influence through the ultimate currency of democratic politics: votes on election day.

This conclusion is reinforced when we turn to the more realistic case in which the middling *I*-group is distributed very unevenly throughout the country. In this scenario, a middling minority could reasonably expect to be a local majority—or at least a decisive voting bloc—in 20 to 30 congressional districts. For the representatives of these districts, the support of the *I*-group amounts to nothing less than the stuff of political survival. In fact, for all our *Carolene* talk about the powerlessness of insular groups, we are perfectly aware of the enormous power such voting blocs have in American politics. The story of the protective tariff is, I suppose, the classic illustration of insularity's power in American history. Over the past half-century, we have been treated to an enormous number of welfare-state variations on the theme of insularity by the farm bloc, the steel lobby, the auto lobby, and others too numerous to mention. In this standard scenario of pluralistic politics, it is precisely the diffuse character of the majority forced to pay the bill for tariffs, agricultural subsidies, and the like, that allows strategically located Congressmen to deliver the goods to their well-organized local constituents. Given these familiar stories, it is really quite remarkable to hear lawyers profess concern that insular interests have too little influence in Congress. Instead, the American system typically deprives *diffuse* groups of their rightful say over the course of legislative policy. If there is anything to *Carolene Products,* then, it cannot be a minority's insularity, taken by itself—something more must be involved.

IV. *DISCRETE* AND INSULAR MINORITIES?

Could that something be the "discreteness" of a *Carolene* minority?

I begin with a question because it is not obvious whether most constitutional lawyers endow the word "discrete" with independent significance in their understanding of the *Carolene* doctrine. Nonetheless, we can conceive the term in a way that adds something important to the overall formula. I propose to define a minority as "discrete" when its members are marked out in ways that make it relatively easy for others to identify them. For instance, there is nothing a black woman may plausibly do to hide the fact that she is black or female. Like it or not, she will have to deal with the social expectations and stereotypes generated by her evident group characteristics. In contrast, other minorities are socially defined in ways that give individual members the chance to avoid easy identification. A homosexual, for example, can keep her sexual preference a very private affair and thereby avoid much of the public opprobrium attached to her minority status. It is for this reason that I shall call homosexuals, and groups like them, "anonymous" minorities and contrast them with "discrete" minorities of the kind paradigmatically exemplified by blacks.

* * *

Carolene takes a straightforward position on this question. In its view, discreteness is a political liability. Once again, however, * * * this is not obvious. * * *

* * * If you are a black in America today, you know there is no way you can avoid the impact of the larger public's views about the significance of blackness. Because exit is not possible, there is only one way to do something about disadvantageous racial stereotypes: complain about them. Among efficacious forms of complaint, the possibility of organized political action will surely rank high.

This is not to say, of course, that individual blacks, or members of other discrete minorities, will necessarily lend their support to interest-group activity. They may, instead, succumb to the temptations of free-riding and thus deprive the group of vital political resources. But even if discreteness is no cure-all for selfishness, it does free a minority from the organizational problem confronting an anonymous group of comparable size. To see my point, compare the problem faced by black political organizers with the one confronting organizers of the homosexual community. As a member of an anonymous group, each homosexual can seek to minimize the personal harm due to prejudice by keeping his or her sexual preference a tightly held secret. Although this is hardly a fully satisfactory response, secrecy does enable homosexuals to "exit" from prejudice in a way that blacks cannot. This means that a homosexual group must confront an organizational problem that does not arise for its black counterpart: somehow the group must induce each anonymous homosexual to reveal his or her sexual preference to the larger public and to bear the private costs this public declaration may involve.

* * * So it would seem that *Carolene Products* is wrong again: a court concerned with pluralist bargaining power should be more, not less, attentive to the claims of anonymous minorities than to those of discrete ones.

V. PREJUDICE

But surely it is time to stop playing *Hamlet* without the Prince. The whole point of *Carolene*'s concern with "discrete and insular minorities" cannot be understood, I am sure you are thinking, without grasping the final term of the formula: prejudice. Indeed, it has been one of my aims to provoke precisely this reaction. By detailing all the ways discrete and insular minorities gain political advantage over diffuse and anonymous groups, I have meant to emphasize how heavy a burden the idea of prejudice must carry in the overall argument for *Carolene Products.* The burden is of two kinds: one empirical, the other conceptual. To take them one at a time, I shall defer all problems involved in conceptualizing prejudice so that we may first focus upon the empirical side of the matter.

A. Questions of Fact

Carolene's empirical inadequacy stems from its underinclusive conception of the impact of prejudice upon American society. It is easy to identify groups in the population that are not discrete and insular but that are nonetheless the victims of prejudice, as that term is commonly understood. Thus, the fact that homosexuals are a relatively anonymous minority has not saved the group from severe prejudice. Nor is sexism a nonproblem merely because women are a diffuse, if discrete, majority. Prejudice is generated by a bewildering variety of social conditions. Although some *Carolene* minorities are seriously victimized, they are not the only ones stigmatized; nor is it obvious that all *Carolene* minorities are stigmatized more grievously than any other non-*Carolene* group. Why should the concern with "prejudice" justify *Carolene*'s narrow fixation upon "discrete and insular" minorities?

The answer seemed easy in a world in which members of the paradigmatic *Carolene* minority group—blacks—were effectively barred from voting and political participation. Something is better than nothing: whatever the organizational problems engendered by anonymity and diffuseness, surely they are not nearly so devastating as total disenfranchisement. As we turn toward the future, however, it is far less clear that such selective perception makes constitutional sense. Nonetheless, I shall give *Carolene* the benefit of the doubt by sketching a "pariah" model of the political process in which *Carolene*'s emphasis on the fate of discrete and insular minorities will still seem empirically plausible. As we move beyond the pariah model, however, anonymous or diffuse minorities will increasingly emerge as the groups that can raise the most serious complaints of pluralist disempowerment.

1. The Pariah Model.—Assume a polity in which middling minorities—in the 10 to 20 percent range—attain majority status in a significant number of congressional districts because of the way their insularity interacts with the geographic biases of the American political system. Nonetheless, the minority representatives these groups elect are entirely ineffective in Congress—because all remaining Congressmen refuse to bargain with them in any way. * * *

Sound implausible? * * * Yet it is only by indulging in something like these strong empirical assumptions that *Carolene* can claim that the effects of prejudice *plainly* outweigh the political advantages enjoyed by minorities that are discrete and insular.

2. Beyond the Pariah Model.—Once we deny the general empirical validity of the pariah model, our assessment of the political impact of a discrete and insular group will invariably be more complex. * * *

* * * I turn to a very different approach to *Carolene* presented by John Hart Ely in his important work, *Democracy and Distrust.* Among its many virtues, the book explicitly recognizes that the conventional *Carolene* wisdom about the powerlessness of discrete and insular minorities is "in need of some reexamination." Yet Dean Ely does not attempt the interest-group analysis that has thus far engaged our energies. Instead, he relies exclusively on a social-psychological approach to the legislative process. On his view, the critical thing about prejudice is the way it allows legislators to stereotype "discrete and insular" minorities. It is this legislative propensity to divide the world into "we-they" categories that, according to Ely, lies at the core of *Carolene*'s concern: "we" legislators will both overestimate the dangers posed by the "they" group and underestimate its similarities to the "we" group. As a consequence, legislation that disadvantages "they" groups will be based on an intolerably distorted perception of social reality.

Even if we were to accept a "we-they" view of legislative psychology, Ely's failure to recognize the limits of the pariah model serves as an independent ground for questioning his conclusions. Quite simply, our efforts in bargaining theory have led us to expect that "middling minorities" of the "discrete and insular" kind will elect a significant number of

Representatives—say 20 to 25—who are extremely responsive to their interests. As long as these politicians are not treated like pariahs, they can become a potent legislative force—trading votes with other legislators to further the objectives of their own constituents. * * * This is more than diffuse or anonymous minorities can expect: *their* representatives may not even *be* at the bargaining table. As soon as he moves beyond the narrow confines of the pariah model, Dean Ely cannot rehabilitate *Carolene*'s exclusive focus on discrete and insular minorities through "we-they" psychology alone.

Dean Ely seems aware of all this. Although *Democracy and Distrust* does not contain a fully developed analysis of minority legislative power, it does hint at an approach different from the one I advance here. Dean Ely suggests that minority politicians may suffer from a distinctive psychological affliction: while other Congressmen act on "we-they" prejudices in favor of their own constituents, minority politicians may accept the very stereotypes they should be challenging. If this point were conceded, Ely's argument would take on a self-sealing quality: no matter how actively minority representatives participated in the bargaining process, they would only reinforce, and never challenge, prevailing prejudices.

Dean Ely shows great restraint in dealing with this suggestion of minority "false consciousness." While he says that "[t]he general idea is one that in some contexts has merit," his book does not, in fact, spend very much space defending and elaborating it. I believe, moreover, that an appeal to "false consciousness" cannot be elaborated in a way that makes constitutional sense.

The first question to ask about "false consciousness" is an empirical one: will the rising generation of minority politicians in fact passively accept debasing stereotypes? I see no reason to project such a grim image upon our future. To the contrary, the classic prejudices are under vigorous challenge by powerful voices emerging from a broad range of discrete and insular communities. * * *

The second question is: even if some social psychologist could "prove" the existence of false consciousness, should the Supreme Court transform this social phenomenon into an assumption of constitutional law? We are dealing here not with an academic scientific inquiry, but with a question of institutional relationships. In branding minority politicians as victims of "false consciousness" on the pages of the *United States Reports,* the Supreme Court would be consigning them to a peculiarly demeaning constitutional status. Henceforth, they—and they alone—would be deemed constitutionally incapable of discharging the representative functions of democratically elected legislators. Such a declaration would make a mockery of *Carolene*'s promise. Rather than attempting to approximate the results of a perfect pluralist democracy, the Court would be protecting minority rights by emphatically impugning the capacity of these very same minorities to engage in democratic politics at all.

* * *

B. Questions of Value

But *Carolene*'s failure to recognize the political predicament of anonymous or diffuse groups that are victims of prejudice is only half the problem; the other half is more conceptual, but no less troubling. The idea of "prejudice" is simply unequal to the task assigned it within the overall *Carolene* analysis. Recall that *Carolene*'s promise is a form of argument that allows a court to say that it is purifying the democratic process rather than imposing its own substantive values upon the political branches. And yet it is just this process orientation that is at risk when a *Carolene* court undertakes to identify the prejudices that entitle a group to special protection from the vagaries of pluralist politics. One person's "prejudice" is, notoriously, another's "principle." How, then, do we identify a group for *Carolene* protection without performing the substantive analysis of constitutional values that *Carolene* hopes to avoid?

The kind of answer required is clear enough. To redeem *Carolene*'s promise, the judicial identification of a prejudice cannot depend upon the substance of the suspect view, but must turn on the way in which legislators come to hold their belief. The process-oriented argument goes something like this: although each of us cannot always expect to convince our legislators, we can at least insist that they treat our claims with respect. At the very least, they should thoughtfully consider our moral and empirical arguments, rejecting them only after conscientiously deciding that they are inconsistent with the public interest. If a group fails to receive this treatment, it suffers a special wrong, one quite distinct from its substantive treatment on the merits. And it is this purely processual kind of prejudice that constitutes the grievance *Carolene* courts may endeavor to remedy without engaging in the suspect task of prescribing substantive values.

* * *

Let me propose a test case. Imagine that, after reading Herbert Wechsler's famous essay,[47] a group of conservative legalists becomes sincerely convinced that *Brown v. Board of Education* could not in fact be based on neutral principles and so does not deserve its place as a cornerstone of our constitutional law. Acting on this conviction, the group begins a campaign advocating a constitutional amendment to repeal *Brown* and generates some modest interest among conservatives across the

[47]Wechsler, *Toward Neutral Principles of Constitutional Law,* 73 Harv.L.Rev. 1 (1959).

country. Arriving in Washington, D.C., with their legal process arguments elaborately developed, the group proceeds to the lobbies of Congress. How do you think the group would be received? Would most Representatives be willing and able to confront the Wechslerian arguments with a thoughtful defense of our constitutional commitment to equality? Or would they respond in a *processually* prejudiced fashion—peremptorily brushing aside the Wechslerians' arguments with a catch-phrase or two that fails to join issue?

This is, in principle, an empirical question—though, like many others, it will never get a good empirical answer. Nonetheless, if my study of politics has taught me anything, I would not expect the agitating Wechslerians to receive a processually unprejudiced response on Capitol Hill. As far as I can tell, any large representative assembly will contain a bewildering variety of human types—from the elaborately thoughtful to the superficially unquestioning. It is simply self-congratulatory to suppose that the members of our own persuasion have reached their convictions in a deeply reflective way, whereas those espousing opinions we hate are superficial. Instead, a thoughtful judge can expect to find an abundance of stereotype-mongers and knee-jerks on *all* sides of *every* important issue—as well as many who have struggled their way to more considered judgments. Given the complexity of the human comedy, a judge is bound on a fool's errand if he imagines that the good guys and bad guys of American politics can be neatly classified according to the seriousness with which they have considered opposing points of view. Processual prejudice is a pervasive problem in the American political system.

But if this is right, *Carolene* cannot justify its concern with discrete and insular minorities without calling on judges to engage in a very different kind of judgment, one dealing with the *substance* of racial and religious prejudice. In doing so, the judge need not try to play the elaborate psychological and political guessing game required to assess the extent to which a statute is the product of a prejudiced refusal to give a respectful hearing to disfavored interests and opinions. Instead, she proceeds to a more familiar judicial inquiry into the nature of the substantive reasons that might plausibly justify the legislature's assertion of authority. If the only plausible reasons for the statute's enactment offend substantive constitutional principles, the groups aggrieved by the statute are declared victims of "prejudice"; if not, not. Although this judicial inquiry into the rational foundations of a statute may sometimes require a focused inquiry into the data available to, or even the subjective opinions of, particular public officials, the critical legal question is of a very different kind: why are the political principles endorsed by some groups judicially recognized as vindicating the constitutionality of a statute, while others are viewed as inadmissible "prejudices" delegitimating a statute's claim to constitutionality?

If *Carolene* somehow hoped to find a shortcut around this substantive inquiry into constitutional values, its journey was fated to fail from the outset. The difference between the things we call "prejudice" and the things we call "principle" is in the end a substantive moral difference. And if the courts are authorized to protect the victims of certain "prejudices," it can only be because the Constitution has placed certain normative judgments beyond the pale of legitimacy.

KIMBERLÉ WILLIAMS CRENSHAW, RACE, REFORM, AND RETRENCHMENT: TRANSFORMATION AND LEGITIMATION IN ANTIDISCRIMINATION LAW

101 HARV.L.REV. 1331, 1369–1381 (1988).

THE CONTEXT DEFINED: RACIST IDEOLOGY AND HEGEMONY

* * *

[T]his Part examines the deep-rooted problem of racist ideology—or white race consciousness—and suggests how this form of consciousness legitimates prevailing injustices and constrains the development of new solutions that benefit Black Americans.

Racist ideology provides a series of rationalizations that suppress the contradiction between American political ideals and Black existence under white supremacy. Not only does racism legitimate the oppression of Blacks, it also helps to define and privilege membership in the white community, creating a basis for identification with dominant interests. Racism serves a consensus-building hegemonic role by designating Black people as separate, visible "others" to be contrasted in every way with all other social groups. Although not consenting to domination, Black people are seen as legitimate objects of antipathy and coercion by whites.

A. The Hegemonic Role of Racism: Establishing the "Other" in American Ideology

Throughout American history, the subordination of Blacks was rationalized by a series of stereotypes and beliefs that made their conditions appear logical and natural.[147] Historically, white supremacy has been

---

[147] *See generally* D. Davis, The Problem of Slavery in the Age of Revolution, 1770–1823 (1975); G. Fredrickson, The Black Image in the White Mind, 1817 to 1914 (1971) [hereinafter G. Fredrickson, The Black Image]; G. Fredrickson, White Supremacy: A Comparative Study in American and South African History (1981) [hereinafter G. Fredrickson, White Supremacy]; W. Jordan, White over Black: American Attitudes Toward the Negro, 1550–1812 (1968); I. Newby, Jim Crow's Defense: Anti–Negro Thought in America 1900–1930 (1968); J. Williamson, The Crucible of Race: Black/White Relations in

premised upon various political, scientific, and religious theories, each of which relies on racial characterizations and stereotypes about Blacks that have coalesced into an extensive legitimating ideology. Today, it is probably not controversial to say that these stereotypes were developed primarily to rationalize the oppression of Blacks. What *is* overlooked, however, is the extent to which these stereotypes serve a hegemonic function by perpetuating a mythology about both Blacks *and* whites even today, reinforcing an illusion of a white community that cuts across ethnic, gender, and class lines.

As presented by * * * scholars [identified with Critical Legal Studies] hegemonic rule succeeds to the extent that the ruling class world view establishes the appearance of a unity of interests between the dominant class and the dominated. Throughout American history, racism has identified the interests of subordinated whites with those of society's white elite. Racism does not support the dominant order simply because all whites want to maintain their privilege at the expense of Blacks, or because Blacks sometimes serve as convenient political scapegoats. Instead, the very existence of a clearly subordinated "other" group is contrasted with the norm in a way that reinforces identification with the dominant group. Racism helps create an illusion of unity through the oppositional force of a symbolic "other." The establishment of an "other" creates a bond, a burgeoning common identity of all non-stigmatized parties—whose identity and interests are defined in opposition to the other.

According to the philosophy of Jacques Derrida, a structure of polarized categories is characteristic of Western thought:

> Western thought * * * has always been structured in terms of dichotomies or polarities: good vs. evil, being vs. nothingness, presence vs. absence, truth vs. error, identity vs. difference, mind vs. matter, man vs. woman, soul vs. body, life vs. death, nature vs. culture, speech vs. writing. These polar opposites do not, however, stand as independent and equal entities. The second term in each pair is considered the negative, corrupt, undesirable version of the first, a fall away from it * * *. In other words, the two terms are not simply opposed in their meanings, but are arranged in a hierarchical order which gives the first term *priority* * * *.[155]

Racist ideology replicates this pattern of arranging oppositional categories in a hierarchical order; historically, whites represented the dominant antinomy while Blacks came to be seen as separate and subordinate. This hierarchy is reflected in the chart below. Note how each

---

the American South Since Emancipation (1984); C. Woodward, The Strange Career of Jim Crow (1958).

[155] J. Derrida, Dissemination viii (B. Johnson trans. 1981) (emphasis in original). * * *

traditional negative image of Blacks correlates with a counter-image of whites:

Historical Oppositional Dualities

WHITE IMAGES	BLACK IMAGES
Industrious	Lazy
Intelligent	Unintelligent
Moral	Immoral
Knowledgeable	Ignorant
Enabling Culture	Disabling Culture
Law-Abiding	Criminal
Responsible	Shiftless
Virtuous/Pious	Lascivious

The oppositional dynamic symbolized by this chart was created and maintained through an elaborate and systematic process. Laws and customs helped create "races" out of a broad range of human traits. In the process of creating races, the categories came to be filled with meaning—Blacks were characterized one way, whites another. Whites became associated with normatively positive characteristics; Blacks became associated with the subordinate, even aberrational characteristics. The operation of this dynamic, along with the important political role of racial oppositionalism, can be illustrated through a few brief historical references.

Edmund Morgan provides vivid illustration of how slaveholders from the seventeenth century onward created and politicized racial categories to maintain the support of non-slaveholding whites.[157] Morgan recounts how the planters "lump[ed] Indians, mulattoes, and Negroes in a single slave class," and how these categories became "an essential, if unacknowledged, ingredient of the republican ideology that enabled Virginians to lead the nation."[158] Having accepted a common interest with slaveholders in keeping Blacks subordinated, even whites who had material reasons to object to the dominance over the slaveholding class could challenge the regime only so far. The power of race consciousness convinced whites to support a system that was opposed to their own economic interests. As George Fredrickson put it, "racial privilege could and did serve as a compensation for class disadvantage."[159]

Domination through race consciousness continued throughout the post-Reconstruction period. Historian C. Vann Woodward has argued that the ruling plantocracy was able to undermine the progressive accomplishments of the Populist movement by stirring up anti-Black sentiment among poor

[157] *See* E. Morgan, American Slavery—American Freedom (1975).

[158] *Id.* at 386.

[159] G. Fredrickson, White Supremacy, *supra* note 147, at 87.

white farmers.[160] Racism was articulated as the "broader ground for a new democracy."[161] As racism formed the new base for a broader notion of democracy, class differences were mediated through reference to a racial community of equality. A tragic example of the success of such race-conscious political manipulation is the career of Tom Watson, leader of the progressive Populist movement of the 1890's. Watson, in his attempts to educate the masses of poor farmers about the destructive role of race-based politics, repeatedly told Black and white audiences, "You are made to hate each other because upon that hatred is rested the keystone of the arch of financial despotism which enslaves you both. You are deceived and blinded that you may not see how this race antagonism perpetuates a monetary system which beggars you both."[163] Yet, by 1906, Watson had joined the movement to disenfranchise Blacks. According to Woodward, Watson had "persuaded himself that only after the Negro was eliminated from politics could Populist principles gain a hearing. In other words, the white men would have to unite before they could divide."[165]

White race consciousness also played a role in the nascent labor movement in the North. Labor historian Herbert Hill has demonstrated that unions of virtually all trades excluded Black workers from their ranks, often entirely barring Black employment in certain fields. Immigrant labor unions were particularly adamant about keeping out Black workers; indeed, it was for the precise purpose of assimilating into the American mainstream that immigrant laborers adopted these exclusionary policies.[168]

The political and ideological role that race consciousness continues to play is suggested by racial polarization in contemporary presidential politics. Several political commentators have suggested that many whites supported Ronald Reagan in the belief that he would correct a perceived policy imbalance that unjustly benefited Blacks,[169] and some argue further that Reagan made a direct racist appeal to white voters.[170] Manning

---

[160] *See* C. Woodward, *supra* note 147, at 68–77.

[161] *Id.* at 76. In the words of Southern Progressive Thomas P. Bailey:

> [The] *disenfranchisement of the negroes has been concomitant with the growth of political and social solidarity among the whites.* The more white men recognize sharply their kinship with their fellow whites, and the more democracy in every sense of the term spreads among them, the more the negro is compelled to "keep his place"—a place that is gradually narrowing in the North as well as in the South.

Id. (emphasis in original).

[163] *See id.* at 44–45.

[165] [*Id.*] at 73–74.

[168] [Hill, *Race and Ethnicity in Organized Labor: The Historical Sources of Resistance to Affirmative Action,* J. Intergroup Rel., Winter 1984, at 5, 6.]

[169] *See, e.g.,* M. Marable, Race and Realignment in American Politics (1985) (unpublished manuscript available in Harvard Law School library).

[170] *See, e.g.,* Howell, *Electoral Politics and Racial Polarization,* 101 Christian Century 1117 (1984); Wilkins, *Smiling Racism,* 23 The Nation 437 (Nov. 3, 1984).

Marable notes, for example, that "[a]ppeals to the 'race consciousness' of white workers were the decisive factor in Reagan's 1984 victory, especially in the South."[171] Reagan received nearly 70% of the white vote whereas 90% of Black voters cast their ballots for Mondale. Similarly, the vast majority of Blacks—82%—disapproved of Reagan's performance, whereas only 32% of whites did.

Even the Democratic Party, which has traditionally relied on Blacks as its most loyal constituency, has responded to this apparent racial polarization by seeking to distance itself from Black interests. Although it has been argued that the racial polarization demonstrated in the 1984 election does not represent a trend of white defections from the Democratic Party, it is significant that, whatever the cause of the Party's inability to attract white votes, Democratic leaders have expressed a willingness to moderate the Party's stand on key racial issues in attempts to recapture the white vote.

B. The Role of Race Consciousness in a System of Formal Equality

The previous section emphasizes the continuity of white race consciousness over the course of American history. This section, by contrast, focuses on the partial transformation of the functioning of race consciousness that occurred with the transition from Jim Crow to formal equality in race law.

Prior to the civil rights reforms, Blacks were formally subordinated by the state. Blacks experienced being the "other" in two aspects of oppression, which I shall designate as symbolic and material. Symbolic subordination refers to the formal denial of social and political equality to all Blacks, regardless of their accomplishments. Segregation and other forms of social exclusion—separate restrooms, drinking fountains, entrances, parks, cemeteries, and dining facilities—reinforced a racist ideology that Blacks were simply inferior to whites and were therefore not included in the vision of America as a community of equals.

Material subordination, on the other hand, refers to the ways that discrimination and exclusion economically subordinated Blacks to whites and subordinated the life chances of Blacks to those of whites on almost every level. This subordination occurs when Blacks are paid less for the same work, when segregation limits access to decent housing, and where poverty, anxiety, poor health care, and crime create a life expectancy for Blacks that is five to six years shorter than for whites.

Symbolic subordination often created material disadvantage by reinforcing race consciousness in everything from employment to education. In fact, the two are generally not thought of separately: separate

---

[171] M. Marable, *supra* note 169, at 34.

facilities were usually inferior facilities, and limited job categorization virtually always brought lower pay and harder work. Despite the pervasiveness of racism, however, there existed even before the civil rights movement a class of Blacks who were educationally, economically, and professionally equal—if not superior—to many whites, and yet these Blacks suffered social and political exclusion as well.

* * *

The response to the civil rights movement was the removal of most formal barriers and symbolic manifestations of subordination. Thus, "White Only" notices and other obvious indicators of the societal policy of racial subordination disappeared—at least in the public sphere. The disappearance of these symbols of subordination reflected the acceptance of the rhetoric of formal equality and signaled the demise of the rhetoric of white supremacy as expressing America's normative vision. In other words, it could no longer be said that Blacks were not included as equals in the American political vision.

Removal of these public manifestations of subordination was a significant gain for all Blacks, although some benefited more than others. The eradication of formal barriers meant more to those whose oppression was primarily symbolic than to those who suffered lasting material disadvantage. Yet despite these disparate results, it would be absurd to suggest that no benefits came from these formal reforms, especially in regard to racial policies, such as segregation, that were partly material but largely symbolic. Thus, to say that the reforms were "merely symbolic" is to say a great deal. These legal reforms and the formal extension of "citizenship" were large achievements precisely because much of what characterized Black oppression was symbolic and formal.

Yet the attainment of formal equality is not the end of the story. Racial hierarchy cannot be cured by the move to facial race-neutrality in the laws that structure the economic, political, and social lives of Black people. White race consciousness, in a new form but still virulent, plays an important, perhaps crucial, role in the new regime that has legitimated the deteriorating day-to-day material conditions of the majority of Blacks.

The end of Jim Crow has been accompanied by the demise of an explicit ideology of white supremacy. The white norm, however, has not disappeared; it has only been submerged in popular consciousness. It continues in an unspoken form as a statement of the positive social norm, legitimating the continuing domination of those who do not meet it. Nor have the negative stereotypes associated with Blacks been eradicated. The rationalizations once used to legitimate Black subordination based on a belief in racial inferiority have now been reemployed to legitimate the domination of Blacks through reference to an assumed cultural inferiority.

* * *

White race consciousness, which includes the modern belief in cultural inferiority, acts to further Black subordination by justifying all the forms of unofficial racial discrimination, injury, and neglect that flourish in a society that is only formally dedicated to equality. In more subtle ways, moreover, white race consciousness reinforces and is reinforced by the myth of equal opportunity that explains and justifies broader class hierarchies.

Race consciousness also reinforces whites' sense that American society is really meritocratic and thus helps prevent them from questioning the basic legitimacy of the free market. Believing both that Blacks are inferior and that the economy impartially rewards the superior over the inferior, whites see that most Blacks are indeed worse off than whites are, which reinforces their sense that the market is operating "fairly and impartially"; those who should logically be on the bottom are on the bottom. This strengthening of whites' belief in the system in turn reinforces their beliefs that Blacks are *indeed* inferior. After all, equal opportunity *is* the rule, and the market *is* an impartial judge; if Blacks are on the bottom, it must reflect their relative inferiority. Racist ideology thus operates in conjunction with the class components of legal ideology to reinforce the status quo, both in terms of class and race.

To bring a fundamental challenge to the way things are, whites would have to question not just their own subordinate status, but also both the economic and the racial myths that justify the status quo. Racism, combined with equal opportunity mythology, provides a rationalization for racial oppression, making it difficult for whites to see the Black situation as illegitimate or unnecessary. If whites believe that Blacks, because they are unambitious or inferior, get what they deserve, it becomes that much harder to convince whites that something is wrong with the entire system. Similarly, a challenge to the legitimacy of continued racial inequality would force whites to confront myths about equality of opportunity that justify for them whatever measure of economic success they may have attained.

Thus, although [Critical Legal Studies scholars] have suggested that legal consciousness plays a central role in legitimating hierarchy in America, the otherness dynamic enthroned within the maintenance and perpetuation of white race consciousness seems to be at least as important as legal consciousness in supporting the dominant order. Like legal consciousness, race consciousness makes it difficult—at least for whites—to imagine the world differently. It also creates the desire for identification with privileged elites. By focusing on a distinct, subordinate "other," whites include themselves in the dominant circle—an arena in which most hold no real power, but only their privileged racial identity.

BIBLIOGRAPHY

Equal Protection Theory

Alexander, *What Makes Wrongful Discrimination Wrong? Biases, Preferences, Stereotypes, and Proxies,* 141 U.Pa.L.Rev. 149 (1992).

Alexander, *Constitutional Theory and Constitutionally Optional Benefits and Burdens*, 11 Const.Comm. 287 (1994).

Bhagwat, *Purpose Scrutiny in Constitutional Analysis*, 85 Calif.L.Rev. 297 (1997).

Cohen, *Is Equal Protection Like Oakland? Equality as a Surrogate for Other Rights,* 59 Tul.L.Rev. 884 (1985).

Delgado, *Two Ways to Think About Race: Reflections in the Id, the Ego and Other Reformist Theories of Equal Protection*, 89 Geo. L.J. 2279 (2001).

D'Amato, *Is Equality a Totally Empty Idea?,* 81 Mich.L.Rev. 600 (1983).

Dorf, *Equal Protection Incorporation*, 88 Va.L.Rev. 951 (2002).

Forbath, *Caste, Class, and Equal Citizenship*, 98 Mich.L.Rev. 1 (1999).

Frank & Munro, *The Original Understanding of "Equal Protection of the Laws",* 1972 Wash.U.L.Q. 421.

Fuentes-Rohwer, Baker*'s Promise, Equal Protection, and the Modern Redistricting Revolution: A Plea for Rationality*, 80 N.Car.L.Rev. 1353 (2002).

Greenawalt, *"Prescriptive Equality": Two Steps Forward*, 110 Harv.L.Rev. 1265 (1997).

Hellman, *The Expressive Dimension of Equal Protection*, 85 Minn.L.Rev. 1 (2000).

Klarman, *An Interpretive History of Modern Equal Protection*, 90 Mich.L.Rev. 213 (1991).

Loffredo, *Poverty, Democracy and Constitutional Law,* 141 U.Pa.L.Rev. 1277 (1993).

Michelman, *On Protecting the Poor Through the Fourteenth Amendment,* 83 Harv.L.Rev. 7 (1969).

Miller, *The True Story of* Carolene Products, 1987 Sup.Ct.Rev. 397.

Nelson, *The Changing Meaning of Equality in Twentieth-Century Constitutional Law*, 52 Wash. & Lee L.Rev. 3 (1995).

Perry, *Modern Equal Protection: A Conceptualization and Appraisal*, 79 Colum.L.Rev. 1023 (1979).

Peters, *Equality Revisited*, 110 Harv.L.Rev. 1210 (1997).

Peters, *Outcomes, Reasons, and Equality*, 80 B.U. L. Rev. 1095 (2000).

Pennock, J. and Chapman, J., IX NOMOS: EQUALITY (1967).

Seidman, Brown *and* Miranda, 80 Calif.L.Rev. 73 (1992).

Selmi, Proving *Intentional Discrimination: The Reality of Supreme Court Rhetoric*, 86 Geo.L.J. 279 (1997).

Siegel, *Why Equal Protection No Longer Protects: The Evolving Forms of Status-Enforcing State Action*, 49 Stan.L.Rev. 1111 (1997).

Simons, *Overinclusion and Underinclusion: A New Model,* 36 U.C.L.A. L.Rev. 447 (1989).

Simons, *The Logic of Egalitarian Norms*, 80 B.U.L.Rev. 693 (2000).

Sunstein, *Public Values, Private Interests, and the Equal Protection Clause,* 1982 Sup.Ct.Rev. 127.

Symposium, *The Origins and Fate of Antisubordination Theory*, Issues in Legal Scholarship (2003), http://www.bepress.com/ils/iss2.

Symposium, *The Scope of Equal Protection*, 2002 U.Chi.L.F. 1.

Tussman and tenBroek, *The Equal Protection of the Laws,* 37 Calif.L.Rev. 341 (1949).

Westen, *The Empty Idea of Equality,* 95 Harv.L.Rev. 537 (1982).

Wilkinson, *The Supreme Court, The Equal Protection Clause, and the Three Faces of Constitutional Equality,* 61 Va.L.Rev. 945 (1975).

Race and the Constitution

Aleinikoff, *The Constitution in Context: The Continuing Significance of Racism,* 63 U.Colo.L.Rev. 325 (1992).

Bell, D., FACES AT THE BOTTOM OF THE WELL: THE PERMANENCE OF RACISM (1992).

Bell, D., RACE, RACISM AND AMERICAN LAW (3d ed. 1992).

Bickel, *The Original Understanding and the Segregation Decision,* 69 Harv.L.Rev. 1 (1955).

Cover, R., JUSTICE ACCUSED (1975).

Delgado, *Recasting the American Race Problem,* 79 Cal.L.Rev. 1389 (1991).

Delgado, *Storytelling for Oppositionists and Others: A Plea for Narrative,* 87 Mich.L.Rev. 2411 (1989).

Dimond, The *Anti-Caste Principle—Toward a Constitutional Standard for Review of Race Cases,* 30 Wayne L.Rev. 1 (1983).

Fairman, C., RECONSTRUCTION AND REUNION, 1864–88, Part I (1971); Part II (1987).

Flagg, *"Was Blind, But Now I See": White Race Consciousness and the Requirement of Discriminatory Intent,* 91 Mich.L.Rev. 953 (1993).

Franklin, J., FROM SLAVERY TO FREEDOM (3d ed. 1967).

Freeman, *Legitimizing Racial Discrimination Through Antidiscrimination Law: A Critical Review of Supreme Court Doctrine,* 62 Minn.L.Rev. 1049 (1978).

Haney López, *Race, Ethnicity, Erasure: The Salience of Race to LatCrit Theory*, 85 Cal.L.Rev. 1143 (1997).

Harris, *Equality Trouble: Sameness and Difference in Twentieth-Century Race Law*, 88 Cal.L.Rev. 1923 (2000).

Hickman, *The Devil and the One Drop Rule: Racial Categories, AfricanAmericans, and the U.S. Census*, 95 Mich.L.Rev. 1161 (1997).

Higginbotham, A., IN THE MATTER OF COLOR (1978).

Hyman, H. and Wiecek, W., EQUAL JUSTICE UNDER LAW: CONSTITUTIONAL DEVELOPMENT, 1835–1875 (1982).

Kaczorowski, *Revolutionary Constitutionalism in the Era of the Civil War and Reconstruction,* 61 N.Y.U.L.Rev. 863 (1986).

Kang, *Cyber-Race*, 113 Harv.L.Rev. 1130 (2000).

Klarman, *Race and the Court in the Progressive Era*, 51 Vand.L.Rev. 881 (1998).

Landsberg, *Race and the Rehnquist Court,* 66 Tulane L.Rev. 1267 (1992).

Maltz, *Slavery, Federalism, and the Structure of the Constitution,* XXXVI Am.J. Legal Hist. 466 (1992).

McNeil, G., GROUNDWORK: CHARLES HAMILTON HOUSTON AND THE STRUGGLE FOR CIVIL RIGHTS (1983).

Oberst, *The Strange Career of Plessy v. Ferguson,* 15 Ariz.L.Rev. 389 (1973).

Robinson, D., SLAVERY IN THE STRUCTURE OF AMERICAN POLITICS, 1765–1820 (1971).

Saunders, *Equal Protection, Class Legislation, and Colorblindness*, 96 Mich.L.Rev. 245 (1997).

Schmidt, *Principle and Prejudice: The Supreme Court and Race in the Progressive Era. Part I: The Heyday of Jim Crow,* 82 Colum.L.Rev. 444 (1982).

Soifer, *Protecting Civil Rights: A Critique of Raoul Berger's History,* 54 N.Y.U.L.Rev. 651 (1979).

Strauss, *The Myth of Colorblindness,* 1986 Sup.Ct.Rev. 99.

Swisher, C., THE TANEY PERIOD, 1835–64 (1974).

Symposium, *We the People: A Celebration of the Bicentennial of the United States Constitution,* 30 Howard L.J. 915 (1987).

Woodward, C., THE STRANGE CAREER OF JIM CROW (1955).

School Desegregation

Balkin, ed., What *Brown v. Board of Education* should have said: the nation's top legal experts rewrite America's landmark civil rights decision (2001).

Bell, *Serving Two Masters: Integration Ideals and Client Interests in School Desegregation Litigation,* 85 Yale L.J. 470 (1976).

Bell, ed., SHADES OF *BROWN*: NEW PERSPECTIVES ON SCHOOL DESEGREGATION (1980).

Bell, Brown v. Board of Education *and the Interest-Convergence Dilemma,* 93 Harv.L.Rev. 518 (1980).

Black, *The Lawfulness of the Segregation Decisions,* 69 Yale L.J. 421 (1960).

Brown, *Has the Supreme Court Allowed the Cure for De Jure Segregation to Replicate the Disease?,* 78 Cornell L.Rev. 1 (1992).

Chang, *The Bus Stops Here: Defining the Constitutional Right of Equal Educational Opportunity and an Appropriate Remedial Process,* 63 B.U.L.Rev. 1 (1983).

Davis, *The Quest for Equal Education in Mississippi: The Implications of* United States v. Fordice, 62 Miss.L.J. 405 (1993).

Devins, *School Desegregation Law in the 1980's: The Courts' Abandonment of* Brown v. Board of Education, 26 Wm. & Mary L.Rev. 7 (1984).

Diamond, R., BEYOND BUSING: INSIDE THE CHALLENGE TO URBAN SEGREGATION (1985).

Dudziak, *Desegregation as a Cold War Imperative,* 41 Stan.L.Rev. 61 (1988).

Fiss, *School Desegregation: The Uncertain Path of the Law,* 4 Phil. & Pub.Aff. 3 (1974).

Fiss, *The Fate of an Idea Whose Time Has Come: Antidiscrimination Law in the Second Decade after* Brown v. Board of Education, 41 U.Chi.L.Rev. 742 (1974).

Gewirtz, *Choice in the Transition: School Desegregation and the Corrective Ideal,* 86 Colum.L.Rev. 728 (1986).

Gewirtz, *Remedies and Resistance,* 92 Yale L.J. 585 (1983).

Goodman, *De Facto School Segregation: A Constitutional and Empirical Analysis,* 60 Calif.L.Rev. 275 (1972).

Graglia, L., DISASTER BY DECREE (1976).

Hayman and Levit, *The Constitutional Ghetto,* 1993 Wis.L.Rev. 627 (1993).

Kirp, D., JUST SCHOOLS (1982).

Kitch, *The Return of Color-Consciousness to the Constitution: Weber, Dayton, and Columbus,* 1979 Sup.Ct.Rev. 1.

Klarman, Brown, *Originalism and Constitutional Theory: A Response to Professor McConnell*, 81 Va.L.Rev. 1881 (1995).

Kluger, R., SIMPLE JUSTICE (1975).

Kujovich, *Equal Opportunity in Higher Education and the Black Public College: The Era of Separate But Equal,* 72 Minn.L.Rev. 29 (1987).

Landsberg, *The Desegregated School System and the Retrogression Plan,* 48 La.L.Rev. 789 (1988).

Liebman, *Desegregation Politics: "All-Out" School Desegregation Explained,* 90 Colum.L.Rev. 1463 (1990).

Macchiarola, et al., *The Judicial System and Equality in Schooling*, 23 Fordham Urb.L.J. 567 (1996).

Marcus, *Learning Together: Justice Marshall's Desegregation Opinions,* 61 Fordham L.Rev. 69 (1992).

McConnell, *Originalism and the Desegregation Decisions*, 81 Va.L.Rev. 947 (1995).

McConnell, *The Originalist Justification for* Brown*: A Reply to Professor Klarman*, 81 Va.L.Rev. 1937 (1995).

Note, *The Courts, HEW, and Southern School Desegregation,* 77 Yale L.J. 321 (1967).

Parker, *The Future of School Desegregation*, 94 Nw.U.L.Rev. 1157 (2000).

Shane, *School Desegregation Remedies and the Fair Governance of Schools,* 132 U.Pa.L.Rev. 1041 (1984).

Symposium, *Brown v. Board of Education*, 20 S.Ill.U.L.J. 1 (1995).

Symposium, *The Resegregation of Southern Schools? A Crucial Moment in the* History *(and the Future) of Public Schooling in America*, 81 N.Car.L.Rev. 1373 (2003).

Tushnet, M., THE NAACP'S LEGAL STRATEGY AGAINST SEGREGATED EDUCATION, 1925–1950 (1987).

Wilkinson, J., FROM *BROWN* TO *BAKKE* (1979).

Chapter VII

EQUALITY AND GENDER

Since the early 1970's, the Supreme Court has subjected governmental actions that discriminate on the basis of gender to "heightened scrutiny." Most recently, the Court has stated that its "skeptical scrutiny" of gender-based discrimination demands an "exceedingly persuasive justification for the government action."[1]

The readings in this Chapter seek to explore the theoretical issues that lie behind the legal doctrine. Are gender classifications as invidious as racial classifications? Does "gender equality" mean a gender-blind legal system? Or should the Equal Protection Clause tolerate gender-based laws that reflect existing differences between the sexes? Are such differences natural (biological) or are they socially created?

Richard Wasserstrom's article sets the stage for analyzing these questions by asking what role gender might play in an ideal society. He suggests that the arguments for taking gender into account based on biological and social differences are not as strong as is normally supposed.

Suzanna Sherry offers grounds for questioning Wasserstrom's assimilationist model. She examines feminist scholarship that suggests that women's moral development and sense of self may differ from men's. Sherry argues that law has been distorted by its reliance on a masculine perspective (that emphasizes autonomy, objectivity, and rights) and its exclusion of a feminine perspective (that would emphasize connection, subjectivity, and responsibility).

The next three excerpts examine the theoretical justifications for constitutional doctrine respecting gender discrimination. John Hart Ely contends that recently enacted gender-based classifications should not be subjected to strict judicial scrutiny.

Wendy Williams analyzes the extent to which current cultural understandings of gender roles may set limits on the work that the Equal Protection Clause can do for gender equality. She argues that the legal strategy of some feminists stressing differences and supporting programs

---

[1]United States v. Virginia, 518 U.S. 515, 531 (1996).

that afford special treatment to women may unwittingly reflect and reinforce traditional cultural notions about the role of women.

Catharine MacKinnon sketches two models of sex discrimination law. The prevailing approach, she asserts, is based on the familiar idea that equality means treating likes alike and unlikes unalike. MacKinnon argues that this "sameness/difference approach" is inadequate because it sets up maleness as the standard against which sameness and difference are to be measured, and it supports dominance of women by approving of distinctions based on differences between the sexes. She proposes a "dominance approach" to gender discrimination which would recognize sex inequalities as matters of imposed status, as the subordination of women to men.

Joan Williams takes issue with "difference feminism" as it is represented in the work of Carol Gilligan (described in Sherry's article) and with Catharine MacKinnon. She argues that to the extent that it is true that women are focused on relationships while men are not, it merely reflects the oppressive realities of the current gender system. The solution is neither the denial of gender differences nor the praise of a special voice or virtue of women; rather, the task is to "deconstruct gender" through a systematic refusal to institutionalize gender in any form.

It is common to describe the constitutional standard in cases involving gender classifications as "intermediate scrutiny." Mary Anne Case argues that the usual formulation of that standard—that a policy be "substantially related to an important governmental objective"—in fact does little work in the Court's analysis in gender cases. Rather, she suggests, the Court will uphold a sex-respecting rule only when it concludes that the rule embodies a "perfect proxy"; rules based on stereotypes—even ones that are, in the main, accurate—will not survive scrutiny.

RICHARD A. WASSERSTROM, RACISM AND SEXISM

PHILOSOPHY AND SOCIAL ISSUES 23–43 (1980).

[W]hat would the good or just society make of an individual's race or sex, and to what degree, if at all, would racial and sexual distinctions ever properly be taken into account there? * * *

* * *

[O]ne conception of a nonracist society is that which is captured by what I shall call the assimilationist ideal: a nonracist society would be one in which the race of an individual would be the functional equivalent of the eye color of individuals in our society today.[25] In our society no basic

[25]There is a danger in calling this ideal the "assimilationist" ideal. That term often suggests the idea of incorporating oneself, one's values, and the like into the dominant group and its practices and values. No part of that idea is meant to be captured by my use of the term. Mine is a stipulative definition.

political rights and obligations are determined on the basis of eye color. No important institutional benefits and burdens are connected with eye color. Indeed, except for the mildest sort of aesthetic preferences, a person would be thought odd who even made private, social decisions by taking eye color into account. * * *

What is a good deal less familiar is an analogous conception of the good society in respect to sexual differentiation—one in which an individual's sex were to become a comparably unimportant characteristic. An assimilationist society in respect to sex would be one in which an individual's sex was of no more significance * * * than is eye color today. There would be no analogue to transsexuality, and, while physiological or anatomical sex differences would remain, they would possess only the kind and degree of significance that today attaches to the physiologically distinct eye colors persons possess.

* * *

* * * [I]t must be acknowledged that to make the assimilationist ideal a reality in respect to sex would involve more profound and fundamental revisions of our institutions and our attitudes than would be the case in respect to race. On the institutional level we would, for instance, have to alter significantly our practices concerning marriage. If a nonsexist society is a society in which one's sex is no more significant than eye color in our society today, then laws which require the persons who are getting married to be of different sexes would clearly be sexist laws.

More importantly, given the significance of role differentiation and ideas about the psychological differences in temperament that are tied to sexual identity, the assimilationist ideal would be incompatible with all psychological and sex-role differentiation. That is to say, in such a society the ideology of the society would contain no proposition asserting the inevitable or essential attributes of masculinity or femininity; it would never encourage or discourage the ideas of sisterhood or brotherhood; and it would be unintelligible to talk about the virtues or the disabilities of being a woman or a man. In addition, such a society would not have any norms concerning the appropriateness of different social behavior depending upon whether one were male or female. There would be no conception of the existence of a set of social tasks that were more appropriately undertaken or performed by males or by females. And there would be no expectation that the family was composed of one adult male and one adult female, rather than, say, just two adults—if two adults seemed the appropriate number. To put it simply, in the assimilationist society in respect to sex, persons would not be socialized so as to see or understand themselves or others as essentially or significantly who they were or what their lives would be like because they were either male or female. And no political rights or social institutions, practices, and norms would mark the physiological differences between males and females as important.

Were sex like eye color, these kinds of distinctions would make no sense. Just as the normal, typical adult is virtually oblivious to the eye color of other persons for all significant interpersonal relationships, so, too, the normal, typical adult in this kind of nonsexist society would be equally as indifferent to the sexual, physiological differences of other persons for all significant interpersonal relationships. Bisexuality, not heterosexuality or homosexuality, would be the typical intimate, sexual relationship in the ideal society that was assimilationist in respect to sex.

To acknowledge that things would be very different is, of course, hardly to concede that they would thereby be undesirable—or desirable for that matter. But still, the problem is, perhaps, with the assimilationist ideal. And the assimilationist ideal is certainly not the only possible, plausible ideal.

There is, for instance, another one that is closely related to, but distinguishable from that of the assimilationist ideal. It can be understood by considering how religion rather than eye color tends to be thought about in our culture today and incorporated within social life today. If the good society were to match the present state of affairs in respect to one's religious identity, rather than the present state of affairs in respect to one's eye color, the two societies would be different, but not very greatly so. In neither would we find that the allocation of basic political rights and duties ever took an individual's religion into account. And there would be a comparable indifference to religion even in respect to most important institutional benefits and burdens—for example, access to employment in the desirable vocations, the opportunity to live where one wished to live, and the like. Nonetheless, in the good society in which religious differences were to some degree socially relevant, it would be deemed appropriate to have some institutions (typically those which are connected in an intimate way with these religions) which did in a variety of ways properly take the religion of members of the society into account. For example, it would be thought both permissible and appropriate for members of a religious group to join together in collective associations which have religious, educational, and social dimensions, and when it came to the employment of persons who were to be centrally engaged in the operation of those religious institutions (priests, rabbis and ministers, for example), it would be unobjectionable and appropriate explicitly to take the religion of job applicants into account. On the individual, interpersonal level, it might also be thought natural and possibly even admirable, were persons to some significant degree to select their associates, friends, and mates on the basis of their religious orientation. So there is another possible and plausible ideal of what the good society would look like in respect to a particular characteristic in which differences based upon that characteristic would be to some degree maintained in some aspects of institutional and interpersonal life. The diversity of the religious beliefs of individuals would be reflected in the society's institutional and ideological fabric in a way in which the diversity of eye color would not be in the assimilationist society. The picture is a more complex, somewhat less easily describable one than that of the assimilationist ideal.

* * *

What opponents of assimilationism and proponents of schemes of strong sexual differentiation seize upon is that sexual difference appears to be a naturally occurring category of obvious and inevitable relevance for the construction of any plausible conception of the nature of the good society. The problems with this way of thinking are twofold. To begin with, a careful and thorough analysis of the social realities would reveal, I believe, that it is the socially created sexual differences which constitute most of our conception of sex differences and which tend in fact to matter the most in the way we live our lives as persons of one sex or the other. For, it is, I think, sex-role differentiation and socialization, not the physiological and related biological differences—if there are any—that make men and women as different as they are from each other, and it is these same sex-role-created differences which are invoked to justify the necessity or the desirability of most sexual differentiation proposed to be maintained at any of the levels of social arrangements and practices described earlier.

It is important, however, not to attach any greater weight than is absolutely necessary to the truth or falsity of this causal claim about the source of the degree of sexual distinctions that exist in our or other cultures. For what is significant, although seldom recognized, is the fact that the answer to that question almost never goes very far in settling the question of what the good society should look like in respect to any particular characteristic of individuals. And the answer certainly does not go as far as many persons appear to believe it does to settle that question of the nature of the good society.

Let us suppose that there are what can be called "naturally occurring" sexual differences and even that they are of such a nature that they are in some sense of direct prima facie social relevance. It is essential to see that this would by no means settle the question of whether in the good society sex should or should not be as minimally significant as eye color. Even if there are major or substantial biological differences between men and women that are in this sense "natural" rather than socially created, this does not determine the question of what the good society can and should make of these differences—without, that is, begging the question by including within the meaning of "major" or "substantial" or "natural" the idea that these are things that ought to be retained, emphasized, or otherwise normally taken into account. It is not easy to see why, without begging the question, it should be thought that this fact, if it is a fact, settles the question adversely to anything like the assimilationist ideal. Persons might think that truths of this sort about nature or biology do affect, if not settle, the question of what the good society should look like for at least two different reasons.

In the first place, they might think the differences are of such a character that they substantially affect what would be *possible* within a good society of human persons. Just as the fact that humans are mortal necessarily limits the features of any possible good society, so, they might argue, the fact that males and females are physiologically or biologically different limits in the same way the features of any possible good society.

In the second place, they might think the differences are of such a character that they are relevant to the question of what would be *desirable* in the good society. That is to say, they might not think that the differences determine or affect to a substantial degree what is possible, but only that the differences are appropriately taken into account in any rational construction of an ideal social existence.

The second reason seems to be a good deal more plausible than the first. For there appear to be very few, if any, respects in which the ineradicable, naturally occurring differences between males and females *must* be taken into account. The industrial revolution has certainly made any of the general differences in strength between the sexes capable of being ignored by the good society for virtually all significant human activities. And even if it were true that women are naturally better suited than men to care for and nurture children, it is also surely the case that men can be taught to care for and nurture children well. Indeed, the one natural or biological fact that seems *required* to be taken into account is the fact that reproduction of the human species requires that the fetus develop *in utero* for a period of months. Sexual intercourse is not necessary, for artificial insemination is available. Neither marriage nor the nuclear family is necessary either for conception or child rearing. Given the present state of medical knowledge and what might be termed the natural realities of female pregnancy, it is difficult to see why any important institutional or interpersonal arrangements are constrained to take the existing biological differences as to the phenomenon of *in utero* pregnancy into account.

But to say all this is still to leave it a wholly open question to what degree the good society *ought* to build upon any ineradicable biological differences, or to create ones in order to construct institutions and sex roles which would thereby maintain a substantial degree of sexual differentiation. The way to answer that question is to consider and assess the arguments for and against doing so. What is significant is the fact that many of the arguments for doing so are less persuasive than they appear to be upon the initial statement of this possibility.

It might be argued, for instance, that the fact of menstruation could be used as a premise upon which to base the case for importantly different social roles for females than for males. But this could only plausibly be proposed if two things were true: first, that menstruation would be debilitating to women and hence relevant to social role even in a culture which did not teach women to view menstruation as a sign of uncleanliness or as a curse; and, second, that the way in which menstruation necessarily affected some or all women was in fact necessarily related in an important way to the role in question. But even if both of these were true, it would still be an open question whether any sexual differentiation ought to be built upon these facts. The society could still elect to develop institutions that would nullify the effect of these natural differences and it would still be an open question whether it ought to do so. Suppose, for example, what seems implausible—that some or all women will not be able to perform a particular task while menstruating, e.g., guard the border of a country. It would be possible, even easy, if the society wanted to, to arrange for substitute guards for the women who were incapacitated. We know that persons are not good guards when they are sleepy, and we make arrangements so that persons alternate guard duty to avoid fatigue. The same could be done for menstruating women, even given the implausibly strong assumptions about menstruation.

The point that is involved here is a very general one that has application in contexts having nothing to do with the desirability or undesirability of maintaining substantial sexual differentiation. It has to do with the fact that humans possess the ability to alter their natural and social environment in distinctive, dramatic, and unique ways. * * *

* * *

There are, though, several other arguments based upon nature, or the idea of the "natural" that also must be considered and assessed. First, it might be argued that if a way of doing something is natural, then it ought to be done that way. Here, what may be meant by "natural" is that this way of doing the thing is the way it would be done if culture did not direct or teach us to do it differently. It is not clear, however, that this sense of "natural" is wholly intelligible; it supposes that we can meaningfully talk about how humans would behave in the absence of culture. And few if any humans have ever lived in such a state. Moreover, even if this is an intelligible notion, the proposal that the natural way to behave is somehow the appropriate or desirable way to behave is strikingly implausible. It is, for example, almost surely natural, in this sense of "natural," that humans would eat their food with their hands, except for the fact that they are, almost always, socialized to eat food differently. Yet, the fact that humans would naturally eat this way, does not seem in any respect to be a reason for believing that that is thereby the desirable or appropriate way to eat food. And the same is equally true of any number of other distinctively human ways of behaving.

Second, someone might argue that substantial sexual differentiation is natural not in the sense that it is biologically determined nor in the sense that it would occur but for the effects of culture, but rather in the sense that substantial sexual differentiation is a virtually universal phenomenon in human culture. By itself, this claim of virtual universality, even if accurate, does not directly establish anything about the desirability or undesirability of any particular ideal. But it can be made into an argument by the addition of the proposition that where there is a widespread, virtually universal social practice or institution, there is probably some good or important purpose served by the practice or institution. Hence, given the fact of substantial sex-role differentiation in all, or almost all, cultures, there is on this view some reason to think that substantial sex-role differentiation serves some important purpose for and in human society.

This is an argument, but it is hard to see what is attractive about it. The premise which turns the fact of sex-role differentiation into any kind of a strong reason for sex-role differentiation is the premise of conservatism. And it is no more or less convincing here than elsewhere. There are any number of practices or institutions that are typical and yet upon reflection seem without significant social purpose. Slavery was once such an institution; war perhaps still is.

More to the point, perhaps, the concept of "purpose" is ambiguous. It can mean in a descriptive sense "plays some role" or "is causally relevant." Or, it can mean in a prescriptive sense "does something desirable" or "has some useful function." If "purpose" is used descriptively in the conservative premise, then the argument says nothing about the continued desirability of sex-role differentiation of the assimilationist ideal. If "purpose" is used prescriptively in the conservative premise, then there is no reason to think that premise is true.

To put it another way, the question that seems fundamentally to be at issue is whether it is desirable to have a society in which sex-role differences are to be retained in the way and to the degree they are today—or even at all. The straightforward way to think about the question is to ask what would be good and what would be bad about a society in which sex functioned like eye color does in our society; or alternatively, what would be good and what would be bad about a society in which sex functioned in the way in which religious identity does today; or alternatively, what would be good and what would be bad about a society in which sex functioned in the way in which it does today. We can imagine what such societies would look like and how they might work. It is hard to see how thinking about answers to this question is substantially advanced by reference to what has typically or always been the case. If it is true, for instance, that the sex-role-differentiated societies that have existed have tended to concentrate power and authority in the hands of males, have developed institutions and ideologies that have perpetuated that concentration, and have restricted and prevented women from living the kinds of lives that persons ought to be able to live for themselves, then this, it seems to me, says far more about what may be wrong with any strongly nonassimilationist ideal than does the conservative premise say what may be right about any strongly nonassimilationist ideal.

* * *

* * * [It remains an open question] whether a society in which sex functioned in the way in which eye color does (a strictly assimilationist society in respect to sex) would be better or worse than one in which sex functioned in the way in which religious identity does in our society (a nonoppressive, more diversified or pluralistic one). For it might be argued that especially in the case of sex and even in the case of race much would be gained and nothing would be lost if the ideal society in respect to these characteristics succeeded in preserving in a nonoppressive fashion the attractive differences between males and females and the comparably attractive differences among ethnic groups. Such a society, it might be claimed, would be less bland, less homogeneous and richer in virtue of its variety.

I do not think there is any easy way to settle this question, but I do think the attractiveness of the appeal to diversity, when sex or race are concerned, is less alluring than is often supposed. The difficulty is in part one of specifying what will be preserved and what will not, and in part one of preventing the reappearance of the type of systemic dominance and subservience that produces the injustice of oppression. Suppose, for example, that it were suggested that there are aspects of being male and aspects of being female that are equally attractive and hence desirable to maintain and perpetuate: the kind of empathy that is associated with women and the kind of self-control associated with men. It does not matter what the characteristic is, the problem is one of seeing why the characteristic should be tied by the social institutions to the sex of the individuals of the society. If the characteristics are genuinely ones that all individuals ought to be encouraged to display in the appropriate circumstances, then the social institutions and ideology ought to endeavor to foster them in all individuals. If it is good for everyone to be somewhat empathetic all of the time or especially empathetic in some circumstances, or good for everyone to have a certain degree of self-control all of the time or a great deal in some circumstances, then there is no reason to preserve institutions which distribute these psychological attributes along sexual lines. And the same is true for many, if not all, vocations, activities, and ways of living. If some, but not all persons would find a life devoted to child rearing genuinely satisfying, it is good, surely, that that option be open to them. Once again, though, it is difficult to see the argument for implicitly or explicitly encouraging, teaching, or assigning to women, as opposed to men, that life simply in virtue of their sex. Thus, while substantial diversity in individual characteristics, attitudes, and ways of life is no doubt an admirable, even important feature of the good society, what remains uncertain is the necessity or the desirability of continuing to link attributes or behaviors such as these to the race or sex of individuals. And for the reasons I have tried to articulate there are significant moral arguments against any conception of the good society in which such connections are pursued and nourished in the systemic fashion required by the existence and maintenance of sex roles.

SUZANNA SHERRY, CIVIC VIRTUE AND THE FEMININE VOICE IN CONSTITUTIONAL ADJUDICATION

72 VA.L.REV. 543, 580–91 (1986).

New studies in a variety of academic disciplines suggest that women in fact may have a unique perspective, a world-view that differs in significant respects from that of men. Feminist scholars in such diverse fields as philosophy, history, sociology, art, and anthropology have identified peculiarly feminine perspectives in those disciplines.[167] Recent work in psychology and in literary theory is particularly illuminating. Psychological studies suggest that women's moral development and concept of self may differ from those of men. Feminist literary theory suggests that women's writing differs from men's in ways that reflect a radically different perspective. Despite the independence of the research and the differences in both topics of investigation and terms of description, the feminine perspective identified in each of these fields is, at its core, a single,

[167]See R. Morgan, The Anatomy of Freedom: Feminism, Physics and Global Politics (1982); N. Noddings, [Caring: A Feminine Approach to Ethics and Moral Education (1984)]; E. Showalter, A Literature of Their Own (1977); P. Spacks, The Female Imagination (1975); Blecki, Feminist Literary Criticism: An Introduction, *in* Feminist Literary Criticism: A Symposium 1 (K. Bordan & F. Rinn eds. 1974); Harding & Hintikka, Introduction, *in* Discovering Reality: Feminist Perspectives on Epistemology, Metaphysics, Methodology, and Philosophy of Science ix (S. Harding & M. Hintikka eds. 1983); O'Brien, Feminist Theory and Dialectical Logic, *in* Feminist Theory: A Critique of Ideology 99 (N. Keohane, M. Rosaldo, & B. Gelpi eds. 1982); Garfunkel, The Improvised Self: Sex Differences in Artistic Identity (Dissertation, Dep't of Psych. & Soc. Rel., Harv. Univ., 1984); Goodman, Women's Studies: The Debate Continues, N.Y. Times Magazine, Apr. 22, 1984, at 39; Kolbert, Scientific Ideas: Women's vs. Men's, N.Y. Times, Oct. 17, 1985, at C1, col. 1; Goleman, Psychology Is Revising Its View of Women, N.Y. Times, Mar. 20, 1984, at C1, col. 1.

common approach. That approach is captured in the tension between women's primary concern with intimacy or connection and men's primary focus on separation or autonomy.[168]

This difference between men and women may influence the manner in which they think about, write about, and practice their disciplines. Thus, it is probable that women's unique perspective on law and jurisprudence, as a function of their different world-view, extends well beyond areas traditionally seen as affecting women, and in fact encompasses all legal issues. Just as women's writing on all subjects—not just on intimacy, domesticity, or women's place in society—reflects a different cast, women's views on the law in general may provide insights and approaches that are less natural to, and therefore less available to, male lawyers and judges.

This different approach to the law makes women a potentially innovative force in the legal community. Because women have been excluded from the mainstream of legal authority and legal change, the legal system, like moral, political, and philosophical discourse, has become "a set of cultural and symbolic forms that view human experience from the distorted and one-sided perspective of a single gender."[170] This is not to suggest merely that the legal structure ignores or minimizes significant gender differences, but rather that because women have been excluded from shaping our legal structure in general, that structure reflects a distorted view of the tension between autonomy and connection and between the individual and society.

What sort of distortion has the masculine paradigm introduced into our legal system? Feminist scholars identify three primary dichotomies between men's and women's thinking: while women emphasize connection,

---

[168]The most persuasive explanation for the differences between men and women is based on differences between boys' and girls' development of an ego or sense of self. Ego development occurs while the child is still quite young and is therefore significantly influenced by the child's primary caretaker. Because, in general, girls are raised by a primary caretaker of the same gender and boys are raised by a primary caretaker of the opposite gender, girls reaffirm their early attachments while boys repudiate them. Thus, women come to see themselves as fundamentally connected and men see themselves as fundamentally detached. See N. Chodorow, [The Reproduction of Mothering: Psychoanalysis and the Sociology of Gender 166–68 (1978)]; C. Gilligan, [In A Different Voice: Psychological Theory and Women's Development 5–23 (1982).] Other explanations for the differences between men and women include the socialization process, the mother's varying reaction to sons and daughters, and biological differences. See, e.g., E. Erikson, Identity, Youth and Crisis (1968); E. Janeway, Man's World, Woman's Place: A Study in Social Mythology (1971); J. Miller, Toward a New Psychology of Women (1976); Flax, The Conflict Between Nurturance and Autonomy in Mother–Daughter Relationships and Within Feminism, Fem. Stud., June 1978, at 171.

[170]O'Brien, supra note 167, at 99. * * *

subjectivity, and responsibility, men emphasize autonomy, objectivity, and rights. * * *

* * *

A brief caveat is in order. First, I am not contending that gender-based differences are universal, only that they are likely enough that the historical exclusion of women from the shaping of the legal system has had a profound impact, which cannot be reversed—or, to a large extent, even recognized—until women begin to participate in that enterprise. Second, I am not limiting my analysis to a feminist perspective: feminists have a particular political agenda that may or may not be shared by all women (and is shared by some men). Rather, this is an analysis of a feminine perspective that encompasses aspects of personality and relationship to the world that have nothing to do with one's political preferences. Finally, I am not suggesting that the feminine perspective is any better than the masculine perspective, just that it is different. The incorporation of a new perspective need not imply a hierarchical ranking; I am arguing merely that the law has been distorted by its one-sided focus and that the feminine perspective described here represents a move toward correcting that distortion. * * *

B. Connection and Autonomy

* * * [T]he feminine perspective views individuals primarily as interconnected members of a community. Nancy Chodorow and Carol Gilligan, in groundbreaking studies on the development of self and morality, have concluded that women tend to have a more intersubjective sense of self than men and that the feminine perspective is therefore more other-directed.[174] Other studies tend to confirm this finding.[175] The essential difference between the male and female perspectives [is that] "[t]he basic feminine sense of self is connected to the world, the basic masculine sense of self is separate."[176] Women thus tend to see others as extensions of themselves rather than as outsiders or competitors.

Gilligan suggests that Kohlberg's description of a morally mature person—a "rational individual aware of values and rights prior to social contracts" who adopts "universal principles of justice," including "respect for the dignity of human beings as individual persons"[178]—instead

---

[174]See N. Chodorow, supra note 168; C. Gilligan, supra note 168. * * *

[175]For example, even at a very young age, female children tend to be more dependent on and reluctant to leave their mothers. See Goldberg & Lewis, Play Behavior in the Year–Old Infant: Early Sex Difference, 40 Child Dev. 21 (1969); Messer & Lewis, Social Class and Sex Differences in the Attachment and Play Behavior of the Year–Old Infant, 18 Merrill–Palmer Q. Behav. & Dev. 295 (1972).

[176]N. Chodorow, supra note 168, at 169 * * *.

[178]Kohlberg, Moral Stages and Moralization: The Cognitive–Developmental Approach,

describes a masculine morality.[179] That masculine perspective embodies the individualism inherent in the modern paradigm. The parallel between the classical paradigm and feminine morality, by contrast, is clearly illustrated by Gilligan's quotation of a typical female response to a moral dilemma:

> By yourself, there is little sense to things. It is like the sound of one hand clapping, the sound of one man or one woman, there is something lacking. *It is the collective that is important to me,* and that collective is based on certain guiding principles, one of which is that *everybody belongs to it,* and that you all come from it. You have to love someone else, because while you may not like them, you are inseparable from them. In a way, it is like loving your right hand. *They are part of you; that other person is part of that giant collection of people that you are connected to.*[180]

Women's emphasis on connection also suggests that the cliche that women are more cooperative and less competitive than men may have some basis in fact. Historically, women have tended to achieve their goals communally; from quilting bees to consciousness-raising sessions, women have banded together rather than striving individually. There are analogous differences between the organization and ideology underlying women's traditional dominion, the family, and men's traditional arena, the market-place: as Frances Olsen notes, the market is based on an individualist ethic and the family on an altruistic ethic.[182]

Some of the most intriguing evidence of a feminine perspective comes from the field of literary criticism, where feminist critics are discovering characteristic differences in both style and substance between male and female authors. In seeking to identify this "uniquely female literary consciousness,"[183] they are discovering indications of a similar tension between autonomy and connection. Male writers typically portray individuals as existing prior to and divorced from society. The male metaphor, and the male travail, is individualist. In contrast, women writers are less apt to focus on purely individual heroism. Unlike the archetypal masculine "coming of age" novel, the developing feminine counterpart describes women's maturation in the context of a group of women, the definition of one "self" from among many "selves[.]" * * *

---

in Moral Development and Behavior: Theory, Research, and Social Issues 34–35 (T. Lickona ed. 1976) (describing the post-conventional level).

[179]See C. Gilligan, supra note 168, at 18–22.

[180]Id. at 160 (some emphasis in original, some added).

[182]Olsen, The Family and the Market: A Study of Ideology and Legal Reform, 96 Harv.L.Rev. 1497, 1505 (1983)[.] * * *

[183]Showalter, Introduction, *in* The New Feminist Criticism: Essays on Women, Literature, and Theory 6 (E. Showalter ed. 1985) * * *.

Feminist literary critics are also beginning to identify some characteristically feminine styles, which also suggest an intersubjective perspective. For example, women writers more frequently use a technique of rotating a novel's perspective from one character to another.[186] This technique is often criticized by male critics, and it may be that women authors are more receptive to the technique because they are better able to perceive not only the relations among characters but also those between themselves and the characters they create. They almost literally "become" their characters (male and female) for the same reason that their intersubjective perspective keeps them from fully separating themselves from others. Males, on the other hand, with their emphasis on autonomy, see the technique as a violation of the ideal of separation.

C. Contextuality and Abstraction

Scholarship in literature and psychology also suggests that women are more contextual and men more abstract. Piaget, for example, found that girls playing children's games tend to treat the rules of the game as less fixed and more flexible than do boys and that girls are more likely to stop a game altogether—thus preserving friendships—if a dispute arises. For boys, development and application of fixed, abstract rules is almost as important as the object of the game itself.[188] Again, Kohlberg's description of moral development (i.e., the development of the masculine perspective) stresses a progression from context-bound judgments to abstract moral principles. Women, on the other hand, in responding to moral dilemmas, tend instead to look to circumstances rather than to abstractions: the right moral response depends on the context.[190]

This concept of feminine reliance on context is borne out in some empirical experiments. For example, the greater familiarity of even young boys with universal principles is well illustrated by a simple experiment in which boys and girls were shown pictures of everyday objects and asked to group related objects:

> [B]oys tend to bracket together objects (or pictures of objects) whose intrinsic characteristics are similar, whereas girls weight more heavily the functional and relational characteristics of the entities to be compared. For instance, boys frequently bracketed together such entities as a truck, a car, and an ambulance, while girls bracketed such entities as a doctor, a hospital bed, and an ambulance.[191]

---

[186]See, e.g., Mellown, Character and Themes in the Novels of Jean Rhys, *in* Contemporary Women Novelists: A Collection of Critical Essays 118, 130 (P. Spacks ed. 1977).

[188]See J. Piaget, The Moral Judgment of The Child 82 (1965); see also Lever, Sex Differences in the Games Children Play, 23 Social Probs. 478 (1976) (similar findings).

[190]See C. Gilligan, supra note 168, at 38.

[191]Hintikka & Hintikka, How Can Language Be Sexist? *in* Discovering Reality: Femi-

The boys focused on the abstraction of "locomotion," seeing the objects as independent units, while the girls emphasized instead the concrete relationships among objects. Other studies confirm that males of all ages are better able to separate discrete objects from their backgrounds and relationships than are females. Males are said to be less field-dependent; that is, they have a greater "ability to overcome the influence of an embedding context."[193]

Moreover, current controversies in philosophy tend to break down along gender lines. Despite exceptions, male philosophers often endorse more abstract and less contextual theories. For example, mainstream discussions of virtue tend to assume that virtues are abstract qualities. Committing murder under dangerous circumstances, though a criminal act, may still constitute an instance of the virtue of courage. Philippa Foot, on the other hand, suggests that virtues are contextual, not abstract: the virtue of courage is exhibited only under circumstances where the act itself can be considered courageous.[194]

* * *

Literary criticism also recognizes the difference between the abstraction of men and the concreteness of women. One critic has suggested, for example, that George Eliot's *Mill on the Floss* illustrates the tension between the male notion of universal maxims and the female unwillingness to differentiate the universal from its particular applications.[199] Women's writing has also been characterized (and criticized) as less linear and unified and more fluid than men's;[200] this again suggests a focus on context rather than on abstract rules of progression. Even feminine literary criticism is more contextual: Elaine Showalter has suggested that one characteristic of feminist criticism is the rejection of (masculine) objective, non-experiential critical theories.[201]

---

nist Perspectives on Epistemology, Metaphysics, Methodology, and Philosophy of Science 139, 145 (S. Harding & M. Hintikka eds. 1983) (footnote omitted).

[193]J. Sherman, On the Psychology of Women: A Survey of Empirical Studies 21 (1971) * * *.

[194]See P. Foot, [Virtues and Vices and Other Essays in Moral Philosophy 15–17 (1978).]

[199]Jacobus, The Question of Language: Men of Maxims and *The Mill on the Floss, in* Writing and Sexual Difference 37, 42 (E. Abel ed. 1982). Jacobus contrasts Eliot's remark, in her novel, that "the man of maxims is the popular representative of the minds that are guided in their moral judgment solely by general rules," with the view of the central character, Maggie Tulliver—"'to lace ourselves up in formulas is to ignore the special circumstances that mark the individual lot.'" Id. (quoting G. Eliot, Mill on the Floss 628 (A. Byatt ed. 1979)).

[200]Gardiner, On Female Identity and Writing By Women, *in* Writing and Sexual Difference 177, 185 (E. Abel ed. 1982); Jacobus, supra note 199, at 39–40.

[201]Showalter, Feminist Criticism in the Wilderness, supra note 183, at 244.

D. Responsibility and Rights

Until recently, the archetypal developmental continuum of individual moral sensibility was believed to be an orderly progression from self-centeredness through other-centeredness to the development of logical, independent, universal principles—rights—that depend neither on one's own needs nor on what others believe is right.[202] Although this progression mirrors male moral development, it fails to reflect the moral growth pattern of women.[203]

Gender-based differences in moral structure, long seen as evidence of women's moral immaturity,[204] may in fact be evidence of a feminine morality that differs in its emphasis from that of males. In her study of moral development, Carol Gilligan found that women tend to view a moral problem as "a problem of care and responsibility in relationships rather than as one of rights and rules."[205] When faced with the moral dilemma of whether a man should steal a drug he cannot afford to save his dying wife, Gilligan found that, while men struggle with the conflicting rights of the parties, women focus on the druggist's "moral obligation to show compassion,"[206] "not on the conflict of rights but on the failure of response."[207] Although men and women may agree that the man ought to steal the drug, men justify it in terms of a resolution between conflicting rights of husband and druggist, and women in terms of the need for more compassion by the druggist in the face of the husband's compassion for his wife.[208] Whether personal or political, the moral structure of "mature" males reflects a paradigm of independent rights, while that of females emphasizes relational responsibilities.

JOHN HART ELY, FACILITATING THE REPRESENTATION OF MINORITIES

Democracy and Distrust 164–170 (1980).

[In this section, Ely considers whether gender-based classifications that disadvantage women should be subject to close judicial scrutiny. We have reprinted Ely's general approach to equal protection in Chapter VII. Recall that he suggests that strict scrutiny is appropriate when there is good reason to suspect that the political process that produced the statute was tainted—either because of ill-will towards the disadvantaged group ("first degree prejudice") or because the legislature is likely to have overestimated the

---

[202]See L. Kohlberg, The Philosophy of Moral Development (1981); Kohlberg, supra note 178.

[203]See C. Gilligan, supra note 168, at 18–22.

[204]See L. Kohlberg, supra note 202 * * *.

[205]C. Gilligan, supra note 168, at 73.

[206]Id. at 54 (quoting a subject of Gilligan's study).

[207]Id.

[208]See, e.g., id. at 29.

accuracy of the generalization upon which the classification is based ("second degree prejudice").]

The case of women is timely and complicated. Instances of first-degree prejudice are obviously rare, but just as obviously exaggerated stereotyping—typically to the effect that women are unsuited to the work of the world and therefore belong at home—has long been rampant throughout the male population and consequently in our almost exclusively male legislatures in particular. It may all be in apparent good humor, even perceived as protective, but it has cost women dearly. Absent a strong demonstration of mitigating factors, therefore, we would have to treat gender-based classifications that act to the disadvantage of women as suspicious. If the stereotyping has been clear, however, so has the noninsularity of the group affected. The degree of contact between men and women could hardly be greater, and neither, of course, are women "in the closet" as homosexuals historically have been. Finally, lest you think I missed it, women have about half the votes, apparently more. As if it weren't enough that they're not discrete and insular, they're not even a minority!

Despite that seeming avalanche of rebuttal, there remains something that seems right in the claim that women have been operating at an unfair disadvantage in the political process, though it's tricky pinning down just what gives rise to that intuition. It is tempting to observe that although women may be a majority, they haven't in any real sense *consented* to the various instances of gender-based legislation. Voters, female and male alike, are typically confronted not with single-issue referenda but rather with packages of attitudes, packages we call candidates. Most women are not injured in any direct way by laws that classify on the basis of sex—depriving women, say, of the opportunity to tend bar, guard railroad crossings, or administer estates—and the fact that they help elect representatives who are unprepared to repeal such laws may mean only that there are other issues about which they feel more strongly. This may indeed be so, but the argument changes the rules. Once we start to shift from a focus on whether something is blocking the opportunity to correct the stereotype reflected in the legislation, to one that attempts to explain why those who have that opportunity have chosen to pursue other goals instead, we begin to lose our way, to permit our disagreement with the substantive merits of the legislation to take the place of what is *constitutionally* relevant, an inability to do anything about it. That answer triggers a more promising inquiry, though—whether it is fair to say that women have "chosen" not to avail themselves of their opportunities either by voting or by personally influencing those men with whom they come in contact, to correct the exaggerated stereotype that many men hold and on the basis of which they have often legislated. A major reason for lack of action on either of these fronts, or so at least it can plausibly be argued, has been that many women have *accepted* the overdrawn stereotype and thus have seen nothing to "correct" by vote or personal persuasion, and by their example may even have acted so as to reinforce it. That could, of course, imply that it wasn't so exaggerated a stereotype after all, but it could mean something else too, that our society, including the women in it, has been so pervasively dominated by men that women quite understandably have accepted men's stereotypes, of women as well as on other subjects.

The general idea is one that in some contexts has merit. A sufficiently pervasive prejudice can block its own correction not simply by keeping its victims "in the closet" but also by convincing even them of its correctness. In *Castaneda v. Partida,* decided in 1977, the Court held that a prima facie case of intentional discrimination against Mexican-Americans in the selection of grand jurors was not constitutionally affected by the fact that Mexican-Americans enjoyed "governing majority" status in the county involved. Concurring, Justice Marshall gave the reason why: "Social scientists agree that members of minority groups frequently respond to discrimination and prejudice by attempting to disassociate themselves from the group, even to the point of adopting the majority's negative attitudes towards the minority."[96] Nor does this insight seem relevant only to numerical minorities: slaves outnumbered masters in the antebellum South, and outnumbered whites generally in some states, but that apparently didn't keep many of them from assimilating much of the mythology used to legitimate their enslavement.

To apply all this to the situation of women in America in 1980, however, is to strain a metaphor past the breaking point. It is true that women do not generally operate as a very cohesive political force, banding together to elect candidates pledged to the "woman's point of view." Constitutional suspiciousness should turn on evidence of blocked access, however, not on the fact that elections are coming out "wrong." There is an infinity of groups that do not act as such in the political marketplace, but we don't automatically infer that they have a "slave mentality." The cause, more often, is that (sensibly or not) the people involved are not in agreement over the significance of their shared characteristic. Thus in assessing suspiciousness it cannot be enough simply to note that a group does not function as a political bloc. A further reference to the surrounding conditions must be had, to see if there are systemic bars (and I'm obviously not suggesting they need be official ones) to access. On that score it seems important that today discussion about the appropriate "place" of women is common among both women and men, and between the sexes as well. The very stereotypes that gave rise to laws "protecting" women by barring them from various

[96] 430 U.S. 482, 503 (1977) (Marshall, J., concurring), citing G. Allport, [The Nature of Prejudice 150–53 (1954).] * * *

activities are under daily and publicized attack, and are the subject of equally spirited defense. (That the common stereotypes are so openly described and debated, as they are not in the case of racial minorities, is itself some evidence of the comparatively free and nonthreatening nature of the interchange.) Given such open discussion of the traditional stereotypes, the claim that the numerical majority is being "dominated," that women are in effect "slaves" who have no realistic choice but to assimilate the stereotypes, is one it has become impossible to maintain except at the most inflated rhetorical level. It also renders the broader argument self-contradictory, since to make such a claim in the context of the current debate one must at least implicitly grant the validity of the stereotype, that women are in effect mental infants who will believe anything men tell them to believe. Many women do seem to prefer the old stereotype to the new liberation. You and I may think that's a mistaken choice. But once we begin regarding serious disagreement with a choice as proof that those who made it aren't in control of their minds, we've torn up the rulebook and made substantive wrongheadedness the test of unconstitutionality.

However, most laws classifying by sex weren't passed this morning or even the day before yesterday: in fact it is rare to see a gender-based classification enacted since the New Deal. In general women couldn't even *vote* until the Nineteenth Amendment was ratified in 1920, and most of these laws probably predate even that: they should be invalidated. Throughout this discussion, however, I have been concerned with factors more subtle than the lack of a vote, and it can at least be argued that until quite recently there persisted throughout America's female population a "*Castaneda*-like" acceptance of the prejudices of males, unventilated by more than token airing of their validity. Given what appropriately makes a classification suspicious, it is not necessarily a unitary question whether discrimination against a certain group should be so regarded, and the case of women seems one where the date of enactment should be important. It surely seems more helpful than anything the Court has come up with on the question of whether those who passed the law in issue were proceeding on the basis of an "archaic and overbroad generalization" or whether, say, they were genuinely trying to protect women from certain physical risks to which in statistical terms they are unusually subject, realized there were counterexamples and estimated their incidence about right, but nonetheless felt the costs of identifying the exceptions were simply too high. * * * Direct attempts to judge whether a given law was generated by an overdrawn stereotype can be dangerously subjective since the face of the statute will inevitably be consistent with either of these descriptions of the decision process, and the legislative history will inevitably be partial and subject to manipulation. The date of passage seems a somewhat more solid datum, one that can at least begin to anchor the judicial inquiry. That's an aside, however, since the date of passage seems unquestionably relevant to what our analysis has suggested is a more promising approach to the question of suspiciousness—one geared to the existence of official or unofficial blocks on the opportunities of those the law disadvantages to counter by argument or example the overdrawn stereotypes we might, from the demography of the decision-making body, otherwise suspect were operative.

The case of women can be further put in perspective by exploring what should follow from a judicial determination that the suspiciousness of a given classification has not been allayed and that it therefore is unconstitutional. Here too the answer is not unitary: we have looked at several indicia of suspiciousness, and their remedial implications differ. Where a law is suspect because of what I have been calling first-degree prejudice, or indeed where it has been infected by a subtler form of stereotyping under conditions where the negatively affected group was barred from effective access at the time of passage *and still is,* the only appropriate remedy is to void the classification and insist—if the legislature wishes to continue to classify—on a different, generally more finely tuned, test of qualification. The obvious alternative to this is to have the judiciary restrike the substantive balance, attempting not to let the prejudices that apparently influenced the legislature play a part, and invalidate the classification only if in some sense it still ends up unacceptable on its merits. You will not be surprised to learn that I regard that approach as quite inappropriate. We can cite occasions on which our judiciary has displayed a lesser susceptibility to bare-knuckled first-degree prejudice than our elected officials, but we also can cite some where it hasn't. Moreover, instances of such prejudice, for reasons it is not necessary to review, are almost invariably instances of self-serving comparison as well. Judges tend to belong to the same broad categories as legislators—most of them, for example, are white heterosexual males comfortably above the poverty line—and there isn't any reason to suppose that they are immune to the usual temptations to self-aggrandizing generalization. When in a given situation you can't be trusted to generalize and I can't be trusted to generalize, the answer, if possible, is not to generalize, which suggests that the Supreme Court has chosen wisely in insisting generally that a classification whose suspiciousness has not been allayed simply cannot be employed. Where in fact it was largely the product of a simple desire to disadvantage those disqualified, it probably will just be abandoned, which seems a desirable outcome. Where, however, a classification of some sort does seem necessary (though the one the legislature employed was constitutionally unacceptable), the remedy of flat-out disallowance will impose costs in both time and money, as it will generally necessitate a somewhat more individualized test of qualification. However, legislatures often incur those costs voluntarily, and courts on other occasions have forced them to do so where constitutionally protected interests will be threatened by an imperfectly fitting classification. The unusual dangers of distortion in situations of self-aggrandizing generalization seem also to demand that we bear the increased costs of more individualized justice.

A case like that of women, where access was blocked in the past but can't responsibly be said to be so any longer, seems different in a way that suggests that a less drastic remedy may be appropriate. In cases of first-degree prejudice, or self-serving stereotyping where the access of the disadvantaged group remains blocked, the alternative of "remanding" the question to the political processes for a "second look" would not be acceptable: we don't give a case back to a rigged jury. Here, however, such a "second look" approach seems to make sense. Technically the Court's judgment would be the same in all situations of unallayed suspiciousness: "due process of lawmaking" having been denied, the law that emerged would have to be declared unconstitutional. The difference would emerge in the event—unlikely, precisely because access is no longer blocked—that the legislature after such a declaration of unconstitutionality reconsidered and repassed the same or a similar law. The fact that due process of lawmaking was denied in 1908 or even in 1939 needn't imply that it was in 1982 as well, and consequently the new law should be upheld as constitutional. In fact I may be wrong in supposing that because women now are in a position to protect themselves they will, that we are thus unlikely to see in the future the sort of official gender discrimination that has marked our past. But if women don't protect themselves from sex discrimination in the future, it won't be because they can't. It will rather be because for one reason or another—substantive disagreement or more likely the assignment of a low priority to the issue—they don't choose to. Many of us may condemn such a choice as benighted on the merits, but that is not a constitutional argument.

WENDY W. WILLIAMS, THE EQUALITY CRISIS: SOME REFLECTIONS ON CULTURE, COURTS, AND FEMINISM

7 WOMEN'S RIGHTS LAW REPT'R 175, 176–200 (1982).

My thesis is that we (feminists) are at a crisis point in our evaluation of equality and women and that perhaps one of the reasons for the crisis is that, having dealt with the easy cases, we (feminists and courts) are now trying to cope with issues that touch the hidden nerves of our most profoundly embedded cultural values.

I will first set the stage for discussion with a brief history of women, equality, and the Supreme Court; second, I will examine what I believe to be evidence that the Supreme Court has, unbeknownst to itself, foundered upon the culturally instilled limits of its ability to dismantle male preserves;

and third, I will speculate that there is also a female preserve, functioning as a hidden hand not only for the courts but for feminists as well, and that this unacknowledged influence may be causing problems for feminist legal theorists.

I. A Brief History of Gender Equality and the Supreme Court

Just before the American Revolution, Blackstone, in the course of his comprehensive commentary on the common law, set forth the fiction that informed and guided the treatment of married women in the English law courts. When a woman married, her legal identity merged into that of her husband; she was civilly dead. She couldn't sue, be sued, enter into contracts, make wills, keep her own earnings, control her own property. She could not even protect her own physical integrity—her husband had the right to chastise her (although only with a switch no bigger than his thumb), restrain her freedom, and impose sexual intercourse upon her against her will.

Beginning in the middle of the nineteenth century, the most severe civil disabilities were removed in this country by state married women's property acts. Blackstone's unities fiction was for the most part replaced by a theory that recognized women's legal personhood but which assigned her a place before the law different and distinct from that of her husband. This was the theory of the separate spheres of men and women, under which the husband was the couple's representative in the public world and its breadwinner; the wife was the center of the private world of the family. Because it endowed women with a place, role, and importance of their own, the doctrine of the separate spheres was an advance over the spousal unities doctrine. At the same time, however, it preserved and promoted the dominance of male over female. The public world of men was governed by law while the private world of women was outside the law, and man was free to exercise his prerogatives as he chose.

* * *

The separate spheres ideology was repudiated by the Supreme Court only [recently]. The engine of destruction was, as a technical matter, the more rigorous standard of review that the Court began applying to sex discrimination cases beginning in 1971.[20] By 1976 the Court was requiring that sex-based classifications bear a "substantial" relationship to an "important" governmental purpose.[21] This standard, announced in *Craig v. Boren*, was not as strong as that used in race cases, but it was certainly a far cry from the rational basis standard that had traditionally been applied to sex-based classifications.

---

[20] In Reed v. Reed, 404 U.S. 71, 75 (1971)[.] * * *

[21] Craig v. Boren, 429 U.S. 190, 197 (1976). * * *

As a practical matter, what the Court did was strike down sex-based classifications that were premised on the old breadwinner-homemaker, master-dependent dichotomy inherent in the separate spheres ideology. Thus, the Supreme Court insisted that women wage earners receive the same benefits for their families under military,[23] social security,[24] welfare,[25] and worker's compensation[26] programs as did male wage earners; that men receive the same child care allowance when their spouses died as women did;[27] that the female children of divorce be entitled to support for the same length of time as male children, so that they too could get the education necessary for life in the public world;[28] that the duty of support through alimony not be visited exclusively on husbands;[29] that wives as well as husbands participate in the management of the community property;[30] and that wives as well as husbands be eligible to administer their deceased relatives' estates.[31]

All this happened in the little more than a decade that has elapsed since 1971. The achievement is not an insubstantial one. Yet it also seems to me that in part what the Supreme Court did was simply to recognize that the real world outside the courtroom had already changed. Woman were in fact no longer chiefly housewife-dependents. The family wage no longer existed; for a vast number of two-parent families, two wage earners were an economic necessity. In addition, many families were headed by a single parent. It behooved the Court to account for this new reality and it did so by recognizing that the breadwinner-homemaker dichotomy was an outmoded stereotype.

II. MEN'S CULTURE: AGGRESSOR IN WAR AND SEX

Of course, not all of the Supreme Court cases involved the breadwinner-homemaker stereotype. The other cases can be grouped in several ways; for my purposes I will place them in two groups. One group is composed of the remedial or compensatory discrimination cases—the cases in which a statute treats women differently and better than men for the purpose of redressing past unequal treatment.[35] The other group, the focus of this

[23] Frontiero v. Richardson, 411 U.S. 677 (1973).

[24] Califano v. Goldfarb, 430 U.S. 199 (1977).

[25] Califano v. Westcott, 443 U.S. 76 (1979).

[26] Wengler v. Druggists Mutual Insurance Co., 446 U.S. 142 (1980).

[27] Weinberger v. Wiesenfeld, 420 U.S. 636 (1975).

[28] Stanton v. Stanton, 421 U.S. 7 (1975).

[29] Orr v. Orr, 440 U.S. 268 (1979).

[30] Kirchberg v. Feenstra, 450 U.S. 455 (1981).

[31] Reed v. Reed, 404 U.S. 71 (1971).

[35] *See, e.g.,* Kahn v. Shevin, 416 U.S. 351 (1974) (Florida statute granting widows but not widowers property tax exemption constitutional because intended to assist sex financially most affected by spousal loss) and Califano v. Webster, 430 U.S. 313 (1977) (Social Security Act section creating benefit calculation formula more favorable to women than men

paper, consists of the cases that don't really seem to fit into any neat category but share a common quality. Unlike the cases discussed above, they do not deal with laws that rest on an economic model of the family that no longer predominates; rather, they concern themselves with other, perhaps more basic, sex-role arrangements. They are what I would call, simply, the "hard" cases, and for the most part, they are cases in which a sex-based classification was upheld by the Court.[36] There are a number of ways one could characterize and analyze them. I want to view them from one of those possible perspectives, namely, what they tell us about the state of our culture with respect to the equality of men and women. What do they say about the cultural limits of the equality principle?

In the 1980–81 Term the Supreme Court decided three sex-discrimination cases. One was *Kirchberg v. Feenstra,*[37] a case which struck down the Louisiana statute that gave husbands total control over the couple's property. That, to my mind, was an easy case. It falls within the line of cases I have already described which dismantle the old separate spheres ideology. The other two cases were *Rostker v. Goldberg,*[38] the case which upheld the male-only draft registration law, and *Michael M. v. Superior Court,*[39] the case upholding the California statutory rape law. They are prime candidates for my hard-cases category.

Justice Rehnquist wrote the opinion of the Court in both *Rostker* and *Michael M.* In *Rostker,* the draft registration case, his reasoning was a simple syllogism. The purpose of the registration, he said, is to identify the draft pool. The purpose of the draft is to provide combat troops. Women are excluded from combat. Thus, men and women are not similarly situated with respect to the draft, and it is therefore constitutional to register males only. Of course, the problem with his syllogism was that one of the

---

held constitutional because intended to compensate women for wage discrimination). * * *

[36]*See, e.g.,* Schlesinger v. Ballard, 419 U.S. 498 (1975) (Court upheld (5–4) law that results in discharge of male officers if twice passed over for promotion, but guarantees female officers 13–year tenure before discharge for lack of promotion); Rostker v. Goldberg, 453 U.S. 57 (1981); Michael M. v. Superior Court, 450 U.S. 464 (1981); Dothard v. Rawlinson, 433 U.S. 321 (1977); Geduldig v. Aiello, 417 U.S. 484 (1974); General Electric Co. v. Gilbert, 429 U.S. 125 (1976); Nashville Gas Co. v. Satty, 434 U.S. 136 (1977). All of these cases were authored either by Justice Stewart or by Justice Rehnquist.

Another case that belongs in this category, even though the gender-based classification was struck down, is the 5–4 decision in Caban v. Mohammed, 441 U.S. 380 (1979). In that case the Court held that a state statute that gave an unwed mother but not an unwed father the right to veto the adoption of her or his child violated the equal protection clause. The Court carefully limited its holding to adoptions of older children who had established a relationship with the father, leaving open the possibility, strongly argued by the dissent, that there were differences between mothers and fathers that would justify a different outcome with respect to the adoption of very young children. * * *

[37]450 U.S. 455 (1981).

[38]453 U.S. 57 (1981).

[39]450 U.S. 464 (1981).

premises—that the purpose of the draft is exclusively to raise combat troops—was and is demonstrably false, but the manipulation of the facts of that case is not what I mean to focus on here.

In *Michael M.*, a 17½-year-old-man and a 16½-year-old woman had sexual intercourse. The 17½-year-old man was prosecuted under California's statutory rape law, which made such intercourse criminal for the man but not the woman. Rehnquist, for a plurality of the Court, accepted the utterly dubious proposition put forward by the State of California that the purpose of the statutory rape statute was to prevent teenage pregnancies. The difference in treatment under the statute is justified, he said, because men and women are not similarly situated with respect to this purpose. Because the young woman is exposed to the risk of pregnancy, she is deterred from sexual intercourse by that risk. The young man, lacking such a natural deterrent, needs a legal deterrent, which the criminal statute provides.

I think that perhaps the outcomes of these two cases—in which the sex-based statutes were upheld—were foregone conclusions and that the only question, before they were decided, was *how* the court would rationalize the outcome. This is perhaps more obvious in the draft case than the statutory rape case, but applies, I think, to both. Let me explain.

Suppose you could step outside our culture, rise above its minutiae, and look at its great contours. Having done so, speculate for a moment about where society might draw the line and refuse to proceed further with gender equality. What does our culture identify as quintessentially masculine? Where is the locus of traditional masculine pride and self-identity? What can we identify in men's cultural experience that most divides it from women's cultural experience? Surely, one rather indisputable answer to that question is "war": physical combat and its modern equivalents. (One could also answer that preoccupation with contact sports is such a difference, but that is, perhaps, just a subset of physical combat.)

Not surprisingly, the Court in *Rostker* didn't come right out and say "We've reached our cultural limits." Yet I did not find it insignificant that even the Justices who dissented on the constitutionality of the draft registration law seemed to concede the constitutionality of excluding women from combat. When Congress considered whether women should be drafted, it was much more forthright about its reasons and those reasons support my thesis. The Senate Armed Services Committee Report states:

> [T]he starting point for any discussion of the appropriateness of registering women for the draft is the question of the proper role of women in combat. The principle that women should not intentionally and routinely engage in combat *is fundamental, and enjoys wide support among our people.*

In addition, the committee expressed three specific reasons for excluding women from combat. First, registering women for assignment to combat "would leave the actual performance of sexually mixed units as an experiment to be conducted in war with unknown risk—a risk that the committee finds militarily unwarranted and dangerous." Second, any attempt to assign women to combat could "affect the national resolve at the time of mobilization." Third, drafting women would "place unprecedented strains on family life." The committee envisioned a young mother being drafted leaving a young father home to care for the family and concluded, "The committee is strongly of the view that such a result * * * is unwise and unacceptable to a large majority of our people." To translate, Congress was worried that (1) sexually mixed units would not be able to function—perhaps because of sex in the foxhole? (2) if women were assigned to combat, the nation might be reluctant to go to war, presumably because the specter of women fighting would deter a protective and chivalrous populace; and (3) the idea that mom could go into battle and dad keep the home fires burning is simply beyond the cultural pale. In short, current notions of acceptable limits on sex-role behavior would be surpassed by putting women into combat.

But what about statutory rape? Not such a clear case, you say. I disagree. Buried perhaps a bit deeper in our collective psyches but no less powerful and perhaps even more fundamental than our definition of man as aggressor in war is man as aggressor in sex. The original statutory rape laws were quite explicitly based on this view. Then, as is true even today, men were considered the natural and proper initiators of sex. In the face of male sexual initiative, women could do one of two things, yield or veto, "consent" or decline. What normal women did not, *should* not, do was to initiate sexual contact, to be the sexual aggressor. The premise underlying statutory rape laws was that young women's chastity was precious and their naivete enormous. Their inability knowingly to consent to sexual intercourse meant that they required protection by laws which made their consent irrelevant but punished and deterred the "aggressive" male.

The Court's opinion, I believe, is implicitly based on stereotypes concerning male sexual aggression and female sexual passivity, despite Justice Rehnquist's express denial of that possibility. His recitation of the facts of the case sets the stage for the sexual gender-role pigeon-holding that follows: "After being struck in the face for rebuffing petitioner's advances, Sharon," we are told, "*submitted* to sexual intercourse with petitioner." Although, in theory, coercion and consent are relevant only to the crime of rape, not to statutory rape, we are thus provided with the details of this particular statutory rape case, details which cast Michael and Sharon as prototypes of the sexually aggressive male and the passive female.

But it is Rehnquist's description of the lower court opinion that most clearly reveals sex role assumptions that lead first the California high court and then the United States Supreme Court to uphold the legislation. He says, "Because *males alone* can 'physiologically cause the result which the law properly seeks to avoid' [pregnancy], the [California Supreme Court] further held that the gender classification was readily justified as a means of identifying *offender* and *victim*."[65] The statement is remarkable for two (related) reasons. The first and most dramatic is the strangeness of the biological concept upon which it is based. Do the justices still believe that each sperm carries a homunculus—a tiny person—who need only be planted in the woman in order to grow? Are they ignorant of ova? Or has sex-role ideology simply outweighed scientific fact? Since no one has believed in homunculi for at least a century, it must be the latter. Driven by the stereotype of male as aggressor/offender and woman as passive victim, even the facts of conception are transformed to fit the image.

The second is the characterization of man and woman as "offender" and "victim." Statutory rape is, in criminal law terms, a clear instance of a victimless crime, since all parties are, by definition, voluntary participants. In what sense, then, can Rehnquist assert that the woman is victim and the man offender? One begins to get an inkling when, later, the Justice explains that the statutory rape law is "protective" legislation: "The statute here protects women from sexual intercourse at an age when those consequences are particularly severe." His preconceptions become manifest when, finally, Rehnquist on one occasion calls the statute a "rape" statute—by omitting the word "statutory" inadvertently exposing his hidden assumptions and underlining the belief structure which the very title of the crime, "statutory rape," lays bare.

What is even more interesting to me than the Court's resolution of these cases is the problem they cause for feminist analysis. The notion that men are frequently the sexual aggressors and that the law ought to be able to take that reality into account in very concrete ways is hardly one that feminists could reject out of hand (I'm thinking here of sexual harassment and forcible rape, among other things): it is therefore an area, like the others I'm about to discuss, in which we need to pay special attention to our impulses lest we inadvertently support and give credence to the very social constructs and behaviors we so earnestly mean to oppose. Should we, for example, defend traditional rape laws on the ground that rape, defined by law as penetration by the penis of the vagina, is a sexual offense the psychological and social consequences of which are so unique, severe, and rooted in age-old power relationships between the sexes that a gender-neutral law would fail in important ways to deal with the world as it really is? Or should we insist that equality theory requires that we reorganize our

---

[65] 450 U.S. at 467 (emphasis added).

understanding of sexual crime, that unwanted sexual intrusion of types other than male-female sexual intercourse can similarly violate and humiliate the victim, and that legislation which defines sexual offenses in gender-neutral terms, because it resists our segregationist urges, and affirms our common humanity, is therefore what feminists should support? These are not easy questions, but they must be answered if feminist lawyers are to press a coherent theory of equality upon the courts in these hard cases.

As for *Rostker v. Goldberg,* the conflicts among feminists were overtly expressed. Some of us felt it essential that we support the notion that a single-sex draft was unconstitutional;[76] others felt that feminists should not take such a position. These latter groups explicitly contrasted the female ethic of nurturance and life-giving with a male ethic of aggression and militarism and asserted that if we argued to the Court that single-sex registration is unconstitutional we would be betraying ourselves and supporting what we find least acceptable about the male world.[77]

To me, this latter argument quite overtly taps qualities that the culture has ascribed to woman-as-childrearer and converts them to a normative value statement, one with which it is easy for us to sympathize. This is one of the circumstances in which the feeling that "I want what he's got but I don't want to be what he's had to be in order to get it" comes quickly to the surface. But I also believe that the reflexive response based on these deeper cultural senses leads us to untenable positions.

The single-sex laws upheld in *Michael M.* and *Rostker* ultimately do damage to women. For one thing, they absolve women of personal responsibility in the name of protection. There is a sense in which women have been victims of physical aggression in part because they have not been

[76]See briefs *amici curiae* of the National Organization for Women, and of a group including Women's Equity Action League, Business and Professional Women, and others, in Rostker v. Goldberg, 453 U.S. 57 (1981).

[77]*See, e.g., A Feminist Opposition to the Draft* (New Haven, Connecticut, 1980) (authors unidentified) in C. MacKinnon, Sexuality and Legality: Toward a Feminist Theory of the State 151–57 (unpublished materials for a course taught at the Stanford Law School, Fall 1980). At the outset, the author(s) state:

> We need at the beginning to differentiate between two kinds of feminism. The one seeks to assimilate women into the traditional institutions of male society. This is the feminism of a small elite. There is another, more broadly based feminism, and this feminism carries with it a fundamental critique of the structure of power in this country.
>
> The one kind of feminism would see the draft as a sign that we have reached equality, or as an opportunity for reaching equality. We consider this to be an extremely narrow notion of equality. We must place the draft in a wider context and see it as an instrument of American policy. The draft, then, is not the only, nor even the primary issue. The real question is what the foreign and domestic policy of this country is, and whether we can assent to it. For a number of reasons we cannot.

Among other grounds for withholding assent, the author or authors "reject the war reflex as an instance of male hysteria; in its essence, feminism is opposed to violence." *Id.* at 151.

permitted to act as anything but victims. For another, do we not acquire a greater right to claim our share from society if we too share its ultimate jeopardies? To me, *Rostker* never posed the question of whether women should be forced as men now are to fight wars, but whether we, like them, must take the responsibility for deciding whether or not to fight, whether or not to bear the cost of risking our lives, on the one hand, or resisting in the name of peace, on the other. And do we not, by insisting upon our differences at these crucial junctures, promote and reinforce the us-them dichotomy that permits the Rehnquists and the Stewarts to resolve matters of great importance and complexity by the simplistic, reflexive assertion that men and women "are simply not similarly situated?"

III. WOMEN'S CULTURE: MOTHER OF HUMANITY

We have looked briefly at the male side of the cultural equation. What are the cultural limits on women's side? Step outside the culture again and speculate. If we find limits and conflicts surrounding the male role as aggressor in war and sex, what will be the trouble spots at the opposite pole? What does the culture identify as quintessentially female? Where does our pride and self-identity lie? Most probably, I think, somewhere in the realm of behaviors and concerns surrounding maternity.

I would expect the following areas to be the places where the move toward equality of the sexes might come into collision with cultural limits, both in judicial opinions and in ourselves: treatment of maternity in the workplace, the tender years presumption, and joint custody of children upon divorce. The issues surrounding pregnancy and maternity are the most difficult from a theoretical point of view and for that reason may be the best illustration of the conflict I am trying to explore.

* * *

Once the Supreme Court took on the task of dismantling the statutory structure built upon the separate spheres ideology, it had to face the question of how to treat pregnancy itself. Pregnancy was, after all, the centerpiece, the linchpin, the essential feature of women's separate sphere. The stereotypes, the generalizations, the role expectations were at their zenith when a woman became pregnant. Gender equality would not be possible, one would think, unless the Court was willing to examine, at least as closely as other gender-related rulemaking, those prescriptions concerning pregnancy itself. On the other hand, the capacity to bear a child is a crucial, indeed definitional, difference between women and men. While it is obvious that the sexes can be treated equally with respect to characteristics that they share, how would it be possible to apply the equality principle to a characteristic unique to women?

So what did the Court do? It drew the line at pregnancy. *Of course* it would take a more critical look at sex discrimination than it had in the past—but, it said, discrimination on the basis of pregnancy is not sex discrimination. Now here was a simple but decisive strategy for avoiding the doctrinal discomfort that inclusion of pregnancy within the magic circle of stricter review would bring with it. By placing pregnancy altogether outside that class of phenomena labeled sex discrimination, the Court need not apply to classifications related to pregnancy the level of scrutiny it had already reserved, in cases such as *Reed v. Reed* and *Frontiero v. Richardson,* for gender classifications. Pregnancy classifications would henceforth be subject only to the most casual review.

The position was revealed for the first time in 1974 in *Geduldig v. Aiello,*[86] a case challenging under the equal protection clause exclusion of pregnancy-related disabilities from coverage by an otherwise comprehensive state disability insurance program. The Court explained, in a footnote, that pregnancy classifications were not sex-based but were, instead, classifications based upon a physical condition and should be treated accordingly[.]

* * *

The second time the Supreme Court said pregnancy discrimination is not sex discrimination was in *General Electric Company v. Gilbert,*[88] decided in 1976. *Gilbert* presented the same basic facts—exclusion of pregnancy-related disabilities from a comprehensive disability program—but this case was brought under Title VII rather than the equal protection clause. The Court nonetheless relied on *Geduldig,* saying that when Congress prohibited "sex discrimination," it didn't mean to include within the definition of that term pregnancy discrimination.

There was, however, an additional theory available in *Gilbert* because it was a Title VII case that was not available in the equal protection case. That theory was that if an employer's rule has a disparate *effect* on women, even though there is no intent to discriminate, it might also violate Title VII. And did the Court find that the exclusion of pregnancy-related disabilities had a disparate effect on women? It did not. Men and women, said Justice Rehnquist, received coverage for the disabilities they had in common. Pregnancy was an *extra* disability, since only women suffered it. To compensate women for it would give them more than men got. So here there was no disparate effect—the exclusion of pregnancy merely insured the basic equality of the program.

The remarkable thing about this statement, like Rehnquist's later assertion in *Michael M.* that only men can "cause" pregnancy, is its peculiarly

[86] 417 U.S. 484.
[88] 429 U.S. 125.

blinkered male vision. After all, men received coverage under General Electric's disability program for disabilities they did not have in common with women, including disabilities linked to exclusively male aspects of the human anatomy. Thus, the only sense in which one can understand pregnancy to be "extra" is in some reverse-Freudian psychological fashion. Under Freud's interpretation, women were viewed by both sexes as inadequate men (men *minus*) because they lacked penises. In Rehnquist's view, woman is now man *plus,* because she shares all his physical characteristics except that she also gets pregnant. Under either of these extravagantly skewed views of the sexes, however, man is the measure against which the anatomical features of woman are counted and assigned value, and when the addition or subtraction is complete, woman comes out behind.

The corollary to *Gilbert* appeared in *Nashville Gas Co. v. Satty,*[94] decided in 1977. There the Court finally found a pregnancy rule that violated Title VII. The rule's chief characteristic was its gratuitously punitive effect. It provided that a woman returning from maternity leave lost all of the seniority she acquired *prior* to her leave. Here, said Rehnquist, we have a case where women are not seeking extra benefits for pregnancy. Here's a case where a woman, now back at work and no longer pregnant, has actually had something taken away from her—her pre-pregnancy seniority—and she therefore suffers a burden that men don't have to bear. This rule therefore has a disproportionate impact on women.

Roughly translated, *Gilbert* and *Satty* read together seemed to stand for the proposition that insofar as a rule deprives a woman of benefits for actual pregnancy, that rule is lawful under Title VII. If, on the other hand, it denies her benefits she had earned while not pregnant (and hence like a man) and now seeks to use upon return to her non-pregnant (male-like) status, it has a disproportionate effect on women and is not lawful.

In summary, then, the Court seems to be of the view that discrimination on the basis of pregnancy isn't sex discrimination. The Court achieves this by, on the one hand, disregarding the "ineluctable link" between gender and pregnancy, treating pregnancy as just another physical condition that the employer or state can manipulate on any arguably rational basis, and on the other hand, using woman's special place in "the scheme of human existence" as a basis for treating her claim to benefits available to other disabled workers as a claim not to equal benefits but to extra benefits, not to equal treatment but to special treatment. The equality principle, according to the Court, cannot be bent to such ends.

In reaction to *Gilbert* and, to a lesser extent, to *Satty,* Congress amended the definitions section of Title VII to provide that discrimination

---

[94] 434 U.S. 136 (1977).

on the basis of pregnancy, childbirth, and related medical conditions was, for purposes of the Act, sex discrimination. The amendment, called the Pregnancy Discrimination Act (PDA),[99] required a rather radical change in approach to the pregnancy issue from that adopted by the Court. In effect, Title VII creates a general presumption that men and women are alike in all relevant respects and casts the burden on the employer to show otherwise in any particular case. The PDA, likewise, rejects the presumption that pregnancy is so unique that special rules concerning it are to be treated as prima facie reasonable. It substitutes the contrary presumption that pregnancy, at least in the workplace context, is like other physical conditions which may affect workers. As with gender classifications in general, it places the burden of establishing pregnancy's uniqueness in any given instance on the employer. The amendment itself specifies how this is to be done:

> [W]omen affected by pregnancy, childbirth, or related medical conditions shall be treated the same for all employment-related purposes, including receipt of benefits under fringe benefit programs, as other persons not so affected but similar in their ability or inability to work * * *.

Under the PDA, employers cannot treat pregnancy less favorably than other potentially disabling conditions, but neither can they treat it more favorably. And therein lies the crisis.

At the time the PDA was passed, all feminist groups supported it. Special treatment of pregnancy in the workplace had always been synonymous with unfavorable treatment; the rules generally had the effect of forcing women out of the work force and back into the home when they became pregnant. By treating pregnancy discrimination as sex discrimination, the PDA required that pregnant women be treated as well as other wage earners who became disabled. The degree to which this assisted women depended on the generosity of their particular employers' sick leave or disability policy, but anything at all was better than what most pregnant women had had before.

The conflict within the feminist community arose because some states had passed legislation which, instead of placing pregnant women at a disadvantage, gave them certain positive protections. Montana, for example, passed a law forbidding employers to fire women who became pregnant and requiring them to give such women reasonable maternity leave.[a] The Miller-Wohl Company, an employer in that state, had a

---

[99]42 U.S.C. § 2000e(k) (Supp. IV 1980).

[a]This article was written before the Supreme Court's decision in *California Federal Savings & Loan Ass'n v. Guerra,* 479 U.S. 272 (1987), which held that a California statute requiring employers to provide leave and reinstatement to women disabled by pregnancy was neither inconsistent with nor pre-empted by the PDA.

particularly ungenerous sick leave policy. Employees were entitled to *no* sick leave in their first year of employment and five days per year thereafter. On August 1, 1979, the company hired a pregnant woman who missed four or five days over the course of the following three weeks because of morning sickness. The company fired her. She asserted her rights under the Montana statute. The company sought declaratory relief in federal court, claiming that Montana's special treatment statute was contrary to the equality principle mandated by the PDA and was therefore invalid under the supremacy clause of the constitution.

Feminists split over the validity of the Montana statute. Some of us felt that the statute was, indeed, incompatible with the philosophy of the PDA. Others of us argued that the PDA was passed to *help* pregnant women, which was also the objective of the Montana statute. Underneath are very different views of what women's equality means; the dispute is therefore one of great significance for feminists.

The Montana statute *was* meant to help pregnant women. It was passed with the best of intentions. The philosophy underlying it is that pregnancy is central to a woman's family role and that the law should take special account of pregnancy to protect that role for the working wife. And those who supported the statute can assert with great plausibility that pregnancy is a problem that men don't have, an extra source of workplace disability, and that women workers cannot adequately be protected if pregnancy is not taken into account in special ways.[110] They might also add that procreation plays a special role in human life, is viewed as a fundamental right by our society, and therefore is appropriately singled out on social policy grounds. The instinct to treat pregnancy as a special case is deeply imbedded in our culture, indeed in every culture. It seems natural, and *right,* to treat it that way.

Yet, at a deeper level, the Supreme Court in cases like *Gilbert,* and the feminists who seek special recognition for pregnancy, are starting from the same basic assumption, namely, that women have a special place in the scheme of human existence when it comes to maternity. Of course, one's view of how that basic assumption cuts is shaped by one's perspective.

---

[110]Some commentators have argued that treating the unique capabilities of women in a special way is not equivalent to granting special, inequitable favors to women. Perhaps the finest articulation of that view is the following passage:

> Uniqueness is a "trap" only in terms of an analysis such as that generated in *Geduldig v. Aiello,* which assumes that maleness is the norm. "Unique" does not necessarily mean uniquely handicapped * * *. To account for pregnancy and breastfeeding is * * * to treat women as equals by respecting the female gender and by ceasing to impose upon women a bifurcated existence; it is to reject antiquated classifications and to restore to women the opportunity to live a continuous life, integrated with respect to career and procreation just as are the lives of men.

Scales. *Towards a Feminist Jurisprudence,* 56 Ind.L.J. 375, 435–36 (1981). * * *

What businessmen, Supreme Court Justices, and feminists make of it is predictably quite different. But the same doctrinal approach that permits pregnancy to be treated *worse* than other disabilities is the same one that will allow the state constitutional freedom to create special *benefits* for pregnant women. The equality approach to pregnancy (such as that embodied in the PDA) necessarily creates not only the desired floor under the pregnant woman's rights but also the ceiling which the *Miller-Wohl* case threw into relief. If we can't have it both ways, we need to think carefully about which way we want to have it.

My own feeling is that, for all its problems, the equality approach is the better one. The special treatment model has great costs. First, as discussed above, is the reality that conceptualizing pregnancy as a special case permits unfavorable as well as favorable treatment of pregnancy. Our history provides too many illustrations of the former to allow us to be sanguine about the wisdom of urging special treatment.

Second, treating pregnancy as a special case divides us in ways that I believe are destructive in a particular political sense as well as a more general sense. On what basis can we fairly assert, for example, that the pregnant woman fired by Miller-Wohl deserved to keep her job when any other worker who got sick for any other reason did not? Creating special privileges of the Montana type has, as one consequence, the effect of shifting attention away from the employer's inadequate sick leave policy or the state's failure to provide important protections to all workers and focusing it upon the unfairness of protecting one class of worker and not others.

Third, as our experience with single-sex protective legislation earlier in this century demonstrated, what appear to be special "protections" for women often turn out to be, at best, a double-edged sword. It seems likely, for example, that the employer who wants to avoid the inconveniences and costs of special protective measures will find reasons not to hire women of childbearing age in the first place.[115]

Fourth, to the extent the state (or employers as proxies for the state) can lay claim to an interest in women's special procreational capacity for "the future well-being of the race," as *Muller v. Oregon* put it in 1908, our freedom of choice about the direction of our lives is more limited than that of men in significant ways. This danger is hardly a theoretical one today. The Supreme Court has recently shown an increased willingness to permit restrictions on abortion in deference to the state's interest in the "potential life" of the fetus, and private employers are adopting policies of exclusion

[115]Title VII does not permit such practices. As a practical matter, however, proof of such motivations is difficult. Actions based on a class sufficiently large to illuminate the hidden motivation are prohibitively expensive and complex.

of women of childbearing capacity in order to protect fetuses from exposure to possibly hazardous substances in the workplace.

More fundamentally, though, this issue, like the others I discussed earlier, has everything to do with how, in the long run, we want to define women's and men's places and roles in society.

Implicit in the PDA approach to maternity issues is a stance toward parenthood and work that is decidedly different from that embodied in the special-treatment approach to pregnancy. For many years, the prototype of the enlightened employer maternity policy was one which provided for a mandatory unpaid leave of absence for the woman employee commencing four or five months before and extending for as long as six months after childbirth. Such maternity leaves were firmly premised on that aspect of the separate spheres ideology which assigned motherhood as woman's special duty and prerogative; employers believed that women should be treated as severed from the labor force from the time their pregnancies became apparent until their children emerged from infancy. Maternity leave was always based upon cultural constructs and ideologies rather than upon biological necessity, upon role expectations rather than irreducible differences between the sexes.

The PDA also has significant ideological content. It makes the prototypical maternity leave policy just described illegal. In its stead, as discussed above, is a requirement that the employer extend to women disabled by pregnancy the same disability or sick leave available to other workers. If the employer chooses to extend the leave time beyond the disability period, it must make such leaves available to male as well as to female parents. Title VII requires sex neutrality with respect to employment practices directed at parents. It does not permit the employer to base policies on the separate spheres ideology. Accordingly, the employer must devise its policies in such a way that women and men can, if they choose, structure the allocation of family responsibilities in a more egalitarian fashion. It forecloses the assumption that women are necessarily and inevitably destined to carry the dual burden of homemaker and wage earner.

Statutes such as the Montana statute challenged in the *Miller-Wohl* case are rooted in the philosophy that women have a special and different role and deserve special and different treatment. Feminists can plausibly and forcibly claim that such laws are desirable and appropriate because they reflect the material reality of women's lives. We can lay claim to such accommodations based on the different pattern of our lives, our commitment to children, our cultural destiny. We can even resort to arguments based on biological imperatives and expect that at least some members of the Supreme Court might lend a sympathetic ear. Justice Stevens suggested one such approach in a footnote to his dissent in *Caban v. Mohammed,*[124] a case invalidating a law that granted to unwed mothers but denied to unwed fathers the right to withhold consent to adoption of their children. He observed:

> [T]here is some sociological and anthropological research indicating that by virtue of the symbiotic relationship between mother and child during pregnancy and the initial contact between mother and child directly after birth a physical and psychological bond immediately develops between the two that is not then present between the infant and the father or any other person. [Citations omitted.]

Justice Stevens' seductive bit of science is useful for making my point, although other illustrations might do as well. Many women who have gone through childbirth have experienced the extraordinary sense of connection to their newborn that the literature calls "bonding." It may be, as some have contended, that the monolithic role women have so long played has been triggered and sustained by this phenomenon, that the effect of this bonding has made it emotionally possible for women to submit to the stringent limitations imposed by law and culture upon the scope and nature of their aspirations and endeavors. On the other hand, it seems entirely possible that the concept of exclusive mother-infant bonding—the latest variation on "maternal instinct"—is a social construct designed to serve ideological ends.

Less than a century ago, doctors and scientists were generally of the view that a woman's intellect, her capacity for education, for reasoning, for public undertakings, was biologically limited. While men were governed by their intellect, women were controlled by their uteruses. No reputable scientist or doctor would make such claims today. But if women are now understood to share with men a capacity for intellectual development, is it not also possible that mother-infant bonding is, likewise, only half the story? What Justice Stevens overlooks is the evidence of the capacity of fathers (the exploration of whose nurturing potential is as new as their opportunity actively to participate in the birth of their children) to "bond" as well.

Again, the question is, are we clinging, without really reflecting upon it, to culturally dictated notions that underestimate the flexibility and potential of human beings of both sexes and which limit us as a class and as individuals?

IV: Conclusion: Confronting Yin and Yang

The human creature seems to be constructed in such a way as to be largely culture bound. We should not, therefore, be surprised that the

[124] 441 U.S. 380 (1979).

creaky old justices on the Supreme Court and we somewhat less creaky feminists sometimes—perhaps often—respond to the same basic characterizations of male and female—although, unquestionably, the justices tend sometimes to do different things with those basic characterizations than feminists would do. At this point, we need to think as deeply as we can about what we want the future of women and men to be. Do we want equality of the sexes—or do we want justice for two kinds of human beings who are fundamentally different? If we gain equality, will we lose the special sense of kinship that grows out of experiences central to our lives and not shared by the other sex? Are feminists defending a separate women's culture while trying to break down the barriers created by men's separate culture? Could we, even if we wanted to, maintain the one while claiming our place within the other? *Michael M.,* which yokes assumptions about male sexual aggression with the conclusion that the sexes are not similarly situated because of women's pregnancy, and the Senate report on the all-male draft, which suggests that what sends men to war and leaves women at home is a fundamental trade-off by which men are assigned to battle and women to child rearing, should give us pause. I for one suspect a deep but sometimes nearly invisible set of complementaries, a yin-yang of sex-role assumptions and assignments so complex and inter-related that we cannot successfully dismantle any of it without seriously exploring the possibility of dismantling it all. The "hard cases"—cases like *Michael M., Rostker, Gilbert, Geduldig, Caban*—give us an opportunity to rethink our basic assumptions about women and men, assumptions sometimes buried beneath our consciousness. They allow us to ask afresh who we are, what we want, and if we are willing to begin to create a new order of things.

CATHARINE A. MACKINNON, DIFFERENCE AND DOMINANCE: ON SEX DISCRIMINATION

FEMINISM UNMODIFIED: DISCOURSES ON LIFE AND LAW, ch. 2 (1987).

What is a gender question a question of? What is an inequality question a question of? These two questions underlie applications of the equality principle to issues of gender, but they are seldom explicitly asked. I think it speaks to the way gender has structured thought and perception that mainstream legal and moral theory tacitly gives the same answer to them both: these are questions of sameness and difference. The mainstream doctrine of the law of sex discrimination that results is, in my view, largely responsible for the fact that sex equality law has been so utterly ineffective at getting women what we need and are socially prevented from having on the basis of a condition of birth: a chance at productive lives of reasonable physical security, self-expression, individuation, and minimal respect and dignity. Here I expose the sameness/difference theory of sex equality, briefly show how it dominates sex discrimination law and policy and underlies its discontents, and propose an alternative that might do something.

* * *

According to the approach to sex equality that has dominated politics, law, and social perception, equality is an equivalence, not a distinction, and sex is a distinction. The legal mandate of equal treatment—which is both a systemic norm and a specific legal doctrine—becomes a matter of treating likes alike and unlikes unlike; and the sexes are defined as such by their mutual unlikeness. Put another way, gender is socially constructed as difference epistemologically; sex discrimination law bounds gender equality by difference doctrinally. A built-in tension exists between this concept of equality, which presupposes sameness, and this concept of sex, which presupposes difference. Sex equality thus becomes a contradiction in terms, something of an oxymoron, which may suggest why we are having such a difficult time getting it.

Upon further scrutiny, two alternate paths to equality for women emerge within this dominant approach, paths that roughly follow the lines of this tension. The leading one is: be the same as men. This path is termed gender neutrality doctrinally and the single standard philosophically. It is testimony to how substance gets itself up as form in law that this rule is considered formal equality. Because this approach mirrors the ideology of the social world, it is considered abstract, meaning transparent of substance; also for this reason it is considered not only to be *the* standard, but *a* standard at all. It is so far the leading rule that the words "equal to" are code for, equivalent to, the words "the same as"—referent for both unspecified.

To women who want equality yet find that you are different, the doctrine provides an alternate route: be different from men. This equal recognition of difference is termed the special benefit rule or special protection rule legally, the double standard philosophically. It is in rather bad odor. Like pregnancy, which always calls it up, it is something of a doctrinal embarrassment. Considered an exception to true equality and not really a rule of law at all, this is the one place where the law of sex discrimination admits it is recognizing something substantive. Together with the Bona Fide Occupational Qualification (BFOQ), the unique physical characteristic exception under ERA policy, compensatory legislation, and sex-conscious relief in particular litigation, affirmative action is thought to live here.

The philosophy underlying the difference approach is that sex is a difference, a division, a distinction, beneath which lies a stratum of human commonality, sameness. The moral thrust of the sameness branch of the doctrine is to make normative rules conform to this empirical reality by granting women access to what men have access to: to the extent that women are no different from men, we deserve what they have. The differences branch, which is generally seen as patronizing but necessary to avoid absurdity, exists to value or compensate women for what we are or have become distinctively as women (by which is meant, unlike men) under existing conditions.

My concern is not with which of these paths to sex equality is preferable in the long run or more appropriate to any particular issue, although most discourse on sex discrimination revolves about these questions as if that were all there is. My point is logically prior: to treat issues of sex equality as issues of sameness and difference *is to take a particular approach.* I call this the difference approach because it is obsessed with the sex difference. The main theme in the fugue is "we're the same, we're the same, we're the same." The counterpoint theme (in a higher register) is "but we're different, but we're different, but we're different." Its underlying story is: on the first day, difference was; on the second day, a division was created upon it; on the third day, irrational instances of dominance arose. Division may be rational or irrational. Dominance either seems or is justified. Difference *is.*

There is a politics to this. Concealed is the substantive way in which man has become the measure of all things. Under the sameness standard, women are measured according to our correspondence with man, our equality judged by our proximity to his measure. Under the difference standard, we are measured according to our lack of correspondence with him, our womanhood judged by our distance from his measure. Gender neutrality is thus simply the male standard, and the special protection rule is simply the female standard, but do not be deceived: masculinity, or maleness, is the referent for both. Think about it like those anatomy models in medical school. A male body is the human body; all those extra things women have are studied in ob/gyn. It truly is a situation in which more is less. Approaching sex discrimination in this way—as if sex questions are difference questions and equality questions are sameness questions—provides two ways for the law to hold women to a male standard and call that sex equality.

* * *

Having been very hard on the difference answer to sex equality questions, I should say that it takes up a very important problem: how to get women access to everything we have been excluded from, while also valuing everything that women are or have been allowed to become or have developed as a consequence of our struggle either not to be excluded from most of life's pursuits or to be taken seriously under the terms that have been permitted to be our terms. It negotiates what we have managed in relation to men. Legally articulated as the need to conform normative standards to existing reality, the strongest doctrinal expression of its sameness idea would prohibit taking gender into account in any way.

Its guiding impulse is: we're as good as you. Anything you can do, we can do. Just get out of the way. I have to confess a sincere affection for this approach. It has gotten women some access to employment and education, the public pursuits, including academic, professional, and blue-collar work; the military; and more than nominal access to athletics. It has moved to change the dead ends that were all we were seen as good for and has altered what passed for women's lack of physical training, which was really serious training in passivity and enforced weakness. It makes you want to cry sometimes to know that it has had to be a mission for many women just to be permitted to do the work of this society, to have the dignity of doing jobs a lot of other people don't even want to do.

* * *

* * * As applied, the sameness standard has mostly gotten men the benefit of those few things women have historically had—for all the good they did us. Almost every sex discrimination case that has been won at the Supreme Court level has been brought by a man. Under the rule of gender neutrality, the law of custody and divorce has been transformed, giving men an equal chance at custody of children and at alimony. Men often look like better "parents" under gender-neutral rules like level of income and presence of nuclear family, because men make more money and (as they say) initiate the building of family units. In effect, they get preferred because society advantages them before they get into court, and law is prohibited from taking that preference into account because that would mean taking gender into account. The group realities that make women more in need of alimony are not permitted to matter, because only individual factors, gender-neutrally considered, may matter. So the fact that women will live their lives, as individuals, as members of the group women, with women's chances in a sex-discriminatory society, may not count, or else it is sex discrimination. The equality principle in this guise mobilizes the idea that the way to get things for women is to get them for men. Men have gotten them. Have women? We still have not got equal pay, or equal work, far less equal pay for equal work, and we are close to losing separate enclaves like women's schools through this approach.

Here is why. In reality, which this approach is not long on because it is liberal idealism talking to itself, virtually every quality that distinguishes men from women is already affirmatively compensated in this society. Men's physiology defines most sports, their needs define auto and health insurance coverage, their socially designed biographies define workplace expectations and successful career patterns, their perspectives and concerns define quality in scholarship, their experiences and obsessions define merit, their objectification of life defines art, their military service defines citizenship, their presence defines family, their inability to get along with each other—their wars and rulerships—defines history, their image defines god, and their genitals define sex. For each of their differences from women, what amounts to an affirmative action plan is in effect, otherwise known as the structure and values of American society. But whenever women are, by this standard, "different" from men and insist on not having it held against us, whenever a difference is used to keep us second class and we refuse to smile about it, equality law has a paradigm trauma and it's crisis time for the doctrine.

What this doctrine has apparently meant by sex inequality is not what happens to us. The law of sex discrimination that has resulted seems to be looking only for those ways women are kept down that have *not* wrapped themselves up as a difference—whether original, imposed, or imagined. Start with original: what to do about the fact that women actually have an ability men still lack, gestating children in utero. Pregnancy therefore is a difference. Difference doctrine says it is sex discrimination to give women what we need, because only women need it. It is not sex discrimination not to give women what we need because then only women will not get what we need.[18] Move into imposed: what to do about the fact that most women are segregated into low-paying jobs where there are no men. Suspecting that the structure of the marketplace will be entirely subverted if comparable worth is put into effect, difference doctrine says that because there is no man to set a standard from which women's treatment is a deviation, there is no sex discrimination here, only sex difference. Never mind that there is no man to compare with because no man would do that job if he had a choice, and of course he has because he is a man, so he won't.

Now move into the so-called subtle reaches of the imposed category, the de facto area. Most jobs in fact require that the person, gender neutral, who is qualified for them will be someone who is not the primary caretaker of a preschool child. Pointing out that this raises a concern of sex in a society in which women are expected to care for the children is taken as day one of taking gender into account in the structuring of jobs. To do that would violate the rule against not noticing situated differences based on gender, so it never emerges that day one of taking gender into account was the day the job was structured with the expectation that its occupant would have no child care responsibilities. Imaginary sex differences—such as

---

[18]This is a reference to the issues raised by several recent cases which consider whether states' attempts to compensate pregnancy leaves and to secure jobs on return constitute sex discrimination. California Federal Savings and Loan Assn. v. Guerra, 758 F.2d 390 (9th Cir.1985), [*aff'd,* 479 U.S. 272 (1987)]; *see also* Miller–Wohl v. Commissioner of Labor, 515 F.Supp. 1264 (D.Montana 1981), *vacated and dismissed,* 685 F.2d 1088 (9th Cir.1982). The position argued in "Difference and Dominance" here suggests that if these benefits are prohibited under Title VII, Title VII is unconstitutional under the equal protection clause.

between male and female applicants to administer estates or between males aging and dying and females aging and dying—I will concede, the doctrine can handle.

I will also concede that there are many differences between women and men. I mean, can you imagine elevating one half of a population and denigrating the other half and producing a population in which everyone is the same? What the sameness standard fails to notice is that men's differences from women are equal to women's differences from men. There is an *equality* there. Yet the sexes are not socially equal. The difference approach misses the fact that hierarchy of power produces real as well as fantasied differences, differences that are also inequalities. What is missing in the difference approach is what Aristotle missed in his empiricist notion that equality means treating likes alike and unlikes unlike, and nobody has questioned it since. Why should you have to be the same as a man to get what a man gets simply because he is one? Why does maleness provide an original entitlement, not questioned on the basis of *its* gender, so that it is women—women who want to make a case of unequal treatment in a world men have made in their image (this is really the part Aristotle missed)—who have to show in effect that they are men in every relevant respect, unfortunately mistaken for women on the basis of an accident of birth?

The women that gender neutrality benefits, and there are some, show the suppositions of this approach in highest relief. They are mostly women who have been able to construct a biography that somewhat approximates the male norm, at least on paper. They are the qualified, the least of sex discrimination's victims. When they are denied a man's chance, it looks the most like sex bias. The more unequal society gets, the fewer such women are permitted to exist. Therefore, the more unequal society gets, the *less* likely the difference doctrine is to be able to do anything about it, because unequal power creates both the appearance and the reality of sex differences along the same lines as it creates its sex inequalities.

The special benefits side of the difference approach has not compensated for the differential of being second class. The special benefits rule is the only place in mainstream equality doctrine where you get to identify as a woman and not have that mean giving up all claim to equal treatment—but it comes close. Under its double standard, women who stand to inherit something when their husbands die have gotten the exclusion of a small percentage of the inheritance tax, to the tune of Justice Douglas waxing eloquent about the difficulties of all women's economic situation.[22] If we're going to be stigmatized as different, it would be nice if the compensation would fit the disparity. Women have also gotten three more years than men get before we have to be advanced or kicked out of the military hierarchy,

[22] Kahn v. Shevin, 416 U.S. 351, 353 (1974).

as compensation for being precluded from combat, the usual way to advance.[23] Women have also gotten excluded from contact jobs in male-only prisons because we might get raped, the Court taking the viewpoint of the reasonable rapist on women's employment opportunities.[24] We also get protected out of jobs because of our fertility. The reason is that the job has health hazards, and somebody who might be a real person some day and therefore could sue—that is, a fetus—might be hurt if women, who apparently are not real persons and therefore can't sue either for the hazard to our health or for the lost employment opportunity, are given jobs that subject our bodies to possible harm. Excluding women is always an option if equality feels in tension with the pursuit itself. They never seem to think of excluding men. Take combat. Somehow it takes the glory out of the foxhole, the buddiness out of the trenches, to imagine us out there. You get the feeling they might rather end the draft, they might even rather not fight wars at all than have to do it with us.

The double standard of these rules doesn't give women the dignity of the single standard; it also does not (as the differences standard does) suppress the gender of its referent, which is, of course, the female gender. I must also confess some affection for this standard. The work of Carol Gilligan on gender differences in moral reasoning[27] gives it a lot of dignity, more than it has ever had, more, frankly, than I thought it ever could have. But she achieves for moral reasoning what the special protection rule achieves in law: the affirmative rather than the negative valuation of that which has accurately distinguished women from men, by making it seem as though those attributes, with their consequences, really are somehow ours, rather than what male supremacy has attributed to us for its own use. For women to affirm difference, when difference means dominance, as it does with gender, means to affirm the qualities and characteristics of powerlessness.

Women have done good things, and it is a good thing to affirm them. I think quilts are art. I think women have a history. I think we create culture. I also know that we have not only been excluded from making what has been considered art; our artifacts have been excluded from setting the standards by which art is art. Women have a history all right, but it is a history both of what was and of what was not allowed to be. So I am critical of affirming what we have been, which necessarily is what we have been permitted, as if it is women's, ours, possessive. As if equality, in spite of everything, already ineluctably exists.

---

[23] Schlesinger v. Ballard, 419 U.S. 498 (1975).

[24] Dothard v. Rawlinson, 433 U.S. 321 (1977); *see also* Michael M. v. Sonoma County Superior Court, 450 U.S. 464 (1981).

[27] Carol Gilligan, *In a Different Voice* (1982).

I am getting hard on this and am about to get harder on it. I do not think that the way women reason morally is morality "in a different voice." I think it is morality in a higher register, in the feminine voice. Women value care because men have valued us according to the care we give them, and we could probably use some. Women think in relational terms because our existence is defined in relation to men. Further, when you are powerless, you don't just speak differently. A lot, you don't speak. Your speech is not just differently articulated, it is silenced. Eliminated, gone. You aren't just deprived of a language with which to articulate your distinctiveness, although you are; you are deprived of a life out of which articulation might come. Not being heard is not just a function of lack of recognition, not just that no one knows how to listen to you, although it is that; it is also silence of the deep kind, the silence of being prevented from having anything to say. Sometimes it is permanent. All I am saying is that the damage of sexism is real, and reifying that into differences is an insult to our possibilities.

So long as these issues are framed this way, demands for equality will always appear to be asking to have it both ways: the same when we are the same, different when we are different. But this is the way men have it: equal and different too. They have it the same as women when they are the same and want it, and different from women when they are different and want to be, which usually they do. Equal and different too would only be parity. But under male supremacy, while being told we get it both ways, both the specialness of the pedestal and an even chance at the race, the ability to be a woman and a person, too, few women get much benefit of either.

* * *

There is an alternative approach, one that threads its way through existing law and expresses, I think, the reason equality law exists in the first place. It provides a second answer, a dissident answer in law and philosophy, to both the equality question and the gender question. In this approach, an equality question is a question of the distribution of power. Gender is also a question of power, specifically of male supremacy and female subordination. The question of equality, from the standpoint of what it is going to take to get it, is at root a question of hierarchy, which—as power succeeds in constructing social perception and social reality—derivatively becomes a categorical distinction, a difference. Here, on the first day that matters, dominance was achieved, probably by force. By the second day, division along the same lines had to be relatively firmly in place. On the third day, if not sooner, differences were demarcated, together with social systems to exaggerate them in perception and in fact, because the systematically differential delivery of benefits and deprivations required making no mistake about who was who. Comparatively speaking, man has been resting ever since. Gender might not even code as difference, might not mean distinction epistemologically, were it not for its consequences for social power.

I call this the dominance approach, and it is the ground I have been standing on in criticizing mainstream law. The goal of this dissident approach is not to make legal categories trace and trap the way things are. It is not to make rules that fit reality. It is critical of reality. Its task is not to formulate abstract standards that will produce determinate outcomes in particular cases. Its project is more substantive, more jurisprudential than formulaic, which is why it is difficult for the mainstream discourse to dignify it as an approach to doctrine or to imagine it as a rule of law at all. It proposes to expose that which women have had little choice but to be confined to, in order to change it.

The dominance approach centers on the most sex-differential abuses of women as a gender, abuses that sex equality law in its difference garb could not confront. It is based on a reality about which little of a systematic nature was known before 1970, a reality that calls for a new conception of the problem of sex inequality. This new information includes not only the extent and intractability of sex segregation into poverty, which has been known before, but the range of issues termed violence against women, which has not been. It combines women's material desperation, through being relegated to categories of jobs that pay nil, with the massive amount of rape and attempted rape—44 percent of all women—about which virtually nothing is done;[30] the sexual assault of children—38 percent of girls and 10 percent of boys—which is apparently endemic to the patriarchal family;[31] the battery of women that is systematic in one quarter to one third of our homes;[32] prostitution, women's fundamental economic condition, what we do when all else fails, and for many women in this country, all else fails often; and pornography, an industry that traffics in female flesh, making sex inequality into sex to the tune of eight billion dollars a year in profits largely to organized crime.

These experiences have been silenced out of the difference definition of sex equality largely because they happen almost exclusively to women. Understand: for this reason, they are considered *not* to raise sex equality

---

[30]Diana Russell and Nancy Howell, "The Prevalence of Rape in the United States Revisited," 8 *Signs: Journal of Women in Culture and Society* 689 (1983) (44 percent of women in 930 households were victims of rape or attempted rape at some time in their lives).

[31]Diana Russell, "The Incidence and Prevalence of Intrafamilial and Extrafamilial Sexual Abuse of Female Children," 7 *Child Abuse & Neglect: The International Journal* 133 (1983).

[32]R. Emerson Dobash and Russell Dobash, *Violence against Wives: A Case against the Patriarchy* (1979); Bruno v. Codd, 90 Misc.2d 1047, 396 N.Y.S.2d 974 (Sup.Ct.1977), *rev'd*, 64 A.D.2d 582, 407 N.Y.S.2d 165 (1st Dep't 1978), *aff'd* 47 N.Y.2d 582, 393 N.E.2d 976, 419 N.Y.S.2d 901 (1979).

issues. Because this treatment is done almost uniquely to women, it is implicitly treated as a difference, the sex difference, when in fact it is the socially situated subjection of women. The whole point of women's social relegation to inferiority as a gender is that for the most part these things aren't done to men. Men are not paid half of what women are paid for doing the same work on the basis of their equal difference. Everything they touch does not turn valueless because they touched it. When they are hit, a person has been assaulted. When they are sexually violated, it is not simply tolerated or found entertaining or defended as the necessary structure of the family, the price of civilization, or a constitutional right.

Does this differential describe the sex difference? Maybe so. It does describe the systematic relegation of an entire group of people to a condition of inferiority and attribute it to their nature. If this differential were biological, maybe biological intervention would have to be considered. If it were evolutionary, perhaps men would have to evolve differently. Because I think it is political, I think its politics construct the deep structure of society. Men who do not rape women have nothing wrong with their hormones. Men who are made sick by pornography and do not eroticize their revulsion are not under-evolved. This social status in which we can be used and abused and trivialized and humiliated and bought and sold and passed around and patted on the head and put in place and told to smile so that we look as though we're enjoying it all is not what some of us have in mind as sex equality.

This second approach—which is not abstract, which is at odds with socially imposed reality and therefore does not look like a standard according to the standard for standards—became the implicit model for racial justice applied by the courts during the sixties. It has since eroded with the erosion of judicial commitment to racial equality. It was based on the realization that the condition of Blacks in particular was not fundamentally a matter of rational or irrational differentiation on the basis of race but was fundamentally a matter of white supremacy, under which racial differences became invidious as a consequence. To consider gender in this way, observe again that men are as different from women as women are from men, but socially the sexes are not equally powerful. To be on the top of a hierarchy is certainly different from being on the bottom, but that is an obfuscatingly neutralized way of putting it, as a hierarchy is a great deal more than that. If gender were merely a question of difference, sex inequality would be a problem of mere sexism, of mistaken differentiation, of inaccurate categorization of individuals. This is what the difference approach thinks it is and is therefore sensitive to. But if gender is an inequality first, constructed as a socially relevant differentiation in order to keep that inequality in place, then sex inequality questions are questions of systematic dominance, of male supremacy, which is not at all abstract and is anything but a mistake.

If differentiation into classifications, in itself, is discrimination, as it is in difference doctrine, the use of law to change group-based social inequalities becomes problematic, even contradictory. This is because the group whose situation is to be changed must necessarily be legally identified and delineated, yet to do so is considered in fundamental tension with the guarantee against legally sanctioned inequality. If differentiation is discrimination, affirmative action, and any legal change in social inequality, is discrimination—but the existing social differentiations which constitute the inequality are not? This is only to say that, in the view that equates differentiation with discrimination, changing an unequal status quo is discrimination, but allowing it to exist is not.

Looking at the difference approach and the dominance approach from each other's point of view clarifies some otherwise confusing tensions in sex equality debates. From the point of view of the dominance approach, it becomes clear that the difference approach adopts the point of view of male supremacy on the status of the sexes. Simply by treating the status quo as "the standard," it invisibly and uncritically accepts the arrangements under male supremacy. In this sense, the difference approach is masculinist, although it can be expressed in a female voice. The dominance approach, in that it sees the inequalities of the social world from the standpoint of the subordination of women to men, is feminist.

If you look through the lens of the difference approach at the world as the dominance approach imagines it—that is, if you try to see real inequality through a lens that has difficulty seeing an inequality as an inequality if it also appears as a difference—you see demands for change in the distribution of power as demands for special protection. This is because the only tools that the difference paradigm offers to comprehend disparity equate the recognition of a gender line with an admission of lack of entitlement to equality under law. Since equality questions are primarily confronted in this approach as matters of empirical fit—that is, as matters of accurately shaping legal rules (implicitly modeled on the standard men set) to the way the world is (also implicitly modeled on the standard men set)—any existing differences must be negated to merit equal treatment. For ethnicity as well as for gender, it is basic to mainstream discrimination doctrine to preclude any true diversity among equals or true equality within diversity.

To the difference approach, it further follows that any attempt to change the way the world actually is looks like a moral question requiring a separate judgment of how things ought to be. This approach imagines asking the following disinterested question that can be answered neutrally as to groups: against the weight of empirical difference, should we treat some as the equals of others, even when they may not be entitled to it because they are not up to standard? Because this construction of the problem is part of what the dominance approach unmasks, it does not arise with the dominance approach, which therefore does not see its own foundations as moral. If sex inequalities are approached as matters of imposed status, which are in need of change if a legal mandate of equality means anything at all, the question whether women should be treated unequally means simply whether women should be treated as less. When it is exposed as a naked power question, there is no separable question of what ought to be. The only real question is what is and is not a gender question. Once no amount of difference justifies treating women as subhuman, eliminating that is what equality law is for. In this shift of paradigms, equality propositions become no longer propositions of good and evil, but of power and powerlessness, no more disinterested in their origins or neutral in their arrival at conclusions than are the problems they address.

* * *

To summarize the argument: seeing sex equality questions as matters of reasonable or unreasonable classification is part of the way male dominance is expressed in law. If you follow my shift in perspective from gender as difference to gender as dominance, gender changes from a distinction that is presumptively valid to a detriment that is presumptively suspect. The difference approach tries to map reality; the dominance approach tries to challenge and change it. In the dominance approach, sex discrimination stops being a question of morality and starts being a question of politics.

You can tell if sameness is your standard for equality if my critique of hierarchy looks like a request for special protection in disguise. It's not. It envisions a change that would make possible a simple equal chance for the first time. To define the reality of sex as difference and the warrant of equality as sameness is wrong on both counts. Sex, in nature, is not a bipolarity; it is a continuum. In society it is made into a bipolarity. Once this is done, to require that one be the same as those who set the standard—those which one is already socially defined as different from—simply means that sex equality is conceptually designed never to be achieved. Those who most need equal treatment will be the least similar, socially, to those whose situation sets the standard as against which one's entitlement to be equally treated is measured. Doctrinally speaking, the deepest problems of sex inequality will not find women "similarly situated" to men. Far less will practices of sex inequality require that acts be intentionally discriminatory. All that is required is that the status quo be maintained. As a strategy for maintaining social power first structure reality unequally, then require that entitlement to alter it be grounded on a lack of distinction in situation; first structure perception so that different equals inferior, then require that discrimination be activated by evil minds who *know* they are treating equals as less.

I say, give women equal power in social life. Let what we say matter, then we will discourse on questions of morality. Take your foot off our necks, then we will hear in what tongue women speak. So long as sex equality is limited by sex difference, whether you like it or don't like it, whether you value it or seek to negate it, whether you stake it out as a grounds for feminism or occupy it as the terrain of misogyny, women will be born, degraded, and die. We would settle for that equal protection of the laws under which one would be born, live, and die, in a country where protection is not a dirty word and equality is not a special privilege.

JOAN C. WILLIAMS, DECONSTRUCTING GENDER

87 MICH.L.REV. 797, 798–799, 837–843 (1989).

I start out, as have many others, from the deep split among American feminists between "sameness" and "difference." The driving force behind the mid-twentieth-century resurgence of American feminism was an insistence on the fundamental similarity of men and women and, hence, their essential equality. Betty Friedan comes to mind as an enormously influential housewife whose focus on men and women as individuals made her intensely hostile to gender stereotyping.[3]

Mid-century feminism, now often referred to somewhat derisively as assimilationism, focused on providing opportunities to women in realms traditionally preserved for men.[4] In the 1980s two phenomena have shifted feminists' attention from assimilationists' focus on how individual women are *like* men to a focus on gender *differences*, on how women as a group differ from men as a group. The first is the feminization of poverty, which dramatizes the chronic and increasing economic vulnerability of women. Feminists now realize that the assimilationists' traditional focus on gender-neutrality may have rendered women more vulnerable to certain gender-related disabilities that have important economic consequences. The second phenomenon that plays a central role in the current feminist imagination is that of career women "choosing" to abandon or subordinate their careers so they can spend time with their small children. These phenomena highlight the fact that deep-seated social differences continue to encourage men and women to make quite different choices with respect to work and family. Thus, "sameness" scholars are increasingly confronted by the existence of gender differences.

---

[3]B. Friedan, The Feminine Mystique (1963). * * *

[4]*See, e.g.,* Wasserstrom, *Racism, Sexism, and Preferential Treatment: An Approach to the Topics,* 24 UCLA L.Rev. 581, 606 (1977). Wasserstrom's comparison of sex to eye color is often criticized by feminists of difference, who argue that something would be lost if sex were treated as a factor as irrelevant as eye color. * * *

Do these challenges to assimilationism prove that we should stop trying to kid ourselves and admit the "real" differences between men and women, as the popular press drums into us day after day, and as the "feminism of difference" appears to confirm? Do such phenomena mean that feminists' traditional focus on gender-neutrality is a bankrupt ideal? I will argue no on both counts, taking an approach quite different from that ordinarily taken by feminists on the sameness side of the spectrum. "Sameness" feminists usually have responded to the feminists of difference by reiterating their basic insight that individual men and women can be very similar. While true, this is not an adequate response to the basic insight of "difference" feminists: that gender exists, that men and women differ as groups. In this article, I try to speak to feminists of difference on their own terms. While I take gender seriously, I disagree with the description of gender provided by difference feminists.

* * *

A. From Gender-Neutrality to Deinstitutionalizing Gender

"Sameness" feminists' focus on the similarities between individual men and individual women led them to advocate "gender-neutral" categories that do not rely on gender stereotypes to differentiate between men and women. Recent feminists have challenged the traditional goal of gender neutrality on the grounds that it mandates a blindness to gender that has left women in a worse position than they were before the mid-twentieth-century challenge to gender roles.

This argument has been made in two different ways. Scholars such as Martha Fineman have argued that liberal feminists' insistence on gender-neutrality in the formulation of "no-fault" divorce laws has led to courts' willful blindness to the ways in which marriage systematically helps men's, and hurts women's, careers.[172] Catharine MacKinnon has generalized this argument. She argues that because women are systematically disadvantaged by their sex, properly designed remedial measures can legitimately be framed by reference to sex.[173]

MacKinnon's "inequality approach" would allow for separate standards for men and women so long as "the policy or practice in question [does not] integrally contribute[ ] to the maintenance of an underclass or a deprived position because of gender status."[174] The strongest form her argument

[172]Fineman, *Implementing Equality: Ideology, Contradiction and Social Change,* 1983 Wis.L.Rev. 789, 791[.]

[173][C. MacKinnon, Sexual Harassment of Working Women—A Case of Sex Discrimination 100–41 (1979) [hereinafter Sexual Harassment]; C. MacKinnon, Feminism Unmodified 35–36 (1987).]

[174]Sexual Harassment, *supra* note [173], at 117. *See* Taub, Book Review, 80 Colum.L.Rev. 1686 (1980).

takes is that adherence to gender roles disadvantages women: Why let liberal feminists' taboo against differential treatment of women eliminate the most effective solution to inequality?

This debate is graced by a core truth and massive confusion. The core truth is that an insistence on gender neutrality by definition precludes protection for women victimized by gender.

The confusion stems from the use of the term gender neutrality. One *could* argue that problems created by the gendered structure of wage labor, or other aspects of the gender system, should not be remedied through the use of categories that identify the protected group by reference to the gender roles that have disadvantaged them. For example, one could argue that workers whose careers were disadvantaged by choices in favor of child care should not be given the additional support they need to "catch up" with their former spouses, on the grounds that the group protected inevitably would be mostly female, and this could reinforce the stereotype that women need special protections. Yet I know of no feminist of any stripe who makes this argument, which would be the position of someone committed to gender neutrality.

Traditionally, feminists have insisted not upon a blindness to gender, but on opposition to the traditional correlation between sex and gender. MacKinnon's crucial divergence is that she accepts the use of sex as a proxy for gender. Thus MacKinnon sees nothing inherently objectionable about protecting workers who have given up ideal worker status[a] due to child-care responsibilities by offering protections to *women.*[175] Her inequality approach allows disadvantages produced by *gender* to be remedied by reference to *sex.* This is in effect an acceptance and a reinforcement of the societal presumption that the social role of primary caretaker is necessarily correlated with possession of a vagina.

MacKinnon's approach without a doubt would serve to reinforce and to legitimize gender stereotypes that are an integral part of the increasingly oppressive gender system. Let's focus on a specific example. Scholars have found that the abolition of the maternal presumption in child-custody decisions has had two deleterious impacts on women.[176] First, in the 90 percent of the cases where mothers received custody, mothers often find themselves bargaining away financial claims in exchange for custody of the children. Even if the father does not want custody, his lawyer often will

[a]By "ideal worker" Williams means the traditional view of an employer that an ideal employee is one without child-care responsibilities. Thus, the concept of "ideal worker" has significantly disadvantaged women in the workplace—eds.

[175]Sexual Harassment, *supra* note [173], at 122–24.

[176]*See* Polikoff, *Why Mothers Are Losing: A Brief Analysis of Criteria Used in Child Custody Determinations,* 7 Women's Rts.L.Rep. 235 (1982); L. Weitzman, [The Divorce Revolution] 217, 310–18 [1985].

advise him to claim it in order to have a bargaining chip with which to bargain down his wife's financial claims. Second, the abolition of the maternal preference has created situations where a father who wants custody often wins even if he was not the primary caretaker prior to the divorce—on the grounds that he can offer the children a better life because he is richer than his former wife. In these circumstances, the ironic result of a mother's sacrifice of ideal worker status for the sake of her children is that she ultimately loses the children.

While these results are no doubt infuriating, do they merit a return to a maternal presumption, as MacKinnon's approach seems to imply? No: the deconstruction of gender, by highlighting the chronic and increasing oppressiveness of the gender system, demonstrates the undesirability of the inequality approach, which would reinforce the gender system in both a symbolic way and a practical one. On a symbolic level, the inequality approach would reinforce and legitimize the traditional assumption that childrearing is "naturally" the province of women. MacKinnon's rule also would reinforce gender mandates in a very concrete way. Say a father chose to give up ideal worker status in order to undertake primary child care responsibility. MacKinnon's rule fails to help him, because the rule is framed in terms of biology, not gender. The result: a strong message to fathers that they should not deviate from established gender roles. MacKinnon's rule operates to reinforce the gender system.

What we need, then, is a rule that avoids the traditional correlation between gender and sex, a rule that is *sex*- but not *gender*-neutral. The traditional goal, properly understood, is really one of *sex*-neutrality, or, more descriptively, one of deinstitutionalizing gender. It entails a systematic refusal to institutionalize gender in any form. This approach mandates not an enforced blindness to gender, but rather a refusal to reinforce the traditional assumption that adherence to gender roles flows "naturally" from biological sex. Reinforcing that assumption reinforces the grip of the gender system as a whole.

For an example that highlights the distinction between gender neutrality and deinstitutionalization, let us return to our "divorce revolution" example. It is grossly unfair for courts suddenly to pretend that gender roles within marriage do not exist once a couple enters the courtroom, and the deinstitutionalization of gender does not require it. What is needed is not a gender-neutral rule but one that avoids the traditional shorthand of addressing gender by reference to sex.

This analysis shows that the traditional commitment, which is really one to deinstitutionalizing gender rather than to gender neutrality, need not preclude rules that protect people victimized by gender. People disadvantaged by gender can be protected by properly naming the group: in this case, not mothers, but anyone who has eschewed ideal worker status to fulfill child-care responsibilities. One court, motivated to clear thinking by a legislature opposed to rules that addressed gender disabilities by reference to sex, has actually framed child-custody rules in this way.[180]

The traditional goal is misstated by the term "gender neutrality." The core feminist goal is not one of pretending gender does not exist. Instead, it is to deinstitutionalize the gendered structure of our society. There is no reason why people disadvantaged by gender need to be suddenly disowned. The deconstruction of gender allows us to protect them by reference to their social roles instead of their genitals.

B. DECONSTRUCTING DIFFERENCE

How can this be done? Certainly the hardest task in the process of deconstructing gender is to begin the long and arduous process of seeing through the descriptions of men and women offered by domesticity. Feminists need to explain exactly how the traditional descriptions of men and women are false. This is a job for social scientists, for a new Carol Gilligan in reverse, who can focus the massive literature on sex stereotyping in a way that dramatizes that Gilligan is talking about metaphors, not actual people. Nonetheless, I offer some thoughts on Gilligan's central imagery: that women are focused on relationships while men are not. As I see it, to the extent this is true, it is merely a restatement of male and female gender roles under the current gender system. Beyond that, it is unconvincing.

This is perhaps easiest to see from Gilligan's description of men as empty vessels of capitalist virtues—competitive and individualistic and espousing liberal ideology to justify this approach to life. Gilligan's description has an element of truth as a description of *gender:* it captures men's sense of entitlement to ideal worker status and their gendered choice in favor of their careers when presented with the choice society sets up between child-care responsibilities and being a "responsible" worker.

Similarly, Gilligan's central claim that women are more focused on relationships reflects gender verities. It is true in the sense that women's lives are shaped by the needs of their children and their husbands—but this is just a restatement of the gender system that has traditionally defined women's social existence in terms of their husbands' need to eliminate child-care and other responsibilities that detract from their ability to function as ideal workers. And when we speak of women's focus on relationships with *men,* we also reflect the underlying reality that the only alternative to marriage for most women—certainly for most mothers—has

[180] *See* Garska v. McCoy, 278 S.E.2d 357, 360–63 (W.Va.1981), *cited in* Williams, *The Equality Crisis: Some Reflections on Culture, Courts, and Feminism,* 7 Women's Rts.L.Rep. 175, 190 n. 80 (1982).

traditionally been poverty, a state of affairs that continues in force to this day.

The kernal of truth in Gilligan's "voices," then, is that Gilligan provides a description of gender differences related to men's and women's different roles with respect to wage labor and child care under the current gender regime. Yet we see these true gender differences through glasses framed by an ideology that distorts our vision. To break free of traditional gender ideology, we need at the simplest level to see how men nurture people and relationships and how women are competitive and powerful. This is a task in which we as feminists will meet considerable resistance, both from inside and outside the feminist movement.

Our difficulty in seeing men's nurturing side stems in part from the word "nurture." Although its broadest definition is "the act of promoting development or growth,"[183] the word derives from nursing a baby, and still has overtones of "something only a mother can do." Yet men are involved in all kinds of relationships in which they promote another's development in a caring way: as fathers, as mentors, as camp counselors, as boy scout leaders. These relationships may have a somewhat different emotional style and tone than do those of women and often occur in somewhat different contexts: that is the gender difference. But a blanket assertion that women are nurturing while men are not reflects more ideology than reality.

So does the related claim that women's voice involves a focus on relationships that is lacking in men. Men focus on relationships, too. How they can be said not to in a culture that deifies romantic love as much as ours does has always mystified me. Perhaps part of what resonates in the claim that men do not focus on relationships is that men *as a group* tend to have a different style than do women: whereas women tend to associate intimacy with self-disclosure, men tend not to. This may be why women forget about the role that relationships play in men's lives, from work relationships, to solidarity based on spectator sports, to time spent "out with the boys." These relationships may not look intimate to women, but they are often important to men.

Ideology not only veils men's needy side, it also veils the competitive nature of many women who want power as avidly as men. "Feminists have long been fiercely critical of male power games, yet we have often ignored or concealed our own conflicts over money, control, position, and recognition * * *. It is time to end the silence."[187] The first step, as these authors note, is to acknowledge the existence of competition in women's lives. Women's desire for control may be exercised in running "a tight ship" on a small income, in tying children to apron strings, or in nagging

[183] The American Heritage Dictionary (William Morris ed. 1970).

[187] Competition: A Feminist Taboo? 1 (V. Miner & H. Longino eds. 1987).

husbands—the classic powerplay of the powerless. Note how these examples tend to deprecate women's desire for power. These are the stereotypes that come to mind because they confirm the ideology that "real" women don't need power. These are ways women's yearning for power has been used as evidence against them, as evidence they are not worthy as wives, as mothers, or as women. Feminists' taboo against competition has only reinforced the traditional view that real women don't need power. Yet women's traditional roles have always required them to be able to wield power with self-confidence and subtlety. Other cultures recognize that dealing with a two-year-old is one of the great recurring power struggles in the cycle of human life. But not ours. We are too wrapped up in viewing childrearing as nurturing, as something opposed by its nature to authoritative wielding of power, to see that nurturing involves a sophisticated use of power in a hierarchical relationship. The differences between being a boss and a mother in this regard are differences in degree as well as in kind.

Moving ever closer to the bone, we need to reassess the role of power in relationships based on romantic love. The notion that a marriage involves complex ongoing negotiations over power may seem shocking. But if we truly are committed to a deconstruction of traditional gender verities, we need to stop blinding ourselves to nurturing outside the home and to power negotiations within it.

MARY ANNE CASE, "THE VERY STEREOTYPE THE LAW CONDEMNS": CONSTITUTIONAL SEX DISCRIMINATION LAW AS A QUEST FOR PERFECT PROXIES

85 CORNELL L.REV. 1447, 1448-1450, 1452-1454, 1457-61 (2000).

[*U.S. v. Virginia* ("*VMI*") marks an] application of the rule that has governed constitutional sex discrimination cases since the early 1970s, a rule quite "simple to articulate" and applied in a way that might satisfy the most rigid of formalists, but one often lurking, as common law rules sometimes do, just below the surface of the decisions applying it. It is my contention that the components of the intermediate scrutiny standard—a practice "substantially related to an important governmental objective"—have rarely been the moving parts in a Supreme Court sex discrimination decision. Rather, the bulk of the work in these decisions has been done by what readers of the opinions may be tempted to treat as mere decorative rhetorical flourish—the proposition that there are constitutional objections to "gross, stereotyped distinctions between the sexes,"[10] that is to say, to "classifications based on sex . . . premised on overbroad generalizations."[11] To determine whether there is unconstitutional sex discrimination, one need

[10]Frontiero v. Richardson, 411 U.S. 677, 685 (1973).

[11]Schlesinger v. Ballard, 419 U.S. 498, 507 (1975).

generally ask only two questions: (1) Is the rule or practice at issue sex-respecting, that is to say, does it distinguish on its face between males and females? and (2) Does the sex-respecting rule rely on a stereotype?

In the constitutional, just as in the statutory, law of sex discrimination, "stereotype" has become a term of art by which is simply meant any imperfect proxy, any overbroad generalization. For a sex-respecting rule to withstand constitutional scrutiny by the Court, it seems to be at least necessary and usually sufficient that it embody some perfect proxy. That is to say, the assumption at the root of the sex-respecting rule must be true of either all women or no women or all men or no men; there must be a zero or a hundred on one side of the sex equation or the other. Even a generalization demonstrably true of an overwhelming majority of one sex or the other does not suffice to overcome the presumption of unconstitutionality the Court has attached to sex-respecting rules: virtually every sex-respecting rule struck down by the Court in the last quarter century embodied a proxy that was overwhelmingly, though not perfectly, accurate.[15] Moreover, overbreadth alone seems to be enough to doom a sex-respecting rule. This is so even though many of the generalizations embodied in sex-respecting rules struck down by the Court are not only overbroad but also "archaic." That is to say, that as well as being descriptively less than perfectly accurate, these generalizations also embody outdated normative stereotypes (i.e., "fixed notions concerning the roles and abilities of males and females"[16] or "the accidental byproduct of a traditional way of thinking about females"[17]).

* * *

I.

PERFECT PROXIES VS. NARROW TAILORING: COMPARING THE REQUIREMENTS

Perhaps the best way of illustrating the difference in the requirements of the prohibition on stereotyping on the one hand and conventional heightened scrutiny on the other is by applying both tests to the facts of the case generally recognized as the first major step toward the construction of today's tiers of scrutiny, *Korematsu v. United States*. Infamously, the Court in *Korematsu* subjected an order banning those of Japanese ancestry from

[15]Thus, for example, in Craig v. Boren, 429 U.S. 190 (1976), though Justice Brennan tried to play games with the math in his majority opinion, more than 90% of those teenagers arrested in Oklahoma for driving while intoxicated were male. See id. at 200 n.8. In Califano v. Goldfarb, 430 U.S. 199 (1977), the evidence indicated that approximately 90% of women and 3% of men in the relevant pool were dependent on their spouses. See id. at 238-39 n.7 (Rehnquist, J., dissenting). These figures are representative, not extraordinary. The exceptions involve proxies, such as those behind sex-based peremptory challenges to jurors, whose accuracy cannot readily be measured.

[16]Mississippi Univ. for Women v. Hogan, 458 U.S. 718, 725 (1982).

[17]Califano, 430 U.S. at 223 (Stevens, J., concurring).

their homes on the West Coast to "the most rigid scrutiny" and nevertheless upheld the order. *Korematsu* is particularly useful as an illustration because it is one of the few race cases in which race is clearly being used as a proxy, specifically, for loyalty to the United States.

If the perfect proxy test is applied to the order in *Korematsu,* it clearly fails the test. The order at issue is clearly both over- and underinclusive. On neither side of the equation does it embody a perfect proxy since there are concededly both loyal Japanese-Americans and disloyal non-Japanese. The difference between this test and the conventional test of strict scrutiny—namely, whether the order is narrowly tailored to meet a compelling governmental interest—is the difference between attention to false positives and false negatives. Whereas the perfect proxy rule asks whether there are any non-traitorous Japanese-Americans and would use a "yes" answer to strike down the rule, avoiding false positives, conventional strict scrutiny, having established that the exclusion of Japanese traitors during a war with Japan is a compelling interest, would instead ask whether there is any rule more narrowly tailored than the exclusion order at issue that would exclude all traitorous Japanese. It seeks to avoid false negatives, but by the least restrictive means. Since there may well be no more narrowly tailored rule that would serve, some rules that might fail the perfect proxy test could nevertheless survive strict scrutiny. This is in fact what happened in *Korematsu,* where the majority acknowledged that, "[i]t was because we could not reject the finding of the military authorities that it was impossible to bring about an immediate segregation of the disloyal from the loyal that we sustained the validity of the . . . order as applying to the whole group.[34]

Among many other things, *Korematsu* may demonstrate how very malleable conventional heightened scrutiny is to judicial manipulation. More importantly, the comparison of the two standards suggests that those commentators who see the standard applied in *VMI* as more exacting than that set forth in the conventional formulation of intermediate scrutiny may be on to something, but this more exacting standard is nothing new. The perfect proxy test has always had the capacity to be more strict even than strict scrutiny. One reason this may not have been obvious in the past may be that, for decades, very few of the race cases to which strict scrutiny was applied involved the use of race as any sort of proxy. Instead, perhaps the most pernicious aspect of the racial classifications at issue in cases from *Brown* to *Loving v. Virginia* was that race was being used for its own sake.

* * *

II.

[34]*Korematsu,* [323 U.S. 214, 219 (1944)] (discussing Hirabayashi v. United States, 320 U.S. 81 (1943), which upheld a similar order imposing a curfew on those of Japanese ancestry).

FINDING PERFECT PROXIES IN SUPREME COURT SEX DISCRIMINATION CASES

In arguing that the rule of decision in constitutional sex discrimination cases has been that of the perfect proxy as described above, I do not mean to indicate endorsement of this rule. Not only do I question whether our concerns about sex equality are appropriately circumscribed by an inquiry only into the closeness of fit of sex-respecting rules, it also seems to me, as it has to many other commentators, that at least some of the perfect proxies found by the Court in upholding sex-respecting rules since the early 1970s are specious.[49] My claim that post-*Frontiero* constitutional sex discrimination cases can be explained by reference to such a rule is a descriptive one, although I address some of its normative implications. Descriptively, while I do not claim that the perfect proxies the Court found are good ones, I do claim (1) that the majority found a perfect proxy in every sex-respecting rule the Court upheld since *Frontiero*, and (2) for every sex-respecting rule struck down since *Frontiero*, no perfect proxy, even a farfetched one, occurred to the court, or to me.

In the years since *Frontiero* [*v. Richardson*], the case in which the Court first expressly noted constitutional opposition to sex-stereotyping, the Court has examined approximately two dozen sex-respecting rules for constitutionality and upheld only about a half dozen. In some of these, the perfect proxy identified was created by another sex-respecting rule whose constitutionality was not before the court; another group involved enduring "[p]hysical differences between men and women"[51] and, in the third group, "[s]ex classifications [were] . . . used to compensate women 'for particular economic disabilities [they have] suffered.'"[52]

Perhaps most notorious is the perfect proxy identified by the plurality

[49] Most obviously, both the law at issue in Michael M. v. Superior Court, 450 U.S. 464 (1981), and the court opinions upholding it, discussed below, rest on stereotypes, as dissenting justices and commentators have made clear. See, e.g., id. at 489 n.2 (Brennan, J., dissenting); Wendy W. Williams, The Equality Crisis: Some Reflections on Culture, Courts, and Feminism, 7 Women's Rts. L. Rep. 175, 186 (1982)

[51] *VMI*, 518 U.S. at 533. This group includes not only *Michael M.*, but also *Parham v. Hughes*, 441 U.S. 347 (1979). In *Parham*, the sex-respecting rule distinguished between the rights of fathers and mothers of illegitimate children not only on the basis of reproductive biology, but also, as with the second group of cases, on the basis of other statutes not before the Court, such as those providing fathers of illegitimate children the opportunity to seek orders of filiation. *See id.* Wendy Williams has criticized this as the "'one discrimination justifies another' approach." Williams, *supra* note 49, at 182 n.50.

[52] *VMI*, 518 U.S. at 533 (quoting Califano v. Webster, 430 U.S. 313, 320 (1977)). The quotations in the text are taken from that portion of the *VMI* opinion in which Justice Ginsburg acknowledged that the "heightened review standard our precedent establishes does not make sex a proscribed classification" and set forth the permissible uses of sex as a classification. Id.

in *Michael M. v. Superior Court*,[53] upholding California's statutory rape law, which criminalized exclusively sexual intercourse with females under the age of eighteen. The statute at issue in *Michael M.* was in several ways a sex-respecting rule: as the California Supreme Court held, it "discriminates on the basis of sex because only females may be victims, and only males may violate the section." For the California Supreme Court, as for the Supreme Court plurality, both halves of this sex distinction rested on a perfect proxy, and hence, the sex distinction embodied in the law was constitutionally permissible. As Justice Rehnquist noted in summarizing the lower court opinion with approval, "the classification was 'supported not by mere social convention but by the immutable physiological fact that it is the female exclusively who can become pregnant.'"[55] Moreover, "males alone can 'physiologically cause the result which the law properly seeks to avoid,' . . . [so] the gender classification was readily justified as a means of identifying offender and victim."[56] Whatever one may think about the archaic nature of Justice Rehnquist's foray into reproductive biology, which conjures up Aristotelian images of homunculi in sperm as well as reinforcing stereotypical notions of female passivity and male activity in sex, he got from it the prefect proxy he seemed to think he needed.

The second group of perfect proxies are no more normatively satisfying. Although * * * Justice Bradley's concurrence in [*Bradwell v. Illinois*] has become the Court's favorite example of what was wrong with earlier views of relations between the sexes, the one aspect of Justice Bradley's opinion that has not been rejected by the modern Court is the notion that one sex discriminatory law can be justified by reference to others not before the court. Just as the legal disabilities of a regime of coverture were used by Justice Bradley to justify Bradwell's exclusion from the bar, so women's exclusion from combat justified both the extra time given women to achieve promotion,[58] and women's exclusion from military registration.[59] And, notwithstanding that the number of women eligible for veterans' preferences in Massachusetts was kept infinitesimally low by "the variety of federal statutes, regulations, and policies that have restricted the number of women who could enlist in the United States Armed Forces, and . . . the simple fact that women have never been subject to a military draft," the Court in *Personnel Administrator v. Feeney* upheld an absolute preference for veterans whose effect was admittedly to keep qualified women out of the upper echelons of the Massachusetts Civil Service.[62] Thus, the combat

---

[53]450 U.S. 464 (1981).

[55][Id. at 467 (quoting [Michael M. v. Superior Court, 601 P.2d 572, 574 (Cal. 1980)].]

[56]Id.

[58]See Schlesinger v. Ballard, 419 U.S. 498 (1975).

[59]See Rostker v. Goldberg, 453 U.S. 57 (1981). * * *

[62][See Personnel Adm'r v. Feeney, 442 U.S. 256, 269-270 (1979).] So-called "women's requisitions" (of the lower echelon, clerical variety) were initially excluded by law from the

exclusion is used to justify both a "benefit" to women (longer time), and women's exemption from the "burden" of draft registration. But, note, of course, that the net result to women includes the resulting deprivation, not only of concrete opportunity as in *Feeney*, but also of citizenship value, inclusion, and respect.

The most interesting group of cases in which a sex-respecting rule was upheld are those in which the purpose of the rule is seen to be to compensate women for discrimination against them as a sex. This group includes *Ballard*, *Califano v. Webster* and *Kahn v. Shevin*. To see how sex can serve as a proxy for discrimination in these cases, it is best to begin with *Ballard*. In this case women were given longer than men to demonstrate their promotability under an "up or out" military regime that mandated discharge for those not promoted within a set time. The justification given was, once again, women's exclusion from combat positions, in which promotability could be demonstrated far more readily. The fact that, notwithstanding the combat exclusion, some women could and did get promoted in the time allowed men did not mean that the proxy was imperfect, because the exclusion still affected all women, even those who by extraordinary effort, luck, or skill managed to overcome its handicap. Similarly, if a rule says a woman must be twice as good as a man to be promoted, and she is twice as good, the discriminatory rule will not have changed the outcome in her case, but she will still not have been exempt from the application of the rule. With this structure of analysis in mind, it becomes easier to see how even the rule in *Kahn*, which gave a $500 annual property tax exemption to widows, but not to widowers, can rely on the perfect proxy of societal discrimination against women, notwithstanding that many female beneficiaries of the exemption may not have suffered identifiable harms from discrimination. As women, they are still surrounded by the ambient level of discrimination against them; just like the military women in *Ballard*, they may be excluded from jobs they neither need nor want, they may succeed despite the exclusion, but they will have been excluded nevertheless. The interesting question posed by these cases and by Justice Ginsburg's reaffirmation in *VMI* that sex-respecting rules will be upheld if they are "used to compensate women 'for particular economic disabilities they have suffered,' . . . 'promote equal employment opportunity,' [or] advance full development of the talent and capacities of our Nation's people,"[67] is what limits, if any, there are on the use of discrimination as a

---

veterans preference and, by the time of *Feeney*, were the sort of "lower paying positions for which males traditionally had not applied." Id. at 270 & n.22.

[67]United States v. Virginia, 518 U.S. 515, 533 (1996).

proxy to justify compensatory or affirmative action schemes for women. Must there be some sort of narrow tailoring, or will any scheme do so long as there is across the board discrimination to serve as a perfect proxy?

BIBLIOGRAPHY

Feminist Jurisprudence

Becker, *Patriarchy and Inequality: Towards a Substantive Feminism*, 1999 U. Chi. Legal F. 21.

DuBois, Dunlap, Gilligan, MacKinnon & Menkel-Meadow, *Feminist Discourse, Moral Values, and the Law—A Conversation,* 34 Buff.L.Rev. 11 (1985).

Finley, *Transcending Equality Theory: A Way Out of the Maternity and the Workplace Debate,* 86 Colum.L.Rev. 1118 (1986).

Gibson, *Childbearing and Childrearing: Feminists and Reform,* 73 Va.L.Rev. 1145 (1987).

Harris, *Race and Essentialism in Feminist Legal Theory,* 42 Stan.L.Rev. 581 (1990).

Littleton, *Reconstructing Sexual Equality,* 75 Cal.L.Rev. 1279 (1987).

Littleton, *Equality and Feminist Legal Theory,* 48 U.Pitt.L.Rev. 1043 (1987).

MacKinnon, *Feminism, Marxism, Method, and the State: An Agenda for Theory,* 7 Signs 515 (1982).

MacKinnon, *Feminism, Marxism, Method, and the State: Toward Feminist Jurisprudence,* 8 Signs 635 (1983).

MacKinnon, C., TOWARD A FEMINIST THEORY OF THE STATE (1989).

Matsuda, *When the First Quail Calls: Multiple Consciousness as Jurisprudential Method,* 11 Women's Rts.L.Rep. 7 (1989).

Minow, M., MAKING ALL THE DIFFERENCE: INCLUSION, EXCLUSION, AND AMERICAN LAW (1990).

Minow, *The Supreme Court 1986 Term—Foreword: Justice Engendered,* 101 Harv.L.Rev. 10 (1987).

Olsen, *Statutory Rape: A Feminist Critique of Rights Analysis,* 63 Tex.L.Rev. 387 (1984).

Olsen, *The Family and the Market: A Study of Ideology and Legal Reform,* 96 Harv.L.Rev. 1497 (1983).

Resnick, *Categorical Federalism: Jurisdiction, Gender and the Globe,* 111 Yale L.J. 619 (2001).

Rhode, JUSTICE AND GENDER: SEX DISCRIMINATION AND THE LAW (1989).

Rifkin, *Toward a Theory of Law and Patriarchy,* 3 Harv.Women's L.J. 83 (1980).

Scales, *Towards a Feminist Jurisprudence,* 56 Ind.L.J. 375 (1981).

Scales, *The Emergence of a Feminist Jurisprudence: An Essay,* 95 Yale L.J. 1371 (1986).

Sunstein, *Feminism and Legal Theory* [review of MacKinnon, FEMINISM UNMODIFIED], 101 Harv.L.Rev. 826 (1988).

Symposium, *Feminist Jurisprudence,* 24 Ga.L.Rev. 759–1044 (1990).

Symposium, *Feminist Jurisprudence—The 1990 Myra Bradwell Day Panel,* 1 Colum.J.Gender & L. 5 (1991).

Taub and Schneider, Perspectives on Women's Subordination and the Role of Law, in THE POLITICS OF LAW 117 (D. Kairys ed. 1982).

West, *Jurisprudence and Gender,* 55 U.Chi.L.Rev. 1 (1988).

West, *The Difference in Women's Hedonic Lives: A Phenomenological Critique of Feminist Legal Theory,* 3 Wisc.Women's L.J. 81 (1987).

Whitman, *Law and Sex* [review of MacKinnon, FEMINISM UNMODIFIED], 86 Mich.L.Rev. 1388 (1988).

Williams, *On Being the Object of Property,* 14 Signs 5 (1988).

Wishik, *To Question Everything: The Inquiries of Feminist Jurisprudence,* 1 Berkeley Women's L.J. 64 (1985).

Wolgast, E., EQUALITY AND THE RIGHTS OF WOMEN (1980).

Gender and the Constitution

Allen, *Autonomy's Magic Wand: Abortion and Constitutional Interpretation,* 72 B.U.L.Rev. 683 (1992).

Brown, Emerson, Falk & Freedman, *The Equal Rights Amendment: A Constitutional Basis for Equal Rights for Women,* 80 Yale L.J. 871 (1971).

Colker, *Anti-Subordination Above All: Sex, Race, and Equal Protection,* 61 N.Y.U.L.Rev. 1003 (1986).

Cruz, *Disestablishing Sex and Gender*, 90 Cal.L.Rev. 997 (2002).

Farina, *Conceiving Due Process,* 3 Yale J.L. & Feminism 189 (1991).

Freedman, *Sex Equality, Sex Differences, and the Supreme Court,* 92 Yale L.J. 913 (1983).

Ginsburg, *Gender and the Constitution,* 44 U.Cin.L.Rev. 1 (1975).

Higgins, *"By Reason of Their Sex": Feminist Theory, Postmodernism, and Justice,* 80 Cornell L. Rev. 1536 (1995).

Higgins, *Democracy and Feminism,* 110 Harv.L.Rev. 1657 (1997).

Karst, *Woman's Constitution,* 1984 Duke L.J. 447.

Kay, *Models of Equality,* 1985 U.Ill.L.Rev. 39.

Kirp, D., M. Yudof, and M. Franks, GENDER JUSTICE (1986).

Law, *Rethinking Sex and the Constitution,* 132 U.Pa.L.Rev. 955 (1984).

Maltz, *Sex Discrimination in the Supreme Court—A Comment on Sex Equality, Sex Differences, and the Supreme Court,* 1985 Duke L.J. 177.

Sullivan, *Constitutionalizing Women's Equality*, 90 Cal.L.Rev. 735 (2002).

Sunstein, *Neutrality in Constitutional Law (With Special Reference to Pornography, Abortion, and Surrogacy)*, 92 Colum.L.Rev. 1 (1992).

Wildman, *The Legitimation of Sex Discrimination: A Critical Response to Supreme Court Jurisprudence*, 63 Or.L.Rev. 265 (1984).

Sex Discrimination and the Law

Abrams, *The New Jurisprudence of Sexual Harassment*, 83 Cornell L. Rev. 1169 (1998).

Austin, *Sapphire Bound!*, 1989 Wis.L.Rev. 539.

Becker, *Obscuring the Struggle: Sex Discrimination, Social Security, and Stone, Seidman, Sunstein & Tushnet's* CONSTITUTIONAL LAW, 89 Colum.L.Rev. 264 (1989).

Becker, *Prince Charming: Abstract Equality*, 1987 Sup.Ct.Rev. 201.

Chamallas, *Deepening the Legal Understanding of Bias: On Devaluation and Biased Prototypes*, 74 S. Cal.L.Rev. 747 (2001).

Dowd, *Maternity Leave: Taking Sex Differences into Account*, 54 Fordham L.Rev. 699 (1986).

Estrich, *Rape*, 95 Yale L.J. 1087 (1986).

Franke, *The Central Mistake of Sex Discrimination Law: The Disaggregation of Sex From Gender*, 144 U.Penn.L.Rev. 1 (1995).

Frug, *Securing Job Equality for Women: Labor Market Hostility to Working Mothers*, 59 B.U.L.Rev. 55 (1979).

Hasday, *The Principle and Practice of Women's "Full Citizenship": A Case Study of Sex-Segregated Public Education*, 101 Mich.L.Rev. 755 (2002).

Kovacic-Fleischer, *United States v. Virginia's New Gender Equal Protection Analysis with Ramifications for Pregnancy, Parenting, and Title VII*, 50 Vand.L.Rev. 845 (1997).

Krieger & Cooney, *The Miller-Wohl Controversy: Equal Treatment, Positive Action and the Meaning of Women's Equality*, 13 Golden Gate U.L.Rev. 513 (1983).

Law, *Women, Work, Welfare, and the Preservation of Patriarchy*, 131 U.Pa. L.Rev. 1249 (1983).

MacKinnon, C., SEXUAL HARASSMENT OF WORKING WOMEN: A CASE STUDY OF SEX DISCRIMINATION (1979).

Powers, *Sex Segregation and the Ambivalent Directions of Sex Discrimination Law*, 1979 Wisc.L.Rev. 55.

Scales-Trent, *Black Women and the Constitution: Finding Our Place, Asserting Our Rights*, 24 Harv.C.R.–C.L.L.Rev. 9 (1989).

Scarborough, *Conceptualizing Black Women's Employment Experiences,* 98 Yale L.J. 1457 (1989).

Schultz, *Telling Stories About Women and Work: Judicial Interpretations of Sex Segregation in the Workplace in Title VII Cases Raising the Lack of Interest Argument,* 103 Harv.L.Rev. 1750 (1990).

Sturm, *Second Generation Employment Discrimination: A Structural Approach*, 101 Colum.L.Rev. 458 (2001).

Symposium, *Comparable Worth,* 20 Mich.J.L.Ref. (1986).

Taub, *Keeping Women in their Place: Stereotyping Per Se as a Form of Employment Discrimination,* 21 B.C.L.Rev. 345 (1980).

Taub, *Review of MacKinnon,* SEXUAL HARASSMENT OF WORKING WOMEN, 80 Colum.L.Rev. 1686 (1980).

Williams, *Equality's Riddle: Pregnancy and the Equal Treatment/Special Treatment Debate,* 13 N.Y.U.Rev.L. & Soc.Change 325 (1985).

Chapter VIII

AFFIRMATIVE ACTION

The readings in this Chapter analyze several different aspects of the affirmative action debate. We begin by asking whether it is ever appropriate to take account of race. Many Americans who sincerely oppose racial discrimination believe that the Constitution requires the government to be colorblind. But this is a position that rules out most forms of affirmative action. In Section A we inspect the arguments for and against colorblindness; we also look at the alternative—race-consciousness. In Section B we examine standards and justifications for evaluating affirmative action programs, most recently addressed by the Supreme Court in cases involving the University of Michigan.[1]

A. COLORBLINDNESS OR RACE-CONSCIOUSNESS

Many people think that the most decent and simple solution to the problem of racial division is to ignore the fact of race. An early statement of this idea is found in Justice Harlan's dissent in *Plessy v. Ferguson:* "There is no caste here. Our Constitution is color-blind, and neither knows nor tolerates classes among citizens."[2] In modern times Alexander Bickel captured the same notion in another memorable phrase: "discrimination on the basis of race is illegal, immoral, unconstitutional, inherently wrong, and destructive of democratic society."[3]

William Van Alstyne is a strong supporter of colorblindness. It is the ideal the Supreme Court rejected in the 19th century, and embraced in *Brown v. Board of Education*[4] (and for 20 years thereafter). In treating all people alike it is self-evidently fair. And because the rule of colorblindness is clear and categorical it cannot be manipulated the way equal protection rules were after the Civil War: courts are not permitted to ask whether racial classifications are "reasonable."

---

[1] Grutter v. Bollinger, 123 S.Ct. 2325 (2003); Gratz v. Bollinger, 123 S.Ct. 2411 (2003).

[2] 163 U.S. 537, 559, 16 S.Ct. 1138, 1146, 41 L.Ed. 256 (1896).

[3] Alexander M. Bickel, The Morality of Consent 133 (1975).

[4] 63 U.S. 537, 559, 16 S.Ct. 1138, 1146, 41 L.Ed. 256 (1896).

Laurence Tribe reads the Court's progress from *Plessy* to *Brown* in a different way. According to Tribe the original intent of the framers of the Fourteenth Amendment tells against colorblindness. And it is not clear that *Brown* enshrines that principle either: we might better understand it as a decision against racial subjugation. That is a holding we could easily square with most kinds of affirmative action.

Tribe is concerned with legal support (in text, intent, and precedent) for the ideal of colorblindness. Neil Gotanda points to a very different kind of problem. Advocates of colorblindness assume that race is at bottom just a question of skin pigment, a sense datum that we can overlook, the way truly colorblind individuals do with shades of red and green. This is not so. Gotanda contends that race is at bottom a social construct rather than an empirical fact. The American system of racial classification incorporates assumptions about white racial purity and black enslaveability that we do not find, for example, in the West Indies or Latin America. The practice of colorblindness will allow us to cover these assumptions up, but they will not go away.

Alexander Aleinikoff makes a case for race-consciousness as an alternative to colorblindness. There is a deep humanism in seeing other races as like ourselves. But we need to go further—to see ourselves as others see us, to realize that our own culture is not a privileged point of view but just one among many. The calls for "black pride" and "black power" in the 1960's were a demand for a reorientation of this sort, and the consequences have been startling.

WILLIAM VAN ALSTYNE, RITES OF PASSAGE: RACE, THE SUPREME COURT, AND THE CONSTITUTION

46 U.CHI.L.REV. 775, 780–784, 788–789, 792 (1979).

A. THE ORIGINAL INTERPRETATION

The first passage for the Court came with the immediate adjudication of race-related cases on the heels of the Civil War amendments. With the exception of a few notable cases striking down the most egregious race regulations,[13] the Supreme Court adopted a wholly tolerant and deferential rendering of all three amendments, imputing to them only the most modest consequences.[14] Federal statutes flatly forbidding racial discrimination by commercial enterprises were held to be excessive, as acts of an unwarranted

[13] *E.g.*, Strauder v. West Virginia, 100 U.S. 303 (1880)[.] *Cf.* Virginia v. Rives, 100 U.S. 313, 319 (1880)[;] *Ex parte* Virginia, 100 U.S. 339 (1880)[.]

[14] *E.g.*, The Slaughter-House Cases, 83 U.S. (16 Wall.) 36 (1873)[.]

color-blind zeal. * * * The cases so disposing of this matter, decided by the Supreme Court in 1883, were ironically entitled *The Civil Rights Cases.*[15]

When regulation by race was the government's own, rather than the practice of private parties, the Court's decisions were nearly as tolerant of legislative discretion as they had been of commercial discrimination in *The Civil Rights Cases*. Allocation by race was not per se forbidden by the Constitution, the Court held, as the consideration of race might be thought by many reasonable persons as sometimes germane to a variety of important social concerns. Thus, the question was not whether political bodies regulated on the basis of race; it was the different question whether the particular regulation by race was constitutionally "reasonable."

* * *

This view of the matter steadily developed between 1873 and the twilight of the 19th century. It was cemented in 1896 in the "separate-but-equal" decision of *Plessy v. Ferguson.*[16] The decision upheld a state law requiring separate passenger cars for white and for black riders: neither was worse off than the other in the quality of accommodations to be furnished to each; neither was more or less protected than the other (rather, each was equally protected) by the racial regulation a legislative body deemed reasonable in the public interest.

There was but one dissent that took a less measured view and would have imposed upon the fourteenth amendment a more categorical imperative. Less flexible than others on the Supreme Court at the time, Justice Harlan was prepared to read into the Civil War amendments what was, to be sure, neither explicitly provided by their terms nor compelled by their compromised legislative history. Proceeding from a more basic premise than that either of these considerations necessarily controlled the matter, Harlan put his finger on the lessons of his own contemporary history. Prior to the Civil War amendments, race was the basis on which status had been determined, worth assigned, entitlements settled, and legal rights measured. It had been iniquitous from the very beginning, and it subsequently proved to be a disaster for the entire country. He believed the enactment of the Civil War amendments should therefore be construed by the Court as altogether disallowing it. Government could not determine worth, assign entitlements, or measure legal rights by race *at all* * * *.

The point of emphasis here is fundamental. It is not that when race is used, all persons identified to each race must be as well regarded as all persons identified to some other race. The thing condemned is not that members of each race must be "equally" protected under laws distinguish-

[15] 109 U.S. 3 (1883)[.]

[16] 163 U.S. 537 (1896).

ing them by their race, nor that they are assigned entitlements unequally on the basis of race. The thing condemned, rather, is the assignment of entitlements by race. It is the impropriety of the *basis* of assignment, not the modicum thus assigned, that constitutes the government's offense:

> These notable additions to the fundamental law [the thirteenth, fourteenth, and fifteenth amendments] were welcomed by the friends of liberty throughout the world. *They removed the race line from our governmental systems.*

The Harlan opinion passed into history at the time, an artifact of mere dissent, discredited by the dominant view that the fourteenth amendment had not withdrawn from legislative bodies a political license to regulate by race. The outcome of the case was taken quite seriously, moreover, as legislatures enacted an ever-enlarging sprawl of race-based laws. Indeed, a half-century later, the dominant legislative response to *Brown v. Board of Education*[22] was one of fury, precisely on this account. For however the Court might phrase the apologetics of that decision, the message as it appeared from the outside was that what was not previously understood to be unconstitutional was now accused of being unconstitutional after all: the use of race to allocate—albeit equally—those facilities deemed most appropriate for persons of that race.

B. The Second Rite of Passage

In the swift consecutive series of per curiam decisions issued by the Supreme Court during the two years following *Brown,* the Court made no further use whatever—indeed, it made no inquiry—as to whether the particular race regulation disadvantaged some more than others. Neither did it ask whether the law stigmatized some more than others, or whether the law was enacted by whites and opposed by blacks, enacted by consent of some of each and opposed by many of each, or whatever. Rather, that line of per curiam decisions appeared more completely to enact Harlan's view that the Civil War amendments altogether "removed the race line from our governmental systems."

Between 1955 and 1976, moreover, virtually every other race-related decision by the Supreme Court appeared to convey this same message. To the reasonably discerning, this appeared true even in instances involving highly controversial judicial decrees that paired racially identifiable schools, redrafted attendance lines, or mandated busing. In each instance, the fulcrum of judicial leverage was an *existing governmental* race line, which the particular judicial order sought to remove. The object was thus to disestablish particular, existing uses of race, not to establish new ones. Indeed, decrees that would subsequently presume to require race-conscious

[22] 347 U.S. 483 (1954).

decisions for any other purpose, for example, to maintain "proportions" or "balances" by race designation, were swiftly reversed.[26]

This second rite of passage was accompanied by consistent developments in the 1960s in the Supreme Court and then, encouragingly, in Congress and the executive branch as well. [Here Van Alstyne discusses the original enacted versions of Title VI and Title VII of the 1964 Civil Rights Act, Executive Order No. 11234, and several other provisions that prohibited racial discrimination period. As of this time, in short, the Court, Congress, and the Executive Branch seemed to be of a common resolve (namely, as Van Alstyne put it, that "we shall not see racism disappear by employing its own ways of classifying people and of measuring their rights [by race]").]

Even when the sole use of race by government was to suggest that race is at least an important political datum—the government itself not presuming to say of what kind of significance—the Supreme Court disallowed the mere encouragement to be "race conscious." A case that expresses that view as well as any other case was *Anderson v. Martin,*[44] decided succinctly and unanimously in 1964. The case involved a state statute that facilitated voter information respecting the racial identification of each candidate for local public office—by designating each candidate's race on each ballot, accurately and truthfully. Voters who might think that datum germane (as a white person to vote white, a black to vote black, a white to vote black, a black to vote white—as each might see a different, but steadfast significance in the idea) could hardly be kept from using it even in the absence of such specific ballot information. As the ballot designation by state law was nonetheless thought objectionable, it could not have been because any candidate was exempt from it, since all were equally subject to it. It must have been, rather, that each was being *individually* disadvantaged insofar as the state thought it appropriate to encourage voters to attribute at least *some* significance to every candidate's race—and that the morality of the Civil War amendments was opposed to the very idea of such encouragement. And this, indeed, was the foundation of the decision in *Anderson v. Martin*: not that a black candidate in particular might be victimized insofar as the state's "truth in candidacy" statute would gratuitously stimulate white bloc votes, but that the state could not thus encourage such racial disadvantaging of *anyone,* white or black.

* * *

[26] *E.g.,* Pasadena City Bd. of Educ. v. Spangler, 427 U.S. 424 (1976). *See also* Dayton Bd. of Educ. v. Brinkman, 433 U.S. 406 (1977); Milliken v. Bradley, 418 U.S. 717 (1974); Keyes v. School Dist. No. 1, 413 U.S. 189 (1973).

[44] 375 U.S. 399 (1964).

In this twenty-year pattern of development, from 1954 to 1974, the Supreme Court's unambiguous lesson thus seemed to be that race was indeed constitutionally withdrawn from the incorrigible temptations of governmental use.

LAURENCE H. TRIBE, "IN WHAT VISION OF THE CONSTITUTION MUST THE LAW BE COLOR-BLIND?"

20 JOHN MARSHALL L.REV. 201–207 (1986).

[M]y focus today will be on the affirmative action controversy as a window into the constitutional and judicial vision—the philosophy of constitutional meaning and judicial role—of those who deem race-specific preferences for minorities to be presumptively invalid, subject only to a narrow exception for judicial relief to identified victims of proven race discrimination. I will call these the "race neutralists." My question is: Why do the race neutralists set themselves against the view, expressed by Justice Blackmun in his separate *Bakke* opinion, that "to get beyond racism, we must first take account of race * * * [a]nd * * * to treat some persons equally, we must * * * treat them differently."[7] In other words, what constitutional sources or theories can the race neutralists invoke?

To begin with, the race neutralists might invoke the notion that *all* racial classifications, the supposedly benign no less than the overtly malign, are "inherently suspect." Now that broad notion itself has a somewhat suspect source: it was given its first explicit articulation in the justly infamous 1944 decision—*Korematsu v. United States*[8]—upholding our government's forced relocation of Japanese-American citizens to concentration camps. Before announcing its result in *Korematsu,* the Supreme Court proclaimed that "*all* legal restrictions which curtail the civil rights of a single racial group are immediately suspect * * *. Courts must subject them to the most rigid scrutiny."[9] It is noteworthy that the Court was speaking there of restricting "civil rights," and *not* of allocating state-created opportunities for individual advancement. More important still, even in *Korematsu* the Supreme Court held that the *point* of strict scrutiny for racial classifications is to detect whether they reflect "[p]ressing public necessity" or merely "racial antagonism."[10] Racial antagonism, of course, is hardly the motive of today's minority set-aside programs.

---

[7]Regents of Univ. of Cal. v. Bakke, 438 U.S. 265, 407 (1978) (Blackmun, J., separate opinion).

[8]323 U.S. 214 (1944).

[9]*Id.* at 216 (emphasis added).

[10]*Id.*

Seeking a sounder source than *Korematsu,* the race neutralists often recur to the first Justice Harlan's dissent in *Plessy v. Ferguson.*[11] Indeed, Solicitor General Charles Fried's argument in *Wygant v. Jackson Board of Education* leans heavily on *Plessy.*[12] The Solicitor General says: "Whether a Plessy is ejected from a railroad coach because he is one-eighth black or laid-off because he is seven-eighths white, the concrete wrong to him is much the same."[13] That may seem counterintuitive, however. For those "wrongs" are *not* self-evidently the same: the actual wrong to Mr. Plessy was a denigration of his moral worth, a perpetuation of slavery, and a reinforcement of his political exclusion; none of this, certainly, can be said of the hypothesized converse harm. Nonetheless, the race neutralists always offer the obligatory quotation from Justice Harlan: "Our Constitution is color-blind." Those who quote the elder Justice Harlan with such abandon should consider the context of the preceding five sentences in that justly famous dissent:

> The white race deems itself to be the dominant race in this country. *And so it is,* in prestige, in achievements, in education, in wealth and in power. So, I doubt not, it will continue to be for all time, if it remains true to its great heritage and holds fast to the principles of constitutional liberty. But in view of the Constitution, in the eye of the law, there is in this country no superior, dominant, ruling class of citizens. There is no caste here. Our Constitution is color-blind * * *.[15]

Perhaps it is anachronistic and even unfair to stress too heavily the manifest racism in Justice Harlan's full statement. But even for this late nineteenth-century proponent of white dominance, the color-blind ideal, it turns out, was only shorthand for the concept that the Fourteenth Amendment prevents our law from enshrining and perpetuating white supremacy. To say that this particular vice is shared, automatically or presumptively, by race-specific minority set-asides strikes many as far-fetched.

So the question remains unanswered: *Why* would anyone equate laying off a white Plessy to make room for a black worker, and ejecting a black Plessy from a railroad coach to maintain white supremacy?

The race neutralists' reply to that question sometimes involves a reference to the "original intention" of the Fourteenth Amendment's Framers.[17]

---

[11]163 U.S. 537 (1896).

[12]See Brief of the United States as Amicus Curiae Supporting Petitioners, Wygant v. Jackson Bd. of Educ., 106 S.Ct. 1842 (1986).

[13]*Id.* at 21.

[15][163 U.S. at 559 (Harlan, J., dissenting) (emphasis added).]

[17]*E.g.,* Reynolds, *Individualism v. Group Rights: The Legacy of Brown,* 93 Yale L.J. 995, 997 (1984) ("History faithfully records that the purpose of the [Thirteenth, Fourteenth and Fifteenth] Amendments was to end forever a system which determined legal rights, measured status, and allocated opportunities on the basis of race, and to erect in its place a regime of race neutrality."). *Compare* Bork, *Original Intent and the Constitution,* 7

But that argument faces an enormous stumbling block. I am not referring to the often-noted historical fact that those same Framers created a Freedman's Bureau to assist former slaves.[18] As the Solicitor General has pointed out, those pieces of nineteenth century legislation were at least partially, if not exclusively, designed to assist *actual victims* of slavery.[19] I am referring to the fact that we know, with as much certainty as such matters ever permit, that the Framers of the Fourteenth Amendment did not think "equal protection of the laws" made *all* racial distinctions in law unconstitutional; they did not intend, for example, to outlaw racially segregated public schools.[20] It involves quite a stretch, then, to take their original intentions as an argument that all race-specific distinctions, even those designed to facilitate practical equality, are either automatically or presumptively unconstitutional.

The necessary response of the race neutralists is, of course, that the Supreme Court was right in *Brown v. Board of Education*—and that the 1954 Court saw the "original intention" more clearly than its 1896 predecessor, when *Brown* rightly held that *all* official distinctions by race are presumptively unconstitutional. But *did* it so hold? That is only the most sweeping and "activist" of at least several equally plausible readings of *Brown.* I will focus upon two such readings, identified as "*Brown*–A" and "*Brown*–B."

> *Brown*–A says that, more than a century after the Civil War, *all* race distinctions must now be banned as inherently "unequal;" in light of modern and more enlightened "values," courts must create a general Fourteenth Amendment right never to be disadvantaged by law on account of one's race, even if this *is* a right the Fourteenth Amendment's authors would not have endorsed.
>
> *Brown*–B says the Fourteenth Amendment's command of "equal protection of the laws" was *always* intended, at its most basic level, to ban the use of law to subjugate a racial group; we now see, as the 1896 Court did not, that racial segregation by law in public schools and other public facilities in fact subjugated blacks, despite its appearance of symmetry and equality, because it stood for white supremacy and therefore denied the minority "equal protection." Thus we are creating no *new* basic right the Fourteenth Amendment's authors would have

---

Humanities 22 (1986) *with* Tribe, *The Holy Grail of Original Intent, id.* at 23.

[18]*See* Schnapper, *Affirmative Action and the Legislative History of the Fourteenth Amendment,* 71 Va.L.Rev. 753, 761, 772–73 (1985) (in practice, under the 1865 Act, most of the Bureau's programs applied only to black freedmen; in addition, the 1866 Act contained explicitly race-conscious measures)

[19]Brief of the United States as Amicus Curiae Supporting Petitioners at 14–15, Wygant v. Jackson Bd. of Educ., 106 S.Ct. 1842 (1986).

[20]*See* Bickel, *The Original Understanding and the Segregation Decision,* 69 Harv.L.Rev. 1, 56 (1955).

rejected; it is not the law that has changed but only our relevant perceptions and understandings.

On the face of it, *Brown*–B seems a more modest, less radical and less strained interpretation than *Brown*–A. Especially when a national, state or local representative body adopts an affirmative action program fully consistent with *Brown*–B, striking that program down as a violation of *Brown*–A seems hard to square with judicial deference to political majorities absent a textually or historically clear constitutional prohibition.

The difficulty deepens when instrumental reasons are added to support the race-neutral position: arguments that racism and race resentments will be exacerbated, and racial stereotypes perpetuated, unless we demand that government be race-blind are properly addressed to political bodies. For if government's actions violate no constitutional command, why are not arguments about their long-term effects best left to the political process?

I can think of only one constitutional command that the race neutralists might invoke to fill this gap and justify their choice of *Brown*–A: a command that law and government must not restrict *any* innocent individual's "liberty," broadly enough defined to include job opportunities and the like, even when such a restriction is justified by a desire to protect others who are equally innocent. And to deprive someone of a benefit, or to impose a burden, merely because of that person's race (and not because of what that specific individual did wrong) violates this command no less when the deprived individual is white than when she is black. But before anyone gravitates to this view, let me make this observation: when the government exercises its power to single out wholly innocent individuals by taking their "private property * * * for public use," the race neutralists do not object that only the *guilty* should ever have to make such focused sacrifices. Indeed, they often *endorse* such property takings outside the affirmative action context—so long as the "innocents" who have been required to make special sacrifices receive "just compensation" for their losses. In assessing the constitutionality and wisdom of affirmative action plans that impose similarly concrete and personalized costs on "innocent" white individuals—losses of seniority, for example—facing questions of just compensation would offer the race neutralists a more moderate alternative to the extremism of *Brown*–A.

So I end with a genuine puzzle: the race neutralists do not in fact put themselves forward, in other respects, as constitutional radicals. First, they purport to respect the historical intentions of the Framers, insofar as those intentions are knowable. Second, they regard basic constitutional norms as alterable only by constitutional amendment, and not by act of judicial improvization. Third, they advocate deference to political majorities when a constitutional prohibition is at best arguable rather than clear. And fourth, they are reluctant to have courts fashion new rights by generalizing, even with the help of the Ninth Amendment, beyond the Constitution's text. Yet on all four of these dimensions, the race neutralists—the constitutional opponents of affirmative action—seem to look the other way.

What has yet to be produced, then, is a cogent explanation of *why* judicial modesty and constitutional strict construction should be abandoned when the subject is affirmative action for racial minorities.

NEIL GOTANDA, A CRITIQUE OF "OUR CONSTITUTION IS COLOR-BLIND"

44 STAN.L.REV. 1, 23–28, 32–34 (1991).

RACIAL CATEGORIES

* * *

A. American Racial Classification: Hypodescent

One way to begin a critique of the American system of racial classification is to ask "Who is Black?" This question rarely provokes analysis; its answer is seen as so self-evident that challenges are novel and noteworthy. Americans no longer have need of a system of judicial screening to decide a person's race; the rules are simply absorbed without explicit articulation.

1. The rule of hypodescent.

American racial classifications follow two formal rules:

> 1) *Rule of recognition:* Any person whose Black-African ancestry is visible is Black.
>
> 2) *Rule of descent:* (a) Any person with a known trace of African ancestry is Black, notwithstanding that person's visual appearance; or, stated differently, (b) the offspring of a Black and a white is Black.

Historians and social scientists have noted the existence of these rules, often summarized as the "one drop of blood" rule, in their analysis of the American system of racial classification. Anthropologist Marvin Harris suggested a name for the American system of social reproduction: "hypodescent."[95]

2. Alternatives to hypodescent.

The American legal system today lacks intermediate or "mixed race" classifications. While the establishment of self-contained Black or white racial categories may seem obvious, an examination of other classification schemes reveals that the American categories are not exhaustive.

Let us posit the two original races: one a "pure Black," the other a "pure white." As interracial reproduction occurs, a multiracial society

[95] Marvin Harris, Patterns of Race in the Americas 37, 56 (1964). * * *

emerges. Four historically documented examples of nonbinary schemes to categorize mixed-race offspring have evolved: Mulatto, Named Fractions, Majoritarian, and Social Continuum. All of these schemes are logically symmetrical, so, at least in theory, neither "pure race" is privileged over the other. Consider each of the schemes in detail:

1. *Mulatto:* All mixed offspring are called mulattoes, irrespective of the percentages or fractions of their Black or white ancestry.[97]

2. *Named Fractions:* Individuals are assigned labels according to the fractional composition of their racial ancestry. Thus, a mulatto is one-half white and one-half Black. A quadroon is one-fourth Black and three-fourths white, a sambo one-fourth white and three-fourths Black, etc.[98]

3. *Majoritarian:* The higher percentage of either white or Black ancestry determines the white or Black label.[99]

4. *Social Continuum:* This is a variation on the Named Fractions scheme: Labels generally correspond to the proportion of white or Black ancestry, but social status is also an important factor in determining which label applies. The result is a much less rigid system of racial classification.[100]

It is worth repeating two observations that apply to all four schemes. First, the use of racial categories presumes that at some time "pure" races existed. Second, because these schemes are symmetrical, nothing in them suggests inequality or subordination between races. [But the] hypodescent rule when combined with color-blind constitutionalism, conveys a complex and powerful ideology that supports. * * *

[B. Racial Subordination]

* * * Under hypodescent, Black parentage is recognized through the generations. The metaphor is one of purity and contamination: White is unblemished and pure, so one drop of ancestral Black blood renders one

---

[97] Laura Foner suggests that in Louisiana and St. Domingue (colonial Haiti), there were three classifications of race: white, Black (mostly slaves), and free colored (mostly mulatto). Laura Foner, The Free People of Color in Louisiana and St. Domingue: A Comparative Portrait of Two Three-Caste Slave Societies, 3 J.Soc.Hist. 406 (1970). Likewise, Eugene Genovese had identified a "three-caste" system in the "Anglo-French Caribbean." E. Genovese, The World The Slaveholders Made [107 (1969)]. These arrangements suggest that the mulatto scheme is consistent with racial categorization techniques existing in other parts of the world.

[98] This type of classification arrangement evolved in parts of the West Indies and Latin America, with additional labels for those with Indian blood. * * *

[99] Ohio followed a majoritarian rule of racial classification for three decades, beginning with Gray v. Ohio, 4 Ohio 353 (1831), and ending with the adoption of the Reconstruction Amendments.

[100] This is the prevailing classification scheme in several Latin American societies. Brazil's system is probably the most widely described. * * *

Black. Black ancestry is a contaminant that overwhelms white ancestry.[101] Thus, under the American system of racial classification, claiming a white racial identity is a declaration of racial purity and an implicit assertion of racial domination. The symmetry of racial categorization systems other than hypodescent brings a sense of objectivity and neutrality to these schemes, and a comparison of hypodescent to symmetrical systems exposes its nonneutral assumptions.

* * *

[*C. The Mutability of Racial Categorization*]

* * *

Modern ways of thinking about racial categories evolved throughout American history. In the early colonial period, racial classifications were highly fluid. Social status often depended as much on the labor status of the individual as on his place of origin. Typically, Africans were brought to the colonies as captives, and Europeans as contractual or indentured servants. * * * There was a hierarchy among those who were not slaves but were also not free. The labels for such labor varied. In Virginia and Maryland, where the English colonists were the dominant group, the various "unfree" were also described as "un-English." The term included French, Africans, and Scots. There were additional labels specific to the African laborers. While the early records are incomplete, there is clear evidence that by the middle 1600s, English colonists maintained some Africans in a status distinguishable from European indentured labor.

Sources from the 1600s variously describe Africans as "heathen," "infidel," and "negro." These terms were attempts to justify the political status of the Africans. The racial classifications differentiated Europeans from the natives of colonized and imperially exploited parts of the world. But the classifications did not indicate a clearly developed belief that slavery was an appropriate condition for Africans.

---

[101] Writer and poet Langston Hughes observed in 1953:

"It's powerful," [Simple] said . . .

> "That one drop of Negro blood—because just one drop of black blood makes a man colored. One drop—you are a Negro! Now, why is that? Why is Negro blood so much more powerful than any other kind of blood in the world? If a man has Irish blood in him, people will say, 'He's part Irish.' If he has a little Jewish blood, they'll say, 'He's half Jewish.' But if he has just a small bit of colored blood in him bam!—He's a Negro!' Not, 'He's part Negro.' No, be it ever so little, if that blood is black, 'He's a Negro!' Now, that is what I do not understand—why our one drop is so powerful. . .. Black is powerful. You can have ninety-nine drops of white blood in your veins down South—but if that other one drop is black, shame on you! Even if you look white, you're black. That drop is powerful."

Langston Hughes, Simple Takes a Wife 85 (1953). * * *

English colonists gradually came to prefer enslaved African labor over indentured Europeans. By the end of the seventeenth century, the number of slaves had increased dramatically.

As slavery became entrenched as the primary source of agricultural labor, slaveholders developed a complementary ideological structure of racial categories that served to legitimate slavery. The formal legal system was tailored to reflect these categories and enforce slave labor. In 1705, the Virginia assembly created the first recognizable slave code. Besides codifying punishment for slaves who stole or ran away, the slave code contained specific rules of descent for classifying offspring. Punishments for Blacks and mulattos differed from those for indentured servants. This institutionalization of racial classifications linked to disparate treatment marked the first formal establishment of racial categories in colonial America.

The new racial classifications offered a basis for legitimating subordination that was unlike the justifications previously employed. By keying official rules of descent to national origin the classification scheme differentiated those who were "enslaveable" from those who were not. Membership in the new social category of "Negro" became itself sufficient justification for enslaveability.

One can, therefore, do more than assert generally that race is not scientific or that race is socially constructed. One can say that our particular system of classification, with its metaphorical construction of racial purity for whites, has a specific history as a badge of enslaveability. As such, the metaphor of purity is not a logical oddity, but an integral part of the construction of the system of racial subordination embedded in American society. Under color-blind constitutionalism, when race is characterized as objective and apolitical, this history is disguised and discounted.

T. ALEXANDER ALEINIKOFF, A CASE FOR RACE-CONSCIOUSNESS

91 COLUM.L.REV. 1060, 1075–1083, 1087–1091, (1991).

A. COLORBLINDNESS AND ANTIDISCRIMINATION LAW

* * *

The allure of colorblindness is strong. It is rooted in the dissenting opinion of the case that ratified American apartheid.[77] And it fits with liberal, individualistic principles that each person should be assessed on individual merits, not upon the basis of group membership. Color-consciousness, under this account, is irrational and immoral because it is so rarely relevant to acceptable purposes.

[77] Plessy v. Ferguson, 163 U.S. 537, 554–55 (1896) (Harlan, J., dissenting).

Colorblindness also has powerful strategic appeal. In a world of white supremacy, most classifications based on race will have the intent or effect of harming blacks. Colorblindness sweeps these away. Furthermore, since whites are likely to look after their own, insisting that blacks get precisely what whites get will materially advance black interests. Colorblindness also keeps white guilt and anxiety at an acceptable level. As Alan Freeman has noted, colorblindness designates as "wrongdoers" only those "racists" who continue to take race into account; colorblind whites are absolved even if they continue to benefit from an unequal state of affairs.[80] Finally, there is the risk that noticing race, even for a "benign" purpose, will only serve to affirm the view of racial differences that supported racial domination in the past.

The opinions in *Croson* and *Metro Broadcasting* show that four Justices believe that colorblindness should be the animating vision for antidiscrimination law. Justice O'Connor's plurality opinion in *Croson* identifies the central constitutional norm as prohibition of the use of racial classifications:

> The Richmond Plan denies certain citizens the opportunity to compete for a fixed percentage of public contracts based solely upon their race. To whatever racial group these citizens belong, their "personal rights" to be treated with equal dignity and respect are implicated by a rigid rule erecting race as the sole criterion in an aspect of public decision-making.[83]

The concurring opinions of Justices Scalia and Kennedy are equally explicit. Justice Scalia writes: "I share the view expressed by Alexander Bickel that ' * * * discrimination on the basis of race is illegal, immoral, unconstitutional, inherently wrong, and destructive of democratic society.'"[84] Justice Kennedy agrees: "The moral imperative of racial neutrality is the driving force of the Equal Protection Clause."[85]

* * *

B. From Colorblindness to Race-Consciousness

[We need to distinguish two varieties of colorblindness.] The first, which I will call "strong colorblindness," argues that race should truly be an irrelevant, virtually unnoticed, human characteristic. Richard Wasserstrom has described this "assimilationist ideal":

---

[80] Freeman, Legitimizing Racial Discrimination Through Antidiscrimination Law: A Critical Review of Supreme Court Doctrine, 62 Minn.L.Rev. 1049, 1054–56, 1067 (1978). * * *

[83] [City of Richmond v. J.A. Croson Co., 109 S.Ct. 706, 721 (1989).] Justices White and Kennedy joined O'Connor with respect to this part of the opinion. Id. at 712.

[84] Id. at 735 (Scalia, J., concurring)[.]

[85] Id. at 734 (Kennedy, J., concurring).

> [A] nonracist society would be one in which the race of an individual would be the functional equivalent of the eye color of individuals in our society today. In our society no basic political rights and obligations are determined on the basis of eye color. No important institutional benefits and burdens are connected with eye color. Indeed, except for the mildest sort of aesthetic preferences, a person would be thought odd who even made private, social decisions by taking eye color into account.[91]

The second type, "weak colorblindness," would not outlaw all recognition of race, but would condemn the use of race as a basis for the distribution of scarce resources or opportunities and the imposition of burdens. Under "weak colorblindness," race might function like ethnicity: an attribute that could have significance for group members, and one that society as a whole could recognize, but not one upon which legal distinctions could be based. * * * Thus, college courses on "African-American literature" might well be permissible under a weak colorblindness regime, but such a regime would not tolerate allocating places in the class based on race or allowing race to be used as a factor in the choice of an instructor. In the sections that follow, I will argue that strong colorblindness is impossible and undesirable, and that weak colorblindness—although perhaps able to be implemented as a legal strategy—is an inadequate response to current manifestations of racial inequality.

1. *Masking Race-Consciousness.*—It is apparently important, as a matter of widespread cultural practice, for whites to assert that they are strongly colorblind, in the sense that they do not notice or act on the basis of race. One can see this at work in such statements as: "I judge each person as an individual." Of course, it cannot be that whites do not notice the race of others. Perhaps what is being said is that the speaker does not begin her evaluation with any preconceived notions. But this too is difficult to believe, given the deep and implicit ways in which our minds are color-coded. To be truly colorblind in this way * * * requires color-consciousness: one must notice race in order to tell oneself not to trigger the usual mental processes that take race into account.

The denial of race-consciousness occasioned by the desire to be strongly colorblind is described in a recent study of a desegregated junior high school by psychologist Janet Schofield. She reports that teachers, apparently concerned that acknowledging racial awareness would be viewed as a sign of prejudice, claimed not to notice the race of their students. In pursuit of colorblindness, teachers rarely used the words "white" or "black," and avoided racial topics and identifications in class.[93]

---

[91] R. Wasserstrom, Philosophy and Social Issues 24 (1980)[.]

[93] Schofield, Causes and Consequences of the Colorblind Perspective, *in* [Prejudice, Discrimination, and Racism 231 (J. Dovidio & S. Gaertner eds. 1986).]

This act of denial is troubling not only because it distorts reality, but also because it will make less accessible the ways in which color-consciousness influences our understanding of the world and of others. Strong colorblindness will perpetuate the white image of blacks by rendering irrelevant the kind of race-based discussion and data necessary for a serious critique of white definitions. Schofield's study documents how teachers' desires to act in a colorblind fashion harmed the educational experience by ignoring or denying race when it would have been appropriate to notice it:

> [One] teacher included George Washington Carver on a list of great Americans from which students could pick individuals to learn about but specifically decided not to mention he was black for fear of raising racial issues. In the best of all worlds, there would be no need to make such mention, because children would have no preconceptions that famous people are generally white. However, in a school where one white child was surprised to learn from a member of our research team that Martin Luther King was black, not white[!], it would seem reasonable to argue that highlighting the accomplishments of black Americans and making sure that students do not assume famous figures are white is a reasonable practice.

* * *

2. *Local Knowledge: Race-Consciousness as Cultural Critique.*—Strong colorblindness, I have argued, is unlikely to produce the result it promises—a world in which race does not matter. In this section, I want to make the case for race-consciousness more direct by focusing on the benefits of race-consciousness in undermining and shifting deep cultural assumptions and ultimately, perhaps, making progress in overcoming racism. In presenting these claims, I hope also to undermine the case for weak colorblindness. To be effective, strategies for attacking racism may well demand affirmative race-conscious governmental policies.

Clifford Geertz, in a collection of his essays entitled *Local Knowledge,* has stated that:

> To see ourselves as others see us can be eye-opening. To see others as sharing a nature with ourselves is the merest decency. But it is from the far more difficult achievement of seeing ourselves amongst others, as a local example of the forms human life has locally taken, a case among cases, a world among worlds, that the largeness of mind, without which objectivity is self-congratulation and tolerance a sham, comes.[101]

Colorblindness operates at Geertz's level of "merest decency." It begins and ends with the observation that there is something, under the skin,

---

[101] C. Geertz, Local Knowledge: Further Essays in Interpretive Anthropology 16 (1983).

common to all human beings. I do not want to discount the deep humanism underlying this perspective. Indeed, it is a significant improvement over the racist ideologies that have been prevalent throughout United States history and that have denied the "inner" equality of the races. But Geertz clearly seeks more than this; he would reorient the usual hierarchical relationship between dominant and subordinate cultures by rotating the axis through its center point, making the vertical horizontal. This shift requires two related transformations: the first is to appreciate the contingency, the nonuniversalism of one's own culture—to view it as an example of "local knowledge;" the second is to recognize and credit the "local knowledges" of other groups. Of course, these two efforts are related. By valorizing the dominated, one is likely to cast doubts on the dominant group's characterizations or definition of the dominated group, which, in turn, tells us something new about the dominant group as well.

[R]ace-consciousness can aid in these cultural transformations. This is, to be sure, hardly a new claim. The calls for "black pride" and "black power" in the 1960s represented a reorienting demand of race-consciousness. * * *

The consequences wrought by the race-conscious advocates were startling. They were able to take the term "black"—which for more than three hundred years had symbolized degradation and stigma—and turn it into an assertion of a group's humanity and solidarity. But African-American self-pride does not necessarily penetrate white cultural norms and narratives. Indeed, a dominant culture can be relatively unconcerned with a subordinated group's definition of itself if that definition either does not get air time or can be dismissed as romantic, self-serving, or fictional.

Rotating the axis helps us to be open to other accounts and perspectives, and in doing so it reminds us of the fictional or constructed nature of "local knowledges"—including our own. Once white Americans shed the false assumption that "they know all they need to know" about African-Americans, they will begin to learn as much about themselves as about others.

* * *

[R]ecognizing race validates the lives and experiences of those who have been burdened because of their race. White racism has made "blackness" a relevant category in our society. Yet colorblindness seeks to deny the continued social significance of the category, to tell blacks that they are no different from whites, even though blacks as blacks are persistently made to feel that difference. Color-consciousness allows for recognition of the distinct and difficult difference that race has made; it facilitates white awareness of the efforts of African-Americans to describe and examine that difference. This is not simply the telling of a story of oppression. Color-consciousness makes blacks subjects and not objects, undermining the durability of white definitions of "blackness." It permits recognition of the strength and adaptive power of a black community able to survive slavery and oppression; and it acknowledges the contributions of black culture—not simply as windows on "the race question" but as distinct (if varied) voices and traditions, worthy of study in their own right.

It is difficult to improve upon Adrienne Rich's insight:

> I used to envy the "colorblindness" which some liberal, enlightened, white people were supposed to possess; raised as I was, where I was, I am and will to the end of my life be acutely, sometimes bitterly, aware of color. Every adult around me in my childhood, white or black, was aware of it; it was a sovereign consciousness, a hushed and compelling secret. But I no longer believe that "colorblindness"—if it even exists—is the opposite of racism; I think it is, in this world, a form of naiveté and moral stupidity. It implies that I would look at a black woman and see her as white, thus engaging in white solipsism to the utter erasure of her particular reality.[131]

Here is the turn of the axis, the recognition of others that helps one to see one's own culture as "a world among worlds."

3. *Weak Colorblindness and Its Costs.*—It is common for advocates of affirmative action to point out that a legal strategy dedicated to "equality of opportunity" is likely to replicate deeply imbedded inequalities. The familiar metaphor is of a race between two runners, one of whom starts many yards back from the starting line, or is encumbered by ankle weights. Color-conscious policies are said to remove the advantage that has for several centuries been granted to whites. The simplicity of this argument should not disguise its soundness or moral power. Unfortunately, however, affirmative action programs based on the objective of overcoming past societal discrimination are deemed to run afoul of the Court's model of weak colorblindness.[134] To the extent race conscious policies help ameliorate material disadvantage due to societal discrimination, the negative injunction of weak colorblindness imposes heavy costs.

Beyond this familiar terrain in the affirmative action debate, there are other advantages to race-conscious programs that also call into question the adequacy of weak colorblindness. [T]here are a number of situations in which it seems eminently reasonable for government decision makers to take race into account. * * * Justice Powell's famous "diversity" argument

---

[131] A. Rich, [Disloyal to Civilization: Feminism, Racism, Gynephobia, *in* On Lies, Secrets, and Silence 275, 300 (1979).]

[134] See, e.g., City of Richmond v. J.A. Croson Co., 109 S.Ct. 706, 720–23 (1989); Wygant v. Jackson Bd. of Educ., 476 U.S. 267, 277–78, 293–94 (1986). * * *

in *Bakke*[137] implicitly acknowledges the reasonableness of some manner of color-conscious decision making in a world in which race has mattered and continues to matter. To the extent that weak colorblindness makes these forms of race-consciousness problematic, it is simply nearsighted social policy.

Most fundamentally, weak colorblindness sacrifices much of the cultural critique that race-consciousness can provide. If the task is to subject dominant views to scrutiny and challenge through the investigation and acceptance of nondominant perspectives, then it would appear sensible to permit decision makers to adopt facilitative programs that necessarily take notice of race. *Metro Broadcasting*[139] is a significant case in this respect. The FCC policies upheld in this case are important not only because they channel economic resources—broadcasting licenses—to African-Americans, but also because these resources both support minority cultural self-definition and provide a means for penetrating mainstream culture.[140] As the Court recognized, "[T]he benefits of [increased] diversity are not limited to the members of minority groups who gain access to the broadcasting industry by virtue of the ownership policies; rather, the benefits redound to all members of the viewing and listening audience."

* * *

To return to a previous example, universities need more than African-American literature classes; they need a diversity of students in all literature classes, and not simply to show white students that students of color can perform as well as white students, but also to help all students become more self-conscious of the underlying assumptions with which they approach the world. To be sure, there are risks. Given the power of imbedded ways of thinking, new information may simply be "processed" in accordance with pre-existing views; or, white students may make the error of assuming that comments by black students express "the" black perspective. But to students and faculty open to a Geertzian moment, the intellectual rewards are enormous.

---

[137] Regents of Univ. of Cal. v. Bakke, 438 U.S. 265, 315–19 (1978).

[139] Metro Broadcasting, Inc. v. FCC, 110 S.Ct. 2997 (1990).

[140] See Williams, *Metro Broadcasting, Inc. v. FCC:* Regrouping in Singular Times, 104 Harv.L.Rev. 525, 537 (1990)[.]

B. JUSTIFICATIONS

In the University of Michigan cases, the Supreme Court stated that "[b]ecause the Fourteenth Amendment 'protect[s] *persons*, not *groups*,' all 'governmental action based on race * * * should be subjected to detailed judicial inquiry to ensure that the *personal* right to equal protection of the laws has not been infringed.'"[1] What governmental interests might justify use of a racial classification?

Richard Posner identifies several possible justifications for affirmative action but rejects each of them. He argues for colorblind policies: the Fourteenth Amendment ought to be read to prohibit the distribution of benefits, no less than burdens, on the basis of race.

Akhil Amar and Neal Katyal argue that a "diversity" justification can sustain affirmative action in education, particularly when one focuses on the democratic benefits of diversity. (Their article was written before the Court's decisions in *Grutter* and *Gratz*; it is worth considering the extent to which their analysis is consistent with the Court's.)

Elizabeth Anderson suggests that affirmative action is best justified as a strategy for achieving integration and thereby furthering democratic values and the goal of equal opportunity. Her argument would provide support for affirmative action outside the context of university admissions—an issue left unresolved in the University of Michigan cases.

Girardeau Spann takes on the *Grutter* and *Gratz* opinions directly. He argues that, despite widespread liberal approval of the cases, *Grutter* and *Gratz* are in fact grounded in the Court's preference for race neutrality and its historical unwillingness to confront systemic societal discrimination. The cases, then, according to Spann, undermine the kinds of racial-balance remedies necessary for achieving racial equality in the United States.

RICHARD A. POSNER, THE *DEFUNIS* CASE AND THE CONSTITUTIONALITY OF PREFERENTIAL TREATMENT OF RACIAL MINORITIES

1974 SUP.CT.REV. 1, 7–12, 15–25.

II. THE REASONABLENESS OF REVERSE DISCRIMINATION

B. Race as a Surrogate for Other, Nonracial Characteristics

A frequently suggested basis for preferential treatment is the desire to increase the diversity of the student body in the hope of thereby enhancing the quality of the students' educational experience. * * *

---

[1] Grutter v. Bollinger, 123 S.Ct. 2325, 2337(2003) (quoting Adarand Constructors, Inc. v. Pena, 515 U.S. 200, 227 (1995)).

For a diversity argument to be convincing, it must identify a differentiating factor that is relevant to the educational experience. It would make no sense to argue that in selecting the entering first-year class a law school should strive for diversity in the height of the students, or in their weight, pulchritude, posture, depth of voice, or blood pressure, or that it should give a preference to (or disfavor) albinos, or people with freckles or double chins. Diversity in these superficial physical respects contributes nothing of value to the legal education of the students. Race *per se*—that is, race completely divorced from certain characteristics that may be strongly correlated with, but do not inevitably accompany, it—is also, and in a similar sense, irrelevant to diversity. There are black people (and Chicanos, Filipinos, etc.) who differ only in the most superficial physical characteristics from whites—who have the same tastes, manners, experiences, aptitudes, and aspirations as the whites with whom one might compare them (here, white law school applicants). To give such people preferential treatment to the end of increasing the diversity of the student body would be equivalent to giving preferential treatment to albinos—were it not that race is frequently correlated with other attributes that are arguably relevant to meaningful diversity, and albinism is not. The average black applicant for admission is more likely than the average white to have known poverty and prejudice first hand, and his experience, communicated to his fellow students (and teachers) both inside and outside of the classroom, might enrich the educational process.

Race in this analysis is simply a proxy for a set of other attributes—relevant to the educational process—with which race, itself irrelevant to the process, happens to be correlated. The use of a racial proxy in making admissions decisions will produce some inaccuracy—blacks will be admitted who lack the attributes that contribute to genuine diversity—but this cost of using a racial proxy may be less than the cost, which is saved, of having to investigate the actual characteristics of each applicant.

The difficulty with this approach is that it closely resembles and could be viewed as imparting legitimacy to the case for regarding discrimination against racial minorities as a proper, because (generally) efficient, form of conduct. There are several possible explanations for the presence of racial and ethnic discrimination. One is sheer irrationality; another is exploitation; another the desire to limit competition. But it may be that most discrimination in today's America can be explained simply by the cost of information. Suppose that a particular racial or ethnic identity is correlated with characteristics that are widely disliked for reasons not patently exploitive, anticompetitive, or irrational. A substantial proportion of the members of the group in question may be loud, or poor, or hostile, or irresponsible, or poorly educated, or dangerously irascible, or ill-mannered, or have different tastes, values, and work habits from our own, or speak an unintelligible patois.[24] To be averse to association (in housing, recreation, schooling, or employment) with an individual because he possessed such a characteristic would not ordinarily be regarded as a sign of prejudice. To be "prejudiced" means, rather, to ascribe to the members of a group defined by a racial or similarly arbitrary characteristic[25] attributes typically or frequently possessed by members of the group without pausing to consider whether the individual member in question has that characteristic—sometimes without being willing even to consider evidence that he does not. The extreme bigot applies an irrebuttable presumption that every member of the group has the characteristic that he dislikes. The moderate bigot applies a rebuttable presumption to the same effect—and all of us are at least moderate bigots in some areas of life.

The history of this country contains examples of the unreasoning type of racial and ethnic prejudice, of exploitive discrimination—illustrated by the treatment of the American Indian in the nineteenth century and by the enslavement of the black—and of the anticompetitive sort as well (*e.g.*, exclusion of women from various occupations). But, today at least, it may be that most prejudice and discrimination are a product of the cost of making individual distinctions within racial and ethnic groups. This is a type of economically efficient conduct similar to a consumer's reluctance to try a new brand or more generally, to carry the process of searching for products beyond the point where the cost of searching is equal to its benefit in enabling a better purchase to be made. It is perfectly rational for an individual to support the exclusion of Armenians, or Jews, or blacks from his club if his experience, whether first or second hand, is that most or very many members of these groups do not have the characteristics that he likes in a social (or business) acquaintance and there is no scarcity of eligible applicants from other groups.

To say that discrimination is often a rational and efficient form of behavior is not to say that it is socially or ethically desirable. "Efficient" must never be confused with "good" or "right." Moreover, there is an important distinction to be drawn between private discrimination and discrimination that is compelled, practiced, or encouraged by the government, or that is practiced by a monopolist. But I am not interested in the normative basis of antidiscrimination policy. My purpose in noting that much discrimination may be applicable in terms of the costs of information

---

[24]The proportion of the racial or ethnic group who actually possess the disfavored characteristic may, of course, be exaggerated, since obtaining accurate information about the characteristics of the average member of the group may be costly too.

[25]An "arbitrary characteristic" in this sense is one whose only significance is as a proxy for some other characteristic. To dislike short people because one finds them repulsive is not prejudice; to dislike short people because one thinks that short people tend to have aggressive personalities is an example of prejudice, assuming that not all short people in fact possess such personalities.

is, rather, to suggest a doubt about the merits of the diversity justification for treating racial minorities preferentially. That justification, it will be recalled, rests on the correlation between racial identity and the possession of characteristics that promote meaningful diversity, and implicitly, therefore, on the cost of ascertaining whether a particular member of the racial group actually possesses the desired characteristic. Could not a policy against hostile discrimination be undermined by a program of benevolent discrimination rooted in the same habit of mind—that of using race or ethnic origin to establish a presumption, in the case of a racially preferential admissions program a conclusive one, that the individual possesses some other attribute as well, that is, some educationally relevant characteristic such as a background of deprivation or a cultural difference? The danger is underscored by the fact that the hostile and the well-disposed discriminators seem to be treating race as a proxy for the same set of characteristics. The characteristics that university admissions officers associate with "black" are the distinctive cultural attributes of many black people who have grown up in an urban slum or in the rural South, and these are the same characteristics that the white bigot ascribes to every black, although he uses a different terminology (*e.g.*, "lazy" rather than "unmotivated").

I am not making the familiar argument that the member of the favored minority is humiliated by being singled out for preferential treatment. He may or may not be. My point is rather that the use of a racial characteristic to establish a presumption that the individual also possesses other, and socially relevant, characteristics exemplifies, encourages, and legitimizes the mode of thought and behavior that underlies most prejudice and bigotry in modern America.

* * *

I have dwelled * * * on the diversity argument for preferential treatment because it is the one argument that seems at first glance not racialistic at all. The argument is not that one race should be preferred over another but that a racial preference will benefit all members of the student body, regardless of race, by enriching the educational experience. Yet if one looks a little more closely at the argument it turns out to rest on a premise fundamentally inconsistent with that of a policy against hostile discrimination, for such a policy, if it is to be effective, requires rejection of administrative convenience as a justification for using racial criteria to allocate benefits or impose burdens.

C. Racial Proportional Representation

Where * * * a racial preference is based squarely on a desire to increase the proportion of lawyers of a particular race, it is no longer possible to argue about whether the preference is a form of racial discrimination and it is more difficult to find a justification based on educational purposes, or for that matter on anything else. Four principal reasons are offered for attempting to achieve at least approximately proportional racial representation in the legal profession: (1) making amends for past discrimination against the minority group; (2) putting the group where it would have been but for the handicaps imposed on its members by past discrimination; (3) improving the level of professional service received by the group; and (4) encouraging the aspirations of its members by the provision of suitable "role models." None of these four reasons would be any more persuasive to an objective observer than the sorts of arguments that could be offered for discriminating against racial minorities.

1. The members of the minority group who receive preferential treatment will often be those who have not been the victims of discrimination while the nonminority people excluded because of the preferences are unlikely to have perpetrated, or to have in any demonstrable sense benefited from,[32] the discrimination. Indian reparations may be a distinct case, based on treaty (equivalent to contractual) obligations enforceable by the heirs of the original beneficiaries against the government; also distinguishable, though in my opinion only tenuously, is the use of racial quotas as part of a decree to remedy unlawful discrimination.[33]

---

[32] One could spend many profitless hours discussing whether [a white applicant to law school] is better or worse off as the result of the history of racial discrimination in this country. Perhaps he is better off because, but for a history of discrimination, there would be a larger pool of qualified black applicants for a law school education. Perhaps he is worse off because, but for the history of discrimination, fewer blacks (and members of other minorities) would be interested in becoming lawyers. Perhaps if there had never been discrimination against blacks, there would never have been slavery in the United States, and without slavery, it is possible, indeed probable, that the black population in the United States would be insignificant, in which event—perhaps—the real income of whites would be higher.

[33] As for example in Swann v. Charlotte—Mecklenburg Bd. of Educ., 402 U.S. 1 (1971). These decisions are difficult to justify because the people adversely affected by the decree are in general different from those who discriminated unlawfully. The remedy does not run against the wrongdoer. A more acceptable remedy would be damages. The costs of a decree imposing a racial quota in a labor market are borne primarily by the white workers (I distinguish the case where the source of the discrimination is the workers themselves or the union representing them) or, in the case of educational discrimination, by children bused to distant or inferior schools. The cost of a damage award, in contrast, would be borne primarily by the owners of the discriminating firm or the taxpayers of the discriminating school district.

In discussions of black reparations, an analogy is frequently drawn to the payment of substantial reparations by Germany to the State of Israel in compensation for Nazi Germany's extermination of millions of European Jews. Among the distinguishing features is the fact that the cost of the German reparations was borne by the German taxpaying public as a whole, rather than by university students, schoolchildren, and members of the working class, who are being asked in this country to subsidize certain racial minorities. But the more important difference is in the degree of felt guilt. If the United States had recently exterminated several millions of blacks, we might be willing to give several billion dollars to some African state that had been established as a refuge for persecuted blacks. Some people

2. Many groups are underrepresented in various occupations for reasons of taste, opportunity, or aptitude unrelated to discrimination. There is no basis for a presumption that but for past discrimination, * * * minorities * * * would supply [a percentage] of the nation's lawyers [proportionate to their representation in the general population.]

3. There is no evidence of which I am aware that a substantial number or proportion of minority-group law school graduates will seek in their professional careers to serve the special needs of their minority group rather than follow the normal patterns of professional advancement.

4. The "role model" argument is similarly *ad hoc* and conjectural. So long as a significant number of members of a minority group enter the legal profession and succeed in it (one of the Justices of the Supreme Court is black, after all), others will know that it is not closed to them. There is no basis for requiring proportional representation.

The reasons advanced for proportional representation are unimpressive. But more disturbing than the lack of solid intellectual foundations are the implications of the underrepresentation approach for the overall structure of society. The ultimate logic of underrepresentation is that the percentage of members of each minority racial and ethnic group in each desirable occupation, and in each level of achievement within the occupation, should be raised to equality with its percentage of the total population (either of the entire nation or, in some versions, of some region or local area). The proponents of proportional representation do not as yet urge adoption of the standard of perfect equality, but there seems to be no logical stopping point short of it within the structure of their argument. This is true despite their soothing assurance that affirmative action is required only in a period of transition to a society in which, all vestiges of discrimination having been eliminated by affirmative action, society can resume a policy of color-blindness. If, as seems more likely than not, occupational preferences and abilities are not randomly distributed across all racial and ethnic groups, then governmental intervention in the labor markets (and in the educational process insofar as it affects occupational choice and success) will have to continue forever if proportional equality in the desirable occupations is to be secured. Consistently implemented, this sort of intervention would, by profoundly distorting the allocation of labor and by driving a wedge between individual merit and economic and professional success, greatly undermine the system of incentives on which a free society depends.

* * *

believe that the American treatment of the black has been comparable in its enormity to Hitler's treatment of the Jews; for them the analogy to German reparations to Israel may be a compelling one. To evaluate such a belief will require more careful studies along the lines of Fogel & Engerman, Time on the Cross: The Economics of American Negro Slavery (1974).

III. THE CONSTITUTIONAL ISSUE

A. Previous Approaches

Twenty-eight *amicus curiae* briefs were submitted to the Supreme Court in the *DeFunis* case,[a] and most of them, rather than provide the Court with additional information not available in the record of the case, discuss points of constitutional doctrine. Yet the variety of constitutional arguments in the multitude of briefs is not great. The briefs supporting DeFunis's position point to the undeniable fact that he was treated less favorably than he would have been if he had been a member of one of the four favored racial groups and argue from this fact that he was a victim of racial discrimination, an unconstitutional form of state action. The opposing briefs argue that racial discrimination is unlawful only when invidious and that DeFunis's treatment carried no implication that being a nonmember of one of the favored groups—*i.e.,* being a white—connotes a despised or inferior status.

Neither argument is persuasive in the form expressed. Discrimination against whites, who constitute the vast majority of our population and who never before (in this country) have, as a group, been subjected to discrimination, is not patently the same phenomenon as the sorts of discrimination involved in previous equal-protection cases involving members of racial or ethnic minorities, or women. But neither is it tenable to argue that discrimination is bad only when the circumstances of its adoption or expression connote invidiousness, exploitation, or hostility, or seek to place a stamp of inferiority on the victims of the discrimination. Suppose that New York City adopted an ordinance (supported by the Jewish members of the City Council) limiting the percentage of Jews who could be teachers in the New York City public school system, and the ordinance was based on a finding that Jews are so able that no merit-based principle of selection could keep them from dominating the school system, but that the resulting concentration of Jews in the public schools had exacerbated racial tensions and had, indeed, promoted anti-Semitism. It is difficult to believe that such an ordinance would or should be upheld against a constitutional challenge, albeit one could argue (though not, in my opinion, persuasively) that the ordinance was not "invidious," since it was premised not on the inferiority of the Jews but indeed on the reverse, and even that the ordinance was in the Jews' best interest.

A distinct argument for the constitutionality of discrimination in favor of minority groups has been made in a recent article by Professor Ely. He argues, along lines similar to those suggested earlier, that a policy of

---

[a] *DeFunis v. Odegaard,* 416 U.S. 312 (1974) (holding moot a challenge to the University of Washington Law School's special admissions program for Blacks, Chicanos, American Indians, and Filipinos).

discrimination, favorable or unfavorable, might be adopted simply because the costs of individualized treatment were thought to exceed its benefits, but that when members of one racial group—such as the white majority of a state legislature—are appraising the costs and benefits of a proposed discrimination against another racial group the comparison is apt to be distorted by conscious or unconscious racial hostility.[37] Hence, he argues, discrimination against a racial minority should be suspect under the Fourteenth Amendment, but discrimination in favor of a minority should not be since it does not involve any danger of majority exploitation of a minority.

There are two fundamental objections to this argument. One—that it misconceives the nature of the political process—I defer for the moment. The other is that it provides a mode of justifying discrimination against racial minorities. Professor Ely accepts the legitimacy of comparing the costs of discriminating against the members of a racial or ethnic minority with the benefits from thereby avoiding the need to make individual distinctions. He only wants assurance that the balance will be accurately struck. He is suspicious that the majority will fail to take adequate account of the costs, or will exaggerate the benefits, of the discriminatory measure, but this suspicion only warrants that the reviewing court satisfy itself that the legislature has in fact assessed the costs and benefits of the discrimination accurately. Suppose the Post Office were able to demonstrate convincingly that blacks had, on average, inferior aptitudes to whites for supervisory positions, that the costs to the postal system of inadequate supervisors were very great, and that the costs of conducting the inquiries necessary to ascertain whether an individual black had the requisite aptitudes were also great in relation to the probability of discovering qualified blacks. It would seem to follow from Ely's analysis that the Post Office could adopt a rule barring blacks from supervisory positions. By condemning only inefficient discriminations, Ely reduces the scope of the Equal Protection Clause to triviality, if I am correct in arguing that most discrimination in contemporary society is caused by the costs of information rather than by irrationality, exploitation, or the suppression of competition.

B. Toward an Objective Constitutional Principle

In order to determine the constitutionality of racially preferential admissions policies, it is first necessary to derive from the Equal Protection Clause some rule, or principle, or standard for applying the constitutional formula (that no state may "deny to any person within its jurisdiction the equal protection of the laws") to racial discrimination. * * *

* * *

[37] Ely, [*The Constitutionality of Reverse Racial Discrimination,* 41 U.Chi.L.Rev. 723,] 729, 732–33 (1974).

[The task] is to derive from the specific purposes of the constitutional framers a rule that, while sufficiently general to avoid constant recourse to the amendment process, is sufficiently precise and objective to limit a judge's exercise of personal whim and preference. The rule I derive on this basis is that the distribution of benefits and costs by government on racial or ethnic grounds is impermissible. Even though it is frequently efficient to sort people by race or ethnic origin, because racial or ethnic identity may be a good proxy for functional classifications, efficiency is rejected as a basis for governmental action in this context. The government is required to incur the additional costs of determining the individual applicant's fitness to hold a particular job, or patronize a particular facility, or be admitted to one of its educational institutions. To permit discrimination to be justified on efficiency grounds, as would Professor Ely, would not only thwart the purpose of the Equal Protection Clause by allowing much, perhaps most, discrimination to continue, but it would give the judges the power to pick and choose among discriminatory measures on the basis of personal values, for the weighing of the relevant costs and benefits would of necessity be largely subjective.

* * *

It remains to consider whether an exception to the rule forbidding discrimination on racial or ethnic grounds can be recognized where the discrimination can be said to be in favor of a racial or ethnic minority, and the race discriminated against is the white race. The exception is inadmissible, because it requires the court not only to consider whether there is discrimination but to decide whether the discrimination harms or hurts a particular racial group, and to weigh the competing claims of different racial groups, and the additional inquiries rob the principle of its precision and objectivity. The Court had no good evidence before it in the *Brown* case that segregated education in fact harmed blacks. The questions critical to the point were not even asked: Would blacks have fared better under a system of no public education (assuming that whites would prefer such a system to integrated public education)? Under a system where students were sorted by IQ? By family income? In later cases the Court stopped asking whether segregation actually hurt the blacks. (Today, of course, some blacks favor segregation.) The antidiscrimination principle is not only more objective, but more compelling, when it is divorced from empirical inquiries into the effects of particular forms of discrimination on the affected groups. The necessary inquiries are intractable and would leave the field open to slippery conjecture. * * * [A] plausible argument could be made that various forms of discrimination nominally against Jews might actually advance the interests of the Jews as a whole, for example by reducing their prominence and visibility in certain areas where the conspicuousness of the Jews may stimulate anti-Semitism. Similar arguments could be made for various forms of conceivably well-intentioned discrimination against blacks (such as "benign" housing quotas, or limitations on the migration of blacks from southern to northern states). The Supreme Court would reject such arguments, but not because they are substantially less compelling than the arguments it accepts when it upholds the constitutionality of governmental action. The arguments about the proper characterization of discrimination nominally in favor of racial minorities have a similar elusiveness. Is the position of the whites in this country so unassailable that they cannot be harmed by racial quotas? Or is the impact of such quotas likely to be concentrated on particular, and perhaps vulnerable, subgroups within the white majority? Do racial quotas actually help the minorities intended to be benefited, or harm them by impairing their self-esteem or legitimating stereotypical thinking about race? Are whites entitled to claim minority status when they are a minority within the political subdivision that enacted the measure discriminating against whites? If so, then by parity of reasoning would blacks lack standing to complain about an ordinance discriminating against them enacted by Newark, New Jersey, or Washington, D.C., or other cities in which blacks are a majority of the population eligible to vote? If these are litigable issues, we do not have a constitutional principle but merely a directive that the judges uphold those forms of racial and ethnic discrimination which accord with their personal values.

AKHIL REED AMAR AND NEAL KUMAR KATYAL, *BAKKE*'S FATE

43 U.C.L.A. L.Rev. 1745, 1771–80 (1996)

II. Policy and Structure

[T]he text and history of the Fourteenth Amendment seem rather open on the question of affirmative action. Textually, exactly what does equal protection require against a backdrop of historic racial inequality? Historically, does the race-consciousness of early bills to help the freedmen—passed by the same Congresses that gave us the Thirteenth and Fourteenth Amendments—permit similar race-conscious policies one hundred years later to eliminate the vestiges of a racial caste system? While text and history may not tell the Court what to do, however, policy and more general structural arguments might.

* * *

A. Quotas Versus Pluses

Our first point concerns quotas versus pluses, or to use Justice O'Connor's phraseology, classifications versus considerations. Race-based classifications impose wooden notions of what it means to be diverse; racial considerations, by contrast, permit and indeed require evaluation of a whole person. From a constitutional standpoint, the distinction between classification and consideration draws upon two separate fairness ideas. First, a classification is unfair to the Allan Bakkes of the world because it automatically excludes them on the basis of their skin color. Because of his pigmentation, Allan Bakke was not even allowed to *compete* for sixteen out of one hundred seats at U.C. Davis. Second, classifications are stigmatizing to *minorities*. Quotas create the impression that minority students are admitted because of the seats wholly set aside for them and only them, and they imply that race is altogether different from other diversity factors in the "normal" and "pure" admissions process.

Using race as one consideration among many, however, minimizes both problems. Minority applicants are not segregated into a separate admissions compartment where their files sit with each other and compete only against one another; instead, they are treated just like other applicants and the kinds of diversity they may offer are assessed alongside other kinds of diversity (of musicians, Texans, chess players, French speakers, and so on). Background and life experience are positive attributes—like growing up Amish—and it is neither unfair to whites nor stigmatizing to minorities to consider these factors so long as they do not become the only or the dominant things that admissions committees look at. If having a distinctive racial experience is viewed in the same way as being bilingual or a good violinist, then the Allan Bakkes of the world may have an easier time understanding the preference. (The bilingual analogy is, we submit, a rather precise one; many—not all, but many—black Americans today must in effect navigate "bilingually" through black America and white America.) If a given minority student understands that she is valued not because of what her ancestors went through two centuries ago, but rather because of what she goes through every day, she may feel less stigma and more self-esteem.

As a practical matter, admissions committees often inevitably know something about the race of an applicant because their goal is to look at a whole person. Just as it is permissible for legislatures to consider their knowledge about racial demographics when they create voting districts because they "always [are] aware of race"[133] in drawing boundaries, it may make sense to permit admissions committees to consider what they will know anyway. To demand otherwise will force admissions committees to evaluate an applicant without ever understanding who that applicant really is. Colleges do not accept an SAT score and a GPA; they accept a whole person.

B. Democratic Diversity in Education

---

[133] [Shaw v. Reno, 509 U.S. 630, 646 (1993).]

The cornerstone of our argument remains democratic diversity. While diversity analogies can be drawn between education and other spheres * * *, we must not lose sight of Justice Powell's vision [in *Bakke*] of the unique democratic value of diversity in education—a message sometimes missed by academics. Kathleen Sullivan, for example, has written that if race is "used as merely one factor in the bidding process [for government contracts] without a preassigned weight," then the "approach would be analogous to the Harvard College admissions plan praised by Justice Powell."[135] But diversity takes on a special meaning in the school. As *Brown v. Board of Education* put it, education is "the very foundation of good citizenship" and "a principal instrument in awakening the [student] to cultural values," preparing her for participation as a political equal in a pluralist democracy.[136] Moreover, university education typically occurs at a distinctive time of life—young adulthood—when people are particularly open to new ideas and when they have a tendency to bond with others. (For similar reasons, this bonding may also occur in places like the Army and the Peace Corps.)

In other words, much of the point of education is to teach students how others think and to help them understand different points of view—to teach students how to be sovereign, responsible, and informed citizens in a heterogeneous democracy. A school admits students, in large part, so that they will be teachers to other students. Again: SAT scores and grades are at best a crude proxy for a student's potential to teach other students—often, an applicant's background and life experience will also be vital components of this potential. If a university wants to teach people about France, the university should admit students from France; if a university wants to teach people about the South, it should admit students from the South. The university experience is thus quite different from the very attenuated interaction between the minority "owner" of a broadcast station and the public in *Metro Broadcasting,* [*Inc. v. FCC*], and even more different from the largely nonexistent contact between the minority and nonminority contractors in *Croson* and *Adarand* [*Constructors, Inc. v. Pena*]. Integrated education democratically benefits students of all races, including white students, by providing a space for people of all races to grow together.

Thus, *Bakke* builds squarely on the rock of *Brown*. *Brown* held that education was sui generis and that even if racial segregation could be tolerated in other spheres, the school was different. Recall that, technically, *Brown* did not explicitly overrule *Plessy*, but simply said that the separate-but-equal rule had "no place" "in the field of public education." * * *

---

[135] Kathleen M. Sullivan, City of Richmond v. J.A. Croson Co.: *The Backlash Against Affirmative Action*, 64 Tul. L. Rev. 1609, 1615-16 n.39 (1990).

[136] Brown v. Board of Educ., 347 U.S. 483, 493 (1954) * * *.

Of course, a contracting set-aside may "diversify" an industry (as could integrated workplaces in the pre-*Brown* era), but the democratic benefits of diversity may not be as strong outside the educational setting. The diversity-in-contracting argument assumes that mingling will somehow occur between firms—a rather heroic or impossible assumption in many contractual settings. In the school context, by contrast, people from different backgrounds are thrown together for four years, and they are there to learn.

Inherent in the concept of diversity-based affirmative action is a recognition of the positive educational value of race and life experience. This differs dramatically from contracting cases involving guardrails and urinals, where affirmative action has no such theory of value. In the contracting arena, a minority is valuable only because the person's race helps secure a contract. Whites may resent the fact that a minority, simply by virtue of her skin color, wins a contract when a white firm could have completed the job at a lower cost. Minorities, for their part, may internalize the belief that they need a handout in order to compete with whites. In education, by contrast, a minority can be intrinsically valuable if she brings a missing element to the school. Because the minority student must still be evaluated on other criteria besides diversity, the school can ensure that it is admitting a student who has the academic prowess to keep up with the rest of the student body—an important consideration because the goal is to encourage intermingling and learning from each other.

Of course, any form of affirmative action for nonwhites risks backlash from whites. But failure to do anything to integrate disadvantaged minorities into mainstream America risks minority backlash—race riots tomorrow, perhaps, and potential democratic breakdown in a generation or two. Affirmative action *in education* contains the best long-run antidote to backlash and enmity among races, by bringing diverse elements of society into a common space, a common conversation. * * * What's more, diversity has a built-in stopping point, an inherent limit on the amount of permissible affirmative action: If a school admits minority students who are not roughly equal to white students, it may actually undermine the democratic benefits of diversity by reinforcing stereotypes of minority students as poor students. A critical mass of students of a particular group may be needed so that other students become aware of the group (and of the diversity within the group), but this by no means requires exact proportionality—or anything like it.

Critics have portrayed diversity as a tool only to help whites understand blacks—or as an exploitative way of adding spice to a white mix. We disagree. Minorities may benefit just as much from diversity as whites do. An African American from rural Georgia, after all, can learn from a white suburbanite from Phoenix, and the suburbanite can learn from the

Georgian. We do not mean to glamorize; we recognize that affirmative action programs may not always work this way. If a diversity program does not, in practice, allow all students to learn from each other, then the program is not serving the state's interest in diversity—and the school should not use the "diversity" slogan to show how the program passes constitutional muster.

We would, for example, be troubled by de facto segregation in university dorms. If schools believe that minorities add to diversity, then they should not encourage different groups to cordon themselves off from each other. Diversity is often tough—it is only natural that people from different backgrounds may find it easier to stick with what is familiar. Doing so, however, blunts the point of diversity-based admissions in the first place—it inhibits the interactive learning process. All of this suggests that schools that permit de facto residential segregation may be estopped from pleading *Bakke* as a defense to affirmative action in admissions. Schools are not required to adopt affirmative action policies—nor are they constitutionally obliged to address self-segregated housing—but if they do choose to adopt diversity programs, then they should live up to the goal of encouraging people to learn from each other.

Of course, diversity cannot function the same way, or be as important, in every academic context. There may be settings where diversity may not have much educational importance at all (graduate school in math, perhaps) and other settings where it will matter a great deal (college, for example). And there is a wide range of places in the middle. But we must be careful not to underestimate the importance of diversity—even in educational settings that, at first blush, seem to have little to gain through diversity. * * *

Our democratic diversity point can perhaps also be recast into remedial language. The Court in *Adarand* and other anti-affirmative action cases has acknowledged that race can indeed be used in narrowly tailored remedies for discrete constitutional violations. Diversity in education may not be narrowly tailored, nor does it respond to discrete violations; but the integration of our universities, great and small, may well be, in Ken Karst's nice phrase, "the best long-term remedy for the private beliefs and behavior that perpetuate the effects of racial caste."[148]

CONCLUSION

* * * There is a proud American tradition of treating education differently from other spheres: Education is different—special—because it teaches Americans how to become full citizens in a heterogeneous, pluralistic scheme of democratic self- government. As Justice Powell wrote

[148] Kenneth L. Karst, *Private Discrimination and Responsibility*: Patterson *in Context*, 1989 Sup. Ct. Rev. 1, 36. * * *

in *Bakke*, "the 'nation's future depends upon leaders trained through wide exposure' to the ideas and mores of students as diverse as this Nation of many peoples."[149] *Adarand*-like set-asides set us apart, but *Bakke*-like affirmative action brings Americans together. Under a Constitution that begins with a vision of We the People coming together in order to form a more perfect union (*e pluribus unum*—out of many, one), this coming together of Americans to teach and to learn from each other is an inspiring event to behold.

ELIZABETH S. ANDERSON, INTEGRATION, AFFIRMATIVE ACTION, AND STRICT SCRUTINY

77 N.Y.U. L.Rev. 1195, 1197–1207, 1217, 1220–26 (2002)

* * *

I. Compensatory Versus Integrative Rationales or Race-Based Affirmative Action

This Article contrasts two competing conceptions of the kind of remedy race-conscious affirmative action programs offer for centuries of systematic, comprehensive legal and social subordination of African Americans. The *compensatory* conception of remediation aims to compensate victims for past discrimination. It waits for wrongs to happen, and compensates the victims after the fact. The *integrative* conception of remediation aims to bring African Americans into the mainstream by dismantling *current* barriers to their advancement. It proactively uses race-conscious means to undo the continuing causes of unjust race-based disadvantage. These two views conceive of the significance of racial segregation differently. The compensatory model represents racial segregation of neighborhoods, schools, and jobs as an *effect* of past discrimination, remediable only to the extent that it was caused by past wrongdoing. The integrative model represents segregation of the major institutions of civil society as a *cause* of unjust racial inequality and a threat to democracy. Segregation is therefore a proper target of direct remediation, whether it is de facto or de jure, whether caused by prior illegal discrimination or not. The integrative model represents race-conscious affirmative action as a forward-looking remedy for segregation, rather than as a backward-looking remedy for discrimination.

Racial integration—the full inclusion and participation as equals of citizens of all races in American institutions—was once viewed as a central goal of the civil rights movement. It was an ideal supported in key desegregation cases following *Brown v. Board of Education*. It informed

[149] Bakke, 438 U.S. at 313 (opinion of Powell, J.) (quoting Keyishian v. Board of Regents, 385 U.S. 589, 603 (1967)).

the Civil Rights Act of 1964. But the courts have turned away from racial integration as a positive ideal for civil society, narrowing their focus merely to remedying discrimination. This narrowing of vision ignores the ways segregation operates as an independent race-based barrier to equality of opportunity that is properly addressed by state intervention. The model of affirmative action defended in this Article regards integration as a *means* for removing barriers to equal opportunity, and to realizing the kind of civil society needed for democracy. * * *

A. Segregation as a Cause of Race-Based Barriers to Equality

Racial segregation in the institutions of American civil society operates at three main levels: residential, educational, and occupational. Residential segregation is the norm for most African Americans. According to a study based on 1980 census results, in the thirty metropolitan areas containing a majority of all blacks in the United States, sixty-eight percent of blacks would have to move to achieve a uniform racial composition across the metropolitan area.[8] The average African American in these cities lives in a census tract that is about two-thirds black, indicating a relatively low probability of contact with whites. This is not simply an "underclass" phenomenon. Rates of residential racial segregation for blacks do not decline with income. Because most K-12 schools draw their students from local neighborhoods, they are also profoundly segregated. One-third of black students attend schools in which less than ten percent of the students are white.[11] In such large states as New York, Michigan, Illinois, and California, less than twenty-five percent of the average black student's classmates are white. In the United States as a whole, fewer than one-third of the average black student's classmates are white. Notwithstanding *Brown*, racial segregation in the schools has been *increasing* in almost every state, even during the 1990s.

Similar, but less drastic, patterns of de facto segregation exist in the job market. Jobs are segregated at the regional, firm, and intrafirm levels. Firms located outside black neighborhoods and beyond the reach of public transportation are significantly less likely to hire black employees.[15] At the

---

[8] Douglas S. Massey & Nancy A. Denton, American Apartheid: Segregation and the Making of the Underclass 64 tbl.3.1 (1993). According to Census 2000 data, in U.S. metropolitan areas as a whole, sixty-five percent of blacks would have to move to attain a uniform distribution, a modest decline since 1980. Lewis Mumford Ctr., Ethnic Diversity Grows, Neighborhood Integration Lags Behind 1-2, 5 (Dec. 18, 2001), http://mumford1.dyndns.org/ cen2000/WholePop/WPreport/MumfordReport.pdf (calculating Index of Dissimilarity, which "captures the degree to which two groups are evenly spread among census tracts in a given city," and presenting chart summarizing black-white segregation.)

[11] Jeffrey Rosen, Bus Stop: The Lost Promise of School Integration, N.Y. Times, Apr. 2, 2000, § 4, at 1.

[15] This is the "spatial mismatch" hypothesis discussed in William Julius Wilson, The

firm level, the race of the owner is a strong predictor of the racial composition of the workforce in privately owned firms. Fifty-eight percent of white-owned firms in major metropolitan areas where minorities live have *no* minority employees at all, whereas eighty-nine percent of black-owned firms have workforces that are at least seventy-five percent minority.[16] The effect of the race of the employer on workforce racial composition is not merely a function of firm location. Even among white-owned firms located in black neighborhoods, one third still have no minority employees. Within the firm, employers practice occupational segregation. One survey of jobs found that half of all job titles were occupied by whites only, and one-quarter of blacks worked in jobs to which only blacks were assigned.[18] A slaughterhouse in North Carolina assigns the butchering jobs to black men, knife work to Mexicans, warehouse jobs to Indians, and mechanic and supervisor positions to whites.[19]

From a compensatory point of view, such patterns of segregation are objectionable as effects of massive, continuing, and illegal private housing and employment discrimination, historic state policies supporting segregation of neighborhoods and schools, officially race-neutral policies that have dramatic racial *effects* (e.g., class-exclusionary zoning), and perhaps also legally permitted expressions of racial antipathy (e.g., white flight). The integrative view focuses more on the *causal impact* of segregation on two core ideals: equality of opportunity and democracy. Segregation is objectionable as a continuing cause of multiple, systematic, mutually reinforcing race-based inequalities, operating independently of and in conjunction with discrimination, in both the economic and political spheres.

1. Equality of Economic Opportunity

Consider, first, how segregation undermines racial equality of economic opportunity, defined as a structure of opportunities in which one's

---

Truly Disadvantaged: The Inner City, the Underclass, and Public Policy (1987). It has been confirmed in multiple studies. See generally Harry J. Holzer & Keith R. Ihlanfeldt, Spatial Factors and the Employment of Blacks at the Firm Level, New Eng. Econ. Rev. May-June 1996, at 65; Keith R. Ihlanfeldt & David J. Sjoquist, Job Accessibility and Racial Differences in Youth Employment Rates, 80 Am. Econ. Rev. 267 (1990); John Kain, The Spatial Mismatch Hypothesis: Three Decades Later, 3 Housing Pol'y Debate 371 (1992); Michael A. Stoll et al., Within Cities and Suburbs: Racial Residential Concentration and the Spatial Distribution of Employment Opportunities Across Sub-Metropolitan Areas, 19 J. Pol'y Analysis & Mgmt. 207 (2000).

[16] Timothy Bates, Banking on Black Enterprise: The Potential of Emerging Firms for Revitalizing Urban Economies 140 (1993).

[18] Donald Tomaskovic-Devey, Gender and Racial Inequality at Work: The Sources and Consequences of Job Segregation 24 (1993).

[19] Charlie LeDuff, At a Slaughterhouse, Some Things Never Die; Who Kills, Who Cuts, Who Bosses Can Depend on Race, N.Y. Times, June 16, 2000, at A1.

racial status has no net causal impact on the value of one's employment, investment, business, and consumption prospects.

Isolation from social networks. Who one knows is at least as important as what one knows in determining one's access to opportunities. At least sixty percent of employers frequently advertise job openings through informal social networks, typically by word-of-mouth through a firm's current employees.[25] Segregation means that whites who get information about job openings are unlikely to know many blacks at work, in school, or in their neighborhoods. Thus, even if whites did not discriminate, blacks would still be excluded from many jobs due to their isolation from the predominantly white social networks of communication and referral that regulate access to mainstream opportunities.

Spatial mismatch of residence from job opportunities. We have seen that residential segregation causes job segregation. This would not lead to systematic disadvantage for African Americans, but for the fact that they live primarily in cities and near suburbs with declining job opportunities, while most job growth has occurred in predominantly white suburbs. The cost per mile of traveling to work is at least fifty percent higher for African Americans than for whites.[29] Housing discrimination imposes barriers to moving where the jobs are located. These factors lead to substantial depression in urban African American wages.

Increased discrimination. Job segregation heightens the salience of race as a marker of employees in ways that encourage unconscious employment discrimination. If a particular job is held only by members of a particular race, the employer's unconscious stereotype of the sort of employee most likely to be suited for that type of job will tend to be racialized. Job segregation is therefore a cause as well as an effect of job discrimination. It is also a cause of racial antipathy in the workplace. Conflicts endemic to the firm's division of labor—for example, between management and labor, or between occupants of different positions in an assembly line who may be inconvenienced by holdups in other parts of the line—become racialized when different races predominate in different positions.

Reduced opportunities for capital accumulation and access to credit. Blacks' confinement to segregated neighborhoods systematically reduces their access to investment opportunities. The middle class invests the largest share of its wealth in housing equity, which amounts to forty-three

[25] See Peter V. Marsden, The Hiring Process: Recruitment Methods, 37 Am. Behav. Scientist 979, 980-85 (1994); id. at 981 (describing how those "who distribute information through interpersonal channels will tend to pass it along to socially similar persons").

[29] Holzer & Ihlanfeldt, supra note 15, at 70

percent of white assets and sixty-three percent of black assets.[33] Because blacks are confined to less-desired neighborhoods, on average the value of their housing grows less than that of whites. Consequently, blacks attain a substantially lower average rate of return on their housing investment than do whites. The current generation of black homeowners has, as a result, suffered a cumulative loss of $58 billion. Because creditworthiness depends on wealth, blacks' lower home values mean they are less able to obtain credit on favorable terms than otherwise equally qualified whites. The current generation of blacks has suffered a cumulative loss of $24 billion due to denial of mortgages and higher mortgage interest rates. Much of this loss can be attributed to residential segregation apart from direct discrimination by lending agents.

Reduced business opportunities. Lack of access to credit is a major cause of low rates of black entrepreneurship.[37] Among all privately owned U.S. businesses, half were started by their owners; the other half were inherited or purchased. By contrast, ninety-four percent of black-owned businesses are self-started (presumably due to the fact that centuries of discrimination and segregation have left blacks with little to inherit). Business startups depend heavily on personal and family wealth, which is leveraged into lines of credit. Residential segregation, by depressing housing appreciation and reducing access to credit, therefore depresses black business startups, upon which black communities disproportionately rely.

Lower access to professional services. African Americans suffer from a far higher burden of disease and mortality than whites while having far less access to medical services. The physician/population ratio in black communities is substantially lower than the U.S. average.[41] This is not just an effect of class. Predominantly black communities are four times more likely to be underserved than communities with the same average income.[42] Professionals are less likely to locate in economically depressed and segregated areas, thereby reducing segregated residents' access to professional services.

2. Democratic Values and Equality of Voice

Racial segregation undermines democratic values as well as equality of economic opportunity. Democracy is a form of governance in which a collective will is forged on the basis of open discussion among equals. It

---

[33] Melvin L. Oliver & Thomas M. Shapiro, Black Wealth/White Wealth: A New Perspective on Racial Inequality 64 (1995).

[37] Thomas D. Boston, Affirmative Action and Black Entrepreneurship 79 (1999).

[41] See Kevin Grumbach et al., Physician Supply and Access to Care in Urban Communities, Health Aff., Jan.-Feb. 1997, at 71.

[42] See Miriam Komaromy et al., The Role of Health Care for Underserved Populations, 334 New Eng. J. Med. 1305, 1306-07 & tbl.1 (1996).

requires a robust civil society in which citizens from all walks of life interact freely on terms of equality. The legitimacy of political outcomes depends on their production through a process of discussion and responsiveness to the interests of all citizens, with no one's voice excluded or ignored because of race. This condition is exceedingly difficult to achieve when the major spheres of civil society—public parks and streets, schools and workplaces—are racially segregated. Again, segregation works its antidemocratic effects through several mechanisms.

Reduced discussion, enhanced mistrust. Segregation reduces opportunities for cross-racial interaction and discussion. It both expresses and reinforces myriad racial antipathies—from hatred, contempt, resentment, and distrust, to discomfort born of unfamiliarity—that interfere with interaction when such opportunities arise. It causes ignorance of the different life circumstances and interests of marginalized groups, enabling policy decisions to be made that disregard the impact on those not present.

Reduced opportunities for political cooperation and sharing of public goods. When racial segregation tracks municipal and district lines, blacks do not have a chance to share in the public services that can be afforded by wealthier whites across district lines. This depresses black access to public goods, which poorer black communities can obtain only at the cost of relatively higher tax burdens. Even middle-class black neighborhoods tend to be in close proximity with poorer areas, so attaining a higher income does not necessarily create a proportional increase in services. Meanwhile, the spatial isolation of black communities within cities makes it more difficult for them to form coalitions with other groups seeking public services because the services provided to blacks need not reach the neighborhoods occupied by other groups.

Policing segregation of public forums. Residential segregation also facilitates and may cause discriminatory policing. If neighborhoods were racially integrated, police could not seize upon someone's race as evidence that their presence is suspicious. Segregation therefore at least makes possible and may cause police to include racial markers in their profile of someone who has no legitimate business in a neighborhood populated by members of a different race. Knowledge that one may be harassed by police for being in the "wrong" neighborhood on account of one's race is a further deterrent to the kind of free and open interracial discussion in civil society that is a prerequisite for realizing democratic ideals.

3. Understanding Discrimination, Segregation, and Integration

Two lessons may be drawn from this brief review of some of the consequences of racial segregation. First, the causal impact of discrimination needs to be reconceived when it takes place in the context of segregation. In the standard discourse on affirmative action, discrimination is viewed as a discrete event, a one-time loss accruing to an individual victim, the effects of which seriously extend no further than her dependents. If the victim is not part of a community segregated from the mainstream, this is a fair model of the causal impact of discrimination. It fits the experience of whites in the United States.

By contrast, when the victim of discrimination belongs to a segregated community, the effects of discrimination spread to other members of the community beyond her family and persist over time. If a firm denies one's neighbor a job due to discrimination, one loses a potential role model, a source of information about job openings at the firm, and a connection who could provide a credible job reference to the firm's owner. This loss is negligible for one who has plenty of other neighbors with connections to mainstream opportunities. But if segregation means one's social network is limited to mostly disadvantaged people like one's neighbor, their disadvantages become one's own. Once these disadvantages become shared, one's community becomes a site of concentrated and self-reinforcing disadvantage, perpetuating the effects of discrimination over time. For African Americans, discrimination is therefore not a discrete one-time loss, because segregation operates as a discrimination "multiplier."

The second lesson is that if racial segregation is part of the problem, then racial integration is part of the solution. Integration is vindicated for its *instrumental* value in dismantling the barriers to equal opportunity and a democratic civil society that are caused by segregation. Integration, in this model, does not mean assimilation. It means effective participation and interaction on terms of equality by members of different races in shared spaces of civil society: at work and school, in the public spaces of neighborhoods, and in the sites of political action and discussion. Here, consideration of the race of participants is not a mere proxy for race-neutral variables, such as being educationally disadvantaged, or even being the victim of discrimination. It is directly, causally relevant to achieving integration and is the most narrowly tailored way to bring about integration. This fact will have substantial implications for considering the constitutionality of race-based affirmative action.

* * *

C. Integration Versus Compensation and Diversity in Educational Contexts

* * *

2. The Diversity Rationale

Should schools * * * try to justify their affirmative action programs on "diversity" grounds? On this defense, schools need racial diversity in the student body to achieve a "robust exchange of ideas."[106] Considered as a purely cognitive end, divorced from the values of democracy and social justice, the "robust exchange of ideas" cannot support the *scope* of racial preferences in college admissions. While it is plausible that the racial diversity of a classroom would enhance discussion of social, political, and cultural subjects by enriching the variety of perspectives voiced, it is hard to see the cognitive relevance of racial diversity to investigations in mathematics, engineering, or the "hard" sciences. Yet schools extend racial preferences in admission to graduate programs in the latter fields. A narrowly academic representation of a school's educational interests undercuts the case for diversity even in the social sciences and humanities. If all that matters is that the whole range of ideas worth considering should be heard, why care about the racial identities of those who voice them? Why can't instructors and reading assignments represent all the diversity of information and opinion students need? If the true educational interest is to ensure that a diversity of opinions be heard in the classroom, schools should select students directly for the ideological diversity they can be expected to bring to the classroom, rather than use race as a crude proxy for this.

* * *

3. Reconfiguring the Mission of Education and Integration

The integrative model of affirmative action offers an alternative rationale for race-sensitive admissions that unites educational with democratic and social justice concerns. It begins with a recognition that Americans live in a profoundly segregated society, a condition inconsistent with a fully democratic society and with equal opportunity. To achieve the latter goals, we need to desegregate—to integrate, that is—to live together as one body of equal citizens. Civil society is the special site where we are supposed do this living together as equals, working out together the terms of our interaction. It is a site still under construction. This construction is hampered by two types of ignorance: Citizens of different races by and large do not know one another and do not know how to live together as equals. Public schools, along with cosmopolitan private colleges and universities, are crucial sites in civil society for citizens of different walks of life to *learn* how to live together on terms of equality. In the United States, they do a remarkably good job teaching citizens of different religions to live together on terms of equality. They have not been able to serve a similar educational function for citizens of different races at the K-12 level, because the

[106] Regents of the Univ. of Cal. v. Bakke, 438 U.S. 265, 313 (Powell, J.) (permitting raceconscious admissions to advance university's compelling interest in "robust exchange of ideas," promoted by diversity in student body).

schools are racially segregated. Colleges and universities provide a nearly unique opportunity for many middle-class Americans to learn how to live in integrated settings. It is a lesson they carry with them later in life, and one rarely learned by whites who attend racially homogeneous colleges. Both blacks and whites tend to continue the patterns of interracial interaction they learned in college. In particular, whites who grew up in predominantly white neighborhoods, but attended colleges with relatively high proportions of minority students, are much more likely to have friends, neighbors, and co-workers of diverse racial backgrounds than their white neighbors who attended colleges with low racial diversity. Without race-conscious admissions, selective colleges cannot achieve integration and thereby teach this lesson to American elites, consistent with their mission of achieving academic excellence on a national or international scale.

The goal of integration on this account is simultaneously educational, democratic, and a matter of social justice. Consider, in this light, one of the forward-looking claims made on behalf of race-conscious admissions: that racial diversity in the student body helps break down racial stereotypes.[119] Our interest in doing so is a matter of justice, of ending societal discrimination. But it is not about compensating for past wrongs. It is about constructing a better future. Members of underrepresented racial groups are admitted under integrative affirmative action programs, not as victims of discrimination, but as agents of integration, contributing to the education of their fellow students.

Our interest in breaking down racial stereotypes is also educational. But it is not a narrowly academic achievement of the sort that could be tested in a recitation of facts or measured in a final exam. Still less is it a matter of adopting politically correct opinions. The stereotypes in question are forms of *practical* incompetence, embodied in clumsy and disrespectful habits that typically inform our behavior in an unconscious way. Breaking them down is a matter of acquiring *practical* knowledge, a skill of engaging with people of different races in a manner that is sensitive to and respectful of their individual differences and social circumstances. This is why this knowledge cannot be obtained solely from curricular materials or from a racially homogeneous faculty. It requires actually interacting with people of different races. Nor can it be obtained from the token numbers of blacks, Latinos, and Native Americans who would populate selective college campuses in the absence of affirmative action. Token numbers are too small to ensure a significant probability that white students will encounter them. Moreover, when members of underrepresented racial groups are present in

[119] Integration, of course, cannot be reduced to this aim. It is about forging interracial cooperation, mutual engagement, friendship and acquaintance, stimulating critical reflection on matters of identity and difference, and much more.

only token numbers, this heightens the salience of their racial identities and primes racial stereotypes. A critical mass of students of a given racial group needs to be present to help people learn to see internal heterogeneity in that group. This explains why the educational interest in racial diversity needs to pay "attention to numbers."[124]

The aim in breaking down racial stereotypes is also a democratic interest. We cannot truly hear what others are saying in democratic dialogue if we process and thereby homogenize what they say through racial stereotypes. Far wider aims are at stake once we recognize that the college campus and classroom are located in civil society, and that they are therefore critical sites for a democratic culture. The central value of democratic culture is not that all the opinions worth considering are heard, but that everyone gets a chance to speak. We cannot identify in advance the opinions that ought to be heard, and then try to select speakers on the ground that they will express those opinions. The authority of conversations about the core contested ideas in our culture—over the contested meanings of cultural practices, historical events, research findings in the human sciences, laws, and public policies—depends on their responsiveness to the input of people from all walks of life who stand in different relations to these phenomena. The realities of segregation and discrimination in America today mean that members of different races come from different walks of life. This is why it matters not just what is said, but who says it. This is what makes the racial inclusiveness of classroom discussion so important.

The integrative model presented here does not reject the diversity defense of affirmative action. It reconfigures that defense so as to join it to the core social justice and democratic concerns that motivate the advocates of affirmative action. "Diversity" should be thought of as another way of talking about integration. The rhetoric of diversity has some advantages. Talk of diversity avoids any insulting suggestion that integration requires assimilation into white-majority ways or pretending, in colorblind mode, that people do not have different racial identities. At the same time, however, tying diversity back to integration reminds us of the realities of segregation and its attendant injustices and hence of what makes racial identities morally relevant in the first place. Moreover, it signals a transformative process of coming together, where both the school and the students are *agents* of social change—in contrast with the connotations of static difference and accommodation that surround the idea of diversity.

The integrative model has several legal advantages over the diversity and compensation models of affirmative action. It makes sense of the scope and weight that educational institutions actually give to race in the

---

[124] Regents of the Univ. of Cal. v. Bakke, 438 U.S. 265, 323 (1978).

admissions process. It thus closes the gap between theory and practice that makes affirmative action programs so vulnerable under strict scrutiny. It also shows how race can be directly relevant to a compelling state interest, rather than a mere proxy for something else, such as diversity of opinions. This makes integration superior to the standard diversity model in its ability to withstand strict scrutiny. It can justify educational affirmative action programs that focus exclusively on integrating marginalized racial groups, without having to adopt an elaborate system considering a myriad of other groups or diversity factors. It avoids the burdensome evidentiary requirements * * * used to effectively preclude compensatory affirmative action in higher education.

GIRARDEAU A. SPANN, THE DARK SIDE OF *GRUTTER*[*]

Forthcoming, CONSTITUTIONAL COMMENTARY (2004)

INTRODUCTION

Liberals have generally cheered the Supreme Court's decision in *Grutter v. Bollinger*[1] as validating the continued use of affirmative action in the struggle against racial injustice. But the Supreme Court's modern race cases rest on a misunderstanding of the nature of contemporary racial discrimination. From *Brown*, to *Bakke*, to *Grutter*, the Court has advanced a colorblind conception of racial equality that treats race-conscious affirmative action as constitutionally suspect, because it deviates from an aspirational baseline of race neutrality that lies at the core of the equal protection clause. However, race neutrality is a hopelessly artificial concept in a Nation like ours, that continues to make race an operative factor in the allocation of nearly all significant societal resources. Rather, it is colorblind race neutrality that should be viewed as constitutionally suspect, because that is what now constitutes the culture's preferred form of racial discrimination. Contemporary "race neutrality" is simply a modern descendent of the more traditional forms of invidious discrimination that have been practiced in the United States since the Nation was founded. And the Supreme Court's current preference for race-neutrality over race-consciousness is a modern descendent of the Court's own tradition of complicity in racial discrimination.

* * *

I. THE COURT'S CONCEPTION OF EQUALITY

[1] 123 S. Ct. 2325 (2003).

The Supreme Court views racial equality as if it were largely synonymous with race neutrality. As a result, the Court treats all racial classifications as constitutionally suspect, and subjects them to strict scrutiny under the equal protection clause, whether they are invidious or benign.[6] The Court's preference for prospective neutrality has the effect of invalidating most uses of race-conscious affirmative action, which in turn makes it difficult to eliminate the existing inequalities that have been produced by centuries of prior discrimination.

A. Race Neutrality

The Supreme Court's fondness for race neutrality is traceable to *Brown v. Board of Education*. *Brown* invalidated the race-conscious, separate-but-equal regime of *Plessy v. Ferguson*, holding that, in our racially stratified society, separate was "inherently unequal." *Brown*, therefore, treated race-conscious governmental classifications as intrinsically objectionable, even if race was used in ways that were hypothetically "equal." But *Brown* also generated a logical dilemma. The Nation's long history of official discrimination left a legacy of existing inequalities that could not be remedied merely through the use of prospective race neutrality. Indeed, the ingrained and often unconscious racial attitudes that caused *Brown* to characterize racial segregation as inherently unequal meant that racial minorities could never make up for the considerable head start that whites had given themselves in the race for economic, political and social resources—unless whites were forced to slow down long enough for racial minorities to catch up. Therefore, the race-neutral society that *Brown* envisioned could come into existence only through use of the race-conscious means that *Brown* found objectionable. *Brown* and its progeny ultimately sought to resolve this dilemma by permitting the use of race-conscious measures only where necessary to remedy past or present constitutional violations. However, *Brown* was unclear about precisely *why* race consciousness offended the Constitution.

The Court's reason for treating race consciousness as constitutionally suspect was fleshed out by Justice Powell's opinion in *Regents of the University of California v. Bakke*.[13] *Bakke* stressed that the problem with racial classifications was that they stereotyped people as members of particular racial groups, rather than treating people as individuals. Moreover, because that was true of *all* racial classifications—whether invidious or benign—all racial classification should be subject to strict scrutiny under the equal protection clause. Affirmative action programs could not therefore use "racial quotas" to achieve "racial balance," because

---

[6] *See Grutter*, 123 S. Ct. at 2337-38; Adarand Constructors v. Peña, 515 U.S. 200, 223-27 (1995).

[13] 438 U.S. 265, 269 (1978) (opinion of Powell, J.).

that would subordinate individual characteristics to group membership in a way that violated the tenets of liberalism on which the equal protection clause rested. Once again, however, the Court's understanding of racial discrimination simply re-posed the *Brown* dilemma. Because someone's race is an important component of his or her individual identity, individualized consideration must necessarily entail some degree of race-conscious consideration. Justice Powell sought to resolve the dilemma by permitting the use of race as a "plus" factor in what was otherwise an individualized assessment of merit. But that could only be done as part of a program that was narrowly tailored to advance a compelling state interest, thereby satisfying the demands of strict scrutiny. Although the *Bakke* "holding" consisted largely of the views of Justice Powell, a five-Justice majority of the Supreme Court endorsed those views in *Grutter v. Bollinger.*[18]

* * *

Grutter reaffirmed the *Bakke* view that diversity could constitute a compelling state interest in an educational context, but it also strongly endorsed *Bakke*'s distaste for racial quotas. In upholding the racial affirmative action program used by the University of Michigan law school, the *Grutter* Court went to great pains to stress that the program was valid because it merely used race as a "plus" factor in "a highly individualized, holistic review of each applicant's file," and did not entail the use of racial quotas that "would amount to outright racial balancing, which is patently unconstitutional." The Court hammered the point home on the same day by invalidating, in *Gratz v. Bollinger*,[32] the separate racial affirmative action program used by the University of Michigan undergraduate college. It found that the undergraduate program's automatic award of a fixed number of points to minority applicants denied "individualized consideration" to each applicant, and had "the effect of making 'the factor of race . . . decisive' for virtually every minimally qualified underrepresented minority applicant." Although it is likely that future affirmative action programs will now be structured to emulate the program upheld in *Grutter*, the Court's insistence on holistic consideration of admissions files may increase the administrative burden imposed on admissions offices enough to reduce the amount of affirmative action that schools can afford to undertake.

The precedential value of *Grutter* is uncertain for at least two reasons. First, the case may or may not be limited to the educational context in which it was decided. Justice Scalia's contrary suggestion notwithstand-

---

[18] *See Grutter*, 123 S. Ct. at 2338-39, 2341-44.

[32] 123 S. Ct. 2411 (2003) (invalidating racial affirmative action program at University of Michigan undergraduate College of Literature, Science and Arts).

ing,[34] diversity may not be recognized as compelling in other contexts such as employment, where the goal is productivity rather than the exchange of intellectual ideas and perspectives. Second, because Justice O'Connor has become the swing vote on the issue of affirmative action, the precedential value of *Grutter* may be limited by both her personal policy preferences and her tenure on the Court. If a more conservative Justice were to replace Justice O'Connor, *Grutter* might be narrowly interpreted or even overruled. If the case were narrowly interpreted, Justice Kennedy's position in *Grutter* might become controlling, and the law of affirmative action could once again revert to its post-*Adarand* status. Affirmative action would remain theoretically permissible, but in actuality, no program would likely be found to survive strict scrutiny. However, it may also be true that considerations of efficiency and collegiality will make the Court reluctant to revisit the racial affirmative action issue in the immediate future. * * *

* * *

B. Societal Discrimination

Liberal celebrations notwithstanding, Justice O'Connor's majority opinion in *Grutter* seems likely to prolong rather than ameliorate the problem of racial discrimination. It holds that affirmative action programs must be narrowly tailored in order to survive strict scrutiny, but it defines narrow tailoring to mean non-responsiveness to the continuing problem of systemic discrimination. Consistent with *Bakke*'s assertion that racial classifications are unconstitutional because they treat people as members of a group rather than as individuals, *Grutter* views racial discrimination as something that is particularized rather than pervasive in nature. Accordingly, it reaffirms prior cases asserting that affirmative action cannot constitutionally be used to remedy general "societal discrimination." This, in turn, allows the Court to treat the concept of racial equality as if it were largely synonymous with the concept of prospective race neutrality. As long as the continuing effects of prior discrimination can be disregarded by denominating them "societal," formal equality can be achieved merely by insisting on prospective colorblindness.

The Supreme Court has repeatedly asserted that the goal of reducing systemic or "societal discrimination" is a constitutionally impermissible goal for race-conscious affirmative action. The Court believes that the pursuit of such a goal would authorize affirmative action programs that were too vast, and too burdensome on innocent whites. Moreover, it would permit the state to utilize quotas to achieve racial balance in a way that was

---

[34] *See Grutter*, 123 S. Ct. at 2349 (Scalia, J. dissenting) (suggesting that diversity justification endorsed by majority could be used to justify affirmative action in public and private employment).

inconsistent with the race-neutrality foundations of *Brown*. Therefore, the Court has historically limited race-conscious affirmative action to narrowly tailored remedies for particularized acts of past discrimination that were supported by reliable legislative, judicial or administrative findings. Although *Grutter* has now authorized the use of affirmative action to promote diversity, it has nevertheless reaffirmed the traditional prohibition on using affirmative action to remedy general societal discrimination.

By ruling race-conscious remedies for societal discrimination out of bounds, the Supreme Court has enabled itself largely to sidestep the dilemma posed by *Brown* and *Bakke*. The Court's reconceptualization of "racial equality" as something that can exist despite the continued systemic effects of past discrimination avoids most needs to authorize the use of race-conscious remedies in the pursuit of equality. Prospective race neutrality typically becomes adequate to satisfy whatever demands the equal protection clause imposes, because the inequalities that cannot be eliminated through race-neutral means typically do not count for equal protection purposes. That sort of reconceptualization is precisely what the Court used to deal with the problem of Northern school desegregation in the post-*Brown* era. Not wanting to force suburban white children to go to school with inner-city black or Latino children, the Supreme Court simply *defined* one-race minority schools to be "desegregated" despite the fact that their racially identifiable character had not changed. Justice Ginsburg's dissenting opinion in *Gratz* offers a striking statistical demonstration of the ways in which societal discrimination continues to make racial minorities an identifiable underclass in American culture.[56] But the Supreme Court has now chosen simply to *define* racial equality as something that takes no cognizance of those inequalities. *Grutter*'s recognition of a constitutionally legitimate interest in educational diversity may superficially seem to be an exception to this characterization. However, I believe that after more careful scrutiny, *Grutter* is better understood as having little to do with the interests of racial minorities.

II. RACE-NEUTRAL DISCRIMINATION

The Supreme Court's preference for race neutrality, rooted in its reluctance to confront the continuing problem of systemic societal discrimination, turns out to be a fairly effective way of engaging in racial discrimination. By reading the Constitution to preserve the racial status quo in the allocation of significant societal resources, the Nation's white majority is able to continue discounting the interests of racial minorities in ways that are too passive to be immediately recognized as oppressive. Even *Grutter* is discriminatory in this sense, because it authorizes only marginal increases

---

[56] *See Gratz*, 123 S. Ct. at 2443-44 (Ginsburg, J., dissenting).

in racial diversity while prohibiting more meaningful systemic change. * * *

A. Passive Oppression

The United States has a long tradition of invidious discrimination against racial minorities, and an equally long tradition of insisting on both the *de jure* and the *de facto* relevance of race in nearly all aspects of American life. It is not surprising, therefore, that the culture's new-found affinity for prospective race neutrality in the post-*Brown* era comes at a time when racial minorities have begun to make economic, political and social gains through the use of race-conscious affirmative action. By arresting those gains, current demands for race neutrality are simply the modern incarnation of the same invidious discrimination that the culture has used to oppress racial minorities in the past. It seems more than a mere coincidence that contemporary voter initiative proposals requiring race neutrality, and even prohibiting the collection of statistical data in racial categories, have been sponsored by political conservatives (who have historically opposed racial minority rights) rather than by political liberals (who have historically favored minority rights).

Similarly, the Supreme Court's refusal to allow even majoritarian political remedies for societal discrimination, fits comfortably within a long tradition of Supreme Court impediments to the advancement of racial equality. It is reminiscent of earlier Supreme Court decisions upholding the appropriation of Indian lands,[59] upholding slavery,[60] upholding official segregation,[61] upholding the exclusion of Japanese-American citizens from their homes,[62] and upholding *de facto* racial segregation.[63] Viewed against this backdrop, the Supreme Court's insistence on defining narrow tailoring to preclude remedies for societal discrimination is more than just curious. The Court's position is itself constitutionally suspect, because it seems to be motivated by a desire to ensure that racial minorities continue to occupy their traditional social status as subordinate to whites. Despite the lofty

---

[59] *See* Johnson v. McIntosh, 21 U.S. (8 Wheat.) 543 (1823) (European discovery of land now constituting United States, and conquest of indigenous Indian inhabitants, divested Indians of title to that land).

[60] *See* Dred Scott v. Sanford, 60 U.S. (19 How.) 397 (1857) (invalidating congressional statute prohibiting slavery in Louisiana Territory

[61] *See* Plessy v. Ferguson, 163 U.S. 537 (1896) (upholding separate-but-equal racial segregation).

[62] *See* Korematsu v. United States, 323 U.S. 214 (1944) (upholding World War II military exclusion order directed at Japanese-American citizens).

[63] *See* Keyes v. Sch. Dist. No. 1, Denver, Colo., 413 U.S. 189, 208-09 (1973) (adopting expansive interpretation of de jure segregation, but reaffirming prohibition on use of race-conscious remedies to eliminate *de facto* segregation); Swann v. Charlotte-Mecklenburg Bd. of Educ., 402 U.S. 1, 17-18 (1971) (same) * * *.

rhetoric that is typically used to advocate it, there is nothing noble about contemporary race neutrality.

The thing that animates the Supreme Court's conception of racial discrimination is a belief that it should be understood as a particularized phenomenon that is unrelated to the statistically disproportionate hardships suffered by racial minorities as a group. However, the most oppressive forms of contemporary discrimination are systemic in nature. They are revealed by racially-correlated statistical disparities, and not by pairing individual discriminators with individual victims. The reason that racial minorities occupy a perpetual underclass in the United States is that they are statistically underrepresented in the allocation of societal resources. And that remains true even though the Supreme Court finds it difficult to identify a particularized cause of that pervasive underrepresentation.

* * *

However, even if one insists on ignoring systemic discrimination and characterizing unconstitutional racial discrimination as the violation of an individual right—as the Supreme Court insists on doing—that characterization is equally applicable to both affirmative action and societal discrimination. To the extent that the burdens of affirmative action can be personified by the harm to one individual white who might have been admitted to a program in the absence of affirmative action, the burdens of societal discrimination can be personified by the harm to one individual black who might have been admitted to a program in the absence of societal discrimination. The only difference is the race of the groups (or individuals) that the Supreme Court decides to protect or abandon. If the victims are white, the Supreme Court will protect them by invalidating the offending affirmative action program. But if the victims are black, the Supreme Court will abandon them and disregard the offending societal discrimination. As it has done so often in the past, the Supreme Court is simply favoring the interests of whites over the interests of racial minorities. In a culture replete with invidious societal discrimination against racial minorities, the Supreme Court has focused its attention on the more marginal burdens that affirmative action imposes on whites. That is called racial discrimination.

* * *

III. RACE-CONSCIOUS EQUALITY

Only vigorous efforts to redistribute societal resources in ways that are unapologetically race-conscious are likely to make any qualitative change in the systemic discrimination that continues to characterize American culture. But *Grutter's* treatment of such racial-balance remedies as inconsistent with a liberal conception of individual rights consigns the concept of affirmative action to a role of marginal utility. Moreover, the lack of any meaningful distinction between the Court's decisions in *Grutter* and *Gratz* makes the Court's racial jurisprudence seem both arbitrary and capricious. And it may be invidious as well.

A. Resource Redistribution

In a culture that was free from racial discrimination, one would expect to see resources distributed in ways that were racially proportional. The maldistribution of resources that exists in contemporary American culture is, therefore, evidence of continuing racial discrimination—either active discrimination, or more passive acquiescence in the lingering effects of past discrimination. Logically, such discrimination must exist either in the selection of the criteria that we use to govern resource allocation; in the manner in which we apply those criteria; or in the training that we provide to satisfy those criteria. This syllogistic conclusion can be avoided only if one believes that racial minorities are inherently inferior to whites in their ability to satisfy our allocation criteria. And that, of course, would be simply another form of racial discrimination.

If we were serious about racial equality, we would want to redistribute societal resources in ways that promoted racial balance. And we would be willing to use racially proportional guidelines and quotas to achieve that racial balance. Race conscious efforts to promote racial balance would enable us to approximate the distribution of resources that would exist in a nondiscriminatory culture, which is something that we have not otherwise been able to achieve. And treating racial balance as an explicit goal would constitute an unambiguous statement of our societal goals and priorities, which would be refreshing in its candor. Racial balance would also constitute a legal standard that was easier for policy makers to implement than the current affirmative action standards, which require policy makers to guess about the Supreme Court's likely response to particular uses of race. In fact, I suspect that most organizations wishing to promote diversity and avoid unconscious racial discrimination have in the past, and would in the future, find racial balancing to be a useful prophylactic technique. But most important, racial balance is likely to offer the only effective protection against the various versions of societal discrimination that are embedded in our more traditional resource allocation criteria. Such societal discrimination is too ingrained, subtle and pervasive to be confronted directly, but is automatically counteracted by the racially proportional allocation of resources.

Rather than facilitating the redistribution of societal resources in a way that would promote racial balance, the Supreme Court has actually held such redistribution to be unlawful. As has been noted, Justice O'Connor's majority opinion in *Grutter* states that such a goal "would amount to outright racial balancing, which is patently unconstitutional."[86] But it is very difficult to see why that should be so. The Court states that it is motivated by a desire to ensure that race-conscious remedies are not too broad, and are not too burdensome on whites. But that is nonresponsive. The whole point of racial balance is to stop giving whites the resources that they have in the past secured through societal discrimination, rather than through more legitimate means. The argument that racial balance is bad because it would burden whites simply entrenches the problem.

A more serious justification for the Court's aversion to racial balancing is that the consideration of race is inconsistent with the right that people possess in a liberal culture to be treated as individuals rather than as members of a racial group. But that argument is ultimately self-consuming. If allocating resources based on race is a denial of individual rights, then refusing to reallocate resources after they have initially been allocated by race is also a denial of individual rights. Once a culture embarks along the path of race-conscious resource allocation—as American culture did with a vengeance—it creates a zero-sum relationship between affirmative action and discrimination that cannot be eliminated until racial balance is restored. Whenever we allocate a resource, we are either allocating it to whites in a way that reinforces societal discrimination, or to racial minorities in a way that ameliorates societal discrimination. There is no middle ground, because there is no such thing as a race-neutral allocation. There is only the pretense of race neutrality that occurs when we elect to use inertia as our preferred form of racial discrimination. Which, of course, is precisely what the Supreme Court has done by reading the Constitution to prohibit race-conscious pursuit of racial balance.

Despite the Supreme Court principle of treating people as individuals rather than as members of a racial group, it should be noted that *Grutter* does *not* prohibit the consideration of race in the allocation of societal resources. *Grutter* holds that race *can* be considered, as long as it is treated as a "plus" factor in a "holistic" evaluation of individual attributes, and is not treated mechanically as a racial quota. In this regard, the Court's approach to race in *Grutter* is similar to its approach in *Miller v. Johnson*,[91] where the Court held that race could be considered as a factor in the redistricting context as long as it was not the "predominant" factor. In both instances, the Supreme Court has adopted a position that is truly curious. It has rejected the polar extremes of prohibiting all consideration of race, or of allowing the express pursuit of racial balance. Instead, it has in effect adopted the position that race can be considered as long as five members of the Court do not think that race has been given too much weight. It is

---

[86] *See Grutter*, 123 S. Ct. at 2339.

[91] 515 U.S. 900 (1995).

striking that the Justices would conclude that the Supreme Court was institutionally more competent than the policymaking arms of American culture to decide on appropriate uses of race, given the Court's historical record on the issue. Moreover, the Court's efforts to distinguish between permissible and impermissible uses of race do not seem to be particularly coherent.

B. Grutter v. Gratz

The Supreme Court purports to distinguish between constitutionally permissible and constitutionally impermissible uses of race in its contrasting *Grutter* and *Gratz* opinions. * * *

* * *

Although the affirmative action programs at issue in *Grutter* and *Gratz* met different constitutional fates, the two programs are analytically indistinguishable. As columnist Michael Kinsley has pointed out, for any individual applicant, race is either dispositive or it is not. This is true no matter how many factors go into an admissions decision. And it is true whether race is used holistically in connection with a flexible admissions process, or mechanically in connection with a mathematical score.[104] Therefore, the differences that exist between the ways in which race was used in *Grutter* and in *Gratz* are simply irrelevant to any constitutionally protected individual right. If it is constitutionally permissible for race to determine the fate of an applicant, that applicant's fate is not changed by the details of the program that gave rise to the consideration of race.

* * *

The real difference between the law school program upheld in *Grutter* and the undergraduate program invalidated in *Gratz* seems to be that the Supreme Court believes that the *Gratz* program gave too much weight to the factor of race, and it did so in a manner that was too transparent. * * * I suspect that in actual operation, both programs would end up admitting largely the same individual minority students, and would therefore have the same general effect on white applicants. But even if I am wrong about this, it is unlikely that differences in the weight given to the factor of race within the range of these two programs could rise to a level of constitutional significance.

There is a real irony in the emphasis that both cases place on the use of points and numerical goals, with *Grutter* finding that such a use of numbers did not play an impermissible role, and *Gratz* finding that it did. The thing that the Court finds troubling about numbers is their potential to serve as

---

[104] *See* Michael Kinsley, *Want Diversity? Think Fuzzy*, WASH. POST, June 25, 2003, at A23. * * *

quotas that insulate minority applicants from competition in order to promote racial balance. But that concern seems backwards. Assuming that minorities are not inherently inferior to whites, we would expect a nondiscriminatory "holistic" admissions program, that was designed to promote diversity, to end up with a racially proportional allocation of seats. However, if a program attempts to use numerical methods to facilitate that goal (as in *Gratz*), the program is unconstitutional because of its resemblance to a quota. Therefore, in order for a program to be constitutionally acceptable (as in *Grutter*), it will have to take great pains to ensure that its consideration of diversity factors does not produce results that make it *look* like quotas were used. The only way to do this reliably is by taking conscious precautions to ensure that the numerical percentages of minority admissions vary from year to year, and do not correspond too closely to the percentages of various racial groups in the applicant pool or in the general population. Thus, the use of a "floating" racial quota will be necessary to ensure that the program looks like a valid holistic program, rather than an invalid quota program that was intended to promote racial balance. Since the institution will have to pay a lot of attention to numbers either way, it is a bit perverse to say that a program is valid only if it gives *more* consideration to numbers in order to create the impression that it gave *less* consideration to numbers. In this regard, the *Gratz* program is probably more honest than the *Grutter* program—which is what makes it unconstitutional. A Supreme Court rule that produces such a result cannot be a proper rule of constitutional law. Unless our goal is to promote disingenuousness. * * *

[T]he argument that we should hide our conscious consideration of race in order to convey the impression that race is a less salient characteristic in contemporary culture than it really is seems counterproductive. The whole point should be to *highlight* our race consciousness so that we can no longer complacently pretend that we live in a race-neutral culture. *Grutter* and *Gratz* allow the continued use of race-conscious affirmative action, but only with the understanding that it will not be used in ways that makes any systemic modifications in the current allocation of resources. The opinions take great pains to ensure that the continuing effects of societal discrimination will remain beyond the reach of race-conscious remedies. And that, in turn, perpetuates the invidious discrimination against racial minorities that has always characterized American culture. The Supreme Court is unwilling to concede that American culture is structurally discriminatory. But the recognition of continuing structural discrimination seems like the most important thing that is at stake in the affirmative action debate. In a sense, *Grutter* and *Gratz* may present the worst of both worlds for racial minorities. They leave open the possibility that affirmative action will sometimes be constitutionally permissible, thereby preventing racial minorities from becoming too unruly. But under the prevailing standards, truly beneficial affirmative action programs will rarely be upheld in reality. That is not a bad strategy for continued racial oppression.

BIBLIOGRAPHY

Adams, *The Last Wave of Affirmative Action*, 1998 Wisc.L.Rev. 1395.

Aleinikoff, *Re-Reading Justice Harlan's Dissent in* Plessy v. Ferguson: *Freedom, Antiracism and Citizenship,* 1992 Ill.L.Rev. 961.

Appiah and Gutmann, COLOR CONSCIOUS, THE POLITICAL MORALITY OF RACE (1996).

Ayres, *Narrow Tailoring,* 43 UCLA L.Rev. 1781 (1996).

Bhagwat, *Affirmative Action and Compelling Interests: Equal Protection Jurisprudence at the Crossroads*, 4 U.Pa.J.Constit. L. 260 (2002).

Bell, *In Defense of Minority Admissions Programs: A Response to Professor Graglia,* 119 U.Pa.L.Rev. 364 (1970).

Belz, H., EQUALITY TRANSFORMED: A QUARTER-CENTURY OF AFFIRMATIVE ACTION (1991).

Blasi, Bakke *as Precedent: Does Mr. Justice Powell Have A Theory?,* 67 Calif.L.Rev. 21 (1979).

Brest and Oshige [McGowan], *Affirmative Action for Whom?,* 47 Stan. L.Rev. 855 (1995).

Brooks, *The Affirmative Action Issue: Law, Policy and Morality,* 22 Conn.L.Rev. 323 (1990).

Bryden, *On Race and Diversity,* 6 Const.Comm. 383 (1989).

Carrington, *Diversity!,* 1992 Utah L.Rev. 1105 (1992).

Carter, REFLECTIONS OF AN AFFIRMATIVE ACTION BABY (1991).

Chang, Discriminatory *Impact, Affirmative Action, and Innocent Victims: Judicial Conservatism or Conservative Justices?,* 91 Colum.L.Rev. 790 (1991).

Chang, Reverse *Racism!: Affirmative Action, The Family, and the Dream That is America,* 23 Hastings Const.L,Q. 1115 (1996).

Chin, *Bakke to the Wall: The Crisis of Bakkean Diversity,* 4 Wm. & Mary Bill of Rights J. 881(1996).

Cohen, *Race and the Constitution,* The Nation, Feb. 8, 1975.

Cohen, *Why Racial Preference is Illegal and Immoral,* Commentary, June 1979, at 40.

Collier, *The New Logic of Affirmative Action*, 45 Duke L.J. 559 (1995).

Days, *Fullilove,* 96 Yale L.J. 453 (1987).

Delgado, *Affirmative Action as a Majoritarian Device: Or, Do You Really Want to Be a* Role *Model?,* 89 Mich.L.Rev. 1222 (1991).

Devins, *Affirmative Action after Reagan,* 68 Tex.L.Rev. 353 (1989).

Devins, Metro Broadcasting, Inc. v. FCC: *Requiem for a Heavyweight,* 69 Tex.L.Rev. 125 (1990).

Duncan, *The Future of Affirmative Action: A Jurisprudential/Legal Critique,* 17 Harv.C.R.–C.L.L.Rev. 503 (1982).

Dworkin, R., TAKING RIGHTS SERIOUSLY ch. 9 (1977).

Eastland, *The Case Against Affirmative Action,* 34 Wm. & Mary L.Rev. 33 (1992).

Edwards and Zaretsky, *Preferential Remedies for Employment Discrimination,* 74 Mich.L.Rev. 1 (1975).

Ellis, *Victim-Specific Remedies: A Myopic Approach to Discrimination,* 13 N.Y.U.Rev.L. & Soc.Change 575 (1985).

Ely, *The Constitutionality of Reverse Racial Discrimination,* 41 U.Chi.L. Rev. 723 (1974).

Epps, *Of Constitutional Seances and Color-blind Ghosts,* 72 N.C.L.Rev. 401 (1994).

Epstein, *The Remote Causes of Affirmative Action, or School Desegregation in Kansas City, Missouri,* 84 Cal.L.Rev. 1101 (1996).

Epstein, *A Rational Basis for Affirmative Action: A Shaky but Classical Liberal Defense*, 100 Mich. L. Rev. 2036 (2002).

EQUALITY AND PREFERENTIAL TREATMENT (M. Cohen, T. Nagel & T. Scanlon eds. 1977).

Fair, *Foreword: Rethinking the Colorblindness Model,* 13 Nat'l Black L.J. 1 (1993).

Fallon, *To Each according to His Ability, From None according to His Race: The Concept of Merit in the Law of Antidiscrimination,* 60 B.U.L.Rev. 815 (1980).

Fallon and Weiler, Firefighters v. Stotts*: Conflicting Models of Racial Justice,* 1984 Sup.Ct.Rev. 1.

Farber and Frickey, *Is* Carolene Products *Dead? Reflections on Affirmative Action and the Dynamics of Civil Rights Legislation,* 79 Cal.L.Rev. 685 (1991).

Forde-Mazrui, *The Constitutional Implications of Race-Neutral Affirmative Action*, 88 Geo.L.J. 2331 (2000).

Foster, *Difference and Equality: A Critical Assessment of the Concept of "Diversity",* 1993 Wis.L.Rev. 105.

Fried, Metro Broadcasting, Inc. v. FCC*: Two Concepts of Equality*, 104 Harv.L.Rev. 107 (1990).

Fullinwinder, R., THE REVERSE DISCRIMINATION CONTROVERSY: A MORAL AND LEGAL ANALYSIS (1980).

Goldman, A., JUSTICE AND REVERSE DISCRIMINATION (1979).

Gottesman, *Twelve Topics to Consider Before Opting for Racial Quotas,* 79 Geo.L.J. 1737 (1991).

Graglia, *Affirmative Action, "Past, Present, and Future",* 22 Ohio N.U.L. Rev. 1207 (1996).

Graglia, Podberesky, Hopwood, *and* Adarand*: Implications for the Future of Race-Based Programs,* 16 N.Ill.U.L.Rev. 287 (1996).

Graglia, *Special Admission of the "Culturally Deprived" to Law School,* 119 U.Pa.L.Rev. 351 (1970).

Greenawalt, K., DISCRIMINATION AND REVERSE DISCRIMINATION (1983).

Greenwalt, *Judicial Scrutiny of "Benign" Racial Preferences in Law School Admissions*) 75 Colum.L.Rev. 559 (1975).

Hall, *Educational Diversity: Viewpoints and Proxies*, 59 Ohio St.L.J. 551 (1998).

Johnson, *Destabilizing Racial Classifications Based on Insights Gleaned from Trademark Law,* 84 Cal.L.Rev. 887 (1996).

Jones, *The Origins of Affirmative Action,* 21 U.C.Davis L.Rev. 383 (1988).

Kahlenberg, *Class-Based Affirmative Action,* 84 Cal.L.Rev. 1037 (1996).

Katz, *The Economics of Discrimination: The Three Fallacies of* Croson, 100 Yale L.J. 103 (1991).

Kennedy, *A Cultural Pluralist Case for Affirmative Action in Legal Academia,* 1990 Duke L.J. 705.

Killenbeck, *Pushing Things Up to Their First Principles: Reflections on the Values of Affirmative Action*, 87 Cal. L. Rev. 1299 (1999).

Kull, A., THE COLOR-BLIND CONSTITUTION (1992).

Lawrence, C. and Matsuda, M., WON'T GO BACK (1997).

Lawrence, *Each Other's Harvest: Diversity's Deeper Meaning,* 3 U.S.F. L.Rev. 757 (1997).

Lawrence, *Two Views of the River: A Critique of the Liberal Defense of Affirmative Action*, 101 Colum.L.Rev. 928 (2001).

Liu, *The Causation Fallacy:* Bakke *and the Basic Arithmetic of Selective Admissions*, 100 Mich.LRev. 1045 (2002).

Malamud, *Class-Based Affirmative Action: Lessons and Caveats*, 74 Tex.L.Rev. 1847 (1996).

Matsuda, *Affirmative Action and Legal Knowledge: Planting Seeds in Plowed-Up Ground,* 11 Harv.Women's L.J. 1 (1988).

Matsuda, *Looking to the Bottom: Critical Legal Studies and Reparations,* 22 Harv.C.R.–C.L.L.Rev. 323 (1987).

Meltzer, *The* Weber *Case: The Judicial Abrogation of the Antidiscrimination Standard in Employment,* 47 U.Chi.L.Rev. 423 (1980).

Mishkin, *The Uses of Ambivalence: Reflections on the Supreme Court and the Constitutionality of Affirmative Action,* 131 U.Pa.L.Rev. 907 (1983).

Moran, *Diversity and Its Discontents: The End of Affirmative Action at Boalt Hall,* 88 Cal. L. Rev. 2241 (2000).

O'Neil, *Preferential Admission: Equalizing the Access of Minority Groups to Higher Education,* 80 Yale L.J. 699 (1975).

Orentlicher, *Affirmative Action and Texas' Ten Percent Solution: Improving Diversity and Quality,* 74 Notre Dame L.Rev. 181 (1998).

Paulsen, *Reverse Discrimination and Law School Faculty Hiring: The Undiscovered Opinion,* 71 Texas L.Rev. 993 (1993).

Peller, *Race Consciousness,* 1990 Duke L.J. 758.

Reynolds, *Individualism vs. Group Rights: The Legacy of Brown,* 93 Yale L.J. 995 (1984).

Rosenfeld, *Affirmative Action, Justice, and Equalities: A Philosophical and Constitutional Appraisal,* 46 Ohio St.L.J. 845 (1985).

Rosenfeld, M., AFFIRMATIVE ACTION AND JUSTICE: A PHILOSOPHICAL AND CONSTITUTIONAL INQUIRY (1991).

Ross, *The Richmond Narratives,* 68 Tex.L.Rev. 381 (1989).

Rubenfeld, *Affirmative Action,* 107 Yale L.J. 427 (1997).

Rutherglen and Ortiz, *Affirmative Action Under the Constitution and Title VII: From Confusion to Convergence,* 35 UCLA L.Rev. 467 (1988).

Sandalow, *Racial Preferences in Higher Education: Political Responsibility and the Judicial Role,* 42 U.Chi.L.Rev. 653 (1975).

Scalia, *The Disease as Cure,* 1979 Wash.U.L.Q. 147.

Schiff, *Reverse Discrimination Redefined as Equal Protection: Orwellian Nightmare in the Enforcement of Civil Rights Law,* 8 Harv.J.L. & Pub.Pol. 627 (1985).

Schnapper, *Affirmative Action and the Legislative History of the Fourteenth Amendment,* 71 Va.L.Rev. 753 (1985).

Schuck, *Affirmative Action: Past, Present, and Future*, 20 Yale L. & Pol'y Rev. 1 (2002).

Schwartz, *The 1986 and 1987 Affirmative Action Cases: It's All Over But the Shouting,* 86 Mich.L.Rev. 524 (1987).

Sedler, *Beyond Bakke: The Constitution and Redressing the Social History of Racism,* 14 Harv.C.R.–C.L.L.Rev. 133 (1979).

Siegel, *The Federal Government's Power to Enact Color-Conscious Laws: An Originalist Inquiry,* 92 Nw.U.L.Rev. 477 (1998).

Siegel, *Discrimination in the Eyes of the Law: How "Color Blindness" Discourse Disrupts and Rationalizes Social Stratification*, 88 Cal. L. Rev. 77 (2000).

Sowell, T., CIVIL RIGHTS: RHETORIC OR REALITY (1987).

Spann, *Affirmative Action and Discrimination*, 39 Howard L.Rev. (1995).

Strauss, *Affirmative Action and the Public Interest,* 1995 Sup.Ct.Rev. 1.

Sturm and Guinier, *The Future of Affirmative Action: Reclaiming the Innovative Ideal,* 84 Cal.L.Rev. 953 (1996).

Symposium, *Affirmative Action,* 26 Wayne L.Rev. 1201–1362 (1980).

Symposium, *Affirmative Action,* 72 Iowa L.Rev. 255–85 (1987).

Symposium, *Affirmative Action: Promise and Problems in the* Search *for Equality,* 43 UCLA L.Rev. 1731 (1996).

Symposium, *Bakke,* 67 Calif.L.Rev. 1–255 (1979).

Symposium, *Bakke,* 14 Harv.C.L.–C.R.L.Rev. 1–327 (1979).

Symposium, *DeFunis,* 75 Colum.L.Rev. 483–602 (1975).

Symposium, *DeFunis,* 60 Va.L.Rev. 917–1011 (1974).

Symposium, *Race Consciousness and Legal Scholarship,* 1992 U.Ill.L.Rev. 945.

Symposium, *Twenty Years After* Bakke*: The Law and Social Science* of *Affirmative Action in Higher Education*, 59 Ohio St. L.J. 663 (1998).

Urofsky, M., A CONFLICT OF RIGHTS: THE SUPREME COURT AND AFFIRMATIVE ACTION (1991).

Wasserstrom, *Racism, Sexism and Preferential Treatment: An Approach to the Topics,* 24 U.C.L.A.L.Rev. 581 (1977).

Williams, *The Survival of Racism Under the Constitution,* 34 Wm. & Mary L.Rev. 7 (1992).

Williams, P., THE ALCHEMY OF RACE AND RIGHTS (1991).

Wright, *Color-Blind Theories and Color-Conscious Remedies*, 47 U.Chi. L.Rev. 213 (1980).

Yoo, *Who Measures the Chancellor's Foot? The Inherent Remedial Authority of the Federal Courts,* 84 Cal.L.Rev. 1121 (1996).

Chapter IX

LIBERTY

It is customary to divide the Constitution's special protections for individuals into two categories—rights and liberties. What makes liberties (like freedom of speech) special is that they entitle a person to *act* in certain ways (to speak). Other rights (like equal protection and the privilege against self-incrimination) promise benefits or forbid harms to essentially passive right-holders. (The only act they perform is the "legal act" of claiming their rights.)[1]

The Constitution guarantees several specific liberties in the First Amendment: freedom of speech, freedom of the press, and the free exercise of religion. These are often taught as a separate course, and are beyond the scope of our subject matter. The Fifth and Fourteenth Amendments also provide that no person shall be deprived of "liberty * * * without due process of law." This brief bit of text conceals several important points. One is that the phrase "due process" has come to mean legislative as well as judicial process. Under some circumstances legislatures are forbidden to pass laws depriving people of liberty. Another is that there are grades of protected liberty. The Supreme Court has said that the term "embrace[s] the right of the citizen to be free in the enjoyment of all his faculties; to be free to use them in all lawful ways[.]"[2] In order to take away most of these liberties the government must have some reason that is not purely arbitrary or vindictive. But there are also a few freedoms picked out by the courts for special protection. In the *Lochner* era this class included freedom of contract. In our time it includes the right of privacy protected in *Roe v. Wade.*

Writings about due process liberty have stressed several important themes. The first is the issue of interpretation. How can the courts find substantive protection in a phrase like "due process?" John Harrison's article which begins this chapter carefully parses the constitutional text in an effort (one that he concedes is mostly unsuccessful) to answer this question. You may want at this point to consult again the readings in Chapter II. As much as any other legal development, the modern doctrine of

---

[1]John H. Garvey, What Are Freedoms For?, ch. 1 (1996).

[2]Allgeyer v. Louisiana, 165 U.S. 578, 589, 17 S.Ct. 427, 431, 41 L.Ed. 832 (1897).

substantive due process has drawn lawyers' attention to the importance of issues of constitutional interpretation.

The readings in the remainder of this Chapter address a different theme, one of value rather than method: have the courts given right answers and convincing reasons in the controversies about due process liberty? Are the current resolutions likely to be stable and enduring? The readings in Section A ask questions like these about so-called "economic due process." Those in Sections B-D deal with the right to privacy.

JOHN HARRISON, SUBSTANTIVE DUE PROCESS AND THE CONSTITUTIONAL TEXT

83 VA. L. REV. 493–494, 504–509, 520–522, 525–527, 530–532, 534–536, 538–540, 558 (1997).

A reader of the Supreme Court's substantive due process cases can come to feel like a moviegoer who arrived late and missed a crucial bit of exposition. Where is the part that explains the connection between this doctrine and the text of the constitutional provisions from which it takes its name?

This is not a piece of exposition that a reader can easily supply. In fact, the whole idea that the Due Process Clauses have anything to do with the substance of legislation, as opposed to the procedures that are used by the government, is subject to the standard objection that because "process" means procedure, substantive due process is not just an error but a contradiction in terms. [Let us consider several possible ways of reconciling the doctrine of substantive due process with the text.]

A. THE CLASSIC INSTANCE

Interpretation often builds on exemplars. One useful way to approach the textual twists and turns that can lead to substantive due process in its varying forms is to understand those forms as variations on a basic reading of the text, a central exemplar. The basic reading addresses the classic instance of an enforcement action in defiance of governing procedural law.

Suppose, for example, that a federal court entered a criminal sentence of imprisonment after ignoring the defendant's demand for a jury trial, or after refusing to hear evidence that was required to be admitted by an act of Congress. Such a criminal sentence would call for (and imprisoning the defendant would impose) a deprivation of liberty without due process of law. A sentence of death entered after such a proceeding would involve a deprivation of life, and a fine would impose a deprivation of property, both without due process of law. The Fifth Amendment forbids this.

It is easy to see the reading of the Due Process Clauses that underlies this conclusion. A judicial sentence requiring that someone be executed, be imprisoned, or pay money leads to a deprivation of life, liberty, or property, respectively. Process can refer to procedures, and the legal procedures enforcing whatever law is at issue are processes "of law." "Process of law" therefore includes the procedures used by courts, and a procedure is not due if it is inconsistent with applicable law, whether constitutional or statutory. * * *

B. No Legislative Deprivations of Life, Liberty, or Property

The first route to substantive due process proceeds from the central exemplar by extending the concept of deprivation of life, liberty, or property to include certain kinds of legislation and by claiming that judicial procedure is not simply an example of due process of law but is its definition. This reading forbids actions by the legislature that constitute deprivations; its principal product is the doctrine of vested rights.

1. Language: Requiring Legislatures to Act Like Courts

If there is going to be substantive due process the relevant Due Process Clause must in some fashion apply to the legislature, not just to the courts and the executive. The first reading to be considered rests on a very straightforward way of applying the Clause to the legislature. This approach requires specific interpretations of two parts of the text.

First, it supposes that a statute can constitute a deprivation of life, liberty, or property—not merely provide for a deprivation, but actually be a deprivation itself. Most statutes provide for deprivations. For example, a statute saying that anyone who commits treason shall suffer death provides that the courts and the executive shall deprive convicted traitors of life. Criminal statutes with lesser sentences provide for deprivation of liberty through imprisonment. The deprivation, however, does not take place unless the sentence is either passed or executed by the judiciary or the executive.

But some laws can be said to be deprivations of property. Every nineteenth century lawyer's favorite example of an unconstitutional statute—albeit one that was thought to be unconstitutional for various different reasons—involves a law that, in Justice Miller's formulation from *Davidson v. New Orleans,* "declares in terms, and without more, that the full and exclusive title of a described piece of land, which is now in A., shall be and is hereby vested in B". . .[39] Such an act of the legislature certainly looks like a deprivation of property. It does not simply provide for a deprivation because it does not set forth the circumstances under which A would lose the property; rather, it operates immediately and of its own force. If a court entered such a decree, most people would say that it had deprived A of property.

---

[39][96 U.S. 97, 102 (1878).]

The second specific textual interpretation this reading requires concerns the phrase "due process of law." It might be reasonable to say that a court had deprived A of property without due process of law if it had entered a decree stating that property that had been A's is now B's without first having conducted a trial. That is so because the primary instance of due process of law is the procedure that the courts normally use in determining people's rights—preeminently notice, hearing, and a decision based on existing law. This concept of due process could be formulated at varying levels of generality. It might entail some specific set of procedures drawn from common law practice, or it might be more abstract, perhaps limited to notice, hearing, and decision according to law. However due process is understood, this way of reading the text would largely prevent the legislature from passing statutes that are deprivations of life, liberty, or property, because legislatures generally do not use anything resembling judicial procedures. They do not normally give people notice, they do not conduct judicial trials before passing statutes, and they rarely, if ever, decide by applying prior law. The whole point of being a legislature is to make law or change it, not to apply existing law. Because legislatures are virtually incapable of acting with due process in the judicial sense, under this reading they may not pass statutes that in and of themselves deprive people of life, liberty, or property.

This reading yields a ban on privative legislation. The details of its content depend on the scope of the concepts of deprivation on one hand, and of liberty and property on the other. On the first concept, it is possible that to constitute a deprivation, an act of the legislature must be as specific as a judicial decree, in the manner of the A-to-B law. Deprivation also could be defined more broadly to include perfectly general laws that take away preexisting rights. Under this latter approach, a statute providing that people could not own automatic weapons would deprive those who owned them at the time of enactment of their property. There is also some play in the concept of deprivation concerning degrees of impairment of property rights. For example, a statute providing that minors may not purchase or own automatic weapons might be said to deprive adult owners of some of their property because it limited their right of alienation. On the other hand, it might not be regarded as a deprivation, as the owners retain all other ownership rights.

Similarly, the concepts of property and liberty can have wide or narrow scope, with varying results for substantive due process doctrine. Property might be limited to vested rights in tangible or intangible property, or it could be conceived very broadly, including virtually everything of value. Liberty too can be broadly or narrowly conceived. Understood most narrowly, liberty is simply freedom from physical restraint, the ability to move about as one chooses. Someone who has been imprisoned has been deprived of liberty in this sense. At its broadest, liberty consists of the ability to do what one likes, free from any restraint, physical or legal. Any law that forbids some type of conduct limits liberty in this sense. Between these two is a sense of liberty that is normally contrasted with license. This last form of liberty might best be characterized as the legal privilege to do as one pleases consistent with the rights of others. A law against murder probably would not be said to deprive anyone of this kind of liberty, but a law against rolling over in bed would be.

2. Doctrine: Vested Rights and More

Different combinations of meanings for deprivation, liberty, and property, together with the definition of due process of law as characteristically judicial procedures, can produce almost all the familiar substantive due process doctrines. If deprivation means specific, decree-like actions and property means vested rights, the result is the earliest and most limited form of the doctrine of vested rights. Under this reading legislation affecting specified property rights is forbidden. Thus, a legislature may not enact an A-to-B law, whereas it may enact a general statute forbidding all ownership of automatic weapons. Under a broader concept of deprivation, no legislative action may interfere with existing property arrangements. This broader concept encompasses general laws. Combined with a concept of property that includes the ability to use one's natural faculties, such an interpretation of deprivation leads to Lochner-style restrictions (and maybe more). The same result obtains if the concept of property is replaced with the intermediate concept of liberty, which includes freedom of contract but not simply doing anything one pleases. * * *

4. Critique: Legislatures Are Not Courts

[This first reading defines] due process quite specifically as the kind of procedures used by courts, or the application of pre-existing law through notice and hearings. [It is not] subject to the classic objection that "process" refers to procedure. [Indeed, its flaw lies in taking "due process of law"] not simply to include appropriate judicial procedures, but to mean appropriate judicial procedures. The phrase "due process of law," however, does not, by itself, connote specifically judicial procedures. Certainly there are legal processes that take place elsewhere than in courts. In particular, legislatures have their own characteristic procedures; the most important procedural rules for Congress are set out in the Constitution itself.[82] While it makes sense to say that a due process provision requires that courts do their work in an appropriately judicial fashion, the application of this principle to legislation would require that legislatures do theirs in an

[82]See, e.g., U.S. Const. art. 1, § 7, cl. 2, 3.

appropriately legislative fashion. It certainly would not forbid them from making or changing law, which is their job. * * *

One response to this critique is that it leads to an unthinkable result because it permits an A-to-B statute. Surely something that looks so much like a judicial decree should be entered only after a judicial hearing. My argument, however, does not necessarily imply that outright legislative confiscations are constitutional. It implies only that they do not violate a due process clause. Certainly if Congress really did purport to adjudicate a case between A and B it would violate Article I, which grants Congress all, but only, legislative power, and Article III, which vests the judicial power only in the courts.

On the other hand, if it is a legitimate exercise of legislative power to transfer property from A to B, or otherwise to divest A of property, then it is silly to say that the legislature should be required to proceed as if it were a court. There is nothing unthinkable about permitting legislatures to legislate through legislative procedures. The real question, one that the Due Process Clauses cannot answer, is whether the legislative power extends to statutes, including A-to-B laws, that directly work deprivations. * * *

C. Due Process of Law and the Form and Substance of Legislative Power

1. *Language: Is Everything a Legislature Does Worthy of the Name "Law"?*

In suggesting that a lawless enforcement procedure was the central example of a failure of due process, I assumed that the procedure involved was "process of law," perhaps on the grounds that it was process undertaken by a government institution, or that it was process based on a statute. Maybe the word "law" is the key. If all deprivations of life, liberty, and property must be with due process of law and if some purported source of authority for a deprivation is not law, then it is possible to say that the deprivation was without due process of law.

There are two senses in which a legislative act might not be law. First, it might fail to have the formal characteristics associated with law. These are usually thought to include generality, prospectivity, publicity, and intelligibility. According to this thinking, only commands consisting of general rules that those subject to them can use in deciding how to act are law. The second sense in which a statute may not qualify as law under this approach rests on more substantive understandings of law. A little quick work along these lines might make the Due Process Clauses vehicles for the notion that the power of American legislatures is inherently limited. The necessary move is to say that something is not law if it is not a valid exercise of legislative power, and then fill in the blank with a notion of what a valid exercise of legislative power is.

It does not matter for this reading whether the deprivation is understood as being worked by a specific enforcement action or directly by a statute. If deprivation refers to a specific action by one of the enforcing branches and certain statutes are not law, then deprivations pursuant to those statutes would not be due process of law because the procedures would be based on something that was not law. Under this approach non-law statutes, although they might be valid in some abstract sense, are unenforceable. Correspondingly, if statutes are understood as working deprivations directly, as in the vested rights approach, then the statutes will not constitute due process of law when they are not law, and their privative effect will be nullified.

2. Doctrine

a. Form: Bills of Attainder, Vested Rights, and a Little More

Formal constraints imposed by this concept of law will generate some but not all of substantive due process as it has developed. To begin with a familiar case, one can easily say that the act of the legislature declaring that the property of A shall be the property of B is not law, both because it is not general and because it is not prospective in that the transfer does not follow from any act of A or B that takes place after the law is adopted. A formal notion of law thus can produce the narrow version of vested rights due process. * * *

Most of modern substantive due process [—the doctrine of incorporation, *Lochner, Roe*—is harder to squeeze out of a formal concept of law.] A ban on criticism of the government is general and prospective, as is a minimum wage law or a ban on abortion. Unless equality completely swallows substance, this understanding of "law" will not produce economic substantive due process, minimum scrutiny, or the doctrine of fundamental rights.

b. Substance: Lochner and Beyond

A requirement that legislation satisfy formal constraints does relatively little to limit the legislature. The substantive approach is much more productive. If legislative power is granted by the people to protect vested rights and not to destroy them, then the due process requirement produces the old doctrine of vested rights. In a more modern mode, if legislatures are not given the power to invade people's privacy, or to interfere with their fundamental rights, or to discriminate arbitrarily among people, due process will produce as much of today's doctrine as one pleases. * * *

4. Critique: "Law" Is What Is Legally Authoritative

[But] this reading of "law" has serious problems. Consider first the Fifth Amendment's Due Process Clause as applied to federal statutes.

According to this approach, the Clause requires the courts to refuse to effect deprivations based on acts of Congress that are not law. The Constitution, however, indicates that there are no such acts of Congress. When a bill has been passed by both Houses and been signed by the President, or when it has been passed by both Houses and lain before the President, unreturned, for ten days (Sundays excepted and unless Congress has prevented its return by adjourning), or when it has been repassed by two-thirds of both Houses after having been returned by the President with his objections, it becomes "a Law." Article VI provides that the "Laws of the United States" made "in Pursuance" of the Constitution are "the supreme Law of the Land." Because properly adopted statutes have been passed as mandated by the Constitution, they are the law.

The original Constitution does more than just affirm that properly enacted federal statutes are law. It also describes as laws things that according to the formally restrictive reading are not: Congress and the states are forbidden to pass any "ex post facto Law." Nowhere in the 1787 document does the word "law" appear in any context that suggests that it refers to some subset of legally binding commands that is defined by formal or substantive criteria.

But what about the principle that unconstitutional statutes are not law? Surely a statute that is inconsistent with the Due Process Clause is in one sense no more law than a duly enacted bill of attainder. Perhaps not, but any attempt to make this into an argument that some statute is in fact inconsistent with the Due Process Clause is question-begging.

This might seem like a mere word game—"law" can have more than one sense—but it is not. In understanding the Constitution, or any legal document, the rational reader postulates a drafter who was trying to make sense. In drafting an amendment to a document that already said that an act of Congress is both a law and the law, no sensible person would try to convey that some acts of Congress are to be disregarded by asking the reader to infer that they are not law, even if there is a different sense of law to which the drafter might be appealing. Such a maneuver is too confusing and too unlikely to be understood to attribute to a rational author. The drafter much more likely would have said that some acts of Congress are invalid when they fail some explicit formal or substantive test. * * *

D. REAL SUBSTANTIVE DUE PROCESS

This reading extends the meaning of the word "due" from "legally required" to "appropriate." Under this approach, standards of propriety come from outside the Constitution and "process of law" extends beyond procedure.

1. Language: Expanded Dueness, Expanded Process of Law

So far I have discussed every part of the Clauses but the word "due." In a legal document, due might mean "legally required" or "in accordance with the applicable law." This sense of due is used in the rule of law application of the Clauses. It does not appear to lead anywhere substantive because it has no independent content. [There is, however,] a sense of what is due that has its own content. It means appropriate, or right, or fitting, whether according to tradition, natural law, or something else. To say that something is due is to say that it conforms to the standards that should be applied to that thing. Here is a word with possibilities.

In light of these possibilities, it seems a waste to limit the requirement of dueness merely to the procedural aspects of government action. That requirement can be extended by rethinking "process of law." The reasoning behind the extension goes like this: A process is an activity. Governments act through law. So, process of law means "what the government does" or "governmental action"—in short, the activity of government. Under this reading the Due Process Clauses provide that no person may be deprived of life, liberty, or property, except by due governmental action. Governmental action includes both statutes and specific enforcement actions, like imprisoning people, so this reading calls for an inclusive sense of deprivation, referring both to changes in the law effected by statutes and to changes in the real world effected by the actions of government officers. Similarly, this reading calls for liberty to refer to both freedom from physical restraint and legal capacities, like freedom of contract.

2. Doctrine: Judicial Supremacy

At last. This is the judicial philosophers' stone, capable of transmuting any attractive but nonconstitutional principle into a constitutional command that can be enforced through judicial review. The efficacy of this magician's tool is so obvious that it is almost a waste of time to show how it can conjure up substantive due process in any of its manifestations. If the main purpose of government is to secure private rights, then it would be completely inappropriate, hence undue, for any government action to interfere with vested rights. If you have a *Lochner*-like view of the appropriate functions of the state, then once again deprivations will be due only when they are in pursuance of those functions. In a system devoted to the protection of other personal freedoms, such as those in the Bill of Rights or the right of privacy, interference with those freedoms is likewise undue. If equality is a basic principle of American government, discrimination is undue and equal protection principles apply through the Fifth Amendment. And so on. * * *

4. Critique: Process and Procedure

Now that the discussion has come to the obvious derivation of substantive due process from the text, it may seem to be time for the obvious answer: Process means procedure. Process differs from substance. Method differs from content. The Legal Process school of jurisprudence takes its name from this distinction and prominent scholars debate whether the Constitution itself should be understood in terms of process or substance. The process of law and the substance of law are two different things, indeed, two contrasting things. To say that the process must meet a standard of dueness is not to say anything about substance.

This obvious answer, while its heart is in the right place, is not adequate. [A] concrete process, proceeding, or procedure can be undue for reasons unrelated to its procedural aspects. That is the sense in which the due process requirement is substantive: Processes are judged, not by their procedural characteristics, but by their substantive consequences, or by the substance of the law that underlies them. In this sense an arrest would be undue if the suspect were charged with violating a statute that was inconsistent with the First Amendment.

[But when] the Constitution regulates the content of rules it does so directly, rather than by referring to the government actions through which they are applied. Article I, Section 9, the federal half of the original Constitution's bill of rights, forbids possible federal statutes by describing their content and telling Congress not to enact them, not by speaking of proceedings in which they should not be enforced. When it means to forbid the enforcement of certain laws, the Constitution does so by describing their content and then banning their enforcement, not simply by purporting to regulate enforcement in general. The Fourteenth Amendment, in the very sentence that contains its Due Process Clause, shows how to bar enforcement of a category of laws that are identified by their content: "No State shall make or enforce any law which shall abridge the privileges or immunities of citizens of the United States." Talking about government action is no more a customary way of referring to the content of rules than is talking about process.

* * *

* * * I have tried to coax the old dragon that we now call substantive due process from its den so that we can examine it in the light of day. Although I have had very little good to say for substantive due process as a reading of the constitutional text, the main point of this effort has not been to prove that all readings are inadmissible. Indeed, it would not be surprising if this discussion has the opposite effect with some readers, suggesting readings that may not have occurred to them and that they might find plausible. Rather, the Article's primary purpose has been to think

about substantive due process from a different perspective, focusing not on the rules that are ultimately derived but on the readings from which they come.

A. ECONOMIC DUE PROCESS

Between 1897[1] and 1937[2] the Supreme Court held unconstitutional a number of state and federal laws regulating wages, hours, working conditions, prices, market entry, and other business practices. Such laws, the Court often said, took away liberty (freedom of contract) guaranteed by the Due Process Clause. It is now generally agreed that the Court's intervention in these cases was a mistake.

Richard Posner's article suggests, though, that the Court may actually have been right in many of its economic due process decisions. He uses the example of *New State Ice Co. v. Liebmann*[3] to argue that the Court had a firmer grasp of economics than some of its contemporary critics. Restrictions on business entry, which the Court today tolerates, may in fact be nothing more than naked preferences that injure consumers as well as producers excluded from the market. But not all of the laws struck down during this period excluded entry into occupations. Some were designed to remedy perceived defects in economic bargaining power. *Lochner* itself is an example. Others dealt with business practices like product standards[4] or fee collection.[5] It is worth considering whether arguments like Posner's can be made against these statutes.

Robert McCloskey asks whether the Court has overcompensated for its mistakes in this area. He reviews the various justifications given for distinguishing economic from "personal" rights, and finds them unconvincing. Perhaps the Court should find some half-way house between its former zeal and its present tolerance that will allow it to provide some check on obvious abuses of the legislative process.

The articles by Robert Brauneis and William Treanor suggest that economic due process is more alive than we have been accustomed to think. The Rehnquist Court has been unusually active in enforcing, through the Due Process Clause, the rule that government regulation may not diminish the value of private property too much. The Court in these cases has invoked the Takings Clause (it has been incorporated in the Fourteenth

[1]Allgeyer v. Louisiana, 165 U.S. 578, 17 S.Ct. 427, 41 L.Ed. 832 (1897).

[2]West Coast Hotel Co. v. Parrish, 300 U.S. 379, 57 S.Ct. 578, 81 L.Ed. 703 (1937).

[3]285 U.S. 262, 52 S.Ct. 371, 76 L.Ed. 747 (1932).

[4]Jay Burns Baking Co. v. Bryan, 264 U.S. 504, 44 S.Ct. 412, 68 L.Ed. 813 (1924) (weight of bread); Weaver v. Palmer Bros. Co., 270 U.S. 402, 46 S.Ct. 320, 70 L.Ed. 654 (1926) (use of "shoddy" in manufacture of bedding).

[5]Adams v. Tanner, 244 U.S. 590, 37 S.Ct. 662, 61 L.Ed. 1336 (1917) (fee collection practices of employment agencies). See generally Wonnell, *Economic Due Process and the Preservation of Competition,* 11 Hastings Const. L.Q. 91 (1983).

Amendment Due Process Clause). But Brauneis argues that the case on which the Court relies for authority, *Pennsylvania Coal Co. v. Mahon*,[6] is itself an old economic due process case. If Brauneis is right, we might want to rethink our assumption that economic due process is dead.

Treanor does not dispute Brauneis's argument that *Mahon* is an economic due process case. But he maintains that Justice Holmes, who wrote the opinion in *Mahon*, was much more willing to defer to legislative judgments than the Court has recently shown itself to be in regulatory takings cases.

RICHARD POSNER, ECONOMIC DUE PROCESS

ECONOMIC ANALYSIS OF LAW 589–593 (3rd ed. 1986).

For a period of 50 years ending in the late 1930s, liberty of contract was a key component of due process under the Fifth and Fourteenth Amendments to the Constitution as interpreted by the Supreme Court, and it was the ground on which the Court invalidated, although fitfully, a number of state and federal statutes regulating economic activity. Classical economic theory was thereby elevated to the status of constitutional principle, for the idea that voluntary transactions almost always promote welfare, and regulations that inhibit such transactions almost always reduce it, is a staple of classical theory. * * *

Although long viewed simply as grotesque distortions of constitutional principle, the liberty of contract decisions recently have attracted some staunch advocates as part of a growing revival of interest in classical economic principles. And although there are grave difficulties in reconciling their position with the philosophy of judicial self-restraint or the interest group theory (and reality) of government, the same can be said about the modern emphasis in constitutional law on personal liberties. The arguments for giving greater protection to personal than to economic liberties are superficial. Thus, while it is said that there was no source for a doctrine of liberty of contract in the text or history of the relevant constitutional provisions, the same criticism can be (and has been) made of the Court's decisions in a wide variety of other constitutional areas. It is also said that economic questions are more difficult for courts to decide than questions involving the rights of criminal defendants, political dissidents, or members of racial minorities—yet in fact less is known about those questions than about conventional economic problems. It is said that economic rights are less important than other rights; even if this is so * * *, it does not follow that the Court should give them no protection at all. It is said that the Court's mistake in the liberty of contract cases was to be out of step with dominant public opinion. But this was true only toward the end of

[6] 260 U.S. 393, 43 S.Ct. 158, 67 L.Ed. 322 (1922).

the era, and is the reason why the era ended when it did. Moreover, the criticism can easily be turned into a compliment to the Court for its steadfastness in the face of contrary popular opinion. It is also said that the victims of economic controls are businessmen well able to protect themselves without the Court's help, unlike the powerless minorities typically involved in a noneconomic constitutional case. Yet as we are about to see, the brunt of the economic legislation challenged during the liberty of contract era was often borne by politically unorganized groups such as consumers. Nor is it correct that racial and religious minorities are unable to compete effectively in the political arena.

* * * [It is also] commonly believed that the liberty of contract decisions reflected a weak grasp of economics. An early criticism based on this view is found in Justice Brandeis's dissenting opinion in *New State Ice Co. v. Liebmann.*[4] The case involved the constitutionality of a state statute that required anyone who wanted to manufacture and sell ice to obtain a certificate of public convenience and necessity and that provided that a certificate would be denied if existing service was adequate. New State, which had such a certificate, sought to enjoin Liebmann, who did not, from entering the ice business in New State's territory. Liebmann's defense was that the statute was unconstitutional. The Court invalidated the statute for reasons with which most economists would concur:

> Stated succinctly, a private corporation here seeks to prevent a competitor from entering the business of making and selling ice * * *. There is no question now before us of any regulation by the state to protect the consuming public either with respect to conditions of manufacture and distribution or to insure purity of products or to prevent extortion. The control here asserted does not protect against monopoly, but tends to foster it. The aim is not to encourage competition, but to prevent it; not to regulate the business, but to preclude persons from engaging in it * * *. It is not the case of a natural monopoly, or of an enterprise in its nature dependent upon the grant of public privileges. The particular requirement before us was evidently not imposed to prevent a practical monopoly of the business, since its tendency is quite to the contrary.

The Court likened the certification provision to an attempt of one shoemaker, under state authority, "to prevent another shoemaker from making or selling shoes because shoemakers already in that occupation can make and sell all the shoes that are needed."

Justice Brandeis's economic argument begins with the proposition that the ice business may be "one which lends itself peculiarly to monopoly"; "the business is conducted in local plants with a market narrowly limited in area" because of the weight and perishability of the product. But the fact

---

[4]285 U.S. 262 (1932).

that a firm has only a local market area does not preclude competition. Brandeis's opinion reveals, moreover, that prior to the passage of the challenged statute there was competition in the ice business in many localities in the state. He argues that "even in those localities the prices of ice were ordinarily uniform," but since, as he stresses elsewhere in his opinion, the product is uniform, one would expect competitive sellers to charge the same price.

* * *

No doubt the real purpose of the statute was to foster cartelization of the Oklahoma ice industry. As Brandeis himself curiously emphasizes,

> Trade journals and reports of association meetings of ice manufacturers bear ample witness to the hostility of the industry to such competition, and to its unremitting efforts, through trade associations, informal agreements, combination of delivery systems, and in particular through the consolidation of plants, to protect markets and prices against competition of any character.

He also notes: "the ice industry as a whole in Oklahoma has acquiesced in and accepted the Act and the status which it creates."

In viewing the case as one in which Liebmann's economic rights were pitted against the interests of the poor people of Oklahoma who could not afford refrigerators, Justice Brandeis got it backwards. The right he would have vindicated was the interest of New State Ice and other established ice companies to be free from competition. The people actually wronged by the statute were the poor, who were compelled to pay more for ice; the well-to-do, as Brandeis pointed out, were more likely to have refrigerators.

If the ice business were a natural monopoly, the Brandeis position might be economically defensible, since * * * the effort of a natural monopolist to maximize his profits by establishing a monopoly price could lead to a wasteful duplication of facilities. Not only is the premise false, however, but it appears from the latter part of Brandeis's opinion that the natural monopoly language of the earlier part is a makeweight and that he was prepared to embrace the sweeping proposition that ruinous competition is a common phenomenon of economic markets and was a major factor behind the great depression of the 1930s. The case was decided in 1931, and although the Oklahoma statute predated the depression, Brandeis discusses extensively, and with apparent approval, the proposition that the philosophy embodied in the Oklahoma limitation on entry into the ice business might be a remedy of general application to the current economic crisis.

The view of the great depression as rooted in the excesses of competition and curable by reducing competition is discredited * * *. Of course, when demand declined during the depression much of the existing industrial capacity, geared as it was to supplying a larger demand, became temporarily excess. But limiting competition would not have increased purchasing power and therefore demand; it would just have impaired the efficiency of economic activity at its reduced level. * * *

Some of the statutes upheld by the Supreme Court in the period when it was guided by liberty of contract notions also were attempts to suppress competition under the guise of promoting the general welfare. In *Muller v. Oregon,*[7] for example, the Court upheld a state statute fixing a maximum work day of 10 hours for women employed in laundries. Unless the state also had a minimum wage law and the wages of women employed in laundries were not significantly higher than the minimum, the statute probably had little effect. Forced to reduce the work day, the employer would compensate by reducing the daily wage. If the employer were prevented from reducing the daily wage, he would treat the statute as having increased the cost of his labor (he gets less output for the same wage) and, under a now-familiar analysis, would adapt by buying a smaller quantity of labor, raising prices, or doing both things. The reduction in employment would harm any workers he laid off who did not have equally good alternative employment opportunities; the increase in prices would harm consumers, and by reducing his output would lead him to further reduce his labor inputs.

Since the Court's repudiation of liberty of contract, it has frequently upheld statutes designed to foster monopoly, such as a state statute that, on grounds of public health, forbade opticians to replace eyeglass frames without a prescription signed by an optometrist or an ophthalmologist[9]—although the statute could have had no purpose other than to increase the incomes of optometrists and ophthalmologists at the expense of opticians and consumers.

ROBERT G. MCCLOSKEY, ECONOMIC DUE PROCESS AND THE SUPREME COURT: AN EXHUMATION AND REBURIAL

1962 SUP.CT.REV. 34, 45–53.

IV. The Doubtful Distinction Between Economic and Civil Rights

* * *

The arguments for demoting economic rights to their modern lowly constitutional status—lowly when compared with "personal rights"—fall

[7]208 U.S. 412 (1908).

[9]See Williamson v. Lee Optical Co., 348 U.S. 483 (1955). For an extreme example of the Court's tolerance see Kotch v. Board of River Port Pilot Commrs., 330 U.S. 552 (1947).

into two categories. First, there is a group of arguments based on judgments about the nature and relative importance of the rights concerned. For example, it is sometimes argued that laws limiting freedom of expression impinge on the human personality more grievously than do laws curbing mere economic liberty, and that the Court is therefore justified in protecting the former more zealously than the latter. The individual has, *qua* individual, "the right to be let alone." The right to free choice in the intellectual and spiritual realm is particularly precious to him. A major difficulty with this formulation is that there is the smell of the lamp about it: it may reflect the tastes of the judges and dons who advance it, rather than the real preferences of the commonality of mortals. Judges and professors are talkers both by profession and avocation. It is not surprising that they would view freedom of expression as primary to the free play of their personalities. But most men would probably feel that an economic right, such as freedom of occupation, was at least as vital to them as the right to speak their minds. Mark Twain would surely have felt constrained in the most fundamental sense, if his youthful aspiration to be a river-boat pilot had been frustrated by a State-ordained system of nepotism.[60] Needless to say, no disparagement of freedom of expression is here intended. But its inarguable importance to the human spirit, on the one hand, does not furnish an adequate ground for downgrading all economic rights, on the other.

So much for a purely individual-centered justification for the disparity between economic rights and other civil liberties. Another suggested rationale looks toward the community rather than the separate individuals within it. Progress, it is said, "is to a considerable extent the displacement of error which once held sway as official truth by beliefs which in turn have yielded to other beliefs."[61] To encourage societal progress, it is important then to protect "those liberties of the individual which history has attested as the indispensable conditions of an open as against a closed society," *e.g.*, freedom of expression.

Presumably this "open society" argument would be relevant no matter how the political system was organized—even a benevolent autocracy must tolerate freedom of expression or risk stagnation. But Alexander Meiklejohn has contended that the point takes on an extra dimension when applied to popular government, to democracy as the West understands that term. In any political system, so the argument runs, the ruler must be fully informed if he is to govern well, and he cannot be fully informed when someone else is deciding what ideas he shall be allowed to hear. In a democracy the people are sovereign, and it follows that they and no one else must decide what and whom they will listen to. And it further follows

[60]Kotch v. Pilot Commissioners, 330 U.S. 552 (1947).

[61]Frankfurter, J., concurring, in Kovacs v. Cooper, 336 U.S. 77 at 95.

that the Constitution must protect any freedoms that help the people to acquire "the intelligence, integrity, sensitivity, and generous devotion to the general welfare that, in theory, casting a ballot is assumed to express."[63] In short, the special importance of certain civil rights derives from their special relationship to the process of self-government. Other rights, including the economic, can be abridged when the legislature deems abridgment desirable.

Some such reasoning probably underlies the related point implied by Mr. Justice Stone in the first paragraph of his famous "footnote four"[64] and by Mr. Justice Frankfurter in the concluding words of the first flag-salute opinion[65] (though neither would of course have followed Professor Meiklejohn in the absolutist conclusions he drew). Stone suggested that judicial scrutiny would be especially exacting when legislation restricted "those political processes which can ordinarily be expected to bring about repeal of undesirable legislation," and Frankfurter intimated that the crucial question is whether "all the effective means of inducing political changes are left free from interference." These pronouncements may rest partly on Professor Meiklejohn's point that the governors must be fully informed; but they also seem to involve a separable idea: that a majoritarian system must, in the name of both justice and progress, preserve the right of a present minority to make its views the views of the majority. A businessman's price may be controlled by the mandate of a popularly elected legislature, but, if his right to work politically for repeal of the control law is untrammeled, the fundamentals of a just democratic policy are still maintained and so is the fluidity of the sociopolitical order.

The whole "open society" line of argument in its various forms is convincing enough as a justification for protecting the free trade in ideas. If one feels the need to explain why the free speech guarantees are important, these explanations will do pretty well for a start. But they are rather less satisfactory as the basis for a policy of *not* protecting economic freedom, of regarding it as unimportant in a democratic system. For one thing, it is not entirely clear why liberty of economic choice is less indispensable to the "openness" of a society than freedom of expression. Few historians would deny that the growth of entrepreneurial and occupational freedom helped to promote material progress in England in the eighteenth and nineteenth centuries and in America after the Civil War (although they might of course argue that the price paid for this progress was unconscionably high). It is one thing to argue that economic liberty must be subject to rational control in the "public interest"; it is quite another to say in effect that it is not

[63]Meiklejohn, *The First Amendment Is an Absolute,* [1961] Supreme Court Review 245, 255.

[64]United States v. Carolene Products Co., 304 U.S. 144, 152 (1938).

[65]Minersville School Dist. v. Gobitis, 310 U.S. 586, 600 (1940).

liberty at all and that the proponent of the "open society" can therefore regard it as irrelevant to progress.

As for the "political process" subthemes of the open-society argument—the Meiklejohn-Stone-Frankfurter rationales just described—they too must be queried insofar as they purport to justify a downgrading of economic rights. In fact, their basic difficulty is that, in exalting the freedoms bearing on the political process, they bypass the question of other freedoms altogether. Meiklejohn's arguments for protecting liberty of expression are cogent, but they do not on their face explain why other, "private," rights should be neglected. A decision to protect Peter does not necessarily involve the decision to abandon Paul. * * *

If Meiklejohn's argument contains the unexamined assumption that the political is primary and almost exclusive, the "Stone—Frankfurter" point described above contains this and an assumption of its own as well: the majoritarian idea in a peculiarly unqualified form. The notion seems to be that the citizen can have nothing really fundamental to complain about in a law if a free majority has enacted it and if he is protected in his right to agitate for its repeal. But this view ascribes a preponderance to the majority will that has certainly not been acknowledged by the American political tradition. In that tradition, it is not assumed that an unjust law becomes just by virtue of majority approval, not even if the victim has the theoretical right to persuade the majority to change its mind. * * *

Furthermore this argument overlooks a difficulty partly recognized by Stone himself in the *Carolene Products* footnote and invoked by him in the first flag-salute case, the problem of "discrete and insular minorities," *i.e.,* those who have no realistic chance of influencing the majority to rescind the law that does them harm. Stone was speaking specifically of religious, national, or racial minorities, and his suggestion was that prejudice against them might curtail the political processes that would ordinarily be expected to protect their rights. Prejudice against Jehovah's Witnesses for their "queerness" makes repressive governmental action more probable, and precisely because of their queerness they are not likely to be numerous enough or influential enough in any given community so that their weight will be felt in the city council. To speak of their power to defend themselves through political action is to sacrifice their civil rights in the name of an amiable fiction. Yet it is not clear why the thrust of this point should be restricted to ethnic and religious minorities. Perhaps it is true that a prosperous corporation can effectively plead its case at the bar of legislative judgment by resort to publicity and direct lobbying. Economic power may be an adequate surrogate for numerical power; no tears need be shed for helpless General Electric. But the scattered individuals who are denied access to an occupation by State-enforced barriers are about as impotent a minority as can be imagined. The would-be barmaids of Michigan[75] or the would-be plumbers of Illinois have no more chance against the entrenched influence of the established bartenders and master plumbers than the Jehovah's Witnesses had against the prejudices of Minersville School District. In fact the Witnesses may enjoy an advantage, for they are at least cohesive; and other "discrete" minorities, such as racial groups, have occasionally displayed respectable capacities to exert political leverage by virtue of their very discreteness. Not so the isolated economic man who belongs to no identifiable group at all.

V. JUDICIAL CAPACITY IN THE REALM OF ECONOMIC REGULATION

* * *

Although the policy of abdication cannot be justified in terms of an analysis of the nature and relative unimportance of the rights concerned, there is a second line of thought that merits consideration. Perhaps the decision to leave economic rights to the tender mercy of the legislative power is based on the idea that the Supreme Court is peculiarly ill-equipped to deal with this subject. No one would argue that the right enshrined in Article IV, the guarantee of a republican form of government, is unimportant. Yet the Court has refused to protect it, because of well-founded doubts about judicial competence to make effective judgments in this field. It may be that similar doubts underlie the policy of abdication in the area of economic affairs.

* * *

There are, of course, economic subjects so recondite that judicial surveillance of them would be anomalous. The choice between "historical cost" and "replacement cost" as a basis for rate making must be made by the legislature, not because it will always choose well, but because the judiciary lacks the knowledge and expertise for distinguishing good from bad in this area. But this point will carry only as far as its logic will bring it, and there are fields of economic regulation less intricate than the problem of public utility rates. To be sure, even the problems raised in these fields may not be simple. A fair evaluation of Oklahoma's need for its anti-optician law would require the Court to make judgments about a complex matter. But this can be said about most questions that reach the Supreme Court in any field. Our problem is not to identify the issues that present difficulties and then to discard them as improper subjects for judicial review. That would be to abandon judicial review in most of the fields where it is now exercised. Our problem is to determine whether economic statutes always or usually involve such extraordinary difficulties that a

[75] Goesaert v. Cleary, 335 U.S. 464 (1948).

modest judiciary must eschew them, even though that same judiciary does claim the competence to judge other, more difficult, issues.

Is it easier for example for the Court to appraise a law empowering a board of censors to ban an "immoral" movie than a law empowering a real estate licensing board to deny a license unless the applicant is of "good moral character"? The two standards would seem to be equally vague and the possibility of arbitrary administrative action would seem to be as menacing in one situation as in the other. * * * Is it easier to see that the State corporate registration law in *N.A.A.C.P. v. Alabama* was being used to facilitate private reprisals against Association members than it is to see that State boards of plumbers, barbers, and morticians sometimes use their publicly granted powers to protect the private financial interests of present guild members to the disadvantage of non-members?

The point is * * * that [these] issues * * * stand on a common level of difficulty and that judicial scrutiny seems as feasible (or unfeasible) for one issue as for the other. And the further, related, point is that there are kinds and kinds of economic subjects and that it is difficult to fashion a generalization that applies to all. Some subjects may be so inscrutable that judicial review cannot fruitfully cope with them; but this is not a justification for avoiding other economic subjects which are no more opaque than the "personal rights" issues that are the standard coinage of judicial discourse these days.

This point likewise applies to the suggestion that the Court, as the relatively weak and non-political branch, simply lacks the power to dictate the economic order, however otherwise competent its members may be. No doubt the Court was presumptuous to imagine, before 1937, that it could hold back such waves as the wage-control movement or the demand for social security. The tide of the welfare state was flowing, and no court could have reversed it. But neither does the judiciary have the practical power to halt any major social developments backed by insistent popular demand. And this would be so whether the development involved economic questions or questions of "personal rights." It was the dimension of the issues in the anti-New Deal cases that made them incongruous for judicial decision, not the mere fact that they were economic in character. No such judicial delusions of grandeur would be implied by enforcement of the requirement that an occupational qualification must be rationally based, or by similar modest applications of substantive due process. The awful will of the sovereign people is not likely to be aroused because the Court has told the morticians of Winnemac that they cannot use State power to maintain a monopoly—or at least no more than it is aroused by other constitutional decisions that issue almost weekly during each Term.

ROBERT BRAUNEIS, "THE FOUNDATION OF OUR 'REGULATORY TAKINGS' JURISPRUDENCE": THE MYTH AND MEANING OF JUSTICE HOLMES'S OPINION IN *PENNSYLVANIA COAL CO. V. MAHON*

106 YALE L.J. 613, 615–616, 666–668, 680–682, 686–688 (1996).

Ten cases and four findings of constitutional infirmity over the last decade would not amount to a trend in, say, First Amendment jurisprudence. But it does in Takings Clause jurisprudence. Before 1986, the Supreme Court's two-hundred-year history arguably reveals no more than four occasions on which the Court found laws to be regulatory takings, triggering the obligation to pay just compensation under the Federal Constitution's Takings Clause although they involved no physical appropriation or destruction of property.[3] Yet the Rehnquist Court has found four regulatory takings in its first ten years.[4] The Court also heard four other regulatory taking cases,[5] and has agreed to hear two more.[6]

Genealogists of this regulatory takings jurisprudence have found their Adam in *Pennsylvania Coal Co. v. Mahon,* a 1922 Supreme Court decision with a majority opinion by Justice Oliver Wendell Holmes. The *Mahon* Court concluded that a Pennsylvania statute prohibiting mining of coal so as to cause surface subsidence was unconstitutional. "The general rule at least," Holmes wrote, "is, that while property may be regulated to a certain extent, if regulation goes too far it will be recognized as a taking." The Holmes opinion, Chief Justice Rehnquist concludes, was "the foundation of our 'regulatory takings' jurisprudence."[10] Holmes, echoes Justice Scalia, invented the idea of the regulatory taking because he recognized that "if the protection against physical appropriations of private property was to be

---

[3]The number here depends upon several definitional issues regarding the term "regulatory takings." Six cases are widely recognized candidates: Loretto v. Teleprompter Manhattan CATV Corp., 458 U.S. 419 (1982); Webb's Fabulous Pharmacies v. Beckwith, 449 U.S. 155 (1980); Kaiser Aetna v. United States, 444 U.S. 164 (1979); Armstrong v. United States, 364 U.S. 40 (1960); Louisville Joint Stock Land Bank v. Radford, 295 U.S. 555 (1935); and the subject of this Article, Pennsylvania Coal Co. v. Mahon, 260 U.S. 393 (1922). However, if takings turning on physical invasions are not regulatory takings, then *Loretto* and *Kaiser Aetna* drop out. * * *

[4]See Dolan v. City of Tigard, 512 U.S. 374 (1994); Lucas v. South Carolina Coastal Council, 505 U.S. 1003 (1992); Nollan v. California Coastal Comm'n, 483 U.S. 825 (1987); Hodel v. Irving, 481 U.S. 704 (1987).

[5]See Concrete Pipe & Prod. v. Construction Laborers Pension Trust, 508 U.S. 602 (1993); Yee v. City of Escondido, 503 U.S. 519 (1992); First English Evangelical Lutheran Church v. County of Los Angeles, 482 U.S. 304 (1987); Keystone Bituminous Coal Ass'n v. DeBenedictis, 480 U.S. 470 (1987).

[6][Here the author cites two cases decided by the Supreme Court the following year: Suitum v. Tahoe Reg'l Planning Agency, 520 U.S. 725 (1997), holding that a regulatory taking claim was ripe for review; and Babbitt v. Youpee, 519 U.S. 234 (1997), which held unconstitutional a provision of the Indian Land Consolidation Act.]

[10]*Keystone,* 480 U.S. at 508 (Rehnquist, C.J., dissenting).

meaningfully enforced, the government's power to redefine the range of interests included in the ownership of property was necessarily constrained by constitutional limits."[11] A bevy of scholars has come to the same conclusion.

[It may come as a surprise to some, then, that] Holmes and the 1922 Court agreed that *Mahon* should be decided under the Contract and Due Process Clauses, not the Takings Clause. At the same time, the Due Process Clause was thought to protect a right of just compensation upon expropriation of property. Holmes's references to the textual basis for the *Mahon* decision, although brief, are quite straightforward. Holmes refers explicitly to the textual basis of the decision once: The police power must be limited, he contends, "*or* the contract and due process clauses are gone." Three coupled references to contract and property rights elsewhere in the opinion underscore this dual textual basis. Later in the opinion, Holmes notes that the Fifth Amendment provides that private property "shall not be taken for [public] use without compensation." He recognizes, however, that *Mahon* is not being decided under the Fifth Amendment, which applies only to the federal government. Holmes notes carefully that "[a] similar assumption is made in the decisions upon the Fourteenth Amendment." The case he cites makes clear—although in 1922 this hardly needed to be made clear—that the pertinent provision of the Fourteenth Amendment was the Due Process Clause.[244] * * *

Although the Contract and Due Process Clauses both had their place in *Mahon,* the Takings Clause did not. In 1896 and 1897, the Court had decided that the Fourteenth Amendment Due Process Clause prevented the states from taking private property for private uses,[249] and required the states to pay just compensation if they took private property for public uses.[250] The Court, however, did not do so on the theory that the Due Process Clause extended the reach of the Takings Clause from the federal government to the states. Rather, the Court used the "fundamental rights" theory later documented and championed by Justices Cardozo and Frankfurter and the second Justice Harlan. As Justice Moody wrote in the 1908 case of *Twining v. New Jersey,* "some of the personal rights safeguarded by the first eight Amendments against National action may also be safeguarded against state action, because a denial of them would be a denial of due process of law," but "[i]f this is so, it is not because those rights are enumerated in the first eight Amendments, but because they are

---

[11]Lucas v. South Carolina Coastal Council, 505 U.S. 1003, 1014 (1992)[.]

[244][260 U.S. 393, 415 (1922) (citing Hairston v. Danville & W. Ry. Co.), 208 U.S. 598, 605 (1908).]

[249][Missouri Pac. Ry. Co. v. Nebraska, 164 U.S. 403 (1896); Fallbrook Irrigation Dist. v. Bradley, 164 U.S. 112 (1896).]

[250]See Chicago, Burlington & Quincy R.R. v. Chicago, 166 U.S. 226, 226 (1897)[.]

of such a nature that they are included in the conception of due process of law." An important corollary of the logical independence of due process principles from the rules of the first eight amendments was that a due process principle might overlap an enumerated rule only in part; the principle and the rule need not be coextensive.

After 1935, *Mahon* appeared to be destined for oblivion, along with many other minor substantive due process cases. For over two decades, it failed to surface in a single Supreme Court majority opinion. [The short explanation of this is that it was a run-of-the-mill due process case, and had gone the way of *Lochner*.] The constitutional revolution of the late 1930s rejected the Due Process Clause as a textual home for substantive economic rights. [*Mahon*] was hopelessly obsolete.

In the post-1937 world, however, a judge who wanted to reestablish some sort of constitutional discourse about the governmental regulation of property rights could find alternative uses for *Mahon*. It might be the best precedent available in support of a discourse that was not vulnerable to charges of either textual or methodological Lochnerism. First, the matter of text. The keys here are Justice Holmes's posthumous reputation as a determined opponent of economic substantive due process and *Mahon's* mention of the Fifth Amendment Takings Clause, which, if not examined too closely, could be taken to indicate reliance on that text. Even as the Court repudiated economic substantive due process, it began to develop the doctrine of incorporation, under which the Fourteenth Amendment Due Process Clause, in addition to retaining a weak substantive component of its own, became a conduit for applying most of the Bill of Rights against the states. The obvious candidate to support a reinvigorated constitutional property discourse was the Fifth Amendment Takings Clause, with its ringing declaration that private "property [shall not] be taken for public use, without just compensation." There could be no doubt that the Takings Clause placed a substantive limitation on government action: "[W]ithout due process of law" might have referred to mere procedure, but "without just compensation" referred to hard cash.

The trickier issue was whether the terms "property" and "taken" could be interpreted broadly enough. Some precedent appeared to hold that "property" was only "taken" within the meaning of the Takings Clause when the government directly appropriated physical things—when government agents forced owners off their land or seized or destroyed their chattels. Other precedents had used just compensation language in reviewing a wider variety of legislation, but the discredited doctrine of substantive due process tainted most of that precedent. * * *

Mahon's reconstruction as a Takings Clause case, rather than a substantive due process case, was fortified in the battle over whether the Constitution mandated a retrospective damages remedy for those temporarily subject to excessively burdensome regulation. By 1980, it was established that the Takings Clause itself entitled an owner whose property had been taken to bring an "inverse condemnation" action, seeking just compensation.[349] Moreover, owners whose property had been taken temporarily—for example, owners whose land or buildings had been taken over by the federal government to be used in the war effort during World War II—could recover just compensation for the period when they had been dispossessed, even after the government returned possession to them.[350] It appeared that if regulations were subject to review under the Takings Clause, the Constitution guaranteed damages for the time during which an excessive regulation was in effect, even if the government agreed to lift the regulation once a court found it to effect a taking. Those opposed to awarding damages for temporary regulatory takings did not question this logic. Rather, they developed the argument that regulations were subject to review only under the Due Process Clause, which did not provide an inverse condemnation action or require interim damages.

Into this debate came *Mahon* and Justice Holmes's comment that "if regulation goes too far it will be recognized as a taking." Did this mean that the Court had decided in 1922 that regulations were reviewable under the Takings Clause? The state courts that had decided against a temporary damages remedy maintained that Justice Holmes had used the word "taking" only in a "metaphorical" sense and that the real issue in *Mahon* was whether the Kohler Act was "an invalid exercise of the police power under the due process clause."[353]

In 1981, however, Justice Brennan rejected this interpretation in his dissent in *San Diego Gas & Electric Co. v. City of San Diego.*[354] While the majority in *San Diego Gas & Electric* held that the Court lacked jurisdiction to decide the temporary damages issue, Justice Brennan, joined by three others, enlisted *Mahon* in support of his conclusion that the Constitution did mandate damages for temporary takings. "[T]he general principle that a regulation can effect a Fifth Amendment 'taking,'" Justice Brennan asserted, "has its source in Justice Holmes' opinion for the Court in *Pennsylvania Coal Co. v. Mahon.*" The state courts were wrong to interpret *Mahon* as merely indicating when a police power regulation would be invalid; the *Mahon* Court "[c]learly . . . contemplated that a regulation could cross the boundary surrounding valid police power exercise and become a Fifth Amendment 'taking.'" If, as Brennan and others assumed,

---

[349]See United States v. Clarke, 445 U.S. 253, 257 (1980).

[350]See, e.g., Kimball Laundry Co. v. United States, 338 U.S. 1 (1949): United States v. General Motors Corp., 323 U.S. 373 (1945).

[353]Fred F. French Investing Co. v. City of New York, 350 N.E.2d 381, 385 (N.Y. 1976); see Agins v. City of Tiburon, 598 P.2d 25, 29 (Cal.1979), aff'd, 447 U.S. 255 (1980)[.]

[354]450 U.S. 621 (1981).

all government action reviewable under the Takings Clause could give rise to liability for temporary damages, then *Mahon,* by reviewing a regulation under that Clause, supported a damages remedy for temporary regulatory takings.

[Then, in the 1987 case of *First English Evangelical Lutheran Church v. County of Los Angeles,*[358]] the Court adopted Justice Brennan's position that the Constitution mandated a damages remedy for temporary regulatory takings, and with it, Brennan's interpretation of *Mahon.* In the view of the *First English* Court, when Holmes stated that " 'if a regulation goes too far it will be recognized as a taking,'" he meant a Fifth Amendment taking, and he meant to acknowledge that the Fifth Amendment provided a damages remedy regardless of whether the government had formally instituted condemnation proceedings. Together, *San Diego Gas & Electric* and *First English* contributed mightily to *Mahon's* reputation as a seminal Takings Clause case.

Mahon's role as support for a damages remedy for temporary regulatory takings depends on two anachronisms. The first is familiar: None of the members of the *Mahon* Court believed that the Fourteenth Amendment "incorporated" the Takings Clause, which continued to apply only to the federal government. Rather, Fourteenth Amendment due process included the fundamental right of just compensation, which happened to be embodied in the Fifth Amendment Takings Clause as well. In addition, a deeper anachronism affected Justice Brennan and the *First English* Court's views about *Mahon* and the issue of damages for temporary regulatory takings. Brennan and the *First English* Court assumed, as did the state courts they opposed, that if a regulation really effected a "taking," then the Constitution required an award of retrospective damages for any period the regulation was in effect. But Justice Holmes and the *Mahon* Court [might] have seen the issue in a different light.

WILLIAM MICHAEL TREANOR, JAM FOR JUSTICE HOLMES: REASSESSING THE SIGNIFICANCE OF *MAHON*

86 GEO. L.J. 813, 822–828, 861, 867–873 (1998).

II. CONCEPTIONS OF *MAHON*

Supreme Court decisions and scholarly writings offer a variety of starkly different visions of the relationship between *Mahon* and the case law that preceded it, as well as of what tests the case embodied. Nonetheless, these different readings all incorporate the view that *Mahon* supports judicial activism in economic matters, and this view has strongly shaped the case law and academic debate.

---

[358] 482 U.S. 304 (1987).

A. FIRST REGULATORY TAKINGS CASE

One standard conception of *Mahon's* place in history is that it was the first case in which the Court interpreted the Takings Clause to bar the uncompensated taking of property through government regulation (as opposed to through some form of physical seizure, such as through eminent domain). In the 1992 case of *Lucas v. South Carolina Coastal Council*,[51] Justice Scalia wrote for the Court:

> Prior to Justice Holmes' exposition in *Pennsylvania Coal Co. v. Mahon*, it was generally though that the Takings Clause reached only a "direct appropriation" of property, to the functional equivalent of a "practical ouster of [the owner's] possession." Justice Holmes recognized in *Mahon*, however, that if the protection against physical appropriations of private property was to be meaningfully enforced, the government's power to redefine the range of interests included in the ownership of property was necessarily constrained by constitutional limits.

* * * There are, in turn, two views about how Holmes thought that tool should be applied.

1. Diminution in Value Test

According to one view, *Mahon* sets forth a diminution in value test under which, if the property owner's loss crosses some unspecified line, compensation is owed. This is both the dominant reading of *Mahon* among commentators, and the principal way in which the Court has read *Mahon*. Moreover, although the Court has been inconsistent in its takings jurisprudence and applied a range of different tests in resolving takings challenges, the diminution in value test is the one that the Court applies most commonly when the challenged regulation targets something other than a nuisance.

Supporting this view of *Mahon* is language in the opinion indicating that courts should focus on the economic loss suffered by the property owner and that compensation is the remedy if the loss is too great. In particular, Holmes observed: "One fact for consideration in determining such limits [to the police power] is the extent of the diminution. When it reaches a certain magnitude, in most if not in all cases there must be an exercise of eminent domain and compensation to sustain the act." He also observed: "The general rule at least is that while property may be regulated to a certain extent, if regulation goes too far it will be recognized as a taking."

Thus stated, however, the diminution in value test is incomplete because it raises the question of how far is "too far?" While proponents of the

---

[51] 505 U.S. 1003 (1992)

diminution in value test do not claim that *Mahon* answers this question, some have contended that, because Holmes focuses on how the Kohler Act affect the coal company's rights, *Mahon* suggests that, at least where the property interest affected by a regulation had in some way been recognized by the law, the question of whether a regulation went "too far" should be determined by focusing on the percentage loss in value of the affected property interest, not the percentage loss in the value of the fee simple as a whole. Professor Margaret Radin has dubbed this approach of focusing on the property interest, not the whole property, "conceptual severance."[60] * * * Where this approach followed in future cases, the range of land use regulations that would violate the Takings Clause would increase enormously because a regulation can make a particular interest valueless even though the effect on the value of property as a whole is relatively small. For example, regulations that bar use of water of mineral rights of that prevent on owner from developing some part of her property might give rise to compenseable takings, even if the overall value of the fee simple did not substantially decline. * * *

2. Balancing Test

Less commonly, commentators and, on one occasion, the Court have read *Mahon* as employing a balancing test, rather than a diminution in value test.[69] While Holmes did not explicitly employ a balancing test, those who find this test in the opinion argue that Holmes's analysis reflects consideration of both the public interest and harm to the property owner.

To say that *Mahon* involved a balancing test is not, however, to say how Holmes intended the balance be struck. The consensus among those who read *Mahon* as embodying a balancing test is that Holmes believed that a large thumb should be placed on the property owner's side of the scale. * * *

A. SUBSTANTIVE DUE PROCESS CASE

While *Mahon* is most commonly described as the first regulatory takings case, others have argued that it is not a regulatory takings case at all, but a substantive due process case "different only in degree" from *Lochner*.

Robert Brauneis recently gave this approach its fullest treatment. "The story of *Mahon*'s reputation and interpretation," he has argued, "is a case study in legal evolution selective borrowing and amnesia." *Mahon* was a "minor substantive due process case." The inquiry is essentially the same

---

[60][Radin, The Liberal Conception of Property: Cross Currents in the Jurisprudence of Takings, 88 Colum. L. Rev. 1667, 1677 (1988)].

[69]In *Keystone*, Justice Stevens, writing for the Court, stated that under *Mahon* the "factors" relevant to constitutionality were the public interest and the diminution in value, implicitly suggesting that the decision embodied a balancing test. [Keystone Bituminous Coal Ass'n v. De Benedictis, 480 U.S. 470, 484,492 (1987).]

under *Mahon* and under *Lochner*. Neither involved a balancing test. Both involved "inquiries into traditional legal categories and legislative purposes." When the Supreme Court "rejected the Due Process Clause as a textual home for substantive economic rights," the case was essentially forgotten: "After 1935, *Mahon* appeared to be destined for oblivion. . . ." Only later was it eventually "rediscovered and to some extent reinvented as the foundation of regulatory jurisprudence." *Mahon* is now widely understood, by Supreme Court Justices and academic commentators alike, to be a landmark: the first 'regulatory takings' case." It has thus been "stripped of its original meaning" as a substantive due process decision. [Holmes intended to require a form of balancing, but with the balance weighted in favor of the government. Only when the public benefit was trivial or nonexistent did he feel that regulations should be invalidated.]

V. RECONCEPTUALIZING *MAHON*

Mahon grows out of Holmes's previous constitutional property decisions and his rejection of the traditional approaches embodied in the case law. The competing schools of thought about the case have failed to understand Holmes's larger project and the case law to which he was responding. As a result, although each approach contains at least a partial truth about the case, the partial truths ultimately serve to obscure rather than reveal. Misunderstanding and disregarding *Mahon*'s background has led to the erroneous conclusion that the case reflects a fairly high degree of judicial oversight of economic regulation. * * *

Mahon is a substantive due process case. It preceded the Supreme Court's acceptance of incorporation. [P]rofessor Brauneis correctly observes: "Holmes's remarks [about] Takings Clause and the Fourteenth Amendment are not sloppy, but quite precise. Holmes refers to the protection afforded by the Takings Clause against the federal government and then states that "[a] similar assumption is made in the decisions upon the 14th Amendment."

Although *Mahon* is technically a substantive due process case, it is not, however, like *Lochner,* and proponents of the substantive due process view of *Mahon* have repeatedly missed this crucial point. * * * Holmes's other decisions reworked and restructured the basic concepts of substantive due process and rejected its formalist approach. * * *

VI. *Mahon* and the Takings Revival

* * * A proper understanding of *Mahon* and, more generally, of Holmes's constitutional property philosophy would have led to a different result in the cases at the heart of the Court's takings revival. The balancing favored by Holmes and the limited inquiry into arbitrariness when government acted as regulator conflict with the mixture of formalism and close scrutiny reflected in recent decisions.

At its most concrete level, a proper understanding of *Mahon* is inconsistent with the diminution in value test (the most commonly applied test in the takings realm), with conceptual severance, and with the continued (if limited) use of the categorical nuisance test exemplified by *Mugler [v. Kansas]*.[315] *Lucas v. South Carolina Coastal Council*[316] best illustrates the shift and its consequences.

David Lucas owned two beachfront lots for which he had paid almost $1,000,000. Thereafter, the South Carolina Beach Management Act was passed and, acting pursuant to that act, the state coastal commission prohibited Lucas from building on the lots, a prohibition that, according to the state trial court, rendered the properties worthless. Ruling for Lucas, the Court held that, when a government regulation takes all economic value from land, compensation is owed unless the regulation bars a common law nuisance or accords with background principle of property law. The elements of the holding reflect Justice Scalia's understanding of, and reliance on, *Mahon*. Justice Scalia traces the diminution in value test back to *Mahon*. The core idea of *Lucas*—that a regulation that takes away all value from land is presumptively a taking—then follows logically from the diminution in value test: that is, if *Mahon*'s concept of "too far" is to have any meaning, loss of "all economically beneficial or productive use of land" must be too far. The nuisance exception reflects Scalia's implicit view that *Mahon* supplemented, rather than displaced, the earlier classic police power case law. This point merits emphasis because it reflects a view at odds with this article's thesis that *Mahon* was fundamentally inconsistent with the case law that preceded it. Scalia and, in dissent, Blackmun offer differing ways to read (and distinguish) the *Mugler* categorical nuisance line of cases. Scalia interprets them narrowly as applying only to common law nuisances: Blackmun reads them as authorizing the government to bar "harmful" activities. No one, however, suggests that there is any tension between *Mugler* and *Mahon*.

As previously observed, Justice Scalia read *Mahon* as adopting a conceptual severance approach and suggested that the Court should apply that approach in future decisions. Thus, when a regulation eliminates a property interest that "has [been] accorded legal recognition and protection"—like the support rights in *Mahon*. [A]nd, in previous decisions, liberal members of the Court have adopted precisely this reading of *Mahon*, although they did not treat it as controlling.

Every point of this analysis conflicts with the contextualized reading of *Mahon* presented here. *Mahon* reflects a balancing test, not a diminution of value test. Thus, government interest comes into play and, because there is

---

[315][123 U.S. 623 (1887) (upholding a state law prohibiting intoxicating beverages).]
[316]505 U.S. 1003 (1992).

something on the other side of the scale, a total loss of value would not necessarily be a taking. Moreover, when the balancing test in *Mahon* is understood in the context of Holmes's other decisions, it becomes clear that the balance is weighted in favor of the government. The state interests advanced—that preserving the beachfront through a development ban would promote the economy through tourism and protect endangered species—are sufficiently substantial to make the statute constitutional; Holmes invalidated regulations only when the public benefit was trivial or nonexistent. At the same time, it should be noted that, were the state seeking to stop a common law nuisance, Holmes's approach would be more favorable to the property owner than Scalia's: while Scalia would automatically uphold the statute, Holmes would still use balancing.

Finally, Holmes's approach is not one of conceptual severance. While in *Mahon* there was a total diminution of a legally recognized property right, that factor did not determine the outcome. Holmes's approach was not categorical; accordingly, to read *Mahon* as embodying a categorical rule is to misread *Mahon*.

The most significant cases in takings revival * * * apart from *Lucas*, are the two "unconstitutional conditions" cases, *Nollan v. California Coastal Commission*,[334] and *Dolan v. City of Tigard*.[335] The unconstitutional conditions doctrine, as applied to the Takings Clause, restricts the conditions that a government can impose on a property owner in exchange for removal of a valid restriction on land use. The doctrine is an important one because it limits a tool that local governments have increasingly used in recent years.

The unconstitutional conditions doctrine received its fullest expression in *Dolan*. There, the court held that there must be both an "essential nexus" between the reason justifying the power to ban and the condition imposed in exchange for lifting the ban. When Tigard, Oregon, granted Florence Dolan permission to expand her hardware store and create a parking lot on the condition that she dedicate land for a bike path the Court found that the "essential nexus" requirement was satisfied, but not the "rough proportionality" requirement, and therefore the town's action was unconstitutional. * * *

Yet, while the Court enlists *Mahon* to support the holding, the low level review that *Mahon* embodies is inconsistent with [this] general position on sovereignty. Holmes believed that, if the state had the power to forbid a certain activity, it could also authorize that activity subject to limitations. * * *

---

[334] 483 U.S. 825 (1987).

[335] 512 U.S. 374 (1994).

The point here is not that *Mahon* itself is inconsistent with the unconstitutional conditions doctrine—it does not discuss that issue—but rather that, in a variety of contexts, the takings revival enlists the spirit of *Mahon*, but *Mahon*, properly understood, fundamentally conflicts with that revival.

If *Mahon* were read as part of Holmes's project of establishing a minimal level of scrutiny for economic regulations, then consistency with Holmes's project would lead to a different approach to these cases. All of these decisions begin from the premise that courts, in reviewing regulatory takings claims, should be significantly more vigilant than when reviewing challenges to regulations brought under the Equal Protection Clause or the Due Process Clause. In contrast, Holmes, in his takings cases, used the same rationality review that he generally used in cases involving substantive due process challenges to economic regulations.

Part of the strength of Holmes's approach lies in the fact that it is more coherent than current case law. That case law incorporates a series of approaches that, as has been often pointed out, conflict with each other, and that make takings law a "mess." In particular, there is an obvious tension between the doctrine that regulation of a common law nuisance can constitutionally destroy all value in a property and the doctrine that all other regulations are reviewed to determine if they diminish value too greatly. Holmes's unified approach does away with this intellectually problematic distinction.

Moreover, his approach allows for greater regulatory freedom to confront new problems and to respond to new conceptions of harm. The *Lucas v. South Carolina Coastal Council* test would prevent a legislature from outlawing an activity that was not a common law nuisance, regardless of its harm, if the regulated property were rendered valueless. It would seem, for example, to require compensation if Congress were to outlaw tobacco planting and property were thereby made worthless. Holmes's approach, in contrast, would uphold such a statute; in using his government-favoring balancing test, a court would find that the state's interest in avoiding the harms associated with smoking would outweigh the property loss caused by the tobacco ban.

Although Holmes never mounted a defense of his position, it can be justified on utilitarian grounds. His balancing reflects a utilitarian calculus: government action is permissible only if its benefits (to society) outweigh its harm (to the individual). A regulation that is clearly unjustified on utilitarian grounds would be held unconstitutional as arbitrary.

Because the balancing test Holmes implicitly adopted favored the government, admittedly, a court applying the test would uphold some government actions that it might feel were problematic. Two reasons, however, justify this weighting. First, it ensures predictability. The Holmesian approach is more constrained than open-ended balancing;

regulations will be upheld unless they essentially transfer property between citizens with little public benefit or useless government acts to benefit its own property. This leads in turn to greater certainty in the average case that the court will not intervene. Second, the weighting is justified on the grounds of majoritarian theory. To quote Horwitz's explanation of Holmes's deference once again: "If law is merely politics, then the legislature should in fact decide."[346] Courts should trump legislatures only when it is unquestionable that the legislature erred.

These are strong arguments. At the same time, there are fundamental problems with Holmes's view. The Takings Clause is, among the clauses in the Bill of Rights, perhaps the one for which balancing is least appropriate. Other constitutional rights necessarily involve a choice between the state and the individual. The Takings Clause uniquely involves something that is quantifiable and fungible. The individual can be made whole when her property is taken in a way that she cannot be when, for example, her speech is curtailed. Therefore, balancing in the takings context merely begs the question. Balancing may tell us that a certain regulation is efficient. It does not tell us who should bear the burden of the regulation—the property owner or society at large.

Similarly, the fact that the balancing test is weighted in favor of the government also ultimately involves a kind of question begging. In other words, if Holmes believed that decision making were inherently political and thus best left to the legislature, that would suggest—not that courts should intervene rarely—but that they should never intervene. The response to this might be that the arbitrariness of the result suggests that the legislative process in fact failed, making any deference to such process inappropriate. Arbitrariness, in other words, suggests corruption (to some extent) of the legislative process and, when the process has been corrupted, courts are under no obligation to defer to it because the decision has no meaningful majoritarian sanction. The problem with this argument is that focus on results in a specific instance is not necessarily a good test of whether the political process has failed.

BIBLIOGRAPHY

Economic Due Process

Brown, *The Fragmented Liberty Clause*, 42 Wm. & Mary L.Rev. 65 (1999).

Chemerinsky, *Substantive Due Process*, 15 Touro L.Rev. 1601 (1999).

Corwin, E., LIBERTY AGAINST GOVERNMENT (1948).

[346][Morton Horwitz, The Transformation of American Law, 1870-1960 (1977), at 142.]

Cushman, *Lost Fidelities*, 41 Wm. & Mary L.Rev. 95 (1999).

Ely, The *Oxymoron Reconsidered: Myth and Reality in the Origins of Substantive Due Process*, 15 Const. Comment. 315 (1999).

Fleming, *Fidelity, Basic Liberties, and the Specter of* Lochner, 41 Wm. & Mary L. Rev. 147 (1999).

Hovenkamp, *The Political Economy of Substantive Due Process,* 40 Stan.L.Rev. 379 (1988).

Levy, *Escaping* Lochner's *Shadow: Toward a Coherent Jurisprudence of Economic Rights*, 73 N.C.L.Rev. 329 (1995).

Miller, *The True Story of* Carolene Products, 1987 Sup.Ct.Rev. 397.

Paul, CONSERVATIVE CRISIS AND THE RULE OF LAW (1969).

Phillips, *The Slow Return of Economic Substantive Due Process*, 49 Syracuse L.Rev. 917 (1999).

Siegan, ECONOMIC LIBERTIES AND THE CONSTITUTION (1980).

Siegan, *Separation of Powers & Economic Liberties*, 70 Notre Dame L.Rev. 415 (1995).

Siegel, *Understanding the* Lochner *Era: Lessons from the Controversy over Railroad and Utility Rate Regulation,* 70 Va.L.Rev. 187 (1984).

Stigler, *The Theory of Economic Regulation,* 2 Bell J.Econ. & Mgmt.Sci. 3 (1971).

Tarrow, Lochner versus New York: *A Political Analysis,* 5 Lab.Hist. 277 (1964).

Wonnell, *Economic Due Process and the Preservation of Competition,* 11 Hast.Const.L.Q. 91 (1983).

The Taking/Regulation Distinction

Ausness, *Regulatory Takings and Wetland Protection in the Post-*Lucas *Era,* 30 Land & Water L.Rev. 349 (1995).

Ausness, *Wild Dunes and Serbonian Bogs,* 70 Denver U.L.Rev. 3 (1993).

Blais, *Takings, Statutes, and the Common Law: Considering Inherent Limitations on Title,* 70 S.Cal.L.Rev. 1 (1996).

Brauneis, *Treanor's* Mahon, 86 Geo. L.J. 907 (1998).

Butler, *The Politics of Takings: Choosing the Appropriate Decisionmaker,* 38 Wm. & Mary L.Rev. 749 (1997).

Byrne, *Regulatory Takings and "Judicial Supremacy",* 51 Ala.L.Rev. 949 (2002).

Clegg, *Reclaiming the Text of the Takings Clause,* 46 S.C.L.Rev. 531 (1995).

Eagle, *Substantive Due Process and Regulatory Takings: A Reappraisal*, 51 Ala.L.Rev. 977(2002).

Epstein, Lucas v. South Carolina Coastal Council: *A Tangled Web of Expectations*, 45 Stan.L.Rev. 1369 (1993).

Epstein, Pennsylvania Coal v. Mahon: *The Erratic Takings Jurisprudence of Justice Holmes*, 86 Geo.L.J. 875 (1998).

Epstein, *Takings, Exclusivity and Speech: The Legacy* of Pruneyard v. Robins, 64 U.Chi.L.Rev. 21 (1997).

Farber, *Public Choice and Just Compensation,* 9 Const.Comm. 279 (1992).

Fischel, W., REGULATORY TAKINGS: LAW, ECONOMICS, AND POLITICS (1995).

Huffman, Dolan v. City of Tigard: *Another Step in the Right Direction,* 25 Envtl.L. 143 (1995).

Kmiec, *At Last, the Supreme Court Solves the Takings Puzzle,* 19 Harv.J.L. & Pub. Pol'y. 147 (1995).

Kmiec, *Inserting the Last Remaining Pieces into the Takings Puzzle,* 38 Wm. & Mary L.Rev. 995 (1997).

Kobach, *The Origins of Regulatory Takings: Setting the Record Straight,* 1996 Utah L.Rev. 1211.

Krier, *The Regulation Machine,* 1 Sup.Ct.Econ.Rev. 1 (1982).

Krotoszynski, *Expropriatory Intent: Defining the Proper Boundaries of Substantive Due Process and the Takings Clause*, 80 N.C. L. Rev. 713 (2002).

Laitos, *Takings and Causation,* 5 Wm. & Mary Bill Rts.J. 359 (1997).

Levmore, *Takings, Torts, and Special Interests,* 77 Va.L.Rev. 1333 (1991).

Mandelker, *New Property Rights Under the Taking Clause*, 81 Marq.L.Rev. (1997).

Mandelker, *Investment-Backed Expectations: Is There a Taking?,* 31 Wash.U.J.Urb. & Contemp.L. 3 (1987).

McUsic, The *Ghost of* Lochner: *Modern Takings Doctrine and Its Impact on Economic Legislation,* 76 B.U.L.Rev. 605 (1996).

Michelman, *Property, Utility and Fairness: Comments on the Ethical Foundations of "Just Compensation" Law,* 80 Harv.L.Rev.1165 (1967).

Riesel and Barshov, *When Does Government Regulation Go "Too Far"?,* 6 Fordham Envtl.L.J. 565 (1995).

Rose, Mahon *Reconstructed: Why the Takings Issue Is Still a Muddle*, 57 S.Cal.L.Rev. 561(1984).

Sax, *Takings and the Police Power*, 74 Yale L.J. 36 (1964).

Sax, *Takings, Private Property and Public Rights,* 81 Yale L.J. 149 (1971).

Schroeder, *Never Jam To-day: On the Impossibility of Takings Jurisprudence,* 84 Geo.L.J. 1531 (1996).

Sidak and Spulber, *Deregulatory Takings and Breach of the Regulatory Contract,* 71 N.Y.U.L.Rev. 851 (1996).

Sullivan, *Substantive Due Process Resurrected Through the Takings Clause:* Nollan, Dolan, *and* Ehrlich, 25 Envtl.L. 155 (1995).

Symposium, *Constitutional Issues in Land Use Regulation,* 8 Hastings Const.L.Q. 449 (1981).

Symposium, *Lucas v. South Carolina Coastal Council,* 45 Stan.L.Rev. 1369 (1993).

Thompson, *Judicial Takings,* 76 Va.L.Rev. 1449 (1990).

Treanor, *The* Armstrong *Principle, the Narratives of Takings, and Compensation Statutes,* 38 Wm. & Mary L.Rev. 1151 (1997).

Treanor, *Understanding* Mahon *in Historical Context,* 86 Geo.L.J. 933 (1998).

Walker, *Property Rights After* Dolan: *The Search for the Madisonian Solution to the Regulatory Takings Conundrum,* 20 Wm. & Mary Envtl.L. & Pol'y Rev. 263 (1996).

Wyeth, *Regulatory Competition and the Takings Clause,* 91 Nw.U.L.Rev. 87 (1996).

B. ABORTION

In *Griswold v. Connecticut*[1] in 1965 the Supreme Court held that a state law forbidding the use of contraceptives violated the Due Process Clause of the Fourteenth Amendment. The Court did not make clear whether it was protecting a right to prevent conception (a liberty properly speaking—a right to act), or a right to privacy in the Fourth Amendment sense (a protection against government snooping). *Roe v. Wade*[2] eight years later was unequivocal. It held that "the Fourteenth Amendment's concept of personal liberty * * * encompass[ed] a woman's decision whether or not to terminate her pregnancy."[3] Since then the courts have been plagued with issues about the scope of this liberty, not just in abortion cases, but also in cases dealing with other family affairs,[4] homosexual behavior,[5] the provision of medical care,[6] and so on.

---

[1]381 U.S. 479, 85 S.Ct. 1678, 14 L.Ed.2d 510 (1965).

[2]410 U.S. 113, 153, 93 S.Ct. 705, 726, 35 L.Ed.2d 147 (1973).

[3]The Court reaffirmed this aspect of *Roe* in Planned Parenthood of Southeastern Pennsylvania v. Casey, 505 U.S. 833, 112 S.Ct. 2791, 120 L.Ed.2d 674 (1992).

[4]Moore v. East Cleveland, 431 U.S. 494, 97 S.Ct. 1932, 52 L.Ed.2d 531 (1977).

[5]Bowers v. Hardwick, 478 U.S. 186, 106 S.Ct. 2841, 92 L.Ed.2d 140 (1986).

[6]Washington v. Glucksberg, 521 U.S. 702, 117 S.Ct. 2258, 138 L.Ed.2d 772 (1997).

The readings in this Section focus on *Roe,* because it is the axis around which these issues revolve. *Roe* has been particularly controversial for two reasons. The first is the difficulty of explaining what makes the freedom to terminate pregnancy a special liberty deserving unusual protection from the courts. The second is the unique quality of the countervailing interest in such cases: the government claims that it is protecting potential (or perhaps actual) human life by restricting abortions.

John Noonan's article asserts that the latter point should be decisive, and that the courts have shied away from confronting it. They have, he argues, dehumanized the unborn child much as nineteenth century courts dehumanized slaves, by treating the idea of a "person" as simply a juridical construct.

Rather than dispute Noonan's assertion, Judith Thomson's famous defense of abortion accepts it as true and asserts that a woman still has a right to decide what shall happen in and to her body. If the fetus is a person it has a right to live, but that is not a right to be kept alive at someone else's expense.

David Strauss points out that Thomson's argument relies on several libertarian assumptions that are hard to justify. Though the law does not usually require people to act as good Samaritans, it does require parents to take care of their children. These duties of care are usually economic or emotional rather than physical (as they are for pregnant women), but it is not obvious that bodily intrusions are more of an imposition than other obligatory parental sacrifices. Strauss concludes that a successful pro-choice argument must make weaker assumptions about the status of fetal life.

John Hart Ely contends that *Roe* is misguided in identifying the right to have an abortion as a "liberty" deserving of special protection. If it were a weaker liberty (like freedom of contract) it would have to yield to the government's interest in protecting the fetus even if the fetus were *not* a person. Nothing in the text or the framers' thinking identifies the woman's action as special. And Ely argues that in this instance—where women's interests conflict with those of fetuses and not men—the political process can be trusted to reach a satisfactory result.

Ruth Bader Ginsburg parries Ely's criticism with one of her own. The real problem with the Court's opinion in *Roe v. Wade,* she charges, is that it invoked the wrong part of the Constitution in support of women's reproductive rights. She contends that the Court would have been on firmer ground, and would have invited less academic criticism and popular outrage, if it had relied upon equal protection rather than due process. In some ways Ginsburg's approach would have been more moderate than the path taken in *Roe*—a fact emphasized by some feminists who criticized her appointment to the Court. In others, though, it may have been more radical.

Consider her suggestion that the government, if it is to govern impartially, must provide public funding for abortions for poor women.

JOHN T. NOONAN, JR., THE ROOT AND BRANCH OF *ROE v. WADE*

63 NEB.L.REV. 668–669, 671–673, 675, 677–679 (1984).

Whoever has the power to define the bearer of constitutional rights has a power that can make nonsense of any particular constitutional right. That this power belongs to the state itself is a point of view associated in jurisprudence with Hans Kelsen. According to Kelsen a person is simply a construct of the law. As he expresses it in *The Pure Theory of Law,* even the apparently natural physical person is a construction of juristic thinking. In this account it appears that just as we personify a corporation for legal purposes so we personify natural physical beings. There are no independent, ontological existences to which we respond as persons. Personhood depends on recognition by the law.[2]

A corollary of that position appears to be what has always seemed to me one of the most terrifying of legal propositions: there is no kind of human behavior that, because of its nature, could not be made into a legal duty corresponding to a legal right. When one thinks of the vast variety of human behavior it is at least startling to think that every variation could be converted into legal duties and legal rights. The proposition becomes terrifying when one thinks of Orwell's *1984* or the actual conduct of the Nazi regime from which Hans Kelsen himself eventually had to flee.

There is one massive phenomenon in the history of our country that might be invoked to support Kelsen's point of view. That phenomenon is the way a very large class of human beings were treated prior to the enactment of the thirteenth and fourteenth amendments. When one looks back at the history of 200 years of slavery in the United States, and looks back at it as a lawyer observing that lawyers had a great deal to do with the classifications that made the phenomenon possible, one realizes that the law, in fact, has been used to create legal rights and legal duties in relation to human behavior that should never have been given a legal form and a legal blessing. To put it bluntly, law was the medium and lawyers were the agents responsible for turning one class of human beings into property. The result was that the property laws of the different states made it smooth and easy to transfer ownership of these human beings. The property laws resolved the questions that occurred at those critical junctions where humanity asserted itself either in the birth of a child to a slave or the death of the owner of a slave. The only question left open for argument was whether the human beings classified as property were realty or personalty.

[2] H. Kelsen, The Pure Theory of Law 95 (M. Knight trans. 2nd ed. 1967).

In the inheritance cases the slave child was treated like the issue of an animal, compared again and again in legal decisions to the issue of livestock.

Gross characterization of human beings in terms that reduced them to animals, or real estate, or even kitchen utensils now may seem so unbelievable that we all can profess shock and amazement that it was ever done. Eminently respectable lawyers were able to engage in this kind of characterization—among them Thomas Jefferson, who co-authored the slave code of Virginia, and Abraham Lincoln who argued on behalf of a slave owner seeking to recover as his property a woman and her four children who had escaped to the free state of Illinois. Looking at such familiar examples and realizing how commonplace it was for lawyers to engage in this kind of fiction, we learn, I think, that law can operate as a kind of magic. All that is necessary is to permit legal legerdemain to create a mask obliterating the human person being dealt with. Looking at the mask—that is looking at the abstract category created by the law—is not to see the human reality on which the mask is imposed.

* * *

[Consider what happened in] *Scott v. Sanford.* Here the black plaintiff attempted to assert his right to freedom in the federal court. The Supreme Court held that the federal statute that should have made him free was an interference with the property rights guaranteed by the Constitution to his owner. The Court applied the due process clause of the fifth amendment—gratuitously reading into this clause a concept of substantive due process—and held the statute invalid. The property mask dropped over Dred Scott was the means by which the Constitution was brought into play. As James Buchanan, the President at the time, happily put it, the Court had achieved "the final settlement" of the question of slavery in the Territories.[12] It was a final settlement curiously like Adolph Hitler's "final solution" of "the Jewish question" in Germany.

Buchanan's description, of course, was inaccurate. The Supreme Court could not resolve an issue that so fundamentally divided the nation. The legal mask was shattered by the Civil War. The thirteenth and fourteenth amendments were adopted. The legal profession forgot about its participation in molding the mask that made slavery possible. It is only in our time that the analogy seems vital.

Kelsen's jurisprudence makes * * * *Dred Scott* a defensible decision: according to it, there is nothing intrinsic in humanity requiring persons to be legally recognized as persons. The relevance of Kelsen's reasoning was acknowledged in a modern case, *Byrn v. New York City Health and*

---

[12] James Buchanan, *Third Annual Message to Congress,* 4 Papers of the Presidents 3085–86 (J. Richardson ed. 1913).

Hospitals Corporation,[13] decided a year before the Supreme Court decided *Roe v. Wade.* In *Byrn,* Robert Byrn was appointed guardian *ad litem* of an unborn child and asserted that child's constitutional right not to be aborted. His position was rejected by the majority of the Court of Appeals of New York, speaking through Judge Charles Breitel. Breitel quoted Kelsen explicitly to support his position that it was a policy determination of the state whether legal personality should be recognized or not. It was, Breitel stated, "not true that the legal order corresponds to the natural order." Breitel did not go as far as Kelsen's statement that natural persons were juristic creations—Breitel seemed to assume that there might be natural persons—but he left the recognition of natural persons to the legislature. As New York, at this time, had already enacted a fairly radical abortion law, he held that the legislature had conclusively made the decision that left the unborn child outside the class of recognized humanity.

* * *

Roe v. Wade itself, decided a year later, was profoundly ambivalent—indeed, to speak bluntly, it was schizoid in its approach to the power of the state to determine who was a person. The opinion was schizoid because the Court wanted to invoke rights that were not dependent on the state—the Court was trying to find a measure by which to invalidate state statutes. The precedents that the Court found to authorize it to act in this area of law were all cases that treated family rights as having a natural basis superior to the law of the state. The cases involved included *Meyer v. Nebraska* and *Pierce v. Society of Sisters,* recognizing a superior right of parents to educate their children; *Skinner v. Oklahoma,* recognizing that a man has a natural right to procreate and so cannot be arbitrarily sterilized by the state; *Loving v. Virginia,* where the natural right to marry was invoked in the course of invalidating a miscegenation statute; and *Griswold v. Connecticut,* where the rights of the married were also asserted, in this case to hold unconstitutional a statute prohibiting the use of contraceptives.

All of these cases rested on the supposition that the family rights being protected were those of persons, and that these persons could not be unmade at will by the state. The natural law fundament of these decisions was camouflaged by their being couched in constitutional language; but the constitutional content was derived from nowhere except the natural law as it had taken shape in the traditions of the United States. At the same time that it invoked such precedents in *Roe,* the Court, when treating of the unborn, felt free to impose its own notions of reality.

In one passage the Court spoke of the unborn before viability as "a theory of life," as though there were competing views as to whether life in

[13] 31 N.Y.2d 194, 286 N.E.2d 887, 335 N.Y.S.2d 390 (1972), *appeal dismissed,* 410 U.S. 949 (1973).

fact existed before viability. The implication could also be found that there was no reality there in the womb but merely theories about what was there. The Court seemed to be uncertain itself and to take the position that if it were unsure, nobody else could be sure. In another passage the Court spoke of life in the womb up to birth as "potential life." This description was accurate if it meant there was existing life with a great deal of development yet to come, as one might say a 5-year-old is "potential life" meaning that he or she is only potentially what he or she will be at twenty-five. The Court's description was inaccurate if the Court meant to suggest that what was in the womb was pure potentiality, a zero that could not be protected by law. To judge from the weight the Court gave the being in the womb—found to be protectable in any degree only in the last two months of pregnancy—the Court itself must have viewed the unborn as pure potentiality or a mere theory before viability. The Court's opinion appeared to rest on the assumption that the biological reality could be subordinated or ignored by the sovereign speaking through the Court.

* * *

The progeny of *Roe* have confirmed the Kelsenite reading of *Roe* that there is no reality that the sovereign must recognize unless the sovereign, acting through the agency of the Court, decides to recognize it. This view would be psychologically incomprehensible if we did not have the history of the creation of the institution of slavery by judges and lawyers. With that history we can see that intelligent and humane lawyers have been able to apply a similar approach to a whole class of beings that they could see—that they were able to create a mask of legal concepts preventing humanity from being visible. A mask is a little easier to impose when the humanity concealed, being in the womb, is not even visible to the naked eye.

Kelsenite logic permits the judges at the apex of a system to dispense with correspondence to reality. The highest court is then free, within the limits that the society in which it functions will tolerate, to be inventive. It may, as the Supreme Court of the United States has sometimes thought, be constrained by the language of the Constitution and the purposes of its makers. Or, as has also sometimes happened, the Court, viewing itself as the final expounder of the Constitution's meaning, will exercise its inventiveness in creating new constitutional doctrine not dependent on text or purposes. Such doctrine—fantasy in the service of ideology—is "the branch" of *Roe v. Wade.* What then becomes possible was illustrated in 1983 by *Akron v. Akron Center for Reproductive Health.* In this case a whole set of constitutional requirements were created on behalf of the claims of an abortion clinic, named with Orwellian aptness, a center for "reproductive health."

* * *

Most strikingly of all, *Akron* held that there could not be a legal requirement that a woman seeking an abortion be informed that the being she wished put to death was a child, that the child was alive, and that the child was human. The Court treated this information as prejudicing the choice of whether to abort or not—as a kind of unfair interference with free choice. The ordinance was bad because it was designed "to influence the woman's informed choice between abortion and childbirth." The holding went beyond the Kelsenite jurisprudential root and any mainline theory of constitutional interpretation. It was, indeed, the invention of a kind of censorship by the Court itself.

* * *

A final provision of the Akron ordinance was that "the remains of the unborn child" be "disposed of in a humane and sanitary manner." The Sixth Circuit Court of Appeals found the word "humane" impermissibly vague in a criminal statute.[43] The ordinance could, the court said, mean to "mandate some sort of 'decent burial' of an embryo at the earliest stages of formation * * *."[44] Justice Powell quoted this analysis and agreed; humane and sanitary burial was beyond the comprehension of a reasonable doctor.

In this conclusion one can observe in the most concrete way the Court's discomfort before reality. The Court cannot uphold a requirement of humane burial without conceding that the being who is to be buried is human. A mask has been placed over this being. Even death cannot remove the mask.

The Court's denial of reality stands in contrast with what Andre Gide has written on the humane burial of an unborn child:

> When morning came, "get rid of that," I said naively to the gardener's wife when she finally came to see how everything was. Could I have supposed that those formless fragments, to which I turning away in disgust was pointing, could I have supposed that in the eyes of the Church they already represented the sacred human being they were being readied to clothe? O mystery of incarnation! Imagine then my stupor when some hours later I saw "it" again. The thing which for me already had no name in any language, now cleaned, adorned, beribboned, laid in a little cradle, awaiting the ritual entombment. Fortunately no one had been aware of the sacrilege I had been about to commit; I had already committed it in thought when I had said get rid of "that." Yes, very happily that ill-considered order had been heard by no one. And, I remained a long time musing before "it." Before that little face with the crushed forehead on which they had carefully hidden the wound. Before this innocent flesh which I, if I had been alone,

---

[43] Akron Center for Reproductive Health v. City of Akron, 651 F.2d 1198, 1211 (1981).

[44] Id.

yielding to my first impulse, would have consigned to the manure heap along with the afterbirth and which religious attentions had just saved from the void. I told no one then of what I felt. Of what I tell here. Was I to think that for a few moments a soul had inhabited this body? It has its tomb in Couvreville in that cemetery to which I wish not to return. Half a century has passed. I cannot truthfully say that I recall in detail that little face. No. What I remember exactly is my surprise, my sudden emotion, when confronted by its extraordinary beauty.[46]

If the Court could respond to Gide and understand what humane and sanitary burial is, it might also perceive the reality of the extraordinary beauty of each human being put to death in the name of the abortion liberty and concealed from legal recognition by a jurisprudence that substitutes a judge's fiat for the truth.

JUDITH JARVIS THOMSON, A DEFENSE OF ABORTION

1 PHIL. & PUB.AFF. 47, 48–62, 65–66 (1971).

I propose * * * that we grant that the fetus is a person from the moment of conception. How does the argument go from here? Something like this, I take it. Every person has a right to life. So the fetus has a right to life. No doubt the mother has a right to decide what shall happen in and to her body; everyone would grant that. But surely a person's right to life is stronger and more stringent than the mother's right to decide what happens in and to her body, and so outweighs it. So the fetus may not be killed; an abortion may not be performed.

It sounds plausible. But now let me ask you to imagine this. You wake up in the morning and find yourself back to back in bed with an unconscious violinist. A famous unconscious violinist. He has been found to have a fatal kidney ailment, and the Society of Music Lovers has canvassed all the available medical records and found that you alone have the right blood type to help. They have therefore kidnapped you, and last night the violinist's circulatory system was plugged into yours, so that your kidneys can be used to extract poisons from his blood as well as your own. The director of the hospital now tells you, "Look, we're sorry the Society of Music Lovers did this to you—we would never have permitted it if we had known. But still, they did it, and the violinist now is plugged into you. To unplug you would be to kill him. But never mind, it's only for nine months. By then he will have recovered from his ailment, and can safely be unplugged from you." Is it morally incumbent on you to accede to this situation? * * *

In this case, of course, you were kidnapped; you didn't volunteer for the operation that plugged the violinist into your kidneys. Can those who

---

[46] A. Gide, Last Journals 95 (R. Stookey trans. 1979).

oppose abortion on the ground I mentioned make an exception for a pregnancy due to rape? Certainly. They can say that persons have a right to life only if they didn't come into existence because of rape; or they can say that all persons have a right to life, but that some have less of a right to life than others, in particular, that those who came into existence because of rape have less. But these statements have a rather unpleasant sound. Surely the question of whether you have a right to life at all, or how much of it you have, shouldn't turn on the question of whether or not you are the product of a rape. And in fact the people who oppose abortion on the ground I mentioned do not make this distinction, and hence do not make an exception in case of rape.

Some won't even make an exception for a case in which continuation of the pregnancy is likely to shorten the mother's life; they regard abortion as impermissible even to save the mother's life. Such cases are nowadays very rare, and many opponents of abortion do not accept this extreme view. All the same, it is a good place to begin: a number of points of interest come out in respect to it.

1. Let us call the view that abortion is impermissible even to save the mother's life "the extreme view." I want to suggest first that it does not issue from the argument I mentioned earlier without the addition of some fairly powerful premises. Suppose a woman has become pregnant, and now learns that she has a cardiac condition such that she will die if she carries the baby to term. What may be done for her? The fetus, being a person, has a right to life, but as the mother is a person too, so has she a right to life. Presumably they have an equal right to life. How is it supposed to come out that an abortion may not be performed? If mother and child have an equal right to life, shouldn't we perhaps flip a coin? Or should we add to the mother's right to life her right to decide what happens in and to her body, which everybody seems to be ready to grant—the sum of her rights now outweighing the fetus' right to life?

The most familiar argument here is the following. We are told that performing the abortion would be directly killing the child, whereas doing nothing would not be killing the mother, but only letting her die. Moreover, in killing the child, one would be killing an innocent person, for the child has committed no crime, and is not aiming at his mother's death. And then there are a variety of ways in which this might be continued. (1) But as directly killing an innocent person is always and absolutely impermissible, an abortion may not be performed. Or, (2) as directly killing an innocent person is murder, and murder is always and absolutely impermissible, an abortion may not be performed. Or, (3) as one's duty to refrain from directly killing an innocent person is more stringent than one's duty to keep a person from dying, an abortion may not be performed. Or, (4) if one's only options are directly killing an innocent person or letting a person die, one must prefer letting the person die, and thus an abortion may not be performed.

Some people seem to have thought that these are not further premises which must be added if the conclusion is to be reached, but that they follow from the very fact that an innocent person has a right to life. But this seems to me to be a mistake, and perhaps the simplest way to show this is to bring out that while we must certainly grant that innocent persons have a right to life, the theses in (1) through (4) are all false. Take (2), for example. If directly killing an innocent person is murder, and thus is impermissible, then the mother's directly killing the innocent person inside her is murder, and thus is impermissible. But it cannot seriously be thought to be murder if the mother performs an abortion on herself to save her life. It cannot seriously be said that she *must* refrain, that she *must* sit passively by and wait for her death. Let us look again at the case of you and the violinist. There you are, in bed with the violinist, and the director of the hospital says to you, "It's all most distressing, and I deeply sympathize, but you see this is putting an additional strain on your kidneys, and you'll be dead within the month. But you *have* to stay where you are all the same. Because unplugging you would be directly killing an innocent violinist, and that's murder, and that's impermissible." If anything in the world is true, it is that you do not commit murder, you do not do what is impermissible, if you reach around to your back and unplug yourself from that violinist to save your life.

* * *

In sum, a woman surely can defend her life against the threat to it posed by the unborn child, even if doing so involves its death. And this shows not merely that the theses in (1) through (4) are false; it shows also that the extreme view of abortion is false, and so we need not canvass any other possible ways of arriving at it from the argument I mentioned at the outset.

* * *

3. Where the mother's life is not at stake, the argument I mentioned at the outset seems to have a much stronger pull. "Everyone has a right to life, so the unborn person has a right to life." And isn't the child's right to life weightier than anything other than the mother's own right to life, which she might put forward as ground for an abortion?

This argument treats the right to life as if it were unproblematic. It is not, and this seems to me to be precisely the source of the mistake.

For we should now, at long last, ask what it comes to, to have a right to life. In some views having a right to life includes having a right to be given at least the bare minimum one needs for continued life. But suppose that what in fact *is* the bare minimum a man needs for continued life is something he has no right at all to be given? If I am sick unto death, and the only thing that will save my life is the touch of Henry Fonda's cool hand on my fevered brow, then all the same, I have no right to be given the touch of Henry Fonda's cool hand on my fevered brow. It would be frightfully nice of him to fly in from the West Coast to provide it. It would be less nice, though no doubt well meant, if my friends flew out to the West Coast and carried Henry Fonda back with them. But I have no right at all against anybody that he should do this for me. * * *

Some people are rather stricter about the right to life. In their view, it does not include the right to be given anything, but amounts to, and only to, the right not to be killed by anybody. But here a related difficulty arises. If everybody is to refrain from killing that violinist, then everybody must refrain from doing a great many different sorts of things. Everybody must refrain from slitting his throat, everybody must refrain from shooting him—and everybody must refrain from unplugging you from him. But does he have a right against everybody that they shall refrain from unplugging you from him? To refrain from doing this is to allow him to continue to use your kidneys. It could be argued that he has a right against us that *we* should allow him to continue to use your kidneys. That is, while he had no right against us that we should give him the use of your kidneys, it might be argued that he anyway has a right against us that we shall not now intervene and deprive him of the use of your kidneys. I shall come back to third-party interventions later. But certainly the violinist has no right against you that *you* shall allow him to continue to use your kidneys. As I said, if you do allow him to use them, it is a kindness on your part, and not something you owe him.

* * *

4. There is another way to bring out the difficulty. In the most ordinary sort of case, to deprive someone of what he has a right to is to treat him unjustly. Suppose a boy and his small brother are jointly given a box of chocolates for Christmas. If the older boy takes the box and refuses to give his brother any of the chocolates, he is unjust to him, for the brother has been given a right to half of them. But suppose that, having learned that otherwise it means nine years in bed with that violinist, you unplug yourself from him. You surely are not being unjust to him, for you gave him no right to use your kidneys, and no one else can have given him any such right. But we have to notice that in unplugging yourself, you are killing him; and violinists, like everybody else, have a right to life, and thus in the view we were considering just now, the right not to be killed. So here you do what he supposedly has a right you shall not do, but you do not act unjustly to him in doing it.

The emendation which may be made at this point is this: the right to life consists not in the right not to be killed, but rather in the right not to be killed unjustly. This runs a risk of circularity, but never mind: it would enable us to square the fact that the violinist has a right to life with the fact that you do not act unjustly toward him in unplugging yourself, thereby killing him. For if you do not kill him unjustly, you do not violate his right to life, and so it is no wonder you do him no injustice.

But if this emendation is accepted, the gap in the argument against abortion stares us plainly in the face: it is by no means enough to show that the fetus is a person, and to remind us that all persons have a right to life—we need to be shown also that killing the fetus violates its right to life, i.e., that abortion is unjust killing. And is it?

I suppose we may take it as a datum that in a case of pregnancy due to rape the mother has not given the unborn person a right to the use of her body for food and shelter. Indeed, in what pregnancy could it be supposed that the mother has given the unborn person such a right? It is not as if there were unborn persons drifting about the world, to whom a woman who wants a child says "I invite you in."

But it might be argued that there are other ways one can have acquired a right to the use of another person's body than by having been invited to use it by that person. Suppose a woman voluntarily indulges in intercourse, knowing of the chance it will issue in pregnancy, and then she does become pregnant; is she not in part responsible for the presence, in fact the very existence, of the unborn person inside her? No doubt she did not invite it in. But doesn't her partial responsibility for its being there itself give it a right to the use of her body? If so, then her aborting it would be more like the boy's taking away the chocolates, and less like your unplugging yourself from the violinist—doing so would be depriving it of what it does have a right to, and thus would be doing it an injustice.

And then, too, it might be asked whether or not she can kill it even to save her own life: If she voluntarily called it into existence, how can she now kill it, even in self-defense?

The first thing to be said about this is that it is something new. Opponents of abortion have been so concerned to make out the independence of the fetus, in order to establish that it has a right to life, just as its mother does, that they have tended to overlook the possible support they might gain from making out that the fetus is *dependent* on the mother, in order to establish that she has a special kind of responsibility for it, a responsibility that gives it rights against her which are not possessed by any independent person—such as an ailing violinist who is a stranger to her.

On the other hand, this argument would give the unborn person a right to its mother's body only if her pregnancy resulted from a voluntary act, undertaken in full knowledge of the chance a pregnancy might result from it. It would leave out entirely the unborn person whose existence is due to rape. Pending the availability of some further argument, then, we would be left with the conclusion that unborn persons whose existence is due to rape have no right to the use of their mothers' bodies, and thus that aborting them is not depriving them of anything they have a right to and hence is not unjust killing.

And we should also notice that it is not at all plain that this argument really does go even as far as it purports to. For there are cases and cases, and the details make a difference. If the room is stuffy, and I therefore open a window to air it, and a burglar climbs in, it would be absurd to say, "Ah, now he can stay, she's given him a right to the use of her house—for she is partially responsible for his presence there, having voluntarily done what enabled him to get in, in full knowledge that there are such things as burglars, and that burglars burgle." It would be still more absurd to say this if I had had bars installed outside my windows, precisely to prevent burglars from getting in, and a burglar got in only because of a defect in the bars. It remains equally absurd if we imagine it is not a burglar who climbs in, but an innocent person who blunders or falls in. * * *

It seems to me that the argument we are looking at can establish at most that there are *some* cases in which the unborn person has a right to the use of its mother's body, and therefore *some* cases in which abortion is unjust killing. There is room for much discussion and argument as to precisely which, if any. But I think we should sidestep this issue and leave it open, for at any rate the argument certainly does not establish that all abortion is unjust killing.

5. There is room for yet another argument here, however. We surely must all grant that there may be cases in which it would be morally indecent to detach a person from your body at the cost of his life. Suppose you learn that what the violinist needs is not nine years of your life, but only one hour: all you need do to save his life is to spend one hour in that bed with him. Suppose also that letting him use your kidneys for that one hour would not affect your health in the slightest. Admittedly you were kidnapped. Admittedly you did not give anyone permission to plug him into you. Nevertheless it seems to me plain you *ought* to allow him to use your kidneys for that hour—it would be indecent to refuse.

* * *

Now some people are inclined to use the term "right" in such a way that it follows from the fact that you ought to allow a person to use your body for the hour he needs, that he has a right to use your body for the hour he needs, even though he has not been given that right by any person or act. They may say that it follows also that if you refuse, you act unjustly toward him. This use of the term is perhaps so common that it cannot be called wrong; nevertheless it seems to me to be an unfortunate loosening of what we would do better to keep a tight rein on. Suppose that box of chocolates I mentioned earlier had not been given to both boys jointly, but was given only to the older boy. There he sits, stolidly eating his way through the box, his small brother watching enviously. Here we are likely to say "You ought not to be so mean. You ought to give your brother some of those chocolates." My own view is that it just does not follow from the truth of this that the brother has any right to any of the chocolates. If the boy refuses to give his brother any, he is greedy, stingy, callous—but not unjust. I suppose that the people I have in mind will say it does follow that the brother has a right to some of the chocolates, and thus that the boy does act unjustly if he refuses to give his brother any. But the effect of saying this is to obscure what we should keep distinct, namely the difference between the boy's refusal in this case and the boy's refusal in the earlier case, in which the box was given to both boys jointly, and in which the small brother thus had what was from any point of view clear title to half.

* * *

So my own view is that even though you ought to let the violinist use your kidneys for the one hour he needs, we should not conclude that he has a right to do so—we should say that if you refuse, you are, like the boy who owns all the chocolates and will give none away, self-centered and callous, indecent in fact, but not unjust. And similarly, that even supposing a case in which a woman pregnant due to rape ought to allow the unborn person to use her body for the hour he needs, we should not conclude that he has a right to do so; we should conclude that she is self-centered, callous, indecent, but not unjust, if she refuses. The complaints are no less grave; they are just different. However, there is no need to insist on this point. If anyone does wish to deduce "he has a right" from "you ought," then all the same he must surely grant that there are cases in which it is not morally required of you that you allow that violinist to use your kidneys, and in which he does not have a right to use them, and in which you do not do him an injustice if you refuse. And so also for mother and unborn child. Except in such cases as the unborn person has a right to demand it—and we were leaving open the possibility that there may be such cases—nobody is morally *required* to make large sacrifices, of health, of all other interests and concerns, of all other duties and commitments, for nine years, or even for nine months, in order to keep another person alive.

* * *

8. My argument will be found unsatisfactory on two counts by many of those who want to regard abortion as morally permissible. First, while I do argue that abortion is not impermissible, I do not argue that it is always

permissible. There may well be cases in which carrying the child to term requires only Minimally Decent Samaritanism of the mother, and this is a standard we must not fall below. I am inclined to think it a merit of my account precisely that it does *not* give a general yes or a general no. It allows for and supports our sense that, for example, a sick and desperately frightened fourteen-year-old schoolgirl, pregnant due to rape, may *of course* choose abortion, and that any law which rules this out is an insane law. And it also allows for and supports our sense that in other cases resort to abortion is even positively indecent. It would be indecent in the woman to request an abortion, and indecent in a doctor to perform it, if she is in her seventh month, and wants the abortion just to avoid the nuisance of postponing a trip abroad. The very fact that the arguments I have been drawing attention to treat all cases of abortion, or even all cases of abortion in which the mother's life is not at stake, as morally on a par ought to have made them suspect at the outset.

Secondly, while I am arguing for the permissibility of abortion in some cases, I am not arguing for the right to secure the death of the unborn child. It is easy to confuse these two things in that up to a certain point in the life of the fetus it is not able to survive outside the mother's body; hence removing it from her body guarantees its death. But they are importantly different. I have argued that you are not morally required to spend nine months in bed, sustaining the life of that violinist; but to say this is by no means to say that if, when you unplug yourself, there is a miracle and he survives, you then have a right to turn round and slit his throat. You may detach yourself even if this costs him his life; you have no right to be guaranteed his death, by some other means, if unplugging yourself does not kill him. There are some people who will feel dissatisfied by this feature of my argument. A woman may be utterly devastated by the thought of a child, a bit of herself, put out for adoption and never seen or heard of again. She may therefore want not merely that the child be detached from her, but more, that it die. Some opponents of abortion are inclined to regard this as beneath contempt—thereby showing insensitivity to what is surely a powerful source of despair. All the same, I agree that the desire for the child's death is not one which anybody may gratify, should it turn out to be possible to detach the child alive.

DAVID A. STRAUSS, ABORTION, TOLERATION, AND MORAL UNCERTAINTY

1992 SUP.CT.REV. 1, 10–16, 18–20 (1993).

THE GOOD SAMARITAN ARGUMENT

[O]ne well-known defense of the pro-choice position (actually, more strongly, a defense of abortion) claims to make it unnecessary to deal with the status of fetal life. The argument is that prohibiting abortion is equivalent to requiring a woman to assume duties of a Good Samaritan of an especially extraordinary form to the fetus.[23] This argument compares the responsibilities assigned to a woman by those who oppose abortion to the responsibilities of a conventional Good Samaritan. We do not require that a conventional Good Samaritan accept burdens comparable to those involved in a pregnancy even when an undoubted human life is at stake. It follows that we should not prohibit abortions even if we assume arguendo that fetal life is equivalent to human life.

[I]n my view the Good Samaritan argument does not succeed. The problem is that this argument depends on two libertarian premises: first, that obligations must be in some way commensurate with voluntary undertakings; and second, that there is a sharp distinction between bodily invasions and other impositions on individuals. These libertarian premises are not obviously true, are difficult to justify, and conflict with strongly held intuitions.

The first premise is needed to meet an obvious and superficial objection to the Good Samaritan argument—that, cases of rape and incest aside, no one becomes pregnant involuntarily. The burdens of pregnancy (it is therefore said), unlike the impositions on a Good Samaritan, are to some extent voluntarily assumed. This argument is insensitive to the many subtle forms of pressure and coercion that call into question the voluntariness of many pregnancies. But the principal answer to this argument offered by the proponents of the Good Samaritan view is that it is, in general, unrealistic and unfair to regard most pregnant women as voluntarily accepting the burdens of pregnancy in any meaningful sense.

That answer seems correct, as far as it goes. But it assumes away the possibility that there are obligations and duties that arise without any voluntary act. They arise by virtue of status or just because one happened to find oneself in a certain position. Obligations to a political community are probably an example; efforts to ground such obligations on voluntary undertakings are difficult to sustain. Obligations *to* a parent or to a sibling are also in this category; they arise, at least in part, by virtue of status, not voluntary acts. One might, therefore, without taking any act of a kind that would ordinarily lead to such strong obligations, find oneself in the position of a parent who has obligations to her own unborn child that she would not have to a stranger.

It might be responded that, while not all obligations have their origin in voluntary acts, the anti-abortion position imposes unique obligations on the mother, obligations of a kind that are never the result of status alone. This

---

[23]First advanced in Judith Jarvis Thomson, *A Defense of Abortion,* 1 Phil. & Pub.Aff. 47 (1971)[.]

response relies on the second libertarian premise, about the distinctiveness of bodily invasions. No one questions that parents have many burdensome obligations to their children, such as the obligation to provide for their economic and emotional support. Weighed just on some sort of quantitative scale (such as how much one would pay to avoid the obligation, other things equal), it is arguable that these burdens are greater than those incurred by a pregnant mother. If pregnancy is an unacceptable obligation to impose on a person, that must be because it involves a physical imposition that is qualitatively different from other parental obligations.

Obviously there is much to the point that physical invasions are peculiarly objectionable. [O]rdinarily we do not insist that people subject themselves to bodily impositions comparable to pregnancy, even when another life is at stake. The law does not require an individual to give up one kidney, for example, to save a stranger's life.

But people have stronger obligations to their children than to strangers, and it may be that parents have a moral obligation to sacrifice their physical integrity, to some degree, for the sake of their children. Parents may not refuse to give up their wealth or their labor, over an extended period, for the sake of their children. Why should a bodily intrusion, such as giving up a kidney, be regarded as necessarily more of an imposition than other parental sacrifices that are unquestionably obligatory? The implicit libertarian premise that bodily intrusion is a peculiarly unacceptable form of burden seems arbitrary.

* * *

In short, a person might have the moral duties of parenthood even though he or she has not taken any voluntary act of a sort that usually has such momentous consequences. Unless the interest in bodily integrity is given enormous significance, beyond what can be easily justified, those duties might include sacrificing one's bodily integrity to save a child's life. * * *

ABORTION AND THE REGIME OF TOLERATION

* * *

If the position that laws forbidding abortion are unconstitutional cannot easily be sustained on the assumption that fetal life is morally equivalent to human life, then that position must be reconciled with the uncertain status of fetal life. The Court in [*Planned Parenthood v. Casey*[a]] seemed to recognize this, and it seemed also to perceive that religious toleration was a useful analogy, although it did not analyze the analogy closely.

---

[a] 112 S.Ct. 2791 (1992).

[There are two] ways in which religious toleration is analogous to the pro-choice position. First, questions about religious belief are characterized by uncertainty. There is no agreed-upon way of deciding the issues with which religious belief is concerned: issues, for example, about the nature of the soul and the afterlife, about the proper spiritual development of human beings and their relationship to some transcendent power. Second, religious issues, although they are issues of the greatest importance, are resolved on the level of the individual, not the level of the state. Religious toleration is therefore a counterexample to the argument made by the dissent in *Casey* that the political process is the proper way to resolve unsettled, but important, issues.

At one time, of course, it was widely accepted that religious issues were to be decided by the state, not by individuals. Indeed, at one time it would have seemed bizarre to say that individuals' spiritual development and the fate of their souls were not among the central concerns of the state. But the development of religious toleration, one of the great advances in Western culture, consisted precisely in deciding that matters of religious belief are to be resolved not at the level of the state, but at the level of each individual.

It might be objected that decisions about religion are different from decisions about abortion because decisions about one's own religious faith do not affect other people. Religiously inspired actions, as distinguished from beliefs, can affect other individuals, and (the argument would go) that is why actions can be regulated. A guarantee of absolute liberty applies only to beliefs, because an individual's belief affects no one else. Since an individual's decision whether to have an abortion affects a being that may have a moral status comparable to that of a human, the analogy to religious toleration does not sustain the pro-choice position.

But this view of religious belief as a private matter is decidedly modern, and slightly skeptical. When the regime of religious toleration arose, the more common view was that one person's religious belief affected others in the most profound ways possible. Aquinas argued for persecution on the ground that "forgers and other malefactors are put to death" and "it is a far graver matter to corrupt the faith which is the life of the soul than to falsify money which sustains temporal life." More fundamentally, the idea that there are matters which are only one person's business is itself a modern artifact. A common justification for persecution was that the duty of love for one's neighbors required that they be saved from false belief and, therefore, from eternal damnation. It was a duty of love to destroy a heretic's body in order to save his or her soul.

These views are not prevalent today, but some people hold them, and—more important—we do not have to establish their falsehood in order to believe that religious liberty is morally imperative. That is, some people believe that we will all be eternally damned if we do not persecute heretics;

and we have no basis for concluding that that belief is false. But we still believe that people have a right to decide for themselves, free from persecution, whether to hold heretical beliefs. This demonstrates that some unsettled issues are to be resolved on the level of the individual, not the level of the state, even if the resolution might affect others besides the individual in the most profound ways possible.

* * *

The question remains: why should the abortion issue be decided on the level of the individual instead of on the level of the state? This is the point at which the status of women, properly emphasized by *Casey,* becomes important. Allowing the abortion decision to be made at the political level, instead of the individual level, would create an impermissible risk of subordinating women.

* * *

First, the political process has a persistent tendency generally to undervalue the interests of women. Although the Court has not given this as a reason for its hostility to gender discrimination, this is the *Carolene Products* explanation—perhaps the most conventional explanation—for requiring a special justification for laws that single out a group. In any event, the persistence of laws and practices that discriminate against women is evidence that their interests are undervalued.

Second, women's bodily integrity, in particular, is systematically undervalued. The Court's opinion in *Casey* alluded to this aspect of women's status. The prevalence of harassment and violence against women, and the widespread social attitudes that implicitly or explicitly condone those practices—for example, the relative respectability of domestic violence and the sexualization of violence against women—are evidence of this.

Third, women are treated as people whose principal responsibility is child bearing and child rearing. They are not seen as full participants in the labor market. The pattern of laws, economic arrangements, and social customs that discourages women from entering the labor market and encourages them to be mothers is evidence that this treatment exists. It is not obvious a priori that this treatment constitutes subordination. But throughout our history—for example, in the opposition to slavery, the exaltation of freedom of contract at the turn of the century, and the centrality of employment discrimination to civil rights issues today—the right to alienate one's labor has been highly valued, and that is evidence that a person is not regarded as fully human in our society unless he or she is allowed to participate in the labor market.

* * *

The Court in *Casey* did not, however, make clear the exact connection between the status of women and the abortion issue. The connection, I believe, is this: the tendency to subordinate women in these three ways disqualifies the political process from resolving the moral uncertainty that is central to the abortion debate. There is too great a danger that if the political process decides the abortion issue, that decision will be an act of subordinating women in one or more of these ways.

JOHN HART ELY, THE WAGES OF CRYING WOLF: A COMMENT ON *ROE v. WADE*

82 YALE L.J. 920, 923–926, 933–939 (1973).

II

Let us not underestimate what is at stake: Having an unwanted child can go a long way toward ruining a woman's life. And at bottom *Roe* signals the Court's judgment that this result cannot be justified by any good that anti-abortion legislation accomplishes. This surely is an understandable conclusion—indeed it is one with which I agree—but ordinarily the Court claims no mandate to second-guess legislative balances, at least not when the Constitution has designated neither of the values in conflict as entitled to special protection. But even assuming it would be a good idea for the Court to assume this function, *Roe* seems a curious place to have begun. Laws prohibiting the use of "soft" drugs or, even more obviously, homosexual acts between consenting adults can stunt "the preferred life styles" of those against whom enforcement is threatened in very serious ways. It is clear such acts harm no one besides the participants, and indeed the case that the participants are harmed is a rather shaky one. Yet such laws survive, on the theory that there exists a societal consensus that the behavior involved is revolting or at any rate immoral. Of course the consensus is not universal but it is sufficient, and this is what is counted crucial, to get the laws passed and keep them on the books. Whether anti-abortion legislation cramps the life style of an unwilling mother more significantly than anti-homosexuality legislation cramps the life style of a homosexual is a close question. But even granting that it does, the *other* side of the balance looks very different. For there is more than simple societal revulsion to support legislation restricting abortion: Abortion ends (or if it makes a difference, prevents) the life of a human being other than the one making the choice.

The Court's response here is simply not adequate. It agrees, indeed it holds, that after the point of viability (a concept it fails to note will become even less clear than it is now as the technology of birth continues to develop) the interest in protecting the fetus is compelling. Exactly why that is the magic moment is not made clear: Viability, as the Court defines it, is achieved some six to twelve weeks after quickening. (Quickening is the point at which the fetus begins discernibly to move independently of the mother and the point that has historically been deemed crucial—to the extent *any* point between conception and birth has been focused on.) But no, it is *viability* that is constitutionally critical: the Court's defense seems to mistake a definition for a syllogism.

> With respect to the State's important and legitimate interest in potential life, the "compelling" point is at viability. This is so because the fetus then presumably has the capacity of meaningful life outside the mother's womb.

With regard to why the state cannot consider this "important and legitimate interest" prior to viability, the opinion is even less satisfactory. The discussion begins sensibly enough: The interest asserted is not necessarily tied to the question whether the fetus is "alive," for whether or not one calls it a living being, it is an entity with the potential for (and indeed the likelihood of) life. But all of arguable relevance that follows are arguments that fetuses (a) are not recognized as "persons in the whole sense" by legal doctrine generally and (b) are not "persons" protected by the Fourteenth Amendment.

To the extent they are not entirely inconclusive, the bodies of doctrine to which the Court adverts respecting the protection of fetuses under general legal doctrine tend to undercut rather than support its conclusion. And the argument that fetuses (unlike, say, corporations) are not "persons" under the Fourteenth Amendment fares little better. The Court notes that most constitutional clauses using the word "persons"—such as the one outlining the qualifications for the Presidency—appear to have been drafted with postnatal beings in mind. (It might have added that most of them were plainly drafted with *adults* in mind, but I suppose that wouldn't have helped.) In addition, "the appellee conceded on reargument that no case can be cited that holds that a fetus is a person within the meaning of the Fourteenth Amendment." (The other legal contexts in which the question could have arisen are not enumerated.)

The canons of construction employed here are perhaps most intriguing when they are contrasted with those invoked to derive the constitutional right to an abortion. But in any event, the argument that fetuses lack constitutional rights is simply irrelevant. For it has never been held or even asserted that the state interest needed to justify forcing a person to refrain from an activity, *whether or not that activity is constitutionally protected,* must implicate either the life or the constitutional rights of another person. Dogs are not "persons in the whole sense" nor have they constitutional rights, but that does not mean the state cannot prohibit killing them: It does not even mean the state cannot prohibit killing them in the exercise of the First Amendment right of political protest. Come to think of it, draft cards aren't persons either.

Thus even assuming the Court ought generally to get into the business of second-guessing legislative balances, it has picked a strange case with which to begin. Its purported evaluation of the balance that produced anti-abortion legislation simply does not meet the issue: That the life plans of the mother must, not simply may, prevail over the state's desire to protect the fetus simply does not follow from the judgment that the fetus is not a person. Beyond all that, however, the Court has no business getting into that business.

III

* * *

* * * In his famous *Carolene Products* footnote, Justice Stone suggested that the interests to which the Court can responsibly give extraordinary constitutional protection include not only those expressed in the Constitution but also those that are unlikely to receive adequate consideration in the political process, specifically the interests of "discrete and insular minorities" unable to form effective political alliances.[84] There can be little doubt that such considerations have influenced the direction, if only occasionally the rhetoric, of the recent Courts. My repeated efforts to convince my students that sex should be treated as a "suspect classification" have convinced me it is no easy matter to state such considerations in a "principled" way. But passing that problem, *Roe* is not an appropriate case for their invocation.

Compared with men, very few women sit in our legislatures, a fact I believe should bear some relevance—even without an Equal Rights Amendment—to the appropriate standard of review for legislation that favors men over women.[85] But *no* fetuses sit in our legislatures. Of course

[84]United States v. Carolene Products Co., 304 U.S. 144, 152 n. 4 (1938).

[85]This is not the place for a full treatment of the subject, but the general idea is this: Classifications by sex, like classifications by race, differ from the usual classification—to which the traditional "reasonable generalization" standard is properly applied—in that they rest on "we-they" generalizations as opposed to a "they-they" generalization. Take a familiar example of the usual approach, Williamson v. Lee Optical Co., 348 U.S. 483 (1955). Of course few legislators are opticians. But few are optometrists either. Thus while a decision to distinguish opticians from optometrists will incorporate a stereotypical comparison of two classes of people, it is a comparison of two "they" stereotypes, *viz.* "They [opticians] are generally inferior to or not so well qualified as *they* [optometrists] are in the following respect(s), which we find sufficient to justify the classification: * * *." However, legislators traditionally have not only not been black (or female); they have been white (and male). A decision to distinguish blacks from whites (or women from men) will therefore have its roots in a comparison between a "we" stereotype and a "they" stereotype, *viz.* "They [blacks or women] are generally inferior to or not so well qualified as *we* [whites or men] are in the following respect(s), which we find sufficient to justify the classification: * * *."

The choice between classifying on the basis of a comparative generalization and attempting to come up with a more discriminating formula always involves balancing the

they have their champions, but so have women. The two interests have clashed repeatedly in the political arena, and had continued to do so up to the date of the opinion, generating quite a wide variety of accommodations. By the Court's lights virtually all of the legislative accommodations had unduly favored fetuses; by its definition of victory, women had lost. Yet in every legislative balance one of the competing interests loses to some extent; indeed usually, as here, they both do. On some occasions the Constitution throws its weight on the side of one of them, indicating the balance must be restruck. And on others—and this is Justice Stone's suggestion—it is at least arguable that, constitutional directive or not, the Court should throw *its* weight on the side of a minority demanding in court more than it was able to achieve politically. But even assuming this suggestion can be given principled content, it was clearly intended and should be reserved for those interests which, *as compared with the interests to which they have been subordinated,* constitute minorities unusually incapable of protecting themselves. Compared with men, women may constitute such a "minority"; compared with the unborn, they do not. I'm not sure I'd know a discrete and insular minority if I saw one, but confronted with a multiple choice question requiring me to designate (a) women or (b) fetuses as one, I'd expect no credit for the former answer.

Of course a woman's freedom to choose an abortion is part of the "liberty" the Fourteenth Amendment says shall not be denied without due process of law, as indeed is anyone's freedom to do what he wants. But "due process" generally guarantees only that the inhibition be procedurally fair and that it have some "rational" connection—though plausible is probably a better word—with a permissible governmental goal. What is unusual about *Roe* is that the liberty involved is accorded a far more stringent protection, so stringent that a desire to preserve the fetus's existence is unable to overcome it—a protection more stringent, I think it fair to say, than that the present Court accords the freedom of the press

increase in fairness which greater individualization will produce against the added costs it will entail. It is no startling psychological insight, however, that most of us are delighted to hear and prone to accept comparative characterizations of groups that suggest that the groups to which *we* belong are in some way superior to others. (I would be inclined to exclude most situations where the "we's" used to be "they's," *cf.* Ferguson v. Skrupa, 372 U.S. 726 (1963), and would therefore agree that the unchangeability of the distinguishing characteristic is indeed relevant, though it is only part of the story.) The danger is therefore greater in we-they situations that we will overestimate the validity of the proposed stereotypical classification by seizing upon the positive myths about our own class and the negative myths about theirs—or indeed the realities respecting some or most members of the two classes—and too readily assuming that virtually the entire membership of the two classes fit the stereotypes and therefore that not many of "them" will be unfairly deprived, nor many of "us" unfairly benefitted, by the proposed classification. In short, I trust your generalizations about the differences between my gang and Wilfred's more than I do your generalizations about the differences between my gang and yours.

explicitly guaranteed by the First Amendment. What is frightening about *Roe* is that this super-protected right is not inferable from the language of the Constitution, the framers' thinking respecting the specific problem in issue, any general value derivable from the provisions they included, or the nation's governmental structure. Nor is it explainable in terms of the unusual political impotence of the group judicially protected vis-à-vis the interest that legislatively prevailed over it. And that, I believe—the predictable early reaction to *Roe* notwithstanding ("more of the same Warren-type activism")—is a charge that can responsibly be leveled at no other decision of the past twenty years. At times the inferences the Court has drawn from the values the Constitution marks for special protection have been controversial, even shaky, but never before has its sense of an obligation to draw one been so obviously lacking.

IV

Not in the last thirty-five years at any rate. For, as the received learning has it, this sort of thing did happen before, repeatedly. From its 1905 decision in *Lochner v. New York* into the 1930's the Court, frequently though not always under the rubric of "liberty of contract," employed the Due Process Clauses of the Fourteenth and Fifth Amendments to invalidate a good deal of legislation. According to the dissenters at the time and virtually all the commentators since, the Court had simply manufactured a constitutional right out of whole cloth and used it to superimpose its own view of wise social policy on those of the legislatures. * * *

It may be objected that *Lochner et al.* protected the "economic rights" of businessmen whereas *Roe* protects a "human right." It should be noted, however, that not all of the *Lochner* series involved economic regulation; that even those that did resist the "big business" stereotype with which the commentators tend to associate them; and that in some of them the employer's "liberty of contract" claim was joined by the employee, who knew that if he had to be employed on the terms set by the law in question, he could not be employed at all. This is a predicament that is economic to be sure, but is not without its "human" dimension. Similarly "human" seems the predicament of the appellees in the 1970 case of *Dandridge v. Williams,* who challenged the Maryland Welfare Department's practice of limiting AFDC grants to $250 regardless of family size or need. * * * It may be, however—at least it is not the sort of claim one can disprove—that the "right to an abortion," or noneconomic rights generally, accord more closely with "this generation's idealization of America" than the "rights" asserted in either *Lochner* or *Dandridge.* But that attitude, of course, is *precisely* the point of the *Lochner* philosophy, which would grant unusual protection to those "rights" that somehow *seem* most pressing, regardless of whether the Constitution suggests any special solicitude for them. The Constitution has little to say about contract, less about abortion, and those who would speculate about which the framers would have been more likely to protect may not be pleased with the answer. The Court continues to disavow the philosophy of *Lochner.* Yet as Justice Stewart's concurrence admits, it is impossible candidly to regard *Roe* as the product of anything else.

RUTH BADER GINSBURG, SOME THOUGHTS ON AUTONOMY AND EQUALITY IN RELATION TO *ROE V. WADE*

63 N.C.L.Rev. 375–386 (1985).

These remarks contrast two related areas of constitutional adjudication: gender-based classification and reproductive autonomy. In both areas, the Burger Court, in contrast to the Warren Court, has been uncommonly active. The two areas are intimately related in this practical sense: the law's response to questions subsumed under these headings bears pervasively on the situation of women in society. * * *

Doctrine in the two areas, however, has evolved in discrete compartments. The High Court has analyzed classification by gender under an equal protection/sex discrimination rubric; it has treated reproductive autonomy under a substantive due process/personal autonomy headline not expressly linked to discrimination against women. The Court's gender classification decisions overturning state and federal legislation, in the main, have not provoked large controversy; the Court's initial 1973 abortion decision, *Roe v. Wade,*[2] on the other hand, became and remains a storm center. *Roe v. Wade* sparked public opposition and academic criticism,[3] in part, I believe, because the Court ventured too far in the change it ordered and presented an incomplete justification for its action. * * *

* * *

[The sex-discrimination decisions of the 1970s] had a spectacular aspect. The race cases that trooped before the Warren Court could be viewed as moving the federal judiciary onto the course set by the Reconstruction Congress a century earlier in the post-Civil War amendments. No similar foundation, set deliberately by actors in the political arena, can account for the Burger Court sex discrimination decisions. Perhaps for that reason, the Court has proceeded cautiously. It has taken no giant step. * * *

The Court's gender-based classification precedent impelled acknowledgement of a middle-tier equal protection standard of review, a level of judicial scrutiny demanding more than minimal rationality but less than a

---

[2] 410 U.S. 113 (1973).

[3] *See, e.g.,* Ely, *The Wages of Crying Wolf: A Comment on* Roe v. Wade, 82 Yale L.J. 920 (1973)[.]

near-perfect fit between legislative ends and means. This movement away from the empty-cupboard interpretation of the equal protection principle in relation to sex equality claims largely trailed and mirrored changing patterns in society—most conspicuously, the emergence of the two-career family. The Court's decisions provoked no outraged opposition in legislative chambers. On the contrary, in a key area in which the Court rejected claims of impermissible sex-based classification, Congress indicated a different view, one more sensitive to discrimination against women.

That area, significantly in view of the Court's approach to reproductive choice, was pregnancy. In 1974 the Court * * * held that a state-operated disability income protection plan could exclude normal pregnancy without offense to the equal protection principle.[28] In a statutory setting as well, under Title VII, the Court later ruled, as it earlier had held in a constitutional context, that women unable to work due to pregnancy or childbirth could be excluded from disability coverage.[29] The classifications in these disability cases, according to the Court, were not gender-based on their face, and were not shown to have any sex-discriminatory effect. All "nonpregnant persons," women along with men, the Court pointed out, were treated alike.

With respect to Title VII, Congress prospectively overruled the Court in 1978. It amended the statute to state explicitly that classification on the basis of sex includes classification on the basis of pregnancy. * * *

Roe v. Wade, in contrast to decisions involving explicit male/female classification, has occasioned searing criticism of the Court, over a decade of demonstrations, a stream of vituperative mail addressed to Justice Blackmun (the author of the opinion), annual proposals for overruling *Roe* by constitutional amendment, and a variety of measures in Congress and state legislatures to contain or curtail the decision. In 1973, when *Roe* issued, abortion law was in a state of change across the nation. There was a distinct trend in the states, noted by the Court, "toward liberalization of abortion statutes." Several states had adopted the American Law Institute's Model Penal Code approach setting out grounds on which abortion could be justified at any stage of pregnancy; most significantly, the Code included as a permissible ground preservation of the woman's physical or mental health. Four states—New York, Washington, Alaska, and Hawaii—permitted physicians to perform first-trimester abortions with virtually no restrictions. This movement in legislative arenas bore some resemblance to the law revision activity that eventually swept through the states establishing no-fault divorce as the national pattern.

---

[28] Geduldig v. Aiello, 417 U.S. 484 (1974).

[29] General Elec. Co. v. Gilbert, 429 U.S. 125 (1976).

The Texas law at issue in *Roe* made it a crime to "procure an abortion" except "by medical advice for the purpose of saving the life of the mother." It was the most extreme prohibition extant. The Court had in close view two pathmarking opinions on reproductive autonomy: first, a 1965 precedent, *Griswold v. Connecticut,*[38] holding inconsistent with personal privacy, somehow sheltered by due process, a state ban on the use of contraceptives even by married couples; second, a 1972 decision, *Eisenstadt v. Baird,*[39] extending *Griswold* to strike down a state prohibition on sales of contraceptives except to married persons by prescription. The Court had already decided *Reed v. Reed,*[40] recognizing the arbitrariness in the 1970s of a once traditional gender-based classification, but it did not further pursue that avenue in *Roe.*

The decision in *Roe* appeared to be a stunning victory for the plaintiffs. The Court declared that a woman, guided by the medical judgment of her physician, had a "fundamental" right to abort a pregnancy, a right the Court anchored to a concept of personal autonomy derived from the due process guarantee. The Court then proceeded to define with precision the state regulation of abortion henceforth permissible. The rulings in *Roe,* and in a companion case decided the same day, *Doe v. Bolton,*[42] were stunning in this sense: they called into question the criminal abortion statutes of every state, even those with the least restrictive provisions.

* * *

[I]n my judgment, *Roe* ventured too far in the change it ordered. The sweep and detail of the opinion stimulated the mobilization of a right-to-life movement and an attendant reaction in Congress and state legislatures. In place of the trend "toward liberalization of abortion statutes" noted in *Roe,* legislatures adopted measures aimed at minimizing the impact of the 1973 rulings, including notification and consent requirements, prescriptions for the protection of fetal life, and bans on public expenditures for poor women's abortions.

Professor Paul Freund explained where he thought the Court went astray in *Roe,* and I agree with his statement. The Court properly invalidated the Texas proscription, he indicated, because "[a] law that absolutely made criminal all kinds and forms of abortion could not stand up; it is not a reasonable accommodation of interests."[53] If *Roe* had left off at that point and not adopted what Professor Freund called a "medical approach," physicians might have been less pleased with the decision, but the

---

[38]381 U.S. 479 (1965)[.]

[39]405 U.S. 438 (1972).

[40]404 U.S. 71 (1971).

[42]410 U.S. 179 (1973).

[53]Freund, *Storms over the Supreme Court,* 69 A.B.A.J. 1474, 1480 (1983)[.]

legislative trend might have continued in the direction in which it was headed in the early 1970s. "[S]ome of the bitter debate on the issue might have been averted," Professor Freund believed; "[t]he animus against the Court might at least have been diverted to the legislative halls." Overall, he thought that the *Roe* distinctions turning on trimesters and viability of the fetus illustrated a troublesome tendency of the modern Supreme Court under Chief Justices Burger and Warren "to specify by a kind of legislative code the one alternative pattern that will satisfy the Constitution."

I commented at the outset that I believe the Court presented an incomplete justification for its action. Academic criticism of *Roe,* charging the Court with reading its own values into the due process clause, might have been less pointed had the Court placed the woman alone, rather than the woman tied to her physician, at the center of its attention. Professor Karst's commentary is indicative of the perspective not developed in the High Court's opinion; he solidly linked abortion prohibitions with discrimination against women.[57] The issue in *Roe,* he wrote, deeply touched and concerned "women's position in society in relation to men."

It is not a sufficient answer to charge it all to women's anatomy—a natural, not man-made, phenomenon. Society, not anatomy, "places a greater stigma on unmarried women who become pregnant than on the men who father their children." Society expects, but nature does not command, that "women take the major responsibility * * * for child care" and that they will stay with their children, bearing nurture and support burdens alone, when fathers deny paternity or otherwise refuse to provide care or financial support for unwanted offspring.

I do not pretend that, if the Court had added a distinct sex discrimination theme to its medically oriented opinion, the storm *Roe* generated would have been less furious. I appreciate the intense divisions of opinion on the moral question and recognize that abortion today cannot fairly be described as nothing more than birth control delayed. The conflict, however, is not simply one between a fetus' interests and a woman's interests, narrowly conceived, nor is the overriding issue state versus private control of a woman's body for a span of nine months. Also in the balance is a woman's autonomous charge of her full life's course—as Professor Karst put it, her ability to stand in relation to man, society, and the state as an independent, self-sustaining, equal citizen.

* * *

I turn, finally, to the plight of the woman who lacks resources to finance privately implementation of her personal choice to terminate her pregnancy. The hostile reaction to *Roe* has trained largely on her.

---

[57] Karst, [*Foreword: Equal Citizenship Under the Fourteenth Amendment,* 91 Harv.L.Rev. 1, 58 (1977).]

Some observers speculated that the seven-two judgment in *Roe* was motivated at least in part by pragmatic considerations—population control concerns, the specter of coat hanger abortions, and concerns about unwanted children born to impoverished women. * * * In a set of 1977 decisions, however, the Court upheld state denial of medical expense reimbursement or hospital facilities for abortions sought by indigent women.[69] Moreover, in a 1980 decision, *Harris v. McRae,*[70] the Court found no constitutional infirmity in the Hyde Amendment, which excluded even medically necessary abortions from Medicaid coverage. After these decisions, the Court was accused of sensitivity only to the Justices' own social milieu—"of creating a middle-class right to abortion."

* * *

Financial need alone, under the Court's jurisprudence, does not identify a class of persons whose complaints of disadvantageous treatment attract close scrutiny. Generally, constitutional claims to government benefits on behalf of the poor have prevailed only when tied to another bark—a right to travel interstate, discrimination because of out-of-wedlock birth, or gender-based discrimination. If the Court had acknowledged a woman's equality aspect, not simply a patient-physician autonomy constitutional dimension to the abortion issue, a majority perhaps might have seen the public assistance cases as instances in which, borrowing a phrase from Justice Stevens, the sovereign had violated its "duty to govern impartially."

* * *

Overall, the Court's *Roe* position is weakened, I believe, by the opinion's concentration on a medically approved autonomy idea, to the exclusion of a constitutionally based sex-equality perspective. I understand the view that for political reasons the reproductive autonomy controversy should be isolated from the general debate on equal rights, responsibilities, and opportunities for women and men. I expect, however, that organized and determined opposing efforts to inform and persuade the public on the abortion issue will continue through the 1980s. In that process there will be opportunities for elaborating in public forums the equal-regard conception of women's claims to reproductive choice uncoerced and unsteered by government.

---

[69]Poelker v. Doe, 432 U.S. 519 (1977)[;] Maher v. Roe, 432 U.S. 464 (1977)[;] Beal v. Doe, 432 U.S. 438 (1977)[.]

[70]448 U.S. 297 (1980).

BIBLIOGRAPHY

Privacy: In General

Beschle, *Defining the Scope of the Constitutional Right to Marry: More than Tradition, Less than Unlimited Autonomy,* 70 Notre Dame L.Rev. 39 (1994).

Hafen, *The Constitutional Status of Marriage, Kinship, and Sexual Privacy—Balancing the Individual and Social Interests,* 81 Mich.L.Rev. 463 (1983).

Johnson, *Constitutional Privacy,* 13 Law & Phil. 161 (1994).

Karst, *Freedom of Intimate Association,* 89 Yale L.J. 624 (1980).

Lupu, *Untangling the Strands of the Fourteenth Amendment,* 77 Mich.L.Rev. 981 (1979).

Mayer, Lochner *Redeemed: Family Privacy After* Troxel *and* Carhart, 48 UCLA L. Rev. 1125 (2001).

Parent, *Privacy, Morality and the Law,* 12 Phil. & Pub.Aff. 269 (1983).

Pennock, J. and Chapman, J., eds., NOMOS XIII: PRIVACY (1971).

Posner, *The Uncertain Protection of Privacy by the Supreme Court,* 1979 Sup.Ct.Rev. 173.

Smolin, The *Jurisprudence of Privacy in a Splintered Supreme Court,* 75 Marquette L.Rev. 975 (1992).

Wellington, *Common Law Rules and Constitutional Double Standards: Some Notes on Adjudication,* 83 Yale L.J. 221 (1973).

Wilkinson & White, *Constitutional Protection for Personal Lifestyles,* 62 Cornell L.Rev. 563 (1977).

Abortion

Brownstein & Dau, *The Constitutional Morality of Abortion,* 33 B.C.L.Rev. 689 (1992).

Clark, *Abortion and the Pied Piper of Compromise*, 68 N.Y.U.L.Rev. 265 (1993).

Cohen, M., T. Nagel, and T. Scanlon, eds., THE RIGHTS AND WRONGS OF ABORTION (1974).

Cruz, "*The Sexual Freedom Cases"? Contraception, Abortion, Abstinence, and the Constitution*, 35 Harv. C.R.-C.L. L. Rev. 299 (2000).

Daly, *Reconsidering Abortion Law: Liberty, Equality, and the New Rhetoric of* Planned Parenthood v. Casey, 45 Am.U.L.Rev. 77 (1996).

Dworkin, R., LIFE'S DOMINION (1993).

Epstein, *Substantive Due Process by Any Other Name: The Abortion Cases,* 1973 Sup.Ct.Rev. 159.

Farber & Nowak, *Beyond the* Roe *Debate: Judicial Experience with the 1980's "Reasonableness" Test,* 76 Va.L.Rev. 519 (1990).

Farrell, *Revisiting* Roe v. Wade: *Substance and Process in the Abortion Debate,* 68 Ind.L.J. 269 (1993).

Farrell-Smith, *Rights-Conflict, Pregnancy, and Abortion,* in BEYOND DOMINATION 265 (C. Gould ed. 1983).

Garfield, J. and Hennessey, P., eds., ABORTION: MORAL AND LEGAL PERSPECTIVES (1984).

Garvey, *The Pope's Submarine,* 31 San Diego L.Rev. 849 (1993).

Glendon, M., ABORTION AND DIVORCE IN WESTERN LAW (1987).

Heymann and Barzelay, *The Forest and the Trees: Roe v. Wade and its Critics,* 53 B.U.L.Rev. 765 (1973).

Kreimer, *The Law of Choice and Choice of Law: Abortion, the Right to Travel, and Extraterritorial Regulation in American Federalism,* 67 N.Y.U.L.Rev. 451 (1992).

Laird, Planned Parenthood v. Casey: *The Role of Stare Decisis*, 57 Mod.L.Rev. 461 (1994).

Law, *Abortion Compromise—Inevitable and Impossible,* 1992 U.Ill.L.Rev. 921 (1993).

Law, *Rethinking Sex and the Constitution,* 132 U.Pa.L.Rev. 955 (1984).

Maltz, *Abortion, Precedent, and the Constitution: A Comment on* Planned Parenthood of Southeastern Pennsylvania v. Casey, 68 Notre Dame L.Rev. 11 (1992).

Mensch and Freeman, *The Politics of Virtue: Animals, Theology and Abortion,* 25 Ga.L.Rev. 923 (1991).

Noonan, J., A PRIVATE CHOICE: ABORTION IN AMERICA IN THE SEVENTIES (1979).

Perry, *Abortion, the Public Morals, and the Police Power: The Ethical Function of Substantive Due Process,* 23 UCLA L.Rev. 689 (1976).

Prygoski, *Abortion and the Right to Die: Judicial Imposition of a Theory of Life,* 23 Seton Hall L.Rev. 67 (1992).

Regan, *Rewriting* Roe v. Wade, 77 Mich.L.Rev. 1569 (1979).

Rubenfeld, *On the Legal Status of the Proposition that "Life Begins at Conception",* 43 Stan.L.Rev. 599 (1991).

Siegel, *Reasoning from the Body: A Historical Perspective on Abortion Regulation and Questions of Equal Protection,* 44 Stan.L.Rev. 261 (1992).

Smolin, *Fourteenth Amendment Unenumerated Rights Jurisprudence: An Essay in Response to* Stenberg v. Carhart, 24 Harv. J.L. & Pub. Pol'y 815 (2001).

Sumner, L., ABORTION AND MORAL THEORY (1981).

Symposium, *Abortion Rights and Public Policy*, 13 St.L.U.Pub.L.Rev. 1 (1993).

Tooley, M., ABORTION AND INFANTICIDE (1983).

Tribe, L., ABORTION, THE CLASH OF ABSOLUTES (1990).

West, *Liberalism and Abortion*, 87 Geo. L.J. 2117 (1999).

Williams, *Gender Wars: Selfless Women in the Republic of Choice,* 66 N.Y.U.L.Rev. 1559 (1991).

C. HOMOSEXUALITY

In *Bowers v. Hardwick*[1] the Supreme Court held that the right to privacy, which earlier cases had found in the Due Process Clause of the Fourteenth Amendment, did not protect homosexual sodomy.

Lawrence v. Texas[2] seventeen years later overruled *Bowers*. The two decisions taken together reflect some remarkable transformations in American constitutional law. *Bowers* held that our history and traditions provide no support for the claim that there is a fundamental right to engage in homosexual conduct. Absent a compelling state interest, it concluded, courts should defer to legislative judgments forbidding such behavior. *Lawrence* assumed that "[p]ersons in a homosexual relationship may seek autonomy for [choices central to personal dignity and autonomy], just as heterosexual persons do." And it held that a contrary state law "furthers no legitimate state interest which can justify its intrusion into the personal and private life of the individual." The Court's about-face poses at least two interesting questions. First, what is the moral foundation for claims about the value of intimate private choices? And second, what are the proper roles of courts and legislatures in arbitrating these claims?

John Garvey examines the standard liberal arguments for a right to privacy and finds them wanting. Some say the right rests on a moral theory (the autonomy theory) that each of us should decide for himself how to act and live. Others say the right is a political device for bracketing questions about which we have irreconcilable differences. But we cannot posit an unqualified right to choose without denying what we all affirm. Many choices (the right to practice optometry) are subject to government control for the flimsiest of reasons. A persuasive argument for freedom must begin

[1] 478 U.S. 186, 106 S.Ct. 2841, 92 L.Ed.2d 140 (1986).

[2] 123 S.Ct. 2472 (2003).

with the assumption that some choices are better or more important than others.

Jed Rubenfeld offers an interesting response to Garvey's challenge. He does not argue that homosexual intimacy is a particularly good or important practice. But he does say that laws against such behavior are especially harmful. This is not because he accepts the "personhood" thesis advanced by Justice Blackmun's dissent (the idea that people should be free to define their own identities by making choices about sexual relations). A person's identity, if there is such a thing, is formed by lots of influences besides his own choices. Rubenfeld instead argues that sodomy laws are unconstitutional because they have a pervasive standardizing effect—forcing homosexuals "into a network of social institutions and relations that will occupy their lives to a substantial degree." In that regard they are like laws forbidding private schools and laws whose consequence is compulsory child-bearing.

Randy Barnett observes that *Lawrence* may signal "nothing short of a constitutional revolution," not for its moral argument about the value of sexual behavior but for its assumption that the government must justify any restriction on personal liberty. Justice Kennedy's opinion abandons the distinction between fundamental rights and other less protected liberty interests which the Court has used since *Griswold v. Connecticut*[3] to fix the level of judicial scrutiny of legislative acts. If Barnett is right, *Lawrence* holds that the government may never criminalize immoral behavior unless it violates the rights of others. Regulating harmless immorality is simply none of the government's business.

The Court's opinion in *Lawrence* lays some stress on the principles observed by European countries under the European Convention on Human Rights.[4] John Finnis argues that the "standard modern European position" actually has two parts. The first (adopted in *Lawrence*) holds that the state has no authority to punish private consensual adult behavior. The second holds that the state does have authority to supervise the public realm or environment—and that in the exercise of that authority it may discourage homosexual conduct. This means, among other things, that homosexual marriage presents a different question than the one resolved in *Lawrence*. Finnis defends this distinction by looking at the general justifying aims of political communities.

Janet Halley asks whether it is right or wise to argue that homosexuality is an immutable status. There are two sides in this debate: essentialists hold that sexual orientation is immutable, constructivists that it is not. And there are pro- and anti-gay forces on each side. Halley points out several

[3] 381 U.S. 479 (1965).

[4] 123 S.Ct. at 2481.

weaknesses in pro-gay essentialism. One is that many forms of discrimination based on immutable characteristics are permissible in our society. (Blind people cannot drive busses.) Another is that homosexuality, whether mutable or not, is expressed through elected behavior, and essentialism does not address the political argument for banning such behavior. Third, essentialists take it for granted that science has already made the genetic case for immutability. This may not be so. And if and when the case is made, we may only have opened the door to genetic responses to the issue of homosexuality.

JOHN H. GARVEY, MEN ONLY

WHAT ARE FREEDOMS FOR? 21–27 (1996).

Michael Hardwick was arrested for violating the Georgia sodomy statute, which forbids any person to engage in oral or anal sex. Hardwick had been charged with drinking in public and missed his court appearance. The arresting officer came to his house with a warrant, was admitted by a house guest, and found Hardwick engaged in oral sex in his bedroom with another man. When the district attorney decided not to prosecute, Hardwick sued for a declaration that the Georgia law was unconstitutional. His complaint was dismissed for failure to state a claim, but was reinstated by the court of appeals. Hardwick was joined as plaintiff by a married couple who claimed that the law deterred them from engaging in similar activity. They were dismissed for lack of standing, and did not pursue their claim beyond the circuit court.

The Supreme Court confined its attention to the law as it applied to Hardwick. In *Bowers v. Hardwick* it held (5–4) that homosexual sodomy was not one of the "fundamental liberties" protected by the due process clause. Such freedoms must be embedded in our traditions, and sodomy—far from being traditionally protected—has been a criminal offense since the bill of rights was adopted in 1791. All fifty states forbade it as recently as 1961; half do so today. Since there was no fundamental right at stake, Georgia could forbid sodomy simply because a majority of the voters found it immoral.

Justice Blackmun, dissenting, said that sodomy should be considered a fundamental freedom. He argued that the ability to "define one's identity" is central to any concept of liberty, and that "individuals define themselves in a significant way through their intimate sexual relationships." We value these relationships precisely because we can "choose [their] form and nature." There is no "right" or "wrong" way to structure them. * * *

Let us consider why someone might be attracted to the idea * * * that freedom protects choices. According to Justice Blackmun sodomy is not an issue of right and wrong. This is not just a peculiar fact about sodomy. No act or form of life is intrinsically right or wrong, good or bad. People used to think otherwise. Aristotle is the standard example. He believed that the good life consists in activity in accordance with moral and intellectual virtue. For him gluttony and other forms of self-indulgence were bad because they were brutish. The glutton lacks the virtue of temperance; he acts more like an animal than a human being. The philosopher, on the other hand, lives the best of lives because he engages in contemplative activity. Some people continue to think this way even today, frequently on the basis of some religious belief. The state of Georgia relied on some such convictions in its defense of the law against sodomy. It pointed out that "traditional Judeo—Christian values proscribe such conduct," noting the condemnations in the old and new testaments and in the theology of Aquinas.

The chief difficulty with these views is that they are controversial. There will always be those, like Hardwick, who see nothing wrong with doing a particular act. If Aristotle (or the people of Georgia) think otherwise they are simply mistaken. And it is no use pointing to scripture or theology to resolve the disagreement. The authority of those sources depends on private revelation rather than on publicly available standards like science and reason. If someone (*X*) has not had the requisite revelation scripture holds no power to convince him.

Hardwick's defenders hold that the only solution for this disagreement is to allow each *X* to decide for himself what is good or bad. But this is not just something we do *faute de mieux*. It is both justifiable and, on some accounts, downright good. Two types of explanations have been offered for it. The first, the autonomy theory, is a moral theory. It holds that no act or form of life is intrinsically good or bad, with this exception—it is good for each *X* to choose how he or she will act and live.

The autonomy theory stresses the idea that each person is an end in himself, a kind of sovereign over a kingdom of one. This is the most basic fact about the moral world. It means that we are all (like sovereign nations) free and equal. The standards of good and bad that apply to me must be ones that I choose, since I alone have legislative jurisdiction over my kingdom. If we get together for political purposes we must treat everyone alike and respect everyone's freedom. It would be wrong to give you two votes and me one (that denies my equality); or to insist that I read only approved books (that denies my freedom). All of us are equal and free to shape our own destinies. And it is good for us to do so. If I am an end in myself, if that is my nature, I've got to make something of myself. I would cast off my humanity by taking orders from someone else. I would be like one of those satellite countries that used to make up the Eastern bloc, with no mind of my own. It is good for me to choose.

This line of argument pervades the discussion of freedom in American law. We lump most of the substantive due process cases together under a general right to autonomy (self-legislation). Influential writers on the first amendment argue that autonomy is the underlying concern behind the protection of free speech. There are even those who contend that the religion clauses are designed to protect our religious autonomy.

The other explanation for protecting personal choices, which is slightly less ambitious, is a political theory rather than an ethical one. It is agnostic about whether some forms of life are better than others. While it might actually be better to live as a rabbi than as a playboy, we cannot form a stable democratic government based on one view or the other. People disagree irreconcilably about the proper answer, and they have strong feelings. To force one opinion upon the minority would be to risk instability. We need to bracket such questions for lawmaking purposes. Freedoms are the device for doing the bracketing: they let people choose the options that appeal to them in matters (like sexual behavior) that count.

Each of these explanations—the autonomy theory and the political theory—provides a persuasive account of why we value freedoms. The first says that we cannot really be human without them. I have no status as a sovereign person if I am constrained by rules that I would not adopt. The second says that we cannot have a society without them. When we conduct politics on a large scale (the nation-state, or even the states of our federal union) it is impossible to legislate morality without alienating a substantial fraction of the population. Political union depends on freedom.

Each theory also explains why constitutional freedoms should protect choices. [F]reedoms are usually understood to have a bilateral character. The same freedoms are used to protect atheism and religion, pornography and Shakespeare, celibacy and sodomy, and so on. How can we value things so contradictory? The autonomy theory offers one answer: perhaps we really value the choice itself, not any particular selection. It is in choosing that we shape our own destiny. This is what Justice Blackmun said about sodomy in *Bowers*. He claimed that we value our intimate sexual relationships because we can "choose [their] form and nature." The political theory offers another: perhaps we value the society that permits the choice. And even though most of us find some choices offensive, it's a package deal. The society can't survive without freedom. Justice Blackmun touched on this point too. He concluded his opinion by saying that suppressing freedom poses a far greater "threat to national cohesion . . . than tolerance of nonconformity could ever do."

The most serious flaw in the idea that freedom is at the service of choice is that it explains too much. It suggests that the law should respect a great variety of choices. But in our system some choices get more protection than others. Consider this simple fact. If Hardwick had been caught engaging in the practice of optometry rather than sodomy, and if Georgia had had a law against it, there is scarcely a judge in America who would have defended his freedom to act as he did. It would make no difference if Hardwick could honestly claim that optometry was central to his conception of self. This suggests that the value of freedom may be tied in some way to the action in question, rather than to the choosing of it. [T]his observation applies to [the actual facts of the case.].

One of the funny aspects of *Bowers v. Hardwick* is its abstract quality. Hardwick's sexual partner was a one-night stand—a schoolteacher from North Carolina who pleaded to reduced charges and left town. The courts showed little interest in him. Hardwick's complaint was equally casual. It merely declared that Hardwick was "a practicing homosexual who regularly engages in private homosexual acts and will do so in the future." The "acts" of sodomy were the focus; the identity of the other actor didn't matter. Hardwick's brief in the Supreme Court said that he "of course claims no right whatever to have any homosexual relationship recognized as a marriage." Justice Blackmun's opinion repeatedly talks about the "private," "intimate," "sensitive" nature of Hardwick's sexual relationship, but with an unacknowledged sense of double entendre. The words suggest a kind of closeness, caring, and sharing typical of people who are in love. But all we can be sure they really mean is that Hardwick and his partner were off by themselves ("private"), engaged in sexual activity ("intimate") that felt good ("sensitive"). What Hardwick's suit asked for was the freedom to reach an orgasm in the particular way that he favored.

I don't mean to assert that that pleasure has no value, but I want to be certain that we recognize it for what it is. It is an event that occurs within the body, rather like the pleasure of eating and drinking, though the sensation is different. A friend of mine says that he thinks of sex like a chocolate milkshake. Lucretius calls this pure sexual pleasure Venus, and distinguishes it from love. He claims, in fact, that the pleasure is greater if we keep the two separate: "Do not think that by avoiding grand passions you are missing the delights of Venus. Rather, you are reaping such profits as carry with them no penalty. Rest assured that this pleasure is enjoyed in a purer form by the healthy than by the love-sick."[19] I don't want to get too involved in a discussion of the accuracy of this observation, but it does make the rather obvious point that we distinguish Venus from erotic love (if I may use that term to designate the more complex attraction that we associate with love). And the most significant difference is that the identity of one's partner matters a lot in one case and not much in the other. C.S. Lewis makes the point nicely in a discussion of heterosexual love, though I would like to assume for the moment that the gender of the beloved is irrelevant.

[19]Lucretius, On the Nature of the Universe 163 (R.E. Latham, trans. 1951).

> [The man pursuing Venus] wants a pleasure for which a woman happens to be the necessary piece of apparatus. How much he cares about the woman as such may be gauged by his attitude to her five minutes after fruition (one does not keep the carton after one has smoked the cigarettes). Now Eros makes a man really want, not a woman, but one particular woman. In some mysterious but quite indisputable fashion the lover desires the Beloved herself, not the pleasure she can give. No lover in the world ever sought the embraces of the woman he loved as the result of a calculation, however unconscious, that they would be more pleasurable than those of any other woman.[20]

The opinions in *Bowers v. Hardwick* spend some time discussing whether Hardwick's action is like adultery or incest, both of which, everyone seems to assume, the state can forbid. But this is a mistake. Adulterous and incestuous relationships, however wrong they are, need not be simple pursuits of orgasmic pleasure. There can also be, mixed with the infidelity and oppression, an element of erotic love. A more apt comparison is prostitution. What the customer seeks is the simple delivery of sexual pleasure for which the prostitute is a necessary piece of apparatus, available for a fee. Or a better analogy still (which controls for the element of exploitation in the case of prostitution) is sodomy with animals. That is what Hardwick's claim is like, if it asks for no more than the right to have an orgasm in the manner he prefers.

I have tried to bring out the difference between Venus and erotic love, and the similarity of Hardwick's claim to the cases of prostitution and bestiality, for the sake of making what I think is a generally accepted point. It is this: we do not put a very high value on the simple act of reaching an orgasm, if that is *all* that one is doing. No one would attack laws against bestiality or prostitution by claiming that they interfere with the fundamental freedom to have an orgasm, and so must be justified by compelling state interests. On the contrary, we view these as debasing activities. Pornography [gets similar treatment. Its defenders] seldom talk about the value of masturbation. Their real concern is that suppression will carry over to legitimate publications.

I do not want to overstate my case. The sexual revolution of the 1960's has had at least this effect: most people do not see Venus, naked and unattached, as evil. Far fewer people today than 30 years ago would condemn masturbation or random couplings (heterosexual or homosexual) as the work of the devil. But at the same time we don't put a high price on them. We do not, for example, raise our children to practice a life of polymorphous sexuality as Marcuse would have had us do.[23] The Supreme

---

[20] C.S. Lewis, The Four Loves, 109–110 (1960).

[23] Herbert Marcuse, Eros and Civilization (1955).

Court has held that unmarried people have a right to buy contraceptives, but it has not suggested that they have any right to use them.[24] Its agenda is more like a program of sterile needles for drug abusers: it wants to prevent people from getting hurt while doing improvident acts.

JED RUBENFELD, THE RIGHT OF PRIVACY

102 HARV.L.REV. 737, 783–787, 792–794, 797–802 (1989).

METHOD

The methodology heretofore universal in privacy analysis has begun with the question, "What is the state trying to forbid?" The proscribed conduct is then delineated and its significance tested through a pre-established conceptual apparatus: for its role in "'the concept of ordered liberty,'" its status as a "fundamental" right, its importance to one's identity, or for any other criterion of fundamentality upon which a court can settle. Suppose instead we began by asking not what is being *prohibited,* but what is being *produced.* Suppose we looked not to the negative aspect of the law—the interdiction by which it formally expresses itself—but at its positive aspect: the real effects that conformity with the law produces at the level of everyday lives and social practices.

* * *

SUBSTANCE

Consider the three principal areas in which the right to privacy has been applied: child-bearing (abortion and contraception), marriage (miscegenation laws, divorce restrictions, and so on), and education of children (*Meyer*[a] and *Pierce*[b]). According to the prevailing method of privacy analysis, certain decisions concerning these matters cannot be proscribed because they are "fundamental." But what is fundamental about these decisions? Are they fundamental in themselves? If, for example, the right to decide whom to marry is inherently fundamental, how is it, for example, that the proscriptions against incestuous and bigamous marriage do not offend it? In fact, a "liberty of fundamental decisions" cannot serve as a constitutional principle any more than could that quite similar quantity—the "liberty of contract"—that animated the *Lochner* jurisprudence. There *is* something fundamental at stake in the privacy decisions, but it is not the proscribed conduct, nor even the freedom of decision—it is not what is being taken away.

---

[24] Carey v. Population Services Int'l, 431 U.S. 678 (1977); Eisenstadt v. Baird, 405 U.S. 438 (1972).

[a] Meyer v. Nebraska, 262 U.S. 390 (1923).

[b] Pierce v. Society of Sisters, 268 U.S. 510 (1925).

The distinctive and singular characteristic of the laws against which the right to privacy has been applied lies in their *productive* or *affirmative* consequences. There are perhaps no legal proscriptions with more profound, more extensive, or more persistent affirmative effects on individual lives than the laws struck down as violations of the right to privacy. Anti-abortion laws, anti-miscegenation laws, and compulsory education laws all involve the forcing of lives into well-defined and highly confined institutional layers. At the simplest, most quotidian level, such laws tend to *take over* the lives of the persons involved: they occupy and preoccupy. They affirmatively and very substantially shape a person's life; they direct a life's development along a particular avenue. These laws do not simply proscribe one act or remove one liberty; they inform the totality of a person's life.

The principle of the right to privacy is not the freedom to do certain, particular acts determined to be fundamental through some ever-progressing normative lens. It is the fundamental freedom not to have one's life too totally determined by a progressively more normalizing state.

Someone might say, I suppose, that anti-abortion or anti-contraception laws do not force women to bear children because women can simply refrain from having sex. Similarly one might say that whites and blacks, confronted by laws forbidding interracial marriage, can simply decline to marry if they do not wish to live with members of their own race.

This is no answer at all. To begin with, it is no answer to the pregnant woman seeking an abortion. More fundamentally, it is no answer because it is merely another attempt to hide behind a factitious focus on the prohibitory aspect of the law. The practical consequence of obeying laws against contraception or interracial marriage is that people become pregnant or marry intraracially. Indeed these laws derive the depth of their affirmative force from the fact that they operate on drives and desires too strong or too subtle for most to resist.

The danger, then, is a particular kind of creeping totalitarianism, an unarmed *occupation* of individuals' lives. That is the danger of which * * * the right to privacy is warning us: a society standardized and normalized, in which lives are too substantially or too rigidly directed. That is the threat posed by state power in our century.

This threat is not unknown to our constitutional jurisprudence. Consider first Justice Jackson's words in *West Virginia State Board of Education v. Barnette,*[187] when, in the midst of the Second World War, the Court struck down a law that required schoolchildren to salute the flag and profess their loyalty to the country:

[187]319 U.S. 624 (1943).

> Struggles to coerce uniformity of sentiment in support of some end thought essential to their time and country have been waged by many good as well as by evil men * * *. As first and moderate attempts to attain unity have failed, those bent on its accomplishment must resort to an ever-increasing severity * * *. Ultimate futility of such attempts to compel coherence is the lesson of every such effort from the Roman drive to stamp out Christianity * * * down to the fast failing efforts of our present totalitarian enemies.

* * *

With this image, however, we have left West Virginia's enforced flag-salute far behind. Or rather we have imagined that flag-salute systematized and ramified into numerous aspects of the child's daily life. We have imagined an existence totally informed or occupied, rather than a single act of enforced loyalty. This distinction is critical: it explains why *Barnette* is not, after all, a right-to-privacy case but rather a first amendment case.

Because of the signal role that speech plays in political freedom and because of the express constitutional guarantee, government in this country can hardly forbid or compel citizens to utter a single opinion without violating their rights. By contrast, in privacy cases, the government must go much further before it transgresses a constitutional limit. Consider now the cases of *Meyer* and *Pierce,* which * * * may be considered the true progenitors of the privacy decisions. Like *Barnette, Meyer* and *Pierce* also involved laws pertaining to the education of children—laws suggestive of a nationalism heightened by war. Yet the statutes struck down in *Meyer* and especially *Pierce* differed significantly from that in *Barnette.*

In *Meyer,* the law at issue prohibited the teaching of "modern" foreign languages to elementary schoolchildren. In *Pierce,* the state had prohibited private elementary schooling altogether, requiring all children between the ages of eight and sixteen to attend public schools. In each of these statutes, the state had gone much further in the effort—using Justice Jackson's phrase—to "coerce uniformity" than had West Virginia in enacting its flag-salute law. It is not that a greater degree of coercion was present; I am not referring to the potential consequences of violating the law. To the contrary, it was the potential consequences of *obeying* the law that mattered. The *Meyer* Court saw the state as attempting to "foster a homogeneous people with American ideals." The Court drew in this connection on images from ancient civilization:

> For the welfare of his Ideal Commonwealth, Plato suggested a law which would provide: "That the wives of our guardians are to be common, and their children are to be common, and no parent is to know his own child, nor any child his parent * * *. The proper officers will take the offspring of the good parents to the pen or fold, and there they will

deposit them with certain nurses who dwell in a separate quarter; but the offspring of the inferior, or of the better when they chance to be deformed, will be put away in some mysterious, unknown place, as they should be." In order to submerge the individual and develop ideal citizens, Sparta assembled the males at seven into barracks and intrusted [sic] their subsequent education and training to official guardians. Although such measures have been deliberately approved by men of great genius, their ideas touching the relation between individual and State were wholly different from those upon which our institutions rest; and it hardly will be affirmed that any legislature could impose such restrictions upon the people of a State without doing violence to both letter and spirit of the Constitution.

* * *

Pierce presented this threat even more starkly because there the state had prohibited all organized elementary education outside the public schools. That the Court was reacting to this threat—and not merely to a deprivation of the "liberty of contract"—cannot be doubted. In language that implicitly derived its force from the same sources on which the Court drew in *Meyer,* the Court struck down the law and held that the "fundamental theory of liberty upon which all governments in this Union repose excludes any general power of the State to *standardize its children.*"

This concept of standardization as applied in *Pierce* is critical for our purposes. It includes both quantitative and qualitative components. The law struck down in *Pierce*—like the Platonic or Spartan regimes described by the *Meyer* Court, but unlike *Barnette* 's flag-salute law—had the effect of affirmatively occupying a substantial portion of the material, day-to-day lives of those individuals subject to it. At the same time, this occupation potentially subjected these individuals to a narrowly directed existence: a regimen, a discipline, a curriculum in which the totality of their personhood or identity could be forcefully compressed into a particular mold.

These two elements—the affirmative occupation of one's time and the directedness of this occupation—are crucial in understanding why the mandatory public schooling law in *Pierce* implicated a constitutional concern, now called the right to privacy, even though no explicit constitutional guarantee could be said to forbid it. Privacy takes its stand at the outer boundaries of the legitimate exercise of state power. It is to be invoked only where the government threatens to take over or occupy our lives—to exert its power in some way over the totality of our lives.

In a few, rare instances this "totalitarian" intervention into a person's life may occur as a result of a single legal prohibition. The burden of elaborating a conception of privacy based on an anti-totalitarian principle is to perceive how a single law may operate positively to take over and direct the totality of our lives.

* * *

DISTINCTIONS

[L]aws against abortion, interracial marriage, * * * and private education all involve a peculiar form of obedience that reaches far beyond mere abstention from the particular proscribed act. It is a form of obedience in which the life of the person forced to obey is thereafter substantially filled up and informed by the living, institutional consequences of obedience. The person finds himself in a new and sharply-defined, but also broadly encompassing institutional role. Because of their affirmative direction of individuals' lives, these roles—whether as mother, spouse, student or family member—have profoundly formative effects on identity and character.

This attribute of the laws discussed above distinguishes them from other proscriptions of unquestionable constitutional validity that might otherwise appear to fall within the ambit of the principles elaborated here. Consider laws against murder. Are such laws not "standardizing" in that they compel all of us to be non-murderers? Do they not operate "on our bodies" in that they work by forbidding us, for example, to pick up a knife and use it in a certain way? And do they not "instrumentalize" us by requiring us to serve the state's interests insofar as we are made thereby to refrain from causing harm to society at large?

* * *

Laws against murder foreclose an avenue; they do not harness us to a given seat and direct us down a single, regulated road. This formulation is not so much a conclusion from logic as from practical, material realities. One may always reformulate propositions to state negatives as positives. Refraining from murder, however, does not fill up one's life in the same way as does bearing a child, attending public school, * * * or marrying only within one's race. Forcing a person to do these latter things goes much further in thrusting him into socially defined, particularized practices and institutions.

This distinction between "negative" and "affirmative" effects of legal rules will no doubt be greeted with skepticism. Yet—to repeat the point—the distinction is not a matter of propositional logic; it is essentially normative. Whether the obligation not to murder is called a negative or affirmative duty makes no difference. The question is the degree to which, and the ways in which, the law informs, shapes, directs, and occupies the actual day-to-day activities of the persons concerned. Power may be understood and experienced as a purely prohibitory force acting upon essentially independent individual lives; it may also, however, appear and act as a force producing those lives from the inside.

The same negative-affirmative distinction directly parallels the essential difference between the anti-totalitarian right to privacy elaborated here and the personhood version of that right [espoused by the dissenters in *Bowers v. Hardwick*]. Formulated propositionally, the two principles seem almost like corollaries. The anti-totalitarian right to privacy, it might be said, prevents the state from imposing on individuals a defined identity, whereas the personhood right to privacy ensures that individuals are free to define their own identities. Is the anti-totalitarian theory of privacy nothing more in reality than a restatement of the personhood idea from another angle?

On the contrary: first, when personhood speaks of the "freedom to define oneself," it speaks for the most part of a chimera. We are all so powerfully influenced by the institutions within which we are raised that it is probably impossible, both psychologically and epistemologically, to speak of defining one's own identity. The point is not to save for the individual an abstract and chimerical right of defining himself; the point is to prevent the state from taking over, or taking undue advantage of, those processes by which individuals are defined in order to produce overly standardized, functional citizens.

Second, because personhood concentrates on the fundamentality of the act or decision at stake in a given case—whether to have a child, whom to marry, and so on—it will produce a different analysis and different results from the anti-totalitarian principle. * * *

* * *

There remains a third and final differentiation to be made between personhood and the right to privacy as understood here. To speak of resisting state-imposed identities—as we have done—does not commit privacy to personhood's central premise: that each individual's defining his identity is an act of such value that it is of constitutional importance. Indeed the right to privacy as developed here may suggest a repudiation of personal identity altogether.

The concept of personal identity—that sense of a unitary, atomic self that we all tend to consider ourselves to "have"—is complex and difficult. It has an almost theological or metaphysical aspect, as if one's "identity" were a kind of hypostatic quantity underlying the multiplicity of his vastly different relations in the world and the mutability of his nature over time. * * * This conception of a unitary personal identity has been radically challenged again and again this century in various fields, including psychoanalysis,[217] literature,[218] and—most recently and surprisingly—analytic philosophy.[219] Personhood, reflecting an essentially liberal philosophy, is obliged to embrace and valorize the idea of a unitary personal identity; the right to privacy is not.

* * *

HOMOSEXUALITY

[Let us consider] *Bowers v. Hardwick* in our new terms. * * * [The] privacy argument against laws forbidding homosexual sex cannot be rested on the claim that they deprive certain persons of something deeply important to them, crucial to their happiness, or even central to their identity. Nor can such laws be attacked on the ground that * * * laws must not impose on individuals any majoritarian values impinging on their autonomy. * * *

Yet laws against homosexual sex have an effect that most laws do not. They forceably channel certain individuals—supposing the law is obeyed—into a network of social institutions and relations that will occupy their lives to a substantial degree.

Most fundamentally, the prohibition against homosexual sex channels individuals' sexual desires into *reproductive* outlets. Although the prohibition does not, like the law against abortions, produce as an imminent consequence compulsory child-bearing, it nonetheless forcibly directs individuals into the pathways of reproductive sexuality, rather than the socially "unproductive" realm of homosexuality. These pathways are further guided, in our society, into particular institutional orbits, chief among which are the nuclear family and the constellation of practices surrounding a heterosexuality that is defined in conscious contradistinction to homosexuality. Indeed it is difficult to separate our society's inculcation of a heterosexual identity from the simultaneous inculcation of a dichotomized complementarity of roles to be borne by men and women. Homosexual couples by necessity throw into question the allocation of specific functions—whether professional, personal, or emotional—between the sexes. It is this aspect of the ban on homosexuality—its central role in the

[217]One of Freud's great theoretical innovations was his tripartite conception of the mind, in which the ego—the "I" of our apperception—is but one of the three strata of subjectivity within each individual. *See generally* S. Freud, New Introductory Lectures on Psychoanalysis 51–71 (J. Strachey trans. 1965) (describing the ego, the id, and the superego). * * *

[218]It is a central theme of Proust's *Remembrance of Things Past* to disabuse us of the illusion of having a singular identity over time, in order (perhaps) for us to regain our past in an even more essential way. *See, e.g.,* 3 M. Proust, Remembrance of Things Past 499 (C. Moncrieff, T. Kilmartin & A. Mayor trans. 1981) [.]

[219]Derek Parfit has made the most powerful arguments within analytic philosophy against the concept of a unitary "I" persisting over time. *See generally* D. Parfit, Reasons and Persons (1984) [.]

maintenance of institutionalized sexual identities and normalized reproductive relations—that have made its *affirmative* or *formative* consequences, as well as the reaction against these consequences, so powerful a force in modern society.

* * *

It is no answer to say that an individual interested in homosexual relations might simply remain celibate. The living force of the law is at issue, not its logical form, and the real force of anti-homosexual laws, if obeyed, is that they enlist and redirect physical and emotional desires that we do not expect people to suppress. Indeed, it is precisely the propensity of such prohibitions to operate on and put to use an individual's most elemental bodily faculties that gives the exertion of power in this area such formative force. We tend to analyze these proscriptions today in terms of the propriety of punishing people for homosexual conduct. We tend, in measuring their morality, to form an image of either the homosexual imprisoned or the homosexual forced to give up his sexual acts. We ought, however, to give up the image of "the homosexual" in the first place and measure the law instead in terms of its creation of heterosexuals (and, in a different way, of homosexuals too) within the standardized parameters of a state-regulated identity.

It should be emphasized that conceiving of the right to privacy as protecting homosexuality for the reasons just discussed is not at all to convert the right to privacy into a general protection of "sexual intimacy," as Justice Blackmun suggested. The point is this: child-bearing, marriage, and the assumption of a specific sexual identity are undertakings that go on for years, define roles, direct activities, operate on or even create intense emotional relations, enlist the body, inform values, and in sum substantially shape the totality of a person's daily life and consciousness. Laws that force such undertakings on individuals may properly be called "totalitarian," and the right to privacy exists to protect against them.

RANDY E. BARNETT, JUSTICE KENNEDY'S LIBERTARIAN REVOLUTION: *LAWRENCE v. TEXAS*

CATO SUPREME COURT REVIEW (2002-2003).

In *Lawrence v. Texas*, the Supreme Court held unconstitutional a Texas law criminalizing sexual relations between persons of the same sex. That would be reason enough to consider the case a landmark decision. But to those schooled in post-New Deal "fundamental rights" jurisprudence, what was most striking about *Lawrence* was the way the Court justified its ruling. If the approach the Court took in the case is followed in other cases in the future, we have in *Lawrence* nothing short of a constitutional revolution, with implications reaching far beyond the "personal liberty" at issue here.

* * *

CONSTITUTIONAL LIBERTY MEETS THE "PROGRESSIVE" MOVEMENT

At the end of the 19th century, as the so-called progressive movement grew in political strength, states passed statutes regulating and restricting all manner of economic activity. * * *

As that sort of legislation gained in popularity, the Supreme Court resisted sporadically, striking down some but not all statutes restricting economic activities. *Lochner v. New York* was the most famous of those cases. There the Supreme Court struck down provisions of a state statute limiting the maximum hours bakeshop employees could work per week. The Court found the provisions violated the "liberty of contract" between employees and employers that was protected, it said, by the "liberty" portion of the Due Process Clause of the Fourteenth Amendment. In other cases, the Court struck down noneconomic legislation as well, such as state laws mandating English-only education of children[4] or requiring parents to send their children to public schools,[5] as arbitrary infringements of liberty.

ENTER THE PRESUMPTION OF CONSTITUTIONALITY

[In 1931] Justice Louis Brandeis adopted a "presumption of constitutionality" when evaluating the exercise of state police powers. In *O'Groman & Young, Inc. v. Hartford Fire Insurance Co.* Brandeis wrote:

> The statute here questioned deals with a subject clearly within the scope of the police power. We are asked to declare it void on the ground that the specific method of regulation prescribed is unreasonable and hence deprives the plaintiff of due process of law. As underlying questions of fact may condition the constitutionality of legislation of this character, the presumption of constitutionality must prevail in the absence of some factual foundation of record for overthrowing the statute.[6]

* * *

[I]nitially the presumption of constitutionality could be rebutted, at least in theory, by those objecting to a statute's constitutionality. By the 1940s, however, the presumption became irrebuttable for all practical purposes, at least in the case of economic regulation. Thus, in the 1956 case

---

[4]Meyer v. Nebraska, 262 U.S. 390 (1923).

[5]Pierce v. Society of Sisters of the Holy Names of Jesus and Mary, 268 U.S. 510 (1925).

[6]282 U.S. 251, 257-58 (1931) (emphasis added).

of *Williamson v. Lee Optical*,[7] the court reversed a lower court that had held unconstitutional portions of a state statute that made it unlawful "for any person not a licensed optometrist or ophthalmologist to fit lenses to a face or to duplicate or replace into frames lenses or other optical appliances, except upon written prescriptive authority of an Oklahoma licensed ophthalmologist or optometrist." The district court had held that such a requirement was not "reasonably and rationally related to the health and welfare of the people." The law thus violated the Due Process Clause by arbitrarily interfering with an optician's right to do business.

Plainly, the trial court was not playing from the post-New Deal playbook.

[But] Justice Douglas's opinion [for the Supreme Court] made clear that when restricting liberty, the legislature need not have had good reasons. It is enough that it *might* have had good reasons:

> The legislature might have concluded that the frequency of occasions when a prescription is necessary was sufficient to justify this regulation of the fitting of eyeglasses. Likewise, . . . the legislature might have concluded that one was needed often enough to require one in every case. Or the legislature may have concluded that eye examinations were so critical, not only for correction of vision but also for detection of latent ailments or diseases, that every change in frames and every duplication of a lens should be accompanied by a prescription from a medical expert. . . .

Consequently, Justice Douglas concluded, "[w]e cannot say that the regulation has no rational relation to that objective and therefore is beyond constitutional bounds." With *Lee Optical* as the norm, what then was left of judicial review?

QUALIFYING THE PRESUMPTION OF CONSTITUTIONALITY: THE THEORY OF FOOTNOTE FOUR

As *Lee Optical* makes plain, post-New Deal deference to state legislatures and to Congress meant that courts simply would not guard against constitutional violations: "For protection against abuses by legislatures the people must resort to the polls, not to the courts," said Douglas. If applied consistently, this deferential attitude would obviously end the entire practice of judicial review. How then did the post-New Deal Court avoid that slippery slope? The answer is found in a single footnote that foreshadows the entire post-New Deal theory of judicial review and constitutional rights.

---

[7]348 U.S. 483 (1956).

I allude, of course, to the famous Footnote Four of the 1938 case of *United States v. Carolene Products Co.*,[8] which concerned legislative restrictions on the sale of a milk substitute that competed with the products of dairy farmers. In the text of his opinion, Justice Harlan Fiske Stone strongly asserted the presumption of constitutionality. [But he followed that passage with a footnote:]

> There may be a narrower scope for operation of the presumption of constitutionality when legislation appears on its face to be within a specific prohibition of the Constitution, such as those of the first ten amendments, which are deemed equally specific when held to be embraced within the Fourteenth.

After *Carolene Products*, legislation was presumed to be constitutional unless one of the three exceptions in Footnote Four was satisfied, in which case the Court would give the statute "heightened scrutiny." Due to the idiosyncrasies of the first eight amendments, this doctrinal maneuver allowed the court to uphold economic regulations, as in *Lee Optical*, while preserving judicial review of such "personal" freedoms as those of speech, assembly, and press. That the personal right to bear arms, explicitly mentioned in the Second Amendment, has not been judicially protected shows the ideological nature of this maneuver, as does the uneven protection of property rights, explicitly mentioned in the Fifth Amendment.

Ironically, in recent years judicial conservatives like Robert Bork and Raoul Berger have been among the most stalwart in their allegiance to the judicial philosophy of Footnote Four. For all the reverence they express toward the Framers of the Constitution, jurisprudentially speaking, they are unreconstructed Roosevelt New Dealers.

ENTER THE UNENUMERATED "RIGHT OF PRIVACY"

Until the 1960's, the Supreme Court was content for the most part to confine judicial review to policing most of the enumerated rights contained in the Bill of Rights, while deferring to legislative power in all other arenas. As just noted, this post-New Deal jurisprudence of (partial) restraint is today the holy grail of judicial conservatives. Their posture came about, in part, in reaction to *Griswold v. Connecticut*,[22] a case in which the Court considered the constitutionality of a state using its police power to ban not only the "personal" liberty to use contraceptives but also the "economic" liberty to sell and distribute them.

The *Griswold* Court struck down the statute for violating an unenumerated right it called the "right of privacy." The task of justifying this extension of judicial review to a right not specified in the Bill of Rights, for the

[8] 304 U.S. 144 (1938).

[22] 381 U.S.479 (1965).

first time since *Carolene Products,* fell to Justice Douglas, author of the *Lee Optical* opinion. He did so by attempting to connect, however tenuously, this unenumerated right to those that are enumerated:

> The foregoing cases suggest that specific guarantees in the Bill of Rights have penumbras, formed by emanations from those guarantees that help give them life and substance. . . . Various guarantees create zones of privacy. * * *

* * *

ENTER "FUNDAMENTAL RIGHTS" v. MERE "LIBERTY INTERESTS"

Nevertheless, "emanations" and "penumbras" could not conceal the fact that the protection of an unenumerated right of privacy was outside the framework of Footnote Four. The beauty of the Footnote Four solution was that it cleanly limited judicial review to enumerated rights, while allowing government free rein in the economic sphere. The problem created by the unenumerated right of privacy, however, was that it now forced upon the Court the messy business of distinguishing those liberties, enumerated and unenumerated, that rebut the presumption of constitutionality from those that do not. The former it called "fundamental rights," while the latter were dubbed mere "liberty interests." But how to tell the difference?

Eventually the Court settled on limiting fundamental rights to those that were in its opinion "implicit in the concept of ordered liberty" and could be grounded in our "traditions and history." As Justice Byron White explained in *Bowers v. Hardwick,* the 1986 decision that upheld a Georgia statute criminalizing sodomy, which *Lawrence* overturned:

> Striving to assure itself and the public that announcing rights not readily identifiable in the Constitution's text involves much more than the imposition of the Justices' own choice of values on the States and the Federal Government, the Court has sought to identify the nature of the rights qualifying for heightened judicial protection. In *Palko v. Connecticut,* . . . it was said that this category includes those fundamental liberties that are "implicit in the concept of ordered liberty," such that "neither liberty nor justice would exist if [they] were sacrificed." A different description of fundamental liberties appeared in *Moore v. East Cleveland,* . . . where they are characterized as those liberties that are "deeply rooted in this Nation's history and tradition.". . . See also *Griswold v. Connecticut*. . .

The outcome of that analysis depends almost entirely, however, on how specifically you define the right being asserted. The more specifically you define the liberty at issue—for example, a "constitutional right of homosexuals to engage in acts of sodomy"—the more difficult a burden this is to meet and the more easily the rights claim can be ridiculed. While "liberty" as a general matter is obviously deeply rooted in our history and traditions, the specific liberty to use contraceptives is not. Nor are many other liberties, especially if unknown at the founding. Even liberties that existed at the founding, like the liberty of self-medication, have not to date been deemed "fundamental" by the Court.

JUSTICE KENNEDY EMPLOYS AN IMPLICIT "PRESUMPTION OF LIBERTY"

Lawrence is potentially revolutionary [because] there is not even the pretense of a "fundamental right" rebutting the "presumption of constitutionality." Justice Kennedy never mentions any presumption to be accorded the Texas statute.

More important, he never tries to justify the sexual liberty of same-sex couples as a fundamental right. Instead, he spends all his energies demonstrating that same-sex sexual freedom is a legitimate aspect of liberty—unlike, for example, actions that violate the rights of others, which are not liberty but license. Not only does this take the Court outside the framework of Footnote Four, it also removes it from the framework of unenumerated fundamental rights that was engrafted upon it in the wake of *Griswold*. Until *Lawrence*, every unenumerated rights case had to establish that the liberty at issue was "fundamental," as opposed to a mere liberty interest.

* * *

Although he never acknowledges it, Justice Kennedy is employing here what I have called a "presumption of liberty" that requires the government to justify its restriction on liberty, instead of requiring the citizen to establish that the liberty being exercised is somehow "fundamental." In this way, once an action is deemed to be a proper exercise of liberty (as opposed to license), the burden shifts to the government.

All that was offered by the government to justify this statute is the judgment of the legislature that the prohibited conduct is "immoral," which for the majority (including, on this issue, Justice O'Connor) is simply not enough to justify the restriction of liberty. Why not? * * *

* * * A legislative judgment of "immorality" means simply that a majority of the legislature disapproves of this conduct. But justifying legislation solely on grounds of morality would entirely eliminate judicial review of legislative powers. How could a court ever adjudicate between a legislature's claim that a particular exercise of liberty is "immoral" and a defendant's contrary claim that it is not?

In practice, therefore, a doctrine allowing legislation to be justified solely on the basis of morality would recognize an unlimited police power in state legislatures. Unlimited power is the very definition of tyranny. While the police power of states may be broad, it was never thought to be unlimited.

DEFENDING *LAWRENCE* FROM JUDICIAL CONSERVATIVES

Given their grounding still rooted in post-New Deal constitutional jurisprudence, the responses of judicial conservatives (not to be equated with all political conservatives) are entirely predictable. Yet each fails upon critical inspection. Three such responses stand out.

First, judicial conservatives argue that all laws restrict some freedom; thus, requiring legislatures to justify to a court their restrictions on liberty would amount to giving judges an unbridled power to strike down laws of which they disapprove. But that is to equate "liberty" and "license," a mistake the Founders never made. Liberty is and always has been the properly defined exercise of freedom. Liberty is and always has been constrained by the rights of others. No one's genuine right to liberty is violated by restricting his or her freedom to rape or murder, because there is no such right in the first place.

That is not to say that the rightful exercise of liberty may never be regulated—or made regular (as opposed to prohibited outright). It is only to say that, as Justice Kennedy implicitly acknowledges, the existence of a right to liberty places a burden on the government to justify any regulations of liberty as necessary and proper. Wrongful behavior that violates the rights of others may justly be prohibited without violating liberty rights—although "wrongful" is not the same as "immoral."

Second, and closely related, the *Lawrence* majority's position, judicial conservatives say, rejects any moral content of law. That is false. As was just explained, wrongful behavior that violates the rights of others may justly be prohibited without violating the liberty rights of others. Because it is usually (but not always) immoral to wrongfully violate the rights of others, the entirely justified prohibition of wrongful behavior also necessarily prohibits much immoral behavior as well. * * *

Finally, judicial conservatives repeatedly assert that there is no textual basis for the protection of a general right to liberty. Unlike "privacy," however, "liberty" is mentioned explicitly in the Due Process Clauses of both the Fifth and Fourteenth Amendments, so this is a much harder argument to sustain. The judicial conservative response is to argue that liberty may properly be restricted so long as "due process" is followed. As Justice Scalia wrote in his dissent: "The Fourteenth Amendment *expressly allows* States to deprive their citizens of liberty, so long as due process of law is provided." This is textually and historically wrong.

Ever since the founding, "due process of law" has included judicial review to ensure that a law is within the proper power of a legislature to enact. * * *

At the federal level, judicial review, which is part of the "due process of law," includes the power to nullify laws that exceed the delegated powers of Congress. * * * In addition, however, federal power is further constrained by the rights retained by the people—both those few that are enumerated and, as affirmed in the Ninth Amendment, those liberty rights that are unenumerated as well. At the state level, the Privileges or Immunities Clause of the Fourteenth Amendment prohibits states such as Texas from infringing the privileges or immunities of U.S. citizens. Those include both the liberty rights or "immunities" retained by the people, and the positive rights or "privileges" created by the Constitution of the United States.

* * *

CONCLUSION: A REMARKABLY SIMPLE RULING

In the end, *Lawrence* is a very simple, indeed elegant, ruling. Justice Kennedy examined the conduct at issue to see if it was properly an aspect of liberty (as opposed to license), and then asked the government to justify its restriction, which it failed to do adequately. The decision would have been far more transparent and compelling if Kennedy had acknowledged what was really happening (though perhaps that would have lost votes by other justices). Without that acknowledgment, the revolutionary aspect of his opinion is concealed and rendered vulnerable to the ridicule of the dissent. Far better would it have been to more closely track the superb amicus briefs of the Cato Institute, which Kennedy twice cited approvingly, and of the Institute for Justice.

If the Court is serious in its ruling, Justice Scalia is right to contend that the shift from privacy to liberty, and away from the New Deal-induced tension between the presumption of constitutionality and fundamental rights, "will have far-reaching implications beyond this case." For example, the medical cannabis cases now wending their way through the Ninth Circuit would be greatly affected if those seeking to use or distribute medical cannabis pursuant to California law did not have to show that their liberty to do so was somehow "fundamental"—and instead the government were forced to justify its restrictions on that liberty. While wrongful behavior (or license) could be prohibited, rightful behavior (or liberty) could be regulated, provided that the regulation was shown to be necessary and proper.

Although it may be possible to cabin this case to the protection of "personal" liberties of an intimate nature—and it is a fair prediction that that is what the Court will attempt—for *Lawrence v. Texas* to be constitutionally revolutionary, the Court's defense of liberty must not be limited to sexual conduct. The more liberties the Court protects, the less ideological it will be and the more widespread political support it will enjoy. Recognizing a robust "presumption of liberty" might also enable the court to transcend the trench warfare over judicial appointments. Both Left and Right would then find their favored rights protected under the same doctrine. When the

Court plays favorites with liberty, as it has since the New Deal, it loses rather than gains credibility with the public, and undermines its vital role as the guardian of the Constitution. If the Court is true to its reasoning, *Lawrence v. Texas* could provide an important step in the direction of a more balanced protection of liberty that could find broad ideological support.

JOHN M. FINNIS, LAW, MORALITY, AND "SEXUAL ORIENTATION"

9 NOTRE DAME J.L. ETHICS & PUB. POL'Y 11—16, 33—34, 36—39 (1995).

I.

During the past thirty years there has emerged in Europe a standard form of legal regulation of sexual conduct. This standard form or scheme, which I shall call the "standard modern [European] position," is accepted by the European Court of Human Rights and the European Commission of Human Rights[.][a] The standard modern European position has two limbs. On the one hand, the state is not authorized to, and does not, make it a punishable offence for adult consenting persons to engage, in private, in immoral sexual acts (for example, homosexual acts). On the other hand, states do have the authority to discourage, say, homosexual conduct and "orientation" (i.e. overtly manifested active willingness to engage in homosexual conduct). And typically, though not universally, they do so. That is to say, they maintain various criminal and administrative laws and policies which have as part of their purpose the discouraging of such conduct. Many of these laws, regulations, and policies discriminate (i.e. distinguish) between heterosexual and homosexual conduct adversely to the latter.

In England, for example, well after Parliament's decriminalization of private adult homosexual conduct by the Sexual Offences Act 1967, the highest court (the House of Lords) reaffirmed that a jury may lawfully convict on a charge of conspiring to corrupt public morals by publishing advertisements by private individuals of their availability for (non-commercial) private homosexual acts. The Court of Appeal has constantly reaffirmed, notably in 1977, 1981 and 1990, that public soliciting of adult males by adult males falls within the statutory prohibition of "importun-[ing] in a public place for an immoral purpose." Parliament has peacefully

[a]The European Court of Human Rights was set up under the Convention for the Protection of Human Rights and Fundamental Freedoms which was drawn up within the Council of Europe. It was opened for signature in Rome on November 4, 1950 and entered into force in September 1953. Protocol No. 11, which came into force on 1 November 1998, amended the Convention by replacing the existing, part-time Court and Commission with a single, full-time Court. [Ed. note.]

accepted both these judicial interpretations of the constitutional, statutory and common law position. It has also voted more than once to maintain the legal position whereby the age of consent for lawful intercourse is 21 for homosexual but 16 for heterosexual intercourse; in February 1994 the House of Commons voted to make the homosexual age of consent 18, which would reduce but retain the differentiation between homosexual and heterosexual conduct. In 1988, Parliament specifically prohibited local governments in England from doing anything to "intentionally promote homosexuality" or "promote the teaching in any maintained school of the acceptability of homosexuality as a pretended family relationship." The provisions of English law relating to marriage and to adoption similarly manifest a purpose or at least a willingness to discourage homosexual conduct and impede its promotion by any form of invitatory activity other than between consenting adults and in a truly private milieu.

The English position as outlined above is in full conformity with the position upheld by the European human rights institutions. When the European Court of Human Rights in 1981 adopted (and in 1988 reaffirmed) the position which Parliament in England had taken in 1967, it ruled that penal prohibition of private adult homosexual activity is not necessary for the securing of the state's legitimate aim of protecting morals.[7] In doing so, the court expressly left unscathed, and in principle confirmed, the decision of March 13, 1980 of the European Commission of Human Rights (and of the Commission on October 12, 1978 and the Council of Ministers by Resolution DH (79) 5 of June 12, 1979) that states can properly prohibit private consensual homosexual acts involving a male under 21 notwithstanding the Convention right of non-discrimination in the legal protection of rights and notwithstanding that the state law in question made 16 the "age of consent" for heterosexual intercourse (and 18 the age of majority for other purposes).

The Commission has subsequently reaffirmed that decision and has declared unarguable ("inadmissible" for further judicial process) complaints made, under the Convention's anti-discrimination provisions, against the longstanding Swiss law which criminalizes homosexual prostitution (male or female) but not heterosexual prostitution.

II.

The standard modern [European] position is consistent with the view that (apart perhaps from special cases and contexts) it is unjust for A to impose any kind of disadvantage on B simply because A believes (perhaps correctly) that B has sexual inclinations (which he may or may not act on) towards persons of the same sex. (Special cases are more likely to arise, for

[7] Dudgeon v. United Kingdom, 45 Eur. Ct H.R. 21 (ser.A) (1981); Norris v. Ireland, 142 Eur. Ct. H.R. 20 (ser.A) (1988).

example, where B's inclination is towards "man-boy love," i.e. pederasty.) The position does not give B the widest conceivable legal protection against such unjust discrimination (just as it generally does not give wide protection against needless acts of adverse private discrimination in housing or employment to people with unpopular or eccentric political views). But the position does not itself encourage, sponsor or impose any such unjust burden. (And it is accompanied by many legal protections for homosexual persons with respect to assaults, threats, unreasonable discrimination by public bodies and officials, etc.)

The concern of the standard modern position itself is not with inclinations but entirely with certain decisions to express or manifest deliberate promotion of, or readiness to engage in, homosexual activity or conduct, including promotion of forms of life (e.g. purportedly marital cohabitation) which both encourage such activity and present it as a valid or acceptable alternative to the committed heterosexual union which the state recognizes as marriage. Subject only to the written or unwritten constitutional requirement of freedom of discussion of ideas, the state laws and state policies which I have outlined are intended to discourage decisions which are thus deliberately oriented towards homosexual conduct and are manifested in public ways.

The standard modern position differs from the position which it replaced, which made adult consensual sodomy and like acts crimes per se. States which adhere to the standard modern position make it clear by laws and policies such as I have referred to that the state has by no means renounced its legitimate concern with public morality and the education of children and young people towards truly worthwhile and against alluring but bad forms of conduct and life. Nor have such states renounced the judgment that a life involving homosexual conduct is bad even for anyone unfortunate enough to have innate or quasi-innate homosexual inclinations.

The difference between the standard modern position and the position it has replaced can be expressed as follows. The standard modern position considers that the state's proper responsibility for upholding true worth (morality) is a responsibility *subsidiary* (auxiliary) to the *primary* responsibility of parents and non-political voluntary associations. The subsidiary character of government is widely emphasized and increasingly accepted, at least in principle, in contemporary European politics. (It was, for example, a cornerstone of the Treaty of Maastricht of 1992.) This conception of the proper role of government has been taken to exclude the state from assuming a directly parental disciplinary role in relation to consenting adults. That role was one which political theory and practice formerly ascribed to the state on the assumption that the role followed by logical necessity from the truth that the state should encourage true worth and discourage immorality. That assumption is now judged to be mistaken (a judgment for which I shall argue in the final part of this lecture).

So the modern theory and practice draws a distinction not drawn in the former legal arrangements—a distinction between (a) supervising the truly private conduct of adults and (b) supervising the *public realm or environment*. The importance of the latter includes the following considerations: (1) this is the environment or public realm in which young people (of whatever sexual inclination) are educated; (2) it is the context in which and by which everyone with responsibility for the well being of young people is helped or hindered in assisting them to avoid bad forms of life; (3) it is the milieu in which and by which all citizens are encouraged and helped, or discouraged and undermined, in their own resistance to being lured by temptation into falling away from their own aspirations to be people of integrated good character, and to be autonomous, self-controlled persons rather than slaves to impulse and sensual gratification.

While the type (a) supervision of truly private adult consensual conduct is now considered to be outside the state's normally proper role[,] type (b) supervision of the moral-cultural-educational environment is maintained as a very important part of the state's justification for claiming legitimately the loyalty of its decent citizens.

III.

The standard modern position is part of a politico-legal order which systematically outlaws many forms of discrimination. Thus the European Convention on Human Rights (model for several dozen constitutions enacted over the past thirty-five years by the British authorities, for nations gaining independence) provides that the protection of the rights it sets out is to be enjoyed without discrimination on any ground such as "sex, race, colour, language, religion, political or other opinion, national or social origin, association with a national minority, property, birth or other status."

But the standard modern position deliberately rejects proposals to include in such lists the item "sexual orientation." The explanation commonly given (correctly, in my opinion) is this. The phrase "sexual orientation" is radically equivocal. Particularly as used by promoters of "gay rights," the phase ambiguously assimilates two things which the standard modern position carefully distinguishes: (I) a psychological or psychosomatic disposition inwardly orienting one *towards* homosexual activity; (II) the deliberate decision so to orient one's public *behavior* as to express or *manifest* one's active interest in and endorsement of homosexual *conduct* and/or forms of life which presumptively involve such conduct.

* * *

[W]hile the standard position accepts that acts of type (I) discrimination are unjust, it judges that there are compelling reasons both to deny that such injustice would be appropriately remedied by laws against "discrimination based on sexual orientation," and to hold that such a "remedy" would work significant discrimination and injustice against (and would indeed damage) families, associations and institutions which have organized themselves to live out and transmit ideals of family life that include a high conception of the worth of truly conjugal sexual intercourse.

It is in fact accepted by almost everyone, on both sides of the political debate, that the adoption of a law framed to prohibit "discrimination on grounds of sexual orientation" would require the prompt abandonment of all attempts by the political community to discourage homosexual conduct by means of educational policies, restrictions on prostitution, non-recognition of homosexual "marriages" and adoptions, and so forth. It is judged (and in my view soundly) that the law itself would perforce have changed from teaching, in many ways, that homosexual conduct is bad to teaching, massively, that it is a type of sexual activity as good as any other * * *.

* * *

VII.

I promised to defend the judgment that the government of political communities is subsidiary, and rationally limited not only by constitutional law and by the moral norms which limit every decent person's deliberation and choice, but also by the inherent limits of its general justifying aim, purpose or rationale. That rationale is, of course, the common good of the political community. And that common good, I shall argue, is not basic, intrinsic or constitutive, but rather is instrumental.

Every community is constituted by the communication and cooperation between its members. To say that a community has a common good is simply to say that communication and cooperation have a point which the members more or less concur in understanding, valuing and pursuing. There are three types of common good which each provide the constitutive point of a distinctive type of open-ended community and directly instantiate a basic human good: (1) the affectionate mutual help and shared enjoyment of the friendship and *communio* of "real friends"; (2) the sharing of husband and wife in married life, united as complementary, bodily persons whose activities make them apt for parenthood—the *communio* of spouses and, if their marriage is fruitful, their children; (3) the *communio* of religious believers cooperating in the devotion and service called for by what they believe to be the accessible truths about the ultimate source of meaning, value and other realities, and about the ways in which human beings can be in harmony with that ultimate source. Other human communities *either* are dedicated to accomplishing a specific goal or set of goals (like a university or hospital) and so are not in the open-ended service of their members, or have a common good which is instrumental rather than basic. * * *

The political community * * * is a community cooperating in the service of a common good which is instrumental, not itself basic. True, it is a good which is "great and godlike"[52] in its ambitious range: "to secure the whole ensemble of material and other conditions, including forms of collaboration, that tend to favor, facilitate, and foster the realization by each individual [in that community] of his or her personal development[.]"[53] True too, its proper range includes the regulation of friendships, marriage, families, and religious associations, as well as of all the many organizations and associations which are dedicated to specific goals or which, like the state itself, have only an instrumental (e.g. an economic) common good. But such regulation of these associations should never (in the case of the associations with a non-instrumental common good) or only exceptionally (in the case of instrumental associations) be intended to take over the formation, direction or management of these personal initiatives and interpersonal associations. Rather, its purpose must be to carry out the subsidiary (i.e. helping, from the Latin *subsidium*, help) function of assisting individuals and groups to coordinate their activities for the objectives and commitments they have chosen, and to do so in ways consistent with the other aspects of the common good of this community, uniquely complex, far-reaching and demanding in its rationale, its requirements of cooperation, and its monopolization of force: the political community.

* * *

Is [this] natural law teaching right? Or should we rather adhere to the uncomplicated theory of Aquinas's treatise *On Princely Government*, that government should command whatever leads people towards their ultimate (heavenly) end, forbid whatever deflects them from it, and coercively deter people from evil-doing and induce them to morally decent conduct?[60] Perhaps the most persuasive short statement of that teaching is still Aristotle's famous attack on theories which, like the sophist Lycophron's, treat the state as a mere mutual insurance arrangement?[61] But in two crucial respects, at least, Aristotle (and with him the tradition) has taken things too easily.

---

[52] Aristotle, Nicomachean Ethics , I,1: 1094b9

[53] John Finnis, Natural Law and Natural Rights 147 (1980)[.]

[60] De Regimine Principum c.14 [.]

[61] * * * Aristotle, Politics, III.5 1280a32, a35, 1280b7-13, b30-31, b34, 1281a1-4.

First: If the object, point or common good of the political community were indeed a self-sufficient life, and if self-sufficiency (*autarcheia*) were indeed what Aristotle defines it to be—a life lacking in nothing, of complete fulfillment—then we would have to say that the political community has a point it cannot hope to achieve, a common good utterly beyond its reach. For subsequent philosophical reflection has confirmed what one might suspect from Aristotle's own manifest oscillation between different conceptions of *eudaimonia* (and thus of *autarcheia*): Integral human fulfillment is nothing less than the fulfillment of (in principle) all human persons in all communities and cannot be achieved in any community short of the heavenly kingdom, a community envisaged not by unaided reason (natural law theory) but only by virtue of divine revelation and attainable only by a divine gift which transcends the capacities of nature. * * *

Second: When Aristotle speaks of "making" people good, he constantly uses the word *poiesis* which he has so often contrasted with *praxis* and reserved for techniques ("arts") of manipulating matter. But helping citizens to choose and act in line with integral human fulfillment must involve something which goes beyond any art or technique. For only individual acting persons can by their own choices make themselves good or evil. Not that their life should or can be individualistic[.] Their choices will involve them in relationships just or unjust, generous or illiberal, vengeful or charitable, with other persons in all these communities. And as members of all these communities they have some responsibility to encourage their fellow-members in morally good and discourage them from morally bad conduct.

To be sure, the political community is a cooperation which undertakes the unique tasks of giving coercive protection to all individuals and lawful associations within its domain, and of securing an economic and cultural environment in which all these persons and groups can pursue their own proper good. To be sure, this common good of the political community makes it far more than a mere arrangement for "preventing mutual injury and exchanging goods." But it is one thing to maintain, as reason requires, that the political community's rationale requires that its public managing structure, the state, should deliberately and publicly identify, encourage, facilitate and support the truly worthwhile (including moral virtue), should deliberately and publicly identify, discourage and hinder the harmful and evil, and should, by its criminal prohibitions and sanctions (as well as its other laws and policies), assist people with parental responsibilities to educate children and young people in virtue and to discourage their vices. It is another thing to maintain that that rationale requires or authorizes the state to direct people to virtue and deter them from vice by making even secret and truly consensual adult acts of vice a punishable offence against the state's laws.

So there was a sound and important distinction of principle which the Supreme Court of the United States overlooked in moving from *Griswold v. Connecticut* (private use of contraceptives by *spouses*) to *Eisenstadt v. Baird* (*public distribution* of contraceptives to *unmarried* people). The truth and relevance of that distinction, and its high importance for the common good, would be overlooked again if laws criminalizing private acts of sodomy between adults were to be struck down by the Court on any ground which would also constitutionally require the law to tolerate the advertising or marketing of homosexual services, the maintenance of places of resort for homosexual activity, or the promotion of homosexualist "lifestyles" via education and public media of communication, or to recognize homosexual "marriages" or permit the adoption of children by homosexually active people, and so forth.

JANET E. HALLEY, SEXUAL ORIENTATION AND THE POLITICS OF BIOLOGY: A CRITIQUE OF THE ARGUMENT FROM IMMUTABILITY

46 STAN. L. REV. 503, 510–513, 516–528 (1994).

Two [recent developments] have contributed to a startling resorgimento of immutability-based arguments among gay-rights advocates notwithstanding their anemic condition in Supreme Court thinking and in the academic literature. First, equal protection law about sexual orientation began to focus on the identity or status of homosexuals—an issue that the pro-gay argument from immutability seems tailored to illuminate. This development began when the Supreme Court held in *Bowers v. Hardwick* that states did not violate federal constitutional guarantees of due process and privacy by criminalizing same-sex sodomy. *Hardwick* was soon followed by a series of federal court holdings that refused to apply heightened equal protection review to discrimination based on sexual orientation because of *Hardwick's* due process holding. They reasoned that, because *Hardwick* permitted states to criminalize same-sex sodomy, and because same-sex sodomy is the "behavior that defines the class of homosexuals," *Hardwick* precluded the application of heightened scrutiny to anti-gay discrimination. "After all," one court reasoned, "there can hardly be more palpable discrimination against a class than making the conduct that defines the class criminal."[32]

These cases challenged gay-rights advocates to convince courts that sodomy alone does not define the class of gay men, lesbians, and bisexuals. Litigators set out to constrain *Hardwick* by framing equal protection cases in which plaintiffs had been subjected to unfavorable treatment not because

[32][Padula v. Webster, 822 F.2d 97, 103 (D.C.Cir.1987).]

of any sexual conduct but because of their public and private identities as gay, lesbian, or bisexual. This strategic choice resulted in an emphasis on military cases notwithstanding the unfavorable deference with which courts typically treat military policy. The military, after all, was in the business of discharging troops based solely on their sexual-orientation identity, and of generating potential plaintiffs with records devoid of any evidence of prohibited (or even disparaged) conduct. In many of the resulting cases, however, courts imputed sodomitical conduct on the basis of identity and denied heightened scrutiny. * * *

A second development [has also] intensified gay-rights advocates' interest in immutability theories: the cultural success of genetics as a source of knowledge about who we are as humans. [But now, bolstered] by citations to recent scientific experiments claiming to show that human sexual orientation rests on a biological substrate, the argument from immutability has become the platform on which many gay-rights advocates prefer to contest post-*Hardwick* courts' equation of homosexual identity with criminalizable sodomy.

[I maintain] that those who wish to premise legal rights of gay men, lesbians, and bisexuals on a biological argument should cease and desist, and should seek instead a common litigation strategy with those in the pro-gay community who resist the argument from immutability. Some distinctions are in order first. [A]n *essentialist* view of homosexual orientation claims that it is a deep-rooted, fixed, and intrinsic feature of individuals. This essentialist view assumes that homosexual orientation is determined (by nature or nurture), not chosen. * * * The *constructivist* view of homosexual orientation claims that it is a contingent, socially malleable trait that arises in a person as she manages her world, its meanings, and her desires. The pro-gay argument from immutability is, on these definitions, essentialist. When the pro-gay argument from immutability adds a reliance on biological causation theories, it merely locates the source of determination in nature.

Neither essentialism nor constructivism is necessarily gay-affirmative. Anti-gay conservatives use both essentialist and constructivist justifications for their discriminatory policies, even as pro-gay advocates use essentialist and constructivist arguments to defeat them. Thus there are four, not two, opposed positions—pro-gay essentialism, pro-gay constructivism, anti-gay essentialism, and anti-gay constructivism—each incorporating its causal theory into its social policy argument:

- *Pro-gay essentialism* holds that because homosexual orientation is fixed, immutable, and definitional, it should be protected from discrimination.

- *Pro-gay constructivism* holds that all forms of sexual orientation are mutable, either across an individual's life, at some important moment of personal choice, or across historical periods, and that social policy on sexual orientation should not impede these variations.

• *Anti-gay essentialism* holds that homosexual orientation is fixed, immutable, and normatively bad or sick, either in itself or in its manifestation, and that society should tailor discrimination against gay men and lesbians to express normative judgments, deter manifestations of homosexual orientation, or cure homosexuals of their illness.

• *Anti-gay constructivism* either emphasizes the mutability of heterosexual orientation, arguing that heterosexuality must be shored up by anti-gay discrimination, or points to the mutability of homosexual orientation, arguing that discrimination should be designed to convert gay men and lesbians to heterosexuality.

Pro-gay activists usually limit their debate to the first two categories—pro-gay essentialism and pro-gay constructivism. But without taking into account the anti-gay positions that these causal theories sometimes support, pro-gay analysis cannot adequately assess the relative merits of essentialism and constructivism.

A. Choice

Anti-gay constructivists say that being gay, lesbian, or bisexual is a choice, and for that reason forms a proper target for a majority that thinks these ways of being are morally bad and seeks to deter people from adopting them. Former Vice President Dan Quayle became the most visible proponent of this position during the 1992 presidential campaign when he announced, "My viewpoint is that it's more of a choice than a biological situation. . . . I think it is a wrong choice."

Most contemporary efforts to justify discrimination against gay men and lesbians rely on former Vice President Quayle's factual assumption. For example, Judge Posner assumes throughout his analysis of homosexuality that, to the extent that society can prevent or deter homosexuality at an acceptable cost, its repression is justified to "make persons who would otherwise become or remain homosexuals happier."[59] As it happens, he concludes that many, but by no means all, forms of discrimination against homosexuals function inefficiently. But other conservative analysts justify capacious regimes of discrimination on the factual assumption that homosexuality is to some extent chosen. Conservative commentator E.L. Pattullo, for example, posits that at least some individuals choose their sexual orientation, and argues on that basis that discrimination against gay men and lesbians, including constraints on their speech, should be tailored

[59]Richard A. Posner, Sex and Reason 308, 303–09 (1992)[.]

to deter such sexual-orientation "waverers" from choosing homosexuality over heterosexuality.[61]

Pro-gay essentialism offers a refutation of this anti-gay constructivist reasoning. It is an exoneration strategy, describing gay men and lesbians as incapable of resisting their sexual orientation and thus not "responsible" for it. Its claim to fairness taps a deep reservoir of intuitive plausibility: that an individual should not be criminally punished or civilly burdened because he or she helplessly bears a disfavored characteristic. Pro-gay essentialism is also a practical strategy, claiming that punishing homosexuality is useless because it cannot be deterred. The argument from immutability may be the only "high concept" argument against anti-gay discrimination in the repertoire of popular debate today.

For a number of reasons, the pro-gay argument from immutability, when advanced as a legal claim, is not the silver bullet its proponents think. [In the first place,] this "folk" form of antidiscrimination reasoning has not survived the exactions of constitutional analysis, which seeks a principled way of distinguishing the many discriminations based on immutable characteristics that we do not find normatively or legally troubling. Second, as many proponents of the argument from immutability concede, the empirical record suggests not that changing someone's sexual orientation is impossible, but that it is so wrenchingly difficult as to be cruel (and thus, in some versions, excessively costly when tallied with the scarcity of effective conversions). Staking the immutability argument on this particular ground is problematic in several ways. The first resort of these arguments is a description of personality or personhood, in which the "traits" associated with homosexual orientation "are so central to a person's identity that it would be abhorrent for government to penalize a person for refusing to change them, regardless of how easy that change might be physically." Personhood arguments transpose the site of immutability from the body to the personality. As Kendall Thomas argues, such a move risks "perpetuat[ing] the psycho-medical conception of the origins and nature of sexual orientation . . . [,] leav[ing] the door open for effective regulation simply by substituting a medical response to homosexual conduct . . . for a legal one."[65] And this modified form of essentialism entirely fails to represent those pro-gay constituencies that deny the centrality of a particularized homosexual orientation to their psychic makeup, whether because they identify as bisexual, because they seek to de-emphasize the gender parameters of sexuality, because they are experimental about sexuality, or because they experience sexuality not as serious self-expressiveness but as play, drag, and ironic self-reflexivity.

---

[61]E.L. Pattullo, *Straight Talk About Gays,* Commentary, Dec. 1992, at 22–23.

[65]Kendall Thomas, *Beyond the Privacy Principle,* 92 Colum.L.Rev. 1431, 1474 (1992)[.]

Moreover, personhood arguments do not establish a rationale for delegitimating popular decisions to sanction voluntary conduct. As philosopher Edward Stein has argued, pro-gay essentialism fails to address the anti-gay argument that homosexuality, whether it is mutable or not, is expressed through elected behavior, ranging from same-sex erotic acts to practices of self-identification.[66] Explaining why rules burdening conduct impinge on elements of life central to personhood would require not a psychiatric or psychological theory of sexuality but a political one. And the justification for these policies need not rest on an assumption that they tend to increase or decrease the amount of homosexuality and heterosexuality being expressed in a society: Anti-gay essentialism might espouse them on an assumption that to do otherwise would indicate approval of the conduct of an immutably defined class. For example, in an argument about gay marriage that he has since modified, Judge Posner noted that "[t]o permit persons of the same sex to marry is to declare, or more precisely to be understood by many people to be declaring, that homosexual marriage is a desirable, even a noble, condition in which to live."[67] Moreover, he offered this justification for prohibiting same-sex marriage on an assumption that heterosexual orientation in those who bear it is immutable.

Finally, anti-gay constructivists are often willing to concede that many, if not most, existing gay men and lesbians cannot switch their sexual orientation. Instead, they tailor their anti-gay social policy to deter new enrollments in the class of homosexuals. For these anti-gay constructivists, the suffering of those who have already and irrevocably made that choice is unimportant—and so it doesn't matter, either, whether that suffering arises from discrimination gay men and lesbians are unable to duck because they cannot change their sexual orientation, or from transformative therapies that cause them anguish. Pattullo, for instance, reasons that even if only some children are sexual orientation "waverers," social policy must "give [them] clear, repeated signals as to society's preference" that they elect heterosexuality. This is the wise thing to do, Pattullo argues, even at the cost of "condemn[ing] youngsters, who from earliest memory know themselves to be gay," and a fortiori at the cost of condemning those who have chosen and now cannot revise their choice. Indeed, the pedagogical design of discrimination under this rationale makes public displays of suffering not merely acceptable but valuable, as the clearest signal of majority preferences imaginable.

An argument from immutability that relies on the futility of, and pain caused by, psychotherapeutic efforts at conversion does not refute a

---

[66]Edward Stein, *The Relevance of Scientific Research About Sexual Orientation to Lesbian and Gay Rights,* in Gay Ethics: Outing, Civil Rights and the Meaning of Science (forthcoming 1994).

[67]Posner, Sex and Reason, [312 (1992).]

program of discrimination actually tailored to prevent people who can choose to become homosexual from doing so in the first place. To refute anti-gay arguments taking this form, a legal argument from immutability needs biological causation. If pro-gay essentialists want to stay in the game, they will have to claim that homosexuality is immutable because it is biologically determined[.]

B. GENES

In the last thirty years, genetics has undergone an astonishing ascendancy among the life sciences. It has broken disciplinary limits it adopted in order to distance itself from Nazi eugenics, and now forthrightly seeks to explain not merely the characteristics of animals and the physiological features of humans, but human behavioral and psychological traits. Pro-gay essentialism rides the coattails of modern genetics' sweeping epistemological authority.

Recent developments in science have been invoked to support the claim that homosexuality is now known, or will soon be known, to be a biologically caused, immutable characteristic. For two reasons, this section will argue, pro-gay essentialists should hesitate to rely on these developments to support the argument from immutability. First, as scientific professionals have amply and repeatedly insisted, behavioral genetics in general, and the homosexuality studies in particular, do not support the claim that homosexual orientation is genetically caused and therefore an immutable characteristic. Second, pro-gay support for genetic explanations of sexual orientation may boomerang by validating the key premises of anti-gay eugenics.

[In another part of her article Halley examines and critiques the methods and claims of the most important recent studies of homosexual orientation. Even if pro-gay essentialists do not choose to heed the arguments offered there, she states,] they should beware of exaggerating the claims that human behavioral genetics can support as a general matter. Science professionals pursuing internal criticism of the behavioral genetics programme emphasize, first, that genetically caused characteristics are not necessarily immutable in the sense that they persist unchanged over time. For example, even if male pattern baldness is entirely genetically caused, it nevertheless emerges only in adulthood and then develops. And behavioral characteristics may exhibit even more complex developmental mutabilities than physical ones.

Nor are genetically caused characteristics necessarily immutable in the sense that they are immune from environmental influence. * * * At the same time, pro-gay essentialism takes some unacceptable risks when that approach borrows the plausibility of modern genetics. On a purely pragmatic level, pro-gay essentialism is just not different enough from anti-essentialism to mount an effective resistance to the development of anti-gay eugenics. Pro-gay essentialism fails to contest the arguments crucial to the discriminatory social policies of both anti-gay essentialism and anti-gay constructivism: that homosexuality is bad either because it is immoral or because it disrupts the social order. Pro-gay essentialism parsimoniously aims at the anti-gay constructivist premise that at least some homosexuality is chosen; but it neglects the second premise, that homosexuality is bad or harmful. Pro-gay constructivists worry that this failure to contest the moral and political meaning assigned to homosexuality leaves pro-gay essentialism vulnerable to cooptation. An anti-gay constructivist could convert to essentialism, maintaining the premise that homosexuality is bad for moral or civic order, agreeing with the important points explicitly made by pro-gay essentialism, and then, without breaking logical stride, undertake an eugenic program to eliminate homosexuals.

Anti-gay eugenics is more than a theoretical danger. Important mainstream scientists have praised the Human Genome Project for its eugenic potential, and researchers on the causes of homosexuality repeatedly acknowledge the possibility of anti-gay eugenics. Moreover, modern genetics aspires not to improve or purify a national or racial gene pool—a task that would require currently unimaginable levels of official participation—but to enable individual parents to prevent the birth of less-than-optimal infants through privately obtained prenatal testing and selective abortion. * * *

Pro-gay essentialism also embodies ideological dangers that could engender concrete political ones. Genetics does not merely describe reality; it also incorporates cultural norms into its premises and diffuses into the wider culture its own implicit norms and epistemological commitments. * * * Genetics thus raises the question of "how the authority for prescribing the meaning of 'normal' is distributed"—a question whose answer will emerge as scientific claims are interpreted and used in culture. One danger of shaping pro-gay legal strategy on genetics is that this pattern developed in genetic medicine will be reiterated in the context of sexuality: Definitions of the normal that exclude homosexuality will already be embedded in the science when it enters culture.

Nor is the danger simply that heterosexuals will get to define the normal as identical with themselves. Heterosexual identity is a complex, indeed unstable phenomenon, as is suggested by studies showing that men affirm their identities as heterosexual even when they acknowledge having recent same-sex contacts. The instability of genetic normality is mirrored in the instability of heterosexuality as a social-representational practice. Social-descriptive concepts that are this manipulable invite, and often receive, opportunistic redefinition in the political sphere. The power to define and redefine who and what the "normal" is, and who and what "heterosexuals" are, can become itself a method of doing politics to secure some aspects of social superordination. The overlap of genetic normality with heterosexual identity doubles the danger.

Despite the danger of the genetics model, however, it would be imprudent for pro-gay constructivists to insist that legal strategy exclude and contradict pro-gay essentialism. [R]obust scientific claims that homosexuality is genetically caused may be made any day now[.] Legal strategy predicated exclusively on pro-gay constructivism would be severely injured if and when researchers show, within the standards of proof that pertain in reputable modern science, that homosexuality as it is currently manifested in our culture is genetically determined. In that event, pro-gay constructivism could maintain its program of legal reform only by successfully attacking the standards of proof that pertain in reputable modem science. Though pro-gay constructivists are entitled to, and should continue to, mount such critiques, it may not be pragmatic to predicate legal strategy on their success.

C. AUTOBIOGRAPHIES

Tom McNaught stated an autobiography in three sentences: "It's not a matter of choice. It's who I am. . . . It's genetic."[90] Pro-gay essentialism makes autobiographical sense to a significant number of gay men and to many, though perhaps fewer, lesbians. But other people who experience anti-gay discrimination tell quite different stories. Some understand themselves to have chosen the form of their desire or the ways in which it structures their lives. Others occupy the hotly contested historical ground that homosexual identity is a product of modernity, not nature or human nature.

Still others worry that the designations "gay" and "lesbian" constrain at the very moment of their application. Among these are self-identified bisexuals, who repeatedly report the difficulty they confront in fitting their lives and experiences into the simple narrative form propounded by Tom McNaught. Other strong currents in the pro-gay movements critique the very impulse to organize around gay and lesbian identity, either because doing so suppresses a sexuality distinct and semi-autonomous from homosexuality, or because it obscures the historical, institutional, and political processes that produce identity. To the extent that these self-articulations are anticategorical, they are increasingly performed under the rubric "queer."

As long as people who suffer anti-gay discrimination differ about whether they were born or became gay—indeed, about whether they are gay—neither a purely essentialist nor a purely constructivist approach can adequately ground pro-gay legal theory. And differ we do, media reports to

---

[90]Tony Rogers, *"Why" of Homosexuality,* Chi. Trib., June 2, 1993, at C2 (quoting Tom McNaught).

the contrary notwithstanding. Immutability offers no theoretical foundation for legal protection of those gay men and lesbians who experience their sexual orientation as contingent, mutable, chosen. This exclusion will only get worse as a distinctive movement of bisexuals takes shape: The fairness theory of pro-gay essentialism does not explain why bisexuals—by hypothesis capable of satisfactory sexual encounters with members of the so-called "opposite" sex—should not be encouraged or forced to do so. But building a new foundation for legal protection on the contrary assumption—that sexual orientation is constructed and not biologically determined—would risk the same exclusion in reverse. An adequate legal theory should protect the entire social class on whose behalf it is articulated.

BIBLIOGRAPHY

Amar, *Attainder and Amendment 2:* Romer's *Rightness,* 95 Mich.L.Rev. 203 (1996).

Arriola, *Sexual Identity and the Constitution: Homosexual Persons as a Discrete and Insular Minority,* 10 Women's Rights L.Rep. 143 (1988).

Cicchino, *Reason and the Rule of Law: Should Bare Assertions of Public Morality Qualify as Legitimate Government Interests for the Purposes of Equal Protection Review?*, 87 Geo L.J. 139 (1998).

Conkle, *The Second Death of Substantive Due Process,* 62 Ind.L.J. 215 (1987).

Coolidge, *Same-Sex Marriage?* Baehr v. Miike *and the Meaning of Marriage,* 38 S.Tex.L.Rev. 1 (1997).

Delgado, *Fact, Norm, and Standard of Review—The Case of Homosexuality,* 10 U.Dayton L.Rev. 575 (1985).

Devlin, P., THE ENFORCEMENT OF MORALS (1965).

Duclos, *Some Complicating Thoughts on Same-Sex Marriage,* 1 Law & Sexuality 31 (1991).

Duncan, *From* Loving *to* Romer*: Homosexual Marriage and Moral Discernment*, 12 B.Y.U. J.Pub.L. 239 (1998).

Duncan, *Wigstock and the Kulturkampf; Supreme Court Storytelling, the Culture War, and* Romer v. Evans, *72* Notre Dame L.Rev. 345 (1997).

Dunlap, *The Lesbian and Gay Marriage Debate,* 1 Law & Sexuality 63 (1991).

Dworkin, R., *Lord Devlin and the Enforcement of Morals,* 75 Yale L.J. 986 (1966).

Eskridge, Hardwick *and Historiography*, 1999 U.Ill.L.Rev. 631 (1999).

Eskridge, *No Promo Homo: The Sedimentation of Antigay Discourse and the Channeling Effect of Judicial Review*, 75 N.Y.U. L.Rev. 1327 (2000).

Eskridge, *Democracy, Kulturkampf, and the Apartheid of the Closet,* 50 Vand.L.Rev. 419 (1997).

Eskridge, *Privacy Jurisprudence and the Apartheid of the Closet, 1946–1961,* 24 Fla.St.U.L.Rev. 703 (1997).

Eskridge, *Public Reason and Political Conflict: Abortion and Homosexuality,* 106 Yale L.J. 2475 (1997).

Eskridge, *A Social Constructionist Critique of Posner's* Sex and Reason: *Steps Toward a Gaylegal Agenda,* 102 Yale L.J. 333 (1992).

Fajer, *Can Two Real Men Eat Quiche Together? Storytelling, Gender-Role Stereotypes, and Legal Protection for Lesbians and Gay Men,* 46 U.Miami L.Rev. 511 (1992).

Farber and Sherry, *The Pariah Principle*, 13 Const.Comm. 257 (1996).

Finnis, *Law, Morality, and "Sexual Orientation",* 69 Notre Dame L.Rev. 1049 (1994).

Goldstein, *History, Homosexuality, and Political Values: Searching for the Hidden Determinants of* Bowers v. Hardwick, 97 Yale L.J. 1073 (1988).

Grey, *Eros, Civilization, and the Burger Court,* 43 L.& Contemp.Probs. 83 (1980).

Hager, *Freedom of Solidarity: Why The Boy Scout Case Was Rightly (But Wrongly) Decided*, 35 Conn.L.Rev. 129 (2002).

Hermann, *Homosexuality and the High Court*, 51 DePaul L.Rev. 1215 (2002).

Hart, H.L.A., LAW, LIBERTY AND MORALITY (1963).

Hunter, *Life after* Hardwick, 27 Harv.C.R.–C.L.L.Rev. 531 (1992).

Jacobs, Romer *Wasn't Built in a Day: The Subtle Transformation in Judicial Argument Over Gay Rights,* 1996 Wis.L.Rev 893.

Khan, *The Invasion of Sexual Privacy*, 23 San Diego L.Rev. 957 (1986).

Law, *Homosexuality and the Social Meaning of Gender,* 1988 Wis.L.Rev. 187.

Lewis, *Introduction*—Commonwealth v. Wasson: *Invalidating Kentucky's Sodomy Statute,* 81 Ky.L.Rev. 423 (1992).

Macedo, *Homosexuality and the Conservative Mind,* 84 Geo.L.J. 261 (1995).

Maroney, Bowers v. Hardwick: *A Case Study in Federalism, Legal Procedure, and Constitutional Interpretation,* 38 Syracuse L.Rev. 1223 (1987).

Note, *Developments in the Law—Sexual Orientation and the Law,* 102 Harv.L.Rev. 1508 (1989).

Ortiz, *Creating Controversy: Essentialism and Constructivism and the Politics of Gay Identity,* 79 Va.L.Rev. 1833 (1993).

Posner, R., SEX AND REASON (1992).

Richards, *Unnatural Acts and the Constitutional Right to Privacy: A Moral Theory,* 45 Fordham L.Rev. 1281 (1977).

Richards, *Sexual Autonomy and the Constitutional Right to Privacy: A Case Study in Human Rights and the Unwritten Constitution,* 30 Hast.L.J. 957 (1979).

Rivera, *Our Straight—Laced Judges: The Legal Position of Homosexual Persons in the United States,* 30 Hast.L.J. 799 (1979).

Sims, *Moving Towards Equal Treatment of Homosexuals,* 23 Pac.L.J. 1543 (1992).

Spindelman, *Reorienting* Bowers v. Hardwick, 79 N.C.L.Rev. 359 (2001).

Stoddard, Bowers v. Hardwick: *Precedent by Personal Predilection,* 54 U.Chi.L.Rev. 648 (1987).

Sunstein, *Homosexuality and the Constitution,* 70 Ind.L.J. 1 (1994)

Sunstein, *Sexual Orientation and the Constitution: A Note on the Relationship Between Due Process and Equal Protection,* 55 U.Chi.L.Rev. 1161 (1988).

Survey on the Constitutional Right to Privacy in the Context of Homosexual Activity, 40 U.Miami L.Rev. 521 (1986).

Symposium, *Gay Rights and the Courts: The Amendment 2 Controversy,* 68 U.Colo.L.Rev. 285 (1997).

Symposium, *Group Conflict and the Constitution: Race, Sexuality, and Religion,* 106 Yale L.J. 2313 (1997)

Symposium, *Law, Community, and Moral Reasoning,* 77 Calif.L.Rev. 475 (1989).

Symposium, *Romer v. Evans,* 6 Wm. & Mary Bill Rts.J. 89 (1997)

Symposium, *Sex, Politics, & the Law: Lesbians and Gay Men Take the Offensive,* 14 N.Y.U.Rev. of L. & Soc.Change 891 (1986).

Symposium, *Symposium on Sexual Orientation,* 9 Notre Dame J.L. Ethics & Pub.Pol'y 1 (1995).

Symposium, *Sexual Morality and the Possibility of "Same-Sex Marriage",* 42 Am.J.Juris. 51 (1997).

Symposium, *The Bill of Rights vs. the Ballot Box: Constitutional Implications of Anti—Gay Ballot Initiatives,* 55 Ohio St.L.J. 491 (1994).

Vieira, Hardwick *and the Right of Privacy,* 55 U.Chi.L.Rev. 1181 (1988).

West, *Taking Preferences Seriously,* 64 Tulane L.Rev. 659 (1990).

D. THE RIGHT TO DIE

The right to die is quite a modern issue. When life was shorter people avoided death. Advances in medical science now enable most of us to reach old age. Machines and drugs can then keep us going indefinitely as our systems wear out. It was possibilities like these that provoked the first kind of problem to reach the Supreme Court. *Cruzan v. Director, Missouri Dept. of Health*[1] involved a patient who was in a persistent vegetative state. The Court assumed, though it did not actually decide, that competent people have a constitutional right to refuse or discontinue lifesaving treatment. It held, though, that a state was entitled to require clear and convincing proof of her wishes before allowing treatment to be withdrawn.

A patient who is conscious and able to express her own desires presents none of these difficulties. But suppose that she wants to commit suicide rather than to decline treatment. Suppose too, to make the issue more poignant, that she is in great physical distress and likely to die shortly in any event. Should we let someone like this make up her own mind about when to die? Should we say that the Constitution gives her that right? The Supreme Court's abortion jurisprudence hinted that it might. The Court said in *Planned Parenthood v. Casey* that "the most intimate and personal choices a person may make in a lifetime, choices central to a person's dignity and autonomy, are central to the liberty protected by the Fourteenth Amendment."[2] Does this observation embrace suicide as well as abortion?

In *Washington v. Glucksberg*[3] the Supreme Court considered an issue one short step removed from this question: whether a state law against assisting suicide violated the Due Process Clause. It held that it did not, against the advice of six of America's most famous moral philosophers. An amicus curiae brief filed by Ronald Dworkin, Thomas Nagel, Robert Nozick, John Rawls, Thomas Scanlon, and Judith Jarvis Thomson asserted that *Casey* recognized a fundamental right to make autonomous decisions about life's most important questions. Ending life is certainly one of these. There are, to be sure, differences between abortion and suicide, but the philosophers argued that they do not warrant outright denial of the latter right.

John Garvey disagrees. The philosophers assume that freedom is a two-way street—that it protects contradictory choices like childbirth and

---

[1]497 U.S. 261, 110 S.Ct. 2841, 111 L.Ed.2d 224(1990).

[2]505 U.S. 833, 851, 112 S.Ct. 2791, 120 L.Ed.2d 674 (1992).

[3]521 U.S. 702, 117 S.Ct. 2258, 138 L.Ed.2d 772 (1997).

abortion, life and death. But why should we make that assumption? For the philosophers, it is because we need to be in control of our own lives. But *is* control the point of life? Garvey argues that that is a thin (and sometimes perverse) ideal, and that courage in the face of death is a greater virtue. He does not argue for punishing suicide. But he says it would be a mistake to raise suicide to the status of a fundamental right on the basis of a weak, controversial, and perhaps mistaken view of life.

Michael McConnell criticizes the philosophers' approach from a different perspective. He thinks that it is risky for courts as institutions to enforce fundamental rights not grounded in the text of the Constitution or deeply rooted in history and tradition. If a practice is widely adopted and long maintained, we have strong evidence that it contributes to the common good and fits our considered sense of right and wrong. The "moral philosophic" approach, by contrast, assumes that judges are wiser, fairer, and more reflective decisionmakers than the rest of us. It also runs an asymmetrical risk of error. When judges refuse to recognize a new fundamental right (as the Court did in *Glucksberg*) we can improve on their decision if our convictions change; when they create new rights (as in *Roe*) we are stuck.

BRIEF FOR RONALD DWORKIN, THOMAS NAGEL, ROBERT NOZICK, JOHN RAWLS, THOMAS SCANLON, AND JUDITH JARVIS THOMSON AS AMICI CURIAE IN *WASHINGTON v. GLUCKSBERG*

Amici are six moral and political philosophers who differ on many issues of public morality and policy. They are united, however, in their conviction that respect for fundamental principles of liberty and justice, as well as for the American constitutional tradition, requires that the decisions of the Courts of Appeals be affirmed. * * *

I. THE LIBERTY INTEREST ASSERTED HERE IS PROTECTED BY THE DUE PROCESS CLAUSE

The Due Process Clause of the Fourteenth Amendment protects the liberty interest asserted by the patient-plaintiffs here.

Certain decisions are momentous in their impact on the character of a person's life—decisions about religious faith, political and moral allegiance, marriage, procreation and death, for example. Such deeply personal decisions pose controversial questions about how and why human life has value. In a free society, individuals must be allowed to make those decisions for themselves, out of their own faith, conscience and convictions. This Court has insisted, in a variety of contexts and circumstances, that this great freedom is among those protected by the Due Process Clause as essential to a community of "ordered liberty." *Palko v. Connecticut,* 302

U.S. 319, 325 (1937). In its recent decision in *Planned Parenthood v. Casey,* 505 U.S. 833, 851 (1992), the Court offered a paradigmatic statement of that principle:

> matters[ ] involving the most intimate and personal choices a person may make in a lifetime, choices central to a person's dignity and autonomy, are central to the liberty protected by the Fourteenth Amendment. * * *

A person's interest in following his own convictions at the end of life is so central a part of the more general right to make "intimate and personal choices" for himself that a failure to protect that particular interest would undermine the general right altogether. Death is, for each of us, among the most significant events of life. As the Chief Justice said in *Cruzan v. Missouri,* 497 U.S. 261, 281 (1990), "[t]he choice between life and death is a deeply personal decision of obvious and overwhelming finality." Most of us see death—whatever we think will follow it—as the final act of life's drama, and we want that last act to reflect our own convictions, those we have tried to live by, not the convictions of others forced on us in our most vulnerable moment.

Different people, of different religious and ethical beliefs, embrace very different convictions about which way of dying confirms and which contradicts the value of their lives. Some fight against death with every weapon their doctors can devise. Others will do nothing to hasten death even if they pray it will come soon. Still others, including the patient-plaintiffs in these cases, want to end their lives when they think that living on, in the only way they can, would disfigure rather than enhance the lives they had created. Some people make the latter choice not just to escape pain. Even if it were possible to eliminate all pain for a dying patient—and frequently that is not possible—that would not end or even much alleviate the anguish some would feel at remaining alive, but intubated, helpless and often sedated near oblivion. * * *

II. THIS COURT'S DECISION [IN *CASEY* COMPELS] RECOGNITION OF A LIBERTY INTEREST HERE

In *Casey,* this Court, in holding that a State cannot constitutionally proscribe abortion in all cases, reiterated that the Constitution protects a sphere of autonomy in which individuals must be permitted to make certain decisions for themselves. The Court began its analysis by pointing out that "[a]t the heart of liberty is the right to define one's own concept of existence, of meaning, of the universe, and of the mystery of human life." Choices flowing out of these conceptions, on matters "involving the most intimate and personal choices a person may make in a lifetime, choices central to personal dignity and autonomy, are central to the liberty protected by the Fourteenth Amendment." "Beliefs about these matters," the Court continued, "could not define the attributes of personhood were they formed under compulsion of the State."

In language pertinent to the liberty interest asserted here, the Court explained why decisions about abortion fall within this category of "personal and intimate" decisions. A decision whether or not to have an abortion, "originat[ing] within the zone of conscience and belief," involves conduct in which "the liberty of the woman is at stake in a sense unique to the human condition and so unique to the law." As such, the decision necessarily involves the very "destiny of the woman" and is inevitably "shaped to a large extent on her own conception of her spiritual imperatives and her place in society." Precisely because of these characteristics of the decision, "the State is [not] entitled to proscribe [abortion] in all instances." Rather, to allow a total prohibition on abortion would be to permit a state to impose one conception of the meaning and value of human existence on all individuals. This the Constitution forbids. * * *

The analysis in *Casey* compels the conclusion that the patient-plaintiffs have a liberty interest in this case that a state cannot burden with a blanket prohibition. Like a woman's decision whether to have an abortion, a decision to die involves one's very "destiny" and inevitably will be "shaped to a large extent on [one's] own conception of [one's] spiritual imperatives and [one's] place in society." Just as a blanket prohibition on abortion would involve the improper imposition of one conception of the meaning and value of human existence on all individuals, so too would a blanket prohibition on assisted suicide. The liberty interest asserted here cannot be rejected without undermining the rationale of *Casey*. * * *

III. STATE INTERESTS DO NOT JUSTIFY A CATEGORICAL PROHIBITION ON ALL ASSISTED SUICIDE

[The government argues that even if a terminally ill adult has a liberty interest at stake in cases like this,] states nevertheless have the right to "override" this liberty interest altogether, because a state could reasonably conclude that allowing doctors to assist in suicide, even under the most stringent regulations and procedures that could be devised, would unreasonably endanger the lives of a number of patients who might ask for death in circumstances when it is plainly not in their interests to die or when their consent has been improperly obtained.

This argument is unpersuasive, however, for at least three reasons. First, in *Cruzan,* this Court noted that its various decisions supported the recognition of a general liberty interest in refusing medical treatment, even when such refusal could result in death. The various risks described by the [government] apply equally to those situations. For instance, a patient kept alive only by an elaborate and disabling life support system might well become depressed, and doctors might be equally uncertain whether the depression is curable: such a patient might decide for death only because he has been advised that he will die soon anyway or that he will never live free of the burdensome apparatus, and either diagnosis might conceivably be mistaken. Relatives or doctors might subtly or crudely influence that decision, and state provision for the decision may (to the same degree in this case as if it allowed assisted suicide) be thought to encourage it. * * *

Indeed, the risks of mistake are overall greater in the case of terminating life support. *Cruzan* implied that a state must allow individuals to make such decisions through an advance directive stipulating either that life support be terminated (or not initiated) in described circumstances when the individual was no longer competent to make such a decision himself, or that a designated proxy be allowed to make that decision. All the risks just described are present when the decision is made through or pursuant to such an advance directive, and a grave further risk is added: that the directive, though still in force, no longer represents the wishes of the patient. The patient might have changed his mind before he became incompetent, though he did not change the directive, or his proxy may make a decision that the patient would not have made himself if still competent. In *Cruzan*, this Court held that a state may limit these risks through reasonable regulation. It did not hold—or even suggest—that a state may avoid them through a blanket prohibition that, in effect, denies the liberty interest altogether.

Second, nothing in the record supports the conclusion that no system of rules and regulations could adequately reduce the risk of mistake. As discussed above, the experience of states in adjudicating requests to have life-sustaining treatment removed indicates the opposite. The [government] has provided no persuasive reason why the same sort of procedures could not be applied effectively in the case of a competent individual's request for physician-assisted suicide.

Third, it is doubtful whether the risks the [government] cites are even of the right character to serve as justification for an absolute prohibition on the exercise of an important liberty interest. The risks fall into two groups. The first is the risk of medical mistake, including a misdiagnosis of competence or terminal illness. To be sure, no scheme of regulation, no matter how rigorous, can altogether guarantee that medical mistakes will not be made. But the Constitution does not allow a state to deny patients a great variety of important choices, for which informed consent is properly deemed necessary, just because the information on which the consent is given may, in spite of the most strenuous efforts to avoid mistake, be wrong. Again, these identical risks are present in decisions to terminate life support, yet they do not justify an absolute prohibition on the exercise of the right.

The second group consists of risks that a patient will be unduly influenced by considerations that the state might deem it not in his best interests to be swayed by, for example, the feelings and views of close family members. But what a patient regards as proper grounds for such a decision normally reflects exactly the judgments of personal ethics—of why his life is important and what affects its value—that patients have a crucial liberty interest in deciding for themselves. Even people who are dying have a right to hear and, if they wish, act on what others might wish to tell or suggest or even hint to them, and it would be dangerous to suppose that a state may prevent this on the ground that it knows better than its citizens when they should be moved by or yield to particular advice or suggestion in the exercise of their right to make fateful personal decisions for themselves. It is not a good reply that some people may not decide as they really wish—as they would decide, for example, if free from the "pressure" of others. That possibility could hardly justify the most serious pressure of all—the criminal law which tells them that they may not decide for death if they need the help of a doctor in dying, no matter how firmly they wish it. * * *

Of course, a state has important interests that justify regulating physician-assisted suicide. It may be legitimate for a state to deny an opportunity for assisted suicide when it acts in what it reasonably judges to be the best interests of the potential suicide, and when its judgment on that issue does not rest on contested judgments about "matters involving the most intimate and personal choices a person may make in a lifetime, choices central to personal dignity and autonomy." *Casey,* 505 U.S. at 851. A state might assert, for example, that people who are not terminally ill, but who have formed a desire to die, are, as a group, very likely later to be grateful if they are prevented from taking their own lives. It might then claim that it is legitimate, out of concern for such people, to deny any of them a doctor's assistance. This Court need not decide now the extent to which such paternalistic interests might override an individual's liberty interest. No one can plausibly claim, however[,] that any such prohibition could serve the interests of any significant number of terminally ill patients. On the contrary, any paternalistic justification for an absolute prohibition of assistance to such patients would of necessity appeal to a widely contested religious or ethical conviction many of them, including the patient-plaintiffs, reject. Allowing that justification to prevail would vitiate the liberty interest.

JOHN H. GARVEY, CONTROL FREAKS

47 DRAKE L. REV. 1–4, 8, 11–17 (1998).

I. AUTONOMY

Let me begin by describing the theory that the Court [rejected in *Wash-*

ington v. Glucksberg.][1] If I had to state it in one sentence, it would be this: freedom is a right to make choices. Here we have a choice between life and death and, the theory holds, we are not free unless we can choose either option. There are other ways of understanding freedom. I will propose a different one later on. But this is a powerful and popular theory, and it warrants close examination. It persuaded Judge Reinhardt and an en banc panel of the Ninth Circuit, whose decision the Supreme Court reversed. And it was supported in the Supreme Court by an amicus brief filed by six of America's best-known moral philosophers. Why would such a distinguished lot of judges and academics insist on a right to commit suicide?

The first clue can be found in the Ninth Circuit's observation that "[d]espite the marvels of technology, Americans frequently die with less dignity than they did in the days when ravaging diseases typically ended their lives quickly. [Many] terminally ill patients . . . die protracted and painful deaths." A protracted and painful death is an awful thing, to be sure. But is it necessarily undignified? The Ninth Circuit assumed that it was. And being a court, not a moral philosophy forum, it probably had in mind the deaths of the plaintiffs, who had sued to invalidate Washington's law against assisted suicide. One of them, Jane Roe, was a sixty-nine-year-old woman with cancer who had less than six months to live. She was bedridden, medicated, and in pain. She also, the court said, suffered from "poor appetite, nausea and vomiting, impaired vision, incontinence of bowel, and general weakness." James Poe, also sixty-nine, was dying of emphysema and heart failure. He was hooked to an oxygen tank at all times and took morphine to calm his fear of suffocation. John Doe, a former painter, was dying of AIDS at the age of forty-four. He was going blind, had chronic infections, grand mal seizures, and extreme fatigue.

The second clue to the court's way of thinking lies in those symptoms that it chose to stress. All of the patients were weak: Jane Roe was bedridden, James Poe was tied to an oxygen tank, and John Doe suffered from extreme fatigue. Sometimes, along with a lack of strength, went a loss of ordinary senses: John Doe suffered from seizures; he and Jane Roe were losing their sight. This was especially difficult for John Doe, who was a painter. The loss of control would occasionally extend to more ordinary and embarrassing functions: Jane Roe suffered from nausea, vomiting, and incontinence. Finally, all these people were of course in pain. Jane Roe's cancer had spread throughout her skeleton, and moving caused her severe pain which medication could not fully alleviate. James Poe took morphine to calm his panic at the feeling of suffocation.

These symptoms signify a loss of control over the patient's own life. As the court put it at one point, each of these people was "reduced at the end of

---

[1] 521 U.S. 702 (1997).

his existence to a childlike state of helplessness, diapered, sedated, incontinent." When the court spoke of dying with dignity, what it meant was dying while still in control—before the onset of helplessness and second childhood. Death is not a very attractive choice in the ordinary case but, the court opined, people might want to choose it rather than lose control over their lives.

This is a coherent theory, but it is not yet a constitutional argument. There is nothing in the language or history of the Constitution suggesting that it was meant to secure to us this measure of control. Indeed, the Due Process Clause suggests the contrary: it protects *life*, liberty, and property against government interference. It does not protect death. There is, however, some legal precedent for the court of appeals' decision. In *Roe v. Wade* the Supreme Court held that a pregnant woman had a constitutional right to end the life inside her, though there continues to be disagreement about whether that life is a fully human person like you and me. In *Planned Parenthood v. Casey* the Court explained why that right was one of the liberties guaranteed us by the Due Process Clause:

> These matters, involving the most intimate and personal choices a person may make in a lifetime, choices central to personal dignity and autonomy, are central to the liberty protected by the Fourteenth Amendment. At the heart of liberty is the right to define one's own concept of existence, of meaning, of the universe, and of the mystery of human life. Beliefs about these matters could not define the attributes of personhood were they formed under compulsion of the State.[28]

This sounds like a bad freshman philosophy paper—the "concept of existence, of meaning, of the universe." But the idea it tries to express is this: it is a good thing for me to be in control of my own life. That is what "autonomy" means—being self-governing. I am only in control if I can make the choices I want. Freedom is the right to make those choices. Indeed, in some ways *Glucksberg* is an easier case than *Roe* and *Casey*. The person who commits suicide takes her own life, of which she is in control. The person who procures an abortion takes the life of another. If that is protected, then a fortiori this case should be.

Let me return now to the thumbnail description of freedom I began with: I said that according to one theory, it is a right to make choices. This means that freedom is a two-way street. Unless I can travel in both directions, I cannot define my "own concept of existence, of meaning, of the universe." Thus, the Supreme Court has said that "[t]he right to speak and the right to refrain from speaking are complementary components of the broader concept of 'individual freedom of mind.'"[31] The First

[28] [505 U.S. 833, 851 (1992).]

[31] Wooley v. Maynard, 430 U.S. 705, 714 (1977) (quoting Board of Educ. v. Barnette,

Amendment freedom to exercise one's religion protects atheists as well as believers.[32] The "concept of personal liberty [protects] a woman's decision whether or not to terminate her pregnancy."[33] And so it should be with life and death: the freedom to live should entail the freedom to "determin[e] the time and manner of one's own death."

I expect that this theory sounds pretty familiar—maybe even self-evident. But the Court rejected it in *Glucksberg*, and so do I. [Garvey suggests a number of difficulties with the autonomy theory, and then proposes an alternative.]

II. COURAGE

Let me turn now from the view of freedom espoused by Judge Reinhardt and the philosophers to the one that I argue for * * *. The former, I have said, is a right to make choices. I have used the metaphor of a two-way street to emphasize the proposition that our choices can go either way (speech-silence; childbirth-abortion; life-death). There is no preferred destination. My own view is very different. I think that freedoms are rights to go in some ways and not others. We might picture them as one-way streets. They might protect childbirth but not abortion, religion but not atheism,[62] life but not death. The right still does important work in this more modest highway system. If I am free to travel west (let us say) on a particular road, my right means that the government may not put up stop signs, speed traps, or bumps to inhibit my progress in that direction. But it can regulate my going the other way.

[That is how I say it is with life and death. It is better to live life out to its natural end than to commit suicide. Our rights in this matter run in one direction but not the other. This is why people do not have the freedom to kill themselves.] We often make the mistake of confusing the virtue of courage with the exercise of power or control. In the movie *The Edge*, Anthony Hopkins plays a rich man who gets stranded in the Alaskan wilderness while on a photographic expedition. Before he can get back home safely, he is obliged to kill a bear with his hands and disarm his own companion, who is intent on taking his life. As he explains early and late in the movie, the rabbit is not afraid of the fox, because the rabbit knows that he is smarter. This is our image of courage: the ability to take control of a difficult situation and bring about the outcome we desire.

---

319 U.S. 624, 637 (1943)).

[32]Torcaso v. Watkins, 367 U.S. 488, 495 (1961).

[33]Roe v. Wade, 410 U.S. 113, 153 (1973).

[62]See Wisconsin v. Yoder, 406 U.S. 205 (1972). Given more space I would qualify this point. As I explain [elsewhere,] we will often want to protect nonreligious actors for religious reasons. See John H. Garvey, What Are Freedoms For? 42–57 (1996). The Church of England should not force either Jews or atheists to attend services on Sunday, chiefly because there is no religious merit in forced observance. Id. at 50, 55–57.

The important part of this picture, however, is not the outcome but the attitude with which one faces death. The character played by Anthony Hopkins is little more than a cartoon figure compared to Oedipus, who fell from kingship to rags but bore his fate to death heroically. *Oedipus at Colonus* tells the story of his last days. Twenty years after he left Thebes, the blinded Oedipus came with Antigone to Colonus in Attica, about a mile from Athens. He tells on his arrival of how he reacted to the knowledge of his fate:

The truth is that at first
My mind was a boiling caldron; nothing so sweet
As death, death by stoning, could have been given me;
Yet no one there would grant me that desire.
It was only later, when my madness cooled,
And I had begun to think my rage excessive,
My punishment too great for what I had done;
Then it was that the city—in its good time!—
Decided to be harsh, and drove me out.[70]

From then until his arrival at Colonus he wandered "blind, bearded and ragged." He had fallen as far as he could from the proud king who unwittingly killed his father and married his mother. He confesses that he is no longer in control. He depends upon Antigone to lead him:

Pity a man's poor carcase and his ghost,
For Oedipus is not the strength he was.
. . .
That must be evident: why, otherwise
Should I need this girl
To lead me, her frailty to put my weight on?[72]

And yet he is an admirable character, above all because he lives out to the end the chorus's injunction: "Whatever God has brought about is to be borne with courage." Even at the end he is no angel. His interviews with Creon and with Polyneices show the anger of his youth and the bitterness of his old age. But he rewards Athens with a blessing for receiving him to die. And when Antigone reflects upon her part in his last days, she seems to strike exactly the right note:

One may long for the past
Though at the time indeed it seemed
Nothing but wretchedness and evil.
Life was not sweet, yet I found it so
When I could put my arms around my father.[74]

---

[70][*Oedipus at Colonus* in 3 Greek Tragedies 130–131 (David Grene & Richmond Lattimore eds. & Robert Fitzgerald Trans., 1968).]

[72]Id. at 116, 118.

[U]nless we have gone through it, we may make the mistake of supposing that caring for the old and feeble, even when their minds begin to fail, is a relationship that only runs one way. When they die courageously they may give us as much as we give them. Oedipus, like Antigone, reflects on this in his last words to his daughters:

> Children, this day your father is gone from you.
> All that was mine is gone. You shall no longer
> Bear the burden of taking care of me—
> I know it was hard, my children.—And yet one word
> Makes all those difficulties disappear:
> That word is love. You never shall have more
> From any man than you have had from me.[75]

Had he had his wish and died at the peak of his misery, Oedipus would have spared himself years of suffering and disgrace. His life would in that sense have finished with a better balance of happiness and pain. But he would not have shown the virtue of courage that redeemed his failures. Sophocles puts his own reflection into the mouth of the messenger who opens the last scene: "[I]ndeed his end was wonderful if mortal's ever was."

I have been trying to make the point that living out the virtue of courage is an act, or more precisely an attitude, that is good in itself. It is not so just for those who choose to see it that way. It is something we all should admire, and if we find ourselves in the unfortunate circumstances where it is called for, we should hope to imitate. This is not a proposition I can prove. It is nonetheless one whose truth I think we can recognize, particularly if we stand it beside the thinner ideal of staying in control, getting what we want, and, at a minimum, avoiding a painful end. It is better, though harder, to live courageously than to die quickly by one's own hand. That is what I mean when I assert that the right to life is a one-way street.

Of course, it is easy for me to say this as I, in the prime of life, reflect on other peoples' misery. I do not condemn those who commit suicide while in the depths of despair or in the thrall of pain. I am making a more modest point. It is simply that although I can understand the temptation of suicide, I do not view it as an act so infused with value that we should classify it as a fundamental right. I would not punish those who attempt it and fail, and I would certainly not attack the estates of those who succeed. But I think we should not encourage or assist people to take that path, and the states are right to punish those who do.

To this point, I have focused only on the virtue of courage at the hour of death. I now want to make two other points. The first is that the consequences of suicide linger back as well as on. The way we die affects the

---

[74]Id. at 183–184.

[75]Id. at 180–181.

way we live. This sounds paradoxical—like talking about Shakespeare's effect on Plutarch. But I mean it in a fairly literal sense. I have already alluded to one facet of this interplay. It is the fashion, in the literature of popular psychology, to talk about the stages of life, as though we spanned so many baseball seasons, each with its own drama and conclusion. But our judgments of people take their whole lives into account. Oedipus at Colonus is the same person as Oedipus Rex. His death redeems his life. It did not look that way when the chorus closed upon him in Oedipus Rex:

> You that live in my ancestral Thebes, behold this Oedipus,—
> him who knew the famous riddles and was a man most masterful;
> not a citizen who did not look with envy on his lot—
> see him now and see the breakers of misfortune swallow him!
> Look upon that last day always. Count no mortal happy till
> he has passed the final limit of his life secure from pain.[77]

At that point, his loss of mastery seemed to spell the end of an enviable life. But his end was further off, and it "was wonderful if ever mortal's was." Our rounded judgment of him is much kinder than the chorus suggested it would be.

Our deaths affect our lives in another, more literal, sense that I have not yet spoken of. I love my children dearly, and it would be my delight in life to have them move in next door to us when they are grown and married. But I began telling them at an early age, "Once you graduate from college, you are out of the house." My older and wiser friends tell me this is a vain hope. Nevertheless, they understand my point, which is this: I would like my children to become self-reliant, to prepare themselves eventually to support themselves, and to live lives of their own. Their typical reaction early on has been one of disbelief. "Dad, you don't really mean that if I couldn't find a job and had no money you would turn me away?" But I have assured them repeatedly that I mean exactly that (or at least I think I do), and that bleak prospect has now become an accepted fact of life—or maybe a regrettable consequence of my hard-heartedness.

The contemplation of our own death is not unlike this. It is a fact that we awaken to at a fairly early age, and the lesson is reinforced from time to time as those close to us die—grandparents, parents, uncles, aunts, friends, brothers, and sisters. Those events figure importantly in the accounts of our lives, but our reflection upon them is itself a subject of common consideration. Think of paintings like Caravaggio's *St. Jerome Writing*[. An] aged St. Jerome wrapped in a red blanket leans on a desk, his pen poised, studying a large book upon which he is writing a commentary. To his right, perched precariously on a couple more books, is a skull silently observing him

[77][*Oedipus Rex* in 1 Greek Tragedies 107, 176 (David Grene & Richmond Lattimore eds. & David Grene trans., 1968).]

through sightless eyes. He seems to ignore it at the moment, but it is surely present in the back of his mind. After all he put it there, as recently as he opened the book it rests upon. It is as relevant to his composition as the text he is poring over—one supposes the vulgate translation of the Bible. I do not imagine, though he is old, that it is the nearness of the event that prompts his reflection on it (as though he were actually doing two things, rather than one, and watching the biological clock to make sure he finished before quitting time). His own bald head has the same shape as the skull; they lean toward each other at the same angle and on about the same level. The one reflects the other. One gets the feeling that they are the same person, one version dressed up a bit more. Jerome's own death is present in his life, while he is in the very act of doing his most important work.

[My point is not just that we worry about the prospect of death.] It is that we think about it in preparation, asking ourselves, as Daniel Callahan has said, "How should I want to live in order that I may die well?"[83] If it is our ambition to maintain control at all costs, even if it means self-destruction to cheat the reaper, that attitude will work its way into our daily life. There are, after all, innumerable reverses that we all must suffer before the end—pain, debility, failure, loss. It is one thing to try our best to overcome them. That is the natural and right reaction. But we will not always prevail. And when we do not, the resolution to deal with death by suicide finds an earlier outlet in a desire to run, or deny our shortcomings. If our dignity depends on our ability to control our bodies, our lives, and our surroundings, as Judge Reinhardt's opinion suggests, we cannot face failure without a loss of self-respect.

Our attitude will be different if we understand that heroes are born from the struggle with necessity. By preparing ourselves to face death with courage, we will make ourselves into the kind of people who can face life with the same attitude. Physical disability, sickness, and pain do not diminish our dignity. On the contrary, much as we rightly dread them, they are occasions for a life of courage.

I said I wanted to make two further points about the virtue of courage before the hour of death. The first had to do with our own lives. The second concerns our dealings with other people. The character we cultivate in anticipation of death affects them too. The preoccupation with self-control that we see in the court of appeals' opinion and the philosophers' brief is often connected with, or grows out of, a conviction that I am the most important person in my life, that you are the most important person in yours, and that the government is only justified in regulating our behavior when it impinges on another's personal space. Acts that are purely self-regarding—and suicide is one of them—are not the government's concern.

---

[83]Daniel Callahan, The Troubled Dream of Life 148 (1993).

I dispute this. I do not think that our lives are strictly our own, and I think that suicide affects the lives of others in several ways, some of which warrant efforts to prevent it. There are, to begin with, the obligations that arise from family and other social responsibilities that we will shirk by leaving. Some, like mine to my wife and children, we undertake voluntarily. Others, to our parents or siblings, for example, we do not. There are, I suppose, some unfortunate people, whose despair at life can be explained at least in part by the absence of such ties, who might object that their debts of that kind have all been satisfied, and it is an interesting question whether they still owe duties to a larger community sufficiently important to warrant their being kept alive. Durkheim reports that in ancient Athens a citizen had to get permission of the Senate before committing suicide—a fact that implies a belief that the state had an interest in insisting on some people's continued service.[85] Fidel Castro in 1964 made the following statement about a man named Augusto Martinez Sanchez, an official of the Cuban revolutionary government who had committed suicide: "We believe that Comrade Martinez could not consciously have committed this act, since every revolutionary knows that he does not have the right to deprive his cause of a life that does not belong to him, and that he can only sacrifice against an enemy."[86] These are not arguments we hear in the United States, and the reason probably is that we take a different view of our relations to the state. But though I prefer our concept of citizenship to these, I am not sure that it is a necessary or a happy feature of ours that we should have no obligation to live for one another.

I pass over this speculation without further comment, because I want to direct attention to two further effects that our suicides may have on others, and that are more closely bound up with the virtue of courage. The first of these is the mundane observation that others may follow our example. In forming our own lives we often look to others whom we admire for a pattern to follow. We are ourselves, though perhaps unwittingly, the objects of this same kind of imitation. It is no statistical anomaly that suicide increases the likelihood of further suicides among family members. Our moral responsibility for these consequences is obviously tempered by the fact that we do not intend them. We are nevertheless aware of them, and that alone (causation plus knowledge) is sometimes a sufficient ground for moral responsibility. To put it in old-fashioned terms, it is bad to cause scandal. The flip side of this is equally worthy of our attention: when we exemplify the virtue of courage in the way we deal with misfortune we set a good example that not only deserves praise but also inspires imitation.

The case of assisted suicide gives a further accent to this observation. The patients in *Glucksberg* wanted not just to end their own lives, but to get

[85]Emile Durkheim, Suicide 330 (John A. Spaulding & George Simpson trans. 1951).

[86]Michael Walzer, Obligations 172 (1970).

the assistance of their doctors in doing so. If we suppose that actions like suicide are purely self-regarding and have no adverse social effects, then doctors and others do no wrong in enabling us to get what we want. But if we bear some moral responsibility for the pattern we offer for others to imitate, we do a further wrong by drawing others in. Their assistance improves our chances of succeeding (that, after all, was the reason for the lawsuit). It also adds respectability to our choice by enlisting more participants in our cause.

The second of the further effects that I had in mind is this: I suggested earlier that the way we die affects the way we live—the character we form in preparation for death is the one we bring to bear on crises short of the last. We should keep that in mind because it affects the goodness of our own lives, not just of our deaths. But it also has spillover effects on the way we see and deal with others. If I think my own dignity depends on my ability to control my mind and body, I will probably make a similar judgment about you. I might consider you less deserving of my respect when you have lost the battle with pain, debility, or mental illness. Opponents of assisted suicide often claim that it is only a short step away from euthanasia. There is more truth to this than we might think. It is not just that the right to choose one's own destiny ("define one's own concept of existence") demands extension to ever larger classes of claimants (even those who, because of mental debility, are unable to assert it for themselves). It is that by equating human dignity with control we invite the conclusion that they can be lost together. Defective newborns, the retarded, the aged and senile, and others who are not autonomous actors may lose our respect as well.

MICHAEL W. MCCONNELL, THE RIGHT TO DIE AND THE JURISPRUDENCE OF TRADITION

1997 UTAH L.REV. 665–669, 681–690.

Like *Brown v. Board of Education* and *Lochner v. New York* before it, *Roe v. Wade* was the galvanizing constitutional decision of a generation. *Roe* stood for the proposition that federal judges can legitimately decide fundamental questions of social policy on the basis of their own normative judgment, even in the face of nearly unanimous contrary determinations under the positive law of the states.

Much of the constitutional scholarship in the decades after *Roe,* and many of the Court's subsequent decisions, can be seen as a reflection on whether such a power, vested in an unelected judiciary, is legitimate. For the most part, in the years after *Roe,* the courts found reason not to repeat the experiment—even in cases, like *Bowers v. Hardwick,* which presented a more compelling argument for a "privacy" right than that in *Roe.* But decisions in this period were based on their particular facts, and no attempt to articulate an alternative constitutional methodology ever commanded five votes. On the one side, Justice Scalia thundered that the courts were usurping authority that, in our democratic system, belongs to representatives of the people. On the other side, Justices Brennan and Blackmun charged that Scalia and his allies would make the Constitution a "stagnant, archaic, hidebound document steeped in the prejudices and superstitions of a time long past." In the middle, Justices Kennedy and O'Connor would (usually) vote for conservative results without being willing to commit themselves to any particular constitutional methodology.

Last Term, the *Roe* era came to an end. *Washington v. Glucksberg,* together with a companion case under the Equal Protection Clause,[10] squarely presented the question of whether federal courts, exercising the power of judicial review, have authority to resolve contentious questions of social policy on the basis of their own normative judgments. In a soft-spoken opinion by Chief Justice Rehnquist that did not even cite *Roe,* a solid majority of the Court answered "no." The Court announced a constitutional jurisprudence of unenumerated rights under the Due Process Clause based not on the normative judgments of courts, but on constitutional text supplemented by the tradition and experience of the nation. *Roe v. Wade* was not reversed on its facts; the abortion right itself remains secure. But the constitutional methodology under which *Roe* was decided has been repudiated. The era of judicial supremacy epitomized by *Roe is* over.

I. THE CONTEXT AND SIGNIFICANCE OF THE *GLUCKSBERG* DECISION

A. Alternative Approaches to Unenumerated Rights

How should our political community resolve conflicts over fundamental issues of justice and the common good where conscientious citizens of good will do not agree? And in particular, what is the role of the courts? These have been the most persistent questions of constitutional law in this century. Two answers have dominated the debate. The first, associated with Justice Hugo Black and, more recently, Judge Robert Bork, is that in the absence of a constitutional norm derived from the text of the Constitution—such as the freedom of speech or the equal protection of the laws—courts have no authority to displace the decisions of the representatives of the people.[11] The command that neither states nor the federal government may "deprive any person of life, liberty, or property, without due process of law," according to this view, means only that deprivations of life, liberty, or property must be carried out with "due process of law"—meaning properly enacted statutes (or common law) administered according to proper pro-

[10] Vacco v. Quill, 521 U.S. 793 (1997)[.]

[11] See Griswold v. Connecticut, 381 U.S. 479, 507–10 (1965) (Black, J., dissenting); Robert Bork, The Tempting of America: The Political Seduction of the Law 118–20 (1990).

cedures. Due process means "process," and "substantive due process," according to this view, is an oxymoron. Any attempt to go beyond the rights enumerated by the Constitution is judicial usurpation.

At the opposite extreme are those judges and scholars who maintain that the open-ended language of the Constitution is an invitation to judges to decide, on the basis of their "own views about political morality,"[15] what liberties Americans should enjoy, and to limit the power of the government to invade those supposed rights in the absence of what the judges deem to be sufficient reasons. This approach goes by different names. * * * I will call it the "moral philosophic" approach. This is the approach toward constitutional law that gave us *Roe v. Wade,* and it is the approach that underlay the circuit court opinions that announced a right to assisted suicide.

The moral philosophic approach dominated constitutional doctrine during two periods of our history. During the first, at the beginning of this century, the courts embraced a political morality based on selective economic libertarianism, striking down such legislation as minimum wage and maximum hour laws on the ground that they served no objective public purpose. With the New Deal, this period came to an abrupt end and its major precedents were overruled. During the second, which began with the Warren Court, the courts embraced a political morality based on selective social libertarianism, striking down legislation regarding such matters as abortion, contraceptives, and pornography in the home. This period lost its steam with the appointment of new, more conservative Justices by President Ronald Reagan in the 1980s, but as a doctrinal matter there was never a sharp break. * * *

B. The Doctrinal Holding of Washington v. Glucksberg

In *Washington v. Glucksberg,*[31] the Court resolved this doctrinal uncertainty by setting forth a method of interpreting the Due Process Clause that falls between these two extremes. The Court began its doctrinal exposition by rejecting the first position: that the Constitution provides no protection for unenumerated rights. "The Due Process Clause guarantees more than fair process, and the 'liberty' it protects includes more than the absence of physical restraint. The Clause also provides heightened protection against government interference with certain fundamental rights and liberty interests." The Court then proceeded to describe what it called "[o]ur established method of substantive-due-process analysis," which squarely rejects the moral philosophic approach. This analysis has three important elements that distinguish it from the alternatives.

---

[15]Ronald Dworkin, Freedom's Law: The Moral Reading of the American Constitution 34 (1996).

[31]521 U.S. 702 (1997).

First, under the Court's analysis, a person challenging a law on substantive due process grounds must satisfy a "threshold requirement" of demonstrating that the "challenged state action implicates a fundamental right." Only then may the court require "more than a reasonable relation to a legitimate state interest to justify the action." This differentiates the Court's approach from one in which the reviewing court balances the state interest against the importance of the individual liberty claim in every case. By imposing this "threshold requirement," the Court "avoids the need for complex balancing of competing interests in every case." It is unnecessary to examine the governmental justification (beyond mere reasonableness) unless the claimant has established that the asserted right is fundamental.

Second, and most significantly, this threshold requirement may be satisfied only by showing either that the asserted right is textually based (like the right to freedom of speech), or that it is "objectively, deeply rooted in this Nation's history and tradition." The Court explained that "[o]ur Nation's history, legal traditions, and practices . . . provide the crucial 'guideposts for responsible decisionmaking'" This is an historical rather than a philosophical inquiry. It depends not on what judges believe the scope of liberty should be, but on what the American people have treated as protected liberty through our history, either through adoption of constitutional text or through longstanding practice. The opinion for the Court illustrated the nature of this inquiry by a detailed examination of the common law and statutory law pertaining to assisted suicide in the United States. Significantly, the Court extended this historical inquiry all the way to the present, examining recent history to satisfy itself that the traditional condemnation of assisted suicide continues to reflect the mores of the nation. Thus, it is not necessary to show that a challenged practice was protected at the time of adoption of the Fourteenth Amendment, but only that it has enjoyed protection over the course of years. Although the Court did not explicitly say so, the opinion implied that even a traditional norm could come to violate substantive due process if it is subsequently abandoned or rejected by a new stable consensus.

Third, the Court insisted that this historical inquiry must be based on "a 'careful description' of the asserted fundamental liberty interest." This means that the "liberty interest" must be described with specificity. Airy generalities like "the right to be left alone," or to make choices "central to personal dignity and autonomy," which mean almost anything or almost nothing, are too imprecise to support legal analysis. Because there are so many conceptions of what these abstractions mean, it would be impossible to determine whether any such traditions exist, or if they exist, what might be included within them.

If the asserted right finds no support in constitutional text or in deeply rooted history and tradition, then it is not "fundamental," and the judicial inquiry comes to an end, save for the requirement, applicable to all laws, that the challenged restriction "be rationally related to legitimate government interests." The effect is to allow the democratic, decentralized institutions of the country to continue to ponder the issue, and to adapt to changing mores and national experience. The Court's approach thus leaves social change and experimentation to the political branches, and reserves to the courts the task of enforcing traditional and enduring principles of justice. As the Chief Justice noted, such a resolution of the constitutional question "permits this debate to continue, as it should in a democratic society."

The traditionalist approach adopted in *Glucksberg* differs sharply from the moral philosophic approach not just in its substance but in its intellectual style. The moral philosophic approach is deductive and theoretical, deriving specific prescriptions from more general theoretical propositions. For example, the Ninth Circuit's argument for recognizing a right to assisted suicide was based on the assertion that this right is encompassed within a supposed right of each individual "to make the 'most intimate and personal choices central to personal dignity and autonomy.'" The traditionalist approach, by contrast, is inductive and experiential. Rather than reasoning down from abstract principles, it reasons up from concrete cases and circumstances. It can be seen as the conservative heir to legal realism: cautious, empirical, flexible, skeptical of claims of overarching theory. * * *

II. A Theoretical, Institutional, and Textual Historical Justification of the *Glucksberg* Approach to Substantive Due Process

I believe the Court's traditionalist approach to adjudication of unenumerated rights claims announced in *Glucksberg* is wise, workable, and firmly grounded in principles of American constitutionalism. It provides a check against particular states or local jurisdictions whose practices contradict what most Americans would deem to be fundamental rights, but does so without licensing courts to second-guess democratic judgments on the basis of their own ideological or philosophical preferences. It must be admitted, however, that Chief Justice Rehnquist's opinion for the Court does not supply much in the way of reasons to support its position. [In the sections that follow I will try to provide an explanation.]

A. Democracy and Conventionalism

It is a postulate of our political system that legitimate government has its origins in the consent of the governed. To be legitimate, therefore, constitutional rulings must trace their authority, in some sense, to decisions of the people. Even if there were reason to suppose that decisions of the nine Supreme Court Justices would likely be wiser and more just than decisions of the people (which there is not), this would not be a sufficient ground for allowing the Justices to base decisions on their own moral and political opinions, since such a government would no longer be a government of the people.

That is why Chief Justice Rehnquist's insistence that constitutional rulings be based either on constitutional text or on longstanding national consensus makes sense. These are two alternative ways of discerning the will of the people. Constitutional text was formally adopted by a supermajority of the people, and deserves respect for that reason. Longstanding consensus similarly reflects a supermajority of the people, expressed through decentralized institutions. No single vote, no single electoral victory, no single jurisdiction suffices to establish a tradition: it requires the acquiescence of many different decision makers over a considerable period of time, subject to popular approval or disapproval. When judges base their decisions either on constitutional text or on longstanding consensus, they do not usurp the right of the people to self-government, but hold the representatives of the people accountable to the deepest and most fundamental commitments of the people.

Moreover, reliance on longstanding consensus is likely to be a more reliable means of reaching a correct result. The problem with decisions based on moral philosophy—like all versions of natural law adjudication—is the uncertain application of theoretical principles to concrete issues. There are limits to the capacity of human reason to reach a definitive answer to many questions of political morality. Unless expressed at a high level of generality, principles of natural law appear arbitrary and contestable rather than natural; but so expressed, the principles are virtually useless for deciding actual matters of controversy.

We might be able to agree on highly generalized principles like "human dignity," "fair play," or "equal concern and respect," but how those abstractions will apply to such specific questions as affirmative action, capital punishment, or proper modes of service of process (to name a few examples) is a matter of disagreement among reasonable people. The attraction of natural law is its seemingly universal reasonableness; but specific applications to specific issues lose that quality of universality. When a court announces that the abstract principle of "equal concern and respect" mandates (or precludes) affirmative action, or the principle of personal autonomy mandates (or precludes) assisted suicide, the judge is not in any realistic sense "applying" natural law, but is merely applying his own opinion about affirmative action or assisted suicide. There is no reason the judge's opinion should prevail over that of the people.

In the absence of any reliable basis for resolving moral and philosophical disagreements of this sort (other than whether a position accords with our own opinion!), courts should look to experience and to stable consensus as an objective basis for decision making. If a practice is adopted by many different communities, and maintained for a considerable period of time, this provides strong evidence that the practice contributes to the common good and accords with the spirit and mores of the people. To be sure, there can be bad, evil, or counterproductive traditions; but if so, one would expect to see a movement away from them. At least, there is more reason to have faith in the product of decentralized decisions, based on experiments and experience over a period of many years, than in the abstract theorizing of particular individuals, even oneself. Imposition of a new, untried, principle will almost certainly have unintended and unpredictable consequences, which is why prudent statesmen are guided by experience rather than by idealistic speculation. * * *

The moral philosophic approach, by contrast, necessarily presupposes that judges are wiser, fairer, more reflective decision makers than those who are more immediately accountable to the public. Alas, there is no evidence to support that presupposition. Indeed, a decentralized process in which many different people, of differing perspectives and walks of life, can participate—directly or indirectly—in the decision making process, is more likely to produce a balanced and sensible conclusion. Federal judges are, almost without exception, well meaning and well educated people. But the courts are a narrow institution, no less prone to prejudice (of a particular sort) than anyone else. Judge Stephen Reinhardt's opinion for the Ninth Circuit dismissed views on assisted suicide contrary to his own as "cruel," "untenable," "disingenuous and fallacious," "meretricious," "ludicrous," and "nihilist." The court praised its own view as "more enlightened." The court characterized hundreds of years of common law precedent as "taboos," linked to superstition; it brushed aside the central text of medical ethics, the Hippocratic Oath, saying that it "does not represent the best or final word on medical or legal controversies today." The Ninth Circuit criticized the conclusions of the American Medical Association and the American Geriatrics Society (among others) as reflecting "a misunderstanding of the proper function of a physician." The sublime arrogance of these judicial pronouncements highlights the danger of allowing courts to set social policy, in defiance of legislatures and referenda, on the basis of their own (often ill-informed) philosophical intuitions.

By relying on the experience and settled judgment of the nation, rather than their own opinions, judges thus keep faith with the democratic postulates of our system, and at the same time are more likely to reach answers that will stand the test of time.

B. The Institutional Dimension

The question of assisted suicide provides an excellent context for consideration of the institutional dimensions of judicial review of novel claims of constitutional right, precisely because of the unambiguous character of the historical record. The case for a right to assisted suicide rested entirely on philosophical, not historical, premises and the case thus highlighted the pitfalls of constitutional decision making based on such premises. Under the moral philosophic approach, courts are instructed to determine for themselves what is the best answer to the problem posed. Indeed, in *Glucksberg,* the Court had the benefit of an unusual amicus curiae brief, signed by six of America's leading political philosophers, which argued that the Court should recognize the right of terminally ill patients to the assistance of doctors in shortening their lives.

But there is every reason for courts to be wary about overturning duly enacted legislation on the basis of untried and uncertain moral and philosophical arguments, where the result is bereft of support in directly relevant constitutional text or in national experience. It may well be true that attitudes about the end of life have changed, or will change, in response to technological developments and their attendant economic and emotional consequences. But no one knows what the actual consequences of various possible policies would be. It would be a grave mistake for the federal courts to leap in and attempt, prematurely, to resolve the issue or to accelerate the pace of change. Even on the heuristic assumption that laws against assisted suicide and euthanasia should be relaxed in some fashion, it is better that reform take place in decentralized and accountable institutions.

A jurisprudence grounded in text and tradition is not hostile to social change, but it assigns the responsibility to determine the pace and direction of change to representative bodies. As Justice Scalia has argued, the argument over traditionalist jurisprudence

> has nothing to do with whether "further progress is to be made" in the "evolution of our legal system." It has to do with whether changes are to be adopted as progressive by the American people or decreed as progressive by the Justices of this Court. Nothing we say today prevents individual States from limiting or entirely abandoning the [traditional position]. And nothing prevents an overwhelming majority of them from doing so, with the consequence that the "traditional notions of fairness" that this Court applies may change.[104]

The great institutional strength of courts is their ability to provide uniform enforcement of legal principles, with consistency across parties, regions, and time periods, treating like cases alike. Where operative principles are in flux and the consequences of new approaches are unpredictable, however, that virtue becomes a vice. Constitutional judicial

[104]Burnham v. Superior Court, 495 U.S. 604, 627 (1990) (Scalia, J., opinion joined by Rehnquist, C.J., and Kennedy, J.) (citations omitted).

review is too inflexible a process to deal sensitively and appropriately with the question of assisted suicide.

First, by locating the right to die in the federal constitution, judicial recognition of such a right would nationalize the issue and eliminate the possibility of state variation and experimentation. Justice Brandeis's characterization of the states as "laboratories of democracy"[105] is no cliché; it is an apt description of one of the principal virtues of a federal system. There was no serious argument in *Glucksberg* that national uniformity is necessary or even desirable. The state of Oregon has undertaken an experiment in physician-assisted suicide[107] that—however misguided it may appear to many of us—will cast light on the practical consequences: on the efficacy of the safeguards against abuse, on the ability of the medical profession to recognize and treat clinical depression and pain in patients requesting suicide, on the robustness of the lines drawn between permitted and forbidden forms of the right to die, and on the danger that death will come to be perceived as a duty owed to family and society. To treat this social policy question as controlled by federal constitutional law is to eliminate the possibility of a multiplicity of approaches, and of regional variation in light of differences in social and moral perceptions. * * *

Second, by their nature constitutional judicial decisions may not be "compromises with social and political pressures." The lines drawn by courts, under the authority of the Constitution, must be defensible at the level of constitutional principle. Yet not every aspect of social life can be governed by crisp and principled rules. Sometimes, the best and most peaceful solution to contentious moral conflicts in society is not to award the brass ring to one side or the other, but to construct compromises that allow each contending force to believe that the system has been responsive to their deeply held convictions. Legislatures are good at that.

Whatever one may think of legislators as moral deliberators, few would dispute that they have the expertise and incentive to resolve social conflict in a way that minimizes political opposition and resistance. The legislative answer may not appear pure from a philosophical or analytical perspective, but it is likely to reduce social discord. And even if legislatures prove unable to forge a stable consensus, contending social forces are more likely to accept the outcome of a process in which their voices were heard than an imposed solution in which their elected representatives were not entitled to a significant role. This is one of the lessons of the abortion decisions.

The right to die is such an issue. The public is seriously divided. Passions run high. The various lines that might be drawn—refusal of treatment versus suicide, assisted suicide versus active euthanasia, terminal illness

[105]New State Ice Co. v. Liebmann, 285 U.S. 262, 311 (1932) (Brandeis, J., dissenting).
[107]Or. Rev. Stat. §§ 127.800 to 127.897 (Supp. 1996).

versus chronic pain or disability, actual consent versus imputed consent, intolerable pain versus other conditions that harm the quality of life, one set of safeguards versus another, and so forth—are, each of them, arbitrary in their own way. Each of them attempts to allow the dying patient some greater degree of control over the circumstances of his death, while at the same time upholding society's obligation to honor life and protect the vulnerable. Each tries to reconcile two honorable impulses that are, in principle, irreconcilable: autonomy and protection. Legislatures, better than courts, can make the compromises necessary to accommodate these conflicting ideals.

Third, and most importantly, courts are seriously constrained in their ability to change their policy in response to experience and criticism. Each decision of the Court is said to be based on an interpretation of the Constitution, and it strains public credulity that the meaning of such an old document would change very rapidly, very often. The doctrine of stare decisis thus creates a heavy presumption in favor of existing doctrine. Stability is a source of judicial strength and legitimacy. But with this strength comes a caution: just as the Court is properly reluctant to jettison a constitutional doctrine that it has embraced, the Court should be reluctant to embrace novel constitutional doctrines that may require modification in the future. As Justice Souter commented, "[a]n unenumerated right should not therefore be recognized, with the effect of displacing the legislative ordering of things, without the assurance that its recognition would prove as durable as the recognition of [textually based constitutional rights]."

Finally, the asymmetrical nature of the risks of judicial error suggests that, in close cases, the courts should defer to legislative judgments. In any case in which a party claims that the decision of our politically responsive institutions is unconstitutional, there are two possible risks. One risk is that the Court will uphold a law that is unconstitutional, thus allowing the continued infringement of constitutional rights. Examples would be *Plessy v. Ferguson,*[112] which upheld Jim Crow legislation segregating private railways, or *Minersville School District v. Gobitis,*[113] which upheld a requirement that Jehovah's Witness schoolchildren be compelled to participate in the flag salute. The opposite risk is that the Court will strike down a law that is constitutional, thus frustrating representative government and, in many cases, infringing statutory rights and protections. Examples would be *Dred Scott v. Sandford,*[114] in which the Court held it was unconstitutional for Congress to bar slavery from the territories, and

[112] 163 U.S. 537 (1896).
[113] 310 U.S. 586 (1940).
[114] 60 U.S. (19 How.) 393 (1857).

Lochner v. New York,[115] in which the Court invalidated maximum hour legislation.

While both types of error have serious consequences, the former can be corrected by political means; the latter cannot. When the Court upholds unjust governmental action, citizens can turn to political means for relief, and legislative branches are able to correct the injustice. The majority of states outlawed transportation segregation notwithstanding *Plessy,* and school boards were free to exempt schoolchildren from the flag salute even if this was not required by *Gobitis.* This provides the seeds for change. When the Court erroneously strikes down legislation, however, it disables the political branches from correcting the error. The only remedies are constitutional amendment, political action to force the Court to reverse its judgment, or (as in the case of *Dred Scott*) violence or civil war. For these reasons, the repeated admonitions by some of the greatest Justices in the Supreme Court's history in favor of a presumption of constitutionality carry great weight. A wise court, recognizing its own fallibility, will stay its hand in close cases where powerful arguments exist on both sides.

Glucksberg is a perfect example. If the Court had affirmed the lower courts' creation of a right to assisted suicide, neither Congress nor the states would have been able to explore contrary policies. Any substantial burden on the exercise of the new "right" would presumably be held invalid. If that judgment proved to be misguided, great injury would have been done to thousands of vulnerable persons in every state in the Union, until the Court brought itself to acknowledge the mistake and reverse the decision. On the other hand, under the Court's actual judgment upholding assisted suicide laws, debate on the issue can proceed in the future. The fifty states will remain free to pass laws allowing assisted suicide or euthanasia in such circumstances and under such safeguards as they may deem advisable. If experiments with liberalized laws on this subject are successful, it is likely that still more states will follow suit. If they prove misguided, these states can reverse course, and the other states will profit by their example.

A jurisprudence based on tradition is responsive to these institutional issues. It leaves room for experimentation and variation among the states, until such time as a stable national consensus has emerged and persisted. Then it may be advisable to force remaining outlier states to conform to the national norm. It allows representative institutions and common law courts to work out broadly acceptable compromises instead of imposing a prematurely "principled" (and therefore rigid) answer to the question. And it allows for adaptation and change. Only when a particular answer has

---

[115] 198 U.S. 45 (1905).

stood the test of time should it be constitutionalized through substantive due process.

Bibliography

Assisted Suicide

Appleton, *Assisted Suicide and Reproductive Freedom: Exploring Some Connections,* 76 Wash.U.L.Q. 15 (1998).

Burt, *Disorder in the Court: Physician-Assisted Suicide and the Constitution*, 82 Minn.L.Rev. 965 (1998).

Chopko and Moses, *Assisted Suicide: Still a Wonderful Life?,* 70 Notre Dame L.Rev. 519 (1995).

Kamisar, *Physician-Assisted Suicide: The Problems Presented by the Compelling, Heartwrenching Case,* 88 J. Crim.L. & Criminology 1121 (1998).

Kreimer, *Does Pro-Choice Mean Pro-Kevorkian? An Essay on* Roe, Casey, *and the Right to Die*, 44 Am.U.L.Rev. 803 (1995).

Law, *Physician-Assisted Death: An Essay on Constitutional Rights and Remedies,* 55 Md.L.Rev. 292 (1996).

Minow, *Which Question?: Which Lie? Reflections on the Physician-Assisted Suicide Cases,* 1997 Sup.Ct.Rev. 1.

Noonan, *Dealing With Death,* 12 Notre Dame J.L. Ethics & Pub. Pol'y 387 (1998).

Orentlicher, *The Legalization of Physician Assisted Suicide: A Very Modest Revolution,* 38 B.C.L.Rev. 443 (1997).

Robinson, *Physician Assisted Suicide: a Constitutional Crisis Resolved*, 12 Notre Dame J.L. Ethics & Pub. Pol'y 369 (1998).

Sunstein, *The Right to Die,* 106 Yale L.J. 1123 (1997).

Symposium, *Physician-Assisted Suicide,* 35 Duq.L.Rev. 1 (1996).

Symposium, *Physician-Assisted Suicide,* 18 Seattle U.L.Rev. 449 (1995).

Symposium, *Physician-Assisted Suicide: Facing Death After* Glucksberg *and* Quill, 82 Minn.L.Rev. 885 (1998).

Symposium, *The Right to Die,* 9 N.D.J.L. Ethics & Pub.Pol'y 345 (1995).

Symposium, *Visions of Death and Dying: Interdisciplinary Perspectives on the Future of Medical Ethics,* 24 Hastings Const.L.Q. 863 (1997).

Refusing Treatment

Buchanan, *The Limits of Proxy Decision-Making,* in R. Sartorious, ed., PATERNALISM 153 (1983).

Burt, R., TAKING CARE OF STRANGERS, ch. 7 (1979).

Burt, *The Ideal of Community in the Work of the President's Commission,* 6 Cardozo L.Rev. 267 (1984).

Callahan, D., SETTING LIMITS: MEDICAL GOALS IN AN AGING SOCIETY (1987).

Dworkin, *The Right to Death,* N.Y.Rev. Books 14 (Jan. 31, 1991).

Emanuel, *A Communal Vision of Care for Incompetent Patients,* 17 Hastings Center Rep. 15 (1987).

Garvey, *Representatives,* in WHAT ARE FREEDOMS FOR? ch. 7 (1996).

Kadish, *Letting Patients Die: Legal and Moral Reflections,* 80 Calif.L.Rev. 857 (1992).

Kamisar, *When Is There a Constitutional "Right to Die"? When Is There No Constitutional "Right to Live"?,* 25 Ga.L.Rev. 1203 (1991).

Mayo, *Constitutionalizing the "Right to Die",* 49 Md.L.Rev. 103 (1990).

Meisel, A., THE RIGHT TO DIE (1989).

Minow, *Beyond State Intervention in the Family: For Baby Jane Doe,* 18 Mich.J.L.Rev. 933 (1985).

Mooney, *Deciding Not To Resuscitate Hospital Patients: Medical and Legal Perspectives,* 1986 U.Ill.L.Rev. 1025.

Note, *Developments in the Law—Medical Technology and the Law,* 103 Harv.L.Rev. 1519 (1990).

Note, *Proxy Decisionmaking for the Terminally Ill: The Virginia Approach,* 70 Va.L.Rev. 1269 (1984).

Note, *State Natural Death Acts: Illusory Protection of Individuals' Life-Sustaining Treatment Decisions,* 29 Harv.J.Legis. 175 (1992).

Rachels, *Active and Passive Euthanasia,* 292 New Eng.J.Med. 78 (1975).

Rhoden, *Litigating Life and Death,* 102 Harv.L.Rev. 375 (1988).

Rhoden, *The Limits of Legal Objectivity,* 68 N.C.L.Rev. 845 (1990).

Roach, *Paradox and Pandora's Box: The Tragedy of Current Right-to-Die Jurisprudence,* 25 U.Mich.J.L.Ref. 133 (1991).

Robertson, Cruzan *and the Constitutional Status of Nontreatment Decisions for Incompetent Patients,* 25 Ga.L.Rev. 1139 (1991).

Russell, O., FREEDOM TO DIE (2d ed. 1977).

Schneider, *Rights Discourse and Neonatal Euthanasia,* 76 Calif.L.Rev. 151 (1988).

Symposium, *Legal Issues Relating to the Elderly,* 42 Hastings L.J. 679 (1991).

Symposium, *Privacy and the Family in Medical Decisions,* 23 J.Family L. 173 (1984–85).

The President's Commission for the Study of Ethical Problems in Medicine and Biomedical and Behavioral Research, DECIDING TO FOREGO LIFE-SUSTAINING TREATMENT (1983).

Vance, *Autonomy's Paradox: Death, Fear, and Advance Directives,* 42 Mercer L.Rev. 1051 (1991).

Wilson, J., DEATH BY DECISION (1975).

Wreen, *Breathing a Little Life Into a Distinction,* 46 Phil.Stud. 395 (1984).

Chapter X

THE PUBLIC–PRIVATE DISTINCTION

To speak very generally, in constitutional law we distinguish private from public actions in two different ways. The first such distinction is one that we dealt with at length in Chapter IX: it holds that some actions are private as a matter of right. They are of no concern to the general public, and the Constitution puts them beyond the government's ability to regulate. The right to privacy protected in cases like *Roe v. Wade* and *Lawrence v. Texas* and claimed in cases like *Glucksberg* is the best illustration of privacy in this sense, but it is not the only example. Many people also think of religion as a private right protected by the Free Exercise Clause, and kept out of the public sphere by the Establishment Clause.

The second public-private distinction is the principal focus of this Chapter. A very large number of actions are private in the more modest sense that they are simply not regulated by the Constitution. These are not things that we have a right (in any strong sense) to do. The government could pass laws forbidding them. But if it does not we can do them without undermining any more fundamental constitutional principle. For example, if I own a deli the Constitution lets me be very selective in hiring a cook: I can discriminate on the basis of religion, gender, or race. Of course the government could pass a law requiring me to be more open-minded, but I have at least this degree of autonomy in running my private life: the default setting (as we might call it) is for freedom of association. Take another example. Broadcasters, unlike newspapers, do not have a First Amendment right to control their own affairs. But the Constitution at least permits them to do so—they can, for example, simply refuse to cover certain issues.[1] If the government wants to it can take away this freedom by making a law or regulation.[2] But once again the default setting is for private autonomy.

---

[1]Columbia Broadcasting System, Inc. v. Democratic Nat'l Committee, 412 U.S. 94, 93 S.Ct. 2080, 36 L.Ed.2d 772 (1973).

[2]Red Lion Broadcasting Co. v. FCC, 395 U.S. 367, 89 S.Ct. 1794, 23 L.Ed.2d 371 (1969).

These two senses of privacy—the strong and the weak—are obviously related. Both of them protect the intimacy of close relationships, autonomy in our personal lives, our ability to be selective and uninhibited in our friendships, and so on. One gives more protection than the other, but there is an obvious family resemblance. These are points that lawyers often overlook, however, because the two ideas have different textual origins and have developed historically in very different ways. Privacy in the strong sense is protected by a list of rights expressly stated (occasionally implied) in the original Constitution, and more especially in the Bill of Rights and other amendments. Privacy in the weak sense is the negative implication of all the clauses that impose constitutional duties on public authorities but not on other people. The First Amendment says that "Congress shall make no law" prohibiting religious freedom or abridging free speech. This permits the rest of us to do as we like. The Fourteenth Amendment says:

> *No State shall make or enforce any law* which shall abridge the privileges or immunities of citizens of the United States; *nor shall any State deprive* any person of life, liberty, or property, without due process of law; *nor deny* to any person within its jurisdiction the equal protection of the laws.

This implies that private actors pursuing their own ends can (at least as far as the Constitution is concerned) treat each other in ways the state cannot. This is why lawyers call privacy in the weak sense the "state action" requirement—to signify that some parts of the Constitution regulate only the action of the state, and leave private actors alone.

In addition to having different textual origins the two senses of privacy have very different histories. The history of the first idea has been one of continual expansion. We tend to think that progress in Constitutional Law consists in the perpetual recognition of more and more rights, giving us ever more protection against government invasion of our private space. The chief reason Constitutional Law books are so fat is that they have tried to keep up with this expansion. The history of the second idea, by contrast, for a long time was one of continual contraction. The courts were willing to find state action at every turn—or to put it the other way around, they used the Constitution to regulate the behavior of private actors. With a little reflection we can see the reason for this apparently wayward behavior. People only lay claim to privacy in the weak sense when their interests conflict with those of people whose rights have a better pedigree. The Constitution permits me to run my deli as I choose; but it gives prospective employees a right to equal protection. It permits broadcasters to control the content of their programming; but it gives political parties a right to freedom of speech. The weak sphere of privacy is just a negative implication from clauses granting rights in the strong sense. So if there is any reason to think that the state has a hand in the activities of deli owners and broadcasters, they are likely to lose out in competition with constitutionally more favored claimants.

Most of the early cases of this kind dealt with race discrimination: the *White Primary Cases,*[3] *Shelley v. Kraemer,*[4] the *Girard College Case,*[5] *Burton v. Wilmington Parking Authority,*[6] *Evans v. Newton*[7] and *Evans v. Abney,*[8] *Reitman v. Mulkey,*[9] and *Moose Lodge No. 107 v. Irvis.*[10] Here the challenged behavior, though arguably private in the weak sense, was also reprehensible. And the challengers, if only they could show some reason to question the integrity of the public-private distinction, had the strongest kind of right to constitutional protection—the guarantee of the Equal Protection Clause. But most of these problems have since been addressed by legislation like the 1964 Civil Rights Act and its successors, which forbid discrimination in many of the areas where the Constitution was once invoked (employment, public accommodations, housing, voting, education, etc.). Nowadays challengers more often attack the public-private distinction in order to extend their rights to due process[11] or freedom of speech.[12] The fact that they have had a lower success rate than earlier claimants reminds us that there are privacy values at stake on both sides of the litigation.

---

[3]Nixon v. Herndon, 273 U.S. 536, 47 S.Ct. 446, 71 L.Ed. 759 (1927); Nixon v. Condon, 286 U.S. 73, 52 S.Ct. 484, 76 L.Ed. 984 (1932); Grovey v. Townsend, 295 U.S. 45, 55 S.Ct. 622, 79 L.Ed. 1292 (1935); Smith v. Allwright, 321 U.S. 649, 64 S.Ct. 757, 88 L.Ed. 987 (1944); Terry v. Adams, 345 U.S. 461, 73 S.Ct. 809, 97 L.Ed. 1152 (1953).

[4]334 U.S. 1, 68 S.Ct. 836, 92 L.Ed. 1161 (1948).

[5]Pennsylvania v. Board of Directors of City Trusts, 353 U.S. 230, 77 S.Ct. 806, 1 L.Ed.2d 792 (1957). See also Pennsylvania v. Brown, 392 F.2d 120 (3d Cir.1968), cert. denied 391 U.S. 921, 88 S.Ct. 1811, 20 L.Ed.2d 657 (1968).

[6]365 U.S. 715, 81 S.Ct. 856, 6 L.Ed.2d 45 (1961).

[7]382 U.S. 296, 86 S.Ct. 486, 15 L.Ed.2d 373 (1966).

[8]396 U.S. 435, 90 S.Ct. 628, 24 L.Ed.2d 634 (1970).

[9]387 U.S. 369, 87 S.Ct. 1627, 18 L.Ed.2d 830 (1967).

[10]407 U.S. 163, 92 S.Ct. 1965, 32 L.Ed.2d 627 (1972).

[11]See, e.g., American Mfrs. Mut. Ins. v. Sullivan, 526 U.S. 40, 119 S.Ct. 977 (1999); DeShaney v. Winnebago County Dept. of Social Services, 489 U.S. 189, 109 S.Ct. 998, 103 L.Ed.2d 249 (1989); NCAA v. Tarkanian, 488 U.S. 179, 109 S.Ct. 454, 102 L.Ed.2d 469 (1988); Tulsa Professional Collection Services, Inc. v. Pope, 485 U.S. 478, 108 S.Ct. 1340, 99 L.Ed.2d 565 (1988); Lugar v. Edmondson Oil Co., 457 U.S. 922, 102 S.Ct. 2744, 73 L.Ed.2d 482 (1982); Blum v. Yaretsky, 457 U.S. 991, 102 S.Ct. 2777, 73 L.Ed.2d 534 (1982); Flagg Bros., Inc. v. Brooks, 436 U.S. 149, 98 S.Ct. 1729, 56 L.Ed.2d 185 (1978); Jackson v. Metropolitan Edison Co., 419 U.S. 345, 95 S.Ct. 449, 42 L.Ed.2d 477 (1974).

[12]Brentwood Academy v. Tennessee Secondary School Ass'n, 531 U.S. 288, 121 S.Ct. 924 (2001);Lebron v. National R.R. Passenger Corp., 513 U.S. 374, 115 S.Ct. 961, 130 L.Ed.2d 902 (1995). San Francisco Arts & Athletics v. USOC, 483 U.S. 522, 107 S.Ct. 2971, 97 L.Ed.2d 427 (1987); Rendell–Baker v. Kohn, 457 U.S. 830, 102 S.Ct. 2764, 73 L.Ed.2d 418 (1982); Hudgens v. NLRB, 424 U.S. 507, 96 S.Ct. 1029, 47 L.Ed.2d 196 (1976); CBS v. Democratic National Committee, 412 U.S. 94, 93 S.Ct. 2080, 36 L.Ed.2d 772 (1973); Lloyd Corporation v. Tanner, 407 U.S. 551, 92 S.Ct. 2219, 33 L.Ed.2d 131 (1972); Amalgamated Food Employees Union v. Logan Valley Plaza, 391 U.S. 308, 88 S.Ct. 1601, 20 L.Ed.2d 603 (1968).

We begin with two pieces examining the legal theories that currently define state action. John Garvey looks at two radical approaches that courts and plaintiffs have suggested for extending constitutional duties to all private actors. One, the *public function* theory, holds that private parties are subject to constitutional constraints when they function like the state in ways that count. (There are actually three versions of this theory. Garvey approves of two of them—those that impose liability where the government conspires with a private actor, or delegates power to a faithless agent. He condemns only the third, which he calls the public interest version.) A second radical theory, the *permission* theory, argues that all private action is taken with the state's permission or control, and therefore should be subject to the same constraints.

Gillian Metzger takes literally what Garvey calls the delegation theory to deal with a phenomenon we see more and more often—government handoffs of programs and activities to private service providers. We have seen this approach suggested for Medicare drug prescription coverage, Social Security reform, and airport security. It has been adopted in the welfare context where private organizations run homeless shelters, provide treatment services, and run Head Start programs. It has drawn attention in the educational arena where the Supreme Court has approved voucher plans that give public funds to help students cover tuition at private schools.[13] Even prisons are now being run by private companies. The Court generally declines to find state action in these cases unless the state is involved in "the specific conduct of which the plaintiff complains."[14] Metzger argues that this is a mistake, and it creates a perverse incentive for the government to ignore the performance of private providers. She suggests that we think about this problem in a different way: hold the government responsible for the delegation of power to private parties, as the early New Deal Court did in cases like *Carter v. Carter Coal.*[15]

The next set of readings asks why we might want the Constitution to control only state action. To that question courts and legal scholars have usually given two kinds of answers. The first is that constitutional controls over private action are undesirable for the same reason that statutory controls are—they inhibit the conduct of intimate affairs, they restrict a person's freedom to live her own life in her own way, and so on. In some ways constitutional controls are worse than ordinary law controls. They are imposed by courts, while ordinary lawmaking is done by legislatures and agencies. (The common law is a significant exception. It, like constitutional law, is made by courts.) It is often easier to make rules through the judicial process than through legislative or administrative processes. Proposals must

---

[13] Zelman v. Simons-Harris, 536 U.S. 639 (2002).

[14] American Manufacturers Mutual Insurance v. Sullivan, 526 U.S. 40, 51 (1999).

[15] 298 U.S. 238 (1936).

have more popular appeal in the latter cases; and at some points the systems are designed to make success difficult. Judges, on the other hand, need only to agree among themselves. This means that sometimes constitutional controls are more likely to be imposed in the first place. Once in place they are also harder to remove. If a court decides that the Constitution forbids deli owners to make arbitrary hiring decisions and this restriction proves very hard to live with, the only remedy is to amend the Constitution, a process that is seldom successful. By contrast, when we regulate deli employment by statute we can change the rules as easily as we made them in the first place.

The second justification given for the state action limitation is that it serves a federalist purpose. Constitutional controls on private action are, after all, federal rules enforced primarily by federal courts. If we leave the control of private action to ordinary law, this will typically (though certainly not always) be law made and enforced by the states. Abolishing the state action limitation, then, would work a substantial transfer of law-making authority from the states to the federal government. Many people think this would be undesirable for the same reasons that unlimited Article I power is undesirable. These reasons are discussed in the series of cases from *M'Culloch v. Maryland*[16] to *United States v. Lopez*[17] and *Printz v. United States.*[18] If we set aside the *risorgimento* of the last few years, these federalist arguments have done little since 1937 to limit Article I power. Is there more reason to think they will limit the reach of the Fourteenth Amendment?

Erwin Chemerinsky reviews and criticizes both of these justifications. He argues that the privacy argument looks at only half the picture. For every private actor ("violator") whose liberty is protected by the state action doctrine, there is another private actor ("victim") who suffers some harm. The doctrine protects my freedom to hire whom I please at my deli, at the expense of qualified job applicants whom I arbitrarily or discriminatorily reject. If we are really interested in maximizing the regime of private liberty, Chemerinsky says, we should look at the merits of these conflicts and hold for the party who has more at stake. As to the argument for state sovereignty, Chemerinsky claims that it has been rendered obsolete by *United States v. Darby*[19] and *Garcia v. San Antonio Metropolitan Transit Authority.*[20] (Would he make the same claim after the Court's decision in *Lopez, Printz, Boerne v. Flores,*[21] and *United States v. Morrison?*[22])

---

[16]17 U.S. (4 Wheat.) 316, 4 L.Ed. 579 (1819).

[17]514 U.S. 549, 115 S.Ct. 1624, 131 L.Ed.2d 626 (1995).

[18]521 U.S. 98, 117 S.Ct. 2365, 138 L.Ed.914 (1997).

[19]312 U.S. 100, 61 S.Ct. 451, 85 L.Ed. 609 (1941).

[20]469 U.S. 528, 105 S.Ct. 1005, 83 L.Ed.2d. 1016 (1985).

[21]521 U.S. 507, 117 S.Ct. 2157, 138 L.Ed.2d.624 (1997).

William Marshall observes that Chemerinsky's cure may be worse than the disease. If what we really want is the regime that maximizes individual liberty, we should not assume that we can get this by allowing the courts to engage in case-by-case balancing of private interests. What's more there is another, often unappreciated, danger in extending the Constitution to cover private cases. All proponents of universal coverage concede that we will have to apply the substantive rules more leniently to private actors. Marshall points out that these new exceptions may leak back into the law governing public authorities.

JOHN H. GARVEY, THE SNAKE

WHAT ARE FREEDOMS FOR? 242–251 (1996).

Near my uncle Michael's house in Indianapolis there is a hardware store (Central Hardware) located by itself in a large building with a parking lot on three sides. It's a pretty big store, part of a chain that has its headquarters in St. Louis, but it's just a hardware store. Does Central Hardware have a duty to allow freedom of speech at its store? Of course it would be bad business to tell customers to shut up. But if I wanted to hand out leaflets against abortion or urge Central's employees to join a union, does the constitution say Central has to let me?

It seems not. The first amendment is addressed to Congress; the fourteenth amendment is addressed to the states. Central is neither of those. It is just a private store. But there are two arguments, neither of them frivolous, for saying that it is covered by the constitution. One is that Central, though it is not actually Congress or a state, is very much like them in the ways that count, so it ought to be subject to similar requirements. I will call this the public function argument. The other assumes that the law governs all aspects of our lives. Central can limit free speech only because the law of Indiana lets it. The first amendment applies to Central Hardware because the state controls (allows) Central's behavior. I will call this the permission argument.

If either of these arguments works, we have gone a long way toward collapsing the distinction between *X* [a private actor] and *Y* [the state] in the jurisprudence of freedom. Central is a private business, the sort of company that usually claims free speech rights. But the public function and permission arguments treat it like a public institution that has free speech duties. They look on Central as a "state actor" (X_Y).

We came to the idea that Central Hardware was performing a public function in three steps. The first happened in 1939 in *Hague v. CIO*. [Mayor] Hague was famous for running people out of town who handed out leaflets or spoke in public about unpleasant subjects, like organized labor.

---

[22] 529 U.S. 598, 120 S.Ct. 1740, 146 L.Ed.2d. 658 (2000).

The Supreme Court held that this violated the first amendment, because people had a free speech right to communicate in public places. Justice Roberts put it thus: "Wherever the title of streets and parks may rest, they have immemorially been held in trust for the use of the public and, time out of mind, have been used for purposes of assembly, communicating thoughts between citizens, and discussing public questions. Such use of the streets and public places has, from ancient times, been a part of the . . . liberties of citizens."[3]

The second step occurred seven years later in *Marsh v. Alabama*. Chickasaw, Alabama was a company town owned by the Gulf Shipbuilding Corporation. Except for that it looked like any other American town: it had houses, streets, sidewalks, sewers, a business block, and a post office. There was even a Mobile County deputy sheriff, paid by the company. Grace Marsh, a Jehovah's Witness, was distributing religious literature on the sidewalk outside the post office when the deputy sheriff asked her to move along. She refused and he arrested her for criminal trespass. The Supreme Court held for Marsh: "The more an owner, for his advantage, opens up his property for use by the public in general, the more do his rights become circumscribed by the . . . constitutional rights of those who use it."[4] The rule then was that the first amendment applied both to towns and to places that were *like* towns.

The third step occurred in 1968 in *Food Employees v. Logan Valley Plaza*. The Logan Valley Mall was a small mall in Altoona, Pennsylvania. When it opened it had only a Sears store and a supermarket, though by the time the case got to the Supreme Court there were seventeen stores in all. The Food Employees Union had picketed the supermarket (in its pickup area) in 1965 for using nonunion labor and the state courts had enjoined this as a trespass. The Supreme Court held that the first amendment applied to the mall, because it was "the functional equivalent of the business district of Chickasaw."[5] It looked like a business district, with roads through the parking lot and sidewalks between the mall buildings. And to an ever-greater extent, the Court pointed out, malls were replacing downtown business districts as people moved to the suburbs. They ought to be treated the same for free speech purposes.

It is not very far from here to the conclusion that Central Hardware too performs a public function. The progression, again, is this: real towns have to allow free speech on streets, sidewalks, and open spaces where there are large audiences; company towns are like real towns; malls are like company towns; Central Hardware is like a mall—it has a big parking area and a lot

[3] 307 U.S. 496, 515 (1939) (opinion of Roberts, J.).

[4] Marsh v. Alabama, 326 U.S. 501, 506 (1946).

[5] Food Employees v. Logan Valley Plaza, 391 U.S 308, 318 (1968).

of people on foot and in cars. And that is what the Eighth Circuit held in 1971. Even though Central had a no-solicitation rule, union organizers could ask employees to sign cards in the parking lot because Central's rule violated the first amendment.[6]

It is easy to see how the courts slid from real towns to hardware stores—from public institutions to private ones—but we still need an explanation. Building streets, sidewalks, and parking lots is something that cities do; why should private actors be subject to the first amendment just because they do the same thing? We can see three arguments in the public function cases. In order from the most modest to the most far-reaching they are the "conspiracy" theory, the "delegation" theory, and the "public interest" theory. Each one explains in a different way why private parties may have to obey constitutional rules.

Under some circumstances the idea that private actors should assume constitutional obligations is not at all controversial. Suppose that the parks in Lexington are segregated by race. After a court orders that they be integrated, the city transfers title to private trustees who maintain the policy of apartheid. Here the city has "gone private" for the purpose of avoiding its constitutional obligations. And even if private owners can ordinarily operate segregated parks, they can't help the city do so.

We might call this the "conspiracy" scenario. The key fact is the city's bad intentions, which the private actor helps the city to realize. And just as one can conspire to commit a crime that one is personally incapable of committing, so the private actor can conspire with the state to violate the constitution. But this explanation doesn't work for all public function cases, including the ones we are looking at. Cities don't conspire with malls and hardware stores to reduce speech in public places. Indeed, cities often resist the construction of malls because they don't want to hurt downtown businesses.

There is a more expansive version of this idea which we might call the "delegation" theory. It goes like this: "when private individuals or groups are endowed by the State with powers or functions governmental in nature, they become agencies or instrumentalities of the State and subject to its constitutional limitations." Here we do not assume that the state has chosen X_Y for the purpose of shirking its constitutional duties. But X_Y gets its power to restrict people's rights from the state. This was the approach the Court used in holding that private parties can't exercise peremptory challenges in a racially discriminatory way. Congress passed a law authorizing litigants to make peremptory challenges. No one argued that Congress—like the city in my last example—was trying to dodge its constitutional duty. But, the

[6]Central Hardware Co. v. NLRB, 439 F.2d 1321 (8th Cir. 1971), rev'd, 407 U.S. 539 (1972).

Court said, "The fact that the government delegates ... this power to private litigants does not change the governmental character of the power exercised."[9]

Here again the justification for extending constitutional duties is that the state is responsible for the harm that occurs. In the conspiracy case the state intentionally causes harm (and X_Y intentionally assists it). In the delegation case the state is guilty of something like bad judgment, misplaced trust, or failure to control its agent. The state has acted like a father who gives his twelve-year-old son a rifle for a birthday present. There is nothing strange about measuring X_Y's behavior against the constitution in cases like these. Though the constitution speaks to the principal (*Y*) and not the agent (X_Y), it limits the authority that can be conferred on the agent.

One difficulty with the delegation theory is that it is often hard to say whether X_Y got its power from the state or not. Consider again the case of peremptory challenges. Although there is a federal law that codifies the right to choose jurors, parties have been making something like peremptory challenges for centuries. This is why the Court has insisted that the power exercised by X_Y must be a traditional public function. If it's something private parties have traditionally done on their own we can't say that the state has delegated the power to them, and the justification for bringing in constitutional standards falls apart. Now, although private parties have long exercised something like peremptory challenges, we might say that even at common law they got their power from the government. After all, the common law is "law," and the jury itself is an institution created by the government. But if the claim were that private nursing homes had to comply with the fourteenth amendment, we could fairly reply that they did not perform a traditional public function.[11]

If we want to identify powers that the government has delegated to private parties, however, it won't be enough to focus on tradition. There are some activities that have traditionally been both public and private. Schools are a good example. Education today is the most important function performed by state governments, but private schools have been around for a long time too, and they don't have their origin in a delegation of power from the state. In *Rendell-Baker v. Kohn* the plaintiff sued a private school for firing her in violation of her first amendment rights. The Court responded that the school was not performing a public function unless it was exercising an exclusive, not just a traditional, prerogative of the state.[12]

---

[9]Edmonson v. Leesville Concrete Co., 500 U.S. 614, 626 (1991).

[11]Blum v. Yaretsky, 457 U.S. 991, 1011–1012 (1982)[.]

[12]457 U.S. 830, 842 (1982)[.]

At this point the notion of a public function becomes a pretty narrow one. There aren't too many things that have been done traditionally and exclusively by the state. Indeed, state action questions only arise when the activity in question (building roads and sidewalks; running a school) is being done by someone else. What's more, it may make no difference to the first amendment claimant whether her freedom is taken away by the state or by a private actor. All that matters to her is that she is not allowed to speak. The Court stressed this point in *Marsh v. Alabama*: "Whether a corporation or a municipality owns or possesses the town the public in either case has an identical interest in the functioning of the community in such manner that the channels of communication remain free."

The strongest version of the public function argument says that this public interest alone justifies imposing constitutional duties on private actors. I will call this the "public interest" theory. It does not dispense altogether with the public/private distinction. Only some people, places, and activities are the subject of public interest; the rest are private. But in the conspiracy and delegation theories the public/private distinction functioned as an axiom: it was an assumption that they built upon. In the public interest theory the public/private distinction is a conclusion: we first decide how far to extend our freedoms, and then we call everything outside that domain private. We don't ask, at the first step, whether the government is involved somehow. It doesn't matter, because constitutional rules can apply to anyone. What we have to decide is whether the interests of those who want to extend freedom outweigh the interests of those who don't. As the Court put it in *Marsh v. Alabama*, "we balance the Constitutional rights of owners of property against those of the people to enjoy freedom of press and religion[.]"

Freedoms don't always win. There are some areas that will be left private. The important question is whether X_Y has the kind of power that we once associated with the state—whether X_Y is the "functional equivalent" of the state. As Justice Stevens put it, "it is no longer possible, if it ever was, to believe that a sharp line can be drawn between private and public actions. . . . The power . . . and the constitutional restrictions on that power are necessary correlatives in our system."[16] The Court held in *Logan Valley* that shopping malls had acquired precisely the kind of power that should subject them to constitutional restrictions: "The large-scale movement of this country's population from the cities to the suburbs has been accompanied by the advent of the suburban shopping center, typically a cluster of individual retail units on a single large privately owned tract. It has been estimated that by the end of 1966 there were between 10,000 and 11,000 shopping centers in the United States and Canada, accounting for

[16]Flagg Bros., Inc. v. Brooks, 436 U.S. 149, 178–179 (1978) (Stevens. J., dissenting).

approximately 37% of the total retail sales in those two countries." Unless all those malls have first amendment duties, the Court concluded, they could squeeze free expression out of a substantial part of the business world.

Notice how the Court, in asking about the extent of the mall's power, looks not just at Logan Valley but at all malls in the United States and Canada. If we take the public interest approach the reach of the first amendment, like the reach of the commerce clause, is an aggregate question. Congress can regulate the crops grown by individual wheat farmers because all such farmers taken together have a substantial effect on interstate commerce. The courts can impose first amendment duties on individual malls because in the aggregate, malls have a substantial effect on free speech. And for the same reason the constitution should reach retail stores in the malls, or stand-alone businesses like Central Hardware: " 'there is no closed class or category of businesses affected with a public interest. . . . The phrase . . . mean[s] no more than that an industry, for adequate reason, is subject to control for the public good.' "

There are, then, three versions of the public function argument. The first two—the conspiracy theory and the delegation theory—are fairly modest. There are persuasive reasons for applying them in a limited number of cases. When they do apply, they impose a derivative form of liability on X_Y: the constitution applies to its activity only because of what the state itself (Y) has done. The third version—the public interest theory—is much more expansive. It holds that we should, as it were, nationalize X_Y's business for first amendment purposes, because we can promote the public good by doing so. It imposes direct liability on X_Y: the constitution regulates its behavior regardless of what Y has done.

* * *

When Grace Marsh got arrested for distributing religious tracts in Chickasaw she was convicted of criminal trespass. The Alabama Code made it a crime to enter or remain on the premises of another after having been warned (as Marsh was) not to do so. One explanation for the Supreme Court's decision to let her off was that Chickasaw was a town just like any other town (the public function argument). But the Court hinted at an alternative explanation which went something like this: "[The fact that this was private property] is not sufficient to justify the State's permitting a corporation to govern a community of citizens so as to restrict their fundamental liberties and the enforcement of such restraint by the application of a state statute." Here the idea is that Chickasaw has constitutional duties because Alabama "permitt[ed]" it to restrict speech, and even "enforce[d]" the town's restrictions.

The Court did not explain what it meant by "permitting," but here are some plausible suggestions:

1. The Gulf Shipbuilding Corporation was an Alabama corporation. The state had granted it a charter that allowed it to do such things as run a company town.

2. Gulf acquired the property in question two years before Marsh was arrested. Marsh claimed that under Alabama common law the sidewalk had been dedicated to public use by Gulf's predecessors; and that in any event their deed conveyed to Gulf no right to exclude her. But as it turned out, Alabama property law was against her on both points. It gave Gulf good title and all the rights the company wanted.

3. Alabama had a law against trespassing that allowed property owners to evict people they didn't like from their property.

4. The Alabama police and the Alabama court system, at Gulf's request, enforced the trespass law against Marsh.

These are examples of state action in a very traditional sense: administrative action, common law, statutory law, prosecution, adjudication. What's more the opposite party in Marsh's lawsuit is the State of Alabama, not Gulf. This seems like a simple case of *X* claiming her rights against *Y*.

But it's more complicated than that. As a result of the Court's decision Gulf is subject to the same first amendment rules as the city of Mobile would be. It has no legal authority to evict Marsh from its property. (Marsh has a first amendment defense to any civil trespass action.) It also has a legal duty not to interfere with her proselytizing: Marsh could collect money damages if Gulf tried to silence her.

What's more, this theory takes us far beyond private actors like Gulf who are big enough to run a company town. It works just as well for you and me. Consider this case. On the edge of Lexington there is a new housing development on what used to be a horse farm. Before the houses could be built the city granted the developer a zoning change from agricultural to residential property and approved the layout of sewers, utilities, roads, and lots. People who buy houses there have to borrow money from banks whose lending practices are supervised by government agencies. Suppose that I bought such a house, and Marsh began handing out leaflets in my front yard. To evict her I would invoke state trespass law, ask a court to enjoin her, and get the sheriff to enforce the injunction. In a sense I, like Gulf Shipbuilding, am able to limit Marsh's freedom of speech only with the state's permission. If we take the permission theory seriously the state has insinuated itself into every detail of our lives. Every step we take is a move in a giant game of Mother May I? There is always state action, and constitutional rules apply to us all in everything we do.

There has to be something wrong with a theory that produces results like that. One influential attempt at explaining what is wrong has focused on what we mean by state *action*—i.e., on what counts as a constraint. Even if we assume that the state is involved in everything everyone does, we might say that only some of its acts bring constitutional rules into play. A state law that forbids leaflets or that gives the sheriff power to license speech is an obvious constraint on freedom. But much of state property and tort law is neutral on the subject of speech. People like me might invoke it to limit speech, or they might not; it's really up to them. And when the state acts neutrally the constitution doesn't come into play. It only applies to laws "prohibiting" the freedom of religion, "abridging" the freedoms of speech and press, etc. Those terms don't encompass neutral action.

But this explanation won't work. The most obvious problem is that it's wrong about neutral action not being a constraint. [Neutral tax laws, for example, are obvious constraints] on people like Marsh. An ordinance against littering is also neutral, but a city can't apply it to Marsh because it constrains her free speech rights. I don't want to overstate the problem. Many such laws are OK. But when they are, it is often because they comply with first amendment rules, not because the first amendment doesn't apply to them. They are constraints; they're just permissible constraints.

This suggests a second way of coping with the overwhelming implications of the permission theory. Suppose we do away with the public/private distinction and concede that the constitution imposes duties on each of us. This does not mean that I violate the constitution whenever I interfere with someone else's freedom of speech. Some constraints are forbidden; others are permitted. What we need to do in each case is to weigh the advantages of extending X_X's freedom against the harm this causes X_Y. I might still be able to evict Marsh from my front yard if the courts gave enough weight to my interest in privacy—including my interest in getting away from religious zealots. Gulf Shipbuilding couldn't evict Marsh because it has no interest in residential privacy. Central Hardware would be a slightly harder case, but it too might lose.

In form the permission theory is like the delegation version of the public function theory. Both hold X_Y derivatively liable because of what Y has done. Typically Y has done no intentional harm to X_X (peremptory challenges aren't designed to promote race discrimination; trespass law is not designed to limit free speech). But there is an enormous difference in coverage between the two theories. The delegation version is designed to cover a few people who have been deputized to do the work of the state (the public function). The permission theory is global. It applies to us all and to many, though not all, of the things we do.

In scope the permission theory looks like the public interest version of the public function theory. Both apply the constitution to lots of private actors, not just the government and a few agents. * * * The reasons for doing this are not identical but they are similar: one says we ought to nationalize private life, the other says we already have. In each case there is also an escape valve, so that not absolutely everything is covered. In the earlier case, constitutional rules are only enforced when there is a sufficient public interest. We ascertain that by balancing the interests of X_X and X_Y (the union and the hardware store). In the latter case we do exactly the same thing.

GILLIAN E. METZGER, PRIVATIZATION AS DELEGATION

103 COLUM.L.REV. 1367 (2003)

* * *

B. The Inadequacies of Current State Action Doctrine

In our system of constitutional government, the absence of state action in most instances of privatization should cause alarm. This absence results not because privatization removes responsibilities from the sphere of governmental endeavor, but because current state action doctrine is significantly underinclusive and ill-equipped to identify and thereby control private exercises of governmental power. Simultaneously, however, current doctrine is also overinclusive, because it makes private actors directly subject to constitutional constraints even when an instance of privatization does not raise the specter of unaccountable governmental power. These flaws combine to create perverse incentives for governments to delegate greater discretionary power over government programs to private actors, which ultimately worsen the threat to constitutional accountability posed by privatization.

1) Inadequate Tests of Governmental Power. One important standard against which to measure the success of current state action doctrine is the extent to which it preserves constitutional controls on the exercise of governmental power. After all, the only reason to even consider applying the Constitution outside of formal governmental institutions is to prevent the public-private divide from eviscerating the fundamental requirement of constitutional accountability. On this measure, current state action doctrine comes up short * * *.

[C]ontrol over third parties' access to governmental resources, specifically government benefits and government-subsidized services, represents governmental power. The Court's state action decisions demonstrate that current doctrine is largely unconcerned with governmental power in this form or more generally with the control over third parties that private entities gain as a result of their roles in government programs.

* * *

More generally, the Court's treatment of close governmental involvement as essentially a prerequisite for finding state action is fundamentally misguided, because such involvement is a very poor litmus test for determining when a private entity should be viewed as wielding governmental power. * * * Focusing on governmental involvement seems logical enough; where the government is closely involved in the actions of its private partners, it is more likely that they are serving as conduits for government decisions and policies rather than as independent decision makers. As a result, these are appropriately viewed as instances of private exercise of governmental power. But this concern gets at only part of the state action concern, that which addresses whether the government is trying to hide behind private action. It omits any inquiry into the nature of the powers exercised by private entities, as well as into whether the government is responsible for enhancing the authority these entities wield over others. Such an inquiry is essential given the way that privatization often not only enhances private actors' power over others, but provides them with forms of authority conventionally understood to constitute governmental power—such as control over government resources, programs, and regulation.

Once the focus shifts to assessing the powers wielded by private entities and away from identifying surreptitious government action, the inadequacy of tying the state action inquiry to identifying close government involvement becomes apparent. The extent of governmental power exercised by private actors is likely to vary inversely rather than directly with governmental involvement. Some minimal governmental involvement in the form of delegation of responsibilities to private actors is needed; but beyond that, the less the government is involved, the more discretion and power private entities have. * * *

The inverse relationship between the extent of governmental involvement and private authority means that current doctrine has it nearly exactly backwards. Private actors given broader discretion in their exercise of governmental power are less likely to be subject to constitutional constraints than those who operate under close government supervision and whose potential for abusive action is thus more curtailed. Indeed, this ill-fit suggests that the Supreme Court has refocused state action doctrine away from ensuring constitutional accountability of governmental power and towards ensuring constitutional accountability of government proper. That is, the Court uses state action doctrine to police against intentional evasion and bad faith by those who are indisputable government actors, but it does not view the doctrine as a safeguard against private actors wielding governmental power outside of constitutional constraints.

Notably, however, governmental involvement is also an inadequate metric even from the perspective of policing government. Government need not be closely involved in the specific decisions of a private entity in order to wield substantial influence over its actions. Instead, government can impose performance incentives or general requirements that as a practical matter mean that its private partners will follow particular courses of action, even though they remain free in theory to do otherwise. Government can also informally control private actors through its ability to cancel or not renew contracts. To the extent current state action doctrine requires governmental involvement in the specific acts being challenged and ignores background involvement unless it rises to the level of pervasive entanglement, the doctrine allows governments to exercise broad authority over a private entity's actions without triggering constitutional protections.

2) Unnecessary Intrusion on Governmental Regulatory Prerogatives. At the same time, however, current state action is also overinclusive. Under standard analysis, private entities are held fully subject to constitutional constraints if they are found to be state actors, even when imposing such liability on private actors is not needed to preserve constitutional accountability.

A good example of this overinclusivity comes from a vacated 1997 Ninth Circuit decision, *Grijalva v. Shalala.*[203] There, MCOs'[a] decisions denying Medicare beneficiaries' requests for medical services were found to constitute governmental action. According to the appeals court, detailed federal requirements for the procedures MCOs must use and the services they must cover, along with the presence of a governmental appeals process for service denials, meant that the MCOs and the federal government were joint participants in implementing Medicare. From a constitutional accountability perspective, holding the MCOs to be state actors seems unnecessary and purely the result of doctrinal rules. The plaintiffs sued only the Secretary of Health and Human Services (HHS), not the MCOs, their goal being to force the Secretary to do a better job at policing the procedures used by MCOs in making coverage decisions. The Secretary, in turn, had disclaimed responsibility for the MCOs' actions, arguing that they were unrelated private entities. State action doctrine thus served as a bridge that allowed the federal government to be charged with responsibility for the MCOs' actions even though the government did not directly participate in specific coverage denials until the appeals level. [Once] the government is [held] liable for private acts, constitutional accountability is assured. Applying constitutional constraints to the private entities or individuals

---

[203] 152 F.3d 115 (9th Cir. 1998), *vacated & remanded*, 526 U.S. 1026 (1999).

[a] An MCO is a managed care organization. [Ed. Note]

involved gives plaintiffs additional defendants, but not additional substantive protection against constitutional violations. * * *

* * *

3) The Perverse Incentives of Current State Action Doctrine. That current doctrine ignores the way governmental power is exercised in the modern administrative state and leads to the unnecessary "constitutionalization" of private actors is perhaps indictment enough. Yet an additional basis for concern exists. The combination of these two features means that current doctrine creates perverse incentives that encourage governments to privatize and to do so in a fashion that allows private entities to exercise government-enhanced power with very little accountability.

At present, state action analysis gives the government the following choices: It can directly implement a program, providing both services and regulatory oversight itself, in which case constitutional constraints are fully applicable. It can also hand over implementation to private entities but remain closely involved in supervising service provision and in program management. [This] will mean not simply that the government's own actions and oversight decisions are subject to constitutional constraints, but also that its private partners may be drawn into the Constitution's orbit. Alternatively, the government can cede direct implementation to private entities and eschew close supervision. Pursuing this route makes it less likely that the government will be held responsible for failing to ensure that its private partners adhere to constitutional constraints or that these partners will be held subject to such constraints if sued independently. Moreover, avoiding constitutional liability under this third option does not require government to surrender all control over programs. Instead, the privatization cases suggest that the government need only forego involvement in specific day-to-day decisions as well as formal institutional control over the private entities to whom implementation responsibilities are given. The government can still "safely" employ general oversight measures and independent accountability mechanisms to ensure that private providers and regulators deliver promised services and serve the public interest.

* * *

C. The Road Not Taken: Private Delegation Doctrine

Private delegation doctrine takes over where state action leaves off. Rather than asking whether ostensibly private actors should be considered public for constitutional purposes, it accepts their private status and asks instead whether the Constitution prohibits governments from delegating certain powers to private actors. These prohibitions vary somewhat according to the level of government involved. When it is state government, the federal constitutional textual basis is the Fourteenth Amendment's Due

Process Clause and the underlying concern is that public power may be abused to achieve particular private aims instead of the public interest. This same due process concern exists in the federal context, but here separation of powers constitutes an additional potential barrier to delegation of power to private actors.

The story of constitutional law's treatment of privatization is not complete without discussion of private delegation doctrine, although the most salient characteristic of current private delegation doctrine is its dormant status. A variety of private delegations came before the Supreme Court in the period from the end of the Nineteenth Century to the beginning of the Twentieth. The New Deal gave sharp focus to the private delegation doctrine, as reliance on private regulation and corporatism represented a cornerstone of President Roosevelt's early efforts to revive the national economy. At first, the Supreme Court responded with hostility to the incorporation of private actors into public regulation. In *Carter v. Carter Coal Company,*[237] the Court invalidated legislation making wage and hour agreements entered into by a majority of miners and large coal producers in a particular region binding on all miners and producers in that area. According to the Court, "in the very nature of things, one person may not be intrusted with the power to regulate the business of another" and allowing a majority of private participants in an industry to do so therefore constituted "clearly arbitrary" interference with the minority's personal liberty and property in violation of due process. But the Court soon effectively reversed course. In *Currin v. Wallace*, it sustained a regulatory scheme under which the Secretary of Agriculture was authorized to impose uniform tobacco standards binding on all tobacco sales in an area if two-thirds of the growers voted in favor of such regulation in a referendum.[238] Similarly, in *Sunshine Anthracite Coal Company v. Adkins* ("*Sunshine*") the Court upheld a later incarnation of the Bituminous Coal Act which allowed local coal producers sitting on local coal boards to set rules governing the sale of coal, with these rules being subject to approval, disapproval or modification by the government's Bituminous Coal Commission.[239] In neither *Currin* nor *Sunshine* did the Court overrule *Carter*. Instead, it held that, unlike *Carter,* these cases did not involve delegation of legislative power to private actors: in *Currin,* because public officials determined the substantive content of regulations and private individuals were limited to deciding whether these regulations would go into effect; and in *Sunshine* because the statute required public officials to review and place an official imprimatur upon the privately devised regulations. * * *

---

[237]298 U.S. 238 (1936).
[238]306 U.S. 1 (1939).
[239]310 U.S. 381 (1940).

Yet while *Carter's* constitutional prohibition on private delegations thus remains alive in theory, it is generally believed to be all but dead in practice. Almost all private delegations are upheld. The Court is satisfied by formal provision for government ratification, however perfunctory. The private delegations that have been sustained often involve substantial direct control over third parties; even seemingly limited delegations that simply grant private entities the power to trigger governmental action, such as the ability to force an administrative hearing or commence a civil penalty action, can be quite significant. Interestingly, many decisions examining private delegations at the federal level use the essentially same framework as is applied to "public" delegations—that is, legislative grants of power to the executive branch—thereby suggesting that the Court sees such private delegations as presenting nothing beyond ordinary separation of powers issues.

* * *

IV. A New Private Delegation Analysis For An Era of Privatized Government

* * *

A. The Case for Rethinking State Action in Private Delegation Terms

* * *

Existing private delegation decisions * * * provide the seeds for a new constitutional analysis of privatization. Like these decisions, the proposed analysis is structural in focus, in that it targets the inquiry on delegations of power to private actors and on the overall system of constraints to which these delegations are subject. Unlike the prior decisions, however, this analysis generally accepts that private actors can exercise the type of power at issue; instead, it focuses on assessing the impact the private delegation has on the constitutional imperative of accountability. The central concern is determining whether a private delegation is structured so as to ensure that private exercises of governmental power do not violate constitutional requirements. Constitutional accountability thus has primacy, because the government is prohibited from delegating governmental power in ways that are not sufficiently constrained. But the government also has flexibility in structuring its relationships with its private partners, because a variety of mechanisms exists by which constitutional constraints can be enforced.

Notwithstanding its emphasis on adequate regulatory protections, two central features make this analysis at bottom a constitutional inquiry. First, the requirement that adequate protections be extended to privatized programs rests ultimately not on political will, but instead on the Constitution itself, which imposes fundamental limits on how government can act.

Second, the Constitution provides the specific substantive content of the protections that regulatory mechanisms must afford, as well as the procedural requirement that these mechanisms must allow for individual enforcement. Even when involvement of private entities affects the substance of constitutional rights, the determination of what protections must be afforded remains a constitutional one; it turns on assessing specifically the constitutional interests at stake, as opposed to simply determining which protections will yield the best policy outcome, "all-things-considered."

Yet under this approach constitutional law will function differently from the standard court-centered image of constitutional adjudication, where the courts bear primary responsibility for enforcing constitutional requirements. Here the courts provide the constitutional baseline, but the task of translating that baseline into practice falls to the elected branches of government. Moreover, this approach transforms the constitutional right being asserted. The claim fundamentally at issue becomes not that the private delegate exercised its powers in ways that violated the plaintiff's constitutional rights, but rather that the private delegation *itself* violates the Constitution because it fails to ensure a sufficient level of constitutional accountability. This latter constitutional claim finds a textual home in the Due Process Clauses because allowing exercises of governmental power outside of constitutional constraints is a violation of the clauses' prohibition on arbitrary government action. But it also can be seen as rooted not in a particular constitutional text, but in the structural Constitution, because—like separation of powers or federalism—the principle of constitutional accountability which this claim embodies is one of the basic structural postulates of our constitutional system.

* * *

C. Application of the Proposed Private Delegation Analysis

To summarize what the proposed private delegation analysis would look like: An individual injured or likely to be injured by a private delegate's action would bring suit against the government (and perhaps the private delegate itself), arguing that the delegation authorizing the private action is unconstitutional because it is inadequately structured to ensure that private exercises of governmental power adhere to constitutional requirements. In assessing the merits of this claim, the court would first determine whether the delegation creates an agency relationship between the private actor and the government. If not, and if the private delegation does not otherwise involve a clear grant of governmental power or power to act on the government's behalf, the plaintiff would lose on the merits.

Where the court finds the existence of such an agency relationship, it would then proceed to assess whether the delegation is adequately structured to preserve constitutional accountability. This requirement is met where some mechanism exists by which the individual can enforce constitutional limits on private exercises of governmental power, such as a statutory surrogate for a constitutional claim or the ability to assert actual constitutional claims against the government. The government becomes a potential target for constitutional challenge when it either sanctions the private delegate's specific actions on administrative review or makes an independent determination as an alternative to private decisionmaking. Other means of satisfying constitutional accountability demands are to structure the delegation so that no private delegate exercises monopolistic or quasi-monopolistic control over access to government benefits, or to delegate only very limited powers. A court may also conclude that a private delegation meets constitutional requirements, even limitations on private delegates equivalent to those that apply to government, because in a particular context the Constitution imposes lesser substantive constraints on private entities wielding governmental authority.

As this description suggests, the claim that a private delegation is inadequately structured to preserve constitutional accountability can take the form of a facial challenge. In some cases, however, the inadequacy of alternative accountability mechanisms will only become apparent through practical application; for example, it may not be clear from the face of governing regulations that certain types of claims are excluded from an administrative complaint system. In such as-applied contexts, plaintiffs would combine their claim for relief under existing accountability mechanisms with the alternative argument that if such relief is unavailable, the delegation is unconstitutional.

If a private delegation creates an agency relationship, or involves delegation of power to act on the government's behalf, and is inadequately structured to ensure that governmental power is ultimately kept within constitutional limits, the delegation is unconstitutional. The usual remedy will be for a court to invalidate the delegation and hold the government responsible for the delegate's unconstitutional acts. But in rare situations, courts may instead apply constitutional constraints directly to the private delegates involved, because doing so represents the only means of ensuring constitutional accountability.

The major question remaining is what difference the proposed private delegation analysis will make in practice. Some sense of an answer comes from examining the different results in past state action cases, summarized in Chart I[.]

CHART I

Case	Current State Action Doctrine	Proposed Private Delegation Analysis	
		Result	**Rationale**
Blum v. Yaretsky	No state action	Unconstitutional private delegation	The delegation to nursing homes of power to determine Medicaid beneficiary's need for nursing services creates an agency relationship, and this delegation is not adequately structured to preserve constitutional accountability: no mechanism exists by which individual beneficiaries can challenge nursing homes' care determinations; in addition, homes exercise quasi-monopoly powers over residents.
Rendell-Baker v. Kohn	No state action	Constitutional private delegation	The delegation to private school of responsibility to provide education to special needs students creates an agency relationship, but at least in regard to teacher terminations, informal state oversight is adequate to preserve constitutional accountability.
West v. Atkins	State action	Unconstitutional private delegation	The delegation to a private doctor to provide medical services to inmates creates an agency relationship, and this delegation is not adequately structured to preserve constitutional accountability: the government undertook no oversight of the doctor's medical decisions; private law remedies such as malpractice suits do not support a claim for failure to provide medical services; and the doctor exercised a monopoly over inmates' access to medical care.
American Mfrs. Mut. Ins. Co. v. Sullivan	No state action	Constitutional private delegation	The statutory authorization for private medical insurers to decline to pay workers' compensation claims absent a finding of medical necessity does not create an agency relationship.

Brentwood Acad. v. Tennessee Secondary Sch. Athletic Ass'n	State action	Unconstitutional private delegation	The prior state delegation of exclusive control over interscholastic athletics, combined with public school officials' *de facto* control of the Association, creates an agency relationship, and this delegation is not adequately structured to preserve constitutional accountability: the Association's decisions were not subjected to governmental review; no alternative means of enforcing constitutional requirements existed; and the Association exercised substantial authority over high school athletics in the state.
San Francisco Arts & Athletics v. United States Olympic Comm.	No state action	Unconstitutional private delegation	Whether Congress' delegation to the USOC of exclusive oversight over amateur sports created an agency relationship with the federal government is a close question: this delegation, as evidenced by Congress' chartering of the USOC and granting it direct access to federal funds, served federal policy goals; however, the government bore no statutory responsibility to provide oversight of amateur sports or of the United States' representation at the Olympics. Regardless, the grant of exclusive oversight represents a clear delegation of governmental power, because the USOC is authorized to regulate amateur athletics and take enforcement action against individual athletes and organizations. While procedural requirements imposed on the USOC by statute may be adequate to meet due process requirements, mechanisms to enforce other constitutional limits appear lacking.

ERWIN CHEMERINSKY, RETHINKING STATE ACTION

80 Nw.U.L.Rev. 503, 535–546, 550–553 (1985).

THE CONTEMPORARY JUSTIFICATIONS FOR THE STATE ACTION DOCTRINE

* * *

Contemporary commentators all offer the same two reasons for requiring state action. First, the doctrine protects individual liberty by defining a zone of private conduct that does not have to comply with the Constitution. Second, limiting the Constitution's protections to state action preserves state sovereignty by giving the states almost complete authority to regulate private behavior. I believe that the state action requirement is unnecessary to achieve these purposes and, in fact, is counterproductive to these goals.

A. Preserving a Zone of Private Autonomy

The state action doctrine frequently is defended on the ground that it "preserves an area of individual freedom by limiting the reach of federal law and federal judicial power."[180] Undoubtedly this is correct; the state action doctrine does preserve the liberty of private parties to ignore the Constitution and the limits contained within it. In considering whether the overall effect of the state action doctrine is to enhance individual liberty, however, we must remember that every time a person's freedom to violate a constitutional right is upheld, a victim's liberty is sacrificed. In each case when a question of state action arises, both the freedom of the violator and the freedom of the victim are at stake. In challenges to private racial discrimination, for example, there is the claimed liberty to discriminate, say, on freedom of association grounds, and the claimed right to be free from discrimination. No matter how a court decides, someone's liberty will be expanded and someone's liberty restricted. To assert that the state action doctrine is desirable because it preserves autonomy and liberty is to look at only one side of the equation.

Furthermore, the state action doctrine is an absurd basis for choosing between the two liberties. The concept of state action completely ignores the competing rights at stake and chooses based entirely on the identity of the actors. There is no reason to believe that the state action doctrine preserves more liberty than it denies because it does not even consider the rights involved. In fact, under the state action doctrine, the rights of the private violator always are favored over the rights of the victims. Therefore, state action enhances freedom only if it is believed that the liberty to violate the Constitution always is more important than the individual rights that are infringed.

---

[180] Lugar v. Edmondson Oil Co., 457 U.S. 922, 936 (1982).

* * *

If the goal is to protect individual freedom, then it is best to decide cases on the merits, without reference to state action. The argument that the state action requirement is necessary to preserve individual autonomy obviously is based on the premise that there is a zone of private conduct that should not be constrained by the Constitution. Accordingly, it would make the most sense to identify the precise rights in that zone and directly protect them. Consider an example frequently mentioned in the literature. It often is suggested that if there were no state action requirement, people could not exclude demonstrators from their living rooms and every dinner party would have to be racially integrated. Such a prospect is antithetical because it offends a belief in privacy and freedom of association. Therefore, the logical way to avoid the harm is to hold directly that, in such circumstances, the rights of privacy and freedom of association outweigh freedom of speech and the right not to be discriminated against. The state action doctrine adds absolutely nothing to the protection of individual liberties. The values hidden in the claim that state action is necessary to preserve personal autonomy can be made explicit and protected openly.

Thus, abandoning the concept of state action does not eliminate the distinction between the public and private realms. Surely everyone believes that there are certain private activities that should be completely uncontrolled by the state. What is suggested is eliminating state action as the dividing line between public and private activities. The state action doctrine is a totally arbitrary basis for separation; the division should be made by focusing on what is substantively desirable to keep private. The emphasis should be on defining the content of the private domain that is immune from state supervision in any form. Simply stated, if the state action requirement is jettisoned, courts will directly balance the competing liberties involved in each case. Such an approach maximizes protection of liberty, replacing the current policy of always choosing to favor the rights of the private violator over those of the victim.

At the very least, state action is unnecessary to protect individual autonomy; direct protection would be at least as effective in upholding personal liberties. In fact, I would suggest that the state action requirement is counterproductive—that individual freedom would be enhanced greatly by eliminating the state action doctrine.

First, allowing the concept of state action to determine when rights are protected undermines liberty by allowing all private invasions of rights, even when the balance completely favors the victims. For example, assume that a utility company with a state-granted monopoly refuses to provide service to blacks. If the holding of *Jackson v. Metropolitan Edison Co.* were followed, a court could not stop the discrimination because there is no state action.[199] Yet, it is hard to imagine any freedom of the utility company that outweighs the harms of the discrimination imposed. Frequently, corporations are allowed to infringe basic rights, even when their freedom is far less important than the liberties infringed.

* * *

Second, eliminating the state action doctrine enhances protection of liberty by focusing attention directly on the valued rights. Obviously, the courts already balance somewhat in determining when state action exists. For example, the state action doctrine is applied more leniently in cases involving allegations of private racial discrimination than in situations when the challenge is to a violation of other rights. This differential approach reflects the courts' unarticulated conclusion that stopping racial discrimination is more important than protecting other rights—that in instances of discrimination the rights of the victim are more important than those of the violator. But this balancing is hidden by the courts, obscured behind the question whether there is state action.

Liberty would best be protected if the courts openly articulated the competing interests that they were balancing. This would force the courts clearly to identify and define the conflicting liberties, enhancing understanding of each of the rights at stake. In dismissing cases for want of state action, the courts fail to describe the liberties of the violators that are preserved by court abstention, and thus the zone of private autonomy protected by the state action doctrine remains undefined. If there are liberties sufficiently important to justify discrimination or infringements of freedom of speech, society is best off if these interests are articulated so that they can be applied in other situations and recognized as a part of personal freedom.

Finally, the state action doctrine does not adequately protect liberties because even if state action is found and private parties are deemed to infringe rights with the impermissible aid of the state, the court does not order the offensive conduct to stop. Rather, the court orders the state only to disengage itself from the challenged activity. Although in some cases the effect is to end the constitutional violation, in other instances the behavior continues, but without the state's involvement. Liberty would be maximized if the court could directly halt the violations of rights.

A different, stronger argument might be made that the state action requirement protects personal autonomy by creating a shield that immunizes certain conduct from any governmental review. Arguably, without a state action doctrine, individuals could be called into court to justify any

---

[199] 419 U.S. 345 (1974). *Jackson* involved a claim that the utility company denied due process by terminating service without providing a hearing. The Supreme Court held that there was no state action.

behavior that interferes with another person's rights. The prospect of such government review is itself a denial of liberty and the state action doctrine is useful because it creates a zone of private activity about which the government may not even inquire.

The flaw in this argument is that it assumes that the state action requirement is necessary to create such a shield. There is no reason why laws and legal doctrines cannot directly create a shield in the absence of a state action doctrine. Balancing need not be done on a case-by-case basis by calling individuals into court in each instance to account for their actions. General rules could be formulated in some areas, where the balance in almost every case will be in a particular direction. For example, a broad rule might be articulated that the associational rights of hosts of private dinner parties always will outweigh the rights of uninvited guests not to be discriminated against. * * *

* * *

B. Preserving a Zone of State Sovereignty

A second contemporary justification for the state action requirement is that it upholds federalism by preserving a zone of state sovereignty. The *Civil Rights Cases* held that federal constitutional rights do not govern individual behavior and, furthermore, that Congress lacks authority to apply them to private conduct:[211] structuring the legal relationships of private citizens was for the state, not the national government. Thus, the state action doctrine protects state sovereignty by leaving governance of individual behavior to state political processes.

This justification for state action assumes, first, that under the Constitution there is a zone of activities completely reserved to state control. The Court in the *Civil Rights Cases* explicitly stated that the tenth amendment creates such a zone of authority, and that congressional regulation of private conduct "is repugnant to the Tenth Amendment." The regulation of private behavior, including protection of civil rights, was seen as a matter entirely of state, not federal, authority.

Thus, the *Civil Rights Cases* reflected a belief in "dual sovereignty"—that there is a domain, which only the states may regulate. The doctrine of "dual sovereignty" dominated constitutional law from the late nineteenth century until 1937. Repeatedly during this era, the Supreme Court struck down congressional economic regulations, holding that they concerned activities which only the states may control.[218] But the experience of the

---

[211] 109 U.S. 3, 11 (1883).

[218] *See, e.g.,* Carter v. Carter Coal Co., 298 U.S. 238 (1936); A.L.A. Schechter Poultry Corp. v. United States, 295 U.S. 495 (1935); Hammer v. Dagenhart, 247 U.S. 251 (1918) (striking down congressional regulations as exceeding congressional power and violating

Depression, the pressure from President Roosevelt's Court-packing plan, and the perceived need for federal government actions led to the complete demise of the concept of dual sovereignty. No longer is it believed that there is a zone of activities which only the states may regulate.[220]

In 1940, in *United States v. Darby,* the Supreme Court declared that the tenth amendment "states but a truism that all is retained which has not been surrendered."[221] In other words, under this view of the tenth amendment, Congress may legislate if it points to an enumerated power as justification for its action. If such authority exists, congressional action is valid, irrespective of the activity regulated. There are no activities that only state governments can regulate. Viewing the state action requirement as a way to protect state sovereignty, thus, is based on the false assumption that there exists a zone of constitutionally reserved state authority.

Second, even if such a zone exists, there is the further assumption that a state's area of control includes determining the protection of individual rights. In particular, it is assumed that state autonomy includes the ability of the state to decide which fundamental rights will not be protected from private interference. The claim must be that under the fourteenth amendment states have the right to decide to do nothing to stop private discrimination or abridgment of free speech. Once it is established that constitutional rights should be protected from private interference, however, then why tolerate a state's refusal to provide protection? State sovereignty provides a justification only if it is believed that a state's rights are more important than individual rights—a premise consistently rejected since the Civil War.

* * *

It might be argued that although Congress has the authority to override state control of private behavior, courts do not have this power. The notion is that states have their institutional interests represented in Congress, and, therefore, the legislature can be trusted best to balance national and state interests.[232] Yet, concluding that courts may not stop private infringements of rights assumes that states have the authority to tolerate the denial of liberty and equality if Congress does not act to restrain them. States clearly have no such authority. * * * If nothing is reserved to the states, then there is no limitation on the judicial power to vindicate rights because of state sovereignty.

---

state sovereignty).

[220] *See* Garcia v. San Antonio Metropolitan Transit Authority, [469 U.S. 528 (1985).]

[221] 312 U.S. 100, 124 (1941). * * *

[232] *Cf.* Garcia v. San Antonio Metropolitan Dist., [469 U.S. 528 (1985)] (political safeguards of federalism are sufficient to protect states' interests); * * * Wechsler, *The Political Safeguards of Federalism,* 54 Colum.L.Rev. 543 (1954) (states' interests are represented in Congress, and, therefore, federalism issues can be left to the legislature).

Furthermore, to conclude that only Congress can compel states to safeguard rights leaves protection of basic liberties to the political process. If Congress does not remedy state denials of liberty, violations of individual freedoms would be unchecked. The argument about state sovereignty is that states, through their political systems, have the authority to structure individual activities. Such deference to majoritarian politics, however, is completely inappropriate when rights are at stake. The whole idea of enshrining rights in a Constitution is to protect them from majority rule. Judicial review to prevent state denials of due process and equal protection therefore is essential.

Finally, eliminating the requirement of state action would not cause a loss of state autonomy. Although states would be compelled to protect rights, they would have great flexibility in choosing the means to be used. State laws would become a major guarantee of liberty, making detailed federal standards unnecessary. Once laws protecting the rights of individuals were well established, federal supervision would be largely unnecessary. Thus, in the long term, more responsibility would shift to state governments, enhancing state sovereignty.

* * *

Doing Away With the State Action Requirement

I have argued that limiting the Constitution's protections to state action is harmful because it permits deprivations of fundamental liberties and that it is completely unnecessary because nothing valuable would be lost without it. The inescapable conclusion is that the doctrine should be banished from American law. The effect of discarding the concept of state action is that the Constitution would be viewed as a code of social morals, not just of governmental conduct, bestowing individual rights that no entity, public or private, could infringe without a compelling justification. Such an approach makes sense especially because the "Constitution was designed to embody and celebrate values and to inculcate proper acceptance of them, as much as to compel governments to abide by them."[250]

Freedom of speech, privacy, and equality are rights of the individual that must be protected from all unjustified deprivations. This does not necessarily mean that protection must come from the Constitution or the federal courts. The legislatures, federal and state, can protect rights from private interference by statute, as Congress did in the area of civil rights. State courts can protect rights through the development of the common law. When protection is afforded in this way, application of the Constitution is unnecessary and would be eliminated—not because of the application of the state action doctrine, but because there is no deprivation of rights.

---

[250]Franz v. United States, 707 F.2d 582, 594 n. 45 (D.C.Cir.1983).

Direct application of the Constitution is necessary only to see if other sources are providing adequate protection. Eliminating the state action requirement would, I hope, encourage legislatures and state courts to fulfill their roles in protecting rights. If no other redress exists, then it would be essential that the federal courts provide protection. * * *

Again, applying constitutional principles to private conduct does not mean that all individual conduct must meet the same standard as that required of the government. Courts would apply traditional principles of constitutional adjudication to determine if sufficiently important justifications exist for the challenged conduct. Essentially, the courts would balance the rights of the violator and victim in deciding the proper result. Thus, the entire inquiry as to state action would be discarded; the only question would be whether a person's rights were unjustifiably infringed.

One objection to eliminating the requirement of state action is that it seemingly would make almost every crime or tort a constitutional violation. Any action denying life, liberty, or property—meaning most crimes and torts—would, arguably, be actionable as a constitutional claim. This objection, however, ignores the fact that if state criminal and tort laws provide adequate remedies, then there is no denial of due process. * * *

* * *

A second objection to eliminating the state action doctrine is that there will be an undesirable increase in the power of the judiciary: if courts are able to redress all private violations of rights, they will have too much control over American society.

* * *

[But] in evaluating the claim that the courts will have too much power, the question is, "too much power compared to what?" The common-law role of the courts was to ensure the vindication of all rights that an individual possesses. Therefore, eliminating the state action doctrine merely would restore the powers that traditionally belonged to the courts. Moreover, in modern society, the most important role courts perform is the protection of rights. Through the removal of the state action requirement, courts would be given precisely the power to accomplish this task.

WILLIAM P. MARSHALL, DILUTING CONSTITUTIONAL RIGHTS: RETHINKING "RETHINKING STATE ACTION"

80 NW.U.L.REV. 558, 561–564, 566–569 (1985).

OF VICTIMS AND VIOLATORS: THE HARMS IN BALANCING CONSTITUTIONAL INTERESTS OF PRIVATE INDIVIDUALS

* * * *Rethinking State Action* is replete with references to constitutional "victims" and "violators." The distinction between victim and violator, however, is not as clear as Professor Chemerinsky would have us believe. In most, if not all, of the cases in which Chemerinsky criticizes the use of the state action doctrine to avoid constitutional inquiry, there are serious constitutional interests present on behalf of the defendant as well as the plaintiff. For example, in *Taylor v. St. Vincent's Hospital,*[18] the plaintiff sought to compel the defendant, a private hospital, to perform a medical procedure that it opposed on religious grounds. Similarly, in *Cook v. Advertiser Co.,*[19] the plaintiffs sought to affect the right of a newspaper to control the content of its publication. Can it rightfully be said that the plaintiffs in these cases were constitutional victims while the defendants were violators?

These are not isolated examples. In defending an eviction motivated by disagreement with a tenant's political beliefs, a landlord can assert the constitutional defenses of due process property rights and rights of association and speech. A rule that entitles the tenant to the premises simply recharacterizes the tenant as the violator and the landlord as the victim of constitutional deprivation. Similarly, in employment cases, employers may be able to raise rights of association in defense against discrimination claims and also will be able to utilize rights of free speech if the refusal to employ is based on political considerations. If an employer loses, is he a constitutional victim?

* * *

* * * Professor Chemerinsky's solution to resolve the inevitable conflicts is that age-old constitutional standby: balancing. For Professor Chemerinsky, the way to assure that both sides receive the fullest constitutional protection is to balance the constitutional interests at stake. He argues that the state action requirement is actually implicit, "obscured" balancing and states, "Liberty would best be protected if the courts openly articulated the competing interests that they were balancing. This would

---

[18]523 F.2d 75 (9th Cir.1975), *cert. denied,* 424 U.S. 948 (1976).

[19]323 F.Supp. 1212 (D.Ala.1971), *aff'd on other grounds,* 458 F.2d 1119 (5th Cir.1972). * * *

force the courts clearly to identify and define the conflicting liberties, enhancing understanding of each of the rights at stake."

But is this "articulated" balancing really possible, and if possible, advisable? How does one articulate valid grounds of decision in choosing between the right of a parent to disinherit his offspring because the latter intends to marry outside of the religion, and the rights of the offspring and putative spouse to be free of religious discrimination? How does one choose between the right of a church to discriminate on religious grounds and the right of a minority seeking admission to that church to be free of discrimination? How, in cases like *St. Vincent's,* can the right to contraceptive surgery be evaluated in relation to the right of a religious hospital to practice medicine according to its theological tenets? More importantly, how are judges going to make consistent decisions with only open-ended balancing as a guideline?

* * * Given the extreme difficulty of choosing between competing rights in the first place, perhaps the decision to insulate private activity from constitutional scrutiny is justified as a way to avoid forcing judges to make impossible decisions.

* * *

Even more critical than the dangers of balancing itself is that the balancing foreseen by Chemerinsky will create a class of constitutional "losers." If one constitutional right is embattled against another, the protection accorded one liberty is going to be diminished. The courts would be forced to articulate priorities in constitutional liberties, with the result that certain liberties eventually might be found to possess only secondary constitutional significance. This in turn may lead to less protection being accorded these rights, even in cases involving "pure" state action.

* * *

Still another difficulty lies in the constitutional balancing process as applied to private law: It inhibits or precludes other sources of legal development. Assume a person, in renting a room in a one-family dwelling, chooses to discriminate because of political differences with the tenant and the court vindicates the landlord's interests under a balancing analysis. What if Congress or a state subsequently enacted a statute prohibiting evictions for political reasons? Because the court's earlier decision was held to be constitutionally mandated, there would be a constitutional bar to the new legislation.

In short, the effect of constitutionalizing private law is to freeze that law. Under existing doctrine, if legislative or common-law rules prove unsatisfactory, they can be changed. On the other hand, a doctrine of constitutional law that imposes judicially created parameters on private conduct places serious constraints on the ability of both the common law and legislatures to respond to social issues.

* * *

THE INEVITABLE DILUTION: REPLACING STATE ACTION WITH ADEQUATE STATE REMEDIES

Professor Chemerinsky's thesis also ignores a practical concern inherent in constitutional jurisprudence: The more broadly rights are drawn, the more difficult it becomes to enforce those rights stringently. In first amendment jurisprudence, for example, although everything we do may be characterized as "expressive," it is nonetheless inappropriate to consider all individual action as constitutionally protected. As Professor Karst has explained, "the danger of such a doctrinal approach is that First Amendment doctrine would become encumbered with new limits and exceptions, because some claims inevitably would be rejected. From these decisions a doctrinal infection would spread, touching even traditional First Amendment concerns."[53] The strength accorded the first amendment, in short, becomes "diluted."

Professor Chemerinsky faces a similar problem in his efforts to apply constitutional principles to private law. Some modifying principle must be adopted in order to make the constitutional protection meaningful. Chemerinsky, as we have seen, does not adopt the approach used in first amendment jurisprudence itself: the exclusion of certain types of expression from full constitutional protection by definition and categorization. Rather, his solution is more surprising.

Professor Chemerinsky argues that if the state provides an adequate remedy, a constitutional violation should not be found. Indeed, he goes so far as to suggest that it "[be assumed] state common law protects natural rights." This is a strange proposition to be advanced by one advocating civil libertarian interests.

Modern civil rights law, in contrast, is predicated on the conclusion in *Monroe v. Pape*[59] that state remedies are inadequate substitutes for constitutional rights. In *Monroe,* Justice Harlan stated, "a deprivation of a constitutional right is significantly different from and more serious than a violation of a state right and therefore deserves a different remedy even though the same act may constitute both a state tort and the deprivation of a constitutional right."

* * *

[53]Karst, *The Freedom of Intimate Association,* 89 Yale L.J. 624, 654–55 n. 140 (1980).
[59]365 U.S. 167 (1961). * * *

The underlying policies and importance of *Monroe* require more development than can be offered here and, in any event, the significance of Professor Chemerinsky's adequate state remedy solution is not in its specifics. Rather, the point is that once constitutional principles are so broadly drawn, some limiting principle becomes necessary. Before adopting Chemerinsky's thesis, then, we must ask whether the cure offered for private infringements of constitutional rights is worth a remedy that undercuts existing constitutional protections against state officials.

BIBLIOGRAPHY

Alexander, *Constitutional Torts, the Supreme Court, and the Law of Noncontradiction: An Essay on* Zinermon v. Burch, 87 Nw.U.L.Rev. 576 (1993).

Alexander and Horton, WHOM DOES THE CONSTITUTION COMMAND? (1988).

Amar and Widawsky, *Child Abuse as Slavery: A Thirteenth Amendment Response to* DeShaney, 105 Harv.L.Rev. 1359 (1992).

Alexander, *Cutting the Gordian Knot: State Action And Self–Help Repossession,* 2 Hast.L.Q. 893 (1975).

Berman, *Cyberspace and the State Action Debate: The Cultural Value of Applying Constitutional Norms to "Private" Regulation,* 71 U.Colo.L. Rev. 1263 (2000).

Bittker and Kaufman, *Taxes and Civil Rights: "Constitutionalizing" the Internal Revenue Code,* 82 Yale L.J. 51 (1972).

Black, *Foreword: "State Action," Equal Protection, and California's Proposition 14,* 81 Harv.L.Rev. 69 (1967).

Blumoff, *Some Moral Implications of Finding No State Action,* 70 Notre Dame L.Rev. 95 (1994).

Bradley, *Untying the State Action Knot,* 7 J. Contemp. Legal Issues 223 (1996).

Buchanan, *A Conceptual History of the State Action Doctrine: The Search for Government Responsibility,* 34 Houston L.Rev. 333 (1997).

Burke and Reber, *State Action, Congressional Power and Creditors' Rights: An Essay on the Fourteenth Amendment,* 46 S.Cal.L.Rev. 1003 (1973).

Chemerinsky, *More Is Not Less: A Rejoinder to Professor Marshall,* 80 Nw.U.L.Rev. 571 (1985).

Choper, *Thoughts on State Action: The "Government Function" and "Power* Theory*" Approaches,* 1979 Wash. U.L.Q. 757.

Colker and Scott, *Dissing States?: Invalidation of State Action During the Rehnquist Era*, 88 Va.L.Rev. 1301 (2002).

Comment, *Tax Incentives as State Action,* 122 U.Pa.L.Rev. 414 (1973).

Epstein, *Classical Liberalism Meets the New Constitutional Order*, 3 Chi.J. Int'l L. 455 (2002).

Eule and Varat, *Transporting First Amendment Norms to the Private Sector: With Every Wish There Comes a Curse*, 45 UCLA L.Rev. 1537 (1998).

Freedman, *Extending Public Law Norms Through Privatization*, 116 Harv.L.Rev. 1285 (2003).

Friendly, H., THE DARTMOUTH COLLEGE CASE AND THE PUBLIC-PRIVATE PENUMBRA (1969).

Garvey, *Another Way of Looking at School Aid,* 1985 Sup.Ct.Rev. 61.

Garvey, *Private Power and the Constitution,* 10 Const. Commentary 301 (1993).

Garvey, *The Boss,* in WHAT ARE FREEDOMS FOR? ch. 14 (1996).

Gavison, *Feminism and the Public/Private Distinction,* 45 Stan.L.Rev. 1 (1992).

Glennon, and Nowak, *A Functional Analysis of the Fourteenth Amendment "State* Action*" Requirement,* 1976 Sup.Ct.Rev. 221.

Henkin, Shelley v. Kraemer: *Notes for a Revised Opinion,* 110 U.Pa.L.Rev. 473 (1962).

Horowitz, *Fourteenth Amendment Aspects of Racial Discrimination in "Private" Housing,* 52 Cal.L.Rev. 1 (1964).

Horowitz, *The Misleading Search for "State Action" Under the Fourteenth Amendment,* 30 S.Cal.L.Rev. 208 (1957).

Karst and Horowitz, Reitman v. Mulkey*: A Telophase of Substantive Equal Protection,* 1967 Sup.Ct.Rev. 39.

Karst and Van Alstyne, *Sit-Ins and State Action—Mr. Justice Douglas, Concurring,* 14 Stan.L.Rev. 762 (1962).

Kay, *The State Action Doctrine, The Public-Private Distinction, and the Independence of Constitutional Law*, 10 Const. Comm. 329 (1993).

Krotoszynski, *Back to the Briarpatch: An Argument in Favor of Constitutional Meta-Analysis in State Action Determinations,* 94 Mich.L.Rev. 302 (1995).

Lewis, *The Meaning of State Action,* 60 Colum.L.Rev. 1083 (1960).

Lewis, Burton v. Wilmington Parking Authority*—A Case Without Precedent,* 61 Colum.L.Rev. 1458 (1961).

Lewis, *The Sit-In Cases: Great Expectations,* 1963 Sup.Ct.Rev. 101.

Madry, *Private Accountability and the Fourteenth Amendment: State Action, Federalism and Congress,* 59 Mo.L.Rev. 499 (1994).

McConnell, *State Action and the Supreme Court's Emerging Consensus on the Line Between Establishment and Private Religious Expression*, 28 Pepp.L.Rev. 681 (2001).

MacKinnon, *Disputing Male Sovereignty: On* United States v. Morrison, 114 Harv.L.Rev. 135 (2000).

Monaghan, *State Law Wrongs, State Law Remedies, and the Fourteenth Amendment,* 86 Colum.L.Rev. 979 (1986).

Nerken, *A New Deal for the Protection of Fourteenth Amendment Rights: Challenging the Doctrinal Bases of the* Civil Rights Cases *and State Action Theory,* 12 Harv.Civ.Rts.–Civ.Lib.L.Rev. 297 (1977).

Note, *State Action: Theories for Applying Constitutional Restrictions to Private Activity,* 74 Colum.L.Rev. 656 (1974).

Parker, *Evans v. Newton and the Racially Restricted Charitable Trust,* 13 How.L.J. 223 (1967).

Pollak, *Racial Discrimination and Judicial Integrity: A Reply to Professor Wechsler,* 108 U.Pa.L.Rev. 1 (1959).

Rowe, *The Emerging Threshold Approach to State Action Determinations: Trying to Make Sense of* Flagg Brothers, Inc. v. Brooks, 69 Geo.L.J. 745 (1981).

Schwartz and Chemerinsky, *Dialogue on State Action*, 16 Touro L.Rev. 775 (2000).

Schwarzschild, *Value Pluralism and the Constitution: In Defense of the State Action Doctrine,* 1988 Sup.Ct.Rev. 129.

Siegel, *Why Equal Protection No Longer Protects: The Evolving Forms of Status-Enforcing State Action,* 49 Stan.L.Rev. 1111 (1997).

St. Antoine, *Color Blindness But Not Myopia: A New Look at State Action, Equal Protection, and "Private" Racial Discrimination,* 59 Mich.L. Rev. 993 (1961).

Strauss, *Due Process, Government Inaction, and Private Wrongs,* 1989 Sup.Ct.Rev. 53.

Sunstein, *State Action is Always Present*, 3 Chi.J.Int'l L. 465 (2002).

Symposium, *The Public/Private Distinction,* 130 U.Pa.L.Rev. 757 (1982).

Thomas, *Liberty and Property in the Patent Law*, 39 Hous.L.Rev. 569 (2002).

Thompson, *Piercing the Veil of State Action: The Revisionist Theory and A Mythical Application To Self-Help Repossession,* 1977 Wis.L.Rev. 1.

Tushnet, Shelley v. Kraemer *and Theories of Equality,* 33 N.Y.L.Sch.L. Rev. 383 (1988).

Tushnet, *State Action, Social Welfare Rights, and the Judicial Role: Some Comparative Observations*, 3 Chi.J.Int'l L. 435 (2002).

Underkuffler, *Vouchers and Beyond: The Individual as Causative Agent in the Establishment Clause Jurisprudence*, 75 Ind.L.J. 167 (2000).

Van Alstyne & Kenneth L. Karst, *State Action,* 14 Stan.L.Rev. 3 (1961).

Van Alstyne, *Mr. Justice Black, Constitutional Review, and the Talisman of State Action,* 1965 Duke L.J. 219.

Wechsler, *Toward Neutral Principles of Constitutional Law,* 73 Harv.L.Rev. 1 (1959).

Wellington, *The Constitution, The Labor Union, and "Governmental Action",* 70 Yale L.J. 345 (1961).

Williams, Mulkey v. Reitman *and State Action,* 14 UCLA L.Rev. 26 (1966).

Williams, *The Twilight of State Action,* 41 Tex.L.Rev. 347 (1963).

Yackle, *The Burger Court, "State Action," and Congressional Enforcement of the Civil War Amendments,* 27 Ala.L.Rev. 479 (1975).

Jefferson & 12th

8:50

3 or 4 James & 5th